CIVIL AIRCRAFT MARKINGS 2018

CIVIL AIRCRAFT MARKINGS 2018

Allan S Wright

Crécy Publishing Ltd

This 69th edition published by Crécy Publishing Ltd 2018

ISBN 9781910809198

Printed in the UK by Martins the Printers

Crecy Publishing Ltd
1a Ringway Trading Est
Shadowmoss Rd
Manchester
M22 5LH
Tel +44 (0)161 499 0024
www.crecy.co.uk

Front cover:
Sukhoi SuperJet 100-95B EI-FWA of
Irish airline CityJet departing Brussels.
CityJet is the first European carrier to
operate the type, EI-FWA was the first
of the 15 of the type on order to enter
service with the airline, which has
options for a further 16 aircraft.
© *Rudi Boigelot, Air Team Images*

.

The familiar 'G' prefixed four-letter registration system was adopted in 1919 after a short-lived spell with serial numbers commencing at K-100. Until July 1928 the UK allocations were issued in the G-Exxx range but, as a result of further international agreements, this series ended at G-EBZZ, the replacement being G-Axxx. From this point registrations were issued in a reasonably orderly manner through to G-AZZZ, the position reached in July 1972. There were, however, two exceptions. In order to prevent possible confusion with signal codes, the G-AQxx sequence was omitted, while G-AUxx was reserved for Australian use originally. In recent years however, individual requests for a mark in the latter range have been granted by the Authorities.

Although the next logical sequence was started at G-Bxxx, it was not long before the strictly applied rules relating to aircraft registration began to be relaxed. Permission was readily given for personalised marks to be issued, incorporating virtually any four-letter combination, while re-registration also became a common feature – a practice almost unheard of in the past. In this book, where this has taken place at some time, all previous UK identities carried appear in parenthesis after the operator's/owner's name. For example, during its career Gazelle G-EROL has also carried the identities G-BBHU, G-ORGE, G-RIFA, G-FDAV and G-NONA.

Some aircraft have also been allowed to wear military markings without displaying their civil identity. In this case the serial number actually carried is shown in parenthesis after the type's name. For example Auster 6A G-ARRX flies in military colours as VF512, its genuine previous identity. As an aid to the identification of such machines, a conversion list is provided.

Other factors caused a sudden acceleration in the number of registrations allocated by the Civil Aviation Authority in the early 1980s. The first surge followed the discovery that it was possible to register plastic bags, and other items even less likely to fly, on payment of the standard fee. This erosion of the main register was checked in early 1982 by the issue of a special sequence for such devices commencing with G-FYAA. Powered hang-gliders provided the second glut of allocations as a result of the decision that these types should be officially registered. Although a few of the early examples penetrated the current in-sequence register, in due course all new applicants were given marks in special ranges, this time G-MBxx, G-MGxx, G-MJxx, G-MMxx, G-MNxx, G-MTxx, G-MVxx, G-MWxx, G-MYxx and G-MZxx. It took some time before all microlights displayed an official mark but gradually the registration was carried, the size and position depending on the dimensions of the component to which it was applied.

There was news of a further change in mid-1998 when the CAA announced that with immediate effect microlights would be issued with registrations in the normal sequence alongside aircraft in other classes. In addition, it meant that owners could also apply for a personalised identity upon payment of the then current fee of £170 from April 1999, a low price for those wishing to display their status symbol. These various changes played their part in exhausting the current G-Bxxx range after some 26 years, with G-BZxx coming into use before the end of 1999. As this batch approached completion the next series to be used began at G-CBxx instead of the anticipated G-CAxx. The reason for this step was to avoid the re-use of marks issued in Canada during the 1920s, although a few have appeared more recently as personalised UK registrations.

Another large increase in the number of aircraft registered resulted from the EU-inspired changes in glider registration. After many years of self-regulation by the British Gliding Association, new gliders must now comply with EASA regulations and hence receive registrations in the main G-Cxxx sequence. The phasing-in of EASA registration for the existing glider fleet was a fairly lengthy process but has now come to an end and by the beginning of 2012 there were over 2,250 examples on the Register.

September 2007 saw the issue of the 50,000th UK aircraft registration with G-MITC being allocated to a Robinson R44 Raven. The total number of aircraft on the Register has risen over the past 25 years from just under 10,000 at the beginning of 1985 to in excess of 21,300 by January 2009. Numbers have fallen back slightly since that time, stabilizing at around 20,000.

The Isle of Man launched its own aircraft register in May 2007 aimed mainly at private and corporate business jets and helicopters and the first to be allocated was Cessna 525B Citation M-ELON. This has now been followed by the Channel Islands Aircraft Registry which was launched by the States of Guernsey on 9 December 2013 and the Jersey Aircraft Registry in November 2015. The M- (Isle of Man), 2- (Guernsey) and TJ- (Jersey) registers can be found at the end of the British Civil Aircraft Registrations section of this book.Also included are some non-airworthy and preserved aircraft which are shown with a star (★) after the type.

Included in this book are details of those overseas airliners most likely to be seen at UK airports on scheduled or charter flights. It is always difficult knowing what to include as at the time of writing the airlines' summer programmes have not been finalised. However, the full fleets of the big European 'national' carriers such as Air France, Lufthansa, SAS and others are listed although it is unlikely that many of their long haul aircraft will visit the UK in any given year. The airline scene is constantly changing and 2017 saw the disappearance among others of Monarch Airlines and Air Berlin whose aircraft have been a common sight throughout Europe for many years. In a further significant move, Easyjet began to transfer many of its Airbuses from the UK on to the Austrian register. Recent years have witnessed the appearance in increasing numbers of newer types such as the Airbus A.350 and A.320/321 NEO, the Boeing 787 Dreamliner and 737MAX and Bombardier CS100/300 whilst the number of DC-9s, DC-10s, MD-11s and early variants of the Boeing 747 have either fallen dramatically or disappeared altogether.

The three-letter codes used by airlines to prefix flight numbers are included for those carriers most likely to appear in the UK. Radio frequencies for the many UK airfields and airports are also listed.

A book of this nature is already out of date before it is published as changes to aircraft registers and airline fleets take place on a daily basis. The 2018 edition includes new allocations to the UK Register up to and including 25 February 2018.

ASW

ACKNOWLEDGEMENTS: Once again thanks are extended to the Registration Department of the Civil Aviation Authority for its assistance and allowing access to its files, thanks are also given to all those who have contributed items for possible use in this edition.

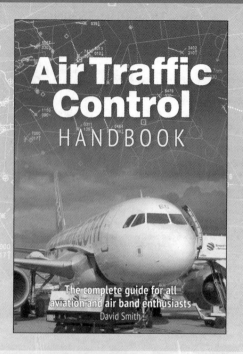

Air Traffic Control Handbook

David Smith

Now in its 10th edition, Air Traffic Control Handbook is the essential guide to modern air traffic control systems and procedures.

Written by an acknowledged expert in the field, Air Traffic Control Handbook covers ATC terminology, procedures, radio frequencies and call signs, together with navigation aids, and approach, weather and aerodrome controls. This fully revised and enlarged hardback edition is illustrated throughout to help the reader understand the intricacies of Air Traffic Control and its jargon and to understand more about this essential aspect of civil aviation.

ISBN: 978 08597 91830 **£17.95**

Available at all good book shops, enthusiast shop and pilot shops

Crecy Publishing Ltd
1a Ringway Trading Est
Shadowmoss Rd
Manchester
M22 5LH
Tel +44 (0)161 499 0024
www.crecy.co.uk

A2-	Botswana		JY-	Jordan
A3-	Tonga		LN-	Norway
A5-	Bhutan		LV-	Argentina
A6-	United Arab Emirates		LX-	Luxembourg
A7-	Qatar		LY-	Lithuania
A8-	Liberia		LZ-	Bulgaria
A9C-	Bahrain		M-	Isle of Man
A40-	Oman		N-	United States of America
AP-	Pakistan		OB-	Peru
B-	China/Taiwan/Hong Kong/Macao		OD-	Lebanon
C-	Canada		OE-	Austria
C2-	Nauru		OH-	Finland
C3-	Andorra		OK-	Czech Republic
C5-	Gambia		OM-	Slovakia
C6-	Bahamas		OO-	Belgium
C9-	Mozambique		OY-	Denmark
CC-	Chile		P-	North Korea
CN-	Morocco		P2-	Papua New Guinea
CP-	Bolivia		P4-	Aruba
CS-	Portugal		PH-	Netherlands
CU-	Cuba		PJ-	Netherlands Antilles
CX-	Uruguay		PK-	Indonesia
D-	Germany		PP-	Brazil
D2-	Angola		PR-	Brazil
D4-	Cape Verde Islands		PT-	Brazil
D6-	Comores Islands		PU-	Brazil
DQ-	Fiji		PZ-	Surinam
E3-	Eritrea		RA-	Russia
E5-	Cook Islands		RDPL-	Laos
E7-	Bosnia and Herzegovina		RP-	Philippines
EC-	Spain		S2-	Bangladesh
EI-	Republic of Ireland		S5-	Slovenia
EK-	Armenia		S7-	Seychelles
EP-	Iran		S9-	São Tomé
ER-	Moldova		SE-	Sweden
ES-	Estonia		SP-	Poland
ET-	Ethiopia		ST-	Sudan
EW-	Belarus		SU-	Egypt
EX-	Kyrgyzstan		SX-	Greece
EY-	Tajikistan		T2-	Tuvalu
EZ-	Turkmenistan		T3-	Kiribati
F-	France, inc Colonies and Protectorates		T7-	San Marino
G-	United Kingdom		T8-	Palau
H4-	Solomon Islands		T9-	Bosnia and Herzegovina
HA-	Hungary		TC-	Turkey
HB-	Switzerland and Liechtenstein		TF-	Iceland
HC-	Ecuador		TG-	Guatemala
HH-	Haiti		TI-	Costa Rica
HI-	Dominican Republic		TJ-	Cameroon
HK-	Colombia		TL-	Central African Republic
HL-	South Korea		TN-	Republic of Congo
HP-	Panama		TR-	Gabon
HR-	Honduras		TS-	Tunisia
HS-	Thailand		TT-	Tchad
HZ-	Saudi Arabia		TU-	Ivory Coast
I-	Italy		TY-	Benin
J2-	Djibouti		TZ-	Mali
J3-	Grenada		UK-	Uzbekistan
J5-	Guinea Bissau		UN-	Kazakhstan
J6-	St. Lucia		UR-	Ukraine
J7-	Dominica		V2-	Antigua
J8-	St. Vincent		V3-	Belize
JA-	Japan		V4	St. Kitts & Nevis
JU-	Mongolia		V5-	Namibia

V6-	Micronesia	3C-	Equatorial Guinea
V7-	Marshall Islands	3D-	Swaziland
V8-	Brunei	3X-	Guinea
VH-	Australia	4K-	Azerbaijan
VN-	Vietnam	4L-	Georgia
VP-A	Anguilla	4O-	Montenegro
VP-B	Bermuda	4R-	Sri Lanka
VP-C	Cayman Islands	4X-	Israel
VP-F	Falkland Islands	5A-	Libya
VP-G	Gibraltar	5B-	Cyprus
VP-L	British Virgin Islands	5H-	Tanzania
VP-M	Montserrat	5N-	Nigeria
VQ-B	Bermuda	5R-	Malagasy Republic (Madagascar)
VQ-H	Saint Helena/Ascension	5T-	Mauritania
VQ-T	Turks & Caicos Islands	5U-	Niger
VT-	India	5V-	Togo
XA-	Mexico	5W-	Western Samoa (Polynesia)
XB-	Mexico	5X-	Uganda
XC-	Mexico	5Y-	Kenya
XT-	Burkina Faso	6O-	Somalia
XU-	Cambodia	6V-	Senegal
XW-	Laos	6Y-	Jamaica
XY-	Myanmar	7O-	Yemen
YA-	Afghanistan	7P-	Lesotho
YI-	Iraq	7Q-	Malawi
YJ-	Vanuatu	7T-	Algeria
YK-	Syria	8P-	Barbados
YL-	Latvia	8Q-	Maldives
YN-	Nicaragua	8R-	Guyana
YR-	Romania	9A-	Croatia
YS-	El Salvador	9G-	Ghana
YU-	Serbia	9H-	Malta
YV-	Venezuela	9J-	Zambia
Z-	Zimbabwe	9K-	Kuwait
Z3-	Macedonia	9L-	Sierra Leone
ZA-	Albania	9M-	Malaysia
ZJ-	Jersey	9N-	Nepal
ZK-	New Zealand	9Q-	Congo Kinshasa
ZP-	Paraguay	9U-	Burundi
ZS-	South Africa	9V-	Singapore
2-	Guernsey	9XR-	Rwanda
3A-	Monaco	9Y-	Trinidad and Tobago
3B-	Mauritius		

(for example PA-28 Piper Type 28)	
A.	Beagle, Auster, Airbus
AAC	Army Air Corps
AA-	American Aviation, Grumman American
AB	Agusta-Bell
AESL	Aero Engine Services Ltd
AG	American General
An	Antonov
ANEC	Air Navigation & Engineering Co
ANG	Air National Guard
AS	Aérospatiale
A.S.	Airspeed
A.W.	Armstrong Whitworth
B.	Blackburn, Bristol, Boeing, Beagle
BA	British Airways
BAC	British Aircraft Company
BAC	British Aircraft Corporation
BAe	British Aerospace
BAPC	British Aviation Preservation Council
BAT	British Aerial Transport
B.K.	British Klemm
BN	Britten-Norman
Bo	Bolkow
Bü	Bücker
CAARP	Co-operatives des Ateliers Aéronautiques de la Région Parisienne
CAC	Commonwealth Aircraft Corporation
CAF	Canadian Air Force
CASA	Construcciones Aeronautics SA
CCF	Canadian Car & Foundry Co
CEA	Centre-Est Aviation
CH.	Chrislea
CHABA	Cambridge Hot-Air Ballooning Association
CLA.	Comper
CP.	Piel
CUAS	Cambridge University Air Squadron
Cycl	Cyclone
D.	Druine
DC-	Douglas Commercial
DH.	de Havilland
DHA.	de Havilland Australia
DHC.	de Havilland Canada
DR.	Jodel (Robin-built)
EE	English Electric
EAA	Experimental Aircraft Association
EMB	Embraer Empresa Brasileira de Aeronautica SA
EoN	Elliotts of Newbury
EP	Edgar Percival
ETPS	Empire Test Pilots School
F.	Fairchild, Fokker
F.A.A.	Fleet Air Arm
FFA	Flug und Fahrzeugwerke AG
FH	Fairchild-Hiller
FrAF	French Air Force
FRED	Flying Runabout Experimental Design
Fw	Focke-Wulf
G.	Grumman
GA	Gulfstream American
GAL.	General Aircraft
GC	Globe Aircraft
GECAS	General Electric Capital Aviation Services
GY	Gardan
H	Helio
HM.	Henri Mignet
HP.	Handley Page
HPR.	Handley Page Reading
HR.	Robin
HS.	Hawker Siddeley
ICA	Intreprinderea de Constructii Aeronau

IHM	International Helicopter Museum
I.I.I.	Iniziative Industriali Italiane
IL	Ilyushin
ILFC	International Lease Finance Corporation
IMCO	Intermountain Manufacturing Co
IWM	Imperial War Museum
KR	Rand-Robinson
L.	Lockheed
L.A.	Luton, Lake
LET	Letecky Narodny Podnik
LLP	Limited Liability Partnership
L.V.G.	Luft-Verkehrs Gesellschaft
M.	Miles, Mooney
MBA	Micro Biplane Aviation
MBB	Messerschmitt-Bölkow-Blohm
McD	McDonnell
MDH	McDonnell Douglas Helicopters
MH.	Max Holste
MHCA	Manhole Cover
MJ	Jurca
MS.	Morane-Saulnier
NA	North American
NC	Nord
NE	North East
P.	Hunting (formerly Percival), Piaggio
PA-	Piper
PC.	Pilatus
PZL	Panstwowe Zaklady Lotnicze
QAC	Quickie Aircraft Co
R.	Rockwell
RAF	Royal Air Force
RAAF	Royal Australian Air Force
RAFGSA	Royal Air Force Gliding & Soaring Association
RCAF	Royal Canadian Air Force
RF	Fournier
R.N.	Royal Navy
S.	Short, Sikorsky
SA,SE,SO	Sud-Aviation, Aérospatiale, Scottish Aviation
SAAB	Svenska Aeroplan Aktieboleg
SC	Short
SCD	Side Cargo Door
SNCAN	Société Nationale de Constructions Aéronautiques du Nord
SOCATA	Société de Construction d'Avions de Tourisme et d'Affaires
SpA	Societa per Azioni
SPP	Strojirny Prvni Petiletky
S.R.	Saunders-Roe, Stinson
SS	Special Shape
ST	SOCATA
SW	Solar Wings
T.	Tipsy
TB	SOCATA
TLAC	The Light Aircraft Company
Tu	Tupolev
UH.	United Helicopters (Hiller)
UK	United Kingdom
USAF	United States Air Force
USAAC	United States Army Air Corps
USN	United States Navy
V.	Vickers-Armstrongs
VLM	Vlaamse Luchttransportmaatschappij
VS.	Vickers-Supermarine
WA	Wassmer
WAR	War Aircraft Replicas
WHE	W.H.Ekin
WS	Westland
Z.	Zlin

Notes	Reg	Type	Owner or Operator
	G-AAAH	DH.60G Moth (replica) (BAPC 168) ★	Yorkshire Air Museum/Elvington
	G-AAAH	DH.60G Moth ★	Science Museum/South Kensington
	G-AACA	Avro 504K (BAPC 177) ★	Brooklands Museum of Aviation/Weybridge
	G-AACN	HP.39 Gugnunc*	Science Museum/Wroughton
	G-AADR	DH.60GM Moth	E. V. Moffatt
	G-AAEG	DH.60G Gipsy Moth	I. B. Grace
	G-AAHI	DH.60G Moth	Nigel John Western Reid Discretionary Settlement 2008
	G-AAHY	DH.60M Moth	D. J. Elliott
	G-AAIN	Parnall Elf II	The Shuttleworth Collection/Old Warden
	G-AAJT	DH.60G Moth	M. R. Paul
	G-AALY	DH.60G Moth	K. M. Fresson
	G-AAMX	DH.60GM Moth ★	RAF Museum/Hendon
	G-AANG	Blériot XI	The Shuttleworth Collection/Old Warden
	G-AANH	Deperdussin Monoplane	The Shuttleworth Collection/Old Warden
	G-AANI	Blackburn Monoplane	The Shuttleworth Collection/Old Warden
	G-AANJ	L.V.G. C VI (7198/18)	Aerospace Museum/Cosford
	G-AANL	DH.60M Moth	R. A. Palmer
	G-AANO	DH.60GMW Gipsy Moth	K. F. Crumplin
	G-AAOK	Curtiss Wright Travel Air 12Q	Shipping & Airlines Ltd
	G-AAOR	DH.60G Moth	B. R. Cox
	G-AAPZ	Desoutter I (mod.)	The Shuttleworth Collection
	G-AATC	DH.80A Puss Moth	R. A. Palmer
	G-AAUP	Klemm L.25-1A	J. I. Cooper
	G-AAWO	DH.60G Moth	Iain Charles Reid Discretionary Settlement 2009
	G-AAXG	DH 60M Moth	S. H. Kidston
	G-AAXK	Klemm L.25-1A ★	C. C. Russell-Vick (stored)
	G-AAYT	DH.60G Moth	P. Groves
	G-AAYX	Southern Martlet	The Shuttleworth Collection
	G-AAZG	DH.60G Moth	E. G. & N. S. C. English
	G-AAZP	DH.80A Puss Moth	R. P. Williams
	G-ABAA	Avro 504K ★	Manchester Museum of Science & Industry
	G-ABAG	DH.60G Moth	A. & P. A. Wood
	G-ABBB	B.105A Bulldog IIA (K2227) ★	RAF Museum/Hendon
	G-ABDA	DH.60G Moth	T. A. Bechtolsheimer
	G-ABDW	DH.80A Puss Moth (VH-UQB) ★	Museum of Flight/East Fortune
	G-ABDX	DH.60G Moth	M. D. Souch
	G-ABEV	DH.60G Moth	S. L. G. Darch
	G-ABHE	Aeronca C.2	N. S. Chittenden
	G-ABJJ	DH.60G Moth	B. R. Cox
	G-ABLM	Cierva C.24 ★	de Havilland Heritage Museum/London Colney
	G-ABLS	DH.80A Puss Moth	T. W. Harris
	G-ABMR	Hart 2 (J9941) ★	RAF Museum/Hendon
	G-ABNT	Civilian C.A.C.1 Coupe	Shipping & Airlines Ltd
	G-ABNX	Redwing 2	Redwing Syndicate
	G-ABOI	Wheeler Slymph ★	Midland Air Museum/Coventry
	G-ABOX	Sopwith Pup (N5195)	C. M. D. & A. P. St. Cyrien
	G-ABSD	DH.60G Moth	M. E. Vaisey
	G-ABUL†	DH.82A Tiger Moth ★	F.A.A. Museum/Yeovilton (G-AOXG)
	G-ABUS	Comper CLA.7 Swift	R. C. F. Bailey
	G-ABVE	Arrow Active 2	Real Aircraft Co
	G-ABWD	DH.83 Fox Moth	M. D. Souch
	G-ABWP	Spartan Arrow	R. T. Blain
	G-ABXL	Granger Archaeopteryx ★	J. R. Granger
	G-ABYA	DH.60G Gipsy Moth	M. J. Saggers
	G-ABZB	DH.60G-III Moth Major	G. M. Turner
	G-ACBH	Blackburn B.2 ★	South Yorkshire Aircraft Museum/Doncaster
	G-ACCB	DH.83 Fox Moth	E. A. Gautrey
	G-ACDA	DH.82A Tiger Moth	J. Turnbull
	G-ACDC	DH.82A Tiger Moth	Tiger Club Ltd
	G-ACDI	DH.82A Tiger Moth	Doublecube Aviation LLP
	G-ACDJ	DH.82A Tiger Moth	R. H. & J. A. Cooper
	G-ACEJ	DH.83 Fox Moth	K. F. Grimminger
	G-ACET	DH.84 Dragon	G. Cormack
	G-ACGS	DH.85 Leopard Moth	M. J. Miller (G-APKH)
	G-ACGT	Avro 594 Avian IIIA ★	Yorkshire Light Aircraft Ltd/Leeds
	G-ACGZ	DH.60G-III Moth Major	N. H. Lemon

Reg	Type	Owner or Operator	Notes
G-ACIT	DH.84 Dragon ★	Science Museum/Wroughton	
G-ACLL	DH.85 Leopard Moth	V. M & D. C. M. Stiles	
G-ACMA	DH.85 Leopard Moth	P. A. Vacher	
G-ACMD	DH.82A Tiger Moth	M. J. Bonnick	
G-ACMN	DH.85 Leopard Moth	M. R. & K. E. Slack	
G-ACNS	DH.60G-III Moth Major	C. T. Parry	
G-ACOJ	DH.85 Leopard Moth	Norman Aeroplane Trust	
G-ACOL	DH.85 Leopard Moth	J. Cresswell	
G-ACSP	DH.88 Comet ★	T. M., M. L., D. A. & P. M. Jones	
G-ACSS	DH.88 Comet ★	The Shuttleworth Collection *Grosvenor House*/Old Warden	
G-ACSS†	DH.88 Comet (replica) ★	G. Gayward (BAPC216)	
G-ACSS†	DH.88 Comet (replica) ★	The Galleria Hatfield (BAPC257)	
G-ACTF	Comper CLA.7 Swift ★	The Shuttleworth Collection/Old Warden	
G-ACUS	DH.85 Leopard Moth	R. A. & V. A. Gammons	
G-ACUU	Cierva C.30A (HM580) ★	G. S. Baker/Duxford	
G-ACUX	S.16 Scion (VH-UUP) ★	Ulster Folk & Transport Museum	
G-ACVA	Kay Gyroplane ★	Museum of Flight/East Fortune	
G-ACWM	Cierva C.30A (AP506) ★	IHM/Weston-super-Mare	
G-ACWP	Cierva C.30A (AP507) ★	Science Museum/South Kensington	
G-ACXB	DH.60G-III Moth Major	D. F. Hodgkinson	
G-ACXE	B.K. L.25C Swallow	I. C. Wakeford	
G-ACYK	Spartan Cruiser III ★	Museum of Flight (front fuselage)/East Fortune	
G-ADAH	DH.89A Dragon Rapide ★	Manchester Museum of Science & Industry *Pioneer*	
G-ADEV	Avro 504K (E3273)	The Shuttleworth Collection/Old Warden (G-ACNB)	
G-ADGP	M.2L Hawk Speed Six	R. A. Mills	
G-ADGT	DH.82A Tiger Moth (BB697)	Finest Hour Warbirds Ltd	
G-ADGV	DH.82A Tiger Moth	M. van Dijk & M. R. Van der Straaten (G-BACW)	
G-ADHD	DH.60G-III Moth Major	M. E. Vaisey	
G-ADIA	DH.82A Tiger Moth	S. J. Beaty	
G-ADJJ	DH.82A Tiger Moth	J. M. Preston	
G-ADKC	DH.87B Hornet Moth	C. G. & S. Winch	
G-ADKK	DH.87B Hornet Moth	S. W. Barratt & A. J. Herbert	
G-ADKL	DH.87B Hornet Moth	J. S. & P. R. Johnson	
G-ADKM	DH.87B Hornet Moth	J. M. O. Miller	
G-ADLY	DH.87B Hornet Moth	Treetops Aircraft LLP	
G-ADMF	BA L.25C Swallow II	D. A. Edwards	
G-ADMT	DH.87B Hornet Moth	D. C. Reid	
G-ADMW	M.2H Hawk Major (DG590) ★	RAF Museum Storage & Restoration Centre/RAF Stafford	
G-ADND	DH.87B Hornet Moth (W9385)	D. M. & S. M. Weston	
G-ADNE	DH.87B Hornet Moth	G-ADNE Group	
G-ADNL	M.5 Sparrowhawk	D. Shew	
G-ADNZ	DH.82A Tiger Moth (DE673)	D. C. Wall	
G-ADOT	DH.87B Hornet Moth ★	de Havilland Heritage Museum/London Colney	
G-ADPC	DH.82A Tiger Moth	P. D. & S. E. Ford	
G-ADPJ	B.A.C. Drone	M. J. Aubrey	
G-ADPS	B.A. Swallow 2	J. F. Hopkins	
G-ADRA	Pietenpol Air Camper	A. J. Mason	
G-ADRG†	Mignet HM.14 (replica) ★	Lower Stondon Transport Museum (BAPC77)	
G-ADRR	Aeronca C.3	C. J. & M. A. Essex	
G-ADRX†	Mignet HM.14 (replica) ★	S. Copeland Aviation Group (BAPC231)	
G-ADRY†	Mignet HM.14 (replica) (BAPC29) ★	Brooklands Museum of Aviation/Weybridge	
G-ADUR	DJ.87B Hornet Moth	C. J. & P. R. Harvey	
G-ADVU†	Mignet HM.14 (replica) ★	North East Aircraft Museum/Usworth (BAPC211)	
G-ADWJ	DH.82A Tiger Moth (BB803)	K. F. Crumplin	
G-ADWO	DH.82A Tiger Moth (BB807) ★	Solent Sky, Southampton	
G-ADWT	M.2W Hawk Trainer	K-F Grimminger	
G-ADXS	Mignet HM.14 ★	Thameside Aviation Museum/Shoreham	
G-ADYS	Aeronca C.3	E. P. & P. A. Gliddon	
G-ADYV†	Mignet HM.14 (replica) ★	P. Ward (BAPC243)	
G-ADZW†	Mignet HM.14 (replica) ★	Solent Sky/Southampton (BAPC253)	
G-AEBB	Mignet HM.14 ★	The Shuttleworth Collection/Old Warden	
G-AEBJ	Blackburn B-2	BAe Systems (Operations) Ltd	

Notes	Reg	Type	Owner or Operator
	G-AEDB	B.A.C. Drone 2	M. J. & S. Honeychurch
	G-AEDU	DH.90 Dragonfly	GAEDU Ltd
	G-AEEG	M.3A Falcon Skysport	P. R. Holloway
	G-AEEH	Mignet HM.14 ★	Aerospace Museum/Cosford
	G-AEFG	Mignet HM.14 (BAPC75) ★	N. H. Ponsford/Breighton
	G-AEFT	Aeronca C.3	N. S. Chittenden
	G-AEGV	Mignet HM.14 ★	Midland Air Museum/Coventry
	G-AEHM	Mignet HM.14 ★	Science Museum/Wroughton
	G-AEJZ	Mignet HM.14 (BAPC120) ★	Aero Venture
	G-AEKR	Mignet HM.14 (BAPC121) ★	Doncaster Museum & Art Gallery
	G-AEKV	Kronfeld Drone ★	Brooklands Museum of Aviation/Weybridge
	G-AEKW	M.12 Mohawk ★	RAF Museum
	G-AELO	DH.87B Hornet Moth	M. J. Miller
	G-AENP	Hawker Hind (K5414) (BAPC78)	The Shuttleworth Collection
	G-AEOA	DH.80A Puss Moth	P. & A. Wood/Old Warden
	G-AEOF†	Mignet HM.14 (BAPC22) ★	Aviodrome/Lelystad, Netherlands
	G-AEOF	Rearwin 8500	Shipping & Airlines Ltd
	G-AEPH	Bristol F.2B (D8096)	The Shuttleworth Collection
	G-AERV	M.11A Whitney Straight	P. W. Bishop
	G-AESB	Aeronca C.3	R. J. M. Turnbull
	G-AESE	DH.87B Hornet Moth	B. R. Cox
	G-AESZ	Chilton D.W.1	R. E. Nerou
	G-AETA	Caudron G.3 (3066) ★	RAF Museum/Hendon
	G-AETG	Aeronca 100	J. Teagle and Partners
	G-AEUJ	M.11A Whitney Straight	R. E. Mitchell
	G-AEVS	Aeronca 100	R. A. Fleming
	G-AEXD	Aeronca 100	M. A. & N. Mills
	G-AEXF	P.6 Mew Gull	Richard Shuttleworth Trustees
	G-AEXT	Dart Kitten II	R. A. Fleming
	G-AEXZ	Piper J-2 Cub	M. & J. R. Dowson
	G-AEZF	S.16 Scion 2 ★	Acebell Aviation/Redhill
	G-AEZJ	P.10 Vega Gull	D. P. H. Hulme
	G-AFAP†	CASA C.352L ★	Aerospace Museum/Cosford
	G-AFBS	M.14A Hawk Trainer 3 ★	G. D. Durbridge-Freeman/Duxford (G-AKKU)
	G-AFCL	B. A. Swallow 2	D. & J. Cresswell
	G-AFDO	Piper J-3F-60 Cub	R. Wald
	G-AFDX	Hanriot HD.1 (HD-75) ★	RAF Museum/Hendon
	G-AFEL	Monocoupe 90A	M. Rieser
	G-AFFD	Percival Type Q Six	G-AFFD Restoration Group
	G-AFFH	Piper J-2 Cub	M. J. Honeychurch
	G-AFFI†	Mignet HM.14 (replica) (BAPC76) ★	Yorkshire Air Museum/Elvington
	G-AFGD	B. A. Swallow 2	South Wales Swallow Group
	G-AFGE	B. A. Swallow 2	A. A. M. & C. W. N. Huke
	G-AFGH	Chilton D.W.1.	M. L. & G. L. Joseph
	G-AFGI	Chilton D.W.1.	K. A. A. McDonald
	G-AFGM	Piper J-4A Cub Coupé	P. H. Wilkinson
	G-AFGZ	DH.82A Tiger Moth	M. R. Paul (G-AMHI)
	G-AFHA	Mosscraft MA.1.	C. V. Butler
	G-AFIN	Chrislea LC.1 Airguard (BAPC203) ★	T. W. J. Carnall
	G-AFIR	Luton LA-4 Minor	Parasol Aircraft Company Ltd
	G-AFIU	Parker CA-4 Parasol ★	The Aeroplane Collection/Hooton Park
	G-AFJB	Foster-Wikner G.M.1. Wicko	J. Dible
	G-AFJR	Tipsy Trainer 1	M. E. Vaisey (stored)
	G-AFJU	M.17 Monarch	Museum of Flight/East Fortune
	G-AFJV	Mosscraft MA.2	C. V. Butler
	G-AFNI	DH.94 Moth Minor	J. Jennings
	G-AFOB	DH.94 Moth Minor	K. Cantwell
	G-AFOJ	DH.94 Moth Minor	A. H. Soper
	G-AFPN	DH.94 Moth Minor	The Moth Minor Group
	G-AFRZ	M.17 Monarch	R. E. Mitchell/Sleap (G-AIDE)
	G-AFSC	Tipsy Trainer 1	D. M. Forshaw
	G-AFSV	Chilton D.W.1A	R. E. Nerou
	G-AFTA	Hawker Tomtit (K1786)	The Shuttleworth Collection
	G-AFTN	Taylorcraft Plus C2 ★	Leicestershire County Council Museums/Snibston
	G-AFUP	Luscombe 8A Silvaire	R. Dispain
	G-AFWH	Piper J-4A Cub Coupé	C. W. Stearn & R. D. W. Norton
	G-AFWI	DH.82A Tiger Moth	J. N. Bailey
	G-AFWT	Tipsy Trainer 1	N. Parkhouse
	G-AFYD	Luscombe 8F Silvaire	J. D. Iliffe

Reg	Type	Owner or Operator	Notes
G-AFYO	Stinson H.W.75	M. Lodge	
G-AFZA	Piper J-4A Cub Coupe	R. A. Benson	
G-AFZE	Heath Parasol	C. J. Essex	
G-AFZK	Luscombe 8A Silvaire	M. G. Byrnes	
G-AFZL	Porterfield CP.50	P. G. Lucas & S. H. Sharpe	
G-AGAT	Piper J-3F-50 Cub	A. S. Bathgate	
G-AGBN	GAL.42 Cygnet 2 ★	Museum of Flight/East Fortune	
G-AGEG	DH.82A Tiger Moth	Norman Aeroplane Trust	
G-AGHY	DH.82A Tiger Moth	P. Groves	
G-AGIV	Piper J-3C-65 Cub	J-3 Cub Group	
G-AGJG	DH.89A Dragon Rapide	M. J. & D. J. T. Miller	
G-AGLK	Auster 5D	M. A. Farrelly & D. K. Chambers	
G-AGMI	Luscombe 8A Silvaire	Oscar Flying Group	
G-AGNJ	DH.82A Tiger Moth	B. P. Borsberry & ptnrs	
G-AGNV	Avro 685 York 1 (TS798) ★	Aerospace Museum/Cosford	
G-AGOS	R.S.4 Desford Trainer (VZ728)	Leicestershire County Council	
G-AGPG	Avro 19 Srs 2 ★	The Aeroplane Collection/Hooton Park	
G-AGPK	DH.82A Tiger Moth (PG657)	T. K. Butcher	
G-AGRU	V.498 Viking 1A ★	Brooklands Museum of Aviation/Weybridge	
G-AGSH	DH.89A Dragon Rapide 6	P. H. Meeson	
G-AGTM	DH.89A Dragon Rapide 6	B. R. Cox	
G-AGTO	Auster 5 J/1 Autocrat	M. J. Barnett & D. J. T. Miller	
G-AGTT	Auster 5 J/1 Autocrat	Parasol Aircraft Company Ltd	
G-AGVG	Auster 5 J/1 Autocrat (modified)	P. J. & S. J. Benest	
G-AGXN	Auster J/1N Alpha	Gentleman's Aerial Touring Carriage Group	
G-AGXU	Auster J/1N Alpha	L. J. Kingscott	
G-AGXV	Auster J/1 Autocrat	M. J. Barnett	
G-AGYD	Auster J/1N Alpha	P. D. Hodson	
G-AGYH	Auster J/1N Alpha	I. M. Staves	
G-AGYT	Auster J/1N Alpha	P. J. Barrett	
G-AGYU	DH.82A Tiger Moth (DE208)	S. A. Firth	
G-AGYY	Ryan ST3KR (27)	H. de Vries/Holland	
G-AGZZ	DH.82A Tiger Moth	M. C. Jordan	
G-AHAG	DH.89A Rapide	Scillonia Airways Ltd	
G-AHAL	Auster J/1N Alpha	Wickenby Aviation	
G-AHAM	Auster J/1 Autocrat	Interna Engineering BVBA/Belgium	
G-AHAN	DH.82A Tiger Moth	G-AHAN Flying Group	
G-AHAO	Auster 5 J/1 Autocrat	R. Callaway-Lewis	
G-AHAP	Auster J/1 Autocrat	W. D. Hill	
G-AHAT	Auster J/1N Alpha ★	Dumfries & Galloway Aviation Museum	
G-AHAU	Auster 5 J/1 Autocrat	Andreas Auster Group	
G-AHBL	DH.87B Hornet Moth	Shipping and Airlines Ltd	
G-AHBM	DH.87B Hornet Moth	P. A. & E. P. Gliddon	
G-AHCL	Auster J/1N Alpha (modified)	N. Musgrave	
G-AHCR	Gould-Taylorcraft Plus D Special	S. F. Griggs	
G-AHEC	Luscombe 8A Silvaire	A. F. Wankowski	
G-AHED	DH.89A Dragon Rapide (RL962) ★	RAF Museum Storage & Restoration Centre/RAF Stafford	
G-AHGW	Taylorcraft Plus D (LB375)	R. Ellingworth	
G-AHGZ	Taylorcraft Plus D (LB367)	P. H. B. Cole	
G-AHHH	Auster J/1 Autocrat	K. Moore & G. J. Molloy	
G-AHHT	Auster J/1N Alpha	South Downs Auster Group	
G-AHIP	Piper J-3C-65 Cub (479712:8-R)	A. D. Pearce	
G-AHIZ	DH.82A Tiger Moth	C.F.G. Flying Ltd	
G-AHKX	Avro 19 Srs 2	The Shuttleworth Collection	
G-AHKY	Miles M.18 Series 2 ★	Museum of Flight/East Fortune	
G-AHLK	Auster 3 (NJ889)	J. H. Powell-Tuck	
G-AHLT	DH.82A Tiger Moth	M. P. Waring	
G-AHNR	Taylorcraft BC-12D	T. M. Buick	
G-AHOO	DH.82A Tiger Moth	J. T. Milsom	
G-AHPZ	DH.82A Tiger Moth	N. J. Wareing	
G-AHRI	DH.104 Dove 1 ★	Newark Air Museum	
G-AHSA	Avro 621 Tutor (K3241)	The Shuttleworth Collection	
G-AHSD	Taylorcraft Plus D (LB323)	K. B. Owen	
G-AHSP	Auster J/1 Autocrat	R. M. Weeks	
G-AHSS	Auster J/1N Alpha	C. W. Tomkins	
G-AHST	Auster J/1N Alpha	A. C. Frost	
G-AHTE	P.44 Proctor V	D. K. Tregilgas	
G-AHTW	A.S.40 Oxford (V3388) ★	Skyfame Collection/Duxford	
G-AHUF	DH.Tiger Moth	Eaglescott Tiger Moth Group	

Notes	Reg	Type	Owner or Operator
	G-AHUG	Taylorcraft Plus D	N. C. Dickinson
	G-AHUI	M.38 Messenger 2A ★	The Aeroplane Collection/Hooton Park
	G-AHUJ	M.14A Hawk Trainer 3 (R1914)	F. Baldanza
	G-AHUN	Globe GC-1B Swift	R. J. Hamlett
	G-AHUV	DH.82A Tiger Moth	A. D. Gordon
	G-AHVU	DH.82A Tiger Moth	A. D. Barton
	G-AHVV	DH.82A Tiger Moth	M. Arter
	G-AHXE	Taylorcraft Plus D (LB312)	J. M. C. Pothecary
	G-AIBE	Fulmar II (N1854) ★	F.A.A. Museum/Yeovilton
	G-AIBH	Auster J/1N Alpha	M. J. Bonnick
	G-AIBM	Auster J/1 Autocrat	R. Greatrex
	G-AIBR	Auster J/1 Autocrat	P. R. Hodson
	G-AIBW	Auster J/1N Alpha	C. R. Sunter
	G-AIBX	Auster J/1 Autocrat	Wasp Flying Group
	G-AIBY	Auster J/1 Autocrat	D. Morris
	G-AICX	Luscombe 8A Silvaire	C. C. & J. M. Lovell
	G-AIDL	DH.89A Dragon Rapide 6 (TX310)	Cirrus Aviation Ltd
	G-AIDN	VS.502 Spitfire Tr.VII (MT818)	Biggin Hill Heritage Hangar Ltd
	G-AIDS	DH.82A Tiger Moth	K. D. Pogmore & T. Dann
	G-AIEK	M.38 Messenger 2A (RG333)	P. E. Beaver
	G-AIFZ	Auster J/1N Alpha	M. D. Ansley
	G-AIGD	Auster V J/1 Autocrat	R. M. D. Saw
	G-AIGF	Auster J/1N Alpha	D. W. Mathie
	G-AIGT	Auster J/1N Alpha	M. J. Miller
	G-AIIH	Piper J-3C-65 Cub	N. G. Busschau & M. S. Pettit
	G-AIJM	Auster J/4	N. Huxtable
	G-AIJS	AusterJ/4	R. J. Lane
	G-AIJT	Auster J/4 Srs 100	Aberdeen Auster Flying Group
	G-AIKE	Auster 5 (NJ728)	Stearman Services Ltd
	G-AIPR	Auster J/4	M. A. & N. Mills
	G-AIPV	Auster J/1 Autocrat	W. P. Miller
	G-AIRC	Auster J/1 Autocrat	K. & C. Jones & C. Morris
	G-AIRK	DH.82A Tiger Moth	J. S. & P. R. Johnson
	G-AISA	Tipsy B Srs 1	J. Pollard
	G-AISC	Tipsy B Srs 1	Wagtail Flying Group
	G-AISS	Piper J-3C-65 Cub	K. W. Wood & F. Watson
	G-AIST	VS.300 Spitfire 1A (P7308/XR-D)	Spitfire The One Ltd
	G-AISX	Piper J-3C-65 Cub (330372)	Cubfly
	G-AITB	A.S.10 Oxford (MP425) ★	RAF Museum/Hendon
	G-AIUA	M.14A Hawk Trainer 3 (T9768)	D. S. Hunt
	G-AIUL	DH.89A Dragon Rapide 6	I. Jones
	G-AIXA	Taylorcraft Plus D (LB264) ★	RAF Museum/Hendon
	G-AIXJ	DH.82A Tiger Moth	D. Green
	G-AIXN	Benes-Mraz M.1C Sokol	Sokol Flying Group Ltd
	G-AIYG	SNCAN Stampe SV.4B	J. E. Henny/Belgium
	G-AIYR	DH.89A Dragon Rapide (HG691)	Spectrum Leisure Ltd
	G-AIYS	DH.85 Leopard Moth	M. R. Paul
	G-AIZE	Fairchild F.24W Argus 2 (FS628) ★	Aerospace Museum/Cosford
	G-AIZG	VS.236 Walrus 1 (L2301) ★	F.A.A. Museum/Yeovilton
	G-AIZU	Auster J/1 Autocrat	C. J. & J. G. B. Morley
	G-AJAD	Piper J-3C-65 Cub	C. R. Shipley
	G-AJAE	Auster J/1N Alpha	D. F. Keller
	G-AJAJ	Auster J/1N Alpha	N. K. Geddes
	G-AJAM	Auster J/2 Arrow	D. A. Porter
	G-AJAP	Luscombe 8A Silvaire	M. Flint
	G-AJAS	Auster J/1N Alpha	P. Ferguson & T. Garner
	G-AJCP	D.31 Turbulent	B. R. Pearson
	G-AJDW	Auster J/1 Autocrat	D. R. Hunt
	G-AJDY	Auster J/1N Alpha (MT182)	W. Bayman
	G-AJEB	Auster J/1N Alpha ★	The Aeroplane Collection/Hooton Park
	G-AJEE	Auster J/1 Autocrat	A. C. Whitehead
	G-AJEH	Auster J/1N Alpha	P. Harrison
	G-AJEI	Auster J/1N Alpha	J. Siddall
	G-AJEM	Auster J/1 Autocrat	A. L. Aish
	G-AJES	Piper J-3C-65 Cub (330485:C-44)	D. E. Jarvis
	G-AJGJ	Auster 5 (RT486)	British Classic Aircraft Restoration Flying Group
	G-AJHS	DH.82A Tiger Moth	Flying Wires/Netherlands
	G-AJIH	Auster J/1 Autocrat (TJ518)	S. Alexander

Reg	Type	Owner or Operator	Notes
G-AJIS	Auster J/1N Alpha	J. J. Hill	
G-AJIT	Auster J/1 Kingsland Autocrat	S. J. Farrant	
G-AJIU	Auster J/1 Autocrat	M. D. Greenhalgh	
G-AJIW	Auster J/1N Alpha	R. J. Guess	
G-AJIX	Auster J/1 Autocrat	S. G. Rule	
G-AJJP	Fairey Jet Gyrodyne (XJ389) ★	Museum of Berkshire Aviation/Woodley	
G-AJJS	Cessna 120	G. A. Robson	
G-AJJT	Cessna 120	Juliet Tango Group	
G-AJJU	Luscombe 8E Silvaire	Enstone Luscombe Group	
G-AJKB	Luscombe 8E Silvaire	T. Carter	
G-AJOC	M.38 Messenger 2A ★	Ulster Folk & Transport Museum	
G-AJOE	M.38 Messenger 2A	P. W. Bishop	
G-AJON	Aeronca 7AC Champion	J. M. Gale	
G-AJOV†	Westland WS-51 Dragonfly ★	Aerospace Museum/Cosford	
G-AJOZ	Fairchild F.24W Argus 2 ★	Yorkshire Air Museum/Elvington	
G-AJPI	Fairchild F.24R-41a Argus 3 (314887)	R. Sijben/Netherlands	
G-AJRB	Auster J/1 Autocrat	Southern Alps Ltd	
G-AJRH	Auster J/1N Alpha ★	Charnwood Museum/Loughborough	
G-AJRS	M.14A Hawk Trainer 3 (P6382:C)	The Shuttleworth Collection	
G-AJTW	DH.82A Tiger Moth (N6965:FL-J)	J. A. Barker	
G-AJUE	Auster J/1 Autocrat	P. H. B. Cole	
G-AJUL	Auster J/1N Alpha	M. J. Crees	
G-AJVE	DH.82A Tiger Moth	R. A. Gammons	
G-AJWB	M.38 Messenger 2A	P. W. Bishop	
G-AJXC	Auster 5 (TJ343)	R. D. Helliar-Symonds, K. A. & S. E. W. Williams	
G-AJXV	Auster 4 (NJ695)	B. A. Farries	
G-AJXY	Auster 4	X-Ray Yankee Group	
G-AJYB	Auster J/1N Alpha	P. J. Shotbolt	
G-AKAT	M.14A Hawk Trainer 3 (T9738)	R. A. Fleming	
G-AKBO	M.38 Messenger 2A	N. P. Lee	
G-AKDF	M.38 Messenger 2A	C. W. P. Turner	
G-AKDK	M.65 Gemini 1A	C. W. P. Turner	
G-AKDN	DHC.1A-1 Chipmunk	K. A. Large & J. Morley	
G-AKDW	DH.89A Dragon Rapide ★	de Havilland Heritage Museum/London Colney	
G-AKEL	M.65 Gemini 1A ★	Ulster Folk & Transport Museum	
G-AKEN	M.65 Gemini 1A	C. W. P. Turner	
G-AKEX	Percival Proctor III	M. Biddulph (G-AKIU)	
G-AKGE	M.65 Gemini 3C ★	Ulster Folk & Transport Museum	
G-AKHP	M.65 Gemini 1A	S. A. Blanchard	
G-AKHU	M.65 Gemini 1A	C. W. P. Turner	
G-AKHZ	M.65 Gemini 7 ★	The Aeroplane Collection/Hooton Park	
G-AKIB	Piper J-3C-90 Cub (480015:M-44)	R. Horner	
G-AKIF	DH.89A Dragon Rapide	Airborne Taxi Services Ltd	
G-AKIN	M.38 Messenger 2A	Sywell Messenger Trust	
G-AKIU	P.44 Proctor V	Air Atlantique Ltd	
G-AKKB	M.65 Gemini 1A	D. R. Gray	
G-AKKH	M.65 Gemini 1A	P. J. Hebdon	
G-AKKR	M.14A Magister (T9707) ★	Museum of Army Flying/Middle Wallop	
G-AKKY	M.14A Hawk Trainer 3 (L6906) ★ (BAPC44)	Museum of Berkshire Aviation/Woodley	
G-AKLW	Short SA.6 Sealand 1 ★	Ulster Folk & Transport Museum	
G-AKOW	Auster 5 (TJ569) ★	Museum of Army Flying/Middle Wallop	
G-AKPF	M.14A Hawk Trainer 3 (N3788)	D. S. Bramwell	
G-AKPI	Auster 5 (TJ207)	M. D. Grinstead	
G-AKRP	DH.89A Dragon Rapide 4	Eaglescott Dominie Group	
G-AKSY	Auster 5 (TJ534)	A. Brier	
G-AKSZ	Auster 5D (modified)	M. A. Farrelly & D. K. Chambers	
G-AKTH	Piper J-3C-65 Cub	G. W. S. Turner	
G-AKTI	Luscombe 8A Silvaire	C. Chambers	
G-AKTK	Aeronca 11AC Chief	A. C. Batchelar	
G-AKTO	Aeronca 7BCM Champion	R. M. Davies	
G-AKTP	PA-17 Vagabond	Golf Tango Papa Group	
G-AKTR	Aeronca 7AC Champion	E. Gordon	
G-AKTS	Cessna 120	M. Isterling	
G-AKTT	Luscombe 8A Silvaire	S. J. Charters	
G-AKUE	DH.82A Tiger Moth	D. F. Hodgkinson	
G-AKUF	Luscombe 8E Silvaire	M. O. Loxton	
G-AKUH	Luscombe 8E Silvaire	A. G. Palmer (G-GIST)	
G-AKUJ	Luscombe 8E Silvaire	P. R. Bentley	

Notes	Reg	Type	Owner or Operator
	G-AKUK	Luscombe 8A Silvaire	O. R. Watts
	G-AKUL	Luscombe 8A Silvaire	K. R. H. Wingate
	G-AKUM	Luscombe 8F Silvaire	D. A. Young
	G-AKUN	Piper J-3F-65 Cub	W. R. Savin
	G-AKUO	Aeronca 11AC Chief	C. V. Dadswell & A. G. Collicot
	G-AKUP	Luscombe 8E Silvaire	D. A. Young
	G-AKUR	Cessna 140	C. G. Applegate
	G-AKUW	Chrislea CH.3 Super Ace 2	R. J. S. G. Clark
	G-AKVF	Chrislea CH.3 Super Ace 2	Aviation Heritage Ltd
	G-AKVM	Cessna 120	P. A. Espin
	G-AKVN	Aeronca 11AC Chief	P. A. Jackson
	G-AKVO	Taylorcraft BC-12D	G-AKVO Flying Group
	G-AKVP	Luscombe 8A Silvaire	J. M. Edis
	G-AKVR	Chrislea CH.3 Skyjeep 4	R. B. Webber
	G-AKVZ	M.38 Messenger 4B	Shipping & Airlines Ltd
	G-AKWS	Auster 5A-160 (RT610)	M. C. Hayes
	G-AKWT	Auster 5 ★	C. Baker
	G-AKXP	Auster 5 (NJ633)	M. J. Nicholson
	G-AKXS	DH.82A Tiger Moth	J. & G. J. Eagles
	G-AKZN	P.34A Proctor 3 (Z7197) ★	RAF Museum/Hendon
	G-ALAH	Miles M.38 Messenger 4A	C. W. P. Turner
	G-ALAR	Miles M.38 Messenger 4A	C. W. P. Turner
	G-ALAX	DH.89A Dragon Rapide ★	Durney Aeronautical Collection/Andover
	G-ALBD	DH.82A Tiger Moth	D. Shew
	G-ALBJ	Auster 5 (TW501)	B. M. Vigor
	G-ALBK	Auster 5	J. S. & J. S. Allison
	G-ALBN	Bristol 173 (XF785) ★	RAF Museum Storage & Restoration Centre/Cardington
	G-ALCK	P.34A Proctor 3 (LZ766) ★	Skyfame Collection/Duxford
	G-ALCU	DH.104 Dove 2 ★	Midland Air Museum/Coventry
	G-ALDG	HP.81 Hermes 4 ★	Duxford Aviation Society (fuselage only)
	G-ALEH	PA-17 Vagabond	A. J. Coker
	G-ALFA	Auster 5	A. E. Jones
	G-ALFU	DH.104 Dove 6 ★	Duxford Aviation Society
	G-ALGA	PA-15 Vagabond	S. T. Gilbert
	G-ALGT	VS.379 Spitfire F.XIVH (RM689)	Rolls-Royce PLC
	G-ALIJ	PA-17 Vagabond	Hampshire Flying Group
	G-ALIW	DH.82A Tiger Moth	F. R. Curry
	G-ALJF	P.34A Proctor 3	J. F. Moore
	G-ALJL	DH.82A Tiger Moth	T. A. Kinnaird
	G-ALJR	Abbott-Baynes Scud III	The Gliding Heritage Centre
	G-ALLF	Slingsby T.30A Prefect (ARK)	J. F. Hopkins & K. M. Fresson
	G-ALMA	Piper J3C-65 Cub	M. J. Butler (G-BBXS)
	G-ALNA	DH.82A Tiger Moth	S. E. Ford
	G-ALND	DH.82A Tiger Moth (N9191)	D. Shew
	G-ALOD	Cessna 140	Condor Aviation International Ltd
	G-ALSP	Bristol 171 Sycamore (WV783) ★	RAF Museum/Hendon
	G-ALSS	Bristol 171 Sycamore (WA576) ★	Dumfries & Galloway Aviation Museum
	G-ALST	Bristol 171 Sycamore (WA577) ★	North East Aircraft Museum/Usworth
	G-ALSW	Bristol 171 Sycamore (WT933) ★	Newark Air Museum
	G-ALSX	Bristol 171 Sycamore (G-48-1) ★	IHM/Weston-super-Mare
	G-ALTO	Cessna 140	T. M. Jones & ptnrs
	G-ALUC	DH.82A Tiger Moth	Tiger Moth Experience Ltd
	G-ALWB	DHC.1 Chipmunk 22A	D. M. Neville
	G-ALWF	V.701 Viscount ★	Duxford Aviation Society RMA Sir John Franklin
	G-ALWS	DH.82A Tiger Moth (N9328)	J. G. Norris
	G-ALWW	DH.82A Tiger Moth	D. E. Findon
	G-ALXT	DH.89A Dragon Rapide ★	Science Museum/Wroughton
	G-ALXZ	Auster 5-150 (NJ689)	P. J. Tyler
	G-ALYB	Auster 5 (RT520) ★	South Yorkshire Aviation Museum/Doncaster
	G-ALYW	DH.106 Comet 1 ★	RAF Exhibition Flight (fuselage converted to 'Nimrod')
	G-ALZE	BN-1F ★	M. R. Short/Solent Sky, Southampton
	G-ALZO	A.S.57 Ambassador ★	Duxford Aviation Society
	G-AMAW	Luton LA-4 Minor	The Real Aeroplane Co.Ltd
	G-AMBB	DH.82A Tiger Moth	J. Eagles
	G-AMCK	DH.82A Tiger Moth	M. R. Masters
	G-AMCM	DH.82A Tiger Moth	J. I. Cooper

Reg	Type	Owner or Operator	Notes
G-AMDA	Avro 652A Anson 1 (N4877:MK-V) ★	Skyfame Collection/Duxford	
G-AMEN	PA-18 Super Cub 95	The G-AMEN Flying Group	
G-AMHF	DH.82A Tiger Moth	A. J. West	
G-AMHJ	Douglas C-47A Dakota 6 (KG651) ★	Assault Glider Association/Shawbury	
G-AMKU	Auster J/1B Aiglet	P. G. Lipman	
G-AMLZ	P.50 Prince 6E ★	The Jetstream Club	
G-AMMS	Auster J/5K Aiglet Trainer	M. C. Jordan	
G-AMNN	DH.82A Tiger Moth	I. J. Perry	
G-AMOG	V.701 Viscount ★	Museum of Flight/East Fortune	
G-AMPG	PA-12 Super Cruiser	D. J. Harrison	
G-AMPI	SNCAN Stampe SV.4C	T. W. Harris	
G-AMPO	Douglas C-47B (FZ626/YS-DH) ★	(gate guardian)/RAF Lyneham	
G-AMPY	Douglas C-47B (KK116)	RVL Aviation Ltd	
G-AMRA	Douglas C-47B	Forderverein Rosinebomber E.V./Germany	
G-AMRF	Auster J/5F Aiglet Trainer	D. A. Hill	
G-AMRK	G.37 Gladiator I (K7985)	The Shuttleworth Collection	
G-AMSG	SIPA 903	S. W. Markham	
G-AMSN	Douglas C-47B ★	Aceball Aviation/Redhill	
G-AMSV	Douglas C-47B Dakota 3	R. Chanrasekhar/India	
G-AMTA	Auster J/5F Aiglet Trainer	J. D. Manson	
G-AMTF	DH.82A Tiger Moth (T7842)	H. A. D. Monro	
G-AMTK	DH.82A Tiger Moth	S. W. McKay & M. E. Vaisey	
G-AMTM	Auster J/1 Autocrat	R. J. Stobo (G-AJUJ)	
G-AMTV	DH.82A Tiger Moth	E. Scurr	
G-AMUF	DHC.1 Chipmunk 21	Redhill Tailwheel Flying Club Ltd	
G-AMUI	Auster J/5F Aiglet Trainer	R. B. Webber	
G-AMVD	Auster 5 (TJ565)	M.Hammond	
G-AMVP	Tipsy Junior	R. A. Fleming	
G-AMVS	DH.82A Tiger Moth	D. Shew	
G-AMYD	Auster J/5L Aiglet Trainer	R. D. Thomasson	
G-AMYJ	Douglas C-47B (KN353) ★	Yorkshire Air Museum/Elvington	
G-AMZI	Auster J/5F Aiglet Trainer	J. F. Moore	
G-AMZT	Auster J/5F Aiglet Trainer	R. B. Webber	
G-ANAF	Douglas C-47B	RVL Aviation Ltd	
G-ANAP	DH.104 Dove 6 ★	Brunel Technical College/Lulsgate	
G-ANBZ	DH.82A Tiger Moth	D. Shew	
G-ANCF	B.175 Britannia 308 ★	Bristol Aero Collection (stored)/Kemble	
G-ANCS	DH.82A Tiger Moth	C. E. Edwards & E. A. Higgins	
G-ANDE	DH.82A Tiger Moth (EM726)	K. M. Perkins	
G-ANDM	DH.82A Tiger Moth	N. J. Stagg	
G-ANDP	DH.82A Tiger Moth	J. McCullough	
G-ANEH	DH.82A Tiger Moth (N6797)	G. J. Wells	
G-ANEL	DH.82A Tiger Moth	Totalsure Ltd	
G-ANEM	DH.82A Tiger Moth	P. J. Benest	
G-ANEN	DH.82A Tiger Moth	G-ANEN Group	
G-ANEW	DH.82A Tiger Moth (NM138)	K. F. Crumplin	
G-ANEZ	DH.82A Tiger Moth	C. D. J. Bland	
G-ANFH	Westland WS-55 Whirlwind ★	IHM/Weston-super-Mare	
G-ANFI	DH.82A Tiger Moth (DE623)	G. P. Graham	
G-ANFL	DH.82A Tiger Moth	Felthorpe Tiger Group Ltd	
G-ANFM	DH.82A Tiger Moth	Reading Flying Group	
G-ANFP	DH.82A Tiger Moth (N9503)	R. Santus	
G-ANFU	Auster 5 (NJ719) ★	North East Aircraft Museum/Usworth	
G-ANHI	DH.82A Tiger Moth	A. D. Barton	
G-ANHK	DH.82A Tiger Moth	T. A. Jackson	
G-ANHR	Auster 5	H. L. Swallow	
G-ANHS	Auster 4 (MT197)	Mike Tango Group	
G-ANHX	Auster 5D (TW519)	T. Taylor	
G-ANIE	Auster 5 (TW467)	R. T. Ingram	
G-ANIJ	Auster 5D (TJ672)	G. M. Rundle	
G-ANIS	Auster 5	J. Clarke-Cockburn	
G-ANJA	DH.82A Tiger Moth (N9389)	A. D. Hodgkinson	
G-ANJD	DH.82A Tiger Moth	D. O. Lewis	
G-ANJI	DH.82A Tiger Moth	D. Shew	
G-ANJK	DH.82A Tiger Moth	H. M. M. Haines	
G-ANKK	DH.82A Tiger Moth (T5854)	Halfpenny Green Tiger Group	
G-ANKT	DH.82A Tiger Moth (T6818)	The Shuttleworth Collection	
G-ANKV	DH.82A Tiger Moth (T7793)	J. A. Cooper	
G-ANKZ	DH.82A Tiger Moth (N6466)	T. D. Le Mesurier	
G-ANLD	DH.82A Tiger Moth	K. Peters	

Notes	Reg	Type	Owner or Operator
	G-ANLS	DH.82A Tiger Moth	P. A. Gliddon
	G-ANLW	Westland WS-51/2 Widgeon ★	Norfolk & Suffolk Museum/Flixton
	G-ANMO	DH.82A Tiger Moth (K4259:71)	K. M. Perkins
	G-ANMY	DH.82A Tiger Moth (DE470)	A. R. & M. A. Baxter
	G-ANNG	DH.82A Tiger Moth	Doublecube Aviation LLP
	G-ANNI	DH.82A Tiger Moth (T6953)	C. E. Ponsford & ptnrs
	G-ANNK	DH.82A Tiger Moth (T7290)	J. Y. Kaye
	G-ANOA	Hiller UH-12A ★	Redhill Technical College
	G-ANOD	DH.82A Tiger Moth	P. G. Watson
	G-ANOH	DH.82A Tiger Moth	N. Parkhouse
	G-ANOK	SAAB S.91C Safir	N. C. Stone
	G-ANOM	DH.82A Tiger Moth	W. J. Pitts
	G-ANON	DH.82A Tiger Moth (T7909)	M. Kelly
	G-ANOO	DH.82A Tiger Moth	R. K. Packman
	G-ANOV	DH.104 Dove 6 ★	Museum of Flight/East Fortune
	G-ANPE	DH.82A Tiger Moth	T. K. Butcher (G-IESH)
	G-ANPK	DH.82A Tiger Moth	A. D. Hodgkinson
	G-ANPP	P.34A Proctor 3	C. P. A. & J. Jeffrey
	G-ANRF	DH.82A Tiger Moth	C. D. Cyster
	G-ANRM	DH.82A Tiger Moth (DF112)	Spectrum Leisure Ltd
	G-ANRN	DH.82A Tiger Moth	J. J. V. Elwes
	G-ANRP	Auster 5 (TW439)	C. L. Petty
	G-ANRX	DH.82A Tiger Moth ★	de Havilland Heritage Museum/London Colney
	G-ANSM	DH.82A Tiger Moth	Douglas Aviation
	G-ANTE	DH.82A Tiger Moth (T6562)	I. L. Cheese
	G-ANTK	Avro 685 York ★	Duxford Aviation Society
	G-ANUO	DH.114 Heron 2D (G-AOXL) ★	Westmead Business Group/Croydon Airport
	G-ANUW	DH.104 Dove 6 ★	Jet Aviation Preservation Group
	G-ANVY	P.31 Proctor 4	J. W. Tregilgas
	G-ANWB	DHC.1 Chipmunk 21	G. Briggs
	G-ANXB	DH.114 Heron 1B ★	Newark Air Museum
	G-ANXC	Auster J/5R Alpine	Alpine Group
	G-ANXR	P.31C Proctor 4 (RM221)	N. H. T. Cottrell
	G-ANZT	Thruxton Jackaroo (T7798)	D. J. Neville & P. A. Dear
	G-ANZU	DH.82A Tiger Moth	M. I. Lodge
	G-ANZZ	DH.82A Tiger Moth (DE974)	T. K. Butcher
	G-AOAA	DH.82A Tiger Moth	R. C. P. Brookhouse
	G-AOBG	Somers-Kendall SK.1	P. W. Bishop
	G-AOBH	DH.82A Tiger Moth (NL750)	P. Nutley
	G-AOBJ	DH.82A Tiger Moth	A. D. Hodgkinson
	G-AOBU	P.84 Jet Provost T.1 (XD693)	T. J. Manna
	G-AOBX	DH.82A Tiger Moth	David Ross Flying Group
	G-AOCP	Auster 5 ★	C. J. Baker (stored)
	G-AOCR	Auster 5D (NJ673)	D. A. Hill
	G-AOCU	Auster 5	S. J. Ball
	G-AODA	Westland S-55 Srs 3 ★	IHM/Weston-super-Mare
	G-AODR	DH.82A Tiger Moth	G-AODR Group (G-ISIS)
	G-AODT	DH.82A Tiger Moth (R5250)	R. A. Harrowven
	G-AOEH	Aeronca 7AC Champion	A. Gregori
	G-AOEI	DH.82A Tiger Moth	C.F.G. Flying Ltd
	G-AOEL	DH.82A Tiger Moth ★	Museum of Flight/East Fortune
	G-AOES	DH.82A Tiger Moth	P. D. & S. E. Ford
	G-AOET	DH.82A Tiger Moth	P. H. Meeson
	G-AOEX	Thruxton Jackaroo	A. T. Christian
	G-AOFE	DHC.1 Chipmunk 22A (WB702)	W. J. Quinn
	G-AOFS	Auster J/5L Aiglet Trainer	P. N. A. Whitehead
	G-AOGA	M.75 Aries ★	Irish Aviation Museum (stored)
	G-AOGI	DH.82A Tiger Moth	W. J. Taylor
	G-AOGR	DH.82A Tiger Moth (XL714)	R. J. S. G. Clark
	G-AOGV	Auster J/5R Alpine	R. E. Heading
	G-AOHY	DH.82A Tiger Moth (N6537)	S. W. Turley
	G-AOHZ	Auster J/5P Autocar	A. J. Kay & R. W. Eaton
	G-AOIM	DH.82A Tiger Moth	R. C. P. Brookhouse
	G-AOIR	Thruxton Jackaroo	K. M. Perkins
	G-AOIS	DH.82A Tiger Moth (R5172)	R. J. Moore & B. S. Floodgate
	G-AOJH	DH.83C Fox Moth	Connect Properties Ltd
	G-AOJJ	DH.82A Tiger Moth (DF128)	JJ Flying Group
	G-AOJK	DH.82A Tiger Moth	P. L. Green
	G-AOJR	DHC.1 Chipmunk 22	G. J-H. Caubergs & N. Marien/Belgium

Reg	Type	Owner or Operator	Notes
G-AOJT	DH.106 Comet 1 (F-BGNX) ★	de Havilland Heritage Museum (fuselage only)	
G-AOKH	P.40 Prentice 1	J. F. Moore	
G-AOKL	P.40 Prentice 1 (VS610)	N. J. Butler	
G-AOKO	P.40 Prentice 1 ★	Aero Venture	
G-AOKZ	P.40 Prentice 1 (VS623) ★	Midland Air Museum/Coventry	
G-AOLK	P.40 Prentice 1 ★	RAF Museum	
G-AOLU	P.40 Prentice 1 (VS356)	N. J. Butler	
G-AORG	DH.114 Heron 2	Duchess of Brittany (Jersey) Ltd	
G-AORW	DHC.1 Chipmunk 22A	S. Maric	
G-AOSK	DHC.1 Chipmunk 22 (WB726)	P. McMillan	
G-AOSY	DHC.1 Chipmunk 22 (WB585:M)	Chippy Sierra Yankee Group	
G-AOTD	DHC.1 Chipmunk 22 (WB588)	S. Piech	
G-AOTF	DHC.1 Chipmunk 23 (Lycoming)	A. C. Darby	
G-AOTI	DH.114 Heron 2D ★	de Havilland Heritage Museum/London Colney	
G-AOTK	D.53 Turbi	J. S. & P. R. Johnson	
G-AOTR	DHC.1 Chipmunk 22	S. J. Sykes	
G-AOTY	DHC.1 Chipmunk 22A (WG472)	Retro Track & Air (UK) Ltd	
G-AOUJ	Fairey Ultra-Light ★	IHM/Weston-super-Mare	
G-AOUO	DHC.1 Chipmunk 22 (Lycoming)	The Royal Air Force Gliding & Soaring Association	
G-AOUP	DHC.1 Chipmunk 22	A. R. Harding	
G-AOUR	DH.82A Tiger Moth ★	Ulster Folk & Transport Museum	
G-AOVF	B.175 Britannia 312F ★	Aerospace Museum/Cosford	
G-AOVS	B.175 Britannia 312F ★	Airport Fire Section/Luton	
G-AOVT	B.175 Britannia 312F ★	Duxford Aviation Society	
G-AOVW	Auster 5	B. Marriott	
G-AOXN	DH.82A Tiger Moth	S. L. G. Darch	
G-AOZH	DH.82A Tiger Moth (K2572)	M. H. Blois-Brooke	
G-AOZL	Auster J/5Q Alpine	R. M. Weeks	
G-AOZP	DHC.1 Chipmunk 22	S. J. Davies	
G-APAF	Auster 5 (TW511)	J. J. J. Mostyn (G-CMAL)	
G-APAH	Auster 5	T. J. Goodwin	
G-APAJ	Thruxton Jackaroo	A. J. Perry	
G-APAL	DH.82A Tiger Moth (N6847)	P. J. Shotbolt	
G-APAM	DH.82A Tiger Moth	R. P. Williams	
G-APAO	DH.82A Tiger Moth (R4922)	H. J. Maguire	
G-APAP	DH.82A Tiger Moth (R5136)	S. E. Ford	
G-APAS	DH.106 Comet 1XB ★	Aerospace Museum/Cosford	
G-APBE	Auster 5	E. G. & G. R. Woods	
G-APBI	DH.82A Tiger Moth	C. J. Zeal	
G-APBO	D.53 Turbi	R. C. Hibberd	
G-APBW	Auster 5	N. Huxtable	
G-APCB	Auster J/5Q Alpine	A. A. Beswick	
G-APCC	DH.82A Tiger Moth	L. J. Rice/Henstridge	
G-APDB	DH.106 Comet 4 ★	Duxford Aviation Society	
G-APEP	V.953C Merchantman ★	Brooklands Museum of Aviation/Weybridge	
G-APFA	D.54 Turbi	F. J. Keitch	
G-APFJ	Boeing 707-436 ★	Museum of Flight/East Fortune	
G-APFU	DH.82A Tiger Moth	C. L. Griffiths	
G-APFV	PA-23-160 Apache	J. L. Thorogood (G-MOLY)	
G-APHV	Avro 19 Srs 2 (VM360) ★	Museum of Flight/East Fortune	
G-APIE	Tipsy Belfair B	D. Beale	
G-APIH	DH.82A Tiger Moth	K. Stewering	
G-APIK	Auster J/1N Alpha	Deadwood Flying Group	
G-APIM	V.806 Viscount ★	Brooklands Museum of Aviation/Weybridge	
G-APIT	P.40 Prentice 1 (VR192) ★	WWII Aircraft Preservation Society/Lasham	
G-APIY	P.40 Prentice 1 (VR249) ★	Newark Air Museum	
G-APIZ	D.31 Turbulent	R. G. Meredith	
G-APJB	P.40 Prentice 1 (VR259)	K. M. Perkins	
G-APJJ	Fairey Ultra-light ★	Midland Aircraft Preservation Society	
G-APJZ	Auster J/1N Alpha	P. G. Lipman	
G-APLG	Auster J/5L Aiglet Trainer ★	Solway Aviation Society	
G-APLO	DHC.1 Chipmunk 22A (WD379)	P. M. Luijken/Netherlands	
G-APLU	DH.82A Tiger Moth	M. E. Vaisey	
G-APMB	DH.106 Comet 4B ★	Gatwick Handling Ltd (ground trainer)	
G-APMH	Auster J/1U Workmaster	M. R. P. Thorogood	
G-APMX	DH.82A Tiger Moth	Foley Farm Flying Group	
G-APMY	PA-23 Apache 160 ★	Aero Venture	
G-APNJ	Cessna 310 ★	Chelsea College/Shoreham	

Notes	Reg	Type	Owner or Operator
	G-APNT	Currie Wot	B. J. Dunford
	G-APNZ	D.31 Turbulent	Turbulent G-APNZ Preservation Society
	G-APPA	DHC.1 Chipmunk 22	M. B.Phillips
	G-APPL	P.40 Prentice 1	S. J. Saggers
	G-APPM	DHC.1 Chipmunk 22 (WB711)	E. H. W. Moore
	G-APRL	AW.650 Argosy 101 ★	Midland Air Museum/Coventry
	G-APRO	Auster 6A	A. F. & H. Wankowski
	G-APRT	Taylor JT.1 Monoplane ★	Newark Air Museum
	G-APSA	Douglas DC-6A	G-APSA Ltd
	G-APSR	Auster J/1U Workmaster	D. & K. Aero Services Ltd
	G-APTR	Auster J/1N Alpha	C. R. Shipley
	G-APTU	Auster 5	G-APTU Flying Group
	G-APTW	Westland WS-51/2 Widgeon ★	North East Aircraft Museum/Usworth
	G-APTY	Beech G.35 Bonanza	G. E. Brennand
	G-APTZ	D.31 Turbulent	J. T. Britcher
	G-APUD	Bensen B.7M (modified) ★	Manchester Museum of Science & Industry
	G-APUE	L.40 Meta Sokol	D. F. P. Finan & P. W. Carlton
	G-APUP	Sopwith Pup (replica) (N5182) ★	RAF Museum/Hendon
	G-APUR	PA-22 Tri-Pacer 160	S. T. A. Hutchinson
	G-APUW	Auster J/5V-160 Autocar	E. S. E. & P. B. Hibbard
	G-APUY	D.31 Turbulent	C. Jones
	G-APVG	Auster J/5L Aiglet Trainer	R. E. Tyers
	G-APVN	D.31 Turbulent	R. Sherwin
	G-APVS	Cessna 170B	N. Simpson Stormin' Norman
	G-APVT	DH.82A Tiger Moth	M. C. Boddington
	G-APVU	L.40 Meta Sokol	S. E. & M. J. Aherne
	G-APVZ	D.31 Turbulent	The Tiger Club (1990) Ltd
	G-APWA	HPR.7 Herald 101 ★	Museum of Berkshire Aviation/Woodley
	G-APWJ	HPR.7 Herald 201 ★	Duxford Aviation Society
	G-APWN	Westland WS-55 Whirlwind 3 ★	Midland Air Museum/Coventry
	G-APWY	Piaggio P.166 ★	Science Museum/Wroughton
	G-APXJ	PA-24 Comanche 250	T. Wildsmith
	G-APXR	PA-22 Tri-Pacer 160	A. Troughton
	G-APXT	PA-22 Tri-Pacer 150 (modified)	A. D. A. Smith
	G-APXU	PA-22 Tri-Pacer 125 (modified)	C. J. Cauwood
	G-APXW	EP.9 Prospector (XM819) ★	Museum of Army Flying/Middle Wallop
	G-APXX	DHA.3 Drover 2 (VH-FDT) ★	WWII Aircraft Preservation Society/Lasham
	G-APYB	Tipsy T.66 Nipper 3	B. O. Smith
	G-APYD	DH.106 Comet 4B ★	Science Museum/Wroughton
	G-APYG	DHC.1 Chipmunk 22	P. A. & J. M. Doyle
	G-APYT	Champion 7FC Tri-Traveller	N. F. O'Neill
	G-APZJ	PA-18 Super Cub 150	S. G. Jones
	G-APZL	PA-22 Tri-Pacer 160	B. Robins
	G-APZX	PA-22 Tri-Pacer 150	H. J. Taggart
	G-ARAD	Luton LA-5 Major ★	North East Aircraft Museum
	G-ARAM	PA-18 Super Cub 150	Skymax (Aviation) Ltd
	G-ARAN	PA-18 Super Cub 150	G-ARAN Group
	G-ARAP	Champion 7EC	J. J. McGonagle
	G-ARAS	Champion 7FC Tri-Traveller	Alpha Sierra Flying Group
	G-ARAW	Cessna 182C Skylane	R. L. McLean & A. J. Homes
	G-ARAX	PA-22-150 Tri-Pacer	C. W. Carnall
	G-ARAZ	DH.82A Tiger Moth (R4959:59)	D. A. Porter
	G-ARBE	DH.104 Dove 8	M. Whale & M. W. A. Lunn
	G-ARBG	Tipsy T.66 Nipper 2	D. Shrimpton
	G-ARBM	Auster V J1B Aiglet	A. D. Hodgkinson
	G-ARBS	PA-22 Tri-Pacer 160 (tailwheel)	S. D. Rowell
	G-ARBV	PA-22 Tri-Pacer 160	L. M. Williams
	G-ARBZ	D.31 Turbulent	J. T. Britcher
	G-ARCF	PA-22 Tri-Pacer 150	M. J. Speakman
	G-ARCS	Auster D6/180	L. I. Bailey
	G-ARCT	PA-18 Super Cub 95	P. Morgan
	G-ARCV	Cessna 175A	R. Francis & C. Campbell
	G-ARCW	PA-23 Apache 160	F. W. Ellis
	G-ARCX	A.W. Meteor 14 ★	Museum of Flight/East Fortune
	G-ARDB	PA-24 Comanche 250	P. Crook
	G-ARDD	CP.301C1 Emeraude	P. J. Huxley & D. Hurst
	G-ARDE	DH.104 Dove 6 ★	T. E. Evans
	G-ARDJ	Auster D.6/180	P. N. A. Whitehead
	G-ARDO	Jodel D.112	W. R. Prescott
	G-ARDS	PA-22 Caribbean 150	S. A. Rennison

Reg	Type	Owner or Operator	Notes
G-ARDY	Tipsy T.66 Nipper 2	J. K. Davies	
G-ARDZ	Jodel D.140A	M. Hales	
G-AREA	DH.104 Dove 8 ★	de Havilland Heritage Museum/London Colney	
G-AREH	DH.82A Tiger Moth	A. J. Hastings & A. Mustard	
G-AREI	Auster 3 (MT438)	R. B. Webber	
G-AREL	PA-22 Caribbean 150	The Caribbean Flying Club	
G-AREO	PA-18 Super Cub 150	E. P. Parkin	
G-ARET	PA-22 Tri-Pacer 160	L. A. Runnalls	
G-AREV	PA-22 Tri-Pacer 160	D. J. Ash	
G-AREX	Aeronca 15AC Sedan	R. J. M. Turnbull	
G-AREZ	D.31 Turbulent	R. E. Garforth	
G-ARFB	PA-22 Caribbean 150	G. Harvey	
G-ARFD	PA-22 Tri-Pacer 160	T. J. Alderdice	
G-ARFI	Cessna 150A	N. M. G. Pearson	
G-ARFO	Cessna 150A	P. M. Fawley	
G-ARFT	Jodel DR.1050	R. Shaw	
G-ARFV	Tipsy T.66 Nipper 2	J. J. Austin	
G-ARGO	PA-22 Colt 108	M. Magrabi	
G-ARGV	PA-18 Super Cub 180	Wolds Gliding Club Ltd	
G-ARGZ	D.31 Turbulent	The Tiger Club (1990) Ltd	
G-ARHB	Forney F-1A Aircoupe	R. E. Dagless	
G-ARHC	Forney F-1A Aircoupe	E. G. Girardey	
G-ARHL	PA-23 Aztec 250	C. J. Freeman	
G-ARHM	Auster 6A (VF557:H)	R. C. P. Brookhouse	
G-ARHR	PA-22 Caribbean 150	A. R. Wyatt	
G-ARHW	DH.104 Dove 8	Aviation Heritage Ltd	
G-ARHX	DH.104 Dove 8 ★	North East Aircraft Museum	
G-ARHZ	D.62 Condor	J. M. Minion & D. F. Evans	
G-ARID	Cessna 172B	Security & Intelligence Exploitation Ltd	
G-ARIF	Ord-Hume O-H.7 Minor Coupé ★	M. J. Aubrey	
G-ARIH	Auster 6A (TW591)	M. C. Jordan	
G-ARIK	PA-22 Caribbean 150	A. Taylor	
G-ARIL	PA-22 Caribbean 150	S. Eustathiou	
G-ARIM	D.31 Turbulent	S. R. P. Harper & J. C. Holland	
G-ARJB	DH.104 Dove 8	M. Whale & M. W. A. Lunn	
G-ARJH	PA-22 Colt 108	F. Vogels/France	
G-ARJR	PA-23 Apache 160G ★	Instructional airframe/Kidlington	
G-ARJS	PA-23 Apache 160G	Bencray Ltd	
G-ARJT	PA-23 Apache 160G	J. H. Ashcroft	
G-ARJU	PA-23 Apache 160G	F. W. & I. F. Ellis	
G-ARKD	CAC CA-18 Mk.22 Mustang P-51D	Classic Flying Machine Collection Ltd	
G-ARKG	Auster J/5G Autocar (A11-301/931)	A. G. Boon & C. L. Towell	
G-ARKJ	Beech N35 Bonanza	G. D. E. Macdonald	
G-ARKK	PA-22 Colt 108	R. D. Welfare	
G-ARKM	PA-22 Colt 108	O. T. Smith	
G-ARKP	PA-22 Colt 108	D. S. White & I. J. Mitchell	
G-ARKS	PA-22 Colt 108	A. J. Silvester	
G-ARLG	Auster D.4/108	Auster D4 Group	
G-ARLK	PA-24 Comanche 250	R. P. Jackson	
G-ARLP	Beagle A.61 Terrier 1	Gemini Flying Group	
G-ARLR	Beagle A.61 Terrier 2	M. Palfreman	
G-ARLU	Cessna 172B Skyhawk ★	Instructional airframe/Irish Air Corps	
G-ARLZ	D.31A Turbulent	A. D. Wilson	
G-ARMC	DHC.1 Chipmunk 22A (WB703)	John Henderson Children's Trust	
G-ARMF	DHC.1 Chipmunk 22A (WZ868:H)	M. Harvey	
G-ARMG	DHC.1 Chipmunk 22A (WK558:DH)	L. J. Irvine	
G-ARMN	Cessna 175B Skylark	Brimpton Aviation Group Ltd	
G-ARMO	Cessna 172B Skyhawk	R. D. Leigh	
G-ARMR	Cessna 172B Skyhawk	T. W. Gilbert	
G-ARMZ	D.31 Turbulent	The Tiger Club (1990) Ltd	
G-ARNB	Auster J/5G Autocar	R. F. Tolhurst	
G-ARNE	PA-22 Colt 108	The Shiny Colt Group	
G-ARNG	PA-22 Colt 108	F. B. Rothera	
G-ARNJ	PA-22 Colt 108	R. A. Keech	
G-ARNK	PA-22 Colt 108 (tailwheel)	S. J. Smith	
G-ARNL	PA-22 Colt 108	M. R. Harrison	
G-ARNO	Beagle A.61 Terrier 1 (VX113)	M. C. R. Wills	
G-ARNP	Beagle A.109 Airedale	S. W. & M. Isbister	
G-ARNY	Jodel D.117	G-ARNY Flying Group	
G-ARNZ	D.31 Turbulent	The Tiger Club (1990) Ltd	

Notes	Reg	Type	Owner or Operator
	G-AROA	Cessna 172B Skyhawk	Phoenix Flying Group
	G-AROC	Cessna 175B	A. J. Symes (G-OTOW)
	G-AROJ	Beagle A.109 Airedale ★	D. J. Shaw (stored)
	G-ARON	PA-22 Colt 108	Security & Intelligence Exploitation Ltd
	G-AROW	Jodel D.140B	A. R. Crome
	G-AROY	Boeing Stearman A75N.1	J. S. Mann
	G-ARPH	HS.121 Trident 1C ★	Museum of Flight/East Fortune
	G-ARPK	HS.121 Trident 1C ★	Manchester Airport Authority
	G-ARPO	HS.121 Trident 1C ★	CAA Fire School/Teesside
	G-ARRD	Jodel DR.1050	R. J. Arnold
	G-ARRE	Jodel DR.1050	R. Weininger
	G-ARRI	Cessna 175B	R. J. Bentley
	G-ARRL	Auster J/1N Alpha	A. C. Ladd
	G-ARRM	Beagle B.206-X ★	Bristol Aero Collection (stored)
	G-ARRO	Beagle A.109 Airedale	M. & S. W. Isbister
	G-ARRS	CP.301A Emeraude	J. F. Sully
	G-ARRU	D.31 Turbulent	D. G. Huck
	G-ARRX	Auster 6A (VF512)	J. E. D. Mackie
	G-ARRY	Jodel D.140B	C. Thomas
	G-ARRZ	D.31 Turbulent	T. A. Stambach
	G-ARSG	Roe Triplane Type IV (replica)	The Shuttleworth Collection/Old Warden
	G-ARTH	PA-12 Super Cruiser	G. R. Trotter
	G-ARTJ	Bensen B.8M ★	Museum of Flight/East Fortune
	G-ARTL	DH.82A Tiger Moth (T7281)	F. G. Clacherty
	G-ARTT	MS.880B Rallye Club	R. N. Scott
	G-ARTZ	McCandless M.4 gyroplane	W. R. Partridge
	G-ARUG	Auster J/5G Autocar	D. P. H. Hulme
	G-ARUI	Beagle A.61 Terrier	T. W. J. Dann
	G-ARUL	LeVier Cosmic Wind	P. G. Kynsey
	G-ARUY	Auster J/1N Alpha	D. K. Tregilgas
	G-ARVM	V.1101 VC10 ★	Brooklands Museum of Aviation/Weybridge
	G-ARVO	PA-18 Super Cub 95	M. P. & S. T. Barnard
	G-ARVT	PA-28 Cherokee 160	S. Hynd
	G-ARVU	PA-28 Cherokee 160	VU Flying Group
	G-ARVV	PA-28 Cherokee 160	G. E. Hopkins
	G-ARVZ	D.62B Condor	A. A. M. Huke
	G-ARWB	DHC.1 Chipmunk 22 (WK611)	Thruxton Chipmunk Flying Club
	G-ARWR	Cessna 172C	Devanha Flying Group
	G-ARWS	Cessna 175C	M. D. Fage
	G-ARXB	Beagle A.109 Airedale	S. W. & M. Isbister
	G-ARXD	Beagle A.109 Airedale	D. Howden
	G-ARXG	PA-24 Comanche 250	R. F. Corstin
	G-ARXH	Bell 47G	T. B. Searle
	G-ARXN	Tipsy Nipper T.66 Srs.2	J. F. Bakewell
	G-ARXP	Luton LA-4 Minor	R. M. Weeks
	G-ARXT	Jodel DR.1050	CJM Flying Group
	G-ARXU	Auster 6A (VF526)	S. D. & S. P. Allen
	G-ARYB	HS.125 Srs 1 ★	Midland Air Museum/Coventry
	G-ARYC	HS.125 Srs 1 ★	de Havilland Heritage Museum/London Colney
	G-ARYD	Auster AOP.6 (WJ358) ★	Museum of Army Flying/Middle Wallop
	G-ARYK	Cessna 172C	Full Sutton Flying Centre Ltd
	G-ARYR	PA-28 Cherokee 180	G-ARYR Flying Group
	G-ARYS	Cessna 172C	G-ARYS Group
	G-ARYV	PA-24 Comanche 250	D. C. Hanss
	G-ARZS	Beagle A.109 Airedale	M. & S. W. Isbister
	G-ARZW	Currie Wot	B. R. Pearson
	G-ASAA	Luton LA-4 Minor	M. J. Aubrey (stored)
	G-ASAI	Beagle A.109 Airedale	K. R. Howden
	G-ASAJ	Beagle A.61 Terrier 2 (WE569)	T. Bailey
	G-ASAL	SA Bulldog Srs 120/124	Pioneer Flying Co Ltd
	G-ASAU	MS.880B Rallye Club	Juliet Tango Group
	G-ASAX	Beagle A.61 Terrier 2	A. D. Hodgkinson
	G-ASAZ	Hiller UH-12E4 (XS165)	Hields Aviation/Sherburn
	G-ASBA	Phoenix Currie Wot	J. M. Lister
	G-ASBH	Beagle A.109 Airedale	D. T. Smollett
	G-ASCC	Beagle E3 Mk 11 (XP254)	R. Warner
	G-ASCD	Beagle A.61 Terrier 2 (TJ704) ★	Yorkshire Air Museum/Elvington
	G-ASCH	Beagle A.61 Terrier 2	G-ASCH Group
	G-ASCM	Isaacs Fury II (K2050)	R. F. Redknap
	G-ASCZ	CP.301A Emeraude	I. Denham-Brown

Reg	Type	Owner or Operator	Notes
G-ASDF	Edwards Gyrocopter ★	B. King	
G-ASDK	Beagle A.61 Terrier 2	J. Swallow (G-ARLM)	
G-ASEA	Luton LA-4A Minor	B. W. Faulkner	
G-ASEB	Luton LA-4A Minor	S. R. P. Harper	
G-ASEO	PA-24 Comanche 250	M. Scott	
G-ASEP	PA-23 Apache 235	J. R. & R. J. Sharpe	
G-ASEU	D.62A Condor	R. A. S. Sutherland	
G-ASFA	Cessna 172D	D. Austin	
G-ASFD	L-200A Morava	M. Emery	
G-ASFL	PA-28 Cherokee 180	G-ASFL Group	
G-ASFR	Bölkow Bö.208A1 Junior	S. T. Dauncey	
G-ASFX	D.31 Turbulent	E. F. Clapham & W. B. S. Dobie	
G-ASGC	V.1151 Super VC10 ★	Duxford Aviation Society	
G-ASHD	Brantly B.2A ★	IHM/Weston-super-Mare	
G-ASHS	SNCAN Stampe SV.4C	J. W. Beaty	
G-ASHT	D.31 Turbulent	C. W. N. Huke	
G-ASHU	PA-15 Vagabond (modified)	The Calybe Flying Group	
G-ASHX	PA-28 Cherokee 180	Powertheme Ltd	
G-ASII	PA-28 Cherokee 180	T. N. & T. R. Hart & R. W. S. Matthews	
G-ASIJ	PA-28 Cherokee 180	A. Wilson	
G-ASIL	PA-28 Cherokee 180	M. J. Pink	
G-ASIS	Jodel D.112	W. R. Prescott	
G-ASIT	Cessna 180	W. J. D. Tollett	
G-ASIY	PA-25 Pawnee 235	Kent Gliding Club Ltd	
G-ASJL	Beech H.35 Bonanza	R. L. Dargue	
G-ASJV	VS.361 Spitfire IX (MH434/PK-K)	Merlin Aviation Ltd	
G-ASJZ	Jodel D.117A	M. A. Watts	
G-ASKC	DH.98 Mosquito 35 (TA719) ★	Skyfame Collection/Duxford	
G-ASKK	HPR.7 Herald 211 ★	Norwich Aviation Museum	
G-ASKL	Jodel D.150	J. M. Graty	
G-ASKP	DH.82A Tiger Moth	Tiger Club (1990) Ltd	
G-ASKT	PA-28 Cherokee 180	T. J. Herbert	
G-ASLV	PA-28 Cherokee 235	S. W. Goodswen	
G-ASMA	PA-30 Twin Comanche 160 C/R	K. Cooper	
G-ASMJ	Cessna F.172E	Aeroscene Ltd	
G-ASML	Luton LA-4A Minor	O. D. Lewis	
G-ASMM	D.31 Tubulent	K. J. Butler	
G-ASMS	Cessna 150A	M. & W. Long	
G-ASMT	Fairtravel Linnet 2	P. Harrison	
G-ASMV	CP.1310-C3 Super Emeraude	D. G. Hammersley	
G-ASMW	Cessna 150D	Dukeries Aviation	
G-ASMY	PA-23 Apache 160 ★	R. D. Forster	
G-ASMZ	Beagle A.61 Terrier 2 (VF516)	Folland Aircraft Ltd	
G-ASNC	Beagle D.5/180 Husky	Peterborough & Spalding Gliding Club Ltd	
G-ASNI	CP.1310-C3 Super Emeraude	Douglas Electronics Industries Ltd	
G-ASNK	Cessna 205	Justgold Ltd	
G-ASNW	Cessna F.172E	G-ASNW Group	
G-ASNY	Campbell-Bensen B.8M gyroplane ★	R. Light & T. Smith	
G-ASOH	Beech 95-B55A Baron	G. Davis & C. Middlemiss	
G-ASOI	Beagle A.61 Terrier 2 (WJ404)	G.D.B. Delmege	
G-ASOK	Cessna F.172E	D. W. Disney	
G-ASOL	Bell 47D ★	North East Aircraft Museum	
G-ASOM	Beagle A.61 Terrier 2	GASOM.org (G-JETS)	
G-ASPF	Jodel D.120	G. W. Street	
G-ASPP	Bristol Boxkite (replica)	The Shuttleworth Collection/Old Warden	
G-ASPS	Piper J-3C-90 Cub	S. Slater	
G-ASPV	DH.82A Tiger Moth (T7794)	R. K. A. Menage	
G-ASRC	D.62C Condor	J. R. Kimberley	
G-ASRK	Beagle A.109 Airedale	M. Wilson	
G-ASRO	PA-30 Twin Comanche 160	D. W. Blake	
G-ASRT	Jodel 150	P. Turton	
G-ASRW	PA-28 Cherokee 180	G. N. Smith	
G-ASSM	HS.125 Srs 1/522 ★	Science Museum/South Kensington	
G-ASSP	PA-30 Twin Comanche 160	P. H. Tavener	
G-ASSS	Cessna 172E	P. R. March & P. Turner	
G-ASST	Cessna 150D	F. R. H. Parker	
G-ASSV	Kensinger KF	C. I. Jefferson	
G-ASSW	PA-28 Cherokee 140	E. R. Curry	
G-ASSY	D.31 Turbulent	C. M. Bracewell	
G-ASTG	Nord 1002 Pingouin II (BG + KM)	R. J. Fray	
G-ASTI	Auster 6A	S. J. Partridge	

Notes	Reg	Type	Owner or Operator
	G-ASTL	Fairey Firefly I (Z2033) ★	F. A. A. Museum/Yeovilton
	G-ASTP	Hiller UH-12C ★	IHM/Weston-super-Mare
	G-ASUB	Mooney M.20E Super 21	S. C. Coulbeck
	G-ASUD	PA-28 Cherokee 180	G-ASUD Group
	G-ASUE	Cessna 150D	D. Huckle
	G-ASUG	Beech E18S ★	Museum of Flight/East Fortune
	G-ASUP	Cessna F.172E	S. A. Williams
	G-ASUS	Jurca MJ.2B Tempete	M. P. Grimshaw
	G-ASVG	CP.301B Emeraude	R. B. McKenzie
	G-ASVM	Cessna F.172E	M. Tobutt
	G-ASVO	HPR.7 Herald 214 ★	Archive Visitor Centre/Shoreham (cockpit section)
	G-ASVZ	PA-28 Cherokee 140	Scillonian Marine Consultants Ltd
	G-ASWJ	Beagle 206 Srs 1 (8449M) ★	Brunel Technical College/Bristol
	G-ASWN	Bensen B.8M	D. R. Shepherd
	G-ASWX	PA-28 Cherokee 180	Gasworks Flying Group Ltd
	G-ASXC	SIPA 903	T. M. Buick (G-DWEL)
	G-ASXD	Brantly B.2B	G-ASXD Group
	G-ASXS	Jodel DR.1050	C. P. Wilkinson
	G-ASXU	Jodel D.120A	G-ASXU Group
	G-ASXX	Avro 683 Lancaster 7 (NX611) ★	Panton Family Trust/East Kirkby
	G-ASYD	BAC One-Eleven 475 ★	Brooklands Museum of Aviation/Weybridge
	G-ASYG	Beagle A.61 Terrier 2 (VX927)	D. & R. L. McDonald
	G-ASYJ	Beech D.95A Travel Air	Crosby Aviation (Jersey) Ltd
	G-ASYP	Cessna 150E	Henlow Flying Group
	G-ASZB	Cessna 150E	Akki Aviation Services Ltd
	G-ASZD	Bölkow Bö.208A2 Junior	D. Allen
	G-ASZE	Beagle A.61 Terrier 2	Historische Flugzeuge/Germany
	G-ASZR	Fairtravel Linnet 2	R. Hodgson
	G-ASZU	Cessna 150E	L. J. Baker & C. Davies
	G-ASZV	Tipsy T.66 Nipper 2	A. M. E. Vervaeke/Belgium
	G-ASZX	Beagle A.61 Terrier 1 (WJ368)	R. B. Webber
	G-ATAG	Jodel DR.1050	T. M. Gamble
	G-ATAS	PA-28 Cherokee 180	G-ATAS Group
	G-ATAU	D.62B Condor	M. C. Burlock
	G-ATAV	D.62C Condor	C. D. Swift
	G-ATBG	Nord 1002 (NJ+C11)	Ardmore Aviation Service
	G-ATBH	Aero 145	P. D. Aberbach
	G-ATBJ	Sikorsky S-61N	British International
	G-ATBL	DH.60G Moth	Comanche Warbirds Ltd
	G-ATBP	Fournier RF-3	D. McNicholl
	G-ATBS	D.31 Turbulent	C. J. L. Wolf
	G-ATBU	Beagle A.61 Terrier 2	T. Jarvis
	G-ATBX	PA-20 Pacer 135	G. D. & P. M. Thomson
	G-ATBZ	Westland WS-58 Wessex 60 ★	IHM/Weston-super-Mare
	G-ATCC	Beagle A.109 Airedale	North East Flight Training Ltd
	G-ATCD	Beagle D.5/180 Husky	T. C. O'Gorman
	G-ATCE	Cessna U.206	Fly High Icarius
	G-ATCJ	Luton LA-4A Minor	A. R. Hutton
	G-ATCL	Victa Airtourer 100	A. D. Goodall
	G-ATCN	Luton LA-4A Minor	The Real Aeroplane Co.Ltd
	G-ATCX	Cessna 182H	K. Sheppard
	G-ATDA	PA-28 Cherokee 160	Aviate Ltd
	G-ATDN	Beagle A.61 Terrier 2 (TW641)	S. J. Saggers
	G-ATDO	Bölkow Bö.208C1 Junior	P. Thompson
	G-ATEF	Cessna 150E	Swans Aviation
	G-ATEM	PA-28 Cherokee 180	G. D. Wyles
	G-ATEP	EAA Biplane ★	E. L. Martin (red)/Guernsey
	G-ATEV	Jodel DR.1050	J. C. Carter & J. L. Altrip
	G-ATEW	PA-30 Twin Comanche 160	J. M. Charlton
	G-ATEX	Victor Airtourer 100	S. Turner
	G-ATEZ	PA-28 Cherokee 140	EFI Aviation Ltd
	G-ATFD	Jodel DR.1050	K. D. Hills
	G-ATFG	Brantly B.2B ★	Museum of Flight/East Fortune
	G-ATFM	Sikorsky S-61N	British International Helicopter Services Ltd
	G-ATFR	PA-25 Pawnee 150	Borders (Milfield) Gliding Club Ltd
	G-ATFV	Agusta-Bell 47J-2A ★	Caernarfon Air World
	G-ATFY	Cessna F.172G	J. M. Vinall
	G-ATGN	Thorn Coal Gas Balloon	British Balloon Museum/Newbury
	G-ATGP	Jodel DR.1050	Madley Flying Group

Reg	Type	Owner or Operator	Notes
G-ATGY	Gardan GY-80 Horizon	D. H. Mackay	
G-ATHA	PA-23 Apache 235 ★	Brunel Technical College/Bristol	
G-ATHD	DHC.1 Chipmunk 22 (WP971)	Spartan Flying Group Ltd	
G-ATHK	Aeronca 7AC Champion	T. C. Barron	
G-ATHN	Nord 1101 Noralpha ★	E. L. Martin (stored)/Guernsey	
G-ATHR	PA-28 Cherokee 180	Azure Flying Club Ltd	
G-ATHT	Victa Airtourer 115	Cotswold Flying Group	
G-ATHU	Beagle A.61 Terrier 1	J. A. L. Irwin	
G-ATHV	Cessna 150F	S. Doyle & R. C. Benyon	
G-ATHZ	Cessna 150F	R. D. Forster	
G-ATIC	Jodel DR.1050	T. A. Major	
G-ATIG	HPR.7 Herald 214 ★	Norwich Airport towing trainer	
G-ATIN	Jodel D.117	C. E. C. & C. M. Hives	
G-ATIR	AIA Stampe SV.4C	A. Trueman	
G-ATIS	PA-28 Cherokee 160	D. Matthews	
G-ATIZ	Jodel D.117	R. A. Smith	
G-ATJA	Jodel DR.1050	Bicester Flying Group	
G-ATJC	Victa Airtourer 100 (modfied)	Aviation West Ltd	
G-ATJG	PA-28 Cherokee 140	D. & J. Albon	
G-ATJL	PA-24 Comanche 260	S. J. Ollier	
G-ATJN	Jodel D.119	Real Hart Flying Group	
G-ATJV	PA-32 Cherokee Six 260	Wingglider Ltd	
G-ATKH	Luton LA-4A Minor	H. E. Jenner	
G-ATKI	Piper J-3C-65 Cub	M. A. Sims	
G-ATKT	Cessna F.172G	R. J. D. Blois	
G-ATKX	Jodel D.140C	Kilo Xray Syndicate	
G-ATLA	Cessna 182J Skylane	J. W. & J. T. Whicher	
G-ATLB	Jodel DR.1050/M1	Le Syndicate du Petit Oiseau	
G-ATLM	Cessna F.172G	N. A. Baxter	
G-ATLP	Bensen B.8M	R. F. G. Moyle	
G-ATLT	Cessna U.206A	Skydive Jersey Ltd	
G-ATLV	Jodel D.120	H. T. & I. A. Robinson	
G-ATMC	Cessna F.150F	M. Biddulph	
G-ATMH	Beagle D.5/180 Husky	J. L. Thorogood	
G-ATMM	Cessna F.150F	Cranfield Aviation Training School	
G-ATNB	PA-28-180 Cherokee	C. K. Delgahawattegedara	
G-ATNE	Cessna F.150F	Cirrus Aircraft UK Ltd & T. & T. Wright	
G-ATNL	Cessna F.150F	Wicklow Wings	
G-ATNV	PA-24-260 Comanche	K. Powell	
G-ATOH	D.62B Condor	Three Spires Flying Group	
G-ATOI	PA-28-140 Cherokee	Rayham Ltd	
G-ATOJ	PA-28-140 Cherokee	British North West Airlines Ltd	
G-ATOK	PA-28-140 Cherokee	ILC Flying Group	
G-ATON	PA-28-140 Cherokee	Stirling Flying Syndicate	
G-ATOO	PA-28-140 Cherokee	Caralair Aviation	
G-ATOP	PA-28-140 Cherokee	P. R. Coombs	
G-ATOR	PA-28-140 Cherokee	Simon Tilling Ltd	
G-ATOT	PA-28-180 Cherokee	Sirius Aviation Ltd	
G-ATOU	Mooney M.20E Super 21	DbProf Doo	
G-ATOY	PA-24 Comanche 260 ★	Museum of Flight/East Fortune	
G-ATPN	PA-28-140 Cherokee	G-ATPN Group	
G-ATPT	Cessna 182J Skylane	C. Beer t/a Papa Tango Group	
G-ATPV	JB.01 Minicab	P. T. Stephenson	
G-ATRG	PA-18 Super Cub 150	Dorset Gliding Club Ltd	
G-ATRK	Cessna F.150F	Falcon Aviation Ltd	
G-ATRL	Cessna F.150F	A. A. W. Stevens	
G-ATRM	Cessna F.150F	K. M. Rigby	
G-ATRW	PA-32-260 Cherokee Six	Pringle Brandon Architects	
G-ATRX	PA-32-260 Cherokee Six	S. P. Vincent	
G-ATSI	Bölkow Bö.208C1 Junior	GATSI Bolkow Ltd	
G-ATSL	Cessna F.172G	Aircraft Engineers Ltd	
G-ATSR	Beech M.35 Bonanza	V. S. E. Norman	
G-ATSZ	PA-30 Twin Comanche 160B	Sierra Zulu Aviation Ltd	
G-ATTB	Wallis WA-116-1 (XR944)	Aerial Media Ltd	
G-ATTI	PA-28 Cherokee 140	A. J. Tobias	
G-ATTK	PA-28 Cherokee 140	G-ATTK Flying Group	
G-ATTN	Piccard HA Balloon ★	Science Museum/South Kensington	
G-ATTR	Bölkow Bö.208C1 Junior	S. Luck	
G-ATTV	PA-28 Cherokee 140	G-ATTV Group	
G-ATTX	PA-28 Cherokee 180	G-ATTX Flying Group	
G-ATUB	PA-28 Cherokee 140	Wicklow Wings	

Notes	Reg	Type	Owner or Operator
	G-ATUF	Cessna F.150F	I. Burnett
	G-ATUG	D.62B Condor	B. L. R. J. Keeping
	G-ATUH	Tipsy T.66 Nipper 1	H. Abraham
	G-ATUI	Bölkow Bö.208C1 Junior	G. J. Ball
	G-ATUL	PA-28 Cherokee 180	Barry Fielding Aviation Ltd
	G-ATVF	DHC.1 Chipmunk 22 (WD327)	ATVF Syndicate
	G-ATVK	PA-28 Cherokee 140	J. Turner
	G-ATVO	PA-28 Cherokee 140	Perryair Ltd
	G-ATVP	Vickers FB.5 Gunbus replica (2345) ★	RAF Museum/Hendon
	G-ATVS	PA-28 Cherokee 180	D. S. Olson
	G-ATVW	D.62B Condor	A. G. & B. N. Stevens
	G-ATVX	Bölkow Bö.208C1 Junior	A. M. Witt
	G-ATWA	Jodel DR.1050	One Twenty Group
	G-ATWB	Jodel D.117	Andrewsfield Whisky Bravo Group
	G-ATWJ	Cessna F.172F	J. P. A. Freeman
	G-ATXA	PA-22 Tri-Pacer 150	I. C. Mills
	G-ATXD	PA-30 Twin Comanche 160B	M. Bagshaw
	G-ATXJ	HP.137 Jetstream 300 ★	Fire Service training airframe/Cardiff
	G-ATXN	Mitchell-Proctor Kittiwake 1	R. G. Day
	G-ATXO	SIPA 903	C. H. Morris
	G-ATXX	McCandless M.4 gyroplane ★	Ulster Folk & Transport Museum
	G-ATXZ	Bölkow Bö.208C1 Junior	M. J. Beardmore
	G-ATYM	Cessna F.150G	Gym Group
	G-ATYN	Cessna F.150G	J. S. Grant
	G-ATYS	PA-28 Cherokee 180	Cherokee Challenge Syndicate
	G-ATZM	Piper J-3C-90 Cub	N. D. Marshall
	G-ATZS	Wassmer Wa.41 Super Baladou IV	I. R. Siddell
	G-ATZZ	Cessna F.150G	L. Prince & A. Meacham (G-DENB)
	G-AVAV	VS Spitfire IXT (MJ772)	Warbird Experiences Ltd
	G-AVAW	D.62B Condor	Condor Aircraft Group
	G-AVBG	PA-28 Cherokee 180	M. C. Plomer-Roberts
	G-AVBH	PA-28 Cherokee 180	Tenterfield (Holdings) Ltd
	G-AVBS	PA-28 Cherokee 180	Bravo Sierra Flying Group
	G-AVBT	PA-28 Cherokee 180	W. T. D. Gillam
	G-AVCM	PA-24 Comanche 260	R. F. Smith
	G-AVCN	BN-26A-8 Islander ★	Britten-Norman Aircraft Preservation Society
	G-AVCV	Cessna 182J Skylane	R. J. Hendry
	G-AVDA	Cessna 182K Skylane	F. W. & I. F. Ellis
	G-AVDF	Beagle B.121 Pup 1	D. I. Collings
	G-AVDS	Beech 65-B80 Queen Air ★	Airport Fire Service/Filton
	G-AVDT	Aeronca 7AC Champion	D. & N. Cheney
	G-AVDV	PA-22-150 Tri-Pacer	L. Beardmore & R. W. Taberner
	G-AVEF	Jodel 150	C. E. Bellhouse
	G-AVEH	SIAI-Marchetti S.205	S. W. Brown
	G-AVEM	Cessna F.150G	N. J. A. Rutherford
	G-AVEN	Cessna F.150G	J. M. Hough
	G-AVEO	Cessna F.150G	G-AVEO Flying Group (G-DENA)
	G-AVER	Cessna F.150G	LAC Flying School
	G-AVEU	Wassmer Wa.41 Baladou IV	The Baladou Flying Group
	G-AVEX	D.62B Condor	R. Manning
	G-AVEY	Currie Super Wot	F. R. Donaldson
	G-AVEZ	HPR.7 Herald 210 ★	Rescue trainer/Norwich
	G-AVFB	HS.121 Trident 2E ★	Duxford Aviation Society
	G-AVFE	HS.121 Trident 2E ★	Belfast Airport Authority
	G-AVFH	HS.121 Trident 2E ★	de Havilland Heritage Museum (fuselage only)/ London Colney
	G-AVFM	HS.121 Trident 2E ★	Brunel Technical College/Bristol
	G-AVFR	PA-28 Cherokee 140	C. Holden & S. Powell
	G-AVFU	PA-32 Cherokee Six 300	Tertium Treuboden Immobilien GmbH/Germany
	G-AVFX	PA-28 Cherokee 140	A. E. Fielding
	G-AVFZ	PA-28 Cherokee 140	G-AVFZ Flying Group
	G-AVGA	PA-24 Comanche 260	G. McD. Moir
	G-AVGC	PA-28 Cherokee 140	L. McIlwain
	G-AVGE	PA-28 Cherokee 140	P. Ruderham & D. Marrani
	G-AVGJ	Jodel DR.1050	I. B. Melville
	G-AVGZ	Jodel DR.1050	A. F. & S. Williams
	G-AVHH	Cessna F.172	Alpha Victor Ltd
	G-AVHL	Jodel DR.105A	Seething Jodel Group
	G-AVHM	Cessna F.150G	R. D. Forster
	G-AVHY	Fournier RF.4D	I. G. K. Mitchell

Reg	Type	Owner or Operator	Notes
G-AVIA	Cessna F.150G	American Airplane Breakers	
G-AVIB	Cessna F.150G	K. W. Wood	
G-AVIC	Cessna F.172★	Leeside Flying Ltd	
G-AVIL	Alon A.2 Aircoupe (VX147)	G. D. J. Wilson	
G-AVIN	MS.880B Rallye Club	R. A. C. Stephens	
G-AVIP	Brantly B.2B	Eaglescott Brantly Group	
G-AVIS	Cessna F.172 ★	J. P. A. Freeman	
G-AVIT	Cessna F.150G	P. Cottrell	
G-AVJF	Cessna F.172H	J. A. & D. T. A. Rees	
G-AVJJ	PA-30 Twin Comanche 160B	A. H. Manser	
G-AVJK	Jodel DR.1050/M1	Juliet Kilo Syndicate	
G-AVJO	Fokker E.III (replica) (422/15)	Flying Aces Movie Aircraft Collection	
G-AVKB	Brochet MB.50 Pipistrelle	R. E. Garforth	
G-AVKD	Fournier RF-4D	Lasham RF4 Group	
G-AVKE	Gadfly HDW.1 ★	IHM/Weston-super-Mare	
G-AVKG	Cessna F.172H	A. J. Austen	
G-AVKI	Slingsby T.66 Nipper 3	T. C. R. Trudgill	
G-AVKK	Slingsby T.66 Nipper 3	C. Watson	
G-AVKP	Beagle A.109 Airedale	D. R. Williams	
G-AVKR	Bölkow Bö.208C1 Junior	L. Hawkins	
G-AVLB	PA-28 Cherokee 140	M. Wilson	
G-AVLC	PA-28 Cherokee 140	P. G. Evans & R. G. Allgood	
G-AVLD	PA-28 Cherokee 140	Flight and Media Enterprises Ltd	
G-AVLE	PA-28 Cherokee 140	G. E. Wright	
G-AVLF	PA-28 Cherokee 140	Woodbine Group	
G-AVLG	PA-28 Cherokee 140	R. J. Everett	
G-AVLI	PA-28 Cherokee 140	Lima India Aviation Group	
G-AVLJ	PA-28 Cherokee 140	Cherokee Aviation Holdings Jersey Ltd	
G-AVLM	Beagle B.121 Pup 3	T. M. & D. A. Jones	
G-AVLN	Beagle B.121 Pup 2	Dogs Flying Group	
G-AVLO	Bölkow Bö.208C1 Junior	E. C. Murgatroyd	
G-AVLT	PA-28-140 Cherokee	Turweston Flying School Ltd (G-KELC)	
G-AVLW	Fournier RF-4D	J. C. A. C. da Silva	
G-AVLY	Jodel D.120A	S. M. S. Smith	
G-AVMA	Gardan GY-80 Horizon 180	Z. R. Hildick	
G-AVMB	D.62B Condor	F. Baldanza	
G-AVMD	Cessna 150G	York Aircraft Leasing Ltd	
G-AVMF	Cessna F. 150G	J. F. Marsh	
G-AVMJ	BAC One-Eleven 510ED ★	European Aviation Ltd (cabin trainer)	
G-AVMK	BAC One-Eleven 510ED ★	Gravesend College (fuselage only)	
G-AVMO	BAC One-Eleven 510ED ★	Museum of Flight/East Fortune	
G-AVMU	BAC One-Eleven 510ED ★	Duxford Aviation Society	
G-AVNC	Cessna F.150G	J. Turner	
G-AVNE	Westland WS-58 Wessex Mk 60 Srs 1 ★	IHM/Weston-super-Mare	
G-AVNN	PA-28 Cherokee 180	G-AVNN Flying Group	
G-AVNO	PA-28 Cherokee 180	November Oscar Flying Group	
G-AVNS	PA-28 Cherokee 180	Fly (Fu Lai) Aviation Ltd	
G-AVNU	PA-28 Cherokee 180	D. Durrant	
G-AVNW	PA-28 Cherokee 180	Len Smith's (Aviation) Ltd	
G-AVNY	Fournier RF-4D	J. B. Giddins (G-IVEL)	
G-AVNZ	Fournier RF-4D	C. D. Pidler	
G-AVOA	Jodel DR.1050	D. A. Willies	
G-AVOD	Beagle D.5/180 Husky	PAW Flying Services Ltd	
G-AVOH	D.62B Condor	Condor Group	
G-AVOM	CEA Jodel DR.221	Avon Flying Group	
G-AVOO	PA-18 Super Cub 150	Dublin Gliding Club Ltd	
G-AVOU	Slingsby T.56 S.E.5A Replica	Sywell SE5 Group	
G-AVOZ	PA-28 Cherokee 180	Oscar Zulu Flying Group	
G-AVPD	Jodel D.9 Bébé ★	S. W. McKay (stored)	
G-AVPI	Cessna F.172H	Air-Tech	
G-AVPJ	DH.82A Tiger Moth	C. C. Silk	
G-AVPM	Jodel D.117	L. B. Clark	
G-AVPN	HPR.7 Herald 213 ★	Yorkshire Air Museum/Elvington	
G-AVPO	Hindustan HAL-26 Pushpak	B. Johns	
G-AVPV	PA-18 Cherokee 180	K. A. Passmore	
G-AVPY	PA-25 Pawnee 235C	Southdown Gliding Club Ltd	
G-AVRK	PA-28 Cherokee 180	Scenic Air Tours North East Ltd	
G-AVRS	Gardan GY-80 Horizon 180	A. G. Fowles & P. J. Tanulak	
G-AVRU	PA-28-Cherokee 180	Lanpro	
G-AVRW	Gardan GY-20 Minicab	Kestrel Flying Group	
G-AVRZ	PA-28 Cherokee 180	RZ Group	

Notes	Reg	Type	Owner or Operator
	G-AVSA	PA-28 Cherokee 180	N. Grantham
	G-AVSB	PA-28 Cherokee 180	G. Cormack
	G-AVSC	PA-28 Cherokee 180	G-AVSC Group
	G-AVSD	PA-28 Cherokee 180	C. B. D. Owen
	G-AVSE	PA-28 Cherokee 180	F. Glendon/Ireland
	G-AVSF	PA-28 Cherokee 180	Monday Club
	G-AVSI	PA-28 Cherokee 140	G-AVSI Flying Group
	G-AVSP	PA-28 Cherokee 180	C. & J. Willis
	G-AVSR	Beagle D.5/180 Husky	S. D. J. Holwill
	G-AVTC	Slingsby Nipper T.66 RA.45 Srs 3	J. Crawford
	G-AVTP	Cessna F.172H	J. Davies
	G-AVTT	Ercoupe 415D	Wright's Farm Eggs Ltd
	G-AVUG	Cessna F.150H	Skyways Flying Group
	G-AVUH	Cessna F.150H	A. G. McLaren
	G-AVUO	Luton LA4 Minor	M. E. Vaisey
	G-AVUS	PA-28 Cherokee 140	P. K. Pemberton
	G-AVUT	PA-28 Cherokee 140	Bencray Ltd
	G-AVUZ	PA-32 Cherokee Six 300	Ceesix Ltd
	G-AVVC	Cessna F.172H	Victor Charlie Flying Group
	G-AVVO	Avro 652A Anson 19 (VL348) ★	Newark Air Museum
	G-AVWA	PA-28 Cherokee 140	SFG Ltd
	G-AVWD	PA-28 Cherokee 140	M. Howells
	G-AVWI	PA-28 Cherokee 140	L. M. Veitch
	G-AVWL	PA-28 Cherokee 140	G-AVWL Group
	G-AVWM	PA-28 Cherokee 140	G-AVWM Group
	G-AVWO	PA-28R Cherokee Arrow 180	Whiskey Oscar Group
	G-AVWR	PA-28R Cherokee Arrow 180	G-AVWR Flying Group
	G-AVWT	PA-28R Cherokee Arrow 180	A. C. Brett
	G-AVWU	PA-28R Cherokee Arrow 180	M. Ali & S. Din
	G-AVWV	PA-28R Cherokee Arrow 180	R. V. Thornton
	G-AVWY	Fournier RF-4D	S. A. W. Becker
	G-AVXA	PA-25 Pawnee 235	S. Wales Gliding Club Ltd
	G-AVXD	Slingsby T.66 Nipper 3	J. A. Brompton
	G-AVXF	PA-28R Cherokee Arrow 180	G-AVXF Group
	G-AVXW	D.62B Condor	C. Willmott
	G-AVXY	Auster AOP.9	G. J. Siddall
	G-AVXZ	PA-28 Cherokee 140 ★	ATC Hayle (instructional airframe)
	G-AVYB	HS.121 Trident 1E-140 ★	SAS training airframe/Hereford
	G-AVYK	Beagle A.61 Terrier 3	R. Burgun
	G-AVYL	PA-28 Cherokee 180	Cotswold Aero Maintenance Ltd
	G-AVYM	PA-28 Cherokee 180	Camborne Insurance Services Ltd
	G-AVYS	PA-28R Cherokee Arrow 180	A. N. Harris
	G-AVYT	PA-28R Cherokee Arrow 180	M. Bonsall
	G-AVYV	Jodel D.120	A. L. Hamer
	G-AVZB	Aero Z-37 Cmelak ★	Science Museum/Wroughton
	G-AVZI	Bölkow Bö.208C1 Junior	C. F. Rogers
	G-AVZP	Beagle B.121 Pup 1	T. A. White
	G-AVZU	Cessna F.150H	R. D. Forster
	G-AVZV	Cessna F.172H	S. E. Waddy
	G-AVZW	EAA Biplane Model P	C. Edmondson
	G-AWAC	Gardan GY-80 Horizon 180	P. B. Hodgson
	G-AWAJ	Beech 95-D55 Baron	B. F. Whitworth
	G-AWAU	Vickers FB.27A Vimy (replica) (F8614) ★	RAF Museum/Hendon
	G-AWAW	Cessna F.150F ★	Science Museum/South Kensington
	G-AWAX	Cessna 150D	Propsnblades BVBA/Belgium
	G-AWAZ	PA-28R Cherokee Arrow 180	A. M. Playford
	G-AWBB	PA-28R Cherokee Arrow 180	P. J. Young
	G-AWBC	PA-28R Cherokee Arrow 180	Anglo Property Services Ltd
	G-AWBE	PA-28 Cherokee 140	B. E. Boyle
	G-AWBG	PA-28 Cherokee 140	I. Herdis
	G-AWBJ	Fournier RF-4D	G. Danhier
	G-AWBM	D.31 Turbulent	J. J. B. Leasor
	G-AWBS	PA-28 Cherokee 140	R. A. Ballard
	G-AWBT	PA-30 Twin Comanche 160B ★	Instructional airframe/Cranfield
	G-AWBU	Morane-Saulnier N (replica) (MS824)	Flying Aces Movie Aircraft Collection
	G-AWBX	Cessna F.150H	R. Nightingale
	G-AWCM	Cessna F.150H	R. Garbett
	G-AWCN	Cessna FR.172E	P. H. Collin
	G-AWCP	Cessna F.150H (tailwheel)	C. E. Mason
	G-AWDA	Slingsby T.66 Nipper 3	H. Abraham

Reg	Type	Owner or Operator	Notes
G-AWDO	D.31 Turbulent	R. N. Crosland	
G-AWDR	Cessna FR.172E	B. A. Wallace	
G-AWDU	Brantly B.2B	N. J. M. Freeman	
G-AWEA	Beagle B.121 Pup Srs.1	T. S. Walker	
G-AWEF	SNCAN Stampe SV.4B	RAF Buchanan	
G-AWEI	D.62B Condor	P. A. Gange	
G-AWEK	Fournier RF-4D	A. F. & M. P. J. Hill	
G-AWEL	Fournier RF-4D	A. B. Clymo	
G-AWEP	Barritault JB-01 Minicab	R. K. Thomas	
G-AWES	Cessna 150H	R. J. Willis	
G-AWEV	PA-28 Cherokee 140	W. J. Layzell	
G-AWEX	PA-28 Cherokee 140	J. W. McLeavy	
G-AWFB	PA-28R Cherokee Arrow 180	J. C. Luke	
G-AWFC	PA-28R Cherokee Arrow 180	A. Simpson	
G-AWFD	PA-28R Cherokee Arrow 180	C. G. Sims	
G-AWFF	Cessna F.150H	R. A. Marven	
G-AWFJ	PA-28R Cherokee Arrow 180	Bavair Ltd	
G-AWFN	D.62B Condor	C. C. Bland	
G-AWFO	D.62B Condor	T. A. & R. E. Major	
G-AWFP	D.62B Condor	S. J. Westley	
G-AWFT	Jodel D.9 Bébé	W. H. Cole	
G-AWFW	Jodel D.117	J. Pool	
G-AWFZ	Beech A23 Musketeer	R. E. Crowe	
G-AWGA	Beagle A.109 Airedale ★	(stored)	
G-AWGK	Cessna F.150H	G. E. Allen	
G-AWGN	Fournier RF-4D	R. J. Grimstead	
G-AWGZ	Taylor JT.1 Monoplane	A. D. Szymanski	
G-AWHB	CASA 2-111D (6J+PR) ★	Aces High Ltd/North Weald	
G-AWHC	Hispano HA.1112 M4L	Air Leasing Ltd	
G-AWHH	Hispano HA.1112 M1L	Anglia Aircraft Restorations Ltd	
G-AWHK	Hispano HA.1112 M1L	Historic Flying Ltd (G-BWUE)	
G-AWHM	Hispano HA.1112 M1L	Air Leasing Ltd	
G-AWHX	Rollason Beta B.2	T. Jarvis	
G-AWHY	Falconar F.11-3	Why Fly Group (G-BDPB)	
G-AWIF	Brookland Mosquito 2	C. A. Reeves	
G-AWII	VS.349 Spitfire VC (AR501)	The Shuttleworth Collection	
G-AWIR	Midget Mustang	R. Ellingworth	
G-AWIT	PA-28 Cherokee 180	G-AWIT Ltd	
G-AWIV	Airmark TSR.3	J. A. Wardlow	
G-AWIW	SNCAN Stampe SV.4B	R. E. Mitchell	
G-AWJE	Slingsby T.66 Nipper 3	K G. G. Howe	
G-AWJV	DH.98 Mosquito TT Mk 35 (TA634) ★	de Havilland Heritage Museum/London Colney	
G-AWJX	Zlin Z.526 Trener Master	M. Baer	
G-AWKD	PA-17 Vagabond	Kilo Delta Flying Group	
G-AWKO	Beagle B.121 Pup 1	J. Martin	
G-AWKP	Jodel DR.253	G-AWKP Group	
G-AWKX	Beech A65 Queen Air ★	(Instructional airframe)/Shoreham	
G-AWLF	Cessna F.172H	Gannet Aviation	
G-AWLG	SIPA 903	S. W. Markham	
G-AWLI	PA-22 Tri-Pacer 150	North Hangar Group	
G-AWLO	Boeing Stearman E75	N. D. Pickard	
G-AWLP	Mooney M.20F	I. C. Lomax	
G-AWLR	Slingsby T.66 Nipper 3	T. D. Reid	
G-AWLS	Slingsby T.66 Nipper 3	G. A. Dunster & B. Gallagher	
G-AWLX	Auster 5 J/2 Arrow	W. J. Taylor	
G-AWLZ	Fournier RF-4D	Nympsfield RF-4 Group	
G-AWMD	Jodel D.11	J. R. Cooper	
G-AWMF	PA-18 Super Cub 150 (modified)	Booker Gliding Club Ltd	
G-AWMN	Luton LA-4A Minor	S. Penfold	
G-AWMR	D.31 Turbulent	B. E. Holz	
G-AWMT	Cessna F.150H	Strategic Synergies Ltd	
G-AWNT	BN-2A Islander	Precision Terrain Surveys Ltd	
G-AWOH	PA-17 Vagabond	A. Lovejoy & K. Downes	
G-AWOT	Cessna F.150H	North East Aviation Ltd	
G-AWOU	Cessna 170B	S. Billington	
G-AWOX	Westland WS-58 Wessex 60 (150225) ★	Paintball Adventure West/Bristol	
G-AWPH	P.56 Provost T.1	J. A. D. Bradshaw	
G-AWPJ	Cessna F.150H	Global Aviation Ltd	
G-AWPN	Shield Xyla	J. P. Gilbert	
G-AWPU	Cessna F.150J	Westair Flying Services Ltd	
G-AWPW	PA-12 Super Cruiser	AK Leasing (Jersey) Ltd	

Notes	Reg	Type	Owner or Operator
	G-AWPZ	Andreasson BA-4B	J. M. Vening
	G-AWRP	Cierva Rotorcraft ★	IHM/Weston-super-Mare
	G-AWRS	Avro 19 Srs. 2 (TX213) ★	North East Aircraft Museum/Usworth
	G-AWRY	P.56 Provost T.1 (XF836)	A. J. House
	G-AWSA	Avro 652A Anson 19 (VL349) ★	Norfolk & Suffolk Aviation Museum/Flixton
	G-AWSH	Zlin Z.526 Trener Master	P. A. Colman
	G-AWSL	PA-28 Cherokee 180D	A. H. & A. H. Brown
	G-AWSM	PA-28 Cherokee 235	Aviation Projects Ltd
	G-AWSN	D.62B Condor	The Condor Club
	G-AWSP	D.62B Condor	M. C. Burlock
	G-AWSS	D.62A Condor	N. J. Butler
	G-AWST	D.62B Condor	J. E. Hobbs
	G-AWSV	Skeeter 12 (XM553)	Maj. M. Somerton-Rayner
	G-AWSW	Beagle D.5/180 Husky (XW635)	Windmill Aviation
	G-AWTL	PA-28 Cherokee 180D	G. B. Stevens
	G-AWTP	Schleicher Ka 6E	R. H. W. Martin
	G-AWTS	Beech A.23 Musketeer	Golf Tango Sierra Ltd
	G-AWTV	Beech 19A Musketeer Sport	J. Whittaker
	G-AWTX	Cessna F.150J	R. D. Forster
	G-AWUB	Gardan GY-201 Minicab	R. A. Hand
	G-AWUE	Jodel DR.1050	K. W. Wood & F. M. Watson
	G-AWUJ	Cessna F.150H	AT Aviation Sales Ltd, L. Gething, J. A. Gibson & R. Gibson
	G-AWUL	Cessna F.150H	A. J. Baron
	G-AWUN	Cessna F.150H	G-AWUN Group
	G-AWUT	Cessna F.150J	Aerospace Resources Ltd
	G-AWUU	Cessna F.150J	D. P. Jones
	G-AWUX	Cessna F.172H	G-AWUX Group
	G-AWUZ	Cessna F.172H	Five Percent Flying Group
	G-AWVA	Cessna F.172H	Barton Air Ltd
	G-AWVC	Beagle B.121 Pup 1	P. I. Meaby
	G-AWVE	Jodel DR.1050/M1	E. A. Taylor
	G-AWVG	AESL Airtourer T.2	C. J. Schofield
	G-AWVN	Aeronca 7AC Champion	Champ Flying Group
	G-AWVZ	Jodel D.112	D. C. Stokes
	G-AWWE	Beagle B.121 Pup 2	Pup Flyers
	G-AWWI	Jodel D.117	J. Pool
	G-AWWN	Jodel DR.1050	M. A. Baker
	G-AWWO	Jodel DR.1050	W. G. Brooks
	G-AWWP	Aerosport Woody Pusher III	M. S. Bird & R. D. Bird
	G-AWWU	Cessna FR.172F	R. Henderson
	G-AWXR	PA-28 Cherokee 180D	Aero Clube da Costa Verde/Portugal
	G-AWXS	PA-28 Cherokee 180D	J. E. Rowley
	G-AWXY	MS.885 Super Rallye	K. Henderson
	G-AWXZ	SNCAN Stampe SV.4C	Bianchi Aviation Film Services Ltd
	G-AWYI	BE.2c replica (687)	M. C. Boddington & S. Slater
	G-AWYJ	Beagle B.121 Pup 2	H. C. Taylor
	G-AWYL	Jodel DR.253B	T. C. Van Lonkhuyzen
	G-AWYO	Beagle B.121 Pup 1	B. R. C. Wild
	G-AWYY	Slingsby T.57 Camel replica (B6401) ★	F.A.A. Museum/Yeovilton
	G-AWZI	HS.121 Trident 3B ★	A. Lee/FAST Museum (nose only)/Farnborough
	G-AWZJ	HS.121 Trident 3B ★	Dumfries & Galloway Museum
	G-AWZK	HS.121 Trident 3B ★	Trident Preservation Society/Manchester
	G-AWZM	HS.121 Trident 3B ★	Science Museum/Wroughton
	G-AWZP	HS.121 Trident 3B ★	Manchester Museum of Science & Industry (nose only)
	G-AWZX	HS.121 Trident 3B ★	BAA Airport Fire Services/Gatwick
	G-AXAB	PA-28 Cherokee 140	Bencray Ltd
	G-AXAN	DH.82A Tiger Moth (EM720)	Duxford Consulting Ltd
	G-AXAT	Jodel D.117A	D. A. White
	G-AXBJ	Cessna F.172H	Atlantic Bridge Aviation Ltd
	G-AXBW	DH.82A Tiger Moth (T5879:RUC-W)	G-AXBW Ltd
	G-AXBZ	DH.82A Tiger Moth	W. J. de Jong Cleyndert
	G-AXCA	PA-28R Cherokee Arrow 200	A. J. Bale
	G-AXCG	Jodel D.117	D. J. Millin
	G-AXCY	Jodel D.117A	R. S. Marom
	G-AXDI	Cessna F.172H	M. F. & J. R. Leusby
	G-AXDK	Jodel DR.315	Delta Kilo Flying Group
	G-AXDN	BAC-Sud Concorde 01 ★	Duxford Aviation Society

Reg	Type	Owner or Operator	Notes
G-AXDV	Beagle B.121 Pup 1	S. R. Hopkins	
G-AXDZ	Cassutt Racer IIIM	A. Chadwick	
G-AXED	PA-25 Pawnee 235	Wolds Gliding Club Ltd	
G-AXEH	B.125 Bulldog 1 ★	Museum of Flight/East Fortune	
G-AXEI	Ward Gnome ★	Real Aeroplane Club/Breighton	
G-AXEO	Scheibe SF.25B Falke	P. F. Moffatt	
G-AXEV	Beagle B.121 Pup 2	D. S. Russell & D. G. Benson	
G-AXFG	Cessna 337D	County Garage (Cheltenham) Ltd	
G-AXFN	Jodel D.119	Aviation Salvage & Recovery Ltd	
G-AXGE	MS.880B Rallye Club	T. R. Scorer	
G-AXGG	Cessna F.150J	A. J. Simpson	
G-AXGP	Piper J-3C-90 Cub (3681)	A. P. Acres	
G-AXGR	Luton LA-4A Minor	B. A. Schlussler	
G-AXGS	D.62B Condor	SAS Flying Group	
G-AXGV	D.62B Condor	AXGV Group	
G-AXGZ	D.62B Condor	G. E. Horder	
G-AXHO	Beagle B.121 Pup 2	L. W. Grundy	
G-AXHP	Piper J-3C-65 Cub (480636:A-58)	Witham (Specialist) Vehicles Ltd	
G-AXHR	Piper J-3C-65 Cub (329601:D-44)	D. J. Dash	
G-AXHV	Jodel D.117A	Derwent Flying Group	
G-AXIA	Beagle B.121 Pup 1	C. K. Parsons	
G-AXIE	Beagle B.121 Pup 2	J. P. Thomas	
G-AXIO	PA-28 Cherokee 140B	R. Wallace	
G-AXIR	PA-28 Cherokee 140B	J. L. Sparks	
G-AXIX	Glos-Airtourer 150	J. C. Wood	
G-AXJB	Omega 84 balloon	Southern Balloon Group	
G-AXJH	Beagle B.121 Pup 2	The Henry Flying Group	
G-AXJI	Beagle B.121 Pup 2	J. B. Bowen & M. Templeman	
G-AXJJ	Beagle B.121 Pup 2	M. L. Jones & ptnrs	
G-AXJO	Beagle B.121 Pup 2	J. A. D. Bradshaw	
G-AXJR	Scheibe SF.25B Falke	Falke Syndicate	
G-AXJV	PA-28 Cherokee 140B	Seahawk Flying Group	
G-AXJX	PA-28 Cherokee 140B	Horizon Aviation Ltd	
G-AXKH	Luton LA-4A Minor	M. E. Vaisey	
G-AXKJ	Jodel D.9	P. A. Gasson	
G-AXKO	Westland-Bell 47G-4A	M. Gallagher	
G-AXKS	Westland Bell 47G-4A ★	Museum of Army Flying/Middle Wallop	
G-AXKX	Westland Bell 47G-4A	R. A. Dale	
G-AXLI	Slingsby T.66 Nipper 3	D. & M. Shrimpton	
G-AXLJ	Slingsby T.66 Nipper 3	R. J. Hodder	
G-AXLS	Jodel DR.105A	Axle Flying Club	
G-AXLZ	PA-18 Super Cub 95	Perryair Ltd	
G-AXMA	PA-24 Comanche 180	B. C. Faulkner	
G-AXMD	Omega O-56 balloon ★	British Balloon Museum/Newbury	
G-AXMT	Bucker Bu.133 Jungmeister	A. J. E. Smith & R. A. Fleming	
G-AXMW	Beagle B.121 Pup 1	DJP Engineering (Knebworth) Ltd	
G-AXMX	Beagle B.121 Pup 2	Bob The Beagle Group	
G-AXNJ	Wassmer Jodel D.120	J. Pool	
G-AXNN	Beagle B.121 Pup 2	Gabrielle Aviation Ltd	
G-AXNP	Beagle B.121 Pup 2	J. W. Ellis & R. J. Hemmings	
G-AXNR	Beagle B.121 Pup 2	AXNR Group	
G-AXNS	Beagle B.121 Pup 2	Derwent Aero Group	
G-AXNW	SNCAN Stampe SV.4C	C. S. Grace	
G-AXNZ	Pitts S.1C Special	November Zulu Group	
G-AXOG	PA-E23 Aztec 250D	G. H. Nolan	
G-AXOH	MS.894 Rallye Minerva	L. C. Clark	
G-AXOJ	Beagle B.121 Pup 2	Pup Flying Group	
G-AXOR	PA-28 Cherokee 180D	Oscar Romeo Aviation Ltd	
G-AXOS	MS.894A Rallye Minerva	R. S. M. Fendt	
G-AXOT	MS.893 Rallye Commodore 180	P. Evans	
G-AXOZ	Beagle B.121 Pup 1	E. G. Williams	
G-AXPA	Beagle B.121 Pup 1	C. B. Copsey	
G-AXPC	Beagle B.121 Pup 2	T. A. White	
G-AXPF	Cessna F.150K	D. R. Marks	
G-AXPG	Mignet HM.293	W. H. Cole (stored)	
G-AXPN	Beagle B.121 Pup 2	P. Wood & R. J. Burgess	
G-AXPZ	Campbell Cricket	W. R. Partridge	
G-AXRC	Campbell Cricket	L. R. Morris	
G-AXRP	SNCAN Stampe SV-4C	C. C. & C. D. Manning (G-BLOL)	
G-AXRR	Auster AOP.9 (XR241)	R. B. Webber	
G-AXRT	Cessna FA.150K (tailwheel)	Aerobat Sp Zoo/Poland	

Notes	Reg	Type	Owner or Operator
	G-AXSC	Beagle B.121 Pup 1	M. P. Whitley
	G-AXSG	PA-28 Cherokee 180	Seagull Aviation Ltd
	G-AXSI	Cessna F.172H	M. H. Asmail (G-SNIP)
	G-AXSM	Jodel DR.1051	T. R. G. & M. S. Barnby
	G-AXSW	Cessna FA.150K	R. J. Whyham
	G-AXSZ	PA-28 Cherokee 140B	White Wings Flying Group
	G-AXTA	PA-28 Cherokee 140B	G-AXTA Aircraft Group
	G-AXTC	PA-28 Cherokee 140B	G-AXTC Group
	G-AXTJ	PA-28 Cherokee 140B	K. Patel
	G-AXTL	PA-28 Cherokee 140B	Bristol and West Aeroplane Club Ltd
	G-AXTO	PA-24 Comanche 260	D. L. Edwards
	G-AXTX	Jodel D.112	C. Sawford
	G-AXUA	Beagle B.121 Pup 1	P. Wood
	G-AXUB	BN-2A Islander	Headcorn Parachute Club Ltd
	G-AXUC	PA-12 Super Cruiser	Weald Air Services Ltd
	G-AXUF	Cessna FA.150K	K. A. O'Connor
	G-AXUJ	Auster J/1 Autocrat	P. Gill (G-OSTA)
	G-AXUK	Jodel DR.1050	Downland Flying Group
	G-AXUM	HP.137 Jetstream 1 ★	Sodeteg Formation/France
	G-AXVB	Cessna F.172H	M. Lazar
	G-AXVK	Campbell Cricket	J. J. Jackson
	G-AXVM	Campbell Cricket	D. M. Organ
	G-AXVN	McCandless M.4	W. R. Partridge
	G-AXWA	Auster AOP.9 (XN437)	C. M. Edwards
	G-AXWT	Jodel D.11	C. S. Jackson
	G-AXWV	Jodel DR.253	R. Friedlander & D. C. Ray
	G-AXWZ	PA-28R Cherokee Arrow 200	Whisky Zulu Group
	G-AXXC	CP.301B Emeraude	R. E. Hughes
	G-AXXV	DH.82A Tiger Moth (DE992)	Fly Tiger Moth Ltd
	G-AXXW	Jodel D.117	R. K. G. Delve
	G-AXYK	Taylor JT.1 Monoplane	G. V. Wright
	G-AXYU	Jodel D.9 Bébé	P. Turton
	G-AXZD	PA-28 Cherokee 180E	Sirius Aviation Ltd
	G-AXZH	Glasflugel H201B Standard Libelle	M. C. Gregorie
	G-AXZM	Slingsby T.66 Nipper 3	G. R. Harlow
	G-AXZO	Cessna 180	B. C. Faulkner
	G-AXZP	PA-E23 Aztec 250D	D. M. Harbottle
	G-AXZT	Jodel D.117	P. Guest
	G-AXZU	Cessna 182N	W. Gollan
	G-AYAB	PA-28 Cherokee 180E	L. Kretschmann
	G-AYAC	PA-28R Cherokee Arrow 200	Fersfield Flying Group
	G-AYAJ	Cameron O-84 balloon	E. T. Hall
	G-AYAL	Omega 56 balloon ★	British Balloon Museum/Newbury
	G-AYAN	Slingsby Motor Cadet III	R. Moyse
	G-AYAR	PA-28 Cherokee 180E	P. McKay
	G-AYAT	PA-28 Cherokee 180E	G-AYAT Flying Group
	G-AYAW	PA-28 Cherokee 180E	North East Flyers Group
	G-AYBG	Scheibe SF.25B Falke	Anglia Sailplanes
	G-AYBP	Jodel D.112	A. Gregori
	G-AYBR	Jodel D.112	I. S. Parker
	G-AYCC	Campbell Cricket	P. I. Jordan
	G-AYCE	Scintex CP.301-C1 Emeraude	A. C. Beech
	G-AYCF	Cessna FA.150K	C. G. Applegarth
	G-AYCG	SNCAN Stampe SV.4C	Tiger Airways
	G-AYCK	AIA Stampe SV.4C	A. A. M. & C. W. M. Huke (G-BUNT)
	G-AYCN	Piper J-3C-65 Cub	W. R. & B. M. Young
	G-AYCO	CEA DR.360	R. H. Underwood
	G-AYCP	Jodel D.112	J. A. Carey
	G-AYCT	Cessna F.172H	J. R. Benson
	G-AYDI	DH.82A Tiger Moth	E. G. & G. R. Woods
	G-AYDR	SNCAN Stampe SV.4C	D. J. Ashley
	G-AYDV	Coates Swalesong SA11	The Real Aeroplane Co.Ltd
	G-AYDW	Beagle A.61 Terrier 2	A. S. Topen
	G-AYDX	Beagle A.61 Terrier 2	T. S. Lee
	G-AYDY	Luton LA-4A Minor	J. Dible/Ireland
	G-AYDZ	Jodel DR.200	Zero One Group
	G-AYEB	Jodel D.112	Echo Bravo Partnership
	G-AYEE	PA-28 Cherokee 180E	Demero Ltd
	G-AYEF	PA-28 Cherokee 180E	Pegasus Flying Group
	G-AYEG	Falconar F-9	R. J. Ripley

Reg	Type	Owner or Operator	Notes
G-AYEH	Jodel DR.1050	T. J. N. H. Palmer	
G-AYEJ	Jodel DR.1050	The Bluebird Flying Group	
G-AYEN	Piper J-3C-65 Cub	P. Warde & C. F. Morris	
G-AYET	MS.892A Rallye Commodore 150	A. T. R. Bingley	
G-AYEW	Jodel DR.1051	J. R. Hope	
G-AYFC	D.62B Condor	A. R. Chadwick	
G-AYFD	D.62B Condor	B. G. Manning	
G-AYFE	D.62C Condor	M. Soulsby	
G-AYFF	D.62B Condor	H. Stuart	
G-AYFJ	MS.880B Rallye Club	Rallye FJ Group	
G-AYFV	Crosby BA-4B	N. J. W. Reid	
G-AYGA	Jodel D.117	J. W. Bowes	
G-AYGB	Cessna 310Q ★	Instructional airframe/Perth	
G-AYGC	Cessna F.150K	Alpha Aviation Group	
G-AYGD	Jodel DR.1051	J. F. M. Barlett & J. P. Liber	
G-AYGE	SNCAN Stampe SV.4C	L. J. & S. Proudfoot	
G-AYGG	Jodel D.120	J. M. Dean	
G-AYGX	Cessna FR.172G	G. W. Marray	
G-AYHA	AA-1 Yankee	N. T. Oakman & G. J. Fricker	
G-AYHX	Jodel D.117A	L. E. Cowling	
G-AYIA	Hughes 369HS	G. D. E. Bilton/Sywell	
G-AYIG	PA-28 Cherokee 140C	G. K. Clarkson	
G-AYII	PA-28R Cherokee Arrow 200	Double India Group	
G-AYIJ	SNCAN Stampe SV.4B	D. Savage	
G-AYJA	Jodel DR.1050	D. M. Blair	
G-AYJB	SNCAN Stampe SV.4C	F. J. M. & J. P. Esson	
G-AYJD	Alpavia-Fournier RF-3	Juliet Delta Group	
G-AYJP	PA-28 Cherokee 140C	Transcourt Ltd and Demero Ltd	
G-AYJR	PA-28 Cherokee 140C	Turweston Flying School	
G-AYJY	Isaacs Fury II	J. G. Norris	
G-AYKD	Jodel DR.1050	K. L. & L. S. Johnson	
G-AYKJ	Jodel D.117A	R. J. Hughes	
G-AYKK	Jodel D.117	J. M. Whitham	
G-AYKS	Leopoldoff L.7 Colibri	W. B. Cooper	
G-AYKT	Jodel D.117	D. I. Walker	
G-AYKW	PA-28 Cherokee 140C	Kilo Whiskey Group	
G-AYKZ	SAI KZ-8	R. E. Mitchell	
G-AYLA	Glos-Airtourer 115	C. P. L. Jenkins	
G-AYLC	Jodel DR.1051	G-AYLC Flying Group	
G-AYLF	Jodel DR.1051 (modified)	R. Twigg	
G-AYLL	Jodel DR.1050	G. Bell	
G-AYLP	AA-1 Yankee	D. Nairn	
G-AYME	Fournier RF-5	Romeo Foxtrot Group	
G-AYMK	PA-28 Cherokee 140C	R. Quinn & B. Hutchinson	
G-AYMP	Currie Wot	R. C. Hibberd	
G-AYMR	Lederlin 380L	P. J. Brayshaw	
G-AYMU	Jodel D.112	M. R. Baker	
G-AYMV	Western 20 balloon	R. G. Turnbull	
G-AYNA	Phoenix Currie Wot	D. R. Partridge	
G-AYNF	PA-28 Cherokee 140C	BW Aviation Ltd	
G-AYNJ	PA-28 Cherokee 140C	A. Andreeva	
G-AYNN	Cessna 185B	Bencray Ltd	
G-AYNP	Westland WS-55 Whirlwind Srs 3 ★	IHM/Weston-super-Mare	
G-AYOW	Cessna 182N	R. Warner	
G-AYOZ	Cessna FA.150L	P. J. Worrall	
G-AYPE	MBB Bö.209 Monsun	Papa Echo Ltd	
G-AYPG	Cessna F.177RG	D. P. McDermott	
G-AYPH	Cessna F.177RG	M. L. & T. M. Jones	
G-AYPJ	PA-28 Cherokee 180	R. B. Petrie	
G-AYPM	PA-18 Super Cub 95 (115373)	A. N. R. Houghton & J. C. Tempest	
G-AYPO	PA-18 Super Cub 95	A. W. Knowles	
G-AYPS	PA-18 Super Cub 95	D. Racionzer & P. Wayman	
G-AYPU	PA-28R Cherokee Arrow 200	Monalto Investments Ltd	
G-AYPV	PA-28 Cherokee 140D	Ashley Gardner Flying Club Ltd	
G-AYPZ	Campbell Cricket	A. Melody	
G-AYRC	Campbell Cricket	B. L. Johnson	
G-AYRG	Cessna F.172K	I. G. Harrison	
G-AYRI	PA-28R Cherokee Arrow 200	J. C. Houdret	
G-AYRL	Sportavia-Putzer SFS31 Milan	A.Hoskins & K. M. Fresson	
G-AYRM	PA-28 Cherokee 140D	M. J. Saggers	
G-AYRO	Cessna FA.150L Aerobat	AJW Construction Ltd	

Notes	Reg	Type	Owner or Operator
	G-AYRS	Jodel D.120A	L. R. H. D'Eath
	G-AYRT	Cessna F.172K	S. Macfarlane
	G-AYRU	BN-2A-6 Islander	Versatile Air Services Ltd
	G-AYSB	PA-30 Twin Comanche 160C	Charles Lock (1963) Ltd
	G-AYSH	Taylor JT.1 Monoplane	C. J. Lodge
	G-AYSK	Luton LA-4A Minor	M. A. Watts
	G-AYSX	Cessna F.177RG	M. Clarke
	G-AYSY	Cessna F.177RG	S. A. Tuer
	G-AYTA	SOCATA MS.880B Rallye Club ★	Manchester Museum of Science & Industry
	G-AYTR	CP.301A Emeraude	M. A. Smith
	G-AYTT	Phoenix PM-3 Duet	R. B. Webber & J. K. Houlgrave
	G-AYTV	Jurca Tempete	C. W. Kirk
	G-AYUB	CEA DR.253B	P. J. Coward, EES Aviation Services Ltd & Forbes Insurance Ltd
	G-AYUH	PA-28 Cherokee 180F	Broadland Flying Group Ltd
	G-AYUJ	Evans VP-1	T. N. Howard
	G-AYUM	Slingsby T.61A Falke	M. H. Simms
	G-AYUN	Slingsby T.61A Falke	G-AYUN Group
	G-AYUP	Slingsby T.61A Falke	P. R. Williams
	G-AYUR	Slingsby T.61A Falke	R. C. Bettany
	G-AYUS	Taylor JT.1 Monoplane	J. G. W. Newton
	G-AYUT	Jodel DR.1050	G. Bell & S. P. Garton
	G-AYUV	Cessna F.172H	Justgold Ltd
	G-AYVP	Woody Pusher	J. R. Wraight
	G-AYWD	Cessna 182N	Wild Dreams Group
	G-AYWH	Jodel D.117A	D. Kynaston
	G-AYWM	Glos-Airtourer Super 150	Star Flying Group
	G-AYWT	AIA Stampe SV.4C	S. T. Carrel
	G-AYXP	Jodel D.117A	G. N. Davies
	G-AYXS	SIAI-Marchetti S205-18R	M. Llewellyn & B. Vincent
	G-AYXT	WS-55 Whirlwind Srs 2 (XK940:911) ★	IHM/Weston-super-Mare
	G-AYXU	Champion 7KCAB Citabria	E. V. Moffatt & J. S. Peplow
	G-AYYO	Jodel DR.1050/M1	Bustard Jodel Group
	G-AYYT	Jodel DR.1050/M1	O. Prince
	G-AYYU	Beech C23 Musketeer	G-AYYU Group
	G-AYZH	Taylor JT.2 Titch	T. Jarvis
	G-AYZI	SNCAN Stampe SV.4C	D. M. & P. A. Fenton
	G-AYZJ	Westland WS-55 Whirlwind HAS.7 ★	Newark Air Museum (XM685)
	G-AYZK	Jodel DR.1050/M1	G. J. McDill
	G-AYZS	D.62B Condor	M. N. Thrush
	G-AYZU	Slingsby T.61A Falke	S. Borthwick
	G-AYZW	Slingsby T.61A Falke	Y-ZW Group
	G-AZAB	PA-30 Twin Comanche 160B	M. Nelson
	G-AZAJ	PA-28R Cherokee Arrow 200B	P. Woulfe
	G-AZAW	Gardan GY-80 Horizon 160	J. W. Foley
	G-AZAZ	Bensen B.8M ★	F.A.A. Museum/Yeovilton
	G-AZBB	MBB Bö.209 Monsun 160FV	J. A. Webb
	G-AZBE	Glos-Airtourer Super 150	607 Group
	G-AZBI	Jodel 150	R. J. Wald
	G-AZBL	Jodel D.9 Bébé	P. A. Gasson
	G-AZBN	Noorduyn AT-16 Harvard IIB (FT391)	Swaygate Ltd
	G-AZBU	Auster AOP.9 (XR246)	Auster Nine Group
	G-AZCB	SNCAN Stampe SV.4C	M. Coward
	G-AZCK	Beagle B.121 Pup 2	P. Crone
	G-AZCL	Beagle B.121 Pup 2	Flew LLP & J. M. Henry
	G-AZCN	Beagle B.121 Pup 2	Snoopy Flying Group
	G-AZCP	Beagle B.121 Pup 1	K. N. St.Aubyn
	G-AZCT	Beagle B.121 Pup 1	J. C. Metcalf
	G-AZCU	Beagle B.121 Pup 1	D. W. Locke
	G-AZCV	Beagle B.121 Pup 2	N. R. W. Long
	G-AZCZ	Beagle B.121 Pup 2	L. Northover
	G-AZDD	MBB Bö.209 Monsun 150FF	Double Delta Flying Group
	G-AZDE	PA-28R Cherokee Arrow 200B	M. Magrabi
	G-AZDG	Beagle B.121 Pup 2	P. J. Beeson
	G-AZDJ	PA-32 Cherokee Six 300	K. J. Mansbridge & D. C. Gibbs
	G-AZDY	DH.82A Tiger Moth	B. A. Mills
	G-AZEE	MS.880B Rallye Club	J. Shelton
	G-AZEF	Jodel D.120	G-AZEF Group
	G-AZEG	PA-28 Cherokee 140D	S. Kennaugh
	G-AZEU	Beagle B.121 Pup 2	G. M. Moir

Reg	Type	Owner or Operator	Notes
G-AZEV	Beagle B.121 Pup 2	A. P. Amor	
G-AZEW	Beagle B.121 Pup 2	D. Ridley	
G-AZEY	Beagle B.121 Pup 2	A. H. Cameron	
G-AZFA	Beagle B.121 Pup 2	P. D. F. Herzberg	
G-AZFC	PA-28 Cherokee 140D	WLS Flying Group	
G-AZFI	PA-28R Cherokee Arrow 200B	G-AZFI Ltd	
G-AZFM	PA-28R Cherokee Arrow 200B	P. J. Jenness	
G-AZGA	Jodel D.120	P. Turton & N. J. Owen	
G-AZGC	SNCAN Stampe SV.4C	D. J. Ashley	
G-AZGE	SNCAN Stampe SV.4C	Tiger Airways	
G-AZGF	Beagle B.121 Pup 2	J. W. Ellis & G. Van Aston	
G-AZGL	MS.894A Rallye Minerva	The Cambridge Aero Club Ltd	
G-AZGY	CP.301B Emeraude	R. H. Braithwaite	
G-AZGZ	DH.82A Tiger Moth (NM181)	R. J. King	
G-AZHB	Robin HR.100/200B	J. P. Armitage	
G-AZHC	Jodel D.112	Aerodel Flying Group	
G-AZHD	Slingsby T.61A Falke	R. J. Shallcrass	
G-AZHH	SA 102.5 Cavalier	M. W. Place	
G-AZHI	Glos-Airtourer Super 150	Flying Grasshoppers Ltd	
G-AZHK	Robin HR.100/200B	T. Woodcock & J. King (G-ILEG)	
G-AZHT	AESL Airtourer (modified)	Aviation West Ltd	
G-AZHU	Luton LA-4A Minor	J. Owen	
G-AZHX	SA Bulldog Srs 100/101	T. W. Harris (G-DOGE)	
G-AZIB	ST-10 Diplomate	W. B. Bateson	
G-AZII	Jodel D.117A	P. Nayeri	
G-AZIJ	Jodel DR.360	D. A. Gathercole	
G-AZIL	Slingsby T.61A Falke	D. W. Savage	
G-AZIP	Cameron O-65 balloon	Dante Balloon Group	
G-AZJC	Fournier RF-5	Seighford RF5 Group	
G-AZJE	Ord-Hume JB-01 Minicab	Kayee Flyers	
G-AZJN	Robin DR.300/140	G. W. Brown	
G-AZJV	Cessna F.172L	G-AZJV Flying Group	
G-AZKE	MS.880B Rallye Club	Profit Invest Sp.Z.O.O./Poland	
G-AZKP	Jodel D.117	J. Pool	
G-AZKR	PA-24 Comanche	S. J. McGovern	
G-AZKS	AA-1A Trainer	I. R. Matterface	
G-AZKW	Cessna F.172L	D. Stewart	
G-AZKZ	Cessna F.172L	R. D. & E. Forster	
G-AZLE	Boeing N2S-5 Kaydet (1102:102)	DH Heritage Flights Ltd	
G-AZLF	Jodel D.120	D. C. O'Dwyer	
G-AZLH	Cessna F.150L	W. Ali	
G-AZLN	PA-28 Cherokee 180F	Enstone Sales & Services Ltd and J. Logan	
G-AZLV	Cessna 172K	G-AZLV Flying Group	
G-AZLY	Cessna F.150L	H. Mackintosh	
G-AZMC	Slingsby T.61A Falke	P. J. R. White	
G-AZMD	Slingsby T.61C Falke	Tandem Gliding Syndicate	
G-AZMJ	AA-5 Traveler	W. R. Partridge	
G-AZMX	PA-28 Cherokee 140 ★	NE Wales Institute of Higher Education (Instructional airframe)/Flintshire	
G-AZMZ	MS.893A Rallye Commodore 150	J. Palethorpe	
G-AZNK	SNCAN Stampe SV.4A	I. Noakes	
G-AZNL	PA-28R Cherokee Arrow 200D	B. P. Liversidge	
G-AZNO	Cessna 182P	N. A. Baxter	
G-AZNT	Cameron O-84 balloon	P. Glydon	
G-AZOA	MBB Bö.209 Monsun 150FF	M. W. Hurst	
G-AZOB	MBB Bö.209 Monsun 150FF	J. A. Webb	
G-AZOE	Glos-Airtourer 150	R. Smith	
G-AZOF	Glos-Airtourer Super 150	R. C. Thursby & C. Goldsmith	
G-AZOG	PA-28R Cherokee Arrow 200D	S. J. Lowe	
G-AZOL	PA-34-200 Seneca II	Stapleford Flying Club Ltd	
G-AZOS	Jurca MJ.5-H1 Sirocco	P. J. Tanulak	
G-AZOU	Jodel DR.1050	Horsham Flying Group	
G-AZOZ	Cessna FRA.150L	A. Mitchell	
G-AZPA	PA-25 Pawnee 235	Black Mountains Gliding Club Ltd	
G-AZPC	Slingsby T.61C Falke	D. Heslop & J. R. Kimberley	
G-AZPF	Fournier RF-5	E. C. Mort	
G-AZPH	Craft-Pitts S-1S Special ★	Science Museum/South Kensington	
G-AZPX	Western O-31 balloon	Zebedee Balloon Service Ltd	
G-AZRA	MBB Bö.209 Monsun 150FF	Alpha Flying Ltd	
G-AZRH	PA-28 Cherokee 140D	Trust Flying Group	
G-AZRI	Payne Free Balloon	C. A. Butter & J. J. T. Cooke	

Notes	Reg	Type	Owner or Operator
	G-AZRK	Fournier RF-5	A. B. Clymo & J. F. Rogers
	G-AZRL	PA-18 Super Cub 95	I. Laws, P. Cooper & R. D. Potter
	G-AZRM	Fournier RF-5	Romeo Mike Group
	G-AZRN	Cameron O-84 balloon	C. J. Desmet/Belgium
	G-AZRS	PA-22 Tri-Pacer 150	R. H. Hulls
	G-AZRZ	Cessna U.206F	Cornish Parachute Club Ltd
	G-AZSA	Stampe et Renard SV.4B	M. R. Dolman
	G-AZSC	Noorduyn AT-16 Harvard IIB (43:SC)	Goodwood Road Racing Co Ltd
	G-AZSF	PA-28R Cherokee Arrow 200D	Smart People Don't Buy Ltd
	G-AZTA	MBB Bö.209 Monsun 150FF	P. A. Grant & E. C. Dugard
	G-AZTF	Cessna F.177RG	R. Burgun
	G-AZTM	AESL Airtourer T2	Victa Restoration Group
	G-AZTS	Cessna F.172L	Eastern Air Executive Ltd
	G-AZTV	Stolp SA.500 Starlet	G. R. Rowland
	G-AZUM	Cessna F.172L	Fowlmere Flyers
	G-AZUY	Cessna E.310L	W. B. Bateson
	G-AZUZ	Cessna FRA.150L	D. J. Parker & J. T. Bonsall
	G-AZVA	MBB Bö.209 Monsun 150FF	M. P. Brinkmann
	G-AZVB	MBB Bö.209 Monsun 150FF	E. & P. M. L. Cliffe
	G-AZVG	AA-5 Traveler	E. Dohrn
	G-AZVI	MS.892A Rallye Commodore	G. C. Jarvis
	G-AZVL	Jodel D.119	J. C. Metcalf
	G-AZVP	Cessna F.177RG	R. Onger
	G-AZWB	PA-28 Cherokee 140	G-AZWB Flying Group
	G-AZWF	SAN Jodel DR.1050	Cawdor Flying Group
	G-AZWS	PA-28R Cherokee Arrow 180	K. M. Turner
	G-AZWT	Westland Lysander IIIA (V9367)	The Shuttleworth Collection
	G-AZWY	PA-24 Comanche 260	Keymer Son & Co Ltd
	G-AZXB	Cameron O-65 balloon	R. J. Mitchener & P. F. Smart
	G-AZXD	Cessna F.172L	A. M. Dinnie
	G-AZXG	PA-23 Aztec 250D ★	Instructional airframe/Cranfield
	G-AZYA	Gardan GY-80 Horizon 160	R. G. Whyte
	G-AZYB	Bell 47H-1 ★	IHM/Weston-super-Mare
	G-AZYD	MS.893A Rallye Commodore	Staffordshire Gliding Club Ltd
	G-AZYF	PA-28-180 Cherokee D	SI Aviation Services Ltd
	G-AZYS	CP.301C-1 Emeraude	C. G. Ferguson & D. Drew
	G-AZYU	PA-23 Aztec 250E	M. E. & M. H. Cromati & F. & N. P. Samuelson
	G-AZYY	Slingsby T.61A Falke	J. A. Towers
	G-AZYZ	Wassmer Wa.51A Pacific	W. A. Stewart
	G-AZZR	Cessna F.150L	D. Petrie
	G-AZZV	Cessna F.172L	ZV Flying Group
	G-AZZZ	DH.82A Tiger Moth	S. W. McKay
	G-BAAD	Evans Super VP-1	The Breighton VP-1 Group
	G-BAAF	Manning-Flanders MF1 (replica)	Aviation Film Services Ltd
	G-BAAI	MS.893A Rallye Commodore	R. D. Taylor
	G-BAAT	Cessna 182P	T. E. Earl
	G-BAAW	Jodel D.119	Alpha Whiskey Flying Group
	G-BABC	Cessna F.150L	P. Tribble
	G-BABD	Cessna FRA.150L (modified)	R. Warner
	G-BABE	Taylor JT.2 Titch	E. R. White
	G-BABG	PA-28 Cherokee 180	R. Nightingale
	G-BABK	PA-34-200 Seneca II	Stapleford Flying Club Ltd
	G-BACB	PA-34-200 Seneca II	Milbrooke Motors Ltd
	G-BACE	Fournier RF-5	G-BACE Fournier Group
	G-BACJ	Jodel D.120	Wearside Flying Association
	G-BACL	Jodel 150	P. I. Morgans
	G-BACN	Cessna FRA.150L	F. Bundy
	G-BACO	Cessna FRA.150L	R. Haverson
	G-BADC	Rollason Beta B.2A	A. P. Grimley
	G-BADH	Slingsby T.61A Falke	M. J. Lake
	G-BADJ	PA-E23 Aztec 250E	K. A. W. Ashcroft
	G-BADM	D.62B Condor	Delta Mike Condor Group
	G-BADV	Brochet MB50	W. B. Cooper
	G-BADW	Pitts S-2A Special	R. E. Mitchell
	G-BADZ	Aerotek Pitts S-2A Special	R. F. Warner
	G-BAEB	Robin DR.400/160	G. D. Jones
	G-BAEE	Jodel DR.1050/M1	R. Little
	G-BAEM	Robin DR.400/125	M. A. Webb
	G-BAEN	Robin DR.400/180	Regent Aero
	G-BAEO	Cessna F.172M	Sherburn Engineering Ltd

Reg	Type	Owner or Operator	Notes
G-BAEP	Cessna FRA.150L (modified)	Peterborough Flying School Ltd	
G-BAER	Cosmic Wind	A. G. Truman	
G-BAET	Piper J-3C-65 Cub (330314)	C. J. Rees	
G-BAEU	Cessna F.150L	G-BAEU Group	
G-BAEV	Cessna FRA.L150L	Hull Aero Club Ltd	
G-BAEW	Cessna F.172M	London Denham Aviation Ltd	
G-BAEY	Cessna F.172M	High Level Photography Ltd	
G-BAEZ	Cessna FRA.150L	Donair Flying Club Ltd	
G-BAFA	AA-5 Traveler	C. F. Mackley	
G-BAFG	DH.82A Tiger Moth	Tiger Moth Experience Ltd	
G-BAFL	Cessna 182P	R. B. Hopkinson & A. S. Pike	
G-BAFT	PA-18 Super Cub 150	C. A. M. Neidt	
G-BAFU	PA-28 Cherokee 140	C. E. Taylor	
G-BAFV	PA-18 Super Cub 95	T. F. & S. J. Thorpe	
G-BAFW	PA-28 Cherokee 140	A. J. Peters	
G-BAFX	Robin DR.400/140	MCRS Aviation	
G-BAGB	SIAI Marchetti SF.260	V. Balzer	
G-BAGC	Robin DR.400/140	J. R. Roberts	
G-BAGF	Jodel D.92 Bébé	J. Hoskins	
G-BAGG	PA-32 Cherokee Six 300E	A. D. Hoy	
G-BAGN	Cessna F.177RG	F. T. Marty	
G-BAGR	Robin DR.400/140	J. D. Last	
G-BAGS	Robin DR.400/180 2+2	M. Whale & M. W. A. Lunn	
G-BAGT	Helio H.295 Courier (66-374:EO)	D. C. Hanss	
G-BAGX	PA-28 Cherokee 140	I. Lwanga	
G-BAGY	Cameron O-84 balloon	P. G. Dunnington	
G-BAHF	PA-28 Cherokee 140	Warwickshire Aviation Ltd	
G-BAHI	Cessna F.150H	MJP Aviation & Sales	
G-BAHJ	PA-24 Comanche 250	K. Cooper	
G-BAHL	Robin DR.400/160	J. B. McVeighty	
G-BAHP	Volmer VJ.22 Sportsman	Seaplane Group	
G-BAHS	PA-28R Cherokee Arrow 200-II	A. R. N. Morris	
G-BAHX	Cessna 182P	M. D. J. Moore	
G-BAIG	PA-34-200-2 Seneca	Mid-Anglia School of Flying	
G-BAIH	PA-28R Cherokee Arrow 200-II	M. G. West	
G-BAIS	Cessna F.177RG	Cardinal Syndicate	
G-BAIW	Cessna F.172M	W. J. Greenfield	
G-BAIZ	Slingsby T.61A Falke	Falke Syndicate	
G-BAJA	Cessna F.177RG	Aviation Facilities Rotterdam BV/Netherlands	
G-BAJB	Cessna F.177RG	J. D. Loveridge	
G-BAJE	Cessna 177	C. Quist	
G-BAJN	AA-5 Traveler	John Wong Aviation Ltd	
G-BAJO	AA-5 Traveler	Montgomery Aviation Ltd	
G-BAJR	PA-28 Cherokee 180	A. C. Sturgeon	
G-BAJZ	Robin DR.400/125	Prestwick Flying Club Ltd	
G-BAKH	PA-28 Cherokee 140	British North West Airlines Ltd	
G-BAKJ	PA-30 Twin Comanche 160B	E. R. & P. M. Jones	
G-BAKM	Robin DR.400/140	D. V. Pieri	
G-BAKN	SNCAN Stampe SV.4C	M. Holloway	
G-BAKR	Jodel D.117	J. Jennings	
G-BAKV	PA-18 Super Cub 150	W. J. Murray	
G-BAKW	Beagle B.121 Pup 2	Cunning Stunts Flying Group	
G-BALD	Cameron O-84 balloon	C. A. Gould	
G-BALF	Robin DR.400/140	G. & D. A. Wasey	
G-BALG	Robin DR.400/180	S. G. Jones	
G-BALH	Robin DR.400/140B	G-BALH Flying Group	
G-BALJ	Robin DR.400/180	D. A. Batt & D. de Lacey-Rowe	
G-BALN	Cessna T.310Q	O'Brien Properties Ltd	
G-BALS	Tipsy Nipper T.66 Srs.3	N. C. Spooner	
G-BAMB	Slingsby T.61C Falke	H. J. Bradley	
G-BAMC	Cessna F.150L	K. Meredith & R. W. Marchant	
G-BAML	Bell 206B Jet Ranger II ★	Aero Venture	
G-BAMR	PA-16 Clipper	R. H. Royce	
G-BAMU	Robin DR.400/160	The Alternative Flying Group	
G-BAMV	Robin DR.400/180	K. Jones	
G-BAMY	PA-28R Cherokee Arrow 200-II	Flying Pig UK Ltd	
G-BANA	Robin DR.221	G. T. Pryor	
G-BANB	Robin DR.400/180	M. Ingvardsen	
G-BANC	Gardan GY-201 Minicab	C. R. Shipley	
G-BANF	Luton LA-4A Minor	N. F. O'Neill	
G-BANU	Wassmer Jodel D.120	C. H. Kilner	

Notes	Reg	Type	Owner or Operator
	G-BANV	Phoenix Currie Wot	A. A. M. & C. W. N. Huke
	G-BANW	CP.1330 Super Emeraude	A. Berry
	G-BANX	Cessna F.172M	Oakfleet 2000 Ltd
	G-BAOJ	MS.880B Rallye Club	G. Jones
	G-BAOM	MS.880B Rallye Club	P. J. D. Feehan
	G-BAOS	Cessna F.172M	Skytrax Aviation Ltd
	G-BAOU	AA-5 Traveler	R. C. Mark
	G-BAPB	DHC.1 Chipmunk 22	R. C. P. Brookhouse
	G-BAPI	Cessna FRA.150L	Marketing Management Services International Ltd
	G-BAPJ	Cessna FRA.150L	T. White
	G-BAPL	PA-23 Turbo Aztec 250E	Donington Aviation Ltd
	G-BAPP	Evans VP-1 Series 2	I. Pearson
	G-BAPR	Jodel D.11	W. Hinchcliffe
	G-BAPS	Campbell Cougar ★	IHM/Weston-super-Mare
	G-BAPV	Robin DR.400/160	J. D. & M. Millne
	G-BAPW	PA-28R Cherokee Arrow 180	J. L. Shields
	G-BAPX	Robin DR.400/160	White Rose Aviators
	G-BAPY	Robin HR.100/210	D. G. Doyle
	G-BARC	Cessna FR.172J	Severn Valley Aviation Group
	G-BARF	Jodel D.112 Club	R. N. Jones
	G-BARH	Beech C.23 Sundowner	G. Moorby & J. Hinchcliffe
	G-BARN	Taylor JT.2 Titch	R. G. W. Newton
	G-BARS	DHC.1 Chipmunk 22 (1377)	J. Beattie & R. M. Scarre
	G-BARZ	Scheibe SF.28A Tandem Falke	K. Kiely
	G-BASH	AA-5 Traveler	BASH Flying Group
	G-BASJ	PA-28-180 Cherokee	Bristol Aero Club
	G-BASN	Beech C.23 Sundowner	Beech G-BASN Group Syndicate
	G-BASO	Lake LA-4 Amphibian	Uulster Seaplane Association Ltd
	G-BASP	Beagle B.121 Pup 1	B. J. Coutts
	G-BATC	MBB Bö.105D	South Georgia Heritage Trust
	G-BATV	PA-28-180D Cherokee	J. N. Rudsdale
	G-BAUC	PA-25 Pawnee 235	Southdown Gliding Club Ltd
	G-BAUH	Jodel D.112	G. A. & D. Shepherd
	G-BAVB	Cessna F.172M	D. G. Smith
	G-BAVH	DHC.1 Chipmunk 22	Portsmouth Naval Gliding Club
	G-BAVL	PA-23 Aztec 250E	S. P. & A. V. Chillott
	G-BAVO	Boeing Stearman N2S (26)	R. C. McCarthy
	G-BAVR	AA-5 Traveler	M. Reusche
	G-BAWG	PA-28R Cherokee Arrow 200-II	Solent Air Ltd
	G-BAWK	PA-28 Cherokee 140	J. P. Nugent
	G-BAXE	Hughes 269A	Reethorpe Engineering Ltd
	G-BAXS	Bell 47G-5	C. R. Johnson
	G-BAXU	Cessna F.150L	Peterborough Flying School Ltd
	G-BAXV	Cessna F.150L	G. E. Fox
	G-BAXY	Cessna F.172M	The Light Aircraft Co.Ltd
	G-BAXZ	PA-28 Cherokee 140	G-BAXZ (87) Syndicate
	G-BAYL	SNCAN Nord 1101 Norecrin ★	(stored)/Chirk
	G-BAYO	Cessna 150L	J. A. & D. T. A. Rees
	G-BAYP	Cessna 150L	Yankee Papa Flying Group
	G-BAYR	Robin HR.100/210	D. G. Doyle
	G-BAZC	Robin DR.400/160	S. G. Jones
	G-BAZM	Jodel D.11	Watchford Jodel Group
	G-BAZS	Cessna F.150L	Full Sutton Flying Centre Ltd
	G-BBAW	Robin HR.100/210	F. A. Purvis
	G-BBAX	Robin DR.400/140	G. J. Bissex & P. H. Garbutt
	G-BBAY	Robin DR.400/140	S. R. Evans
	G-BBBB	Taylor JT.1 Monoplane	M. C. Arnold
	G-BBBC	Cessna F.150L	S. Collins & C. A. Widdowson
	G-BBBI	AA-5 Traveler	R. Madden
	G-BBBN	PA-28 Cherokee 180	Estuary Aviation Ltd
	G-BBBW	FRED Srs 2	M. Palfreman
	G-BBBY	PA-28 Cherokee 140	Ledbury Flying Group
	G-BBCH	Robin DR.400/2+2	S. P. Smith
	G-BBCN	Robin HR.100/210	J. C. King
	G-BBCS	Robin DR.400/140	M. D. Grinstead
	G-BBCY	Luton LA-4A Minor	A. W. McBlain
	G-BBCZ	AA-5 Traveler	A. J. Gomes
	G-BBDC	PA-28-140 Cherokee	N. Wright

Reg	Type	Owner or Operator	Notes
G-BBDE	PA-28R Cherokee Arrow 200-II	R. L. Coleman, R. Johnston, P. Knott & Istec Services Ltd	
G-BBDG	BAC-Aérospatiale Concorde 100 ★	Brooklands Museum	
G-BBDH	Cessna F.172M	J. D. Woodward	
G-BBDL	AA-5 Traveler	M. Kadir	
G-BBDM	AA-5 Traveler	Jackeroo Aviation Group	
G-BBDO	PA-23 Turbo Aztec 250E	J. W. Anstee	
G-BBDP	Robin DR.400/160	Robin Lance Aviation Associates Ltd	
G-BBDT	Cessna 150H	Delta Tango Group	
G-BBDV	SIPA S.903	E. Leggoe	
G-BBEA	Luton LA-4 Minor	D. S. Evans	
G-BBEB	PA-28R Cherokee Arrow 200-II	March Flying Group	
G-BBEC	PA-28 Cherokee 180	P. & M. Corrigan	
G-BBEN	Bellanca 7GCBC Citabria	C. A. G. Schofield	
G-BBFD	PA-28R Cherokee Arrow 200-II	G-BBFD Flying Group	
G-BBFL	Gardan GY-201 Minicab	R. Smith	
G-BBFV	PA-32 Cherokee Six 260	A. M. W. Driskell	
G-BBGI	Fuji FA.200-160	A and P West	
G-BBHF	PA-23-250 Aztec E	Eastern Air Executive Ltd	
G-BBHJ	Piper J-3C-65 Cub	Wellcross Flying Group	
G-BBHK	Noorduyn AT-16 Harvard IIB (FH153)	M. Kubrak	
G-BBHY	PA-28 Cherokee 180	Air Operations Ltd	
G-BBIF	PA-23 Aztec 250E	Marshall of Cambridge Aerospace Ltd	
G-BBIL	PA-28 Cherokee 140	Saxondale Group	
G-BBIO	Robin HR.100/210	R. P. Caley	
G-BBIX	PA-28 Cherokee 140	Sterling Aviation	
G-BBJI	Isaacs Spitfire (RN218)	S. Vince	
G-BBJU	Robin DR.400/140	P. F. Moderate	
G-BBJV	Cessna F.177RG	P. R. Powell	
G-BBJX	Cessna F.150L	York Aircraft Leasing Ltd	
G-BBJY	Cessna F.172M	D. G. Wright	
G-BBJZ	Cessna F.172M	M. W. Barlow	
G-BBKA	Cessna F.150L	Aviolease Ltd	
G-BBKB	Cessna F.150L	Justgold Ltd	
G-BBKG	Cessna FR.172J	R. Wright	
G-BBKI	Cessna F.172M	C. W. & S. A. Burman	
G-BBKL	CP.301A Emeraude	P. J. Swain	
G-BBKX	PA-28 Cherokee 180	DRA Flying Club Ltd	
G-BBKY	Cessna F.150L	F. W. Astbury	
G-BBKZ	Cessna 172M	KZ Flying Group	
G-BBLH	Piper J-3C-65 Cub (31145:G-26)	Shipping & Airlines Ltd	
G-BBLS	AA-5 Traveler	A. Grant	
G-BBLU	PA-34-200 Seneca II	R. H. R. Rue	
G-BBMB	Robin DR.400/180	K. Wade & N. Clark	
G-BBMH	EAA. Sports Biplane Model P.1	G-BBMH Flying Group	
G-BBMN	DHC.1 Chipmunk 22	R. Steiner	
G-BBMO	DHC.1 Chipmunk 22 (WK514)	Mike Oscar Group	
G-BBMR	DHC.1 Chipmunk 22 (WB763:14)	P. J. Wood	
G-BBMT	DHC.1 Chipmunk 22	MT Group	
G-BBMV	DHC.1 Chipmunk 22 (WG348)	Boultbee Vintage Ltd	
G-BBMW	DHC.1 Chipmunk 22 (WK628)	G. Fielder & A. Wilson	
G-BBMZ	DHC.1 Chipmunk 22	G-BBMZ Chipmunk Syndicate	
G-BBNA	DHC.1 Chipmunk 22 (Lycoming)	Coventry Gliding Club Ltd	
G-BBNC	DHC.1 Chipmunk T.10 (WP790) ★	de Havilland Heritage Museum/London Colney	
G-BBND	DHC.1 Chipmunk 22 (WD286)	Bernoulli Syndicate	
G-BBNI	PA-34-200 Seneca II	D. H. G. Penney	
G-BBNJ	Cessna F.150L	G. E. Fox	
G-BBNT	PA-31-350 Navajo Chieftain	Atlantic Bridge Aviation Ltd	
G-BBNZ	Cessna F.172M	J. H. Sandham Aviation	
G-BBOA	Cessna F.172M	Cirrus Aviation Ltd	
G-BBOH	Pitts S-1S Special	P. H. Meeson	
G-BBOL	PA-18 Super Cub 150	N. Moore	
G-BBOO	Thunder Ax6-56 balloon	K. Meehan Tigerjack	
G-BBOR	Bell 206B JetRanger 2	G. D. B. Budworth	
G-BBPP	PA-28 Cherokee 180	Big Red Kite Ltd (G-WACP)	
G-BBPS	Jodel D.117	V. F. Flett	
G-BBRA	PA-23 Aztec 250D	Sulafat OU/Estonia	
G-BBRB	DH.82A Tiger Moth (DF198)	R. Barham	
G-BBRC	Fuji FA.200-180	BBRC Ltd	
G-BBRI	Bell 47G-5A	Alan Mann Aviation Group Ltd	
G-BBRN	Procter Kittiwake 1 (XW784/VL)	H. M. Price	

Notes	Reg	Type	Owner or Operator
	G-BBRZ	AA-5 Traveler	B. McIntyre
	G-BBSA	AA-5 Traveler	Usworth 84 Flying Associates Ltd
	G-BBSS	DHC.1A Chipmunk 22	Coventry Gliding Club Ltd
	G-BBSW	Pietenpol Air Camper	J. K. S. Wills
	G-BBTB	Cessna FRA.150L	S. E. Waddy
	G-BBTG	Cessna F.172M	Jetstream Aero
	G-BBTH	Cessna F.172M	Ormand Flying Club Ltd
	G-BBTJ	PA-23 Aztec 250E	J. A. & R. H. Cooper
	G-BBTK	Cessna FRA.150L	Cleveland Flying School Ltd
	G-BBTY	Beech C23 Sundowner	G-BBTY Group
	G-BBUJ	Cessna 421B	Aero VIP Companhia de Transportes & Servicios Aereos SA/Portugal
	G-BBUT	Western O-65 balloon	R. G. Turnbull
	G-BBUU	Piper J-3C-65 Cub	C. Stokes
	G-BBVF	SA Twin Pioneer Srs 3 ★	Museum of Flight/East Fortune
	G-BBVO	Isaacs Fury II (K5682)	S. Vince
	G-BBXB	Cessna FRA.150L	D. C. Somerville
	G-BBXK	PA-34-200 Seneca	A. Elliott (G-FBPL)
	G-BBXW	PA-28-151 Cherokee Warrior	Bristol Aero Club
	G-BBXY	Bellanca 7GCBC Citabria	R. R. L. Windus
	G-BBYB	PA-18 Super Cub 95	Perryair Ltd
	G-BBYH	Cessna 182P	Ramco (UK) Ltd
	G-BBYM	HP.137 Jetstream 200 ★	Aerospace Museum/Cosford (G-AYWR)
	G-BBYP	PA-28 Cherokee 140	P. J. Terry
	G-BBYU	Cameron O-56 balloon ★	British Balloon Museum
	G-BBZH	PA-28R-200 Cherokee Arrow II	S. I. Tugwell
	G-BBZN	Fuji FA.200-180	D. Kynaston & ptnrs
	G-BBZV	PA-28R Cherokee Arrow 200-II	P. B. Mellor
	G-BCAH	DHC.1 Chipmunk 22 (WG316)	Century Aviation Ltd
	G-BCAP	Cameron O-56 balloon ★	Balloon Preservation Group/Lancing
	G-BCAR	Thunder Ax7-77 balloon ★	British Balloon Museum/Newbury
	G-BCAZ	PA-12 Super Cruiser	J. Forshaw
	G-BCBG	PA-23 Aztec 250E	M. Vetter
	G-BCBH	Fairchild 24R-46A Argus III	H. Mackintosh
	G-BCBJ	PA-25 Pawnee 235	Deeside Gliding Club (Aberdeenshire) Ltd
	G-BCBL	Fairchild 24R-46A Argus III (HB751)	F. J. Cox
	G-BCBR	AJEP/Wittman W.8 Tailwind	D. P. Jones
	G-BCBX	Cessna F.150L	P. Lodge & J. G. McVey
	G-BCCE	PA-23 Aztec 250E	Golf Charlie Echo Ltd
	G-BCCF	PA-28 Cherokee 180	Charlie Foxtrot Aviation
	G-BCCK	AA-5 Traveler	Prospect Air Ltd
	G-BCCR	CP.301A Emeraude (modified)	I. Taberer
	G-BCCX	DHC.1 Chipmunk 22 (Lycoming)	Charlie X-Ray Syndicate Ltd
	G-BCCY	Robin HR.200/100	Sky Ferry LLC
	G-BCDK	Partenavia P.68B	Amazon Air Services
	G-BCDL	Cameron O-42 balloon	D. P. & Mrs B. O. Turner Chums
	G-BCDN	F.27 Friendship Mk 200 ★	Instructional airframe/Norwich
	G-BCDY	Cessna FRA.150L	Leased Flight Ltd
	G-BCEE	AA-5 Traveler	P. J. Marchant
	G-BCEN	BN-2A-26 Islander	Britten-Norman Ltd
	G-BCEP	AA-5 Traveler	Sandown Aircraft Group G-BCEP
	G-BCER	Gardan GY-201 Minicab	A. N. Barley
	G-BCEU	Cameron O-42 balloon	P. Glydon
	G-BCEY	DHC.1 Chipmunk 22 (WG465)	Gopher Flying Group
	G-BCFO	PA-18-150 Super Cub	D. J. Ashley (G-MUDI)
	G-BCFR	Cessna FRA.150L	Foxtrot Romeo Group
	G-BCFW	SAAB 91D Safir	D. R. Williams
	G-BCGB	Bensen B.8	A. Melody
	G-BCGC	DHC.1 Chipmunk 22 (WP903)	Henlow Chipmunk Group
	G-BCGH	SNCAN NC.854S	P. L. Lovegrove
	G-BCGI	PA-28 Cherokee 140	D. H. G. Penny
	G-BCGJ	PA-28 Cherokee 140	Demero Ltd & Transcourt Ltd
	G-BCGM	Jodel D.120	S. M. Kenyon-Roberts
	G-BCGN	PA-28 Cherokee 140	C. F. Hessey
	G-BCGS	PA-28R Cherokee Arrow 200	The Shoreham Arrow Group
	G-BCGW	Jodel D.11	G. H. Chittenden
	G-BCHL	DHC.1 Chipmunk 22A (WP788)	Shropshire Soaring Ltd
	G-BCHP	CP.1310-C3 Super Emeraude	P. Purdey (G-JOSI)
	G-BCHT	Schleicher ASK.16	Dunstable K16 Group
	G-BCIH	DHC.1 Chipmunk 22 (WD363)	P. J. Richie

Reg	Type	Owner or Operator	Notes
G-BCIJ	AA-5 Traveler	C. M. Heck	
G-BCIR	PA-28-151 Warrior	Reborn Aviation Ltd	
G-BCJM	PA-28 Cherokee 140	J. G. McVey & P. Lodge	
G-BCJN	PA-28 Cherokee 140	Bristol and Wessex Aeroplane Club Ltd	
G-BCJO	PA-28R Cherokee Arrow 200	R. Ross	
G-BCJP	PA-28 Cherokee 140	S. Turton	
G-BCKN	DHC.1A Chipmunk 22 (Lycoming)	Coventry Gliding Club Ltd	
G-BCKS	Fuji FA.200-180AO	G. J. Ward	
G-BCKT	Fuji FA.200-180	A. G. Dobson	
G-BCKU	Cessna FRA.150L	Forge Consulting Ltd	
G-BCKV	Cessna FRA.150L	M. Bonsall	
G-BCLI	AA-5 Traveler	G-BCLI Group	
G-BCLS	Cessna 170B	M. J. Whiteman-Haywood	
G-BCLU	Jodel D.117	D. H. G. Cotter	
G-BCMD	PA-18 Super Cub 95	P. Stephenson	
G-BCMJ	Squarecraft Cavalier SA.102-5	N. F. Andrews	
G-BCMT	Isaacs Fury II	R.W. Burrows	
G-BCNC	Gardan GY-201 Minicab	J. R. Wraight	
G-BCNP	Cameron O-77 balloon	P. Spellward	
G-BCNX	Piper J-3C-65 Cub (540)	C. M. L. Edwards	
G-BCNZ	Fuji FA.200-160	Y. A. Soojeri	
G-BCOB	Piper J-3C-65 Cub (329405:A-23)	C. Marklew-Brown	
G-BCOI	DHC.1 Chipmunk 22 (WP870:12)	M. J. Diggins	
G-BCOM	Piper J-3C-65 Cub	Dougal Flying Group	
G-BCOO	DHC.1 Chipmunk 22	Double Oscar Chipmunk Group	
G-BCOR	SOCATA Rallye 100ST	Oscar Romeo Group	
G-BCOU	DHC.1 Chipmunk 22 (WK522)	Loweth Flying Group	
G-BCOY	DHC.1 Chipmunk 22	Coventry Gliding Club Ltd	
G-BCPD	Gardan GY-201 Minicab	P. R. Cozens	
G-BCPG	PA-28R Cherokee Arrow 200-II	A. J. B. Borak & E. J. Burgham	
G-BCPH	Piper J-3C-65 Cub (329934:B-72)	G. Earl	
G-BCPJ	Piper J-3C-65 Cub	J. W. Widdows	
G-BCPN	AA-5 Traveler	G-BCPN Group	
G-BCPU	DHC.1 Chipmunk 22 (WP973)	P. Green	
G-BCRB	Cessna F.172M	Wingstask 1995Ltd	
G-BCRE	Cameron O-77 balloon ★	Balloon Preservation Group/Lancing	
G-BCRL	PA-28-151 Warrior	Romeo Lima Flying Club	
G-BCRR	AA-5B Tiger	S. Waite	
G-BCRX	DHC.1 Chipmunk 22 (WD292)	P. J. Tuplin & M. I. Robinson	
G-BCSA	DHC.1 Chipmunk 22 (Lycoming)	Shenington Gliding Club Ltd	
G-BCSL	DHC.1 Chipmunk 22	Chipmunk Flyers Ltd	
G-BCTF	PA-28-151 Warrior	I. J. Hiatt	
G-BCTI	Schleicher ASK 16	Tango India Syndicate	
G-BCTK	Cessna FR.172J	M. G. E. Morton	
G-BCUB	Piper J-3C-65 Cub	S. L. Goldspink	
G-BCUF	Cessna F.172M	Howell Plant Hire & Construction	
G-BCUH	Cessna F.150M	G-BCUH Group	
G-BCUJ	Cessna F.150M	Thaxair Ltd	
G-BCUL	SOCATA Rallye 100ST	C. A. Ussher & Fountain Estates Ltd	
G-BCUO	SA Bulldog Srs 120/122	Cranfield University	
G-BCUS	SA Bulldog Srs 120/122	Falcon Group	
G-BCUV	SA Bulldog Srs 120/122 (XX704)	Flew LLP	
G-BCUW	Cessna F.177RG	S. J. Westley	
G-BCUY	Cessna FRA.150M	J. C. Carpenter	
G-BCVB	PA-17 Vagabond	A. T. Nowak	
G-BCVC	SOCATA Rallye 100ST	W. Haddow	
G-BCVE	Evans VP-2	D. Masterson & D. B. Winstanley	
G-BCVF	Practavia Pilot Sprite	A. C. Barber	
G-BCVG	Cessna FRA.150L	G-BCVG Flying Group	
G-BCVH	Cessna FRA.150L	C. Quist	
G-BCVJ	Cessna F.172M	Rothland Ltd	
G-BCVY	PA-34-200T Seneca II	Topex Ltd	
G-BCWB	Cessna 182P	M. F. Oliver & A. J. Mew	
G-BCWH	Practavia Pilot Sprite	A. T. Fines	
G-BCWK	Alpavia Fournier RF-3	T. J. Hartwell	
G-BCXB	SOCATA Rallye 100ST	A. & E. A. Wiseman	
G-BCXE	Robin DR.400/2+2	Weald Air Services Ltd	
G-BCXJ	Piper L-4J Cub (480752:E-39)	A. J. Blackford	
G-BCXN	DHC.1 Chipmunk 22 (WP800)	G. M. Turner	
G-BCYH	DAW Privateer Mk. 3	G-BCYH Group	
G-BCYK	Avro CF.100 Mk 4 Canuck (18393) ★	Imperial War Museum/Duxford	

43

Notes	Reg	Type	Owner or Operator
	G-BCYM	DHC.1 Chipmunk 22 (WK577)	G-BCYM Group
	G-BCYR	Cessna F.172M	D. M. Lockley
	G-BDAD	Taylor JT.1 Monoplane	S. Woodgate & R. Pike
	G-BDAG	Taylor JT.1 Monoplane	R. L. Soutar & R. C. Bunce
	G-BDAH	Evans VP-1	G. H. J. Geurts
	G-BDAI	Cessna FRA.150M	B. K. & W. G. Ranger
	G-BDAK	Rockwell Commander 112	M. C. Wilson
	G-BDAM	RT-16 Harvard IIB	Black Star Aviation Ltd
	G-BDAO	SIPA S.91	S. B. Churchill
	G-BDAP	AJEP Tailwind	D. G. Kelly
	G-BDAR	Evans VP-1	R. F. Powell
	G-BDAY	Thunder Ax5-42S1 balloon	J. F. Till
	G-BDBD	Wittman W.8 Tailwind	P. A. Hall
	G-BDBF	FRED Srs 2	G. E. & R. E. Collins
	G-BDBI	Cameron O-77 balloon	C. Jones
	G-BDBS	Short SD3-30 ★	Ulster Aviation Society
	G-BDBU	Cessna F.150M	S. Collins
	G-BDBV	Jodel D.11A	Seething Jodel Group
	G-BDBZ	Westland WS-55 Whirlwind (XJ398) ★	Aeroventure/Doncaster
	G-BDCD	Piper J-3C-85 Cub (480133:B-44)	Cubby Cub Group
	G-BDCI	CP.301A Emeraude	D. L. Sentence
	G-BDCO	Beagle B.121 Pup Series 1	M. R. Badminton
	G-BDDF	Jodel D.120	J. V. Thompson
	G-BDDG	Jodel D.112	J. Pool & D. G. Palmer
	G-BDDS	PA-25 Pawnee 235	Black Mountains Gliding Club
	G-BDDX	Whittaker MW2B Excalibur ★	Cornwall Aero Park/Helston
	G-BDDZ	CP.301A Emeraude	E. C. Mort
	G-BDEC	SOCATA Rallye 100ST	J. Fingleton
	G-BDEH	Jodel D.120A	N. J. Cronin
	G-BDEI	Jodel D.9 Bébé	The Noddy Flying Group
	G-BDEX	Cessna FRA.150M	A. P. F. Tucker
	G-BDEY	Piper J-3C-65 Cub	A. V. Williams
	G-BDFB	Currie Wot	J. Jennings
	G-BDFH	Auster AOP.9 (XR240)	R. B. Webber
	G-BDFR	Fuji FA.200-160	C. B. Mellor
	G-BDFU	Dragonfly MPA Mk 1 ★	Museum of Flight/East Fortune
	G-BDFX	Taylorcraft Auster 5	A. D. Pearce
	G-BDFY	AA-5 Traveler	Grumman Group
	G-BDGB	Gardan GY-20 Minicab	T. W. Slater
	G-BDGM	PA-28-151 Cherokee Warrior	M. Lee
	G-BDGY	PA-28-140 Cherokee	J. Eagles
	G-BDHK	Piper J-3C-65 Cub (329417)	Knight Flying Group
	G-BDIE	Rockwell Commander 112	J. McAleer & R. J. Adams
	G-BDIG	Cessna 182P	J. Lee & A. Horton
	G-BDIH	Jodel D.117	T. A. S. Rayner
	G-BDIX	DH.106 Comet 4C ★	Museum of Flight/East Fortune
	G-BDJD	Jodel D.112	The Real Aeroplane Company Ltd
	G-BDJG	Luton LA-4A Minor	Luton Minor Group
	G-BDJP	Piper J-3C-90 Cub	S. T. Gilbert
	G-BDJR	SNCAN Nord NC.858	P. L. Lovegrove
	G-BDKC	Cessna A185F	Lude & Invergarry Farm Partnership
	G-BDKD	Enstrom F-28A	P. J. Price
	G-BDKH	CP.301A Emeraude	R. K. Griggs
	G-BDKM	SIPA 903	S. W. Markham
	G-BDKW	Rockwell Commander 112A	G-BDKW Group
	G-BDLO	AA-5A Cheetah	D. Kryl
	G-BDLT	Rockwell Commander 112	I. Parkinson
	G-BDLY	K & S SA.102.5 Cavalier	P. R. Stevens
	G-BDMS	Piper J-3C-65 Cub (FR886)	A. T. H. Martin
	G-BDMW	Jodel DR.100A	Vectis Gliding Club Ltd
	G-BDNC	Taylor JT.1 Monoplane	J. A. Corina
	G-BDNG	Taylor JT.1 Monoplane	P. D. J. Brown
	G-BDNT	Jodel D.92 Bébé	R. J. Stobo
	G-BDNU	Cessna F.172M	J. & K. G. McVicar
	G-BDNW	AA-1B Trainer	N. A. Baxter
	G-BDNX	AA-1B Trainer	N. Clark
	G-BDOD	Cessna F.150M	OD Group
	G-BDOG	SA Bulldog Srs 200	D. C. Bonsall
	G-BDOL	Piper J-3C-65 Cub	L. R. Balthazor
	G-BDPA	PA-28-151 Warrior	J. H. Sandham Aviation

Reg	Type	Owner or Operator	Notes
G-BDPJ	PA-25 Pawnee 235B	Glider FX	
G-BDRD	Cessna FRA.150M	CBM Associates Consulting Ltd	
G-BDRG	Taylor JT.2 Titch	D. R. Gray	
G-BDRK	Cameron O-65 balloon	R. J. Mitchener & P. F. Smart	
G-BDSB	PA-28-181 Archer II	Testair Ltd	
G-BDSF	Cameron O-56 balloon	J. H. Greensides	
G-BDSH	PA-28 Cherokee 140 (modified)	The Wright Brothers Flying Group	
G-BDSK	Cameron O-65 balloon	Southern Balloon Group *Carousel II*	
G-BDSM	Slingsby T.31B Cadet III	F. C. J. Wevers/Netherlands	
G-BDTB	Evans VP-1	C. J. Riley	
G-BDTL	Evans VP-1 series 2	S. A. Daniels	
G-BDTU	Omega III gas balloon	R. G. Turnbull	
G-BDTV	Mooney M.20F	F. Laufenstein/Germany	
G-BDTX	Cessna F.150M	F. W. & I. F. Ellis	
G-BDUI	Cameron V-56 balloon	D. J. W. Johnson	
G-BDUL	Evans VP-1 Srs.2	J. C. Lindsay	
G-BDUM	Cessna F.150M	P. B. Millington	
G-BDUN	PA-34-200T Seneca II	T. W. R. Case	
G-BDUO	Cessna F.150M	B. A. Nicholson & S. J. Anderson	
G-BDUY	Robin DR.400/140B	J. G. Anderson	
G-BDUZ	Cameron V-56 balloon	Zebedee Balloon Service	
G-BDVA	PA-17 Vagabond	I. M. Callier	
G-BDVB	PA-15 (PA-17) Vagabond	B. P. Gardner	
G-BDVC	PA-17 Vagabond	A. R. Caveen	
G-BDWE	Flaglor Scooter	P. King	
G-BDWH	SOCATA Rallye 150ST	M. A. Jones	
G-BDWJ	SE-5A (replica) (F8010:Z)	D. W. Linney	
G-BDWM	Mustang scale replica (414673:LH-I))	D. C. Bonsall	
G-BDWP	PA-32R-300 Cherokee Lance	T. F. Jueschke	
G-BDWY	PA-28-140 Cherokee E	N. Donohue	
G-BDXX	SNCAN NC.858S	K. M. Davis	
G-BDYG	P.56 Provost T.1 (WV493) ★	Museum of Flight/East Fortune	
G-BDZA	Scheibe SF.25E Super Falke	Hereward Flying Group	
G-BDZD	Cessna F.172M	M. Watkinson	
G-BDZG	Slingsby T.59H Kestrel	R. E. Gretton	
G-BEAB	Jodel DR.1051	R. C. Hibberd	
G-BEAC	PA-28 Cherokee 140	R. Murray & A. Bagley-Murray	
G-BEAD	WG.13 Lynx ★	Instructional airframe/Middle Wallop	
G-BEAH	Auster J/2 Arrow	Bedwell Hey Flying Group	
G-BEBC	Westland WS-55 Whirlwind 3 (XP355) ★	Norwich Aviation Museum	
G-BEBN	Cessna 177B	S. K. Gheyi	
G-BEBR	GY-201 Minicab	A. R. Hawes	
G-BEBS	Andreasson BA-4B	T. D. Wood	
G-BEBU	Rockwell Commander 112A	I. Hunt	
G-BEBZ	PA-28-151 Warrior	P. E. Taylor	
G-BECB	SOCATA Rallye 100ST	D. H. Tonkin	
G-BECK	Cameron V-56 balloon	N. H. & A. M. Ponsford	
G-BECN	Piper J-3C-65 Cub (480480:E-44)	CN Cub Group	
G-BECT	CASA 1.131E Jungmann 2000 (A-57)	Alpha 57 Group	
G-BECW	CASA 1.131E Jungmann 2000 (A-10)	C. M. Rampton	
G-BECZ	CAARP CAP-10B	The London Aerobatic Company Ltd	
G-BEDA	CASA 1-131E Jungmann Srs.2000	L. Atkin	
G-BEDB	Nord 1203 Norecrin ★	B. F. G. Lister (stored)/Chirk	
G-BEDF	Boeing B-17G-105-VE (124485:DF-A)	B-17 Preservation Ltd	
G-BEDG	Rockwell Commander 112	G-BEDG Group	
G-BEDJ	Piper J-3C-65 Cub (44-80594)	R. Earl	
G-BEDV	V.668 Varsity T.1 (WJ945) ★	Duxford Aviation Society	
G-BEEE	Thunder Ax6-56A balloon ★	British Balloon Museum/Newbury	
G-BEEH	Cameron V-56 balloon	Sade Balloons Ltd	
G-BEEI	Cameron N-77 balloon	A. P. Griffiths	
G-BEER	Isaacs Fury II (K2075)	C. E. Styles	
G-BEFA	PA-28-151 Warrior	K. T. Langstone & M. Lawrynowicz	
G-BEFF	PA-28 Cherokee 140F	Flightpath Flying Club Ltd	
G-BEGG	Scheibe SF.25E Super Falke	G-BEGG Motorfalke	
G-BEHH	PA-32R Cherokee Lance 300	K. Swallow	
G-BEHU	PA-34-200T Seneca II	G. Y. Phillips	
G-BEHV	Cessna F.172M	Leading Edge Flight Training Ltd	
G-BEIF	Cameron O-65 balloon	C. Vening	
G-BEIG	Cessna F.150M	R. D. Forster	
G-BEII	PA-25 Pawnee 235D	Burn Gliding Club Ltd	

Notes	Reg	Type	Owner or Operator
	G-BEIP	PA-28-181 Archer II	A. Reckermann
	G-BEIS	Evans VP-1	D. L. Haines
	G-BEJK	Cameron S-31 balloon	Rango Balloon and Kite Company
	G-BEKM	Evans VP-1	G. J. McDill
	G-BEKN	Cessna FRA.150M	Peterborough Flying School Ltd
	G-BEKO	Cessna F.182Q	G. J. & F. J. Leese
	G-BELT	Cessna F.150J	R. J. Whyham (G-AWUV)
	G-BEMB	Cessna F.172M	Stocklaunch Ltd
	G-BEMW	PA-28-181 Archer II	Touch & Go Ltd
	G-BEMY	Cessna FRA.150M	J. R. Power
	G-BEND	Cameron V-56 balloon	Dante Balloon Group
	G-BENJ	Rockwell Commander 112B	BENJ Flying Group
	G-BEOE	Cessna FRA.150M	W. J. Henderson
	G-BEOH	PA-28R-201T Turbo Arrow III	Gloucestershire Flying Club
	G-BEOI	PA-18 Super Cub 150	Southdown Gliding Club Ltd
	G-BEOK	Cessna F.150M	D. M. Cloke
	G-BEOL	Short SC.7 Skyvan 3 variant 100	Liberty Aviation Ltd
	G-BEOX	Lockheed 414 Hudson IV (A16-199) ★	RAF Museum/Hendon
	G-BEOY	Cessna FRA.150L	J. N. Ponsford
	G-BEOZ	A.W.650 Argosy 101 ★	Aeropark/East Midlands
	G-BEPV	Fokker S.11-1 Instructor (174)	S. W. & M. Isbister & C. Tyers
	G-BEPY	Rockwell Commander 112B	T. L. Rippon
	G-BERA	SOCATA Rallye 150ST	A. C. Stamp
	G-BERI	Rockwell Commander 114	G-BERI Group
	G-BERN	Saffrey S-330 balloon	B. Martin
	G-BERT	Cameron V-56 balloon	E. C. Barker
	G-BERY	AA-1B Trainer	I. R. Matterface
	G-BETD	Robin HR.200/100	C. L. Wilsher
	G-BETE	Rollason B.2A Beta	T. M. Jones
	G-BETF	Cameron 'Champion' SS balloon ★	British Balloon Museum/Newbury
	G-BETM	PA-25 Pawnee 235D	Yorkshire Gliding Club (Pty) Ltd
	G-BEUA	PA-18 Super Cub 150	London Gliding Club (Pty) Ltd
	G-BEUD	Robin HR.100/285R	E. A. & L. M. C. Payton
	G-BEUI	Piper J-3C-65 Cub	Mudsville Flyers
	G-BEUM	Taylor JT.1 Monoplane	Condor Aviation International Ltd
	G-BEUP	Robin DR.400/180	MCRS Aviation
	G-BEUU	PA-18 Super Cub 95	C. Gartland
	G-BEUX	Cessna F.172N	Zentelligence Ltd
	G-BEUY	Cameron N-31 balloon	J. J. Daly
	G-BEVB	SOCATA Rallye 150ST	L. Clarke
	G-BEVC	SOCATA Rallye 150ST	Wolds Flyers Syndicate
	G-BEVG	PA-34-200T Seneca II	M. Klies
	G-BEVO	Sportavia-Pützer RF-5	M. Hill
	G-BEVP	Evans VP-2	G. Moscrop & R. C. Crowley
	G-BEVS	Taylor JT.1 Monoplane	D. Hunter
	G-BEVT	BN-2A Mk III-2 Trislander	Aurigny Air Services Ltd
	G-BEWN	DH.82A Tiger Moth	H. D. Labouchere
	G-BEWO	Zlin Z.326 Trener Master	T. Cooper
	G-BEWR	Cessna F.172N	Aerotech Solent Ltd
	G-BEWX	PA-28R-201 Arrow III	Three Greens Arrow Group
	G-BEWY	Bell 206B JetRanger 3	Polo Aviation Ltd (G-CULL)
	G-BEXJ	BN-2A-26 Islander	Channel Islands Air Search Ltd
	G-BEXN	AA-1C Lynx	Just Plane Trading Ltd
	G-BEXW	PA-28-181 Cherokee	J. O'Keeffe
	G-BEYA	Enstrom 280C	P. H. Jackson
	G-BEYB	Fairey Flycatcher (replica) (S1287) ★	F.A.A. Museum/Yeovilton
	G-BEYF	HPR.7 Herald 401 ★	Jet Heritage Museum/Bournemouth
	G-BEYL	PA-28 Cherokee 180	Yankee Lima Group
	G-BEYT	PA-28 Cherokee 140	J. N. Plange
	G-BEYV	Cessna T.210M	P. Middleton
	G-BEYZ	Jodel DR.1051/M1	M. L. Balding
	G-BEZC	AA-5 Traveler	Easter Flying Group
	G-BEZE	Rutan Vari-Eze	S. K. Cockburn
	G-BEZF	AA-5 Traveler	The G-BEZF Flying Group
	G-BEZG	AA-5 Traveler	M. D. R. Harling
	G-BEZH	AA-5 Traveler	The ZH Group
	G-BEZI	AA-5 Traveler	C. J. & L. Campbell
	G-BEZK	Cessna F.172H	S. Jones
	G-BEZL	PA-31-310 Turbo Navajo C	2 Excel Aviation Ltd
	G-BEZO	Cessna F.172M	Staverton Flying School @ Skypark Ltd
	G-BEZP	PA-32 Cherokee Six 300D	T. P. McCormack & J. K. Zealley

Reg	Type	Owner or Operator	Notes
G-BEZV	Cessna F.172M	Insch Flying Group	
G-BEZY	Rutan Vari-Eze	J. P. Kynaston	
G-BEZZ	Jodel D.112	G-BEZZ Jodel Group	
G-BFAF	Aeronca 7BCM Champion (7797)	D. A. Crompton	
G-BFAP	SIAI-Marchetti S.205-20R	A. O. Broin	
G-BFAS	Evans VP-1	A. I. Sutherland	
G-BFAW	DHC.1 Chipmunk 22 (WP848)	M. L. J. Goff	
G-BFAX	DHC.1 Chipmunk 22 (WG422)	S. R. Symonds	
G-BFBA	Jodel DR.100A	R. E. Nicholson	
G-BFBE	Robin HR.200/100	A. C. Pearson	
G-BFBM	Saffery S.330 balloon	B. Martin	
G-BFBR	PA-28-161 Warrior II	Phoenix Aviation	
G-BFBY	Piper J-3C-65 Cub (329707:S-44)	M. Shaw	
G-BFCT	Cessna Tu.206F	D. I. Schellingerhout	
G-BFDC	DHC.1 Chipmunk 22 (WG475)	N. F. O'Neill	
G-BFDE	Sopwith Tabloid (replica) (168) ★	RAF Museum/Hendon	
G-BFDF	SOCATA Rallye 235E	M. A. Wratten	
G-BFDI	PA-28-181 Archer II	Truman Aviation Ltd	
G-BFDK	PA-28-161 Warrior II	S. T. Gilbert	
G-BFDL	Piper J-3C-65 Cub (454537:J-04)	B. A. Nicholson	
G-BFDO	PA-28R-201T Turbo Arrow III	D. J. Blackburn & J. Driver	
G-BFEB	Jodel 150	G-BFEB Syndicate	
G-BFEF	Agusta-Bell 47G-3B1	I. F. Vaughan	
G-BFEH	Jodel D.117A	M. D. Mold	
G-BFEK	Cessna F.152	Staverton Flying School @ Skypark Ltd	
G-BFEV	PA-25 Pawnee 235	Yorkshire Gliding Club (Proprietary) Ltd	
G-BFFE	Cessna F.152-II	A. J. Hastings	
G-BFFP	PA-18 Super Cub 150 (modified)	East Sussex Gliding Club Ltd	
G-BFFW	Cessna F.152	Stapleford Flying Club Ltd	
G-BFGD	Cessna F.172N-II	Wannabe Flyers	
G-BFGG	Cessna FRA.150M	J. M. Machin	
G-BFGH	Cessna F.337G	S. Findlay	
G-BFGK	Jodel D.117	A. D. Eastwood	
G-BFGL	Cessna FA.152	E-Pane Ltd	
G-BFGS	MS.893E Rallye 180GT	Chiltern Flyers Ltd	
G-BFGZ	Cessna FRA.150M	C. M. Barnes	
G-BFHH	DH.82A Tiger Moth	P. & T. J. Harrison	
G-BFHI	Piper J-3C-65 Cub	N. Glass & A. J. Richardson	
G-BFHP	Champion 7GCAA Citabria	M. Walker & M. R. Keen	
G-BFHR	Jodel DR.220/2+2	B. Carter	
G-BFHU	Cessna F.152-II	M. Bonsall	
G-BFHX	Evans VP-1	D. A. Milstead	
G-BFIB	PA-31 Turbo Navajo	2 Excel Aviation Ltd	
G-BFID	Taylor JT.2 Titch Mk III	D. J. Howell	
G-BFIE	Cessna FRA.150M	J. P. A. Freeman	
G-BFIG	Cessna FR.172K XPII	K. Rogan	
G-BFIN	AA-5A Cheetah	Aircraft Engineers Ltd	
G-BFIP	Wallbro Monoplane 1909 (replica) ★	Norfolk & Suffolk Aviation Museum/Flixton	
G-BFIT	Thunder Ax6-56Z balloon	J. A. G. Tyson	
G-BFIU	Cessna FR.172K XP	A. R. Greenly	
G-BFIV	Cessna F.177RG	C. Fisher & M. L. Miller	
G-BFIX	Thunder Ax7-77A balloon	S. J. Owen	
G-BFIY	Cessna F.150M	Blackbushe Flying Club Ltd	
G-BFJR	Cessna F.337G	City North Ltd	
G-BFJZ	Robin DR.400/140B	Airpull Aviation SL	
G-BFKB	Cessna F.172N	Shropshire Flying Group	
G-BFKL	Cameron N-56 balloon	Merrythought Toys Ltd *Merrythought*	
G-BFLU	Cessna F.152	Swiftair Maintenance Ltd	
G-BFLX	AA-5A Cheetah	A. M. Verdon	
G-BFLZ	Beech 95-A55 Baron	D. Pye	
G-BFMF	Cassutt Racer IIIM	T. D. Gardner	
G-BFMG	PA-28-161 Warrior II	Andrewsfield Aviation Ltd	
G-BFMH	Cessna 177B	Aerofoil Aviation Ltd	
G-BFMK	Cessna FA.152	The Leicestershire Aero Club Ltd	
G-BFMR	PA-20 Pacer 125	J. Knight	
G-BFMX	Cessna F.172N	M. Rowe	
G-BFNG	Jodel D.112	NG Group	
G-BFNI	PA-28-161 Warrior II	Lion Services	
G-BFNK	PA-28-161 Warrior II	Parachuting Aircraft Ltd	
G-BFNM	Globe GC-1B Swift	M. J. Butler	
G-BFOE	Cessna F.152	Redhill Air Services Ltd	

Notes	Reg	Type	Owner or Operator
	G-BFOF	Cessna F.152	Ionian Aviation Ltd
	G-BFOG	Cessna 150M	Wicklow Wings
	G-BFOJ	AA-1 Yankee	J. J. N. Carpenter
	G-BFOP	Jodel D.120	J. K. Cook & E. Leggoe
	G-BFOU	Taylor JT.1 Monoplane	G. Bee
	G-BFOV	Cessna F.172N	D. J. Walker
	G-BFPA	Scheibe SF.25B Falke	M. V. Hearns & P. Wigginton
	G-BFPH	Cessna F.172K	Linc-Air Flying Group
	G-BFPO	Rockwell Commander 112B	Doerr International Ltd
	G-BFPP	Bell 47J-2 Ranger	M. R. Masters
	G-BFPR	PA-25 Pawnee 235D	The Windrushers Gliding Club Ltd
	G-BFPS	PA-25 Pawnee 235D	C. A. M. M. Neidt
	G-BFPZ	Cessna F.177RG Cardinal	O. C. Baars
	G-BFRI	Sikorsky S-61N	British International
	G-BFRR	Cessna FRA.150M	Romeo Romeo Flying Group
	G-BFRS	Cessna F.172N	Aerocomm Ltd
	G-BFRV	Cessna FA.152	Cristal Air Ltd
	G-BFRY	PA-25 Pawnee 260	Yorkshire Gliding Club (Pty) Ltd
	G-BFSA	Cessna F.182Q	Delta Lima Flying Group
	G-BFSC	PA-25 Pawnee 235D	Essex Gliding Club Ltd
	G-BFSD	PA-25 Pawnee 235D	Deeside Gliding Club (Aberdeenshire) Ltd
	G-BFSR	Cessna F.150J	W. Ali
	G-BFSS	Cessna FR.172G	Albedale Farms Ltd
	G-BFSY	PA-28-181 Archer II	Downland Aviation
	G-BFSZ	PA-28-161 Warrior II	R. J. Whyham (G-KBPI)
	G-BFTC	PA-28R-201T Turbo Arrow III	Top Cat Flying Group
	G-BFTF	AA-5B Tiger	F. C. Burrow Ltd
	G-BFTG	AA-5B Tiger	D. Hepburn & G. R. Montgomery
	G-BFTH	Cessna F.172N	T. W. Oakley
	G-BFTX	Cessna F.172N	Tri Society
	G-BFUB	PA-32RT-300 Lance II	J. Lowndes
	G-BFUD	Scheibe SF.25E Super Falke	SF25E Syndicate
	G-BFVG	PA-28-181 Archer II	C. J. P. Mrziglod
	G-BFVH	DH.2 (replica) (5964)	S. W. Turley
	G-BFVS	AA-5B Tiger	G-BFVS Flying Group
	G-BFVU	Cessna 150L	A. N. Mole
	G-BFWB	PA-28-161 Warrior II	Mid-Anglia School of Flying
	G-BFWD	Currie Wot (C3009)	A. Foan
	G-BFXF	Andreasson BA.4B	P. N. Birch
	G-BFXG	D.31 Turbulent	XG Group
	G-BFXK	PA-28 Cherokee 140	G-BFXK Owners Ltd
	G-BFXL	Albatros D.5a replica (D5397/17) ★	F.A.A. Museum/Yeovilton
	G-BFXR	Jodel D.112	R. G. Marshall
	G-BFXS	Rockwell Commander 114	Romeo Whiskey Ltd
	G-BFXW	AA-5B Tiger	A. M. & J. D. Arnold
	G-BFXX	AA-5B Tiger	W. R. Gibson
	G-BFYA	MBB Bö.105DB	Wessex Aviation Ltd
	G-BFYI	Westland-Bell 47G-3B1	K. P. Mayes
	G-BFYK	Cameron V-77 balloon	L. E. Jones
	G-BFYL	Evans VP-2	F. C. Handy
	G-BFYO	SPAD XIII (replica) (4513:1) ★	American Air Museum/Duxford
	G-BFYW	Slingsby T.65A Vega	S. A. Whitaker
	G-BFZB	Piper J-3C-85 Cub (480723:E5-J)	M. S. Pettit
	G-BFZD	Cessna FR.182RG	A. R. Harris
	G-BFZH	PA-28R Cherokee Arrow 200	Aircraft Engineers Ltd
	G-BFZM	Rockwell Commander 112TC	J. A. Hart & R. J. Lamplough
	G-BFZO	AA-5A Cheetah	G-BFZO Flying Group
	G-BGAA	Cessna 152 II	PJC Leasing Ltd
	G-BGAB	Cessna F.152 II	TG Aviation Ltd
	G-BGAE	Cessna F.152 II	Aerolease Ltd
	G-BGAJ	Cessna F.182Q II	B. & C. Blumberg
	G-BGAX	PA-28 Cherokee 140	G-BGAX Group
	G-BGAZ	Cameron V-77 balloon	C. J. Madigan & D. H. McGibbon
	G-BGBE	Jodel DR.1050	J. A. & B. Mawby
	G-BGBF	Druine D.31 Turbulent	T. A. Stambach
	G-BGBG	PA-28-181 Archer II	Harlow Printing Ltd
	G-BGBI	Cessna F.150L	BI Flying Group
	G-BGBK	PA-38-112 Tomahawk	Smart People Don't Buy Ltd
	G-BGBV	Slingsby T65A Vega	M. P. Day
	G-BGBW	PA-38-112 Tomahawk	Smart People Don't Buy Ltd

Reg	Type	Owner or Operator	Notes
G-BGCB	Slingsby T.65A Vega	G. Wright & F. J. Bradley	
G-BGCM	AA-5A Cheetah	R. W. Walker	
G-BGCO	PA-44-180 Seminole	BAE Systems (Operations) Ltd	
G-BGCU	Slingsby T.65A Vega	K. Challinor	
G-BGCY	Taylor JT.1 Monoplane	M. R. Punter	
G-BGEF	Jodel D.112	G. G. Johnson	
G-BGEH	Monnett Sonerai II	E. C. Murgatroyd	
G-BGEI	Baby Great Lakes	D. H. Greenwood	
G-BGES	Phoenix Currie Super Wot	N. M. Bloom	
G-BGFF	FRED Srs 2	I Pearson & P. C. Appleton	
G-BGFG	AA-5A Cheetah	A. J. Williams	
G-BGFJ	Jodel D.9 Bébé	R. J. Stobo	
G-BGFX	Cessna F.152	Redhill Air Services Ltd	
G-BGGA	Bellanca 7GCBC Citabria	L. A. King	
G-BGGB	Bellanca 7GCBC Citabria	D. A. Payne	
G-BGGC	Bellanca 7GCBC Citabria	P. J. F. H. De Coninck	
G-BGGD	Bellanca 8GCBC Scout	Bidford Gliding & Flying Club Ltd	
G-BGGE	PA-38-112 Tomahawk	Smart People Don't Buy Ltd	
G-BGGI	PA-38-112 Tomahawk	Smart People Don't Buy Ltd	
G-BGGM	PA-38-112 Tomahawk	G. E. Fox	
G-BGGO	Cessna F.152	East Midlands Flying School Ltd	
G-BGGP	Cessna F.152	East Midlands Flying School Ltd	
G-BGHF	Westland WG.30 ★	IHM/Weston-super-Mare	
G-BGHJ	Cessna F.172N	Air Plane Ltd	
G-BGHM	Robin R.1180T	P. Price	
G-BGHS	Cameron N-31 balloon	G. Gray	
G-BGHT	Falconar F-12	C. R. Coates	
G-BGHU	NA T-6G Texan (115042:TA-042)	C. E. Bellhouse	
G-BGHY	Taylor JT.1 Monoplane	J. H. Mangan	
G-BGHZ	FRED Srs 2	A. J. Perry	
G-BGIB	Cessna 152 II	Redhill Air Services Ltd	
G-BGIG	PA-38-112 Tomahawk	Leading Edge Flight Training Ltd	
G-BGIU	Cessna F.172H	S. J. Windle	
G-BGIY	Cessna F.172N	Leading Edge Flight Training Ltd	
G-BGKO	Gardan GY-20 Minicab	Condor Aviation International Ltd	
G-BGKS	PA-28-161 Warrior II	Fly with the Best Ltd	
G-BGKT	Auster AOP.9 (XN441)	Kilo Tango Group	
G-BGKU	PA-28R-201 Arrow III	Aerolease Ltd	
G-BGKV	PA-28R-201 Arrow III	R. N. Mayle	
G-BGKY	PA-38-112 Tomahawk	APB Leasing Ltd	
G-BGKZ	Auster J/5F Aiglet Trainer	R. B. Webber	
G-BGLA	PA-38-112 Tomahawk	J. T. Mountain	
G-BGLB	Bede BD-5B ★	Science Museum/Wroughton	
G-BGLF	Evans VP-1 Srs 2	B. A. Schlussler	
G-BGLG	Cessna 152	Cloud Global Ltd	
G-BGLO	Cessna F.172N	General Aero Equipment Ltd	
G-BGLZ	Stits SA-3A Playboy	W. Hinchcliffe	
G-BGME	SIPA 903	M. Emery (G-BCML)	
G-BGMJ	Gardan GY-201 Minicab	G-BGMJ Group	
G-BGMP	Cessna F.172G	B. M. O'Brien	
G-BGMR	Gardan GY-20 Minicab	P. A. Hall	
G-BGMS	Taylor JT.2 Titch	M. A. J. Spice	
G-BGMT	SOCATA Rallye 235E	C. G. Wheeler & M. Faulkner	
G-BGND	Cessna F.172N	A. J. M. Freeman	
G-BGNT	Cessna F.152	Aerolease Ltd	
G-BGNV	GA-7 Cougar	D. D. Saint	
G-BGOG	PA-28-161 Warrior II	W. D. Moore & F. J. Morris	
G-BGOL	PA-28R-201T Turbo Arrow III	R. G. Jackson	
G-BGON	GA-7 Cougar	S. J. Green	
G-BGOR	AT-6D Harvard III (14863)	A. P. Wilson & M. B. Levy	
G-BGPB	CCF T-6J Texan (1747)	Aircraft Spares & Materials Ltd	
G-BGPD	Piper J-3C-65 Cub (479744:M-49)	P. R. Whiteman	
G-BGPH	AA-5B Tiger	Shipping & Airlines Ltd	
G-BGPI	Plumb BGP-1	B. G. Plumb	
G-BGPJ	PA-28-161 Warrior II	W. Lancs Warrior Co Ltd	
G-BGPL	PA-28-161 Warrior II	Transcourt Ltd	
G-BGPM	Evans VP-2	Condor Aviation International Ltd	
G-BGPN	PA-18 Super Cub 150	A. R. Darke	
G-BGRE	Beech A200 Super King Air	Killinchy Aerospace Holdings Ltd	
G-BGRI	Jodel DR.1051	R. G. Hallam	
G-BGRM	PA-38-112 Tomahawk	V. Baltzopoulos	

Notes	Reg	Type	Owner or Operator
	G-BGRO	Cessna F.172M	Cammo Aviation
	G-BGRR	PA-38-112 Tomahawk	S. P. Vincent
	G-BGRT	Steen Skybolt	F. Ager
	G-BGRX	PA-38-112 Tomahawk	N. M. Robinson
	G-BGSA	Morane MS.892E-150	B. Huda & P. W. Osborne
	G-BGSJ	Piper J-3C-65 Cub (236657)	M. A. V. Gatehouse
	G-BGSV	Cessna F.172N	Southwell Air Services Ltd
	G-BGSW	Beech F33 Debonair	J. J. Noakes
	G-BGSY	GA-7 Cougar	P. J. K. Luthaus
	G-BGTC	Auster AOP.9 (XP282)	Terranne Auster Group
	G-BGTF	PA-44-180 Seminole	M. J. Edgeworth (G-OPTC)
	G-BGTI	Piper J-3C-65 Cub	A. P. Broad
	G-BGUB	PA-32 Cherokee Six 300E	D. P. & E. A. Morris
	G-BGVB	Robin DR.315	K. Hartmann
	G-BGVE	CP.1310-C3 Super Emeraude	R. Whitwell
	G-BGVH	Beech 76 Duchess	Velco Marketing
	G-BGVN	PA-28RT-201 Arrow IV	John Wailing Ltd
	G-BGVS	Cessna F.172M	Enterprise Purchasing Ltd
	G-BGVY	AA-5B Tiger	R. J. C. Neal-Smith
	G-BGVZ	PA-28-181 Archer II	M. & W. Walsh
	G-BGWC	Robin DR.400/180	S. A. Cook & G. C. Bremner
	G-BGWM	PA-28-181 Archer II	Thames Valley Flying Club Ltd
	G-BGWO	Jodel D.112	G-BGWO Group
	G-BGWZ	Eclipse Super Eagle ★	F.A.A. Museum/Yeovilton
	G-BGXA	Piper J-3C-65 Cub (329471:F-44)	P. King
	G-BGXC	SOCATA TB10 Tobago	M. H. & S. H. Cundey
	G-BGXD	SOCATA TB10 Tobago	Whitewest Ltd
	G-BGXO	PA-38-112 Tomahawk	Goodwood Terrena Ltd
	G-BGXR	Robin HR.200/100	J. R. Cross
	G-BGXS	PA-28-236 Dakota	G-BGXS Group
	G-BGXT	SOCATA TB10 Tobago	J. L. Alexander
	G-BGYH	PA-28-161 Warrior II	Tayside Aviation Ltd
	G-BGYN	PA-18 Super Cub 150	B. J. Dunford
	G-BHAA	Cessna 152 II	Herefordshire Aero Club Ltd
	G-BHAD	Cessna A.152	Cirrus Aviation Ltd
	G-BHAI	Cessna F.152	ACS Aviation Ltd
	G-BHAJ	Robin DR.400/160	Rowantask Ltd
	G-BHAV	Cessna F.152	T. M. & M. L. Jones
	G-BHAX	Enstrom F-28C-UK-2	PVS (Barnsley) Ltd
	G-BHAY	PA-28RT-201 Arrow IV	Alpha Yankee Ltd
	G-BHBA	Campbell Cricket	S. N. McGovern
	G-BHBE	Westland-Bell 47G-3B1 (Soloy)	T. R. Smith (Agricultural Machinery) Ltd
	G-BHBG	PA-32R Cherokee Lance 300	Teamtischer GmbH/Germany
	G-BHBT	Marquart MA.5 Charger	Bravo Tango Group
	G-BHCC	Cessna 172M	D. Wood-Jenkins
	G-BHCE	Jodel D.112	Charles Echo Group
	G-BHCM	Cessna F.172H	J. Dominic
	G-BHCP	Cessna F.152	Eastern Air Executive Ltd
	G-BHCZ	PA-38-112 Tomahawk	J. E. Abbott
	G-BHDD	V.668 Varsity T.1 (WL626:P) ★	Aeropark/East Midlands
	G-BHDE	SOCATA TB10 Tobago	P. A. Parry & J. C. Parker
	G-BHDK	Boeing B-29A-BN (461748:Y) ★	Imperial War Museum/Duxford
	G-BHDM	Cessna F.152 II	Big Red Kite Ltd
	G-BHDP	Cessna F.182Q II	Zone Travel Ltd
	G-BHDS	Cessna F.152 II	Redmosaic Formacao de Technicos de Aeronaves Unipessoal
	G-BHDV	Cameron V-77 balloon	P. Glydon
	G-BHDX	Cessna F.172N	D. M. Hobson
	G-BHDZ	Cessna F.172N	H. Mackintosh
	G-BHED	Cessna FA.152	Skytrek Flying School Ltd
	G-BHEG	Jodel 150	D. M. Griffiths
	G-BHEK	CP.1315-C3 Super Emeraude	D. B. Winstanley
	G-BHEL	Jodel D.117	D. W. & S. J. McAllister
	G-BHEN	Cessna FA.152	Leicestershire Aero Club Ltd
	G-BHEU	Thunder Ax7-65 balloon	J. A. W. Dyer
	G-BHEV	PA-28R Cherokee Arrow 200	7-Up Group
	G-BHFC	Cessna F.152	JH Sandham Aviation
	G-BHFE	PA-44-180 Seminole	Transport Command Ltd
	G-BHFG	SNCAN Stampe SV.4C	A. D. R. Northeast & S. A. Cook
	G-BHFH	PA-34-200T Seneca II	Andrews Professional Colour Laboratories Ltd

Reg	Type	Owner or Operator	Notes
G-BHFI	Cessna F.152	BAe (Warton) Flying Club	
G-BHFJ	PA-28RT-201T Turbo Arrow IV	S. A. Cook & D. R. Northeast	
G-BHFK	PA-28-151 Warrior	G-BHFK Flying Group	
G-BHGC	PA-18 Super Cub 150	C. R. Dacey	
G-BHGF	Cameron V-56 balloon	P. Smallward	
G-BHGJ	Jodel D.120	M. Devlin	
G-BHGO	PA-32 Cherokee Six 260	W. J. Henry	
G-BHGY	PA-28R Cherokee Arrow 200	Truman Aviation Ltd	
G-BHHE	Jodel DR.1051/M1	D. Dunn	
G-BHHG	Cessna F.152 II	TG Aviation Ltd	
G-BHHH	Thunder Ax7-65 balloon	J. M. J. Roberts	
G-BHHK	Cameron N-77 balloon ★	British Balloon Museum	
G-BHHN	Cameron V-77 balloon	Itchen Valley Balloon Group	
G-BHIB	Cessna F.182Q	M. S. Williams	
G-BHII	Cameron V-77 balloon	R. V. Brown	
G-BHIJ	Eiri PIK-20E-1 (898)	P. J. Shout & I. P. Freestone	
G-BHIN	Cessna F.152	Sussex Flying Club Ltd	
G-BHIR	PA-28R Cherokee Arrow 200	Factorcore Ltd	
G-BHIS	Thunder Ax7-65 balloon	Hedgehoppers Balloon Group	
G-BHIY	Cessna F.150K	N. J. Butler	
G-BHJF	SOCATA TB10 Tobago	T. W. Marsh	
G-BHJI	Mooney M.20J	Otomed APS/Denmark	
G-BHJK	Maule M5-235C Lunar Rocket	M. K. H. Bell	
G-BHJN	Fournier RF-4D	RF-4 Group	
G-BHJO	PA-28-161 Warrior II	G-BHJO Group	
G-BHJS	Partenavia P.68B	Flew LLP	
G-BHJU	Robin DR.400/2+2	Ageless Aeronautics	
G-BHKR	Colt 12A balloon ★	British Balloon Museum/Newbury	
G-BHKT	Jodel D.112	G. Dawes	
G-BHLE	Robin DR.400/180	A. V. Harmer	
G-BHLH	Robin DR.400/180	G-BHLH Group	
G-BHLJ	Saffery-Rigg S.200 balloon	I. A. Rigg	
G-BHLT	DH.82A Tiger Moth	R. C. P. Brookhouse	
G-BHLU	Fournier RF-3	A. C. Bell	
G-BHLW	Cessna 120	Moray Flying Group	
G-BHLX	AA-5B Tiger	M. D. McPherson	
G-BHMA	SIPA 903	H. J. Taggart	
G-BHMG	Cessna FA.152	North Weald Flying Group Ltd	
G-BHMJ	Avenger T.200-2112 balloon	R. Light Lord Anthony 1	
G-BHMK	Avenger T.200-2112 balloon	P. Kinder Lord Anthony 2	
G-BHMT	Evans VP-1	J. Hoskins	
G-BHMY	F.27 Friendship Mk.200 ★	Norwich Aviation Museum	
G-BHNC	Cameron O-65 balloon	D. & C. Bareford	
G-BHNK	Jodel D.120A	G. J. Prisk	
G-BHNO	PA-28-181 Archer II	HJK Asset Management Ltd	
G-BHNP	Eiri PIK-20E-1	D. A. Sutton	
G-BHNV	Westland-Bell 47G-3B1	S. W. Hutchinson	
G-BHNX	Jodel D.117	M. J. A. Trudgill	
G-BHOA	Robin DR.400/160	T. L. Trott	
G-BHOL	Jodel DR.1050	S. J. Pearson	
G-BHOM	PA-18 Super Cub 95	D. R. & R. M. Lee	
G-BHOR	PA-28-161 Warrior II	Oscar Romeo Flying Group	
G-BHOT	Cameron V-65 balloon	Dante Balloon Group	
G-BHOZ	SOCATA TB9 Tampico	Fosseway Flying Club Ltd	
G-BHPK	Piper J-3C-65 Cub (238410:A-44)	L-4 Group	
G-BHPL	CASA 1.131E Jungmann 1000 (E3B-350:05-97)	A. Burroughes	
G-BHPS	Jodel D.120A	Papa Sierra Syndicate	
G-BHPZ	Cessna 172N	O'Brien Properties Ltd	
G-BHRC	PA-28-161 Warrior II	Sherwood Flying Club Ltd	
G-BHRH	Cessna FA.150K	Merlin Flying Club Ltd	
G-BHRK	Colt Saucepan 56 SS balloon	D. P. Busby	
G-BHRO	Rockwell Commander 112	M. G. Cookson	
G-BHRR	CP.301A Emeraude	T. Brown	
G-BHSB	Cessna 172N	J. W. Cope & M. P. Wimsey	
G-BHSD	Scheibe SF.25E Super Falke	K. E. Ballington	
G-BHSE	Rockwell Commander 114	604 Sqdn Flying Group Ltd	
G-BHSL	CASA 1-131E Jungmann	H. I. Taylor	
G-BHSY	Jodel DR.1050	T. R. Allebone	
G-BHTA	PA-28-236 Dakota	Dakota Ltd	
G-BHTC	Jodel DR.1050/M1	B. R. Hunter	

Notes	Reg	Type	Owner or Operator
	G-BHTG	Thunder Ax6-56 Bolt balloon	The British Balloon Museum & Library Ltd
	G-BHUB	Douglas C-47A (315509:W7-S) ★	Imperial War Museum/Duxford
	G-BHUE	Jodel DR.1050	M. J. Harris
	G-BHUG	Cessna 172N	L. Marriott & R. Wainwright
	G-BHUI	Cessna 152	South Warwickshire School of Flying Ltd
	G-BHUM	DH.82A Tiger Moth	S. G. Towers
	G-BHUU	PA-25 Pawnee 235	Booker Gliding Club Ltd
	G-BHVB	PA-28-161 Warrior II	Falcon Flying Services
	G-BHVF	Jodel 150A	Groupe Ariel
	G-BHVP	Cessna 182Q	The G-BHVP Flying Group
	G-BHVR	Cessna 172N	Victor Romeo Group
	G-BHVV	Piper J-3C-65 Cub	T. Kattinger
	G-BHWA	Cessna F.152	DSFT Ltd
	G-BHWB	Cessna F.152	Lincoln Enterprises Ltd
	G-BHWY	PA-28R Cherokee Arrow 200-II	Kilo Foxtrot Flying Group
	G-BHWZ	PA-28-181 Archer II	M. A. Abbott
	G-BHXA	SA Bulldog Srs 120/1210	Air Plan Flight Equipment Ltd
	G-BHXB	SA Bulldog Srs 120/1210	XB Group (G-JWCM)
	G-BHXD	Jodel D.120	R. E. Guscott
	G-BHXS	Jodel D.120	Plymouth Jodel Group
	G-BHXY	Piper J-3C-65 Cub (44-79609:44-S)	F. W. Rogers
	G-BHYA	Cessna R.182RG II	J.-P. Jarier
	G-BHYC	Cessna 172RG II	BHM Aviation
	G-BHYD	Cessna R.172K XP II	A. J. House
	G-BHYI	SNCAN Stampe SV.4A	D. Hicklin
	G-BHYP	Cessna F.172M	Avior Ltd
	G-BHYR	Cessna F.172M	G-BHYR Group
	G-BHYV	Evans VP-1	J. L. Van Wijk/Belgium
	G-BHZE	PA-28-181 Archer II	Zegruppe Ltd
	G-BHZH	Cessna F.152	Fly NQY Pilot Training
	G-BHZK	AA-5B Tiger	ZK Group
	G-BHZO	AA-5A Cheetah	PG Air
	G-BHZR	SA Bulldog Srs 120/1210	J. G. McTaggart
	G-BHZT	SA Bulldog Srs 120/1210	D. M. Curties
	G-BHZU	Piper J-3C-65 Cub	P. F. Durnford
	G-BHZV	Jodel D.120A	G-BHZV Group
	G-BIAC	SOCATA Rallye 235E	B. Brou
	G-BIAH	Jodel D.112	K. J. Steele
	G-BIAI	WMB.2 Windtracker balloon	I. Chadwick
	G-BIAP	PA-16 Clipper	G-BIAP Flying Group
	G-BIAR	Rigg Skyliner II balloon	I. A. Rigg
	G-BIAU	Sopwith Pup (replica) (N6452) ★	F.A.A. Museum/Yeovilton
	G-BIAX	Taylor JT.2 Titch	P. J. Hebdon & C. S. Hales
	G-BIAY	AA-5 Traveler	A. J. Black
	G-BIBA	SOCATA TB9 Tampico	TB Aviation Ltd
	G-BIBO	Cameron V-65 balloon	D. M. Hoddinott
	G-BIBS	Cameron P-20 balloon	Cameron Balloons Ltd
	G-BIBT	AA-5B Tiger	Bravo Tango Ltd
	G-BIBX	WMB.2 Windtracker balloon	I. A. Rigg
	G-BICD	Auster 5	T. R. Parsons
	G-BICE	NA AT-6C Harvard IIA (41-33275:CE)	C. M. L. Edwards
	G-BICG	Cessna F.152 II	M. A. Khan
	G-BICM	Colt 56A balloon	M. R. Stokoe
	G-BICP	Robin DR.360	B. McVeighty
	G-BICR	Jodel D.120A	T. W. J. Carnall & M. B. Blackmore
	G-BICS	Robin R.2100A	Chiltern Flying Group
	G-BICU	Cameron V-56 balloon	Black Pearl Balloons
	G-BICW	PA-28-161 Warrior II	Charlie Whisky Flying Group
	G-BIDD	Evans VP-1	J. Hodgkinson
	G-BIDG	Jodel 150A	D. R. Gray
	G-BIDH	Cessna 152 II	Hull Aero Club Ltd (G-DONA)
	G-BIDI	PA-28R-201 Arrow III	S. Jameson
	G-BIDJ	PA-18A Super Cub 150	S. M. Hart
	G-BIDK	PA-18 Super Cub 150	Y. Leysen
	G-BIDO	CP.301A Emeraude	A. R. Plumb
	G-BIDV	Colt 14A balloon ★	British Balloon Museum/Newbury
	G-BIDW	Sopwith 11⁄2 Strutter (replica) (A8226) ★	RAF Museum/Hendon
	G-BIDX	Jodel D.112	P. Turton
	G-BIEN	Jodel D.120A	M. J. Sharp
	G-BIEO	Jodel D.112	R. S. & S. C. Solley

Reg	Type	Owner or Operator	Notes
G-BIES	Maule M5-235C Lunar Rocket	William Proctor Ltd	
G-BIET	Cameron O-77 balloon	G. M. Westley	
G-BIEY	PA-28-151 Warrior	M. J. Isaac	
G-BIFB	PA-28-150 Cherokee C	D. H. G. Penney	
G-BIFO	Evans VP-1 Srs.2	G. W. Hancox	
G-BIFP	Colt 56A balloon	J. W. Adkins	
G-BIFY	Cessna F.150L	North Weald Flying Group Ltd	
G-BIGJ	Cessna F.172M	Cirrus Aviation Ltd	
G-BIGK	Taylorcraft BC-12D	R. A. Benson	
G-BIGL	Cameron O-65 balloon	P. L. Mossman	
G-BIGR	Avenger T.200-2112 balloon	R. Light	
G-BIGX	Bensen B.8M	W. C. Turner	
G-BIHD	Robin DR.400/160	R. C. Boll	
G-BIHF	SE-5A (replica) (F943)	C. J. Zeal	
G-BIHI	Cessna 172M	D. H. G. Penney	
G-BIHO	DHC.6 Twin Otter 310	Isles of Scilly Skybus Ltd	
G-BIHT	PA-17 Vagabond	N. F. Andrews	
G-BIHU	Saffrey S.200 balloon	B. L. King	
G-BIHX	Bensen B.8M	P. P. Willmott	
G-BIIA	Fournier RF-3	C. H. Dennis	
G-BIID	PA-18 Super Cub 95	D. A. Lacey	
G-BIIF	Fournier RF-4D	K. M. Fresson (G-BVET)	
G-BIIK	MS.883 Rallye 115	N. J. Garbett	
G-BIIO	BN-2T Islander	Islander Aircraft Ltd	
G-BIIT	PA-28-161 Warrior II	Tayside Aviation Ltd	
G-BIIZ	Great Lakes 2T-1A Sport Trainer	Airborne Adventures Ltd	
G-BIJB	PA-18 Super Cub 150	James Aero Ltd	
G-BIJD	Bölkow Bö.208C Junior	J. D. Day	
G-BIJE	Piper J-3C-65 Cub	R. L. Hayward & A. G. Scott	
G-BIJS	Luton LA-4A Minor	C. C. & J. M. Lovell	
G-BIJU	CP-301A Emeraude	Eastern Taildraggers Flying Group (G-BHTX)	
G-BIJV	Cessna F.152 II	Falcon Flying Services	
G-BIJW	Cessna F.152 II	Falcon Flying Services	
G-BIJX	Cessna F.152 II	Falcon Flying Services	
G-BIKB	Boeing 757-236F	DHL Air Ltd	
G-BIKE	PA-28R Cherokee Arrow 200	R. Taylor	
G-BIKX	Boeing 757-236F	DHL Air Ltd	
G-BIKZ	Boeing 757-236F	DHL Air Ltd	
G-BILB	WMB.2 Windtracker balloon	B. L. King	
G-BILE	Scruggs BL.2B balloon	P. D. Ridout	
G-BILG	Scruggs BL.2B balloon	P. D. Ridout	
G-BILH	Slingsby T.65C Vega	P. Woodcock	
G-BILI	Piper J-3C-65 Cub (454467:J-44)	G-BILI Flying Group	
G-BILR	Cessna 152 II	APB Leasing Ltd	
G-BILS	Cessna 152 II	Mona Flying Club	
G-BILU	Cessna 172RG	Full Sutton Flying Centre Ltd	
G-BILZ	Taylor JT.1 Monoplane	A. Petherbridge	
G-BIMK	Tiger T.200 Srs 1 balloon	M. K. Baron	
G-BIMM	PA-18 Super Cub 150	Spectrum Leisure Ltd	
G-BIMN	Steen Skybolt	R. J. Thomas	
G-BIMT	Cessna FA.152	Staverton Flying School @ Skypark Ltd	
G-BIMX	Rutan Vari-Eze	D. G. Crow	
G-BIMZ	Beech 76 Duchess	Firfax Aviation Ltd	
G-BINL	Scruggs BL.2B balloon	P. D. Ridout	
G-BINM	Scruggs BL.2B balloon	P. D. Ridout	
G-BINR	Unicorn UE.1A balloon	Unicorn Group	
G-BINS	Unicorn UE.2A balloon	Unicorn Group	
G-BINT	Unicorn UE.1A balloon	D. E. Bint	
G-BINX	Scruggs BL.2B balloon	P. D. Ridout	
G-BINY	Oriental balloon	J. L. Morton	
G-BIOA	Hughes 369D	AH Helicopter Services Ltd	
G-BIOB	Cessna F.172P	High Level Photography Ltd	
G-BIOC	Cessna F.150L	K. Rowell	
G-BIOI	Jodel DR.1051/M	A. A. Alderdice	
G-BIOK	Cessna F.152	N. Foster	
G-BIOM	Cessna F.152	J. B. P. E. Fernandes	
G-BIOU	Jodel D.117A	M. R. Routh	
G-BIPA	AA-5B Tiger	Tri-Star Developments Ltd	
G-BIPH	Scruggs BL.2B balloon	C. M. Dewsnap	
G-BIPI	Everett gyroplane	J. G. Farina	
G-BIPN	Fournier RF-3	G-BIPN Group	

Notes	Reg	Type	Owner or Operator
	G-BIPT	Jodel D.112	C. R. Davies
	G-BIPV	AA-5B Tiger	Echo Echo Ltd
	G-BIPW	Avenger T.200-2112 balloon	B. L. King
	G-BIRD	Pitts S-1D Special	N. E. Smith
	G-BIRE	Colt 56 Bottle SS balloon	D. M. Hoddinott
	G-BIRI	CASA 1.131E Jungmann 1000	D. Watt
	G-BIRL	Avenger T.200-2112 balloon	R. Light
	G-BIRP	Arena Mk 17 Skyship balloon	A. S. Viel
	G-BIRT	Robin R.1180TD	W. D'A. Hall
	G-BIRW	MS.505 Criquet (F+IS) ★	Museum of Flight/East Fortune
	G-BISG	FRED Srs 3	T. Littlefair
	G-BISH	Cameron V-65 balloon	P. J. Bish
	G-BISL	Scruggs BL.2B balloon	P. D. Ridout
	G-BISM	Scruggs BL.2B balloon	P. D. Ridout
	G-BISS	Scruggs BL.2C balloon	P. D. Ridout
	G-BIST	Scruggs BL.2C balloon	P. D. Ridout
	G-BISX	Colt 56A balloon	C. D. Steel
	G-BITA	PA-18 Super Cub 150	P. T. Shaw
	G-BITE	SOCATA TB10 Tobago	N. A. Baxter
	G-BITF	Cessna F.152 II	G-BITF Owners Group
	G-BITH	Cessna F.152 II	J. R. Hyde (G-TFSA)
	G-BITK	FRED Srs 2	I. Pearson
	G-BITO	Jodel D.112D	A. Dunbar
	G-BITY	FD.31T balloon	A. J. Bell
	G-BIUP	SNCAN NC.854S	S. A. Richardson
	G-BIUY	PA-28-181 Archer II	Redhill Air Services Ltd
	G-BIVA	Robin R.2112	Victor Alpha Group
	G-BIVB	Jodel D.112	P. B. Readings
	G-BIVC	Jodel D.112	T. D. Wood
	G-BIVF	CP.301C-3 Emeraude	E. Stephenson
	G-BIVK	Bensen B.8M	M. J. Atyeo
	G-BIWB	Scruggs RS.5000 balloon	P. D. Ridout
	G-BIWC	Scruggs RS.5000 balloon	P. D. Ridout
	G-BIWF	Warren balloon	P. D. Ridout
	G-BIWG	Zelenski Mk 2 balloon	P. D. Ridout
	G-BIWJ	Unicorn UE.1A balloon	B. L. King
	G-BIWN	Jodel D.112	C. R. Coates & P. K. Morley
	G-BIWR	Mooney M.20F	M. Broady
	G-BIWU	Cameron V-65 balloon	L. P. Hooper
	G-BIWY	Westland WG.30 ★	Instructional airframe/Yeovil
	G-BIXA	SOCATA TB9 Tampico	W. Maxwell
	G-BIXB	SOCATA TB9 Tampico	B. G. Adams
	G-BIXL	P-51D Mustang (472216:HO-M)	R. W. Tyrrell
	G-BIXN	Boeing Stearman A75N1 (FJ777)	V. S. E. Norman
	G-BIXW	Colt 56B balloon	N. A. P. Bates
	G-BIXX	Pearson Srs 2 balloon	D. Pearson
	G-BIXZ	Grob G-109	C. Beck
	G-BIYI	Cameron V-65 balloon	Sarnia Balloon Group
	G-BIYJ	PA-18 Super Cub 95	N. J. Butler
	G-BIYK	Isaacs Fury II	S. M. Roberts
	G-BIYR	PA-18 Super Cub 150 (R-151)	Delta Foxtrot Flying Group
	G-BIYU	Fokker S.11.1 Instructor (E-15)	Fokker Syndicate
	G-BIYW	Jodel D.112	R. C. Hibberd
	G-BIYX	PA-28 Cherokee 140	W. B. Bateson
	G-BIYY	PA-18 Super Cub 95	A. E. & W. J. Taylor
	G-BIZE	SOCATA TB9 Tampico	B. Higgins
	G-BIZF	Cessna F.172P	R. S. Bentley
	G-BIZG	Cessna F.152	M. A. Judge
	G-BIZK	Nord 3202 (78)	A. I. Milne
	G-BIZM	Nord 3202	Global Aviation Ltd
	G-BIZO	PA-28R Cherokee Arrow 200	Bristol Flying Club Ltd
	G-BIZR	SOCATA TB9 Tampico	R. A. Danby (G-BSEC)
	G-BIZV	Piper L-18C Super Cub	J. P. Nugent
	G-BIZW	Champion 7GCBC Citabria	G. Read & Sons
	G-BIZY	Jodel D.112	T. R. Fray
	G-BJAD	FRED Srs 2 ★	Newark (Nottinghamshire & Lincolnshire) Air Museum
	G-BJAE	Lavadoux Starck AS.80	D. J. & S. A. E. Phillips/Coventry
	G-BJAF	Piper J-3C-65 Cub	P. J. Cottle
	G-BJAG	PA-28-181 Archer II	C. R. Chubb

Reg	Type	Owner or Operator	Notes
G-BJAJ	AA-5B Tiger	Draycott Tiger Club	
G-BJAL	CASA 1.131E Jungmann 1000	G-BJAL Group	
G-BJAO	Bensen B.8M	A. P. Lay	
G-BJAP	DH.82A Tiger Moth (K2587)	K. Knight	
G-BJAS	Rango NA.9 balloon	A. Lindsay	
G-BJAY	Piper J-3C-65 Cub (44-79790)	D. W. Finlay	
G-BJBK	PA-18 Super Cub 95	M. S. Bird	
G-BJBM	Monnett Sonerai I	I. Pearson	
G-BJBO	Jodel DR.250/160	Wiltshire Flying Group	
G-BJBW	PA-28-161 Warrior II	152 Group	
G-BJCA	PA-28-161 Warrior II	Falcon Flying Services Ltd	
G-BJCF	CP.1310-C3 Super Emeraude	R. N. R. Bellamy	
G-BJCI	PA-18 Super Cub 150 (modified)	The Borders (Milfield) Gliding Club Ltd	
G-BJCW	PA-32R-301 Saratoga SP	Golf Charlie Whisky Ltd	
G-BJDE	Cessna F.172M	M. Rowntree & S. Bridgeman	
G-BJDF	MS.880B Rallye 100T	C. J. dos Santos Prado	
G-BJDJ	HS.125 Srs 700B	TAG Farnborough Engineering Ltd (G-RCDI)	
G-BJDK	European E.14 balloon	Aeroprint Tours	
G-BJDW	Cessna F.172M	Hardman Aviation Ltd	
G-BJEC	BN-2T Turbine Islander	Islander Aircraft Ltd (G-SELX)	
G-BJED	BN-2T Turbine Islander	Islander Aircraft Ltd (G-MAFF)	
G-BJEF	BN-2B-26 Islander	Islander Aircraft Ltd	
G-BJEI	PA-18 Super Cub 95	E. M. Cox	
G-BJEJ	BN-2T Turbine Islander	Islander Aircraft Ltd	
G-BJEL	SNCAN NC.854	C. A. James	
G-BJEV	Aeronca 11AC Chief (897)	M. B. Blackmore	
G-BJEX	Bölkow Bö.208C Junior	G. D. H. Crawford	
G-BJFC	European E.8 balloon	P. D. Ridout	
G-BJFE	PA-18 Super Cub 95	P. H. Wilmot-Allistone	
G-BJFM	Jodel D.120	J. V. George	
G-BJGM	Unicorn UE.1A balloon	D. Eaves & P. D. Ridout	
G-BJGY	Cessna F.172P	K. & S. Martin	
G-BJHB	Mooney M.20J	Zitair Flying Club Ltd	
G-BJHK	EAA Acro Sport	M. R. Holden	
G-BJHV	Voisin Replica ★	Brooklands Museum of Aviation/Weybridge	
G-BJIA	Allport balloon	D. J. Allport	
G-BJIC	Dodo 1A balloon	P. D. Ridout	
G-BJID	Osprey 1B balloon	P. D. Ridout	
G-BJIG	Slingsby T.67A	A. D. Hodgkinson	
G-BJIV	PA-18 Super Cub 180	Yorkshire Gliding Club (Pty) Ltd	
G-BJLC	Monnett Sonerai IIL	P. O. Yeo	
G-BJLX	Cremer balloon	P. W. May	
G-BJLY	Cremer balloon	P. Cannon	
G-BJML	Cessna 120	R. A. Smith	
G-BJMR	Cessna 310R	J. H. Sandham Aviation	
G-BJMW	Thunder Ax8-105 balloon	G. M. Westley	
G-BJMX	Jarre JR.3 balloon	P. D. Ridout	
G-BJMZ	European EA.8A balloon	P. D. Ridout	
G-BJNA	Arena Mk 117P balloon	P. D. Ridout	
G-BJND	Osprey Mk 1E balloon	A. Billington & D. Whitmore	
G-BJNG	Slingsby T.67AM	D. F. Hodgkinson	
G-BJNY	Aeronca 11CC Super Chief	P. I. & D. M. Morgans	
G-BJNZ	PA-23 Aztec 250F	J. A. D. Richardson (G-FANZ)	
G-BJOB	Jodel D.140C	T. W. M. Beck & M. J. Smith	
G-BJOE	Jodel D.120A	D. R. Gibby	
G-BJOH	Britten-Norman BN-2T Islander	Islander Aircraft Ltd (G-SRAY/G-OPBN)	
G-BJOT	Jodel D.117	R. A. Kilbride	
G-BJOV	Cessna F.150K	G-BJOV Flying Group	
G-BJPI	Bede BD-5G	M. D. McQueen	
G-BJRA	Osprey Mk 4B balloon	E. Osborn	
G-BJRG	Osprey Mk 4B balloon	A. E. de Gruchy	
G-BJRH	Rango NA.36 balloon	N. H. Ponsford	
G-BJRP	Cremer balloon	M. D. Williams	
G-BJRR	Cremer balloon	M. D. Williams	
G-BJRV	Cremer balloon	M. D. Williams	
G-BJSS	Allport balloon	D. J. Allport	
G-BJST	CCF T-6J Harvard IV (KF729)	G-BJST Group	
G-BJSV	PA-28-161 Warrior II	Flevo Aviation BV/Netherlands	
G-BJSW	Thunder Ax7-65 balloon	J. Edwards	
G-BJSZ	Piper J-3C-65 Cub	S. T. Gilbert	
G-BJTB	Cessna A.150M	Cirrus Aviation Ltd	

Notes	Reg	Type	Owner or Operator
	G-BJTP	PA-18 Super Cub 95 (115302:TP)	G. J. Molloy
	G-BJTY	Osprey Mk 4B balloon	A. E. de Gruchy
	G-BJUB	BVS Special 01 balloon	P. G. Wild
	G-BJUD	Robin DR.400/180R	Lasham Gliding Society Ltd
	G-BJUR	PA-38-112 Tomahawk	Smart People Don't Buy Ltd
	G-BJUS	PA-38-112 Tomahawk	J. D. Williams
	G-BJUV	Cameron V-20 balloon	P. Spellward
	G-BJVH	Cessna F.182Q	R. Beggs
	G-BJVJ	Cessna F.152	Henlow Flying Club
	G-BJVK	Grob G-109	J. M. & J. R. Kimberley
	G-BJVM	Cessna 172N	R. D. Forster
	G-BJVS	CP.1310-C3 Super Emeraude	D. Barrow
	G-BJVU	Thunder Ax6-56 Bolt balloon	N. R. Beckwith
	G-BJWH	Cessna F.152 II	J. D. Baines
	G-BJWI	Cessna F.172P	Falcon Flying Services Ltd
	G-BJWT	Wittman W.10 Tailwind	R. F. Lea
	G-BJWV	Colt 17A balloon	D. T. Meyes
	G-BJWW	Cessna 172N	D. Westoby
	G-BJWX	PA-18 Super Cub 95	R. A. G. Lucas
	G-BJWY	S-55 Whirlwind HAR.21(WV198) ★	Solway Aviation Museum/Carlisle
	G-BJWZ	PA-18 Super Cub 95	G-BJWZ Syndicate
	G-BJXA	Slingsby T.67A	P. K. Pemberton (G-GFAA)
	G-BJXB	Slingsby T.67A	D. Pegley
	G-BJXK	Fournier RF-5	RF5 Syndicate
	G-BJXR	Auster AOP.9 (XR267)	I. Churm & J. Hanson
	G-BJXX	PA-23 Aztec 250E	V. Bojovic
	G-BJXZ	Cessna 172N	T. M. Jones
	G-BJYD	Cessna F.152 II	N. J. James
	G-BJYF	Colt 56A balloon	S. Seguineau
	G-BJYK	Jodel D.120A	Dream Machine Flying Group
	G-BJZB	Evans VP-2	VW Flyers
	G-BJZN	Slingsby T.67A	ZN Group
	G-BJZR	Colt 42A balloon	Selfish Balloon Group
	G-BKAE	Jodel D.120	Bumble Bee Group
	G-BKAF	FRED Srs 2	N. Glass
	G-BKAM	Slingsby T.67M Firefly160	R. C. B. Brookhouse
	G-BKAO	Jodel D.112	A. J. Wright & H. G. Mayes
	G-BKAY	Rockwell Commander 114	D. L. Bunning
	G-BKAZ	Cessna 152	Cloud Global Ltd
	G-BKBD	Thunder Ax3 balloon	D. W. Westlake
	G-BKBF	MS.894A Rallye Minerva 220	BKBF Flying Group
	G-BKBK	SNCAN Stampe SV-4A	D. J. Pearson
	G-BKBP	Bellanca 7GCBC Scout	M. G. & J. R. Jefferies
	G-BKBS	Bensen B8MV	L. Harrison
	G-BKBV	SOCATA TB10 Tobago	G-BKBV Group
	G-BKBW	SOCATA TB10 Tobago	Merlin Aviation
	G-BKCC	PA-28 Cherokee 180	DR Flying Club Ltd
	G-BKCE	Cessna F.172P II	The Leicestershire Aero Club Ltd
	G-BKCI	Brügger MB.2 Colibri	M. R. Walters
	G-BKCJ	Oldfield Baby Lakes	B. L. R. J. Keeping
	G-BKCV	EAA Acro Sport II	R. J. Bower
	G-BKCW	Jodel D.120	Dundee Flying Group (G-BMYF)
	G-BKCX	Mudry/CAARP CAP-10B	G. N. Davies
	G-BKCZ	Jodel D.120A	I. K. Ratcliffe
	G-BKDC	Monnett Sonerai II	K. J. Towell
	G-BKDH	Robin DR.400/120	Marine & Aviation Ltd
	G-BKDJ	Robin DR.400/120	S. Pritchard & I. C. Colwell
	G-BKDK	Thunder Ax7-77Z balloon	A. J. Byrne
	G-BKDP	FRED Srs 3	M. Whittaker
	G-BKDR	Pitts S-1S Special	L. E. Richardson
	G-BKDT	SE-5A (replica) (F943) ★	Yorkshire Air Museum/Elvington
	G-BKDX	Jodel DR.1050	D. G. T. & R. J. Ward
	G-BKER	SE-5A (replica) (F5447:N)	N. K. Geddes
	G-BKET	PA-18 Super Cub 95	N. J. F. Campbell
	G-BKEV	Cessna F.172M	Derby Arrows
	G-BKEW	Bell 206B JetRanger 3	G. Birchmore, R. J. Palmer & R. Toghill
	G-BKEY	FRED Srs 3	G. S. Taylor
	G-BKFC	Cessna F.152 II	C. Walton Ltd
	G-BKFG	Thunder Ax3 Maxi Sky Chariot balloon	S. G. Whatley
	G-BKFI	Evans VP-1	A. S. Watts

Reg	Type	Owner or Operator	Notes
G-BKFK	Isaacs Fury II	P. T. Catanach	
G-BKFR	CP.301C Emeraude	Devonshire Flying Group	
G-BKFW	P.56 Provost T.1 (XF597)	A. J. House	
G-BKGA	MS.892E Rallye 150GT	C. J. Spradbery	
G-BKGB	Jodel D.120	B. A. Ridgway	
G-BKGC	Maule M.6-235	K. V. Marks	
G-BKGD	Westland WG.30 Srs.100 ★	IHM/Weston-super-Mare	
G-BKGL	Beech D.18S (1164:64)	A. N. R. Houghton	
G-BKGM	Beech D.18S	Bristol Airways Ltd	
G-BKGW	Cessna F.152-II	Leicestershire Aero Club Ltd	
G-BKHG	Piper J-3C-65 Cub (479766:D-63)	T. W. Harris	
G-BKHW	Stoddard-Hamilton Glasair IIRG	D. W. Rees	
G-BKHY	Taylor JT.1 Monoplane	B. C. J. O'Neill	
G-BKHZ	Cessna F.172P	L. R. Leader	
G-BKIB	SOCATA TB9 Tampico	G. J. Vickers	
G-BKIC	Cameron V-77 balloon	C. A. Butler	
G-BKIF	Fournier RF-6B	Tiger Airways	
G-BKII	Cessna F.172M	Sealand Aerial Photography Ltd	
G-BKIJ	Cessna F.172M	Cirrus Aviation Ltd	
G-BKIK	Cameron DG-19 airship ★	Balloon Preservation Group/Lancing	
G-BKIR	Jodel D.117	R. Shaw & D. M. Hardaker	
G-BKIS	SOCATA TB10 Tobago	D. Hoare	
G-BKIT	SOCATA TB9 Tampico	P. J. Dunglinson	
G-BKIU	Colt 17A Cloudhopper balloon	S. R. J. Pooley	
G-BKIX	Cameron V-31 Air Chair balloon	K. J. & M. E. Gregory	
G-BKIY	Thunder Ax3 balloon ★	Balloon Preservation Group/Lancing	
G-BKIZ	Cameron V-31 balloon	A. P. S. Cox	
G-BKJB	PA-18 Super Cub 135	K. E. Burnham	
G-BKJS	Jodel D.120A	T. J. Nicholson	
G-BKJW	PA-23 Aztec 250E	Alan Williams Entertainments Ltd	
G-BKKN	Cessna 182R	R A. Marven	
G-BKKO	Cessna 182R	R. A. Dean	
G-BKKP	Cessna 182R	D. Jaffa	
G-BKKZ	Pitts S-1D Special	P. G. Gabriele	
G-BKLO	Cessna F.172M	Stapleford Flying Club Ltd	
G-BKMA	Mooney M.20J Srs 201	Foxtrot Whisky Aviation	
G-BKMB	Mooney M.20J Srs 201	G-BKMB Flying Group	
G-BKMG	Handley Page O/400 (replica)	The Paralyser Group	
G-BKMT	PA-32R-301 Saratoga SP	P. Ashworth	
G-BKNO	Monnett Sonerai IIL	S. Hardy	
G-BKNZ	CP.301A Emeraude	A. K. Halvorsen	
G-BKOA	SOCATA MS.893E Rallye 180GT	M. Jarrett	
G-BKOB	Z.326 Trener Master	A. L. Rae	
G-BKOK	BN-2B-26 Islander	Cormack (Aircraft Services) Ltd	
G-BKOT	Wassmer WA.81 Piranha	B. J. Griffiths	
G-BKOU	P.84 Jet Provost T.3 (XN637)	G-BKOU/2 Ltd	
G-BKPA	Hoffmann H-36 Dimona	R. S. Skinner	
G-BKPB	Aerosport Scamp	J. M. Brightwell	
G-BKPC	Cessna A.185F	C. Taylor & P. C. Hambilton	
G-BKPD	Viking Dragonfly	E. P. Browne & G. J. Sargent	
G-BKPS	AA-5B Tiger	A. E. T. Clarke	
G-BKPX	Jodel D.120A	D. M. Garrett & C. A. Jones	
G-BKPY	SAAB 91B/2 Safir (56321:U-AB) ★	Newark Air Museum	
G-BKPZ	Pitts S-1T Special	D. A. Slater	
G-BKRA	NA T-6G Texan (51-15227)	First Air Ltd	
G-BKRF	PA-18 Super Cub 95	T. F. F. van Erck	
G-BKRH	Brügger MB.2 Colibri	T. C. Darters	
G-BKRK	SNCAN Stampe SV.4C	Strathgadie Stampe Group	
G-BKRL	Chichester-Miles Leopard ★	Bournemouth Aviation Museum	
G-BKRN	Beechcraft D.18S (43-35943)	A. A. Marshall & P. L. Turland	
G-BKRU	Crossley Racer	S. Alexander	
G-BKSC	Saro Skeeter AOP.12 (XN351) ★	R. A. L. Falconer	
G-BKSE	QAC Quickie Q.1	M. D. Burns	
G-BKST	Rutan Vari-Eze	R. Towle	
G-BKSX	SNCAN Stampe SV.4C	C. A. Bailey & J. A. Carr	
G-BKTA	PA-18 Super Cub 95	M. J. Dyson	
G-BKTH	CCF Hawker Sea Hurricane IB (Z7015)	The Shuttleworth Collection	
G-BKTM	PZL SZD-45A Ogar	Hinton Ogar Group	
G-BKTZ	Slingsby T.67M Firefly	Formation Flying Ltd (G-SFTV)	
G-BKUE	SOCATA TB9 Tampico	Fife TB9ers	
G-BKUI	D.31 Turbulent	E. Shouler	

Notes	Reg	Type	Owner or Operator
	G-BKUR	CP.301A Emeraude	T. Harvey
	G-BKVC	SOCATA TB9 Tampico	J. P. Gough
	G-BKVF	FRED Srs 3	I. Pearson
	G-BKVG	Scheibe SF.25E Super Falke	G-BKVG Ltd
	G-BKVK	Auster AOP.9 (WZ662)	J. K. Houlgrave
	G-BKVL	Robin DR.400/160	G. D. Jones
	G-BKVM	PA-18 Super Cub 150 (115684)	M. C. Curtis
	G-BKVP	Pitts S-1D Special	S. A. Smith
	G-BKVW	Airtour 56 balloon	L. D. & H. Vaughan
	G-BKVY	Airtour B-31 balloon	Cloud Nine Balloon Group
	G-BKWD	Taylor JT.2 Titch	J. F. Sully
	G-BKWR	Cameron V-65 balloon	Window on the World Ltd
	G-BKXA	Robin R.2100	M. Wilson
	G-BKXF	PA-28R Cherokee Arrow 200	G. Booth
	G-BKXJ	Rutan VariEze	K. O. Miller (G-TIMB)
	G-BKXM	Colt 17A balloon	R. G. Turnbull
	G-BKXN	ICA-Brasov IS-28M2/80HP	A. Phillips
	G-BKXO	Rutan LongEz	L. T. O'Connor & R. L. Soutar
	G-BKXP	Auster AOP.6	M. A. Farrelly & D. K. Chambers
	G-BKXR	D.31A Turbulent	G-BKXR Turbulent Group
	G-BKZM	Isaacs Fury	L. C. Wells
	G-BKZT	FRED Srs 2	U. Chakravorty
	G-BLAC	Cessna FA.152	W. Ali
	G-BLAF	Stolp SA.900 V-Star	A. T. Lane
	G-BLAI	Monnett Sonerai 2L	T. Simpon
	G-BLAM	Jodel DR.360	J. S. Dalton
	G-BLAT	Jodel 150	G-BLAT Flying Group
	G-BLCH	Colt 65D balloon	R. S. Breakwell
	G-BLCI	EAA Acro Sport	M. R. Holden
	G-BLCT	Jodel DR.220 2+2	F. N. P. Maurin
	G-BLCU	Scheibe SF.25B Falke	Charlie Uniform Syndicate
	G-BLDB	Taylor JT.1 Monoplane	J. P. J. Hefford
	G-BLDG	PA-25 Pawnee 260C	Ouse Gliding Club Ltd
	G-BLDK	Robinson R22	Flight Academy (Gyrocopters) Ltd
	G-BLDN	Rand-Robinson KR-2	P. R. Diffey
	G-BLDV	BN-2B-26 Islander	Loganair Ltd
	G-BLES	Stolp SA.750 Acroduster Too	R. K. Woodland
	G-BLFI	PA-28-181 Archer II	Fly Elstree Ltd
	G-BLGH	Robin DR.300/180R	Booker Gliding Club Ltd
	G-BLGS	SOCATA Rallye 180T	A. Waters
	G-BLGV	Bell 206B JetRanger 3	Heliflight (UK) Ltd
	G-BLHH	Jodel DR.315	S. J. Luck
	G-BLHJ	Cessna F.172P	J. H. Sandham Aviation
	G-BLHM	PA-18 Super Cub 95	A. G. Edwards
	G-BLHN	Robin HR.100/285	K. A. & L. M. C. Payton
	G-BLHR	GA-7 Cougar	H. Mackintosh & R. Ellingworth
	G-BLHS	Bellanca 7ECA Citabria	Devon & Somerset Flight Training Ltd
	G-BLHW	Varga 2150A Kachina	J. B. Webb
	G-BLID	DH.112 Venom FB.50 (J-1605) ★	P. G. Vallance Ltd
	G-BLIT	Thorp T-18 CW	R. M. Weeks
	G-BLIW	P.56 Provost T.51 (WV514)	A. D. M. & K. B. Edie
	G-BLIX	Saro Skeeter Mk 12 (XL809)	K. M. Scholes
	G-BLJM	Beech 95-B55 Baron	A. H. G. Herbst
	G-BLJO	Cessna F.152	Redhill Air Services Ltd
	G-BLKA	DH.112 Venom FB.54 (WR410:N) ★	Fishburn Historic Aviation Centre
	G-BLKM	Jodel DR.1051	Kilo Mike Group
	G-BLLA	Bensen B.8M	K. T. Donaghey
	G-BLLB	Bensen B.8M	D. H. Moss
	G-BLLD	Cameron O-77 balloon	G. Birchall
	G-BLLH	Jodel DR.220A 2+2	J. & J. K. Houlgrave
	G-BLLO	PA-18 Super Cub 95	M. F. Watts
	G-BLLP	Slingsby T.67B	Air Navigation and Trading Co Ltd
	G-BLLR	Slingsby T.67B	R. L. Brinklow
	G-BLLS	Slingsby T.67B	Parish Planes Ltd
	G-BLLW	Colt 56B balloon	C. J. Dunkley
	G-BLLZ	Rutan LongEz	R. S. Stoddart-Stones
	G-BLMA	Zlin 326 Trener Master	G. P. Northcott
	G-BLMC	Avro 698 Vulcan B.2A ★	Aeropark/East Midlands
	G-BLMG	Grob G.109B	G-BLMG Group
	G-BLMI	PA-18-95 Super Cub (R-55)	T. F. F. Van Erck

Reg	Type	Owner or Operator	Notes
G-BLMN	Rutan LongEz	K. W. Taylor	
G-BLMP	PA-17 Vagabond	C. W. Thirtle	
G-BLMR	PA-18 Super Cub 150	M. Vickers	
G-BLMT	PA-18 Super Cub 135	I. S. Runnalls	
G-BLMW	T.66 Nipper 3	S. L. Millar	
G-BLMZ	Colt 105A balloon	M. D. Dickinson	
G-BLNI	BN-2B-26 Islander	Islander Aircraft Ltd	
G-BLNO	FRED Srs 3	L. W. Smith	
G-BLOR	PA-30 Twin Comanche 160	M. C. Jordan	
G-BLOS	Cessna 185A (also flown with floats)	G. P. Harrington & J. R. Chapman	
G-BLOT	Colt Ax6-56B balloon	H. J. Anderson	
G-BLPB	Turner TSW Hot Two Wot	Papa Bravo Group	
G-BLPE	PA-18 Super Cub 95	A. A. Haig-Thomas	
G-BLPF	Cessna FR.172G	S. Culpin	
G-BLPG	Auster J/1N Alpha (16693:693)	Annic Marketing (G-AIZH)	
G-BLPH	Cessna FRA.150L	J. D. Baines	
G-BLPI	Slingsby T.67B	RAF Wyton Flying Group Ltd	
G-BLPP	Cameron V-77 balloon	G. B. Davies	
G-BLRC	PA-18 Super Cub 135	Supercub Group	
G-BLRF	Slingsby T.67C	R. C. Nicholls	
G-BLRL	CP.301C-1 Emeraude	A. M. Smith	
G-BLSD	DH.112 Venom FB.54 (J-1758) ★	R. Lamplough/North Weald	
G-BLSX	Cameron O-105 balloon	B. J. Petteford	
G-BLTC	D.31A Turbulent	S. J. Butler	
G-BLTM	Robin HR.200/100	Troughton Engineering Aircraft Maintenance Ltd	
G-BLTN	Thunder Ax7-65 balloon	V. Michel	
G-BLTR	Scheibe SF.25B Falke	V. Mallon/Germany	
G-BLTS	Rutan LongEz	R. W. Cutler	
G-BLTV	Slingsby T.67B	R. L. Brinklow	
G-BLTW	Slingsby T.67B	Cheshire Air Training Services Ltd	
G-BLTY	Westland WG.30 Srs 160	D. Brem-Wilson	
G-BLUE	Colt 77A balloon	D. P. Busby	
G-BLUJ	Cameron V-56 balloon	G. R. Preece	
G-BLUV	Grob G.109B	109 Flying Group	
G-BLUX	Slingsby T.67M Firefly 200	R. L. Brinklow	
G-BLUZ	DH.82B Queen Bee (LF858)	The Bee Keepers Group	
G-BLVA	Airtour AH-31 balloon	D. L. Peltan & S. Church	
G-BLVB	Airtour AH-56 balloon	J. J. Daly	
G-BLVI	Slingsby T.67M Firefly Mk II	M. L. Scott	
G-BLVK	CAARP CAP-10B	R. W. H. Cole	
G-BLVL	PA-28-161 Warrior II	TG Aviation Ltd	
G-BLVS	Cessna 150M	D. H. G. Penney	
G-BLVW	Cessna F.172H	R. Holloway	
G-BLWD	PA-34-200T Seneca 2	Bencray Ltd	
G-BLWF	Robin HR.100/210	M. D. Parker	
G-BLWH	Fournier RF-6B-100	F. J. Hodson & C. C. Rollings	
G-BLWM	Bristol M.1C (replica) (C4994) ★	RAF Museum/Hendon	
G-BLWP	PA-38-112 Tomahawk	APB Leasing Ltd	
G-BLWT	Evans VP-1	M. W. Olliver	
G-BLWY	Robin R.2160D	Pure Aviation Support Services Ltd	
G-BLXA	SOCATA TB20 Trinidad	A. Durose	
G-BLXG	Colt 21A balloon	D. P. Busby	
G-BLXH	Fournier RF-3	R. H. W. A. Westerhuis	
G-BLXI	CP.1310-C3 Super Emeraude	W. D. Garlick	
G-BLXO	Jodel 150	M. T. Parsonage	
G-BLXS	Aerospatiale AS.332L Super Puma	Vector Aerospace Financial Services Ireland Ltd	
G-BLXT	Eberhardt S.E.5E	R. S. Grace	
G-BLYD	SOCATA TB20 Trinidad	Yankee Delta Corporation Ltd	
G-BLZA	Scheibe SF.25B Falke	Zulu Alpha Syndicate	
G-BLZH	Cessna F.152 II	P. D'Costa	
G-BLZJ	Aerospatiale AS.332L Super Puma	Airbus Helicopters (G-PUMJ)	
G-BLZP	Cessna F.152	East Midlands Flying School Ltd	
G-BMAD	Cameron V-77 balloon	M. A. Stelling	
G-BMAO	Taylor JT.1 Monoplane	N. D. Plumb	
G-BMAX	FRED Srs 2	D. A. Arkley	
G-BMAY	PA-18 Super Cub 135	R. W. Davies	
G-BMBB	Cessna F.150L	S. Collins	
G-BMBJ	Schempp-Hirth Janus CM	BJ Flying Group	
G-BMBZ	Scheibe SF.25E Super Falke	K. E. Ballington	
G-BMCC	Thunder Ax7-77 balloon	D. P. Busby	

Notes	Reg	Type	Owner or Operator
	G-BMCD	Cameron V-65 balloon	R. Lillyman
	G-BMCG	Grob G.109B	D. K. R. Draper
	G-BMCI	Cessna F.172H	A. B. Davis
	G-BMCN	Cessna F.152	Cristal Air Ltd
	G-BMCS	PA-22 Tri-Pacer 135	T. A. Hodges
	G-BMCV	Cessna F.152	M. Bonsall
	G-BMCX	AS.332L Super Puma	Airbus Helicopters
	G-BMDB	SE-5A (replica) (F235:B)	D. E. Blaxland
	G-BMDD	Cadet Motor Glider	A. R. Hutton
	G-BMDE	Pietenpol AirCamper	P. B. Childs
	G-BMDJ	Price Ax7-77S balloon	R. A. Benham
	G-BMDP	Partenavia P.64B Oscar 200	J. L. Sparks
	G-BMDS	Jodel D.120	J. V. Thompson
	G-BMEA	PA-18 Super Cub 95	M. J. Butler
	G-BMEH	Jodel 150 Special Super Mascaret	R. J. & C. J. Lewis
	G-BMET	Taylor JT.1 Monoplane	M. K. A. Blyth
	G-BMEU	Isaacs Fury II	I. G. Harrison
	G-BMEX	Cessna A.150K	Cotswold Flying School Ltd
	G-BMFD	PA-23 Aztec 250F	Giles Aviation Ltd (G-BGYY)
	G-BMFG	Dornier Do.27A-4	M. P. Wood
	G-BMFI	PZL SZD-45A Ogar	S. L. Morrey
	G-BMFN	QAC Quickie Tri-Q 200	R. F. Thomson
	G-BMFP	PA-28-161 Warrior II	Aerobility
	G-BMFU	Cameron N-90 balloon	J. J. Rudoni
	G-BMFY	Grob G.109B	P. J. Shearer
	G-BMGB	PA-28R Cherokee Arrow 200	G-BMGB Group
	G-BMGC	Fairey Swordfish Mk II (W5856)	F.A.A. Museum/Yeovilton
	G-BMGG	Cessna 152 II	Falcon Flying Services
	G-BMGR	Grob G.109B	G-BMGR Group
	G-BMHA	Rutan LongEz	S. F. Elvins
	G-BMHC	Cessna U.206F	H. and R. Morley
	G-BMHL	Wittman W.8 Tailwind	H. J. Bennet
	G-BMHS	Cessna F.172M	N. J. Robins
	G-BMHT	PA-28RT-201T Turbo Arrow	G-BMHT Flying Group
	G-BMID	Jodel D.120	G-BMID Flying Group
	G-BMIG	Cessna 172N	R. B. Singleton-McGuire
	G-BMIM	Rutan LongEz	V. E. Jones
	G-BMIO	Stoddard-Hamilton Glasair RG	G-BMIO Group
	G-BMIP	Jodel D.112	F. J. E. Brownsill
	G-BMIR	Westland Wasp HAS.1 (XT788) ★	Park Aviation Supply/Charlwood
	G-BMIV	PA-28R-201T Turbo Arrow III	Firmbeam Ltd
	G-BMIW	PA-28-181 Archer II	Oldbus Ltd
	G-BMIX	SOCATA TB20 Trinidad	Falcon Flying Group
	G-BMIY	Oldfield Baby Great Lakes	J. B. Scott (G-NOME)
	G-BMIZ	Robinson R22 Beta	Heli Air Ltd
	G-BMJA	PA-32R-301 Saratoga SP	J. Cottrell
	G-BMJB	Cessna 152	Endrick Aviation LLP
	G-BMJD	Cessna 152 II	Donair Flying Club Ltd
	G-BMJJ	Cameron Watch 75 SS balloon	D. P. Busby
	G-BMJL	Rockwell Commander 114	D. J. & S. M. Hawkins
	G-BMJM	Evans VP-1 Series 2	C. J. Clarke
	G-BMJN	Cameron O-65 balloon	P. M. Traviss
	G-BMJO	PA-34-220T Seneca III	Fastnet Jet Alliance Ltd
	G-BMJY	Yakovlev C18M (07)	W. A. E. Moore
	G-BMKB	PA-18 Super Cub 135	Cubair Flight Training Ltd
	G-BMKC	Piper J-3C-65 Cub (329854:R-44)	P. R. Monk
	G-BMKF	Jodel DR.221	S. T. & L. A. Gilbert
	G-BMKJ	Cameron V-77 balloon	R. C. Thursby
	G-BMKK	PA-28R-200 Cherokee Arrow II	P. M. Murray
	G-BMKP	Cameron V-77 balloon	R. Bayly
	G-BMKR	PA-28-161 Warrior II	Steve Batchelor Ltd (G-BGKR)
	G-BMKX	Cameron Elephant 77 SS balloon	A. Smith
	G-BMKY	Cameron O-65 balloon	A. R. Rich
	G-BMLJ	Cameron N-77 balloon	C. J. Dunkley
	G-BMLK	Grob G.109B	Brams Syndicate
	G-BMLL	Grob G.109B	G-BMLL Flying Group
	G-BMLS	PA-28R-201 Arrow III	R. M. Shorter
	G-BMLT	Pietenpol Air Camper	W. E. R. Jenkins
	G-BMLX	Cessna F.150L	J. P. A. Freeman
	G-BMMF	FRED Srs 2	R. C. Thomas
	G-BMMI	Pazmany PL.4A	P. I. Morgans

Reg	Type	Owner or Operator	Notes
G-BMMJ	Siren Pik-30	LRU Group	
G-BMMK	Cessna 182P	Lambley Flying Group	
G-BMMM	Cessna 152 II	Falcon Flying Services Ltd	
G-BMMP	Grob G.109B	G-BMMP Ltd	
G-BMMV	ICA-Brasov IS-28M2A	C. D. King & C. I. Roberts	
G-BMMW	Thunder Ax7-77 balloon	P. A. George	
G-BMOE	PA-28R Cherokee Arrow 200	Piper Leasing Ltd	
G-BMOF	Cessna U206G	Wild Geese Parachute Ltd	
G-BMOG	Thunder Ax7-77 balloon	R. M. Boswell	
G-BMOH	Cameron N-77 balloon	I. M. Taylor	
G-BMOK	ARV Super 2	R. E. Griffiths	
G-BMOL	PA-23 Aztec 250D	LDL Enterprises (G-BBSR)	
G-BMPC	PA-28-181 Archer II	C. J. & R. J. Barnes	
G-BMPD	Cameron V-65 balloon	R. P. E. Phillips	
G-BMPL	Optica Industries OA.7 Optica	J. K. Edgley	
G-BMPP	Cameron N-77 balloon	The Sarnia Balloon Group	
G-BMPR	PA-28R-201 Arrow III	Sterling Aviation	
G-BMPS	Strojnik S-2A	G. J. Green	
G-BMPY	DH.82A Tiger Moth	N. M. Eisenstein	
G-BMRA	Boeing 757-236F	DHL Air Ltd	
G-BMRB	Boeing 757-236F	DHL Air Ltd	
G-BMRD	Boeing 757-236F	DHL Air Ltd	
G-BMRE	Boeing 757-236F	DHL Air Ltd	
G-BMRF	Boeing 757-236F	DHL Air Ltd	
G-BMRG	Boeing 757-236F	DHL Air Ltd	
G-BMRH	Boeing 757-236F	DHL Air Ltd	
G-BMRI	Boeing 757-236F	DHL Air Ltd	
G-BMRJ	Boeing 757-236F	DHL Air Ltd	
G-BMSA	Stinson HW-75 Voyager	P. Fraser-Bennison (G-MIRM/G-BCUM)	
G-BMSB	VS.509 Spitfire IX (MJ627:9G-P)	Warbird Experiences Ltd (G-ASOZ)	
G-BMSC	Evans VP-2	R. S. Acreman	
G-BMSD	PA-28-181 Archer II	R. E. Parsons	
G-BMSE	Valentin Taifun 17E	D. O'Donnell	
G-BMSL	Clutton FRED Series 3	G. Smith	
G-BMTA	Cessna 152 II	ACS Aviation Ltd	
G-BMTB	Cessna 152 II	Stapleford Flying Club Ltd	
G-BMTC	AS.355F1 Twin Squirrel	RCR Aviation Ltd (G-SASU/G-BSSM/G-BKUK/G-EPOL)	
G-BMTJ	Cessna 152 II	The Pilot Centre Ltd	
G-BMTU	Pitts S-1E Special	N. A. A. Pogmore	
G-BMTX	Cameron V-77 balloon	J. A. Langley	
G-BMUG	Rutan LongEz	A. G. Sayers	
G-BMUJ	Colt Drachenfisch balloon	Virgin Airship & Balloon Co Ltd	
G-BMUO	Cessna A.152	Redhill Air Services Ltd	
G-BMUT	PA-34-200T Seneca II	M. Iqbal	
G-BMUU	Thunder Ax7-77 balloon	A. R. Hill	
G-BMUZ	PA-28-161 Warrior II	Pilot Traing & Testing Ltd	
G-BMVB	Cessna F.152	W. Ali	
G-BMVL	PA-38-112 Tomahawk	Flightpathblackpool Ltd	
G-BMVU	Monnett Moni	Stacey Aviation Ltd	
G-BMWF	ARV Super 2	D. L. Aspinall	
G-BMWR	Rockwell Commander 112	T. A. Stoate	
G-BMWU	Cameron N-42 balloon	I. Chadwick	
G-BMXA	Cessna 152 II	ACS Aviation Ltd	
G-BMXB	Cessna 152 II	Devon & Somerset Flight Training Ltd	
G-BMXC	Cessna 152 II	MK Aero Support Ltd	
G-BMYC	SOCATA TB10 Tobago	A. Sapnagis & E. Juskauskas	
G-BMYG	Cessna FA.152	Central Horizon Partnership LLC	
G-BMYI	AA-5 Traveler	W. C. & S. C. Westran	
G-BMYU	Jodel D.120	J. A. Northen	
G-BMZF	WSK-Mielec LiM-2 (MiG-15bis) (01420) ★	F.A.A. Museum/Yeovilton	
G-BMZN	Everett gyroplane	P. A. Gardner	
G-BMZS	Everett gyroplane	M. A. Cload	
G-BMZW	Bensen B.8MR	P. D. Widdicombe	
G-BMZX	Wolf W-11 Boredom Fighter	N. Wright	
G-BNAI	Wolf W-II Boredom Fighter (146-11083)	C. M. Bunn	
G-BNAJ	Cessna 152 II	Galair Ltd	
G-BNAN	Cameron V-65 balloon	Rango Balloon and Kite Company	
G-BNAW	Cameron V-65 balloon	A. Walker	
G-BNBU	Bensen B.8MV	B. A. Lyford	

Notes	Reg	Type	Owner or Operator
	G-BNCB	Cameron V-77 balloon	E. K. Read
	G-BNCM	Cameron N-77 balloon	C. A. Stone
	G-BNCR	PA-28-161 Warrior II	Airways Aero Associations Ltd
	G-BNCS	Cessna 180	C. Elwell Transport Ltd
	G-BNCX	Hawker Hunter T.7 (XL621) ★	Brooklands Museum of Aviation/Weybridge
	G-BNDP	Brügger MB.2 Colibri	J. M. Boden
	G-BNDR	SOCATA TB10 Tobago	J-M Segonne
	G-BNDT	Brügger MB.2 Colibri	G. D. Gunby & P. Coman
	G-BNEE	PA-28R-201 Arrow III	Britannic Management Aviation
	G-BNEL	PA-28-161 Warrior II	NM Flight ervices Ltd
	G-BNEO	Cameron V-77 balloon	J. G. O'Connell
	G-BNEV	Viking Dragonfly	N. W. Eyre
	G-BNFP	Cameron O-84 balloon	M. Clarke
	G-BNFR	Cessna 152 II	A. Jahanfar
	G-BNFV	Robin DR.400/120	J. P. A. Freeman
	G-BNGE	Auster AOP.6 (TW536)	K. A. Hale
	G-BNGJ	Cameron N-77 balloon	S. W. K. Smeeton
	G-BNGO	Thunder Ax7-77 balloon	J. S. Finlan
	G-BNGT	PA-28-181 Archer II	A. Soojeri
	G-BNGV	ARV Super 2	N. A. Onions & L. J. Russell
	G-BNGW	ARV Super 2	Southern Gas Turbines Ltd
	G-BNGY	ARV Super 2	J. & P. Morris (G-BMWL)
	G-BNHB	ARV Super 2	N. A. Onions
	G-BNHJ	Cessna 152 II	The Pilot Centre Ltd
	G-BNHK	Cessna 152 II	Wayfarers Flying Group
	G-BNHL	Colt beer glass SS balloon	M. R. Stokoe
	G-BNHN	Colt Ariel Bottle SS balloon ★	British Balloon Museum
	G-BNHT	Fournier RF-3	G-BNHT Group
	G-BNID	Cessna 152 II	MK Aero Support Ltd
	G-BNII	Cameron N-90 balloon	Topless Balloon Group
	G-BNIK	Robin HR.200/120	G-BNIK Group
	G-BNIN	Cameron V-77 balloon	Cloud Nine Balloon Group
	G-BNIO	Luscombe 8A Silvaire	M. Richardson & R. C. Dyer
	G-BNIP	Luscombe 8A Silvaire	M. J. Diggins
	G-BNIU	Cameron O-77 balloon	M. E. Dubois/France
	G-BNIV	Cessna 152 II	Smart People Dont Buy Ltd
	G-BNIW	Boeing Stearman PT-17	Skymax (Aviation) Ltd
	G-BNJB	Cessna 152 II	Aerolease Ltd
	G-BNJC	Cessna 152 II	Stapleford Flying Club Ltd
	G-BNJH	Cessna 152 II	ACS Aviation Ltd
	G-BNJT	PA-28-161 Warrior II	Hawarden Flying Group
	G-BNJX	Cameron N-90 balloon	Mars UK Ltd
	G-BNKC	Cessna 152 II	Herefordshire Aero Club Ltd
	G-BNKD	Cessna 172N	R. Nightingale
	G-BNKE	Cessna 172N	Kilo Echo Flying Group
	G-BNKH	PA-38-112 Tomahawk	M. C. R. Sims
	G-BNKI	Cessna 152 II	RAF Halton Aeroplane Club Ltd
	G-BNKP	Cessna 152 II	Spectrum Leisure Ltd
	G-BNKR	Cessna 152 II	Airways Aero Associations Ltd
	G-BNKS	Cessna 152 II	APB Leasing Ltd
	G-BNKT	Cameron O-77 balloon	A. A. Brown
	G-BNKV	Cessna 152 II	Cristal Air Ltd
	G-BNLJ	Boeing 747-436	British Airways
	G-BNLK	Boeing 747-436	British Airways
	G-BNLN	Boeing 747-436	British Airways
	G-BNLO	Boeing 747-436	British Airways
	G-BNLP	Boeing 747-436	British Airways
	G-BNLY	Boeing 747-436	British Airways
	G-BNMB	PA-28-151 Warrior	Aviation, Advice & Consulting Ltd
	G-BNMD	Cessna 152 II	T. M. Jones
	G-BNME	Cessna 152 II	M. Bonsall
	G-BNMF	Cessna 152 II	Redhill Air Services Ltd
	G-BNMH	Pietenpol Air Camper	N. M. Hitchman
	G-BNMI	Colt Flying Fantasy SS balloon	Air 2 Air Ltd
	G-BNML	Rand-Robinson KR-2	P. J. Brookman
	G-BNMO	Cessna TR.182RG	T. W. Gale & S. R. Whitling
	G-BNMX	Thunder Ax7-77 balloon	P. Coman
	G-BNNE	Cameron N-77 balloon	R. D. Allen, L. P. Hooper & M. J. Streat
	G-BNNO	PA-28-161 Warrior II	Tor Financial Consulting Ltd
	G-BNNT	PA-28-151 Warrior	S. T. Gilbert
	G-BNNU	PA-38-112 Tomahawk	J. G. McVey & P. Lodge

Reg	Type	Owner or Operator	Notes
G-BNNX	PA-28R-201T Turbo Arrow III	Professional Flying Ltd	
G-BNNY	PA-28-161 Warrior II	Falcon Flying Services	
G-BNNZ	PA-28-161 Warrior II	Falcon Flying Services Ltd	
G-BNOB	Wittman W.8 Tailwind	D. G. Hammersley	
G-BNOF	PA-28-161 Warrior II	Tayside Aviation Ltd	
G-BNOH	PA-28-161 Warrior II	Sherburn Aero Club Ltd	
G-BNOJ	PA-28-161 Warrior II	BAE (Warton) Flying Club	
G-BNOM	PA-28-161 Warrior II	J. H. Sandham Aviation	
G-BNON	PA-28-161 Warrior II	Tayside Aviation Ltd	
G-BNOP	PA-28-161 Warrior II	BAE (Warton) Flying Club	
G-BNPE	Cameron N-77 balloon	R. N. Simpkins	
G-BNPF	Slingsby T.31M	S. Luck & ptnrs	
G-BNPH	P.66 Pembroke C.1 (WV740)	M. A. Stott	
G-BNPM	PA-38-112 Tomahawk	Papa Mike Aviation	
G-BNPO	PA-28-181 Archer II	Threeshires Flying NPAS Ltd	
G-BNPV	Bowers Fly-Baby 1B (1801/18)	A. Berry	
G-BNPY	Cessna 152 II	G. Tennant	
G-BNRA	SOCATA TB10 Tobago	Double D Airgroup	
G-BNRG	PA-28-161 Warrior II	Glenn Aviation Ltd	
G-BNRL	Cessna 152 II	Corvalis Aircraft Leasing Ltd	
G-BNRP	PA-28-181 Archer II	PA-28 Warrior Ltd	
G-BNRR	Cessna 172P	Wentworth Productions	
G-BNRW	Colt 69A balloon	D. Charles	
G-BNRX	PA-34-200T Seneca II	Sky Zone Servicos Aereos Lds/Portugal	
G-BNRY	Cessna 182Q	K. F. & S. J. Farey	
G-BNSG	PA-28R-201 Arrow III	Odhams Air Services Ltd	
G-BNSL	PA-38-112 Tomahawk II	J. G. McVey & P. Lodge	
G-BNSM	Cessna 152 II	Cornwall Flying Club Ltd	
G-BNSN	Cessna 152 II	The Pilot Centre Ltd	
G-BNSR	Slingsby T.67M Firefly Mk II	Slingsby SR Group	
G-BNST	Cessna 172N	CSG Bodyshop	
G-BNSU	Cessna 152 II	Falcon Flying Services Ltd	
G-BNSY	PA-28-161 Warrior II	Fedex Aviation Ltd	
G-BNSZ	PA-28-161 Warrior II	O. H. Hogan	
G-BNTD	PA-28-161 Warrior II	DSFT Ltd	
G-BNTP	Cessna 172N	Westnet Ltd	
G-BNTZ	Cameron N-77 balloon	Balloon Team	
G-BNUL	Cessna 152 II	Big Red Kite Ltd	
G-BNUN	Beech 95-58PA Baron	SMB Aviation Ltd	
G-BNUO	Beech 76 Duchess	Pace Projects Ltd and Professional Flight Simulation Ltd	
G-BNUT	Cessna 152 Turbo	Stapleford Flying Club Ltd	
G-BNUY	PA-38-112 Tomahawk II	D. C. Storey	
G-BNVB	AA-5A Cheetah	M. E. Hicks	
G-BNVE	PA-28-181 Archer II	Take Flight Aviation Ltd	
G-BNVT	PA-28R-201T Turbo Arrow III	Victor Tango Group	
G-BNWA	Boeing 767-336ER	British Airways	
G-BNWB	Boeing 767-336ER	British Airways	
G-BNWX	Boeing 767-336ER	British Airways	
G-BNWZ	Boeing 767-336ER	British Airways	
G-BNXE	PA-28-161 Warrior II	M. S. Brown	
G-BNXL	Glaser-Dirks DG.400	J. Mjels	
G-BNXM	PA-18 Super Cub 95	K. A. A. McDonald & N. G. Rhind	
G-BNXU	PA-28-161 Warrior II	Friendly Warrior Group	
G-BNXV	PA-38-112 Tomahawk	W. B. Bateson	
G-BNXX	SOCATA TB20 Trinidad	J. M. Thorpe	
G-BNXZ	Thunder Ax7-77 balloon	Hale Hot Air Balloon Group	
G-BNYD	Bell 206B JetRanger 3	Aerospeed Ltd	
G-BNYK	PA-38-112 Tomahawk	J. G. McVey & P. Lodge	
G-BNYL	Cessna 152 II	V. J. Freeman	
G-BNYM	Cessna 172N	Kestrel Syndicate	
G-BNYO	Beech 76 Duchess	Skies Airline Training AB/Sweden	
G-BNYP	PA-28-181 Archer II	G-BNYP Group	
G-BNYZ	SNCAN Stampe SV.4E	Bianchi Film Aviation Services Ltd	
G-BNZB	PA-28-161 Warrior II	Falcon Flying Services Ltd	
G-BNZC	DHC.1 Chipmunk 22 (18671:671)	The Shuttleworth Collection	
G-BNZK	Thunder Ax7-77 balloon	T. D. Marsden	
G-BNZL	Rotorway Scorpion 133	J. R. Wraight	
G-BNZM	Cessna T.210N	A. J. M. Freeman	
G-BNZN	Cameron N-56 balloon	P. Lesser	
G-BNZO	Rotorway Executive	J. S. David	

Notes	Reg	Type	Owner or Operator
	G-BNZZ	PA-28-161 Warrior II	Providence Aviation Ltd
	G-BOAA	BAC-Aérospatiale Concorde 102 ★	Museum Of Flight East Fortune (G-N94AA)
	G-BOAB	BAC-Aérospatiale Concorde 102 ★	Preserved at Heathrow (G-N94AB)
	G-BOAC	BAC-Aérospatiale Concorde 102 ★	Displayed in viewing area Manchester International (G-N81AC)
	G-BOAF	BAC-Aérospatiale Concorde 102 ★	Bristol Aero Collection/Filton (G-N94AF)
	G-BOAH	PA-28-161 Warrior II	Aircraft Engineers Ltd
	G-BOAI	Cessna 152 II	Aviation Spirit Ltd
	G-BOAL	Cameron V-65 balloon	N. H. & A. M. Ponsford
	G-BOAU	Cameron V-77 balloon	G. T. Barstow
	G-BOBA	PA-28R-201 Arrow III	Bravo Aviation Ltd
	G-BOBR	Cameron N-77 balloon	I. R. F. Worsman
	G-BOBT	Stolp SA.300 Starduster Too	G-BOBT Group
	G-BOBV	Cessna F.150M	M. L. Brown & P. L. Hill
	G-BOBY	Monnett Sonerai II	R. G. Hallam
	G-BOCI	Cessna 140A	Charlie India Aviators
	G-BOCK	Sopwith Triplane (replica) (N6290)	The Shuttleworth Collection
	G-BOCL	Slingsby T.67C	Richard Brinklow Aviation Ltd
	G-BOCM	Slingsby T.67C	Richard Brinklow Aviation Ltd
	G-BOCN	Robinson R22 Beta	HQ Aviation Ltd
	G-BOCU	PA-34-220T Seneca III	Advanced Aircraft Leasing (Teesside) Ltd
	G-BODB	PA-28-161 Warrior II	Sherburn Aero Club Ltd
	G-BODD	PA-28-161 Warrior II	CG Aviation Ltd
	G-BODE	PA-28-161 Warrior II	Sherburn Aero Club Ltd
	G-BODI	Glasair III Model SH-3R	A. P. Durston
	G-BODO	Cessna 152	Enstone Sales and Services Ltd
	G-BODR	PA-28-161 Warrior II	Airways Aero Associations Ltd
	G-BODS	PA-38-112 Tomahawk	T. W. Gilbert
	G-BODT	Jodel D.18	The Jodel Syndicate
	G-BODU	Scheibe SF.25C Falke ⌐	Hertfordshire County Scout Council
	G-BODY	Cessna 310R	Reconnaissance Ventures Ltd
	G-BODZ	Robinson R22 Beta	Langley Aviation Ltd
	G-BOEE	PA-28-181 Archer II	J. C. & G. M. Brinkley
	G-BOEH	Jodel DR.340	B. W. Griffiths
	G-BOEK	Cameron V-77 balloon	R. I. M. Kerr & ptnrs
	G-BOEM	Pitts S-2A	M. Murphy
	G-BOEN	Cessna 172M	R. Kolozsi
	G-BOER	PA-28-161 Warrior II	B. Boult
	G-BOET	PA-28RT-201 Arrow IV	B. C. Chambers (G-IBEC)
	G-BOFC	Beech 76 Duchess	Odhams Air Services Ltd
	G-BOFE	PA-34-200T Seneca II	Atlantic Flight Training Ltd
	G-BOFL	Cessna 152 II	S. A. Abid
	G-BOFW	Cessna A.150M	Golf Fox Whisky Group
	G-BOFY	PA-28 Cherokee 140	R. A. Brown
	G-BOFZ	PA-28-161 Warrior II	Pilot Traing & Testing Ltd
	G-BOGI	Robin DR.400/180	A. L. M. Shepherd
	G-BOGK	ARV Super 2	M. K. Field
	G-BOGM	PA-28RT-201T Turbo Arrow IV	G. Marsango
	G-BOGO	PA-32R-301T Saratoga SP	Diff Air KFT
	G-BOHA	PA-28-161 Warrior II	Phoenix Aviation
	G-BOHD	Colt 77A balloon	D. B. Court
	G-BOHH	Cessna 172N	Staverton Flying School @ Skypark Ltd
	G-BOHI	Cessna 152 II	Cirrus Aviation Ltd
	G-BOHJ	Cessna 152 II	M. Power
	G-BOHM	PA-28 Cherokee 180	B. F. Keogh & R. A. Scott
	G-BOHO	PA-28-161 Warrior II	Egressus Flying Group
	G-BOHR	PA-28-151 Warrior	R. M. E. Garforth
	G-BOHV	Wittman W.8 Tailwind	D. H. Greenwood
	G-BOHW	Van's RV-4	R. C. St. H. Mason
	G-BOIB	Wittman W.10 Tailwind	C. R. Nash
	G-BOIC	PA-28R-201T Turbo Arrow III	S. P. Donoghue
	G-BOID	Bellanca 7ECA Citabria	D. Mallinson
	G-BOIG	PA-28-161 Warrior II	GFT Warrior Group
	G-BOIK	Air Command 503 Commander	F. G. Shepherd
	G-BOIL	Cessna 172N	Upperstack Ltd
	G-BOIO	Cessna 152	Sandham Aviation
	G-BOIR	Cessna 152	APB Leasing Ltd
	G-BOIT	SOCATA TB10 Tobago	Naval Aviation Ltd
	G-BOIV	Cessna 150M	India Victor Group
	G-BOIX	Cessna 172N	J. W. N. Sharpe

Reg	Type	Owner or Operator	Notes
G-BOIY	Cessna 172N	S. Smith	
G-BOIZ	PA-34-200T Seneca II	OCTN Trust	
G-BOJB	Cameron V-77 balloon	S. R. Skinner	
G-BOJI	PA-28RT-201 Arrow IV	Arrow Two Group	
G-BOJM	PA-28-181 Archer II	R. P. Emms	
G-BOJS	Cessna 172P	Paul's Planes Ltd	
G-BOJW	PA-28-161 Warrior II	Phoenix Aviation	
G-BOJZ	PA-28-161 Warrior II	Falcon Flying Services	
G-BOKA	PA-28-201T Turbo Dakota	CBG Aviation Ltd	
G-BOKB	PA-28-161 Warrior II	Apollo Aviation Advisory Ltd	
G-BOKF	Air Command 532 Elite	J. K. Padden	
G-BOKH	Whittaker MW7	I. Pearson	
G-BOKW	Bolkow Bo.208C Junior	The Bat Group	
G-BOKX	PA-28-161 Warrior II	Turweston Flying Club Ltd	
G-BOKY	Cessna 152 II	D. F. F. & J. E. Poore	
G-BOLB	Taylorcraft BC-12-65	C. E. Tudor	
G-BOLC	Fournier RF-6B-100	Devon & Somerset RF Group	
G-BOLD	PA-38-112 Tomahawk	G-BOLD Group	
G-BOLE	PA-38-112 Tomahawk	Smart People Don't Buy Ltd	
G-BOLG	Bellanca 7KCAB Citabria	B. R. Pearson	
G-BOLI	Cessna 172P	Boli Flying Club	
G-BOLL	Lake LA-4 Skimmer	M. C. Holmes	
G-BOLN	Colt 21A balloon	G. Everett	
G-BOLO	Bell 206B JetRanger	Hargreaves Leasing Ltd	
G-BOLR	Colt 21A balloon	C. J. Sanger-Davies	
G-BOLS	FRED Srs 2	I. F. Vaughan	
G-BOLT	Rockwell Commander 114	I. R. Harnett	
G-BOLU	Robin R.3000/120	P. J. R. White & J. M. Smith	
G-BOLV	Cessna 152 II	A. J. Gomes	
G-BOLW	Cessna 152 II	G-BOLW Flying Group	
G-BOLY	Cessna 172N	Lima Yankee Flying Group	
G-BOMB	Cassutt Racer IIIM	D. Hart	
G-BOMO	PA-38-112 Tomahawk II	APB Leasing Ltd	
G-BOMP	PA-28-181 Archer II	A. Flinn	
G-BOMS	Cessna 172N	Penchant Ltd	
G-BOMU	PA-28-181 Archer II	R. J. Houghton	
G-BOMY	PA-28-161 Warrior II	Sunrise Global Asset Management Ltd	
G-BOMZ	PA-38-112 Tomahawk	G-BOMZ Aviation	
G-BONC	PA-28RT-201 Arrow IV	I. H. Finegan	
G-BONG	Enstrom F-28A-UK	G. E. Heritage	
G-BONP	CFM Streak Shadow	G. J. Chater	
G-BONR	Cessna 172N	D. I. Craikl	
G-BONS	Cessna 172N	R. W. Marchant & K. Meredith	
G-BONU	Slingsby T.67B	R. L. Brinklow	
G-BONW	Cessna 152 II	LAC Flying School	
G-BONY	Denney Kitfox Model 1	R. Dunn	
G-BONZ	Beech V35B Bonanza	R. H. Townsend	
G-BOOB	Cameron N-65 balloon	P. J. Hooper	
G-BOOC	PA-18 Super Cub 150	S. A. C. Whitcombe	
G-BOOD	Slingsby T.31M Motor Tutor	D. G. Bilcliffe	
G-BOOE	GA-7 Cougar	S. J. Olechnowicz	
G-BOOF	PA-28-181 Archer II	Blackbushe Flying Club Ltd	
G-BOOG	PA-28RT-201T Turbo Arrow IV	Katheros Ltd	
G-BOOH	Jodel D.112	T. K. Duffy	
G-BOOL	Cessna 172N	A. van Rooijen/Belgium	
G-BOOW	Aerosport Scamp	D. A. Weldon/Ireland	
G-BOOX	Rutan LongEz	I. R. Wilde	
G-BOOZ	Cameron N-77 balloon	J. E. F. Kettlety	
G-BOPA	PA-28-181 Archer II	Flyco Ltd	
G-BOPC	PA-28-161 Warrior II	Aeros Ltd	
G-BOPD	Bede BD-4	S. T. Dauncey	
G-BOPH	Cessna TR.182RG	J. M. Mitchell	
G-BOPO	Brooklands OA.7 Optica	J. K. Edgley	
G-BOPR	Brooklands OA.7 Optica	Aeroelvira Ltd	
G-BOPT	Grob G.115	Composite Mast Engineering & Technology Ltd	
G-BOPU	Grob G.115	J. L. Sparks	
G-BORB	Cameron V-77 balloon	M. H. Wolff	
G-BORD	Thunder Ax7-77 balloon	Western Region British Balloon and Airship Club Ltd	
G-BORE	Colt 77A balloon	J. D. & C. J. Medcalf	
G-BORG	Campbell Cricket	R. L. Gilmore	

Notes	Reg	Type	Owner or Operator
	G-BORK	PA-28-161 Warrior II	Turweston Flying Club Ltd (G-IIIC)
	G-BORL	PA-28-161 Warrior II	Westair Flying Services Ltd
	G-BORM	HS.748 Srs 2B ★	Airport Fire Service/Exeter
	G-BORN	Cameron N-77 balloon	I. Chadwick
	G-BORW	Cessna 172P	Briter Aviation Ltd
	G-BORY	Cessna 150L	D. H. G. Penney
	G-BOSE	PA-28-181 Archer II	G-BOSE Group
	G-BOSJ	Nord 3400 (124)	A. I. Milne
	G-BOSM	Jodel DR.253B	A. G. Stevens
	G-BOSN	AS.355F1 Ecureuil II	Helicopter & Pilot Services Ltd
	G-BOSO	Cessna A.152	Redhill Air Services Ltd
	G-BOTD	Cameron O-105 balloon	J. Taylor
	G-BOTF	PA-28-151 Warrior	G-BOTF Group
	G-BOTG	Cessna 152 II	Donington Aviation Ltd
	G-BOTH	Cessna 182Q	P. G. Guilbert
	G-BOTI	PA-28-151 Warrior	Falcon Flying Services
	G-BOTK	Cameron O-105 balloon	N. Woodham
	G-BOTN	PA-28-161 Warrior II	Apollo Aviation Advisory
	G-BOTO	Bellanca 7ECA Citabria	G-BOTO Group
	G-BOTP	Cessna 150J	R. F. Finnis & C. P. Williams
	G-BOTU	Piper J-3C-65 Cub	T. L. Giles
	G-BOTV	PA-32RT-300 Lance II	Robin Lance Aviation Association Ltd
	G-BOTW	Cameron V-77 balloon	M. R. Jeynes
	G-BOUE	Cessna 172N	Swift Group
	G-BOUF	Cessna 172N	B. P. & M. I. Sneap
	G-BOUJ	Cessna 150M	The UJ Flying Group
	G-BOUK	PA-34-200T Seneca II	C. J. & R. J. Barnes
	G-BOUM	PA-34-200T Seneca II	Sky Zone Services Aereos Lda
	G-BOUT	Colomban MC.12 Cri-Cri	C. K. Farley
	G-BOUV	Bensen B.8MR	L. R. Phillips
	G-BOUZ	Cessna 150G	Atlantic Bridge Aviation Ltd
	G-BOVB	PA-15 Vagabond	J. R. Kimberley
	G-BOVK	PA-28-161 Warrior II	Tayside Aviation Ltd
	G-BOVU	Stoddard-Hamilton Glasair III	E. Andersen
	G-BOVX	Hughes 269C	L. J. J. Leeman
	G-BOWB	Cameron V-77 balloon	R. A. Benham
	G-BOWM	Cameron V-56 balloon	R. S. Breakwell
	G-BOWN	PA-12 Super Cruiser	T. L. Giles
	G-BOWO	Cessna R.182	P. E. Crees (G-BOTR)
	G-BOWP	Jodel D.120A	T. E. Cummins
	G-BOWV	Cameron V-65 balloon	R. A. Harris
	G-BOWY	PA-28RT-201T Turbo Arrow IV	J. S. Develin & Z. Islam
	G-BOXA	PA-28-161 Warrior II	Channel Islands Aero Club (Jersey) Ltd
	G-BOXC	PA-28-161 Warrior II	M. A. Lee
	G-BOXG	Cameron O-77 balloon	Aociazione Sportiva Dilettantistica Experience/Italy
	G-BOXH	Pitts S-1S Special	G-BOXH Group
	G-BOXJ	Piper J-3C-65 Cub (479897)	A. Bendkowski
	G-BOXR	GA-7 Cougar	London School of Flying Ltd
	G-BOXT	Hughes 269C	Goldenfly Ltd
	G-BOXV	Pitts S-1S Special	C. Waddington
	G-BOXW	Cassutt Racer Srs IIIM	D. I. Johnson
	G-BOYB	Cessna A.152	W. Ali
	G-BOYC	Robinson R22 Beta	Yorkshire Helicopters
	G-BOYF	Sikorsky S-76B	Darley Stud Management Co Ltd
	G-BOYH	PA-28-151 Warrior	R. Nightingale
	G-BOYI	PA-28-161 Warrior II	Aviation Advice & Consulting Ltd
	G-BOYL	Cessna 152 II	Redhill Air Services Ltd
	G-BOYM	Cameron O-84 balloon	M. P. Ryan
	G-BOYO	Cameron V-20 balloon	J. L. Hilditch & T. Ward
	G-BOYV	PA-28R-201T Turbo Arrow III	P. Lodge
	G-BOYX	Robinson R22 Beta	R. Towle
	G-BOZI	PA-28-161 Warrior II	Aerolease Ltd
	G-BOZO	AA-5B Tiger	J. Le Moignan
	G-BOZR	Cessna 152 II	Adam Russell Ltd
	G-BOZS	Pitts S-1C Special	S. D. Blakey
	G-BOZV	CEA DR.340 Major	C. J. Turner & S. D. Kent
	G-BOZW	Bensen B.8M	M. E. Wills
	G-BOZY	Cameron RTW-120 balloon	Magical Adventures Ltd
	G-BOZZ	AA-5B Tiger	Dolphin Property (Management) Ltd

Reg	Type	Owner or Operator	Notes
G-BPAA	Acro Advanced	B. O. & F. A. Smith	
G-BPAB	Cessna 150M	AB Group	
G-BPAF	PA-28-161 Warrior II	S. T. & T. W. Gilbert	
G-BPAJ	DH.82A Tiger Moth	J. M. Hodgson & J. D. Smith (G-AOIX)	
G-BPAL	DHC.1 Chipmunk 22 (WG350)	K. F. & P. Tomsett (G-BCYE)	
G-BPAW	Cessna 150M	G-BPAW Group	
G-BPAY	PA-28-181 Archer II	White Waltham Airfield Ltd	
G-BPBJ	Cessna 152 II	W. Shaw & P. G. Haines	
G-BPBK	Cessna 152 II	Swiftair Maintenance Ltd	
G-BPBM	PA-28-161 Warrior II	Redhill Air Services Ltd	
G-BPBO	PA-28RT-201T Turbo Arrow IV	G. N. Broom & T. R. Lister	
G-BPBP	Brügger MB.2 Colibri	D. A. Preston	
G-BPCA	BN-2B-26 Islander	Loganair Ltd (G-BLNX)	
G-BPCF	Piper J-3C-65 Cub	B. M. O'Brien	
G-BPCI	Cessna R.172K	N. A. Bairstol	
G-BPCK	PA-28-161 Warrior II	Compton Abbas Airfield Ltd	
G-BPCL	SA Bulldog Srs 120/128 (HKG-6)	Isohigh Ltd	
G-BPCR	Mooney M.20K	T. & R. Harris	
G-BPCX	PA-28-236 Dakota	Blue Yonder Aviation Ltd	
G-BPDE	Colt 56A balloon	J. E. Weidema/Netherlands	
G-BPDJ	Chris Tena Mini Coupe	J. J. Morrissey	
G-BPDM	CASA 1.131E Jungmann 2000(781-32)	J. D. Haslam	
G-BPDT	PA-28-161 Warrior II	Channel Islands Aero Club (Jersey) Ltd	
G-BPDV	Pitts S-1S Special	G-BPDV Syndicate	
G-BPEM	Cessna 150K	D. Wright	
G-BPEO	Cessna 152 II	Swiftair Maintenance Ltd	
G-BPES	PA-38-112 Tomahawk II	Smart People Don't Buy Ltd	
G-BPEZ	Colt 77A balloon	J. W. Adkins	
G-BPFD	Jodel D.112	M. & S. Mills	
G-BPFH	PA-28-161 Warrior II	Aircraft Engineers Ltd	
G-BPFI	PA-28-181 Archer II	S. D. Hodgson	
G-BPFL	Davis DA-2	P. E. Barker	
G-BPFM	Aeronca 7AC Champion	C. C. Burton	
G-BPFZ	Cessna 152 II	Devon and Somerset Flight Training Ltd	
G-BPGD	Cameron V-65 balloon	Gone With The Wind Ltd	
G-BPGE	Cessna U.206C	Scottish Parachute Club	
G-BPGH	EAA Acro Sport II	R. Clark & A. C. May	
G-BPGK	Aeronca 7AC Champion	P. J. Clegg	
G-BPGT	Colt AS-80 Mk II airship	P. Porati/Italy	
G-BPGU	PA-28-181 Archer II	G. Underwood	
G-BPGZ	Cessna 150G	J. B. Scott	
G-BPHG	Robin DR.400/180	B. Brenton	
G-BPHH	Cameron V-77 balloon	C. D. Aindow	
G-BPHI	PA-38-112 Tomahawk	Flying Fox Aviation	
G-BPHO	Taylorcraft BC-12	P. A. Durrans	
G-BPHP	Taylorcraft BC-12-65	J. M. Brightwell	
G-BPHR	DH.82A Tiger Moth (A17-48)	N. Parry	
G-BPHU	Thunder Ax7-77 balloon	R. P. Waite	
G-BPHX	Cessna 140	M. J. Medland	
G-BPHZ	MS.505 Criquet (DM+BK)	Aero Vintage Ltd	
G-BPIF	Bensen-Parsons 2-place gyroplane	B. J. L. P. & W. J. A. L. de Saar	
G-BPII	Denney Kitfox	Dolphin Flying Group	
G-BPIP	Slingsby T.31 Motor Cadet III	V. K. Meers	
G-BPIR	Scheibe SF.25E Super Falke	A. P. Askwith	
G-BPIU	PA-28-161 Warrior II	Golf India Uniform Group	
G-BPIV	B.149 Bolingbroke Mk IVT (L6739)	Blenheim (Duxford) Ltd	
G-BPIZ	AA-5B Tiger	D. A. Horsley	
G-BPJG	PA-18 Super Cub 150	N. P. Shields	
G-BPJS	PA-28-161 Cadet	Redhill Air Services Ltd	
G-BPJW	Cessna A.150K	G. Duck	
G-BPJZ	Cameron O-160 balloon	M. L. Gabb	
G-BPKF	Grob G.115	Swiftair Maintenance Ltd	
G-BPKK	Denney Kitfox Mk 1	F. McDonagh	
G-BPKM	PA-28-161 Warrior II	Pure Aviation Support Services Ltd	
G-BPKT	Piper J.5A Cub Cruiser	A. J. Greenslade	
G-BPLH	Jodel DR.1051	C. K. Farley	
G-BPLM	AIA Stampe SV.4C	C. J. Jesson	
G-BPLV	Cameron V-77 balloon	J. Jacquet/France	
G-BPLZ	Hughes 369HS	M. A. & R. J. Fawcett	
G-BPME	Cessna 152 II	London School of Flying Ltd	
G-BPMF	PA-28-151 Warrior	Mike Foxtrot Group	

Notes	Reg	Type	Owner or Operator
	G-BPML	Cessna 172M	N. A. Bilton
	G-BPMM	Champion 7ECA Citabria	J. McCullough
	G-BPMU	Nord 3202B	E. C. Murgatroyd (G-BIZJ)
	G-BPMW	QAC Quickie Q.2	P. M. Wright (G-OICI/G-OGKN)
	G-BPNI	Robinson R22 Beta	G. J. Collins
	G-BPNO	Zlin Z.326 Trener Master	A. Gibson, M. N. King & A T Aviation Sales Ltd
	G-BPOA	Gloster Meteor T.7 (WF877) ★	39 Restoration Group
	G-BPOB	Sopwith Camel F.1 (replica) (B2458:R)	Flying Aces Movie Aircraft Collection
	G-BPOM	PA-28-161 Warrior II	POM Flying Group
	G-BPOS	Cessna 150M	Hull Aero Club Ltd
	G-BPOT	PA-28-181 Archer II	P. S. Simpson
	G-BPOU	Luscombe 8A Silvaire	J. L. Grayer
	G-BPPE	PA-38-112 Tomahawk	First Air Ltd
	G-BPPF	PA-38-112 Tomahawk	Bristol Strut Flying Group
	G-BPPJ	Cameron A-180 balloon	D. J. Farrar
	G-BPPK	PA-28-151 Warrior	Damarah Ltd
	G-BPPO	Luscombe 8A Silvaire	P. Dyer
	G-BPPP	Cameron V-77 balloon	Sarnia Balloon Group
	G-BPPZ	Taylorcraft BC-12D	G. C. Smith
	G-BPRC	Cameron 77 Elephant SS balloon	A. Schneider/Germany
	G-BPRD	Pitts S-1C Special	M. W. Bodger
	G-BPRI	AS.355F1 Twin Squirrel	MW Helicopters Ltd (G-TVPA)
	G-BPRJ	AS.355F1 Twin Squirrel	PLM Dollar Group Ltd
	G-BPRL	AS.355F1 Twin Squirrel	MW Helicopters Ltd
	G-BPRM	Cessna F.172L	BJ Aviation Ltd (G-AZKG)
	G-BPRX	Aeronca 11AC Chief	A. F. Kutz
	G-BPRY	PA-28-161 Warrior II	White Wings Aviation Ltd
	G-BPSO	Cameron N-90 balloon	J. Oberprieler/Germany
	G-BPSR	Cameron V-77 balloon	K. J. A. Maxwell
	G-BPTA	Stinson 108-2	M. L. Ryan
	G-BPTD	Cameron V-77 balloon	J. Lippett
	G-BPTE	PA-28-181 Archer II	A. J. Gomes
	G-BPTG	Rockwell Commander 112TC	B. Ogunyemi
	G-BPTI	SOCATA TB20 Trinidad	N. Davis
	G-BPTL	Cessna 172N	M. J. Spittal
	G-BPTS	CASA 1.131E Jungmann 1000 (E3B-153:781-75)	E. P. Parkin
	G-BPTV	Bensen B.8	C. Munro
	G-BPTZ	Robinson R22 Beta	Kuki Helicopter Sales Ltd and S. J. Nicholls
	G-BPUA	EAA Sport Biplane	D. A. Whitmore & N. P. Lambe
	G-BPUB	Cameron V-31 balloon	M. T. Evans
	G-BPUF	Thunder Ax6-56Z balloon	R. C. & M. A. Trimble (G-BHRL)
	G-BPUL	PA-18 Super Cub 150	C. D. Duthy-James & B. M. Reed
	G-BPUM	Cessna R.182RG	R. C. Chapman
	G-BPUP	Whittaker MW7	J. H. Beard
	G-BPUR	Piper J-3L-65 Cub (379994 52/J)	G. R. J. Caunter
	G-BPUU	Cessna 140	D. R. Speight
	G-BPVA	Cessna 172F	South Lancashire Flyers Group
	G-BPVE	Bleriot IX (replica) (1)	Bianchi Aviation Film Services Ltd
	G-BPVH	Cub Aircraft J-3C-65 Prospector	D. E. Cooper-Maguire
	G-BPVI	PA-32-301 Saratoga SP	M. T. Coppen
	G-BPVK	Varga 2150A Kachina	M. W. Oliver
	G-BPVN	PA-32R-301T Turbo Saratoga SP	O. Green
	G-BPVO	Cassutt Racer IIIM	J. B. Wilshaw
	G-BPVW	CASA 1.131E Jungmann 2000	C. & J-W. Labeij/Netherlands
	G-BPVZ	Luscombe 8E Silvaire	S. M. Thomas & A. P. Wilkie
	G-BPWE	PA-28-161 Warrior II	Warrior BPWE Ltd
	G-BPWG	Cessna 150M	GB Pilots Wilsford Group
	G-BPWK	Sportavia-Putzer Fournier RF-5B	G-BPWK Group
	G-BPWL	PA-25 Pawnee 235	M. H. Sims
	G-BPWM	Cessna 150L	P. D. Button
	G-BPWN	Cessna 150L	R. J. Grantham
	G-BPWP	Rutan LongEz (modified)	D. A. Field
	G-BPWR	Cessna R.172K	J. A. & D. T. A. Rees
	G-BPWS	Cessna 172P	Chartstone Ltd
	G-BPXA	PA-28-181 Archer II	Cherokee Flying Group
	G-BPXE	Enstrom 280C Shark	A. Healy
	G-BPXJ	PA-28RT-201T Turbo Arrow IV	E. Swift
	G-BPXX	PA-34-200T Seneca II	Yorkshire Aviation Ltd
	G-BPYJ	Wittman W.8 Tailwind	J. P. & Y. Mills
	G-BPYK	Thunder Ax7-77 balloon	P. J. Waller

Reg	Type	Owner or Operator	Notes
G-BPYL	Hughes 369D	Morcorp (BVI) Ltd	
G-BPYN	Piper J-3C-65 Cub	The Aquila Group	
G-BPYR	PA-31-310 Turbo Navajo	Excel Aviation Ltd	
G-BPYS	Cameron O-77 balloon	D. J. Goldsmith	
G-BPYT	Cameron V-77 balloon	M. H. Redman	
G-BPYY	Cameron A-180 balloon	G. D. Fitzpatrick	
G-BPZB	Cessna 120	Cessna 120 Group	
G-BPZC	Luscombe 8A Silvaire	C. C. & J. M. Lovell	
G-BPZD	SNCAN NC.858S	Zula Delta Syndicate	
G-BPZE	Luscombe 8E Silvaire	M. A. Watts	
G-BPZM	PA-28RT-201 Arrow IV	M. D. Darragh (G-ROYW/G-CRTI)	
G-BPZY	Pitts S-1C Special	J. S. Mitchell	
G-BRAA	Pitts S-1C Special	Haverfordwest Pitts	
G-BRAK	Cessna 172N	Falcon Flying Services Ltd	
G-BRAM	Mikoyan MiG-21PF (503) ★	FAST Museum/Farnborough	
G-BRAR	Aeronca 7AC Champion	R. B. Armitage	
G-BRBA	PA-28-161 Warrior II	C. Bonello & W. Richens	
G-BRBC	NA T-6G Texan	A. P. Murphy	
G-BRBD	PA-28-151 Warrior	Compton Abbas Airfield Ltd	
G-BRBE	PA-28-161 Warrior II	KN Singles and Twins Aviation	
G-BRBG	PA-28 Cherokee 180	P. M. Carter	
G-BRBH	Cessna 150H	Horizon Aircraft Engineering Ltd	
G-BRBI	Cessna 172N	Skyhawk Flying Group	
G-BRBJ	Cessna 172M	J. H. Sandham Aviation	
G-BRBK	Robin DR.400/180	A. D. Friday	
G-BRBL	Robin DR.400/180	U. A. Schliessler & R. J. Kelly	
G-BRBM	Robin DR.400/180	R. W. Davies	
G-BRBN	Pitts S-1S Special	G-BRBN Flying Group	
G-BRBO	Cameron V-77 balloon	D. Joly	
G-BRBP	Cessna 152	The Pilot Centre Ltd	
G-BRBV	Piper J-4A Cub Coupe	P. Clarke	
G-BRBW	PA-28 Cherokee 140	Air Navigation and Trading Co Ltd	
G-BRBX	PA-28-181 Archer II	Trent 199 Flying Group	
G-BRCA	Jodel D.112	R. C. Jordan	
G-BRCD	Cessna A.152	D. J. Hockings	
G-BRCE	Pitts S-1C Special	M. P. & S. T. Barnard	
G-BRCJ	Cameron H-20 balloon	P. A. Sweatman	
G-BRCM	Cessna 172L	D. C. C. Handley & D. A. Williams	
G-BRCT	Denney Kitfox Mk 2	M. L. Roberts	
G-BRCV	Aeronca 7AC Champion	J. Davies	
G-BRCW	Aeronca 11AC Chief	R. B. Griffin	
G-BRDD	Avions Mudry CAP-10B	T. A. Smith	
G-BRDF	PA-28-161 Warrior II	White Waltham Airfield Ltd	
G-BRDG	PA-28-161 Warrior II	Falcon Flying Services	
G-BRDJ	Luscombe 8A Silvaire	G-BRDJ Group	
G-BRDM	PA-28-161 Warrior II	White Waltham Airfield Ltd	
G-BRDO	Cessna 177B	Cardinal Aviation	
G-BRDV	Viking Wood Products Spitfire Prototype replica (K5054) ★	Solent Sky, Southampton	
G-BRDW	PA-24 Comanche 180	I. P. Gibson	
G-BREA	Bensen B.8MR	D. J. Martin	
G-BREB	Piper J-3C-65 Cub	J. R. Wraight	
G-BREH	Cameron V-65 balloon	M. Ptaszynski	
G-BREL	Cameron O-77 balloon	R. A. Patey	
G-BRER	Aeronca 7AC Champion	M. Hough	
G-BREU	Montgomerie-Bensen B.8MR	J. S. Firth	
G-BREX	Cameron O-84 balloon	W. S. Calvert	
G-BREY	Taylorcraft BC-12D	BREY Group	
G-BREZ	Cessna 172M	R. G. Rutty	
G-BRFB	Rutan LongEz	N. M. Robbins	
G-BRFC	Percival P.57 Sea Prince T.Mk.1 (WP321)	M. A. Stott	
G-BRFF	Colt 90A balloon	Amber Valley Aviation	
G-BRFI	Aeronca 7DC Champion	S. J. Ball	
G-BRFJ	Aeronca 11AC Chief	J. M. Mooney	
G-BRFM	PA-28-161 Warrior II	Swiftair Maintenance Ltd	
G-BRFO	Cameron V-77 balloon	Hedge Hoppers Balloon Group	
G-BRFW	Montgomerie-Bensen B.8 2-seat	A. J. Barker	
G-BRFX	Pazmany PL.4A	D. E. Hills	
G-BRGD	Cameron O-84 balloon	P. A. Davies	
G-BRGE	Cameron N-90 balloon	Oakfield Farm Products Ltd	

Notes	Reg	Type	Owner or Operator
	G-BRGF	Luscombe 8E Silvaire	J. A. Coutts
	G-BRGI	PA-28 Cherokee 180	R. A. Buckfield
	G-BRGT	PA-32 Cherokee Six 260	A. A. Mattacks & T. J. W. Hood
	G-BRGW	Gardan GY-201 Minicab	R. G. White
	G-BRHA	PA-32RT-300 Lance II	Lance G-BRHA Group
	G-BRHO	PA-34-200 Seneca	Transair (CI) Ltd
	G-BRHP	Aeronca O-58B Grasshopper (31923)	R. B. McComish
	G-BRHR	PA-38-112 Tomahawk	London School of Flying Ltd
	G-BRHX	Luscombe 8E Silvaire	J. Lakin
	G-BRHY	Luscombe 8E Silvaire	R. A. Keech
	G-BRIE	Cameron N-77 balloon	S. F. Redman
	G-BRIH	Taylorcraft BC-12D	M. J. Medland
	G-BRIJ	Taylorcraft F-19	E. N. L. Troffigue
	G-BRIK	T.66 Nipper 3	Clipgate Nipper Group
	G-BRIL	Piper J-5A Cub Cruiser	D. J. Bone
	G-BRIO	Turner Super T-40A	S. Bidwell
	G-BRIV	SOCATA TB9 Tampico Club	S. J. Taft
	G-BRIY	Taylorcraft DF-65 (42-58678:IY)	S. R. Potts
	G-BRJA	Luscombe 8A Silvaire	A. D. Keen
	G-BRJC	Cessna 120	J. Hodgson
	G-BRJK	Luscombe 8A Silvaire	M. Richardson & R. C. Dyer
	G-BRJL	PA-15 Vagabond	A. R. Williams
	G-BRJN	Pitts S-1C Special	W. Chapel
	G-BRJV	PA-28-161 Cadet	Pilot Traing & Testing Ltd
	G-BRJX	Rand-Robinson KR-2	J. R. Bell
	G-BRJY	Rand-Robinson KR-2	R. E. Taylor
	G-BRKC	Auster J/1 Autocrat	J. W. Conlon
	G-BRKH	PA-28-236 Dakota	T. A. White
	G-BRKL	Cameron H-34 balloon	B. J. Newman
	G-BRKR	Cessna 182R	D. Horan
	G-BRKW	Cameron V-77 balloon	T. J. Parker
	G-BRKY	Viking Dragonfly Mk II	Polar Bear Services Ltd
	G-BRLB	Air Command 532 Elite	F. G. Shepherd
	G-BRLF	Campbell Cricket (replica)	J. L. G. McLane
	G-BRLG	PA-28RT-201T Turbo Arrow IV	N. R. Quirk
	G-BRLI	Piper J-5A Cub Cruiser	D. J. M. Eardley
	G-BRLL	Cameron A-105 balloon	P. A. Sweatman
	G-BRLO	PA-38-112 Tomahawk	Pilot Training & Testing Ltd
	G-BRLP	PA-38-112 Tomahawk	Highland Aviation Training Ltd
	G-BRLR	Cessna 150G	D. Bull & T. Adams
	G-BRLS	Thunder Ax7-77 balloon	J. R. Palmer
	G-BRMA	WS-51 Dragonfly HR.5 (WG719) ★	IHM/Weston-super-Mare
	G-BRMB	Bristol192 Belvedere HC.1 ★	IHM/Weston-super-Mare
	G-BRME	PA-28-181 Archer II	Falcon Flying Services Ltd
	G-BRMT	Cameron V-31 balloon	B. Reed
	G-BRMU	Cameron V-77 balloon	P. Spellward
	G-BRMV	Cameron O-77 balloon	P. D. Griffiths
	G-BRNC	Cessna 150M	G-BRNC Group
	G-BRND	Cessna 152 II	T. M. & M. L. Jones
	G-BRNE	Cessna 152 II	Redhill Air Services Ltd
	G-BRNK	Cessna 152 II	D. C. & M. Bonsall
	G-BRNN	Cessna 152 II	Eastern Air Executive Ltd
	G-BRNT	Robin DR.400/180	C. E. Ponsford & ptnrs
	G-BRNU	Robin DR.400/180	November Uniform Travel Syndicate Ltd
	G-BRNV	PA-28-181 Archer II	D. N. F. Barrington-Bullock
	G-BRNW	Cameron V-77 balloon	N. Robertson & G. Smith
	G-BRNX	PA-22 Tri-Pacer 150	S. N. Askey
	G-BROE	Cameron N-65 balloon	A. I. Attwood
	G-BROG	Cameron V-65 balloon	R. Kunert
	G-BROJ	Colt 31A balloon	N. J. Langley
	G-BROO	Luscombe 8E Silvaire	P. R. Bush
	G-BROP	Van's RV-4	K. Keen & N. Huxtable (G-NADZ)
	G-BROR	Piper J-3C-65 Cub	White Hart Flying Group
	G-BROX	Robinson R22 Beta	Phoenix Helicopter Academy Ltd
	G-BROY	Cameron V-77 balloon	R. Rebosio
	G-BROZ	PA-18 Super Cub 150	P. G. Kynsey
	G-BRPE	Cessna 120	C. G. Applegarth
	G-BRPF	Cessna 120	M. A. Potter
	G-BRPG	Cessna 120	I. C. Lomax
	G-BRPH	Cessna 120	R. Kelvey
	G-BRPK	PA-28 Cherokee 140	G-BRPK Group

Reg	Type	Owner or Operator	Notes
G-BRPL	PA-28-140 Cherokee	British North West Airlines Ltd	
G-BRPM	T.66 Nipper 3	J. H. H. Turner	
G-BRPP	Brookland Hornet (modified)	B. J. L. P. & W. J. A. L. de Saar	
G-BRPR	Aeronca O-58B Grasshopper (31952)	A. F. Kutz	
G-BRPS	Cessna 177B	W. Parent	
G-BRPT	Rans S.10 Sakota	J. A. Harris	
G-BRPV	Cessna 152	Eastern Air Executive Ltd	
G-BRPX	Taylorcraft BC-12D	G-BRPX Group	
G-BRPY	PA-15 Vagabond	C. S. Whitwell	
G-BRPZ	Luscombe 8A Silvaire	C. A. Flint	
G-BRRA	VS.361 Spitfire LF.IX (MK912:SH-L)	Peter Monk Ltd	
G-BRRB	Luscombe 8E Silvaire	CAV Aircraft Services Ltd	
G-BRRF	Cameron O-77 balloon	K. P. & G. J. Storey	
G-BRRK	Cessna 182Q	Werewolf Aviation Ltd	
G-BRRP	Pitts S-1S Special	T. Q. Short (G-WAZZ)	
G-BRRR	Cameron V-77 balloon	K. P. & G. J. Storey	
G-BRRU	Colt 90A balloon	Reach For The Sky Ltd	
G-BRSA	Cameron N-56 balloon	C. M. Duggan	
G-BRSD	Cameron V-77 balloon	M. E. Granger	
G-BRSF	VS.361 Spitfire HF.9c (RR232)	M. B. Phillips	
G-BRSL	Cameron N-56 balloon	S. Budd	
G-BRSO	CFM Streak Shadow	I. Pearson	
G-BRSP	Air Command 532 Elite	G. M. Hobman	
G-BRSW	Luscombe 8A Silvaire	Bloody Mary Aviation	
G-BRSX	PA-15 Vagabond	Sierra Xray Group	
G-BRSY	Hatz CB-1	B. Doyle	
G-BRTD	Cessna 152 II	152 Group	
G-BRTJ	Cessna 150F	T. O"Driscoll	
G-BRTL	Hughes 369E	Road Tech Computer Systems Ltd	
G-BRTP	Cessna 152 II	R. Lee	
G-BRTT	Schweizer 269C	Fairthorpe Ltd	
G-BRTW	Glaser-Dirks DG.400	I. J. Carruthers	
G-BRTX	PA-28-151 Warrior	T. Mahmood	
G-BRUB	PA-28-161 Warrior II	Flytrek Ltd	
G-BRUD	PA-28-181 Archer II	Falcon Flying Services	
G-BRUG	Luscombe 8E Silvaire	N. W. Barratt	
G-BRUJ	Boeing Stearman A.75N1 (6136:205)	R. L. McDonald	
G-BRUM	Cessna A.152	A. J. Gomes	
G-BRUN	Cessna 120	J. W. Wolfe (G-BRDH)	
G-BRUO	Taylor JT.1 Monoplane	S. T. S. Bygrave	
G-BRUV	Cameron V-77 balloon	T. W. & R. F. Benbrook	
G-BRUX	PA-44-180 Seminole	M. Ali	
G-BRVB	Stolp SA.300 Starduster Too	K. G. F. Radenbach	
G-BRVE	Beech D.17S	Patina Ltd	
G-BRVF	Colt 77A balloon	J. Adkins	
G-BRVG	NA SNJ-7 Texan (27)	D. Gilmour/Intrepid Aviation Co	
G-BRVH	Smyth Model S Sidewinder	B. D. Deleporte	
G-BRVI	Robinson R22 Beta	York Helicopters	
G-BRVJ	Slingsby T.31 Motor Cadet III	B. Outhwaite	
G-BRVL	Pitts S-1C Special	M. F. Pocock	
G-BRVO	AS.350B Ecureuil	Rotorhire LLP	
G-BRVZ	Jodel D.117	L. Holland	
G-BRWA	Aeronca 7AC Champion	S. J. Donno	
G-BRWB	NA T-6G Texan (526)	R. Clifford	
G-BRWD	Robinson R22 Beta	Heli Air Ltd	
G-BRWP	CFM Streak Shadow	T. McDonald & D. Brunton	
G-BRWR	Aeronca 11AC Chief	A. W. Crutcher	
G-BRWT	Scheibe SF.25C Falke	Booker Gliding Club Ltd	
G-BRWU	Luton LA-4A Minor	R. A. Benson	
G-BRWV	Brügger MB.2 Colibri	M. P. Wakem	
G-BRXA	Cameron O-120 balloon	R. J. Mansfield	
G-BRXD	PA-28-181 Archer II	Xraydelta Ltd	
G-BRXE	Taylorcraft BC-12D	B. T. Morgan & W. J. Durrad	
G-BRXF	Aeronca 11AC Chief	Aeronca Flying Group	
G-BRXG	Aeronca 7AC Champion	X-Ray Golf Flying Group	
G-BRXH	Cessna 120	BRXH Group	
G-BRXL	Aeronca 11AC Chief (42-78044)	P. L. Green	
G-BRXP	SNCAN Stampe SV.4C (modified)	T. Brown	
G-BRXS	Howard Special T Minus	F. A. Bakir	
G-BRXU	Aerospatiale AS.332L Super Puma	Airbus Helicopters	
G-BRXW	PA-24 Comanche 260	L. J. & M. A. Hounsome	

Notes	Reg	Type	Owner or Operator
	G-BRXY	Pietenpol Air Camper	P. S. Ganczakowski
	G-BRZA	Cameron O-77 balloon	S. J. Nichols & N. M. Benjamin
	G-BRZB	Cameron A-105 balloon	Headland Services Ltd
	G-BRZD	Hapi Cygnet SF-2A	P. A. Gasson
	G-BRZF	Enstrom 280C Shark	M. Richardson (G-IDUP)
	G-BRZG	Enstrom F-28A	R. Windley
	G-BRZK	Stinson 108-2	D. A. Gathercole
	G-BRZL	Pitts S-1D Special	T. R. G. Barnby
	G-BRZS	Cessna 172P	YP Flying Group
	G-BRZW	Rans S.10 Sakota	D. L. Davies
	G-BRZX	Pitts S-1S Special	Zulu Xray Group
	G-BSAH	BN-2T Turbine Islander	Islander Aircraft Ltd
	G-BSAI	Stoddard-Hamilton Glasair III	K. J. & P. J. Whitehead
	G-BSAJ	CASA 1.131E Jungmann 2000	P. G. Kynsey
	G-BSAK	Colt 21A balloon	M. D. Mitchell
	G-BSAS	Cameron V-65 balloon	P. Donkin
	G-BSAV	Thunder Ax7-77 balloon	I. G. & C. A. Lloyd
	G-BSAW	PA-28-161 Warrior II	Compton Abbas Airfield Ltd
	G-BSAZ	Denney Kitfox Mk 2	A. J. Lloyd
	G-BSBA	PA-28-161 Warrior II	Falcon Flying Services Ltd
	G-BSBG	CCF Harvard IV (20310:310)	A. P. St. John
	G-BSBR	Cameron V-77 balloon	R. P. Wade
	G-BSBT	Piper J-3C-65 Cub	A. R. Elliott
	G-BSBV	Rans S.10 Sakota	S. Bain
	G-BSCC	Colt 105A balloon	A. F. Selby
	G-BSCE	Robinson R22 Beta	Kuki Helicopter Sales Ltd
	G-BSCG	Denney Kitfox Mk 2	D. J. Couzens
	G-BSCH	Denney Kitfox Mk 2	R. Windley
	G-BSCI	Colt 77A balloon	S. C. Kinsey
	G-BSCK	Cameron H-24 balloon	J. D. Shapland
	G-BSCM	Denney Kitfox Mk 2	H. D. Colliver (G-MSCM)
	G-BSCN	SOCATA TB20 Trinidad	T. W. Gilbert
	G-BSCO	Thunder Ax7-77 balloon	F. J. Whalley
	G-BSCP	Cessna 152 II	Moray Flying Club (1990) Ltd
	G-BSCS	PA-28-181 Archer II	A. C. Renouf
	G-BSCV	PA-28-161 Warrior II	Southwood Flying Group
	G-BSCW	Taylorcraft BC-65	G. Johnson
	G-BSCY	PA-28-151 Warrior	Take Flight Aviation Ltd
	G-BSCZ	Cessna 152 II	The RAF Halton Aeroplane Club Ltd
	G-BSDA	Taylorcraft BC-12D	A. D. Pearce
	G-BSDD	Denney Kitfox Mk 2	C. Morris
	G-BSDH	Robin DR.400/180	G-BSDH Group
	G-BSDK	Piper J-5A Cub Cruiser	J. E. Mead
	G-BSDN	PA-34-200T Seneca II	S. J. Green
	G-BSDO	Cessna 152 II	Cloud Global Ltd
	G-BSDP	Cessna 152 II	Paul's Planes Ltd
	G-BSDS	Boeing Stearman E75 (118)	L. W. Scattergood
	G-BSDW	Cessna 182P	Clipper Data Ltd
	G-BSDX	Cameron V-77 balloon	G. P. & S. J. Allen
	G-BSDZ	Enstrom 280FX	C. D. Meek
	G-BSEA	Thunder Ax7-77 balloon	B. T. Lewis
	G-BSED	PA-22 Tri-Pacer 160 (modified)	M. D. N. Fisher
	G-BSEE	Rans S.9	D. A. Karniewicz
	G-BSEF	PA-28 Cherokee 180	I. D. Wakeling
	G-BSEH	Cameron V-77 balloon	L. M. P. Vernackt/Belgium
	G-BSEJ	Cessna 150M	J. R. Nicholas
	G-BSEL	Slingsby T.61G Super Falke	D. G. Holley
	G-BSER	PA-28 Cherokee 160	Yorkair Ltd
	G-BSEU	PA-28-181 Archer II	Herefordshire Aero Club Ltd
	G-BSEV	Cameron O-77 balloon	P. B. Kenington
	G-BSEX	Cameron A-180 balloon	Heart of England Balloons
	G-BSEY	Beech A36 Bonanza	P. Malam-Wilson
	G-BSFA	Aero Designs Pulsar	P. F. Lorriman
	G-BSFD	Piper J-3C-65 Cub (16037)	P. E. S. Latham
	G-BSFE	PA-38-112 Tomahawk II	Leading Edge Flight Training Ltd
	G-BSFF	Robin DR.400/180R	Lasham Gliding Society Ltd
	G-BSFP	Cessna 152T	The Pilot Centre Ltd
	G-BSFR	Cessna 152 II	Galair Ltd
	G-BSFW	PA-15 Vagabond	J. R. Kimberley
	G-BSFX	Denney Kitfox Mk 2	F. Colman

Reg	Type	Owner or Operator	Notes
G-BSGD	PA-28 Cherokee 180	R. J. Cleverley	
G-BSGF	Robinson R22 Beta	Heliyorks Ltd	
G-BSGG	Denney Kitfox Mk 2	S. E. Lyden	
G-BSGH	Airtour AH-56B balloon	A. R. Hardwick	
G-BSGJ	Monnett Sonerai II	J. L. Loweth	
G-BSGS	Rans S.10 Sakota	M. R. Parr	
G-BSGT	Cessna T.210N	E. A. T. Brenninkmeyer	
G-BSHA	PA-34-200T Seneca II	Justgold Ltd	
G-BSHC	Colt 69A balloon	Magical Adventures Ltd	
G-BSHH	Luscombe 8E Silvaire	CAV Aircraft Services Ltd	
G-BSHO	Cameron V-77 balloon	D. J. Duckworth & J. C. Stewart	
G-BSHP	PA-28-161 Warrior II	Pilot Training and Testing Ltd	
G-BSHR	Cessna F.172N	Deep Cleavage Ltd (G-BFGE)	
G-BSHY	EAA Acro Sport I	R. J. Hodder	
G-BSIC	Cameron V-77 balloon	R. Parr	
G-BSIF	Denney Kitfox Mk 2	S. M. Dougan	
G-BSIG	Colt 21A Cloudhopper balloon	C. J. Dunkley	
G-BSII	PA-34-200T Seneca II	R. Knowles	
G-BSIJ	Cameron V-77 balloon	G. B. Davies	
G-BSIM	PA-28-181 Archer II	Falcon Flying Services Ltd	
G-BSIO	Cameron 80 Shed SS balloon	R. E. Jones	
G-BSIU	Colt 90A balloon	S. Travaglia/Italy	
G-BSIY	Schleicher ASK.14	P. W. Andrews	
G-BSIZ	PA-28-181 Archer II	AJW Construction Ltd	
G-BSJX	PA-28-161 Warrior II	Bulldog Aviation Ltd	
G-BSJZ	Cessna 150J	J. M. Vinall	
G-BSKA	Cessna 150M	GS Aviation (Europe) Ltd	
G-BSKG	Maule MX-7-180	A. J. Lewis	
G-BSKW	PA-28-181 Archer II	R. J. Whyham	
G-BSLA	Robin DR.400/180	A. B. McCoig	
G-BSLH	CASA 1.131E Jungmann 2000	M. A. Warden	
G-BSLJ	Denney Kitfox	J. A. Budd	
G-BSLK	PA-28-161 Warrior II	Take Flight Aviation Ltd	
G-BSLM	PA-28 Cherokee 160	Fly (Fu Lai) Aviation Ltd	
G-BSLT	PA-28-161 Warrior II	CG Aviation Ltd	
G-BSLU	PA-28 Cherokee 140	Merseyflight Air Training School	
G-BSLV	Enstrom 280FX	B. M. B Roumier	
G-BSLW	Bellanca 7ECA Citabria	Condor Aviation International Ltd	
G-BSLX	WAR Focke-Wulf Fw 190 (replica) (4+)	S. Freeman	
G-BSME	Bölkow Bö.208C1 Junior	D. J. Hampson	
G-BSMM	Colt 31A balloon	P. Spellward	
G-BSMN	CFM Streak Shadow	D. R. C. Pugh	
G-BSMT	Rans S-10 Sakota	T. D. Wood	
G-BSMV	PA-17 Vagabond (modified)	A. Cheriton	
G-BSNE	Luscombe 8E Silvaire	O. R. Watts	
G-BSNF	Piper J-3C-65 Cub	D. A. Hammant	
G-BSNG	Cessna 172N	A. J. & P. C. MacDonald	
G-BSNT	Luscombe 8A Silvaire	Luscombe Quartet	
G-BSNU	Colt 105A balloon	Gone Ballooning	
G-BSNX	PA-28-181 Archer II	Redhill Air Services Ltd	
G-BSOE	Luscombe 8A Silvaire	R. G. Downhill	
G-BSOF	Colt 25A balloon	J. M. Bailey	
G-BSOG	Cessna 172M	Gloster Aero Group	
G-BSOJ	Thunder Ax7-77 balloon	R. J. S. Jones	
G-BSOK	PA-28-161 Warrior II	G. E. Fox	
G-BSOM	Glaser-Dirks DG.400	P. Ryland	
G-BSON	Green S.25 balloon	J. J. Green	
G-BSOO	Cessna 172F	The Oscar Oscar Group	
G-BSOR	CFM Streak Shadow Srs SA	A. Parr	
G-BSOU	PA-38-112 Tomahawk II	Leading Edge Flight Training Ltd	
G-BSOX	Luscombe 8AE Silvaire	R. Dauncey	
G-BSOZ	PA-28-161 Warrior II	Pactum Company Ltd	
G-BSPA	QAC Quickie Q.2	G. V. McKirdy & B. K. Glover	
G-BSPC	Jodel D.140C	B. E. Cotton	
G-BSPE	Cessna F.172P	T. W. Williamson	
G-BSPG	PA-34-200T Seneca II	Andrews Professional Colour Laboratories Ltd	
G-BSPK	Cessna 195A	A. G. & D. L. Bompas	
G-BSPL	CFM Streak Shadow Srs SA	G. L. Turner	
G-BSPN	PA-28R-201T Turbo Arrow III	Wendex Vehicle Rental Ltd	
G-BSRH	Pitts S-1C Special	T. L. & T. W. Davis	
G-BSRI	Lancair 235	P. M. Harrison	

Notes	Reg	Type	Owner or Operator
	G-BSRK	ARV Super 2	J. Svenson
	G-BSRL	Campbell Cricket Mk.4 gyroplane	M. Brudnicki
	G-BSRP	Rotorway Executive	R. J. Baker
	G-BSRR	Cessna 182Q	C. M. Moore
	G-BSRT	Denney Kitfox Mk 2	S. J. Walker
	G-BSRX	CFM Streak Shadow	I. P. Freestone
	G-BSSA	Luscombe 8E Silvaire	Luscombe Flying Group
	G-BSSB	Cessna 150L	D. T. A. Rees
	G-BSSC	PA-28-161 Warrior II	Sky Blue Flight Training
	G-BSSF	Denney Kitfox Mk 2	F. W. Astbury
	G-BSSI	Rans S.6 Coyote II	W. McDowell (G-MWJA)
	G-BSSK	QAC Quickie Q.2	R. Greatrex
	G-BSSP	Robin DR.400/180R	Soaring (Oxford) Ltd
	G-BSST	BAC-Sud Concorde 002 ★	F.A.A. Museum/Yeovilton
	G-BSSV	CFM Streak Shadow	R. W. Payne
	G-BSSY	Polikarpov Po-2 (28)	Richard Shuttleworth Trustees
	G-BSTC	Aeronca 11AC Chief	J. Armstrong & D. Lamb
	G-BSTE	AS.355F2 Twin Squirrel	Oscar Mayer Ltd
	G-BSTI	Piper J-3C-65 Cub	J. A. Scott
	G-BSTK	Thunder Ax8-90 balloon	M. Williams
	G-BSTL	Rand-Robinson KR-2	C. S. Hales & N. Brauns
	G-BSTM	Cessna 172L	G-BSTM Group
	G-BSTO	Cessna 152 II	M. A. Stott
	G-BSTP	Cessna 152 II	LAC Aircraft Ltd
	G-BSTR	AA-5 Traveler	J. C. M. Alty
	G-BSTT	Rans S.6 Coyote II	D. G. Palmer
	G-BSTX	Luscombe 8A Silvaire	R. J. Bentley
	G-BSTZ	PA-28 Cherokee 140	Air Navigation & Trading Co Ltd
	G-BSUA	Rans S.6 Coyote II	A. J. Todd
	G-BSUB	Colt 77A balloon	E. Stephens
	G-BSUD	Luscombe 8A Silvaire	Luscombe Quartet
	G-BSUF	PA-32RT-300 Lance II	R. Knappe
	G-BSUK	Colt 77A balloon	T. Knight
	G-BSUO	Scheibe SF.25C Falke	Portmoak Falke Syndicate
	G-BSUV	Cameron O-77 balloon	I. R. F. Worsman
	G-BSUW	PA-34-200T Seneca II	W. Ali
	G-BSUX	Carlson Sparrow II	N. & S. Wise
	G-BSUZ	Denney Kitfox Mk 3	J. D. Randall
	G-BSVB	PA-28-181 Archer II	Veebee Aviation Ltd
	G-BSVE	Binder CP.301S Smaragd	Smaragd Flying Group
	G-BSVG	PA-28-161 Warrior II	Airways Aero Associations Ltd
	G-BSVH	Piper J-3C-65 Cub	G. J. Digby
	G-BSVM	PA-28-161 Warrior II	EFG Flying Services
	G-BSVN	Thorp T-18	M. D. Moaby
	G-BSVP	PA-23-250 Aztec F	S. G. Spier
	G-BSVR	Schweizer 269C	M. K. E. Askham
	G-BSVS	Robin DR.400/100	D. McK. Chalmers
	G-BSWB	Rans S.10 Sakota	F. A. Hewitt
	G-BSWC	Boeing Stearman E75 (112)	D. A. Jack
	G-BSWF	PA-16 Clipper	GW Evans Ltd
	G-BSWG	PA-17 Vagabond	M. J. Benham
	G-BSWH	Cessna 152 II	Airspeed Aviation Ltd
	G-BSWL	Slingsby T.61F Venture T.2	G-BSWL Group
	G-BSWM	Slingsby T.61F Venture T.2	Venture Gliding Group
	G-BSWR	BN-2T-26 Turbine Islander	Police Service of Northern Ireland
	G-BSWV	Cameron N-77 balloon	S. Charlish
	G-BSXA	PA-28-161 Warrior II	Falcon Flying Services
	G-BSXB	PA-28-161 Warrior II	S. R. Mendes
	G-BSXC	PA-28-161 Warrior II	Cristal Air Ltd
	G-BSXD	Soko P-2 Kraguj (30146)	Airfield Aviation Ltd
	G-BSXI	Mooney M.20E	D. H. G. Penney
	G-BSXM	Cameron V-77 balloon	C. A. Oxby
	G-BSXT	Piper J-5A Cub Cruiser	Great American Flyers
	G-BSYF	Luscombe 8A Silvaire	V. R. Leggott
	G-BSYG	PA-12 Super Cruiser	Fat Cub Group
	G-BSYH	Luscombe 8A Silvaire	N. R. Osborne
	G-BSYJ	Cameron N-77 balloon	Chubb Fire Ltd
	G-BSYO	Piper J-3C-90 Cub	C. R. Reynolds (G-BSMJ/G-BRHE)
	G-BSYU	Robin DR.400/180	P. D. Smoothy
	G-BSYV	Cessna 150M	E-Plane Ltd
	G-BSYY	PA-28-161 Warrior II	Aerobility

Reg	Type	Owner or Operator	Notes
G-BSYZ	PA-28-161 Warrior II	F. C. P. Hood	
G-BSZB	Stolp SA.300 Starduster Too	P. J. B. Lewis	
G-BSZF	Jodel DR.250/160	J. B. Randle	
G-BSZJ	PA-28-181 Archer II	M. L. A. Pudney & R. D. Fuller	
G-BSZM	Montgomerie-Bensen B.8MR	P. C. W. Raine	
G-BSZO	Cessna 152	A. Jahanfar	
G-BSZT	PA-28-161 Warrior II	Golf Charlie Echo Ltd	
G-BSZV	Cessna 150F	C. A. Davis	
G-BSZW	Cessna 152	S. T. & T. W. Gilbert	
G-BTAK	EAA Acrosport II	A. D. Friday	
G-BTAL	Cessna F.152 II	Herefordshire Aero Club Ltd	
G-BTAM	PA-28-181 Archer II	Tri-Star Farms Ltd	
G-BTAW	PA-28-161 Warrior II	Piper Flying Group	
G-BTAZ	Evans VP-2 ★	Norwich Aviation Museum	
G-BTBA	Robinson R22 Beta	Elite Helicopters	
G-BTBC	PA-28-161 Warrior II	M. A. Khan	
G-BTBG	Denney Kitfox Mk 2	A. S. Cadney	
G-BTBH	Ryan ST3KR (854)	R. C. Piper	
G-BTBJ	Cessna 190	P. W. Moorcroft	
G-BTBL	Montgomerie-Bensen B.8MR	AES Radionic Surveillance Systems	
G-BTBU	PA-18 Super Cub 150	S. D. Edwards	
G-BTBV	Cessna 140	A. M. A. C. White	
G-BTBW	Cessna 120	K. U. Platzer/Germany	
G-BTBY	PA-17 Vagabond	F. M. Ward	
G-BTCB	Air Command 582 Sport	G. Scurrah	
G-BTCE	Cessna 152	S. T. Gilbert	
G-BTCH	Luscombe 8E Silvaire Deluxe	M. W. Orr	
G-BTCI	PA-17 Vagabond	T. R. Whittome	
G-BTCJ	Luscombe 8E Silvaire	D. Snook	
G-BTCZ	Cameron Chateau 84 balloon	Balleroy Developpement SAS	
G-BTDA	Slingsby T.61G Falke	G-BTDA Group	
G-BTDC	Denney Kitfox Mk 2	R. Dunn	
G-BTDD	CFM Streak Shadow	The Adventurous SSDR Group	
G-BTDE	Cessna C-165 Airmaster	R. H. Screen	
G-BTDF	Luscombe 8A Silvaire	G. Johnson	
G-BTDI	Robinson R22	S. Klinge	
G-BTDN	Denney Kitfox Mk 2	J. Bennett & D. Rudd	
G-BTDR	Aero Designs Pulsar	A. & P. Kingsley-Dobson	
G-BTDT	CASA 1.131E Jungmann 2000	Cirrus Aircraft UK Ltd	
G-BTDV	PA-28-161 Warrior II	Falcon Flying Services Ltd	
G-BTDW	Cessna 152 II	J. H. Sandham Aviation	
G-BTDZ	CASA 1.131E Jungmann 2000	R. J. & M. Pickin	
G-BTEL	CFM Streak Shadow	J. E. Eatwell	
G-BTES	Cessna 150H	C. Burt-Brown & J. Taylor	
G-BTET	Piper J-3C-65 Cub	City of Oxford Flying Group	
G-BTEW	Cessna 120	A. I. & J. H. Milne	
G-BTFC	Cessna F.152 II	Aircraft Engineers Ltd	
G-BTFE	Bensen-Parsons 2-seat gyroplane	A. Corleanca	
G-BTFG	Boeing Stearman A75N1 (441)	TG Aviation Ltd	
G-BTFJ	PA-15 Vagabond	A. G. Thomas & R. Ellingworth	
G-BTFK	Taylorcraft BC-12D	M. Ward	
G-BTFL	Aeronca 11AC Chief	BTFL Group	
G-BTFO	PA-28-161 Warrior II	Flyfar Ltd	
G-BTFP	PA-38-112 Tomahawk	M. Lee	
G-BTFT	Beech 58 Baron	Fastwing Air Charter Ltd	
G-BTFU	Cameron N-90 balloon	J. J. Rudoni & A. C. K. Rawson	
G-BTFV	Whittaker MW7	C. R. Buckle	
G-BTGD	Rand-Robinson KR-2 (modified)	B M. Neary	
G-BTGI	Rearwin 175 Skyranger	J. M. Fforde	
G-BTGJ	Smith DSA-1 Miniplane	Aviation Salvage & Recovery Ltd	
G-BTGL	Light Aero Avid Flyer	J. S. Clair-Quentin	
G-BTGM	Aeronca 7AC Champion	Heligan Champ Group	
G-BTGO	PA-28 Cherokee 140	Demero Ltd & Transcourt Ltd	
G-BTGR	Cessna 152 II	A. J. Gomes	
G-BTGS	Stolp SA.300 Starduster Too	G. N. Elliott & ptnrs (G-AYMA)	
G-BTGT	CFM Streak Shadow	I. Heunis (G-MWPY)	
G-BTGW	Cessna 152 II	Stapleford Flying Club Ltd	
G-BTGX	Cessna 152 II	Stapleford Flying Club Ltd	
G-BTGY	PA-28-161 Warrior II	Stapleford Flying Club Ltd	
G-BTGZ	PA-28-181 Archer II	Nick Deyong Ltd	

Notes	Reg	Type	Owner or Operator
	G-BTHE	Cessna 150L	General Technics Ltd
	G-BTHF	Cameron V-90 balloon	N. J. & S. J. Langley
	G-BTHK	Thunder Ax7-77 balloon	M. S.Trend
	G-BTHM	Thunder Ax8-105 balloon	Montgolfieres Club de L'Orme/France
	G-BTHP	Thorp T.211	M. Gardner
	G-BTHX	Colt 105A balloon	I. J. Wadey
	G-BTHY	Bell 206B JetRanger 3	Suffolk Helicopters Ltd
	G-BTIE	SOCATA TB10 Tobago	D. J. & S. N. Taplin
	G-BTIF	Denney Kitfox Mk 3	D. S. Lally
	G-BTIG	Montgomerie-Bensen B.8MR	G. H. Leeming
	G-BTII	AA-5B Tiger	G-BTII Group
	G-BTIJ	Luscombe 8E Silvaire	S. J. Hornsby
	G-BTIL	PA-38-112 Tomahawk	B. J. Pearson
	G-BTIM	PA-28-161 Cadet	White Waltham Airfield Ltd
	G-BTIV	PA-28-161 Warrior II	Warrior Group
	G-BTJA	Luscombe 8E Silvaire	N. C. Wildey
	G-BTJB	Luscombe 8E Silvaire	M. Loxton
	G-BTJC	Luscombe 8F Silvaire	M. Colson
	G-BTJD	Thunder Ax8-90 S2 balloon	P. Richardson
	G-BTJH	Cameron O-77 balloon	M. Saveri
	G-BTJL	PA-38-112 Tomahawk	A5E Ltd
	G-BTJO	Thunder Ax9-140 balloon	G. P. Lane
	G-BTJS	Montgomerie-Bensen B.8MR	B. F. Pearson
	G-BTJX	Rans S.10 Sakota	J. A. Harris
	G-BTKA	Piper J-5A Cub Cruiser	M. J. Walker
	G-BTKB	Renegade Spirit 912	P. J. Calvert
	G-BTKD	Denney Kitfox Mk 4	R. A. Hills
	G-BTKL	MBB Bö.105DB-4	Helicom Ltd
	G-BTKP	CFM Streak Shadow	G-BTKP Group
	G-BTKT	PA-28-161 Warrior II	Biggin Hill Flying Club Ltd
	G-BTKV	PA-22 Tri-Pacer 160	R. A. Moore
	G-BTKW	Cameron O-105 balloon	L. J. Whitelock
	G-BTKX	PA-28-181 Archer II	D. J. Perkins
	G-BTLB	Wassmer Wa.52 Europa	Hampshire Flying Group
	G-BTLG	PA-28R Cherokee Arrow 200	S. A. Thomas
	G-BTLL	Pilatus P.3-03	R. E. Dagless
	G-BTLP	AA-1C Lynx	Partlease Ltd
	G-BTMA	Cessna 172N	R. F. Wondrak
	G-BTMK	Cessna R.172K XPII	K. E. Halford
	G-BTMO	Colt 69A balloon	Cameron Balloons Ltd
	G-BTMP	Campbell Cricket	P. W. McLaughlin
	G-BTMR	Cessna 172M	Hull Aero Club Ltd
	G-BTMV	Everett Srs 2 gyroplane	L. Armes
	G-BTNA	Robinson R22 Beta	HQ Aviation Ltd
	G-BTNC	AS.365N-2 Dauphin 2	Multiflight Ltd
	G-BTNH	PA-28-161 Warrior II	Falcon Flying Services Ltd (G-DENH)
	G-BTNO	Aeronca 7AC Champion	J. M. Farquhar
	G-BTNR	Denney Kitfox Mk 3	High Notions Flying Group
	G-BTNT	PA-28-151 Warrior	Azure Flying Club Ltd
	G-BTNV	PA-28-161 Warrior II	B. Somerville & P. A. Teasdale
	G-BTNW	Rans S.6-ESA Coyote II	Coyote Ugly Group
	G-BTOG	DH.82A Tiger Moth	TOG Group
	G-BTOL	Denney Kitfox Mk 3	P. J. Gibbs
	G-BTON	PA-28 Cherokee 140	R. Nightingale
	G-BTOO	Pitts S-1C Special	T. L. Davis
	G-BTOP	Cameron V-77 balloon	J. J. Winter
	G-BTOT	PA-15 Vagabond	Vagabond Flying Group
	G-BTOU	Cameron O-120 balloon	J. J. Daly
	G-BTOW	SOCATA Rallye 180GT	M. Jarrett
	G-BTOZ	Thunder Ax9-120 S2 balloon	H. G. Davies
	G-BTPJ	BAe ATP	West Atlantic Aircraft Management AB
	G-BTPL	BAe ATP	West Atlantic Aircraft Management AB
	G-BTPT	Cameron N-77 balloon	H. J. Andrews
	G-BTPV	Colt 90A balloon	C. J. Wootton & J. S. Russon
	G-BTPX	Thunder Ax8-90 BALLOON	B. J. Ross
	G-BTRC	Light Aero Avid Speedwing	H. Bishop
	G-BTRF	Aero Designs Pulsar	P. F. Crosby & C. Smith
	G-BTRG	Aeronca 65C Super Chief	Condor Aviation International Ltd
	G-BTRI	Aeronca 11CC Super Chief	A. F. Wankowski & H. Wankowska
	G-BTRK	PA-28-161 Warrior II	Stapleford Flying Club Ltd
	G-BTRL	Cameron N-105 balloon	J. Lippett

Reg	Type	Owner or Operator	Notes
G-BTRR	Thunder Ax7-77 balloon	P. J. Wentworth	
G-BTRS	PA-28-161 Warrior II	Airwise Flying Group	
G-BTRT	PA-28R Cherokee Arrow 200-II	Romeo Tango Group	
G-BTRU	Robin DR.400/180	R. H. Mackay	
G-BTRW	Slingsby T.61F Venture T.2	RW Group	
G-BTRY	PA-28-161 Warrior II	M. A. Wood	
G-BTRZ	Jodel D.18	A. P. Aspinall	
G-BTSC	Evans VP-2	I. Pearson	
G-BTSJ	PA-28-161 Warrior II	Coastal Air (SW) Ltd	
G-BTSN	Cessna 150G	Wicklow Wings	
G-BTSP	Piper J-3C-65 Cub	A. Corcoran	
G-BTSR	Aeronca 11AC Chief	J. M. Miller	
G-BTSV	Denney Kitfox Mk 3	R. J. Folwell	
G-BTSX	Thunder Ax7-77 balloon	A. J. Gregory	
G-BTSY	EE Lightning F.6 (XR724) ★	Lightning Association	
G-BTSZ	Cessna 177A	Henlow Aviation Ltd	
G-BTTD	Montgomerie-Bensen B.8MR	A. J. P. Herculson	
G-BTTL	Cameron V-90 balloon	M. J. Axtell	
G-BTTR	Aerotek Pitts S-2A Special	Yellowbird Adventures Syndicate	
G-BTTW	Thunder Ax7-77 balloon	T. D. Gibbs	
G-BTTY	Denney Kitfox Mk 2	B. J. Clews	
G-BTTZ	Slingsby T.61F Venture T.2	Upwood Motorglider Group	
G-BTUA	Slingsby T.61F Venture T.2	Shenington Gliding Club	
G-BTUB	Yakovlev C.11	G. G. L. James	
G-BTUC	EMB-312 Tucano ★	Ulster Aviation Heritage	
G-BTUG	SOCATA Rallye 180T	D. Moore & L. C. Clark	
G-BTUH	Cameron N-65 balloon	J. S. Russon	
G-BTUK	Aerotek Pitts S-2A Special	S. H. Elkington	
G-BTUL	Aerotek Pitts S-2A Special	Intui Ltd	
G-BTUM	Piper J-3C-65 Cub	G-BTUM Syndicate	
G-BTUR	PA-18 Super Cub 95 (modified)	P. S. Gilmour	
G-BTUS	Whittaker MW7	C. T. Bailey	
G-BTUW	PA-28-151 Warrior	T. S. Kemp	
G-BTUZ	American General AG-5B Tiger	Meadowland Aviation Ltd	
G-BTVA	Thunder Ax7-77 balloon	M. Mansfield	
G-BTVC	Denney Kitfox Mk 2	G. C. Jiggins	
G-BTVE	Hawker Demon I (K8203)	Demon Displays Ltd	
G-BTVW	Cessna 152 II	Madalena Cruel Lda/Portugal	
G-BTVX	Cessna 152 II	S. J. Nicholls	
G-BTWB	Denney Kitfox Mk 3	C. J. Scott (G-BTTM)	
G-BTWC	Slingsby T.61F Venture T.2 (ZA656)	621 Venture Syndicate	
G-BTWD	Slingsby T.61F Venture T.2	York Gliding Centre	
G-BTWE	Slingsby T.61F Venture T.2	Aston Down G-BTWE Syndicate	
G-BTWF	DHC.1 Chipmunk 22 (WK549)	J. A. Simms	
G-BTWI	EAA Acro Sport I	J. O'Connell	
G-BTWJ	Cameron V-77 balloon	C. Gingell & M. Holden-Wadsworth	
G-BTWL	WAG-Aero Acro Sport Trainer	F. E. Tofield	
G-BTWY	Aero Designs Pulsar	R. Bishop	
G-BTWZ	Rans S.10 Sakota	J. T. Phipps	
G-BTXD	Rans S.6-ESA Coyote II	A. I. Sutherland	
G-BTXF	Cameron V-90 balloon	G. Thompson	
G-BTXI	Noorduyn AT-16 Harvard IIB (FE695)	Patina Ltd	
G-BTXK	Thunder Ax7-65 balloon	A. F. Selby	
G-BTXM	Colt 21A Cloudhopper balloon	H. J. Andrews	
G-BTXX	Bellanca 8KCAB Decathlon	Tatenhill Aviation Ltd	
G-BTXZ	Zenair CH.250	G-BTXZ Group	
G-BTYC	Cessna 150L	Polestar Aviation Ltd	
G-BTYH	Pottier P.80S	R. D. Boor	
G-BTYI	PA-28-181 Archer II	S. W. Hedges	
G-BTYT	Cessna 152 II	Cristal Air Ltd	
G-BTYX	Cessna 140	R. F. Richards	
G-BTYY	Curtiss Robertson C-2 Robin	R. W. Hatton	
G-BTZA	Beech F33A Bonanza	G-BTZA Group	
G-BTZB	Yakovlev Yak-50 (10 yellow)	Airborne Services Ltd	
G-BTZD	Yakovlev Yak-1 (1342)	Historic Aircraft Collection Ltd	
G-BTZE	LET Yakovlev C.11 (52)	A. Balk, F. Fraundienst & R. Steinberger	
G-BTZO	SOCATA TB20 Trinidad	J. F. Busby	
G-BTZP	SOCATA TB9 Tampico	M. W. Orr	
G-BTZS	Colt 77A balloon	P. T. R. Ollivere	
G-BTZV	Cameron V-77 balloon	J. W. Tyrell	
G-BTZX	Piper J-3C-65 Cub	ZX Cub Group	

Notes	Reg	Type	Owner or Operator
	G-BTZY	Colt 56A balloon	R. J. Maud
	G-BTZZ	CFM Streak Shadow	T. Garnham
	G-BUAB	Aeronca 11AC Chief	J. Reed
	G-BUAG	Jodel D.18	P. A. Silcox
	G-BUAI	Everett Srs 3 gyroplane	D. Stevenson
	G-BUAM	Cameron V-77 balloon	N. Florence
	G-BUAO	Luscombe 8A Silvaire	G-BUAO Group
	G-BUAR	Westland Seafire Mk.III (PP972:II-5)	Air Leasing Ltd
	G-BUAT	Thunder Ax9-120 balloon	S. W. K. Smeeton
	G-BUAV	Cameron O-105 balloon	D. & T. Dorrell
	G-BUBG	BN-2B-2T Turbine Islander	G. Cormack (G-JSPC)
	G-BUBL	Thunder Ax8-105 balloon ★	British Balloon Museum/Newbury
	G-BUBN	BN-2B-26 Islander	Isles of Scilly Skybus Ltd
	G-BUBP	BN-2B-26 Islander	Isles of Scilly Skybus Ltd
	G-BUBS	Lindstrand LBL-77B balloon	M. Saveri
	G-BUBT	Stoddard-Hamilton Glasair IIS RG	AAA Partners Ltd
	G-BUBY	Thunder Ax8-105 Series 2 balloon	D. W. Torrington
	G-BUCA	Cessna A.150K	R. J. Whyham
	G-BUCC	CASA 1.131E Jungmann 2000 (BU+CC)	R. N. Crosland (G-BUEM)
	G-BUCG	Schleicher ASW.20L (modified)	W. B. Andrews
	G-BUCH	Stinson V-77 Reliant	Sopwith Court Ltd
	G-BUCI	Auster AOP.9 (XP242)	Historic Aircraft Flight Reserve Collectio
	G-BUCK	CASA 1.131E Jungmann 1000 (BU+CK)	Jungmann Flying Group
	G-BUCM	Hawker Sea Fury FB.11	Patina Ltd
	G-BUCO	Pietenpol Air Camper	A. James
	G-BUCT	Cessna 150L	Air Navigation & Trading Co.Ltd
	G-BUDA	Slingsby T.61F Venture T.2	G-BUDA Syndicate
	G-BUDC	Slingsby T.61F Venture T.2 (ZA652)	G. M. Hall
	G-BUDE	PA-22 Tri-Pacer 135 (tailwheel)	P. Robinson
	G-BUDI	Aero Designs Pulsar	R. W. L. Oliver
	G-BUDK	Thunder Ax7-77 balloon	W. Evans
	G-BUDL	Auster 3 (NX534)	L. R. Leek
	G-BUDN	Cameron 90 Shoe SS balloon	Magical Adventures Ltd
	G-BUDO	PZL-110 Koliber 150	A. S. Vine
	G-BUDR	Denney Kitfox Mk 3	J. M. Pipping
	G-BUDS	Rand-Robinson KR-2	B. L. R. J. Keeping
	G-BUDT	Slingsby T.61F Venture T.2	G-BUDT Group
	G-BUDU	Cameron V-77 balloon	T. M. G. Amery
	G-BUDW	Brügger MB.2 Colibri	S. P. Barrett (G-GODS)
	G-BUEC	Van's RV-6	A. H. Harper
	G-BUED	Slingsby T.61F Venture T.2	Venture Syndicate
	G-BUEF	Cessna 152 II	Channel Aviation
	G-BUEG	Cessna 152 II	P. Rudd
	G-BUEI	Thunder Ax8-105 balloon	P. J. Hooper
	G-BUEK	Slingsby T.61F Venture T.2	G-BUEK Group
	G-BUEN	VPM M-14 Scout	C. R. Gordon
	G-BUEP	Maule MX-7-180	N. J. B. Bennett
	G-BUEW	Rans S-6 Coyote II	C. Cheeseman (G-MWYE)
	G-BUFG	Slingsby T.61F Venture T.2	G. W. Withers
	G-BUFH	PA-28-161 Warrior II	Solent School of Flying
	G-BUFR	Slingsby T.61F Venture T.2	Buckminster Gliding Club Ltd
	G-BUFY	PA-28-161 Warrior II	Bickertons Aerodromes Ltd
	G-BUGJ	Robin DR.400/180	W. E. R. Jenkins
	G-BUGL	Slingsby T.61F Venture T.2	S. L. Hoy
	G-BUGP	Cameron V-77 balloon	R. Churcher
	G-BUGS	Cameron V-77 balloon	S. J. Dymond
	G-BUGT	Slingsby T.61F Venture T.2	York Gliding Centre (Operations) Ltd
	G-BUGV	Slingsby T.61F Venture T.2	Oxfordshire Sportflying Ltd
	G-BUGW	Slingsby T.61F Venture T.2	Holdcroft Aviation Services Ltd & Transcourt Ltd
	G-BUGY	Cameron V-90 balloon	Dante Balloon Group
	G-BUGZ	Slingsby T.61F Venture T.2	Dishforth Flying Group
	G-BUHA	Slingsby T.61F Venture T.2 (ZA634:C)	Saltby Flying Group
	G-BUHM	Cameron V-77 balloon	P. T. Lickorish
	G-BUHO	Cessna 140	W. B. Bateson
	G-BUHR	Slingsby T.61F Venture T.2	The Northumbria Gliding Club Ltd
	G-BUHS	Stoddard-Hamilton Glasair SH TD-1	T. F. Horrocks
	G-BUHU	Cameron N-105 balloon	M. Rate
	G-BUHZ	Cessna 120	The Cessna 140 Group
	G-BUIF	PA-28-161 Warrior II	Pilot Training & Testing Ltd
	G-BUIG	Campbell Cricket (replica)	R. H. Braithwaite

Reg	Type	Owner or Operator	Notes
G-BUIH	Slingsby T.61F Venture T.2	The Falcon Gliding Group	
G-BUIJ	PA-28-161 Warrior II	D. J. Taplin	
G-BUIK	PA-28-161 Warrior II	D. S. Lawer	
G-BUIL	CFM Streak Shadow	A. A. Castleton	
G-BUIN	Thunder Ax7-77 balloon	P. C. Johnson	
G-BUIP	Denney Kitfox Mk 2	S. Porter	
G-BUIR	Light Aero Avid Speedwing Mk 4	G. J. Fry	
G-BUIZ	Cameron N-90 balloon	J. S. Russon	
G-BUJA	Slingsby T.61F Venture T.2	The Burn Gliding Club Ltd	
G-BUJB	Slingsby T.61F Venture T.2	Falke Syndicate	
G-BUJE	Cessna 177B	FG93 Group	
G-BUJH	Colt 77B balloon	B. Fisher	
G-BUJI	Slingsby T.61F Venture T.2	Solent Venture Syndicate	
G-BUJJ	Avid Speedwing	P. P. Trangmar	
G-BUJK	Montgomerie-Bensen B.8MR	S. P. Debrikasaan	
G-BUJM	Cessna 120	K. G. Grayson	
G-BUJN	Cessna 172N	Warwickshire Aviation Ltd	
G-BUJO	PA-28-161 Warrior II	Falcon Flying Services	
G-BUJP	PA-28-161 Warrior II	Phoenix Aviation	
G-BUJV	Light Aero Avid Speedwing Mk 4	C. Thomas	
G-BUJX	Slingsby T.61F Venture T.2	York Gliding Centre Ltd	
G-BUJZ	Rotorway Executive 90 (modified)	M. P. Swoboda	
G-BUKB	Rans S.10 Sakota	M. K. Blatch	
G-BUKF	Denney Kitfox Mk 4	Kilo Foxtrot Group	
G-BUKH	D.31 Turbulent	G. Haye	
G-BUKI	Thunder Ax7-77 balloon	Virgin Balloon Flights	
G-BUKK	Bücker Bü 133C Jungmeister (U-80)	B. R. Cox	
G-BUKO	Cessna 120	Peregrine Flying Group	
G-BUKP	Denney Kitfox Mk 2	C. J. Thompson	
G-BUKR	MS.880B Rallye Club 100T	G-BUKR Flying Group	
G-BUKU	Luscombe 8E Silvaire	Silvaire Flying Group	
G-BUKY	CCF Harvard 4M (52-8543)	A. Stendel	
G-BUKZ	Evans VP-2	P. R. Farnell	
G-BULB	Thunder Ax7-77 balloon	A. Lutz	
G-BULC	Light Aero Avid Flyer Mk 4	C. Nice	
G-BULG	Van's RV-4	V. D. Long	
G-BULJ	CFM Streak Shadow	D. R. Stansfield	
G-BULL	SA Bulldog Srs 120/128 (HKG-5)	Bulldog Aeros Ltd	
G-BULN	Colt 210A balloon	H. G. Davies	
G-BULO	Luscombe 8A Silvaire	B. W. Foulds	
G-BULR	PA-28-140 Cherokee B	D. H. G. Penny	
G-BULT	Campbell Cricket	A. T. Pocklington	
G-BULY	Light Aero Avid Flyer	C. Coleman	
G-BULZ	Denney Kitfox Mk 2	T. G. F. Trenchard	
G-BUMP	PA-28-181 Archer II	M. J. Green & D. Major	
G-BUNB	Slingsby T.61F Venture T.2	Wessex Ventures 2016	
G-BUNC	PZL-104 Wilga 35	R. F. Goodman	
G-BUNG	Cameron N-77 balloon	A. Kaye	
G-BUNO	Lancair 320	J. Softley	
G-BUOA	Whittaker MW6-S Fatboy Flyer	H. N. Graham	
G-BUOB	CFM Streak Shadow	J. M. Hunter	
G-BUOD	SE-5A (replica) (B595:W)	M. D. Waldron/Belgium	
G-BUOF	D.62B Condor	D. W. Collins	
G-BUOL	Denney Kitfox Mk 3	P. Dennington	
G-BUON	Light Aero Avid Aerobat	T. P. Beare	
G-BUOR	CASA 1.131E Jungmann 2000	M. I. M. S. Voest/Netherlands	
G-BUOS	VS.394 Spitfire FR.XVIII (SM845:R)	Spitfire Ltd	
G-BUOW	Aero Designs Pulsar XP	T. J. Hartwell	
G-BUPA	Rutan LongEz	N. G. Henry	
G-BUPB	Stolp SA.300 Starduster Too	J. R. Edwards & J. W. Widdows	
G-BUPC	Rollason Beta B.2	C. A. Rolph	
G-BUPF	Bensen B.8R	P. W. Hewitt-Dean	
G-BUPH	Colt 25A balloon	M. E. White	
G-BUPM	VPM M-16 Tandem Trainer	A. Kitson	
G-BUPP	Cameron V-42 balloon	C. L. Schoeman	
G-BUPR	Jodel D.18	R. W. Burrows	
G-BUPU	Thunder Ax7-77 balloon	R. C. Barkworth & D. G. Maguire/USA	
G-BUPV	Great Lakes 2T-1A	R. J. Fray	
G-BUPW	Denney Kitfox Mk 3	S. G. Metcalfe	
G-BURH	Cessna 150E	B. Russel	
G-BURI	Enstrom F-28C	D. W. C. Holmes	

Notes	Reg	Type	Owner or Operator
	G-BURL	Colt 105A balloon	J. E. Rose
	G-BURP	Rotorway Executive 90	N. K. Newman
	G-BURR	Auster AOP.9 (WZ706)	Annic Aviation
	G-BURZ	Hawker Nimrod II (K3661:362)	Historic Aircraft Collection Ltd
	G-BUSN	Rotorway Executive 90	J. P. McEnroe
	G-BUSR	Aero Designs Pulsar	S. S. Bateman & R. A. Watts
	G-BUSS	Cameron 90 Bus SS balloon	Magical Adventures Ltd
	G-BUSV	Colt 105A balloon	H. C. J. Williams
	G-BUSW	Rockwell Commander 114	M. J. P. Lynch
	G-BUTB	CFM Streak Shadow	H. O. Maclean
	G-BUTD	Van's RV-6	B. S. Carpenter
	G-BUTF	Aeronca 11AC Chief	A. W. Crutcher
	G-BUTG	Zenair CH.601HD	A. Brown
	G-BUTH	CEA DR.220 2+2	Phoenix Flying Group
	G-BUTJ	Cameron O-77 balloon	C. & P. Collins
	G-BUTK	Murphy Rebel	A. J. Gibson
	G-BUTM	Rans S.6-116 Coyote II	J. D. Sinclair-Day
	G-BUTT	Cessna FA150K	Ag-Raum GmbH/Germany (G-AXSJ)
	G-BUTX	CASA 1.133C Jungmeister (ES.1-4)	S. R. Stead
	G-BUTY	Brügger MB.2 Colibri	R. M. Lawday
	G-BUTZ	PA-28 Cherokee 180C	L. M. Sidwell (G-DARL)
	G-BUUA	Slingsby T.67M Firefly Mk II	Heartland Aviation Ltd
	G-BUUC	Slingsby T.67M Firefly Mk II	Swiftair Maintenance Ltd
	G-BUUE	Slingsby T.67M Firefly Mk II	J. R. Bratty
	G-BUUF	Slingsby T.67M Firefly Mk II	Tiger Airways
	G-BUUI	Slingsby T.67M Firefly Mk II	Bustard Flying Club Ltd
	G-BUUJ	Slingsby T.67M Firefly Mk II	Blue Skies Group
	G-BUUK	Slingsby T.67M Firefly Mk II	Avalanche Aviation Ltd
	G-BUUL	Slingsby T.67M Firefly Mk II	Air Ministry Aviation Ltd
	G-BUUU	Cameron Bottle SS balloon ★	British Balloon Museum/Newbury
	G-BUUX	PA-28 Cherokee 180D	Aero Group 78
	G-BUVA	PA-22-135 Tri-Pacer	Oaksey VA Group
	G-BUVB	Colt 77A balloon	K. J. & M. E. Gregory
	G-BUVM	CEA DR.250/160	G-BUVM Group
	G-BUVN	CASA 1.131E Jungmann 2000(BI-005)	W. Van Egmond/Netherlands
	G-BUVO	Cessna F.182P	Romeo Mike Flying Group (G-WTFA)
	G-BUVR	Christen A.1 Husky	Aviat Aircraft (UK) Ltd
	G-BUVT	Colt 77A balloon	N. A. Carr
	G-BUVW	Cameron N-90 balloon	L. J. Whitelock
	G-BUVX	CFM Streak Shadow	Light Aircraft Holdings Ltd
	G-BUWE	SE-5A (replica) (C9533:M)	Airpark Flight Centre Ltd
	G-BUWF	Cameron N-105 balloon	R. E. Jones
	G-BUWH	Parsons 2-seat gyroplane	R. V. Brunskill
	G-BUWI	Lindstrand LBL-77A balloon	G. A. Chadwick
	G-BUWK	Rans S.6-116 Coyote II	R. Warriner
	G-BUWL	Piper J-4A	M. L. Ryan
	G-BUWR	CFM Streak Shadow	T. Harvey
	G-BUWS	Denney Kitfox Mk 2	J. E. Brewis
	G-BUWT	Rand-Robinson KR-2	G. Bailey-Woods
	G-BUWU	Cameron V-77 balloon	T. R. Dews
	G-BUXC	CFM Streak Shadow SA-M	N. R. Beale
	G-BUXI	Steen Skybolt	Leipzig Aviators Group
	G-BUXK	Pietenpol Air Camper	B. M. D. Nelson
	G-BUXL	Taylor JT.1 Monoplane	P. J. Hebdon
	G-BUXW	Thunder Ax8-90 S2 balloon	N. T. Parry
	G-BUXX	PA-17 Vagabond	R. H. Hunt
	G-BUXY	PA-25 Pawnee 235	Bath, Wilts & North Dorset Gliding Club Ltd
	G-BUYB	Aero Designs Pulsar	A. R. Thorpe
	G-BUYC	Cameron 80 Concept balloon	R. P. Cross
	G-BUYE	Aeronca 7AC Champion	A. A. Gillon
	G-BUYF	Falcon XP	M. J. Hadland
	G-BUYK	Denney Kitfox Mk 4	M. S. Shelton
	G-BUYL	RAF 2000GT gyroplane	M. H. J. Goldring
	G-BUYO	Colt 77A balloon	S. F. Burden/Netherlands
	G-BUYS	Robin DR.400/180	G-BUYS Flying Group
	G-BUYU	Bowers Fly-Baby 1A (1803/18)	R. C. Piper
	G-BUYY	PA-28 Cherokee 180	G-BUYY Group
	G-BUZA	Denney Kitfox Mk 3	G. O. Newell
	G-BUZB	Aero Designs Pulsar XP	S. M. Macintyre
	G-BUZG	Zenair CH.601HD	G. Cox
	G-BUZH	Aero Designs Star-Lite SL-1	B. A. Lyford

Reg	Type	Owner or Operator	Notes
G-BUZK	Cameron V-77 balloon	Zebedee Balloon Service Ltd	
G-BUZM	Light Aero Avid Flyer Mk 3	D. W. Bowman	
G-BUZO	Pietenpol Air Camper	D. A. Jones	
G-BUZR	Lindstrand LBL-77A balloon	Lindstrand Technologies Ltd	
G-BUZT	Kolb Twinstar Mk 3	J. A. G. Robb	
G-BUZZ	Agusta-Bell 206B JetRanger 2	Skypark (UK) Ltd	
G-BVAB	Zenair CH.601HDS	B. N. Rides	
G-BVAC	Zenair CH.601HD	J. A. Tyndall	
G-BVAF	Piper J-3C-65 Cub	G-BVAF Group	
G-BVAH	Denney Kitfox Mk.3	S. Allinson	
G-BVAI	PZL-110 Koliber 150	A. J. Verlander	
G-BVAM	Evans VP-1 Series 2	The Breighton VP-1 Group	
G-BVAW	Staaken Z-1 Flitzer (D-692)	L. R. Williams	
G-BVBF	PA-28-151 Warrior	R. K. Spence	
G-BVBJ	Colt Flying Coffee Jar SS balloon	The British Balloon Museum & Library Ltd	
G-BVBK	Colt Flying Coffe Jar SS balloon	M. E. White	
G-BVCA	Cameron N-105 balloon	Kent Ballooning	
G-BVCG	Van's RV-6	A. W. Shellis	
G-BVCL	Rans S.6-116 Coyote II	A. M. Colman	
G-BVCN	Colt 56A balloon	G. A. & I. Chadwick & S. Richards	
G-BVCO	FRED Srs 2	BCVO Group	
G-BVCP	Piper CP.1 Metisse	B. M. Diggins	
G-BVCS	Aeronca 7BCM Champion	A. C. Lines	
G-BVCT	Denney Kitfox Mk 4	A. F. Reid	
G-BVCY	Cameron H-24 balloon	A. C. K. Rawson & J. J. Rudoni	
G-BVDB	Thunder Ax7-77 balloon	M. K. Bellamy (G-ORDY)	
G-BVDC	Van's RV-3	R. S. Hatwell	
G-BVDF	Cameron Doll 105 SS balloon	A. Kaye & K-H Gruenauer	
G-BVDG	VPM M-15	R. F. G. Moyle	
G-BVDH	PA-28RT-201 Arrow IV	J. Goldstein	
G-BVDI	Van's RV-4	J. G. Gorman & H. Tallini	
G-BVDJ	Campbell Cricket (replica)	S. Jennings	
G-BVDO	Lindstrand LBL-105A balloon	K. Graham	
G-BVDP	Sequoia F.8L Falco	N. M. Turner	
G-BVDR	Cameron O-77 balloon	M. D. Sullivan-Gould	
G-BVDT	CFM Streak Shadow	A. Harner	
G-BVDW	Thunder Ax8-90 balloon	S. C. Vora	
G-BVDX	Cameron V-90 balloon	R. K. Scott	
G-BVDY	Cameron 60 Concept balloon	P. Baker/Ireland	
G-BVDZ	Taylorcraft BC-12D	M. W. Jackman	
G-BVEA	Mosler Motors N.3 Pup	M. T. Taylor (G-MWEA)	
G-BVEH	Jodel D.112	M. L. Copland	
G-BVEL	Evans VP-1 Srs.2	M. J. & S. J. Quinn	
G-BVEN	Cameron 80 Concept balloon	B. J. & M. A. Alford	
G-BVEP	Luscombe 8A Master	B. H. Austen	
G-BVER	DHC.2 Beaver 1 (XV268)	Seaflite Ltd (G-BTDM)	
G-BVEV	PA-34-200 Seneca	M. Ali	
G-BVEY	Denney Kitfox Mk 4-1200	J. H. H. Turner	
G-BVEZ	P.84 Jet Provost T.3A (XM479)	Newcastle Jet Provost Group	
G-BVFA	Rans S.10 Sakota	J. C. Longmore & S. M. Hall	
G-BVFB	Cameron N-31 balloon	P. Lawman	
G-BVFF	Cameron V-77 balloon	R. J. Kerr & G. P. Allen	
G-BVFM	Rans S.6-116 Coyote II	F. B. C. de Beer	
G-BVFO	Light Aero Avid Speedwing	T. G. Solomon	
G-BVFR	CFM Streak Shadow	J. H. Pope & S. G. Smith	
G-BVFS	Slingsby T.31M	S. R. Williams	
G-BVFU	Cameron 105 Sphere SS balloon	Stichting Phoenix/Netherlands	
G-BVFZ	Maule M5-180C Lunar Rocket	R. C. Robinson	
G-BVGA	Bell 206B JetRanger3	Bucklefields Business Developments Ltd	
G-BVGB	Thunder Ax8-105 S2 balloon	E. K. Read	
G-BVGE	WS-55 Whirlwind HAR.10 (XJ729)	A. D. Whitehouse	
G-BVGF	Shaw Europa	T. C. Hyde	
G-BVGH	Hawker Hunter T.7 (XL573)	M. Stott	
G-BVGI	Pereira Osprey II	D. Westoby	
G-BVGJ	Cameron C-80 balloon	J. M. J. & V. F. Roberts	
G-BVGK	Lindstrand LBL Newspaper SS balloon	H. Holmqvist	
G-BVGO	Denney Kitfox Mk 4-1200	P. Madden	
G-BVGP	Bücker Bü 133 Jungmeister (U-95)	T. A. Bechtolsheimer	
G-BVGT	Auster J/1 (modified)	K. D. & C. S. Rhodes	
G-BVGW	Luscombe 8A Silvaire	H. E. Simons	

Notes	Reg	Type	Owner or Operator
	G-BVGY	Luscombe 8E Silvaire	P. Chandler
	G-BVGZ	Fokker Dr.1 (replica) (152/17)	R. A. Fleming
	G-BVHC	Grob G.115D-2 Heron	Aeros Holdings Ltd
	G-BVHD	Grob G.115D-2 Heron	J. A. Woodcock
	G-BVHE	Grob G.115D-2 Heron	Tayside Aviation Ltd
	G-BVHG	Grob G.115D-2 Heron	KFZ Kogl Alexander EU/Austria
	G-BVHI	Rans S.10 Sakota	J. D. Amos
	G-BVHK	Cameron V-77 balloon	C. M. Duggan & M. J. Axtell
	G-BVHL	Nicollier HN.700 Menestrel II	G. W. Lynch
	G-BVHM	PA-38-112 Tomahawk	G. E. Fox (G-DCAN)
	G-BVHO	Cameron V-90 balloon	N. W. B. Bews
	G-BVHR	Cameron V-90 balloon	G. P. Walton
	G-BVHS	Murphy Rebel	S. T. Raby
	G-BVHV	Cameron N-105 balloon	K. F. Lowry
	G-BVIE	PA-18 Super Cub 95 (modified)	J. C. Best (G-CLIK/G-BLMB)
	G-BVIK	Maule MXT-7-180 Star Rocket	Graveley Flying Group
	G-BVIL	Maule MXT-7-180 Star Rocket	K. & S. C. Knight
	G-BVIS	Brügger MB.2 Colibri	B. H. Shaw
	G-BVIV	Light Aero Avid Speedwing	S. Styles
	G-BVIW	PA-18-Super Cub 150	I. H. Logan
	G-BVIZ	Shaw Europa	M. Dovey
	G-BVJG	Cyclone AX3/K	J. Gilroy (G-MYOP)
	G-BVJK	Glaser-Dirks DG.800A	Birkett Air Services Ltd
	G-BVJN	Shaw Europa	H. F. Maccoll
	G-BVJT	Cessna F.406	Nor Leasing
	G-BVJU	Evans VP-1	BVJU Flying Club & Associates
	G-BVJX	Marquart MA.5 Charger	J. D. Bally
	G-BVKF	Shaw Europa	J. R. F. Bennett
	G-BVKK	Slingsby T.61F Venture T.2	Buckminster Gliding Club Ltd
	G-BVKL	Cameron A-180 balloon	Dragon Balloon Co Ltd
	G-BVKM	Rutan Vari-Eze	J. P. G. Lindquist/Switzerland
	G-BVKU	Slingsby T.61F Venture T.2	G-BVKU Syndicate
	G-BVLA	Lancair 320	K. W. Scrivens
	G-BVLD	Campbell Cricket (replica)	S. J. Smith
	G-BVLF	CFM Starstreak Shadow SS-D	J. C. Pratelli
	G-BVLG	AS.355F1 Twin Squirrel	PLM Dollar Group PLC
	G-BVLN	Aero Designs Pulsar XP	D. A. Campbell
	G-BVLR	Van's RV-4	RV4 Group
	G-BVLT	Bellanca 7GCBC Citabria	Slade Associates
	G-BVLU	D.31 Turbulent	C. D. Bancroft
	G-BVLV	Shaw Europa	Euro 39 Group
	G-BVLX	Slingsby T.61F Venture T.2	Wessex Ventures 2016
	G-BVMA	Beech 200 Super King Air	Dragonfly Aviation Services Ltd (G-VPLC)
	G-BVMJ	Cameron 95 Eagle SS balloon	R. D. Sargeant
	G-BVMM	Robin HR.200/100	P. J. V. Dibble
	G-BVMN	Ken Brock KB-2 gyroplane	G-BVMN Group
	G-BVMR	Cameron V-90 balloon	I. R. Comley
	G-BVNG	DH.60G-III Moth Major	P. & G. Groves
	G-BVNI	Taylor JT-2 Titch	P. M. Jones
	G-BVNS	PA-28-181 Archer II	Scottish Airways Flyers (Prestwick) Ltd
	G-BVNU	FLS Aerospace Sprint Club	S. R. Evans
	G-BVNY	Rans S.7 Courier	S. Hazleden
	G-BVOC	Cameron V-90 balloon	A. R. Hardwick
	G-BVOH	Campbell Cricket (replica)	A. Kitson
	G-BVOI	Rans S.6-116 Coyote II	S. J. Taft
	G-BVOP	Cameron N-90 balloon	October Gold Ballooning Ltd
	G-BVOR	CFM Streak Shadow	J. M. Chandler
	G-BVOS	Shaw Europa	Durham Europa Group
	G-BVOW	Shaw Europa	H. P. Brooks
	G-BVOY	Rotorway Executive 90	R. Horner
	G-BVOZ	Colt 56A balloon	British School of Ballooning
	G-BVPA	Thunder Ax8-105 S2 balloon	J. Fenton
	G-BVPD	CASA 1.131E Jungmann 2000	Bucker Group
	G-BVPM	Evans VP-2 Coupé	P. Marigold
	G-BVPS	Jodel D.112	P. J. Brookman
	G-BVPV	Lindstrand LBL-77B balloon	P. G. Hill
	G-BVPW	Rans S.6-116 Coyote II	T. B. Woolley
	G-BVPX	Bensen B.8 (modified) Tyro Gyro	A. W. Harvey
	G-BVPY	CFM Streak Shadow	A. J. Grant
	G-BVRA	Shaw Europa	N. M. Robbins
	G-BVRH	Taylorcraft BL.65	M. J. Kirk

Reg	Type	Owner or Operator	Notes
G-BVRL	Lindstrand LBL-21A balloon	T. J. Orchard & M. E. Banks	
G-BVRU	Lindstrand LBL-105A balloon	D. K. Hempleman-Adams	
G-BVRV	Van's RV-4	A. Troughton	
G-BVRZ	PA-18 Super Cub 95	R. W. Davison	
G-BVSB	TEAM mini-MAX	D. G. Palmer	
G-BVSD	SE.3130 Alouette II (V-54)	M. J. Cuttell	
G-BVSF	Aero Designs Pulsar	R. J. & J. A. Freestone	
G-BVSG	BN-2B-20 Islander	Britten-Norman Ltd	
G-BVSK	BN-2T Turbine Islander	G. Cormack	
G-BVSM	RAF2000	A van Rooijen/Belgium	
G-BVSN	Light Aero Avid Speedwing	D. N. Smith & G. Everett	
G-BVSP	P.84 Jet Provost T.3A	Weald Aviation Services Ltd	
G-BVSS	Jodel D.150	M. F. R. B. Collett & M. S. C. Ball	
G-BVST	Jodel D.150	A. Shipp	
G-BVSX	TEAM mini-MAX 91	J. A. Sephton	
G-BVSZ	Pitts S-1E (S) Special	H. J. Morton	
G-BVTC	P.84 Jet Provost T.5A (XW333)	Global Aviation Ltd	
G-BVTL	Colt 31A balloon	A. Lindsay	
G-BVTM	Cessna F.152 II	RAF Halton Aeroplane Club (G-WACS)	
G-BVTV	Rotorway Executive 90	P. M. Scheiwiller	
G-BVTW	Aero Designs Pulsar	R. J. Panther	
G-BVTX	DHC.1 Chipmunk 22A (WP809)	N. P. Woods	
G-BVUA	Cameron O-105 balloon	Wickers World Ltd	
G-BVUC	Colt 56A balloon	J. F. Till	
G-BVUG	Betts TB.1 (Stampe SV.4C)	H. F. Fekete (G-BEUS)	
G-BVUH	Thunder Ax6-65B balloon	H. J. M. Lacoste	
G-BVUK	Cameron V-77 balloon	H. G. Griffiths & W. A. Steel	
G-BVUM	Rans S.6-116 Coyote II	M. A. Abbott	
G-BVUN	Van's RV-4	D. J. Harvey	
G-BVUT	Evans VP-1 Srs. 2	M. J. Barnett	
G-BVUU	Cameron C-80 balloon	T. M. C. McCoy	
G-BVUV	Shaw Europa	R. J. Mills	
G-BVUZ	Cessna 120	R. W. Maxted	
G-BVVB	Carlson Sparrow II	L. M. McCullen	
G-BVVE	Jodel D.112	M. Balls	
G-BVVG	Nanchang CJ-6A (68)	Nanchang CJ6A Group	
G-BVVH	Shaw Europa	M. Giudici	
G-BVVI	Hawker Audax I (K5600)	Aero Vintage Ltd	
G-BVVK	DHC.6 Twin Otter 310	Loganair Ltd	
G-BVVL	EAA Acro Sport II	G-BVVL Syndicate	
G-BVVM	Zenair CH.601HD	D. F. Hurn	
G-BVVN	Brügger MB.2 Colibri	N. F. Andrews	
G-BVVP	Shaw Europa	B. A. Fawkes	
G-BVVR	Stits SA-3A Playboy	J. H. Prendergast	
G-BVVS	Van's RV-4	E. G. & N. S. C. English	
G-BVVU	Lindstrand LBL Four SS balloon	Magical Adventures Ltd/USA	
G-BVVW	Yakovlev Yak-52	M. Blackman	
G-BVVZ	Corby CJ-1 Starlet	P. V. Flack	
G-BVWB	Thunder Ax8-90 S2 balloon	M. A. Stelling & K. C. Tanner	
G-BVWI	Cameron light bulb SS balloon	M. E. White	
G-BVWM	Shaw Europa	A. Head	
G-BVWW	Lindstrand LBL-90A balloon	J. D. A. Shields	
G-BVWZ	PA-32-301 Saratoga	Ambar Kelly Ltd	
G-BVXA	Cameron N-105 balloon	R. E. Jones	
G-BVXC	EE Canberra B.6 (WT333) ★	Classic Aviation Projects Ltd/Bruntingthorpe	
G-BVXD	Cameron O-84 balloon	C. J. Dunkley	
G-BVXK	Yakovlev Yak-52 (26 grey)	A. R. Dent	
G-BVXM	AS.350B Ecureuil	RCR Aviation Ltd	
G-BVYF	PA-31-350 Navajo Chieftain	J. A. Rees & D. T. Rees (G-SAVE)	
G-BVYG	CEA DR.300/180	PA Technologies Ltd	
G-BVYM	CEA DR.300/180	London Gliding Club (Pty) Ltd	
G-BVYO	Robin R.2160 Alpha Sport	Smart People Don't Buy Ltd	
G-BVYP	PA-25 Pawnee 235B	Bidford Gliding & Flying Club Ltd	
G-BVYX	Light Aero Avid Speedwing Mk 4	C. A. Simmonds	
G-BVYY	Pietenpol Air Camper	T. F. Harrison	
G-BVYZ	Stemme S.10V	L. Gubbay	
G-BVZJ	Rand-Robinson KR-2	G. M. Rundle	
G-BVZN	Cameron C-80 balloon	S. J. Clarke	
G-BVZO	Rans S.6-116 Coyote II	P. J. Brion	
G-BVZR	Zenair CH.601HD	R. A. Perkins	
G-BVZT	Lindstrand LBL-90A balloon	J. Edwards	

Notes	Reg	Type	Owner or Operator
	G-BVZX	Cameron H-34 balloon	R. H. Etherington
	G-BVZY	Mooney M.20R Ovation	Hansengroup LTD
	G-BVZZ	DHC.1 Chipmunk 22 (WP795)	Portsmouth Naval Gliding Club
	G-BWAB	Jodel D.14	R. G. Fairall
	G-BWAC	Waco YKS-7	D. N. Peters
	G-BWAD	RAF 2000GT gyroplane	A. Melody
	G-BWAF	Hawker Hunter F.6A (XG160:U) ★	Bournemouth Aviation Museum/Bournemouth
	G-BWAH	Montgomerie-Bensen B.8MR	J. B. Allan
	G-BWAI	CFM Streak Shadow	C. M. James
	G-BWAN	Cameron N-77 balloon	I. Chadwick
	G-BWAO	Cameron C-80 balloon	R. D. Allen
	G-BWAP	FRED Srs 3	G. A. Shepherd
	G-BWAR	Denney Kitfox Mk 3	M. J. Downes
	G-BWAT	Pietenpol Air Camper	P. W. Aitchison
	G-BWAU	Cameron V-90 balloon	K. M. & A. M. F. Hall
	G-BWAW	Lindstrand LBL-77A balloon	D. Bareford
	G-BWBI	Taylorcraft F-22A	R. T. G. Preston
	G-BWBO	Lindstrand LBL-77A balloon	T. J. Orchard
	G-BWBZ	ARV-1 Super 2	M. P. Holdstock
	G-BWCA	CFM Streak Shadow	I. C. Pearson
	G-BWCK	Everett Srs 2 gyroplane	N. M. Gent
	G-BWCS	P.84 Jet Provost T.5 (XW293:Z)	J. H. Ashcroft
	G-BWCT	Tipsy T.66 Nipper 1	R. Targonski
	G-BWCY	Murphy Rebel	A. J. Glading
	G-BWDH	Cameron N-105 balloon	M. W. Shepherd
	G-BWDO	Sikorsky S-76B	Trustair Ltd
	G-BWDP	Shaw Europa	S. Attubato
	G-BWDS	P.84 Jet Provost T.3A (XM424)	AT Aviation Sales Ltd, D. C. Cooper & J. A. Gibson
	G-BWDX	Shaw Europa	J. Robson
	G-BWDZ	Sky 105-24 balloon	M. T. Wiltshire
	G-BWEB	P.84 Jet Provost T.5A (XW422:3)	Flight Test Support
	G-BWEE	Cameron V-42 balloon	J. A. Hibberd/Netherlands
	G-BWEF	SNCAN Stampe SV.4C	Acebell G-BWEF Syndicate (G-BOVL)
	G-BWEG	Shaw Europa	J. W. Kelly
	G-BWEM	VS.358 Seafire L.IIIC (RX168)	Aircraft Spares & Materials Ltd
	G-BWEN	Macair Merlin GT	D. A. Hill
	G-BWEU	Cessna F.152 II	Eastern Air Executive Ltd
	G-BWEW	Cameron N-105 balloon	Unipart Balloon Club
	G-BWEY	Bensen B.8	F. G. Shepherd
	G-BWEZ	Piper J-3C-65 Cub (436021)	Edenfield Aero
	G-BWFG	Robin HR.200/120B	T. J. Lowe
	G-BWFH	Shaw Europa	G. C. Grant
	G-BWFJ	Evans VP-1	G. Robson
	G-BWFK	Lindstrand LBL-77A balloon	C. J. Wootton & J. S. Russon
	G-BWFL	Cessna 500 Citation 1	A. Manku & P. J. Kelly (G-JTNC/G-OEJA)
	G-BWFM	Yakovlev Yak-50	Fox Mike Group
	G-BWFN	Hapi Cygnet SF-2A	I. P. Manley
	G-BWFO	Colomban MC.15 Cri-Cri	K. D. & C. S. Rhodes
	G-BWFT	Hawker Hunter T.8M (XL602)	G. I. Begg
	G-BWFX	Shaw Europa	A. D. Stewart
	G-BWFZ	Murphy Rebel	S. Irving (G-SAVS)
	G-BWGF	P.84 Jet Provost T.5A (XW325)	G-JPVA Ltd
	G-BWGJ	Chilton DW.1A	T. J. Harrison
	G-BWGL	Hawker Hunter T.8C (XJ615)	Stichting Hawker Hunter Foundation/Netherlands
	G-BWGO	Slingsby T.67M Firefly 200	R. Gray
	G-BWGY	HOAC Katana DV.20	Stemme UK Ltd
	G-BWHA	Hawker Hurricane IIB (Z5252)	Historic Flying Ltd
	G-BWHD	Lindstrand LBL-31A balloon	M. R. Noyce & R. P. E. Phillips
	G-BWHI	DHC.1 Chipmunk 22A (WK624)	E. H. N. M. Clare
	G-BWHK	Rans S.6-116 Coyote II	S. J. Wakeling
	G-BWHP	CASA 1.131E Jungmann (S4+A07)	J. F. Hopkins
	G-BWHR	Tipsy Nipper T.66 Srs 1	L. R. Marnef
	G-BWHS	RAF 2000 gyroplane	B. J. Payne
	G-BWHU	Westland Scout AH.1 (XR595)	N. J. F. Boston
	G-BWID	D.31 Turbulent	N. Huxtable
	G-BWII	Cessna 150G	J. D. G. Hicks (G-BSKB)
	G-BWIJ	Shaw Europa	R. Lloyd
	G-BWIK	DH.82A Tiger Moth (NL985)	H. M. M. Haines

Reg	Type	Owner or Operator	Notes
G-BWIL	Rans S-10	G. Forde	
G-BWIP	Cameron N-90 balloon	O. J. Evans	
G-BWIV	Shaw Europa	T. G. Ledbury	
G-BWIX	Sky 120-24 balloon	J. M. Percival	
G-BWIZ	QAC Quickie Tri-Q 200	M. C. Davies	
G-BWJG	Mooney M.20J	A. Mass	
G-BWJH	Shaw Europa	I. R. Willis	
G-BWJM	Bristol M.1C (replica) (C4918)	The Shuttleworth Collection	
G-BWJY	DHC.1 Chipmunk 22 (WG469)	AT Aviation Sales Ltd	
G-BWKE	Cameron AS-105 GD airship	S. A. Sorn	
G-BWKT	Stephens Akro Laser	P. D. Begley	
G-BWKW	Thunder Ax8-90 balloon	Gone With The Wind Ltd	
G-BWKZ	Lindstrand LBL-77A balloon	J. H. Dobson	
G-BWLD	Cameron O-120 balloon	D. Pedri/Italy	
G-BWLF	Cessna 404	Reconnaisance Ventures Ltd (G-BNXS)	
G-BWLJ	Taylorcraft DCO-65 (42-35870/129)	B. J. Robe	
G-BWLL	Murphy Rebel	F. W. Parker	
G-BWLM	Sky 65-24 balloon	W. J. Brogan	
G-BWLW	Avid Speed Wing Mk.4	P. G. Hayward (G-XXRG)	
G-BWLY	Rotorway Executive 90	P. W. & I. P. Bewley	
G-BWMB	Jodel D.119	C. Hughes	
G-BWMC	Cessna 182P	Aeroplane Views	
G-BWMF	Gloster Meteor T.7 (WA591)	Aviation Heritage Ltd	
G-BWMH	Lindstrand LBL-77B balloon	W. C. Wood	
G-BWMI	PA-28RT-201T Turbo Arrow IV	R. W. Pascoe	
G-BWMJ	Nieuport 17/2B (replica) (N1977:8)	J. P. Gilbert	
G-BWMK	DH.82A Tiger Moth (T8191)	K. F. Crumplin	
G-BWMN	Rans S.7 Courier	D. C. Stokes	
G-BWMO	Oldfield Baby Lakes	D. Maddocks (G-CIII)	
G-BWMS	DH.82A Tiger Moth	Stichting Vroege Vogels/Netherlands	
G-BWMU	Cameron 105 Monster Truck SS balloon	Magical Adventures Ltd/Canada	
G-BWMX	DHC.1 Chipmunk 22 (WG407:67)	407th Flying Group	
G-BWMY	Cameron Bradford & Bingley SS balloon	Magical Adventures Ltd/USA	
G-BWNB	Cessna 152 II	South Warwickshire School of Flying Ltd	
G-BWNC	Cessna 152 II	South Warwickshire School of Flying Ltd	
G-BWND	Cessna 152 II	South Warwickshire School of Flying Ltd	
G-BWNI	PA-24 Comanche 180	B. V. & J. B. Haslam	
G-BWNJ	Hughes 269C	L. R. Fenwick	
G-BWNK	D,H,C,1 Chipmunk 22 (WD390)	WD390 Group	
G-BWNM	PA-28R Cherokee Arrow 180	M. & R. C. Ramnial	
G-BWNO	Cameron O-90 balloon	T. Knight	
G-BWNP	Cameron 90 Club SS balloon	H. Cusden & J. Edwards	
G-BWNS	Cameron O-90 balloon	I. C. Steward	
G-BWNT	DHC.1 Chipmunk 22 (WP901)	J. Willis & S. Monk	
G-BWNU	PA-38-112 Tomahawk	Kemble Aero Club Ltd	
G-BWNY	Aeromot AMT-200 Super Ximango	M. Powell-Brett	
G-BWNZ	Agusta A109C	South Acre Aviation Ltd	
G-BWOB	Luscombe 8F Silvaire	S. Forde	
G-BWOF	P.84 Jet Provost T.5	Techair London Ltd	
G-BWOH	PA-28-161 Cadet	Redhill Air Services Ltd	
G-BWOI	PA-28-161 Cadet	Parachuting Aircraft Ltd	
G-BWOK	Lindstrand LBL-105G balloon	C. J. Sanger-Davies	
G-BWOR	PA-18 Super Cub 135	G. Cormack	
G-BWOT	P.84 Jet Provost T.3A	D. Bryan	
G-BWOV	Enstrom F-28A	P. A. Goss	
G-BWOY	Sky 31-24 balloon	C. Wolstenholme	
G-BWPC	Cameron V-77 balloon	H. Vaughan	
G-BWPE	Murphy Renegade Spirit UK	J. Hatswell/France	
G-BWPH	PA-28-181 Archer II	D. R. Lewis	
G-BWPJ	Steen Skybolt	A. J. Hurran	
G-BWPP	Sky 105-24 balloon	Sarnia Balloon Group	
G-BWPS	CFM Streak Shadow SA	P. J. Mogg	
G-BWPT	Cameron N-90 balloon	G.Everett	
G-BWRA	Sopwith LC-1T Triplane (replica) (N500)	J. G. Brander (G-PENY)	
G-BWRC	Light Aero Avid Speedwing	J. E. Cox	
G-BWRO	Europa	R. A. Darley	
G-BWRR	Cessna 182Q	A. & R. Reid	
G-BWRS	SNCAN Stampe SV.4C	G. P. J. M. Valvekens/Belgium	
G-BWSB	Lindstrand LBL-105A balloon	R. Calvert-Fisher	
G-BWSD	Campbell Cricket	R. F. G. Moyle	
G-BWSG	P.84 Jet Provost T.5 (XW324/K)	J. Bell	

Notes	Reg	Type	Owner or Operator
	G-BWSH	P.84 Jet Provost T.3A (XN498)	Global Aviation Ltd
	G-BWSI	K & S SA.102.5 Cavalier	B. W. Shaw
	G-BWSJ	Denney Kitfox Mk 3	J. C. Holland
	G-BWSL	Sky 77-24 balloon	E. J. Briggs
	G-BWSN	Denney Kitfox Mk 3	R. J. Mitchell
	G-BWSU	Cameron N-105 balloon	A. M. Marten
	G-BWSV	Yakovlev Yak-52 (43)	M. W. Fitch
	G-BWTE	Cameron O-140 balloon	T. G. Church
	G-BWTG	DHC.1 Chipmunk 22 (WB671:910)	R. G. T. de Man/Netherlands
	G-BWTJ	Cameron V-77 balloon	A. J. Montgomery
	G-BWTK	RAF 2000 GTX-SE gyroplane	L. P. Rolfe
	G-BWTO	DHC.1 Chipmunk 22 (WP984)	Skycraft Services Ltd
	G-BWTW	Mooney M.20C	T. J. Berry
	G-BWUH	PA-28-181 Archer III	Phoenix Aviation
	G-BWUJ	Rotorway Executive 162F	Southern Helicopters Ltd
	G-BWUN	DHC.1 Chipmunk 22 (WD310)	E. H. W. Moore
	G-BWUP	Shaw Europa	V. Goddard
	G-BWUS	Sky 65-24 balloon	N. A. P. Bates
	G-BWUT	DHC.1 Chipmunk 22 (WZ879)	Herbert Aviation Ltd
	G-BWUU	Cameron N-90 balloon	Bailey Balloons Ltd
	G-BWUV	DHC.1 Chipmunk 22A (WK640)	A. C. Darby
	G-BWVB	Pietenpol Air Camper	G. Oldfield & A. T. Marshall
	G-BWVC	Jodel D.18	A. H. Simmonds
	G-BWVF	Pietenpol Air Camper	N. Clark
	G-BWVI	Stern ST.80	I. Pearson
	G-BWVN	Whittaker MW7	G. W. S. Turner
	G-BWVR	Yakovlev Yak-52 (52 yellow)	I. Parkinson
	G-BWVS	Shaw Europa	D. R. Bishop
	G-BWVT	DHA.82A Tiger Moth	N. L. MacKaness
	G-BWVU	Cameron O-90 balloon	J. Atkinson
	G-BWVY	DHC.1 Chipmunk 22 (WP896)	N. Gardner
	G-BWVZ	DHC.1 Chipmunk 22A (WK590)	D. Campion/Belgium
	G-BWWA	Ultravia Pelican Club GS	J. S. Aplin
	G-BWWB	Shaw Europa	WB Group
	G-BWWC	DH.104 Dove 7 (XM223)	Air Atlantique Ltd
	G-BWWE	Lindstrand LBL-90A balloon	T. J. Wilkinson
	G-BWWF	Cessna 185A	T. N. Bartlett & S. M. C. Harvey
	G-BWWK	Hawker Nimrod I (S1581)	Patina Ltd
	G-BWWL	Colt Flying Egg SS balloon	Magical Adventures Ltd/USA
	G-BWWN	Isaacs Fury II (K8303:D)	J. S. Marten-Hale
	G-BWWU	PA-22 Tri-Pacer 150	K. M. Bowen
	G-BWWW	BAe Jetstream 3102	British Aerospace PLC
	G-BWWY	Lindstrand LBL-105A balloon	C. D. Monk
	G-BWXA	Slingsby T.67M Firefly 260	Power Aerobatics Ltd
	G-BWXB	Slingsby T.67M Firefly 260	Power Aerobatics Ltd
	G-BWXF	Slingsby T.67M Firefly 260	L3 CTS Airline and Academy Training Ltd
	G-BWXJ	Slingsby T.67M Firefly 260	D. I. Stanbridge
	G-BWXP	Slingsby T.67M Firefly 260	M. Haller & T. Bock
	G-BWXS	Slingsby T.67M Firefly 260	Power Aerobatics Ltd
	G-BWXT	Slingsby T.67M Firefly 260	Cranfield University
	G-BWXV	Slingsby T.67M Firefly 260	W. Hillick
	G-BWYB	PA-28 Cherokee 160	A. J. Peters
	G-BWYD	Europa	S. Styles
	G-BWYI	Denney Kitfox Mk3	A. J. Glading
	G-BWYK	Yakovlev Yak-50	A. Marangoni
	G-BWYN	Cameron O-77 balloon	W. H. Morgan (G-ODER)
	G-BWYO	Sequoia F.8L Falco	M. C. R. Sims
	G-BWYR	Rans S.6-116 Coyote II	D. A. Lord
	G-BWYU	Sky 120-24 balloon	Aerosauras Balloons Ltd
	G-BWZA	Shaw Europa	T. G. Cowlishaw
	G-BWZG	Robin R.2160	Sherburn Aero Club Ltd
	G-BWZJ	Cameron A-250 balloon	Balloon Club of Great Britain
	G-BWZU	Lindstrand LBL-90B balloon	Iseo Mongolfiere SAS di Rossi Paolo EC/Italy
	G-BWZY	Hughes 269A	R. R. Orr (G-FSDT)
	G-BXAB	PA-28-161 Warrior II	TG Aviation Ltd (G-BTGK)
	G-BXAC	RAF 2000 GTX-SE gyroplane	J. A. Robinson
	G-BXAF	Pitts S-1D Special	N. J. Watson
	G-BXAJ	Lindstrand LBL-14A balloon	Oscair Project AB/Sweden
	G-BXAK	Yakovlev Yak-52 (44 black)	A. M. Holman-West
	G-BXAN	Scheibe SF-25C Falke	C. Falke Syndicate

Reg	Type	Owner or Operator	Notes
G-BXAO	Avtech Jabiru SK	P. J. Thompson	
G-BXAU	Pitts S-1 Special	L. Westnage	
G-BXAX	Cameron N-77 balloon ★	Balloon Preservation Group	
G-BXAY	Bell 206B JetRanger 3	Viewdart Ltd	
G-BXBB	PA-20 Pacer 150	M. E. R. Coghlan	
G-BXBK	Avions Mudry CAP-10B	S. Skipworth	
G-BXBL	Lindstrand LBL-240A balloon	J. Fenton	
G-BXBU	Avions Mudry CAP-10B	J. Mann	
G-BXBZ	PZL-104 Wilga 80	J. H. Sandham Aviation	
G-BXCA	Hapi Cygnet SF-2A	J. D. C. Henslow	
G-BXCC	PA-28-201T Turbo Dakota	Greer Aviation Ltd	
G-BXCD	TEAM mini-MAX 91A	A. Maltby	
G-BXCG	Jodel DR.250/160	P.G. Morris	
G-BXCJ	Campbell Cricket (replica)	A. G. Peel	
G-BXCN	Sky 105-24 balloon	Nottingham Hot-Air Balloon Club	
G-BXCO	Colt 120A balloon	J. R. Lawson	
G-BXCT	DHC.1 Chipmunk 22 (WB697)	Wickenby Aviation	
G-BXCU	Rans S.6-116 Coyote II	N. A. Preston	
G-BXCV	DHC.1 Chipmunk 22 (WP929)	Ardmore Aviation Services Ltd/Hong Kong	
G-BXCW	Denney Kitfox Mk 3	D. R. Piercy	
G-BXDA	DHC.1 Chipmunk 22 (WP860)	D. P. Curtis	
G-BXDB	Cessna U.206F	D. A. Howard (G-BMNZ)	
G-BXDE	RAF 2000GTX-SE gyroplane	P. D. Annison	
G-BXDG	DHC.1 Chipmunk 22 (WK630)	Felthorpe Flying Group	
G-BXDH	DHC.1 Chipmunk 22 (WD331)	Royal Aircraft Establishment Aero Club Ltd	
G-BXDI	DHC.1 Chipmunk 22 (WD373)	A. M. Dinnie & D. J. Spicer	
G-BXDN	DHC.1 Chipmunk 22 (WK609)	W. D. Lowe, G. James & L. A. Edwards	
G-BXDO	Rutan Cozy	Cozy Group	
G-BXDR	Lindstrand LBL-77A balloon	A. J. & A. R. Brown	
G-BXDS	Bell 206B JetRanger III	Aerospeed Limited (G-TAMF/G-OVBJ)	
G-BXDU	Aero Designs Pulsar	S. I. Hatherall	
G-BXDV	Sky 105-24 balloon	N. A. Carr	
G-BXDY	Shaw Europa	S. Attubato & D. G. Watts	
G-BXDZ	Lindstrand LBL-105A balloon	D. J. & A. D. Sutcliffe	
G-BXEC	DHC.1 Chipmunk 22 (WK633)	A. J. Robinson & M. J. Miller	
G-BXEF	Europa	C. Busuttil-Reynard	
G-BXEJ	VPM M-16 Tandem Trainer	AES Radionic Surveillance Systems	
G-BXEN	Cameron N-105 balloon	E. Ghio/Italy	
G-BXES	P.66 Pembroke C.1 (XL954)	C. Keane	
G-BXEX	PA-28-181 Archer II	Nottingham Archer Syndicate	
G-BXEZ	Cessna 182P	Forhawk Ltd	
G-BXFB	Pitts S-1 Special	J. F. Dowe	
G-BXFC	Jodel D.18	M. Godbold	
G-BXFE	Avions Mudry CAP-10B	Avion Aerobatic Ltd	
G-BXFG	Shaw Europa	A. Rawicz-Szczerbo	
G-BXFK	CFM Streak Shadow	T. J. Searle	
G-BXFN	Colt 77A balloon	Charter Ballooning Ltd	
G-BXGD	AS.350B2 Ecureuil	PLM Dollar Group Ltd	
G-BXGG	Sky 90-24 balloon	Servo & Electronic Sales Ltd	
G-BXGG	Shaw Europa	D. J. Joyce	
G-BXGL	DHC.1 Chipmunk 22	N. P. Marriott	
G-BXGM	DHC.1 Chipmunk 22 (WP928:D)	Chipmunk G-BXGM Group	
G-BXGO	DHC.1 Chipmunk 22 (WB654:U)	T. J. Orchard	
G-BXGP	DHC.1 Chipmunk 22 (WZ882)	Eaglescott Chipmunk Group	
G-BXGS	RAF 2000 gyroplane	D. W. Howell	
G-BXGT	I.I.I. Sky Arrow 650T	J. S. C. Goodale	
G-BXGV	Cessna 172R	G-BXGV Skyhawk Group	
G-BXGX	DHC.1 Chipmunk 22 (WK586:V)	The Real Flying Co.Ltd	
G-BXGY	Cameron V-65 balloon	Dante Balloon Group	
G-BXGZ	Stemme S.10V	G. S. Craven & A. J. Garner	
G-BXHA	DHC.1 Chipmunk 22 (WP925)	H. M. & S. Roberts	
G-BXHF	DHC.1 Chipmunk 22 (WP930:J)	Hotel Fox Syndicate	
G-BXHH	AA-5A Cheetah	P. G. Hayward	
G-BXHJ	Hapi Cygnet SF-2A	I. J. Smith	
G-BXHL	Sky 77-24 balloon	C. Timbrell	
G-BXHO	Lindstrand Telewest Sphere SS balloon	Magical Adventures Ltd	
G-BXHR	Stemme S.10V	J. H. Rutherford	
G-BXHT	Bushby-Long Midget Mustang	K. Manley	
G-BXHU	Campbell Cricket Mk 6	B. F. Pearson	
G-BXHY	Shaw Europa	Jupiter Flying Group	
G-BXIA	DHC.1 Chipmunk 22 (WB615)	WB615 Group	

Notes	Reg	Type	Owner or Operator
	G-BXIE	Colt 77B balloon	I. R. Warrington
	G-BXIF	PA-28-161 Warrior II	Piper Flight Ltd
	G-BXIG	Zenair CH.701 STOL	S. Ingram
	G-BXIH	Sky 200-24 balloon	Kent Ballooning
	G-BXII	Shaw Europa	D. A. McFadyean
	G-BXIJ	Shaw Europa	P. N. Birch
	G-BXIM	DHC.1 Chipmunk 22 (WK512)	A. B. Ashcroft & P. R. Joshua
	G-BXIT	Zebedee V-31 balloon	Zebedee Balloon Service Ltd
	G-BXIW	Sky 105-24 balloon	A. G. A. Barclay-Faulkner
	G-BXIX	VPM M-16 Tandem Trainer	P. P. Willmott
	G-BXIY	Blake Bluetit (BAPC37)	M. J. Aubrey
	G-BXIZ	Lindstrand LBL-31A balloon	Lakeside Lodge Golf Centre
	G-BXJB	Yakovlev Yak-52	Yak Display Group
	G-BXJD	PA-28-180C Cherokee	S. Atherton
	G-BXJG	Lindstrand LBL-105B balloon	W. C. Wood
	G-BXJH	Cameron N-42 balloon	D. M. Hoddinott
	G-BXJM	Cessna 152	ACS Aviation Ltd
	G-BXJN	Eurocopter AS.350BB Ecureuil	FB Heliservices Ltd
	G-BXJO	Cameron O-90 balloon	Dragon Balloon Co Ltd
	G-BXJS	Schempp-Hirth Janus CM	Janus Syndicate
	G-BXJT	Sky 90-24 balloon	J. G. O'Connell
	G-BXJY	Van's RV-6	J. P. Kynaston
	G-BXJZ	Cameron C-60 balloon	N. J. & S. J. Bettin
	G-BXKF	Hawker Hunter T.7(XL577/V)	R. F. Harvey
	G-BXKL	Bell 206B JetRanger 3	Top Shop LLP
	G-BXKM	RAF 2000 GTX-SE gyroplane	E. Mangles
	G-BXKU	Colt AS-120 Mk II airship	D. C. Chipping/Portugal
	G-BXKW	Slingsby T.67M Firefly 200	J-F Jansen & A. Huygens
	G-BXKX	Auster V	J. A. Sephton
	G-BXLF	Lindstrand LBL-90A balloon	S. McMahon & J. Edwards
	G-BXLG	Cameron C-80 balloon	S. M. Anthony
	G-BXLK	Shaw Europa	R. J. Sheridan
	G-BXLN	Fournier RF-4D	P. W. Cooper & M. R. Fox
	G-BXLO	P.84 Jet Provost T.4 (XR673/L)	Century Aviation Ltd
	G-BXLP	Sky 90-24 balloon	D. Bedford & J. Edwards
	G-BXLS	PZL-110 Koliber 160A	P. R. Powell
	G-BXLT	SOCATA TB200 Tobago XL	C., G. & J. Fisher & D. Fitton
	G-BXLW	Enstrom F.28F	Rhoburt Ltd
	G-BXLY	PA-28-151 Warrior	Pilot Training and Testing Ltd (G-WATZ)
	G-BXMV	Scheibe SF.25C Falke 1700	K. E. Ballington
	G-BXMX	Currie Wot	R. B. Griffin
	G-BXMY	Hughes 269C	R. D. Masters
	G-BXNC	Shaw Europa	J. K. Cantwell
	G-BXNN	DHC.1 Chipmunk 22 (WP983:B)	E. N. Skinner
	G-BXNS	Bell 206B JetRanger 3	Aerospeed Ltd
	G-BXOA	Robinson R22 Beta	Swift Helicopter Services Ltd
	G-BXOC	Evans VP-2	Condor Aviation International Ltd
	G-BXOF	Diamond Katana DA20-A1	Aircraft Engineers Ltd
	G-BXOI	Cessna 172R	E. J. Watts
	G-BXOJ	PA-28-161 Warrior III	Tayside Aviation Ltd
	G-BXOM	Isaacs Spitfire	S. Vince
	G-BXON	Auster AOP.9	A. G. Thomas
	G-BXOT	Cameron C-70 balloon	Dante Balloon Group
	G-BXOU	CEA DR.360	J. A. Lofthouse
	G-BXOX	AA-5A Cheetah	R. L. Carter & P. J. Large
	G-BXOY	QAC Quickie Q.235	C. C. Clapham
	G-BXOZ	PA-28-181 Archer II	Spritetone Ltd
	G-BXPC	Diamond Katana DA20-A1	Cubair Flight Training Ltd
	G-BXPD	Diamond Katana DA20-A1	Cubair Flight Training Ltd
	G-BXPI	Van's RV-4	B. M. Diggins
	G-BXPM	Beech 58 Baron	Whitehouse Retail Ltd
	G-BXPP	Sky 90-24 balloon	S. A. Nother
	G-BXPT	Ultramagic H-77 balloon	Aerobility
	G-BXRA	Avions Mudry CAP-10B	Cole Aviation Ltd
	G-BXRB	Avions Mudry CAP-10B	T. T. Duhig
	G-BXRC	Avions Mudry CAP-10B	Group Alpha
	G-BXRF	CP.1310-C3 Super Emeraude	D. T. Gethin
	G-BXRO	Cessna U.206G	Wild Geese Parachute Ltd
	G-BXRP	Schweizer 269C	Findelta Pty Ltd
	G-BXRS	Westland Scout AH.1 (XW613)	C. J. Marsden
	G-BXRT	Robin DR.400-180	T. P. Usborne

Reg	Type	Owner or Operator	Notes
G-BXRV	Van's RV-4	Cleeve Flying Grouip	
G-BXRY	Bell 206B JetRanger	Twylight Management Ltd	
G-BXRZ	Rans S.6-116 Coyote II	M. P. Hallam	
G-BXSC	Cameron C-80 balloon	Murray Rene Ltd	
G-BXSD	Cessna 172R	R. Paston	
G-BXSE	Cessna 172R	MK Aero Support Ltd	
G-BXSG	Robinson R22 Beta II	Rivermead Aviation Ltd	
G-BXSH	Glaser-Dirks DG.800B	D. Crimmins	
G-BXSI	Avtech Jabiru SK	P. F. Gandy	
G-BXSP	Grob G.109B	Deeside Grob Group	
G-BXSR	Cessna F172N	SR Sharing	
G-BXST	PA-25 Pawnee 235C	Staffordshire Gliding Club Ltd	
G-BXSU	TEAM mini-MAX 91A	I. Pearson (G-MYGL)	
G-BXSV	SNCAN Stampe SV.4C	P. A. Greenhalgh	
G-BXSX	Cameron V-77 balloon	D. R. Medcalf	
G-BXSY	Robinson R22 Beta II	N. M. G. Pearson	
G-BXTB	Cessna 152	Pilot Training & Testing Ltd	
G-BXTD	Shaw Europa	P. R. Anderson	
G-BXTF	Cameron N-105 balloon	C. J. Dunkley	
G-BXTG	Cameron N-42 balloon	P. M. Watkins & S. M. M. Carden	
G-BXTI	Pitts S-1S Special	A. Schmer	
G-BXTO	Hindustan HAL-6 Pushpak	P. Q. Benn	
G-BXTS	Diamond Katana DA20-A1	Airbourne Aviation Ltd	
G-BXTT	AA-5B Tiger	J. Ducray	
G-BXTW	PA-28-181 Archer III	Davison Plant Hire	
G-BXTY	PA-28-161 Cadet	Flew LLP	
G-BXTZ	PA-28-161 Cadet	Flew LLP	
G-BXUA	Campbell Cricket Mk.5	A. W. Harvey	
G-BXUC	Robinson R22 Beta	Rivermead Aviation Ltd/Switzerland	
G-BXUF	Agusta-Bell 206B JetRanger 3	SJ Contracting Services Ltd	
G-BXUG	Lindstrand Baby Bel SS balloon	K-H. Gruenauer/Germany	
G-BXUH	Lindstrand LBL-31A balloon	R. A. Lovell	
G-BXUI	Glaser-Dirks DG.800B	J. Le Coyte	
G-BXUO	Lindstrand LBL-105A balloon	Lindstrand Technologies Ltd	
G-BXUU	Cameron V-65 balloon	M. D. Freeston & S. Mitchell	
G-BXUW	Cameron Colt 90A balloon	V. Beardall	
G-BXUX	Brandli Cherry BX-2	M. F. Fountain	
G-BXVA	SOCATA TB200 Tobago XL	M. Goehen	
G-BXVB	Cessna 152 II	PJC (Leasing) Ltd	
G-BXVG	Sky 77-24 balloon	M. Wolf	
G-BXVK	Robin HR.200/120B	B. A. Mills	
G-BXVM	Van's RV-6A	J. C. Lomax	
G-BXVO	Van's RV-6A	R. Marsden	
G-BXVP	Sky 31-24 balloon	S. I. Williams & H. G. Griffiths	
G-BXVR	Sky 90-24 balloon	P. Hegarty	
G-BXVS	Brügger MB.2 Colibri	G. T. Snoddon	
G-BXVT	Cameron O-77 balloon	R. P. Wade	
G-BXVU	PA-28-161 Warrior II	D. C. & M. Brooks	
G-BXVV	Cameron V-90 balloon	Adeilad Cladding	
G-BXVX	Rutan Cozy	G. E. Murray	
G-BXVY	Cessna 152	Stapleford Flying Club Ltd	
G-BXWB	Robin HR.100/200B	Yorkshire Land Ltd	
G-BXWG	Sky 120-24 balloon	M. E. White	
G-BXWH	Denney Kitfox Mk.4-1200	M. G. Porter	
G-BXWK	Rans S.6-ESA Coyote II	M. Taylor	
G-BXWL	Sky 90-24 balloon	E. J. Briggs	
G-BXWO	PA-28-181 Archer II	J. S. Develin & Z. Islam	
G-BXWP	PA-32 Cherokee Six 300	D. F. Scrimshaw	
G-BXWR	CFM Streak Shadow	M. A. Hayward (G-MZMI)	
G-BXWT	Van's RV-6	R. C. Owen	
G-BXWU	FLS Aerospace Sprint 160	Aeroelvia Ltd	
G-BXWV	FLS Aerospace Sprint 160	Aeroelvia Ltd	
G-BXWX	Sky 25-16 balloon	C. O'N. Davis	
G-BXXG	Cameron N-105 balloon	R. N. Simpkins	
G-BXXH	Hatz CB-1	R. D. Shingler	
G-BXXI	Grob G.109B	Malcolm Martin Flying Group	
G-BXXJ	Colt Flying Yacht SS balloon	Magical Adventures Ltd/USA	
G-BXXK	Cessna FR.172N	Flybai SL/Spain	
G-BXXL	Cameron N-105 balloon	C. J. Dunkley	
G-BXXO	Lindstrand LBL-90B balloon	G. P. Walton	
G-BXXP	Sky 77-24 balloon	T. R. Wood	

Notes	Reg	Type	Owner or Operator
	G-BXXS	Sky 105-24 balloon	S. A. Sorn
	G-BXXT	Beech 76 Duchess	Air Navigation & Trading Co.Ltd
	G-BXXU	Colt 31A balloon	Sade Balloons Ltd
	G-BXXW	Enstrom F-28F	D. A. Marks (G-SCOX)
	G-BXYE	CP.301-C1 Emeraude	D. T. Gethin
	G-BXYF	Colt AS-105 GD airship	LN Flying Ltd
	G-BXYI	Cameron H-34 balloon	S. P. Harrowing
	G-BXYJ	Jodel DR.1050	G-BXYJ Group
	G-BXYM	PA-28 Cherokee 235	B. Guenther
	G-BXYO	PA-28RT-201 Arrow IV	D. Atherton
	G-BXYP	PA-28RT-201 Arrow IV	G. I. Cooper
	G-BXYT	PA-28RT-201 Arrow IV	Falcon Flying Services Ltd
	G-BXZB	Nanchang CJ-6A (2632019)	R. Davy, J. L. Swallow & P. Lloyd
	G-BXZF	Lindstrand LBL-90A balloon	S. McGuigan
	G-BXZI	Lindstrand LBL-90A balloon	C. M. Morley
	G-BXZK	MDH MD-900 Explorer	Specialist Aviation Services Ltd
	G-BXZO	Pietenpol Air Camper	P. J. Cooke
	G-BXZU	Micro Aviation Bantam B.22-S	M. E. Whapham & R. W. Hollamby
	G-BXZV	CFM Streak Shadow	D. J. S. Maclean
	G-BXZY	CFM Streak Shadow Srs DD	G. L. Turner
	G-BYAV	Taylor JT.1 Monoplane	R. D. Boor
	G-BYAW	Boeing 757-204ER	TUI Airways Ltd
	G-BYAY	Boeing 757-204ER	TUI Airways Ltd
	G-BYAZ	CFM Streak Shadow	A. G. Wright
	G-BYBD	Cessna F.172H	R. Macbeth-Seath (G-OBHX/G-AWMU)
	G-BYBF	Robin R.2160i	D. J. R. Lloyd-Evans
	G-BYBH	PA-34-200T Seneca II	Aero Club Frosinone ASD/Italy
	G-BYBI	Bell 206B JetRanger 3	Castle Air Ltd
	G-BYBJ	Medway Hybred 44XLR	M. Gardner
	G-BYBK	Murphy Rebel	P. R. Goodwill
	G-BYBL	Gardan GY-80 Horizon 160D	Bluewing Flying Group
	G-BYBM	Avtech Jabiru SK	P. H. Thomas
	G-BYBP	Cessna A.185F	G. M. S. Scott
	G-BYBS	Sky 80-16 balloon	B. K. Rippon
	G-BYBU	Renegade Spirit UK	M. E. Gilman
	G-BYBV	Mainair Rapier	M. W. Robson
	G-BYBY	Thorp T.18C Tiger	P. G. Mair
	G-BYBZ	Jabiru SK	P. J. Whitehouse
	G-BYCA	PA-28-140 Cherokee D	Go Fly Oxford Ltd
	G-BYCJ	CFM Shadow Srs DD	P. I. Hodgson
	G-BYCL	Raj Hamsa X'Air Jabiru(1)	A. A. Ross
	G-BYCM	Rans S.6-ES Coyote II	E. W. McMullan
	G-BYCN	Rans S.6-ES Coyote II	T. J. Croskery
	G-BYCS	Jodel DR.1051	G. A. Stops
	G-BYCT	Aero L-29A Delfin	M. P. Grimshaw & M. C. Hall
	G-BYCW	Mainair Blade 912	P. C. Watson
	G-BYCX	Westland Wasp HAS.1	C. J. Marsden
	G-BYCY	I.I.I. Sky Arrow 650T	K. A. Daniels
	G-BYCZ	Avtech Jabiru SK	T. Herbert
	G-BYDB	Grob G.115B	A. R. Willis & A. P. Shoobert
	G-BYDG	Beech C24R Sierra	H. Loeffert & R. Kolb/Germany
	G-BYDJ	Colt 120A balloon	D. K. Hempleman-Adams
	G-BYDK	SNCAN Stampe SV.4C	Bianchi Aviation Film Services Ltd
	G-BYDL	Hawker Hurricane IIB (Z5207)	K-F Grimminger
	G-BYDV	Van's RV-6	B. F. Hill
	G-BYDY	Beech 58 Baron	Pilot Services Flying Group Ltd
	G-BYDZ	Pegasus Quantum 15-912	S. J. Ward
	G-BYEA	Cessna 172P	M. Gates
	G-BYEC	Glaser-Dirks DG.800B	P. D. Craven
	G-BYEE	Mooney M.20K	G. Mexias
	G-BYEH	CEA Jodel DR.250	S. T. Scully
	G-BYEJ	Scheibe SF-28A Tandem Falke	D. Shrimpton
	G-BYEK	Stoddard Hamilton Glastar	T. A. Reed
	G-BYEL	Van's RV-6	D. Millar
	G-BYEM	Cessna R.182 RG	Bickertons Aerodromes Ltd
	G-BYEO	Zenair CH.601HDS	J. R. Clarke
	G-BYER	Cameron C-80 balloon	J. M. Langley
	G-BYEW	Pegasus Quantum 15-912	R. S. Matheson
	G-BYEY	Lindstrand LBL-21 Silver Dream balloon	Oscair Project Ltd/Sweden
	G-BYFA	Cessna F.152 II	Redhill Air Services Ltd (G-WACA)

Reg	Type	Owner or Operator	Notes
G-BYFF	Pegasus Quantum 15-912	T. A. Willcox	
G-BYFI	CFM Starstreak Shadow SA	J. A. Cook	
G-BYFJ	Cameron N-105 balloon	R. J. Mercer	
G-BYFK	Cameron Printer 105 SS balloon	Mobberley Balloon Collection	
G-BYFL	Diamond HK.36 TTS	Seahawk Gliding Club	
G-BYFM	Jodel DR.1050M-1 (replica)	A. J. Roxburgh	
G-BYFR	PA-32R-301 Saratoga II HP	ATT Aviation Holding Ltd	
G-BYFT	Pietenpol Air Camper	G. Everett	
G-BYFV	TEAM mini-MAX 91	W. E. Gillham	
G-BYFX	Colt 77A balloon	Wye Valley Aviation Ltd	
G-BYFY	Avions Mudry CAP-10B	R. N. Crosland	
G-BYGA	Boeing 747-436	British Airways	
G-BYGB	Boeing 747-436	British Airways	
G-BYGC	Boeing 747-436	British Airways	
G-BYGD	Boeing 747-436	British Airways	
G-BYGE	Boeing 747-436	British Airways	
G-BYGF	Boeing 747-436	British Airways	
G-BYGG	Boeing 747-436	British Airways	
G-BYHC	Cameron Z-90 balloon	T. J. Wilkinson	
G-BYHE	Robinson R22 Beta	Helimech Ltd	
G-BYHG	Dornier 328-100	Loganair Ltd	
G-BYHH	PA-28-161 Warrior III	Stapleford Flying Club Ltd	
G-BYHI	PA-28-161 Warrior II	T. W. & W. S. Gilbert	
G-BYHJ	PA-28R-201 Arrow	Flew LLP	
G-BYHK	PA-28-181 Archer III	T-Air Services	
G-BYHL	DHC.1 Chipmunk 22 (WG308)	M. R. & I. D. Higgins	
G-BYHO	Mainair Blade 912	P. G. Evans	
G-BYHP	CEA DR.253B	HP Flying Group	
G-BYHR	Pegasus Quantum 15-912	I. D. Chantler	
G-BYHS	Mainair Blade 912	Telzor Group	
G-BYHT	Robin DR.400/180R	Deeside Robin Group	
G-BYHU	Cameron N-105 balloon	Ezmerelda Balloon Syndicate	
G-BYHV	Raj Hamsa X'Air 582	M. G. Adams	
G-BYHY	Cameron V-77 balloon	P. Spellward	
G-BYIA	Avtech Jabiru SK	M. D. Doyle	
G-BYIB	Rans S.6-ES Coyote II	S. McLatchie	
G-BYID	Rans S.6-ES Coyote II	R. M. Watson	
G-BYIE	Robinson R22 Beta II	K. W. Horobin	
G-BYII	TEAM mini-MAX	G. Wilkinson	
G-BYIJ	CASA 1.131E Jungmann 2000	R. N. Crosland	
G-BYIK	Shaw Europa	D. Allen	
G-BYIN	RAF 2000 gyroplane	J. R. Legge	
G-BYIO	Colt 105A balloon	N. Charbonnier/Italy	
G-BYIP	Aerotek Pitts S-2A Special	D. P. Heather-Hayes	
G-BYIR	Aerotek Pitts S-1S Special	S. Kramer	
G-BYIS	Pegasus Quantum 15-912	D. J. Ramsden	
G-BYIU	Cameron V-90 balloon	H. Micketeit/Germany	
G-BYIV	Cameron PM-80 balloon	A. Schneider/Germany	
G-BYIW	Cameron PM-80 balloon	T. Gleixner/Switzerland	
G-BYIX	Cameron PM-80 balloon	A. Schneider/Germany	
G-BYJA	RAF 2000 GTX-SE	C. R. W. Lyne	
G-BYJB	Mainair Blade 912	R. G. Mason	
G-BYJC	Cameron N-90 balloon	A. G. Merry	
G-BYJD	Avtech Jabiru UL	K. McKay	
G-BYJE	TEAM Mini-MAX 91	T. A. Willcox	
G-BYJF	Thorpe T.211	M. J. Newton	
G-BYJH	Grob G.109B	Grob GJH Group	
G-BYJI	Shaw Europa	M. Gibson (G-ODTI)	
G-BYJK	Pegasus Quantum 15-912	S. J. Wilson	
G-BYJL	Aero Designs Pulsar	A. Young	
G-BYJN	Lindstrand LBL-105A balloon	B. Meeson	
G-BYJO	Rans S.6-ES Coyote II	P. D. Smalley	
G-BYJP	Aerotek Pitts S-1S Special	Eaglescott Pitts Group	
G-BYJR	Lindstrand LBL-77B balloon	B. M. Reed	
G-BYJS	SOCATA TB20 Trinidad	A. P. Bedford	
G-BYJT	Zenair CH.601HD	AV8 Flying Group	
G-BYJW	Cameron Sphere 105 balloon	Balleroy Developpement SAS	
G-BYJX	Cameron C-70 balloon	John Aimo Balloons SAS/Italy	
G-BYKA	Lindstrand LBL-69A balloon	B. Meeson	
G-BYKB	Rockwell Commander 114	D. L. Macdonald	
G-BYKC	Mainair Blade 912	A. Williams	

Notes	Reg	Type	Owner or Operator
	G-BYKD	Mainair Blade 912	D. C. Boyle
	G-BYKF	Enstrom F-28F	Merlin Group LLC
	G-BYKG	Pietenpol Air Camper	K. B. Hodge
	G-BYKJ	Westland Scout AH.1	Austen Associates
	G-BYKK	Robinson R44	Dragonfly Aviation
	G-BYKL	PA-28-181 Archer II	Transport Command Ltd
	G-BYKP	PA-28R-201T Turbo Arrow IV	AT Aviation Sales Ltd
	G-BYKT	Pegasus Quantum 15-912	N. J. Howarth
	G-BYKU	BFC Challenger II	P. A. Tarplee
	G-BYKX	Cameron N-90 balloon	C. O'N. Davis
	G-BYLB	D. H. 82A Tiger Moth	D. F. Sargant
	G-BYLC	Pegasus Quantum 15-912	G. P. D. Coan
	G-BYLD	Pietenpol Air Camper	S. Bryan
	G-BYLF	Zenair CH.601HDS Zodiac	S. Plater
	G-BYLI	Nova Vertex 22 hang glider	M. Hay
	G-BYLJ	Letov LK-2M Sluka	J. G. & W. H. McMinn
	G-BYLO	T.66 Nipper Srs 1	M. J. A. Trudgill
	G-BYLP	Rand-Robinson KR-2	C. S. Hales
	G-BYLS	Bede BD-4	P. J. Greenrod
	G-BYLT	Raj Hamsa X'Air 582	T. W. Phipps
	G-BYLW	Lindstrand LBL-77A balloon	Associazione Gran Premio Italiano
	G-BYLX	Lindstrand LBL-105A balloon	Italiana Aeronavi/Italy
	G-BYLY	Cameron V-77 balloon (1)	R. Bayly/Italy (G-ULIA)
	G-BYLZ	Rutan Cozy	W. S. Allen
	G-BYMB	Diamond Katana DA20-C1	S. Staniulis & M. Zakaras
	G-BYMD	PA-38-112 Tomahawk II	M. A. Petrie
	G-BYMF	Pegasus Quantum 15-912	G. R. Stockdale
	G-BYMI	Pegasus Quantum 15	J. Drewe
	G-BYMJ	Cessna 152	PJC (Leasing) Ltd
	G-BYMN	Rans S.6-ESA Coyote II	R. J. P. Herivel
	G-BYMR	Raj Hamsa X'Air R100(3)	W. Drury
	G-BYMW	Boland 52-12 balloon	C. Jones
	G-BYNA	Cessna F.172H	D. M. White (G-AWTH)
	G-BYND	Pegasus Quantum 15	W. J. Upton
	G-BYNE	Pilatus PC-6/B2-H4 Turbo Porter	ASD Sprl/Belgium
	G-BYNF	NA-64 Yale I (3349)	R. S. Van Dijk
	G-BYNK	Robin HR.200/160	Penguin Flight Group
	G-BYNM	Mainair Blade 912	D. E. Ashton
	G-BYNN	Cameron V-90 balloon	Cloud Nine Balloon Group
	G-BYNP	Rans S.6-ES Coyote II	C. J. Lines
	G-BYNS	Avtech Jabiru SK	D. K. Lawry
	G-BYNU	Cameron Thunder Ax7-77 balloon	B. Fisher
	G-BYNW	Cameron H-34 balloon	IS. J. Roake & M. A. Stelling
	G-BYNX	Cameron RX-105 balloon	Cameron Balloons Ltd
	G-BYNY	Beech 76 Duchess	M. D. Darragh
	G-BYOB	Slingsby T.67M Firefly 260	Stapleford Flying Club Ltd
	G-BYOD	Slingsby T.67C	D. I. Stanbridge
	G-BYOG	Pegasus Quantum 15-912	A. C. Tyler
	G-BYOH	Raj Hamsa X'Air 582 (5)	J. Owen
	G-BYOI	Sky 80-16 balloon	D. J. Tofton
	G-BYOJ	Raj Hamsa X'Air 582 (1)	T. C. Ellison
	G-BYON	Mainair Blade	J. Masters & B. Allen
	G-BYOO	CFM Streak Shadow	G. R. Eastwood
	G-BYOR	Raj Hamsa X'Air 582(7)	R. Dilkes
	G-BYOS	Mainair Blade 912	K. Worthington
	G-BYOT	Rans S.6-ES Coyote II	G-BYOT Syndicate
	G-BYOV	Pegasus Quantum 15-912	M. Howland
	G-BYOW	Mainair Blade	P. Szymanski & P. Gadek
	G-BYOX	Cameron Z-90 balloon	Ballooning Network Ltd
	G-BYOZ	Mainair Rapier	G. P. Hodgson
	G-BYPB	Pegasus Quantum 15-912	Cloudbase Paragliding Ltd
	G-BYPF	Thruster T.600N	T. R. Villa
	G-BYPH	Thruster T.600N	D. M. Canham
	G-BYPJ	Pegasus Quantum 15-912	Airmasters (UK) Ltd
	G-BYPM	Shaw Europa XS	G. F.Stratton
	G-BYPN	MS.880B Rallye Club	R. Edwards and D. & S. A. Bell
	G-BYPO	Raj Hamsa X'Air 582 (1)	W. Parker
	G-BYPR	Zenair CH.601HD Zodiac	N. Surman
	G-BYPU	PA-32R-301 Saratoga SP	GOBOB Flying Group
	G-BYPW	Raj Hamsa X'Air 583 (3)	P. J. Kimpton
	G-BYPY	Ryan ST3KR (001)	T. Curtis-Taylor

Reg	Type	Owner or Operator	Notes
G-BYPZ	Rans S.6-116 Super 6	R. A. Blackbourne	
G-BYRC	Westland WS-58 Wessex HC.2 (XT671)	D. Brem-Wilson	
G-BYRG	Rans S.6-ES Coyote II	S. J. Macmillan	
G-BYRJ	Pegasus Quantum 15-912	J. & R. Thompson	
G-BYRK	Cameron V-42 balloon	R. Kunert	
G-BYRO	Mainair Blade	T. W. Thiele	
G-BYRR	Mainair Blade 912	W. J. Dowty	
G-BYRU	Pegasus Quantum 15-912	L. M. Westwood	
G-BYRV	Raj Hamsa X'Air 582 (1)	A. D. Russell	
G-BYRX	Westland Scout AH.1 (XT634)	Edwalton Aviation Ltd	
G-BYRY	Slingsby T.67M Firefly 200	J. Clowes	
G-BYSE	Agusta-Bell 206B JetRanger 2	C. I. Motors Ltd (G-BFND)	
G-BYSF	Avtech Jabiru UL	Jabber 430	
G-BYSG	Robin HR.200/120B	Grosvenor Aircraft	
G-BYSI	WSK-PZL Koliber 160A	J. & D. F. Evans	
G-BYSJ	DHC.1 Chipmunk 22 (WB569:R)	Propshop Ltd	
G-BYSM	Cameron A-210 balloon	Adventure Balloons Ltd	
G-BYSP	PA-28-181 Archer II	Take Flight Aviation Ltd	
G-BYSV	Cameron N-120 balloon	S. Simmington	
G-BYSX	Pegasus Quantum 15-912	K. A. Landers	
G-BYSY	Raj Hamsa X'Air 582 (1)	A. Cochrane	
G-BYTB	SOCATA TB20 Trinidad	Watchman Aircraft Ltd	
G-BYTC	Pegasus Quantum 15-912	J. C. & J. E. Munro-Hunt	
G-BYTI	PA-24 Comanche 250	M. Carruthers & G. Auchterlonie	
G-BYTJ	Cameron C-80 balloon	J. D. Smallridge	
G-BYTK	Avtech Jabiru UL	G. R. Phillips	
G-BYTL	Mainair Blade 912	D. A. Meek & T.J. Burrow	
G-BYTM	Dyn' Aero MCR-01	I. Lang	
G-BYTN	DH.82A Tiger Moth (N6720:VX)	Tiger Leasing Company Ltd	
G-BYTR	Raj Hamsa X'Air 582 (1)	L. A. Dotchin	
G-BYTS	Montgomerie-Bensen B.8MR gyroplane	C. Seaman	
G-BYTU	Mainair Blade 912	A. S. R. Galley	
G-BYTV	Avtech Jabiru SPL-450	M. W. T. Wilson	
G-BYTW	Cameron O-90 balloon	Sade Balloons Ltd	
G-BYTX	MW6-S Fat Boy Flyer	J. K. Ewing	
G-BYTZ	Raj Hamsa X'Air 582 (1)	J. R. Kinder	
G-BYUB	Grob G.115E Tutor	Babcock Aerospace Ltd	
G-BYUC	Grob G.115E Tutor	Babcock Aerospace Ltd	
G-BYUD	Grob G.115E Tutor	Babcock Aerospace Ltd	
G-BYUE	Grob G.115E Tutor	Babcock Aerospace Ltd	
G-BYUF	Grob G.115E Tutor	Babcock Aerospace Ltd	
G-BYUH	Grob G.115E Tutor	Babcock Aerospace Ltd	
G-BYUI	Grob G.115E Tutor	Babcock Aerospace Ltd	
G-BYUJ	Grob G.115E Tutor	Babcock Aerospace Ltd	
G-BYUK	Grob G.115E Tutor	Babcock Aerospace Ltd	
G-BYUL	Grob G.115E Tutor	Babcock Aerospace Ltd	
G-BYUM	Grob G.115E Tutor	Babcock Aerospace Ltd	
G-BYUN	Grob G.115E Tutor	Babcock Aerospace Ltd	
G-BYUO	Grob G.115E Tutor	Babcock Aerospace Ltd	
G-BYUR	Grob G.115E Tutor	Babcock Aerospace Ltd	
G-BYUS	Grob G.115E Tutor	Babcock Aerospace Ltd	
G-BYUU	Grob G.115E Tutor	Babcock Aerospace Ltd	
G-BYUV	Grob G.115E Tutor	Babcock Aerospace Ltd	
G-BYUW	Grob G.115E Tutor	Babcock Aerospace Ltd	
G-BYUX	Grob G.115E Tutor	Babcock Aerospace Ltd	
G-BYUY	Grob.G.115E Tutor	Babcock Aerospace Ltd	
G-BYUZ	Grob G.115E Tutor	Babcock Aerospace Ltd	
G-BYVA	Grob G.115E Tutor	Babcock Aerospace Ltd	
G-BYVB	Grob G.115E Tutor	Babcock Aerospace Ltd	
G-BYVC	Grob G.115E Tutor	Babcock Aerospace Ltd	
G-BYVD	Grob G.115E Tutor	Babcock Aerospace Ltd	
G-BYVE	Grob G.115E Tutor	Babcock Aerospace Ltd	
G-BYVF	Grob G.115E Tutor	Babcock Aerospace Ltd	
G-BYVG	Grob G.115E Tutor	Babcock Aerospace Ltd	
G-BYVH	Grob G.115E Tutor	Babcock Aerospace Ltd	
G-BYVI	Grob G.115E Tutor	Babcock Aerospace Ltd	
G-BYVK	Grob G.115E Tutor	Babcock Aerospace Ltd	
G-BYVL	Grob G.115E Tutor	Babcock Aerospace Ltd	
G-BYVM	Grob G.115E Tutor	Babcock Aerospace Ltd	
G-BYVO	Grob G.115E Tutor	Babcock Aerospace Ltd	
G-BYVP	Grob G.115E Tutor	Babcock Aerospace Ltd	

Notes	Reg	Type	Owner or Operator
	G-BYVR	Grob G.115E Tutor	Babcock Aerospace Ltd
	G-BYVU	Grob G.115E Tutor	Babcock Aerospace Ltd
	G-BYVW	Grob G.115E Tutor	Babcock Aerospace Ltd
	G-BYVY	Grob G.115E Tutor	Babcock Aerospace Ltd
	G-BYVZ	Grob G.115E Tutor	Babcock Aerospace Ltd
	G-BYWA	Grob G.115E Tutor	Babcock Aerospace Ltd
	G-BYWB	Grob G.115E Tutor	Babcock Aerospace Ltd
	G-BYWD	Grob G.115E Tutor	Babcock Aerospace Ltd
	G-BYWF	Grob G.115E Tutor	Babcock Aerospace Ltd
	G-BYWG	Grob G.115E Tutor	Babcock Aerospace Ltd
	G-BYWH	Grob G.115E Tutor	Babcock Aerospace Ltd
	G-BYWI	Grob G.115E Tutor	Babcock Aerospace Ltd
	G-BYWK	Grob G.115E Tutor	Babcock Aerospace Ltd
	G-BYWL	Grob G.115E Tutor	Babcock Aerospace Ltd
	G-BYWM	Grob G.115E Tutor	Babcock Aerospace Ltd
	G-BYWO	Grob G.115E Tutor	Babcock Aerospace Ltd
	G-BYWR	Grob G.115E Tutor	Babcock Aerospace Ltd
	G-BYWS	Grob G.115E Tutor	Babcock Aerospace Ltd
	G-BYWU	Grob G.115E Tutor	Babcock Aerospace Ltd
	G-BYWV	Grob G.115E Tutor	Babcock Aerospace Ltd
	G-BYWW	Grob G.115E Tutor	Babcock Aerospace Ltd
	G-BYWX	Grob G.115E Tutor	Babcock Aerospace Ltd
	G-BYWY	Grob G.115E Tutor	Babcock Aerospace Ltd
	G-BYWZ	Grob G.115E Tutor	Babcock Aerospace Ltd
	G-BYXA	Grob G.115E Tutor	Babcock Aerospace Ltd
	G-BYXC	Grob G.115E Tutor	Babcock Aerospace Ltd
	G-BYXD	Grob G.115E Tutor	Babcock Aerospace Ltd
	G-BYXE	Grob G.115E Tutor	Babcock Aerospace Ltd
	G-BYXF	Grob G.115E Tutor	Babcock Aerospace Ltd
	G-BYXG	Grob G.115E Tutor	Babcock Aerospace Ltd
	G-BYXH	Grob G.115E Tutor	Babcock Aerospace Ltd
	G-BYXI	Grob G.115E Tutor	Babcock Aerospace Ltd
	G-BYXJ	Grob G.115E Tutor	Babcock Aerospace Ltd
	G-BYXK	Grob G.115E Tutor	Babcock Aerospace Ltd
	G-BYXL	Grob G.115E Tutor	Babcock Aerospace Ltd
	G-BYXM	Grob G.115E Tutor	Babcock Aerospace Ltd
	G-BYXO	Grob G.115E Tutor	Babcock Aerospace Ltd
	G-BYXP	Grob G.115E Tutor	Babcock Aerospace Ltd
	G-BYXS	Grob G.115E Tutor	Babcock Aerospace Ltd
	G-BYXT	Grob G.115E Tutor	Babcock Aerospace Ltd
	G-BYXW	Medway Eclipser	G. A. Hazell
	G-BYXX	Grob G.115E Tutor	Babcock Aerospace Ltd
	G-BYXZ	Grob G.115E Tutor	Babcock Aerospace Ltd
	G-BYYA	Grob G.115E Tutor	Babcock Aerospace Ltd
	G-BYYB	Grob G.115E Tutor	Babcock Aerospace Ltd
	G-BYYC	Hapi Cygnet SF-2A	G. H. Smith
	G-BYYE	Lindstrand LBL-77A balloon	Virgin Balloon Flights
	G-BYYG	Slingsby T.67C	The Pathfinder Flying Club Ltd
	G-BYYJ	Lindstrand LBL-25A balloon	G-BYYJ Go Hopping
	G-BYYL	Avtech Jabiru SPL-450	D. Licheri & S. Langley
	G-BYYM	Raj Hamsa X'Air 582 (1)	J. Pozniak
	G-BYYN	Pegasus Quantum 15-912	R. J. Bullock
	G-BYYO	PA-28R -201 Arrow III	Stapleford Flying Club Ltd
	G-BYYP	Pegasus Quantum 15	D. A. Linsey-Bloom
	G-BYYR	Raj Hamsa X'Air 582 (4)	T. D. Bawden
	G-BYYT	Avtech Jabiru UL 450	S. Turnbull
	G-BYYX	TEAM mini-MAX 91	P. J. Bishop
	G-BYYY	Pegasus Quantum 15-912	R. D. C. Hayter
	G-BYZA	AS.355F2 Twin Squirrel	PLM Dollar Group Ltd
	G-BYZB	Mainair Blade	A. M. Thornley
	G-BYZF	Raj Hamsa X'Air 582 (1)	R. P. Davies
	G-BYZL	Cameron GP-65 balloon	P. Thibo
	G-BYZO	Rans S.6-ES Coyote II	S. McGarr
	G-BYZR	I.I.I. Sky Arrow 650TC	G-BYZR Flying Group
	G-BYZS	Avtech Jabiru UL-450	G. J. Stafford
	G-BYZT	Nova Vertex 26	M. Hay
	G-BYZU	Pegasus Quantum 15	D. W. C. Beer
	G-BYZV	Sky 90-24 balloon	P. Farmer
	G-BYZW	Raj Hamsa X'Air 582 (2)	H. C. Lowther
	G-BYZX	Cameron R-90 balloon	D. K. Hempleman-Adams
	G-BYZY	Pietenpol Aircamper	D. M. Hanchett

Reg	Type	Owner or Operator	Notes
G-BZAE	Cessna 152	Tatenhill Aviation Ltd	
G-BZAH	Cessna 208B Grand Caravan	Army Parachute Association	
G-BZAI	Pegasus Quantum 15	S. A. Holmes	
G-BZAK	Raj Hamsa X'Air 582 (1)	L. M. Devine	
G-BZAL	Mainair Blade 912	J. Potts	
G-BZAM	Europa	N. M. Graham	
G-BZAP	Avtech Jabiru UL-450	I. J. Grindley & D. R. Griffiths	
G-BZAR	Denney Kitfox 4-1200 Speedster	N. J. France (G-LEZJ)	
G-BZAS	Isaacs Fury II (K5673)	N. C. Stone	
G-BZBC	Rans S.6-ES Coyote II	A. J. Baldwin	
G-BZBE	Cameron A-210 balloon	Border Ballooning Ltd	
G-BZBF	Cessna 172M	W. G. E. James	
G-BZBH	Thunder Ax6-65 balloon	P. J. Hebdon & A. C. Fraser	
G-BZBJ	Lindstrand LBL-77A balloon	P. T. R. Ollivere	
G-BZBL	Lindstrand LBL-120A balloon	A. G. A. Barclay-Faulkner	
G-BZBO	Stoddard-Hamilton Glasair III	M. B. Hamlett/France	
G-BZBP	Raj Hamsa X'Air 582 (1)	J. L. B. Roy	
G-BZBR	Pegasus Quantum 15-912	S. Rawlings	
G-BZBS	PA-28-161 Warrior III	White Waltham Airfield Ltd	
G-BZBT	Cameron H-34 Hopper balloon	P. Lesser	
G-BZBW	Rotorway Executive 162F	G-BZBW Group	
G-BZBX	Rans S.6-ES Coyote II	P. J. Taylor	
G-BZBZ	Jodel D.9	D. C. Unwin	
G-BZDA	PA-28-161 Warrior III	White Waltham Airfield Ltd	
G-BZDC	Mainair Blade	E. J. Wells & P. J. Smith	
G-BZDD	Mainair Blade 912	B. J. Fallows	
G-BZDE	Lindstrand LBL-210A balloon	Toucan Travel Ltd	
G-BZDF	CFM Streak Shadow SA	P. D. Beckwith	
G-BZDH	PA-28R Cherokee Arrow 200-II	G-BZDH Ltd	
G-BZDK	X'Air 582(2)	J. Bagnall	
G-BZDM	Stoddard-Hamilton Glastar	F. G. Miskelly	
G-BZDN	Cameron N-105 balloon	I. R. Warrington & P. A. Foot	
G-BZDP	SA Bulldog Srs 120/121 (XX551:E)	R. M. Raikes	
G-BZDR	Tri-R Kis	D. F. Sutherland	
G-BZDS	Pegasus Quantum 15-912	M. Tomlinson	
G-BZDT	Maule MXT-7-180	Strongcrew Ltd	
G-BZDV	Westland Gazelle HT.2	D. A. Gregory	
G-BZEA	Cessna A.152	Blueplane Ltd	
G-BZEB	Cessna 152	Blueplane Ltd	
G-BZEC	Cessna 152	Redhill Air Services Ltd	
G-BZED	Pegasus Quantum 15-912	D. Crozier	
G-BZEG	Mainair Blade	R. P. Cookson	
G-BZEJ	Raj Hamsa X'Air 582 (7)	H-Flight X'Air Flying Group	
G-BZEL	Mainair Blade 912	M. Law	
G-BZEN	Avtech Jabiru UL-450	J. R. Hunt	
G-BZEP	SA Bulldog Srs 120/121 (XX561:7)	R. C. Skinner	
G-BZER	Raj Hamsa X'Air 582(2)	N. P. Lloyd & H. Lloyd-Jones	
G-BZES	Rotorway Executive 90	Southern Helicopters Ltd (G-LUFF)	
G-BZEU	Raj Hamsa X'Air 582 (2)	W. J. McCarroll	
G-BZEW	Rans S.6-ES Coyote II	M. J. Wooldridge	
G-BZEY	Cameron N-90 balloon	G. L. Forde	
G-BZEZ	CFM Streak Shadow	G. J. Pearce	
G-BZFB	Robin R.2112A	K. M. Perkins	
G-BZFC	Pegasus Quantum 15-912	G. Addison	
G-BZFD	Cameron N-90 balloon	C. D. & E. Gingell	
G-BZFG	Sky 105 balloon	Virgin Airship & Balloon Co Ltd	
G-BZFH	Pegasus Quantum 15-912	J. C. R. Davies	
G-BZFI	Avtech Jabiru UL	B. S. Lapthorn	
G-BZFK	Team Minimax	I. Pearson	
G-BZFN	SA Bulldog Srs 120/121 (XX667:16)	Risk Logical Ltd	
G-BZFS	Mainair Blade 912	B. V. Davies	
G-BZFT	Murphy Rebel	R. M. Pols	
G-BZGA	DHC.1 Chipmunk 22 (WK585)	Compton Abbas Airfield Ltd	
G-BZGB	DHC.1 Chipmunk 22 (WZ872:E)	G. Briggs	
G-BZGF	Rans S.6-ES Coyote II	C. A. Purvis	
G-BZGH	Cessna F.172N	R. B. J. Tyrrell	
G-BZGJ	Thunder Ax10-180 S2 balloon	Merlin Balloons	
G-BZGL	NA OV-10B Bronco (99+26)	Liberty Aviation Ltd	
G-BZGM	Mainair Blade 912	D. Avery	
G-BZGO	Robinson R44	Flight Academy (Gyrocopters) Ltd	
G-BZGS	Mainair Blade 912	M. W. Holmes	

Notes	Reg	Type	Owner or Operator
	G-BZGT	Avtech Jabiru SPL-450	A. G. Bridger
	G-BZGV	Lindstrand LBL-77A balloon	J. H. Dryden
	G-BZGW	Mainair Blade	M. Liptrot
	G-BZGY	Dyn'Aéro CR.100	B. Appleby
	G-BZGZ	Pegasus Quantum 15-912	D. W. Beech
	G-BZHA	Boeing 767-336ER	British Airways
	G-BZHB	Boeing 767-336ER	British Airways
	G-BZHC	Boeing 767-336ER	British Airways
	G-BZHE	Cessna 152	Andrewsfield Aviation Ltd
	G-BZHF	Cessna 152	Modi Aviation Ltd
	G-BZHG	Tecnam P92 Echo	R. W. F. Boarder
	G-BZHJ	Raj Hamsa X'Air 582 (7)	R. W. Carbutt
	G-BZHL	Noorduyn AT-16 Harvard IIB	R. H. Cooper & S. Swallow
	G-BZHN	Pegasus Quantum 15-912	A. M. Sirant
	G-BZHO	Pegasus Quantum 15	G-BZHO Group
	G-BZHR	Avtech Jabiru UL-450	N. Morrison
	G-BZHT	PA-18A Super Cub 150	C. G. Bell
	G-BZHU	Wag-Aero Sport Trainer	Teddy Boys Flying Group
	G-BZHV	PA-28-181 Archer III	R. M. & T. A. Limb
	G-BZHX	Thunder Ax11-250 S2 balloon	Wizard Balloons Ltd
	G-BZHY	Mainair Blade 912	A. Brier
	G-BZIA	Raj Hamsa X'Air 700 (1)	J. L. Pritchett
	G-BZIC	Lindstrand LBL Sun SS balloon	Life Less Ordinary AB/Sweden
	G-BZID	Montgomerie-Bensen B.8MR	A. Gault
	G-BZIG	Thruster T.600N	K. M. Jones
	G-BZIH	Lindstrand LBL-31A balloon	H. & L. D. Vaughan
	G-BZII	Extra EA.300/1	BZII Ltd
	G-BZIJ	Robin DR.400/500	Rob Airways Ltd
	G-BZIL	Colt 120A balloon	Champagne Flights
	G-BZIM	Pegasus Quantum 15-912	M. J. Stalker
	G-BZIO	PA-28-161 Warrior III	White Waltham Airfield Ltd
	G-BZIP	Montgomerie-Bensen B.8MR	V. G. Freke
	G-BZIS	Raj Hamsa X'Air 582 (2)	J. Boniface
	G-BZIT	Beech 95-B55 Baron	Propellorhead Aviation Ltd
	G-BZIV	Avtech Jabiru UL-450	A. Parr
	G-BZIW	Pegasus Quantum 15-912	J. M. Hodgson
	G-BZIX	Cameron N-90 balloon	M. Stefanini & P. Marmugi/Italy
	G-BZIY	Raj Hamsa X'Air 582 (2)	K. W. Hogg
	G-BZIZ	Ultramagic H-31 balloon	C. J. Davies
	G-BZJC	Thruster T.600N	P. D. Snowdon
	G-BZJD	Thruster T.600T	C. C. Belcher
	G-BZJH	Cameron Z-90 balloon	Egroup SRL/Italy
	G-BZJI	Nova X-Large 37 paraplane	M. Hay
	G-BZJM	VPM M-16 Tandem Trainer	A. Phillips & J. K. Padden
	G-BZJN	Mainair Blade 912	K. Roberts
	G-BZJO	Pegasus Quantum 15	D. Minnock
	G-BZJR	Montgomerie-Bensen B.8MR	G. Golding (G-IPFM)
	G-BZJV	CASA 1-131E Jungmann 1000	R. A. Cumming
	G-BZJW	Cessna 150F	P. Ligertwood
	G-BZJZ	Pegasus Quantum 15	S. Baker
	G-BZKC	Raj Hamsa X'Air 582 (11)	K. P. Puckey
	G-BZKD	Stolp Starduster Too	P. & C. Edmunds
	G-BZKE	Lindstrand LBL-77B balloon	H. Cresswell
	G-BZKF	Rans S.6-ES Coyote II	S. Cartwright & D. G. Stothard
	G-BZKL	PA-28R-201 Arrow III	M. A. & M. H. Cromati
	G-BZKO	Rans S-6-ES Coyote II	B. N. & P. Ringland
	G-BZKU	Cameron Z-105 balloon	N. A. Fishlock
	G-BZKV	Cameron Sky 90-24 balloon	D. P. Busby
	G-BZKW	Ultramagic M-77 balloon	Slowfly Montgolfiere SNC/Italy
	G-BZLC	WSK-PZL Koliber 160A	G. F. Smith
	G-BZLE	Rans S.6-ES Coyote II	G. Spittlehouse
	G-BZLF	CFM Shadow Srs CD	D. W. Stacey
	G-BZLG	Robin HR.200/120B	Flew LLP
	G-BZLH	PA-28-161 Warrior II	Pilot Training and Testing Ltd
	G-BZLK	Slingsby T.31M Motor Tutor	G. Smith
	G-BZLL	Pegasus Quantum 15-912	P. F. Willey
	G-BZLP	Robinson R44	Polar Helicopters Ltd
	G-BZLS	Cameron Sky 77-24 balloon	D. W. Young
	G-BZLU	Lindstrand LBL-90A balloon	A. E. Lusty
	G-BZLV	Avtech Jabiru UL-450	G. Dalton
	G-BZLX	Pegasus Quantum 15-912	M. C. Wright

Reg	Type	Owner or Operator	Notes
G-BZLY	Grob G.109B	G-BZLY Group	
G-BZLZ	Pegasus Quantum 15-912	J. Hill	
G-BZMB	PA-28R-201 Arrow III	Thurrock Arrow Group	
G-BZMC	Avtech Jabiru UL	D. Maddison	
G-BZMD	SA Bulldog Srs 120/121 (XX554)	Mad Dog Flying Group	
G-BZME	SA Bulldog Srs 120/121 (XX698:9)	XX698 Bulldog Group	
G-BZMF	Rutan LongEz	Go-Ez Group	
G-BZMH	SA Bulldog Srs 120/121 (XX692:A)	M. E. J. Hingley	
G-BZMJ	Rans S-6-ES Coyote II	R. J. G. Clark	
G-BZML	SA Bulldog Srs 120/121 (XX693:07)	I. D. Anderson	
G-BZMM	Robin DR.400/180R	Cairngorm Gliding Club	
G-BZMS	Mainair Blade	S. Elmazouri	
G-BZMW	Pegasus Quantum 15-912	Jarvy Enterprises Ltd	
G-BZMY	SPP Yakovlev Yak C-11 (I)	A. M. Holman-West	
G-BZMZ	CFM Streak Shadow	J. F. F. Fouche	
G-BZNC	Pegasus Quantum 15-912	D. E. Wall	
G-BZND	Sopwith Pup Replica (N5199)	M. J. Goddard	
G-BZNE	Beech B300 Super King Air	Skyhopper LLP	
G-BZNF	Colt 120A balloon	M. Torio/Italy	
G-BZNH	Rans S-6-ES Coyote II	K. J. Underwood	
G-BZNI	Bell 206B Jet Ranger II	Heli Consultants Ltd (G-ODIG/G-NEEP)	
G-BZNJ	Rans S-6-ES Coyote II	R. A. McKee	
G-BZNK	Morane Saulnier MS.315-D2 (354)	R. H. Cooper & S. Swallow	
G-BZNM	Pegasus Quantum 15	L. L. Perry	
G-BZNN	Beech 76 Duchess	Flew LLP	
G-BZNP	Thruster T.600N	P. D. Twissell	
G-BZNS	Mainair Blade	T. M. Shaw	
G-BZNT	Aero L-29 Delfin	T. Traaholt	
G-BZNU	Cameron A-300 balloon	Balloon School (International) Ltd	
G-BZNV	Lindstrand LBL-31A balloon	G. R. Down	
G-BZNW	Isaacs Fury II (K2048)	S. M. Johnston	
G-BZNY	Shaw Europa XS	W. J. Harrison	
G-BZOB	Slepcev Storch (6G-ED)	P. J. Clegg	
G-BZOE	Pegasus Quantum 15	B. Dale	
G-BZOF	Montgomerie-Bensen B.8MR gyroplane	S. J. M. Ledingham	
G-BZOI	Nicollier HN.700 Menestrel II	S. J. McCollum	
G-BZOL	Robin R.3000/140	M. A. Stott	
G-BZON	SA Bulldog Srs 120/121 (XX528:D)	D. J. Critchley	
G-BZOO	Pegasus Quantum 15-912	A. J. Maxfield	
G-BZOR	TEAM mini-MAX 91	T. P. V. Sheppard	
G-BZOU	Pegasus Quantum 15-912	M. A. Bradford	
G-BZOV	Pegasus Quantum 15-912	D. Turner	
G-BZOW	Whittaker MW7	G. W. Peacock	
G-BZOX	Cameron Colt 90B balloon	D. J. Head	
G-BZOZ	Van's RV-6	M. & S. Sheppard	
G-BZPA	Mainair Blade 912S	J. McGoldrick	
G-BZPD	Cameron V-65 balloon	P. Spellward	
G-BZPF	Scheibe SF-24B Motorspatz	D. & M. Shrimpton	
G-BZPG	Beech C24R Sierra 200	Peter J. Ward Nurseryman Ltd	
G-BZPH	Van's RV-4	G-BZPH RV-4 Group	
G-BZPI	SOCATA TB20 Trinidad	A. Setterfield	
G-BZPK	Cameron C-80 balloon	D. L. Homer	
G-BZPN	Mainair Blade 912S	G. R. Barker	
G-BZPS	SA Bulldog Srs 120/121 (XX658:07)	A. J. Robinson & M. J. Miller	
G-BZPW	Cameron V-77 balloon	J. Vonka	
G-BZPX	Ultramagic S-105 balloon	Scotair Balloons	
G-BZPY	Ultramagic H-31 balloon	Scotair Balloons	
G-BZPZ	Mainair Blade	R. A. W. Young	
G-BZRF	Percival P.56 Provost T.Mk.1	P. B. Childs	
G-BZRJ	Pegasus Quantum 15-912	D. A. Hutchinson	
G-BZRO	PA-30 Twin Comanche C	Gloucester Comanche Group	
G-BZRP	Pegasus Quantum 15-912	M. F. Sheerman-Chase	
G-BZRR	Pegasus Quantum 15-912	BZRR Syndicate	
G-BZRS	Eurocopter EC 135T2	Babcock Mission Critical Services Onshore Ltd	
G-BZRV	Van's RV-6	N. M. Hitchman	
G-BZRW	Mainair Blade 912S	G. J. E. Alcorn	
G-BZRY	Rans S.6-ES Coyote II	A. G. Smith	
G-BZRZ	Thunder Ax11-250 S2 balloon	A. C. K. Rawson & J. J. Rudoni	
G-BZSB	Pitts S-1S Special	A. D. Ingold	
G-BZSC	Sopwith Camel F.1 (replica) (D1851)	The Shuttleworth Collection	
G-BZSE	Hawker Hunter T.8B (WV322:Y)	Canfield Hunter Ltd	

Notes	Reg	Type	Owner or Operator
	G-BZSG	Pegasus Quantum 15-912	A. J. Harris
	G-BZSH	Ultramagic H-77 balloon	P. M. G. Vale
	G-BZSI	Pegasus Quantum 15	G. M. Dinsdale
	G-BZSM	Pegasus Quantum 15	G. Jenkinson
	G-BZSO	Ultramagic M-77C balloon	C. C. Duppa-Miller
	G-BZSP	Stemme S.10	A. Flewelling & L. Bleaken
	G-BZSS	Pegasus Quantum 15-912	M. Eddy
	G-BZST	Jabiru SPL-450	M. D. Tulloch
	G-BZSX	Pegasus Quantum 15-912	G. Reid
	G-BZSZ	Avtech Jabiru UL-450	T. J. Heaton
	G-BZTA	Robinson R44	Jarretts Motors Ltd
	G-BZTC	TEAM mini-MAX 91	G. G. Clayton
	G-BZTD	Thruster T.600T 450 JAB	J. Bainbridge
	G-BZTH	Shaw Europa	D. J. Shipley
	G-BZTK	Cameron V-90 balloon	E. Appollodorus
	G-BZTM	Mainair Blade	I. Stanulet
	G-BZTN	Europa XS	P. R. Norwood
	G-BZTR	Mainair Blade	A. R. Lynn
	G-BZTS	Cameron 90 Bertie Bassett SS balloon	Trebor Bassett Ltd
	G-BZTU	Mainair Blade 912	C. T. Halliday
	G-BZTV	Mainair Blade 912S	R. D. McManus
	G-BZTW	Hunt Wing Avon 582 (1)	T. S. Walker
	G-BZTX	Mainair Blade 912	K. A. Ingham
	G-BZTY	Avtech Jabiru UL	R. P. Lewis
	G-BZUB	Mainair Blade	J. Campbell
	G-BZUC	Pegasus Quantum 15-912	J. J. D. Firmino do Carmo
	G-BZUD	Lindstrand LBL-105A balloon	D. Venegoni/Italy
	G-BZUE	Pagasus Quantum 15-912	D. T. Richardson
	G-BZUF	Mainair Rapier	B. Craig
	G-BZUG	RL.7A XP Sherwood Ranger	J. G. Boxall
	G-BZUH	Rans S.6-ES Coyote II	R. A. Darley
	G-BZUI	Pegasus Quantum 15-912	A. P. Slade
	G-BZUL	Avtech Jabiru UL	J. G. Campbell
	G-BZUP	Raj Hamsa X'Air Jabiru(3)	M. T. Sheelan
	G-BZUU	Cameron C-90 balloon	D. C. Ball
	G-BZUV	Cameron H-24 balloon	J. N. Race
	G-BZUX	Pegasus Quantum 15	C. Gorvett
	G-BZUY	Van's RV-6	D. J. Butt
	G-BZUZ	Hunt Avon-Blade R.100 (1)	C. F. Janes
	G-BZVA	Zenair CH.701UL	M. W. Taylor
	G-BZVB	Cessna FR.172H	Victor Bravo Group Ltd (G-BLMX)
	G-BZVI	Nova Vertex 24 hang glider	M. Hay
	G-BZVJ	Pegasus Quantum 15	R. Blackhall
	G-BZVK	Raj Hamsa X'Air 582 (2)	R. J. Hamilton
	G-BZVM	Rans S.6-ES Coyote II	D. P. Sudworth
	G-BZVN	Van's RV-6	Syndicate RV6 G-BZVN
	G-BZVR	Raj Hamsa X'Air 582 (4)	R. F. E. Berry
	G-BZVT	I.I.I. Sky Arrow 650T	D. J. Goldsmith
	G-BZVU	Cameron Z-105 balloon	Ballooning Network Ltd
	G-BZVV	Pegasus Quantum 15-912	S. Smith & J. Giladjian
	G-BZVW	Ilyushin IL-2 Stormovik	S. Swallow & R. H. Cooper
	G-BZVX	Ilyushin IL-2 Stormovik	S. Swallow & R. H. Cooper
	G-BZWB	Mainair Blade 912	O. M. Blythin & L. G. Penson
	G-BZWC	Raj Hamsa X'Air Falcon 912 (1)	J. Webb
	G-BZWG	PA-28 Cherokee 140	D. Lea
	G-BZWJ	CFM Streak Shadow	T. A. Morgan
	G-BZWK	Avtech Jabiru SK	M. Housley
	G-BZWM	Pegasus XL-Q	D. T. Evans
	G-BZWN	Van's RV-8	A. J. Symms & R. D. Harper
	G-BZWR	Mainair Rapier	M. A. Steele
	G-BZWS	Pegasus Quantum 15-912	G-BZWS Syndicate
	G-BZWT	Technam P.92-EM Echo	R. F. Cooper
	G-BZWU	Pegasus Quantum 15-912	M. D. Evans
	G-BZWV	Steen Skybolt	D. E. Blaxland
	G-BZWX	Whittaker MW5D Sorcerer	J. Bate
	G-BZWZ	Van's RV-6	Bizzywizzy Group
	G-BZXB	Van's RV-6	R. A. Pritchard & G. W. Cunningham
	G-BZXC	SA Bulldog Srs 120/121 (XX538:A, 03) ★	Carnegie College
	G-BZXI	Nova Philou 26 hang glider	M. Hay
	G-BZXK	Robin HR.200/120B	Flew LLP
	G-BZXM	Mainair Blade 912	S. Dolan

Reg	Type	Owner or Operator	Notes
G-BZXN	Avtech Jabiru UL-450	D. A. Hall & A. G. Sparshott	
G-BZXO	Cameron Z-105 balloon	J. Dyer	
G-BZXP	Kiss 400-582 (1)	A. Fairbrother	
G-BZXR	Cameron N-90 balloon	F. R. Battersby	
G-BZXS	SA Bulldog Srs 120/121 (XX631:W)	K. J. Thompson	
G-BZXT	Mainair Blade 912	D. Squire	
G-BZXV	Pegasus Quantum 15-912	P. I. Oliver	
G-BZXW	VPM M-16 Tandem Trainer	P. J. Troy-Davies (G-NANA)	
G-BZXX	Pegasus Quantum 15-912	D. J. Johnston & D. Ostle	
G-BZXY	Robinson R44	Flight Checks Ltd	
G-BZXZ	SA Bulldog Srs 120/121 (XX629:V)	C. N. Wright	
G-BZYA	Rans S.6-ES Coyote II	M. Lockett & G. Deakin	
G-BZYD	Westland Gazelle AH.1 (XZ329)	Aerocars Ltd	
G-BZYG	Glaser-Dirks DG.500MB	R. C. Bromwich	
G-BZYI	Nova Phocus 123 hang glider	M. Hay	
G-BZYK	Avtech Jabiru UL	M. F. Farrer	
G-BZYN	Pegasus Quantum 15-912	J. Cannon	
G-BZYR	Cameron N-31 balloon	C. J. Sanger-Davies	
G-BZYS	Micro Aviation Bantam B.22-S	D. L. Howell	
G-BZYU	Whittaker MW6 Merlin	B. J. Syson	
G-BZYV	Snowbird Mk.V 582 (1)	Snowbird Community Projects CIC	
G-BZYX	Raj Hamsa X'Air 700 (1A)	A. M. Sutton	
G-BZYY	Cameron N-90 balloon	M. E. Mason	
G-BZZD	Cessna F.172M	R. H. M. Richardson-Bunbury (G-BDPF)	
G-CAHA	PA-34-200T Seneca II	Tayside Aviation Ltd	
G-CALL	PA-23 Aztec 250F	J. D. Moon	
G-CAMM	Hawker Cygnet (replica)	Richard Shuttleworth Trustees	
G-CAMR	BFC Challenger II	P. R. A. Walker	
G-CAPI	Mudry/CAARP CAP-10B	PI Group (G-BEXR)	
G-CAPX	Avions Mudry CAP-10B	H. J. Pessall	
G-CBAD	Mainair Blade 912	J. Stocking	
G-CBAF	Lancair 320	L. H. & M. van Cleeff	
G-CBAK	Robinson R44	Phoenix Building Systems Ltd	
G-CBAL	PA-28-161 Warrior II	CBAL Flying Group	
G-CBAN	SA Bulldog Srs 120/121 (XX668:1)	A. C. S. Reynolds	
G-CBAP	Zenair CH.601ULA	G. D. Summers	
G-CBAR	Stoddard-Hamilton Glastar	Fishburn Flyers	
G-CBAS	Rans S.6-ES Coyote II	S. Stockill	
G-CBAT	Cameron Z-90 balloon	British Telecommunications PLC	
G-CBAU	Rand-Robinson KR-2	C. B. Copsey	
G-CBAV	Raj Hamsa X'Air V.2 (1)	D. W. Stamp & G. J. Lampitt	
G-CBAW	Cameron A-300 balloon	Bailey Balloons Ltd	
G-CBAX	Tecnam P92-EA Echo	L. Collier	
G-CBAZ	Rans S.6-ES Coyote II	E. S. Wills	
G-CBBB	Pegasus Quantum 15-912	F. A. Dimmock	
G-CBBC	SA Bulldog Srs 120/121 (XX515:4)	Bulldog Support Ltd	
G-CBBF	Beech 76 Duchess	Flew LLP	
G-CBBG	Mainair Blade	B. Donnan	
G-CBBH	Raj Hamsa X'Air 582 (11)	D. J. Lewis	
G-CBBK	Robinson R22	R. J. Everett	
G-CBBL	SA Bulldog Srs 120/121 (XX550:Z)	A. Cunningham	
G-CBBM	Savannah VG Jabiru (1)	J. Pavelin	
G-CBBN	Pegasus Quantum 15-912	G-CBBN Flying Group	
G-CBBO	Whittaker MW5D Sorcerer	P. J. Gripton	
G-CBBP	Pegasus Quantum 15-912	A. C. Richards	
G-CBBS	SA Bulldog Srs 120/121 (XX694:E)	D. R. Keene	
G-CBBT	SA Bulldog Srs 120/121 (XX695:3)	K. A. Johnston	
G-CBBW	SA Bulldog Srs 120/121 (XX619:T)	S. E. Robottom-Scott	
G-CBCB	SA Bulldog Srs 120/121 (XX537:C)	M. W. Minary The General Aviation Trading Co Ltd	
G-CBCD	Pegasus Quantum 15	I. A. Lumley	
G-CBCF	Pegasus Quantum 15-912	P. A. Bromley	
G-CBCH	Zenair CH.701UL	I. J. McNally	
G-CBCI	Raj Hamsa X'Air 582 (2)	R. McKie	
G-CBCK	Tipsy T.66 Nipper Srs 3	J. Laszio (G-TEDZ)	
G-CBCL	Stoddard-Hamilton Glastar	D. W. Parfrey	
G-CBCM	Raj Hamsa X'Air 700 (1A)	C. Childs	
G-CBCP	Van's RV-6A	G-CBCP Group	
G-CBCR	SA Bulldog Srs 120/121 (XX702:P)	D. Wells	

Notes	Reg	Type	Owner or Operator
	G-CBCX	Pegasus Quantum 15	The Microlight School (Lichfield) Ltd
	G-CBCY	Beech C24R Sierra Super	J. Waldie
	G-CBCZ	CFM Streak Shadow SLA	J. O'Malley-Kane
	G-CBDC	Thruster T.600N 450-JAB	J. A. Walker
	G-CBDD	Mainair Blade 912	G. Hird
	G-CBDG	Zenair CH.601HD	R. E. Lasnier
	G-CBDH	Flight Design CT2K	S. J. Goate
	G-CBDI	Denney Kitfox Mk.2	J. G. D. Barbour
	G-CBDJ	Flight Design CT2K	P. J. Walker
	G-CBDK	SA Bulldog Srs 120/121 (XX611:7)	J. N. Randle
	G-CBDL	Mainair Blade	T. R. Villa
	G-CBDM	Tecnam P92-EM Echo	J. J. Cozens
	G-CBDN	Mainair Blade	T. Peckham
	G-CBDP	Mainair Blade 912	S. T. Hayes
	G-CBDU	Quad City Challenger II	E. J. Brooks
	G-CBDV	Raj Hamsa X'Air 582	U. J. Anderson
	G-CBDX	Pegasus Quantum 15	P. Sinkler
	G-CBDZ	Pegasus Quantum 15-912	P. Smith
	G-CBEB	Kiss 400-582 (1)	M. Harris
	G-CBEE	PA-28R Cherokee Arrow 200	IHC Ltd
	G-CBEF	SA Bulldog Srs 120/121 (XX621:H)	A. L. Butcher & F. W. Sandwell
	G-CBEH	SA Bulldog Srs 120/121 (XX521:H)	J. E. Lewis
	G-CBEI	PA-22 Colt 108	D. Sharp
	G-CBEJ	Colt 120A balloon	Airxcite Ltd
	G-CBEK	SA Bulldog Srs 120/121 (XX700:17)	T. Wakeman & B. C. Faulkner
	G-CBEL	Hawker Fury F.Mk.11 (SR661)	Anglia Aircraft Restorations Ltd
	G-CBEM	Mainair Blade	K. W. Bodley
	G-CBEN	Pegasus Quantum 15-912	A. T. Cook
	G-CBES	Shaw Europa XS	D. J. Shipley
	G-CBEU	Pegasus Quantum 15-912	Fula Ltd
	G-CBEV	Pegasus Quantum 15-912	P. C. Smith
	G-CBEW	Flight Design CT2K	Cruise Flight Group
	G-CBEX	Flight Design CT2K	A. G. Quinn
	G-CBEY	Cameron C-80 balloon	M. N. Hume
	G-CBEZ	Robin DR.400/180	K. V. Field
	G-CBFA	Diamond DA40 Star	Lyrastar Ltd
	G-CBFE	Raj Hamsa X'Air V.2 (1)	A. R. Rainford
	G-CBFJ	Robinson R44	F. Klinge
	G-CBFK	Murphy Rebel	P. J. Gibbs
	G-CBFM	SOCATA TB21 Trinidad	Exec Flight Ltd
	G-CBFN	Robin DR.100/200B	Foxtrot November Group
	G-CBFO	Cessna 172S	P. Warren-Gray
	G-CBFP	SA Bulldog Srs 120/121 (XX636:Y)	R. Nisbet
	G-CBFU	SA Bulldog Srs 120/121 (XX628:9)	J. R. & S. J. Huggins
	G-CBFW	Bensen B.8	A. J. Thomas
	G-CBFX	Rans S.6-ES Coyote II	O. C. Rash
	G-CBGB	Zenair CH.601UL	J. F. Woodham
	G-CBGC	SOCATA TB10 Tobago	P. J. Wills
	G-CBGD	Zenair CH.701UL	I. S. Walsh
	G-CBGE	Tecnam P92-EM Echo	J. P. Spiteri
	G-CBGG	Pegasus Quantum 15	T. E. Davies
	G-CBGH	Teverson Bisport	Phoenix Flyers
	G-CBGJ	Aeroprakt A.22 Foxbat	E. Smyth & T. G. Fitzpatrick
	G-CBGL	MH.1521M Broussard	K. M. Perkins
	G-CBGO	Murphy Maverick 430	K. J. Miles & R. Withall
	G-CBGP	Ikarus C.42 FB UK	C. F. Welby
	G-CBGR	Avtech Jabiru UL-450	M. D. Brown
	G-CBGU	Thruster T.600N 450-JAB	B. R. Cardosi
	G-CBGV	Thruster T.600N 450	West Flight Aviators
	G-CBGW	Thruster T.600N 450-JAB	A. R. Pluck
	G-CBGX	SA Bulldog Srs 120/121 (XX622:B)	Bulldog GX Group
	G-CBGZ	Westland Gazelle HT.2 (ZB646:59/CU)	D. Weatherhead Ltd
	G-CBHA	SOCATA TB10 Tobago	Oscar Romeo Aviation Ltd
	G-CBHC	RAF 2000 GTX-SE gyroplane	R. Barton
	G-CBHG	Mainair Blade 912S	C. R. Buckle
	G-CBHI	Shaw Europa XS	Alpha Syndicate
	G-CBHJ	Mainair Blade 912	A. W. Leadley
	G-CBHK	Pegasus Quantum 15 (HKS)	I. R. Price
	G-CBHM	Mainair Blade 912	S. A. Mercer
	G-CBHN	Pegasus Quantum 15-912	A. N. Bellis
	G-CBHO	Gloster Gladiator II (N5719)	Retro Track & Air (UK) Ltd

Reg	Type	Owner or Operator	Notes
G-CBHP	Corby CJ-1 Starlet	K. M. Hodson	
G-CBHR	Lazer Z200	The G-CBHR Group	
G-CBHU	RL.5A Sherwood Ranger	D. J. Seymour	
G-CBHW	Cameron Z-105 balloon	Bristol Chamber of Commerce, Industry & Shipping	
G-CBHX	Cameron V-77 balloon	A. Hook	
G-CBHY	Pegasus Quantum 15-912	D. W. Allen	
G-CBHZ	RAF 2000 GTX-SE gyroplane	M. P. Donnelly	
G-CBIB	Flight Design CT2K	T. R. Villa	
G-CBIC	Raj Hamsa X'Air V2 (2)	J. T. Blackburn & D. R. Sutton	
G-CBID	SA Bulldog Srs 120/121(XX549:6)	The Red Dog Group	
G-CBIE	Flight Design CT2K	H. D. Colliver	
G-CBIF	Avtech Jabiru SPL-450	A. G. Sindrey	
G-CBII	Raj Hamsa X'Air 582(8)	S. G. Young	
G-CBIJ	Ikarus C.42 FB UK Cyclone	J. A. Smith	
G-CBIL	Cessna 182K	E. Bannister (G-BFZZ)	
G-CBIM	Lindstrand LBL-90A balloon	R. K. Parsons	
G-CBIN	TEAM mini-MAX 91	A. R. Mikolaczyk	
G-CBIP	Thruster T.600N 450-JAB	D. R. Seabrook	
G-CBIR	Thruster T.600N 450-JAB	S. Langtry	
G-CBIS	Raj Hamsa X'Air 582 (2)	P. T. W. T. Derges	
G-CBIT	RAF 2000 GTX-SE gyroplane	Terrafirma Services Ltd	
G-CBIV	Skyranger 912 (1)	J. N. Whelan	
G-CBIX	Zenair CH.601UL	R. A. & B. M. Roberts	
G-CBIY	Aerotechnik EV-97 Eurostar	S. J. Smith	
G-CBIZ	Pegasus Quantum 15-912	B. Cook	
G-CBJD	Stoddard-Hamilton Glastar	K. F. Farey	
G-CBJE	RAF 2000 GTX-SE gyroplane	V. G. Freke	
G-CBJG	DHC.1 Chipmunk 20 (1373)	C. J. Rees	
G-CBJH	Aeroprakt A.22 Foxbat	H. Smith	
G-CBJL	Kiss 400-582 (1)	R. E. Morris	
G-CBJM	Avtech Jabiru SP-470	G. R. T. Elliott	
G-BCJN	RAF 2000 GTX-SE	G. W. Duffill	
G-CBJO	Pegasus Quantum 15-912	A. E. Kemp	
G-CBJP	Zenair CH.601UL	R. E. Peirse	
G-CBJR	Aerotechnik EV-97A Eurostar	Madley Flying Group	
G-CBJS	Cameron C-60 balloon	N. Ivison	
G-CBJT	Mainair Blade	M. A. Hartill	
G-CBJV	Rotorway Executive 162F	P. W. Vaughan	
G-CBJW	Ikarus C.42 Cyclone FB UK	E. Foster & J. H. Peet	
G-CBJX	Raj Hamsa X'Air Falcon J22	R. D. Bateman	
G-CBJY	Jabiru UL-450	M. A. Gould	
G-CBJZ	Westland Gazelle HT.3	K. G. Theurer/Germany	
G-CBKA	Westland Gazelle HT.3 (XZ937:Y)	J. Windmill	
G-CBKB	Bücker Bü 181C Bestmann	W. R. & G. D. Snadden	
G-CBKD	Westland Gazelle HT.2	Flying Scout Ltd	
G-CBKF	Easy Raider J2.2 (1)	D. A. Karniewicz	
G-CBKG	Thruster T.600N 450 JAB	M. C. Henry	
G-CBKK	Ultramagic S-130 balloon	Hayrick Ltd	
G-CBKL	Raj Hamsa X'Air Jabiru(2)	G. Baxter & G. Ferries	
G-CBKM	Mainair Blade 912	T. E. Robinson	
G-CBKN	Mainair Blade 912	D. S. Clews	
G-CBKO	Mainair Blade 912S	S. J. Taft	
G-CBKR	PA-28-161 Warrior III	Yeovil Auto Tuning	
G-CBKU	Ikarus C.42 Cyclone FB UK	C. Blackburn	
G-CBKW	Pegasus Quantum 15-912	A. Sharma	
G-CBKY	Avtech Jabiru SP-470	I. A.Lavey	
G-CBLA	Aero Designs Pulsar XP	J. P. Kynaston	
G-CBLB	Technam P.92-EM Echo	R. Lewis-Evans	
G-CBLD	Mainair Blade 912S	N. E. King	
G-CBLE	Robin R.2120U	Flew LLP	
G-CBLF	Raj Hamsa X'Air 582 (11)	B. J. Harper & P. J. Soukup	
G-CBLK	Hawker Hind	Aero Vintage Ltd	
G-CBLL	Pegasus Quantum 15-912	P. D. Alford	
G-CBLM	Mainair Blade 912	A. S. Saunders	
G-CBLN	Cameron Z-31 balloon	J. R. Lawson	
G-CBLO	Lindstrand LBL-42A balloon	D. G. Such	
G-CBLP	Raj Hamsa X'Air Falcon	A. C. Parsons	
G-CBLS	Fiat CR.42	Fighter Collection Ltd	
G-CBLT	Mainair Blade 912	C. R. Brown	
G-CBLW	Raj Hamsa X'Air Falcon 582(3)	R. G. Halliwell	

Notes	Reg	Type	Owner or Operator
	G-CBLY	Grob G.109B	G-CBLY Syndicate
	G-CBLZ	Rutan LongEz	S. K. Cockburn
	G-CBMB	Cyclone Ax2000	T. H. Chadwick
	G-CBMC	Cameron Z-105 balloon	B. R. Whatley
	G-CBMD	IDA Bacau Yakovlev Yak-52 (10 yellow)	Nova Trust Agency SRL
	G-CBME	Cessna F.172M	Skytrax Aviation Ltd
	G-CBMI	Yakovlev Yak-52	I. D. Jones
	G-CBMK	Cameron Z-120 balloon	G. Davies
	G-CBML	DHC.6 Twin Otter 310	Isles of Scilly Skybus Ltd
	G-CBMM	Mainair Blade 912	W. L. Millar
	G-CBMO	PA-28 Cherokee 180	T. Rawlings
	G-CBMP	Cessna R.182	Orman (Carrolls Farm) Ltd
	G-CBMR	Medway Eclipser	D. S. Blofeld
	G-CBMT	Robin DR.400/180	A. C. Williamson
	G-CBMU	Whittaker MW6-S Fat Boy Flyer	A. M. Witt
	G-CBMV	Pegasus Quantum 15	I. Davis
	G-CBMZ	Aerotechnik EV-97 Eurostar	J. C. O'Donnell
	G-CBNC	Mainair Blade 912	K. L. Smith
	G-CBNF	Rans S.7 Courier	I. M. Ross
	G-CBNG	Robin R.2112	E. W. Russell & R. K. Galbally
	G-CBNI	Lindstrand LBL-180A balloon	K. W. Scott
	G-CBNJ	Raj Hamsa X'Air 582 (11)	D. Squire
	G-CBNL	Dyn'Aéro MCR-01 Club	D. H. Wilson
	G-CBNO	CFM Streak Shadow	P. J. Porter
	G-CBNT	Pegasus Quantum 15-912	R. Davies
	G-CBNV	Rans S.6-ES Coyote II	M. J. A. New & A. Clift
	G-CBNW	Cameron N-105 balloon	Bailey Balloons
	G-CBNX	Mongomerie-Bensen B.8MR	A. C. S. M. Hart
	G-CBNZ	TEAM hi-MAX 1700R	A. P. S. John
	G-CBOC	Raj Hamsa X'Air 582 (5)	A. J. McAleer
	G-CBOE	Hawker Hurricane IIB (AG244)	K. F. Grimminger
	G-CBOF	Shaw Europa XS	I. W. Ligertwood
	G-CBOG	Mainair Blade 912S	OG Group
	G-CBOM	Mainair Blade 912	G. Suckling
	G-CBOO	Mainair Blade 912S	H. Moore
	G-CBOP	Avtech Jabiru UL-450	E. Bentley
	G-CBOR	Cessna F.172N	R. P. Rochester
	G-CBOS	Rans S.6-ES Coyote II	J. T. Athulathmudali
	G-CBOV	Mainair Blade 912	M. A. Pantling
	G-CBOW	Cameron Z-120 balloon	Ballooning Network Ltd
	G-CBOY	Pegasus Quantum 15-912	G. K. Smith
	G-CBOZ	IDA Bacau Yakovlev Yak-52	M. J. Babbage
	G-CBPD	Ikarus C.42 Cyclone FB UK	Waxwing Group
	G-CBPE	SOCATA TB10 Tobago	A. F. Welch
	G-CBPI	PA-28R-201 Arrow III	M. L. Roland
	G-CBPM	Yakovlev Yak-50 (50 black)	P. W. Ansell
	G-CBPR	Avtech Jabiru UL-450	N. R. Andrew
	G-CBPU	Raj Hamsa X'Air R100(3)	R. Power
	G-CBPV	Zenair CH.601UL	C. J. Meadows
	G-CBPW	Lindstrand LBL-105A balloon	P. Donkin
	G-CBRB	Ultramagic S-105 balloon	I. S. Bridge
	G-CBRC	Jodel D.18	P. J.Gripton
	G-CBRD	Jodel D.18	J. D. Haslam
	G-CBRE	Mainair Blade 912	L. M. Marsh
	G-CBRJ	Mainair Blade 912S	R. W. Janion
	G-CBRK	Ultramagic M-77 balloon	R. Gower
	G-CBRM	Mainair Blade	M. H. Levy
	G-CBRR	Aerotechnik EV-97A Eurostar	T. O. Powley & M. S. Turner
	G-CBRT	Murphy Elite	T. W. Baylie
	G-CBRV	Cameron C-90 balloon	C. J. Teall
	G-CBRW	Aerostar Yakovlev Yak-52 (50 grey)	Max-Alpha Aviation GmbH/Germany
	G-CBRX	Zenair CH.601UL Zodiac	C. J. Meadows
	G-CBRZ	Kiss 400-582(1)	J. J. Ryan/Ireland
	G-CBSF	Westland Gazelle HT.2	Falcon Aviation Ltd
	G-CBSI	Westland Gazelle HT.3 (XZ934:U)	P. S. Unwin
	G-CBSK	Westland Gazelle HT.3 (ZB627:A)	Falcon Flying Group
	G-CBSL	IDA Bacau Yakovlev Yak-52 (67 red)	E. Martin
	G-CBSO	PA-28-181 Archer II	Archer One Ltd
	G-CBSS	IDA Bacau Yakovlev Yak-52	E. J. F. Verhellen/Belgium
	G-CBSU	Avtech Jabiru UL	K. R. Crawley
	G-CBSV	Montgomerie-Bensen B.8MR	J. A. McGill

Reg	Type	Owner or Operator	Notes
G-CBSZ	Mainair Blade 912S	P. J. Nolan	
G-CBTB	I.I.I. Sky Arrow 650TS	S. Woolmington	
G-CBTD	Pegasus Quantum 15-912	D. Baillie	
G-CBTE	Mainair Blade 912S	K. R. Hine	
G-CBTK	Raj Hamsa X'Air 582 (5)	M. T. Slater	
G-CBTM	Mainair Blade	K. G. Osborne	
G-CBTN	PA-31 Navajo C	Durban Aviation Services Ltd	
G-CBTO	Rans S.6-ES Coyote II	D. Wakefield	
G-CBTR	Lindstrand LBL-120A balloon	R. H. Etherington	
G-CBTS	Gloster Gamecock (replica)	Retro Track & Air (UK) Ltd	
G-CBTT	PA-28-181 Archer II	Cedar Aviation Ltd (G-BFMM)	
G-CBTW	Mainair Blade 912	J. R. Davis	
G-CBTX	Denney Kitfox Mk.2	G. I. Doake	
G-CBUA	Extra EA.230	R. F.Pooler	
G-CBUC	Raj Hamsa X'Air 582 (5)	R. S. Noremberg & P. B. J. Eveleigh	
G-CBUD	Pegasus Quantum 15-912	G. N. S. Farrant	
G-CBUF	Flight Design CT2K	N. A. Thomas	
G-CBUG	Technam P.92-EM Echo	D. R. Garside	
G-CBUI	Westland Wasp HAS.1 (XT420:606)	C. J. Marsden	
G-CBUJ	Raj Hamsa X'Air 582 (10)	R. G. Herrod	
G-CBUK	Van's RV-6A	P. G. Greenslade	
G-CBUN	Barker Charade	D. R. Wilkinson & T. Coldwell	
G-CBUO	Cameron O-90 balloon	W. J. Treacy & P. M. Smith	
G-CBUP	VPM M-16 Tandem Trainer	J. S. Firth	
G-CBUS	Pegasus Quantum 15	J. Liddiard	
G-CBUU	Pegasus Quantum 15-912	N. A. Hobson	
G-CBUW	Cameron Z-133 balloon	Balloon School (International) Ltd	
G-CBUX	Cyclone AX2000	A. J. Sharratt	
G-CBUY	Rans S.6-ES Coyote II	S. T. Cadywould	
G-CBUZ	Pegasus Quantum 15	D. G. Seymour	
G-CBVA	Thruster T.600N 450	J. H. Brady	
G-CBVB	Robin R.2120U	Flew LLP	
G-CBVC	Raj Hamsa X'Air 582 (5)	J. Rivera	
G-CBVD	Cameron C-60 balloon	Phoenix Balloons Ltd	
G-CBVE	Raj Hamsa X'Air Falcon 912(1)	T. A. England	
G-CBVF	Murphy Maverick	H. A. Leek	
G-CBVG	Mainair Blade 912S	J. S. M. Collado	
G-CBVH	Lindstrand LBL-120A balloon	Alba Ballooning Ltd	
G-CBVM	Aerotechnik EV-97 Eurostar	M. Sharpe	
G-CBVN	Pegasus Quik	RIKI Group	
G-CBVR	Best Off Skyranger 912 (2)	S. H. Lunney	
G-CBVS	Best Off Skyranger 912 (1)	S. C. Cornock	
G-CBVU	PA-28R Cherokee Arrow 200-II	S. Crowley	
G-CBVV	Cameron N-120 balloon	John Aimo Balloons SAS/Italy	
G-CBVX	Cessna 182P	P. & A. de Weerdt	
G-CBVY	Ikarus C.42 Cyclone FB UK	Grandpa's Flying Group	
G-CBVZ	Flight Design CT2K	O. W. Achurch	
G-CBWA	Flight Design CT2K	J. Paterson	
G-CBWD	PA-28-161 Warrior III	J. Wright	
G-CBWE	Aerotechnik EV-97 Eurostar	J. & C. W. Hood	
G-CBWG	Aerotechnik EV-97 Eurostar	C. Long & M. P. & T. Middleton	
G-CBWI	Thruster T. 600N 450	M. Afzal	
G-CBWJ	Thruster T. 600N 450	J. K. Clayton & K. D. Smith	
G-CBWK	Ultramagic H-77 balloon	S. J. Stevens	
G-CBWN	Campbell Cricket Mk.6	A. G. W. Davis	
G-CBWO	Rotorway Executive 162F	S. Abbott	
G-CBWP	Shaw Europa	T. W. Greaves	
G-CBWS	Whittaker MW6 Merlin	K. R. Emery	
G-CBWV	Falconar F-12A Cruiser	A. Ackland	
G-CBWW	Skyranger 912 (2)	A. Gilruth	
G-CBWY	Raj Hamsa X'Air 582 (6)	J. C. Rose	
G-CBWZ	Robinson R22 Beta	J. Fleming	
G-CBXB	Lindstrand LBL-150A balloon	M. A. Webb	
G-CBXC	Ikarus C.42 Cyclone FB UK	J. A. Robinson	
G-CBXE	Easy Raider J2.2 (3)	A. K. Day	
G-CBXF	Easy Raider J2.2 (2)	M. R. Grunwell	
G-CBXG	Thruster T.600N 450	Newtownards Microlight Group	
G-CBXJ	Cessna 172S	Steptoe & Son Properties Ltd	
G-CBXK	Robinson R22 Mariner	Whizzard Helicopters	
G-CBXM	Mainair Blade	B. A. Coombe	
G-CBXN	Robinson R22 Beta II	N. M. G. Pearson	

Notes	Reg	Type	Owner or Operator
	G-CBXR	Raj Hamsa X-Air Falcon 582 (1)	J. F. Heath
	G-CBXS	Skyranger 912 (2)	The Ince Skyranger Group
	G-CBXU	TEAM miniMAX 91A	D. Crowhurst
	G-CBXW	Shaw Europa XS	R. G. Fairall
	G-CBXZ	Rans S.6-ES Coyote II	A. Faehndrich
	G-CBYB	Rotorway Executive 162F	Clark Contracting
	G-CBYD	Rans S.6-ES Coyote II	R. Burland
	G-CBYF	Mainair Blade	J. Ayre
	G-CBYH	Aeroprakt A.22 Foxbat	G. C. Moore
	G-CBYI	Pegasus Quantum 15-503	The G-BCYI Group
	G-CBYM	Mainair Blade	D. Reid
	G-CBYN	Shaw Europa XS	G. M. Tagg
	G-CBYO	Pegasus Quik	G-CBYO Syndicate
	G-CBYP	Whittaker MW6-S Fat Boy Flyer	W. G. Reynolds
	G-CBYS	Lindstrand LBL-21 balloon France	B. M. Reed/France
	G-CBYT	Thruster T.600N 450	P. McAteer
	G-CBYU	PA-28-161 Warrior II	Stapleford Flying Club Ltd
	G-CBYV	Pegasus Quantum 15-912	G-CBYV Syndicate
	G-CBYW	Hatz CB-1	T. A. Hinton
	G-CBYZ	Tecnam P92-EM Echo-Super	B. Weaver
	G-CBZA	Mainair Blade	M. Lowe
	G-CBZD	Mainair Blade	G. P. J. Davies
	G-CBZE	Robinson R44	Alps (Scotland) Ltd
	G-CBZG	Rans S.6-ES Coyote II	S.G. Young
	G-CBZH	Pegasus Quik	M. P. Chew
	G-CBZJ	Lindstrand LBL-25A balloon	Pegasus Ballooning
	G-CBZK	Robin DR.400/180	A. C. Fletcher
	G-CBZL	Westland Gazelle HT.3	Armstrong Aviation Ltd
	G-CBZM	Avtech Jabiru SPL-450	M. E. Ledward
	G-CBZN	Rans S.6-ES Coyote II	K. Stevens
	G-CBZP	Hawker Fury 1 (K5674)	Historic Aircraft Collection
	G-CBZR	PA-28R-201 Arrow III	Folada Aero & Technical Services Ltd
	G-CBZS	Aurora	J. Lynden
	G-CBZT	Pegasus Quik	S. M. Smith
	G-CBZW	Zenair CH.701 STOL	S. Richens
	G-CBZX	Dyn' Aero MCR-01 ULC	A. C. N. Freeman & M. P. Wilson
	G-CBZZ	Cameron Z-275 balloon	A. C. K. Rawson & J. J. Rudoni
	G-CCAB	Mainair Blade	A. J. Morris
	G-CCAC	Aerotech EV-97 Eurostar	D. C. Lugg
	G-CCAD	Mainair Pegasus Quik	M. Richardson
	G-CCAE	Avtech Jabiru UL-450	D. Logan
	G-CCAF	Best Off Skyranger 912 (1)	M. Scott
	G-CCAG	Mainair Blade 912	A. Robinson
	G-CCAK	Zenair CN.601HD	G and J E Trading Ltd
	G-CCAL	Technam P.92-EA Echo	G. Hawkins
	G-CCAP	Robinson R22 Beta II	D. Baker, M. Healer & H. Price
	G-CCAR	Cameron N-77 balloon	D. P. Turner
	G-CCAS	Pegasus Quik	Caunton Alpha Syndicate
	G-CCAT	AA-5A Cheetah	Rate 1 Aero Ltd (G-OAJH/G-KILT/G-BJFA)
	G-CCAV	PA-28-181 Archer II	Archer II Ltd
	G-CCAW	Mainair Blade 912	I. G. Molesworth
	G-CCAY	Cameron Z-42 balloon	P. Stern
	G-CCAZ	Mainair Pegasus Quik	J. P. Floyd
	G-CCBA	Skyranger R.100	Fourstrokes Group
	G-CCBB	Cameron N-90 balloon	S. C. A. & L. D. Craze
	G-CCBC	Thruster T.600N 450	M. K. Boydle
	G-CCBF	Maule M.5-235C	E. van Veenen (G-NHVH)
	G-CCBG	Skyranger Swift 912(1)	K. Wileman
	G-CCBH	PA-28 Cherokee 236	J. R. Hunt & M. Kenny
	G-CCBI	Raj Hamsa X'Air 582(11)	N. Byrne
	G-CCBJ	Skyranger 912 (2)	J. d'Rozario
	G-CCBK	Aerotechnik EV-97 Eurostar	B. S. Waycott
	G-CCBM	Aerotechnik EV-97 Eurostar	P. W. Nestor & B. Hunter
	G-CCBN	Scale Replica SE-5a (80105/19)	A. Schweisthal
	G-CCBR	Jodel D.120	A. Dunne & M. Munnelly
	G-CCBT	Cameron Z-90 balloon	I. J. Sharpe
	G-CCBW	Sherwood Ranger	A. L. Virgoe
	G-CCBX	Raj Hamsa X'Air 133 (2)	S. Hunt
	G-CCBY	Avtech Jabiru UL-450	D. M. Goodman
	G-CCBZ	Aero Designs Pulsar	J. M. Keane

Reg	Type	Owner or Operator	Notes
G-CCCA	VS.509 Spitfire Tr.IX (PV202)	Historic Flying Ltd (G-TRIX)	
G-CCCB	Thruster T.600N 450	J. Hartland	
G-CCCD	Mainair Pegasus Quantum 15	R. N. Gamble	
G-CCCE	Aeroprakt A.22 Foxbat	P. Sykes	
G-CCCF	Thruster T.600N 450	P. R. Norman	
G-CCCG	Mainair Pegasus Quik	J. W. Sandars	
G-CCCH	Thruster T.600N 450	G. Scullion	
G-CCCJ	Nicollier HN.700 Menestrel II	G. A. Rodmell	
G-CCCK	Skyranger 912 (2)	P. R. Butler	
G-CCCM	Skyranger 912 (2)	Connel Gliding Group	
G-CCCO	Aerotechnik EV-97A Eurostar	D. R. G. Whitelaw	
G-CCCR	Sky Ranger 912(2)	D. C. Nixon	
G-CCCU	Thruster T.600N 450	A. F. Cashin	
G-CCCV	Raj Hamsa X'Air Falcon 133 (1)	G. J. Boyer	
G-CCCW	Pereira Osprey 2	D. J. Southward	
G-CCCY	Skyranger 912 (2)	A. Watson	
G-CCDB	Mainair Pegasus Quik	P. K. Dale	
G-CCDC	Rans S-6-ES Coyote II	J. A. Matthews	
G-CCDD	Mainair Pegasus Quik	G. Clark	
G-CCDF	Mainair Pegasus Quik	R. P. McGann	
G-CCDG	Skyranger 912 (1)	Freebird Group	
G-CCDH	Skyranger 912 (2)	C. F. Rogers	
G-CCDJ	Raj Hamsa X'Air Falcon 582 (2)	A. L. Lyons	
G-CCDK	Pegasus Quantum 15-912	D. Bishop	
G-CCDL	Raj Hamsa X'Air Falcon 582 (2)	C. Surman	
G-CCDM	Mainair Blade	A. R. Smith	
G-CCDO	Mainair Pegasus Quik	S. T. Welsh	
G-CCDP	Raj Hamsa X'Air R.100 (3)	B. Moore & M. V. Daly	
G-CCDS	Nicollier HN.700 Menestrel II	B. W. Gowland	
G-CCDU	Tecnam P92-EM Echo	G. P. & P. T. Willcox	
G-CCDV	Thruster T.600N 450	G. C. Hobson	
G-CCDX	Aerotechnik EV-97 Eurostar	G-CCDX Syndicate 2013	
G-CCDY	Skyranger 912 (2)	I. Brumpton	
G-CCDZ	Pegasus Quantum 15-912	R. D. Leigh	
G-CCEA	Mainair Pegasus Quik	G. D. Ritchie	
G-CCEB	Thruster T600N 450	C. P. Whitwell	
G-CCED	Zenair CH.601UL	R. P. Reynolds	
G-CCEF	Shaw Europa	C. P. Garner	
G-CCEH	Skyranger 912 (2)	ZC Owners	
G-CCEJ	Aerotechnik EV-97 Eurostar	J. R. Iveson	
G-CCEK	Kiss 400-582 (1)	J. L. Stone	
G-CCEL	Avtech Jabiru UL	F. McMullan	
G-CCEM	Aerotechnik EV-97 Eurostar	Oxenhope Flying Group	
G-CCEN	Cameron Z-120 balloon	R. Hunt	
G-CCES	Raj Hamsa X'Air 3203(1)	G. V. McCloskey	
G-CCET	Nova Vertex 28 hang glider	M. Hay	
G-CCEU	RAF 2000 GTX-SE gyroplane	N. G. Dovaston	
G-CCEW	Mainair Pegasus Quik	A. B. Mackinnon	
G-CCEY	Raj Hamsa X'582 (11)	I. G. Poutney	
G-CCEZ	Easy Raider J2.2	P. J Clegg	
G-CCFC	Robinson R44 II	Hawker Aviation Ltd	
G-CCFD	BFC Challenger II	W. Oswald	
G-CCFE	Tipsy Nipper T.66 Srs 2	N. S. Dell	
G-CCFG	Dyn'Aéro MCR-01 Club	P. H. Milward	
G-CCFI	PA-32 Cherokee Six 260	P. McManus & N. Whelan	
G-CCFJ	Kolb Twinstar Mk.3	S. Buckland	
G-CCFK	Shaw Europa	C. R. Knapton	
G-CCFL	Mainair Pegasus Quik	T. E. Thomas	
G-CCFO	Pitts S-1S Special	R. J. Anderson	
G-CCFS	Diamond DA40D Star	R. H. Butterfield	
G-CCFT	Mainair Pegasus Quantum 15-912	D. P. Gawlowski	
G-CCFU	Diamond DA40D Star	Jetstream Aviation Training & Services SA/Greece	
G-CCFV	Lindstrand LBL-77A balloon	Lindstrand Media Ltd	
G-CCFW	WAR Focke-Wulf Fw.190	D. B. Conway	
G-CCFX	EAA Acrosport 2	G. Cameron	
G-CCFY	Rotorway Executive 162F	A. & A. Thomas	
G-CCFZ	Ikarus C.42 FB UK	B. W. Drake	
G-CCGA	Medway EclipseR	G. Cousins	
G-CCGB	TEAM mini-MAX	A. D, Pentland	
G-CCGC	Mainair Pegasus Quik	C. A. McLean & D. T. McAfee	

Notes	Reg	Type	Owner or Operator
	G-CCGF	Robinson R22 Beta	Glenntrade Ltd
	G-CCGG	Jabiru Aircraft Jabiru J400	A. Simmers
	G-CCGH	Supermarine Aircraft Spitfire Mk.26 (AB196)	Cokebusters Ltd
	G-CCGK	Mainair Blade	C. M. Babiy & M. Hurn
	G-CCGM	Kiss 450-582 (1)	J. Howarth
	G-CCGO	Medway Raven X	D. A. Coupland
	G-CCGS	Dornier 328-100	Loganair Ltd
	G-CCGU	Van's RV-9A	B. J. Main & ptnrs
	G-CCGW	Shaw Europa	D. Buckley
	G-CCGY	Cameron Z-105 balloon	Cameron Balloons Ltd
	G-CCHH	Pegasus Quik	Pegasus XL Group
	G-CCHI	Mainair Pegasus Quik	M. R. Starling
	G-CCHL	PA-28-181 Archer iii	Archer Three Ltd
	G-CCHM	Kiss 450-582(1)	M. J. Jessup
	G-CCHN	Corby CJ.1 Starlet	G. Evans
	G-CCHO	Mainair Pegasus Quik	M. Allan
	G-CCHP	Cameron Z-31 balloon	M. H. Redman
	G-CCHR	Easy Raider 583 (1)	S. Wilkes
	G-CCHS	Raj Hamsa X'Air 582	N. H. Gokul
	G-CCHV	Mainair Rapier	B. J. Wesley
	G-CCHX	Scheibe SF.25C Falke	Lasham Gliding Society Ltd
	G-CCID	Jabiru Aircraft Jabiru J430	B. J. Robe & F. Patterson
	G-CCIF	Mainair Blade	A. R. Vincent & P. W. Dunn
	G-CCIH	Mainair Pegasus Quantum 15	J. Hill
	G-CCII	ICP Savannah Jabiru (3)	D. Chaloner
	G-CCIJ	PA-28R Cherokee Arrow 180	S. A. Hughes
	G-CCIK	Skyranger 912 (2)	M. D. Kirby
	G-CCIR	Van's RV-8	N. W. Charles
	G-CCIS	Scheibe SF.28A Tandem Falke	Cornwall Aviation Heritage Centre Ltd
	G-CCIT	Zenair CH.701UL	J. A. R. Hughes
	G-CCIU	Cameron N-105 balloon	W. W. Leitlein
	G-CCIV	Mainair Pegasus Quik	G. H. Ousby
	G-CCIW	Raj Hamsa X'Air 582 (2)	A. Evans
	G-CCIY	Skyranger 912 (2)	L. F. Tanner
	G-CCIZ	PZL-110 Koliber 160A	J. P. Nugent
	G-CCJA	Skyranger 912 (2)	G. R. Barker
	G-CCJB	Zenair CH.701 STOL	M. A. Franklin
	G-CCJD	Pegasus Quantum 15	P. Clark
	G-CCJH	Lindstrand LBL-90A balloon	J. R. Hoare
	G-CCJI	Van's RV-6	A. Jenkins
	G-CCJJ	Medway Pirana	J. K. Sargent
	G-CCJK	Aerostar Yakovlev Yak-52	G-CCJK Group
	G-CCJL	Supermarine Spitfire XXVI (PV303)	M. W. Hanley & P. M. Whitaker
	G-CCJM	Mainair Pegasus Quik	The Quik Group
	G-CCJN	Rans S.6ES Coyote II	W. A. Ritchie
	G-CCJO	ICP-740 Savannah Jabiru 4	R. & I. Fletcher
	G-CCJT	Skyranger 912 (2)	Juliet Tango Group
	G-CCJU	ICP MXP-740 Savannah Jabiru (4)	Savannah Flying Group
	G-CCJV	Aeroprakt A.22 Foxbat	J. Keats
	G-CCJW	Skyranger 912 (2)	J. R. Walter
	G-CCJX	Shaw Europa XS	J. S. Baranski
	G-CCJY	Cameron Z-42 balloon	D. J. Griffin
	G-CCKF	Best Off Skyranger 912 (1)	M. Johnson
	G-CCKG	Best Off Skyranger 912 (2)	C. E. Penny
	G-CCKH	Diamond DA40D Star	Flying Time Ltd
	G-CCKJ	Raj Hamsa X'Air 133 (3)	G. A. Davidson
	G-CCKL	Aerotechnik EV-97A Eurostar	G-CCKL Group
	G-CCKM	Mainair Pegasus Quik	J. P. Quinlan
	G-CCKN	Nicollier HN.700 Menestrel II	C. R. Partington
	G-CCKO	Mainair Pegasus Quik	G. Bennett & L. A. Harper
	G-CCKP	Robin DR.400/120	Duxford Flying Group
	G-CCKR	Pietenpol Air Camper	P. G. Humphrey
	G-CCKT	Hapi Cygnet SF-2	P. W. Abraham
	G-CCKV	Isaacs Fury II (K7271)	G. Smith
	G-CCKW	PA-18 Super Cub 135	Kronos BVBA/Belgium (G-GDAM)
	G-CCKZ	Customcraft A-25 balloon	P. A. George
	G-CCLF	Best Off Skyranger 912 (2)	J. Donaldson
	G-CCLG	Lindstrand LBL-105A balloon	M. A. Derbyshire
	G-CCLH	Rans S.6-ES Coyote II	K. R. Browne
	G-CCLJ	PA-28-140 Cherokee Cruiser	A. M. George
	G-CCLM	Mainair Pegasus Quik	T. A. A. Frohawk

Reg	Type	Owner or Operator	Notes
G-CCLO	Ultramagic H-77 balloon-	S. J. M. Hornsby	
G-CCLP	ICP MXP-740 Savannah	C. J. Powell & A. H. Watkins	
G-CCLR	Schleicher Ash 26E	A. Darby & R. N. John	
G-CCLS	Comco Ikarus C.42 FB UK	B. D. Wykes	
G-CCLU	Best Off Skyranger 912	C. M. Babiy	
G-CCLW	Diamond DA40D Star	Shacklewell Diamond Group	
G-CCLX	Mainair Pegasus Quik	T. D. Welburn	
G-CCMC	Jabiru Aircraft Jabiru UL 450	K. J. Simpson	
G-CCMD	Mainair Pegasus Quik	J. T. McCormack	
G-CCME	Mainair Pegasus Quik	Caunton Graphites Syndicate	
G-CCMH	M.2H Hawk Major	J. A. Pothecary	
G-CCMJ	Easy Raider J2.2 (1)	G. F. Clews	
G-CCMK	Raj Hamsa X'Air Falcon	M. J. J. Clutterbuck	
G-CCML	Mainair Pegasus Quik	D. Renton	
G-CCMM	Dyn'Aéro MCR-01 ULC Banbi	J. D. Harris	
G-CCMN	Cameron C-90 balloon	A.E. Austin	
G-CCMO	Aerotechnik EV-97 Eurostar	IBFC EV97 Group	
G-CCMP	Aerotechnik EV-97A Eurostar	E. K. McAlinden	
G-CCMR	Robinson R22 Beta	G. F. Smith	
G-CCMS	Mainair Pegasus Quik	Barton Charlie Charlie Group	
G-CCMT	Thruster T.600N 450	G. L. Logan	
G-CCMU	Rotorway Executive 162F	A. J. Thomas	
G-CCMW	CFM Shadow Srs.DD	K. H. Creed	
G-CCMX	Skyranger 912 (2)	S. G. Weaver	
G-CCMZ	Best Off Skyranger 912 (2)	D. D. Appleford	
G-CCNA	Jodel DR.100A (Replica)	R. Everitt	
G-CCNC	Cameron Z-275 balloon	J. D. & K. Griffiths	
G-CCND	Van's RV-9A	K. S. Woodard	
G-CCNE	Mainair Pegasus Quantum 15	G. D. Barker	
G-CCNF	Raj Hamsa X'Air Falcon 912(2)	R. E. Williams	
G-CCNG	Flight Design CT2K	S. Gaiety & P. Wayman	
G-CCNH	Rans S.6ES Coyote II	J. E. Howard	
G-CCNJ	Skyranger 912 (2)	J. D. Buchanan	
G-CCNL	Raj Hamsa X'Air Falcon 133(1)	S. E. Vallance	
G-CCNM	Mainair Pegasus Quik	F. J. Thorne & J. Flynn	
G-CCNP	Flight Design CT2K	North East Flying Club Ltd	
G-CCNR	Skyranger 912 (2)	P. Horsley	
G-CCNS	Skyranger 912 (2)	D. Murdoch, P. V. Griffiths & F. Gallacher	
G-CCNT	Ikarus C.42 FB80	November Tango Group	
G-CCNW	Mainair Pegasus Quantum Lite	P. A. Peckover	
G-CCNX	CAB CAP-10B	Arc Input Ltd	
G-CCNZ	Raj Hamsa X'Air 133 (1)	J. M. Walsh	
G-CCOB	Aero C.104 Jungmann	C. W. Tomkins	
G-CCOC	Mainair Pegasus Quantum 15	C. M. Ayres	
G-CCOF	Rans S.6-ESA Coyote II	A. C. Bell	
G-CCOG	Mainair Pegasus Quik	D. P. Clarke	
G-CCOH	Raj Hamsa X'Air Falcon Jabiru(3)	D. R. Sutton	
G-CCOK	Mainair Pegasus Quik	C. Curtin	
G-CCOM	Westland Lysander IIIA (V9312)	Propshop Ltd	
G-CCOP	Ultramagic M-105 balloon	M. E. J. Whitewood	
G-CCOR	Sequoia F.8L Falco	D. J. Thoma	
G-CCOT	Cameron Z-105 balloon	Airborne Adventures Ltd	
G-CCOU	Mainair Pegasus Quik	D. E. J. McVicker	
G-CCOV	Shaw Europa XS	B. C. Barton	
G-CCOW	Mainair Pegasus Quik	D. Coppin, T. Lewis & A. Taylor	
G-CCOY	NA AT-6D Harvard II	Classic Flying Machine Collection Ltd	
G-CCOZ	Monnett Sonerai II	W. H. Cole	
G-CCPC	Mainair Pegasus Quik	S. M. Oliver	
G-CCPD	Campbell Cricket Mk.4	T. H. Geake	
G-CCPE	Steen Skybolt	C. Moore	
G-CCPF	Skyranger 912 (2)	J. R. M. Macpherson	
G-CCPG	Mainair Pegasus Quik	A.W. Lowrie	
G-CCPH	EV-97 TeamEurostar UK	A. H. Woolley	
G-CCPJ	EV-97 TeamEurostar UK	J. S. Webb	
G-CCPL	Skyranger 912 (2)	CCPL Group	
G-CCPM	Mainair Blade 912	P. S. Davies	
G-CCPN	Dyn'Aéro MCR-01 Club	J. C. Thompson	
G-CCPP	Cameron 70 Concept balloon	Sarnia Balloon Group	
G-CCPS	Ikarus C.42 FB100 VLA	H. Cullens	
G-CCPT	Cameron Z-90 balloon	Charter Ballooning Ltd	
G-CCPV	Jabiru J400	J. R. Lawrence	

Notes	Reg	Type	Owner or Operator
	G-CCRB	Kolb Twinstar Mk.3 (modified)	N. R. Pettigrew
	G-CCRC	Cessna Tu.206G	D. M. Penny
	G-CCRF	Mainair Pegasus Quantum 15	C. J. Middleton
	G-CCRG	Ultramagic M-77 balloon	M. Cowling
	G-CCRI	Raj Hamsa X'Air 582 (5)	D. K. Beaumont
	G-CCRJ	Shaw Europa	F. M. Ward
	G-CCRK	Luscombe 8A Silvaire	J. R. Kimberley
	G-CCRN	Thruster T.600N 450	R. Locke & A. W. Ambrose
	G-CCRP	Thruster T.600N 450	M. M. Lane (G-ULLY)
	G-CCRR	Skyranger 912 (1)	M. S. N. Alam
	G-CCRS	Lindstrand LBL-210A balloon	Bailey Balloons Ltd
	G-CCRT	Mainair Pegasus Quantum 15	N. Mitchell
	G-CCRV	Skyranger 912 (1)	N. C. Milnes & A. Jopp
	G-CCRW	Mainair Pegasus Quik	M. L. Cade
	G-CCRX	Jabiru UL-450	M. Everest
	G-CCSD	Mainair Pegasus Quik	S. J. M. Morling
	G-CCSF	Mainair Pegasus Quik	D. G. Barnes & A. Sorah
	G-CCSG	Cameron Z-275 balloon	Wickers World Ltd
	G-CCSH	Mainair Pegasus Quik	G. Carr
	G-CCSI	Cameron Z-42 balloon	IKEA Ltd
	G-CCSL	Mainair Pegasus Quik	A. J. Harper
	G-CCSN	Cessna U.206G	K. Brady
	G-CCSP	Cameron N-77 balloon	D. Berg
	G-CCSR	Aerotechnik EV-97A Eurostar	Sierra Romeo Flying Group
	G-CCSS	Lindstrand LBL-90A balloon	British Telecom
	G-CCST	PA-32R-301 Saratoga	A. R. Whibley
	G-CCSW	Nott PA balloon	J. R. P.Nott
	G-CCSX	Best Off Skyranger 912(1)	T. Jackson
	G-CCSY	Mainair Pegasus Quik	G. J. Gibson
	G-CCTA	Zenair CH.601UL Zodiac	P. Moore
	G-CCTC	Mainair Pegasus Quik	D. R. Purslow
	G-CCTD	Mainair Pegasus Quik	R. N. S. Taylor
	G-CCTE	Dyn'Aéro MCR-01 Banbi	C. J. McInnes
	G-CCTF	Aerotek Pitts S-2A Special	Stampe and Pitts Flying Group
	G-CCTG	Van's RV-3B	A. Donald
	G-CCTH	EV-97 TeamEurostar UK	B. M. Davis
	G-CCTI	EV-97 TeamEurostar UK	Flylight Airsports Ltd
	G-CCTM	Mainair Blade	J. N. Hanso
	G-CCTO	EV-97 Eurostar	H. Cooke& B. Robertson
	G-CCTP	EV-97 Eurostar	P. E. Rose
	G-CCTR	Skyranger 912	G. Lampit & D. W. Stamp
	G-CCTS	Cameron Z-120 balloon	F. R. Hart
	G-CCTT	Cessna 172S	Highland Aviation Training Ltd
	G-CCTU	Mainair Pegasus Quik	N. J. Lindsay
	G-CCTV	Rans S.6ESA Coyote II	B. Swindon
	G-CCTW	Cessna 152	R. J. Dempsey
	G-CCTZ	Mainair Pegasus Quik 912S	S. Baker
	G-CCUA	Mainair Pegasus Quik	J. B. Crawford
	G-CCUB	Piper J-3C-65 Cub	G. Cormack
	G-CCUC	Best Off Skyranger J2.2(1)	R. Marrs
	G-CCUE	Ultramagic T-180 balloon	N. J. Dunnington
	G-CCUF	Skyranger 912(2)	R. E. Parker
	G-CCUI	Dyn'Aéro MCR-01 Banbi	J. T. Morgan
	G-CCUL	Shaw Europa XS	Europa 6
	G-CCUR	Mainair Pegasus Quantum 15-912	D. W. Power & D. James
	G-CCUT	Aerotechnik EV-97 Eurostar	Doctor and the Medics
	G-CCUY	Shaw Europa	N. Evans
	G-CCUZ	Thruster T.600N 450	Fly 365 Ltd
	G-CCVA	Aerotechnik EV-97 Eurostar	K. J. Scott
	G-CCVE	Raj Hamsa X'Air Jabiru (3)	G. J. Slater
	G-CCVF	Lindstrand LBL-105 balloon	Alan Patterson Design
	G-CCVH	Curtiss H-75A-1 (82:8)	The Fighter Collection
	G-CCVI	Zenair CH.701 SP	P. J. Bunce
	G-CCVJ	Raj Hamsa X'Air Falcon Jabiru (3)	I. S. Doig
	G-CCVK	Aerotechnik EV-97 TeamEurostar UK	J. Holditch
	G-CCVL	Zenair CH.601XL Zodiac	A. Y-T. Leungr & G. Constantine
	G-CCVM	Van's RV-7A	J. G. Small
	G-CCVN	Jabiru SP-470	Teesside Aviators Group
	G-CCVP	Beech 58	Richard Nash Cars Ltd
	G-CCVR	Skyranger 912(2)	M. J. Batchelor
	G-CCVS	Van's RV-6A	T. Knight & S. Thomas (G-CCVC)

Reg	Type	Owner or Operator	Notes
G-CCVU	Robinson R22 Beta II	J. H. P. S. Sargent	
G-CCVW	Nicollier HN.700 Menestrel II	B. F. Enock	
G-CCVX	Mainair Tri Flyer 330	J. A. Shufflebotham	
G-CCVZ	Cameron O-120 balloon	T. M. C. McCoy	
G-CCWC	Skyranger 912	G-CCWC Flying Group	
G-CCWL	Mainair Blade	M. S. Eglin	
G-CCWM	Robin DR.400/180	D. M. Scorer	
G-CCWO	Mainair Pegasus Quantum 15-912	R. Fitzgerald	
G-CCWP	Aerotechnik EV-97 TeamEurostar UK	Airsports	
G-CCWU	Skyranger 912(1)	A. R. Young	
G-CCWV	Mainair Pegasus Quik	C. Buttery	
G-CCWW	Mainair Pegasus Quantum 15-912	Whisky Whisky Syndicate	
G-CCWZ	Raj Hamsa X'Air Falcon Jabiru(3)	The Norman Group	
G-CCXA	Boeing Stearman A75N-1 Kaydet (669)	Skymax (Aviation) Ltd	
G-CCXB	Boeing Stearman B75N1	C. D. Walker	
G-CCXC	Avion Mudry CAP-10B	J. E. Keighley	
G-CCXD	Lindstrand LBL-105B balloon	Silver Ghost Balloon Club	
G-CCXF	Cameron Z-90 balloon	B. J. Workman	
G-CCXG	SE-5A (replica) (C5430)	C. Morris	
G-CCXH	Skyranger J2.2	M. J. O'Connor	
G-CCXK	Pitts S-1S Special	P. G. Bond	
G-CCXM	Skyranger 912(1)	R. D. Jordan	
G-CCXN	Skyranger 912(1)	G. D. P. Clouting	
G-CCXO	Corgy CJ-1 Starlet	S. C. Ord	
G-CCXP	ICP Savannah Jabiru	B. J. Harper	
G-CCXS	Montgomerie-Bensen B.8MR	A. Morgan	
G-CCXT	Mainair Pegasus Quik	C. F. Yaxley	
G-CCXU	Diamond DA40D Star	R. J. & L. Hole	
G-CCXV	Thruster T.600N 450	R. Kelly	
G-CCXW	Thruster T.600N 450	D. J. Atkinson	
G-CCXX	AG-5B Tiger	P. D. Lock	
G-CCXZ	Mainair Pegasus Quik	J. D. Rickard	
G-CCYB	Escapade 912(1)	B. E. & S. M. Renehan	
G-CCYC	Robinson R44 II	J. Butler	
G-CCYE	Mainair Pegasus Quik	P. M. Scrivener	
G-CCYG	Robinson R44 II	Mosswood Carsavan Park	
G-CCYI	Cameron O-105 balloon	S. Bitti/Italy	
G-CCYJ	Mainair Pegasus Quik	G. M. Cruise-Smith	
G-CCYL	MainairPegasus Quantum 15	A. M. Goulden	
G-CCYM	Skyranger 912	I. Pilton	
G-CCYO	Christen Eagle II	P. C. Woolley	
G-CCYP	Colt 56A balloon	Magical Adventures Ltd	
G-CCYR	Ikarus C.42 FB80	Airbourne Aviation Ltd	
G-CCYS	Cessna F.182Q	S. Dyson	
G-CCYU	Ultramagic S-90 balloon	J. Francis	
G-CCYX	Bell 412	RCR Aviation Ltd	
G-CCYY	PA-28-161 Warrior II	Flightcontrol Ltd	
G-CCYZ	Dornier EKW C3605	CW Tomkins Ltd	
G-CCZA	SOCATA MS.894A Rallye Minerva 220	R. N. Aylett	
G-CCZB	Mainair Pegasus Quantum 15	A. Johnson	
G-CCZD	Van's RV-7	A. P. Hatton & E. A. Stokes	
G-CCZJ	Raj Hamsa X' Air Falcon 582	S. Uzochukwu & C. R. Stevens	
G-CCZK	Zenair CH.601 UL Zodiac	R. J. Hopkins & J. Lonergan	
G-CCZL	Ikarus C-42 FB80	Shadow Aviation Ltd	
G-CCZM	Skyranger 912S	Skyranger Group	
G-CCZN	Rans S.6-ES Coyote II	R. D. Proctor	
G-CCZO	Mainair Pegasus Quik	P. G. Penhaligan	
G-CCZR	Medway Raven Eclipse R	S. P. D. Hill	
G-CCZS	Raj Hamsa X'Air Falcon 582	S. Siddiqui	
G-CCZT	Van's RV-9A	Zulu Tango Flying Group	
G-CCZV	PA-28-151 Warrior	London School of Flying Ltd	
G-CCZW	Mainair Pegasus Blade	D. Sisson	
G-CCZX	Robin DR.400/180	Exeter Aviation Ltd	
G-CCZY	Van's RV-9A	A. Hutchinson	
G-CCZZ	Aerotechnik EV-97 Eurostar	B. M Starck & J. P. Aitken	
G-CDAA	Mainair Pegasus Quantum 15-912	G. E. Parker	
G-CDAB	Glasair Super IISRG	W. L. Hitchins	
G-GDAC	Aerotechnik EV-97 TeamEurostar	C. R. Cousins	
G-CDAD	Lindstrand LBL-25A balloon	G. J. Madelin	
G-CDAE	Van's RV-6A	The Alpha Echo Group	

Notes	Reg	Type	Owner or Operator
	G-CDAI	Robin DR.400/140B	D. Hardy & J. Sambrook
	G-CDAL	Zenair CH.601UL Zodiac	R. J. Howell
	G-CDAO	Mainair Pegasus Quantum 15 -912	J. C. Duncan
	G-CDAP	Aerotechnik EV-97 TeamEurostar UK	L. N. Givens
	G-CDAR	Mainair Pegasus Quik	E. Schoonbrood
	G-CDAT	ICP MXP-740 Savannah Jabiru	G. M. Railson
	G-CDAX	Mainair Pegasus Quik	L. Hurman
	G-CDAY	Skyranger 912	Redlands Skyranger Group
	G-CDAZ	Aerotechnik EV-97 Eurostar	K. M. Howell
	G-CDBA	Skyranger 912(1)	P. J. Brennan
	G-CDBB	Mainair Pegasus Quik	K. J. Whitehead
	G-CDBD	Jabiru J400	I. D. Rutherford
	G-CDBE	Montgomerie-Bensen B.8M	P. Harwood
	G-CDBG	Robinson R22 Beta	Jepar Rotorcraft
	G-CDBJ	Yakovlev Yak-3	C. E. Bellhouse
	G-CDBK	Rotorway Executive 162F	R. S. Snell
	G-CDBM	Robin DR.400/180	C. M. Simmonds
	G-CDBO	Skyranger 912	G-CDBO Flying Group
	G-CDBR	Stolp SA.300 Starduster Too	R. J. Warren
	G-CDBU	Ikarus C.42 FB100	S. E. Meehan
	G-CDBV	Skyranger 912S	C. R. Burgess & T. Smith
	G-CDBX	Shaw Europa XS	P. B. Davey
	G-CDBY	Dyn'Aero MCR-01 ULC	A. Thornton
	G-CDBZ	Thruster T.600N 450	BZ Flying Group
	G-CDCC	Aerotechnik EV-97 Eurostar	J. R. Tomlin
	G-CDCD	Van's RVF-9A	RV9ers
	G-CDCE	Avions Mudry CAP-10B	The Tiger Club (1990) Ltd
	G-CDCF	Mainair Pegasus Quik	P. Thaxter
	G-CDCG	Ikarus C.42 FB UK	N. E. Ashton
	G-CDCH	Skyranger 912(1)	G-CDCH Group
	G-CDCI	Pegasus Quik	R. J. Allarton
	G-CDCK	Mainair Pegasus Quik	R. Solomons
	G-CDCM	Ikarus C.42 FB UK	S. T. Allen
	G-CDCO	Ikarus C.42 FB UK	R. Urquhart
	G-CDCP	Avtech Jabiru J400	J. Cherry
	G-CDCR	Savannah Jabiru(1)	T. Davidson
	G-CDCS	PA-12 Super Cruiser	C. W. Tomkins
	G-CDCT	Aerotechnik EV-97 TeamEurostar UK	G. R. Nicholson
	G-CDCV	Robinson R44 II	3GR Comm Ltd
	G-CDCW	Escapade 912 (1)	P. Nicholls
	G-CDDA	SOCATA TB20 Trinidad	Z. Clean
	G-CDDB	Grob/Schempp-Hirth CS-11	J. M. A. Pring
	G-CDDG	PA-26-161 Warrior II	Aviation Advice and Consulting Ltd
	G-CDDH	Raj Hamsa X'Air Falcon	G. Loosley
	G-CDDI	Thruster T.600N 450	R. Nayak
	G-CDDK	Cessna 172M	Flight & Media Enterprises Ltd
	G-CDDL	Cameron Z-350 balloon	Adventure Balloons Ltd
	G-CDDN	Lindstrand LBL 90A balloon	Flying Enterprises
	G-CDDO	Raj Hamsa X'Air 133(2)	S. Bain
	G-CDDP	Lazer Z.230	G-CDDP Flying Group
	G-CDDR	Skyranger 582(1)	A. Greenwell & A. Carver
	G-CDDS	Zenair CH.601HD	D. J. Hunter
	G-CDDU	Skyranger 912(2)	R. Newton & P. A. Burton
	G-CDDW	Aeroprakt A.22 Foxbat	A. Assiaian
	G-CDDX	Thruster T.600N 450	B. S. P. Finch
	G-CDDY	Van's RV-8	D. F. Clorley
	G-CDEA	SAAB 2000	Eastern Airways
	G-CDEB	SAAB 2000	Eastern Airways
	G-CDEF	PA-28-161 Cadet	Western Air (Thruxton) Ltd
	G-CDEH	ICP MXP-740 Savannah	D. C. Crawley
	G-CDEM	Raj Hamsa X' Air 133	R. J. Froud
	G-CDEN	Mainair Pegasus Quantum 15 912	J. D. J. Spragg
	G-CDEO	PA-28 Cherokee 180	Perranporth Flying Club Ltd
	G-CDEP	Aerotechnik EV-97 TeamEurostar	Echo Papa Group
	G-CDET	Culver LCA Cadet	J. Gregson
	G-CDEU	Lindstrand LBL-90B balloon	N. Florence & P. J. Marshall
	G-CDEV	Escapade 912 (1)	Banana Group
	G-CDEW	Pegasus Quik	K. M. Sullivan
	G-CDEX	Shaw Europa	K. Martindale
	G-CDFD	Scheibe SF.25C Falke	The Royal Air Force Gliding and Soaring Association

Reg	Type	Owner or Operator	Notes
G-CDFG	Mainair Pegasus Quik	D. Gabbott	
G-CDFJ	Skyranger 912(1)	B. H. Goldsmith	
G-CDFK	Jabiru UL-450	J. C. Eagle	
G-CDFL	Zenair CH.601UL	Caunton Zodiac Group	
G-CDFM	Raj Hamsa X'Air 582 (5)	W. A. Keel-Stocker	
G-CDFN	Thunder Ax7-77 balloon	E. Rullo/Italy	
G-CDFO	Pegasus Quik	The Foxtrot Oscars	
G-CDFP	Skyranger 912 (1)	R. Potter	
G-CDFR	Mainair Pegasus Quantum 15	P. D. J. Davies	
G-CDFU	Rans S.6-ES Coyote II	G. Mudd	
G-CDGA	Taylor JT.1 Monoplane	R. M. Larimore	
G-CDGB	Rans S.6-116 Coyote	S. Penoyre	
G-CDGC	Pegasus Quik	A. T. K. Crozier	
G-CDGD	Pegasus Quik	I. D. & V. A. Milne	
G-CDGE	Edge XT912-IIIB	M & G Flight	
G-CDGF	Ultramagic S-105 balloon	D. & K. Bareford	
G-CDGH	Rans S.6-ES Coyote	A. L. Virgoe	
G-CDGI	Thruster T600N 450	P. A. Pilkington	
G-CDGN	Cameron C-90 balloon	M. C. Gibbons	
G-CDGO	Pegasus Quik	J. C. Townsend	
G-CDGP	Zenair CH 601XL	B. & P. J. Chandler	
G-CDGR	Zenair CH 701UL	I. A. R. Sim	
G-CDGS	AG-5B Tiger	M. R. O'B. Thompson	
G-CDGT	Montgomerie-Parsons Two Place g/p	J. B. Allan	
G-CDGU	VS.300 Spitfire I (X4276)	Peter Monk Ltd	
G-CDGW	PA-28-181 Archer III	Rutland Flying Group	
G-CDGX	Pegasus Quantum 15-912	S. R. Green	
G-CDGY	VS.349 Spitfire Mk VC	Aero Vintage Ltd	
G-CDHA	Best Off Skyranger 912S(1)	A. T. Cameron	
G-CDHC	Slingsby T67C	Brimpton Flying Group	
G-CDHE	Skyranger 912(2)	C. A. S. Powell	
G-CDHF	PA-30 Twin Comanche B	M. Large	
G-CDHG	Mainair Pegasus Quik	T. W. Pelan	
G-CDHJ	Lindstrand LBL-90B balloon	Lindstrand Hot Air Balloons Ltd	
G-CDHM	Pegasus Quantum 15	M. R. Smith	
G-CDHN	Lindstrand LBL-317A balloon	Bailey Balloons Ltd	
G-CDHO	Raj Hamsa X'Air 133 (1)	S. B. Walters & P. Osborne	
G-CDHR	Ikarus C.42 FB80	J. Bainbridge	
G-CDHU	Best Off Skyranger Swift 912 (1)	G-CDHU Group	
G-CDHX	Aeroprakt A.22 Foxbat	N. E. Stokes	
G-CDHY	Cameron Z-90 balloon	D. M. Roberts	
G-CDHZ	Nicollier HN.700 Menestrel II	G. E. Whittaker	
G-CDIA	Thruster T.600N 450	IA Flying Group	
G-CDIB	Cameron Z-350Z balloon	Ballooning Network Ltd	
G-CDIF	Mudry CAP-10B	J. D. Gordon	
G-CDIG	Aerotechnik EV-97 Eurostar	P. D. Brisco & J. Young	
G-CDIH	Cameron Z-275 balloon	Bailey Balloons Ltd	
G-CDIJ	Best Off Skyranger 912 (2)	K. C. Yeates	
G-CDIL	Pegasus Quantum 15-912	C. M. Russell	
G-CDIO	Cameron Z-90 balloon	Slowfly Montgolfiere SNC/Italy	
G-CDIR	Mainair Pegasus Quantum 15-912	M. Crane	
G-CDIT	Cameron Z-105 balloon	Bailey Balloons Ltd	
G-CDIU	Skyranger 912S(1)	Darley Moor Flyers Club	
G-CDIX	Ikarus C.42 FB.100	T. G. Greenhill & J. G. Spinks	
G-CDIY	Aerotechnik EV-97A Eurostar	R. E. Woolsey	
G-CDIZ	Escapade 912(3)	E. G. Bishop & E. N. Dunn	
G-CDJB	Van's RV-4	J. K. Cook	
G-CDJD	ICP MXP-740 Savannah Jabiru (4)	D. W. Mullin	
G-CDJE	Thruster T.600N 450	R. J. Stamp	
G-CDJF	Flight Design CT2K	P. A. James	
G-CDJG	Zenair 601UL Zodiac	G-CDJG Group	
G-CDJI	UltraMagic M-120 balloon	S. J. Roake	
G-CDJJ	IAV Yakovlev Yak-52	J. J. Miles	
G-CDJK	Ikarus C.42 FB 80	Cornish Aviation Ltd	
G-CDJL	Avtech Jabiru J400	J. Gardiner	
G-CDJN	RAF 2000 GTX-SE gyroplane	D. J. North	
G-CDJO	DH.82A Tiger Moth	D. Dal Bon	
G-CDJP	Best Off Skyranger 912(2)	I. A. Cunningham	
G-CDJR	Aerotechnik EV-97 TeamEurostar	K. C. Lye & M. D. White	
G-CDJU	CASA 1.131E Jungmann Srs.1000	P. Gaskell	
G-CDJV	Beech A.36 Bonanza	Atlantic Bridge Aviation Ltd	

Notes	Reg	Type	Owner or Operator
	G-CDJX	Cameron N-56 balloon	Cameron Balloons Ltd
	G-CDJY	Cameron C-80 balloon	British Airways PLC
	G-CDKA	SAAB 2000	Eastern Airways
	G-CDKB	SAAB 2000	Eastern Airways
	G-CDKE	Rans S6-ES Coyote II	J. E. Holloway
	G-CDKF	Escapade 912 (1)	K. R. Butcher
	G-CDKH	Skyranger 912S (1)	C. Lenaghan
	G-CDKI	Skyranger 912S (1)	J. M. Hucker
	G-CDKK	Mainair Pegasus Quik	P. M. Knight
	G-CDKL	Escapade 912 (2)	G-CDKL Group
	G-CDKM	Pegasus Quik	P. Lister
	G-CDKN	ICP MXP-740 Savannah Jabiru (4)	T. Wicks
	G-CDKO	ICP MXP-740 Savannah Jabiru (4)	K. Arksey
	G-CDKP	Avtech Jabiru UL-D Calypso	Rochester Microlights Ltd
	G-CDKX	Skyranger J.2 .2 (1)	E. Lewis
	G-CDLA	Mainair Pegasus Quik	C. R. Stevens & B. Mills
	G-CDLC	CASA 1.131E Jungmann 2000	R. D. Loder
	G-CDLD	Mainair Pegasus Quik 912S	W. Williams
	G-CDLG	Skyranger 912 (2)	CDLG Skyranger Group
	G-CDLI	Airco DH.9 (E8894)	Aero Vintage Ltd
	G-CDLJ	Mainair Pegasus Quik	J. S. James & R. S. Keyser
	G-CDLK	Skyranger 912S	L. E. Cowling
	G-CDLL	Dyn'Aéro MCR-01 ULC	R. F. Connell
	G-CDLR	ICP MXP / 740 Savannah Jabiru (4)	K. J. Barnard
	G-CDLS	Jabiru Aircraft Jabiru J400	Teesside Aviators Group
	G-CDLW	Zenair ZH.601UL Zodiac	W. A. Stphen
	G-CDLY	Cirrus SR20	Talama/France
	G-CDLZ	Mainair Pegasus Quantum 15-912	Lima Zulu Owner Syndicate
	G-CDMA	PA-28-151 Warrior	Wingtask 1995 Ltd
	G-CDMC	Cameron Z-105 balloon	A-Gas (ORB) Ltd
	G-CDMD	Robin DR.400/500	P. R. Liddle
	G-CDME	Van's RV-7	W. H. Greenwood
	G-CDMF	Van's RV-9A	J. R. Bowden
	G-CDMH	Cessna P.210N	A. M. Holman-West
	G-CDMJ	Mainair Pegasus Quik	M. J. R. Dean
	G-CDMK	Montgomerie-Bensen B8MR	P. Rentell
	G-CDML	Mainair Pegasus Quik	P. O'Rourke
	G-CDMN	Van's RV-9	G. J. Smith
	G-CDMO	Cameron S Can-100 balloon	A. Schneider/Germany
	G-CDMP	Best Off Skyranger 912(1)	J. A. Charlton
	G-CDMS	Ikarus C,42 FB 80	Airbourne Aviation Ltd
	G-CDMT	Zenair CH.601XL Zodiac	H. Drever
	G-CDMV	Best Off Skyranger 912S(1)	D. O'Keeffe & K. E. Rutter
	G-CDMX	PA-28-161 Warrior II	Westshore Investments LLC
	G-CDMY	PA-28-161 Warrior II	Redhill Air Services Ltd
	G-CDNA	Grob G.109A	Army Gliding Association
	G-CDND	GA-7 Cougar	C. J. Chaplin
	G-CDNE	Best Off Skyranger Swift 912S(1)	St. Michael's Skyranger Syndicate
	G-CDNF	Aero Design Pulsar 3	D. Ringer
	G-CDNG	Aerotechnik EV-97 TeamEurostar UK	G-CDNG New Syndicate
	G-CDNH	Mainair Pegasus Quik	T. P. R. Wright
	G-CDNM	Aerotechnik EV-97 TeamEurostar UK	H. C. Lowther
	G-CDNO	Westland Gazelle AH.1 (XX432)	CJ Helicopters
	G-CDNP	Aerotechnik EV-97 TeamEurostar UK	Eaglescott Eurostar Group
	G-CDNS	Westland Gazelle AH.1 (XZ321)	Falcon Aviation Ltd
	G-CDNT	Zenair CH.601XL Zodiac	W. McCormack
	G-CDNW	Ikarus C.42 FB UK	W. Gabbott
	G-CDNY	Jabiru SP-470	G. Lucey
	G-CDOA	EV-97 TeamEurostar UK	Mainair Microlight School Ltd
	G-CDOB	Cameron C-90 balloon	G. T. Holmes
	G-CDOC	Mainair Quik GT450	R. J. Carver
	G-CDOK	Ikarus C.42 FB 100	M Aviation Ltd
	G-CDOM	Mainair Pegasus Quik	G-CDOM Flying Group
	G-CDON	PA-28-161 Warrior II	G-CDON Group
	G-CDOO	Mainair Pegasus Quantum 15-912	O. C. Harding
	G-CDOP	Mainair Pegasus Quik	G-CDOP Syndicate
	G-CDOT	Ikarus C.42 FB 100	A. C. Anderson
	G-CDOV	Skyranger 912(2)	N. Grugan
	G-CDOY	Robin DR.400/180R	Lasham Gliding Society Ltd
	G-CDOZ	EV-97 TeamEurostar UK	Wizards of Oz
	G-CDPA	Alpi Pioneer 300	N. D. White

Reg	Type	Owner or Operator	Notes
G-CDPB	Skyranger 982(1)	N. S. Bishop	
G-CDPD	Mainair Pegasus Quik	M. D. Vearncombe	
G-CDPE	Skyranger 912(2)	I. M. Hull	
G-CDPG	Crofton Auster J1-A	G-CDPG Group	
G-CDPH	Tiger Cub RL5A LW Sherwood Ranger ST	O. C. Pope	
G-CDPL	EV-97 TeamEurostar UK	C. I. D. H Garrison	
G-CDPN	Ultramagic S-105	D. J. MacInnes	
G-CDPP	Ikarus C42 FB UK	H. M. Owen	
G-CDPS	Raj Hamsa X'Air 133	C. G., M. & N. Chambers	
G-CDPV	PA-34-200T Seneca II	Globebrow Ltd	
G-CDPW	Mainair Pegasus Quantum 15-912	Hadair	
G-CDPY	Shaw Europa	A. Burrill	
G-CDPZ	Flight Design CT2K	M. E. Henwick	
G-CDRC	Cessna 182Q	Concorde Investments Ltd	
G-CDRD	AirBorne XT912-B Edge/Streak III-B	Fly NI Ltd	
G-CDRF	Cameron Z-90 balloon	Chalmers Ballong Corps	
G-CDRG	Mainair Pegasus Quik	S. P. Adams	
G-CDRH	Thruster T.600N	Carlisle Thruster Group	
G-CDRI	Cameron O-105 balloon	Snapdragon Balloon Group	
G-CDRJ	Tanarg/Ixess 15 912S(1)	P. D. Gregory	
G-CDRN	Cameron Z-225 balloon	Adventure Balloons Ltd	
G-CDRO	Ikarus C42 F880	Airbourne Aviation Ltd	
G-CDRP	Ikarus C42 FB80	D. S. Parker	
G-CDRR	Mainair Pegasus Quantum 15-912	M. I. White	
G-CDRS	Rotorway Executive 162F	R. C. Swann	
G-CDRT	Mainair Pegasus Quik	R. Tetlow	
G-CDRU	CASA 1.131E Jungmann 2000	P. Cunniff	
G-CDRV	Van's RV-9A	R. J. Woodford	
G-CDRW	Mainair Pegasus Quik	C. J. Meadows	
G-CDRY	Ikarus C42 FB100 VLA	R. J. Mitchell	
G-CDRZ	Baloney Kubicek BB22 balloon	Club Amatori del Volo in Mongolfiera/Italy	
G-CDSA	Mainair Pegasus Quik	F. R. Simpson	
G-CDSB	Alpi Pioneer 200	T. A. & P. M. Pugh	
G-CDSC	Scheibe SF.25C Rotax-Falke	Devon & Somerset Motorglider Group	
G-CDSD	Alpi Pioneer 300	P. G. Leonard	
G-CDSF	Diamond DA40D Star	Flying Time Ltd	
G-CDSH	ICP MXP-740 Savannah CAMIT(1)	G. Miller	
G-CDSK	Reality Escapade Jabiru(3)	R. H. Sear	
G-CDSM	P & M Aviation Quik GT450	S. L. Cogger	
G-CDSN	Raj Hamsa X'Air Jabiru(3)	R. J. Spence	
G-CDSS	Mainair Pegasus Quik	R. N. S. Taylor	
G-CDST	Ultramagic N-250 balloon	Adventure Balloons Ltd	
G-CDSW	Ikarus C.42 FB UK	Deanland Flight Training Ltd	
G-CDSX	EE Canberra T.Mk.4 (VN799) ★	Classic Air Force/Newquay	
G-CDTA	EV-97 TeamEurostar UK	R. D. Stein	
G-CDTB	Mainair Pegasus Quantum 15-912	D. W. Corbett	
G-CDTG	Diamond DA.42 Twin Star	CTC Aviation Group Ltd	
G-CDTH	Schempp-Hirth Nimbus 4DM	M. A. V. Gatehouse	
G-CDTI	Messerschmitt Bf.109E (4034)	Rare Aero Ltd	
G-CDTJ	Escapade Jabiru(1)	M. E. Gilbert	
G-CDTL	Avtech Jabiru J-400	M. I. Sistern	
G-CDTO	P & M Quik GT450	A. R. Watt	
G-CDTP	Skyranger 912S (1)	P. M. Whitaker	
G-CDTR	P & M Quik GT450	S. M. Furner	
G-CDTT	Savannah Jabiru(4)	M. J. Day	
G-CDTU	EV-97 TeamEurostar UK	G-CDTU Group	
G-CDTV	Tecnam P2002 EA Sierra	S. A. Noble	
G-CDTX	Cessna F.152	Blueplane Ltd	
G-CDTY	Savannah Jabiru (5)	D. A. Cook	
G-CDTZ	Aeroprakt A.22 Foxbat	Colditz Group	
G-CDUE	Robinson R44 1	Southport Golf Complex Ltd	
G-CDUH	P & M Quik GT450	N. F. Taylor	
G-CDUJ	Lindstrand LBL 31A balloon	R. G. Griffin	
G-CDUK	Ikarus C.42 FB UK	J. Molinari	
G-CDUL	Skyranger 912S (2)	M. B. Wallbutton & M. P. D. Cook	
G-CDUS	Skyranger 912S (1)	G. Devlin & J. Northage	
G-CDUT	Jabiru J400	T. W. & A. Pullin.	
G-CDUU	P & M Quik GT450	Caunton Charlie Delta Group	
G-CDUV	Savannah Jabiru(5)	D. M. Blackman	
G-CDUW	Aeronca C3	N. K. Geddes	
G-CDUY	Thunder & Colt 77A balloon	G. Birchall	

Notes	Reg	Type	Owner or Operator
	G-CDVA	Skyranger 912 (1)	S. J. Dovey
	G-CDVB	Agusta A.109E Power	Leonardo SpA/Italy
	G-CDVC	Agusta A109E Power	Leonardo SpA/Italy
	G-CDVD	EV-97 Eurostar	The Northern Flying Group
	G-CDVG	Pegasus Quik	C. M. Lewis
	G-CDVH	Pegasus Quantum 15	J. Clark
	G-CDVI	Ikarus C42 FB80	Airbourne Aviation Ltd
	G-CDVJ	Montgomerie-Bensen B8MR	D. J. Martin
	G-CDVK	Savannah Jabiru (5)	M. Peters
	G-CDVL	Alpi Pioneer 300	J. D. Clabon
	G-CDVN	P & M Quik GT450	P. Warrener
	G-CDVO	P & M Quik	D. Sykes
	G-CDVR	P & M Quik GT450	M. J. King
	G-CDVS	Europa XS	J. F. Lawn
	G-CDVT	Van's RV-6	P. J. Wood
	G-CDVU	Aeroteknik EV-97 TeamEurostar	M. R. Smith
	G-CDVV	SA Bulldog Srs. 120/121 (XX626:02, W)	W. H. M. Mott
	G-CDVZ	P & M Quik GT450	S. M. Green & M. D. Peacock
	G-CDWB	Skyranger 912(2)	D. R. Hammond
	G-CDWD	Cameron Z-105 balloon	Bristol University Ballooning Society
	G-CDWE	Nord NC.856 Norvigie	J. R. Davison
	G-CDWG	Dyn'Aéro MCR-01 Club	A. W. Lowrie
	G-CDWI	Ikarus C42 FB80	The Scottish Flying Club
	G-CDWJ	Flight Design CTSW	G. P. Rood
	G-CDWK	Robinson R44	B. Morgan
	G-CDWM	Skyranger 912S (1)	J. McCluskey & D. R. Devlin
	G-CDWN	Ultramagic N-210 balloon	S. R. Seager
	G-CDWO	P & M Quik GT450	G. W. Carwardine
	G-CDWR	P & M Quik GT450	I. C. Macbeth
	G-CDWT	Flight Design CTSW	R. Scammell
	G-CDWU	Zenair CH.601UL Zodiac	J. White
	G-CDWW	P & M Quik GT450	J. H. Bradbury
	G-CDWX	Lindstrand LBL 77A balloon	LSB Public Relations Ltd
	G-CDWZ	P & M Quik GT450	Oakley Flyers
	G-CDXD	Medway SLA100 Executive	A. J. Baker & G. Withers
	G-CDXF	Lindstrand LBL 31A balloon	R. K. Worsman
	G-CDXG	P & M Pegasus Quantum 15-912	I. C. Braybrook
	G-CDXI	Cessna 182P	B. G. McBeath
	G-CDXJ	Jabiru J400	J. C. Collingwood
	G-CDXK	Diamond DA42 Twin Star	A. M. Healy
	G-CDXL	Flight Design CTSW	A. K. Paterson
	G-CDXN	P & M Quik GT450	D. J. Brookfield
	G-CDXP	Aeroteknik EV-97 Eurostar	R. J. Crockett
	G-CDXR	Replica Fokker DR.1 (403/17)	P. B. Dickinson
	G-CDXS	Aeroteknik EV-97 Eurostar	T. R. James
	G-CDXT	Van's RV-9	T. M. Storey
	G-CDXU	Chilton DW.1A	M. Gibbs & J. Pollard
	G-CDXV	Campbell Cricket Mk.6A	T. L. Morley
	G-CDXW	Cameron Orange 120 SS balloon	You've Been Tangoed
	G-CDXY	Skystar Kitfox Mk.7	D. E. Steade
	G-CDYB	Rans S.6-ES Coyote II	P. J. Hellyer
	G-CDYD	Ikarus C42 FB80	C42 Group
	G-CDYG	Cameron Z-105 balloon	Slowfly Montgolfiere SNC/Italy
	G-CDYL	Lindstrand LBL-77A balloon	S. Morge
	G-CDYM	Murphy Maverick 430	C. J. Gresham
	G-CDYO	Ikarus C42 FB80	A. R. Hughes
	G-CDYP	Aeroteknik EV-97 TeamEurostar UK	R. V. Buxton & R. Cranborne
	G-CDYR	Bell 206L-3 LongRanger III	Yorkshire Helicopters
	G-CDYT	Ikarus C42 FB80	P. Bayliss
	G-CDYU	Zenair CH.701UL	A. Gannon
	G-CDYX	Lindstrand LBL-77B balloon	H. M. Savage
	G-CDYY	Alpi Pioneer 300	B. Williams
	G-CDYZ	Van's RV-7	Holden Group Ltd
	G-CDZA	Alpi Pioneer 300	J. F. Dowe
	G-CDZB	Zenair CH.601UL Zodiac	L. J. Dutch
	G-CDZG	Ikarus C42-FB80	Mainair Microlight School Ltd
	G-CDZO	Lindstrand LBL-60X balloon	R. D. Parry
	G-CDZR	Nicollier HN.700 Menestrel II	S. J. Bowles & C. Antrobus
	G-CDZS	Kolb Twinstar Mk.3 Extra	P. J. Nolan & K. V. Hill
	G-CDZU	ICP MXP-740 Savannah Jabiru (5)	P. J. Cheyney & A. H. McBreen
	G-CDZW	Cameron N-105 balloon	Backetorp Byggconsult AB

Reg	Type	Owner or Operator	Notes
G-CDZY	Medway SLA 80 Executive	Medway Microlights	
G-CDZZ	Rotorsport UK MT-03	H. E. Simons	
G-CEAK	Ikarus C42 FB80	Barton Heritage Flying Group	
G-CEAM	Aerotechnik EV-97 TeamEurostar UK	Flylight Airsports Ltd	
G-CEAN	Ikarus C42 FB80	M. D. Grinstead	
G-CEAO	Jurca MJ.5 Sirocco	P. S. Watts	
G-CEAR	Alpi Pioneer 300	R. S. Swift	
G-CEAT	Zenair CH.601HDS Zodiac	T. B. Smith	
G-CEAU	Robinson R44	Mullahead Property Co Ltd	
G-CEAY	Ultramagic H-42 balloon	J. D. A. Shields	
G-CEBA	Zenair CH.601XL Zodiac	Lamb Holm Flyers	
G-CEBC	ICP MXP-740 Savannah Jabiru (5)	H. C. Lowther	
G-CEBE	Schweizer 269C-1	Millburn World Travel Services Ltd	
G-CEBF	Aerotechnik EV-97A Eurostar	M. Lang	
G-CEBG	Balóny Kubícek BB26 balloon	P. M. Smith	
G-CEBH	Tanarg 912S/Bionix 15	G. McAnelly	
G-CEBI	Kolb Twinstar Mk.3	R. W. Livingstone	
G-CEBL	Balóny Kubícek BB20GP balloon	Associazione Sportiva Aerostatica Lombada/Italy	
G-CEBM	P & M Quik GT450	R. L. Davies	
G-CEBO	Ultramagic M-65C balloon	M. G. Howard	
G-CEBP	EV-97 TeamEurostar UK	M. J. Morson	
G-CEBT	P & M Quik GT450	N. J. Paine	
G-CEBW	P-51D Mustang	Iceni International Ltd	
G-CEBZ	Zenair CH.601UL Zodiac	W. J. Miazek	
G-CECA	P & M Quik GT450	A. Weatherall	
G-CECC	Ikarus C42 FB80	M. J. Black	
G-CECD	Cameron C-90 balloon	S. P. Harrowing	
G-CECE	Jabiru UL-D	ST Aviation Ltd	
G-CECF	Just/Reality Escapade Jabiru (3)	M. M. Hamer	
G-CECG	Jabiru UL-D	A. N. C. P. Lester	
G-CECH	Jodel D.150	W. R. Prescott	
G-CECI	Pilatus PC-6/B2-H4 Turbo Porter	P. Leal	
G-CECJ	Aeromot AMT-200S Super Ximango	G-CECJ Syndicate	
G-CECK	ICP MXP-740 Savannah Jabiru (5)	J. F. Boyce	
G-CECL	Ikarus C42 FB80	C. Lee	
G-CECP	Best Off Skyranger 912(2)	I. D. Woodall, B. P. Lycett & D. W. Buggins	
G-CECS	Lindstrand LBL-105A balloon	R. P. Ashfo	
G-CECV	Van's RV-7	D. M. Stevens	
G-CECY	EV-97 Eurostar	M. R. M. Welch	
G-CECZ	Zenair CH.601XL Zodiac	Bluebird Aviation	
G-CEDB	Reality Escapade Jabiru (5)	R. F. Morton	
G-CEDC	Ikarus C42 FB100	L. M. Call	
G-CEDE	Flight Design CTSW	M. B. Hayter	
G-CEDF	Cameron N-105 balloon	Bailey Balloons Ltd	
G-CEDI	Best Off Skyranger 912(2)	P. J. Hopkins	
G-CEDJ	Aero Designs Pulsar XP	P. F. Lorriman	
G-CEDL	TEAM Minimax 91	A. J. Weir	
G-CEDN	Pegasus Quik	Microlight Flight Lessons	
G-CEDO	Raj Hamsa X'Air Falcon 133(2)	OCTN Trust	
G-CEDT	Tanarg/Ixess 15 912S (1)	N. S. Brayn	
G-CEDV	Evektor EV-97 TeamEurostar UK	G-CEDV Flying Group	
G-CEDX	Evektor EV-97 TeamEurostar UK	Delta X-Ray Group	
G-CEDZ	Best Off Skyranger 912(2)	J. E. Walendowski & I. Bell	
G-CEEC	Raj Hamsa X'Air Hawk	G-CEEC Group	
G-CEED	ICP MXP-740 Savannah Jabiru(5)	A. C. Thompson	
G-CEEG	Alpi Pioneer 300	D. McCormack	
G-CEEI	P & M Quik GT450	S. G. Brown	
G-CEEJ	Rans S-7S Courier	R. Dunn	
G-CEEK	Cameron Z-105 balloon	T. R. Wood & J. Campbell	
G-CEEL	Ultramagic S-90 balloon	San Paolo Company SRL	
G-CEEN	PA-28-161 Cadet	T. J. Harry & B. Coren	
G-CEEO	Flight Design CTSW	E. McCallum	
G-CEEP	Van's RV-9A	B. M. Jones	
G-CEER	ELA 07R	F. G. Shepherd	
G-CEES	Cameron C-90 balloon	P. C. May	
G-CEEU	PA-28-161 Cadet	White Waltham Airfield Ltd	
G-CEEW	Ikarus C42 FB100	B. Metcalfe & P. McCusker	
G-CEEX	ICP MXP-740 Savannah Jabiru(5)	G. M. Teasdale	
G-CEEZ	PA-28-161 Warrior III	Skies Aviation Academy PC/Greece	

Notes	Reg	Type	Owner or Operator
	G-CEFA	Ikarus C42 FB100 VLA	Ikarus Group
	G-CEFB	Ultramagic H-31 balloon	M. Ekeroos
	G-CEFC	Super Marine Spitfire 26 (RB142)	D. R. Bishop
	G-CEFJ	Sonex	R. W. Chatterton
	G-CEFK	Evektor EV-97 TeamEurostar UK	P. Morgan
	G-CEFM	Cessna 152	Westair Flying Services Ltd
	G-CEFP	Jabiru J430	R. W. Brown
	G-CEFS	Cameron C-100 balloon	Gone With The Wind Ltd
	G-CEFT	Whittaker MW5-D Sorcerer	A. M. R. Bruce
	G-CEFV	Cessna 182T Skylane	A.H, D. H, P. M, & R. H. Smith
	G-CEFY	ICP MXP-740 Savannah Jabiru(4)	B. Hartley
	G-CEFZ	EV-97 TeamEurostar uk	Robo Flying Group
	G-CEGG	Lindstrand LBL-25A Cloudhopper balloon	M. W. A. Shemitt
	G-CEGH	Van's RV-9A	M. E. Creasey
	G-CEGI	Van's RV-8	D. R. Fraser & R. Tye
	G-CEGJ	P & M Quik GT450	Flylight Airsports Ltd
	G-CEGK	ICP MXP-740 Savannah VG Jabiru(1)	A. & C. Kimpton
	G-CEGL	Ikarus C42 FB80	G-CEGL Flying Group
	G-CEGO	Evektor EV-97A Eurostar	N. J. Keeling, R. F. McLachlan & J. A. Charlton
	G-CEGP	Beech 200 Super King Air	DO Systems Ltd (G-BXMA)
	G-CEGS	PA-28-161 Warrior II	Parachuting Aircraft Ltd
	G-CEGT	P & M Quik GT450	S. J. Fisher
	G-CEGU	PA-28-151 Warrior	White Waltham Airfield Ltd
	G-CEGV	P & M Quik GT450	S. P. A. Morris
	G-CEGW	P & M Quik GT450	A. Beatty
	G-CEGZ	Ikarus C42 FB80	C42 Swift Instruction Group
	G-CEHA	Avro RJ85	Triangle (Funding One) Ltd
	G-CEHC	P & M Quik GT450	G-CEHC Syndicate
	G-CEHD	Best Off Skyranger 912(2)	R. Higton
	G-CEHE	Medway SLA 100 Executive	R. P. Stoner
	G-CEHG	Ikarus C42 FB100	C. J. Hayward & C. Walters
	G-CEHI	P & M Quik GT450	A. Costello
	G-CEHL	EV-97 TeamEurostar UK	A. C. Richards
	G-CEHM	Rotorsport UK MT-03	1013 Aviation Ltd
	G-CEHN	Rotorsport UK MT-03	B. N. Trowbridge
	G-CEHR	Auster AOP.9	C. R. Wheeldon & M. H. Bichan
	G-CEHS	CAP.10B	M. D. Wynne
	G-CEHT	Rand KR-2	P. P. Geoghegan
	G-CEHV	Ikarus C42 FB80	P. G. Brooks
	G-CEHW	P & M Quik GT450	G-CEHW Group
	G-CEHX	Lindstrand LBL-9A balloon	P. Baker
	G-CEHZ	Edge XT912-B/Streak III-B	J. Daly
	G-CEIA	Rotorsport UK MT-03	M. P Chetwynd-Talbot
	G-CEIB	Yakovlev Yak-18A (03)	R. A. Fleming
	G-CEID	Van's RV-7	A. Moyce
	G-CEIE	Flight Design CTSW	G. Hardman
	G-CEIG	Van's RV-7	W. K. Wilkie
	G-CEII	Medway SLA80 Executive	P. T. M. Kroef
	G-CEIL	Reality Escapade 912(2)	T. N. Crawley
	G-CEIS	Jodel DR.1050	G. R. Richardson
	G-CEIT	Van's RV-7	W. Jones & I. R. Court
	G-CEIV	Tanarg/Ixess 15 912S(2)	W. O. Fogden
	G-CEIW	Europa	R. Scanlan
	G-CEIX	Alpi Pioneer 300	I. M. Walton
	G-CEIY	Ultramagic M-120 balloon	N. Banducci/Italy
	G-CEIZ	PA-28-161 Warrior II	IZ Aviation
	G-CEJA	Cameron V-77 balloon	G. Gray (G-BTOF)
	G-CEJC	Cameron N-77 balloon	M. Cooper
	G-CEJD	PA-28-161 Warrior III	Western Air (Thruxton) Ltd
	G-CEJE	Wittman W.10 Tailwind	R. A. Povall
	G-CEJG	Ultramagic M-56 balloon	Dragon Balloon Co.Ltd
	G-CEJI	Lindstrand LBL-105A balloon	Richard Nash Cars Ltd
	G-CEJJ	P & M Quik GT450	G. McLaughlin & I. D. Baxter
	G-CEJN	Mooney M.20F	G. R. Wakeley
	G-CEJW	Ikarus C42 FB80	M. I. Deeley
	G-CEJX	P & M Quik GT450	P. Stewart & A. J. Huntly
	G-CEJY	Aerospool Dynamic WT9 UK	R. G. Bennett
	G-CEJZ	Cameron C-90 balloon	M. J. Woodcock
	G-CEKC	Medway SLA100 Executive	M. J. Woollard
	G-CEKD	Flight Design CTSW	M. W. Fitch

Reg	Type	Owner or Operator	Notes
G-CEKE	Robin DR400/180	M. F. Cuming	
G-CEKG	P & M Quik GT450	C. R. Whitton	
G-CEKI	Cessna 172P	N. Houghton	
G-CEKJ	Evektor EV-97A Eurostar	C. W. J. Vershoyle-Greene	
G-CEKK	Best Off Sky Ranger Swift 912S(1)	M. S. Schofield	
G-CEKO	Robin DR400/100	Exavia Ltd	
G-CEKS	Cameron Z-105 balloon	Phoenix Balloons Ltd	
G-CEKT	Flight Design CTSW	Charlie Tango Group	
G-CEKV	Europa	K. Atkinson	
G-CEKW	Jabiru J430	J430 Syndicate	
G-CELE	Boeing 737-377	Jet.com (G-MONN)	
G-CELF	Boeing 737-377	Jet 2.com	
G-CELG	Boeing 737-377	Jet 2.com	
G-CELH	Boeing 737-330	Jet 2.com	
G-CELI	Boeing 737-330	Jet 2.com	
G-CELM	Cameron C-80 balloon	L. Greaves	
G-CELO	Boeing 737-33AQC	Jet 2.com	
G-CELS	Boeing 737-377	Jet 2.com	
G-CELV	Boeing 737-377	Jet 2.com	
G-CELX	Boeing 737-377	Jet 2.com	
G-CELY	Boeing 737-377	Jet 2 com	
G-CEMA	Alpi Pioneer 200	R. W. Skelton & A. Daraskevicius	
G-CEMB	P & M Quik GT450	D. W. Logue	
G-CEMC	Robinson R44 Raven II	Express Charters Ltd	
G-CEME	Evektor EV-97 Eurostar	F. W. McCann	
G-CEMF	Cameron C-80 balloon	Linear Communications Consultants Ltd	
G-CEMG	Ultramagic M-105 balloon	Comunicazione In Volo SRL/Italy	
G-CEMI	Europa XS	B. D. A. Morris	
G-CEMM	P & M Quik GT450	M. A. Rhodes	
G-CEMO	P & M Quik GT450	T. D. Stock	
G-CEMR	Mainair Blade 912	J. A. Sweeney	
G-CEMT	P & M Quik GT450	M. Tautz	
G-CEMU	Cameron C-80 balloon	J. G. O'Connell	
G-CEMV	Lindstrand LBL-105A balloon	R. G. Turnbull	
G-CEMX	P & M Pegasus Quik	S. J. Meehan	
G-CEMY	Alpi Pioneer 300	J. C. A. Garland & P. F. Salter	
G-CEMZ	Pegasus Quik	P. G. Eastlake	
G-CENA	Dyn'Aero MCR-01 ULC Banbi	I. N. Drury	
G-CENB	Evektor EV-97 TeamEurostar UK	K. J. Gay	
G-CEND	Evektor EV-97 TeamEurostar UK	Flylight Airsports Ltd	
G-CENE	Flight Design CTSW	The CT Flying Group	
G-CENG	SkyRanger 912(2)	R. A. Knight	
G-CENH	Tecnam P2002-EA Sierra	M. W. Taylor	
G-CENJ	Medway SLA 951	M. Ingleton	
G-CENK	Schempp-Hirth Nimbus 4DT	G-CENK Syndicate	
G-CENL	P & M Quik GT450	P. Von Sydow & S. Baker	
G-CENM	Evektor EV-97 Eurostar	N. D. Meer	
G-CENN	Cameron C-60 balloon	C. J. Y. Holvoet	
G-CENO	Aerospool Dynamic WT9 UK	J. H. Sands	
G-CENP	Ace Magic Laser	A. G. Curtis	
G-CENS	SkyRanger Swift 912S(1)	J. Spence	
G-CENV	P & M Quik GT450	Mid Anglia Microlights Ltd	
G-CENW	Evektor EV-97A Eurostar	Southside Flyers	
G-CENX	Lindstrand LBL-360A	Wickers World Ltd	
G-CENZ	Aeros Discus/Alize	A. M. Singhvi	
G-CEOB	Pitts S-1 Special	N. J. Radford	
G-CEOC	Tecnam P2002-EA Sierra	M. Nicholas	
G-CEOG	PA-28R-201 Arrow	A. J. Gardiner	
G-CEOH	Raj Hamsa X'Air Falcon ULP(1)	J. C. Miles	
G-CEOI	Cameron C-60 balloon	A. Pieber	
G-CEOJ	Eurocopter EC 155B	Starspeed Ltd	
G-CEOL	Flylight Lightfly/Aeros Discus 15T	J. M. Pearce	
G-CEOM	Jabiru UL-450	J. R. Caylow	
G-CEON	Raj Hamsa X'Air Hawk	K. S. Campbell	
G-CEOO	P & M Quik GT450	S. Moran	
G-CEOP	Aeroprakt A22-L Foxbat	G. F. Elvis	
G-CEOS	Cameron C-90 balloon	British School of Ballooning	
G-CEOT	Dudek ReAction Sport/Bailey Quattro 175	J. Kelly	
G-CEOU	Lindstrand LBL-31A balloon	R. D. Allen	
G-CEOW	Europa XS	R. W. Wood	
G-CEOX	Rotorsport UK MT-03	A. J. Saunders	

Notes	Reg	Type	Owner or Operator
	G-CEOY	Schweizer 269C-1	Whitearrow Associates Ltd
	G-CEOZ	Paramania Action GT26/PAP Chariot Z	A. M. Shepherd
	G-CEPL	Super Marine Spitfire Mk.26 (P9398)	S. R. Marsh
	G-CEPM	Jabiru J430	T. R. Sinclair
	G-CEPP	P & M Quik GT450	W. M. Studley
	G-CEPR	Cameron Z-90 balloon	Sport Promotion SRL/Italy
	G-CEPU	Cameron Z-77 balloon	G. Forgione/Italy
	G-CEPV	Cameron Z-77 balloon	John Aimo Balloons SAS/Italy
	G-CEPW	Alpi Pioneer 300	N. K. Spedding
	G-CEPX	Cessna 152	Devon & Somerset Flight Training Ltd
	G-CEPY	Ikarus C42 FB80	L. A. Hosegood
	G-CEPZ	DR.107 One Design	S. Malakova
	G-CERB	SkyRanger Swift 912S(1)	J. J. Littler
	G-CERC	Cameron Z-350 balloon	Ballooning Network Ltd
	G-CERD	D.H.C.1 Chipmunk 22	A. C. Darby
	G-CERE	Evektor EV-97 TeamEurostar UK	D. A. Abel
	G-CERF	Rotorsport UK MT-03	P. J. Robinson
	G-CERH	Cameron C-90 balloon	A. Walker
	G-CERI	Shaw Europa XS	S. J. M. Shepherd
	G-CERK	Van's RV-9A	P. E. Brown
	G-CERN	P & M Quik GT450	P. M. Jackson
	G-CERP	P & M Quik GT450	RP Syndicate
	G-CERT	Mooney M.20K	M. Simon
	G-CERV	P & M Quik GT450	N. F. Taylor
	G-CERW	P & M Pegasus Quik	D. J. Cornelius
	G-CERX	Hawker 850XP	Hangar 8 Management Ltd
	G-CERY	SAAB 2000	Eastern Airways
	G-CERZ	SAAB 2000	Eastern Airways
	G-CESA	Replica Jodel DR.1050	T. J. Bates
	G-CESD	SkyRanger Swift 912S(1)	B. R. Trotman
	G-CESH	Cameron Z-90 balloon	A. P. Jay
	G-CESI	Aeroprakt A22-L Foxbat	D. N. L. Howell
	G-CESJ	Raj Hamsa X'Air Hawk	J. Bolton & R. Shewan
	G-CESM	TL2000UK Sting Carbon	R. D. Myles
	G-CESR	P & M Quik GT450	G. Kerr & A. Shields
	G-CEST	Robinson R44	Startrade Heli Gmbh & Co KG/Germany
	G-CESV	EV-97 TeamEurostar UK	W. D. Kyle & T. J. Dowling
	G-CESW	Flight Design CTSW	J. Whiting
	G-CESZ	CZAW Sportcruiser	G. Glover
	G-CETB	Robin DR.400/180	QR Flying Club
	G-CETD	PA-28-161 Warrior III	AJW Construction Ltd
	G-CETE	PA-28-161 Warrior III	Aerodynamics Malaga SL/Spain
	G-CETF	Flight Design CTSW	I. Epton
	G-CETK	Cameron Z-145 balloon	R. H. Etherington
	G-CETL	P & M Quik GT450	J. I. Greenshields
	G-CETM	P & M Quik GT450	G-CETM Flying Group
	G-CETN	Hummel Bird	A. A. Haseldine
	G-CETO	Best Off Sky Ranger Swift 912S(1)	S. C. Stoodley
	G-CETP	Van's RV-9A	D. Boxall & S. Hill
	G-CETR	Ikarus C42 FB80	Cloudbase Paragliding Ltd
	G-CETS	Van's RV-7	TS Group
	G-CETT	Evektor EV-97 TeamEurostar UK	P. Thompson
	G-CETU	Best Off Sky Ranger Swift 912S(1)	A. Raithby & N. McCusker
	G-CETV	Best Off Sky Ranger Swift 912S(1)	C. J. Johnson
	G-CETX	Alpi Pioneer 300	J. M. P. Ree
	G-CETY	Rans S-6-ES Coyote II	J. North
	G-CETZ	Ikarus C42 FB100	G-CETZ Group
	G-CEUF	P & M Quik GT450	G. T. Snoddon
	G-CEUH	P & M Quik GT450	W. Brownlie
	G-CEUJ	SkyRanger Swift 912S(1)	The CUEJ Group
	G-CEUL	Ultramagic M-105 balloon	R. A. Vale
	G-CEUM	Ultramagic M-120 balloon	Skydive Chatteris Club Ltd
	G-CEUN	Orlican Discus CS	The Royal Air Force Gliding and Soaring Association
	G-CEUU	Robinson R44 II	A. Stafford-Jones
	G-CEUV	Cameron C-90 balloon	A. M. Holly
	G-CEUW	Zenair CH.601XL Zodiac	P. Connolly
	G-CEUZ	P & M Quik GT450	P. M. Williamson
	G-CEVA	Ikarus C42 FB80	The Scottish Flying Group
	G-CEVB	P & M Quik GT450	C. Traher
	G-CEVC	Van's RV-4	P. A. Brook

Reg	Type	Owner or Operator	Notes
G-CEVD	Rolladen-Schneider LS3	R. M. Theil	
G-CEVE	Centrair 101A	T. P. Newham	
G-CEVH	Cameron V-65 balloon	J. A. Atkinson	
G-CEVJ	Alpi Pioneer 200-M	K. Worthington	
G-CEVK	Schleicher Ka 6CR	K. E. & O. J. Wilson	
G-CEVM	Tecnam P2002-EA Sierra	J. A. Ellis	
G-CEVN	Rolladen-Schneider LS7	N. Gaunt & B. C. Toon	
G-CEVO	Grob G.109B	T.J. Wilkinson	
G-CEVP	P & M Quik GT450	P. J. Lowe	
G-CEVS	EV-97 TeamEurostar UK	Golf Victor Sierra Flying Group	
G-CEVT	Dudek Reaction 27/Bailey Quattro 175	J. Kelly	
G-CEVU	Savannah VG Jabiru(4)	I. C. May	
G-CEVV	Rolladen-Schneider LS3	LS3 307 Syndicate	
G-CEVW	P & M Quik GT450	R. W. Sutherland	
G-CEVX	Aeriane Swift Light PAS	P. Trueman	
G-CEVY	Rotorsport UK MT-03	Silver Birch Pet Jets Ltd	
G-CEVZ	Centrair ASW-20FL	B. Watkins	
G-CEWC	Schleicher ASK-21	London Gliding Club Proprietary Ltd	
G-CEWD	P & M Quik GT450	S. C. Key	
G-CEWE	Schempp-Hirth Nimbus 2	T. Clark	
G-CEWF	Jacobs V35 Airchair balloon	G. F. & I. Chadwick & M. G. Roberts	
G-CEWH	P & M Quik GT450	G-CEWH Syndicate	
G-CEWI	Schleicher ASW-19B	S. R. Edwards	
G-CEWK	Cessna 172S	S. Howe	
G-CEWL	Alpi Pioneer 200	R. W. H. Watson	
G-CEWM	DHC.6 Twin Otter 300	Isles of Scilly Skybus Ltd	
G-CEWN	Diamond DA-42 Twin Star	Halsbury Travel Ltd	
G-CEWO	Schleicher Ka 6CR	D. P. Westcott	
G-CEWP	Grob G.102 Astir CS	G-CEWP Flying Group	
G-CEWR	Aeroprakt A22-L Foxbat	C. S. Bourne & G. P. Wiley	
G-CEWS	Zenair CH.701SP	D. L. Aspinall & G. E. MacCuish	
G-CEWT	Flight Design CTSW	K. Tuck	
G-CEWU	Ultramagic H-77 balloon	P. C. Waterhouse	
G-CEWW	Grob G.102 Astir CS	The South Wales Gliding Club Ltd	
G-CEWX	Cameron Z-350 balloon	Celador Radio (South West) Ltd	
G-CEWY	Quicksilver GT500	R. J. Scott	
G-CEWZ	Schempp-Hirth Discus bT	J. F. Goudie	
G-CEXL	Ikarus C42 FB80	Syndicate C42-1	
G-CEXM	Best Off Sky Ranger Swift 912S(1)	A. F. Batchelor	
G-CEXN	Cameron A-120 balloon	Dragon Balloon Company Ltd	
G-CEXO	PA-28-161 Warrior III	Pilot Traning & Testing Ltd	
G-CEXP	HPR.7 Herald 209 ★	Towing and rescue trainer/Gatwick	
G-CEXX	Rotorsport UK MT-03	D. Goh	
G-CEYC	DG Flugzeugbau DG-505 Elan Orion	Scottish Gliding Union Ltd	
G-CEYE	PA-32R-300 Cherokee Lance	D. C. McH. Wilson	
G-CEYG	Cessna 152	C. M. de C. C. Cabral/Portugal	
G-CEYH	Cessna 152	Cornwall Flying Club Ltd	
G-CEYK	Europa XS	A. B. Milne	
G-CEYL	Bombardier BD-700-1A10 Global Express	TAG Aviation (UK) Ltd	
G-CEYM	Van's RV-6	R. B. Skinner	
G-CEYN	Grob G.109B	G-CEYN Flying Group	
G-CEYP	North Wing Design Stratus/ATF	J. S. James	
G-CEYR	Rotorsport UK MT-03	S. R. Voller	
G-CEYY	EV-97 TeamEurostar UK	N. J. James	
G-CEZA	Ikarus C42 FB80	P. J. Morton & D. E. Bassett	
G-CEZB	Savannah VG Jabiru(1)	W. E. Dudley	
G-CEZD	EV-97 TeamEurostar	G. P. Jones	
G-CEZE	Best Off Sky Ranger Swift 912S	J. A. Williams	
G-CEZF	EV-97 TeamEurostar UK	D. J. Dick	
G-CEZH	Aerochute Dual	G. Stokes	
G-CEZI	PA-28-161 Cadet	Redhill Air Services Ltd	
G-CEZK	Stolp S.750 Acroduster Too	R. I. M. Hague	
G-CEZL	PA-28-161 Cadet	Chalrey Ltd	
G-CEZM	Cessna 152	Cristal Air Ltd	
G-CEZO	PA-28-161 Cadet	Redhill Air Services Ltd	
G-CEZR	Diamond DA.40D Star	Flying Time Ltd	
G-CEZS	Zenair CH.601HDS Zodiac	V. D. Asque	
G-CEZT	P & M Aviation Quik GT450	A. A. Greig	
G-CEZU	CFM Streak Shadow SA	A. W. Hodder	
G-CEZW	Jodel D.150 Mascaret	J. C. Carter	
G-CEZX	P & M Aviation Quik GT450	Zulu Xray Group	

Notes	Reg	Type	Owner or Operator
	G-CEZZ	Flight Design CTSW	J. A. Lynch
	G-CFAJ	Glaser-Dirks DG-300 Elan	N. L. J. Everett
	G-CFAK	Rotorsport UK MT-03	R. M. Savage
	G-CFAM	Schempp-Hirth Nimbus 3/24.5	Nimbus III Syndicate J15
	G-CFAO	Rolladen-Schneider LS4	V. R. Roberts
	G-CFAP	Interplane ZJ-Viera	P. I. Passmore
	G-CFAR	Rotorsport UK MT-03	P. M. Twose
	G-CFAS	Escapade Jabiru(3)	C. G. N. Boyd
	G-CFAT	P & M Aviation Quik GT450	I. F. Bruce
	G-CFAV	Ikarus C42 FB80	Deanland Flight Training Ltd
	G-CFAW	Lindstrand LBL-35A Cloudhopper balloon	A. Walker
	G-CFAX	Ikarus C42 FB80	R. E. Parker & B. Cook
	G-CFAY	Sky 120-24 balloon	G. B. Lescott
	G-CFBA	Schleicher ASW-20BL	C. R. Little
	G-CFBB	Schempp-Hirth Standard Cirrus	N. Wall
	G-CFBC	Schleicher ASW-15B	G-CFBC Group
	G-CFBE	Ikarus C42 FB80	K. H. Denham
	G-CFBF	Lindstrand LBL 203T Hiflyer gas balloon	S and D Leisure (Europe) Ltd
	G-CFBH	Glaser-Dirks DG-100G Elan	IBM Gliding Club
	G-CFBJ	Rotorsport UK MT-03	P. S. Ball
	G-CFBL	Best Off Sky Ranger Swift 912S(1)	D. Hennings & M. A. Azeem
	G-CFBM	P & M Quantum 15-912	G-CFBM Flying Group
	G-CFBN	Glasflugel Mosquito B	S. R. & J. Nash
	G-CFBT	Schempp-Hirth Ventus bT	P. R. Stafford-Allen
	G-CFBV	Schleicher ASK-21	London Gliding Club Proprietary Ltd
	G-CFBW	DG-100G Elan	G-CFBW Syndicate
	G-CFBY	Best Off Sky Ranger Swift 912S(1)	K. Washbourne
	G-CFCA	Schempp-Hirth Discus b	P. Lund
	G-CFCB	Centrair 101	T. J. Berriman & M. Phillimore
	G-CFCC	Cameron Z-275 balloon	Ballooning Network Ltd
	G-CFCD	SkyRanger Swift 912S(1)	D. & L. Payn
	G-CFCE	Raj Hamsa X'Air Hawk	B. M. Tibenham
	G-CFCF	Aerochute Dual	C. J. Kendal & S. G. Smith
	G-CFCI	Cessna F.172N	J. Blacklock
	G-CFCJ	Grob G.102 Astir CS	A. J. C. Beaumont & P. Hardwick
	G-CFCK	Best Off Sky Ranger 912S(1)	J. Smith
	G-CFCL	Rotorsport UK MT-03	D. D. Taylor
	G-CFCM	Robinson R44	Newmarket Plant Hire Ltd
	G-CFCN	Schempp-Hirth Standard Cirrus	P. C. Bunniss
	G-CFCP	Rolladen-Schneider LS6-a	M. A. Hall
	G-CFCR	Schleicher Ka-6E	R. F. Whittaker
	G-CFCS	Schempp-Hirth Nimbus 2C	J. Luck & P. Dolling
	G-CFCT	EV-97 TeamEurostar UK	Sutton Eurostar Group
	G-CFCV	Schleicher ASW-20	I. R. Gallacher
	G-CFCW	Rotorsport UK MT-03	C. M. Jones
	G-CFCX	Rans S-6-ES Coyote II	D. & S. Morrison
	G-CFCY	Best Off Sky Ranger Swift 912S(1)	M. E. & T. E. Simpson
	G-CFCZ	P & M Quik GT450	P. K. Dale
	G-CFDA	Schleicher ASW-15	N. B. Coggins
	G-CFDE	Schempp-Hirth Ventus bT	K. W. Clarke
	G-CFDF	Ultramagic S-90 balloon	Edinburgh University Hot Air Balloon Club
	G-CFDG	Schleicher Ka 6CR	Delta-Golf Group
	G-CFDI	Van's RV-6	M. D. Challoner
	G-CFDJ	EV-97 TeamEurostar UK	J. D. J. Spragg & M. Jones
	G-CFDK	Rans S-6-ES Coyote II	Conair Sports Ltd
	G-CFDL	P & M QuikR	N. A. Higgins
	G-CFDM	Schempp-Hirth Discus b	J. L. & T. G. M. Whiting
	G-CFDN	Best Off Sky Ranger Swift 912S(1)	Hadair Fixed Wing Flyers
	G-CFDO	Flight Design CTSW	D. McCabe & M. Harris
	G-CFDP	Flight Design CTSW	N. Fielding
	G-CFDS	TL2000UK Sting Carbon	A. G. Cummings
	G-CFDT	Aerola Alatus-M	M. J. Reader-Hoer & G. Rainey
	G-CFDX	PZL-Bielsko SZD-48-1 Jantar Standard 2	A. Phillips
	G-CFDY	P &M Quik GT450	C. N. Thornton
	G-CFDZ	Flight Design Exxtacy/Alize	N. C. O. Watney
	G-CFEA	Cameron C-90 balloon	A. M. Holly
	G-CFEB	Cameron C-80 balloon	N. Edmunds
	G-CFED	Van's RV-9	E. W. Taylor
	G-CFEE	Evektor EV-97 Eurostar	G-CFEE Flying Group
	G-CFEF	Grob G.102 Astir CS	Oxford University Gliding Club

Reg	Type	Owner or Operator	Notes
G-CFEG	Schempp-Hirth Ventus b/16.6	J. R. Eccles	
G-CFEH	Centrair 101 Pegase	Booker Gliding Club Ltd	
G-CFEI	RAF 2000 GTX-SE	C. J. Watkinson	
G-CFEJ	Schempp-Hirth Discus b	Lima Charlie Syndicate	
G-CFEK	Cameron Z-105 balloon	R. M. Penny (Plant Hire and Demolition) Ltd	
G-CFEL	EV-97A Eurostar	J. A. Crook	
G-CFEI	RAF 2000 GTX-SE	A. M. Wells	
G-CFEM	P & M Aviation Quik GT450	A. M. King	
G-CFEN	PZL-Bielsko SZD-50-3 Puchacz	The Northumbria Gliding Club Ltd	
G-CFEO	EV-97 Eurostar	J. B. Binks	
G-CFER	Schempp-Hirth Discus b	S. R. Westlake	
G-CFES	Schempp-Hirth Discus b	M. J. Spittal	
G-CFET	Van's RV-7	J. Astor	
G-CFEV	P & M Pegasus Quik	W. T. Davis	
G-CFEX	P & M Quik GT450	H. Wilson	
G-CFEY	Aerola Alatus-M	M. S. Hayman	
G-CFEZ	CZAW Sportcruiser	J. F. Barber & J. R. Large	
G-CFFA	Ultramagic M-90 balloon	Proxim SPA/Italy	
G-CFFB	Grob G.102 Astir CS	R. Millins	
G-CFFC	Centrair 101A	G. R. Hudson	
G-CFFE	EV-97 TeamEurostar UK	R. W. Osborne	
G-CFFF	Pitts S-1S Special	P. J. Roy	
G-CFFG	Aerochute Dual	G. J. Pemberton	
G-CFFJ	Flight Design CTSW	R. Germany	
G-CFFL	Lindstrand LBL-317A balloon	Bailey Balloons Ltd	
G-CFFN	P & M Quik GT450	S. D. Cox	
G-CFFO	P & M Quik GT450	D. Ben-Lamri & R. Wade	
G-CFFS	Centrair 101A	R. C. Verdier	
G-CFFT	Schempp-Hirth Discus b	Goalrace Ltd	
G-CFFU	Glaser-Dirks DG-101G Elan	FFU Group	
G-CFFV	PZL-Bielsko SZD-51-1 Junior	Herefordshire Gliding Club Ltd	
G-CFFX	Schempp-Hirth Discus b	P. J. Richards	
G-CFFY	PZL-Bielsko SZD-51-1 Junior	Scottish Gliding Union Ltd	
G-CFGA	VS Spitfire VIII	Aviation Heritage Foundation Ltd	
G-CFGB	Cessna 680 Citation Sovereign	Keepflying LLP	
G-CFGC	Aeros Discus 15T	D. P. Dixon	
G-CFGD	P & M Quik GT450	D. J. Revell	
G-CFGE	Stinson 108-1 Voyager (108-1601:H)	Windmill Aviation	
G-CFGF	Schempp-Hirth Nimbus 3T	R. E. Cross	
G-CFGG	Rotorsport UK MT-03	G-CFGG Flying Group	
G-CFGH	Jabiru J160	S. M. Spencer	
G-CFGJ	VS.300 Spitfire I (N3200)	Imperial War Museum	
G-CFGK	Grob G.102 Astir CS	P. Allingham	
G-CFGM	Ikarus C42 FB80	G. P. Burns	
G-CFGO	Best Off Sky Ranger Swift 912S	R. G. Hearsey	
G-CFGP	Schleicher ASW-19	A. E. Prime	
G-CFGR	Schleicher ASK-13	Edensoaring Ltd	
G-CFGT	P & M Aviation Quik GT450	A. C. McAllister	
G-CFGU	Schempp-Hirth Standard Cirrus	G-CFGU Syndicate	
G-CFGV	P & M Quik GT450	R. Bennett	
G-CFGX	EV-97 TeamEurostar UK	Golf XRay Group	
G-CFGY	Rotorsport UK MT-03	A. R. Hawes	
G-CFGW	Centrair 101A	L. P. Smith	
G-CFGZ	Flight Design CTSW	G. R. Cassie	
G-CFHB	Micro Aviation B.22J Bantam	P. Rayson	
G-CFHC	Micro Aviation B.22J Bantam	M. Russell	
G-CFHD	Schleicher ASW-20 BL	196 Syndicate	
G-CFHF	PZL-Bielsko SZD-51-1	Black Mountains Gliding Club	
G-CFHG	Schempp-Hirth Mini Nimbus C	187 Syndicate	
G-CFHI	Van's RV-9	J. R. Dawe	
G-CFHK	Aeroprakt A22-L Foxbat	R. Bellew	
G-CFHL	Rolladen-Schneider LS4	G-CFHL Syndicate	
G-CFHM	Schleicher ASK-13	Lasham Gliding Society Ltd	
G-CFHN	Schleicher K 8B	The Nene Valley Gliding Club Ltd	
G-CFHO	Grob G.103 Twin Astir II	The Surrey Hills Gliding Club Ltd	
G-CFHP	Ikarus C42 FB80	ACornwall Microlights	
G-CFHR	Schempp-Hirth Discus b	Q5 Syndicate	
G-CFHS	Tchemma T01/77 balloon	J. Dyer	
G-CFHU	Robinson R22 Beta	Cameron and Brown Partnership	
G-CFHW	Grob G.102 Astir CS	D. J. Wedlock & D. Brown	
G-CFHX	Schroeder Fire Balloons G22/24 balloon	T. J. Ellenrieder	

Notes	Reg	Type	Owner or Operator
	G-CFHY	Fokker Dr.1 Triplane replica (556/17)	P. G. Bond
	G-CFHZ	Schleicher Ka 6CR	P. J. Howarth
	G-CFIA	Best Off Sky Ranger Swift 912S(1)	D. Lamb & N. Elahi
	G-CFIC	Jodel DR.1050/M1	J. H. & P. I. Kempton
	G-CFID	Tanarg/Ixess 15 912S	D. Smith
	G-CFIE	Rotorsport UK MT-03	The India Echo Flyers
	G-CFIF	Christen Eagle II	CFG Flying Group
	G-CFIG	P & M Aviation Quik GT450	J. Whitfield
	G-CFIH	Piel CP.1320	A. R. Wade
	G-CFII	DH.82A Tiger Moth	S. Deane
	G-CFIJ	Christen Eagle II	V. Kiminius
	G-CFIK	Lindstrand LBL-60X balloon	L. Sambrook
	G-CFIL	P & M Aviation Quik GT450	S. N. Catchpole
	G-CFIM	P & M Aviation Quik GT450	D. M. Broom
	G-CFIO	Cessna 172S	Skytrek Air Services
	G-CFIT	Ikarus C42 FB100	G-CFIT Group
	G-CFIU	CZAW Sportcruiser	G. Everett & D. Smith
	G-CFIW	Balony Kubicek BB20XR balloon	I. S. Bridge
	G-CFIZ	Best Off Sky Ranger 912(2)	J. A. Hartshorne
	G-CFJB	Rotorsport UK MT-03	N. J. Hargreaves
	G-CFJC	Sikorsky S-76C	Bristow Helicopters Ltd
	G-CFJF	Schempp-Hirth SHK-1	J. F. Mills
	G-CFJG	Best Off Sky Ranger Swift 912S(1)	E. E. Colley
	G-CFJH	Grob G.102 Astir CS77	D. B. Harrison
	G-CFJI	Ultramagic M-105 balloon	Club Aerostatico Wind & Fire/Italy
	G-CFJJ	Best Off Sky Ranger Swift 912S(1)	J. J. Ewing
	G-CFJK	Centrair 101A	D. Lewis
	G-CFJL	Raj Hamsa X'Air Hawk	G. L. Craig
	G-CFJM	Rolladen-Schneider LS4-a	I. G. Sullivan
	G-CFJN	Diamond DA.40D Star	Airways Aviation Academy Ltd
	G-CFJO	Diamond DA.40D Star	Airways Aviation Academy Ltd
	G-CFJR	Glaser-Dirks DG-300 Club Elan	W. Palmer & H. Inigo-Jones
	G-CFJS	Glaser-Dirks DG-300 Club Elan	K. L. Goldsmith
	G-CFJU	Raj Hamsa X'Air Hawk	J. Beattie
	G-CFJV	Schleicher ASW-15	D. J. Price
	G-CFJW	Schleicher K7	K7 Group
	G-CFJX	DG-300 Elan	Crown Service Gliding Club
	G-CFJZ	Schempp-Hirth SHK-1	B. C. Irwin & R. H. Hanna
	G-CFKA	Rotorsport UK MT-03	M. J. L. Carter
	G-CFKB	CZAW Sportcruiser	KB Flying Group
	G-CFKD	Raj Hamsa X'Air Falcon Jabiru(2)	J. C. Dawson
	G-CFKE	Raj Hamsa X'Air Hawk	J. F. Northey & S. P. Read
	G-CFKG	Rolladen-Schneider LS4-a	G-CFKG Group
	G-CFKH	Zenair CH.601XL Zodiac	C. Long
	G-CFKJ	P & M Aviation Quik GT450	E. Avery & J. Witcombe
	G-CFKL	Schleicher ASW-20 BL	J. Ley
	G-CFKM	Schempp-Hirth Discus b	Lasham Gliding Society Ltd
	G-CFKN	Lindstrand GA22 Mk.II airship	Lindstrand Technologies Ltd
	G-CFKO	P & M Quik GT450	A. Maudsley
	G-CFKP	Performance Designs Barnstormer/Voyager	G. P. Foyle
	G-CFKR	P & M Pegasus Quik	R. D. Ballard
	G-CFKS	Flight Design CTSW	L. I. Bailey
	G-CFKT	Schleicher K 8B	FKT Group
	G-CFKU	P & M Aviation Quik GT450	P. W. Frost
	G-CFKW	Alpi Pioneer 200	A. B. Dean
	G-CFKX	Cameron Z-160 balloon	Ballooning in Tuscany SRL
	G-CFKY	Schleicher Ka 6CR	J. A. Timmis
	G-CFKZ	Europa XS	W. Aspden & P. H. Wiltshire
	G-CFLA	P & M Aviation Quik GT450	P. H. Woodward
	G-CFLC	Glaser-Dirks DG-300 Club Elan	J. L.Hey
	G-CFLD	Ikarus C42 FB80	M. R. Badminton
	G-CFLE	Schempp-Hirth Discus b	D. A. Humphreys
	G-CFLF	Rolladen-Schneider LS4-a	D. Lamb
	G-CFLG	CZAW Sportcruiser	G. R. Greensall
	G-CFLH	Schleicher K8B	The South Wales Gliding Club Ltd
	G-CFLI	Europa Aviation Europa	A. & E. Bennett
	G-CFLK	Cameron C-90 balloon	J. R. Rivers-Scott
	G-CFLL	EV-97 Eurostar	I. Galea
	G-CFLM	P & M Pegasus Quik	The JAG Flyers
	G-CFLN	Best Off Sky Ranger Swift 912S(1)	D. Bletcher
	G-CFLO	Rotorsport UK MT-03	K. J. Jamieson

Reg	Type	Owner or Operator	Notes
G-CFLP	D.31 Turbulent	Eaglescott Turbulent Group	
G-CFLR	P & M Aviation Quik GT450	S. J. Baker	
G-CFLS	Schleicher Ka 6CR	University College London Union	
G-CFLU	SAAB 2000	Eastern Airways	
G-CFLV	SAAB 2000	Eastern Airways	
G-CFLW	Schempp-Hirth Standard Cirrus 75	J. Pack	
G-CFLX	DG-300 Club Elan	Felix Flying Group	
G-CFLZ	Scheibe SF-27A Zugvogel V	J. C. Gazzard	
G-CFMA	BB03 Trya/BB103	P. D. Curtis	
G-CFMB	P & M Aviation Quik GT450	Countermine Technologies PLC	
G-CFMC	Van's RV-9A	G-CFMC Flying Group	
G-CFMD	P & M Aviation Quik GT450	M. J. C. & S. A. C. Curtis	
G-CFMH	Schleicher ASK-13	Lasham Gliding Society Ltd	
G-CFMI	Best Off Sky Ranger 912(1)	P. Shelton	
G-CFMM	Cessna 172S	Fastnet Jet Alliance Ltd	
G-CFMN	Schempp-Hirth Ventus cT	FMN Glider Syndicate	
G-CFMO	Schempp-Hirth Discus b	P. D. Bagnall	
G-CFMP	Europa XS	M. P. Gamble	
G-CFMR	Ultramagic V-14 balloon	P. Baker	
G-CFMS	Schleicher ASW-15	D. A. Logan	
G-CFMT	Schempp-Hirth Standard Cirrus	G-CFMT Group	
G-CFMU	Schempp-Hirth Standard Cirrus	T. J. Williamson	
G-CFMV	Aerola Alatus-M	P. J. Wood	
G-CFMW	Scheibe SF-25C	The Windrushers Gliding Club Ltd	
G-CFMX	PA-28-161 Warrior II	Stapleford Flying Club Ltd	
G-CFMY	Rolladen-Schneider LS7	G-CFMY Group	
G-CFNB	Cameron TR-70 balloon	P. Bals	
G-CFNC	Flylight Dragonfly	W. G. Minns	
G-CFND	Schleicher Ka 6E	C. Scutt	
G-CFNE	PZL-Bielsko SZD-38A Jantar 1	T. Robson, J. Murray & I. Gordon	
G-CFNF	Robinson R44 II	Kuki Helicopter Sales Ltd	
G-CFNH	Schleicher ASW-19	S. N. & P. E. S. Longland	
G-CFNI	Airborne Edge XT912-B/Streak III-B	Fly NI Ltd	
G-CFNK	Slingsby T.65A Vega	I. P. Goldstraw	
G-CFNL	Schempp-Hirth Discus b	A. S. Ramsay & P. P. Musto	
G-CFNM	Centrair 101B Pegase	D. T. Hartley	
G-CFNO	Best Off Sky Ranger Swift 912S(1)	P. R. Hanman	
G-CFNP	Schleicher Ka 6CR	P. Pollard-Wilkins	
G-CFNR	Schempp-Hirth Discus b	C. J. Short	
G-CFNS	Glaser-Dirks DG-300 Club Elan	FNS Syndicate	
G-CFNT	Glaser-Dirks DG-600	G-CFNT Group	
G-CFNU	Rolladen Schneider LS4-a	R. J. Simpson	
G-CFNW	CZAW Sportcruiser	N. D. McAllister & M. Owen	
G-CFNW	EV-97 TeamEurostar UK	The Scottish Aero Club Ltd	
G-CFNX	ixess 13 (modified/Buggy 582 Trike)	A. E. Barron	
G-CFNY	Flylight Dragonfly	C. Moore	
G-CFNZ	Airborne Edge XT912-B/Streak III-B	N. C. Grayson	
G-CFOB	Schleicher ASW-15B	G. J. Chisholm	
G-CFOC	Glaser-Dirks DG200/17	R. Robinson	
G-CFOF	Scheibe SF-27A Zugvogel V	J. H. B. Jones	
G-CFOG	Ikarus C42 FB UK	P. D. Coppin	
G-CFOI	Cessna 172N	P. Fearon	
G-CFOJ	Eurocopter EC.155 B1	Starspeed Ltd	
G-CFOM	Scheibe SF27A	A. Ruddle & P. DrakeK. A. Ford	
G-CFON	Wittman W8 Tailwind	G-CFON Group	
G-CFOO	P & M Aviation Quik R	Microavionics	
G-CFOP	Cameron Hopping Bag 120 SS balloon	J. Ravibalan	
G-CFOR	Schleicher K 8B	Dorset Gliding Club Ltd	
G-CFOS	Flylight Dragonfly	C. G. Langham	
G-CFOT	PZL-Bielsko SZD-48-3 Jantar Standard 3	T. Greenwood	
G-CFOU	Schleicher K7	Eaglescott ASK7 Group	
G-CFOV	CZAW Sportcruiser	J. G. Murphy	
G-CFOW	Best Off Sky Ranger Swift 912S(1)	Oscar Whiskey Syndicate	
G-CFOX	Marganski MDM-1	M. Makari	
G-CFOY	Schempp-Hirth Discus b	J. W. Slater, R. F. Dowty & B. K. Atkins	
G-CFOZ	Rolladen-Schneider LS1-f	L51 Group	
G-CFPA	CZAW Sportcruiser	T. W. Lorimer	
G-CFPB	Schleicher ASW-15B	G-CFPB Syndicate	
G-CFPD	Rolladen-Schneider LS7	LS7 Group	
G-CFPE	Schempp-Hirth Ventus cT	R. Palmer	
G-CFPG	AMS-Flight Carat A	B. J. L. Bollen	

Notes	Reg	Type	Owner or Operator
	G-CFPH	Centrair ASW-20F	G-CFPH Group
	G-CFPI	P & M Aviation Quik GT450	E. J. Douglas
	G-CFPJ	CZAW Sportcruiser	S. R. Winter
	G-CFPL	Schempp-Hirth Ventus c	R. V. Barrett
	G-CFPM	PZL-Bielsko SZD-51-1 Junior	Kent Gliding Club Ltd
	G-CFPN	Schleicher ASW-20	J. C. M. Docherty
	G-CFPP	Schempp-Hirth Nimbus 2B	R. Jones & D. W. North
	G-CFPR	P & M Quik R	J. A. Horn
	G-CFPS	Sky 25-16 balloon	G. B. Lescott
	G-CFPT	Schleicher ASW-20	L. Hornsey and L. Weeks Syndicate
	G-CFPW	Glaser-Dirks DG-600	P. B. Gray
	G-CFRC	Schempp-Hirth Nimbus 2B	Tim and Martin Nimbus 2B Group
	G-CFRE	Schleicher Ka 6E	R. A. Foreshew
	G-CFRF	Lindstrand LBL-31A	RAF Halton Hot Air Balloon Club
	G-CFRH	Schleicher ASW-20CL	J. N. Wilton
	G-CFRI	Ultramagic N-355 balloon	Kent Ballooning
	G-CFRJ	Schempp-Hirth Standard Cirrus	J. H. B. Jones
	G-CFRK	Schleicher ASW-15B	P. R. Boet
	G-CFRM	SkyRanger Swift 912S(1)	R. K. & T. A. Willcox
	G-CFRN	Rotorsport UK MTO Sport	R. Marks
	G-CFRP	Centrair 101A Pegase	L. Bourne
	G-CFRR	Centrair 101A	G-CFRR Syndicate
	G-CFRS	Scheibe Zugvogel IIIB	G-CFRS Flying Group
	G-CFRT	EV-97 TeamEurostar UK	K. A. O'Neill
	G-CFRV	Centrair 101A	J. D. Hubberstey
	G-CFRW	Schleicher ASW-20L	R. M. Green
	G-CFRX	Centrair 101A	S. Woolrich
	G-CFRY	Zenair CH 601UL	C. K. Fry
	G-CFRZ	Schempp-Hirth Standard Cirrus	S. G. Lapworth
	G-CFSB	Tecnam P2002-RG Sierra	W. J. Gale and Son
	G-CFSD	Schleicher ASK-13	Edensoaring Ltd
	G-CFSF	P & M Aviation QuikR	C. J. Gordon
	G-CFSG	Van's RV-9	Foley Farm Flying Group
	G-CFSH	Grob G.102 Astir CS Jeans	Buckminster Gliding Club Ltd
	G-CFSJ	Jabiru J160	S. Langley
	G-CFSK	Dyn'Aero MCR-01 VLA Sportster	A. Daraskevicius
	G-CFSL	Kubicek BB-26Z balloon	M. R. Jeynes
	G-CFSO	Flylight Dragonfly/Aeros Discus 15T	M. F. J. Armstrong
	G-CFSR	DG-300 Elan	A. P. Montague
	G-CFSS	Schleicher Ka 6E	FSS Syndicate
	G-CFST	Schleicher ASH-25E	D. Tucker & K. H. Lloyd
	G-CFSW	Skyranger Swift 912S(1)	C. T. Hanbury-Tenison
	G-CFSX	Savannah VG Jabiru(1)	M. E. Caton
	G-CFTA	Ace Magic Laser	P and M Aviation Ltd
	G-CFTB	Schleicher Ka 6CR	B. T. Green & M. W. Bennett
	G-CFTC	PZL-Bielsko SZD-51-1 Junior	Seahawk Gliding Club
	G-CFTD	Schleicher ASW-15B	A. A. Thornburn
	G-CFTG	P & M Aviation Quik R	A. V. Cosser
	G-CFTH	PZL-Bielsko SZD-50-3 Puchacz	Buckminster Gliding Club Ltd
	G-CFTI	Evektor EV-97A Eurostar	R. J. Dance
	G-CFTJ	Aerotechnik EV-97A Eurostar	C. B. Flood
	G-CFTK	Grob G.102 Astir CS Jeans	Ulster Gliding Club Ltd
	G-CFTL	Schleicher ASW-20CL	J. S. & S. V. Shaw
	G-CFTM	Cameron C-80 balloon	P. A. Meecham
	G-CFTN	Schleicher K 8B	Mendip Gliding Club Ltd
	G-CFTO	Ikarus C42 FB80	Fly Hire Ltd
	G-CFTP	Schleicher ASW-20CL	D. J. Pengilley
	G-CFTR	Grob G.102 Astir CS77	The University of Nottingham Students Union
	G-CFTS	Glaser-Dirks DG-300 Club Elan	FTS Syndicate
	G-CFTT	Van's RV-7	J. A. Paley
	C-CFTU	Flylight Dragonfly	R. J. Cook
	G-CFTV	Rolladen-Schneider LS7-WL	D. Hilton
	G-CFTW	Schempp-Hirth Discus b	230 Syndicate
	G-CFTX	Jabiru J160	J. Williamson & J. King
	G-CFTY	Rolladen-Schneider LS7-WL	J. A. Thomson & A. Burgess
	G-CFTZ	Evektor EV-97 Eurostar	TZ Flyers
	G-CFUA	Van's RV-9A	I. M. Macleod
	G-CFUB	Schleicher Ka 6CR	C. Boyd
	G-CFUD	Skyranger Swift 912S(1)	G-CFUD Group
	G-CFUE	Alpi Pioneer 300 Hawk	A. Dayani
	G-CFUF	Ultramagic N-300 balloon	Virgin Balloon Flights

Reg	Type	Owner or Operator	Notes
G-CFUG	Grob G.109B	Portsmouth Naval Gliding Centre	
G-CFUH	Schempp-Hirth Ventus c	C. G. T. Huck & S. E. Lucas	
G-CFUI	Hunt Wing/Avon 503(4)	R. F. G. Moyle	
G-CFUJ	Glaser-Dirks DG-300 Elan	FUJ Syndicate 2015	
G-CFUL	Schempp-Hirth Discus b	Discus 803 Syndicate	
G-CFUN	Schleicher ASW-20CL	C. A. Bailey	
G-CFUP	Schempp-Hirth Discus b	Lasham Gliding Society Ltd	
G-CFUR	Schempp-Hirth Ventus cT	A. P. Carpenter	
G-CFUS	PZL-Bielsko SZD-51-1 Junior	Scottish Gliding Union Ltd	
G-CFUT	Glaser-Dirks DG-300 Club Elan	P. E. Newman	
G-CFUU	DG-300 Club Elan	S. K. Ruffell	
G-CFUV	Rolladen-Schneider LS7-WL	G. J. Hoile	
G-CFUW	Rotorsport UK MTO Sport	D. A. Robertson	
G-CFUX	Cameron C-80 balloon	A. E. Still	
G-CFUY	PZL-Bielsko SZD-50-3 Puchacz	The Bath, Wilts and North Dorset Gliding Club	
G-CFUZ	CZAW Sportcruiser	M. Gislam	
G-CFVA	P & M Quik GT450	Countermine Technologies PLC	
G-CFVC	Schleicher ASK-13	Mendip Gliding Club Ltd	
G-CFVE	Schempp-Hirth Nimbus 2	L. Mitchell	
G-CFVH	Rolladen-Schneider LS7	C. C. & J. C. Marshall	
G-CFVJ	Cvjetkovic CA-65 Skyfly	D. Hunter	
G-CFVK	Best Off Skyranger 912(2)	Flylight Airsports Ltd	
G-CFVL	Scheibe Zugvogel IIIB	The G-CFVL Flying Group	
G-CFVM	Centrair 101A Pegase	S. H. North	
G-CFVN	Centrair 101A Pegase	K. Samuels	
G-CFVP	Centrair 101A Pegase	Foxtrot Victor Papa Group	
G-CFVR	Europa XS	G-CFVR Group	
G-CFVT	Schempp-Hirth Nimbus 2	I. Dunkley	
G-CFVU	Schleicher ASK-13	Edensoaring Ltd	
G-CFVV	Centrair 101A Pegase	Cambridge Gliding Club Ltd	
G-CFVW	Schempp-Hirth Ventus bT	J. F. de Hollander	
G-CFVX	Cameron C-80 balloon	A. Hornshaw	
G-CFVY	Cameron A-120 balloon	C. A. Petre	
G-CFVZ	Schleicher Ka 6E	N. R. Bowers	
G-CFWA	Schleicher Ka 6CR	C. C. Walley	
G-CFWB	Schleicher ASK-13	Cotswold Gliding Club	
G-CFWC	Grob G.103C Twin III Acro	The South Wales Gliding Club Ltd	
G-CFWD	Rotorsport UK MTO Sport	Gower Gyronautics	
G-CFWF	Rolladen-Schneider LS7	G. B. Hibberd	
G-CFWH	Scheibe SF27A	A. S. Carter	
G-CFWI	Kubicek BB-22Z balloon	V. Gounon	
G-CFWJ	P & M Quik GT450	T. Porter & D. Whiteley	
G-CFWK	Schempp-Hirth Nimbus-3DT	29 Syndicate	
G-CFWL	Schleicher K8B	D. S. Downton	
G-CFWM	Glaser-Dirks DG-300 Club Elan	FWM Group	
G-CFWN	P & M Quik GT450	G-CFWN Group	
G-CFWP	Schleicher ASW-19B	A. Zuchora	
G-CFWR	Best Off Sky Ranger 912(2)	C. G. Le Boutillier	
G-CFWS	Schleicher ASW-20C	662 Syndicate	
G-CFWT	PZL-Bielsko SZD-50-3 Puchacz	Coventry Gliding Club Ltd	
G-CFWU	Rolladen-Schneider LS7-WL	H. Macdonald	
G-CFWV	Van's RV-7	S. J. Carr & D. K. Sington	
G-CFWW	Schleicher ASH-25E	N. A. C. Norman	
G-CFWY	Centrair 101A Pegase	G. M. Dodwell & J. Randall	
G-CFXA	Grob G.104 Speed Astir IIB	Ringmer Speedy Syndicate	
G-CFXB	Schleicher K 8B	R. Sansom & M. A. Keller	
G-CFXC	Schleicher Ka 6E	G. E. Pook	
G-CFXD	Centrair 101A Pegase	D. G. England & R. Banks	
G-CFXF	Magni M-16C Tandem Trainer	M. W. King	
G-CFXG	Flylight Dragonfly	C. A. Mason	
G-CFXK	Flylight Dragonfly	N. R. Pettigrew	
G-CFXM	Schempp-Hirth Discus bT	G. R. E. Bottomley	
G-CFXN	CZAW Sportcruiser	H. Bishop	
G-CFXO	PZL-Bielsko SZD-50-3 Puchacz	Coventry Gliding Club Ltd	
G-CFXP	Lindstrand LBL-105A balloon	Shaun Bradley Project Services Ltd	
G-CFXR	Lindstrand LBL-105A balloon	Lindstrand Media Ltd	
G-CFXS	Schleicher Ka 6E	D. P. Aherne	
G-CFXT	Naval Aircraft Factory N3N-3	R. H. & J. A. Cooper	
G-CFXU	Schleicher Ka-6E	Xray Uniform Group	
G-CFXW	Schleicher K8B	The South Wales Gliding Club Ltd	
G-CFXX	P & M Quik R	M. C. Shortman	

Notes	Reg	Type	Owner or Operator
	G-CFXY	Schleicher ASW-15B	E. L. Youle
	G-CFXZ	P & M Quik R	M. Naylor
	G-CFYA	PZL-Bielsko SZD-50-3 Puchacz	Cairngorm Gliding Club
	G-CFYB	Rolladen-Schneider LS7	A. T. Macdonald & V. P. Haley
	G-CFYC	Schempp-Hirth Ventus b	J. M. Brooke
	G-CFYD	Aeroprakt A22-L Foxbat	A. P. Fenn
	G-CFYE	Scheibe Zugvogel IIIB	P. G. H. Purdie
	G-CFYF	Schleicher ASK-21	London Gliding Club Proprietary Ltd
	G-CFYG	Glasflugel Club Libelle 205	FYG Syndicate
	G-CFYH	Rolladen-Schneider LS4-a	G. W. & C. A. Craig
	G-CFYI	Grob G.102 Astir CS	S. R. Hill, A. H. Kay & D. A. Spencer
	G-CFYJ	Schempp-Hirth Standard Cirrus	W. Blackburn
	G-CFYK	Rolladen-Schneider LS7-WL	J. Bayford
	G-CFYL	PZL-Bielsko SZD-50-3 Puchacz	Deesside Gliding Club (Aberdeenshire) Ltd
	G-CFYM	Schempp-Hirth Discus bT	T. Wright
	G-CFYN	Schempp-Hirth Discus b	N. White & P. R. Foulger
	G-CFYO	P & M Quik R	M. A. Sandwith
	G-CFYP	FBM & W Silex M/Flyke/Monster	A. J. R. Carver
	G-CFYR	LET L-23 Super Blanik	G-CFYR Group
	G-CFYS	Dynamic WT9 UK	E. M. Middleton
	G-CFYU	Glaser-Dirks DG-100 Elan	J. Hunt
	G-CFYV	Schleicher ASK-21	The Bristol Gliding Club Proprietary Ltd
	G-CFYW	Rolladen-Schneider LS7	J. Douglass
	G-CFYX	Schempp-Hirth Discus b	D. A. Salmon
	G-CFYY	Schleicher ASK-13	Lasham Gliding Society Ltd
	G-CFYZ	Schleicher ASH-25	171 Syndicate
	G-CFZB	Glasflugel H201B Standard Libelle	J. C. Meyer
	G-CFZD	Jabiru J430	C. J. Judd & A. Macknish
	G-CFZF	PZL-Bielsko SZD-51-1 Junior	Devon and Somerset Gliding Club Ltd
	G-CFZH	Schempp-Hirth Ventus c	FZH Group
	G-CFZI	Savannah Jabiru (5)	J. T., A. L. & O. D. Lewis
	G-CFZJ	VS.388 Seafire F.46	C. T. Charleston
	G-CFZK	Schempp-Hirth Standard Cirrus	S. Lucas & R. Burgoyne
	G-CFZL	Schleicher ASW-20 CL	A. L. & R. M. Housden
	G-CFZO	Schempp-Hirth Nimbus 3	954 Syndicate
	G-CFZP	PZL-Bielsko SZD-51-1 Junior	PA Technologies Ltd
	G-CFZR	Schleicher Ka 6CR	A. J. Randalls
	G-CFZT	Ace Magic Laser	J. E. Orbell
	G-CFZW	Glaser-Dirks DG-300 Club Elan	D. O'Flanagan & G. Stilgoe
	G-CFZX	Rotorsport UK MTO Sport	Gyro-I Ltd
	G-CFZZ	LET L-33 Solo	The Andreas L33 Group
	G-CGAA	Flylight Dragonfly	G. Adkins
	G-CGAB	AB Sportine LAK-12 Lietuva	W. T. Emery
	G-CGAC	P & M Quik GT450	G. Brockhurst
	G-CGAD	Rolladen-Schneider LS3	J. D. Brister
	G-CGAF	Schleicher ASK-21	Lasham Gliding Society Ltd
	G-CGAG	Scleicher ASK-21	Stratford on Avon Gliding Club Ltd
	G-CGAH	Schempp-Hirth Standard Cirrus	J. W. Williams
	G-CGAI	Raj Hamsa X'Air Hawk	R. G. Cheshire
	G-CGAJ	Alpi Pioneer 400	C. Rusalen
	G-CGAK	Acrosport II	P. D. Sibbons
	G-CGAL	P & M Quik R	R. A. Keene
	G-CGAM	Schleicher ASK-21	T. R. Dews
	G-CGAN	Glasflugel H301 Libelle	M. D. Butcher
	G-CGAO	DHC.1 Chipmunk 22 (1350)	G-CGAO Group
	G-CGAP	Schempp-Hirth Ventus bT	J. R. Greenwell
	G-CGAR	Rolladen-Schneider LS6-c	A. Warbrick
	G-CGAS	Schempp-Hirth Ventus cT	G. M. J. Monaghan
	G-CGAT	Grob G.102 Astir CS	N. J. Hooper & S. J. Chapman
	G-CGAU	Glasflugel H201B Standard Libelle	G-CGAU Group
	G-CGAV	Scheibe SF-27A Zugvogel V	Golf Alpha Victor Group
	G-CGAX	PZL-Bielsko SZD-55-1 Promyk	I. D. Macro & P. Gold
	G-CGAZ	P & M Aviation Quik R	G-CGAZ Syndicate
	G-CGBB	Schleicher ASK-21	University of Edinburgh Sports Union
	G-CGBD	PZL-Bielsko SZD-50-3	The Northumbria Gliding Club Ltd
	G-CGBF	Schleicher ASK-21	London Gliding Club Pty Ltd
	G-CGBG	Rolladen-Schneider LS6-18w	C. Villa
	G-CGBH	Raj Hamsa X'Air Hawk	S. E. McEwen
	G-CGBJ	Grob G.102 Astir CS	Banbury Gliding Club Ltd
	G-CGBL	Rolladen-Schneider LS7-WL	P. A. Roche

Reg	Type	Owner or Operator	Notes
G-CGBM	Flight Design CTSW	M. S. Hammond	
G-CGBN	Schleicher ASK-21	Essex and Suffolk Gliding Club Ltd	
G-CGBO	Rolladen-Schneider LS6	G-CGBO Syndicate	
G-CGBR	Rolladen-Schneider LS6-c	V. L. Brown	
G-CGBS	Glaser-Dirks DG-300 Club Elan	A. Gillanders & M. C. Chalmers	
G-CGBU	Centrair 101A Pegase	D. J. Arblaster	
G-CGBV	Schleicher ASK-21	Wolds Gliding Club Ltd	
G-CGBY	Rolladen-Schneider LS7-WL	B. N. Searle	
G-CGBZ	Glaser-Dirks DG-500 Elan Trainer	G. N. Turner	
G-CGCA	Schleicher ASW-19B	Deeside Gliding Club (Aberdeenshire) Ltd	
G-CGCC	PZL-Bielsko SZD-51-1 Junior	Coventry Gliding Club Ltd	
G-CGCD	Schempp-Hirth Standard Cirrus	Cirrus Syndicate	
G-CGCE	Magni M16C Tandem Trainer	A. J. A. Fowler	
G-CGCF	Schleicher ASK-23	Cotswold Gliding Club	
G-CGCH	CZAW Sportcruiser	C. Harrison	
G-CGCI	Sikorsky S-92A	Bristow Helicopters Ltd	
G-CGCK	PZL-Bielsko SZD-50-3 Puchacz	Kent Gliding Club Ltd (G-BTJV)	
G-CGCL	Grob G.102 Astir CS	Southdown Gliding Club Ltd	
G-CGCM	Rolladen-Schneider LS6-c	G. R. Glazebrook	
G-CGCN	MCR-01 Club	D. J. Smith	
G-CGCO	Schempp-Hirth Cirrus VTC	S. V. Jones	
G-CGCP	Schleicher Ka-6CR	A. Gibb & C. Johnson	
G-CGCR	Schleicher ASW-15B	ASW15B 748 Group	
G-CGCS	Glasflugel Club Libelle 205	D. G. Coats	
G-CGCT	Schempp-Hirth Discus b	Banbury Gliding Club Ltd	
G-CGCU	PZL-Bielsko SZD-50-3 Puchacz	Darlton Gliding Club Ltd	
G-CGCV	Raj Hamsa X'Air Hawk	K. Buckley & B. L. Prime	
G-CGCW	Skyranger Swift 912(1)	R. Wilkinson	
G-CGCX	Schleicher ASW-15	R. L. Horsnell	
G-CGDA	Rolladen-Schneider LS3-17	J. S. Romanes	
G-CGDB	Schleicher K 8B	T. A. Odom	
G-CGDC	Rotorsport UK MTO Sport	R. E. Derham & T. R. Kingsley	
G-CGDD	Bolkow Phoebus C	G. C. Kench	
G-CGDE	Schleicher Ka 6CR	K6 Syndicate	
G-CGDF	Schleicher Ka 6BR	H. Marshall & D. Pask	
G-CGDG	Cameron C-80 balloon	J. Braeckman/Belgium	
G-CGDH	Europa XS	G-CGDH Group	
G-CGDI	EV-97A Eurostar	D. Street	
G-CGDK	Schleicher K 8B	Dartmoor Gliding Society	
G-CGDL	P & M Quik R	S. C. Reeve	
G-CGDM	Sonex Sonex	P. Johnson	
G-CGDN	Rolladen-Schneider LS3-17	S. J. Glassett	
G-CGDO	Grob G.102 Astir CS	P. Lowe & R. Bostock	
G-CGDR	Schempp-Hirth Discus CS	D. Daniels	
G-CGDS	Schleicher ASW-15B	B. Birk & P. A. Crouch	
G-CGDT	Schleicher ASW-24	Tango 54 Syndicate	
G-CGDV	CSA Sportcruiser	Delta Victor Group	
G-CGDW	CSA PS-28 Sportcruiser	Onega Ltd	
G-CGDX	Orlican Discus CS	D. Bieniasz	
G-CGDY	Schleicher ASW-15B	K. P. Russell	
G-CGDZ	Schleicher ASW-24	J. M. Norman	
G-CGEA	Schleicher Ka 6CR	J. McShane	
G-CGEB	Grob G.102 Astir CS77	T. R. Dews	
G-CGEC	Flight Design CTLS	S. Munday	
G-CGEE	Glasflugel H201B Standard Libelle	D. Plumb & S. J. Maddison	
G-CGEG	Schleicher K 8B	Darlton Gliding Club Ltd	
G-CGEH	Schleicher ASW-15B	D. K. Tappenden	
G-CGEI	Cessna 550 Citation Bravo	Rushbury Enterprises Ltd	
G-CGEJ	Alpi Pioneer 200-M	D. E. Foster	
G-CGEK	Ace Magic Laser	T. Smith	
G-CGEL	PZL-Bielsko SZD-50-3	The Northumbria Gliding Club Ltd	
G-CGEM	Schleicher Ka 6CR	GEM Syndicate	
G-CGEO	CSA Sportcruiser	The Jester Flying Group	
G-CGEP	Schempp-Hirth Standard Cirrus	C. J. Owen & P. S. Harvey	
G-CGER	Cameron Z-105 balloon	M. Casaburo/Italy	
G-CGEU	Flylight Dragonfly	I. Hesling-Gibson	
G-CGEV	Heliopolis Gomhouria Mk.6 (CG+EV)	A. Brier	
G-CGEW	Rotorsport UK MTO Sport	G. W. Libby & C. W. Rose	
G-CGEX	P & M Quik GT450	M. D. Howe	
G-CGEY	Julian CD Dingbat	A. H. H. Mole	
G-CGEZ	Raj Hamsa X'Air Hawk	M. Howes & B. J. Ellis	

Notes	Reg	Type	Owner or Operator
	G-CGFB	BB03 Trya/BB103	B. J. Fallows
	G-CGFG	Cessna 152	Shoreham Flying Club Ltd
	G-CGFH	Cessna T182T Turbo Skylane	H. Riffkin
	G-CGFK	Ace Magic Laser	B. B. Adams
	G-CGFN	Cameron C-60 balloon	G. J. Madelin
	G-CGFO	Ultramagic H-42 balloon	D. G. SuchJ
	G-CGFP	Pietenpol Aircamper	M. D. Waldron
	G-CGFR	Lindstranbd LBL HS-120 airship	D. Duke
	G-CGFU	Schempp-Hirth Mini-Nimbus C	S. Foster
	G-CGFY	Lindstrand LBL-105A balloon	G. J. Grimes
	G-CGFZ	Thruster T.600N 450	K. J. Crompton
	G-CGGD	Eurocopter AS365N2 Dauphin 2	Multiflight Ltd
	G-CGGE	Cameron Z-275 balloon	Wickers World Ltd
	G-CGGF	Robinson R44 II	G. Stroud
	G-CGGG	Robinson R44	K. Hayes (G-SJDI)
	G-CGGK	Westland Wasp HAS Mk.1	The Real Aeroplane Co.Ltd
	G-CGGM	EV-97 TeamEurostar UK	Golf Mike Group
	G-CGGO	Robin DR.400-180 Regent	G. I. J. Thomson & R. A. Hawkins
	G-CGGP	Autogyro MTOSport	J. Taylforth & G. P. Gibson
	G-CGGS	Robinson R44 II	Oakfield Investments Ltd
	G-CGGT	P & M Quik GT450	A. H. Beveridge
	G-CGGV	Rotorsport UK MTO Sport	S. Morris
	G-CGGW	Rotorsport UK MTO Sport	P. Adams
	G-CGGY	UltraMagic N-425 balloon	Adventure Balloons Ltd
	G-CGGZ	UltraMagic S-90 balloon	P. Lawman
	G-CGHA	P & M Quik R	C. A. Green
	G-CGHB	NAMC CJ-6A (61367)	M. J. Harvey
	G-CGHG	P & M Quik GT450	J. & K. D. McAlpine
	G-CGHH	P & M Quik R	C. Pyle & N. Richardson
	G-CGHJ	Staaken Z-21A Flitzer	D. J. Ashley
	G-CGHK	Alpi Pioneer 300 Hawk	D. J. Ashley
	G-CGHL	Rotorsport UK MTOSport	C. S. Mackenzie
	G-CGHN	Aeros Discus/Alize	R. Simpson & N. Sutton
	G-CGHR	Magic Laser	N. P. Power
	G-CGHT	Dyn'Aero MCR-01 Banbi	R. P. Trives (G-POOP)
	G-CGHU	Hawker Hunter T.Mk.8C	Hawker Hunter Aviation Ltd
	G-CGHV	Raj Hamsa X'Air Hawk	H. Adams
	G-CGHW	Czech Sport Aircraft Sportcruiser	Sportcruiser 290 Ltd
	G-CGHZ	P & M Quik R	J. Rockey
	G-CGIA	Paramania Action/Adventure	A. E. C. Phillips
	G-CGIB	Magic Cyclone	S. B. Walters
	G-CGIC	Rotorsport MTO Sport	J. Harmon
	G-CGID	PA-31-350 Navajo Chieftain	T. Michaels
	G-CGIE	Flylight Dragonfly	N. S. Brayn
	G-CGIF	Flylight Dragonfly	R. D. Leigh
	G-CGIG	Lindstrand LBL-90A balloon	M. R. Stokoe
	G-CGIH	Cameron C-90 balloon	A. Sweet & P. Gunning-Stevenson
	G-CGIJ	Agusta Westland AW139	HM Coastguard
	G-CGIK	Isaacs Spitfire	A. J. Harpley
	G-CGIL	CZAW Sportcruiser	G-CGIL Group
	G-CGIM	Ace Aviation Magic Laser	C. Royle
	G-CGIN	Paramania Action GT/Adventure	A. E. C. Phillips
	G-CGIO	Medway SLA100 Executive	G-CGIO Syndicate
	G-CGIR	CZAW Sportcruiser	J. Greenhaigh
	G-CGIR	Remos GX	L. R. Marks & J. A. Pereira
	G-CGIS	Cameron Parachutist 110 SS balloon	K-H. Gruenauer (G-RIPS)
	G-CGIV	Kolb Firefly	W. A. Emmerson
	G-CGIX	Rotorsport UK MTO Sport	J. W. G. Andrews
	G-CGIY	Piper J3C-65 (330244:C-46)	R. C. Cummings
	G-CGIZ	Flight Design CTSW	J. Hilton
	G-CGJB	Schempp-Hirth Duo Discus T	G. J. Basey
	G-CGJC	Rotorsport UK MTO Sport	J. C. Collingwood
	G-CGJE	VS.361 Spitfire IX	Historic Flight Ltd
	G-CGJF	Fokker E.111 Replica	I. Brewster
	G-CGJI	Best Off Skyranger 912S(1)	Flylight Airsports Ltd
	G-CGJJ	P & M Quik R	Juliet Juliet Group
	G-CGJL	CZAW Sportcruiser	S. Catalano
	G-CGJM	Skyranger Swift 912S(1)	J. P. Metcalfe
	G-CGJN	Van's RV-7	E. K. Coventry
	G-CGJP	Van's RV-10	G-CGIP Group
	G-CGJS	CZAW Sportcruiser	J. M. Tiley

Reg	Type	Owner or Operator	Notes
G-CGJT	CZAW Sportcruiser	D. F. Toller	
G-CGJW	RAF 2000 GTX-SE	J. J. Wollen	
G-CGJX	SA.341B Gazelle AH Mk.1	The Gazelle Squadron Display Team	
G-CGJZ	SA.341D Gazelle HT Mk.3 (XZ933)	The Gazelle Squadron Display Team	
G-CGKD	Grob G115E Tutor	Babcock Aerospace Ltd	
G-CGKE	Grob G115E Tutor	Babcock Aerospace Ltd	
G-CGKG	Grob G115E Tutor	Babcock Aerospace Ltd	
G-CGKH	Grob G115E Tutor	Babcock Aerospace Ltd	
G-CGKK	Grob G115E Tutor	Babcock Aerospace Ltd	
G-CGKL	Grob G115E Tutor	Babcock Aerospace Ltd	
G-CGKM	Grob G115E Tutor	Babcock Aerospace Ltd	
G-CGKN	Grob G115E Tutor	Babcock Aerospace Ltd	
G-CGKO	Grob G115E Tutor	Babcock Aerospace Ltd	
G-CGKP	Grob G115E Tutor	Babcock Aerospace Ltd	
G-CGKR	Grob G115E Tutor	Babcock Aerospace Ltd	
G-CGKS	Grob G115E Tutor	Babcock Aerospace Ltd	
G-CGKT	Grob G115E Tutor	Babcock Aerospace Ltd	
G-CGKU	Grob G115E Tutor	Babcock Aerospace Ltd	
G-CGKW	Grob G115E Tutor	Babcock Aerospace Ltd	
G-CGKX	Grob G115E Tutor	Babcock Aerospace Ltd	
G-CGKY	Cessna 182T	T. A. E. Dobell	
G-CGKZ	Best Off Sky Ranger Swift 912S(1)	T. Swinson	
G-CGLB	Airdrome Dream Classic	R. D. Leigh	
G-CGLC	Czech Sport Aircraft Sportcruiser	M. A. Ulrick	
G-CGLE	Flylight Dragonfly	B. Skelding	
G-CGLF	Magni M-16C Tandem Trainer	J. S. Walton	
G-CGLG	P & M Quik GT450	P. H. Evans	
G-CGLI	Alpi Pioneer 200M	B. A. Lyford	
G-CGLJ	TL 2000UK Sting Carbon	L. A. James	
G-CGLK	Magni M-16C Tandem Trainer	R. M. Savage	
G-CGLM	Rotorsport UK MTO Sport	D. S. T. Harris	
G-CGLN	Jabiru J430	A. J. Thomas	
G-CGLO	P & M Quik R	R. H. Lowndes	
G-CGLP	CZAW Sportcruiser	P. S. Tanner	
G-CGLR	Czech Sport Aircraft Sportcruiser	G-CGLR Group	
G-CGLT	Czech Sport Aircraft Sportcruiser	I. Jalowiecki	
G-CGLY	Rotorsport UK Calidus	R. J. Steel	
G-CGLZ	TL 2000UK Sting Carbon	Newtownards Microlight Group	
G-CGMA	Ace Magic Laser	J. N. Hanson	
G-CGMD	Rotorsport UK Calidus	W. H. Morgan	
G-CGMF	Cessna 560XL Citation XLS	NAL Asset Management Ltd	
G-CGMG	Van's RV-9	D. J. Bone	
G-CGMH	Jodel D150A Mascaret	M. Hales	
G-CGMI	P & M Quik GT450	W. G. Reynolds	
G-CGML	TL 2000UK Sting Carbon	G. T. Leedham	
G-CGMM	CZAW Sportcruiser	TAF and Co	
G-CGMN	Best Off Sky Ranger Swift 912S	G-CGMN Flying Group	
G-CGMO	Ace Magic Laser	G. J. Latham	
G-CGMP	CZAW Sportcruiser	R. Hasler	
G-CGMR	Colt Bibendum-110 balloon	Mobberley Balloon Collection (G-GRIP)	
G-CGMV	Roko Aero NG 4HD	Roko NG4	
G-CGMW	Alpi Pioneer 200M	M. S. McCrudden	
G-CGMZ	P & M Quik R	M. J. Hyde	
G-CGNA	Cameron Super FMG-100 balloon	Cameron Balloons Ltd	
G-CGNC	Rotorsport UK MTO Sport	Bath Leasing & Supplies Ltd	
G-CGNE	Robinson R44 II	Heli Air Ltd	
G-CGNG	CZAW Sportcruiser	H. M. Wooldridge	
G-CGNH	Reality Escapade Jabiru(3)	J. M. Ingram	
G-CGNI	Ikarus C42 FB80	S. Conion	
G-CGNJ	Cameron Z-105 balloon	Loughborough Students Union Hot Air Balloon Club	
G-CGNK	P & M Quik GT450	G. W. Hillidge	
G-CGNM	Magni M-16C Tandem Trainer	Evolo Ltd	
G-CGNN	Montgomerie-Bensen B.8MR	P. M. Ryder	
G-CGNO	P & M Quik GT450	A. Fern	
G-CGNS	Sky 65-24 balloon	R. L. Bovell	
G-CGNV	Reality Escapade	P. M. Noonan	
G-CGNW	Scheibe SF-25C Falke	Army Gliding Association	
G-CGNX	Rotorsport UK MTO Sport	L. McCallum	
G-CGNY	Cessna 340A	B. Ban	
G-CGNZ	Europa XS	R. Vianello	

Notes	Reg	Type	Owner or Operator
	G-CGOA	Cessna 550 Citation II	XJC Ltd (G-JMDW)
	G-CGOB	P & M Quik R	P & M Aviation Ltd
	G-CGOD	Cameron N-77 balloon	Trinity Balloons
	G-CGOG	Evektor EV-97 Eurostar	D. C. & S. G. Emmons
	G-CGOH	Cameron C-80 balloon	Lindstrand Media Ltd
	G-CGOI	Stewart S-51 Mustang (413926 E2-S)	K. E. Armstrong
	G-CGOJ	Jodel D.11	J. Laszio
	G-CGOK	Ace Magic Cyclone	T. H. Lee
	G-CGOL	Jabiru J430	J. F. Woodham
	G-CGOM	Flight Design MC	R. C. W. Parkinson
	G-CGOR	Jodel D.18	R. D. Cook
	G-CGOS	PA-28-161 Warrior III	S. H. B. Smith
	G-CGOT	Rotorsport UK Calidus	P. Slater
	G-CGOU	Sikorsky S-76C	Bristow Helicopters Ltd
	G-CGOV	Raj Hamsa X'Air Falcon 582(2)	L. Fee
	G-CGOW	Cameron Z-77 balloon	J. F. Till
	G-CGOX	Raj Hamsa X'Air Hawk	W. B. Russell
	G-CGOZ	Cameron GB-1000 free gas balloon	Cameron Balloons Ltd
	G-CGPA	Ace Magic Cyclone	A. Williams
	G-CGPB	Magni M-24C	D. Beevers
	G-CGPC	P & M Pegasus Quik	D. W. Watson & E. McCallum
	G-CGPD	Ultramagic S-90 balloon	S. J. Farrant
	G-CGPE	P & M Quik GT450	E. H. Gatehouse
	G-CGPF	Flylight Dragonfly	R. G. Morris
	G-CGPG	Rotosport UK MTO Sport	H. A. Batchelor
	G-CGPH	Ultramagic S-50 balloon	C. D. Harding
	G-CGPI	Eurocopter EC135 T2+	Babcock Mission Critical Services Onshore Ltd (G-TAGG)
	G-CGPJ	Robin DR.400-140	W. H. Cole & P. Dass
	G-CGPK	Rotorsport UK MT-03	Ellis Flying Group (G-RIFS)
	G-CGPL	Sonex Sonex	P. C. Askew
	G-CGPN	SOCATA MS.880B Rallye Club	J. Fingleton
	G-CGPO	TL2000UK Sting Carbon	G. A. Squires
	G-CGPR	Czech Sport Aircraft Pipersport	J. T. Langford
	G-CGPS	EV-97 Eurostar SL	P. R. Jenson & R. A. Morris
	G-CGPV	Cameron C-80 balloon	D. G. Such & M. Tomlin
	G-CGPW	Raj Hamsa X'Air Hawk	G. J. Langston
	G-CGPX	Zenair CH.601XL Zodiac	A. James
	G-CGPY	Boeing A75L 300 Stearman	M. P. Dentith
	G-CGPZ	Rans S-4 Coyote	G. J. Jones
	G-CGRB	Flight Design CTLS	The Romeo Bravo Group
	G-CGRC	P & M Quik R	R. J. Cook
	G-CGRJ	Carnet Paramotor	M. Carnet
	G-CGRM	VS.329 Spitfire Mk.IIA	M. R. Oliver
	G-CGRN	Pazmany PL-4A	G. Hudson
	G-CGRR	P & M Quik	M. W. Scott
	G-CGRS	P & M Quik	J. Crosby
	G-CGRV	DG Flugzeugbau DG-1000M	BR Aviation Ltd
	G-CGRW	P & M Quik	P. M. Coppola
	G-CGRX	Cessna F.172N	J. Woods
	G-CGRY	Magni M-24C	Pollards Wholesale Ltd
	G-CGRZ	Magni M-24C	R. S. B. O'Kane
	G-CGSA	Flylight Dragonfly	G. Sykes
	G-CGSC	Quad City Challenger II	L. Gregory
	G-CGSD	Magni M-16C	The Gyrocopter Company UK Ltd
	G-CGSG	Cessna 421C	J. R. Shannon
	G-CGSH	Evektor EV-97 TeamEurostar UK	D. B. Medland
	G-CGSI	Zenair CH.601HDS Zodiac	E. McHugh
	G-CGSJ	Bombardier BD700-1A10 Global Express	Abbeville Holdings Ltd
	G-CGSO	P & M Quik GT450	Light Vending Ltd
	G-CGSP	Cessna 152	C. M. de CamposCosta Cabral
	G-CGSU	Cassutt Racer IIIM	M. J. Saggers
	G-CGSW	Flylight Motorfloater	M. P. Wimsey
	G-CGSX	Aeroprakt A22-L Foxbat	P. J. Trimble
	G-CGSZ	Schempp-Hirth Ventus 2CM	D. B. Smith
	G-CGTC	BN-2T-4S Islander	Police Service of Northern Ireland
	G-CGTD	EV-97 TeamEurostar UK	R. J. Butler
	G-CGTE	Cherry BX-2	D.Roberts
	G-CGTF	AutoGyro MT-03	N. R. Osborne
	G-CGTJ	AS.332L2 Super Puma	Airbus Helicopters
	G-CGTK	Magni M-24C	S. Brogden

Reg	Type	Owner or Operator	Notes
G-CGTL	Alpi Pioneer 300	M. S. Ashby	
G-CGTM	Cessna 172S	Skytrek Air Services	
G-CGTR	Best Off Sky Ranger Nynja 912S(1)	M. Jenvey	
G-CGTS	Cameron A-140 balloon	A. A. Brown	
G-CGTT	EV-97 Eurostar SL	D. L. Walker	
G-CGTU	P & M Quik GT450	I. G. R. Christie	
G-CGTV	MXP-740 Savannah VG Jabiru(1)	B. L. Cook & P. Etherington	
G-CGTW	Flylight MotorFloater	S. J. Varden	
G-CGTX	CASA 1-131E Jungmann Srs 2000	G. Hunter & T. A. S. Rayner	
G-CGTY	Cameron Z-250 balloon	Airxcite Ltd	
G-CGTZ	Reality Escapade Kid	P. K. Jenkins	
G-CGUD	Lindstrand LBL-77A balloon	I. J. Sharpe	
G-CGUE	Aeroprakt A-22-L Foxbat	A. T. Hayward	
G-CGUG	P & M Quik R	J. D. Lawrance	
G-CGUI	Clutton FRED Srs.II	I. Pearson	
G-CGUK	VS.300 Spitfire 1A (X4650)	Comanche Warbirds Ltd	
G-CGUO	DH.83C Fox Moth	Airtime Aerobatics Ltd	
G-CGUP	P & M Quik GT450	D. J. Allen	
G-CGUR	P & M QuikR	M. J. Williams	
G-CGUT	Balloon Works Firefly 9B-15	J. N. Uhrmann	
G-CGUU	Sky Ranger Nynja 912S(1)	J. A. Hunt	
G-CGUV	Balloon Works Firefly 9B-15	J. N. Uhrmann	
G-CGUW	Tecnam P2002-EA Sierra	D. J. Burton	
G-CGUY	Rotorsport UK Calidus	R. F. Harrison	
G-CGVA	Aeroprakt A-22-L Foxbat	M. E. Gilman	
G-CGVC	PA-28-181 Archer III	Western Air (Thruxton) Ltd	
G-CGVD	Van's RV-12	B. Gorvett	
G-CGVE	Raj Hamsa X'Air Hawk	D. J. Baird	
G-CGVG	Flight Design CTSW	B. Cook	
G-CGVH	Flylight Motorfloater	P. F. Mayes	
G-CGVJ	Europa XS	D. Glowa	
G-CGVK	Autogyro UK Calidus	B & H Mouldings Ltd	
G-CGVP	EV-97 Eurstar	G. R. Pritchard	
G-CGVS	Raj Hamsa X'Air Hawk	D. Matthews	
G-CGVT	EV-97 TeamEurostar UK	Mainair Microlight School Ltd	
G-CGVV	Cameron Z-90 Balloon	John Aimo Balloons SAS/Italy	
G-CGVX	Europa	M. P. Sambrook	
G-CGVY	Cameron Z-77 balloon	M. P. Hill	
G-CGVZ	Zenair CH.601XL Zodiac	K. A. Dilks	
G-CGWA	Ikarus C42 FB80 Bravo	I. A. MacAdam	
G-CGWB	Agusta AW139	CHC Scotia Ltd/HM Coastguard	
G-CGWC	Ultramagic H-31 balloon	K. Dodman	
G-CGWD	Robinson R-44	J. M. Potter	
G-CGWE	EV-97A Eurostar	W. S. Long	
G-CGWF	Van's RV-7	M. S. Hill	
G-CGWG	Van's RV-7	G. Waters	
G-CGWH	CZAW Sportcruiser	R. E. & N. G. Nicholson	
G-CGWI	Spitfire Mk.26 (BL927:JH-I)	Bertha Property LLP	
G-CGWK	Ikarus C42 FB80	J. R. Wilkinson	
G-CGWL	Sky Ranger Nynja 912S(1)	Exodus Airsports Ltd	
G-CGWM	Dragonfly Lite	P. A. Gardner	
G-CGWN	Dragonfly Lite	J. Williams	
G-CGWO	Tecnam P2002-JF Sierra	Shropshire Aero Club Ltd	
G-CGWP	Aeroprakt A22-L Foxbat	P. K. Goff	
G-CGWR	Nord NC.856A Norvigie	R. B. McLain	
G-CGWS	Raj Hamsa X'Air Hawk	I. S. McNulty	
G-CGWT	Best Off Sky Ranger Swift 912(1)	N. A. & P. A. Allwood	
G-CGWU	UltraMagic S-90 balloon	P. Pruchnickj & R. P. Allan	
G-CGWV	Embraer EMB-145MP	Eastern Airways	
G-CGWX	Cameron C-90 balloon	J. D. A. Shields	
G-CGWZ	P & M QuikR	P. J. Lomax & J. A. Robinson	
G-CGXB	Glasair Super IIS RG	P. J. Brion	
G-CGXC	Flylight Dragonfly	R. M. Anderson	
G-CGXE	P & M Quik GT450	B. D. Searle	
G-CGXF	North Wing Stratus/Skycycle	I. D. Smith	
G-CGXG	Yakovlev Yak-3M (100)	Chameleon Technologies Ltd	
G-CGXI	Ikarus C42 FB80	G. V. Aggett	
G-CGXL	Robin DR.400/180	M. F. Ashton (G-GLKE)	
G-CGXN	American Legend Cub	P. L. Gaze	
G-CGXO	Lindstrand LBL-105A balloon	Aerosaurus Balloons Ltd	
G-CGXP	Grob G.109B	S. M. Rathband	

Notes	Reg	Type	Owner or Operator
	G-CGXR	Van's RV-9A	Solway Flyers 2010 Ltd
	G-CGXT	Kowacs Midgie	J. P. Kovacs
	G-CGXV	P & M Quik R	A. Nikulin
	G-CGXW	Grob G.109B	I. B. Kennedy
	G-CGXX	ICP MXP-740 Savannah HKS(1)	P. Hayward
	G-CGXY	Flylight Dragonfly	A. I. Lea
	G-CGXZ	AutoGyro MTO Sport	G-CGXZ Flying Group
	G-CGYA	Stoddard-Hamilton Glasair III	Aerocars Ltd
	G-CGYB	EV-97 TeamEurostar UK	J. Waite
	G-CGYC	Aeropro Eurofox 912(S)	J. C. Taylor
	G-CGYD	Fairey Firefly TT.1	Propshop Ltd
	G-CGYF	Gloster Gamecock II	Retro Track & Air (UK) Ltd
	G-CGYG	Aeropro Eurofox 912(S)	Highland Gliding Club Ltd
	G-CGYH	Magni M-24C	J. L. Ward
	G-CGYI	Van's RV-12	M. J. Poole
	G-CGYJ	VS.361 Spitfire HF.IX (TD314)	K. M. Perkins
	G-CGYO	Van's RV-6A	G. & N. Kieswetter
	G-CGYP	Best Off Sky Ranger 912(2)	Yankee Papa Group
	G-CGYR	Avro RJ-85	Trident Turboprop (Dublin) Ltd
	G-CGYT	Flylight Dragonfly	C. Jones
	G-CGYW	Sikorsky S-92A	Bristow Helicopters Ltd
	G-CGYX	AutoGyro Cavalon	K. Hall
	G-CGYY	MXP-740 Savannah VG Jabiru(1)	Carlisle Skyrangers
	G-CGYZ	P & M Quik GT450	M. Florence
	G-CGZE	Rotorsport UK MTO Sport	Rufforth No.1 Gyro Syndicate
	G-CGZF	EV-97 TeamEurostar UK	B. P. Keating
	G-CGZG	AutoGyro MTO Sport	Highland Aviation Training Ltd
	G-CGZI	SOCATA TB-21 Trinidad TC	K. B. Hallam
	G-CGZJ	ITV Dakota XL	C. J. Lines
	G-CGZM	AutoGyro MTO Sport	J. W. Cope
	G-CGZN	Dudek Synthesis 31/Nirvana Carbon	P. M. Jones
	G-CGZP	Curtiss P-40F Kittyhawk (41-19841 X-17)	The Fighter Collection
	G-CGZR	Cameron Z-350 balloon	Ballooning Network Ltd
	G-CGZT	Aeroprakt A22-L Foxbat	D. Jessop
	G-CGZU	VS.361 Spitfire F.IXc (LZ842:EF-F)	M. A. Bennett
	G-CGZV	Europa XS	I. M. Moxon
	G-CGZW	Scheibe SF-25C Falke	Airborne Services International Ltd
	G-CGZY	EV-97 TeamEurostar UK	K. J. Ward & F. A. Thompson
	G-CGZZ	Kubicek BB22E balloon	A. M. Holly
	G-CHAB	Schleicher Ka 6CR	J. March
	G-CHAC	PZL-Bielsko SZD-50-3 Puchacz	Peterborough and Spalding Gliding Club Ltd
	G-CHAD	Aeroprakt A.22 Foxbat	DJB Foxbat
	G-CHAE	Glasflugel H205 Club Libelle	E. A. & S. R. Scothern
	G-CHAF	PZL-Bielsko SZD-50-3 Puchacz	Seahawk Gliding Club
	G-CHAG	Guimbal Cabri G2	European Helicopter Importers Ltd
	G-CHAH	Shaw Europa	T. Higgins
	G-CHAJ	Cirrus SR22	H. T. D. Flower
	G-CHAM	Cameron 90 Pot SS balloon	Pendle Balloon Company
	G-CHAN	Robinson R22 Beta	Aztec Aviators Ltd
	G-CHAO	Rolladen-Schneider LS6-b	Cloud Nine Syndicate
	G-CHAP	Robinson R44	Brierley Lifting Tackle Co Ltd
	G-CHAR	Grob G.109B	The Royal Air Force Gliding and Soaring Association
	G-CHAS	PA-28-181 Archer II	G-CHAS Flying Group
	G-CHAU	Cameron C-80 balloon	G. G. Cannon & P. Haworth
	G-CHAW	Replica Fokker EIII	S. W. C. Duckworth
	G-CHAX	Schempp-Hirth Standard Cirrus	C. Keating & R. Jarvis
	G-CHAY	Rolladen-Schneider LS7	N. J. Leaton
	G-CHBA	Rolladen-Schneider LS7	LS7 Crew
	G-CHBB	Schleicher ASW-24	London Gliding Club Propietary Ltd
	G-CHBC	Rolladen-Schneider LS6-c	A. Crowden
	G-CHBD	Glaser-Dirks DG-200	HBD Syndicate
	G-CHBE	Glaser-Dirks DG-300 Club Elan	DG 356 Group
	G-CHBF	Schempp-Hirth Nimbus 2C	J. A. Clark
	G-CHBG	Schleicher ASW-24	Imperial College of Science, Technology and Medicine
	G-CHBH	Grob G.103C Twin III Acro	Imperial College of Science, Technology and Medicine
	G-CHBK	Grob G.103 Twin Astir II	S. Naylor
	G-CHBL	Grob G.102 Astir CS77	Bidford Gliding & Flying Club Ltd

Reg	Type	Owner or Operator	Notes
G-CHBM	Grob G.102 Astir CS77	A. C. E. Walton-Smith & M. A. Rees-Boughton	
G-CHBO	Schleicher Ka 6CR	S. Oram	
G-CHBS	PZL-Bielsko SZD-41A Jantar Standard 1	P. J. Chaisty & D. Hendry	
G-CHBT	Grob G.102 Astir CS Jeans	Astir Syndicate	
G-CHBU	Centrair ASW-20F	M. Staljan, S. Brogger & C. Behrendt	
G-CHBV	Schempp-Hirth Nimbus 2B	G. J. Evison & R. Beezer	
G-CHBW	Jurca Spitfire (AD370:PJ-C)	T. A. Major	
G-CHBX	Lindstrand LBL-77A balloon	K. Hull	
G-CHBY	Agusta AW.139	Bristow Helicopters Ltd	
G-CHBZ	TL2000UK Sting Carbon	C. R. Ashley	
G-CHCF	AS.332L-2 Super Puma	Lombard North Central PLC	
G-CHCG	AS.332L-2 Super Puma	Airbus Helicopters Ltd	
G-CHCH	AS.332L-2 Super Puma	Airbus Helicopters Ltd	
G-CHCI	AS.332L-2 Super Puma	Lombard North Central PLC	
G-CHCK	Sikorsky S-92A	CHC Scotia Ltd	
G-CHCL	EC.225LP Super Puma	Wilmington Trust SP Services (Dublin) Ltd	
G-CHCM	EC.225LP Super Puma	CHC Scotia Ltd	
G-CHCS	Sikorsky S-92A	CHC Scotia Ltd	
G-CHCU	AS.332L2 Super Puma II	Airbus Helicopters Ltd	
G-CHCY	EC.225LP Super Puma	Airbus Helicopters Ltd	
G-CHDA	Pilatus B4-PC11AF	HDA Syndicate	
G-CHDB	PZL-Bielsko SZD-51-1 Junior	Stratford on Avon Gliding Club Ltd	
G-CHDD	Centrair 101B Pegase 90	591 Glider Syndicate	
G-CHDE	Pilatus B4-PC11AF	I. L. Pattingale	
G-CHDH	Lindstrand LBL-77A balloon	Lindstrand Media Ltd	
G-CHDJ	Schleicher ASW-20CL	G. E. G. Lambert & L. M. M. Sebreights	
G-CHDK	Magni M-16C Tandem Trainer	J. Gledhill	
G-CHDL	Schleicher ASW-20	D. Reeves & B. D. Allen	
G-CHDM	P & M QuikR	A. Sheveleu	
G-CHDN	Schleicher K 8B	Upward Bound Trust	
G-CHDP	PZL-Bielsko SZD-50-3 Puchacz	Heron Gliding Club	
G-CHDR	DG-300 Elan	R. Robins	
G-CHDU	PZL-Bielsko SZD-51-1 Junior	Cambridge Gliding Club Ltd	
G-CHDV	Schleicher ASW-19B	ASW Aviation	
G-CHDX	Rolladen-Schneider LS7-WL	D. Holborn & R. T. Halliburton	
G-CHDY	Schleicher K 8B	V. Mallon	
G-CHDZ	Cameron O-120 balloon	R. J. Mansfield	
G-CHEB	Shaw Europa	I. C. Smit & P. Whittingham	
G-CHEC	PZL-Bielsko SZD-55-1	D. Pye	
G-CHED	Flylight Dragonfly	G. W. Cameron	
G-CHEE	Schempp-Hirth Discus b	A. Henderson	
G-CHEF	Glaser-Dirks DG-500 Elan Trainer	Yorkshire Gliding Club (Proprietary) Ltd	
G-CHEG	AB Sportine Aviacija LAK-12	J. M. Caldwell, D. Cockburn, Z. Kmita & R. G. Parker	
G-CHEH	Rolladen-Schneider LS7-WL	P. Candler	
G-CHEJ	Schleicher ASW-15B	A. F. F. Webb	
G-CHEK	PZL-Bielsko SZD-51-1	Cambridge Gliding Club Ltd	
G-CHEL	Colt 77B balloon	Chelsea Financial Services PLC	
G-CHEM	PA-34-200T Seneca II	London Executive Aviation Ltd	
G-CHEN	Schempp-Hirth Discus b	G-CHEN Group	
G-CHEO	Schleicher ASW-20	M. J. Williamson	
G-CHEP	PZL-Bielsko SZD-50-3 Puchacz	Peterborough and Spalding Gliding Club Ltd	
G-CHER	PA-38-112 Tomahawk II	G. E. Fox	
G-CHEW	Rolladen-Schneider LS6-c18	D. N. Tew	
G-CHEX	Aero Designs Pulsar	M. R. Punter	
G-CHFA	Schempp-Hirth Ventus b/16.6	A. K. Lincoln	
G-CHFB	Schleicher Ka-6CR	R. J. Shepherd	
G-CHFC	P & M Quik GTR	A. Niarchos	
G-CHFD	Agusta AW.109SP	Flight Charter Services Pty Ltd	
G-CHFF	Schempp-Hirth Standard Cirrus	Foxtrot 2 Group	
G-CHFG	Van's RV-6	RV Flying Group	
G-CHFH	PZL-Bielsko SZD-50-3	Trent Valley Gliding Club Ltd	
G-CHFK	PA-32-360 Cherokee Six	Aerobility	
G-CHFL	Scheibe SF-25C Falke	Staffordshire Gliding Club Ltd	
G-CHFM	Cameron Z-120 balloon	David Hathaway Transport Ltd	
G-CHFO	P & M Quik GTR	M. Bailey	
G-CHFP	Hawker Sea Fury T.Mk.20 (WG655)	N. Grey	
G-CHFT	Tanarg Bionix 15 912S(1)	N. C. Stubbs	
G-CHFU	P & M Quik GTR	P. H. J. Fenn	
G-CHFV	Schempp-Hirth Ventus B/16.6	A. Cliffe & B. Pearson	
G-CHFW	Schleicher K 8B	Oxford Gliding Co.Ltd	

Notes	Reg	Type	Owner or Operator
	G-CHFX	Schempp-Hirth Nimbus 4T	R. F. Barber
	G-CHFZ	Best Off Sky Ranger Nynja 912S(1)	Skyview Systems Ltd
	G-CHGA	P & M Quik GTR	Flying for Freedom Ltd
	G-CHGB	Grob G.102 Astir CS	The Windrushers Gliding Club Ltd
	G-CHGE	EV-97 TeamEurostar UK	J. R. Mackay
	G-CHGF	Schleicher ASW-15B	HGF Flying Group
	G-CHGG	Schempp-Hirth Standard Cirrus	HGG Flying Group
	G-CHGI	Beech A.36 Bonanza	Aeronav87 Maintenance
	G-CHGJ	Flylight MotorFloater Fox 16T	A. Brooks
	G-CHGK	Schempp-Hirth Discus bT	P. W. Berridge
	G-CHGL	Bell 206B JetRanger II	Vantage Aviation Ltd (G-BPNG/G-ORTC)
	G-CHGM	Groppo Trail	J. Walker
	G-CHGN	Ace Aviation Easy Riser Spirit	Tideswell Trading Ltd
	G-CHGO	AB Sportine Aviacija LAK-12	P. Raymond & J-M Peuffier
	G-CHGP	Rolladen-Schneider LS6-c	D. J. Miller
	G-CHGR	AB Sportline Aviacija LAK-12	M. R. Garwood
	G-CHGS	Schempp-Hirth Discus b	G-CHGS Syndicate
	G-CHGT	FFA Diamant 16.5	T. E. Lynch
	G-CHGU	Ace Aviation Easy Riser Touch	T. A. Dobbins
	G-CHGV	Glaser-Dirks DG500/22 Elan	Hotel Golf Victor Syndicate
	G-CHGW	Centrair ASW-20F	P. J. Coward
	G-CHGX	AB Sportine LAK-12 Lietuva	M. Jenks
	G-CHGY	Schleicher ASW-27-18	G-CHGY Flying Group
	G-CHGZ	Schempp-Hirth Discus bT	G. C. Bell
	G-CHHB	Aeroprakt A22-LS Foxbat	A. J. L. Gordon
	G-CHHC	Cameron A-300 balloon	Wickers World Ltd
	G-CHHD	RL7A XP Sherwood Ranger	R. Simpson
	G-CHHF	Sikorsky S-92A	Bristow Helicopters Ltd
	G-CHHH	Rolladen-Schneider LS6-c	P. H. Rackham
	G-CHHI	Van's RV-7	M. G. Jefferies
	G-CHHJ	Aeropro Eurofox 912	K. J. Watt
	G-CHHK	Schleicher ASW-19B	P. Lysak & R. Hubrecht
	G-CHHL	Cameron C-80 balloon	H. G. Griffiths & W. A. Steel
	G-CHHN	Schempp-Hirth Ventus b/16.6	Ventus 979 Syndicate
	G-CHHO	Schempp-Hirth Discus bT	97Z Syndicate
	G-CHHP	Schempp-Hirth Discus b	F. R. Knowles
	G-CHHR	PZL-Bielsko SZD-55-1 Promyk	J. R. Sayce
	G-CHHS	Schleicher ASW-20	P.J. Rocks & D. Britt
	G-CHHT	Rolladen-Schneider LS6-c	D. Wilson
	G-CHHU	Rolladen-Schneider LS6-c	445 Syndicate
	G-CHHV	Junqua Ibis RJ.03	J. J. R. Joubert
	G-CHHW	AB Sportine LAK-12	A. J. Dibdin
	G-CHHX	Wassmer WA.26P Squale	M. H. Gagg
	G-CHHY	Ace Magic Laser	S. W. Walker
	G-CHHZ	Schempp-Hirth Cirrus	B. J. Dawson & S. E. Richardson
	G-CHIA	North American SNJ-5 Texan (85061:7F 061)	The Warplane Flying Company Ltd
	G-CHIB	Lindstrand LBL-77A balloon	Cameron Balloons Ltd
	G-CHID	Eurofox 912(1)	A. P. Scott & P. David
	G-CHIE	Dudek Nucleon 34/Flymecc Mini Trike	J. M. Keen
	G-CHIG	Grob G.109B	Southdown Gliding Club Ltd
	G-CHIH	Aeropro Eurofox 912(S)	Banbury Gliding Club Ltd
	G-CHII	CASA 1-131E Jungmann Srs 1000	J. A. Sykes
	G-CHIJ	Ikarus C42 FB80	G. E. Cole
	G-CHIK	Cessna F.152	Stapleford Flying Club Ltd (G-BHAZ)
	G-CHIM	Ultramagic H-31 balloon	G. B. Lescott
	G-CHIP	PA-28-181 Archer II	J. A. Divis
	G-CHIR	Van's RV-7	F. Sharples
	G-CHIS	Robinson R22	A. R. Collett
	G-CHIT	AutoGyro MTO Sport	N. G. H. Staunton
	G-CHIV	P & M Quik R	G-CHIV Syndicate
	G-CHIW	Raj Hamsa X'Air Hawk	M. D. Boley
	G-CHIX	Robin DR.400/500	P. A. & R. Stephens
	G-CHIY	Flylight MotorFloater	S. Polley
	G-CHIZ	Flylight Dragonfly	J. Paterson
	G-CHJB	Flylight Dragonfly	Celtic Solutions Ltd
	G-CHJC	Rolladen-Schneider LS6-c	J. M. Whelan
	G-CHJD	Schleicher Ka 6E	The Ruby Syndicate
	G-CHJE	Schleicher K 8B	Staffordshire Gliding Club Ltd
	G-CHJF	Rolladen-Schneider LS6-c	J. L. Bridge
	G-CHJG	Evektor EV-97 TeamEurostar UK	P. A. Bass
	G-CHJJ	Medway Clipper-80	J. Bulpin

Reg	Type	Owner or Operator	Notes
G-CHJK	Cessna T.206H Turbo Stationair	G. G. Weston	
G-CHJL	Schempp-Hirth Discus bT	Discus JL Group	
G-CHJM	Cameron C-80 balloon	C. L. Smith	
G-CHJN	Schempp-Hirth Standard Cirrus	P. M. Hardingham	
G-CHJO	Bushby-Long Midget Mustang M-1	R. J. Hodder	
G-CHJP	Schleicher Ka-6CR	D. M. Cornelius	
G-CHJR	Glasflugel H201B Standard Libelle	R. P. G. Hayhoe	
G-CHJS	Schleicher ASW-27-18E	J. D. Spencer	
G-CHJT	Centrair ASW-20F	M. S. R. Broadway & A. F. Irwin	
G-CHJV	Grob G.102 Astir CS	Cotswold Gliding Club	
G-CHJW	P & M Quik GTR	A. C. Rowlands	
G-CHJX	Rolladen-Schneider LS6-c	M. R. Haynes & P. Robinson	
G-CHJY	Schempp-Hirth Standard Cirrus	Cirrus-459 Group	
G-CHJZ	Luscombe 8E Silvaire Deluxe	Narli Aviation Ltd	
G-CHKA	Orlican Discus CS	R. W. & M. P. Weaver	
G-CHKB	Grob G.102 Astir CS77	C. D. Woodward	
G-CHKC	Schempp-Hirth Standard Cirrus	J. M. Hilll	
G-CHKD	Schempp-Hirth Standard Cirrus	Stratocirrus Owners Club	
G-CHKF	Grob G.109B	CHKF Group	
G-CHKG	Best Off Skyranger Nynja 912S(1)	D. L. Turner	
G-CHKH	Schleicher ASW-28	D. Bradley	
G-CHKI	Sikorsky S-92A	Bristow Helicopters Ltd	
G-CHKK	Schleicher K8B	Tweeetie Bird	
G-CHKM	Grob G.102 Astir CS Jeans	Essex and Suffolk Gliding Club Ltd	
G-CHKN	Kiss 400-582(1)	P. J. Higgins	
G-CHKO	Best Off Skyranger Swift 912S(1)	A. E. Kemp & B. Hetherington	
G-CHKR	Jastreb Standard Cirrus G/81	N. A. White	
G-CHKS	Jastreb Standard Cirrus G/81	S. J. Glasset	
G-CHKT	Balony Kubicek BB22E balloon	D. L. Beckwith	
G-CHKU	Schempp-Hirth Standard Cirrus	T. J. Wheeler & T. M. O'Sullivan	
G-CHKV	Scheibe Zugvogel IIIA	Dartmoor Gliding Society Ltd	
G-CHKW	Robinson R44	G. Riddell	
G-CHKX	Rolladen-Schneider LS4-B	G-CHKX Flying Group	
G-CHKY	Schempp-Hirth Discus b	M. T. Davis	
G-CHKZ	CARMAM JP 15-36AR Aiglon	T. A. & A. J. Hollings	
G-CHLB	Rolladen-Schneider LS4-b	E. G. Leach & K. F. Rogers	
G-CHLC	Pilatus B4-PC11AF	E. Lockhart	
G-CHLD	AutoGyro MTO Sport	D. L. Sivyer	
G-CHLE	Cameron A-160 balloon	Virgin Baloon Flights	
G-CHLH	Schleicher K 8B	Shenington Gliding Club	
G-CHLI	Cosmik Aviation Superchaser	Cosmik Aviation Ltd	
G-CHLK	Glasflugel H.301 Libelle	D. T. Bray	
G-CHLM	Schleicher ASW-19B	J. R. Paskins	
G-CHLN	Schempp-Hirth Discus CS	Portsmouth Naval Gliding Centre	
G-CHLP	Schleicher ASK-21	Southdown Gliding Club Ltd	
G-CHLS	Schempp-Hirth Discus b	R. Roberts	
G-CHLV	Schleicher ASW-19B	P. J. Belcher & R. I. Brickwood	
G-CHLY	Schempp-Hirth Discus CS	S. J. Pearce	
G-CHLZ	Best Off Skyranger LS 912(1)	S. K. Ridge	
G-CHMA	PZL-Bielsko SZD-51-1 Junior	The Welland Gliding Club Ltd	
G-CHMB	Glaser-Dirks DG-300 Elan	A. D. & P. Langlands	
G-CHMD	DG Flugzeugbau LS8-T	G. B. Monslow & A. P. Balkwill	
G-CHME	Glaser-Dirks DG-300 Elan	A. G. Gibbs	
G-CHMG	ICA IS-28B2	A. Sutton, R. Maksymowicz & A. J. Palfreyman	
G-CHMH	Schleicher K8B	Shenington Gliding Club	
G-CHMI	Lindstrand LBL-105A balloon	J. A. Lawton	
G-CHMK	Rolladen-Schneider LS6-18W	R. C. Hodge	
G-CHML	Schempp-Hirth Discus CS	I. D. Bateman	
G-CHMM	Glasflugel 304B	A. F. Greenhalgh	
G-CHMN	Raj Hamsa X'Air Falcon Jabiru(1)	F. C. Claydon	
G-CHMO	Orlican Discus CS	S. Barter	
G-CHMP	Bellanca 7ACA Champ	I. J. Langley	
G-CHMR	Embraer EMB-145MP	Eastern Airways	
G-CHMS	Glaser-Dirks DG-100	P. S. Medlock	
G-CHMT	Glasflugel Mosquito B	J. Taberham	
G-CHMU	CARMAM JP-15/36AR Aiglon	G-CHMU Group	
G-CHMV	Schleicher ASK-13	The Windrushers Gliding Club Ltd	
G-CHMW	Evektor EV-97 Eurostar SL	A. Wright & S. A. Ivell	
G-CHMX	Rolladen-Schneider LS4-a	L Couval	
G-CHMY	Schempp-Hirth Standard Cirrus	HMY Syndicate	
G-CHMZ	Fedorov ME7 Mechta	R. Andrews	

Notes	Reg	Type	Owner or Operator
	G-CHNA	Glaser-Dirks DG-500/20 Elan	G-CHNA Group
	G-CHNB	Scheibe SF-28A	J. M. Alonso
	G-CHNC	Schleicher ASK-19B	T. J. Highton
	G-CHND	Ultramagic H-65	N. Dykes
	G-CHNF	Schempp-Hirth Duo Discus	Booker Gliding Club Ltd
	G-CHNH	Schempp-Hirth Nimbus 2C	A. J. & M. J. W. Harris
	G-CHNI	Magni M-24C	A. Smith
	G-CHNK	PZL-Bielsko SZD-51-1 Junior	Booker Gliding Club Ltd
	G-CHNM	Standard Cirrus G/81	A. N. Mayer & C. R. I. Emson
	G-CHNO	Cameron C-60 balloon	J. F. Till
	G-CHNR	P & M Quik GTR	R. M. Powell
	G-CHNS	Agusta AW.139	Bristow Helicopters Ltd
	G-CHNT	Schleicher ASW-15	K. Tunnicliff
	G-CHNU	Schempp-Hirth Nimbus 4DT	D. E. Findon
	G-CHNV	Rolladen-Schneider LS4-b	S. K. Armstrong & P. H. Dixon
	G-CHNW	Schempp-Hirth Duo Discus	G-CHNW Group
	G-CHNY	Centrair 101A Pegase	M. O. Breen
	G-CHNZ	Centrair 101A Pegase	C. R. & R. H. Partington
	G-CHOA	Bell 206B-3 JetRanger III	Haverholme Farm Partnership
	G-CHOD	Schleicher ASW-20	S. E. Archer-Jones & A. Duerden
	G-CHOE	Robin DR400/140B	YP Flying Group
	G-CHOF	CARMAM M100S	M. A. Farrelly
	G-CHOG	AB Sportine LAK-12	J. M. Pursey
	G-CHOI	ReplicaWhite Monoplane 1912 Canard Pusher	J. Aubert
	G-CHOJ	Cameron A-375 balloon	Ballooning in Tuscany SRL
	G-CHOO	Ikarus C42 FB80	M. J. Reed
	G-CHOP	Westland-Bell 47G-3B1	Leamington Hobby Centre Ltd
	G-CHOR	Schempp-Hirth Discus b	G-CHOR Syndicate
	G-CHOT	Grob G.102 Astir CS77	Southdown Gliding Club Ltd
	G-CHOU	EV-97 TeamEurostar UK	R. A. Betts
	G-CHOX	Shaw Europa XS	Chocs Away Ltd
	G-CHOY	Schempp-Hirth Mini Nimbus C	A. H. Sparrow
	G-CHOZ	Rolladen-Schneider LS6-18W	U2 Syndicate
	G-CHPA	Robinson R22 Beta	Rivermead Aviation Ltd/Switzerland
	G-CHPC	Schleicher ASW-20 CL	B. L. Liddard & P. J. Williams
	G-CHPD	Rolladen-Schneider LS6-c18	R. E. Robertson
	G-CHPE	Schleicher ASK-13	Dumfries and District Gliding Club
	G-CHPG	Cirrus SR-20	AT Aviation Sales Ltd, G. Greenfield & K. M. O'Sullivan
	G-CHPH	Schempp-Hirth Discus CS	I. N & S. G. Hunt
	G-CHPI	DHC.1 Chipmunk Mk.22	J. A. Da Silva Costa
	G-CHPL	Rolladen-Schneider LS4-b	Southdown Gliding Club Ltd
	G-CHPO	Schleicher Ka-6CR	A. P. Frost
	G-CHPS	Best Off SkyRanger 582(1)	J. A. Gregorig
	G-CHPT	Federov ME7 Mechta	Midland Gliding Club Ltd
	G-CHPV	Schleicher ASK-21	Scottish Gliding Union Ltd
	G-CHPW	Schleicher ASK-21	Scottish Gliding Union Ltd
	G-CHPX	Schempp-Hirth Discus CS	G-CHRS Group
	G-CHPY	DHC.1 Chipmunk 22 (WB652:V)	Devonair Executive Business Travel Ltd
	G-CHPZ	P & M Quik GT450	D. J. Shippen
	G-CHRC	Glaser-Dirks DG500/20 Elan	DG500-390 Syndicate
	G-CHRD	Flylight Dragonlite	I. A. Barclay
	G-CHRE	Nicollier HN.700 Menestrel II	M. K. A. Blyth
	G-CHRG	PZL-Bielsko SZD-51-1 Junior	PA Technologies Ltd
	G-CHRH	Schempp-Hirth Discus 2cT	C. Hyett
	G-CHRJ	Schleicher K 8B	Romeo Juliet K8 Group
	G-CHRL	Schempp-Hirth Standard Cirrus	M. Oleksiewicz
	G-CHRM	Ikarus C42 FB80 Bravo	Tebs Group
	G-CHRN	Schleicher ASK-18	K. Richards
	G-CHRS	Schempp-Hirth Discus CS	M. Santopinto
	G-CHRT	EV-97 TeamEurostar UK	A. J. Ferguson & T. W. Pawson
	G-CHRU	Flylight Dragonlite Fox	J. R. Kendall
	G-CHRV	Van's RV-7	R. E. Tyers
	G-CHRW	Schempp-Hirth Duo Discus	802 Syndicate
	G-CHRX	Schempp-Hirth Discus a	A. Spirling
	G-CHSB	Glaser-Dirks DG-303 Elan	P. J. Britten
	G-CHSD	Schempp-Hirth Discus b	G-CHSD Group
	G-CHSE	Grob G.102 Astir CS77	Hotel Sierra Echo Group
	G-CHSG	Scheibe SF27A	HSG Syndicate
	G-CHSH	Scheibe Zugvogel IIIB	G-CHSH Group
	G-CHSI	Ellipse Fuji/Pulma 2000	H. J. Mayer

Reg	Type	Owner or Operator	Notes
G-CHSK	Schleicher ASW-20CL	751 Syndicate	
G-CHSM	Schleicher ASW-13	Staffordshire Gliding Club Ltd	
G-CHSN	Schleicher Ka-6CR	Needwood Forest Gliding Club Ltd	
G-CHSO	Schempp-Hirth Discus b	Midland Gliding Club Ltd	
G-CHSP	UltraMagic M-65C balloon	S. Bareford	
G-CHSS	Ikarus C42 FB80 Bravo	A. P. Burch	
G-CHST	Van's RV-9A	R. J. Charles	
G-CHSU	Eurocopter EC 135T1	2 Excel Aviation Ltd	
G-CHSX	Scheibe SF-27A	Essex & Suffolk Gliding Club Ltd	
G-CHSY	Aeroprakt A22-LS Foxbat	J. D. Reed	
G-CHTA	AA-5A Cheetah	K. T. Pierce (G-BFRC)	
G-CHTB	Schempp-Hirth Janus	Janus G-CHTB Syndicate	
G-CHTC	Schleicher ASW-15B	S. J. Glassett	
G-CHTD	Grob G.102 Astir CS	S. Waldie	
G-CHTE	Grob G.102 Astir CS77	J. P. W. Towill	
G-CHTF	AB Sportline LAK-12	M. Tolson	
G-CHTH	Zenair CH.701SP	S. C. Richards & R. E. Lasnier	
G-CHTI	Van's RV-12	M. & N. D. Stannard	
G-CHTJ	Schleicher ASK-13	Queen's University Gliding Club	
G-CHTK	Hawker Sea Hurricane 1B (P2921/GZ-L)	Warbird Experiences Ltd (G-TWTD)	
G-CHTL	Schempp-Hirth Arcus T	38 Syndicate	
G-CHTM	Rolladen-Schneider LS8-18	M. J. Chapman	
G-CHTO	Rans S-7S	A. G. Bell	
G-CHTR	Grob G.102 Astir CS	I. P. & D. M. Wright	
G-CHTS	Rolladen-Schneider LS8-18	P. T. Cunnison	
G-CHTU	Schempp-Hirth Cirrus	Open Cirrus Group	
G-CHTV	Schleicher ASK-21	Cambridge Gliding Club Ltd	
G-CHTX	Voltair 86	Hartlepool College of Further Education	
G-CHTZ	Airbus A.330-243	Thomas Cook Airlines Ltd (G-WWBM)	
G-CHUA	Schleicher ASW-19B	G. D. Vaughan	
G-CHUC	Denney Kitfox Model 2	Silver Fox Group	
G-CHUD	Schleicher ASK-13	London Gliding Club Propietary Ltd	
G-CHUE	Schleicher ASW-27	M. J. Smith	
G-CHUF	Schleicher ASK-13	The Welland Gliding Club Ltd	
G-CHUG	Shaw Europa	C. M. Washington	
G-CHUH	Schempp-Hirth Janus	B. J. Biskup	
G-CHUJ	Centrair ASW-20F	J. A. Heanen	
G-CHUK	Cameron O-77 balloon	A. Hook	
G-CHUN	Grob G.102 Astir CS Jeans	Staffordshire Gliding Club Ltd	
G-CHUO	Federov ME7 Mechta	J. D. A. Cooper & W. H. Ollis	
G-CHUP	Aeropro Eurofox 912(S)	B Walker & Co (Dursley) Ltd	
G-CHUR	Schempp-Hirth Cirrus	M. Rossiter & J. A. Stillwagon	
G-CHUS	Scheibe SF27A Zugvogel V	SF27 HUS Syndicate	
G-CHUT	Centrair ASW-20F	S. R. Phelps	
G-CHUU	Schleicher ASK-13	Upward Bound Trust	
G-CHUX	P & M Aviation QuikR	A. J. Trye	
G-CHUY	Schempp-Hirth Ventus cT	P. R. Gammell	
G-CHUZ	Schempp-Hirth Discus bT	G. Starling	
G-CHVB	P & M Aviation Quik R	Victor Bravo Group	
G-CHVC	Cameron C-60 balloon	B. G. Jones	
G-CHVG	Schleicher ASK-21	Rattlesden Gliding Club Ltd	
G-CHVH	Pilatus B4-PC11AF	London Gliding Club Proprietary Ltd	
G-CHVI	Cameron Z-210 balloon	A-Gas (Orb) Ltd	
G-CHVJ	VS.349 Spitfire Vb	G. N. S. Farrant	
G-CHVK	Grob G.102 Astir CS	R. Duke & M. Burridge	
G-CHVM	Glaser-Dirks DG-300	Glider Syndicate 303	
G-CHVO	Schleicher ASK-13	R. Brown	
G-CHVP	Schleicher ASW-20	G. P. Northcott	
G-CHVR	Schempp-Hirth Discus b	Yorkshire Gliding Club (Proprietary) Ltd	
G-CHVS	ICP MXP-740 Savannah VG Jabiru(1)	Sandtoft Ultralights	
G-CHVU	Rolladen-Schneider LS8-a	R. Engelhardt	
G-CHVV	Rolladen-Schneider LS4-b	A. J. Bardgett	
G-CHVY	Ikarus C42 FB80	G-CHVY Syndicate	
G-CHUW	Rolladen-Schneider LS8-18	S8 Group	
G-CHVX	Centrair ASW-20F	D. Coker	
G-CHVW	Scleicher ASK-13	Rattlesden Gliding Club Ltd	
G-CHVZ	Schempp-Hirth Standard Cirrus	ABC Soaring	
G-CHWA	Schempp-Hirth Ventus 2c	C. Garton	
G-CHWB	Schempp-Hirth Duo Discus	Lasham Gliding Society Ltd	
G-CHWC	Glasflugel Standard Libelle 201B	R. P. Hardcastle	
G-CHWD	Schempp-Hirth Standard Cirrus	M. R. Hoskins	

Notes	Reg	Type	Owner or Operator
	G-CHWE	Lindstrand LBL-77A balloon	B. P. Witter
	G-CHWF	Jastreb Standard Cirrus G/81	Team Cirrus 2ZC
	G-CHWG	Glasflugel Standard Libelle 201B	M. R. Fox
	G-CHWH	Schempp-Hirth Ventus cT	M. J. Philpott
	G-CHWI	APEV Demoichelle	G. R. Moore
	G-CHWJ	Guimbal Cabri G2	European Helicopter Importers Ltd
	G-CHWK	Aerochute Hummerchute	W. A. Kimberlin
	G-CHWL	Rolladen-Schneider LS8-18	D. S. Lodge
	G-CHWM	AutoGyro Cavalon	Devon Autogyro Ltd
	G-CHWN	Ikarus C42 FB100 Bravo	J. J. Greenshields
	G-CHWO	P & M Aviation Quik GTR	M. J. Robbins
	G-CHWP	Glaser-Dirks DG-100G Elan	HWP Group
	G-CHWS	Rolladen-Schneider LS8-18	G. E. & H. B. Chalmers
	G-CHWT	Schleicher K 8B	Shenington Gliding Club
	G-CHWW	Grob G.103A Twin II Acro	Crown Service Gliding Club
	G-CHXA	Scheibe Zugvogel IIIB	G-CHXA Group
	G-CHXB	Grob G.102 Astir CS77	K. Lafferty
	G-CHXD	Schleicher ASW-27	J. Quartermaine & M. Jerman
	G-CHXE	Schleicher ASW-19B	I. J. Fisher
	G-CHXF	Cameron A-140 balloon	Gone With The Wind Ltd
	G-CHXG	CZAW Sportcruiser	R. J. Warne
	G-CHXH	Schempp-Hirth Discus b	Deesside Gliding Club (Aberdeenshire) Ltd
	G-CHXJ	Schleicher ASK-13	Cotswold Gliding Club
	G-CHXK	Scheibe SF-25A Falke 2000	Stratford on Avon Gliding Club Ltd
	G-CHXL	Van's RV-6	S. C. Parsons & R. W. Marchant
	G-CHXM	Grob G.102 Astir CS	University of Bristol Students Union
	G-CHXN	Balony Kubicek BB20GP balloon	D. R. Medcalf
	G-CHXO	Schleicher ASH-25	The Eleven Group
	G-CHXP	Schleicher ASK-13	Dartmoor Gliding Society
	G-CHXR	Schempp-Hirth Ventus cT	560 Group
	G-CHXS	Cameron C-90 balloon	Dribuild Ltd
	G-CHXT	Rolladen-Schneider LS-4a	P. N. Murray
	G-CHXU	Schleicher ASW-19B	UCLU
	G-CHXV	Schleicher ASK-13	Aquila Gliding Club Ltd
	G-CHXW	Rolladen-Schneider LS8-18	W. Aspland
	G-CHXZ	Rolladen-Schneider LS4	N. Croxford
	G-CHYB	Grob G.109B	Morgan Airborne LLP
	G-CHYC	Westlake Altair AX4-31/12 balloon	D. W. Westlake
	G-CHYD	Schleicher ASW-24	E. S. Adlard
	G-CHYE	DG-505 Elan Orion	The Bristol Gliding Club Proprietary Ltd
	G-CHYF	Rolladen-Schneider LS8-18	R. E. Francis
	G-CHYG	Sikorsky S-92A	Bristow Helicopters Ltd
	G-CHYH	Rolladen-Schneider LS3-17	B. Silke
	G-CHYJ	Schleicher ASK-21	Highland Gliding Club Ltd
	G-CHYK	Centrair ASW-20FL	K. H. Bates
	G-CHYN	CCF Harvard 4	Victoria Group Holdings Ltd
	G-CHYO	Ace Magic Laser	D. R. Purslow
	G-CHYP	PZL-Bielsko SZD-50-3 Puchacz	Rattlesden Gliding Club Ltd
	G-CHYR	Schleicher ASW-27	A. J. Manwaring
	G-CHYS	Schleicher ASK-21	Army Gliding Association
	G-CHYT	Schleicher ASK-21	Army Gliding Association
	G-CHYU	Schempp-Hirth Discus CS	Army Gliding Association
	G-CHYY	Schempp-Hirth Nimbus 3DT	G-CHYY Syndicate
	G-CHYZ	Skystar Vixen	M. J. Turner
	G-CHZB	PZL-Swidnik PW-5 Smyk	The Burn Gliding Club Ltd
	G-CHZD	Schleicher ASW-15B	C. P. Ellison & S. Barber
	G-CHZE	Schempp-Hirth Discus CS	Darlton Gliding Club Ltd
	G-CHZG	Rolladen-Schneider LS8-18	M. J. & T. J. Webb
	G-CHZH	Schleicher Ka 6CR	C. Hankinson
	G-CHZI	Cessna 172RG	Aeroplano-Planeamento Exploracao e Manutencao de Aeronaves Lda/Portugal
	G-CHZJ	Schempp-Hirth Standard Cirrus	P. Mucha
	G-CHZK	Europa XS	P. J. Harrod
	G-CHZL	Zenair CH.601XL Zodiac	S. F. Beardsell
	G-CHZM	Rolladen-Schneider LS4-a	J. M. Bevan
	G-CHZO	Schleicher ASW-27	Lima Zulu Group
	G-CHZP	Cessna 152	Aeroplano-Planeamento Exploracao e Manutencao de Aeronaves Lda/Portugal
	G-CHZR	Schleicher ASK-21	K21 HZR Group
	G-CHZS	Zenair CH.601HDS	G. Addison

Reg	Type	Owner or Operator	Notes
G-CHZT	Groppo Trail	A. Strachan & B. J. Main	
G-CHZU	Schempp-Hirth Standard Cirrus	D. J. Richmond	
G-CHZV	Schempp-Hirth Standard Cirrus	S. M. Cass	
G-CHZW	P & M Aviation Quik GTR	N. J. Braund	
G-CHZX	Schleicher K 8B	K8B Boys Club	
G-CHZY	Rolladen-Schneider LS4-a	N. P. Wedi	
G-CHZZ	Schleicher ASW-20L	LD Syndicate	
G-CIAA	Mitchinson Safari	S. A. Labib	
G-CIAB	Avion Riot/Samba	Avian Ltd	
G-CIAC	HOAC DV.20 Katana	LOC Aircraft/Belgium	
G-CIAE	Cameron TR-70 balloon	Cameron Balloons Ltd	
G-CIAF	TL3000 Sirius	P. H. Ronfell	
G-CIAI	Schempp-Hirth Arcus T	G-CIAI Group	
G-CIAJ	Hawker Hart B4A	Westh Flyg AB/Sweden	
G-CIAK	Groppo Trail	I. Markham	
G-CIAL	Cameron Z-77 balloon	A. A. Osman	
G-CIAM	PA-28-181 Archer III	J. Mendonca-Caridad	
G-CIAN	Unicorn Ax6 balloon	G. A. & I. Chadwick	
G-CIAO	I.I.I. Sky Arrow 1450-L	G. Arscott	
G-CIAP	Cameron Z-77 balloon	A. A. Osman	
G-CIAR	P & M Aviation Quik GTR	C. R. Paterson	
G-CIAU	Bombardier CL600-1A11 Challenger 600	Inflite Aviation (IOM) Ltd	
G-CIAV	Ace Magic Cyclone	D. M. Pecheur	
G-CIAW	Ikarus C42 FB80	Salex Design Services Ltd	
G-CIAX	CZAW Sportcruiser	A. G. Higgins	
G-CIAY	Cameron C-70 balloon	R. P. Wade	
G-CIAZ	Aeropro Eurofox 912(1)	M. P. Dale	
G-CIBA	Cameron N-145 balloon	J. D. Smith	
G-CIBB	Cessna F.172H	D. R. Godfrey	
G-CIBC	Aeropro Eurofox 912(S)	M. P. Brockington	
G-CIBF	Aeropro Eurofox 912(S)	The Borders (Milfield) Gliding Club Ltd	
G-CIBH	Van's RV-8A	W. B. Blair-Hickman	
G-CIBI	Lindstrand LBL-90A balloon	A. J. & S. J. M. Boyle	
G-CIBJ	Colomban MC-30 Luciole	R. A. Gardiner	
G-CIBL	AutoGyro Cavalon	A. C. R. & J. Drayton	
G-CIBM	Van's RV-8	G. P. Williams	
G-CIBN	Cameron Z-90 balloon	B. J. Newman	
G-CIBO	Cessna 180K	CIBO Ops Ltd	
G-CIBP	Cameron Z-77 balloon	A. A. Osman	
G-CIBR	P & M Quik GT450	K. D. Smith	
G-CIBT	P & M Quik R	G-CIBT Syndicate	
G-CIBU	Jabiru J160	D. J. Bly	
G-CIBV	Best Off Skyranger Swift 912S(1)	PPL (UK) Ltd	
G-CIBW	Westland Scout AH.1 (XT626)	Historic Aircraft Flight Trust	
G-CIBX	Cameron Z-31 balloon	A. E. Austin	
G-CIBZ	Aeropro Eurofox 912(S1)	K. N. Rigley & D. Thorpe	
G-CICA	Europa Aviation Europa XS	R. J. Grainger	
G-CICC	Cessna 152	The Pilot Centre Ltd	
G-CICD	Colt 105A balloon	Mobberley Balloon Collection	
G-CICF	Ikarus C42 FB80	D. Durrans	
G-CICG	Ikarus C42 FB80	G-CICG Group	
G-CICH	Sikorsky S-92A	Bristow Helicopters Ltd	
G-CICK	VS.509 Spitfire T IX	K. M. Perkins	
G-CICM	Rotorsport UK Calidus	F. Hammond	
G-CICN	Agusta-Bell Sioux H. Mk.1 (XT131)	Historic Aircraft Flight Trust	
G-CICO	UltraMagic H-42 balloon	A. M. Holly	
G-CICP	de Havilland DHC-2 Beaver AL.Mk.1 (XP820)	Historic Aircraft Flight Trust	
G-CICR	Auster AOP.Mk.1 (XR244)	Historic Aircraft Flight Trust	
G-CICT	Schempp-Hirth Ventus 2cT	S. G. Jones (G-ZENN)	
G-CICU	Raj Hamsa X'Air Hawk	X'Air Group	
G-CICW	Rotorsport UK MTO Sport	J. Owen	
G-CICX	Flylight Dragonlite Fox	C. M. James	
G-CICY	PZL-Bielsko SZD-50-3 Puchasz	Deeside Gliding Club (Aberdeenshire) Ltd	
G-CIDB	Flylight Dragon Chaser	D. M. Broom	
G-CIDC	Yakovlev Yak-18T	D. M. Cue	
G-CIDD	Bellanca 7ECA Citabria	B. F. L. & T. A. Hodges	
G-CIDF	Autogyro MTOSport	K. J. Whitehead	
G-CIDG	P & M Aviation Quik GTR	G. N. Kenny	
G-CIDH	Cameron C-80 balloon	P. C. Johnson	
G-CIDK	Eurocopter EC225LP Super Puma	Wilmington Trust SP Services (Dublin) Ltd	

Notes	Reg	Type	Owner or Operator
	G-CIDM	Eurocopter EC225LP Super Puma	Wilmington Trust SP Services (Dublin) Ltd
	G-CIDO	Glaser-Dirks DG-600/18M	S. S. M. Turner
	G-CIDP	Sonex	P. I. Marshall
	G-CIDS	Ikarus C42 FB100	P. H. J. Fenn
	G-CIDT	Schleicher ASH-25E	G. D. E. Macdonald (G-KIGR)
	G-CIDU	Balony Kubicek BB22E balloon	A. M. Daniels
	G-CIDW	Aerotechnik EV-97 Eurostar	D. Workman
	G-CIDX	Sonex Sonex	J. P. Dilks
	G-CIDY	P & M Quik GTR	G. P. Wade
	G-CIDZ	EV-97 Eurostar SL Microlight	Delta Zulu Group
	G-CIEA	Rolladen-Schneider LS4-b	T. Zorn
	G-CIEB	AutoGyro MTO Sport	K. A. Hastie
	G-CIEC	SAAB 2000	Eastern Airways
	G-CIED	Aeros Fox 16T/RIP1	R. J. Ripley
	G-CIEE	Ikarus C42 FB100	Hadair
	G-CIEF	Aeropro Eurofox 912(S)	Darlton Eurofox Group
	G-CIEG	P & M Quik R	Flying Group G-CIEG
	G-CIEH	Aeropro Eurofox 912(S)	Lakes Gliding Club
	G-CIEI	Lindstrand LBL-HS-110 balloon	Lindstrand Asia Ltd (G-TRIB)
	G-CIEJ	AutoGyro MTO Sport	G-CIEJ Group
	G-CIEK	Flylight Dragonlite Fox	P. A. Marks
	G-CIEL	Cessna 560XL Citation Excel	Enerway Ltd
	G-CIEM	P & M Quik R	S. P. T. Magnus-Hannaford
	G-CIEN	Super Marine Spitfire Mk.26 (PL788)	A. G. Counsell
	G-CIEP	Flylight Dragon Chaser	R. Urquhart
	G-CIER	Cameron Z-160 balloon	J. Taylor
	G-CIET	Lindstrand LBL-31A balloon	C. A. Butter & S. I. Williams
	G-CIEW	AutoGyro Cavalon	Rotorsport Sales & Service Ltd
	G-CIEX	SA.341G Gazelle AH.Mk.1	Gazelle Flying Group
	G-CIEY	Westland SA.341G Gazelle AH.Mk.1	Gazelle Flying Group A
	G-CIEZ	Bucker Bu.181B-1 Bestmann	A. C. Whitehead
	G-CIFA	Aeropro Eurofox 912(1)	J. R. Elcocks
	G-CIFB	Aerochute Dual	J. D. Abraham
	G-CIFC	SOCATA TB-200 Tobago XL	Lincoln Aero Club Ltd
	G-CIFD	Titan T-51 Mustang (2106638/E9-R)	B. J. Chester-Master
	G-CIFE	Beech B.200 Super King Air	Number Seven (Aviation) Ltd (G-RAFJ)
	G-CIFF	P &M Quik GT450	Light Flight Fox Fox Group
	G-CIFH	Cameron N-275 balloon	MSJ Ballooning Ltd
	G-CIFI	Cameron Z-77 balloon	A. M. Holly (G-UKFT)
	G-CIFK	Raj Hamsa X'Air Hawk	E. B. Toulson
	G-CIFL	Van's RV-6	A. J. Maxwell
	G-CIFM	Flylight Dragon Chaser	J. P. McCall
	G-CIFN	Ikarus C42 FB80	K. J. A. Farrance
	G-CIFO	Aeropro Eurofox 912(S)	Herefordshire Gliding Club Ltd
	G-CIFP	Cameron Frog-90 SS balloon	Lindstrand Asia Ltd
	G-CIFS	Lindstrand LBL-150A balloon	Lindstrand Asia Ltd
	G-CIFT	Autogyro MTO Sport	J. Reade & Sons
	G-CIFU	Rolladen-Schneider LS4	N. A. Taylor
	G-CIFV	P & M Quik GTR	R. Higton
	G-CIFX	Ultramagic M-105 balloon	E. C. Meek
	G-CIFY	PA-28-181 Archer III	D. S. Gould (G-GFPA)
	G-CIFZ	Ikarus C42 FB80	Air Cornwall
	G-CIGA	Ultramagic H-42 balloon	A. S. Davidson
	G-CIGB	Stinson L-1 Vigilant	G. & P. M. Turner
	G-CIGC	P & M Quik R	W. G. Craig
	G-CIGD	Cessna F.172M	D. S. Sime & D. M. Collins (G-ENII)
	G-CIGE	DHC-1 Chipmunk 22 (WK634:902)	Skyblue Aero Services Ltd
	G-CIGF	Slingsby T.61F Venture T.Mk.2	M. F. Cuming
	G-CIGG	P & M Quik GTR	N. J. Lister
	G-CIGH	Max Holste MH.1521M Broussard	R. A. Fleming
	G-CIGI	Lindstrand LBL-77A balloon	Lindstrand Media Ltd
	G-CIGJ	Cameron Z-90 balloon	Atlantic Ballooning BVBA/Belgium
	G-CIGN	Cameron Z-90 balloon	Elgas SRL/Italy
	G-CIGP	Cessna F.172N	Flugzeugreparatur Damme GmbH/Germany
	G-CIGR	Groppo Trail	D. H. Pattison
	G-CIGS	Autogyro MTOSport	E. A. Blomfield-Smith
	G-CIGT	Best Off Skyranger Swift 912S(1)	N. S. Wells
	G-CIGU	Aerochute Dual	B. Griffiths
	G-CIGV	Hewing Demoiselle 15/Aeros Fox 16T	R. B. Hewing
	G-CIGW	BRM Aero Bristell NG5 Speed Wing	J. R. Frohnsdorff
	G-CIGY	Westland-Bell 47G-3B1	M. L. Romeling (G-BGXP)

Reg	Type	Owner or Operator	Notes
G-CIGZ	Sikorsky S-92A	Bristow Helicopters Ltd	
G-CIHA	P & M Quik R	S. D. Hitchcock	
G-CIHB	Colomban LC-30 Luciole	S. Kilpin	
G-CIHC	Cameron Z-105 balloon	First Flight	
G-CIHD	BAe Jetstream 4100	Airtime AB/Sweden	
G-CIHE	BAe Jetstream 4100	Airtime AB/Sweden	
G-CIHF	Schempp-Hirth Discus 2a	B. J. Flewett	
G-CIHG	Cameron Z-90 balloon	I. Parsons	
G-CIHH	AutoGyro MTO Sport	A. D. Gordon	
G-CIHI	Cameron V-77 balloon	P. Spellward	
G-CIHL	P & M Quik GTR	T. G. Jackson	
G-CIHM	Schleicher ASW-28018E	S. A. Kerby	
G-CIHO	Cameron Z-77 balloon	Lighter Than Air Ltd	
G-CIHT	Flylight Dragonlite Fox	M. D. Harper	
G-CIHV	Best Off Skyranger Nynja 912(1)	A. Dawson	
G-CIHW	AutoGyro Cavalon	A. E. Polkey & R. I. Broadhead	
G-CIHY	P & M Pegasus Quik	A. P. & G. M. Douglas-Dixon	
G-CIHZ	P & M Quik GTR	B. Michnay	
G-CIIA	P & M Quik R	K. A. Forsyth	
G-CIIB	Aerochute Dual	P. Dean	
G-CIIC	PA-18-150 Super Cub	Bianchi Aviation Film Services Ltd (G-PULL)	
G-CIID	BFC Challenger II Long Wing	J. A. Evans	
G-CIIE	Cameron Z-56 balloon	Pearl Balloon SPRL/Belgium	
G-CIIH	P & M Quik GTR	B. Dossett	
G-CIIK	Yakovlev Yak-55	Yak 55 2014 Ltd	
G-CIIL	BRM Aero Bristell NG5 Speed Wing	D. F. P. Finan	
G-CIIM	Cessna F.172N	Surrey Aviation Ltd	
G-CIIN	Ikarus C42 FB100	R. S. O'Carroll	
G-CIIO	Curtis P-40C Warhawk (39-160:160 10AB)	Patina Ltd	
G-CIIP	Aviad Zigolo MG12	Sprite Aviation Services Ltd	
G-CIIR	Cessna FRA.150L	N. Concannon	
G-CIIT	Best Off Skyranger Swift 912S(1)	G-CIIT Flying Group	
G-CIIU	TLAC Sherwood Ranger ST	S. K. Moeller	
G-CIIV	AMS-Flight Apis M	J. A. Harris	
G-CIIW	Piper J3L-65 Cub	S. D. R. Dray	
G-CIIX	Ultramagic M-105 balloon	E. C. Meek	
G-CIIY	Robinson R22	A. G. Littara/Italy	
G-CIIZ	Flylight Dragonlite Fox	J. Lane	
G-CIJA	P & M Quik GT450	A. Jackson	
G-CIJB	Cameron Z-90 balloon	J. Bennett & Son (Insurance Brokers) Ltd	
G-CIJE	Alisport Silent 2 Electro	B. J. Harrison	
G-CIJF	Schempp-Hirth Duo Discus T	Lasham Gliding Society Ltd	
G-CIJG	La Mouette Samson/Atos-VR	A. J. Hollidge	
G-CIJH	Alisport Silent Club	R. J. Marshall	
G-CIJI	Gefa-Flug AS105 GD Airship	Alex Air Media Ltd	
G-CIJJ	Cameron O-31 balloon	M. J. Woodcock	
G-CIJK	Zenair CH.750	N. M. Goodacre	
G-CIJL	Cameron Z-105 balloon	B. T. Harris	
G-CIJM	Cameron N-133 balloon	Border Ballooning Ltd	
G-CIJN	Boeing Stearman E-75 Kaydet (317)	R. D. King	
G-CIJO	P & M Quik GTR	B. N. Montila	
G-CIJR	P & M Pegasus Quantum 15-912	T. A. Chambers	
G-CIJS	Cessna F.152	R. M. D. C. C. Cabral	
G-CIJT	Best Off Skyranger Nynja 912S(1)	G-CIJT Group	
G-CIJU	Cessna 177RG	H. A. Ermert	
G-CIJV	CASA 1-133 Jungmeister (LG+01)	R. A. Cumming	
G-CIJW	Agusta AW139	Bristow Helicopters Ltd	
G-CIJX	Agusta AW139	Bristow Helicopters Ltd	
G-CIJY	Wittman W.10 Tailwind	P. Mather	
G-CIJZ	Zenair CH.750	M. Henderson	
G-CIKA	P & M Quik Lite	C. M. Wilkinson	
G-CIKB	Schempp-Hirth Duo Discus T	P. Morrison & N. Jones	
G-CIKC	Cameron D-77 airship	Cameron Balloons Ltd	
G-CIKD	Alisport Silent 2 Targa	B. N. Searle	
G-CIKE	Aeroprakt A22-LS Foxbat Supersport 600	C. A. Pollard	
G-CIKG	Rotorsport UK Calidus	Gyronimo Ltd	
G-CIKH	Eurofox 914	Deeside Gliding Club (Aberdeenshire) Ltd	
G-CIKI	P & M Pegasus Quik	D. Brown	
G-CIKJ	Ace Aviation Easy Riser Spirit	P. Jones	
G-CIKK	Ace Magic Laser	D. R. Cooper	
G-CIKL	Ultramagic S-70 balloon	L. J. Watts	

Notes	Reg	Type	Owner or Operator
	G-CIKM	Diamond DA.42 Twin Star	Cloud Global Ltd & S. G. Jones
	G-CIKN	Lindstrand LBL-150A balloon	Helena Maria Fragoso Dos Santos SA/Portugal
	G-CIKO	Agusta AW139	Bristow Helicopters Ltd
	G-CIKR	Best Off Skyranger Nynja 912S(1)	A. M. Wilkes
	G-CIKS	Slingsby T.67 Mk.II Firefly	R. C. P. Brookhouse
	G-CIKT	Evektor EV-97 TeamEurostar UK	J. R. Grigg
	G-CIKU	Flylight Dragonfly	N. S. Brayn
	G-CIKV	Flylight Foxcub	M. P. Wimsey
	G-CIKW	Aeros Ant/Discus	I. M. Vass
	G-CIKX	Robinson R66	LSET Hire LLP
	G-CIKZ	Cameron Z-90 balloon	Ufttools-Uftlas BVBA/Belgium
	G-CILA	Aeropro Eurofox 912(1)	D. S. Runnalls
	G-CILB	SAlisport Silent 2 Electro	H. G. Nicklin & R. Butt
	G-CILD	Pruett Pusher VP-1	J. A. Cooper
	G-CILG	Van's RV-7A	D. Perl
	G-CILI	Replica Nieuport 11 (A126)	R. E. Peirse
	G-CILL	BRM Aero Bristell NG5	J. Edgeworth
	G-CILM	Cameron Z-77 balloon	Morson Group Ltd
	G-CILN	Agusta Westland AW.139	Bristow Helicopters Ltd
	G-CILO	Cameron TR-70 balloon	A. Collett
	G-CILP	Agusta Westland AW.139	Bristow Helicopters Ltd
	G-CILR	Guimbal Cabri G2	European Helicopter Importers Ltd
	G-CILS	Rolladen-Schneider LS10-st	W. M. Coffee
	G-CILT	Ikarus C42 FB100	Boston Wings Ltd
	G-CILU	Guimbal Cabri G2	European Helicopters Importers Ltd
	G-CILV	Dragon Chaser	C. J. Johnson
	G-CILW	Ace Aviation Easy Riser Touch	A. Voyce
	G-CILX	Stolp V-Star	S. R. Green
	G-CILY	Ikarus C42 FB80	G. R. Shipman
	G-CILZ	Cameron Z-140 balloon	Atlantic Ballooning BVBA/Belgium
	G-CIMB	Cessna 177RG	A. R. Willis
	G-CIMC	Hoffmann H.36 Dimona	East Sussex Gliding Club Ltd
	G-CIMD	Alpi Pioneer 400	F. A. Cavacuiti
	G-CIME	Balony Kubicek BB30Z balloon	A. Pasin
	G-CIMG	Aerochute Dual	M. R. Gaylor
	G-CIMH	P & M Quik Lite	G-CIMH Syndicate
	G-CIMI	Grob G.115	M. Kostiuk
	G-CIMK	P & M Quik Lite	N. R. Beale
	G-CIML	Eurofox 912(S)	G-CIML Eurofox Flying Group
	G-CIMM	Cessna T.182 Turbo Skylane II	A. W. Oliver (G-PDHJ)
	G-CIMN	Zenair CH.750	D. A. G. Johnson
	G-CIMO	Sportavia-Putzer RF5B Sperber	G-CIMO Operating Group
	G-CIMP	Scheibe SF.25C Falke	W. B. Andrews
	G-CIMS	Aeropro Eurofox 912(1)	C. M. Sperring
	G-CIMT	Autogyro Cavalon	M. L. Watson
	G-CIMV	Groppo Trail	A. Batters
	G-CIMW	Cameron O-31 balloon	B. Geeraerts
	G-CIMX	Westland Scout AH.Mk.1 (XW283)	G. P. Hinkley
	G-CIMY	Sadler Vampire SV2	I. P. Freestone
	G-CIMZ	Robinson R44 II	JMR Aviation LLP
	G-CINA	Cessna 152	Swiftair Maintenance Ltd
	G-CINB	Ace Magic Laser	M. F. McLean
	G-CINC	Magnaghi Sky Arrow 650 TCNS	Spectrum Aviation Ltd
	G-CIND	Cameron C-70 balloon	Gone with the Wind Ltd
	G-CINF	Cessna 182M	Aero-Club Braunschweig EV/Germany
	G-CING	Sherwood Ranger ST	J. North & P. K. Goff
	G-CINH	P & M Quik R	P. Martin
	G-CINI	Rans S7S	D. R. P. Mole
	G-CINJ	Milholland Legal Eagle	N. S. Jeffrey
	G-CINK	Grob G.109	The Lyveden Motor Gliding Syndicate
	G-CINL	Skyranger Swift 912(S)1	B. Richardson
	G-CINM	Grob G.109B	Grob 109B Motorglider Syndicate G-CINM
	G-CINN	Cameron Z-31 balloon	Turner Balloons Ltd
	G-CINO	Grob G.109B	T. R. Dews
	G-CINU	Eurocopter EC225LP Super Puma	Omni Helicopters International SA
	G-CINV	Aeroprakt A22-LS Foxbat	J. P. Mimnagh
	G-CINX	Van's RV-7	R. Barnwell
	G-CINZ	Magic Cyclone	T. W. Lorimer
	G-CIOA	Murphy Rebel	O. P. Sparrow
	G-CIOC	Boeing A75N1 Stearman	Skymax (Aviation) Ltd

Reg	Type	Owner or Operator	Notes
G-CIOD	P & M Quik Lite	C. R. Buckle	
G-CIOF	Aeropro Eurofox 912(S)	Yorkshire Gliding Club (Proprietary) Ltd	
G-CIOG	Fresh Breeze Bullix Trike/Relax	D. Burton	
G-CIOI	Aerospatiale AS.332L Super Puma	Vector Aerospace International Ltd	
G-CIOJ	Aeropro Eurofox 912(IS)	A. C. S. Paterson	
G-CIOK	Skyranger Swift 912(S)(1)	J. de Pree & B. Janson	
G-CIOL	P &M Quik GTR	D. L. Clark	
G-CIOM	Magni M24C Orion	C. R. Lear	
G-CIOO	Van's RV-7	M. Albert-Recht	
G-CIOP	Aerospatiale AS.355F Ecureuil 2	RCR Aviation Ltd	
G-CIOR	Nicollier HN.700 Menestrel II	R. C. & R. P. C. Teverson	
G-CIOS	MD Helicopters MD.900 Explorer	Specialist Aviation Services Ltd (G-SASO)	
G-CIOU	Cameron Z-70 balloon	R. J. Mansfield	
G-CIOV	Ultramagic H-31 balloon	Murray Rene Ltd	
G-CIOW	Westland SA.341C Gazelle HT Mk.2	S. Atherton	
G-CIOX	Flylight Foxcub	P. J. Cheyney	
G-CIOY	Beech G.36 Bonanza	J. Feeny	
G-CIOZ	Ikarus C42 FB100	J. R. Gardiner	
G-CIPA	P & M Pegasus Quik	B. J. Harrison	
G-CIPB	Messerschmitt Bf109E-4	Biggin Hill Heritage Hangar Ltd	
G-CIPD	Cameron O-31 balloon	Gone with the Wind Ltd	
G-CIPE	Boeing Stearman A75N-1 Kaydet	Retro Track and Air (UK) Ltd	
G-CIPF	Alisport Silent 2 Electro	Media Technice Ltd	
G-CIPG	BRM Aero Bristell NG5 Speed Wing	G-CIPG Syndicate	
G-CIPJ	DH.83 Fox Moth	B. K. Broady	
G-CIPL	Van's RV-9	M. W. Meynell	
G-CIPM	P & M Quik R	M. R. Niznik	
G-CIPN	Robinson R22	P. P. M. Brotto/Italy	
G-CIPO	Ikarus C42 FB80	J. Richards	
G-CIPP	AutoGyro Calidus	Dragon Gyrocopters	
G-CIPR	Skyranger Nynja 912(1)	J. M. Ross	
G-CIPS	Eurofox 912(1)	P. Stretton	
G-CIPT	BRM Aero Bristell NG5 Speed Wing	A. J. Radford	
G-CIPU	Cessna F.172F	G. Hinz/Germany	
G-CIPW	Agusta Westland AW.139	Bristow Helicopters Ltd	
G-CIPX	Agusta Westland AW.139	Bristow Helicopters Ltd	
G-CIPY	Cessna F.172 II	Swiftair Maintenance Ltd	
G-CIPZ	Pazmany PL-4	J. J. Hill	
G-CIRB	EV-97 Eurostar SL	R. J. Garbutt	
G-CIRC	Such BM60-20 balloon	D. G. Such	
G-CIRE	Corby CJ-1 Starlet	J. Evans	
G-CIRF	Advance Alpha 5/Parajet Zenith Paramotor	R. Frankham	
G-CIRG	Airbus Helicopters AS350B3 Ecureuil	Airbus Helicopters UK Ltd	
G-CIRH	Magni M16C Tandem Trainer	Willy Rose Technology Ltd	
G-CIRI	Cirrus SR20	Cirrus Flyers Group	
G-CIRK	Alisport Silent 2 Electro	C. H. Appleyard	
G-CIRL	Ultramagic S-90 balloon	M. A. Scholes & D. J. Day	
G-CIRM	Van's RV-12	P. J. Hynes	
G-CIRN	Cameron Z-120 balloon	D. Gusse	
G-CIRO	Cessna F.172H	H. G. Stroemer	
G-CIRP	Aeropro Eurofox 912(S)	GS Aviation (Europe) Ltd	
G-CIRR	Ryan ST3KR	A. J. Montgomery	
G-CIRT	AutoGyro MTOSport	M. Pugh & J. Gleeson	
G-CIRU	Cirrus SR20	Cirrent BV/Netherlands	
G-CIRV	Van's RV-7	R. J. Fray	
G-CIRW	Cessna FA.150K	Air Navigation and Trading Company Ltd	
G-CIRX	Cameron Z-150 balloon	Phoenix Balloons Ltd	
G-CIRY	EV-97 Eurostar SL	Hotel Victor Flying Group	
G-CIRZ	Ikarus C42 FB80	Mainair Microlight School Ltd	
G-CISA	Sprite Stinger	Sprite Aviation Services Ltd	
G-CISB	Sackville AH56 balloon	T. J. Wilkinson	
G-CISC	Sackville AH77 balloon	T. J. Wilkinson	
G-CISD	Sackville AH31 balloon	T. J. Wilkinson	
G-CISE	Aero Designs Pulsar XP	S. C. Goozee	
G-CISF	Quad City Challenger II	S. A. Beddus	
G-CISG	Ikarus C42 FB80	C. W. Good	
G-CISH	Thatcher CX4	P. J. Watson	
G-CISI	P & M Quik GTR	Kent County Scout Council	
G-CISJ	Ultramagic H-31 balloon	R. P. Wade	
G-CISK	Embraer EMB-145LR	Eastern Airways	
G-CISL	Cameron C-70 balloon	S. Lundin	

Notes	Reg	Type	Owner or Operator
	G-CISM	P & M Quik Lite	P & M Aviation Ltd
	G-CISN	Flylight Foxcub	G. Nicholas
	G-CISO	Cessna 150G	Enterprise Purchasing Ltd
	G-CISR	Flying K Sky Raider 1	J. A. Harris
	G-CISS	Ikarus C42 FB80	R. O'Malley-White
	G-CIST	P & M Quik GT450	G. J. Prisk
	G-CISU	CM Sunbird	C. W. Mitchinson
	G-CISV	VS.349 Spitfire Vb (R9649)	Comanche Warbirds Ltd
	G-CISW	La Mouette Samson 12	N. Pain
	G-CISX	Cessna 172M	M. A. Lorne
	G-CISZ	Van's RV-7	D. C. Hanss
	G-CITC	Apollo Delta Jet 2	P. Broome
	G-CITD	Sportavia-Putzer Fournier RF-5	G-CITD Group
	G-CITE	Grob G.102 Astir CS Jeans	The Bath, Wilts & North Dorset Gliding Club Ltd
	G-CITF	EV-97 Eurostar SL	J. C. Rose
	G-CITG	Skyranger Nynja 912S(1)	A. C. & B. A. Aiken
	G-CITH	Eans S-6-ES Coyote II	J. P. Colton
	G-CITK	Alisport Silent 2 Targa	B. T. Green
	G-CITL	Ace Magic Cyclone	J. R. Kendall
	G-CITM	Magni M16C Tandem Trainer	A. G. Jones
	G-CITN	P-51D-25-NA Mustang	P. Earthey
	G-CITO	P & M Quik	M. P. Jackson
	G-CITP	Grumman AA-1B Trainer	Have a Look SPRL/Belgium
	G-CITR	Cameron Z-105 balloon	A. Kaye
	G-CITS	Groppo Trail	D. A. Buttress
	G-CITT	Mooney M.20J Model 201	J. M. Tiley
	G-CITU	Kobra Basik/Ozone Spark	T. A. Dobbins
	G-CITV	AutoGyro Cavalon	N. R. W. Whitling
	G-CITW	Extra EA.400	LAC Marine Ltd
	G-CITX	AutoGyro MTOSport	Blue Thunder Ltd
	G-CITY	PA-31-350 Navajo Chieftain	Blue Sky Investments Ltd
	G-CIUA	Ultramagic B-70 balloon	K. W. Graham
	G-CIUB	Cameron Z-90 balloon	G. Forster
	G-CIUD	ACLA Sirocco SW FT	D. H. Lewis (G-ROCO)
	G-CIUE	CASA 1-131E Jungmann Srs 2000	R. A. Fleming
	G-CIUF	Aviad Zigolo MG12	D. J. Pilkington
	G-CIUG	Aeropro Eurofox 3K	J. A. Thomas & J. V. Clewer
	G-CIUH	Cessna 152	J. M. Perfettini
	G-CIUI	Best Off Skyranger 912(2)	Wexair Group
	G-CIUK	Cameron O-65 balloon	Cameron Balloons Ltd
	G-CIUM	PA-12 Super Cruiser	J. Havers & S. James
	G-CIUN	Flylight Foxcub	C. I. Chegwen
	G-CIUO	Ekolot KR-010 ELF	P. V. Griffiths
	G-CIUP	Europa XS	P. C. Matthews & P. Bridges
	G-CIUR	Proairsport Glow	Proairsport Ltd
	G-CIUT	DAR Solo 120	J. B. Silverstone
	G-CIUU	Cessna F.152	DSFT Ltd
	G-CIUW	AT-16 Harvard IIB	J. Brown
	G-CIUX	Auster AOP.Mk.9 (WZ679)	R. Warner
	G-CIUY	Bell 206L-3 Long Ranger III	Volantair LLP
	G-CIUZ	P & M Quik GTR	S. Spyrou
	G-CIVA	Boeing 747-436	British Airways
	G-CIVB	Boeing 747-436	British Airways
	G-CIVC	Boeing 747-436	British Airways
	G-CIVD	Boeing 747-436	British Airways
	G-CIVE	Boeing 747-436	British Airways
	G-CIVF	Boeing 747-436	British Airways
	G-CIVG	Boeing 747-436	British Airways
	G-CIVH	Boeing 747-436	British Airways
	G-CIVI	Boeing 747-436	British Airways
	G-CIVJ	Boeing 747-436	British Airways
	G-CIVK	Boeing 747-436	British Airways
	G-CIVL	Boeing 747-436	British Airways
	G-CIVM	Boeing 747-436	British Airways
	G-CIVN	Boeing 747-436	British Airways
	G-CIVO	Boeing 747-436	British Airways
	G-CIVP	Boeing 747-436	British Airways
	G-CIVR	Boeing 747-436	British Airways
	G-CIVS	Boeing 747-436	British Airways
	G-CIVT	Boeing 747-436	British Airways

Reg	Type	Owner or Operator	Notes
G-CIVU	Boeing 747-436	British Airways	
G-CIVV	Boeing 747-436	British Airways	
G-CIVW	Boeing 747-436	British Airways	
G-CIVX	Boeing 747-436	British Airways	
G-CIVY	Boeing 747-436	British Airways	
G-CIVZ	Boeing 747-436	British Airways	
G-CIWA	Skyranger Swift 912(1)	S. D. Lilley	
G-CIWB	Van's RV-6	C. G. Price	
G-CIWC	Raj Hamsa X'Air Hawk	G. A. J. Salter	
G-CIWD	TLAC Sherwood Ranger ST	A. R. Pitcher	
G-CIWE	Balony Kubicek BB-22Z balloon	O. J. Webb	
G-CIWF	EC.225LP Super Puma	Babcock Mission Critical Services Offshore Ltd	
G-CIWG	Aeropro Eurofox 912(IS)	A. Hegner	
G-CIWH	Agusta-Bell 206B-3 Jet Ranger III	P. Rosati	
G-CIWI	EV-97 Eurostar SL	J. S. Holden	
G-CIWL	Techpro Merlin 100UL	Sprite Aviation Services Ltd	
G-CIWN	Such BM42-16 balloon	D. G. Such	
G-CIWO	AS.350B3 Ecureuil	R & J Helicopters LLP	
G-CIWP	Ikarus C42 FB100	P. D. Ashley	
G-CIWS	Zenair CH.601ULA	A. M. Hemmings	
G-CIWT	Ikarus C42 FB80	J. W. Lorains	
G-CIWU	McDonnell Douglas MD.369E	Century Aviation (Training) Ltd	
G-CIWV	Van's RV-7	J. W. Baker	
G-CIWW	Sackville BM-56 balloon	T. J. Wilkinson	
G-CIWX	Sackville 65 balloon	T. J. Wilkinson	
G-CIWY	Sackville 90 balloon	T. J. Wilkinson	
G-CIWZ	Sackville 6BM-34 balloon	T. J. Wilkinson	
G-CIXA	Dudek Nucleon 31	P. Sinkler	
G-CIXB	Grob G.109B	G-CIXB Syndicate	
G-CIXD	Cameron A-105 balloon	K. R. Karlstrom	
G-CIXE	Moravan Zlin Z-326 Trener Master	J. J. B. Leasor	
G-CIXG	Phantom X1	K. B. Woods	
G-CIXH	Schempp-Hirth Ventus 2a	O. Walters	
G-CIXI	Polaris FIB	Pirates Cove Flyers	
G-CIXJ	Curtiss P-36C Hawk	Patina Ltd	
G-CIXK	Titan T-51B Mustang (KH570/5J-X)	J. M. Gammidge	
G-CIXL	Air Creation Ifun 13 Pixel 250XC	S. C. Reeve	
G-CIXM	Supermarine Spitfire Mk.26 (PL793)	S. W. Markham	
G-CIXN	CFM Shadow Series E	U. J. Anderson	
G-CIXP	Cessna 152	C. M. de C. C. Cabral	
G-CIXR	Cameron Z-77 balloon	Airship and Balloon Company Ltd	
G-CIXS	Zenair CH.701SP	S. Foreman	
G-CIXT	Flylight Foxcub	A. G. Cummings	
G-CIXU	Cameron Z-77 balloon	Airship and Balloon Company Ltd	
G-CIXV	Embraer ERJ170-100LR	Eastern Airways	
G-CIXW	Embraer ERJ170-100LR	Eastern Airways	
G-CIXX	AutoGyro Cavalon	M. J. Taylor	
G-CIXY	Ikarus C42 FB80	London Light Flight Ltd	
G-CIXZ	P & M Quik R	N. H. N. Douglas	
G-CIYB	CEA Jodel DR.1051M1	Axis Technology and Development Ltd	
G-CIYC	Flylight Foxcub	J. M. Mooney	
G-CIYE	Eurocopter EC.225LP Super Puma	Leonardo SpA/Norway	
G-CIYG	Airbike Light Sport	N. Allen	
G-CIYH	Eurocopter EC.225LP Super Puma	Leonardo SpA/Norway	
G-CIYJ	MD Helicopter Inc Hughes 369E	Studwelders Holdings Ltd	
G-CIYK	Free Spirit Biplane	J. C. Greenslade	
G-CIYL	Aeropro Eurofox 912iS(1)	R. M. Cornwell	
G-CIYM	Yakovlev Yak-18T	P. Ringenbach	
G-CIYN	Skyranger Nynja 912S(1)	R. W. Sutherland	
G-CIYO	Groppo Trail	A. McIvor	
G-CIYP	Aeropro Eurofox 912(1)	J. Andrews	
G-CIYR	Lindstrand LTL-177T Skyflyer gas balloon	Lindstrand Technologies Ltd	
G-CIYT	Flugastol	F. B. Rich	
G-CIYU	AutoGyro Calidus	P. M. Bidston	
G-CIYV	Van's RV-9A	M. S. Ashby	
G-CIYX	Embraer EMB-145LR	Eastern Airways	
G-CIYY	TLAC Sherwood Ranger XP	M. R. M. Welch	
G-CIYZ	P & M Quik R	R. Keene & Sons	
G-CIZA	Spacek SD-1 Minisport	P. Smith	
G-CIZB	Magni M-24C Orion	J. E. Fallis	
G-CIZD	P & M Quik GT450	D. Orton	

Notes	Reg	Type	Owner or Operator
	G-CIZE	Cameron O-56 balloon	P. Spellward
	G-CIZF	Ozone Indy/Paramotor Flyer Trike	M. R. Gaylor
	G-CIZG	Robinson R66	Buildrandom Ltd
	G-CIZI	PA-32RT-300 Lance II	Papier Volant SAS/France
	G-CIZL	P & M Quik R	East Fortune Flyers
	G-CIZM	Cameron Z-210 balloon	The Balloon Company Ltd
	G-CIZN	J-5B Cub Cruiser	M. Howells
	G-CIZO	PA-28-161 Cadet	Falcon Flying Services Ltd
	G-CIZP	AutoGyro Cavalon Pro	C. Coffield
	G-CIZR	Van's RV-9	M. L. Martin
	G-CIZS	Tipsy Nipper T.66 Series 2	N. D. Dykes
	G-CIZT	Ace Magic Cyclone	T. Robinson
	G-CIZU	EV-97 Eurostar SL	A. Parker
	G-CIZV	P & M Quik R	G-CIZV Syndicate
	G-CIZW	Alisport Silent 2 Electro	P. C. Jarvis & C. C. Redrup
	G-CIZY	PA-34-200T Seneca II	BAR Aviation Rentals Ltd
	G-CJAF	Cessna 182T	C. S. Ringer
	G-CJAI	P & M Quik GT450	J. C. Kitchen
	G-CJAJ	P & M Quik GT450	D. Al-Bassam
	G-CJAK	Skyranger Nynja 912S(1)	A. K. Birt
	G-CJAL	Schleicher Ka 6E	JAL Syndicate
	G-CJAM	Ikarus C42 FB80	G. C. Linley
	G-CJAO	Schempp-Hirth Discus b	O. Kahn
	G-CJAP	Ikarus C42 FB80	B. H. J. Van der Berg
	G-CJAR	Schempp-Hirth Discus bT	C. J. H. Donnelly
	G-CJAS	Glasflugel Standard Libelle 201B	M. J. Collett
	G-CJAT	Schleicher K8B	Wolds Gliding Club Ltd
	G-CJAU	White Sports Monoplane	J. Aubert
	G-CJAV	Schleicher ASK-21	Wolds Gliding Club Ltd
	G-CJAW	Glaser-Dirks DG-200/17	F. Friend
	G-CJAX	Schleicher ASK-21	Wolds Gliding Club Ltd
	G-CJAY	Mainair Pegasus Quik GT450	J. C. Kitchen
	G-CJAZ	Grob G.102 Astir CS Jeans	M. R. Dews
	G-CJBA	Alisport Silent 2 Electro	B. A. Fairston & A. Stotter
	G-CJBC	PA-28 Cherokee 180	J. B. Cave
	G-CJBD	Spacek SD-1 Minisport	D. Cox
	G-CJBE	Ikarus C42 FB80	J. H. Bradbury
	G-CJBH	Eiriavion PIK-20D	G. A. Darby
	G-CJBI	Aeropro Eurofox 912(iS)	M. B. Z. de Ferranti
	G-CJBJ	Schempp-Hirth Standard Cirrus	S. T. Dutton
	G-CJBK	Schleicher ASW-19B	D. Caielli & P. Deane
	G-CJBL	Flylight Foxtug	R. W. Twamley
	G-CJBM	Schleicher ASK-21	The Burn Gliding Club Ltd
	G-CJBN	Sackville BM-65 balloon	B. J. Newman
	G-CJBO	Rolladen-Schneider LS8-18	L7 Syndicate
	G-CJBP	Flylight Foxcub	Flylight Airsports Ltd
	G-CJBR	Schempp-Hirth Discus b	G-CJBR Group
	G-CJBT	Schleicher ASW-19B	G. Dennis
	G-CJBU	BRM Aero Bristell NG5 Speed Wing	H. R. Pearson
	G-CJBV	IAV Bacau Yak-52	R. J. Harper
	G-CJBW	Schempp-Hirth Discus bT	G-CJBW Syndicate
	G-CJBX	Rolladen-Schneider LS4-a	P. W. Lee
	G-CJBZ	Grob G.102 Astir CS	The Royal Air Force Gliding Association
	G-CJCD	Schleicher ASW-24	R. A. Cheetham
	G-CJCE	Ultramagic M-77C	Murray Rene Ltd
	G-CJCF	Grob G.102 Astir CS77	The Northumbria Gliding Club Ltd
	G-CJCG	PZL-Swidnik PW-5 Smyk	K. Cullen, S. Kinnear & M. Walsh
	G-CJCH	AB Sportine Aviacija LAK-19T	LAK 19T Syndicate
	G-CJCJ	Schempp-Hirth Standard Cirrus	G-CJCJ Syndicate
	G-CJCK	Schempp-Hirth Discus bT	G. A. Friedrich
	G-CJCL	EV-97B Eurostar SL	F. Omaraie-Hamdanie
	G-CJCM	Schleicher ASW-27	Zulu Glasstek Ltd
	G-CJCN	Schempp-Hirth Standard Cirrus 75	G. D. E. Macdonald
	G-CJCO	Ikarus C42 FB80	GS Aviation (Europe) Ltd
	G-CJCR	Grob G.102 Astir CS	B. J. Harrison
	G-CJCS	Balony Kubicek BB-60Z balloon	South Down Ballooning Ltd
	G-CJCT	Schempp-Hirth Nimbus 4T	E. W. Richards
	G-CJCU	Schempp-Hirth Standard Cirrus B	R. A. Davenport
	G-CJCW	Grob G.102 Astir CS77	Essex Gliding Club Ltd
	G-CJCX	Schempp-Hirth Discus bT	A. D. Johnson

Reg	Type	Owner or Operator	Notes
G-CJCZ	Schleicher Ka 6CR	G. R. Bonny	
G-CJDA	Ikarus C42 FB80	Mainair Microlight School Ltd	
G-CJDB	Cessna 525 Citationjet	Breed Aircraft Ltd	
G-CJDC	Schleicher ASW-27	T. A. Sage	
G-CJDD	Glaser-Dirks DG-200/17	N. P. Harrison	
G-CJDE	Rolladen-Schneider LS8-18	Army Gliding Association	
G-CJDG	Rolladen-Schneider LS6-b	R. H. & A. Moss	
G-CJDJ	Rolladen-Schneider LS3	S. Wilkinson & B. J. R. Moate	
G-CJDK	Rolladen-Schneider LS8-18	B. Bredenbeck	
G-CJDL	Pipistrel Apis 15M M FES	M. E. Hughes	
G-CJDM	Schleicher ASW-15B	J. D. Morris	
G-CJDN	Cameron C-90 balloon	N. Ivison	
G-CJDP	Glaser-Dirks DG-200/17	The Owners of JDP	
G-CJDR	Schleicher ASW-15	S. Mudaliar	
G-CJDS	Schempp-Hirth Standard Cirrus 75	P. Nicholls	
G-CJDV	DG Flugzeugbau DG-300 Elan Acro	M. K. Lavender	
G-CJDW	Magni M-16C Tandem Trainer	A. Brown & W. J. Whyte	
G-CJDX	Wassmer WA-28	R. Hutchinson	
G-CJEA	Rolladen-Schneider LS8-18	M. W. Durham	
G-CJEB	Schleicher ASW-24	P. C. Scholz	
G-CJEC	PZL-Bielsko SZD-50-3 Puchasz	Cambridge Gliding Club Ltd	
G-CJED	Schempp-Hirth Nimbus 3/24.5	J. Edyvean	
G-CJEE	Schleicher ASW-20L	B. Pridgeon	
G-CJEH	Glasflugel Mosquito B	M. J. Vickery	
G-CJEI	UltraMagic M-77 balloon	British Telecommunications PLC	
G-CJEJ	Best Off Skyranger Nynja 912(1)	Attitude Airsports Nynja G-CJEJ	
G-CJEK	Guimbal Cabri G2	I. C. Macdonald	
G-CJEL	Schleicher ASW-24	S. M. Chapman	
G-CJEP	Rolladen-Schneider LS4-b	C. F. Carter & N. Backes	
G-CJER	Schempp-Hirth Standard Cirrus 75	C. Parvin	
G-CJES	Cameron TR-77 balloon	International Merchandising, Promotion and Services	
G-CJEU	Glasflugel Standard Libelle	D. B. Johns	
G-CJEW	Schleicher Ka 6CR	W. J. Prince	
G-CJEX	Schempp-Hirth Ventus 2a	D. S. Watt	
G-CJEY	Flylight Dragon Combat 12T	D. J. Cross	
G-CJEZ	Glaser-Dirks DG-100	R. Kehr	
G-CJFA	Schempp-Hirth Standard Cirrus	P. M. Sheahan	
G-CJFC	Schempp-Hirth Discus CS	C. J. Tooze	
G-CJFE	Schempp-Hirth Janus CE	A. Cordonnier	
G-CJFG	Aeriane Swift Light PAS	M. Jackson	
G-CJFH	Schempp-Hirth Duo Discus	The Royal Air Force Gliding and Soaring Association	
G-CJFI	Ace Magic Cyclone	W. P. Byrne	
G-CJFJ	Schleicher ASW-20CL	A. M. McDermott	
G-CJFN	DHC.8-402Q Dash Eight	NAC Aviation 23 Ltd	
G-CJFO	Diamond DA.42 Twin Star	Kerrington (Grove Lodge) Ltd	
G-CJFP	Dudek Synthesis LT29	P. A. Sadowski	
G-CJFS	Pulse SSDR	D. Stephens	
G-CJFT	Schleicher K-8B	The Surrey Hills Gliding Club Ltd	
G-CJFU	Schleicher ASW-19B	M. T. Stanley	
G-CJFW	Ace As-tec 15	M. J. Pollard	
G-CJFX	Rolladen-Schneider LS8-a	J. E. Gatfield	
G-CJFZ	Fedorov ME7 Mechta	R. J. Colbourne	
G-CJGA	Cameron Z-90 balloon	Sport Promotion SRL	
G-CJGB	Schleicher K 8B	Edensoaring Ltd	
G-CJGC	Cameron Z-105 balloon	GSM Aeropanorami SRL/Italy	
G-CJGD	Scleicher K 8B	R. E. Pettifer & C. A. McLay	
G-CJGE	Schleicher ASK-21	M. R. Wall	
G-CJGF	Schempp-Hirth Ventus c	R. D. Slater	
G-CJGG	P & M Quik GT450	J. M. Pearce	
G-CJGH	Schempp-Hirth Nimbus 2C	G-CJGH Syndicate	
G-CJGI	Boeing 787-9	Norwegian Air Shuttle	
G-CJGJ	Schleicher ASK-21	Midland Gliding Club Ltd	
G-CJGK	Eiri PIL-200	The Four Aces	
G-CJGL	Schempp-Hirth Discus CS	The Royal Air Force Gliding and Soaring Association	
G-CJGM	Schempp-Hirth Discus CS	The Royal Air Force Gliding and Soaring Association	
G-CJGN	Schempp-Hirth Standard Cirrus	P. A. Shuttleworth	
G-CJGO	Lindstrand LTL Racer 65 balloon	Lindstrand Technologies Ltd	

Notes	Reg	Type	Owner or Operator
	G-CJGP	Breezer M400	R. M. Cornwell
	G-CJGR	Schempp-Hirth Discus bT	S. P. Wareham & G. W. Kemp
	G-CJGS	Rolladen-Schneider LS8-18	T. Stupnik
	G-CJGT	AMS-Flight Apis M	R. G. Parker & A. Spencer
	G-CJGU	Schempp-Hirth Mini-Nimbus B	N. D. Ashton
	G-CJGV	Flylight Foxcub	R. A. Chapman
	G-CJGW	Schleicher ASK-13	Darlton Gliding Club Ltd
	G-CJGX	Schleicher K 8B	Andreas K8 Group
	G-CJGY	Schempp-Hirth Standard Cirrus	P. J. Shout
	G-CJGZ	Glasflugel Standard Libelle 201B	D. A. Joosten
	G-CJHB	CSA PS-28 Cruiser	The Little Aeroplane Company Ltd
	G-CJHC	Kolb Firefly	D. J. Pilkington
	G-CJHE	Astir CS77	Aero Club de Portugal
	G-CJHF	Aeroprpo Eurofox 912(iS)	BGC Eurofox Group
	G-CJHG	Grob G.102 Astir CS	P. L. E. Zelazowski
	G-CJHJ	Glasflugel Standard Libelle 201B	N. P. Marriott
	G-CJHK	Schleicher K8B	East Sussex Gliding Club Ltd
	G-CJHL	Schleicher Ka 6E	J. R. Gilbert
	G-CJHM	Schempp-Hirth Discus b	J. C. Thwaites
	G-CJHN	Grob G.102 Astir CS Jeans	Astir Syndicate
	G-CJHO	Schleicher ASK-18	RAF Gliding and Soaring Association
	G-CJHP	Flight Design CTSW	S. J. Reader
	G-CJHR	Centrair SNC34C Alliance	The Borders (Milfield) Gliding Club Ltd
	G-CJHS	Schleicher ASW-19B	JHS Syndicate
	G-CJHT	Aeropro Eurofox 3K	GS Aviation (Europe) Ltd
	G-CJHV	Lindstrand LTL Series 1-31 balloon	Lindstrand Technologies Ltd
	G-CJHW	Glaser-Dirks DG-200	A. W. Thornhill & S. Webster
	G-CJHY	Rolladen-Schneider LS8-18	S. J. Eyles
	G-CJHZ	Schleicher ASW-20	T. J. Stanley
	G-CJIA	Lindstrand LTL Series 2-70 balloon	Lindstrand Technologies Ltd
	G-CJIB	Alisport Silent 2 Electro	F. Pilkington
	G-CJIC	Van's RV-12	N. W. Wilkinson
	G-CJID	Alisport Silent 2	A. K. Carver
	G-CJIE	Flylight Foxcub	M. J. Pollard
	G-CJIG	Lindstrand LTL Series 1-70 balloon	A. M. Holly
	G-CJIH	Lindstrand LTL Series 1-105 balloon	Southern Plasticlad Ltd
	G-CJII	TLAC Sherwood Ranger ST	D. H. Pattison
	G-CJIK	Cameron Z-77 balloon	P. Greaves
	G-CJIL	Sackville BM-90 balloon	B. Mead
	G-CJIN	Boeing Stearman A75L300	R. D. Leigh
	G-CJIO	Rans S-6-S-116 Super Six	D. Bedford
	G-CJIP	Aero 31 AM9 balloon	C. J. Sanger-Davies
	G-CJIR	Rotorway Executive 162F	Southern Helicopters Ltd (G-ESUS)
	G-CJIS	Eurocopter EC225LP Super Puma	Wilmington Trust SP Services (Dublin) Ltd
	G-CJIT	Ikarus C42 FB100	K. Thomas
	G-CJIU	Lindstrand 9T Tethered gas balloon	Lindstrand Technologies Ltd
	G-CJIX	Cameron O-31 balloon	D. J. Head
	G-CJJA	EV-97 Eurostar SL	Purple Aviation Ltd
	G-CJJB	Rolladen-Schneider LS4	M. Tomlinson
	G-CJJC	Lindstrand LTL Series 1-105 balloon	A. M. Holly
	G-CJJD	Schempp-Hirth Discus bT	D. Wilson & C. O'Boyle
	G-CJJE	Schempp-Hirth Discus a	A. Soffici
	G-CJJH	DG Flugzeugbau DG-800S	J. S. Weston
	G-CJJJ	Schempp-Hirth Standard Cirrus	J-P. M. Roots
	G-CJJK	Rolladen-Schneider LS8-18	A. D. Roch
	G-CJJL	Schleicher ASW-19B	G-CJJL Group
	G-CJJN	Robin HR.100/210 Safari II	The G-CJJN Syndicate
	G-CJJP	Schempp-Hirth Duo Discus	494 Syndicate
	G-CJJS	PA-28-151 Cherokee Warrior	Phil Short Electrical Ltd (G-VIVS)
	G-CJJT	Schleicher ASW-27	Portsmouth Naval Gliding Centre
	G-CJJV	Van's RV-12	B. F. Hill
	G-CJJW	Lambert Mission M108	D. S. James
	G-CJJX	Schleicher ASW-15B	A. Snell
	G-CJJY	Aerochute SSDR	G. R. Britton
	G-CJJZ	Schempp-Hirth Discus bT	S. J. C. Parker
	G-CJKA	Schleicher ASK-21	East Sussex Gliding Club Ltd
	G-CJKB	PZL-Swidnik PW-5 Smyk	A. J. Spray
	G-CJKE	PZL-Swidnik PW-5 Smyk	D. Hertzberg
	G-CJKF	Glaser-Dirks DG-200	D. O. Sandells
	G-CJKG	Schleicher ASK-18	The Royal Air Force Gliding and Soaring Association

Reg	Type	Owner or Operator	Notes
G-CJKH	Ultramagic M-120 balloon	Cold Climate Expeditions Ltd	
G-CJKI	Ultramagic S-90 balloon	M. P. Rowley	
G-CJKJ	Schleicher ASK-21	The Royal Air Force Gliding and Soaring Association	
G-CJKK	Schleicher ASK-21	Army Gliding Association	
G-CJKM	Glaser-Dirks DG200/17	G. F. Coles & E. W. Russell	
G-CJKN	Rolladen-Schneider LS8-18	790 Syndicate	
G-CJKO	Schleicher ASK-21	The Royal Air Force Gliding and Soaring Association	
G-CJKP	Rolladen-Schneider LS4-b	C. E. P. Mills	
G-CJKS	Schleicher ASW-19B	R. J. P. Lancaster	
G-CJKT	Schleicher ASK-13	The Royal Air Force Gliding and Soaring Association	
G-CJKU	Schleicher ASK-18	Derbyshire & Lancashire Gliding Club Ltd	
G-CJKV	Grob G.103A Twin II Acro	The Welland Gliding Club Ltd	
G-CJKW	Grob G.102 Astir CS77	The Bath, Wilts and North Dorset Gliding Club Ltd	
G-CJKY	Schempp-Hirth Ventus cT	G. V. Matthews & M. P. Osborn	
G-CJKZ	Schleicher ASK-21	The Royal Air Force Gliding and Soaring Association	
G-CJLA	Schempp-Hirth Ventus 2cT	S. G. Jones	
G-CJLB	Agusta Westland AW139	Bristow Helicopters Ltd	
G-CJLC	Schempp-Hirth Discus CS	The Royal Air Force Gliding and Soaring Association	
G-CJLD	Lambert Mission M108	P. R. Mailer	
G-CJLF	Schleicher ASK-13	V. Mallon	
G-CJLH	Rolladen-Schneider LS4	JLH Syndicate	
G-CJLI	PA-28-161 Warrior II	Smart People Don't Buy Ltd	
G-CJLJ	Rolladen-Schneider LS4-b	Army Gliding Association	
G-CJLK	Rolladen-Schneider LS7	D. N. Munro & J. P. W. Roche-Kelly	
G-CJLL	Robinson R44 II	R. D. J. Alexander	
G-CJLM	Denney Kitfox 4-1050 Speedster	C. Kinder & T. Neale	
G-CJLN	Rolladen-Schneider LS8-18	The Royal Air Force Gliding and Soaring Association	
G-CJLO	Schleicher ASK-13	Bowland Forest Gliding Club Ltd	
G-CJLP	Schempp-Hirth Discus CS	The Royal Air Force Gliding and Soaring Association	
G-CJLS	Schleicher K-8B	E. Ustenler	
G-CJLT	Cameron O-84 balloon	T. M. Lee	
G-CJLU	Spacek SD-1 Minisport	J. Krajca	
G-CJLV	Schleicher Ka 6E	J. C. Cooper	
G-CJLW	Schempp-Hirth Discus CS	The Royal Air Force Gliding and Soaring Association	
G-CJLX	Schempp-Hirth Standard Cirrus	J. Hunneman	
G-CJLY	Schleicher ASW-27	L. M. Astle & P. C. Piggott	
G-CJLZ	Grob G.103A Twin II Acro	21 Syndicate	
G-CJMA	Schleicher ASK-18	The Royal Air Force Gliding and Soaring Association	
G-CJMF	BRM Aero Bristell NG5 Speed Wing	G. E. Collard	
G-CJMG	PZL-Bielsko SZD-51-1 Junior	Kent Gliding Club Ltd	
G-CJMJ	Schleicher ASK-13	The Royal Air Force Gliding and Soaring Association	
G-CJMK	Schleicher ASK-18	The Royal Air Force Gliding and Soaring Association	
G-CJML	Grob G.102 Astir CS77	The Royal Air Force Gliding and Soaring Association	
G-CJMN	Schempp-Hirth Nimbus 2	R. A. Holroyd	
G-CJMO	Rolladen-Schneider LS8-18	D. J. Langrick	
G-CJMP	Schleicher ASK-13	East Sussex Gliding Club Ltd	
G-CJMS	Schleicher ASK-21	The Royal Air Force Gliding and Soaring Association	
G-CJMU	Rolladen-Schneider LS8-18	R. Lorenz	
G-CJMV	Schempp-Hirth Nimbus-2C	G. Tucker & K. R. Walton	
G-CJMW	Schleicher ASK-13	The Royal Air Force Gliding and Soaring Association	
G-CJMX	Schleicher ASK-13	The Nene Valley Gliding Club Ltd	
G-CJMY	PZL-Bielsko SZD-51-1 Junior	Highland Gliding Club Ltd	
G-CJMZ	Schleicher ASK-13	Devon & Somerset Gliding Club Ltd	
G-CJNA	Grob G.102 Astir CS Jeans	Shenington Gliding Club	
G-CJNB	Rolladen-Schneider LS8-18	P. M. Barnes	

Notes	Reg	Type	Owner or Operator
	G-CJNC	Eurocopter MBB-BK117 C-2	The Milestone Aviation Asset Holding Group No.8 Ltd
	G-CJND	Eurocopter MBB-BK117 C-2	The Milestone Aviation Asset Holding Group No.8 Ltd
	G-CJNG	Glasflugel Standard Libelle 201B	N. C. Burt & G. V. Tanner
	G-CJNH	P & M Quik R	N. Hammerton
	G-CJNI	Agusta Westland AW139	Bristow Helicopters Ltd
	G-CJNJ	Rolladen-Schneider LS8-18	A. B. Laws
	G-CJNK	Rolladen-Schneider LS8-18	Army Gliding Association
	G-CJNL	Jodel DR.1050M Replica	M. G. Dolphin
	G-CJNN	Schleicher K 8B	Buckminster Gliding Club Ltd
	G-CJNO	Glaser-Dirks DG-300 Elan	Yankee Kilo Group
	G-CJNP	Rolladen-Schneider LS6-b	E. & P. S. Fink & L. Armbrust
	G-CJNR	Glasflugel Mosquito B	L. S. Hitchins & R. A. Markham
	G-CJNT	Schleicher ASW-19B	T. R. Edwards
	G-CJNU	Techpro Merlin 100UL	B. S. Carpenter
	G-CJNZ	Glaser-Dirks DG-100	G. Synedercombe
	G-CJOA	Schempp-Hirth Discus b	K. A. Jarrett
	G-CJOB	Schleicher K 8B	JQB Syndicate
	G-CJOC	Schempp-Hirth Discus bT	S. G. Jones
	G-CJOD	Rolladen-Schneider LS8-18	The Royal Air Force Gliding and Soaring Association
	G-CJOE	Schempp-Hirth Standard Cirrus	D. I. Bolsdon & P. T. Johnson
	G-CJOF	Bombardier BD100-1A10 Challenger 350	London Executive Aviation Ltd
	G-CJOI	Cameron O-31 balloon	Cameron Balloons Ltd
	G-CJOJ	Schleicher K 8B	M. P. Webb
	G-CJOK	HpH Glasflugel 304 MS Shark	JOK Syndicate
	G-CJOL	Eurofox 3K	S. B. & L. S. Williams
	G-CJOM	Eurofox 3K	G. R. Postans
	G-CJON	Grob G.102 Astir CS77	The Royal Air Force Gliding and Soaring Association
	G-CJOO	Schempp-Hirth Duo Discus	185 Syndicate
	G-CJOP	Centrair 101A Pegase	P. A. Woodcock
	G-CJOR	Schempp-Hirth Ventus 2cT	A. M. George & N. A. Maclean
	G-CJOS	Schempp-Hirth Standard Cirrus	G-CJOS Group
	G-CJOT	Ikarus C42 FB80	The Cherhill Gang
	G-CJOV	Schleicher ASW-27	J. W. White
	G-CJOW	Schempp-Hirth Cirrus VTC	North Wales Gliding Club Ltd
	G-CJOX	Schleicher ASK-21	Southdown Gliding Club Ltd
	G-CJOY	Zenair CH.601HDS Zodiac	G. M. Johnson
	G-CJOZ	Schleicher K 8B	Derbyshire and Lancashire Gliding Club Ltd
	G-CJPA	Schempp-Hirth Duo Discus	Coventry Gliding Club Ltd
	G-CJPB	Skyranger Swift 581(1)	T. W. Thiele
	G-CJPC	Schleicher ASK-13	Shalbourne Soaring Society Ltd
	G-CJPD	Cameron O-56 balloon	Cameron Balloons Ltd
	G-CJPE	Skyranger Nynja 912S(1)	R. J. Sutherland & M. J. Stolworthy
	G-CJPG	Cameron C-80 balloon	P. R. Audenaert
	G-CJPI	HPH Glasflugel 304MS Shark	T. P. Docherty
	G-CJPJ	Grob G.104 Speed Astir IIB	M. A. Jones
	G-CJPK	Sgian Dubh	Sgian Dubh Flying Group
	G-CJPL	Rolladen-Schneider LS8-18	I. A. Reekie
	G-CJPM	Grob G.102 Astir CS Jeans	G-CJPM Syndicate
	G-CJPN	Cessna 152	M. Magrabi
	G-CJPO	Schleicher ASK-18	The Royal Air Force Gliding and Soaring Association
	G-CJPP	Schempp-Hirth Discus b	S. R. Thompson
	G-CJPR	Rolladen-Schneider LS8-18	D. M. Byass & J. A. McCoshim
	G-CJPT	Schleicher ASW-27	R. C. Willis-Fleming
	G-CJPV	Schleicher ASK-13	Cyprus Gliding Group/Cyprus
	G-CJPW	Glaser-Dirks DG-200	A. Kitchen & R. Truchan
	G-CJPX	Schleicher ASW-15	M. G. & R. G. Garrish
	G-CJPY	Schleicher ASK-13	The Royal Air Force Gliding and Soaring Association
	G-CJPZ	Schleicher ASK-18	The Royal Air Force Gliding and Soaring Association
	G-CJRA	Rolladen-Schneider LS8-18	J. Williams
	G-CJRB	Schleicher ASW-19B	J. W. Baxter
	G-CJRC	Glaser-Dirks DG-300 Elan	P. J. Sillett
	G-CJRD	Grob G.102 Astir CS	The Vale of The White Horse Gliding Centre Ltd
	G-CJRE	Scleicher ASW-15	R. A. Starling
	G-CJRF	PZL-Bielsko SZD-50-3 Puchacz	Wolds Gliding Club Ltd

Reg	Type	Owner or Operator	Notes
G-CJRG	Schempp-Hirth Standard Cirrus	N. J. Laux	
G-CJRJ	PZL-Bielsko SZD-50-3 Puchacz	Derbyshire & Lancashire Gliding Club Ltd	
G-CJRK	Cameron Z-31 balloon	BWS Standfast Fire and Security Systems	
G-CJRL	Glaser-Dirks DG-100G Elan	P. Lazenby	
G-CJRM	Grob G.102 Astir CS	A. R. Moore	
G-CJRN	Glaser-Dirks DG-200/17	T. G. Roberts	
G-CJRO	Cameron Z-105 balloon	BWS Standfast Fire and Security Systems	
G-CJRR	Schempp-Hirth Discus bT	N. A. Hays	
G-CJRS	BRM Aero Bristell NG5 Speed Wing	A. Watt	
G-CJRT	Schempp-Hirth Standard Cirrus	N. G. Henry	
G-CJRU	Schleicher ASW-24	C. D. Bingham	
G-CJRV	Schleicher ASW-19B	R. E. Corner	
G-CJRX	Schleicher ASK-13	The Royal Air Force Gliding and Soaring Association	
G-CJRZ	Ikarus C42 FB80	D. W. Cross	
G-CJSA	Nanchang NAMC CJ-6A	J. N. Ware & M. Elmes	
G-CJSB	Republic RC-3 Seabee	J. A. & R. H. Cooper	
G-CJSC	Schempp-Hirth Nimbus-3DT	S. G. Jones	
G-CJSD	Grob G.102 Astir CS	The Royal Air Force Gliding and Soaring Association	
G-CJSE	Schempp-Hirth Discus b	Imperial College of Science, Technology and Medicine	
G-CJSF	PA-28R-180 Cherokee Arrow	Y. N. Dimitrov & V. I. Genchev (G-SBMM/G-BBEL)	
G-CJSG	Schleicher Ka 6E	A. J. Emck	
G-CJSH	Grob G.102 Club Astir IIIB	Lasham Gliding Society Ltd	
G-CJSK	Grob G.102 Astir CS	Sierra Kilo Group	
G-CJSL	Schempp-Hirth Ventus cT	D. Latimer	
G-CJSM	Van's RV-8	S. T. G. Lloyd	
G-CJSN	Schleicher K 8B	Cotswold Gliding Club	
G-CJSP	PA-28-180 Cherokee Archer	J. R. Wright	
G-CJSR	Steen Skybolt	S. L. Millar	
G-CJSS	Schleicher ASW-27	G. K. & S. R. Drury	
G-CJST	Rolladen-Schneider LS1-c	A. M. Walker	
G-CJSU	Rolladen-Schneider LS8-18	J. G. Bell	
G-CJSV	Schleicher ASK-13	The Royal Air Force Gliding and Soaring Association	
G-CJSX	AMS-Flight DG-500	Oxford Gliding Company Ltd	
G-CJSY	Sackville BM-34 balloon	B. J. Newman	
G-CJSZ	Schleicher ASK-18	C. Weston	
G-CJTA	Autogyro MTOSport	R. Brain	
G-CJTB	Schleicher ASW-24	T. Davies	
G-CJTC	AutoGyro Calidus	C. J. Rose	
G-CJTD	Techpro Aviation Merlin 100UL	J. Murphy	
G-CJTE	Aeropro Eurofox 3K	C. M. Theakstone	
G-CJTG	Hoffman H36 Dimona II	Dimona Syndicate	
G-CJTH	Schleicher ASW-24	R. J. & J. E. Lodge	
G-CJTI	Aerochute Industries Hummerchute	I. Davies	
G-CJTJ	Schempp-Hirth Mini-Nimbus B	R. A. Bowker	
G-CJTK	DG Flugzeugbau DG-300 Elan Acro	A. Drury	
G-CJTM	Rolladen-Schneider LS8-18	A. D. Holmes	
G-CJTN	Glaser-Dirks DG-300 Elan	A. D. Noble & P. R. Gardiner	
G-CJTO	Glasflugel H303A Mosquito	I. W. Myles	
G-CJTP	Schleicher ASW-20L	C. A. Sheldon & R. Abercrombie	
G-CJTS	Schempp-Hirth Cirrus VTC	G-CJTS Cirrus Group	
G-CJTT	Aerochute Industries Hummerchute	D. Townsend	
G-CJTU	Schempp-Hirth Duo Discus T	JTU Syndicate	
G-CJTW	Glasflugel Mosquito B	B. L. C. Gordon	
G-CJTX	EV-97 Eurostar SL	G-TX Group	
G-CJTY	Rolladen-Schneider LS8-a	JTY Syndicate	
G-CJUB	Schempp-Hirth Discus CS	Coventry Gliding Club Ltd	
G-CJUD	Denney Kitfox Mk 3	S. Nixon & J. E. Jeffrey	
G-CJUF	Schempp-Hirth Ventus 2cT	M. H. B. Pope	
G-CJUJ	Schleicher ASW-27	T. K. Gooch	
G-CJUK	Grob G.102 Astir CS	P. Freer & S. J. Calvert	
G-CJUL	Boeing 787-9	Norwegian Air UK Ltd	
G-CJUM	Schempp-Hirth Duo Discus T	2 UP Group	
G-CJUN	Schleicher ASW-19B	M. P. S. Roberts	
G-CJUO	Cameron Z-42 balloon	Atlantic Ballooning BVBA/Belgium	
G-CJUR	Valentin Mistral C	East Sussex Gliding Club Ltd	
G-CJUT	Skyranger Nynja 912S(1)	A. Jackson	

Notes	Reg	Type	Owner or Operator
	G-CJUU	Schempp-Hirth Standard Cirrus	A. R. Jones
	G-CJUV	Schempp-Hirth Discus b	Lasham Gliding Society Ltd
	G-CJUX	Aviastroitel AC-4C	R. J. Walton
	G-CJUY	SNS-8 Hiperlight	R. H. Cooper
	G-CJUZ	Schleicher ASW-19B	J. M. Hough
	G-CJVA	Schempp-Hirth Ventus 2cT	M. S. Armstrong
	G-CJVB	Schempp-Hirth Discus bT	C. J. Edwards
	G-CJVC	PZL-Bielsko SZD-51-1 Junior	York Gliding Centre Ltd
	G-CJVD	Team Minimax 1600	D. R. Thompson
	G-CJVE	Eiriavion PIK-20D	S. R. Wilkinson
	G-CJVF	Schempp-Hirth Discus CS	J. Hodgson
	G-CJVG	Schempp-Hirth Discus bT	P. M. Holland & M. J. Beaumont
	G-CJVH	Lindstrand LTL Series 1-105 balloon	Lindstrand Technologies Ltd
	G-CJYI	PA-28-140 Cherokee E	N. Butler
	G-CJVK	Skyranger Nynja 912S(1)	R. J. Speight
	G-CJVL	DG-300 Elan	A. T. Vidion & M. S. Hoy
	G-CJVM	Schleicher ASW-27	G. K. Payne
	G-CJVN	Lindstrand Racer 65 balloon	Lindstrand Technologies Ltd
	G-CJVO	Lindstrand Racer 56 balloon	Lindstrand Technologies Ltd
	G-CJVP	Glaser-Dirks DG-200	M. S. Howey & S. Leadbeater
	G-CJVS	Schleicher ASW-28	A. & G. S. J. Bambrook
	G-CJVU	Standard Cirrus CS-11-75L	P. L. Turner
	G-CJVV	Schempp-Hirth Janus C	J50 Syndicate
	G-CJVW	Schleicher ASW-15	Channel Gliding Club
	G-CJVX	Schempp-Hirth Discus CS	G-CJVX Syndicate
	G-CJVZ	Schleicher ASK-21	Yorkshire Gliding Club (Proprietary) Ltd
	G-CJWA	Schleicher ASW-28	J. R. Klunder
	G-CJWB	Schleicher ASK-13	East Sussex Gliding Club Ltd
	G-CJWD	Schleicher ASK-21	London Gliding Club Proprietary Ltd
	G-CJWE	Harvard 4	Cirrus Aircraft UK Ltd
	G-CJWG	Schempp-Hirth Nimbus 3	880 Group
	G-CJWH	Lindstrans LTL series 1-90 balloon	Flintnine Fasteners Ltd
	G-CJWI	Streak Shadow (modified)	J. A. Harris
	G-CJWJ	Schleicher ASK-13	The Royal Air Force Gliding and Soaring Association
	G-CJWK	Schempp-Hirth Discus bT	722 Syndicate
	G-CJWL	Hawker Hunter Mk.58A	Hawker Hunter Aviation Ltd
	G-CJWM	Grob G.103 Twin Astir II	The South Wales Gliding Club Ltd
	G-CJWN	Airbus Helicopters EC.225LP Super Puma	Vertical Aviation No.1 Ltd
	G-CJWO	VS Spitfire LFVB	R. M. B. Parnall
	G-CJWP	Bolkow Phoebus B1	A. Fidler
	G-CJWR	Grob G.102 Astir CS	Cairngorm Gliding Club
	G-CJWT	Glaser-Dirks DG-200	K. R. Nash
	G-CJWU	Schempp-Hirth Ventus bT	B. C. P. & C. Crook
	G-CJWW	Spitfire Mk.26	M. R. Overall
	G-CJWX	Schempp-Hirth Ventus 2cT	M. M. A. Lipperheide & S. G. Olender
	G-CJWY	Cameron O-31 balloon	Cameron Balloons Ltd
	G-CJXA	Schempp-Hirth Nimbus 3	Y44 Syndicate
	G-CJXB	Centrair 201B Marianne	A. C. Cherry
	G-CJXC	Wassmer WA28	A. P. Montague
	G-CJXD	Ultramagic H-77 balloon	C. G. Dobson
	G-CJXE	Lindstrand LTL series 1-120 balloon	N. R. Beckwith
	G-CJXF	Skyranger Swift 912(1)	R. J. Heath
	G-CJXG	Eiriavion PIK-20D	W5 Group
	G-CJXH	Embraer EMB-500 Phenom 100	Affinity Flying Training Services Ltd
	G-CJXI	Cameron A-300 balloon	Bailey Balloons Ltd
	G-CJXJ	Cameron Z-105 balloon	Bristol University Hot Air Ballooning Society
	G-CJXK	Cameron O-31 balloon	A. P. Jay
	G-CJXL	Schempp-Hirth Discus CS	J. Hall
	G-CJXM	Schleicher ASK-13	The Windrushers Gliding Club
	G-CJXN	Centrair 201B	C. E. Metcalfe & G. R. Davey
	G-CJXO	Flylight Dragonfly	P. C. Knowles
	G-CJXP	Glaser-Dirks DG-100	N. L. Morris
	G-CJXR	Schempp-Hirth Discus b	Cambridge Gliding Club Ltd
	G-CJXT	Schleicher ASW-24B	JXT Syndicate
	G-CJXW	Schempp-Hirth Duo Discus T	R. A. Beatty & R. R. Bryan
	G-CJXX	Pilatus B4-PC11AF	C. B. Shepperd
	G-CJXY	Neukom Elfe S4A	Rufforth Elfe S4A Syndicate
	G-CJYC	Grob G.102 Astir CS	R. A. Christie
	G-CJYD	Schleicher ASW-27	M. Kries
	G-CJYE	Schleicher ASK-13	North Wales Gliding Club Ltd

Reg	Type	Owner or Operator	Notes
G-CJYF	Schempp Hirth Discus CS	C. D. Sword	
G-CJYH	Grob G.120TP-A	Affinity Flying Training Services Ltd	
G-CJYJ	Cameron O-31 balloon	P. Spellward	
G-CJYK	Boeing B75N1 Stearman	R. Redmond	
G-CJYL	AB Sportine Aviacija LAK-12	A. Camerotto	
G-CJYM	Ultramagic S-90 balloon	M. A. Wrigglesworth	
G-CJYO	Glaser-Dirks DG-100G Elan	A. M. Booth	
G-CJYP	Grob G.102 Club Astir II	Bravo One Two Group	
G-CJYR	Schempp-Hirth Duo Discus T	CJYR Flying Group	
G-CJYS	Schempp-Hirth Mini Nimbus C	A. Jenkins	
G-CJYU	Schempp-Hirth Ventus 2cT	The Royal Air Force Gliding and Soaring Association	
G-CJYV	Schleicher K8B	Club Agrupacion de Pilotos del Sureste/Spain	
G-CJYW	Schleicher K8B	Club Agrupacion de Pilotos del Sureste/Spain	
G-CJYX	Rolladen-Schneider LS3-17	D. Meyer-Beeck & V. G. Diaz	
G-CJYY	Spitfire Mk.26	D. A. Whitmore	
G-CJYZ	Cameron Z-120 balloon	MSJ Ballooning Ltd	
G-CJZB	Glaser-Dirks DG-500 Elan Orion	The Borders (Milfield) Gliding Club Ltd	
G-CJZD	Aeropro Eurofox 912(S)	R. Maddocks-Born	
G-CJZE	Schleicher ASK-13	Bowland Forest Gliding Club Ltd	
G-CJZG	Schempp-Hirth Discus bT	I. K. G. Mitchell	
G-CJZH	Schleicher ASW-20 CL	A. K. Bartlett	
G-CJZK	Glaser-Dirks DG-505 Elan Orion	Devon and Somerset Gliding Club Ltd	
G-CJZL	Schempp-Hirth Mini Nimbus B	J. F. Wells	
G-CJZM	Schempp-Hirth Ventus 2a	S. Crabb	
G-CJZN	Schleicher ASW-28	C. J. Davison	
G-CJZO	RAF BE2e replica (A2943)	O. Wulff	
G-CJZP	RAF BE.2e replica (A2767)	D. A. Whitmore	
G-CJZU	Jodel D.150	P. T. Catanach	
G-CJZV	PA-28RT-201T Turbo Arrow IV	Associazone Sportiva Aeronautica/Italy	
G-CJZW	Van's RV-12	M. A. N. Newall	
G-CJZY	Grob G.102 Standard Astir III	Lasham Gliding Society Ltd	
G-CJZZ	Rolladen-Schneider LS7	C. L. Rogers	
G-CKAA	Whittaker MW9 Plank	M. W. J. Whittaker	
G-CKAB	Eurofox 912(IS)	R. M. Cornwell	
G-CKAC	Glaser-Dirks DG-200	N. Frost	
G-CKAE	Centrair 101A Pegase	J. P. Gilbert	
G-CKAF	Embraer RJ145EP	bmi regional	
G-CKAG	Embraer RJ145EP	bmi regional	
G-CKAI	Griffin RG28 balloon	R. G. Griffin	
G-CKAL	Schleicher ASW-28	D. A. Smith	
G-CKAM	Glasflugel Club Libelle 205	P. A. Cronk & R. C. Tallowin	
G-CKAN	PZL-Bielsko SZD-50-3 Puchacz	The Bath Wilts and North Dorset Gliding Club Ltd	
G-CKAO	Lindstrand LTL Series 1-17 balloon	Lindstrand Technologies Ltd	
G-CKAP	Schempp-Hirth Discus CS	H. A. Johnston & R. Gollings	
G-CKAR	Schempp-Hirth Duo Discus T	977 Syndicate	
G-CKAS	Schempp-Hirth Ventus 2cT	KAS Club	
G-CKAT	Cessna F.152	A. S. Bamrah	
G-CKAU	DG Flugzeugbau DG-303 Elan Acro	G. Earle	
G-CKAX	AMS-Flight DG-500 Elan Orion	York Gliding Centre Ltd	
G-CKAY	Grob G.102 Astir CS	P. Fowler & R. G. Skerry	
G-CKAZ	Embraer EMB-505 Phenom 300	Golconda Aircraft Leasing LLP	
G-CKBA	Centrair 101A Pegase	KBA Pegase 101A Syndicate	
G-CKBB	Sopwith 7F1 Snipe replica (F2367)	The Vintage Aviator Ltd	
G-CKBC	Rolladen-Schneider LS6-c18	A. W. Lyth	
G-CKBD	Grob G.102 Astir CS	Astir KBD Syndicate	
G-CKBE	Van's RV-8	B. E. Smith	
G-CKBF	AMS-Flight DG-303 Elan	G. A. Burtenshaw	
G-CKBG	Schempp-Hirth Ventus 2cT	D. Martin& R. Bollom	
G-CKBH	Rolladen-Schneider LS6	F. C. Ballard & P. Walker	
G-CKBJ	Ultramagic H-31 balloon	R. D. Parry	
G-CKBL	Grob G.102 Astir CS	Norfolk Gliding Club Ltd	
G-CKBM	Schleicher ASW-28	P. J. Brown	
G-CKBN	PZL-Bielsko SZD-55-1 Promyk	G-CKBN Group	
G-CKBO	Eurocopter EC225LP Super Puma	Wilmington Trust SP Services (Dublin) Ltd	
G-CKBP	Smudger 77 balloon	C. E. Smith	
G-CKBR	Nott AN4 gas balloon	J. R. P. Nott	
G-CKBT	Schempp-Hirth Standard Cirrus	P. R. Johnson	
G-CKBU	Schleicher ASW-28	G. C. Metcalfe	

Notes	Reg	Type	Owner or Operator
	G-CKBV	Schleicher ASW-28	P. Whipp
	G-CKBW	Cessna 150M	Associazione Sportiva Aeronautica/Italy
	G-CKBX	Schleicher ASW-27	M. Wright
	G-CKBY	Eurocopter AS.365N3 Dauphin 2	Babcock Mission Critical Services Offshore Ltd
	G-CKCB	Rolladen-Schneider LS4-a	The Bristol Gliding Club Proprietary Ltd
	G-CKCC	Cameron Z-105 balloon	First Flight
	G-CKCD	Schempp-Hirth Ventus 2cT	R. S. Jobar & S. G. Jones
	G-CKCE	Schempp-Hirth Ventus 2cT	Ventus 24 Group
	G-CKCF	Scintex CP.301C-1 Emeraude	N. C. Scanlan
	G-CKCH	Schempp-Hirth Ventus 2cT	J. J. Pridal
	G-CKCI	Guimbal Cabri G2	D. Robson
	G-CKCJ	Schleicher ASW-28	M. McHugo
	G-CKCK	Enstrom 280FX	C. M. Parkinson
	G-CKCL	Cessna 182T	CE Ventures Ltd
	G-CKCM	Glasflugel Standard Libelle 201B	F. Sleigh & G. K. Drury
	G-CKCN	Schleicher ASW-27	W. J. Head
	G-CKCP	Grob G.102 Astir CS	Norfolk Gliding Club Ltd
	G-CKCR	AB Sportine Aviacija LAK-17A	M. Kessler/Italy
	G-CKCT	Schleicher ASK-21	Kent Gliding Club Aircraft Ltd
	G-CKCU	Embraer EMB-500 Phenom 100	Affinity Flying Training Services Ltd
	G-CKCV	Schempp-Hirth Duo Discus T	WE4 Group
	G-CKCX	Leonardo AW169	Waypoint Asset Euro 1G Ltd
	G-CKCY	Schleicher ASW-20	K. W. Payne
	G-CKCZ	Schleicher ASK-21	Booker Gliding Club Ltd
	G-CKDA	Schempp-Hirth Ventus 2B	D. J. Eade
	G-CKDB	Schleicher Ka 6CR	Banbury Gliding Club Ltd
	G-CKDD	Aeropro Eurofox 2K	H. I. Tindall
	G-CKDE	Grob G.109B	Navboys Ltd
	G-CKDF	Schleicher ASK-21	Portsmouth Naval Gliding Centre
	G-CKDG	BB03 Tyra/BB103	Z. G. Nagygyorgy
	G-CKDJ	Sonex	S. Rance
	G-CKDK	Rolladen-Schneider LS4-a	M. C. & P. A. Ridger
	G-CKDL	Robinson R.22 Beta II	Elicast SRL/Italy
	G-CKDM	Zenair CH.750	M. R. Cleveley
	G-CKDN	Schleicher ASW-27B	J. S. McCullagh
	G-CKDO	Schempp-Hirth Ventus 2cT	M. W. Edwards
	G-CKDP	Schleicher ASK-21	Kent Gliding Club Aircraft Ltd
	G-CKDR	PZL-Bielsko SZD-48-3 Jantar Standard 3	G. Hyrkowski
	G-CKDS	Schleicher ASW-27	A. W. Gillett & G. D. Morris
	G-CKDT	Cameron C-80 balloon	W. Thijs
	G-CKDU	Glaser-Dirks DG-200/17	J. M. Knight
	G-CKDV	Schempp-Hirth Ventus B/16.6	M. A. Codd
	G-CKDW	Schleicher ASW-27	C. Colton
	G-CKDX	Glaser-Dirks DG-200	Delta X Ray Group
	G-CKDY	Glaser-Dirks DG-100	503 Syndicate
	G-CKEA	Schempp-Hirth Cirrus 18	S. G. Jessup
	G-CKEB	Schempp-Hirth Standard Cirrus	R. H. Buzza
	G-CKED	Schleicher ASW-27B	A. & R. Maskell
	G-CKEE	Grob G.102 Astir CS	Essex and Suffolk Gliding Club Ltd
	G-CKEF	Embraer EMB-500 Phenom 100	Affinity Flying Training Services Ltd
	G-CKEG	Cameron Z-105 balloon	First Flight
	G-CKEH	Kolb Twister Mk.III Xtra	The Darley Tail Draggers
	G-CKEI	Diamond DA.40NG Star	D. B. Smith
	G-CKEJ	Schleicher ASK-21	London Gliding Club Proprietary Ltd
	G-CKEK	Schleicher ASK-21	Devon and Somerset Gliding Club Ltd
	G-CKEP	Rolladen-Schneider LS6-b	J. Stellmacher & S. Tschorn/Germany
	G-CKER	Schleicher ASW-19B	W. A. Bowness & E. Richards
	G-CKES	Schempp-Hirth Cirrus 18	D. Judd & N. Hawley
	G-CKET	Rolladen-Schneider LS8-t	M. B. Jefferyes & J. C. Taylor
	G-CKEV	Schempp-Hirth Duo Discus	The Royal Air Force Gliding and Soaring Association
	G-CKEY	PA-28-161 Warrior II	Warwickshire Aviation Ltd
	G-CKEZ	DG Flugzeugbau LS8	D. A. Jesty
	G-CKFA	Schempp-Hirth Standard Cirrus 75	University of the West of England, Bristol Higher Education Corporation
	G-CKFB	Schempp-Hirth Discus-2T	P. L. & P. A. G. Holland
	G-CKFD	Schleicher ASW-27B	W. T. Craig
	G-CKFE	Eiriavion PIK-20D	G. E. Rabe
	G-CKFF	Zenair CH.701SP	G. Kingaby
	G-CKFG	Grob G.103A Twin II Acro	The Surrey Hills Gliding Club Ltd

Reg	Type	Owner or Operator	Notes
G-CKFH	Schempp-Hirth Mini Nimbus	C. J. Friar	
G-CKFI	Cameron Drop-95 balloon	Belvoir Fruit Farms Ltd	
G-CKFJ	Schleicher ASK-13	York Gliding Centre Ltd	
G-CKFK	Schempp-Hirth Standard Cirrus 75	P. R. Wilkinson	
G-CKFL	Rolladen-Schneider LS4	D. O'Brien & D. R. Taylor	
G-CKFN	DG Flugzeugbau DG1000	Yorkshire Gliding Club (Proprietary) Ltd	
G-CKFP	Schempp-Hirth Ventus 2cxT	D. A. Smith	
G-CKFR	Schleicher ASK-13	Club Acrupacion de Pilotos del Sureste/Spain	
G-CKFS	Schleicher ASK-14	J. Pool	
G-CKFT	Schempp-Hirth Duo Discus T	Duo Discus Syndicate	
G-CKFV	DG Flugzeugbau LS8-t	G. A. Rowden & K. I. Arkley	
G-CKFW	Mauchline Quaich	Quaich Flying Group	
G-CKFX	Centrair 101AP Pegase	G-CKFX Flying Group	
G-CKFY	Schleicher ASK.21	Cambridge Gliding Club	
G-CKFZ	Ultramagic M-77 balloon	E. C. Meek	
G-CKGA	Schempp-Hirth Ventus 2cxT	D. R. Campbell	
G-CKGB	Schempp-Hirth Ventus 2cxT	R. Henz/Germany	
G-CKGC	Schempp-Hirth Ventus 2cxT	C. P. A. Jeffery	
G-CKGD	Schempp-Hirth Ventus 2cxT	C. Morris	
G-CKGF	Schempp-Hirth Duo Discus T	Duo 233 Group	
G-CKGG	Grob G.109B	R. Banks	
G-CKGH	Grob G.102 Club Astir II	D. C. & K. J. Mockford	
G-CKGI	Ultramagic M-77C balloon	D. J. L. Gillespie	
G-CKGJ	Nicollier HN.700 Menestrel II	J. R., S. J. & T. M. Rickett	
G-CKGK	Schleicher ASK-21	The Royal Air Force Gliding & Soaring Association	
G-CKGL	Schempp-Hirth Ventus 2cT	T. R. Dews	
G-CKGM	Centrair 101A Pegase	S. France	
G-CKGS	Ikarus C42 FB80	GS Aviation (Europe) Ltd	
G-CKGV	Schleicher ASW-20	A. H. Reynolds	
G-CKGX	Schleicher ASK-21	Coventry Gliding Club Ltd	
G-CKGY	Scheibe Bergfalke IV	B. R. Pearson	
G-CKHB	Rolladen-Schneider LS3	C. J. Cole	
G-CKHC	DG Flugzeugbau DG.505	G-CKHC Group	
G-CKHD	Schleicher ASW-27B	R. L. Smith	
G-CKHE	AB Sportine Aviacija LAK-17AT	V. S. Bettle	
G-CKHH	Schleicher ASK-13	The South Wales Gliding Club Ltd	
G-CKHI	P & M Quik R	G-CKHI Syndicate	
G-CKHJ	Ultramagic H-31 balloon	G. A. Board	
G-CKHK	Schempp-Hirth Duo Discus T	Duo Discus Syndicate	
G-CKHL	Boeing 787-9	Norwegian Air UK Ltd	
G-CKHM	Centrair 101A Pegase 90	J. A. Tipler	
G-CKHN	PZL SZD-51-1 Junior	The Nene Valley Gliding Club Ltd	
G-CKHO	Flight Design CT-Supralight	J. A. Horn	
G-CKHR	PZL-Bielsko SZD-51-1 Junior	Wolds Gliding Club Ltd	
G-CKHS	Rolladen-Schneider LS7-WL	M. Lawson & D. Wallis	
G-CKHU	Balony Kubicek BB17XR balloon	Balloon Flight	
G-CKHV	Glaser-Dirks DG-100	G-CKHV Trust	
G-CKHW	PZL SZD-50-3 Puchacz	Derbyshire and Lancashire Gliding Club Ltd	
G-CKHY	P &M Hyper GTR	E. J. Douglas	
G-CKHZ	Aeriane Swift Light PAS	W. True	
G-CKIE	Cessna 172S	Western Air (Thruxton) Ltd	
G-CKIF	Cessna 172S	Western Air (Thruxton) Ltd	
G-CKIG	Flylight Fox Tug	D. T. Mackenzie	
G-CKIH	Agusta A.109S Grand	Heli Delta BV/Netherlands	
G-CKIN	Lindstrand LTL Series 1-105 balloon	A. M. Holly	
G-CKIO	PA-28-151 Cherokee Warrior	Falcon Flying Services Ltd	
G-CKIP	Cessna 172N	Aero Club de Leiria/Portugal	
G-CKIS	Aero Designs Pulsar XP	D. R. Piercy	
G-CKIT	Cameron C-60 balloon	Turner Balloons Ltd	
G-CKIU	Scheibe SF-25C Rotax-Falke	The Burn Gliding Club Ltd	
G-CKIX	Aeropro Eurofox 3K	R. Mulford	
G-CKIY	Best Off Skyranger Nynja 912S(1)	D. Lamb & N. Elahi	
G-CKIZ	Eurofly Minifox	N. R. Beale	
G-CKJB	Schempp-Hirth Ventus bT	KJB Group	
G-CKJC	Schempp-Hirth Nimbus 3T	A. C. Wright	
G-CKJE	DG Flugzeugbau LS8-18	M. D. Wells	
G-CKJF	Schempp-Hirth Standard Cirrus	T. W. Arscott	
G-CKJG	Schempp-Hirth Cirrus VTC	C. Nobbs & A. R. Blanchard	
G-CKJH	Glaser-Dirks DG.300 Elan	Yorkshire Gliding Club	
G-CKJI	Best Off Skyranger Nynja 912S(1)	Flylight Airsports Ltd	

Notes	Reg	Type	Owner or Operator
	G-CKJJ	DG Flugzeugbau DG-500 Elan Orion	Ulster Gliding Club Ltd
	G-CKJL	Scleicher ASK-13	Lincolnshire Gliding Club Ltd
	G-CKJM	Schempp-Hirth Ventus cT	G-CKJM Group
	G-CKJN	Schleicher ASW-20	R. Logan
	G-CKJO	Lindstrand 9T tethered gas balloon	Lindstrand Technologies Ltd
	G-CKJP	Schleicher ASK-21	The Royal Air Force Gliding and Soaring Association
	G-CKJR	Leonardo AW169	Waypoint Asset Co 5A Ltd
	G-CKJS	Schleicher ASW-28-18E	G-CKJS Syndicate
	G-CKJT	Ultramagic H-42 balloon	J. Taylor
	G-CKJV	Schleicher ASW-28-18E	A. C. Price
	G-CKJZ	Schempp-Hirth Discus bT	G-CKJZ Group
	G-CKKB	Centrair 101A Pegase	D. M. Rushton
	G-CKKC	DG Flugzeugbau DG-300 Elan Acro	Charlie Kilo Kilo Charlie Syndicate
	G-CKKE	Schempp-Hirth Duo Discus T	P. Foster
	G-CKKF	Schempp-Hirth Ventus 2cT	A. R. MacGregor
	G-CKKG	TL3000 Sirius	W. F. Hughes
	G-CKKH	Schleicher ASW-27	P. L. Hurd
	G-CKKL	Boeing 787-9	Norwegian Air UK
	G-CKKO	Ultramagic H-77 balloon	I. C. Steward
	G-CKKP	Schleicher ASK-21	Bowland Forest Gliding Club Ltd
	G-CKKR	Schleicher ASK-13	The Windrushers Gliding Club Ltd
	G-CKKV	DG Flugzeugbau DG-1000S	Les Ailes d'Issoudun/France
	G-CKKX	Rolladen-Schneider LS4-A	B. W. Svenson
	G-CKKY	Schempp-Hirth Duo Discus T	P. D. Duffin
	G-CKLA	Schleicher ASK-13	Booker Gliding Club Ltd
	G-CKLC	Glasflugel H206 Hornet	W. Ellis
	G-CKLD	Schempp-Hirth Discus 2cT	797 Syndicate
	G-CKLE	Autogyro MTOsport 2017	Rotorsport Sales and Service Ltd
	G-CKLG	Rolladen-Schneider LS4	P. M. Scheiwiller
	G-CKLI	PA-28R-180 Cherokee Arrow	Exavia Ltd
	G-CKLK	Autogyro MTOsport 2017	Rotorsport Sales and Service Ltd
	G-CKLL	Waco YKS-7	K. D. Pearce
	G-CKLN	Rolladen-Schneider LS4-A	Army Gliding Association
	G-CKLP	Scleicher ASW-28-18	P. E. Baker
	G-CKLS	Rolladen-Schneider LS4	Wolds Gliding Club Ltd
	G-CKLT	Schempp-Hirth Nimbus 3/24.5	G. N. Thomas
	G-CKLV	Schempp-Hirth Discus 2cT	KLV Syndicate
	G-CKLW	Schleicher ASK-21	Yorkshire Gliding Club
	G-CKLY	DG Flugzeugbau DG-1000T	G-CKLY Flying Group
	G-CKLZ	Boeing 787-9	Norwegian Air UK Ltd
	G-CKMA	DG Flugzeugbau LS8-T	W. J. Morecraft
	G-CKMB	AB Sportline Aviacija LAK-19T	D. J. McKenzie
	G-CKMD	Schempp-Hirth Standard Cirrus	S. A. Crabb
	G-CKME	DG Flugzeugbau LS8-T	S. M. Smith
	G-CKMF	Centrair 101A Pegase	D. L. M. Jamin
	G-CKMG	Glaser-Dirks DG-101G Elan	R. A. Johnson
	G-CKMH	Kavanagh Balloons EX-65 balloon	Border Ballooning Ltd
	G-CKMI	Schleicher K8C	V. Mallon
	G-CKMJ	Schleicher Ka 6CR	V. Mallon
	G-CKMK	Sportine Aviacija LAK-17AT	B. N. Searle
	G-CKML	Schempp-Hirth Duo Discus T	G-CKML Group
	G-CKMM	Schleicher ASW-28-18E	R. G. Munro
	G-CKMN	Lindstrand LTL Series 1-105 balloon	M. A. Derbyshire
	G-CKMO	Rolladen-Schneider LS7-WL	R. D. Payne
	G-CKMP	AB Sportine Aviacija LAK-17A	J. L. McIver
	G-CKMS	Lindstrand LBL 400A balloon	Flying Circus SRL/Spain
	G-CKMT	Grob G103C	Essex & Suffolk Gliding Club Ltd
	G-CKMU	Boeing 787-9	Norwegian Air UK Ltd
	G-CKMV	Rolladen-Schneider LS3-17	S. Procter & M. P. Woolmer
	G-CKMW	Schleicher ASK-21	The Royal Air Force Gliding & Soaring Association
	G-CKMX	Van's RV-7	S. J. Cummins
	G-CKMZ	Schleicher ASW-28-18E	R. J. Woodhams
	G-CKNA	Boeing 787-9	Norwegian Air UK
	G-CKNB	Schempp-Hirth Standard Cirrus	S. Potter
	G-CKNC	Caproni Calif A21S	Calif 240 Syndicate
	G-CKND	DG Flugzeugbau DG-1000T	KND Group
	G-CKNE	Schempp-Hirth Standard Cirrus 75-VTC	G. D. E. Macdonald
	G-CKNF	DG Flugzeugbau DG-1000T	DG 1000 Syndicate
	G-CKNG	Schleicher ASW-28-18E	NG209 Group

Reg	Type	Owner or Operator	Notes
G-CKNK	Glaser-Dirks DG.500	Cotswold Gliding Club	
G-CKNL	Schleicher ASK-21	Buckminster Gliding Club Ltd	
G-CKNM	Scleicher ASK-18	Derbyshire & Lancashire Gliding Club Ltd	
G-CKNO	Schempp-Hirth Ventus 2cxT	R. T. Starling	
G-CKNR	Schempp-Hirth Ventus 2cxT	R. J. Nicholls	
G-CKNS	Rolladen-Schneider LS4-A	I. R. Willows	
G-CKNV	Schleicher ASW-28-18E	The KNV Group	
G-CKNX	Ozone Buzz Z4 ML/Parajet VI Macro Trike	I. T. Callaghan	
G-CKNY	Boeing 787-9	Norwegian Air UK Ltd	
G-CKNZ	Boeing 787-9	Norwegian Air UK Ltd	
G-CKOD	Schempp-Hirth Discus BT	M. W. Talbot & D. Ascroft	
G-CKOE	Schleicher ASW-27-18	R. C. Bromwich	
G-CKOF	Boeing 787-9	Norwegian Air UK Ltd	
G-CKOG	Boeing 787-9	Norwegian Air UK Ltd	
G-CKOH	DG Flugzeugbau DG-1000T	A. D. & P. Langlands	
G-CKOI	AB Sportine Aviacija LAK-17AT	C. G. Corbett	
G-CKOK	Schempp-Hirth Discus 2cT	P. Topping	
G-CKOL	Schempp-Hirth Duo Discus T	Oscar Lima Syndicate	
G-CKOM	Schleicher ASW-27-18	P. G. Whipp	
G-CKON	Schleicher ASW-27-18E	J. P. Gorringe	
G-CKOO	Schleicher ASW-27-18E	G-CKOO Flying Group	
G-CKOR	Glaser-Dirks DG-300 Elan	D. Jokinen & W. Xu	
G-CKOT	Schleicher ASK-21	Ulster Gliding Club Ltd	
G-CKOU	AB Sportine Aviacija LAK-19T	PAC LAK Syndicate	
G-CKOW	DG-505 Elan Orion	Southdown Gliding Club Ltd	
G-CKOX	AMS-Flight DG-505 Elan Orion	Seahawk Gliding Club	
G-CKOY	Schleicher ASW-27-18E	G-CKOY Group	
G-CKOZ	Schleicher ASW-27-18E	E. W. Johnston	
G-CKPA	AB Sportline Aviacija LAK-19T	M. J. Hargreaves	
G-CKPC	Cameron Z-77 balloon	A. A. Osman	
G-CKPE	Schempp-Hirth Duo Discus	Portsmouth Naval Gliding Centre	
G-CKPF	Champion 7GCBC Citabria	C. F. Dukes	
G-CKPG	Schempp-Hirth Discus 2cT	G. Knight & P. Rowden	
G-CKPI	Aerospatiale SA.319B Alouette III	S. Atherton	
G-CKPJ	Neukom S-4D Elfe	S. Szladowski	
G-CKPK	Schempp-Hirth Ventus 2cxT	I. C. Lees	
G-CKPM	DG Flugzeugbau LS8-T	S. P. Woolcock	
G-CKPN	PZL-Bielsko SZD-51-1 Junior	Rattlesden Gliding Club Ltd	
G-CKPO	Schempp-Hirth Duo Discus xT	KPO Syndicate	
G-CKPP	Schleicher ASK-21	The Gliding Centre	
G-CKPR	Cameron TR-65 balloon	Cameron Balloons Ltd	
G-CKPS	Aerospatiale AS.350B2 Ecureuil	Helitrain Ltd	
G-CKPU	Schleicher ASW-27-18E	C. S. & M. E. Newland-Smith	
G-CKPV	Schempp-Hirth HS.7 Mini-Nimbus B	D. K. McCarthy	
G-CKPX	ZS Jezow PW-6U	North Wales Gliding Club Ltd	
G-CKPY	Schempp-Hirth Duo Discus xT	Duo-Discus Syndicate	
G-CKPZ	Schleicher ASW-20	T. C. J. Hogarth	
G-CKRB	Schleicher ASK-13	Derbyshire and Lancashire Gliding Club Ltd	
G-CKRC	Schleicher ASW-28-18E	J. T. Garrett	
G-CKRD	Schleicher ASW-27-18E	R. F. Thirkell	
G-CKRE	La Mouette Samson/Atos-VR	J. S. Prosser	
G-CKRF	DG-300 Elan	G. A. King	
G-CKRH	Grob G.103 Twin Astir II	Staffordshire Gliding Club Ltd	
G-CKRI	Schleicher ASK-21	Kent Gliding Club Aircraft Ltd	
G-CKRJ	Schleicher ASW-27-18E	J. J. Marshall	
G-CKRK	Guimbal Cabri G2	European Helicopter Importers Ltd	
G-CKRL	Europa XS	D. M. Cope	
G-CKRO	Schempp-Hirth Duo Discus T	Duo Discus Syndicate KRO	
G-CKRP	Grob G.120TP-A	Affinity Flying Training Services Ltd	
G-CKRR	Schleicher ASW-15B	D. T. Edwards	
G-CKRU	ZS Jezow PW-6U	Essex Gliding Club Ltd	
G-CKRV	Schleicher ASW-27-18E	Z. Marczynski	
G-CKRW	Schleicher ASK-21	The Royal Air Force Gliding and Soaring Association	
G-CKRX	Jezow PW-6U	Essex Gliding Club Ltd	
G-CKRY	Grob G.120TP-A	Affinity Flying Training Services Ltd	
G-CKRZ	Skyranger Nynja 912S(1)	R. J. Clarke	
G-CKSA	Airbus EC.135 T3	Airbus Helicopters UK Ltd	
G-CKSB	Airbus EC.135 T3	Airbus Helicopters UK Ltd	
G-CKSC	Czech Sport Aircraft Sportcruiser	Czechmate Syndicate	
G-CKSD	Rolladen-Schneider LS8-a	J. H. Cox & K. A. Fox	

Notes	Reg	Type	Owner or Operator
	G-CKSE	Cessna 208B Grand Caravan	Wingglider Ltd
	G-CKSG	Avro RJ100	Trident Turboprop (Dublin) DAC
	G-CKSK	Pilatus B4-PC11	K. Steinmair
	G-CKSL	Schleicher ASW-15B	Sierra Lima Group
	G-CKSM	Schempp-Hirth Duo Discus T	J. H. May & S. P. Ball
	G-CKSP	PA-28-180 Cherokee Archer	Italian Wings ASD/Italy
	G-CKSR	Boeing Stearman D75N	T. W. Gilbert
	G-CKST	Boeing Stearman B75N1	T. W. Gilbert
	G-CKSU	Boeing Stearman A75	T. W. Gilbert
	G-CKSV	Boeing Stearman A75	T. W. Gilbert
	G-CKSW	Cameron O-26 balloon	S. G. Whatley
	G-CKSX	Schleicher ASW-27-18E	M. C. Foreman
	G-CKSY	Rolladen-Schneider LS-7-WL	ICKSY Syndicate
	G-CKSZ	Cameron Sport 90 balloon	Cameron Balloons Ltd
	G-CKTA	Aerochute Hummerchute	G. Stokes
	G-CKTB	Schempp-Hirth Ventus 2cT	M. H. Player
	G-CKTC	Schleicher Ka 6CR	B. Brannigan
	G-CKTD	Colomban MC-30 Luciole	D. K. Lawry
	G-CKTE	Aeropro Eurofox 3K	R. J. Bird
	G-CKTF	Van's RV-6A	D. Bennett
	G-CKTH	Boeing 737-3YO	Onexp ApS & TAG Aviation (Stansted) Ltd (G-IGOA)
	G-CKTJ	Lindstrand LTL Racer 65 balloon	A. M. Holly
	G-CKTK	Denney Kitfox Model 4-1200	I. J. M. Donnelly
	G-CKTL	Aerochute Hummerchute	R. D. Knight
	G-CKTM	Pitts S-1 Special	R. Farrer
	G-CKTN	BRM Aero Bristell NG5 Speed Wing	E. O. Ridley & T. H. Crow
	G-CKTO	Avro RJ100	Aero Partners Ltd
	G-CKTP	Ultramagic M-90 balloon	Proximm SPA/Italy
	G-CKTR	Tecnam P2006T	Vandermeer Holdings Ltd
	G-CKTS	Jodel D.9 Bebe	R. A. Yates
	G-CKTT	P & M Quik GTR	M. K. Ashmore
	G-CKTU	Ultramagic M-90 balloon	Proximm SPA/Italy
	G-CKTV	Lindstrand LTL Series 1-105 balloon	A. M. Holly
	G-CKTW	Cameron O-31 balloon	M. & S. Mitchell
	G-CKTX	Van's RV-7	M. M. McElrea
	G-CKTY	Avro RJ100	Trident Turboprop (Dublin) DAC
	G-CKTZ	Cameron Z-77 balloon	A. A. Osman
	G-CKUA	Cameron Z-77 balloon	A. A. Osman
	G-CKUB	Cessna 560XL Citation XLS+	Catreus Ltd
	G-CKUC	Beech C90A King Air	J. M. Gottlieb
	G-CKUE	VS.361 Spitfire LF.XVIe	C. F. T. Van Eerd
	G-CKUH	CZAW Sportcruiser	K. Rogan
	G-CKUJ	ATEC 212 Solo	Mission Capital Ltd
	G-CKUK	Ultramagic Shemilt Eco 50 balloon	Thames Valley Balloons Ltd
	G-CKUL	Ace As-Tec 13	G. L. Logan
	G-CKUM	Swing XWing/Xcitor paratrike	D. Burton
	G-CKUN	Bareford DB-6R balloon	D. Bareford
	G-CKUO	Aeroprakt A22-LS Foxbat	P. Gosney
	G-CKUR	Skyranger Swift 912(1)	R. F. Pearce
	G-CKUS	Conway Viper	D. B. Conway
	G-CKUU	PA-23-250 Aztec	G. Scillieri
	G-CKUV	PA-34-220T Seneca V	Craigard Property Trading Ltd (G-VYND)
	G-CKUX	Magic Laser	L. P. Harper
	G-CKVA	BN-2T Islander	Britten-Norman Aircraft Ltd
	G-CKVC	Rotorsport UK Cavalon	H2E Energy Ltd
	G-CKVD	Rolladen-Schneider LS-1f	G. M. Spreckley
	G-CKVE	Aero 31 AM9 balloon	A. Marshall
	G-CKVF	Aeroprakt A22-LS Foxbat	R. J. Davey
	G-CKVJ	Titan T-51 Mustang	Euro Aviation Ltd
	G-CKVP	Rotorsport UK Calidus	P. M. Bidston
	G-CKVX	Breezer M400	M. W. Houghton
	G-CKVZ	Rotorsport UK Cavalon Pro	Autogyro GmbH
	G-CKWM	Van's RV-8	C. A. G. Schofield
	G-CKWW	Cameron Sport 50 balloon	Cameron Balloons Ltd
	G-CKWZ	Grob G.109B	T. R. Dews
	G-CKZT	PA-28-235 Cherokee Pathfinder	U. Chakravorty
	G-CLAA	Boeing 747-446F	Cargologicair Ltd
	G-CLAB	Boeing 747-83QF	Cargologicair Ltd
	G-CLAC	PA-28-161 Warrior II	G-CLAC Group

Reg	Type	Owner or Operator	Notes
G-CLAD	Cameron V-90 balloon	Adeilad Cladding	
G-CLAL	Ikarus C42 FB100	C. I. Law	
G-CLAV	Shaw Europa	G. Laverty	
G-CLAX	Jurca MJ.5 Sirocco	G. S. Williams (G-AWKB)	
G-CLAY	Bell 206B JetRanger 3	Tiger Properties (Kent) Ltd (G-DENN)	
G-CLBA	Boeing 747-428ERF	Cargologicair Ltd	
G-CLBZ	Cessna FR.172J	E. Marinoni	
G-CLEA	PA-28-161 Warrior II	Freedom Aviation Ltd	
G-CLEE	Rans S.6-ES Coyote II	P. S. Chapman	
G-CLEM	Bölkow Bö.208A2 Junior	G-CLEM Group (G-ASWE)	
G-CLEO	Zenair CH.601HD	K. M. Bowen	
G-CLES	Scheicher ASW-27-18E	A. P. Brown	
G-CLEU	Glaser-Dirks DG-200	S. F. Tape	
G-CLFB	Rolladen-Schneider LS4-A	K2 Syndicate	
G-CLFC	Mainair Blade	P. E. Jackson	
G-CLFH	Schleicher ASW-20C	T. Fordwich-Gorefly & P. Armstrong	
G-CLFX	Schempp-Hirth Duo Discus T	M. G. Lynes & S. Holland	
G-CLFZ	Schleicher ASW-18E	C. F. Cownden & J. P. Davies	
G-CLGC	Schempp-Hirth Duo Discus	London Gliding Club Proprietary Ltd	
G-CLGL	Schempp-Hirth Ventus 2c	S. C. Williams	
G-CLGR	Glasflugel Club Libelle 205	LGR Libelle Group	
G-CLGT	Rolladen-Schneider LS4	C. B. & N. M. Hill	
G-CLGU	Schleicher ASW-27-18	T. J. Scott	
G-CLGW	Centrair 101A Pegase	M. White	
G-CLGZ	Schempp-Hirth Duo Discus T	P. Dolan & D. R. Irving	
G-CLHF	Scheibe Bergfalke IV	Andreas Gliding Club Ltd	
G-CLHG	Schempp-Hirth Discus b	S. J. Edinborough	
G-CLIC	Cameron A-105 balloon	M. Arno	
G-CLIF	Ikarus C42 FB UK	E. R. Sims	
G-CLIN	Ikarus C42 FB100	J. O'Halloran	
G-CLJE	Schleicher ASH-25M	A. Hegner	
G-CLJM	Cessna F.172G	N. Guglielmo/Italy	
G-CLJP	Cessna F.172G	C. Marti	
G-CLJZ	Schleicher ASH-31Mi	J. C. Thompson	
G-CLKF	Schempp-Hirth Cirrus VTC	E. C. Wright	
G-CLKG	Schempp-Hirth Janus CM	Lakes Janus Group	
G-CLKK	Schleicher ASH-31 Mi	Zulu Glasstek Ltd	
G-CLKU	Schleicher Ka 6E	K. Richards	
G-CLLB	Schempp-Hirth Discus 2cT	R. P. Das	
G-CLLC	HpH Glasflugel 304 Shark	F16 Group	
G-CLLH	HpH Glasflugel 304 Shark	J. Haigh	
G-CLLL	Schleicher ASW-27-18E	I. P. Hick	
G-CLLT	Grob G.102 Standard Astir II	Staffordshire Gliding Club Ltd	
G-CLLX	Schempp-Hirth Duo Discus T	B. D. Scougall	
G-CLLY	Rolladen-Schneider LS6-C18	P. W. Brown	
G-CLMD	AB Sportine Aviacija LAK-17B FES	R. C. Bromwich	
G-CLME	Schempp-Hirth Ventus 2cT	Gransden Ventus LME Group	
G-CLMF	Glaser-Dirks DG-200	P. H. Whitehouse	
G-CLMO	Schleicher ASW-28-18E	B. Bobrovnikov	
G-CLMV	Glasflugel 304 SJ Shark	G. J. Bowser	
G-CLMY	Glaser-Dirks DG-300	LMY Glider Syndicate	
G-CLNE	Schleicher ASH-31 Mi	T. P. Jenkinson	
G-CLNG	Schleicher ASW-27-18	G-CLNG Flying Group	
G-CLOC	Schleicher ASK-13	P. Sharpe	
G-CLOE	Sky 90-24 balloon	J. L. M. Van Hoesel	
G-CLOG	Schleicher ASW-27-18E	R. E. D. Bailey	
G-CLOL	Schleicher ASK-21	Lasham Gliding Society Ltd	
G-CLON	HPH Glasflugel 304S Shark	P. D. Ruskin	
G-CLOO	Grob G.103 Twin Astir	R. G. J. Tait	
G-CLOS	PA-34-200 Seneca II	R. A. Doherty	
G-CLOV	Schleicher ASK-21	Scottish Gliding Union Ltd	
G-CLPB	Rolladen-Schneider LS6c-18W	C. J. Harrison	
G-CLPE	Schempp-Hirth Discus bT	R. A. Braithwaite	
G-CLPL	Rolladen-Schneider LS7-WL	W. M. Davies	
G-CLPU	Schleicher ASW-27-18E	A. R. J. Hughes	
G-CLPV	Schleicher ASK-21	Portsmouth Naval Gliding Centre	
G-CLPX	Grob G.103C Twin III Acro	The Windrushers Gliding Club Ltd	
G-CLPZ	Jonker JS-MD Single	Bailey Aviation	
G-CLRA	Schleicher ASW-27-18E	C. A. Hunt & C. P. J. Gibson	
G-CLRC	Schleicher ASW-27-18E	W. R. Tandy	
G-CLRD	PZL-Bielsko SZD-51-1 Junior	Devon & Somerset Gliding Club Ltd	

Notes	Reg	Type	Owner or Operator
	G-CLRE	Schleicher Ka 6BR	B. Bay
	G-CLRF	Schleicher ASW-27-18E	C. G. Starkey
	G-CLRH	HPH Glasflugel 304S Shark	The Shark Group
	G-CLRJ	Schempp-Hirth Discus bT	M. S. Smith
	G-CLRK	Sky 77-24 balloon	William Clark & Son (Parkgate) Ltd
	G-CLRN	Glaser-Dirks DG-100G Elan	DG100 Group
	G-CLRO	Glaser-Dirks DG-300 Elan	P. E. Kerman
	G-CLRP	Schempp-Hirth Janus B	S. M. Grant & W. I. H. Hall
	G-CLRS	Schleicher ASW-27-18E	G-CLRS Flying Group
	G-CLRT	Schleicher ASK-21	Cotswold Gliding Club
	G-CLRY	Rolladen Schneider LS4	S. O. Boye
	G-CLRZ	Rolladen-Schneider LS-1f	KC Group
	G-CLSG	Rolladen-Schneider LS4-b	C. Marriott & C. Taunton
	G-CLSH	Schleicher ASK-21	Lasham Gliding Society Ltd
	G-CLSJ	HPH Glasflugel 304S Shark	C. M. Lewis
	G-CLSL	Glaser-Dirks DG-500 Elan Trainer	Needwood Forest Gliding Club Ltd
	G-CLSO	Schempp-Hirth Nimbus 3T	R. S. Rose
	G-CLSR	Grob G103 Twin Astir	The Nene Valley Gliding Club Ltd
	G-CLSW	Schleicher ASW-20BL	A. Docherty
	G-CLSY	Schempp-Hirth SHK-1	J. R. Stiles
	G-CLSZ	DG Flugzeugbau DG-800B	M. Roberts
	G-CLTA	HpH Glasflugel 304ES	R. E. Cross
	G-CLTC	Schempp-Hirth Janus CE	C. A. Willson & P. J. D. Smith
	G-CLTD	Schleicher K.8B	G. D. Western
	G-CLTF	Schempp-Hirth Discus a	L. Runhaar
	G-CLTG	Glaser-Dirks DG-100	L. B. Roberts
	G-CLTJ	Sportine Aviacija LAK-17B FES	J. T. Newbery
	G-CLTK	Grob G-103 Twin Astir Trainer	B. J. Biskup
	G-CLTL	Schleicher ASW-19B	J. P. Salt
	G-CLTO	Schleicher ASW-27-18E	J. Pack
	G-CLTP	Rolladen-Schneider LS3-17	F. C. Roles
	G-CLTS	Schempp-Hirth Arcus T	M. C. Boik
	G-CLTW	Glasflugel 304ES	S. Murdoch & A. Holswilder
	G-CLTX	Sportine Aviacija LAK-17B FES Mini	D. R. Bennett
	G-CLUD	Grob G.102 Club Astir IIIB	Lasham Gliding Society Ltd
	G-CLUE	PA-34-200T Seneca II	P. Wilkinson
	G-CLUG	Schleicher K.8B	The Windrushers Gliding Club Ltd
	G-CLUK	Schleicher ASK-23B	London Gliding Club Proprietary Ltd
	G-CLUP	Schleicher ASH-25E	A. K. Laylee & G. G. Dale
	G-CLUV	Schleicher ASK-23B	Midland Gliding Club Ltd
	G-CLUX	Cessna F.172N	G. Fox
	G-CLVJ	DG Flugzeugbau DG-505 Elan Orion	Coventry Gliding Club Ltd
	G-CLWN	Cameron Clown SS balloon	Magical Adventures Ltd (G-UBBE)
	G-CMBR	Cessna 172S	C. M. B. Reid
	G-CMBS	MDH MD-900 Explorer	Specialist Aviation Services Ltd
	G-CMCL	Agusta Westland AW169	CMCL Limited Partnership
	G-CMDG	P & M Quik R	M. D. Greaves & C. Fender
	G-CMED	SOCATA TB9 Tampico	Aero-Club Diepholz EV/Germany
	G-CMEW	Aerospool Dynamic WT9 UK	M. W. Frost
	G-CMKL	Van's RV-12	K. L. Sangster
	G-CMNK	DHC.1 Chipmunk 22	A. D. & N. Barton
	G-CMOR	Skyranger 912(2)	P. J. Tranmer
	G-CMOS	Cessna T.303 Crusader	C. J. Moss
	G-CMPA	PA-28RT-201Arrow IV	J. T. E. Buwalda (G-BREP)
	G-CMPC	Titan T-51 Mustang	J. A. Carey
	G-CMRA	Eurocopter AS.355N Ecureuil 2	Cheshire Helicopters Ltd
	G-CMSN	Robinson R22 Beta	Kuki Helicopter Sales Ltd (G-MGEE//G-RUMP)
	G-CMTO	Cessna 525 Citation M2	Golconda Aircraft Leasing LLP
	G-CMWK	Grob G.102 Astir CS	J. Schaper
	G-CNAB	Avtech Jabiru UL	G-CNAB Group
	G-CNCN	Rockwell Commander 112CA	G. R. Frost
	G-CNHB	Van's RV-7	M. E. Wood
	G-CNWL	MD.900 Explorer	Specialist Aviation Services Ltd (G-CIGX)
	G-COAI	Cranfield A.1	Cranfield University (G-BCIT)
	G-COBO	ATR-72-212A	Aurigny Air Services Ltd
	G-COBS	Diamond DA.42 M-NG	Thales UK Ltd
	G-COCO	Cessna F.172M	P. C. Sheard & R. C. Larder

Reg	Type	Owner or Operator	Notes
G-CODA	Hughes 369E	Studwelders Holdings Ltd (G-CIYJ)	
G-COGS	Bell 407	HC Services Ltd	
G-COIN	Bell 206B JetRanger 2	J. P. Niehorster	
G-COLA	Beech F33C Bonanza	Airport Direction Ltd (G-BUAZ)	
G-COLF	BRM Bristell NG-5 Speed Wing	C. Firth	
G-COLI	Rotorsport UK MT-03	G. D. Smith	
G-COLR	Colt 69A balloon ★	British School of Ballooning/Lancing	
G-COLS	Van's RV-7A	C. Terry	
G-COLY	Aeropro Eurofox 912(S)	C. J. Norman	
G-COMB	PA-30 Twin Comanche 160B	M. Bonsall (G-AVBL)	
G-COMP	Cameron N-90 balloon	Computacenter Ltd	
G-CONA	Flight Design CTLS	R. A. Eve (G-CGED)	
G-CONB	Robin DR.400/180	T. N. Clark (G-BUPX)	
G-CONC	Cameron N-90 balloon	A. A. Brown	
G-CONL	SOCATA TB10 Tobago	J. M. Huntington	
G-CONN	Eurocopter EC.120B Colibri	M. J. Connors (G-BZMK)	
G-CONR	Champion 7GCBC Scout	Aerofoyle Group	
G-CONS	Groppo Trail	G. Constantine	
G-CONV	Convair CV-440-54 ★	Reynard Nursery/Carluke	
G-COOT	Taylor Coot A	P. M. Napp	
G-COPP	Schleicher ASW-27-18E	G. D. Coppin	
G-COPR	Robinson R44 II	BML Utility Contractors Ltd	
G-COPS	Piper J-3C-65 Cub	R. W. Sproat	
G-CORA	Shaw Europa XS	A. P. Gardner (G-ILUM)	
G-CORB	SOCATA TB20 Trinidad	Corvid Aviation Ltd	
G-CORD	Slingsby T.66 Nipper 3	P. S. Gilmour (G-AVTB)	
G-CORS	Noorduyn AT-16-ND Harvard IIB	Propshop Ltd	
G-CORW	PA-28-180 Cherokee C	R. P. Osborne & C. A. Wilson (G-AVRY)	
G-COSF	PA-28-161 Warrior II	PA-28 Warrior Ltd	
G-COSY	Lindstrand LBL-56A balloon	M. H. Read & J. E. Wetters	
G-COTH	MD-900 Explorer	Specialist Aviation Services Ltd	
G-COTT	Cameron 60 Cottage SS balloon	Dragon Balloon Co Ltd	
G-COUZ	Raj Hamsa X'Air 582(2)	D. J. Tully	
G-COVA	PA-26-161 Warrior III	Coventry (Civil) Aviation Ltd (G-CDCL)	
G-COVC	PA-28-161 Warrior II	Coventry (Civil) Aviation Ltd	
G-COVE	Avtech Jabiru UL	A. A. Rowson	
G-COVZ	Cessna F.150M	R. A. Doherty (G-BCRT)	
G-COXI	Xtremeair XA42	ABD Networks LLP	
G-COXS	Aeroprakt A.22 Foxbat	S. Cox	
G-COZI	Rutan Cozy III	R. Machin	
G-CPAO	Eurocopter EC.135P2+	Police & Crime Commissioner for West Yorkshire	
G-CPAS	Eurocopter EC.135P2+	Police & Crime Commissioner for West Yorkshire	
G-CPCD	CEA DR.221	P. J. Taylor	
G-CPDA	DH.106 Comet 4C (XS235) ★	C. Walton Ltd/Bruntingthorpe	
G-CPDW	Avions Mudry CAP.10B	Hilfa Ltd	
G-CPEU	Boeing 757-236	TUI Airways Ltd	
G-CPEV	Boeing 757-236	TUI Airways Ltd	
G-CPFC	Cessna F.152 II	Falcon Flying Services Ltd	
G-CPII	Avions Mudry CAP-231	Dep Promotions Ltd	
G-CPLG	AutoGyro Cavalon Pro	Commotion Aviation Ltd	
G-CPLH	Guimbal Cabri G2	Helicentre Aviation Ltd	
G-CPMK	DHC.1 Chipmunk 22 (WZ847)	P. A. Walley	
G-CPMS	SOCATA TB20 Trinidad	N. G. P. White	
G-CPMW	PA-32R-301 Saratoga II HP	P. M. Weaver	
G-CPOL	AS.355F1 Twin Squirrel	MW Helicopters Ltd	
G-CPPG	Alpi Pioneer 400	P. B. Godfrey	
G-CPPM	North American Harvard II	S. D. Wilch	
G-CPRR	Cessna 680 Citation Sovereign	Bookajet Aircraft Management Ltd	
G-CPSS	Cessna 208B Grand Caravan	Army Parachute Association	
G-CPTM	PA-28-151 Warrior	T. J. & C. Mackay (G-BTOE)	
G-CPXC	Avions Mudry CAP-10C	JRW Aerobatics Ltd	
G-CRAB	Skyranger 912 (2)	J. O. Williams	
G-CRAR	CZAW Sportcruiser	J. S. Kinsey	
G-CRBV	Balóny Kubíček BB26 balloon	Charter Ballooning Ltd	
G-CRES	Denney Kitfox Mk 3	C. F. O'Neill	
G-CREY	SeaRey Amphibian	K. M. & M. Gallagher & A. F. Reid	
G-CRIC	Colomban MC.15 Cri-Cri	R. S. Stoddart-Stones	

Notes	Reg	Type	Owner or Operator
	G-CRIK	Colomban MC.15 Cri-Cri	N. Huxtable
	G-CRIL	Rockwell Commander 112B	Rockwell Aviation Group
	G-CRIS	Taylor JT.1 Monoplane	C. R. Steer
	G-CRJW	Schleicher ASW-27-18	R. J. Welford
	G-CRLA	Cirrus SR20	Aero Club Heidelberg EV/Germany
	G-CRNL	Fairchild M62A-4 Cornell	CRNL Aviation Ltd (G-CEVL)
	G-CRNS	Dassault Falcon 7X	TAG Aviation (UK) Ltd
	G-CROL	Maule MXT-7-180	J. R. Pratt
	G-CROP	Cameron Z-105 balloon	W. Roussell & J. Tyrell
	G-CROW	Robinson R44	Longmoore Ltd
	G-CROY	Shaw Europa	M. T. Austin
	G-CRSR	Czech Sport Aircraft Sportcruiser	G-CRSR Flying Group
	G-CRSS	Guimbal Cabri G2	MTC Helicopters Ltd
	G-CRUI	CZAW Sportcruiser	J. Massey
	G-CRUM	Westland Scout AH.1 (XV137)	G-CRUM Group
	G-CRUZ	Cessna T.303	J. R. Tubb
	G-CRVC	Van's RV-14	C. C. Cooper
	G-CRWZ	CZAW Sportcruiser	P. B. Lowry
	G-CRZA	CZAW Sportcruiser	I. M. Mackay
	G-CRZE	Ultramagic M-105 balloon	Fresh Air Ltd
	G-CRZR	Czech Sport PS-28 Cruiser	S. J. Newman & S. P. Rawlinson (G-EGHA)
	G-CSAM	Van's RV-9A	B. G. Murray
	G-CSAV	Thruster T.600N 450	D. J. N. Brown
	G-CSAW	CZAW Sportcruiser	B. C. Fitzgerald-O'Connor
	G-CSBD	PA-28-236 Dakota	GCSBD Group Ltd (G-CSBO)
	G-CSBM	Cessna F.150M	Blackbushe Flying Club Ltd
	G-CSCS	Cessna F.172N	L. E. Winstanley & J. M. Grainger
	G-CSDJ	Avtech Jabiru UL	M. Smith
	G-CSDR	Corvus CA22	Crusader Syndicate
	G-CSEE	Balony Kubicek BB20ED balloon	Fairfax Aviation Ltd
	G-CSFC	Cessna 150L	Go Fly Oxford Aircraft Rentals Ltd
	G-CSFT	PA-23 Aztec 250D ★	Aces High Ltd (G-AYKU)
	G-CSGT	PA-28-161 Warrior II	C. P. Awdry (G-BPHB)
	G-CSHB	Czech Sport PS-28 Cruiser	P. Moodie & D. Gilham
	G-CSIX	PA-32 Cherokee Six 300	A. J. Hodge
	G-CSKW	Van's RV-7	G-CSKW Group (G-CDJW)
	G-CSMD	Agusta A.109A	Jetcom SRL/Italy
	G-CSMK	Aerotechnik EV-97 Eurostar	R. Frey
	G-CSPR	Van's RV-6A	P. J. Pengilly
	G-CSPT	Gippsaero GA8 Airvan	Downlock Ltd
	G-CSUE	Savannah VG Jabiru (5)	J. R. Stratton & R. K. Stephens
	G-CSZM	Zenair CH.601XL Zodiac	C. Budd
	G-CTAB	Bellanca 7GCAA Citabria	M. R. Keen & M. Walker (G-BFHP)
	G-CTAG	Rolladen-Schneider LS8-18	C. D. R. Tagg
	G-CTAM	Cirrus SR22	M. R. Munn
	G-CTAV	Aerotechnik EV-97 Eurostar	P. Simpson
	G-CTCB	Diamond DA42 Twin Star	L3 CTS Airline and Academy Training Ltd (G-CDTG)
	G-CTCC	Diamond DA42 Twin Star	L3 CTS Airline and Academy Training Ltd (G-OCCZ)
	G-CTCD	Diamond DA42 Twin Star	L3 CTS Airline and Academy Training Ltd
	G-CTCE	Diamond DA42 Twin Star	L3 CTS Airline and Academy Training Ltd
	G-CTCF	Diamond DA42 Twin Star	L3 CTS Airline and Academy Training Ltd
	G-CTCG	Diamond DA42 Twin Star	I. Annenskiy
	G-CTCH	Diamond DA42 Twin Star	L3 CTS Airline and Academy Training Ltd
	G-CTCL	SOCATA TB10 Tobago	Double S Group (G-BSIV)
	G-CTDH	Flight Design CT2K	A. D. Thelwall
	G-CTDW	Flight Design CTSW	H. D. Colliver
	G-CTED	Van's RV-7A	Tapeformers Ltd
	G-CTEE	Flight Design CTSW	P. J. Clegg (G-CLEG)
	G-CTEL	Cameron N-90 balloon	M. R. Noyce
	G-CTFL	Robinson R44	Heli Air Scotland Ltd (G-CLOT)
	G-CTFS	Westland SA.341C Gazelle HT2	RSE 15119 Ltd (G-OJCO/G-LEDR/G-CBSB)
	G-CTIO	SOCATA TB20 Trinidad	I. R. Hunt
	G-CTIX	VS.509 Spitfire T.IX (PT462)	Propshop Ltd
	G-CTKL	Noorduyn AT-16 Harvard IIB (54137)	M. R. Simpson
	G-CTLS	Flight Design CTLS	D. J. Haygreen
	G-CTNG	Cirrus SR20	J. Crackett
	G-CTOY	Denney Kitfox Mk 3	J. I. V. Hill

Reg	Type	Owner or Operator	Notes
G-CTRL	Robinson R22 Beta	Central Helicopters Ltd	
G-CTSL	Flight Design CT-Supralight	G. D. Alcock & J. Lander	
G-CTTS	English Electric Canberra B.Mk.2	Vulcan to the Sky Trust (G-BVWC)	
G-CTUG	PA-25 Pawnee 235	Portsmouth Naval Gliding Centre Ltd	
G-CTWO	Schempp-Hirth Standard Cirrus	R. J. Griffin	
G-CTZO	SOCATA TB20 Trinidad GT	G-CTZO Group	
G-CUBA	PA-32R-301T Turbo Saratoge	M. Atlass	
G-CUBB	PA-18 Super Cub 180	East Sussex Gliding Club Ltd	
G-CUBI	PA-18 Super Cub 125	G. T. Fisher	
G-CUBJ	PA-18 Super Cub 150 (18-5395:CDG)	R. C. W. King	
G-CUBN	PA-18 Super Cub 150	N. J. R. Minchin	
G-CUBS	Piper J-3C-65 Cub	S. M. Rolfe (G-BHPT)	
G-CUBW	WAG-Aero Acro Trainer	B. G. Plumb & A. G. Bourne	
G-CUBY	Piper J-3C-65 Cub	J. Slade (G-BTZW)	
G-CUCU	Colt 180A balloon	S. R. Seage	
G-CUDY	Enstrom 480B	Eastern Atlantic Helicopters Ltd (G-REAN)	
G-CUGC	Schleicher ASW-19B	Cambridge University Gliding Club (G-CKEX)	
G-CUMU	Schempp-Hirth Discus b	C. E. Fernando	
G-CUPP	Pitts S-2A	Avmarine Ltd	
G-CURV	Avid Speedwing	K. S. Kelso	
G-CUTE	Dyn'Aéro MCR-01	J. M. Keane	
G-CUTH	P & M Quik R	A. R. & S. Cuthbertson	
G-CVAL	Ikarus C42 FB100	K. H. Denham	
G-CVBA	Rolladen-Schneider LS6-18W	A. S. J. & S. J. Pepler	
G-CVBF	Cameron A-210 balloon	Virgin Balloon Flights Ltd	
G-CVET	Flight Design CTLS	AAA Dev LLP (G-CGVR)	
G-CVII	Dan Rihn DR.107 One Design	One Design Group	
G-CVIX	DH.110 Sea Vixen D.3 (XP924)	Naval Aviation Ltd	
G-CVLN	Autogyro Cavalon	N. A. Quintin (G-CIAT)	
G-CVMI	PA-18-150 Super Cub	C. Watson	
G-CVST	Jodel D.140E	M. P. de Gruchy Lambert	
G-CVXN	Cessna F.406 Caravan	Caledonian Airborne Systems Ltd (G-SFPA)	
G-CVZT	Schempp-Hirth Ventus 2cT	A. & M. C. Conboy	
G-CWAG	Sequoia F. 8L Falco	D. R. Austin	
G-CWAL	Raj Hamsa X'Air 133	L. R. Morris	
G-CWAY	Ikarus C42 FB100	M. Conway	
G-CWBM	Phoenix Currie Wot	G-CWBM Group (G-BTVP)	
G-CWCD	Beech B.200GT Super King Air	Clowes Estates Ltd	
G-CWDW	Cessna 182T	R. A. S. White (G-PCBC)	
G-CWEB	P & M Quik GT450	G-CWEB Syndicate	
G-CWFC	PA-38-112 Tomahawk ★	Cardiff-Wales Flying Club Ltd (G-BRTA)	
G-CWFS	Tecnam P2002-JF Sierra	S. Adey	
G-CWIC	Mainair Pegasus Quik	G-CWIC Group	
G-CWLC	Schleicher ASH-25	G-CWLC Group	
G-CWMC	P & M Quik GT450	A. R. Hughes	
G-CWMT	Dyn'Aéro MCR-01 Bambi	A. D. Heath	
G-CWOW	Balony Kubicek BB45Z balloon	Skybus Ballooning	
G-CWTD	Aeroprakt A22 Foxbat	Newtownards Microlight Group	
G-CWTT	Cessna 182T	S. B. Turner	
G-CXCX	Cameron N-90 balloon	Cathay Pacific Airways (London) Ltd	
G-CXDZ	Cassutt Speed Two	J. A. H. Chadwick	
G-CXIP	Thruster T.600N	R. J. Howells	
G-CXIV	Thatcher CX4	I. B. Melville	
G-CXLS	Cessna 560 XL Citation XLS	Aviation Beauport (G-PKRG)	
G-CXSM	Cessna 172R	S. Eustathiou (G-BXSM)	
G-CXTE	BRM Aero Bristell NG5 Speed Wing	M. Langmead	
G-CYGI	HAPI Cygnet SF-2A	B. Brown	
G-CYLL	Sequoia F.8L Falco	N. J. Langrick & A. J. Newall	
G-CYMA	GA-7 Cougar	Cyma Petroleum (UK) Ltd (G-BKOM)	
G-CYPC	Cessna 208B Grand Caravan	The Cyprus Combined Services Parachute Club	
G-CYPM	Cirrus SR22	I. C. Fisher	
G-CYRA	Kolb Twinstar Mk. 3 (Modified)	S. J. Fox (G-MYRA)	
G-CYRL	Cessna 182T	S. R. Wilson	
G-CZAC	Zenair CH.601XL	K. W. Eskins	

BRITISH CIVIL AIRCRAFT MARKINGS

Notes	Reg	Type	Owner or Operator
	G-CZAG	Sky 90-24 balloon	D. S. Tree
	G-CZAW	CZAW Sportcruiser	G. N. Smith
	G-CZCZ	Avions Mudry CAP-10B	M. Farmer
	G-CZMI	Best Off Skyranger Swift 912(1)	D. G. Baker
	G-CZNE	BN-2B-20 Islander	Skyhopper LLP (G-BWZF)
	G-CZOS	Cirrus SR20	W. R. M. Beesley
	G-CZSC	CZAW Sportcruiser	F. J. Wadia
	G-DAAN	Eurocopter EC 135P2+	Devon Air Ambulance Trading Co.Ltd
	G-DAAZ	PA-28RT-201T Turbo Arrow IV	Fifty Two Management Ltd
	G-DACA	P.57 Sea Prince T.1 (WF118) ★	P. G. Vallance Ltd/Charlwood
	G-DACE	Corben Baby Ace D	G. N. Holland (G-BTSB)
	G-DACF	Cessna 152 II	T. M. & M. L. Jones (G-BURY)
	G-DADA	Rotorsport UK MT-03	J. C. Hilton-Johnson
	G-DADD	Reality Escapade 912(2)	P. S. Balmer
	G-DADG	PA-18-150 Super Cub	F. J. Cox
	G-DADJ	Glaser-Dirks DG-200	M. A. Hunton
	G-DADZ	CZAW Sportcruiser	Meon Flying Group
	G-DAGF	EAA Acrosport II	D. A. G. Fraser
	G-DAGJ	Zenair CH.601HD Zodiac	D. A. G. Johnson
	G-DAGN	Ikarus C42 FB80	N. L. James
	G-DAIR	Luscombe 8A Silvaire	D. F. Soul (G-BURK)
	G-DAJB	Boeing 757-2T7	Icelandair/Iceland
	G-DAKA	PA-28-236 Dakota	M. M. Zienkiewicz
	G-DAKK	Douglas C-47A	R. G. T. de Man
	G-DAKM	Diamond DA40D Star	K. MacDonald
	G-DAKO	PA-28-236 Dakota	M. H. D. Smith
	G-DAMB	Sequoia F.8L Falco	S. O. Foxlee (G-OGKB)
	G-DAME	Vans RV-7	H. Manners
	G-DAMS	Best Off Skyranger Nynja 912S(1)	Dambusters Ltd
	G-DAMY	Shaw Europa	U. A. Schliessler & R. J. Kelly
	G-DANA	Jodel DR.200 (replica)	Cheshire Eagles (G-DAST)
	G-DANB	Sherwood Ranger ST	W. A. Douthwaite
	G-DAND	SOCATA TB10 Tobago	Coventry Aviators Flying Group
	G-DANP	Van's RV-7	D. T. Pangbourne
	G-DANY	Avtech Jabiru UL	D. A. Crosbie
	G-DASG	Schleicher ASW-27-18E	E. Alston
	G-DASH	Rockwell Commander 112	M. J. P. Lynch (G-BDAJ)
	G-DASS	Ikarus C.42 FB100	E. Wright
	G-DATR	Agusta-Bell 206B-3 JetRanger 3	P. J. Spinks (G-JLEE/G-JOKE/G-CSKY/G-TALY)
	G-DAVB	Aerosport Scamp	D. R. Burns
	G-DAVD	Cessna FR.172K	P. Ferguson , S. Copeland & S. Maddock
	G-DAVE	Jodel D.112	I. D. Worthington
	G-DAVM	Akrotech Europe CAP.10B	D. Moorman
	G-DAVS	AB Sportine Aviacija LAK-17AT	G-DAVS Syndicate
	G-DAWG	SA Bulldog Srs 120/121 (XX522)	S. J. Wood
	G-DAYI	Europa	A. F. Day
	G-DAYO	Beech A36 Bonanza	Exeter Aviation Ltd
	G-DAYP	Beech B.300C Super King Air	Gama Aviation (Asset 2) Ltd
	G-DAYS	Europa	R. M. F. Pereira
	G-DAYZ	Pietenpol Air Camper	T. W. J. Carnall & M. B. Blackmore
	G-DAZO	Diamond DA.20-A1 Katana	Cubair Flight Training Ltd
	G-DAZZ	Van's RV-8	Wishangar RV8
	G-DBCA	Airbus A.319-131	British Airways plc
	G-DBCB	Airbus A.319-131	British Airways plc
	G-DBCC	Airbus A.319-131	British Airways plc
	G-DBCD	Airbus A.319-131	British Airways plc
	G-DBCE	Airbus A.319-131	British Airways plc
	G-DBCF	Airbus A.319-131	British Airways plc
	G-DBCG	Airbus A.319-131	British Airways plc
	G-DBCH	Airbus A.319-131	British Airways plc
	G-DBCI	Airbus A.319-131	British Airways plc
	G-DBCJ	Airbus A.319-131	British Airways plc
	G-DBCK	Airbus A.319-131	British Airways plc
	G-DBDB	VPM M-16 Tandem Trainer	K. Kerr (G-IROW)
	G-DBEN	Schleicher ASW-15	Oscar 8 Syndicate
	G-DBIN	Medway SLA 80 Executive	J. A. Lynch
	G-DBJD	PZL-Bielsko SZD-9BIS Bocian 1D	Bertie the Bocian Glider Syndicate
	G-DBKL	VS.379 Spitfire F.Mk.XIV	P. M. Andrews

Reg	Type	Owner or Operator	Notes
G-DBND	Schleicher Ka 6CR	Lincolnshire Gliding Club Ltd	
G-DBNH	Schleicher Ka 6CR	The Bath, Wilts and North Dorset Gliding Club Ltd	
G-DBNK	Eurocopter EC.120B Colibri	Tesschoob Ltd (G-PERF)	
G-DBOD	Cessna 172S	Goodwood Road Racing Co Ltd	
G-DBOL	Schleicher Ka 6CR	G-DBOL Group	
G-DBRT	Slingsby T.51 Dart	C. W. Logue	
G-DBRU	Slingsby T.51 Dart	P. S. Whitehead	
G-DBRY	Slingsby T.51 Dart	G. B. Marshall	
G-DBSA	Slingsby T.51 Dart	K. P. Russell	
G-DBSL	Slingsby T.51 Dart	G-DBSL Group	
G-DBTJ	Schleicher Ka 6CR	I. G. Robinson	
G-DBTM	Schleicher Ka 6CR	The Nene Valley Gliding Club Ltd	
G-DBUZ	Schleicher Ka 6CR	J. J. Hartwell	
G-DBVB	Schleicher K7	Dartmoor Gliding Society Ltd	
G-DBVH	Slingsby T.51 Dart 17R	R. D. Brister	
G-DBVR	Schleicher Ka 6CR	A. L. Hoskin	
G-DBVX	Schleicher Ka 6CR	Y. Marom	
G-DBVZ	Schleicher Ka 6CR	G-DBVZ Group	
G-DBWC	Schleicher Ka 6CR	T. W. Humphrey	
G-DBWJ	Slingsby T.51 Dart 17R	M. F. Defendi	
G-DBWM	Slingsby T.51 Dart 17R	P. L. Poole	
G-DBWO	Slingsby T.51 Dart	C. R. Stacey	
G-DBWP	Slingsby T-51 Dart 17R	R. Johnson	
G-DBWS	Slingsby T-51 Dart 17R	R. D. Broome	
G-DBXG	Slingsby T.51 Dart 17R	J. M. Whelan	
G-DBXT	Schleicher Ka 6CR	C. I. Knowles	
G-DBYC	Slingsby T.51 Dart 17R	R. L. Horsnell & N. A. Jaffray	
G-DBYG	Slingsby T-51 Dart 17R	J. R. G. Furnell	
G-DBYL	Schleicher Ka 6CR	The Surrey Hills Gliding Club Ltd	
G-DBYM	Schleicher Ka 6CR	K. S. Smith	
G-DBYU	Schleicher Ka-6CR	G. B. Sutton	
G-DBYX	Schleicher Ka-6E	I. Bannister	
G-DBZF	Slingsby T.51 Dart 17R	S. Rhenius	
G-DBZJ	Slingsby T.51 Dart 17R	S. Foster	
G-DBZX	Schleicher Ka 6CR	B. Brockwell	
G-DCAE	Schleicher Ka 6E	J. R. & P. R. Larner	
G-DCAG	Schleicher Ka 6E	715 Syndicate	
G-DCAM	Eurocopter AS.355NP Ecureuil 2	Cameron Charters LLP	
G-DCAO	Schempp-Hirth SHK-1	M. G. Entwisle & M. Watt	
G-DCAS	Schleicher Ka 6E	R. F. Tindall	
G-DCAZ	Slingsby T-51 Dart 17R	D. A. Bullock & Man L. C.	
G-DCBA	Slingsby T-51 Dart 17R	K. T. Kreis	
G-DCBI	Schweizer 269C-1	P. T. Shaw	
G-DCBM	Schleicher Ka 6CR	R. J. Shepherd	
G-DCBP	SZD-24C Foka	The Gliding Heritage Centre	
G-DCBW	Schleicher ASK-13	Stratford on Avon Gliding Club Ltd	
G-DCBY	Schleicher Ka 6CR	R. G. Appleboom	
G-DCCA	Schleicher Ka 6E	R. K. Forrest	
G-DCCB	Schempp-Hirth SHK-1	CCB Syndicate	
G-DCCD	Schleicher Ka 6E	Charlie Charlie Delta Group	
G-DCCE	Schleicher ASK-13	Oxford Gliding Co.Ltd	
G-DCCG	Schleicher Ka 6E	R. J. Playle	
G-DCCJ	Schleicher Ka 6CR	S. Badby	
G-DCCL	Schleicher Ka 6E	A. Sanders	
G-DCCM	Schleicher ASK-13	The Burn Gliding Club Ltd	
G-DCCP	Schleicher ASK-13	Lima 99 Syndicate	
G-DCCR	Schleicher Ka 6E	G-DCCR Syndicate	
G-DCCT	Schleicher ASK-13	East Sussex Gliding Club Ltd	
G-DCCU	Schleicher Ka 6E	J. L. Hasker	
G-DCCV	Schleicher Ka 6E	B. J. Darton	
G-DCCW	Schleicher ASK-13	Midland Gliding Club Ltd	
G-DCCX	Schleicher ASK-13	Trent Valley Gliding Club Ltd	
G-DCCY	Schleicher ASK-13	Mendip Gliding Club Ltd	
G-DCCZ	Schleicher ASK-13	The Windrushers Gliding Club Ltd	
G-DCDA	Schleicher Ka 6E	R. E. Musselwhite & D. C. Kirby-Smith	
G-DCDB	Bell 407	A. P. Morrin	
G-DCDC	Lange E1 Antares	J. D. Williams	
G-DCDF	Schleicher Ka 6E	CDF Syndicate	
G-DCDG	FFA Diamant 18	J. Cashin & D. McCarty	

Notes	Reg	Type	Owner or Operator
	G-DCDO	Ikarus C42 FB80	M. Cheetham
	G-DCDW	Diamant 18	D. R. Chapman
	G-DCDZ	Schleicher Ka 6E	J. R. J. Minns
	G-DCEB	PZL-Bielsko SZD-9BIS Bocian 1E	G-DCEB Syndicate
	G-DCEC	Schempp-Hirth Cirrus	C. Coville & P. J. Little
	G-DCEM	Schleicher Ka 6E	S. G. Jessup
	G-DCEN	PZL-Bielsko SZD-30 Pirat	Essex & Suffolk Gliding Club Ltd
	G-DCEO	Schleicher Ka 6E	C. L. Lagden & J. C. Green
	G-DCEW	Schleicher Ka 6E	J. W. Richardson and Partners Group
	G-DCFA	Schleicher ASK-13	Dorset Gliding Club Ltd
	G-DCFF	Schleicher K 8B	Derbyshire and Lancashire Gliding Club Ltd
	G-DCFG	Schleicher ASK-13	The Nene Valley Gliding Club Ltd
	G-DCFK	Schempp-Hirth Cirrus	P. D. Whitters
	G-DCFL	Schleicher Ka 6E	D. M. Cornelius
	G-DCFS	Glasflugel Standard Libelle 201B	J. E. Hoy
	G-DCFW	Glasflugel Standard Libelle 201B	R. A. Robertson
	G-DCFX	Glasflugel Standard Libelle 201B	A. S. Burton
	G-DCFY	Glasflugel Standard Libelle 201B	C. W. Stevens
	G-DCGB	Schleicher Ka 6E	P. M. Turner & S. C. Male
	G-DCGD	Schleicher Ka 6E	Charlie Golf Delta Group
	G-DCGE	Schleicher Ka 6E	O. J. Anderson & B. Silke
	G-DCGH	Schleicher K 8B	K7 (1971) Syndicate
	G-DCGM	FFA Diamant 18	J. G. Batch
	G-DCGO	Schleicher ASK-13	Oxford Gliding Company Ltd
	G-DCGT	Schempp-Hirth SHK-1	T. Callier
	G-DCGY	Schempp-Hirth Cirrus	S. H. Fletcher
	G-DCHB	Schleicher Ka 6E	577 Syndicate
	G-DCHC	Bolkow Phoebus C	H. Nolz
	G-DCHG	PZL-Bielsko SZD-30 Pirat	Pirat Syndicate
	G-DCHJ	Bolkow Phoebus C	D. C. Austin
	G-DCHL	PZL-Bielsko SZD-30	P. M. Harrison
	G-DCHT	Schleicher ASW-15	P. G. Roberts & J. M. Verrill
	G-DCHU	Schleicher K 8B	G-DCHU Syndicate
	G-DCHW	Schleicher ASK-13	Dorset Gliding Club Ltd
	G-DCHZ	Schleicher Ka 6E	S. Sullivan & P. K. Bunnage
	G-DCII	Agusta Westland AW139	Executive Jet Charter Ltd
	G-DCJB	Bolkow Phoebus C	R. Idle
	G-DCJF	Schleicher K-8B	G. Smith
	G-DCJJ	Bolkow Phoebus C	P. N. Maddocks
	G-DCJK	Schempp-Hirth SHK-1	R. H. Short
	G-DCJM	Schleicher K-8B	Midland Gliding Club Ltd
	G-DCJN	Schempp-Hirth SHK-1	R. J. Makin
	G-DCJR	Schempp-Hirth Cirrus	C. Thirkell
	G-DCJY	Schleicher Ka 6CR	CJY Syndicate
	G-DCKD	PZL-Bielsko SZD-30	Pirat Flying Group
	G-DCKK	Cessna F.172N	KK Group
	G-DCKL	Schleicher Ka 6E	BGA1603 Owners Syndicate
	G-DCKP	Schleicher ASW-15	M. Laity
	G-DCKR	Schleicher ASK-13	Midland Gliding Club Ltd
	G-DCKV	Schleicher ASK-13	Black Mountains Gliding Club
	G-DCKY	Glasflugel Standard Libelle 201B	B. B. Hughes
	G-DCKZ	Schempp-Hirth Standard Cirrus	G. I. Bustin
	G-DCLM	Glasflugel Standard Libelle 201B	R. L. Smith
	G-DCLO	Schempp-Hirth Cirrus	Bravo Delta Group
	G-DCLP	Glasflugel Standard Libelle 201B	D. Heaton
	G-DCLT	Schleicher K7	Dartmoor Gliding Society
	G-DCLV	Glasflugel Standard Libelle 201B	T. J. McHugh
	G-DCLZ	Schleicher Ka 6E	G-DCLZ Flying Group
	G-DCMI	Mainair Pegasus Quik	F. Omaraie-Hamdanie
	G-DCMK	Schleicher ASK-13	Black Mountains Gliding Club
	G-DCMN	Schleicher K 8B	The Bristol Gliding Club Proprietary Ltd
	G-DCMO	Glasflugel Standard Libelle 201B	M. E. Wolff & L. C. Wood
	G-DCMR	Glasflugel Standard Libelle 201B	J. M. Oatridge & A. Elliott
	G-DCMS	Glasflugel Standard Libelle 201B	Libelle 602 Syndicate
	G-DCMV	Glasflugel Standard Libelle 201B	M. Izdorczak
	G-DCMW	Glasflugel Standard Libelle 201B	D. Williams
	G-DCNC	Schempp-Hirth Standard Cirrus	Cirrus 273 Syndicate
	G-DCNE	Glasflugel Standard Libelle 201B	C. J. Davison
	G-DCNG	Glasflugel Standard Libelle 201B	M. C. J. Gardner
	G-DCNJ	Glasflugel Standard Libelle 201B	P. I. Jameson
	G-DCNM	PZL-Bielsko SZD-9bis Bocian 1E	Bocian Syndicate

Reg	Type	Owner or Operator	Notes
G-DCNP	Glasflugel Standard Libelle 201B	I. G. Carrick & D. J. Miles	
G-DCNS	Slingsby T.59A Kestrel	J. R. Greenwell	
G-DCNW	Slingsby T.59F Kestrel	S. R. Watson	
G-DCNX	Slingsby T.59F Kestrel	M. Boxall	
G-DCOC	PZL-Bielsko SZD-30 Pirat	The Surrey Hills Gliding Club Ltd	
G-DCOE	Van's RV-6	R. E. Welch	
G-DCOI	Agusta Westland AW.139	Executive Jet Charter Ltd	
G-DCOJ	Slingsby T.59A Kestrel	T. W. Treadaway	
G-DCOR	Schempp-Hirth Standard Cirrus	H. R. Ford	
G-DCOY	Schempp-Hirth Standard Cirrus	RPG	
G-DCPB	Eurocopter MBB-BK 117C-1	Police & Crime Commissioner for West Yorkshire	
G-DCPD	Schleicher ASW-17	A. J. Hewitt	
G-DCPF	Glasflugel Standard Libelle 201B	P. J. A. Wickes	
G-DCPJ	Schleicher KA6E	The K6 Group	
G-DCPM	Glasflugel Standard Libelle 201B	P. E. Jessop & A. M. Carpenter	
G-DCPU	Schempp-Hirth Standard Cirrus	P. J. Ketelaar	
G-DCRB	Glasflugel Standard Libelle 201B	A. I. Mawer	
G-DCRH	Schempp-Hirth Standard Cirrus	P. E. Thelwall	
G-DCRN	Schempp-Hirth Standard Cirrus	N. McLaughlin	
G-DCRO	Glasflugel Standard Libelle 201B	G-DCRO Group	
G-DCRS	Glasflugel standard Libelle 201B	J. R. Hiley & P. S. Isaacs	
G-DCRV	Glasflugel Standard Libelle 201B	G. G. Dale	
G-DCRW	Glasflugel Standard Libelle 201B	T. Fletcher	
G-DCSB	Slingsby T.59F Kestrel	W. Fischer	
G-DCSD	Slingsby T.59D Kestrel	L. P. Davidson	
G-DCSF	Slingsby T.59F Kestrel 19	R. Birch	
G-DCSI	Robinson R44 II	Cotswold Ventures Ltd (G-TGDL)	
G-DCSJ	Glasflugel Standard Libelle 201B	P. J. Gill	
G-DCSK	Slingsby T.59D Kestrel	Kestrel CSK Group	
G-DCSN	Pilatus B4-PC11AF	J. S. Firth	
G-DCSP	Pilatus B4-PC11	G-DCSP Group	
G-DCSR	Glasflugel Standard Libelle 201B	Glasgow and West of Scotland Gliding Club	
G-DCTB	Schempp-Hirth Standard Cirrus	S. E. McCurdy	
G-DCTJ	Slingsby T.59D Kestrel	J. Young & R. J. Aylesbury	
G-DCTL	Slingsby T.59D Kestrel	E. S. E. Hibbard	
G-DCTM	Slingsby T.59D Kestrel	C. Swain	
G-DCTO	Slingsby T.59D Kestrel	G-DCTO Gliding Syndicate	
G-DCTP	Slingsby T.59D Kestrel	D. C. Austin	
G-DCTR	Slingsby T.59D Kestrel	K. M. Charlton	
G-DCTT	Schempp-Hirth Standard Cirrus	E. Sparrow	
G-DCTU	Glasflugel Standard Libelle 201B	P. M. Davies & R. Cobb	
G-DCTV	PZL-Bielsko SZD-30	Black Mountains Gliding Club	
G-DCTX	PZL-Bielsko SZD-30	J. R. Sniadowski	
G-DCUB	Pilatus B4-PC11	G-DCUB Group	
G-DCUC	Pilatus B4-PC11	G. M. Cumner	
G-DCUD	Yorkshire Sailplanes YS53 Sovereign	T. J. Wilkinson	
G-DCUJ	Glasflugel Standard Libelle 201B	J. Poley & D. T. Collins	
G-DCUS	Schempp-Hirth Cirrus VTC	R. C. Graham	
G-DCUT	Pilatus B4 PC11AF	A. L. Walker	
G-DCVE	Schempp-Hirth Cirrus VTC	S. Hardy	
G-DCVG	Pilatus B4-PC11AF	M. Kempf	
G-DCVK	Pilatus B4-PC11AF	J. P. Marriott	
G-DCVL	Glasflugel Standard Libelle 201B	J. Williams	
G-DCVP	PZL-Bielsko SZD-9bis Bocian 1E	Portmoak CVP Group	
G-DCVR	PZL-Bielsko SZD-30 Pirat	M. T. Pitorak	
G-DCVV	Pilatus B4-PC11AF	Syndicate CVV	
G-DCVW	Slingsby T.59D Kestrel	J. J. Green & J. A. Tonkin	
G-DCVY	Slingsby T.59D Kestrel	N. Dickenson	
G-DCWB	Slingsby T.59D Kestrel	Kestrel 677 Syndicate	
G-DCWD	Slingsby T.59D Kestrel	G. J. Palmer	
G-DCWE	Glasflugel Standard Libelle 201B	L. J. Maksymowicz	
G-DCWF	Slingsby T.59D Kestrel	P. F. Nicholson	
G-DCWG	Glasflugel Standard Libelle 201B	Libelle 322 Group	
G-DCWH	Schleicher ASK-13	York Gliding Centre Ltd	
G-DCWJ	Schleicher K7	M. P. Webb	
G-DCWP	PZL-Bielsko SZD-36A Cobra 15	P. Kalcher	
G-DCWR	Schempp-Hirth Cirrus VTC	CWR Group	
G-DCWS	Schempp-Hirth Cirrus VTC	Cirrus G-DCWS Syndicate	
G-DCWT	Glasflugel Standard Libelle 201B	A. A. Tills	
G-DCWX	Glasflugel Standard Libelle	A. Coatsworth	

Notes	Reg	Type	Owner or Operator
	G-DCWY	Glasflugel Standard Libelle 201B	S. J. Taylor
	G-DCWZ	Glasflugel Standard Libelle 201B	Syndicate Maul/Rakowski/Germany
	G-DCXH	PZL-Bielsko SZD-36A Cobra 15	J. Dudzik
	G-DCXI	Slingsby T.61F Venture T.2	611 Vintage Flight (G-BUDB)
	G-DCXK	Glasflugel Standard Libelle 201B	J. C. Richards
	G-DCXM	Slingsby T.59D Kestrel	W. H. Dyozinski
	G-DCXV	Yorkshire Sailplanes YS-53 Sovereign	The Gliding Heritage Centre
	G-DCYA	Pilatus B4 PC-11	B4-072 Group
	G-DCYD	PZL-Bielsko SZD-30 Pirat	G-DCYD Group
	G-DCYG	Glasflugel H201B Standard Libelle	R. J. Barsby & G. Wheldon
	G-DCYM	Schempp-Hirth Standard Cirrus	K. M. Fisher
	G-DCYO	Schempp-Hirth Standard Cirrus	P. Summers & M. J. Layton
	G-DCYP	Schempp-Hirth Standard Cirrus	A. F. Scott
	G-DCYT	Schempp-Hirth Standard Cirrus	W. A. L. Leader
	G-DCYZ	Schleicher K 8B	Oxford Gliding Co.Ltd
	G-DCZD	Pilatus B4 PC-11AF	T. Dale
	G-DCZE	PZL-Bielsko SZD-30	L. A. Bean
	G-DCZG	PZL-Bielsko SZD-30	J. T. Pajdak
	G-DCZJ	PZL-Bielsko SZD-30	Lincolnshire Gliding Club Ltd
	G-DCZN	Schleicher ASW-15B	J. R. Walters
	G-DCZR	Slingsby T.59D Kestrel	R. P. Brisbourne
	G-DCZU	Slingsby T.59D Kestrel	Kestrel 826 Syndicate
	G-DDAC	PZL-Bielsko SZD-36A	R. J. A. Colenso
	G-DDAJ	Shempp-Hirth Nimbus 2	North Devon Gliding Club Nimbus Group
	G-DDAN	PZL-Bielsko SZD-30	J. M. A. Shannon
	G-DDAP	SZL-Bielsko SZD-30	Delta Alpha Papa Group
	G-DDAS	Schempp-Hirth Standard Cirrus	G. Goodenough
	G-DDAY	PA-28R-201T Turbo Arrow III	G-DDAY Group (G-BPDO)
	G-DDBB	Slingsby T.51 Dart 17R	A. L. R. Roth
	G-DDBC	Pilatus B4-PC11	J. H. France & G. R. Harris
	G-DDBD	Shaw Europa XS	B. Davies
	G-DDBG	ICA IS-29D	P. S. Whitehead
	G-DDBK	Slingsby T.59D Kestrel	523 Syndicate
	G-DDBN	Slingsby T.59D Kestrel	G. K. Hutchinsonl
	G-DDBP	Glasflugel Club Libelle 205	K. Fuks
	G-DDBS	Slingsby T.59D Kestrel	K. Millar
	G-DDBV	PZL-Bielsko SZD-30	The Surrey Hills Gliding Club Ltd
	G-DDCA	PZL-Bielsko SZD-36A Cobra 15	J. Young & J. R. Aylesbury
	G-DDCC	Glasflugel Standard Libelle 201B	G-DDCC Syndicate
	G-DDCW	Schleicher Ka 6CR	B. W. Rendall
	G-DDDA	Schempp-Hirth Standard Cirrus	G-DDDA Group
	G-DDDB	Schleicher ASK-13	Shenington Gliding Club
	G-DDDE	PZL-Bielsko SZD-38A Jantar 1	Jantar One Syndicate
	G-DDDK	PZL-Bielsko SZD-30 Pirat	Buckminster Gliding Club Ltd
	G-DDDL	Schleicher K8B	Lakes Gliding Club Ltd
	G-DDDM	Schempp-Hirth Cirrus	DDM Syndicate
	G-DDDR	Schempp-Hirth Standard Cirrus	J. D. Ewence
	G-DDDY	P & M Quik GT450	J. W. Dodson
	G-DDEB	Slingsby T.59D Kestrel	J. L. Smoker
	G-DDEG	ICA IS-28B2	P. S. Whitehead
	G-DDEO	Glasflugel H205 Club Libelle	716 Group
	G-DDEP	Schleicher Ka-6CR	G. D. & L. A. Ferguson
	G-DDEV	Schleicher Ka-6CR	DEV Group
	G-DDEW	ICA-Brasov IS-29D	P. S. Whitehead
	G-DDFC	Schempp-Hirth Standard Cirrus	C. E. Fisher & I. Helme
	G-DDFE	Molino PIK-20B	M. A. Roff-Jarrett
	G-DDFK	Molino PIK-20B	B. H. & M. J. Fairclough
	G-DDFL	PZL-Bielsko SZD-38A Jantar 1	G-DDFL Group
	G-DDFR	Grob G.102 Astir CS	The Windrushers Gliding Club Ltd
	G-DDFU	PZL-Bielsko SZD-38A Jantar 1	Jantar 38A Group
	G-DDGA	Schleicher K-8B	The Welland Gliding Club Ltd
	G-DDGE	Schempp-Hirth Standard Cirrus	T. P. Brown
	G-DDGG	Schleicher Ka 6E	N. F. Holmes & F. D. Platt
	G-DDGJ	Champion 8KCAB	Western Air (Thruxton) Ltd
	G-DDGK	Schleicher Ka 6CR	R. G. Olsen
	G-DDGV	Breguet 905S Fauvette	J. N. Lee
	G-DDGX	Schempp-Hirth Standard Cirrus 75	USKGC Group
	G-DDGY	Schempp-Hirth Nimbus 2	Nimbus 195 Group
	G-DDHA	Schleicher K 8B	Shalborne Soaring Society Ltd
	G-DDHE	Slingsby T.53B	Aviation Preservation Society of Scotland

Reg	Type	Owner or Operator	Notes
G-DDHG	Schleicher Ka 6CR	M. W. Roberts	
G-DDHH	Eiriavion PIK-20B	D. M. Steed	
G-DDHJ	Glaser-Dirks DG-100	G. E. McLaughlin	
G-DDHK	Glaser-Dirks DG-100	K. Dillon & R. Allcoat	
G-DDHL	Glaser-Dirks DG-100	DHL Syndicate	
G-DDHT	Schleicher Ka 6E	I. Deans & N. Worrell	
G-DDHW	Schempp-Hirth Nimbus 2	M. J. Carruthers & D. Thompson	
G-DDHX	Schempp-Hirth Standard Cirrus B	J. Franke	
G-DDHZ	PZL-Bielsko SZD-30	Peterborough and Spalding Gliding Club	
G-DDJB	Schleicher K-8B	Portsmouth Naval Gliding Centre	
G-DDJD	Grob G.102 Astir CS	G-DDJD Group	
G-DDJF	Schempp-Hirth Duo Discus T	R. J. H. Fack	
G-DDJK	Schleicher ASK-18	Dorset Gliding Club Ltd	
G-DDJN	Eiriavion PIK-20B	M. Ireland & S. Lambourne	
G-DDJR	Schleicher Ka 6CR	K6CR Syndicate	
G-DDJX	Grob G.102 Astir CS	Trent Valley Gliding Club Ltd	
G-DDKC	Schleicher K 8B	Yorkshire Gliding Club (Proprietary) Ltd	
G-DDKD	Glasflugel Hornet	Hornet Syndicate	
G-DDKE	Schleicher ASK-13	The South Wales Gliding Club Ltd	
G-DDKG	Schleicher Ka 6CR	C. B. Woolf	
G-DDKL	Schempp-Hirth Nimbus 2	G. J. Croll	
G-DDKM	Glasflugel Hornet	R. S. Lee	
G-DDKR	Grob G.102 Astir CS	Oxford Gliding Co.Ltd	
G-DDKS	Grob G.102 Astir CS	Oxford Gliding Co.Ltd	
G-DDKU	Grob G.102 Astir CS	Delta Kilo Uniform Syndicate	
G-DDKV	Grob G.102 Astir CS	T. J. Ireson	
G-DDKW	Grob G.102 Astir CS	M. A. Sandwith	
G-DDKX	Grob G.102 Astir CS	The South Wales Gliding Club Ltd	
G-DDLA	Pilatus B4 PC-11	P. R. Seddon	
G-DDLB	Schleicher ASK-18	B. A. Fairston & A. Stotter	
G-DDLC	Schleicher ASK-13	Lasham Gliding Society Ltd	
G-DDLE	Schleicher Ka 6E	P. J. Abbott & J. Banks	
G-DDLG	Schempp-Hirth Standard Cirrus 75	S. Naylor	
G-DDLH	Grob G.102 Astir CS77	M. D. & M. E. Saunders	
G-DDLJ	Eiriavion PIK-20B	G. K. Stanford	
G-DDLM	Grob G.102 Astir CS	M. Newby & W. H. Ollis	
G-DDLP	Schleicher Ka 6CR	J. R. Crosse	
G-DDLS	Schleicher K 8B	North Devon Gliding Club	
G-DDLY	Eiriavion PIK-20D	M. Conrad	
G-DDMB	Schleicher K 8B	Crown Service Gliding Club	
G-DDMG	Schleicher K 8B	Dorset Gliding Club Ltd	
G-DDMH	Grob G.102 Astir CS	C. K. Lewis	
G-DDMK	Schempp-Hirth SHK-1	D. Breeze	
G-DDML	Schleicher K-7	Dumfries and District Gliding Club	
G-DDMM	Schempp-Hirth Nimbus 2	T. Linee	
G-DDMN	Glasflugel Mosquito	DMN Group	
G-DDMO	Schleicher Ka 6E	R. C. Sharman	
G-DDMP	Grob G.102 Astir CS	Kingswood Syndicate	
G-DDMR	Grob G.102 Astir CS	Mendip Gliding Club Ltd	
G-DDMS	Glasflugel Standard Libelle 201B	G-DDMS Group	
G-DDMU	Eiriavion PIK-20D	P. Goodchild	
G-DDMV	NA T-6G Texan (493209)	K. M. Perkins	
G-DDMX	Schleicher ASK-13	Dartmoor Gliding Society Ltd	
G-DDNC	Grob G.102 Astir CS	Norfolk Gliding Club Ltd	
G-DDND	Pilatus B4-PC11AF	DND Group	
G-DDNE	Grob G.102 Astir CS77	621 Astir Syndicate	
G-DDNG	Schempp-Hirth Nimbus 2	Nimbus 265 Syndicate	
G-DDNK	Grob G.102 Astir CS	G-DDNK Group	
G-DDNU	PZL-Bielsko SZD-42-1 Jantar 2	C. D. Rowland & D. Chalmers-Brown	
G-DDNV	Schleicher ASK-13	Channel Gliding Club	
G-DDNW	Schleicher Ks 6CR	G-DDNW Group	
G-DDNX	Schleicher Ka 6CR	Black Mountains Gliding Club	
G-DDNZ	Schleicher K 8B	Southampton University Gliding Club	
G-DDOA	Schleicher ASK-13	Essex and Suffolk Gliding Club Ltd	
G-DDOC	Schleicher Ka 6CR	W. St. G. V. Stoney	
G-DDOE	Grob G.102 Astir CS77	Heron Gliding Club	
G-DDOF	Schleicher Ka 6CR	A. J. Watson	
G-DDOG	SA Bulldog Srs 120/121 (XX524:04)	Deltaero Ltd	
G-DDOK	Schleicher Ka 6E	R. S. Hawley & S. Y. Duxbury	
G-DDOU	Eiriavion PIK-20D	J. M. A. Shannon	
G-DDOX	Schleicher K-7	The Nene Valley Gliding Club Ltd	

Notes	Reg	Type	Owner or Operator
	G-DDPA	Schleicher ASK-18	M. J. Huddart
	G-DDPH	Schempp-Hirth Mini-Nimbus B	J. W. Murdoch
	G-DDPJ	Grob G.102 Astir CS77	DPJ Syndicate
	G-DDPK	Glasflugel H303A Mosquito	H. Nolz
	G-DDPL	Eiriavion PIK-20D	437 Syndicate
	G-DDPO	Grob G.102 Astir CS77	Yorkshire Gliding Club (Proprietary) Ltd
	G-DDPY	Grob G.102 Astir CS77	C. A. Bailey
	G-DDRA	Schleicher Ka 6CR	K6CR Group Shobdon
	G-DDRB	Glaser-Dirks DG-100	DRB Syndicate
	G-DDRD	Schleicher Ka 6CR	Essex & Suffolk Gliding Club Ltd
	G-DDRE	Schleicher Ka 6CR	DRE Syndicate
	G-DDRJ	Schleicher ASK-13	Lasham Gliding Society Ltd
	G-DDRL	Scheibe SF26A	T. A. Lipinski
	G-DDRM	Schleicher K 7	K7 DRM Syndicate
	G-DDRN	Glasflugel H303A Mosquito	K. J. King
	G-DDRO	Grob G.103 Twin Astir	Twin Astir 258 Syndicate
	G-DDRP	Pilatus B4-PC11	DRP Syndicate
	G-DDRT	Eiriavion PIK-20D	P. J. Seymour
	G-DDRV	Schleicher K 8B	DRV Syndicate
	G-DDRW	Grob G.102 Astir CS	The Royal Air Force Gliding & Soaring AssociationI
	G-DDRY	Schleicher Ka 6CR	M. K. Bradford
	G-DDRZ	Schleicher K-8B	East Sussex Gliding Club Ltd
	G-DDSB	Schleicher Ka-6E	G. B. Griffiths
	G-DDSF	Schleicher K-8B	University of Edinburgh Sports Union
	G-DDSG	Schleicher Ka 6CR	S. McGuirk
	G-DDSH	Grob G.102 Astir CS77	Astir 648 Syndicate
	G-DDSJ	Grob G.103 Twin Astir II	Herefordshire Gliding Club Ltd
	G-DDSL	Grob G.103 Twin Astir	DSL Group
	G-DDSP	Schempp-Hirth Mini Nimbus B	DDSP Group
	G-DDST	Schleicher ASW-20L	A. R. Winton
	G-DDSU	Grob G.102 Astir CS77	Bowland Forest Gliding Club Ltd
	G-DDSV	Pilatus B4-PC11AF	G. M. Drinkell
	G-DDSX	Schleicher ASW-19B	G-DDSX Group
	G-DDSY	Schleicher Ka-6CR	W. S. H. Taylor
	G-DDTA	Glaser-Dirks DG-200	M. Rose
	G-DDTC	Schempp-Hirth Janus B	Darlton Gliding Club Ltd
	G-DDTE	Schleicher ASW-19B	G. R. Purcell
	G-DDTG	Schempp-Hirth SHK-1	M. W. Roberts
	G-DDTK	Glasflugel Mosquito B	P. France
	G-DDTM	Glaser-Dirks DG-200	M. C. Bailey
	G-DDTN	Schleicher K 8B	C. G. & G. N. Thomas
	G-DDTP	Schleicher ASW-20	T. S. & S. M. Hills
	G-DDTS	CARMAM M-100S	J. P. Dyne
	G-DDTU	Schempp-Hirth Nimbus 2B	J. SA. Castle
	G-DDTV	Glasflugel Mosquito B	D. R. Allan
	G-DDTW	PZL-Bielsko SZD-30 Pirat	NDGC Pirat Syndicate
	G-DDTX	Glasflugel Mosquito B	P. T. S. Nash
	G-DDTY	Glasflugel H303 Mosquito B	W. H. L. Bullimore
	G-DDUB	Glasflugel H303 Mosquito B	Mosquito G-DDUB Syndicate
	G-DDUE	Schleicher ASK-13	Norfolk Gliding Club Ltd
	G-DDUF	Schleicher K 8B	M. Staljan
	G-DDUH	Scheibe L-Spatz 55	R. J. Aylesbury & J. Young
	G-DDUK	Schleicher K-8B	The Bristol Gliding Club Propietary Ltd
	G-DDUL	Grob G.102 Astir CS77	M. G. Dodd & K. Nattrass
	G-DDUR	Schleicher Ka 6CR	B. N. Bromley
	G-DDUS	Schleicher Ka 6E	D.E. Findon
	G-DDUT	Schleicher ASW-20	M. E. Doig & E. T. J. Murphy
	G-DDUY	Glaser-Dirks DG-100	R. L. & K. P. McLean
	G-DDVB	Schleicher ASK-13	Essex and Suffolk Gliding Club Ltd
	G-DDVC	Schleicher ASK-13	Staffordshire Gliding Club Ltd
	G-DDVG	Schleicher Ka-6CR	G-DDVG Banana Group
	G-DDVH	Schleicher Ka 6E	M. A. K. Cropper
	G-DDVK	PZL-Bielsko SZD-48 Jantar Standard 2	R. Goodchild
	G-DDVL	Schleicher ASW-19	J. Gavin, P. K. Newman & G. Prophet
	G-DDVM	Glasflugel H205 Club Libelle	M. A. Field
	G-DDVN	Eiriavion PIL-20D-78	P. A. & T. P. Bassett
	G-DDVP	Schleicher ASW-19	VP Syndicate
	G-DDVS	Schempp-Hirth Standard Cirrus	J. C. & T. J. Milner
	G-DDVV	Schleicher ASW-20L	D. M. Hurst & C. J. Bishop
	G-DDVX	Schleicher ASK-13	Shenington Gliding Club

Reg	Type	Owner or Operator	Notes
G-DDVY	Schempp-Hirth Cirrus	M. G. Ashton & G. Martin	
G-DDVZ	Glasflugel H303 Mosquito B	R. M. Spreckley	
G-DDWB	Glasflugel H303 Mosquito B	D. T. Edwards	
G-DDWC	Schleicher Ka 6E	C. Hitchings	
G-DDWJ	Glaser-Dirks DG-200	A. P. Kamp & P. R. Desmond	
G-DDWL	Glasflugel Mosquito B	H. A. Stanford	
G-DDWN	Schleicher K7 Rhonadler	L. R. & J. E. Merritt	
G-DDWP	Glasflugel Mosquito B	I. H. Murdoch	
G-DDWR	Glasflugel Mosquito B	C. D. Lovell	
G-DDWS	Eiriavion PIK-20D	D. G. Slocombe	
G-DDWT	Slingsby T.65C Vega	A. P. Grimley	
G-DDWU	Grob G.102 Astir CS	Astir G-DDWU Syndicate	
G-DDWW	Slingsby T.65A Vega	M. Finnie & B. Grice	
G-DDWZ	Schleicher ASW-19B	P. Woodcock	
G-DDXB	Schleicher ASW-20	81 Syndicate	
G-DDXD	Slingsby T.65A Vega	G-DDXD Flying Group	
G-DDXE	Slingsby T.65A Vega	H. K. Rattray	
G-DDXF	Slingsby T.65A Vega	B. A. Walker	
G-DDXG	Slingsby T.65A Vega	P. J. Smith	
G-DDXH	Schleicher Ka 6E	D. E. Findon	
G-DDXJ	Grob G.102 Astir CS77	DXJ Syndicate	
G-DDXK	Centrair ASW-20F	E. & A. Townsend	
G-DDXL	Schempp-Hirth Standard Cirrus	A. C. Bridges	
G-DDXN	Glaser-Dirks DG-200	J. A. Johnston	
G-DDXT	Schempp-Hirth Mini-Nimbus C	M. J. Love	
G-DDXW	Glasflugel Mosquito B	B. L. C. Gordon	
G-DDXX	Schleicher ASW-19B	Cotswold Gliding Club	
G-DDYC	Schleicher Ka 6CR	F. J. Bradley	
G-DDYE	Schleicher ASW-20L	P. J. L. Howell	
G-DDYF	Grob G.102 Astir CS77	York Gliding Centre Ltd	
G-DDYH	Glaser-Dirks DG-200	P. Johnson	
G-DDYJ	Schleicher Ka 6CR	Upward Bound Trust	
G-DDYL	CARMAM JP 15-36AR	J. M. Caldwell	
G-DDYR	Schleicher K7	University of the West of England Gliding Club	
G-DDYU	Schempp-Hirth Nimbus -2C	C. B. Shepperd	
G-DDZA	Slingsby T.65A Vega	A. W. Roberts	
G-DDZB	Slingsby T.65A Vega	A. L. Maitland	
G-DDZF	Schempp-Hirth Standard Cirrus	G-DDZF Group	
G-DDZM	Slingsby T.65A Vega	A. Mattano	
G-DDZN	Slingsby T.65A Vega	D. A. White	
G-DDZP	Slingsby T.65A Vega	M. T. Crews	
G-DDZR	IS-28B2	Lakes Gliding Club Ltd	
G-DDZT	Eiriavion PIK-20D	PIK-20D 106 Group	
G-DDZU	Grob G.102 Astir CS	P. Clarke	
G-DDZV	Scheibe SF-27A	N. Newham	
G-DDZW	Schleicher Ka 6CR	S. W. Naylor	
G-DDZY	Schleicher ASW-19B	M. C. Fairman	
G-DEAE	Schleicher ASW-20L	R. Burghall	
G-DEAF	Grob G.102 Astir CS77	The Borders (Milfield) Gliding Club Ltd	
G-DEAG	Slingsby T.65A Vega	P. Hadfield	
G-DEAH	Schleicher Ka 6E	R. J. King	
G-DEAJ	Schempp-Hirth Nimbus 2	A. O'Keefe	
G-DEAK	Glasflugel H303 Mosquito B	T. A. L. Barnes	
G-DEAM	Schempp-Hirth Nimbus 2B	Alpha Mike Syndicate	
G-DEAN	Solar Wings Pegasus XL-Q	IM. G. J. Bridges (G-MVJV)	
G-DEAR	Eiriavion PIK-20D	G-DEAR Group	
G-DEAT	Eiriavion PIK-20D	D. J. Knights	
G-DEAU	Schleicher K7	The Welland Gliding Club Ltd	
G-DEAV	Schempp-Hirth Mini-Nimbus C	G. D. H. Crawford	
G-DEAW	Grob G.102 Astir CS77	EAW Group	
G-DEBT	Pioneer 300	N. J. T. Tonks & A. J. Lloyd	
G-DEBX	Schleicher ASW-20	S. M. Economou & R. M Harris	
G-DECC	Schleicher Ka 6CR	Redwing	
G-DECJ	Slingsby T.65A Vega	J. E. B. Hart	
G-DECL	Slingsby T.65A Vega	J. M. Sherman	
G-DECM	Slingsby T.65A Vega	F. Wilson	
G-DECO	Dyn'Aéro MCR-01 Club	A. P. Wheelwright & A. W. Bishop	
G-DECP	Rolladen-Schneider LS3-17	LS3-17 ECP Syndicate	
G-DECR	P & M Quik R	D. J. Lawrence	
G-DECS	Glasflugel H303 Mosquito B	G. Richardson	

Notes	Reg	Type	Owner or Operator
	G-DECW	Schleicher ASK-21	Norfolk Gliding Club Ltd
	G-DECZ	Schleicher ASK-21	Booker Gliding Club Ltd
	G-DEDG	Schleicher Ka 6CR	S. J. Wood
	G-DEDH	Glasflugel H303 Mosquito B	B. L. Liddiard
	G-DEDJ	Glasflugel H303 Mosquito B	D. M. Ward
	G-DEDK	Schleicher K7 Rhonadler	Cyprus Gliding Group
	G-DEDM	Glaser-Dirks DG-200	D. Watson
	G-DEDN	Glaser-Dirks DG-100G	DG 280 Syndicate
	G-DEDU	Schleicher ASK-13	Channel Gliding Club
	G-DEDX	Slingsby T.65D Vega	G. Kirkham
	G-DEDY	Slingsby T.65D Vega	G. Spelman & J. Shaw
	G-DEDZ	Slingsby T.65C Vega	R. C. R. Copley
	G-DEEA	Slingsby T.65C Vega	S. J. Harrison
	G-DEEC	Schleicher ASW-20L	D. Beams
	G-DEED	Schleicher K-8B	The Windrushers Gliding Club Ltd
	G-DEEF	Rolladen-Schneider LS3-17	Echo Echo Foxtrot Group
	G-DEEG	Slingsby T.65C Vega	Vega Syndicate
	G-DEEO	Schleicher ASW-19	K. Kiely
	G-DEEJ	Schleicher ASW-20L	EEJ Syndicate
	G-DEEK	Schempp-Hirth Nimbus 2C	G. D. Palmer
	G-DEEM	Schleicher K-8	The South Wales Gliding Club Ltd
	G-DEEN	Schempp-Hirth Standard Cirrus 75	G-DEEN Flying Group
	G-DEEO	Grob G.102 Club Astir II	G-DEEO Group
	G-DEEP	Wassmer WA.26P Squale	Wassmer G-DEEP Group
	G-DEES	Rolladen-Schneider LS3-17	J. B. Illidge
	G-DEEW	Schleicher Ka 6CR	S. M. Dodds
	G-DEEX	Rolladen-Schneider LS3-17	G-DEEX Group
	G-DEEZ	Denney Kitfox Mk.3	J. D. & D. Cheesman
	G-DEFA	Schleicher ASW-20L	Eight Eighties Syndicate
	G-DEFB	Schempp-Hirth Nimbus 2C	G. D. Palmer
	G-DEFE	Centrair ASW-20F	W. A. Horne & D. A. Mackenzie
	G-DEFF	Schempp-Hirth Nimbus 2C	J. W. L. Clarke and P. J. D. Smith
	G-DEFS	Rolladen-Schneider LS3	A. Twigg
	G-DEFV	Schleicher ASW-20	A. R. McKillen
	G-DEFW	Slingsby T.65C Sport Vega	H. Yildiz
	G-DEFZ	Rolladen-Schneider LS3-a	EFZ Syndicate
	G-DEGE	Rolladen-Schneider LS3-a	EGE Glider Syndicate
	G-DEGF	Slingsby T.65D Vega	Shalbourne Soaring Society Ltd
	G-DEGH	Slingsby T.65C Vega	P. Thomas
	G-DEGJ	Slingsby T.65C Vega	Sport Vega Syndicate
	G-DEGK	Schempp-Hirth Standard Cirrus	D. A. Parker
	G-DEGN	Grob G.103 Twin Astir II	Staffordshire Gliding Club Ltd
	G-DEGP	Schleicher ASW-20L	S. Pozerskis
	G-DEGS	Schempp-Hirth Nimbus 2CS	A. Klapa
	G-DEGT	Slingsby T.65D Vega	G-DEGT Group
	G-DEGW	Schempp-Hirth Mini-Nimbus C	I. F. Barnes and Partners
	G-DEGX	Slingsby T.65C Vega	Haddenham Vega Syndicate
	G-DEGZ	Schleicher ASK-21	Black Mountains Gliding Club
	G-DEHC	Eichelsdorfer SB-5B	J. A. Castle
	G-DEHG	Slingsby T.65C Vega	S. R. Hopkins
	G-DEHH	Schempp-Hirth Ventus a	L. B. Roberts
	G-DEHK	Rolladen-Schneider LS4	S. Eyles
	G-DEHM	Schleicher Ka 6E	J. B. Symonds
	G-DEHO	Schleicher ASK-21	Lasham Gliding Society Ltd
	G-DEHP	Schempp-Hirth Nimbus 2C	D. J. King
	G-DEHT	Schempp-Hirth Nimbus 2C	M. V. Boydon
	G-DEHU	Glasflugel 304	F. Townsend
	G-DEHY	Slingsby T.65D Vega	C. J. A. Rosales
	G-DEHZ	Schleicher ASW-20L	G-DEHZ Syndicate
	G-DEJA	ICA IS-28B2	M. H. Simms
	G-DEJB	Slingsby T.65C Vega	D. Tait & I. G. Walker
	G-DEJC	Slingsby T-65C Vega	I. Powis
	G-DEJD	Slingsby T.65D Vega	R. L. & K. P. McLean
	G-DEJE	Slingsby T-65C Vega	Crown Service Gliding Club
	G-DEJF	Schleicher K 8B	Cotswold Gliding Club
	G-DEJH	Eichelsdorfer SB-5E	Edensoaring Ltd
	G-DEJR	Schleicher ASW-19B	J. C. M. Docherty
	G-DEJY	PZL-Bielsko SZD-9bis Bocian 1D	G-DEJY Group
	G-DEKA	Cameron Z-90 balloon	P. G. Bogliaccino
	G-DEKC	Schleicher Ka 6E	M. N. K. Willcox
	G-DEKF	Grob G.102 Club Astir III	The Bristol Gliding Club Proprietary Ltd

Reg	Type	Owner or Operator	Notes
G-DEKG	Schleicher ASK-21	Army Gliding Association	
G-DEKJ	Schempp-Hirth Ventus b	I. J. Metcalfe	
G-DEKS	Scheibe SF27A Zugvogel V	T. Emms	
G-DEKU	Schleicher ASW-20L	A. J. Gillson	
G-DEKV	Rolladen-Schneider LS4	S. L. Helstrip	
G-DEKW	Schempp-Hirth Nimbus 2B	V. Luscombe-Mahoney	
G-DEKX	Schleicher Ka 6E	D. S. Downton	
G-DELA	Schleicher ASW-19B	S. G. Jones	
G-DELB	Robinson R-22 Beta ★	Aero Venture	
G-DELD	Slingsby T65C Vega	ELD Syndicate	
G-DELF	Aero L-29A Delfin	Komo-Sky KFT/Hungary	
G-DELG	Schempp-Hirth Ventus b/16.6	A. G. Machin	
G-DELN	Grob G.102 Astir CS Jeans	Bowland Forest Gliding Club Ltd	
G-DELO	Slingsby T.65D Vega	I. Sim & I. Surley	
G-DELR	Schempp-Hirth Ventus b	I. D. Smith	
G-DELU	Schleicher ASW-20L	V. Derrick	
G-DELZ	Schleicher ASW-20L	D. A. Fogden	
G-DEME	Glaser-Dirks DG-200/17	E. D. Casagrande	
G-DEMF	Rolladen-Schneider LS4	R. N. Johnston & M. C. Oggelsby	
G-DEMG	Rolladen-Schneider LS4	Stratford on Avon Gliding Club	
G-DEMH	Cessna F.172M (modified)	M. Hammond (G-BFLO)	
G-DEMN	Slingsby T.65D Vega	J. C. Jenks	
G-DEMP	Slingsby T.65C Vega	G. Winch	
G-DEMR	Slingsby T.65C Vega	Llantysilio Team	
G-DEMT	Rolladen-Schneider LS4	M. R. Fox	
G-DEMU	Glaser-Dirks DG-202/17	A. Butterfield & N. Swinton	
G-DEMZ	Slingsby T65A Vega	K. Western (G-BGCA)	
G-DENC	Cessna F.150G	G-DENC Cessna Group (G-AVAP)	
G-DEND	Cessna F.150M	Wicklow Wings (G-WAFC/G-BDFI)	
G-DENI	PA-32-300 Cherokee Six	A. Bendkowski (G-BAIA)	
G-DENJ	Schempp-Hirth Ventus b/16.6	S. Boyden	
G-DENM	BB03 Trya	D. A. Morgan	
G-DENO	Glasflugel Standard Libelle 201B	D. M. Bland	
G-DENS	Binder CP.301S Smaragd	Garston Smaragd Group	
G-DENU	Glaser-Dirks DG-100G	435 Syndicate	
G-DENV	Schleicher ASW-20L	R. D. Hone	
G-DENX	PZL-Bielsko SZD-48 Jantar Standard 2	J. M. Hire	
G-DENY	Robinson R44 II	S. P. Denneny	
G-DEOB	PZL-Bielsko SZD-30	R. M. Golding	
G-DEOD	Grob G.102 Astir CS77	D. S. Fenton	
G-DEOE	Schleicher ASK-13	Essex Gliding Club Ltd	
G-DEOF	Schleicher ASK-13	K13-DEOF Syndicate	
G-DEOJ	Centrair ASW-20FL	C. J. Bowden	
G-DEOK	Centrair 101A Pegase	J. V. D. Hoek & J. Hunt	
G-DEOM	Carman M100S	S. W. Hutchinson	
G-DEON	Schempp-Hirth Nimbus 3	117 Syndicate	
G-DEOT	Grob G.103A Twin II Acro	R. Tyrrell	
G-DEOU	Pilatus B4-PC11AF	C. Noon	
G-DEOV	Schempp-Hirth Janus C	Burn Gliding Club Ltd	
G-DEOW	Schempp-Hirth Janus C	383 Syndicate	
G-DEOX	Carmam M-200 Foehn	B. S. Goodspeed	
G-DEOZ	Schleicher K 8B	Cotswold Gliding Club	
G-DEPD	Schleicher ASK-21	London Gliding Club Proprietary Ltd	
G-DEPE	Schleicher ASW-19B	P. A. Goulding	
G-DEPF	Centrair ASW-20FL	323 Syndicate	
G-DEPG	CARMAM M100S	J. Kohlmetz	
G-DEPP	Schleicher ASK-13	Mendip Gliding Club Ltd	
G-DEPS	Schleicher ASW-20L	C. Beveridge	
G-DEPT	Schleicher K-8B	R. McEvoy	
G-DEPU	Glaser-Dirks DG-101G Elan	J. F. Rogers	
G-DEPX	Schempp-Hirth Ventus b/16.6	M. E. S. Thomas	
G-DERA	Centrair ASW-20FL	R. J. Lockett	
G-DERH	Schleicher ASK-21	The Burn Gliding Club Ltd	
G-DERJ	Schleicher ASK-21	The Royal Air Force Gliding and Soaring Association	
G-DERR	Schleicher ASW-19B	University of Edinburgh Sports Union	
G-DERS	Schleicher ASW-19B	Booker Gliding Club Ltd	
G-DERU	Schempp-Hirth Nimbus 3/25.5	Verein fur Streckenegelflug Leipzig/Roitzshjora EV/Germany	
G-DERV	Cameron Truck SS balloon	J. M. Percival	
G-DERX	Centrair 101A Pegase	I. P. Freestone	

Notes	Reg	Type	Owner or Operator
	G-DESB	Schleicher ASK-21	Oxford University Gliding Club
	G-DESC	Rolladen-Schneider LS4	J. Crawford & J. M. Staley
	G-DESH	Centrair 101A	J. E. Moore
	G-DESJ	Schleicher K8B	Bowland Forest Gliding Club Ltd
	G-DESO	Glaser-Dirks DG-300 Elan	G. R. P. Brown
	G-DESU	Schleicher ASK-21	Banbury Gliding Club Ltd
	G-DETA	Schleicher ASK-21	P. Hawkins
	G-DETG	Rolladen-Schneider LS4	K. J. Woods
	G-DETJ	Centrair 101A	S. C. Phillips
	G-DETM	Centrair 101A	J. E. Masheder & A. Carden
	G-DETV	Rolladen-Schneider LS4	P. Fabian
	G-DETY	Rolladen-Schneider LS4	D. T. Staff
	G-DETZ	Schleicher ASW-20CL	The 20 Syndicate
	G-DEUC	Schleicher ASK-13	North Wales Gliding Club Ltd
	G-DEUD	Schleicher ASW-20C	R. Tietema
	G-DEUF	PZL-Bielsko SZD-50-3	Shalbourne Soaring Society Ltd
	G-DEUH	Rolladen-Schneider LS4	F. J. Parkinson
	G-DEUJ	Schempp-Hirth Ventus b/16.6	S. C. Renfrew
	G-DEUK	Centrair ASW-20FL	P. A. Clark
	G-DEUP	Agusta A.109S Grand	Castle Air Ltd (G—FUFU)
	G-DEUS	Schempp-Hirth Ventus b/16.6	R. J. Whitaker
	G-DEUV	PZL-Bielsko SZD-42-2 Jantar 2B	G. V. McKirdy
	G-DEUY	Schleicher ASW-20BL	ASW20BL-G-DUEY Group
	G-DEVF	Schempp-Hirth Nimbus 3T	A. G. Leach
	G-DEVH	Schleicher Ka 10	C. W. & K. T. Matten
	G-DEVJ	Schleicher ASK-13	Lasham Gliding Society Ltd
	G-DEVK	Grob G.102 Astir CS	Peterborough and Spalding Gliding Club Ltd
	G-DEVL	Eurocopter EC 120B	P. Richardson
	G-DEVM	Centrair 101A	Seahawk Gliding Club
	G-DEVO	Centrair 101A	G-DEVO Pegase Glider
	G-DEVP	Schleicher ASK-13	Lasham Gliding Society Ltd
	G-DEVS	PA-28 Cherokee 180	180 Group (G-BGVJ)
	G-DEVV	Schleicher ASK-23	Midland Gliding Club Ltd
	G-DEVW	Schleicher ASK-23	London Gliding Club Proprietary Ltd
	G-DEVX	Schleicher ASK-23	London Gliding Club Proprietary Ltd
	G-DEWE	P & M Flight Design CTSW	A. R. Hughes
	G-DEWG	Grob G.103A Twin II Acro	Herefordshire Gliding Club Ltd
	G-DEWI	Rotorsport UK MTO Sport	D. V. Nockels
	G-DEWP	Grob G.103A Twin II Acro	Bowland Forest Gliding Club Ltd
	G-DEWR	Grob G.103A Twin II Acro	The Bristol Gliding Club Proprietary Ltd
	G-DEWZ	Grob G.103A Twin II Acro	T. R. Dews
	G-DEXA	Grob G.103A Twin II Acro	Trent Valley Gliding Club Ltd
	G-DEXP	ARV Super 2	R. W. Clarke
	G-DEXT	Robinson R44 II	Berkley Properties Ltd
	G-DFAF	Schleicher ASW-20L	G-DFAF Group
	G-DFAR	Glasflugel H205 Club Libelle	R. G. Appleboom
	G-DFAT	Schleicher ASK-13	Dorset Gliding Club Ltd
	G-DFAW	Schempp-Hirth Ventus b/16.6	J. Hanlon
	G-DFBD	Schleicher ASW-15B	J. J. Mion
	G-DFBE	Rolladen-Schneider LS6	J. B. Van Woerden
	G-DFBJ	Schleicher K 8B	Bidford Gliding & Flying Club Ltd
	G-DFBM	Schempp-Hirth Nimbus 3/24.5	D. Gardiner
	G-DFBO	Schleicher ASW-20BL	A. M. Cridge
	G-DFBR	Grob G.102 Astir CS77	Essex Gliding Club Ltd
	G-DFBY	Schempp-Hirth Discus b	D. Latimer
	G-DFCD	Centrair 101A	G. J. Bass
	G-DFCK	Schempp-Hirth Ventus b	S. A. Adlard
	G-DFCM	Glaser-Dirks DG-300	A. Davis & I. D. Roberts
	G-DFCW	Schleicher ASK-13	Lasham Gliding Society Ltd
	G-DFCY	Schleicher ASW-15	M. R. Shaw
	G-DFDF	Grob G.102 Astir CS	W. D. Harrop
	G-DFDO	Evektor EV-97 Eurostar SL	Dodo Group
	G-DFDW	Glaser-Dirks DG-300	C. M. Hadley
	G-DFEB	Grob G.102 Club Astir III	Lasham Gliding Society Ltd
	G-DFEO	Schleicher ASK-13	Lasham Gliding Society Ltd
	G-DFEX	Grob G.102 Astir CS77	Loughborough Students Union Gliding Club
	G-DFFP	Schleicher ASW-19B	Foxtrot Papa Group
	G-DFGJ	Schleicher Ka 6CR	G. D. S. Caldwell
	G-DFGT	Glaser-Dirks DG-300 Elan	T. J. Gray
	G-DFHS	Schempp-Hirth Ventus cT	154 Group

Reg	Type	Owner or Operator	Notes
G-DFHY	Scheibe SF-27A	J. M. Pursey	
G-DFJO	Schempp-Hirth Ventus cT	FJO Syndicate	
G-DFKI	Westland Gazelle HT.2	D. J. Fravigar (G-BZOT)	
G-DFKX	Schleicher Ka 6CR	J. E. Herring	
G-DFMG	Schempp-Hirth Discus b	J. R. Day	
G-DFOG	Rolladen-Schneider LS7	R. B. Porteous	
G-DFOV	CARMAM JP 15-36AR Aiglon	M. Howley	
G-DFOX	AS.355F1 Ecureuil II	RCR Aviation Ltd (G-NAAS/G-BPRG/G-NWPA)	
G-DFRA	Rolladen-Schneider LS6-b	79 Syndicate	
G-DFSA	Grob G.102 Astir CS	Astir 498 Syndicate	
G-DFTF	Schleicher Ka-6CR	J. Preller	
G-DFTJ	PZL-Bielsko SZD-48-1 Jantar Standard 2	P. Nock	
G-DFUF	Scheibe SF-27A Zugvogel V	R. J. Savage	
G-DFUN	Van's RV-6	G-DFUN Flying Group	
G-DFWJ	Rolladen-Schneider LS7-WL	J. F. Waumans	
G-DFXE	Rolladen-Schneider LS7	Booker Gliding Club Ltd	
G-DFXR	Sportine Aviacija LAK-12	M. C. Bailey	
G-DGAJ	Glaser-Dirks DG-300 Club Elan	S. Lewis	
G-DGAL	Ikarus C42 FB80 Bravo	D. & P. A. Gall	
G-DGAV	P & M Quik R	G. P. Jones	
G-DGAW	Schleicher Ka 6CR	H. C. Yorke & D. Searle	
G-DGBT	Chimera Dragon GBT 1170	Chimera Aviation Ltd	
G-DGDJ	Rolladen-Schneider LS4-a	450 Syndicate	
G-DGDW	Scheibe SF-27A Zugvogel V	G. Wardle	
G-DGEF	Schleicher Ka 6CR	Lee K6CR Group	
G-DGFD	Robinson R44 II	Macrae Aviation Ltd (G-CGNF)	
G-DGFY	Flylight Dragonfly	M. R. Sands	
G-DGHI	Dyn'Aéro MCR-01 Club	J. M. Keane	
G-DGIO	Glaser-Dirks DG-100G Elan	DG1 Group	
G-DGIV	Glaser-Dirks DG.800B	S. M. Tilling & P. G. Noonan	
G-DGKB	Centrair ASW-20F	J. Archer	
G-DGMT	III Sky Arrow 650 T	A. Powell	
G-DGPS	Diamond DA-42 Twin Star	Flight Calibration Services Ltd	
G-DGRE	Guimbal Cabri G2	Helicentre Aviation Ltd	
G-DGSC	CZAW Sportcruiser	Sierra Charlie Group	
G-DGST	Beech 95-B55 Baron	CE Ventures Ltd (G-BXDF)	
G-DHAA	Glasflugel H201B Standard Libelle	D. J. Jones & R. N. Turner	
G-DHAD	Glasflugel H201B Standard Libelle	R. Hines	
G-DHAH	Aeronca 7BCM Champion	Alpha Hotel Group (G-JTYE)	
G-DHAL	Schleicher ASK-13	The Windrushers Gliding Club Ltd	
G-DHAM	Robinson R44 II	D. B. Hamilton	
G-DHAP	Schleicher Ka 6E	M.Fursedon & T. Turner	
G-DHAT	Glaser-Dirks DG-200/17	G-DHAT Group	
G-DHCA	Grob G.103 Twin Astir	Midland Gliding Club Ltd	
G-DHCC	DHC.1 Chipmunk 22 (WG321:G)	Liberty Aviation Ltd	
G-DHCE	Schleicher ASW-19B	A. M. Wilmot	
G-DHCF	PZL-Bielsko SZD-50-3	Shalbourne Soaring Society Ltd	
G-DHCJ	Grob G.103A Twin II Acro	Peterborough and Spalding Gliding Club Ltd	
G-DHCL	Schempp-Hirth Discus b	A. I. Lambe	
G-DHCO	Glasflugel Standard Libelle 201B	M. J. Birch	
G-DHCR	PZL-Bielsko SZD-51-1	East Sussex Gliding Club Ltd	
G-DHCU	DG-300 Club Elan	R. B. Hankey & J. B. Symonds	
G-DHCV	Schleicher ASW-19B	R. C. May	
G-DHCW	PZL-Bielsko SZD-51-1	Deeside Gliding Club (Aberdeenshire) Ltd	
G-DHCX	Schleicher ASK-21	Devon and Somerset Gliding Club Ltd	
G-DHCZ	DHC.2 Beaver 1	Propshop Ltd (G-BUCJ)	
G-DHDH	Glaser-Dirks DG-200	Delta Hotel Syndicate	
G-DHDV	DH.104 Dove 8 (VP981)	K. M. Perkins	
G-DHEB	Schleicher Ka 6CR	J. Burrow	
G-DHEM	Schempp-Hirth Discus CS	473 Syndicate	
G-DHER	Schleicher ASW-19B	R. R. Bryan	
G-DHES	Centrair 101A	G. H. Lawrence & G. S. Sanderson	
G-DHET	Rolladen-Schneider LS6-c18	A. Lake & M. D. Langford	
G-DHEV	Schempp-Hirth Cirrus	L. K. Nazar	
G-DHGL	Schempp-Hirth Discus b	E. A. Martin	
G-DHGS	Robinson R22 Beta	Helimech Ltd	
G-DHGY	SZD-24C Foka	S. J. Glassett	
G-DHHD	PZL-Bielsko SZD-51-1	Scottish Gliding Union Ltd	

Notes	Reg	Type	Owner or Operator
	G-DHHF	North American AT-6 Harvard II	DH Heritage Flights Ltd
	G-DHJH	Airbus A.321-211	Thomas Cook Airlines Ltd
	G-DHKA	Boeing 757-23N	DHL Air Ltd
	G-DHKB	Boeing 757-256	DHL Air Ltd
	G-DHKC	Boeing 757-256	DHL Air Ltd
	G-DHKD	Boeing 757-23N	DHL Air Ltd
	G-DHKE	Boeing 757-23N	DHL Air Ltd
	G-DHKF	Boeing 757-236	DHL Air Ltd (G-TCBB)
	G-DHKG	Boeing 757-236	DHL Air Ltd (G-TCBC)
	G-DHKH	Boeing 757-28A	DHL Air Ltd (G-FCLI)
	G-DHKI	Boeing 757-28A	DHL Air Ltd (G-STRY)
	G-DHKJ	Boeing 757-28A	DHL Air Ltd
	G-DHKK	Boeing 757-28A	DHL Air Ltd
	G-DHKL	Schempp-Hirth Discus bT	M. A. Thorne
	G-DHKM	Boeing 757-223	DHL Air Ltd
	G-DHKN	Boeing 757-223	DHL Air Ltd
	G-DHKX	Boeing 757-23APF	DHL Air Ltd
	G-DHLE	Boeing 767-3JHF	DHL Air Ltd
	G-DHLF	Boeing 767-3JHF	DHL Air Ltd
	G-DHLG	Boeing 767-3JHF	DHL Air Ltd
	G-DHLH	Boeing 767-3JHF	DHL Air Ltd
	G-DHMM	PA-34-200T Seneca II	Cristal Air Ltd (G-BEJV)
	G-DHMP	Schempp-Hirth Discus b	T. Janikowski
	G-DHNX	Rolladen-Schneider LS4-b	M. B. Margetson & P. R. Wilson
	G-DHOC	Scheibe Bergfalke II-55	R. Karch
	G-DHOK	Schleicher ASW-20CL	S. D. Minson
	G-DHOP	Van's RV-9A	C. Partington
	G-DHPA	Issoire E-78 Silene	P. Woodcock
	G-DHPM	OGMA DHC.1 Chipmunk 20 (1365)	P. Meyrick
	G-DHPR	Schempp-Hirth Discus b	Knibbs Johnson Syndicate
	G-DHRR	Schleicher ASK-21	Lakes Gliding Club Ltd
	G-DHSJ	Schempp-Hirth Discus b	D. Byrne
	G-DHSR	AB Sportine LAK-12 Lietuva	G. Forster
	G-DHTG	Grob G.102 Astir CS	Trent Valley Gliding Club Ltd
	G-DHUK	Schleicher Ka 6CR	Essex Gliding Club Ltd
	G-DHYL	Schempp-Hirth Ventus 2a	M. J. Cook
	G-DHYS	Titan T-51 Mustang (414907:CY-S)	D. Houghton
	G-DHZF	DH.82A Tiger Moth (N9192)	M. R. Johnson (G-BSTJ)
	G-DHZP	Rolladen-Schneider LS8-18	A. D. May & D. J. Bennett
	G-DIAT	PA-28 Cherokee 140	G. D. Jones (G-BCGK)
	G-DICA	SIAI Marchetti S.208	P. di Carlo/Italy
	G-DICK	Thunder Ax6-56Z balloon	R. D. Sargeant
	G-DIDG	Van's RV-7	B. R. Alexander
	G-DIDO	Agusta A109E Power	Castle Air Ltd
	G-DIDY	Thruster T600T 450	A. M. Brooks
	G-DIGA	Robinson R66	Helicopter & Pilot Services Ltd
	G-DIGI	PA-32 Cherokee Six 300	D. Stokes
	G-DIGS	Hughes 369HE	AT Aviation Sales Ltd (G-DIZZ)
	G-DIGZ	Hughes 369D	Mackinnon Construction Ltd (G-MCDD)
	G-DIII	Pitts S-2B Special	J. A. Coutts (G-STUB)
	G-DIKY	Murphy Rebel	Stoke Golding Flyers
	G-DIME	Rockwell Commander 114	H. B. Richardson
	G-DINA	AA-5B Tiger	Portway Aviation Ltd
	G-DINO	Pegasus Quantum 15	R. D. J. Buchanan (G-MGMT)
	G-DINS	Boeing Stearman A75N1 (44)	M. V. Linney (G-RJAH)
	G-DIPI	Cameron 80 Tub SS balloon	C. G. Dobson
	G-DIPM	PA-46-350P Malibu Mirage	MAS Mix Ltd
	G-DIPZ	Colt 17A Cloudhopper balloon	C. G. Dobson
	G-DIRK	Glaser-Dirks DG.400	Romeo-Kilo Gliding Club
	G-DISA	SA Bulldog Srs 120/125	I. W. Whiting
	G-DISO	Jodel 150	P. K. Morley & C. R. Coates
	G-DISP	AutoGyro Calidus	P. J. Troy-Davies
	G-DIWY	PA-32 Cherokee Six 300	IFS Chemicals Ltd
	G-DIXY	PA-28-181 Archer III	Modern Air (UK) Ltd
	G-DIZI	Reality Escapade 912(2)	J. C. Carter
	G-DIZO	Jodel D.120A	N. M. Harwood (G-EMKM)
	G-DIZY	PA-28R-201T Turbo Arrow III	Dizy Aviation Ltd
	G-DJAA	Schempp-Hirth Janus B	Bidford Gliding & Flying Club Ltd
	G-DJAB	Glaser-Dirks DG-300 Elan	I. G. Johnston

Reg	Type	Owner or Operator	Notes
G-DJAC	Schempp-Hirth Duo Discus	G-DJAC Group	
G-DJAD	Schleicher ASK-21	The Borders (Milfield) Gliding Club Ltd	
G-DJAH	Schempp-Hirth Discus b	S. C. Moss	
G-DJAN	Schempp-Hirth Discus b	N. F. Perren	
G-DJAY	Avtech Jabiru UL-450	L. C. Rowson & J. M. Naylor	
G-DJBC	Ikarus C42 FB100	Bluecool Water Dispensers	
G-DJBX	Aeropro Eurofox 912(IS)	D. J. Barrott	
G-DJCR	Varga 2150A Kachina	M. Legge (G-BLWG)	
G-DJET	Diamond DA42 Twin Star	Diamond Executive Aviation Ltd	
G-DJGG	Schleicher ASW-15B	J. P. N. Haxell	
G-DJHP	Valentin Mistral C	P. B. Higgs	
G-DJJA	PA-28-181 Archer II	Interactive Aviation Ltd	
G-DJLL	Schleicher ASK-13	Bidford Gliding & Flying Club Ltd	
G-DJMC	Schleicher ASK-21	The Royal Air Force Gliding and Soaring Association	
G-DJMD	Schempp-Hirth Discus b	G-DJMD Syndicate	
G-DJNC	ICA-Brasov IS-28B2	Delta Juliet November Group	
G-DJNE	DG Flugzeugbau DG-808C	J. N. Ellis (G-DGRA)	
G-DJNH	Denney Kitfox Mk 3	P. Dennington	
G-DJSM	Eurocopter AS.350B3 Ecureuil	Meoble Estate (G-CICZ)	
G-DJST	Ixess 912(1)	K. Buckley & B. L. Prime	
G-DJVY	Scintex CP.1315-C3 Super Emeraude	A. P. Goodwin	
G-DJWS	Schleicher ASW-15B	S. P. Collier	
G-DKBA	DKBA AT 0301-0 balloon	I. Chadwick	
G-DKDP	Grob G.109	P. Wardell	
G-DKEM	Bell 407	True Course Helicopter Ltd	
G-DKEN	Rolladen-Schneider LS4-a	K. L. Sangster and B. Lytollis	
G-DKEY	PA-28-161 Warrior II	PA-28 Warrior Ltd	
G-DKFU	Schempp-Hirth Ventus 2cxT	R. L. Watson (G-CKFU)	
G-DKGF	Viking Dragonfly ★	(stored)/Enstone	
G-DKGM	Cameron O-56 balloon	Gone with the Wind Ltd (G-CKAD)	
G-DKNY	Robinson R44 II	Williamair Ltd	
G-DKTA	PA-28-236 Dakota	G. Beattie & C. J. T. Kitchen	
G-DLAF	Bristell NG5 Speed Wing	A. French & G. Dangerfield	
G-DLAK	Cessna 208 Caravan 1	Eggesford Ltd	
G-DLAL	Beech E90 King Air	Penylan Ltd	
G-DLCB	Shaw Europa	G. F. Perry	
G-DLDL	Robinson R22 Beta	Helimech Ltd	
G-DLEE	SOCATA TB9 Tampico Club	D. A. Lee (G-BPGX)	
G-DLFN	Aero L-29 Delfin	AMP Aviation Ltd	
G-DLOE	Schleicher ASW-27-18E	J. E. Gatfield	
G-DLOM	SOCATA TB20 Trinidad	P. A Rieck	
G-DLOT	Glasflugel 304S	Shark G-DLOT Syndicate	
G-DLOW	Grob G.103 Twin II	The Vale of the White Horse Gliding Centre Ltd	
G-DLTR	PA-28 Cherokee 180E	M. A. J. Spiers (G-AYAV)	
G-DLTY	HpH Glasflugel 304 ES	B. D. Michael & J. M. Gilbey	
G-DLUT	HpH Glasflugel 304 ES	A. R. Fish	
G-DLUX	Eurocopter EC.120B Colibri	EBG (Helicopters) Ltd (G-IGPW/G-CBRI)	
G-DMAC	Avtech Jabiru SP-430	C. J. Pratt	
G-DMAH	SOCATA TB20 Trinidad	William Cook Holdings Ltd	
G-DMBO	Van's RV-7	C. J. Goodwin	
G-DMCA	Douglas DC-10-30 ★	Forward fuselage/Manchester Airport Viewing Park	
G-DMCI	Ikarus C42 FB100	C-More Flying School Ltd	
G-DMCS	PA-28R Cherokee Arrow 200-II	Arrow Associates (G-CPAC)	
G-DMCT	Flight Design CT2K	A. M. Sirant	
G-DMCW	Magni M-24C	B. A. Carnegie (G-CGVF)	
G-DMEE	Cameron Z-105 balloon	Airship & Balloon Company Ltd	
G-DMES	Cameron Minion 105 SS balloon	Airship & Balloon Company Ltd	
G-DMEZ	Cameron Minion 105 SS balloon	Airship & Balloon Company Ltd	
G-DMND	Diamond DA42 Twin Star	Flying Time Ltd	
G-DMNG	Diamond DA.42M-NG Twin Star	Diamond Executive Aviation Ltd (G-PEEK)	
G-DMON	Xtremeair XA-42 Sbach 342	R. M. Hockey	
G-DMPI	Agusta A.109E Power	D E & M C Pipe Partnership (G-FVIP/G-HCFC)	
G-DMPL	Van's RV-7A	P. J. & W. M. Hodgkins	
G-DMPP	Diamond DA42M-NG Twin Star	Diamond Executive Aviation Ltd	
G-DMSS	Westland Gazelle HT.3 (XW858:C)	G. Wood	

Notes	Reg	Type	Owner or Operator
	G-DMWW	CFM Shadow Srs DD	M. Whittle
	G-DNBH	Raj Hamsa X'Air Hawk	D. N. B. Hearn
	G-DNGR	Colt 31A balloon	G. J. Bell
	G-DKNY	Ikarus C42 FB80	D. N. K. & M. A. Symon
	G-DLBR	Airbus Helicopters EC.175B	Klaret Sky Leasing Ltd
	G-DLRA	BN-2T Islander	Britten-Norman Ltd (G-BJYU)
	G-DLRL	Glasflugel 304S Shark	M. P. Brooks
	G-DNOP	PA-46-350P Malibu Mirage	Campbell Aviation Ltd
	G-DOBS	Van's RV-8	BS Flying Group
	G-DOCB	Boeing 737-436 ★	Cranfield University instructional airframe
	G-DODB	Robinson R22 Beta	Durham Flying Syndicate
	G-DODD	Cessna F.172P-II	M. D. Darragh
	G-DODG	Aerotechnik EV-97A Eurostar	J. Jones
	G-DOEA	AA-5A Cheetah	T. M. Buick (G-RJMI)
	G-DOFY	Bell 206B JetRanger 3	First Fence Ltd
	G-DOGG	SA Bulldog Srs 120/121 (XX638)	P. Sengupta
	G-DOGI	Robinson R22 Beta	Phoenix Helicopter Academy Ltd (G-BVGS)
	G-DOGZ	Horizon 1	M. J. Nolan
	G-DOIG	CZAW Sportcruiser	P. N. Bailey
	G-DOIN	Skyranger 912(S)1	M. Geczy
	G-DOLF	AS.365N3 Dauphin II	Executive Jet Charter Ltd
	G-DOLI	Cirrus SR20	Furness Asset Management Ltd
	G-DOLS	PA-28-236 Dakota	P. J. Crowther (G-FRGN)
	G-DOLY	Cessna T.303	KW Aviation Ltd (G-BJZK)
	G-DOMS	Aerotechnik EV-97A Eurostar	R. K. & C. A. Stewart
	G-DONE	Bell 505 Jet Ranger X	Simpson Heli Charters Ltd
	G-DONI	AA-5B Tiger	D. F. Smith (G-BLLT)
	G-DONK	Ultramagic M-77 balloon	K. R. Holzer
	G-DONT	Xenair CH.601XL Zodiac	J. A. Kentzer
	G-DORN	EKW C-3605	Yak UK Ltd
	G-DORS	Eurocopter EC 135T3	Premier Fund Leasing
	G-DORY	Cameron Z-315 balloon	P. Baker
	G-DOSB	Diamond DA42 Twin Star	DO Systems Ltd
	G-DOSC	Diamond DA42 Twin Star	DO Systems Ltd
	G-DOTS	Dornier Do.27A-4	ILiberty Aviation Ltd
	G-DOTT	CFM Streak Shadow	R. J. Bell
	G-DOTW	Savannah VG Jabiru(1)	I. W. Gardner
	G-DOTY	Van's RV-7	D. F. Daines
	G-DOUZ	Van's RV-12	J and G Aerospace Ltd
	G-DOVE	Cessna 182Q	P. Puri
	G-DOVE†	D. H. 104 Devon C.2 (VP967) ★	E. Surrey College/Gatton Point, Redhill (G-KOOL)
	G-DOVS	Robinson R44 II	J. Watt
	G-DOWN	Colt 31A balloon	M. Williams
	G-DOZI	Ikarus C.42 FB100	D. A. Izod
	G-DOZZ	Best Off Sky Ranger Swift 912S(1)	J. P. Doswell
	G-DPER	M & D Flugzeugbau JS-MD	M. P. Clark
	G-DPRV	Van's RV-7A	D. H. Pattison
	G-DPYE	Robin DR400/500	O. Houssard
	G-DRAM	Cessna FR.172F (floatplane)	H. R. Mitchell
	G-DRAT	Slingsby T.51 Dart 17R	W. R. Longstaff
	G-DRAW	Colt 77A balloon	A. G. Odell
	G-DRCC	EV-97 TeamEurostar UK	Sanctuary Medical Ltd (G-SLNM)
	G-DRCS	Schleicher ASH-25E	C. R. Smithers
	G-DRDR	Cirrus SR22T	P. Orton
	G-DREG	Superchaser	N. R. Beale
	G-DREI	Fokker DR.1 Triplane Replica	P. M. Brueggemann
	G-DRGC	P & M Quik GT450	D. R. G. Cornwell
	G-DRGL	PA-18-135 Super Cub	Goodwood Road Racing Company Ltd (G-BLIH)
	G-DRGS	Cessna 182S	Walter Scott & Partners Ltd
	G-DRIO	Jodel DR.1050M	B. N. Stevens (G-BXIO)
	G-DRMM	Shaw Europa	T. J. Harrison
	G-DROL	Robinson R44 II	M. R. Lord (G-OPDG)
	G-DROP	Cessna U.206C	K. Brady (G-UKNO/G-BAMN)

Reg	Type	Owner or Operator	Notes
G-DRPK	Reality Escapade	P. A. Kirkham	
G-DRPO	Cameron Z-105 balloon	Datum RPO Ltd	
G-DRRT	Slingsby T.51 Dart 17R	L. W. Whittington (G-DBXH)	
G-DRSV	CEA DR.315 (modified)	R. S. Voice	
G-DRTA	Boeing 737-85P	Jet 2.com	
G-DRTB	Boeing 737-85N	Jet 2.com	
G-DRYS	Cameron N-90 balloon	C. A. Butter	
G-DRZM	CEA DR.360	P. K. Kaufeler	
G-DSAA	Leonardo AW169	SAS (Dorset and Somerset) Ltd	
G-DSFT	PA-28R Cherokee Arrow 200-II	J. Jones (G-LFSE/G-BAXT)	
G-DSGC	PA-25 Pawnee 235C	Devon & Somerset Gliding Club Ltd	
G-DSID	PA-34-220T Seneca III	I. M. Worthington	
G-DSJT	Cessna 182T	D. S. J. Tait	
G-DSKI	Aerotechnik EV-97 Eurostar	G-DSKI Group	
G-DSKY	Diamond DA.42 Twin Star	J. M. Pirrie (G-CDSZ)	
G-DSLL	Pegasus Quantum 15-912	D. T. Evans	
G-DSMA	P & M Aviation Quik R	D. Young & F. Hogarth	
G-DSOO	Glaser-Dirks DG-500M	Twin Astir Syndicate	
G-DSPK	Cameron Z-140	Bailey Balloons Ltd	
G-DSPL	Diamond DA40 Star	Dynamic Signal Processing Ltd (G-GBOS)	
G-DSPZ	Robinson R44 II	Focal Point Communications Ltd	
G-DSRV	Van's RV-7	D. W. Murcott & S. J. Boynett	
G-DSTN	Bell 206L Long Ranger	D. S. Dryden (G-CYRS)	
G-DSVN	Rolladen-Schneider LS8-18	A. R. Paul	
G-DTAR	P & M Aviation Quik GT450	The Scottish Aero Club Ltd	
G-DTCP	PA-32R-300 Cherokee Lance	R. S. Cook (G-TEEM)	
G-DTFF	Cessna T.182T Turbo Skylane	Ridgway Aviation Ltd	
G-DTFT	CSA PS-28 Cruiser	Pilot Training & Testing Ltd	
G-DTOY	Ikarus C.42.FB100	C. W. Laske	
G-DTSM	EV-97 TeamEurostar UK	J. R. Stothart	
G-DTUG	Wag-Aero Super Sport	D. A. Bullock	
G-DUBI	Lindstrand LBL-120A balloon	M. B. Vennard	
G-DUDE	Van's RV-8	J. J. Cooke & R. A. Seeley	
G-DUDI	Rotorsport UK MTO Sport	Cloud 9 Gyro Flight Ltd	
G-DUDZ	Robin DR.400/180	W. J. Lee (G-BXNK)	
G-DUFF	Rand Robinson KR-2	J. I. B. Duff	
G-DUGE	Ikarus C42 FB UK	D. Stevenson	
G-DUNK	Cessna F172M Skyhawk	Devon and Somerset Flight Training Ltd	
G-DUNS	Lindstrand LBL-90A balloon	A. Murphy	
G-DUOT	Schempp-Hirth Duo Discus T	G-DUOT Soaring Group	
G-DURO	Shaw Europa	W. R. C. Williams-Wynne	
G-DURX	Thunder 77A balloon	P. Coman & D. J. Stagg	
G-DUSK	DH.115 Vampire T.11 (XE856) ★	Bournemouth Aviation Museum	
G-DUST	Stolp SA.300 Starduster Too	A. R. R. Holden	
G-DUVL	Cessna F.172N	G-DUVL Flying Group	
G-DVAA	Eurocopter EC135 T2+	Devon Air Ambulance Trading Co.Ltd	
G-DVBF	Lindstrand LBL-210A balloon	Virgin Balloon Flights	
G-DVCI	Ultramagic H-31 balloon	Davinci Associates Ltd	
G-DVIP	Agusta A.109E Power	Castle Air Ltd	
G-DVMI	Van's RV-7	North West RV Flyers	
G-DVON	DH.104 Devon C.2 (VP955)	C. L. Thatcher	
G-DVOR	Diamond DA.62	Flight Calibration Services Ltd	
G-DVOY	CZAW Sportcruiser	J. Devoy (G-TDKI)	
G-DVTA	Cessna T.206H	D. Parker	
G-DWCB	Chilton DW.1A	C. M. Barnes	
G-DWCE	Robinson R44 II	3CR Comm Ltd	
G-DWIA	Chilton D.W.1A	D. Elliott	
G-DWIB	Chilton D.W.1B (replica)	J. Jennings	
G-DWMS	Avtech Jabiru UL-450	B. J. Weighell	
G-DWRU	Chilton DW.1A	K. J. Steele	
G-DXLT	Schempp-Hirth Duo Discus xLT	G-DXLT Group	
G-DXTR	Beech B.200 Super King Air	Synergy Aviation Ltd (G-RIOO)	
G-DYKE	Dyke JD.2 Delta	M. S. Bird	
G-DYLN	Pilatus PC-12/47E	Oriens Leasing Ltd	

Notes	Reg	Type	Owner or Operator
	G-DYNA	Dynamic WT9 UK	J. C. Stubbs
	G-DYNM	Aerospool Dynamic WT9 UK	November Mike Group
	G-DZDZ	Rolladen-Schneider LS4	I. MacArthur
	G-DZKY	Diamond DA.40D Star	Go 2 Aviation Ltd (G-CEZP)
	G-DZZY	Champion 8KCAB	Paul's Planes Ltd
	G-EAGA	Sopwith Dove (replica)	A. Wood
	G-EAOU†	Vickers Vimy (replica)(NX71MY)	Greenco (UK) Ltd
	G-EASD	Avro 504L	G. M. New
	G-EASQ†	Bristol Babe (replica) (BAPC87) ★	Bristol Aero Collection (stored)/Kemble
	G-EAVX	Sopwith Pup (B1807)	K. A. M. Baker
	G-EBED†	Vickers 60 Viking (replica) (BAPC114)★	Brooklands Museum of Aviation/Weybridge
	G-EBHB	Avro 504K	T. W. Harris
	G-EBHX	DH.53 Humming Bird	The Shuttleworth Collection
	G-EBIA	RAF SE-5A (F904)	The Shuttleworth Collection
	G-EBIB	RAF SE-5A ★	Science Museum/South Kensington
	G-EBIC	RAF SE-5A (F938) ★	RAF Museum/Hendon
	G-EBIR	DH.51	The Shuttleworth Collection
	G-EBJE	Avro 504K (E449) ★	RAF Museum/Hendon
	G-EBJG	Parnall Pixie IIIH	Midland Aircraft Preservation Society
	G-EBJI	Hawker Cygnet (replica)	C. J. Essex
	G-EBJO	ANEC IIH	The Shuttleworth Collection
	G-EBKY	Sopwith Pup (9917)	The Shuttleworth Collection
	G-EBLV	DH.60 Cirrus Moth	British Aerospace PLC
	G-EBMB	Hawker Cygnet I ★	RAF Museum/Cosford
	G-EBNV	English Electric Wren	The Shuttleworth Collection
	G-EBQP	DH.53 Humming Bird (J7326) ★	P. L. Kirk & T. G. Pankhurst
	G-EBWD	DH.60X Hermes Moth	The Shuttleworth Collection
	G-EBZM	Avro 594 Avian IIIA ★	Manchester Museum of Science & Industry
	G-EBZN	DH.60X Moth	J. Hodgkinson (G-UAAP)
	G-ECAC	Alpha R21620U	Bulldog Aviation Ltd
	G-ECAD	Cessna FA.152	Andrewsfield Aviation Ltd & Corvalis Aircraft Leasing Ltd (G-JEET/G-BHMF)
	G-ECAE	Royal Aircraft Factory SE.5A	West Flyg AB/Sweden
	G-ECAF	Robin HR.200-120B	Bulldog Aviation Ltd (G-BZET)
	G-ECAG	Robin HR.200-120B	Bulldog Aviation Ltd (G-MFLD/G-BXDT)
	G-ECAK	Cessna F.172M	Bulldog Aviation Ltd (G-BENK)
	G-ECAM	EAA Acrosport II	C. England
	G-ECAN	DH.84 Dragon	Norman Aeroplane Trust
	G-ECAP	Robin HR.200-120B	Bulldog Aviation Ltd (G-NSOF)
	G-ECAR	Robin HR.200-120B	Bulldog Aviation Ltd (G-MFLB/G-BXOR)
	G-ECBI	Schweizer 269C-1	Iris Aviation Ltd
	G-ECDB	Schleicher Ka 6E	C. W. R. Neve
	G-ECDS	DH.82A Tiger Moth	N. C. Wilson
	G-ECDX	DH.71 Tiger Moth (replica)	Airtime Aerobatics Ltd
	G-ECEA	Schempp-Hirth Cirrus	CEA Group
	G-ECGC	Cessna F.172N	D. H. G. Penney
	G-ECGO	Bölkow Bö.208C1 Junior	P. Norman
	G-ECHB	Dassault Falcon 900DX	TAG Aviation (UK) Ltd
	G-ECJM	PA-28R-201T Turbo Arrow III	Regishry Ltd (G-FESL/G-BNRN)
	G-ECKB	Escapade 912(2)	C. M. & C. P. Bradford
	G-ECLW	Glasflugel Standard Libelle 201B	R. Harkness & S. Leach
	G-ECMK	PA-18-150 Super Cub	Shacklewell Super Cub Group
	G-ECNX	Cessna F.177RG	V. Haack
	G-ECOA	DHC.8-402 Dash Eight	Flybe.com
	G-ECOB	DHC.8-402 Dash Eight	Flybe.com
	G-ECOC	DHC.8-402 Dash Eight	Flybe.com
	G-ECOD	DHC.8-402 Dash Eight	Flybe.com
	G-ECOE	DHC.8-402 Dash Eight	Flybe.com
	G-ECOF	DHC.8-402 Dash Eight	Flybe.com
	G-ECOG	DHC.8-402 Dash Eight	Flybe.com
	G-ECOH	DHC.8-402 Dash Eight	Flybe.com
	G-ECOI	DHC.8-402 Dash Eight	Flybe.com
	G-ECOJ	DHC.8-402 Dash Eight	Flybe.com
	G-ECOK	DHC.8-402 Dash Eight	Flybe.com
	G-ECOL	Schempp-Hirth Nimbus 2	M. Upex & L. I. Rigby
	G-ECOM	DHC.8-402 Dash Eight	Flybe.com
	G-ECOO	DHC.8-402 Dash Eight	Flybe.com

Reg	Type	Owner or Operator	Notes
G-ECOP	DHC.8-402 Dash Eight	Flybe.com	
G-ECOR	DHC.8-402 Dash Eight	Flybe.com	
G-ECOT	DHC.8-402 Dash Eight	Flybe.com	
G-ECOX	Grega GN.1 Air Camper	H. C. Cox	
G-ECPA	Glasflugel H201B Standard Libelle	M. J. Witton	
G-ECRM	Slingsby T.67M Firefly Mk II	CRM Aviation Europe Ltd (G-BNSP)	
G-ECTF	Comper CLA.7 Swift Replica	P. R. Cozens	
G-ECUB	PA-18 Super Cub 150	G-ECUB Flying Group (G-CBFI)	
G-ECVB	Pietenpol Air Camper	J. M. O. Taylor	
G-ECVZ	Staaken Z-1S Flitzer	J. Cresswell	
G-ECXL	PZL-Bielsko SZD-30 Pirat	Charlie X-Ray Lima Group	
G-EDAV	SA Bulldog Srs 120/121 (XX534:B)	Edwalton Aviation Ltd	
G-EDBD	PZL-Bielsko SZD-30 Pirat	S. P. Burgess	
G-EDDD	Schempp-Hirth Nimbus 2	C. A. Mansfield (G-BKPM)	
G-EDDS	CZAW Sportcruiser	C. P. Davis	
G-EDDV	PZL-Bielsko SZD-38A Jantar 1	S. R. Bruce	
G-EDEE	Comco Ikarus C.42 FB100	C. L. & D. Godfrey	
G-EDEL	PA-32-300 Cherokee Six D	I. Blamire	
G-EDEN	SOCATA TB10 Tobago	Group Eden	
G-EDEO	Beech B.24R Sierra 200	P. Schirrmeister	
G-EDFS	Pietenpol Air Camper	J. V. Comfort	
G-EDGA	PA-28-161 Warrior II	The RAF Halton Aeroplane Club Ltd	
G-EDGE	Jodel 150	A. D. Edge	
G-EDGI	PA-28-161 Warrior II	H. K. & T. W. Gilbert	
G-EDGK	Cessna TR.182	A. Hasenmuller/Germany	
G-EDGY	Flight Test Edge 540	C. R. A. Scrope	
G-EDLY	Airborne Edge 912/Streak IIIB	M. & P. L. Eardley	
G-EDMC	Pegasus Quantum 15-912	R. Frost	
G-EDMK	Boeing A75 N1 Stearman	T. W. Harris	
G-EDNA	PA-38-112 Tomahawk	Pure Aviation Support Services Ltd	
G-EDRE	Lindstrand LBL 90A balloon	Edren Homes Ltd	
G-EDRV	Van's RV-6A	P. R. Sears	
G-EDTO	Cessna FR.172F	N. G. Hopkinson	
G-EDVK	RH78 Tiger Light	M. Peters (G-MZGT)	
G-EDVL	PA-28R Cherokee Arrow 200-II	Redhill Air Services Ltd (G-BXIN)	
G-EDYO	PA-32-260 Cherokee Six	McCarthy Aviation Ltd	
G-EDZZ	Ikarus C42 FB100 Bravo	Microavionics UK Ltd	
G-EEAA	Pietenpol Air Camper	P. G. Humphrey	
G-EEAD	Slingsby T.65A Vega	A. P. P. Scorer & P. Nayeri	
G-EEBA	Slingsby T.65A Vega	J. A. Cowie & K. Robertson	
G-EEBF	Schempp-Hirth Mini Nimbus C	M. Pingel	
G-EEBK	Schempp-Hirth Mini Nimbus C	R. A. Foreshew	
G-EEBL	Schleicher ASK-13	Derbyshire and Lancashire Gliding Club Ltd	
G-EEBN	Centrair ASW-20FL	S. MacArthur & R. Carlisle	
G-EEBR	Glaser-Dirks DG200/17	S. E. Marples	
G-EEBS	Scheibe Zugvogel IIIA	G-EEBS Syndicate	
G-EEBZ	Schleicher ASK-13	Bidford Gliding & Flying Club Ltd	
G-EECC	Aerospool Dynamic WT9 UK	C. V. Ellingworth	
G-EECK	Slingsby T65A Vega	Vega G-EECK 2014	
G-EECO	Lindstrand LBL-25A balloon	A. Jay	
G-EEDE	Centrair ASW-20F	G. M. Cumner	
G-EEEK	Extra EA.300/200	A. R. Willis	
G-EEER	Schempp-Hirth Mini Nimbus C	D. J. Uren	
G-EEEZ	Champion 8KCAB	P. J. Webb	
G-EEFA	Cameron Z-90 balloon	A. Murphy	
G-EEFK	Centrair ASW-20FL	J. Gale	
G-EEFT	Schempp-Hirth Nimbus 2B	S. A. Adlard	
G-EEGL	Christen Eagle II	M. P. Swoboda & S. L. Nicholson	
G-EEGU	PA-28-161 Warrior II	Tor Financial Consulting Ltd	
G-EEHA	Sonex	T. J. Fane de Salis	
G-EEJE	PA-31 Navajo B	J. P. Nugent	
G-EEKA	Glaser-Dirks DG-202/17	D. M. Betts	
G-EEKI	Sportine Aviacija LAK-17B FES	M. G. Lynes	
G-EEKK	Cessna 152	A. D. R. Northeast (G-BNSW)	
G-EEKX	P & M Aviation Quik	D. Subhani	
G-EEKY	PA-28-140 Cherokee B	J. L. Sparks	
G-EEKZ	P & M Quik GTR	D. Subhani	
G-EELS	Cessna 208B Caravan 1	Glass Eels Ltd	
G-EELT	Rolladen-Schneider LS4	ELT Syndicate	

Notes	Reg	Type	Owner or Operator
	G-EELY	Schleicher Ka 6CR	K6 ELY Syndicate
	G-EENI	Shaw Europa	M. P. Grimshaw
	G-EENK	Schleicher ASK-21	Cotswold Gliding Club
	G-EENO	Cessna T.210NTurbo Centurion II	F. Renner
	G-EENT	Glasflugel 304	M. Hastings & P. D. Morrison
	G-EENW	Schleicher ASW-20L	G-EENW Group
	G-EENZ	Schleicher ASW-19B	C. J. & G. J. Walker
	G-EEPJ	Pitts S-1S Special	R. J. Porter
	G-EERV	Van's RV-6	M. Crunden & C. B. Stirling
	G-EERY	Robinson R22	EGB (Helicopters) Ltd
	G-EESA	Shaw Europa	C. Deith (G-HIIL)
	G-EESY	Rolladen-Schneider LS4	S. G. D. Gaze
	G-EETF	Cessna F.177RG	P. F. A. Oberkonig/Germany
	G-EETG	Cessna 172Q Cutlass	A. Kiernan
	G-EETH	Schleicher K.8B	Bowland Forest Gliding Club Ltd
	G-EEUP	SNCAN Stampe SV.4C	A. M. Wajih
	G-EEVL	Grob G.102 Astir CS77	L. F. Escartin/Spain
	G-EEVY	Cessna 170A	Fly by Wire Flying Group
	G-EEWZ	Mainair Pegasus Quik	A. J. Roche
	G-EEYE	Mainair Blade 912	B. J. Egerton
	G-EEZR	Robinson R44	Geezer Aviation LLP
	G-EEZS	Cessna 182P	F. T. M. Tarczykowski
	G-EEZZ	Zenair CH.601XL Zodiac	S. Michaelson
	G-EFAM	Cessna 182S Skylane	G-EFAM Flying Group
	G-EFAO	Scintex CP.301-C1 Emeraude	T. A. S. Rayner
	G-EFBP	Cessna FR.172K	E. C. Bellamy
	G-EFCG	Aeropro Eurofox 912(S)	C. A. White
	G-EFCM	PA-28-180 Cherokee D	2 Excel Aviation Ltd
	G-EFFH	Cessna T.210L Turbo Centurion	R. Paletar
	G-EFGH	Robinson R22 Beta	K. R. Hoer/Germany
	G-EFIZ	Pitts S-2B Special	R. S. Goodwin & G. V. Paino
	G-EFJD	MBB Bo.209 Monsun	A. H. & F. A. Macaskill
	G-EFLT	Glasflugel Standard Libelle 201B	P. A. Tietema
	G-EFLY	Centrair ASW-20FL	G. E. Smith
	G-EFNH	Cessna FR.182	C. J. & V. J. Crawford
	G-EFOF	Robinson R22 Beta	Helicopter & Pilot Services Ltd
	G-EFON	Robinson R22 II	Burton Aviation Ltd (G-SCHO)
	G-EFOX	Eurofox 912(2)	C. J. Parsons
	G-EFRP	Bower Fly Baby 1A	R. A. Phillips (G-BFRD)
	G-EFSD	Eurofox 912(IS)	S. E. Dancaster
	G-EFSF	Cessna FR.172K	A. Vaughan
	G-EFSM	Slingsby T.67M Firefly 260	Anglo Europe Aviation Ltd (G-BPLK)
	G-EFTE	Bölkow Bö.207	B. Morris & R. L. Earl
	G-EFTF	AS.350B Ecureuil	T French & Son (G-CWIZ/G-DJEM/G-ZBAC/G-SEBI/G-BMCU)
	G-EFUN	Bishop & Castelli E-Go	Giocas Ltd
	G-EGAG	SOCATA TB20 Trinidad	D. & E. Booth
	G-EGAL	Christen Eagle II	Eagle Partners
	G-EGBJ	PA-28-161 Warrior II	Aviation Advice & Consulting Ltd (G-CPFM/G-BNNS)
	G-EGBP	American Champion 7ECA Citabria Aurora	Freedom Aviation Ltd (G-IRGJ)
	G-EGBS	Van's RV-9A	Shobdon RV-9A Group
	G-EGCA	Rans S-6-ES Coyote II	P. A. Linford
	G-EGEG	Cessna 172R	C. D. Lever
	G-EGEL	Christen Eagle II	G-EGEL Flying Group
	G-EGES	Lindstrand LBL Triangle balloon	Lighter Than Air Ltds
	G-EGEN	Piel CP301A Emeraude	Croft Aviators Flying Group
	G-EGGI	Ikarus C.42FB UK	J. S. D. Llewellyn
	G-EGGS	Robin DR.400/180	G-EGGS Syndicate
	G-EGGZ	Best Off Sky Ranger Swift 912S(1)	J. C. Sheardown
	G-EGIA	UltraMagic M-65C balloon	A. Dizioli/Italy
	G-EGIB	PA-28-181 Archer II	P. A. Venton
	G-EGIL	Christen Eagle II	Smoke On Go Ltd
	G-EGJA	SOCATA TB20 Trinidad	Kraydon Services Ltd
	G-EGJJ	P & M Quik GTR	M. D. Bowen
	G-EGKB	BAe 125 Srs 800B	Mountfitchet Aircraft Ltd (G-IFTF/G-RCEJ/G-GEIL)
	G-EGLA	Cessna 172M	Cornwall Flying Club Ltd (G-CGFJ)
	G-EGLE	Christen Eagle II	D. Thorpe
	G-EGLK	CSA PS-28 Cruiser	D. J. & L. Medcraft & Yonder Plains Ltd

Reg	Type	Owner or Operator	Notes
G-EGLL	PA-28-161 Warrior II	Airways Aero Associations Ltd (G-BLEJ)	
G-EGLS	PA-28-181 Archer III	M. Wallace	
G-EGLT	Cessna 310R	RVL Aviation Ltd (G-BHTV)	
G-EGPG	PA-18-135 Super Cub	G. Cormack (G-BWUC)	
G-EGRV	Van's RV-8	B. M. Gwynnett (G-PHMG)	
G-EGSJ	Jabiru J400	C. N. & K. J. Stephen (G-MGRK)	
G-EGSL	Cessna F.152	Corvalis Aircraft Leasing Ltd	
G-EGSR	Van's RV-7A	P. S. Gilmour & C. A. Acland	
G-EGSS	Raytheon Hawker 800XP	Interflight (Air Charter) Ltd (G-JMAX)	
G-EGTB	PA-28-161 Warrior II	Tayside Aviation Ltd (G-BPWA)	
G-EGUR	Jodel D.140B	S. H. Williams	
G-EGVA	PA-28R-200 Cherokee Arrow	Social Infrastructure Ltd	
G-EGVO	Dassault Falcon 900EX	TAG Aviation (UK) Ltd	
G-EGWN	American Champion 7ECA	Freedom Aviation Ltd	
G-EHAA	MDH MD-900 Explorer	Specialist Aviation Services Ltd (G-GNAA)	
G-EHAV	Glasflugel Standard Libelle 201B	A. & M. Truelove	
G-EHAZ	PA-28-161 Warrior III	Freedom Aviation Ltd (G-CEEY)	
G-EHBJ	CASA 1.131E Jungmann 2000	E. P. Howard	
G-EHCB	Schempp-Hirth Nimbus 3DT	G-EHCB Group	
G-EHCC	PZL-Bielsko SZD-50-3 Puchacz	Heron Gliding Club	
G-EHCZ	Schleicher K8B	The Windrushers Gliding Club Ltd	
G-EHDS	CASA 1.131E Jungmann 2000	I. C. Underwood (G-DUDS)	
G-EHEH	Lindstrand LTL Series 1 balloon	A. M. Holly	
G-EHEM	MDH MD-900 Explorer	Specialist Aviation Services Ltd (G-LNCT)	
G-EHGF	PA-28-181 Archer II	G. P. Robinson	
G-EHIC	Jodel D.140B	G-EHIC Group	
G-EHLX	PA-28-181 Archer II	ASG Leasing Ltd	
G-EHMF	Isaacs Fury II	M. W. Bodger	
G-EHMJ	Beech S35 Bonanza	A. J. Daley	
G-EHMM	Robin DR.400/180R	Booker Gliding Club Ltd	
G-EHMS	MD Helicopters MD-900	London's Air Ambulance Ltd	
G-EHOT	Cessna 172	U. P. Beewen/Germany	
G-EHRU	Cessna 175	Die Netzschmiede GmbH/Germany	
G-EHTT	Schleicher ASW-20CL	HTT Syndicate	
G-EHXP	Rockwell Commander 112A	A. L. Stewart	
G-EHZT	Zlin Z.526F Trener Master	E. H. Haulage Ltd	
G-EIAP	Jodel DR.1050	P. M. Irvine	
G-EICK	Cessna 172S	Centenary Flying Group	
G-EIKY	Shaw Europa	J. D. Milbank	
G-EINI	Europa XS	K. J. Burns (G-KDCC)	
G-EISG	Beech A36 Bonanza	R. J. & B. Howard	
G-EISO	SOCATA MS.892A Rallye Commodore 150*	Sammy Miller Motorcycle Museum/Nrew Milton	
G-EITE	Luscombe 8F Silvaire	C. P. Davey	
G-EIVC	Cessna F.182Q	C. R. Wagner	
G-EIWT	Cessna FR.182RG	K. McConnell	
G-EIZO	Eurocopter EC 120B	Blok (UK) Ltd	
G-EJAC	Mudry CAP.232	G. C. J. Cooper, P. Varinot & E. Vazeille (G-OGBR)	
G-EJAE	GlaserDirks DG-200	D. L. P. H. Waller	
G-EJAR	Airbus A.319-111	EasyJet Airline Co Ltd	
G-EJAS	Skystar Kitfox Model 7	D. A. Holl	
G-EJBI	Bolkow Bo.207	A. A. R. Moore	
G-EJEL	Cessna 550 Citation II	Futura Finances	
G-EJGO	Z.226HE Trener	S. K. T. & C. M. Neofytou	
G-EJHH	Schempp-Hirth Standard Cirrus	L. T. Merr-Taylor	
G-EJIM	Schempp-Hirth Discus 2cT	J. K. Weeks	
G-EJOC	AS.350B Ecureuil	CK's Supermarket Ltd (G-GEDS/G-HMAN/G-SKIM/G-BIVP)	
G-EJRS	PA-28-161 Cadet	Carlisle Flight Traing Ltd	
G-EJTC	Robinson R44	N. Parkhouse	
G-EJWI	Flight Design CTLS	D. D. J. Rossdale	
G-EKEY	Schleicher ASW-20 CL	A. P. Nisbet	
G-EKIM	Alpi Pioneer 300	Targett Aviation Ltd	
G-EKIR	PA-28-262 Cadet	Aeros Holdings Ltd	
G-EKKL	PA-28-161 Warrior II	Perryair Ltd	
G-EKOS	Cessna FR.182 RG	S. Charlton	

Notes	Reg	Type	Owner or Operator
	G-ELAM	PA-30 Twin Comanche160B	Hangar 39 Ltd (G-BAWU/G-BAWV)
	G-ELDR	PA-32 Cherokee Six 260	G-ELDR Cherokee 6 Group
	G-ELEE	Cameron Z-105 balloon	M. A. Stelling
	G-ELEN	Robin DR.400/180	Foster ELEN Group
	G-ELIS	PA-34-200T Seneca II	A. Gougas (G-BOPV)
	G-ELIZ	Denney Kitfox Mk 2	A. J. Ellis
	G-ELKA	Christen Eagle II	J. T. Matthews
	G-ELKE	Cirrus SR-20	S. Auer/Germany
	G-ELKI	Diamond DA.40 NG Star	Euro Aircraft Leasing Ltd
	G-ELKO	Diamond DA.42 NG Twin Star	Euro Aircraft Leasing Ltd
	G-ELKS	Avid Speedwing Mk 4	R. A. Budd & S. Grant
	G-ELLA	PA-32R-301 Saratoga IIHP	C. C. W. Hart
	G-ELLE	Cameron N-90 balloon	D. J. Stagg
	G-ELLI	Bell 206B JetRanger 3	A. Chatham
	G-ELMH	NA AT-6D Harvard III (42-84555:EP-H)	M. Hammond
	G-ELRT	Sopwith Pup	T. A. Bechtolsheimer
	G-ELSB	Robin DR.400-180R	Cambridge Gliding Club Ltd
	G-ELSE	Diamond DA.42 Twin Star	R. Swann
	G-ELSI	Tanarg/Ixess 15 912S(1)	C. R. Buckle
	G-ELUE	PA-28-161 Warrior II	Freedom Aviation Ltd
	G-ELUN	Robin DR.400/180R	Cotswold DR.400 Syndicate
	G-ELUT	PA-28R Cherokee Arrow 200-II	Green Arrow Europe Ltd
	G-ELUX	Rolladen-Schneider LS8-18	M. Davis
	G-ELVN	Van's RV-7A	G. P. Elvin
	G-ELWK	Van's RV-12	J. Devlin
	G-ELXE	Cessna 182T	O. Petrov
	G-ELYS	Cessna FA.150K	Skyworthy Hire (G-BIBN)
	G-ELZN	PA-28-161 Warrior II	ZN Flying Group
	G-ELZY	PA-28-161 Warrior II	Redhill Air Services Ltd
	G-EMAA	Eurocopter EC 135T2	Babcock Mission Critical Services Onshore Ltd
	G-EMAC	Robinson R22 Beta	P. M. Phillips (G-CBDB)
	G-EMBI	Embraer RJ145EP	bmi regional
	G-EMBJ	Embraer RJ145EP	bmi regional
	G-EMBN	Embraer RJ145EP	bmi regional
	G-EMBO	Embraer RJ145EP	Aircraft Solutions ERJ-145 LLC
	G-EMCA	Commander Aircraft 114B	S. Roberts
	G-EMDM	Diamond DA40-P9 Star	D. J. Munson
	G-EMEA	Airbus EC175B	CHC Scotia Ltd
	G-EMEB	Airbus EC175B	CHC Scotia Ltd
	G-EMHC	Agusta A109E Power	Burton Aviation Ltd
	G-EMHE	Agusta A109S Grand	East Midlands Helicopters
	G-EMHK	MBB Bö.209 Monsun 150FV	C. Elder (G-BLRD)
	G-EMHN	Agusta A.109S Grand	Burton Aviation Ltd
	G-EMID	Eurocopter EC 135P2	Police & Crime Commissioner for West Yorkshire
	G-EMIN	Shaw Europa	S. A. Lamb
	G-EMJA	CASA 1.131E Jungmann 2000	C. R. Maher
	G-EMKT	Cameron Z-105 balloon	Webster Adventures Ltd
	G-EMLE	Aerotechnik EV-97 Eurostar	A. R. White
	G-EMLS	Cessna T210L Turbo Centurion	I. K. F. Simcock
	G-EMLY	Pegasus Quantum 15	S. J. Reid
	G-EMMM	Diamond DA40 Star	A. J. Leigh
	G-EMMX	P & M Quik GT450	A. W. Buchan
	G-EMMY	Rutan Vari-Eze	M. J. Tooze
	G-EMOL	Schweizer 269C-1	Bliss Aviation Ltd
	G-EMPP	Diamond DA.42M Twin Star	Diamond Executive Aviation Ltd (G-DSPY)
	G-EMSA	Czech Sport Aircraft Sportcruiser	A. C. & M. A. Naylor
	G-EMSI	Shaw Europa	P. W. L. Thomas
	G-EMSY	DH.82A Tiger Moth	G-EMSY Group (G-ASPZ)
	G-ENAA	Supermarine Spitfire Mk.26B (EN130:FN-A)	G-ENAA Syndicate
	G-ENBW	Robin DR.400-180R	P. S. Carder & B. Elliott
	G-ENCE	Partenavia P.68B	Exeter Flights Ltd (G-OROY/G-BFSU)
	G-ENEA	Cessna 182P	Air Ads Ltd
	G-ENEE	CFM Streak Shadow SA	A. L. & S. Roberts
	G-ENGO	Steen Skybolt	R. G. Fulton
	G-ENGR	Head AX8-105 balloon	Royal Engineers Balloon Club
	G-ENHP	Enstrom 480B	H. J. Pelham
	G-ENIA	Staaken Z-21 Flitzer	A. F. Wankowski
	G-ENID	Reality Escapade ULP(1)	Q. Irving

Reg	Type	Owner or Operator	Notes
G-ENIE	Tipsy T.66 Nipper 3	M. J. Freeman	
G-ENIO	Pitts S-2C Special	Advanced Flying (London) Ltd	
G-ENNA	PA-28-161 Warrior II	Falcon Flying Serices Ltd (G-ESFT)	
G-ENNI	Robin R.3000/180	W. Schmidt	
G-ENOA	Cessna F.172F	M. K. Acors (G-ASZW)	
G-ENRE	Avtech Jabiru UL	P. R. Turton	
G-ENRI	Lindstrand LBL-105A balloon	P. G. Hall	
G-ENST	CZAW Sportcruiser	Enstone Flyers	
G-ENSX	Robinson R44 II	M. Duggan (G-CLII)	
G-ENTS	Van's RV-9A	L. G. Johnson	
G-ENTT	Cessna F.152 II	C. & A. R. Hyett (G-BHHI)	
G-ENTW	Cessna F.152 II	London School of Flying Ltd (G-BFLK)	
G-ENVO	MBB Bo.105CBS-4	F. C. Owen	
G-ENZO	Cameron Z-105 balloon	Garelli VI SPA	
G-EOFW	Pegasus Quantum 15-912	G-EOFW Microlight Group	
G-EOGE	Gefa-Flug AS105GD airship (hot air)	George Brazil 2015 Ltd	
G-EOHL	Cessna 182L	Branton Knight Ltd	
G-EOID	Aeroprakt A22-L Foxbat	J. Pearce	
G-EOIN	Zenair CH.701UL	G-EOIN Group	
G-EOJB	Robinson R44 II	Difuria Contractors Ltd (G-EDES)	
G-EOLD	PA-28-161 Warrior II	Fly Welle Ltd	
G-EOLE	Cameron O-84 balloon	McCornick, Van Haarne and Co	
G-EOMI	Robin HR.200/120B	LAC Aircraft Ltd	
G-EOPH	Cameron C-90 balloon	A. J. Cherrett	
G-EORG	PA-38-112 Tomahawk	Control Developments (UK) Ltd	
G-EORJ	Shaw Europa	P. E. George	
G-EPAR	Robinson R22 Beta II	Jepar Rotorcraft	
G-EPIC	Jabiru UL-450	T. Chadwick	
G-EPOC	Jabiru UL-450	S. Cope	
G-EPSN	Ultramagic M-105 balloon	G. Everett	
G-EPTL	PA-28RT-201T Turbo Arrow IV	J. R. Wright	
G-EPTR	PA-28R Cherokee Arrow 200-II	ACS Aviation Ltd	
G-EPYW	PA-28-181 Archer II	LAC Aircraft Ltd	
G-ERAS	Cameron O-31 balloon	A. A. Laing	
G-ERBE	Cessna P.210N	J. Luschnig	
G-ERCO	Ercoupe 415D	E. G. Girardey	
G-ERDA	Staaken Z-21A Flitzer	J. Cresswell	
G-ERDS	DH.82A Tiger Moth	W. A. Gerdes	
G-ERDW	Enstrom F-28F Falcon	G. Wolfshohl/Germany	
G-ERFC	S.E.5A replica	R. A. Palmer	
G-ERFS	PA-28-161 Warrior II	Steptoe and Son Properties Ltd	
G-ERIC	Rockwell Commander 112TC	E. N. Struys	
G-ERIE	Raytheon Beech 400A	Atlantic Bridge Aviation Ltd	
G-ERIW	Staaken Z-21 Flitzer	R. I. Wasey	
G-ERJA	Embraer RJ145EP	Falak Lease Nine Ltd	
G-ERJR	Agusta A109C	3GRCOMM Ltd (G-DBOY)	
G-ERKN	Eurocopter EC.350B3 Ecureuil	Jet Helicopters Ltd (G-ORKI)	
G-ERLI	Cessna 510 Citation Mustang	Catreus AOC Ltd	
G-ERMO	ARV Super 2	A. R. Hawes (G-BMWK)	
G-ERNI	PA-28-181 Archer II	J. Gardener & N. F. P. Hopwood (G-OSSY)	
G-EROB	Europa XS	R. J. Bull (G-RBJW)	
G-EROE	Avro 504K Replica	British Aviation 100	
G-EROL	Westland SA.341G Gazelle 1	MW Helicopters Ltd (G-NONA/G-FDAV/ G-RIFA/G-ORGE/G-BBHU)	
G-EROS	Cameron H-34 balloon	Evening Standard Co Ltd	
G-ERRI	Lindstrand LBL-77A balloon	S. M. Jones	
G-ERRY	AA-5B Tiger	M. Reischi	
G-ERTE	Skyranger 912S (1)	A. P. Trumper	
G-ERTI	Staaken Z-21A Flitzer	A. M. Wyndham	
G-ERYR	P & M Aviation Quik GT450	R. D. Ellis	
G-ESCA	Escapade Jabiru (1)	G. W. E. & R. H. May	
G-ESCC	Escapade 912	G. & S. Simons	
G-ESCP	Escapade 912(1)	A. Palmer	
G-ESET	Eurocopter EC.130B4 Ecureuil	Cyclix LLP	
G-ESGA	Reality Escapade	I. Bamford	
G-ESKA	Escapade 912	C. G. Thompson	
G-ESME	Cessna R.182 II (15211)	G. C. Cherrington (G-BNOX)	

Notes	Reg	Type	Owner or Operator
	G-ESNA	Embraer EMB-550 Legacy 500	Air Charter Scotland Ltd
	G-ESSL	Cessna R.182	J. W. F. Russell
	G-ESTR	Van's RV-6	J. P. M. & P. White
	G-ETAT	Cessna 172S	I. R. Malby
	G-ETBT	PA-38-112 Tomahawk	Highland Aviation Training Ltd
	G-ETBY	PA-32 Cherokee Six 260	G-ETBY Group (G-AWCY)
	G-ETDC	Cessna 172P	The Moray Flying Club
	G-ETGO	Groppo Trail Mk.2	S. Taylor & S. E. Gribble
	G-ETIM	Eurocopter EC 120B	Tenterfield (Holdings) Ltd
	G-ETIN	Robinson R22 Beta	HQ Aviation Ltd
	G-ETIV	Robin DR.400/180	C. A. Prior
	G-ETKT	Robinson R44 II	McClaren Construction Ltd
	G-ELTX	PA-28R-200 Cherokee Arrow II	LX Avionics Ltd
	G-ETME	Nord 1002 Pingouin (KG+EM)	S. H. O'Connell
	G-ETNT	Robinson R44	Irwin Plant Hire
	G-ETPE	Airbus AS.350B3 Ecureuil	Airbus Helicopters UK Ltd
	G-ETPF	Airbus AS.350B3 Ecureuil	QinetiQ Ltd
	G-ETPG	Airbus AS.350B3 Ecureuil	Airbus Helicopters UK Ltd
	G-ETPH	Airbus AS.350B3 Ecureuil	Airbus Helicopters UK Ltd
	G-ETUG	Aeropro Eurofox 912(S)	The Nortumbria Gliding Club Ltd
	G-ETVS	Alpi Pioneer 300 Hawk	V. Serazzi
	G-ETWO	Guimbal Cabri G2	European Helicopter Importers Ltd
	G-EUAB	Europa XS	A. D. Stephens
	G-EUAN	Jabiru UL-D	M. Wade & M. Lusted
	G-EUFO	Rolladen-Schneider LS7-WL	G. D. Alcock & M. J. Mingay
	G-EUJG	Avro 594 Avian IIIA	R. I. & D. E. Souch
	G-EUKS	Westland Widgeon III	R. I. Souch
	G-EUNA	Airbus A.318-112	British Airways
	G-EUNB	Airbus A.318-112	Titan Airways Ltd
	G-EUNG	Europa NG	D. I. Stanbridge
	G-EUNI	Beech B200 Super King Air	Universita Telematica E-Campus (G-TAGH)
	G-EUOA	Airbus A.319-131	British Airways
	G-EUOB	Airbus A.319-131	British Airways
	G-EUOC	Airbus A.319-131	British Airways
	G-EUOD	Airbus A.319-131	British Airways
	G-EUOE	Airbus A.319-131	British Airways
	G-EUOF	Airbus A.319-131	British Airways
	G-EUOG	Airbus A.319-131	British Airways
	G-EUOH	Airbus A.319-131	British Airways
	G-EUOI	Airbus A.319-131	British Airways
	G-EUPA	Airbus A.319-131	British Airways
	G-EUPB	Airbus A.319-131	British Airways
	G-EUPC	Airbus A.319-131	British Airways
	G-EUPD	Airbus A.319-131	British Airways
	G-EUPE	Airbus A.319-131	British Airways
	G-EUPF	Airbus A.319-131	British Airways
	G-EUPG	Airbus A.319-131	British Airways
	G-EUPH	Airbus A.319-131	British Airways
	G-EUPJ	Airbus A.319-131	British Airways
	G-EUPK	Airbus A.319-131	British Airways
	G-EUPL	Airbus A.319-131	British Airways
	G-EUPM	Airbus A.319-131	British Airways
	G-EUPN	Airbus A.319-131	British Airways
	G-EUPO	Airbus A.319-131	British Airways
	G-EUPP	Airbus A.319-131	British Airways
	G-EUPR	Airbus A.319-131	British Airways
	G-EUPS	Airbus A.319-131	British Airways
	G-EUPT	Airbus A.319-131	British Airways
	G-EUPU	Airbus A.319-131	British Airways
	G-EUPV	Airbus A.319-131	British Airways
	G-EUPW	Airbus A.319-131	British Airways
	G-EUPX	Airbus A.319-131	British Airways
	G-EUPY	Airbus A.319-131	British Airways
	G-EUPZ	Airbus A.319-131	British Airways
	G-EUSO	Robin DR.400/140 Major	Airpull Aviation SL/Spain
	G-EUUA	Airbus A.320-232	British Airways
	G-EUUB	Airbus A.320-232	British Airways
	G-EUUC	Airbus A.320-232	British Airways
	G-EUUD	Airbus A.320-232	British Airways

Reg	Type	Owner or Operator	Notes
G-EUUE	Airbus A.320-232	British Airways	
G-EUUF	Airbus A.320-232	British Airways	
G-EUUG	Airbus A.320-232	British Airways	
G-EUUH	Airbus A.320-232	British Airways	
G-EUUI	Airbus A.320-232	British Airways	
G-EUUJ	Airbus A.320-232	British Airways	
G-EUUK	Airbus A.320-232	British Airways	
G-EUUL	Airbus A.320-232	British Airways	
G-EUUM	Airbus A.320-232	British Airways	
G-EUUN	Airbus A.320-232	British Airways	
G-EUUO	Airbus A.320-232	British Airways	
G-EUUP	Airbus A.320-232	British Airways	
G-EUUR	Airbus A.320-232	British Airways	
G-EUUS	Airbus A.320-232	British Airways	
G-EUUT	Airbus A.320-232	British Airways	
G-EUUU	Airbus A.320-232	British Airways	
G-EUUV	Airbus A.320-232	British Airways	
G-EUUW	Airbus A.320-232	British Airways	
G-EUUX	Airbus A.320-232	British Airways	
G-EUUY	Airbus A.320-232	British Airways	
G-EUUZ	Airbus A.320-232	British Airways	
G-EUXC	Airbus A.321-231	British Airways	
G-EUXD	Airbus A.321-231	British Airways	
G-EUXE	Airbus A.321-231	British Airways	
G-EUXF	Airbus A.321-231	British Airways	
G-EUXG	Airbus A.321-231	British Airways	
G-EUXH	Airbus A.321-231	British Airways	
G-EUXI	Airbus A.321-231	British Airways	
G-EUXJ	Airbus A.321-231	British Airways	
G-EUXK	Airbus A.321-231	British Airways	
G-EUXL	Airbus A.321-231	British Airways	
G-EUXM	Airbus A.321-231	British Airways	
G-EUYA	Airbus A.320-232	British Airways	
G-EUYB	Airbus A.320-232	British Airways	
G-EUYC	Airbus A.320-232	British Airways	
G-EUYD	Airbus A.320-232	British Airways	
G-EUYE	Airbus A.320-232	British Airways	
G-EUYF	Airbus A.320-232	British Airways	
G-EUYG	Airbus A.320-232	British Airways	
G-EUYH	Airbus A.320-232	British Airways	
G-EUYI	Airbus A.320-232	British Airways	
G-EUYJ	Airbus A.320-232	British Airways	
G-EUYK	Airbus A.320-232	British Airways	
G-EUYL	Airbus A.320-232	British Airways	
G-EUYM	Airbus A.320-232	British Airways	
G-EUYN	Airbus A.320-232	British Airways	
G-EUYO	Airbus A.320-232	British Airways	
G-EUYP	Airbus A.320-232	British Airways	
G-EUYR	Airbus A.320-232	British Airways	
G-EUYS	Airbus A.320-232	British Airways	
G-EUYT	Airbus A.320-232	British Airways	
G-EUYU	Airbus A.320-232	British Airways	
G-EUYV	Airbus A.320-232	British Airways	
G-EUYW	Airbus A.320-232	British Airways	
G-EUYX	Airbus A.320-232	British Airways	
G-EUYY	Airbus A.320-232	British Airways	
G-EVAA	Autogyro Cavalon	J. W. Payne	
G-EVAJ	Best Off Skyranger 912S(1)	A. B. Gridley	
G-EVBF	Cameron Z-350 balloon	Virgin Balloon Flights	
G-EVEE	Robinson R44	EFL Helicopters Ltd (G-REGE)	
G-EVEN	Cirrus SR22	Glemmestad Invest AS (G-CGRD)	
G-EVET	Cameron 80 Concept balloon	M. D. J. Walker	
G-EVEY	Thruster T.600N 450-JAB	The G-EVEY Flying Group	
G-EVIB	Cirrus SR22	P. Bishop	
G-EVIE	PA-28-181 Warrior II	Tayside Aviation Ltd (G-ZULU)	
G-EVIG	Evektor EV-97 TeamEurostar UK	A. S. Mitchell	
G-EVII	Schempp-Hirth Ventus 2cT	Ventus G-EVII Syndicate	
G-EVLE	Rearwin 8125 Cloudster	W. D. Gray (G-BVLK)	
G-EVMK	deHavilland DHC-2 Beaver 1	T. W. Harris	
G-EVPI	Evans VP-1 Srs 2	C. P. Martyr	
G-EVRO	Aerotechnik EV-97 Eurostar	J. E. Rourke	

Notes	Reg	Type	Owner or Operator
	G-EVSL	Aerotechnik EV-97 Eurostar SL	M. Vouros
	G-EVSW	Evektor EV-97 Sportstar	I. Shulver
	G-EVTO	PA-28-161 Warrior II	Redhill Air Services Ltd
	G-EWAD	Robinson R44 II	MG Helicopters Ltd
	G-EWAN	Prostar PT-2C	C. G. Shaw
	G-EWBC	Avtec Jabiru SK	E. W. B. Comber
	G-EWEN	Aeropro Eurofox 912(S)	M. H. Talbot
	G-EWES	Pioneer 300	D. A. Ions
	G-EWEW	AB Sportine Aviacija LAK-19T	J. B. Strzebrakowski
	G-EWIZ	Pitts S-2E Special	R. S. Goodwin
	G-EWME	PA-28 Cherokee 235	R. J. Clarke
	G-EXAM	PA-28RT-201T Turbo Arrow IV	RR. S. Urquhart & A. Cameron
	G-EXCC	Carbon Cub EX-2	M. S. Colebrook
	G-EXEC	PA-34-200 Seneca	Sky Air Travel Ltd
	G-EXES	Shaw Europa XS	D. Barraclough
	G-EXEX	Cessna 404	Reconnaissance Ventures Ltd
	G-EXGC	Extra EA.300/200	P. J. Bull
	G-EXHL	Cameron C-70 balloon	R. K. Gyselynck
	G-EXII	Extra EA.300	S. Landi
	G-EXIL	Extra EA.300/S	G-Force Aerobatics LLP
	G-EXIT	MS.893E Rallye 180GT	G-EXIT Group
	G-EXLC	Extra EA.300/L	Cirrus Aircraft UK Ltd
	G-EXLL	Zenair CH.601	M. R. Brumby
	G-EXLT	Extra EA.300/LT	J. W. Marshall
	G-EXPL	Champion 7GCBC Citabria	Aero-Club Paris Nord/France
	G-EXTR	Extra EA.260	Principia Aerobatics LLP
	G-EXXL	Zenair CH.601XL Zodiac	J. H. Ellwood
	G-EYAK	Yakovlev Yak-50 (50 yellow)	P. N. A. Whitehead
	G-EYCO	Robin DR.400/180	M. J. Hanlon
	G-EYOR	Van's RV-6	S. I. Fraser
	G-EZAA	Airbus A.319-111	easyJet Airline Co.Ltd
	G-EZAB	Airbus A.319-111	easyJet Airline Co.Ltd
	G-EZAC	Airbus A.319-111	easyJet Airline Co.Ltd
	G-EZAF	Airbus A.319-111	easyJet Airline Co.Ltd
	G-EZAG	Airbus A.319-111	easyJet Airline Co.Ltd
	G-EZAI	Airbus A.319-111	easyJet Airline Co.Ltd
	G-EZAJ	Airbus A.319-111	easyJet Airline Co.Ltd
	G-EZAK	Airbus A.319-111	easyJet Airline Co.Ltd
	G-EZAL	Airbus A.319-111	easyJet Airline Co.Ltd
	G-EZAM	Airbus A.319-111	easyJet Airline Co.Ltd (G-CCKA)
	G-EZAN	Airbus A.319-111	easyJet Airline Co.Ltd
	G-EZAO	Airbus A.319-111	easyJet Airline Co.Ltd
	G-EZAP	Airbus A.319-111	easyJet Airline Co.Ltd
	G-EZAR	Pegasus Quik	D. McCormack
	G-EZAS	Airbus A.319-111	easyJet Airline Co.Ltd
	G-EZAT	Airbus A.319-111	easyJet Airline Co.Ltd
	G-EZAU	Airbus A.319-111	easyJet Airline Co.Ltd
	G-EZAV	Airbus A.319-111	easyJet Airline Co.Ltd
	G-EZAW	Airbus A.319-111	easyJet Airline Co.Ltd
	G-EZAX	Airbus A.319-111	easyJet Airline Co.Ltd
	G-EZAZ	Airbus A.319-111	easyJet Airline Co.Ltd
	G-EZBA	Airbus A.319-111	easyJet Airline Co.Ltd
	G-EZBB	Airbus A.319-111	easyJet Airline Co.Ltd
	G-EZBC	Airbus A.319-111	easyJet Airline Co.Ltd
	G-EZBD	Airbus A.319-111	easyJet Airline Co.Ltd
	G-EZBE	Airbus A.319-111	easyJet Airline Co.Ltd
	G-EZBF	Airbus A.319-111	easyJet Airline Co.Ltd
	G-EZBH	Airbus A.319-111	easyJet Airline Co.Ltd
	G-EZBI	Airbus A.319-111	easyJet Airline Co.Ltd
	G-EZBJ	Airbus A.319-111	easyJet Airline Co.Ltd
	G-EZBK	Airbus A.319-111	easyJet Airline Co.Ltd
	G-EZBN	Airbus A.319-111	easyJet Airline Co.Ltd
	G-EZBO	Airbus A.319-111	easyJet Airline Co.Ltd
	G-EZBR	Airbus A.319-111	easyJet Airline Co.Ltd
	G-EZBU	Airbus A.319-111	easyJet Airline Co.Ltd
	G-EZBV	Airbus A.319-111	easyJet Airline Co.Ltd
	G-EZBW	Airbus A.319-111	easyJet Airline.Co.Ltd

Reg	Type	Owner or Operator	Notes
G-EZBX	Airbus A.319-111	easyJet Airline Co.Ltd	
G-EZBZ	Airbus A.319-111	easyJet Airline Co.Ltd	
G-EZDA	Airbus A.319-111	easyJet Airline Co.Ltd	
G-EZDC	Airbus A.319-111	easyJet Airline Co Ltd (G-CCKB)	
G-EZDD	Airbus A.319-111	easyJet Airline Co.Ltd	
G-EZDF	Airbus A.319-111	easyJet Airline Co.Ltd	
G-EZDG	Rutan Vari-Eze	Varieze Flying Group (G-EZOS)	
G-EZDH	Airbus A.319-111	easyJet Airline Co.Ltd	
G-EZDI	Airbus A.319-111	easyJet Airline Co.Ltd	
G-EZDJ	Airbus A.319-111	easyJet Airline Co.Ltd	
G-EZDK	Airbus A.319-111	easyJet Airline Co.Ltd	
G-EZDL	Airbus A.319-111	easyJet Airline Co.Ltd	
G-EZDM	Airbus A.319-111	easyJet Airline Co.Ltd	
G-EZDN	Airbus A.319-111	easyJet Airline Co.Ltd	
G-EZDS	Airbus A.319-111	easyJet Airline Co.Ltd	
G-EZDV	Airbus A.319-111	easyJet Airline Co.Ltd	
G-EZDY	Airbus A.319-111	easyJet Airline Co.Ltd	
G-EZDZ	Airbus A.319-111	easyJet Airline Co.Ltd	
G-EZEB	Airbus A.319-111	easyJet Airline Co Ltd	
G-EZEG	Airbus A.319-111	easyJet Airline Co.Ltd	
G-EZEL	Westland SA.341G Gazelle 1	W. R. Pitcher (G-BAZL)	
G-EZES	Airbus A.319-111	easyJet Airline Co.Ltd	
G-EZEV	Airbus A.319-111	easyJet Airline Co.Ltd	
G-EZEY	Airbus A.319-111	easyJet Airline Co.Ltd	
G-EZEZ	Airbus A.319-111	easyJet Airline Co Ltd	
G-EZFA	Airbus A.319-111	easyJet Airline Co.Ltd	
G-EZFB	Airbus A.319-111	easyJet Airline Co.Ltd	
G-EZFC	Airbus A.319-111	easyJet Airline Co.Ltd	
G-EZFF	Airbus A.319-111	easyJet Airline Co.Ltd	
G-EZFH	Airbus A.319-111	easyJet Airline Co.Ltd	
G-EZFJ	Airbus A.319-111	easyJet Airline Co.Ltd	
G-EZFL	Airbus A.319-111	easyJet Airline Co.Ltd	
G-EZFM	Airbus A.319-111	easyJet Airline Co.Ltd	
G-EZFP	Airbus A.319-111	easyJet Airline Co.Ltd	
G-EZFT	Airbus A.319-111	easyJet Airline Co.Ltd	
G-EZFU	Airbus A.319-111	easyJet Airline Co.Ltd	
G-EZFV	Airbus A.319-111	easyJet Airline Co.Ltd	
G-EZFW	Airbus A.319-111	easyJet Airline Co.Ltd	
G-EZFX	Airbus A.319-111	easyJet Airline Co.Ltd	
G-EZFY	Airbus A.319-111	easyJet Airline Co.Ltd	
G-EZFZ	Airbus A.319-111	easyJet Airline Co.Ltd	
G-EZGA	Airbus A.319-111	easyJet Airline Co.Ltd	
G-EZGB	Airbus A.319-111	easyJet Airline Co.Ltd	
G-EZGC	Airbus A.319-111	easyJet Airline Co.Ltd	
G-EZGD	Airbus A.319-111	easyJet Airline Co.Ltd	
G-EZGE	Airbus A.319-111	easyJet Airline Co.Ltd	
G-EZGF	Airbus A.319-111	easyJet Airline Co.Ltd	
G-EZIH	Airbus A.319-111	easyJet Airline Co.Ltd	
G-EZII	Airbus A.319-111	easyJet Airline Co.Ltd	
G-EZIJ	Airbus A.319-111	easyJet Airline Co.Ltd	
G-EZIK	Airbus A.319-111	easyJet Airline Co.Ltd	
G-EZIL	Airbus A.319-111	easyJet Airline Co.Ltd	
G-EZIM	Airbus A.319-111	easyJet Airline Co.Ltd	
G-EZIN	Airbus A.319-111	easyJet Airline Co.Ltd	
G-EZIO	Airbus A.319-111	easyJet Airline Co.Ltd	
G-EZIP	Airbus A.319-111	easyJet Airline Co.Ltd	
G-EZIR	Airbus A.319-111	easyJet Airline Co.Ltd	
G-EZIS	Airbus A.319-111	easyJet Airline Co.Ltd	
G-EZIT	Airbus A.319-111	easyJet Airline Co.Ltd	
G-EZIV	Airbus A.319-111	easyJet Airline Co.Ltd	
G-EZIW	Airbus A.319-111	easyJet Airline Co.Ltd	
G-EZIX	Airbus A.319-111	easyJet Airline Co.Ltd	
G-EZIY	Airbus A.319-111	easyJet Airline Co.Ltd	
G-EZIZ	Airbus A.319-111	easyJet Airline Co.Ltd	
G-EZMK	Airbus A.319-111	easyJet Airline Co.Ltd	
G-EZNC	Airbus A.319-111	easyJet Airline Co.Ltd (G-CCKC)	
G-EZNM	Airbus A.319-111	easyJet Airline Co.Ltd	
G-EZOA	Airbus A.320-214	easyJet Airline Co.Ltd	
G-EZOB	Airbus A.320-214	easyJet Airline Co.Ltd	
G-EZOC	Airbus A.320-214	easyJet Airline Co.Ltd	
G-EZOD	Airbus A.320-214	easyJet Airline Co.Ltd	

Notes	Reg	Type	Owner or Operator
	G-EZOF	Airbus A.320-214	easyJet Airline Co.Ltd
	G-EZOG	Airbus A.320-214	easyJet Airline Co.Ltd
	G-EZOI	Airbus A.320-214	easyJet Airline Co.Ltd
	G-EZOK	Airbus A.320-214	easyJet Airline Co.Ltd
	G-EZOM	Airbus A.320-214	easyJet Airline Co.Ltd
	G-EZON	Airbus A.320-214	easyJet Airline Co.Ltd
	G-EZOO	Airbus A.320-214	easyJet Airline Co.Ltd
	G-EZOP	Airbus A.320-214	easyJet Airline Co.Ltd
	G-EZOT	Airbus A.320-214	easyJet Airline Co.Ltd
	G-EZOU	Airbus A.320-214	easyJet Airline Co.Ltd
	G-EZOW	Airbus A.320-214	easyJet Airline Co.Ltd
	G-EZOX	Airbus A.320-214	easyJet Airline Co.Ltd
	G-EZOY	Airbus A.320-214	easyJet Airline Co.Ltd
	G-EZOZ	Airbus A.320-214	easyJet Airline Co.Ltd
	G-EZPB	Airbus A.320-214	easyJet Airline Co.Ltd
	G-EZPC	Airbus A.320-214	easyJet Airline Co.Ltd
	G-EZPD	Airbus A.320-214	easyJet Airline Co.Ltd
	G-EZPE	Airbus A.320-214	easyJet Airline Co.Ltd
	G-EZPF	Airbus A.320-214	easyJet Airline Co.Ltd
	G-EZPG	Airbus A.319-111	easyJet Airline Co.Ltd
	G-EZPI	Airbus A.320-214	easyJet Airline Co.Ltd
	G-EZPO	Airbus A.320-214	easyJet Airline Co.Ltd
	G-EZPS	Airbus A.320-214	easyJet Airline Co.Ltd
	G-EZPT	Airbus A.320-214	easyJet Airline Co.Ltd
	G-EZPW	Airbus A.320-214	easyJet Airline Co.Ltd
	G-EZPY	Airbus A.320-214	easyJet Airline Co.Ltd
	G-EZRA	Airbus A.320-214	easyJet Airline Co.Ltd
	G-EZRD	Airbus A.320-214	easyJet Airline Co.Ltd
	G-EZRG	Airbus A.320-214	easyJet Airline Co.Ltd
	G-EZRH	Airbus A.320-214	easyJet Airline Co.Ltd
	G-EZRI	Airbus A.320-214	easyJet Airline Co.Ltd
	G-EZRJ	Airbus A.320-214	easyJet Airline Co.Ltd
	G-EZRK	Airbus A.320-214	easyJet Airline Co.Ltd
	G-EZRL	Airbus A.320-214	easyJet Airline Co.Ltd
	G-EZRM	Airbus A.320-214	easyJet Airline Co.Ltd
	G-EZRN	Airbus A.320-214	easyJet Airline Co.Ltd
	G-EZRO	Airbus A.320-214	easyJet Airline Co.Ltd
	G-EZRP	Airbus A.320-214	easyJet Airline Co.Ltd
	G-EZRR	Airbus A.320-214	easyJet Airline Co.Ltd
	G-EZRS	Airbus A.320-214	easyJet Airline Co.Ltd
	G-EZRT	Airbus A.320-214	easyJet Airline Co.Ltd
	G-EZRU	Airbus A.320-214	easyJet Airline Co.Ltd
	G-EZTA	Airbus A.320-214	easyJet Airline Co.Ltd
	G-EZTB	Airbus A.320-214	easyJet Airline Co.Ltd
	G-EZTC	Airbus A.320-214	easyJet Airline Co.Ltd
	G-EZTD	Airbus A.320-214	easyJet Airline Co.Ltd
	G-EZTE	Airbus A.320-214	easyJet Airline Co.Ltd
	G-EZTG	Airbus A.320-214	easyJet Airline Co.Ltd
	G-EZTH	Airbus A.320-214	easyJet Airline Co.Ltd
	G-EZTK	Airbus A.320-214	easyJet Airline Co.Ltd
	G-EZTM	Airbus A.320-214	easyJet Airline Co.Ltd
	G-EZTR	Airbus A.320-214	easyJet Airline Co.Ltd
	G-EZTT	Airbus A.320-214	easyJet Airline Co.Ltd
	G-EZTY	Airbus A.320-214	easyJet Airline Co.Ltd
	G-EZTZ	Airbus A.320-214	easyJet Airline Co.Ltd
	G-EZUA	Airbus A.320-214	easyJet Airline Co.Ltd
	G-EZUB	Zenair CH.601HD Zodiac	J. R. Davis
	G-EZUC	Airbus A.320-214	easyJet Airline Co.Ltd
	G-EZUD	Airbus A.320-214	easyJet Airline Co.Ltd
	G-EZUF	Airbus A.320-214	easyJet Airline Co.Ltd
	G-EZUG	Airbus A.320-214	easyJet Airline Co.Ltd
	G-EZUH	Airbus A.320-214	easyJet Airline Co.Ltd
	G-EZUJ	Airbus A.320-214	easyJet Airline Co.Ltd
	G-EZUK	Airbus A.320-214	easyJet Airline Co.Ltd
	G-EZUL	Airbus A.320-214	easyJet Airline Co.Ltd
	G-EZUM	Airbus A.320-214	easyJet Airline Co.Ltd
	G-EZUN	Airbus A.320-214	easyJet Airline Co.Ltd
	G-EZUO	Airbus A.320-214	easyJet Airline Co.Ltd
	G-EZUP	Airbus A.320-214	easyJet Airline Co.Ltd
	G-EZUR	Airbus A.320-214	easyJet Airline Co.Ltd
	G-EZUS	Airbus A.320-214	easyJet Airline Co.Ltd

Reg	Type	Owner or Operator	Notes
G-EZUT	Airbus A.320-214	easyJet Airline Co.Ltd	
G-EZUW	Airbus A.320-214	easyJet Airline Co.Ltd	
G-EZUZ	Airbus A.320-214	easyJet Airline Co.Ltd	
G-EZVS	Colt 77B balloon	A. J. Lovell	
G-EZWA	Airbus A.320-214	easyJet Airline Co.Ltd	
G-EZWB	Airbus A.320-214	easyJet Airline Co.Ltd	
G-EZWC	Airbus A.320-214	easyJet Airline Co.Ltd	
G-EZWD	Airbus A.320-214	easyJet Airline Co.Ltd	
G-EZWE	Airbus A.320-214	easyJet Airline Co.Ltd	
G-EZWF	Airbus A.320-214	easyJet Airline Co.Ltd	
G-EZWG	Airbus A.320-214	easyJet Airline Co.Ltd	
G-EZWH	Airbus A.320-214	easyJet Airline Co.Ltd	
G-EZWI	Airbus A.320-214	easyJet Airline Co.Ltd	
G-EZWJ	Airbus A.320-214	easyJet Airline Co.Ltd	
G-EZWL	Airbus A.320-214	easyJet Airline Co.Ltd	
G-EZWM	Airbus A.320-214	easyJet Airline Co.Ltd	
G-EZWN	Airbus A.320-214	easyJet Airline Co.Ltd	
G-EZWP	Airbus A.320-214	easyJet Airline Co.Ltd	
G-EZWR	Airbus A.320-214	easyJet Airline Co.Ltd	
G-EZWS	Airbus A.320-214	easyJet Airline Co.Ltd	
G-EZWT	Airbus A.320-214	easyJet Airline Co.Ltd	
G-EZWU	Airbus A.320-214	easyJet Airline Co.Ltd	
G-EZWV	Airbus A.320-214	easyJet Airline Co.Ltd	
G-EZWX	Airbus A.320-214	easyJet Airline Co.Ltd	
G-EZWY	Airbus A.320-214	easyJet Airline Co.Ltd	
G-EZWZ	Airbus A.320-214	easyJet Airline Co.Ltd	
G-EZXO	Colt 56A balloon	K. Jakobsson/Sweden	
G-EZZA	Shaw Europa XS	J. C. R. Davey	
G-EZZE	CZAW Sportcruiser	C. Turner	
G-EZZL	Westland Gazelle HT.3	Regal Group UK (G-CBKC)	
G-EZZY	Evektor EV-97A Eurostar	D. P. Creedy	
G-FABA	PA-31-350 Navajo Chieftain	Atlantic Bridge Aviation Ltd (G-OJIL)	
G-FABO	Bombardier CL600-2B16 Challenger 604	Hangar 8 Management Ltd	
G-FACE	Cessna 172S	Oxford Aviation Services Ltd	
G-FADF	PA-18-150 Super Cub	A. J. Neale	
G-FAEJ	Cessna 182A	C. Keller, S. Koch & B. Schmiedel/Germany	
G-FAIR	SOCATA TB10 Tobago	A. J. Gomes	
G-FAJC	Alpi Pioneer 300 Hawk	M. Clare	
G-FAJM	Robinson R44 II	Ryvoan Aviation Ltd	
G-FALC	Aeromere F.8L Falco	D. M. Burbridge (G-AROT)	
G-FAME	Starstreak Shadow SA-II	C. R. Buckle	
G-FANL	Cessna FR.172K XP-II	J. A. Rees	
G-FARE	Robinson R44 II	Toriamos Ltd/Ireland	
G-FARL	Pitts S-1E Special	J. P. Barrenechea	
G-FARO	Aero Designs Star-Lite SL.1	S. C. Goozee	
G-FARR	Jodel 150	S. J. Farr	
G-FARY	QAC Quickie Tri-Q	A. Bloomfield	
G-FATB	Rockwell Commander 114B	James D. Pearce & Co	
G-FATE	Falco F8L	G-FATE Flying Group	
G-FAZT	Stoddard-Hamilton Glasair II-SRG	C. Bruce	
G-FBAR	Diamond DA.40 Star	Exceedingly Ltd	
G-FBAT	Aeroprakt A.22 Foxbat	J. Jordan	
G-FBCY	Skystar Kitfox Mk 7	A. Bray (G-FBOY)	
G-FBEF	Embraer ERJ190-200LR	Flybe.com	
G-FBEG	Embraer ERJ190-200LR	Flybe.com	
G-FBEH	Embraer ERJ190-200LR	Flybe.com	
G-FBEI	Embraer ERJ190-200LR	Flybe.com	
G-FBEJ	Embraer ERJ190-200LR	Flybe.com	
G-FBEK	Embraer ERJ190-200LR	Flybe.com	
G-FBEL	Embraer ERJ190-200LR	Flybe.com	
G-FBEM	Embraer ERJ190-200LR	Flybe.com	
G-FBEN	Embraer ERJ190-200LR	Flybe.com	
G-FBII	Ikarus C.42 FB100	F. Beeson	
G-FBJA	Embraer ERJ170-200STD	Flybe.com	
G-FBJB	Embraer ERJ170-200STD	Flybe.com	
G-FBJC	Embraer ERJ170-200STD	Flybe.com	
G-FBJD	Embraer ERJ170-200STD	Flybe.com	
G-FBJE	Embraer ERJ170-200STD	Flybe.com	
G-FBJF	Embraer ERJ170-200STD	Flybe.com	

Notes	Reg	Type	Owner or Operator
	G-FBJG	Embraer ERJ170-200STD	Flybe.com
	G-FBJH	Embraer ERJ170-200STD	Flybe.com
	G-FBJI	Embraer ERJ170-200STD	Flybe.com
	G-FBJJ	Embraer ERJ170-200STD	Flybe.com
	G-FBJK	Embraer ERJ170-200STD	Flybe.com
	G-FBKB	Cessna 510 Citation Mustang	Wijet
	G-FBKC	Cessna 510 Citation Mustang	Wijet
	G-FBKE	Cessna 510 Citation Mustang	Wijet
	G-FBKF	Cessna 510 Citation Mustang	Wijet
	G-FBKG	Cessna 510 Citation Mustang	Wijet
	G-FBKH	Cessna 510 Citation Mustang	Wijet
	G-FBKK	Cessna 510 Citation Mustang	Wijet
	G-FBLK	Cessna 510 Citation Mustang	Wijet
	G-FBNK	Cessna 510 Citation Mustang	Wijet
	G-FBRN	PA-28-181 Archer II	G. E. Fox
	G-FBSS	Aeroprakt A22-LS Foxbat	S. R. V. McNeill
	G-FBTT	Aeroprakt A22-L Foxbat	J. Toner & J. Coyle
	G-FBWH	PA-28R-180 Cherokee Arrow	K. McElhinney
	G-FBXA	Aerospatiale ATR-72-212A	Flybe Ltd/SAS
	G-FBXB	Aerospatiale ATR-72-212A	Flybe Ltd/SAS
	G-FBXC	Aerospatiale ATR-72-212A	Flybe Ltd/SAS
	G-FBXD	Aerospatiale ATR-72-212A	Flybe Ltd/SAS
	G-FBXE	Aerospatiale ATR-72-212A	Flybe Ltd/SAS
	G-FCAC	Diamond DA.42 Twin Star	AJW Construction Ltd (G-ORZA)
	G-FCAV	Schleicher ASK-13	M. F. Cuming
	G-FCCC	Schleicher ASK-13	Shenington Gliding Club
	G-FCKD	Eurocopter EC 120B	Red Dragon Management LLP
	G-FCOM	Slingsby T.59F Kestrel	P. A. C. Wheatcroft & A. G. Truman
	G-FCSL	PA-32-350 Navajo Chieftain	Culross Aerospace Ltd (G-CLAN)
	G-FCSP	Robin DR.400/180	N. W. McConachie
	G-FCTK	DH.82C Tiger Moth	A. J. Palmer
	G-FCUK	Pitts S-1C Special	H. C. Luck & M. J. Saggers
	G-FCUM	Robinson R44 II	Barnes Holdings Ltd
	G-FDDY	Schleicher Ka 6CR	M. D. Brooks
	G-FDHB	Bristol Scout Model C Replica (1264)	Bristol Scout Group
	G-FDHS	Leonardo AW109SP Grand New	Knaresborough Aviation LLP
	G-FDPS	Aviat Pitts S-2C Special	Flights and Dreams Ltd
	G-FDZA	Boeing 737-8K5	TUI Airways Ltd
	G-FDZB	Boeing 737-8K5	TUI Airways Ltd
	G-FDZD	Boeing 737-8K5	TUI Airways Ltd
	G-FDZE	Boeing 737-8K5	TUI Airways Ltd
	G-FDZF	Boeing 737-8K5	TUI Airways Ltd
	G-FDZG	Boeing 737-8K5	TUI Airways Ltd
	G-FDZJ	Boeing 737-8K5	TUI Airways Ltd
	G-FDZR	Boeing 737-8K5	TUI Airways Ltd
	G-FDZS	Boeing 737-8K5	TUI Airways Ltd
	G-FDZT	Boeing 737-8K5	TUI Airways Ltd
	G-FDZU	Boeing 737-8K5	TUI Airways Ltd
	G-FDZW	Boeing 737-8K5	TUI Airways Ltd
	G-FDZX	Boeing 737-8K5	TUI Airways Ltd
	G-FDZY	Boeing 737-8K5	TUI Airways Ltd
	G-FDZZ	Boeing 737-8K5	TUI Airways Ltd
	G-FEAB	PA-28-181 Archer III	Feabrex Ltd
	G-FEBB	Grob G.104 Speed Astir IIB	G-FEBB Syndicate
	G-FEBJ	Schleicher ASW-19B	I. R. Willows
	G-FECO	Grob G.102 Astir CS77	Stratford on Avon Gliding Club
	G-FEED	Cameron Z-90 balloon	O. Rosellino/Italy
	G-FEEF	Jodel DR.220-2 + 2	M. Juhrig
	G-FEET	Mainair Pegasus Quik	M. P. Duckett
	G-FEGN	PA-28-236 Dakota	P. J. Vacher
	G-FELC	Cirrus SR22	F. Rossello
	G-FELD	Rotorsport UK MTO Sport	S. Pearce
	G-FELL	Shaw Europa	M. C. Costin & J. A. Inglis
	G-FELT	Cameron N-77 balloon	R. P. Allan
	G-FELX	CZAW Sportcruiser	T. F. Smith
	G-FERN	Mainair Blade 912	S. Worthington
	G-FERV	Rolladen-Schneider LS4	S. Walker
	G-FESB	Pipistrel Apis 15M M FES	P. C. Piggott

Reg	Type	Owner or Operator	Notes
G-FESS	Pegasus Quantum 15-912	P. M. Fessi (G-CBBZ)	
G-FEST	AS.350B Ecureuil	Wavendon Social Housing Ltd	
G-FESX	Schempp-Hirth Discus 2C FES	K. S. McPhee & P. K. Carpenter	
G-FEVS	PZL-Bielsko SZD-50-3 Puchacz	Norfolk Gliding Club Ltd	
G-FEWG	Fuji FA.200-160	Cirrus UK Training Ltd (G-BBNV)	
G-FEZZ	Bell 206B JetRanger II	R. J. Myram	
G-FFAB	Cameron N-105 balloon	B. J. Hammond	
G-FFAF	Cessna F.150L	R. J. Fletcher	
G-FFBG	Cessna F.182Q	D. P. Edwards	
G-FFEN	Cessna F.150M	D. A. Abel	
G-FFFA	P & M PulsR	Flying For Freedom Ltd	
G-FFFB	P & M Quik GTR	Flying for Freedom Ltd	
G-FFFC	Cessna 510 Citation Mustang	Wijet	
G-FFFF	Zenair CH.750	J. Bate	
G-FFFT	Lindstrand LBL-31A balloon	W. Rousell & J. Tyrrell	
G-FFIT	Pegasus Quik	R. G. G. Pinder	
G-FFMV	Diamond DA.42 M-NG Twin Star	Cobham Leasing Ltd	
G-FFOX	Hawker Hunter T.7B (WV318:D)	Swift Composites Ltd	
G-FFRA	Dassault Falcon 20DC	FR Aviation Ltd	
G-FFUN	Pegasus Quantum 15	M. D. & R. M. Jarvis	
G-FFWD	Cessna 310R	T. S. Courtman (G-TVKE/G-EURO)	
G-FGAZ	Schleicher Ka 6E	P. W. Graves	
G-FGID	Vought FG-1D Corsair (KD345:130-A)	Patina Ltd	
G-FGSI	Montgomerie-Bensen B8MR	F. G. Shepherd	
G-FGXP	Bell 407	Pink Time Ltd	
G-FHAS	Scheibe SF.25E Super Falke	Upwood Motorglider Group	
G-FIAT	PA-28 Cherokee 140	Demero Ltd & Transcourt Ltd (G-BBYW)	
G-FIBS	AS.350BA Ecureuil	Maceplast Romania SA/Romania	
G-FIBT	Robinson R44 II	G. Mazza & A. Curnis/Italy	
G-FICA	PA-28RT-201 Arrow IV	G. E. Entrup-Otte & W. F.-J. Wagener	
G-FICH	Guimbal Cabri G2	Helicentre Aviation Ltd	
G-FICS	Flight Design CTSW	J. I. Spring, A. S. Harris & D. R. Green	
G-FIDL	Thruster T.600T 450 Jab	T. A. Colman (G-CBIO)	
G-FIDO	Best Off Skyranger Nynja 912S(1)	P. D. Hollands	
G-FIFA	Cessna 404 Titan	RVL Aviation Ltd (G-TVIP/G-KIWI/G-BHNI)	
G-FIFE	Cessna FA.152	The Moray Flying Club (1990) (G-BFYN)	
G-FIFI	SOCATA TB20 Trinidad	C. P. H. Palmer-Brown (G-BMWS)	
G-FIFT	Ikarus C.42 FB 100	A. R. Jones	
G-FIFY	Colomban MC-30 Luciole	I. J. M. Donnelly	
G-FIGA	Cessna 152	Bowen-Air Ltd	
G-FIGB	Cessna 152	A. J. Gomes	
G-FIII	Extra EA.300/L	M. & R. M. Nagel (G-RGEE)	
G-FIJJ	Cessna F.177RG	Fly 177 SARL/France (G-AZFP)	
G-FILE	PA-34-200T Seneca	G-FILE Group	
G-FINA	Cessna F.150L	A. Boyd (G-BIFT)	
G-FIND	Cessna F.406	Reconnaissance Ventures Ltd	
G-FINT	Piper L-4B Grasshopper	G. & H. M. Picarella	
G-FINZ	I.I.I Sky Arrow 650T	C. A. Bloom	
G-FION	Titan T-51 Mustang	A. A. Wordsworth	
G-FITY	Europa XS	D. C. A. Moore	
G-FIXX	Van's RV-7	P. C. Hambilton	
G-FIZY	Shaw Europa XS	G. J. P. Skinner (G-DDSC)	
G-FIZZ	PA-28-161 Warrior II	G-FIZZ Group	
G-FJET	Cessna 550 Citation II	London Executive Aviation Ltd (G-DCFR/ G-WYLX/G-JETD)	
G-FJMS	Partenavia P.68B	J. B. Randle (G-SVHA)	
G-FJTH	Aeroprakt A.22 Foxbat	B. Gurling	
G-FKNH	PA-15 Vagabond	M. J. Mothershaw	
G-FKOS	PA-28-181 Archer II	M. K. Johnson	
G-FLAG	Colt 77A balloon	B. A. Williams	
G-FLAV	PA-28-161 Warrior II	G. E. Fox	
G-FLAX	Aeropro Eurofox 914	Lleweni Parc Ltd	
G-FLBA	DHC.8-402 Dash Eight	Flybe.com	
G-FLBB	DHC.8-402 Dash Eight	Flybe.com	

Notes	Reg	Type	Owner or Operator
	G-FLBC	DHC.8-402 Dash Eight	Flybe.com
	G-FLBD	DHC.8-402 Dash Eight	Flybe.com
	G-FLBE	DHC.8-402 Dash Eight	Flybe.com
	G-FLBK	Cessna 510 Citation Mustang	Wijet
	G-FLBY	Ikarus C42 FB100 Bravo	Fly by Light
	G-FLCA	Fleet Model 80 Canuck	S. P. Evans
	G-FLCN	Dassault Falcon 900B	XJC Ltd
	G-FLCT	Hallam Fleche	R. G. Hallam
	G-FLDG	Skyranger 912	A. J. Gay
	G-FLEA	SOCATA TB10 Tobago	N. J. Thomas
	G-FLEE	ZJ-Viera	P. C. Piggott
	G-FLEW	Lindstrand LBL-90A balloon	H. C. Loveday
	G-FLGT	Lindstrand LBL-105A balloon	Ballongaventyr I. Skane AB/Sweden
	G-FLIA	AutoGyro Calidus	P. Davies
	G-FLIK	Pitts S-1S Special	R. P. Millinship
	G-FLIP	Cessna FA.152	South East Area Flying Section (G-BOES)
	G-FLIS	Magni M.16C	M. L. L. Temple
	G-FLIT	Rotorway Executive 162F	R. S. Snell
	G-FLKE	Scheibe SF.25C Falke	The Royal Air Force Gliding & Soaring Association
	G-FLKS	Scheibe SF.25C Falke	London Gliding Club Propietary Ltd
	G-FLKY	Cessna 172S	M. E. Falkingham
	G-FLOE	Robinson R66	Freechase Ventures Ltd
	G-FLOR	Shaw Europa	A. F. C. van Eldik
	G-FLOW	Cessna 172N	P. H. Archard
	G-FLOX	Shaw Europa	DPT Group
	G-FLPI	Rockwell Commander 112	J. B. Thompson
	G-FLTC	BAe 146-300	E3205 Trading Ltd (G-JEBH/G-BVTO/G-NJID)
	G-FLUZ	Rolladen-Schneider LS8-18	D. M. King
	G-FLXS	Dassault Falcon 2000LX	TAG Aviation (UK) Ltd
	G-FLYA	Mooney M.20J	B. Willis
	G-FLYB	Ikarus C.42 FB100	M. D. Stewart
	G-FLYC	Ikarus C.42 FB100	Solent Flight Ltd
	G-FLYF	Mainair Blade 912	D. G. Adley
	G-FLYG	Slingsby T.67C	G. Laden
	G-FLYI	PA-34-200 Seneca II	Falcon Flying Services Ltd (G-BHVO)
	G-FLYJ	EV-97 Eurostar SL	The Scottish Aero Club Ltd
	G-FLYK	Beech B.200 Super King Air	D. T. A. Rees
	G-FLYM	Ikarus C42 FB100	R. S. O'Carroll
	G-FLYO	EV-97 Eurostar SL	C. Berbec
	G-FLYP	Beagle B.206 Srs 2	R. H. Ford & A. T. J. Darrah (G-AVHO)
	G-FLYT	Shaw Europa	K. F. & R. Richardson
	G-FLYW	Beech B.200 Super King Air	J. A. Rees (G-LIVY/G-PSTR)
	G-FLYX	Robinson R44 II	HQ Aviation Ltd
	G-FLYY	BAC.167 Strikemaster 80A	High G Jets Ltd
	G-FLZR	Staaken Z-21 Flitzer	I. V. Staines
	G-FMAM	PA-28-151 Warrior (modified)	Air Training Club Aviation Ltd (G-BBXV)
	G-FMBS	Inverted US 12	W. P. Wright
	G-FMGB	Cameron Z-90 balloon	A. M. Holly
	G-FMGG	Maule M5-235C Lunar Rocket	S. Bierbaum (G-RAGG)
	G-FMKA	Diamond HK.36TC Super Dimona	G. P. Davis
	G-FMLY	Commander 114B	PNG Air Ltd (G-VICS)
	G-FNAV	PA-31-350 Navajo Chieftain	Flight Calibration Services Ltd (G-BFFR)
	G-FNEY	Cessna F.177RG	F. Ney
	G-FNLD	Cessna 172N	Papa Hotel Flying Group
	G-FOFO	Robinson R44 II	A. Pickup
	G-FOGG	Cameron N-90 balloon	J. P. E. Money-Kyrle
	G-FOGI	Shaw Europa XS	B. Fogg
	G-FOKK	Fokker DR1 (replica) (477/17)	P. D. & S. E. Ford
	G-FOKR	Fokker E.III (replica) (422/15)	R. D. Myles
	G-FOKS	Aeropro Eurofox 912(S)	E. R. Scougall
	G-FOKX	Eurofox 912(S)	Trent Valley Eurofox Group
	G-FOKZ	Aeropro Eurofox 912(IS)	R. J. Evans
	G-FOLI	Robinson R22 Beta II	Paul D. White Ltd
	G-FOLY	Aerotek Pitts S-2A Modified	C. T. Charleston
	G-FOOT	Robinson R44 I	Autorotation Ltd
	G-FOPP	Lancair 320	Great Circle Design Ltd
	G-FORA	Schempp-Hirth Ventus cT	P. Clay

Reg	Type	Owner or Operator	Notes
G-FORD	SNCAN Stampe SV.4C	P. H. Meeson	
G-FORZ	Pitts S-1S Special	N. W. Parkinson	
G-FOSY	MS.880B Rallye Club	A. G. Foster (G-AXAK)	
G-FOWL	Colt 90A balloon	M. R. Stokoe	
G-FOXA	PA-28-161 Cadet	Leicestershire Aero Club Ltd	
G-FOXB	Aeroprakt A.22 Foxbat	G. D. McCullough	
G-FOXC	Denney Kitfox Mk 3	T. Willford & R. M. Bremner	
G-FOXD	Denney Kitfox Mk 2	P. P. Trangmar	
G-FOXF	Denney Kitfox Mk 4	M. S. Goodwin	
G-FOXG	Denney Kitfox Mk 2	M. V. Hearns	
G-FOXI	Denney Kitfox	I. M. Walton	
G-FOXL	Zenair CH.601XL Zodiac	R. W. Taylor	
G-FOXM	Bell 206B JetRanger 2	Hessle Dock Company Ltd (G-STAK/G-BNIS)	
G-FOXO	Aeropro Eurofox 912(S)	S. E. Coles	
G-FOXS	Denney Kitfox Mk 2	G-FOXS Darley Tail Draggers	
G-FOXT	Aeros Ant/Fox 13TL	R. Bower	
G-FOXU	Aeropro Eurofox 912S(1)	C. D. Waldron	
G-FOXW	Aeropro Eurofox 912(1)	A. P. Whitmarsh	
G-FOXX	Denney Kitfox	M. D. Gregory	
G-FOXZ	Denney Kitfox	S. C. Goozee	
G-FOZY	Van's RV-7	M. G. Forrest (G-COPZ)	
G-FOZZ	Beech A36 Bonanza	Edelweiss Media GmbH/Austria	
G-FPEH	Guimbal Cabri G2	Paul D. White Ltd	
G-FPIG	PA-28-151 Warrior	G. F. Strain (G-BSSR)	
G-FPLD	Beech 200 Super King Air	Thales UK Ltd	
G-FPSA	PA-28-161 Warrior II	Falcon Flying Services (G-RSFT/G-WARI)	
G-FRAD	Dassault Falcon 20E	Cobham Leasing Ltd (G-BCYF)	
G-FRAF	Dassault Falcon 20E	FR Aviation Ltd	
G-FRAG	PA-32 Cherokee Six 300E	T. A. Houghton	
G-FRAH	Dassault Falcon 20DC	FR Aviation Ltd	
G-FRAI	Dassault Falcon 20E	FR Aviation Ltd	
G-FRAJ	Dassault Falcon 20E	FR Aviation Ltd	
G-FRAK	Dassault Falcon 20DC	FR Aviation Ltd	
G-FRAL	Dassault Falcon 20DC	FR Aviation Ltd	
G-FRAN	Piper J-3C-90 Cub(480321:H-44)	Essex L-4 Group (G-BIXY)	
G-FRAO	Dassault Falcon 20DC	FR Aviation Ltd	
G-FRAP	Dassault Falcon 20DC	FR Aviation Ltd	
G-FRAR	Dassault Falcon 20DC	FR Aviation Ltd	
G-FRAS	Dassault Falcon 20C	FR Aviation Ltd	
G-FRAT	Dassault Falcon 20C	FR Aviation Ltd	
G-FRAU	Dassault Falcon 20C	FR Aviation Ltd	
G-FRAW	Dassault Falcon 20ECM	FR Aviation Ltd	
G-FRCE	Folland Gnat T.Mk.1 (XS104)	Red Gnat Ltd	
G-FRCX	P & M Quik GTR	G-FRCX Syndicate	
G-FRDM	Boeing Stearman B75N1	T. W. Gilbert	
G-FRDY	Dynamic WT9 UK	J. A. Lockert	
G-FRGT	P & M Quik GT450	G-FRGT Group	
G-FRJB	Britten Sheriff SA-1 ★	Aeropark	
G-FRNK	Skyranger 912(2)	D. L. Foxley & G. Lace	
G-FROM	Ikarus C.42 FB100	G-FROM Group	
G-FRRN	Leonardo AW109SP Grand New	Harrier Enterprises Ltd	
G-FRSX	VS.388 Seafire F.46 (LA564)	Seafire Displays Ltd	
G-FRYA	Robinson R44 II	Bryanair (G-EJRC)	
G-FRYI	Beech 200 Super King Air	London Executive Aviation Ltd (G-OAVX/ G-IBCA/G-BMCA)	
G-FRYL	Beech 390 Premier 1	Hawk Air Ltd	
G-FSAR	Agusta Westland AW189	British International Helicopter Services Ltd	
G-FSBW	Aeropro Eurofox 912S(1)	N. G. Heywood	
G-FSEU	Beech 200 Super King Air	Nimbus Air Ltd	
G-FSZY	TB-10 Tobago	P. J. Bentley	
G-FTAX	Cessna 421C	Gold Air International Ltd (G-BFFM)	
G-FTIL	Robin DR.400/180R	RAF Wyton Flying Club Ltd	
G-FTUS	Ultramagic F-12 Paquete balloon	A. M. Holly	
G-FUEL	Robin DR.400/180	S. L. G. Darch	
G-FUKM	Westland Gazelle AH.1 (ZA730)	Falcon Aviation Ltd	
G-FULL	PA-28R Cherokee Arrow 200-II	Stapleford Flying Club Ltd (G-HWAY/G-JULI)	

Notes	Reg	Type	Owner or Operator
	G-FUND	Thunder Ax7-65Z balloon	G. B. Davies
	G-FUNN	Plumb BGP-1A	J. Riley
	G-FURI	Isaacs Fury II	S. M. Johnston
	G-FURZ	Best Off Sky Ranger Nynja 912S(1)	D. J. Tomlin
	G-FUSE	Cameron N-105 balloon	S. A. Lacey
	G-FUUN	Silence SA.180 Twister	A. W. McKee
	G-FUZZ	PA-18 Super Cub 95 (51-15319)	G. W. Cline
	G-FVEE	Monnett Sonerai 1	J. S. Baldwin
	G-FVEL	Cameron Z-90 balloon	Fort Vale Engineering Ltd
	G-FWJR	Ultramagic M-56 balloon	Harding and Sons Ltd
	G-FWKS	Tanarg/Ixess 15 912S(1)	M. A. Coffin (G-SYUT)
	G-FWPW	PA-28-236 Dakota	P. A. & F. C. Winters
	G-FXAR	Raytheon 400XT	Flexjet Ltd
	G-FXBT	Aeroprakt A.22 Foxbat	R. H. Jago
	G-FXCR	Raytheon 400A	Flexjet Ltd
	G-FXER	Raytheon 400A	Flexjet Ltd
	G-FXII	VS.366 Spitfire F.XII (EN224)	Air Leasing Ltd
	G-FXKR	Raytheon 400XT	Flexjet Ltd
	G-FXPR	Raytheon 400XT	Flexjet Ltd
	G-FYAN	Williams Westwind MLB	M. D. Williams
	G-FYAO	Williams Westwind MLB	M. D. Williams
	G-FYAU	Williams Westwind Mk 2 MLB	M. D. Williams
	G-FYAV	Osprey Mk 4E2 MLB	C. D. Egan & C. Stiles
	G-FYBX	Portswood Mk XVI MLB	I. Chadwick
	G-FYCL	Osprey Mk 4G MLB	P. J. Rogers
	G-FYCV	Osprey Mk 4D MLB	M. Thomson
	G-FYDF	Osprey Mk 4DV	K. A. Jones
	G-FYDI	Williams Westwind Two MLB	M. D. Williams
	G-FYDN	European 8C MLB	P. D. Ridout
	G-FYDO	Osprey Mk 4D MLB	N. L. Scallan
	G-FYDP	Williams Westwind Three MLB	M. D. Williams
	G-FYDS	Osprey Mk 4D MLB	N. L. Scallan
	G-FYEK	Unicorn UE.1C MLB	D. & D. Eaves
	G-FYEO	Eagle Mk 1 MLB	M. E. Scallan
	G-FYEV	Osprey Mk 1C MLB	M. E. Scallan
	G-FYEZ	Firefly Mk 1 MLB	M. E. & N. L. Scallan
	G-FYFI	European E.84DS MLB	M. Stelling
	G-FYFJ	Williams Westland 2 MLB	M. D. Williams
	G-FYFN	Osprey Saturn 2 MLB	J. & M. Woods
	G-FYFW	Rango NA-55 MLB	Rango Balloon and Kite Company
	G-FYFY	Rango NA-55RC MLB	Rango Balloon and Kite Company
	G-FYGC	Rango NA-42B MLB	L. J. Wardle
	G-FYGJ	Airspeed 300 MLB	N. Wells
	G-FYGM	Saffrey/Smith Princess MLB	A. Smith
	G-FZZA	General Avia F22-A	W. A. Stewart
	G-FZZI	Cameron H-34 balloon	Magical Adventures Ltd
	G-GAAL	Cessna 560XL Citation XLS	London Executive Aviation Ltd (G-DEIA)
	G-GAAZ	Cessna F.172N	M. Baumeister
	G-GABI	Lindstrand LBL-35A Cloudhopper balloon	R. D. Sargeant
	G-GABS	Cameron TR-70 balloon	N. M. Gabriel
	G-GABY	Bombardier BD-700-1A10 Global Express	Emperor Aviation Ltd
	G-GACA	P.57 Sea Prince T.1 (WP308:572CU) ★	P. G. Vallance Ltd/Charlwood
	G-GACB	Robinson R44 II	S. P. Barker
	G-GAEA	Aquila AT01	KH Air BV/Netherlands
	G-GAEC	Aquila AT-01-100A	KH Air BV/Netherlands
	G-GAED	Aquila AT-01-100A	KH Air BV/Netherlands
	G-GAEE	Tecnam P2010	KH Air BV/Netherlands
	G-GAFT	PA-44-180 Seminole	Bravo Aviation Ltd
	G-GAGE	Cameron Z-105 balloon	A. J. Thompson
	G-GAII	Hawker Hunter GA.11 (XE685)	Hawker Hunter Aviation Ltd
	G-GAJB	AA-5B Tiger	G-GAJB Group (G-BHZN)
	G-GALA	PA-28 Cherokee 180E	J. Harrison
	G-GALB	PA-28-161 Warrior II	Gamston Flying School Ltd
	G-GAMA	Beech 58 Baron	Gama Aviation (UK) Ltd (G-WWIZ/G-BBSD)
	G-GAME	Cessna T.303	German Automotive Ltd

Reg	Type	Owner or Operator	Notes
G-GAND	Agusta-Bell 206B Jet Ranger	R. Henderson (G-AWMK)	
G-GAOH	Robin DR.400 / 2 +2	M. A. Stott	
G-GAOM	Robin DR.400 / 2+2	P. M. & P. A. Chapman	
G-GARE	Cessna 560XL Citation XLS	Virtus Aviation Ltd	
G-GARI	Ace Aviation Touch/Buzz	G. B. Shaw	
G-GASP	PA-28-181 Archer II	G-GASP Flying Group	
G-GAST	Van's RV-8	G. M. R. Abrey	
G-GATH	Airbus A.320-232	British Airways	
G-GATJ	Airbus A.320-232	British Airways	
G-GATK	Airbus A.320-232	British Airways	
G-GATL	Airbus A.320-232	British Airways	
G-GATM	Airbus A.320-232	British Airways	
G-GATN	Airbus A.320-232	British Airways	
G-GATP	Airbus A.320-232	British Airways	
G-GATR	Airbus A.320-232	British Airways	
G-GATS	Airbus A.320-232	British Airways	
G-GATT	Robinson R44 II	B. W. Faulkner	
G-GATU	Airbus A.320-232	British Airways	
G-GAVA	BAe Jetstream 3102	A C Aviation Wales Ltd (G-CCPW)	
G-GAVH	P & M Quik	I. J. Richardson	
G-GAWA	Cessna 140	C140 Group (G-BRSM)	
G-GAXC	Robin R2160 Alpha Sport	D. D. McMaster	
G-GAZA	Aérospatiale SA.341G Gazelle 1	The Auster Aircraft Co Ltd (G-RALE/G-SFTG)	
G-GAZN	P & M Quik GT450	C. Hughes	
G-GAZO	Ace Magic Cyclone	G. J. Pearce	
G-GAZZ	Aérospatiale SA.341G Gazelle 1	Cheqair Ltd	
G-GBAO	Robin R1180TD	J. Toulorge	
G-GBAS	Diamond DA.62	Flight Calibration Services Ltd	
G-GBBB	Schleicher ASH-25	ASH25 BB Glider Syndicate	
G-GBBT	Ultramagic M-90 balloon	S. J. Chatfield	
G-GBCC	Ikarus C42 FB100	I. R. Westrope	
G-GBEE	Mainair Pegasus Quik	G. S. Bulpitt	
G-GBET	Ikarus C42 FB UK	G. P. Masters (G-BDBMK/G-MROY)	
G-GBFI	Kreimendahl K-10 Shoestring	T. Jarvis	
G-GBFF	Cessna F.172N	AKM Aviation Ltd	
G-GBFR	Cessna F.177RG	Airspeed Aviation Ltd	
G-GBGA	Scheibe SF.25C Falke	The Royal Air Force Gliding and Soaring Association	
G-GBGB	Ultramagic M.105 balloon	S. A. Nother	
G-GBGF	Cameron Dragon SS balloon	Magical Adventures Ltd (G-BUVH)	
G-GBHB	SOCATA TB-10 Tobago	B. A. Mills	
G-GBHI	SOCATA TB-10 Tobago	J. H. Garrett-Cox	
G-GBJP	Mainair Pegasus Quantum 15	K. S. Reardon	
G-GBLP	Cessna F.172M	Aviate Scotland Ltd (G-GWEN)	
G-GBMM	Agusta A109S Grand	Hadleigh Patners LLP (G-GRND)	
G-GBNZ	Eurofox 912(iS)	C. F. Pote	
G-GBOB	Alpi Pioneer 300 Hawk	R. E. Burgess	
G-GBPP	Rolladen-Schneider LS6-c18	G. J. Lyons & R. Sinden	
G-GBRB	PA-28 Cherokee 180C	Bravo Romeo Group	
G-GBRU	Bell 206B JetRanger 3	R. A. Fleming Ltd (G-CDGV)	
G-GBRV	Van's RV-9A	G. Carter & K. L. Chorley (G-THMB)	
G-GBSL	Beech 76 Duchess	M. H. Cundsy (G-BGVG)	
G-GBTL	Cessna 172S	BTL IT Solutions Ltd	
G-GBTV	Eurocopter AS.355N Ecureuil II	Cheshire Helicopters Ltd	
G-GBUE	Robin DR.400/120A	J. A. Kane (G-BPXD)	
G-GBUN	Cessna 182T	G. M. Bunn	
G-GBUV	Robin DR400/120	Aero Club de Valenciennes/France	
G-GBVX	Robin DR400/120A	N. Foster	
G-GCAC	Europa XS T-G	W. G. Miller	
G-GCAT	PA-28 Cherokee 140B	Group Cat (G-BFRH)	
G-GCCL	Beech 76 Duchess	Aerolease Ltd	
G-GCDA	Cirrus SR20	S. James	
G-GCDB	Cirrus SR20	S. James	
G-GCEA	Pegasus Quik	K. & P. Bailey	
G-GCFM	Diamond DA.40D Star	V. Babaca	
G-GCIY	Robin DR.400-140B	M. S. Lonsdale	
G-GCJA	Rolladen-Schneider LS8-18	N. T. Mallender	
G-GCJH	Aerospool Dynamic WT9 UK	C. J. Harling	
G-GCKI	Mooney M.20K	B. Barr	

Notes	Reg	Type	Owner or Operator
	G-GCMW	Grob G.102 Astir CS	M. S. F. Wood
	G-GCOY	SOCATA TB-9 Tampico	B. C. Costin & N. J. Richardson
	G-GCRT	Robin DR400/120	Aero Club de Valenciennes/France
	G-GCUF	Robin DR400/160	A. Davis & S. Clayton
	G-GCVV	Cirrus SR22	Daedalus Aviation (Services) Ltd
	G-GCWS	Cessna 177	B. A. Mills
	G-GCYC	Cessna F.182Q	The Cessna 180 Group
	G-GDAC	AA-5A Cheetah	Flight & Media Enterprises Ltd
	G-GDAV	Robinson R44 II	G. H. Weston
	G-GDEF	Robin DR.400/120	J. M. Shackleton
	G-GDER	Robin R.1180TD	Berkshire Aviation Services Ltd
	G-GDFB	Boeing 737-33A	Jet 2
	G-GDFC	Boeing 737-8K2	Jet 2
	G-GDFD	Boeing 737-8K5	Jet 2
	G-GDFE	Boeing 737-3Q8	Jet 2
	G-GDFF	Boeing 737-85P	Jet 2
	G-GDFG	Boeing 737-36Q	Jet 2
	G-GDFH	Boeing 737-3Y5	Jet 2
	G-GDFJ	Boeing 737-804	Jet 2 (G-CDZI)
	G-GDFK	Boeing 737-36N	Jet 2 (G-STRE/G-XBHX)
	G-GDFL	Boeing 737-36N	Jet 2
	G-GDFM	Boeing 737-36N	Jet 2
	G-GDFN	Boeing 737-33V	Jet 2 (G-EZYH)
	G-GDFO	Boeing 737-3U3	Jet 2 (G-THOP)
	G-GDFP	Boeing 737-8Z9	Jet 2
	G-GDFR	Boeing 737-8Z9	Jet 2
	G-GDFS	Boeing 737-86N	Jet 2
	G-GDFT	Boeing 737-36Q	Jet 2 (G-TOYM/G-OHAJ)
	G-GDFU	Boeing 737-8K5	Jet 2
	G-GDFV	Boeing 737-85F	Jet 2
	G-GDFW	Boeing 737-8K5	Jet 2
	G-GDFX	Boeing 737-8K5	Jet 2
	G-GDFY	Boeing 737-86Q	Jet 2
	G-GDFZ	Boeing 737-86Q	Jet 2
	G-GDHI	Boeing 737-8K5	Jet 2
	G-GDIA	Cessna F.152	Skytrek Flying School Ltd
	G-GDJF	Robinson R44 II	Berkley Properties Ltd (G-DEXT)
	G-GDKR	Robin DR400/140B	Hampshire Flying Group
	G-GDMW	Beech 76 Duchess	Flew LLP
	G-GDOG	PA-28R Cherokee Arrow 200-II	The Mutley Crew Group (G-BDXW)
	G-GDRV	Van's RV-6	J. R. S. Heaton & R. Feather
	G-GDSG	Agusta A109E Power	Palmhall Ltd
	G-GDSO	Autogyro Cavalon	P. Setterfield
	G-GDTU	Avions Mudry CAP-10B	R. W. H. Cole
	G-GECO	Hughes 369HS	N. Duggan (G-ATVEE/G-GCXK)
	G-GEEP	Robin R.1180TD	Aiglon Flying Group
	G-GEHL	Cessna 172S	Ebryl Ltd
	G-GEHP	PA-28RT-201 Arrow IV	Aeros Leasing Ltd
	G-GEJS	Extra EA300/LT	G. Sealey
	G-GELI	Colt 31A balloon	S. F. Burden (G-CDFI)
	G-GEMM	Cirrus SR20	Schmolke Grosskuechensysteme GmbH
	G-GEMS	Thunder Ax8-90 Srs 2 balloon	Kraft Bauprojekt GmbH/Germany
	G-GEMX	P & M Quik GT450	A. R. Oliver
	G-GEOF	Pereira Osprey 2	G. Crossley
	G-GEOS	Diamond HK.36 TTC-ECO	University Court (School of Geosciences) of the Super Dimona University of Edinburgh
	G-GERI	Robinson R44 1	Robraven Ltd
	G-GERS	Robinson R44 II	M. Virdee
	G-GERT	Van's RV-7	C. R. A. Scrope
	G-GETU	Leonardo AW169	Jetheli Ltd
	G-GEZZ	Bell 206B JetRanger II	Rivermead Aviation Ltd
	G-GFCA	PA-28-161 Cadet	Aviation, Advice & Consulting Ltd
	G-GFCB	PA-28-161 Cadet	Bristol and Wessex Aeroplane Club Ltd
	G-GFEY	PA-34-200T Seneca II	M. R. Badminton
	G-GFIB	Cessna F.152 II	Westair Flying Services Ltd (G-BPIO)
	G-GFID	Cessna 152 II	Pure Aviation Support Services Ltd (G-BORJ)
	G-GFIE	Cessna 152	J. L. Sparks (G-CEUS)
	G-GFIG	Cessna 152	The Pilot Centre Ltd (G-BNOZ)

Reg	Type	Owner or Operator	Notes
G-GFKY	Zenair CH.250	R. G. Kelsall	
G-GFLY	Cessna F.150L	Hangar 1 Ltd	
G-GFNO	Robin ATL	M. J. Pink	
G-GFRA	PA-28RT-201T Turbo Arrow IV	Ravenair Aircraft Ltd (G-LROY/G-BNTS)	
G-GFSA	Cessna 172R Skyhawk	Atlantic Flight Training Ltd	
G-GFTA	PA-28-161 Warrior III	One Zero Three Ltd	
G-GFZG	PA-28-140 Cherokee E	B. A. Mills	
G-GGDV	Schleicher Ka 6E	East Sussex Gliding Club Ltd	
G-GGGG	Thunder Ax7-77A balloon	T. A. Gilmour	
G-GGHZ	Robin ATL	M. J. Pink	
G-GGJK	Robin DR.400/140B	Headcorn Jodelers	
G-GGRH	Robinson R44	Heli Air Ltd	
G-GGRN	PA-28R-201 Cherokee Arrow III	P. Sharpe	
G-GGRR	SA Bulldog Srs 120/121 (XX614:V)	D. J. Sharp (G-CBAM)	
G-GGRV	Van's RV-8	C. F. O'Neill	
G-GGTT	Agusta-Bell 47G-4A	P. R. Smith	
G-GGZZ	Aviat A-1B Husky	J. A. S. Everett	
G-GHEE	Aerotechnik EV-97 Eurostar	P. R. Howson	
G-GHER	AS.355N Ecureuil II	Gallagher Air LLP	
G-GHKX	PA-28-161 Warrior II	Pilot Training and Testing Ltd	
G-GHOP	Cameron Z-77 balloon	Lakeside Lodge Golf Centre	
G-GHOW	Cessna F.182Q	Southern Counties Aviation Ltd	
G-GHRW	PA-28RT-201 Arrow IV	P. Cowley (G-ONAB/G-BHAK)	
G-GHZJ	SOCATA TB9 Tampico	P. K. Hayward	
G-GIAS	Ikarus C42 FB80	North East Aviation Ltd	
G-GIBB	Robinson R44 II	Tingdene Aviation Ltd	
G-GIBI	Agusta A.109E Power	Gazelle Management Services Ltd	
G-GIBP	Moravan Zlin Z.526 Trener Master	D. G. Cowden	
G-GIDY	Shaw Europa XS	Gidy Group	
G-GIFF	Balony Kubicek BB26XR balloon	A. M. Holly & The Lord Mayor's Appeal	
G-GIGA	Vulcanair P68C	Apem Aviation Ltd	
G-GIGZ	Van's RV-8	N. G. Rhind & K. A. A. McDonald	
G-GILB	Cessna 510 Citation Mustang	Catreus AOC Ltd	
G-GIPC	PA-32R-301 Saratoga SP	GIPC Flying Group	
G-GIRY	AG-5B Tiger	Romeo Yankee Flying Group	
G-GIVE	Cameron A-300 balloon	Wickers World Ltd	
G-GIWT	Shaw Europa XS	A. Twigg	
G-GJCD	Robinson R22 Beta	J. C. Lane	
G-GKAT	Enstrom 280C	D. G. Allsop & A. J. Clark	
G-GKFC	RL-5A LW Sherwood Ranger	G. L. Davies (G-MYZI)	
G-GKKI	Avions Mudry CAP 231EX	Kilo India Group	
G-GKRC	Cessna 180K	W. J. Pitts	
G-GKUE	SOCATA TB-9 Tampico Club	R. S. McMaster	
G-GLAA	Eurocopter EC135 T2	PDG Helicopters	
G-GLAB	Eurocopter EC135 T2+	PLM Dollar Group Ltd (G-CFFR)	
G-GLAD	Gloster G.37 Gladiator II (N5903:H)	Patina Ltd	
G-GLAK	AB Sportine LAK-12	C. Roney	
G-GLAW	Cameron N-90 balloon	N. D. Humphries	
G-GLED	Cessna 150M	G-GLED Group	
G-GLHI	Skyranger 912	S. F. Winter	
G-GLID	Schleicher ASW-28-18E	S. Bovin and Compagnie Belge d'Assurances Aviation	
G-GLII	Great Lakes 2T-1A-2	T. J. Richardson	
G-GLOB	Bombardier BD700-1A10 Global Express	Execujet (UK) Ltd	
G-GLOC	Extra EA.300/200	The Cambridge Aero Club Ltd	
G-GLSA	EV-97 Eurostar SL	LSA1 Group	
G-GLST	Great Lakes Sport Trainer	T. Boehmerle & A. Hofmann	
G-GLUC	Van's RV-6	P. Shoesmith & J. M. Whitham	
G-GLUE	Cameron N-65 balloon	L. J. M. Muir & G. D. Hallett	
G-GMAA	Learjet 45	Gama Aviation (UK) Ltd	
G-GMAD	Beech B.300C Super King Air 350C	Gama Aviation (Asset 2) Ltd	
G-GMAE	Beech B.200 Super King Air	Gama Aviation (UK) Ltd	
G-GMAX	SNCAN Stampe SV.4C	G. H. Stinnes (G-BXNW)	
G-GMCM	AS.350B3 Ecureuil	T. J. Morris Ltd	

Notes	Reg	Type	Owner or Operator
	G-GMCT	Beech A.33 Bonanza	MCT Agentur GmbH/Germany
	G-GMGH	Robinson R66	M. G. Holland
	G-GMIB	Robin DR400/500	St. David's Farm & Equine Practice
	G-GMKE	Robin HR200/120B	Nogaro Ltd
	G-GMMR	BAe. 125 Srs 800B	Hadleigh Partners LLP (G-OGFS/G-GRGA/ G-DCTA/G-OSPG/G-ETOM/BVFC/G-TPHK/ G-FDSL)
	G-GMOX	Cessna 152	Staverton Flying School @ Skypark Ltd
	G-GMPX	MDH MD-900 Explorer	Specialist Aviation Services Ltd
	G-GMSI	SOCATA TB9 Tampico	M. L. Rhodes
	G-GNJW	Ikarus C.42	N. C. Pearse
	G-GNRV	Van's RV-9A	N. K. Beavins
	G-GNSS	Diamond DA.62	Flight Calibration Services Ltd
	G-GNTB	SAAB SF.340A	Loganair Ltd
	G-GNTF	SAAB SF.340A	Loganair Ltd
	G-GOAC	PA-34-200T Seneca II	Sky Zone Servicos Aereos Lda/Portugal
	G-GOAL	Lindstrand LBL-105A balloon	I. Chadwick
	G-GOBD	PA-32R-301 Saratoga IIHP	Saratoga Group (G-OARW)
	G-GOCX	Cameron N-90 balloon	P. Rossi/Italy
	G-GODV	CAP Aviation CAP232	G-GODV Group
	G-GOER	Bushby-Long Midget Mustang	C. Antrobus
	G-GOES	Robinson R44-II	Helicentre Ltd
	G-GOFF	Extra EA.300/LC	George J. Goff Ltd
	G-GOFR	Ultramagic M-105 balloon	Associazione Vivere Paestum/Italy
	G-GOGB	Lindstrand LBL ,90A	J. Dyer (G-CDFX)
	G-GOGW	Cameron N-90 balloon	S. E. Carroll
	G-GOHI	Cessna 208 Caravan 1 amphibian	S. Ulrich
	G-GOLA	Zenair CH.701SP	J. D. Hayward
	G-GOLF	SOCATA TB10 Tobago	B. Lee
	G-GOLX	Europa XS	LX Avionics Ltd (G-CROB)
	G-GOMS	Robinson R66	Bri-Stor Systems Ltd
	G-GOOF	Flylight Dragonfly	M. G. Preston
	G-GOPR	Cameron Z-90 balloon	Flying Enterprises
	G-GORA	Robin DR.400-160	Robin Flying Club Ltd
	G-GORD	Robin DR.401	J. G. Bellerby (G-JSMH)
	G-GORE	CFM Streak Shadow	P. F. Stares
	G-GORV	Van's RV-8	G-GORV Group
	G-GOSL	Robin DR.400/180	R. M. Gosling (G-BSDG)
	G-GOSS	Jodel DR.221	Avon Flying Group
	G-GOTC	GA-7 Cougar	U. Guddat
	G-GOTH	PA-28-161 Warrior III	Stamp Aviation Ltd
	G-GOUP	Robinson R22 Beta	AKP Aviation Ltd (G-DIRE)
	G-GOWF	Eurocopter EC.135 T2+	Babcock Mission Critical Services Onshore Ltd
	G-GOXC	HpH Glasflugel 304S Shark	S. A. W. Becker
	G-GOYA	Bombardier BD700-1A10 Global Express	TAG Aviation (UK) Ltd
	G-GPAG	Van's RV-6	S. J. Perkins & D. Dobson
	G-GPAT	Beech 76 Duchess	Folada Aero & Technical Services Ltd
	G-GPEG	Sky 90-24 balloon	R. Cains-Collinson
	G-GPMW	PA-28RT-201T Turbo Arrow IV	Calverton Flying Group Ltd
	G-GPPN	Cameron TR-70 balloon	Backetorp Byggconsult AB
	G-GPSI	Grob G.115	Swiftair Maintenance Ltd
	G-GPSR	Grob G.115	Swiftair Maintenance Ltd (G-BOCD)
	G-GPSX	Grob G.115	Swiftair Maintenance Ltd
	G-GPWE	Ikarus C42 FB100	P. W. Ellis
	G-GREC	Sequoia F.8L Falco	J. D. Tseliki
	G-GREY	PA-46-350P Malibu Mirage	S. T. Day & S. C. Askham
	G-GRIN	Van's RV-6	E. Andersen
	G-GRIZ	PA-18-135 Super Cub (modified)	P. N. Elkington (G-BSHV)
	G-GRLS	Skyranger Swift 912S(1)	British Microlight Aircraft Association Ltd
	G-GRLW	Jabiru J400	R. L. Wood (G-NMBG)
	G-GRMN	Aerospool Dynamic WT9 UK	I. D. Worthington
	G-GROE	Grob G.115A	M. B. Blackmore
	G-GROL	Maule MXT-7-180	D. C. Croll & ptnrs
	G-GROW	Cameron N-77 balloon	Derbyshire Building Society
	G-GRPA	Ikarus C.42 FB100	G-GRPA Group
	G-GRRR	SA Bulldog Srs 120/122	Horizons Europe Ltd (G-BXGU)
	G-GRVE	Van's RV-6	G-GRVE Group
	G-GRVY	Van's RV-8	A. Page

Reg	Type	Owner or Operator	Notes
G-GRWL	Lilliput Type 4 balloon	A. E. & D. E. Thomas	
G-GRYN	Rotorsport UK Calidus	Rotorsport Sales & Service Ltd	
G-GRYZ	Beech F33A Bonanza	J. Kawadri & M. Kaveh	
G-GRZZ	Robinson R44 II	Kuki Helicopter Sales Ltd	
G-GSAL	Fokker E.III Reolica (416/15)	Grass Strip Aviation Ltd	
G-GSCV	Ikarus C42 FB UK	T. J. Gayton-Polley	
G-GSFS	Cessna 152	Staverton Flying School @ Skypark Ltd	
G-GSGS	HpH Glasflugel 304 ES	G. E. Smith	
G-GSPY	Robinson R44 II	Percy Wood Leisure Ltd	
G-GSST	Grob G.102 Astir CS77	770 Group	
G-GSVI	Gulfstream 650	Executive Jet Charter Ltd	
G-GSYL	PA-28RT-201T Turbo Arrow IV	S. J. Sylvester (G-DAAH)	
G-GSYS	PA-34-220T Seneca V	R. Schilling	
G-GTAX	PA-31-350 Navajo Chieftain	Hadagain Investments Ltd (G-OIAS)	
G-GTBT	Pilatus B4-PC11AF	T. Geissel (G-DCUO)	
G-GTFB	Magni M-24C	Rotormurf Ltd	
G-GTFC	P & M Quik	A. J. Fell	
G-GTGT	P & M Quik GT.450	C. W. Brown	
G-GTHM	PA-38-112 Tomahawk	D. R. Clyde	
G-GTJD	P & M Quik GT450	A. J. Bacon	
G-GTOM	Alpi Pioneer 300	S. C. Oliphant & J. Watkins	
G-GTRE	P & M Quik GTR	M. J. Austin	
G-GTRR	P & M Quik GTR	M. R. Wallis	
G-GTRX	P & M Quik GTR	N. Matthews	
G-GTSD	P & M Quik GT450	P. Bayliss	
G-GTSO	P & M Quik GT450	C. Bayliss	
G-GTTP	P & M Quik GT450	S. E. Powell	
G-GTWO	Schleicher ASW-15	J. M. G. Carlton & R. Jackson	
G-GUAR	PA-28-161 Warrior II	B. A. Mills	
G-GUCK	Beech C23 Sundowner 180	G-GUCK Flying Group (G-BPYG)	
G-GULP	I.I.I. Sky Arrow 650T	L. J. Betts	
G-GULZ	Christen Eagle II	T. N. Jinks	
G-GUMM	Aviat A-1B	A. E. Poulson (G-LTMM)	
G-GUNS	Cameron V-77 balloon	J. Jacquet/France	
G-GUNZ	Van's RV-8	Cirrus Aircraft UK Ltd	
G-GURU	PA-28-161 Warrior II	Avro-Marine Ltd	
G-GUSS	PA-28-151 Warrior	The Sierra Flying Group (G-BJRY)	
G-GVFR	SOCATA TB-20 Trinidad	J. J. Toomey & J. G. Gleeson (G-CEPT/G-BTEK)	
G-GVPI	Evans VP-1 srs.2	G. Martin	
G-GVSL	Evektor EV-97 Eurostar SL	G. Verity	
G-GWAA	Eurocopter EC.135 T2	Babcock Mission Critical Services Onshore Ltd (G-WMAS)	
G-GWAC	Eurocopter EC.135 T2+	Babcock Mission Critical Services Onshore Ltd (G-WASN)	
G-GWFT	Rans S-6-ES Coyote II	The Georgia Williams Trust	
G-GWIZ	Colt Clown SS balloon	Magical Adventures Ltd	
G-GWYN	Cessna F.172M	G. Dunne	
G-GXLS	Cessna 560XL Citation XLS	London Executive Aviation Ltd	
G-GYAK	Yakovlev Yak-50	O. Luehring	
G-GYAT	Gardan GY-80 Horizon 180	Rochester GYAT Flying Group	
G-GYAV	Cessna 172N	Southport & Merseyside Aero Club (1979) Ltd	
G-GYRA	AutoGyro Calidus	W. C. Walters & D. B. Roberts	
G-GYRO	Campbell Cricket	J. W. Pavitt	
G-GYTO	PA-28-161 Warrior III	White Waltham Airfield Ltd	
G-GZDO	Cessna 172N	Eagle Flying Ltd	
G-GZIP	Rolladen-Schneider LS8-18	D. S. S. Haughton	
G-GZOO	Gulfstream G200	NAL Asset Management Ltd	
G-HAAH	Schempp-Hirth Ventus 2cT	V66 Syndicate	
G-HAAR	Eurofox 912(S)	Longside Flying Group	
G-HAAT	MDH MD.900 Explorer	Specialist Aviation Services Ltd (G-GMPS)	
G-HABI	Best Off SkyRanger 912S(1)	J. Habicht	

Notes	Reg	Type	Owner or Operator
	G-HABT	Supermarine Aircraft Spitfire Mk.26 (BL735:BT-A)	Wright Grumman Aviation Ltd
	G-HACE	Van's RV-6A	G-HACE Group
	G-HACK	PA-18 Super Cub 150	Intrepid Aviation Co
	G-HACS	Tecnam P2002-JF	The RAF Halton Aeroplane Club Ltd
	G-HADD	P & M Quik R	T. J. Barker
	G-HAEF	EV-97 TeamEurostar UK	RAF Microlight Flying Association
	G-HAFG	Cessna 340A	Pavilion Aviation Ltd
	G-HAFT	Diamond DA42 Twin Star	Airways Aviation Academy Ltd
	G-HAGL	Robinson R44 II	HQ Aviation Ltd
	G-HAHU	Yakovlev Yak-18T	A. Leftwich
	G-HAIB	Aviat A-1B Husky	H. Brockmueller
	G-HAIG	Rutan LongEz	P. R. Dalton
	G-HAIR	Robin DR.400/180	S. P. Copson
	G-HAJJ	Glaser-Dirks DG.400	W. G. Upton & J. G. Kosak
	G-HALC	PA-28R Cherokee Arrow 200	Halcyon Aviation Ltd
	G-HALJ	Cessna 140	A. R. Wills
	G-HALL	PA-22 Tri-Pacer 160	F. P. Hall (G-ARAH)
	G-HALS	Robinson R44 II	Paul D. White Ltd (G-CEKA)
	G-HALT	Mainair Pegasus Quik	J. McGrath
	G-HAMI	Fuji FA.200-180	HAMI Group (G-OISF/G-BAPT)
	G-HAMP	Bellanca 7ACA Champ	R. J. Grimstead
	G-HAMR	PA-28-161 Warrior II	CG Aviation Ltd
	G-HAMS	Pegasus Quik	D. R. Morton
	G-HAMW	Aeropro Eurofox 3K	M. D. Hamwee
	G-HANC	Robinson R22	S. Hancock (G-CHIS)
	G-HANG	Diamond DA42 Twin Star	Airways Aviation Academy Ltd
	G-HANS	Robin DR.400 2+2	The Cotswold Aero Club Ltd
	G-HANY	Agusta-Bell 206B JetRanger 3	Heliflight (UK) Ltd (G-ESAL/G-BHXW/G-JEKP)
	G-HAPE	Pietenpol Aircamper	J. P. Chape
	G-HAPI	Lindstrand LBL-105A balloon	Adventure Balloons Ltd
	G-HAPY	DHC.1 Chipmunk 22A (WP803)	Astrojet Ltd
	G-HARA	Sikorsky S-76C	Air Harrods Ltd (G-WIWI)
	G-HARD	Dyn'Aéro MCR-01 ULC	N. A. Burnet
	G-HARE	Cameron N-77 balloon	D. H. Sheryn & C. A. Buck
	G-HARG	Embraer EMB-550 Legacy 500	Centreline AV Ltd
	G-HARI	Raj Hamsa X'Air V2 (2)	J. Blackburn
	G-HARN	PA-28-181 Archer II	Busaviation Ltd (G-DENK/G-BXRJ)
	G-HARR	Robinson R22 Beta	Sloane Helicopters Ltd
	G-HART	Cessna 152 (tailwheel)	Taildraggers Flying Group (G-BPBF)
	G-HARY	Alon A-2 Aircoupe	M. B. Willis (G-ATWP)
	G-HATB	AutoGyro MTOSport	N. J. Bent
	G-HATD	DH.115 Vampire T.55	Aviation Heritage Ltd
	G-HATF	Thorp T-18CW	A. T. Fraser
	G-HATZ	Hatz CB-1	S. P. Rollason
	G-HAUL	Westland WG.30 Srs 300 ★	IHM/Weston-super-Mare
	G-HAUT	Schempp-Hirth Mini Nimbus C	A. D. Peacock
	G-HAYS	Skyranger Swift 912S(1)	G. Hayes (G-CFBS)
	G-HAYY	Czech Sport Aircraft Sportcruiser	Sportcrew YY
	G-HAZA	Diamond DA.42NG Twin Star	R. W. F. Jackson
	G-HAZD	Cameron Z-56 balloon	L. S. Crossland-Clarke
	G-HBBC	DH.104 Dove 8	Roger Gawn 2007 Family Trust (G-ALFM)
	G-HBBH	Ikarus C42 FB100	Golf Bravo Hotel Group
	G-HBEE	Lindstrand LTL Series 2-80 balloon	R. P. Waite
	G-HBEK	Agusta A109C	HPM Investments Ltd (G-RNLD/G-DATE)
	G-HBJT	Eurocopter EC.155B1	Starspeed Ltd
	G-HBMW	Robinson R22	G. Schabana/Germany (G-BOFA)
	G-HBOS	Scheibe SF-25C Rotax-Falke	Coventry Gliding Club Ltd
	G-HCAC	Schleicher Ka 6E	Ka 6E 994 Group
	G-HCAT	Sindlinger Hawker Hurricane	G. S. Jones
	G-HCBW	Sequoia Falco F.8L	R. A. F. Buchanan
	G-HCCF	Vans RV-8A	S. M. E. Solomon
	G-HCEN	Guimbal Cabri G2	Helicentre Aviation Ltd
	G-HCPD	Cameron C-80 balloon	H. Crawley& P. Dopson
	G-HCSA	Cessna 525A CJ2	Bookajet Aircraft Management Ltd
	G-HDAE	DHC.1 Chipmunk 22 (WP964)	Airborne Classics Ltd
	G-HDBV	MD MD-900 Explorer	Heli Delta BV/Netherlands (G-SASH)
	G-HDEF	Robinson R44 II	Arena Aviation Ltd (G-LOCO/G-TEMM)

Reg	Type	Owner or Operator	Notes
G-HDEW	PA-32R-301 Saratoga SP	D. P. Wood	
G-HDIX	Enstrom 280FX	K. & M. A. Payne	
G-HDMD	MDH Douglas MD-900 Explorer	Heli Delta BV/Netherlands (G-CEMS)	
G-HDTV	Agusta A109A-II	Castle Air Ltd (G-BXWD)	
G-HEAD	Colt Flying Head SS balloon	Ikeair	
G-HEAN	AS.355NP Ecureuil 2	Brookview Developments Ltd	
G-HEBB	Schleicher ASW-27-18E	G-HEBB Group	
G-HEBO	BN-2B-20 Islander	Islander Aircraft Ltd (G-BUBK)	
G-HEBS	BN-2B-26 Islander	Hebridean Air Services Ltd (G-BUBJ)	
G-HEBZ	BN-2A-26 Islander	Cormack (Aircraft Services) Ltd (G-BELF)	
G-HECB	Fuji FA.200-160	H. E. W. E. Bailey (G-BBZO)	
G-HECK	Robinson R44 II	Helivation Aviation Ltd (G-ILLG)	
G-HEDL	Extra EA.300/LC	H. J. R. Aylott	
G-HEFF	Stemme S12	J. Heffernan	
G-HEHE	Eurocopter EC.120B Colibri	HE Group Ltd	
G-HEKK	RAF 2000 GTX-SE gyroplane	C. J. Watkinson (G-BXEB)	
G-HEKL	Percival Mew Gull Replica	D. Beale	
G-HELA	SOCATA TB10 Tobago	Future Flight	
G-HELE	Bell 206B JetRanger 3	B. E. E. Smith (G-OJFR)	
G-HELL	Sonex	T. J. Shaw	
G-HELN	Piper PA-18-95 Super Cub	Helen Group	
G-HEMC	Airbus Helicopters MBB BK-117D-2	Babcock Mission Critical Services Onshore Ltd	
G-HEMN	Eurocopter EC135 T2+	Babcock Mission Critical Services Onshore Ltd	
G-HEMZ	Agusta A109S Grand	Sloane Helicopters Ltd	
G-HENT	SOCATA Rallye 110ST	G. Dolan	
G-HENY	Cameron V-77 balloon	R. S. D'Alton	
G-HEOI	Eurocopter EC135 P2+	Police & Crime Commisioner for West Yorkshire	
G-HERC	Cessna 172S	Cambridge Aero Club Ltd	
G-HERD	Lindstrand LBL-77B balloon	S. W. Herd	
G-HEVR	Ikarus C42 FB80	Deanland Flight Training Ltf	
G-HEWI	Piper J-3C-90 Cub	Denham Grasshopper Group (G-BLEN)	
G-HEWZ	Hughes 369HS	A. S. Mackenzie (G-LEEJ)	
G-HEXE	Colt 17A balloon	A. Dunnington	
G-HEYY	Cameron 72 Bear SS balloon	Magical Adventures Ltd	
G-HFBM	Curtiss Robin C-2	D. M. Forshaw	
G-HFCB	Cessna F.150L	J. H. Francis	
G-HFCL	Cessna F.152	Devon & Somerset Flight Training Ltd (G-BGLR)	
G-HFCT	Cessna F.152	Stapleford Flying Club Ltd	
G-HFLY	Robinson R44 II	Helifly (UK) Ltd	
G-HFRH	DHC-1 Chipmunk 22 (WK635)	P. M. Jacobs	
G-HGPI	SOCATA TB20 Trinidad	M. J. Jackson	
G-HGRB	Robinson R44	Nick Cook Plant Hire Ltd (G-BZIN)	
G-HHAA	HS. Buccaneer S.2B (XX885)	Hawker Hunter Aviation Ltd	
G-HHAC	Hawker Hunter F.58 (J-4021)	Hawker Hunter Aviation Ltd (G-BWIU)	
G-HHDR	Cessna 182T	I. D. Brierley	
G-HHEM	Leonardo AW169	Essex & Herts Air Ambulance Trust	
G-HHII	Hawker Hurricane 2B (BE505: XP-L)	Hawker Restorations Ltd (G-HRLO)	
G-HHPM	Cameron Z-105 balloon	J. Armstrong	
G-HIAL	Viking DHC-6-400 Twin Otter	Loganair Ltd	
G-HIBM	Cameron N-145 balloon	Alba Ballooning Ltd	
G-HICU	Schleicher ASW-27-18E	N. Hoare	
G-HIEL	Robinson R22 Beta	Helimech Ltd	
G-HIJK	Cessna 421C	DO Systems Ltd (G-OSAL)	
G-HIJN	Ikarus C.42 FB80	G. P. Burns	
G-HILI	Van's RV-3B	A. G. & E. A. Hill	
G-HILO	Rockwell Commander 114	Alpha Golf Flying Group	
G-HILS	Cessna F.172H	LS Flying Group (G-AWCH)	
G-HILT	SOCATA TB10 Tobago	L. Windle	
G-HILY	Zenair CH.600 Zodiac	K. V. Hill (G-BRII)	
G-HILZ	Van's RV-8	A. G. & E. A. Hill	
G-HIMM	Cameron Z-105 balloon	C. M. D. Haynes	
G-HIND	Maule MT-7-235	M. A. Ashmole	
G-HINZ	Avtec Jabiru SK	P. J. Jackson	
G-HIOW	Airbus Helicopters EC.135T3	Babcock Mission Critical Services Onshore Ltd	

Notes	Reg	Type	Owner or Operator
	G-HIPE	Sorrell SNS-7 Hiperbipe	D. G. Curran (G-ISMS)
	G-HIRE	GA-7 Cougar	London Aerial Tours Ltd (G-BGSZ)
	G-HITI	Airbus Helicopters AS.350B3 Ecureuil	Elstree Ink Ltd
	G-HITL	Airbus AS.350B3 Ecureuil	Airbus Helicopters UK Ltd (G-CKPH)
	G-HITM	Raj Hamsa X'Air 582 (1)	I. Johnson & J. Hennegan
	G-HITT	Hawker Hurricane 1 (P3717:SW-P)	H. Taylor
	G-HIUP	Cameron A-250 balloon	J. D. & K. Griffiths
	G-HIVE	Cessna F.150M	Peterborough Flying School Ltd (G-BCXT)
	G-HIYA	Best Off Skyranger 912(2)	R. D. & C. M. Parkinson
	G-HIZZ	Robinson R22 II	Flyfare (G-CNDY/G-BXEW)
	G-HJSM	Schempp-Hirth Nimbus 4DM	G. Paul (G-ROAM)
	G-HJSS	AIA Stampe SV.4C (modified)	H. J. Smith (G-AZNF)
	G-HKAA	Schempp-Hirth Duo Discus T	J. Randall
	G-HKCC	Robinson R66	HQ Aviation Ltd
	G-HKCF	Enstrom 280C-UK	HKC Helicopter Services (G-MHCF/G-GSML/ G-BNNV)
	G-HKHM	Hughes 369B	HQ Aviation Ltd
	G-HLCF	Starstreak Shadow SA-II	F. E. Tofield
	G-HLCM	Leonardo AW109SP Grand New	Helicom
	G-HLEE	Best Off Sky Ranger J2.2(1)	P. G. Hill
	G-HLMB	Schempp-Hirth Ventus-2b	U. Hoefinghoff/Germany
	G-HLOB	Cessna 172S	Goodwood Road Racing Co.Ltd
	G-HLSA	Agusta AW109SP Grand New	London Southend Airport Company Ltd (G-HCOM)
	G-HMCA	EV-97 TeamEurostar UK	RAF Microlight Flying Association
	G-HMCB	Skyranger Swift 912S(1)	R. W. Goddin
	G-HMCD	Ikarus C42 FB80	B. Murkin
	G-HMCE	Ikarus C42 FB80	RAF Microlight Flying Association
	G-HMCF	EV-97 Eurostar SL mictolight	RAF Microlight Flying Association
	G-HMCH	EV-97 Eurostar SL	RAF Microlight Flying Association
	G-HMDX	MDH MD-900 Explorer	Specialist Aviation Services Ltd
	G-HMEC	Robinson R22	Helimech Ltd (G-BWTH)
	G-HMED	PA-28-161 Warrior III	Eglinton Flying Club Ltd
	G-HMEI	Dassault Falcon 900	Executive Jet Group Ltd
	G-HMHM	Rotorsport UK MTO Sport	R. M. Kimbell
	G-HMJB	PA-34-220T Seneca III	W. B. Bateson
	G-HMPS	CZAW Sportcruiser	H. & P. Shedden
	G-HMPT	Agusta-Bell 206B JetRanger 2	Yorkshire Helicopters
	G-HMSJ	Robin DR.400/140B	SJ Aircraft
	G-HNGE	Ikarus C42 FB80	Compton Abbas Airfield Ltd
	G-HNPN	Embraer EMB-505 Phenom 300	Flairjet Ltd
	G-HNTR	Hawker Hunter T.7 (XL571:V) ★	Yorkshire Air Museum/Elvington
	G-HOBO	Denney Kitfox Mk 4	L. J. James
	G-HOCA	Robinson R44 II	JRS Aviation Ltd
	G-HODN	Kavanagh Balloons E-120 balloon	A. C. C. Hodgson
	G-HODR	Skyranger Swift 912S(1)	A. W. Hodder
	G-HOFF	P & M Aviation Quik GT450	L. Mazurek
	G-HOFM	Cameron N-56 balloon	Magical Adventures Ltd
	G-HOGS	Cameron 90 Pig SS balloon	Magical Adventures Ltd
	G-HOJO	Schempp-Hirth Discus 2a	S. G. Jones
	G-HOLA	PA-28-201T Turbo Dakota	D. Ash (G-BNYB)
	G-HOLD	Robinson R44 II	Mignini and Petrini Spa/Italy
	G-HOLE	P & M Quik GT450	B. Birtle (G-CEBD)
	G-HOLI	Ultramagic M-77 balloon	G. Everett
	G-HOLM	Eurocopter EC.120B Colibri	Oxford Air Services Ltd
	G-HONG	Slingsby T.67M Firefly 200	Jewel Aviation and Technology Ltd
	G-HONI	Robinson R22 Beta	Elstree Helicopters (G-SEGO)
	G-HONK	Cameron O-105 balloon	M. A. Green
	G-HONO	Just Superstol	C. A. Ho
	G-HONY	Lilliput Type 1 Srs A balloon	A. E. & D. E. Thomas
	G-HOON	Pitts S-1S Special	J. Wood
	G-HOPA	Lindstrand LBL-35A balloon	S. F. Burden/Netherlands
	G-HOPE	Beech F33A Bonanza	Hope Aviation Ltd
	G-HOPR	Lindstrand LBL-25A balloon	K. C. Tanner
	G-HOPY	Van's RV-6A	R. C. Hopkinson

Reg	Type	Owner or Operator	Notes
G-HORK	Pioneer 300 Hawk	R. Y. Kendal	
G-HOSS	Beech F33A	T. D. Broadhurst	
G-HOTA	EV-97 TeamEurostar UK	W. Chang	
G-HOTB	Eurocopter EC155 B1	Airbus Helicoptrers UK Ltd (G-CEXZ)	
G-HOTC	AutoGyro MTOSport	G. Hotchen (G-CINW)	
G-HOTM	Cameron C-80 balloon	M. G. Howard	
G-HOTR	P & M Quik GTR	M. E. Fowler	
G-HOTY	Bombardier CL600-2B16 Challenger 604	Jet Exchange Ltd	
G-HOTZ	Colt 77B balloon	C. J. & S. M. Davies	
G-HOUR	Max Holste MH.1521 C1 Broussard	Bremont Watch Company Ltd	
G-HOUS	Colt 31A balloon ★	The British Balloon Museum and Library	
G-HOWD	Magni M-24C Orion	J. P. & M. G. Howard	
G-HOWI	Cessna F.182Q	H. Poulson	
G-HOWL	RAF 2000 GTX-SE gyroplane	C. J. Watkinson	
G-HOXN	Van's RV-9	XRay November Flying Club	
G-HPCB	Ultramagic S-90 balloon	D. A. Rawlings	
G-HPDM	Agusta A.109E Power	Adonby International Ltd (G-DPPF)	
G-HPIN	Bell 429	Harpin Ltd	
G-HPJT	HpH Glasflugel 304S	P. D. Harvey	
G-HPOL	MDH MD-902 Explorer	Draper Gain Aviation Ltd	
G-HPSF	Rockwell Commander 114B	R. W. Scandrett	
G-HPSL	Rockwell Commander 114B	M. B. Endean	
G-HPUX	Hawker Hunter T.7 (XL587)	Hawker Hunter Aviation Ltd	
G-HPWA	Van's RV-8	M. de Ferranti	
G-HRAF	Schleicher ASK-13	Upward Bound Trust (G-DETS)	
G-HRDB	Agusta A.109S Grand	Freshair UK Ltd	
G-HRDY	Cameron Z-105 balloon	Flying Enterprises	
G-HRIO	Robin HR.100/120	Eule Industrial Robotics GmbH/Germany	
G-HRLE	Tecnam P2008-JC	P. J. Harle (G-OTUK)	
G-HRLI	Hawker Hurricane 1 (V7497)	Hawker Restorations Ltd	
G-HRND	Cessna 182T	R. H. Wicks	
G-HROI	Rockwell Commander RC.112	Intereuropean Aviation Ltd	
G-HRVD	CCF Harvard IV	P. Earthy (G-BSBC)	
G-HRVS	Van's RV-8	D. J. Harvey	
G-HRYZ	PA-28-180 Cherokee Archer	Gama Engineering Ltd (G-WACR/G-BCZF)	
G-HSDL	Westland Gazelle AH. Mk 1	Howard Stott Demolition Ltd	
G-HSEB	Pegasus Quantum 15-912	D. Gwyther (G-BYNO)	
G-HSKE	Aviat A-18 Husky	R. B. Armitage & S. L. Davis	
G-HSKI	Aviat A-1B	C. J. R. Flint	
G-HSOO	Hughes 369HE	Century Aviation Ltd (G-BFYJ)	
G-HSTH	Lindstrand LBL. HS-110 balloon	C. J. Sanger-Davies	
G-HSVI	Cessna FR.172J	S. J. Sylvester	
G-HSXP	Raytheon Hawker 850XP	Fowey Services Ltd	
G-HTAX	PA-31-350 Navajo Chieftain	Hadagain Investments Ltd	
G-HTEC	Cameron Z-31 balloon	Airborne Adventures Ltd	
G-HTEK	Ultramagic M-77 balloon	Airborne Adventures Ltd	
G-HTFU	Gippsland GA8-TC 320 Airvan	Skydive London Ltd	
G-HTML	P & M Aviation Quik R	Skywards Aviation Consultants	
G-HTRL	PA-34-220T Seneca III	Techtest Ltd (G-BXXY)	
G-HTWE	Rans S6-116	G. R. Hill	
G-HUBB	Partenavia P.68B	Ravenair Aircraft Ltd	
G-HUBY	Embraer EMB-135BJ Legacy	London Executive Aviation Ltd	
G-HUCH	Cameron 80 Carrots SS balloon	Magical Adventures Ltd (G-BYPS)	
G-HUDS	P & M Quik GTR	S. J. M. Morling	
G-HUET	ATR42-500	Aurigny Air Services Ltd	
G-HUEW	Shaw Europa XS	C. R. Wright	
G-HUEY	Bell UH-1H	MX Jets Ltd	
G-HUEZ	Hughes 369E	Falcon Helicopters Ltd (G-WEBI)	
G-HUFF	Cessna 182P	Highfine Ltd	
G-HUKA	MDH Hughes 369E	B. P. Stein (G-OSOO)	
G-HUKS	Balony Kubicek BB22XR balloon	Wharf Farm Ltd	
G-HULK	Skyranger 912(2)	L. C. Stockman	
G-HULL	Cessna F.150M	Wicklow Wings	
G-HUME	EAA Acrosport II	G. Home	
G-HUMH	Van's RV-9A	D. F. Daines	
G-HUMM	Bell 407	Century Aviation Ltd	

Notes	Reg	Type	Owner or Operator
	G-HUNI	Bellanca 7GCBC Scout	R. G. Munro
	G-HUPW	Hawker Hurricane 1 (R4118:UP-W)	J. Brown
	G-HURI	CCF Hawker Hurricane XIIA (P3700:RF-E)	Historic Aircraft Collection Ltd
	G-HUSK	Aviat A-1B	G. D. Ettlmayr
	G-HUTY	Van's RV-7	S. A. Hutt
	G-HUXY	Cessna 152	Iris Aviation Ltd
	G-HVBF	Lindstrand LBL-210A balloon	Virgin Balloon Flights
	G-HVER	Robinson R44 II	Equation Associates Ltd
	G-HVRZ	Eurocopter EC 120B	J. S. Tobias
	G-HWAA	Eurocopter EC135T2	Babcock Mission Critical Services Onshore Ltd
	G-HWKS	Robinson R44	Nugent Aviation Ltd (G-ETFF/G-HSLJ)
	G-HWKW	Hughes 369E	Flitwick Helicopters Ltd
	G-HXJT	Glasflugel 304 S Shark	H. Hingley
	G-HXTD	Robin DR.400/180	S. R. Evans
	G-HYBD	Gramex Song	University of Cambridge
	G-HYLA	Balony Kubicek BB26E balloon	J. A. Viner
	G-HYLT	PA-32R-301 Saratoga SP	T. G. Gordon
	G-HYND	Robinson R44	Heli Air Scotland Ltd
	G-IACA	Sikorsky S-92A	Bristow Helicopters Ltd
	G-IACB	Sikorsky S-92A	Bristow Helicopters Ltd
	G-IACC	Sikorsky S-92A	Bristow Helicopters Ltd
	G-IACD	Sikorsky S-92A	Bristow Helicopters Ltd
	G-IACE	Sikorsky S-92A	Bristow Helicopters Ltd
	G-IACF	Sikorsky S-92A	Bristow Helicopters Ltd
	G-IACY	Avions Transport ATR-72-212A	Eastern Airways
	G-IAGI	SOCATA TB-9 Tampico	B. Smith
	G-IAGL	Eurocopter EC.120B Colibri	AGL Helicopters (G-UYFI)
	G-IAGO	Groppo Trail Mk.2	J. Jones & J. W. Armstrong
	G-IAHS	EV-97 TeamEurostar UK	I. A. Holden
	G-IAJJ	Robinson R44 II	O'Connor Utilities Ltd
	G-IAJS	Ikarus C.42 FB UK	A. J. Slater
	G-IAMP	Cameron H-34 balloon	W. D. Mackinnon
	G-IANB	Glaser-Dirks DG-800B	I. S. Bullous
	G-IANC	SOCATA TB10 Tobago	Rougham Flying Group (G-BIAK)
	G-IANH	SOCATA TB10 Tobago	Severn Valley Aero Group
	G-IANI	Shaw Europa XS T-G	W. D. Dewey
	G-IANJ	Cessna F.150K	J. A. & D. T. A. Rees (G-AXVW)
	G-IANN	Kolb Twinstar Mk 3	I. Newman & P. Read
	G-IANW	AS.350B3 Ecureuil	Milford Aviation Services Ltd
	G-IANZ	P & M Quik GT450	I. W. Harriman
	G-IARC	Stoddard-Hamilton Glastar	A. A. Craig
	G-IART	Cessna 182F	Aeroclub of Attica/Greece
	G-IASA	Beech B.200 Super King Air	IAS Medical Ltd
	G-IASB	Beech B.200GT Super King Air	IAS Medical Ltd
	G-IASM	Beech B.200 Super King Air	MIAW LLP (G-OEAS)
	G-IBAZ	Ikarus C.42 FB100	B. R. Underwood
	G-IBBS	Shaw Europa	R. H. Gibbs
	G-IBCF	Cameron Z-105 balloon	Cash 4 Cars
	G-IBED	Robinson R22A	Brian Seedle Helicopters Blackpool (G-BMHN)
	G-IBEE	Pipistrel Apis	Fly About Aviation Ltd
	G-IBFC	BFC Challenger II	S. D. Puddle
	G-IBFF	Beech A23-24 Musketeer Super	J. Lankfer (G-AXCJ)
	G-IBFP	VPM .M.16 Tandem Trainer	B. F. Pearson
	G-IBFW	PA-28R-201 Arrow III	Archer Four Ltd
	G-IBIG	Bell 206B JetRanger 3	D. W. Bevan (G-BORV)
	G-IBII	Pitts S-2A Special	First Light Aviation Ltd (G-XATS)
	G-IBLP	P & M Quik GT450	C. Zizzo
	G-IBMS	Robinson R44	BMS Holdings Ltd
	G-IBNH	Westland Gazelle HT Mk.2 (XW853)	Buckland Newton Hire Ltd (G-SWWM)
	G-IBSY	VS.349 Spitfire Mk.VC (EE602/DV-V)	Anglia Aircraft Restorations Ltd (G-VMIJ)
	G-IBUZ	CZAW Sportcruiser	G. L. Fearon
	G-ICAS	Pitts S-2B Special	J. C. Smith
	G-ICBM	Stoddard-Hamilton Glasair III Turbine	G. V. Walters & D. N. Brown

Reg	Type	Owner or Operator	Notes
G-ICDM	Jabiru UL-450	D. J. R. Wenham (G-CEKM)	
G-ICDP	Cessna F.150L	P. Morton	
G-ICEI	Leonardo AW169	Iceland Foods Ltd	
G-ICES	Thunder Ax6-56 balloon ★	British Balloon Museum & Library Ltd	
G-ICGA	PA-28-140 Cherokee E	M. Lalik/Poland	
G-ICLC	Cessna 150L	HUB2YOU SA/Belgium	
G-ICMT	Evektor EV-97 Eurostar	R. Haslam	
G-ICMX	Cessna 182P	E. Bilda/Germany	
G-ICOM	Cessna F.172M	N. J. Yeoman (G-BFXI)	
G-ICON	Rutan LongEz	S. J. & M. A. Carradice	
G-ICRS	Ikarus C.42 FB UK Cyclone	Ikarus Flying Group Ltd	
G-ICRV	Van's RV-7	I. A. Coates	
G-ICSG	AS.355F1 Twin Squirrel	RCR Aviation Ltd (G-PAMI/G-BUSA)	
G-ICUT	Maule MX-7-180A Super Rocket	R. A. Smith	
G-ICWT	Pegasus Quantum 15-912	Whisky Tango Group	
G-IDAY	Skyfox CA-25N Gazelle	G. G. Johnstone	
G-IDEB	AS.355F1 Ecureuil 2	MW Helicopters Ltd (G-ORMA/G-SITE/G-BPHC)	
G-IDER	Orlican Discus CS	S. G. Jones	
G-IDHC	Cessna 172N	Aero-Club Maritime	
G-IDII	Dan Rihn DR.107 One Design	C. Darlow	
G-IDLE	Airbus Helicopters AS.350B3 Ecureuil	Airbus Helicopters UK Ltd (G-CJZA)	
G-IDMG	Robinson R44	B. Davis	
G-IDOL	Evektor EV-97 Eurostar	K. Handley	
G-IDRS	Van's RV-8	T. I. Williams	
G-IDTO	PA-28RT-201T Turbo Arrow IV	Aeronautix BV/Netherlands	
G-IDYL	AutoGyro Cavalon	J. M. & M. J. Newman	
G-IEEF	Raj Hamsa X'Air Hawk	P. J. Sheehy	
G-IEIO	PA-34-200T Seneca II	Sky Zone Servicos Aereos Lda	
G-IEJH	Jodel 150A	A. Turner & D. Worth (G-BPAM)	
G-IENN	Cirrus SR20	Transcirrus BV/Netherlands (G-TSGE)	
G-IFAB	Cessna F.182Q	Bristol & West Aeroplane Club Ltd	
G-IFBP	AS.350B2 Ecureuil	Frank Bird Aviation	
G-IFFR	PA-32 Cherokee Six 300	Brendair (G-BWVO)	
G-IFFY	Flylight Dragonfly	R. D. Leigh	
G-IFIF	Cameron TR-60 balloon	M. G. Howard	
G-IFIK	Cessna 421C	T. Geither/Germany	
G-IFIT	PA-31-350 Navajo Chieftain	Dart Group PLC (G-NABI/G-MARG)	
G-IFLE	Aerotechnik EV-97 TeamEurostar UK	M. R. Smith	
G-IFLI	AA-5A Cheetah	M. Vilcins	
G-IFLP	PA-34-200T Seneca II	ACS Aviation Ltd	
G-IFOS	Ultramagic M-90 balloon	I. J. Sharpe	
G-IFRH	Agusta A109C	Helicopter & Pilot Services Ltd	
G-IFTE	HS.125 Srs 700B	Interflight (Air Charter) Ltd (G-BFVI)	
G-IFWD	Schempp-Hirth Ventus cT	C. J. Hamilton	
G-IGBI	Game Composites GB1	Game Composites Ltd	
G-IGEL	Cameron N-90 balloon	Computacenter Ltd	
G-IGGL	SOCATA TB10 Tobago	Cavendish Aviation UK Ltd (G-BYDC)	
G-IGHT	Van's RV-8	E. A. Yates	
G-IGIA	AS.350B3 Ecureuil	Faloria Ltd	
G-IGIE	SIAI Marchetti SF.260	Flew LLP	
G-IGIS	Bell 206B JetRanger II	C. J. Edwards (G-CHGL/G-BPNG/G-ORTC)	
G-IGLE	Cameron V-90 balloon	G-IGLE Group	
G-IGLI	Schempp-Hirth Duo Discus T	C. Fox	
G-IGLL	AutoGyro MTO Sport	I. M. Donnellan	
G-IGLY	P & M Aviation Quik GT450	R. D. Leigh	
G-IGLZ	Champion 8KCAB	Robin Flying Club Ltd	
G-IHAR	Cessna 172P	MN Solutions (Cambridge) Ltd	
G-IHCI	Europa	I. H. Clarke (G-VKIT)	
G-IHHI	Extra EA.300/SC	Airdisplays.com Ltd	
G-IHOP	Cameron Z-31 balloon	N. W. Roberts	
G-IHOT	Aerotechnik EV-97 Eurostar UK	Exodos Airsports Ltd	
G-IHXD	Cessna F.150M	Air Navigation & Trading Co.Ltd	
G-IIAC	Aeronca 11AC Chief	N. Jamieson (G-BTPY)	
G-IIAI	Mudry CAP.232	DEP Promotions Ltd	

Notes	Reg	Type	Owner or Operator
	G-IIAN	Aero Designs Pulsar	I. G. Harrison
	G-IICC	Van's RV-4	P. R. Fabish & J. C. Carter (G-MARX)
	G-IICT	Schempp-Hirth Ventus 2Ct	P. McLean
	G-IICX	Schempp-Hirth Ventus 2cxT	M. J. M. Turnbull
	G-IIDC	Midget Mustang	D. Cooke (G-IIMT/G-BDGA)
	G-IIDD	Van's RV-8	D. J. C. Davidson
	G-IIDI	Extra EA.300/L	Power Aerobatics Ltd (G-XTRS)
	G-IIDR	Ikarus C42 FB100	D. M. Richards
	G-IIDW	Flylight Dragon Combat 12T	I. D. Wildgoose
	G-IIDY	Aerotek Pitts S-2B Special	The S-2B Group (G-BPVP)
	G-IIEX	Extra EA.300/L	S. G. Jones
	G-IIFI	Xtremair XA41	Attitude Aerobatics Ltd
	G-IIFM	Edge 360	F. L. McGee
	G-IIFX	Marganski MDM-1	Glider FX
	G-IIGI	Van's RV-4	T. D. R. Hardy
	G-IIHI	Extra 300/SC	M. M. Choim
	G-IIHX	Bushby-Long Midget Mustang	M. C. Huxtable
	G-IIHZ	Avions Murdy CAP 231	J. Taylor & R. Bates (G-OZZO)
	G-IIID	Dan Rihn DR.107 One Design	D. A. Kean
	G-IIIE	Aerotek Pitts S-2B Special	R. M. C. R. de Aguiar/Portugal
	G-IIIF	Xtremeair XA-41	Airtime Aerobatics Ltd
	G-IIIG	Boeing Stearman A75N1 (309)	Stearman G-IIIG Group /Belgium (G-BSDR)
	G-IIII	Aerotek Pitts S-2B Special	M. Milhaud
	G-IIIJ	American Champion 8GCBC	J. D. May
	G-IIIK	Extra EA.300/SC	Extra 300SC LLP
	G-IIIL	Pitts S-1T Special	J. O. Vize
	G-IIIM	Stolp SA.100 Starduster	H. Mackintosh
	G-IIIN	Pitts S-1C Special	R. P. Evans
	G-IIIO	Schempp-Hirth Ventus 2CM	S. J. Clark
	G-IIIP	Pitts S-1D Special	R. S. Grace (G-BLAG)
	G-IIIR	Pitts S-1S Special	R. Farrer
	G-IIIT	Aerotek Pitts S-2A Special	The Aerobatics Co LLP
	G-IIIV	Pitts Super Stinker 11-260	S. D. Barnard & A. N. R. Houghton
	G-IIIX	Pitts S-1S Special	D. S. T. Eggleton (G-LBAT/G-UCCI/G-BIYN)
	G-IIIY	Boeing A75N1 Stearman	Aero-Super-Batics Ltd
	G-IIJC	Midget Mustang	D. C. Landy (G-CEKU)
	G-IIJI	Xtremeair XA-42 Sbach 342	G. H. Willson
	G-IILL	Vans RV-7	G-IILL Group
	G-IILY	Robinson R44 I	Twylight Management Ltd (G-DCSG/G-TRYG)
	G-IIMI	Extra EA.300/L	Firebird Aerobatics Ltd
	G-IINI	Van's RV-9A	N. W. Thomas
	G-IINK	Cirrus SR22	N. P. Kingdon
	G-IIOO	Schleicher ASW-27-18E	M. Clarke
	G-IIPI	Steen Skybolt	J. Burglass (G-BVXE/G-LISA)
	G-IIPT	Robinson R22 Beta	Swift Helicopter Services Ltd (G-FUSI)
	G-IIRG	Stoddard-Hamilton Glasair IIS RG	A. C. Lang
	G-IIRI	Xtreme Air Sbach 300	One Sky Aviation LLP
	G-IIRP	Mudry CAP.232	R. J. Pickin
	G-IIRV	Van's RV-7	R. C. W. King
	G-IIRW	Van's RV-8	G. G. Ferriman
	G-IISC	Extra EA.300/SC	G-IISC Group
	G-IITC	Mudry CAP.232	Skyboard Aerobatics Ltd
	G-IIXF	Van's RV-7	C. A. & S. Noujaim
	G-IIXI	Extra EA.300/L	B. Nielsen
	G-IIXX	Parsons 2-seat gyroplane	J. M. Montgomerie
	G-IIYK	Yakovlev Yak-50	Eaglescott Yak 50 Group
	G-IIYY	Cessna 421C	H-J Simon
	G-IIZI	Extra EA.300	M. G. Jefferies
	G-IJAC	Light Aero Avid Speedwing Mk 4	I. J. A. Charlton
	G-IJAG	Cessna 182T Skylane	AG Group
	G-IJBB	Enstrom 480	R. P. Bateman (G-LIVA/G-PBTT)
	G-IJMC	Magni M-16 Tandem Trainer	R. F. G. Moyle (G-POSA/G-BVJM)
	G-IJOE	PA-28RT-201T Turbo Arrow IV	J. H. Bailey
	G-IKAH	Slingsby T.51 Dart 17R	K. A. Hale
	G-IKBP	PA-28-161 Warrior II	NWMAS Leasing Ltd
	G-IKES	Stoddard-Hamilton GlaStar	M. Stow
	G-IKEV	Jabiru UL-450	S. A. Wilson & P. J. Findlay
	G-IKON	Van's RV-4	N. C. Spooner
	G-IKOS	Cessna 550 Citation Bravo	Medox Enterprises Ltd

Reg	Type	Owner or Operator	Notes
G-IKRK	Shaw Europa	K. R. Kesterton	
G-IKRS	Ikarus C42 FB UK	K. J. Warburton	
G-IKUS	Ikarus C42 FB UK	W. P. Hearn	
G-ILBO	Rolladen-Schneider LS3-A	J. P. Gilbert	
G-ILBT	Cessna 182T	G. E. Gilbert	
G-ILDA	VS.361 Spitfire HF.IX (SM520 : KJ-1)	Boultbee Vintage LLP (G-BXHZ)	
G-ILEE	Colt 56A balloon	B. W. Smith	
G-ILES	Cameron O-90 balloon	G. N. Lantos	
G-ILEW	Schempp Hirth Arcus M	Lleweni Parc Ltd	
G-ILHR	Cirrus SR22	L. H. Robinson	
G-ILIB	PZL-Bielsko SZD-36A	D. Poll	
G-ILLE	Boeing Stearman A75L3 (379)	M. Minkler	
G-ILLR	Avro RJ100	Cello Aviation Ltd (G-CFAC)	
G-ILLY	PA-28-181 Archer II	R. A. & G. M. Spiers	
G-ILLZ	Europa XS	R. S. Palmer	
G-ILPD	SIAI Marchetti F.260C	M. Mignini/Italy	
G-ILRS	Ikarus C.42 FB UK Cyclone	J. J. Oliver	
G-ILSE	Corby CJ-1 Starlet	S. Stride	
G-ILUA	Alpha R2160I	A. R. Haynes	
G-ILYA	Agusta-Bell 206B Jet Ranger II	Horizontal Attitude Ltd (G-MHMH/G-HOLZ/ G-CDBT)	
G-ILZZ	PA-31 Navajo	T. D. Nathan & I. Kazi	
G-IMAB	Europa XS	K. Richards	
G-IMAD	Cessna 172P	Superior Air SA	
G-IMAG	Colt 77A balloon ★	Balloon Preservation Group	
G-IMBI	QAC Quickie 1	P. Churcher (G-BWIT)	
G-IMBO	CEA Jodel DR.250/160	Training & Leisure Consultants Ltd	
G-IMCD	Van's RV-7	I. G. McDowell	
G-IMEA	Beech 200 Super King Air	2 Excel Aviation Ltd (G-OWAX)	
G-IMEC	PA-31 Navajo C	FAS Rhodos Air/Greece (G-BFOM)	
G-IMEL	Rotary Air Force RAF 2000 GTX-SE	N. A. Smith	
G-IMHK	P & M Quik R	J. Waite	
G-IMME	Zenair CH.701SP	T. R. Sinclair	
G-IMMI	Escapade Kid	C. Summerfield & R. K. W. Moss	
G-IMMY	Robinson R44	Eli SRL/Italy	
G-IMNY	Escapade 912	D. S. Bremner	
G-IMOK	Hoffmann HK-36R Super Dimona	A. L. Garfield	
G-IMPS	Skyranger Nynja 912S	B. J. Killick	
G-IMPX	Rockwell Commander 112B	G. Valluzzi/Italy	
G-IMUP	Tanarg/Ixess 15 912S (1)	C. R. Buckle	
G-INCA	Glaser-Dirks DG.400	C. Rau	
G-INCE	Skyranger 912(2)	A. B. Shayes	
G-INDC	Cessna T.303	J-Ross Developments Ltd	
G-INDI	Pitts S-2C Special	L. Coesens	
G-INDX	Robinson R44	Toppesfield Ltd	
G-INDY	Robinson R44	Lincoln Aviation	
G-INES	Zenair CH.650B	P. W. Day & N. J. Brownlow	
G-INGA	Thunder Ax8-84 balloon	M. L. J. Ritchie	
G-INGS	American Champion 8KCAB	Scotflight Ltd	
G-INII	Pitts S-1 Special	C. Davidson (G-BTEF)	
G-INJA	Ikarus C42 FB UK	C. E. Walls	
G-INKO	Cessna 172R	L. Salvatore	
G-INNI	Jodel D.112	K. Dermott	
G-INNY	SE-5A (replica) (F5459:Y)	D. A. Porter	
G-INSR	Cameron N-90 balloon	P. J. Waller	
G-INTS	Van's RV-4	H. R. Carey	
G-INTV	AS.355F2 Ecureuil 2	Arena Aviation Ltd (G-JETU)	
G-IOFR	Lindstrand LBL-105A balloon	RAF Halton Hot Air Balloon Club	
G-IOIA	I.I.I. Sky Arrow 650T	G-IOIA Group	
G-IOOI	Robin DR.400-160	N. B. Mason & R. P. Jones	
G-IOOK	Agusta A.109E	Hundred Percent Aviation Ltd (G-VIPE)	
G-IOOP	Christen Eagle II	A. P. S. Maynard	
G-IOOZ	Agusta A109S Grand	Castle Air Ltd	
G-IORG	Robinson R22 Beta	G. J. Collins	
G-IORV	Van's RV-10	J. E. Howe	
G-IOSI	Jodel DR.1051	D. C. & M. Brooks	
G-IOSL	Van's RV-9	S. Leach (G-CFIX)	

209

Notes	Reg	Type	Owner or Operator
	G-IOSO	Jodel DR.1050	A. E. Jackson
	G-IOWE	Shaw Europa XS	P. G. & S. J. Jeffers
	G-IPAT	Jabiru SP	Fly Jabiru Scotland
	G-IPAV	PA-32R-301T Saratoga IITC	Tofana Aviation Ltd
	G-IPAX	Cessna 560XL Citation Excel	Pacific Aviation Ltd
	G-IPEN	UltraMagic M-90 balloon	G. Holtam
	G-IPEP	Beech 95-B55 Baron	P. E. T. Price (G-FABM)
	G-IPIG	Elan 550/Pegasus Cosmos Fly Away 01	R. Frankham
	G-IPII	Steen Skybolt	J. Burglass
	G-IPJF	Robinson R44 II	Specialist Group International Ltd (G-RGNT/G-DMCG)
	G-IPKA	Alpi Pioneer 300	M. E. Hughes
	G-IPLY	Cessna 550 Citation Bravo	International Plywood (Aviation) Ltd (G-OPEM)
	G-IPOD	Europa XS	J. Wighton (G-CEBV)
	G-IPPL	Cessna F.172M	Aeroclub Schweighofen Wissembourg EV
	G-IPSI	Grob G.109B	D. G. Margetts (G-BMLO)
	G-IPUP	Beagle B.121 Pup 2	T. S. Walker
	G-IRAF	RAF 2000 GTX-SE gyroplane	Condor Aviation International Ltd
	G-IRAK	SOCATA TB-10 Tobago	Flying Feather Ltd
	G-IRAL	Thruster T600N 450	J. Giraldez
	G-IRAP	Bombardier BD-700-1A10 Global Express	TAG Aviation (UK) Ltd (G-CJME)
	G-IRAR	Van's RV-9	IPGI Ltd
	G-IRAY	Best Off Skyranger 912S(1)	G. R. Breadon
	G-IRED	Ikarus C42 FB100	Deanland Flight Training Ltd
	G-IREN	SOCATA TB-20 Trinidad GT	Chios Aeroclub
	G-IRIS	AA-5B Tiger	H. de Libouton (G-BIXU)
	G-IRJX	Avro RJX-100 ★	Manchester Heritage Museum
	G-IRLE	Schempp-Hirth Ventus cT	D. J. Scholey
	G-IRLY	Colt 90A balloon	Ballooning in Tuscany SRL/Italy
	G-IRLZ	Lindstrand LBL-60X balloon	A. M. Holly
	G-IROB	SOCATA TB-10 Tobago	R. Evans
	G-IROJ	Magni M-16 Tandem Trainer	A. G. Jones
	G-IRON	Shaw Europa XS	T. M. Clark
	G-IROS	Rotorsport UK Calidus	M. P. Kemp & W. Perry
	G-IROX	Magni M-24C Orion	A. J. Roxburgh
	G-IRPC	Cessna 182Q	A. T. Jeans (G-BSKM)
	G-IRPW	Europa XS	R. P. Wheelwright
	G-IRTM	DG Flugzeugbau DG-1000M	Morgan Land Sea & Air LLP
	G-IRTY	VS.361 Spitfire LF.IX	Boultbee Flight Academy LLP
	G-IRYC	Schweizer 269-1	Virage Helicopter Academy LLP
	G-ISAC	Isaacs Spitfire (TZ164:OI-A)	A. James
	G-ISAR	Cessna 421C	Skycab Ltd (G-BHKJ)
	G-ISAX	PA-28-181 Archer III	Spectrum Flying Group
	G-ISBD	Alpi Pioneer 300 Hawk	B. Davies
	G-ISCD	Czech Sport Aircraft Sportcruiser	P. W. Shepherd
	G-ISDB	PA-28-161 Warrior II	K. Bartholomew (G-BWET)
	G-ISDN	Boeing Stearman A75N1 (14)	D. R. L. Jones
	G-ISEH	Cessna 182R	D. Jaffa (G-BIWS)
	G-ISEL	Best Off Skyranger 912 (2)	P. A. Robertson
	G-ISEW	P & M Quik GT450	R. & T. Raffle
	G-ISHA	PA-28-161 Warrior III	LAC Flying School
	G-ISLC	BAe Jetstream 3202	Oberbank Leasing GmbH/Austria
	G-ISLF	Aerospatiale ATR-42-500	Blue Islands Ltd
	G-ISLH	Aerospatiale ATR-42-320	Blue Islands Ltd
	G-ISLI	Aerospatiale ATR-72-212A	Blue Islands Ltd
	G-ISLK	Aerospatiale ATR-72-212A	Blue Islands Ltd
	G-ISLL	Aerospatiale ATR-72-212A	Blue Islands Ltd
	G-ISLY	Cessna 172S	RMACF Aviation (G-IZZS)
	G-ISMA	Van's RV-7	S. Marriott (G-STAF)
	G-ISMO	Robinson R22 Beta	Kuki Helicopter Sales Ltd
	G-ISOB	Cameron O-31 balloon	C. G. Dobson
	G-ISPH	Bell 206B JetRanger 2	Blades Aviation (UK) LLP (G-OPJM)
	G-ISRV	Van's RV-7	I. A. Sweetland
	G-ISSG	DHC.6-310 Twin Otter	Isles of Scilly Skybus Ltd
	G-ISSV	Eurocopter EC 155B1	Bristow Helicopters Ltd
	G-ISZA	Aerotek Pitts S-2A Special	T. J. B. Dugan (G-HISS/G-BLVU)

Reg	Type	Owner or Operator	Notes
G-ITAF	SIAI-Marchetti SF.260AM	N. A. Whatling	
G-ITAR	Magni M-16C Tandem Trainer	Hartis Autogyro Syndicate	
G-ITBT	Alpi Pioneer 300 Hawk	F. Paolini	
G-ITII	Aerotech Pitts S-2A Special	P. J. Kirkpatrick	
G-ITOI	Cameron N-90 balloon	Flying Pictures Ltd	
G-ITOR	Robinson R44 II	MV Commercial Ltd	
G-ITOY	Robin DR.400-140B	Neal Cavalier-Smith Group (G-MHSJ)	
G-ITPH	Robinson R44 II	Helicopter Services Europe Ltd	
G-ITST	Europa	I. Tucker	
G-ITSU	Embraer EMB-500 Phenom 100	Sovereign Business Jets Ltd (G-RUBO)	
G-ITVM	Lindstrand LBL-105A balloon	Elmer Balloon Team	
G-ITWB	DHC.1 Chipmunk 22	I. T. Whitaker-Bethe	
G-IUII	Aerostar Yakovlev Yak-52	Cosmos Technology Ltd	
G-IUMB	Schleicher ASW-20L	M. S. Szymkowicz	
G-IVAL	CAB CAP-10B	H. Thomas	
G-IVAN	Shaw TwinEze	A. M. Aldridge	
G-IVAR	Yakovlev Yak-50	A. H. Soper	
G-IVEN	Robinson R44 II	OKR Group/Ireland	
G-IVER	Shaw Europa XS	I. Phillips	
G-IVES	Shaw Europa	D. G. Lewendon (G-JOST)	
G-IVET	Shaw Europa	K. J. Fraser	
G-IVII	Van's RV-7	M. A. N. Newall	
G-IVIP	Agusta A109E Power	Castle Air Ltd (G-VIRU)	
G-IVOR	Aeronca 11AC Chief	South Western Aeronca Group	
G-IWFC	Agusta AW109SP Grand	GB Helicopters	
G-IWIN	Raj Hamsa X'Air Hawk	C. G. & M. G. Chambers	
G-IWIZ	Flylight Dragonfly	I. White	
G-IWON	Cameron V-90 balloon	D. P. P. Jenkinson (G-BTCV)	
G-IWRB	Agusta A109A-II	Skyhost ApS (G-VIPT)	
G-IXII	Christen Eagle II	Eagle II Group (G-BPZI)	
G-IXXI	Schleicher ASW-27-18E	G. P. Stingemore	
G-IXXY	Magic Cyclone	L. Hogan	
G-IYRO	RAF2000 GTX-SE	G. Golding (G-BXDD)	
G-IZIT	Rans S.6-116 Coyote II	D. J. Flower	
G-IZOB	Eurocopter EC.120B Colibri	Beechview Developments Ltd	
G-IZRV	Van's RV-12	D. J. Mountain & H. W. Hall	
G-IZZI	Cessna T.182T	W. E. Davis	
G-IZZZ	Champion 8KCAB	Leased Flight Ltd	
G-JAAB	Avtech Jabiru UL	I. A. Smith	
G-JABB	Avtech Jabiru UL	R. J. Sutherland	
G-JABE	Jabiru Aircraft Jabiru UL-D	Rochester Microlights Ltd	
G-JABI	Jabiru Aircraft Jabiru J400	K. & M. A. Payne	
G-JABJ	Jabiru Aircraft Jabiru J400	South Essex Flying Group	
G-JABS	Avtech Jabiru UL-450	Jabiru Flying Group	
G-JABU	Jabiru J430	S. D. Miller	
G-JABY	Avtech Jabiru UL-450	N. J. Wakeling	
G-JABZ	Avtech Jabiru UL-450	G-JABZ Group	
G-JACA	PA-28-161 Warrior II	The Pilot Centre Ltd	
G-JACB	PA-28-181 Archer III	P. R. Coe (G-PNNI)	
G-JACH	PA-28-181 Archer III	Alderney Flight Training Ltd (G-IDPH)	
G-JACO	Avtech Jabiru UL	C. Denham	
G-JACS	PA-28-181 Archer III	Modern Air (UK) Ltd	
G-JADJ	PA-28-181 Archer III	P. D. Wheelen	
G-JADW	Ikarus C42 FB80	G-JADW Group	
G-JAEE	Van's RV-6A	J. A. E. Edser	
G-JAES	Bell 206B JetRanger 3	Associazione Croce Italia Area Flegrea/Italy (G-STOX/G-BNIR)	
G-JAFS	PA-32R-301 Saratoga II HP	Countrywide Aviation (G-VMFC)	
G-JAFT	Diamond DA.42 Twin Star	Airways Aviation Academy Ltd	
G-JAGA	Embraer EMB-505 Phenom 300	London Executive Aviation Ltd	
G-JAGS	Cessna FRA.150L	RAF Marham Aero Club (G-BAUY)	
G-JAGY	Europa XS	J. S. Chaggar	
G-JAIR	Mainair Blade	G. Spittlehouse	
G-JAJA	Robinson R44 II	J. D. Richardson	
G-JAJB	AA-5A Cheetah	D. Hadlow & Partners Flying Group	

Notes	Reg	Type	Owner or Operator
	G-JAJK	PA-31-350 Navajo Chieftain	Blue Sky Investments Ltd (G-OLDB/G-DIXI)
	G-JAJP	Avtech Jabiru UL	J. Anderson
	G-JAKF	Robinson R44 Raven II	J. G. Froggatt
	G-JAKI	Mooney M.20R	D. M. Abrahamson
	G-JAKS	PA-28 Cherokee 160	K. Harper (G-ARVS)
	G-JAKX	Cameron Z-69 balloon	J. A. Hibberd
	G-JALS	Cessna 560XL Citation XLS+	Air Charter Scotland Ltd
	G-JAME	Zenair CH 601UL	J. J. Damp (G-CDFZ)
	G-JAMM	Guimbal Cabri G2	A Woodward Aviation Ltd
	G-JAMP	PA-28-151 Warrior	Lapwing Flying Group Ltd (G-BRJU)
	G-JAMY	Shaw Europa XS	J. P. Sharp
	G-JAMZ	P & M QuikR	S. Cuthbertson
	G-JANA	PA-28-181 Archer II	S. Hoo-Hing
	G-JANB	Colt Flying Bottle SS balloon	Justerini & Brooks Ltd
	G-JANF	BRM Aero Bristell NG5 Speed Wing	G-JANF Group
	G-JANI	Robinson R44	JT Helicopters Ltd
	G-JANN	PA-34-220T Seneca III	D. J. Whitcombe
	G-JANS	Cessna FR.172J	R. G. Scott
	G-JANT	PA-28-181 Archer II	Janair Aviation Ltd
	G-JAOC	Best Off Sky Ranger Swift 912S(1)	R. L. Domiczew
	G-JAPK	Grob G.130A Twin II Acro	Cairngorm Gliding Club
	G-JARM	Robinson R44	J. Armstrong
	G-JASE	PA-28-161 Warrior II	Mid-Anglia School of Flying
	G-JASS	Beech B200 Super King Air	Atlantic Bridge Aviation Ltd
	G-JAVO	PA-28-161 Warrior II	Victor Oscar Ltd (G-BSXW)
	G-JAWC	Pegasus Quantum 15-912	M. J. Flower
	G-JAWZ	Pitts S-1S Special	A. R. Harding
	G-JAXS	Avtech Jabiru UL	S. R. Hughes
	G-JAYI	Auster J/1 Autocrat	R. Greatrex
	G-JAYK	Robinson R44 II	HQ Aviation Ltd (G-MACU/G-SEFI)
	G-JAYS	Skyranger 912S(1)	K. O'Connor & T. L. Whitcombe
	G-JAYZ	CZAW Sportcruiser	J. Williams
	G-JBAN	P & M Quik GT450	A. Nourse
	G-JBAS	Neico Lancair 200	A. Slater
	G-JBAV	EV-97 Eurostar SL	JB Aviation Ltd
	G-JBBB	Eurocopter EC120B Colibri	Bartram Land Ltd
	G-JBBZ	AS.350B3 Ecureuil	D. Donnelly
	G-JBCB	Agusta A.109E Power	Castle Air Ltd (G-PLPL/G-TMWC)
	G-JBDB	Agusta-Bell 206B JetRanger	Aerospeed Ltd (G-OOPS/G-BNRD)
	G-JBDH	Robin DR.400/180	W. A. Clark
	G-JBEN	Mainair Blade 912	G. J. Bentley
	G-JBKA	Robinson R44	J. G. Harrison
	G-JBLZ	Cessna 550 Citation Bravo	Executive Aviation Services Ltd
	G-JBRD	Mooney M.20K	R. J. Doughton
	G-JBRE	Rotorsport UK MT-03	P. A. Remfry
	G-JBRN	Cessna 182S	Ngaio Aviation (G-RITZ)
	G-JBRS	Van's RV-8	C. Jobling
	G-JBSP	Avtech Jabiru SP-470	M. D. Beeby and C. K. & C. R. James
	G-JBTR	Van's RV-8	Double Whisky Flying Group
	G-JBUZ	Robin DR400/180R Remorqueur	D. A. Saywell
	G-JBVP	Aeropro Eurofox 3K	J. A. Valentine & B. J. Partridge
	G-JCIH	Van's RV-7A	M. A. Hughes & D. F. Chamberlain
	G-JCJC	Colt Flying Jeans SS balloon	Magical Adventures Ltd
	G-JCKT	Stemme S.10VT	M. B. Jefferyes & J. C. Taylor
	G-JCOP	Eurocopter AS.350B3 Ecureuil	Optimum Ltd
	G-JCUB	PA-18 Super Cub 135	Vintage Aircraft Flying Group
	G-JCWM	Robinson R44 II	M. L. J. Goff
	G-JCWS	Reality Escapade 912(2)	J. C. W. Seward
	G-JDBC	PA-34-200T Seneca II	JD Aviation Ltd (G-BDEF)
	G-JDEL	Jodel 150	K. F. & R. Richardson (G-JDLI)
	G-JDOG	Cessna 305C Bird Dog (24541/BMG)	BC Arrow Ltd
	G-JDPB	PA-28R-201T Turbo Arrow III	BC Arrow Ltd (G-DNCS)
	G-JDRD	Alpi Pioneer 300	Anvilles Flying Group
	G-JEBS	Cessna 172S	Integrated Hi-Tech Ltd
	G-JECI	DHC.8-402 Dash Eight	Flybe.com
	G-JECJ	DHC.8-402 Dash Eight	Flybe.com
	G-JECK	DHC.8-402 Dash Eight	Flybe.com

Reg	Type	Owner or Operator	Notes
G-JECL	DHC.8-402 Dash Eight	Flybe.com	
G-JECM	DHC.8-402 Dash Eight	Flybe.com	
G-JECN	DHC.8-402 Dash Eight	Flybe.com	
G-JECO	DHC.8-402 Dash Eight	Flybe.com	
G-JECP	DHC.8-402 Dash Eight	Flybe.com	
G-JECR	DHC.8-402 Dash Eight	Flybe.com	
G-JECX	DHC.8-402 Dash Eight	Flybe.com	
G-JECY	DHC.8-402 Dash Eight	Flybe.com	
G-JECZ	DHC.8-402 Dash Eight	Flybe.com	
G-JEDH	Robin DR.400/180	J. B. Hoolahan	
G-JEDM	DHC.8-402 Dash Eight	Flybe.com	
G-JEDP	DHC.8-402 Dash Eight	Flybe.com	
G-JEDR	DHC.8-402 Dash Eight	Flybe com	
G-JEDS	Andreasson BA-4B	S. B. Jedburgh (G-BEBT)	
G-JEDT	DHC.8-402 Dash Eight	Flybe com	
G-JEDU	DHC.8-402 Dash Eight	Flybe com	
G-JEDV	DHC.8-402 Dash Eight	Flybe.com	
G-JEDW	DHC.8-402 Dash Eight	Flybe.com	
G-JEEP	Evektor EV-97 Eurostar	G-JEEP Group (G-CBNK)	
G-JEFA	Robinson R44	Simlot Ltd	
G-JEJE	RAF 2000 GTX-SE gyroplane	A. F. Smallacombe	
G-JEJH	Jodel DR.1050 Ambassadeur	Bredon Hill Flying Group	
G-JEMI	Lindstrand LBL-90A balloon	J. A. Lawton	
G-JEMM	Jodel DR.1050	D. W. Garbe	
G-JEMP	BRM Aero Bristell NG5 Speed Wing	W. Precious	
G-JEMS	Ultramagic S-90 balloon	D. J. , J. E. & L. V. McDonald	
G-JEMZ	Ultramagic H-31 balloon	J. A. Atkinson	
G-JENA	Mooney M.20K	Jena Air Force	
G-JENK	Ikarus C42 FB80	G-JENK Chatteris 2015	
G-JERO	Shaw Europa XS	P. Jenkinson & N. Robshaw	
G-JERR	Aeropro Eurofox 3K	J. Robertson	
G-JESS	PA-28R-201T Turbo Arrow III	R. E. Trawicki (G-REIS)	
G-JETH	Hawker Sea Hawk FGA.6 (XE489) ★	P. G. Vallance Ltd/Charlwood	
G-JETM	Gloster Meteor T.7 (VZ638) ★	P. G. Vallance Ltd/Charlwood	
G-JETV	HPH Glasflugel 304S Shark	Sierra Hotel Shark Group	
G-JETX	Bell 206B JetRanger 3	G-JETX Aviation LLP	
G-JEWL	Van's RV-7	H. A. & J. S. Jewell	
G-JEZZ	Skyranger 912S(1)	C. Callicott	
G-JFAN	P & M Quik R	P. R. Brooker & G. R. Hall	
G-JFDI	Dynamic WT9 UK	S. Turnbull	
G-JFER	Rockwell Commander 114B	Helitrip Charter LLP (G-HPSE)	
G-JFLO	Aerospool Dynamic WT9 UK	J. Flood	
G-JFLY	Schleicher ASW-24	Cambridge Gliding Club Ltd	
G-JFMK	Zenair CH.701SP	J. D. Pearson	
G-JFRV	Van's RV-7A	J. H. Fisher	
G-JFWI	Cessna F.172N	Skyhawk II Ltd	
G-JGAR	Robinson R44 II	Garratt Aviation Ltd (G-DMRS)	
G-JGBI	Bell 206L-4 LongRanger	Dorbcrest Homes Ltd	
G-JGCA	VS.361 Spitfire LF.IXe (TE517)	P. R. Monk (G-CCIX/G-BIXP)	
G-JGMN	CASA 1.131E Jungmann 2000	P. D. Scandrett	
G-JGSI	Pegasus Quantum 15-912	G-JGSI Group	
G-JHAA	Csameron Z-90 balloon	C. L. Thompson	
G-JHAC	Cessna FRA.150L	J. H. A. Clarke (G-BACM)	
G-JHDD	Czech Sport Aircraft Sportcruiser	G-JHDD Syndicate	
G-JHEW	Robinson R22 Beta	Heli Air Ltd	
G-JHKP	Shaw Europa XS	J. E. S. Turner	
G-JHLE	P & M Quik GTR	A. D. Carr	
G-JHLP	Flylight Dragon Chaser	N. L. Stammers	
G-JHMP	SOCATA TB-20 Trinidad	D. M. Hook	
G-JHNY	Cameron A.210 balloon	Bailey Balloons Ltd	
G-JHPC	Cessna 182T	J. R. Turner	
G-JHYS	Shaw Europa	G-JHYS Group	
G-JIBO	BAe Jetstream 3102	K. Beaumont (G-OJSA/G-BTYG)	
G-JIFI	Schempp-Hirth Duo Discus T	620 Syndicate	
G-JIII	Stolp SA.300 Starduster Too	VT10 Aero Company	
G-JIIL	Pitts S-2AE Special	A. M. Southwell	
G-JIMB	Beagle B.121 Pup 1	K. D. H. Gray & P. G. Fowler (G-AWWF)	

Notes	Reg	Type	Owner or Operator
	G-JIMC	Van's RV-7	J. Chapman
	G-JIMH	Cessna F.152 II	D. J. Howell (G-SHAH)
	G-JIMM	Shaw Europa XS	J. Cherry
	G-JIMP	Messerschmitt Bf 109G-2	M. R. Oliver
	G-JIMZ	Van's RV-4	R. Tyrer
	G-JINI	Cameron V-77 balloon	I. R. Warrington
	G-JINX	Silence SA.180 Twister	P. M. Wells
	G-JJAB	Jabiru J400	K. Ingebrigsten
	G-JJAN	PA-28-181 Archer II	Blueplane Ltd
	G-JJEN	PA-28-181 Archer III	K. M. R. Jenkins
	G-JJET	Cessna 510 Citation Mustang	Fly Vectra Ltd
	G-JJFB	Eurocopter EC.120B Colibri	J. G. Rhoden
	G-JJIL	Extra EA.300/L	M. M. Choim
	G-JJSI	BAe 125 Srs 800B	Gama Leasing Ltd (G-OMGG)
	G-JKAT	Robinson R22	J. N. Kenwright (G-WIZY/G-BMWX)
	G-JKAY	Robinson R44	Dydb Marketing Ltd
	G-JKEE	Diamond DA.42NG Twin Star	Morgan Land and Sea Ltd
	G-JKEL	Van's RV-7	J. D. Kelsall (G-LNNE)
	G-JKHT	Robinson R22	J K Helicopter Training Ltd (G-OTUA/G-LHCA)
	G-JKKK	Cessna 172S	P. Eaton
	G-JKMH	Diamond DA42 Twin Star	Flying Time Ltd
	G-JKMI	Diamond DA42 Twin Star	Flying Time Ltd (G-KELV)
	G-JKMJ	Diamond DA42 Twin Star	Skies Aviation Academy PC
	G-JKRV	Schempp-Hirth Arcus T	Syndicate 291
	G-JLAT	Aerotechnik EV-97 Eurostar	N. E. Watts
	G-JLCA	PA-34-200T Seneca II	Tayside Aviation Ltd (G-BOKE)
	G-JLHS	Beech A36 Bonanza	I. G. Meredith
	G-JLIA	Cameron O-90 balloon	M. Thompson
	G-JLIN	PA-28-161 Cadet	JH Sandham Aviation
	G-JLRW	Beech 76 Duchess	Gem Aviation Ltd
	G-JLSP	Extra EA.300/LC	J. M. Lynch & S. A. Perkes
	G-JMAA	Boeing 757-3CQ	Thomas Cook Airlines Ltd
	G-JMAB	Boeing 757-3CQ	Thomas Cook Airlines Ltd
	G-JMAC	BAe Jetstream 4100 ★	Jetstream Club, Liverpool Marriott Hotel South, Speke (G-JAMD/G-JXLI)
	G-JMAL	Jabiru UL-D	I. D. Cracknell & P. Bennett
	G-JMAN	Mainair Blade 912S	S. T. Cain
	G-JMBJ	Magni M24C Orion	B. Lesslie
	G-JMBO	Embraer EMB-505 Phenom 300	Catreus AOC Ltd
	G-JMBS	Agusta A109S Grand	Castle Air Ltd
	G-JMCB	Boeing 737-436	Atlantic Airlines Ltd (G-GBTA/G-BVHA)
	G-JMCH	Boeing 737-476	Atlantic Airlines Ltd (G-RAJG)
	G-JMCJ	Boeing 737-436	Atlantic Airlines Ltd (G-DOCW)
	G-JMCK	Boeing 737-4D7	Atlantic Airlines Ltd
	G-JMCL	Boeing 737-322	Atlantic Airlines Ltd
	G-JMCM	Boeing 737-3YO	Atlantic Airlines Ltd
	G-JMCO	Boeing 737-3TOF	Atlantic Airlines Ltd
	G-JMCP	Boeing 737-3TO	Atlantic Airlines Ltd
	G-JMCR	Boeing 737-4YO	Atlantic Airlines Ltd
	G-JMCS	Boeing 737-4YO	Atlantic Airlines Ltd
	G-JMCT	Boeing 737-3YO	Atlantic Airlines Ltd (G-ZAPV/G-IGOC)
	G-JMCU	Boeing 737-301SF	Atlantic Airlines Ltd
	G-JMCV	Boeing 737-4K5	Atlantic Airlines Ltd
	G-JMCX	Boeing 737-406	Atlantic Airlines Ltd
	G-JMCY	Boeing 737-4Q8	Atlantic Airlines Ltd
	G-JMCZ	Boeing 737-4K5	Atlantic Airlines Ltd
	G-JMDI	Schweizer 269C	J. M. Heath (G-FLAT)
	G-JMGP	Aero L-39ZO Albatros	SARL Jet Concept/France
	G-JMKE	Cessna 172S	M. C. Plomer-Roberts & H. White
	G-JMNN	CASA 1-131E Jungmann	B. S. Charters
	G-JMOG	Boeing 757-330	Thomas Cook Airlines Ltd
	G-JMON	Agusta A109A-II	Falcon Aviation Ltd (G-RFDS/G-BOLA)
	G-JMOS	PA-34-220T Seneca V	Moss Aviation LLP
	G-JMRT	Ikarus C42 FB80	Kennedy Tuck Air Ltd
	G-JMRV	Van's RV-7	J. W. Marshall
	G-JNAR	Ace Easy Rider Touch	D. Reckitt

Reg	Type	Owner or Operator	Notes
G-JNAS	AA-5A Cheetah	C. J. Williams	
G-JNET	Robinson R22 Beta	R. L. Hartshorn	
G-JNMA	VS.379 Spitfire FR.Mk.XIVe	P. M. Andrews	
G-JNNB	Colt 90A balloon	N. A. P. Godfrey	
G-JNSC	Schempp-Hirth Janus CT	D. S. Bramwell	
G-JNSH	Robinson R22	Hawes Bates LLP	
G-JNUS	Schempp-Hirth Janus C	N. A. Peatfield	
G-JOBA	P & M Quik GT450	S. P. Durnall	
G-JOBS	Cessna T182T	Tech Travel Ltd (G-BZVF)	
G-JODB	Jodel D.9 Bebe	M. R. Routh	
G-JODE	Jodel D.150	B. R. Vickers	
G-JODL	Jodel D.1050/M	D. Silsbury	
G-JOED	Lindstrand LBL-77A balloon	G. R. Down	
G-JOHA	Cirrus SR20	N. Harris	
G-JOID	Cirrus SR20	I. F. Doubtfire	
G-JOJO	Cameron A-210 balloon	A. C. Rawson & J. J. Rudoni	
G-JOKR	Extra EA.300/L	C. Jefferies	
G-JOLY	Cessna 120	B. V. Meade	
G-JONG	Rotorway Executive 162F	Central of Coalville Ltd	
G-JONL	CZAW Sportcruiser	J. R. Linford	
G-JONM	PA-28-181 Archer III	J. H. Massey	
G-JONO	Colt 77A balloon★	British Balloon Museum and Library	
G-JONT	Cirrus SR22	J. A. Green	
G-JONX	Aeropro Eurofox 912(1)	A. J. South	
G-JONY	Cyclone AX2000 HKS	S and A Logistics Ltd	
G-JONZ	Cessna 172P	M. Guinee	
G-JOOL	Mainair Blade 912	P. C. Collins	
G-JORD	Robinson R44 II	Overby Ltd	
G-JOTA	Beech B.90 King Air	Jota Aircraft Leasing Ltd (G-OJRO)	
G-JOTB	Beech C.90 King Air	Jota Aircraft Leasing Ltd	
G-JOTR	Avro RJ-85	Jota Aviation Ltd (G-CHFE)	
G-JOTS	Avro RJ-100	Jota Aviation Ltd	
G-JOYT	PA-28-181 Archer II	John K. Cathcart Ltd (G-BOVO)	
G-JOYZ	PA-28-181 Archer III	Zulu Group	
G-JOZI	AS.350BA Ecureuil	WW Medical Facilities Ltd	
G-JPBA	Van's RV-6	S. B. Austin	
G-JPEG	BN-2A-20 Islander	Apem Aviation Ltd (G-BEDW)	
G-JPIT	Pitts S-2S Special	R. S. Goodwin	
G-JPJR	Robinson R44 II	Longstop Investments Ltd	
G-JPMA	Avtech Jabiru UL	A. J. Thomas	
G-JPOT	PA-32R-301 Saratoga SP	The Big 6 Flyers Ltd (G-BIYM)	
G-JPRO	P.84 Jet Provost T.5A (XW433)	J. A. Campbell	
G-JPTV	P.84 Jet Provost T.5A (XW354)	Century Aviation Ltd	
G-JPWM	Skyranger 912 (2)	R. S. Waters & M. Pittock	
G-JRBC	PA-28-140 Cherokee	N. Livni	
G-JRCR	Bell 206L-1 LongRanger II	RSCP Management Ltd (G-EYRE/G-STVI)	
G-JREE	Maule MX-7-180	C. R. P. Briand	
G-JRER	Tecnam P2006T	3GRCOMM Ltd	
G-JRLR	Sackville BM-65 balloon	J. S. Russon	
G-JRME	Jodel D.140E	Sapphire Leasing Ltd	
G-JROO	Agusta-Bell 206B JetRanger II	GH Byproducts (Derby) Ltd (G-VJMJ/G-PEAK/ G-BLJE)	
G-JRSH	Cirrus SR22T	Lismore Instruments Ltd	
G-JRVB	Van's RV-8	J. W. Salter	
G-JRXI	Bell 505 Jet Ranger X	Helicompany Ltd	
G-JSAK	Robinson R22 Beta II	Tukair Aircraft Charter	
G-JSAT	BN-2T Turbine Islander	Chewton Glen Aviation (G-BVFK)	
G-JSAW	Robinson R66	J. S. A. Wood	
G-JSCA	PA-28RT-201 Arrow IV	G-JSCA Flying Group (G-ICSA)	
G-JSEY	Bollonbau Worner NL-STU/1000	M. Leblanc	
G-JSFC	Tecnam P2008-JC	Stapleford Flying Club Ltd	
G-JSIC	M & D Flugzeugbau JS-MD Single	A. G. W. Hall & K. Barker	
G-JSKY	Ikarus C42 FB80	M. S. Westman	
G-JSMA	Gloster Meteor T.Mk.7.5 (WL419)	Martin-Baker Aircraft Company Ltd	
G-JSPL	Avtech Jabiru UL-450	R. S. Cochrane	
G-JSPR	Glaser-Dirks DG400	J. Mjels	
G-JSRK	HpH Glasflugel 304S Shark	Great White Syndicate	

Notes	Reg	Type	Owner or Operator
	G-JSRV	Van's RV-6	J. Stringer
	G-JSSD	HP.137 Jetstream 3001 ★	Museum of Flight/East Fortune
	G-JSSE	Dassault Falcon 900B	XJC Ltd
	G-JTBX	Bell 206B Jet Ranger III	Skywest Aviation Ltd (G-EWAW/G-DORB)
	G-JTPC	Aeromot AMT-200 Super Ximango	G. J. & J. T. Potter
	G-JTSA	Robinson R44 II	S. Novotny
	G-JUDD	Avtech Jabiru UL-450	N. Morrisen
	G-JUDE	Robin DR.400/180	Bravo India Flying Group Ltd
	G-JUDY	AA-5A Cheetah	R. E. Dagless
	G-JUFS	SOCATA TB-9 Tampico	N. J. Richardson & B. C. Costin
	G-JUGE	Aerotechnik EV-97 TeamEurostar UK	I. A. Baker
	G-JUGS	Autógyro MTOSport	S. J. M. Hornsby
	G-JUJU	Chilton DW1A	D. C. Reid
	G-JULE	P & M Quik GT450	G. Almond
	G-JULL	Stemme S.10VT	J. P. C. Fuchs
	G-JULU	Cameron V-90 balloon	J. M. Searle
	G-JULZ	Shaw Europa XS	J. S. Firth
	G-JUNG	CASA 1.131E Jungmann 1000 (E3B-143)	J. A. Sykes
	G-JUNO	Fokker D.VII Replica	S. J. Green
	G-JURG	Rockwell Commander 114A	M. G. Wright
	G-JUST	Beech F33A Bonanza	N. M. R. Richards
	G-JVBF	Lindstrand LBL-210A balloon	Virgin Balloon Flights
	G-JVBP	Aerotechnik EV-97 Team Eurostar UK	Otherton Blue Skies Syndicate
	G-JVET	Aeropro Eurofox 912(IS)	J. S. G. Down
	G-JWBI	Agusta-Bell 206B JetRanger 2	The Cloudy Bay Trading Company (G-RODS/ G-NOEL/G-BCWN)
	G-JWDB	Ikarus C.42 FB80	A. R. Hughes
	G-JWDS	Cessna F.150G	G. Sayer (G-AVNB)
	G-JWDW	Ikarus C42 FB80	D. A. & J. W. Wilding
	G-JWIV	Jodel DR.1051	C. M. Fitton
	G-JWJW	CASA 1-131E Jungmann Srs.2000	J. W. & J. T. Whicher
	G-JWMA	Gloster Meteor T.Mk.7	Martin-Baker Aircraft Co.Ltd
	G-JWNW	Magni M-16C Tandem Trainer	J. A. Ingram
	G-JWRN	Robinson R44 II	Heritage Automotive Holdings LTD (G-JSCH)
	G-JWXS	Shaw Europa XS T-G	J. Wishart
	G-JXTC	BAe Jetstream 3108★	University of Glamorgan instructional airframe (G-LOGT/G-BSFH)
	G-JYRO	Rotorsport UK MT-03	A. Richards
	G-JZBA	Boeing 737-800	Jet 2.com
	G-JZBB	Boeing 737-800	Jet 2.com
	G-JZBC	Boeing 737-800	Jet 2.com
	G-JZBD	Boeing 737-800	Jet 2.com
	G-JZBE	Boeing 737-800	Jet 2.com
	G-JZBF	Boeing 737-800	Jet 2.com
	G-JZBG	Boeing 737-800	Jet 2.com
	G-JZBH	Boeing 737-800	Jet 2.com
	G-JZBI	Boeing 737-800	Jet 2.com
	G-JZBJ	Boeing 737-800	Jet 2.com
	G-JZHA	Boeing 737-8K5	Jet 2.com
	G-JZHB	Boeing 737-8K5	Jet 2.com
	G-JZHC	Boeing 737-8K5	Jet 2.com
	G-JZHD	Boeing 737-808	Jet 2.com
	G-JZHE	Boeing 737-8K2	Jet 2.com
	G-JZHF	Boeing 737-8K2	Jet 2.com
	G-JZHG	Boeing 737-85P	Jet 2.com
	G-JZHH	Boeing 737-85P	Jet 2.com
	G-JZHJ	Boeing 737-8MG	Jet 2.com
	G-JZHK	Boeing 737-8MG	Jet 2.com
	G-JZHM	Boeing 737-8MG	Jet 2.com
	G-JZHN	Boeing 737-8MG	Jet 2.com
	G-JZHO	Boeing 737-8MG	Jet 2.com
	G-JZHP	Boeing 737-8MG	Jet 2.com
	G-JZHR	Boeing 737-8MG	Jet 2.com

Reg	Type	Owner or Operator	Notes
G-JZHS	Boeing 737-8MG	Jet 2.com	
G-JZHT	Boeing 737-8MG	Jet 2.com	
G-JZHU	Boeing 737-8MG	Jet 2.com	
G-JZHV	Boeing 737-8MG	Jet 2.com	
G-JZHW	Boeing 737-8MG	Jet 2.com	
G-JZHX	Boeing 737-8MG	Jet 2.com	
G-JZHY	Boeing 737-8MG	Jet 2.com	
G-JZHZ	Boeing 737-8MG	Jet 2.com	
G-KAAT	MDH MD-902 Explorer	Specialist Aviation Services Ltd (G-PASS)	
G-KAEW	Fairey Gannet AEW Mk.3	M. Stott	
G-KAFT	Diamond DA40D Star	Airways Aviation Academy Ltd	
G-KAIR	PA-28-181 Archer II	G. Fox	
G-KALI	PA-28-140 Cherokee F	Akki Aviation Services Ltd (G-BASL)	
G-KALP	Schleicher ASW-24	H. E. Gokalp	
G-KALS	Bombardier BD-100-1A10	Volar Ltd	
G-KAMP	PA-18 Super Cub 135	G. Cormack	
G-KAMY	AT-6D Harvard III (8084)	Orion Enterprises Ltd	
G-KANZ	Westland Wasp HAS.1 (NZ3909)	T. J. Manna	
G-KAOM	Scheibe SF.25C Falke	Falke G-KAOM Syndicate	
G-KAOS	Van's RV-7	J. L. Miles	
G-KAPW	P.56 Provost T.1 (XF603)	The Shuttleworth Collection	
G-KARA	Brügger MB.2 Colibri	C. L. Hill (G-BMUI)	
G-KARE	Pilatus PC-12/47E	Graham Aircraft Hire Ltd	
G-KARI	Fuji FA.200-160	E. T. Leonardus	
G-KARK	Dyn'Aéro MCR-01 Club	M. J. Dawson	
G-KARN	Rotorway Executive 90	U. G. P. Nimz (G-VART/G-BSUR)	
G-KART	PA-28-161 Warrior II	Romeo Tango Aviation Ltd	
G-KASW	Rotorsport UK Calidus	R. A. Clarkson	
G-KASX	VS.384 Seafire Mk.XVII (SX336)	T. J. Manna (G-BRMG)	
G-KATI	Rans S.7 Courier	C. E. Hunt	
G-KATT	Cessna 152 II	C. M. de C. C. Cabral/Portugal (G-BMTK)	
G-KATZ	Flight Design CT2K	A. N. D. Arthur	
G-KAWA	Denney Kitfox Mk 2	J. K. Ewing	
G-KAXF	Hawker Hunter F.6A (N-294)	Stichting Dutch Hawker Hunter Foundation/Netherlands	
G-KAXT	Westland Wasp HAS.1 (XT787)	T. E. Martin	
G-KAXW	Westland Scout AH.1 (XW612)	Orion Enterprises Ltd (G-BXRR)	
G-KAYD	Boeing Stearman A75N1	R. H. Butterfield	
G-KAYH	Extra EA.300/L	F. M. H. Versteegh/Belgium	
G-KAYI	Cameron Z-90 balloon	Snow Business International Ltd	
G-KAYS	Hughes 369E	Transair (UK) Ltd (G-CIMJ/G-RISK)	
G-KAZB	Sikorsky S-76C	Bristow Helicopters Ltd	
G-KAZI	Mainair Pegasus Quantum 15-912	Fairlight Engineering Ltd	
G-KBOJ	Autogyro MTOSport	K. M. G. Barnett	
G-KBOX	Flight Design CTSW	G. N. S. Farrant	
G-KBWP	Schempp-Hirth Arcus T	G-KBWP Gliding Group	
G-KCHG	Schempp-Hirth Ventus Ct	J. Burrow	
G-KCIG	Sportavia RF-5B	Deeside Fournier Group	
G-KCIN	PA-28-161 Cadet	The Pilot Centre Ltd (G-CDOX)	
G-KCWJ	Schempp-Hirth Duo Discus T	G-KCWJ Group	
G-KDCD	Thruster T.600N 450	M. N. Watson	
G-KDEY	Scheibe SF.25E Super Falke	Falke Syndicate	
G-KDIX	Jodel D.9 Bébé	S. J. Johns	
G-KDOG	SA Bulldog Srs 120/121 (XX624:E)	S. R. Tilling	
G-KEAM	Schleicher ASH 26E	I. W. Paterson	
G-KEAY	AutoGyro MTO Sport	R. Keay	
G-KEDK	Schempp-Hirth Discus bT	S. G. Vardigans	
G-KEEF	Commander Aircraft 112A	K. D. Pearse	
G-KEEN	Stolp SA.300 Starduster Too	Sharp Aerobatics Ltd/Netherlands	
G-KEES	PA-28 Cherokee 180	C. N. Ellerbrook	
G-KEJY	Aerotechnik EV-97 TeamEurostar UK	D. Young	
G-KELI	Robinson R44 Raven II	Manor Corporate Ltd	
G-KELL	Van's RV-6	K. A. Keigher	
G-KELP	Aeroprakt A22-LS Foxbat	J. F. Macknay	
G-KELS	Van's RV-7	F. W. Hardiman	
G-KELX	Van's RV-6	P. J. McMahon (G-HAMY)	

Notes	Reg	Type	Owner or Operator
	G-KELZ	Van's RV-8	B. F. Hill (G-DJRV)
	G-KEMC	Grob G.109	Norfolk Gliding Club Ltd
	G-KEMI	PA-28-181 Archer III	Modern Air (UK) Ltd
	G-KENB	Air Command 503 Commander	K. Brogden
	G-KENC	Ikarus C42 FB100	K. Clark
	G-KENG	Rotorsport UK MT-03	K. A. Graham
	G-KENK	Cameron TR-70 balloon	K. R. Karlstrom
	G-KENM	Luscombe 8EF Silvaire	M. G. Waters
	G-KENW	Robin DR400/500	K. J. White
	G-KENZ	Rutan Vari-Eze	K. M. McConnel I (G-BNUI)
	G-KEPE	Schempp-Hirth Nimbus 3DT	Nimbus Syndicate PE
	G-KEPP	Rans S.6-ES Coyote II	R. G. Johnston
	G-KESS	Glaser-Dirks DG-400	M. T. Collins & T. Flude
	G-KEST	Steen Skybolt	G-KEST Syndicate
	G-KESY	Slingsby T.59D Kestrel	C. J., K. A. & P. J. Teagle
	G-KETH	Agusta-Bell 206B JetRanger 2	DAC Leasing Ltd
	G-KEVA	Ace Magic Cyclone	K. A. Armstrong
	G-KEVB	PA-28-181 Archer III	Victor Bravo Flying Ltd
	G-KEVG	Rotorsport UK MT-03	C. J. Morton
	G-KEVH	Avtech Jabiru UL-450	K. L. Harris (G-CBPP)
	G-KEVI	Jabiru J400	The Jabo Club
	G-KEVK	Flight Design CTSW	K. Kirby
	G-KEVL	Rotorway Executive 162F	K. D. Longhurst (G-CBIK)
	G-KEVS	P 7 M Quik GT450	I. A. Macadam
	G-KEVZ	P & M Quik R	K. Mallin
	G-KEWT	Ultramagic M.90 balloon	R. D. Parry
	G-KEYS	PA-23 Aztec 250F	Giles Aviation Ltd
	G-KEYY	Cameron N-77 balloon	S. M. Jones (G-BORZ)
	G-KFBA	Valentin Taifun 17E	M. T. Collins
	G-KFCA	Ikarus C42 FB80	D. Young
	G-KFLY	Flight Design CTSW	G. WF. Morton & J. J. Brutnell (G-LFLY)
	G-KFOG	Van's RV-7	K. Fogarty
	G-KFOX	Denney Kitfox	R. A. Hampshire
	G-KFVG	Schempp-Hirth Arcus M	M. T. Burton
	G-KGAO	Scheibe SF.25C Falke 1700	Falke 2000 Group
	G-KGAW	Scheibe SF.25C	The Windrushers Gliding Club Ltd
	G-KGMM	Schempp-Hirth Ventus 2cT	G. Smith
	G-KHCC	Schempp-Hirth Ventus Bt	J. L. G. McLane
	G-KHCG	AS.355F2 Ecureuil II	CE Aviation UK Ltd (G-SDAY/G-SYPA/G-BPRE)
	G-KHEA	Scheibe SF.25B Falke	R. J. Hale
	G-KHEH	Grob G.109B	M. P. & T. L. Whitcombe
	G-KHOP	Zenair CH.601HDS Zodiac	K. Hopkins
	G-KHPI	Schleicher ASW-28-18E	J. C. Ferguson
	G-KHRE	MS.893E Rallye 150SV	Kingsmuir Group
	G-KIAB	Scheibe SF.25C Falke 2000	L. Ingram
	G-KIAN	PA-28R-201 Arrow III	M. Al-Souri
	G-KIAU	Scheibe SF.25C Falke 2000	L. Ingram
	G-KICK	Pegasus Quantum 15-912	G. van der Gaag
	G-KIDD	Jabiru J430	R. L. Lidd (G-CEBB)
	G-KIEV	DKBA AT 0300-0 balloon	The Volga Balloon Team
	G-KIII	Extra EA.300/L	Extra 200 Ltd
	G-KIMA	Zenair CH.601XL Zodiac	D. Joy
	G-KIMB	Robin DR.300/140	S. Eustace
	G-KIMH	Rotorsport UK MTO Sport	P. B. Harrison
	G-KIMI	PA-46-500TP Malibu Meridian	S. N. Mitchell & M. Konstantinovic
	G-KIMK	Partenavia P.68B	R. Turrell & P. Mason (G-BCPO)
	G-KIMM	Shaw Europa XS	R. A. Collins
	G-KIMS	Ikarus C42 FB100	J. W. D. Blythe
	G-KIMY	Robin DR.400/140B	J. H. Wood
	G-KIMZ	PA-28-160 Cherokee D	B. McCready (G-AWDP)
	G-KINL	Grumman FM-2 Wildcat	T. W. Harris (G-CHPN)
	G-KINT	Scheibe SF.25C Falke 2000	G-KINT Syndicate
	G-KIRB	Europa XS	P. Handford (G-OIZI)
	G-KIRC	Pietenpol Air Camper	M. Kirk (G-BSVZ)
	G-KIRT	Stoddard-Hamilton GlaStar	K. Luby
	G-KISP	Rolladen-Schneider LS10-st	J. J. Shaw & D. G. Pask

Reg	Type	Owner or Operator	Notes
G-KISS	Rand-Robinson KR-2	E. A. Rooney	
G-KITH	Alpi Pioneer 300	K. G. Atkinson	
G-KITI	Pitts S-2E Special	The Roland Pitch Group	
G-KITO	PA-24-260 Comanche B	A. Costi	
G-KITS	Shaw Europa	J. R. Evernden	
G-KIZZ	Kiss 450-582	D. L. Price	
G-KJBS	CSA Sportcruiser	S. M. Lowe	
G-KJJR	Schempp-Hirth Ventus 2cT	R. J. L. Maisonpierre	
G-KJTT	Cessna 182A	F. Actis	
G-KKAM	Schleicher ASW-22BLE	D. P. Taylor	
G-KKER	Avtech Jabiru UL-450	M. A. Coffin	
G-KKEV	DHC.8-402 Dash Eight	Flybe.com	
G-KKKK	SA Bulldog Srs 120/121 (XX513:10)	M. Cowan (G-CCMI)	
G-KKTG	Cessna 182R	The TG Flying Group	
G-KLAW	Christen Eagle II	The Eagle Group	
G-KLNE	Hawker 900XP	Saxonair Charter Ltd	
G-KLNH	Leonardo AW109SP Grand New	Saxonair Charter Ltd	
G-KLNP	Eurocopter EC120B Colibri	Quinto Crane & Plant Ltd	
G-KLNW	Cessna 510 Citation Mustang	Saxonair Charter Ltd	
G-KLTB	Lindstrand LTL Series 1-90 balloon	A. M. Holly	
G-KLYE	Best Off Sky Ranger Swift 912S(1)	M. G. Allen	
G-KMAK	P & M Quik GT450	K. I. Making	
G-KMBB	Scheibe SF-25D Falke	K. P. & R. L. McLean	
G-KMFW	Glaser-Dirks DG-800B	D. C. W. Sanders	
G-KMIR	Schleicher ASH-31 Mi	M. Woodcock	
G-KMJK	DG Flugzeugbau DG-808C	M. J. Kingsley	
G-KMKM	AutoGyro MTO Sport	O. & T. Brooking	
G-KMLA	Cirrus SR20	KML Aviation OY/Finland	
G-KMRV	Van-s RV-9A	G. K. Mutch	
G-KNCG	PA-32-301FT 6X	Sportsdata Services & Take Flight Aviation Ltd	
G-KNEE	Ultramagic M-77C balloon	M. A.Green	
G-KNEK	Grob G.109B	Syndicate 109	
G-KNIB	Robinson R22 Beta II	C. G. Knibb	
G-KNOW	PA-32 Cherokee Six 300	C. S. Higgins	
G-KNYS	Cessna 208B Grand Caravan	Parachuting Caravan Leasing Ltd	
G-KNYT	Robinson R44	Brosters Environmental Ltd	
G-KOBH	Schempp-Hirth Discus bT	C. F. M. Smith & K. Neave	
G-KOCO	Cirrus SR22	R. Fitzgerald	
G-KOFM	Glaser-Dirks DG.600/18M	A. Mossman	
G-KOKL	Hoffmann H-36 Dimona	Dimona Group	
G-KOLB	Kolb Twinstar Mk 3A	Condor Aviation International Ltd	
G-KOLI	WSK PZL-110 Koliber 150	G-KOLI Group	
G-KONG	Slingsby T.67M Firefly 200	N. A. & O. O'Sullivan	
G-KORE	Sportavia SFS31 Milan	J. R. Edyvean	
G-KOTA	PA-28-236 Dakota	M. D. Rush	
G-KOVU	Cessna FA.150K	Pilot Training and Testing Ltd (G-FMSG/ G-POTS/ G-AYUY)	
G-KOYY	Schempp-Hirth Nimbus 4T	D. Pitman	
G-KPTN	Dassault Falcon 50	Tri-Leg Leasing Ltd	
G-KRBN	Embraer EMB-505 Penom 300	Catreus AOC Ltd	
G-KRBY	Van's RV-8	P. Kirby	
G-KRES	Stoddard-Hamilton Glasair IIS RG	A. D. Murray	
G-KRIB	Robinson R44 II	Cribarth Helicopters	
G-KRII	Rand-Robinson KR-2	M. R. Cleveley	
G-KRMA	Cessna 425 Corsair	Speedstar Holdings Ltd	
G-KRUZ	CZAW Sportcruiser	A. W. Shellis & P. Whittingham	
G-KRWR	Glaser-Dirks DG-600/18M	A. D. W. Hislop	
G-KSFR	Bombardier BD-100-1A10 Challenger	The Lily Partnership LLP	
G-KSHI	Beech A36 Bonanza	Hangar 11 Collection	
G-KSIR	Stoddard-Hamilton Glasair IIS RG	K. M. Bowen	
G-KSIX	Schleicher Ka 6E	C. D. Sterritt	
G-KSKS	Cameron N-105 balloon	Kiss the Sky Ballooning	

Notes	Reg	Type	Owner or Operator
	G-KSKY	Sky 77-24 balloon	J. W. Dale
	G-KSSA	MDH MD-900 Explorer	Specialist Aviation Services Ltd
	G-KSSC	Leonardo AW169	Specialist Aviation Services Ltd
	G-KSSH	MDH MD-900 Explorer	Specialist Aviation Services Ltd (G-WMID)
	G-KSST	Agusta AW.169	Specialist Aviation Services Ltd
	G-KSSX	Schleicher ASW-27-18E	L. M. Brady
	G-KSVB	PA-24 Comanche 260	Knockin Flying Club Ltd
	G-KTEE	Cameron V-77 balloon	A. Ruitenburg
	G-KTOW	Ikarus C42 FB100	Mayfly G-KTOW Ltd
	G-KTTY	Denney Kitfox Model 3	B. J. Finch (G-LESJ)
	G-KTWO	Cessna 182T	S. J. G. Mole
	G-KUBE	Robinson R44 II	Helicopter Services Ltd (G-VEIT)
	G-KUGG	Schleicher ASW-27-18E	J. W. L. Otty
	G-KUIK	Mainair Pegasus Quik	P. Nugent
	G-KUIP	CZAW Sportcruiser	A. J. Kuipers
	G-KULA	Best Off Skyranger 912S(1)	G. S. Cridland
	G-KUPP	Flight Design CTSW	Cloudbase Group
	G-KURK	J-3C-65 Cub	M. J. Kirk
	G-KURT	Jurca MJ.8 Fw190	S. D. Howes
	G-KUTI	Flight Design CTSW	D. F. & S. M. Kenny
	G-KUTU	Quickie Q.2	R. Nash
	G-KUUI	J-3C-65 Cub	V. S. E. Norman
	G-KVAN	Flight Design CTSW	K. Brown (G-IROE)
	G-KVBF	Cameron A-340HL balloon	Virgin Balloon Flights
	G-KVIP	Beech 200 Super King Air	Capital Air Ambulance Ltd
	G-KWAK	Scheibe SF.25C	Mendip Gliding Club Ltd
	G-KWFL	EV-97 Eurostar SL	Aqueous 1st Kwikflow Ltd
	G-KWIC	Mainair Sports Pegasus Quik	D. Seiler
	G-KWKI	QAC Quickie Q.200	R. Greatrex
	G-KWKR	P and M Aviation QuikR	L. G. White
	G-KWKX	P & M Quik R	M. G. Evans
	G-KXMS	Schempp-Hirth Ventus cT	A. J. McNamara
	G-KXXI	Schleicher ASK-21	Shenington Gliding Club
	G-KYLA	Cirrus SR22	J. Bannister
	G-KYLE	Thruster T600N 450	RM Aviation Ltd
	G-KYTE	Piper PA-28-161 Warrior II	G. Whitlow (G-BRRN)
	G-KYTT	PA-18-150 Super Cub	F. Actis
	G-LAAC	Cameron C-90 balloon	Directorate Army Aviation
	G-LAAI	Druine D.5 Turbi	D. Silsbury
	G-LABS	Shaw Europa	P. J. Tyler
	G-LACB	PA-28-161 Warrior II	LAC Flying School
	G-LACD	PA-28-181 Archer III	Phoenix Flight Training Ltd (G-BYBG)
	G-LACR	Denney Kitfox	C. M. Rose
	G-LADD	Enstrom 480	Foscombe Transport LLP
	G-LADS	Rockwell Commander 114	D. F. Soul
	G-LAFT	Diamond DA40D Star	Airways Aviation Academy Ltd
	G-LAGR	Cameron N-90 balloon	J. R. Clifton
	G-LAIN	Robinson R22 Beta	Startrade GmbH/Germany
	G-LAIR	Stoddard-Hamilton Glasair IIS FT	A. I.O'Broin & S. T. Raby
	G-LAKE	Lake LA-250 Renegade	Lake Aviation Ltd
	G-LAKI	Jodel DR.1050	D. Evans (G-JWBB)
	G-LALA	Cessna FA.150K	L. J. Liveras
	G-LALE	Embraer EMB-135BJ Legacy	Bookajet Aircraft Management Ltd
	G-LAMM	Shaw Europa	S. A. Lamb
	G-LAMP	Cameron 110 Lampbulb SS balloon	D. M. Hoddinott
	G-LAMS	Cessna F.152 II	APB Leasing Ltd
	G-LANC	Avro 683 Lancaster X (KB889) ★	Imperial War Museum/Duxford
	G-LANE	Cessna F.172N	M. J. Hadley
	G-LANS	Cessna 182T	G. Robinson
	G-LAOL	PA-28RT-201 Arrow IV	Arrow Flying Group
	G-LARA	Robin DR.400/180	K. D. & C. A. Brackwell
	G-LARD	Robinson R66	Perry Farming Company
	G-LARE	PA-39 Twin Comanche 160 C/R	Glareways (Neasden) Ltd
	G-LARK	Helton Lark 95	Lark Group

Reg	Type	Owner or Operator	Notes
G-LARR	AS.350B3 Squirrel	TSL Contractors Ltd	
G-LASN	Skyranger J2.2(1)	A. J. Coote	
G-LASR	Stoddard-Hamilton Glasair II	G. Lewis	
G-LASS	Rutan Vari-Eze	J. Mellor	
G-LATE	Falcon 2000EX	Executive Jet Charter Ltd	
G-LAUD	Cessna 208 Caravan 1	Laudale Estate LLP	
G-LAVE	Cessna 172R	M. L. Roland (G-BYEV)	
G-LAWX	Sikorsky S-92A	Starspeed Ltd	
G-LAZL	PA-28-161 Warrior II	Highland Aviation Training Ltd	
G-LAZR	Cameron O-77 balloon	Wickers World Ltd	
G-LAZZ	Stoddard-Hamilton Glastar	C. R. & R. H. Partington	
G-LBAC	Evektor EV-97 TeamEurostar UK	G. Burder & A. Cox	
G-LBDC	Bell 206B JetRanger III	Heli Logistics Ltd	
G-LBMM	PA-28-161 Warrior II	M. A. Jones	
G-LBRC	PA-28RT-201 Arrow IV	D. J. V. Morgan	
G-LBSB	Beech B.300C King Air	Gama Aviation (Asset 2) Ltd	
G-LBUK	Lindstrand LBL-77A balloon	D. E. Hartland	
G-LBUZ	Aerotechnick EV-97A Eurostar	D. P. Tassart	
G-LCFC	Agusta A109S Grand	Celio Del Rey Co.Ltd	
G-LCGL	Comper CLA.7 Swift (replica)	R. A. Fleming	
G-LCKY	Flight Design CTSW	G. D. Honey	
G-LCLE	Colomban MC-30 Luciole	J. A. Harris	
G-LCMW	TL 2000UK Sting Carbon	B. J. Tyre	
G-LCPL	AS.365N-2 Dauphin 2	Charterstyle Ltd	
G-LCPX	Eurocopter EC155 B1	Charterstyle Ltd (G-WINV/G-WJCJ)	
G-LCUB	PA-18 Super Cub 95	The Tiger Club 1990 Ltd (G-AYPR)	
G-LCYD	Embraer ERJ170-100STD	BA Cityflyer Ltd	
G-LCYE	Embraer ERJ170-100STD	BA Cityflyer Ltd	
G-LCYF	Embraer ERJ170-100STD	BA Cityflyer Ltd	
G-LCYG	Embraer ERJ170-100STD	BA Cityflyer Ltd	
G-LCYH	Embraer ERJ170-100STD	BA Cityflyer Ltd	
G-LCYI	Embraer ERJ170-100STD	BA Cityflyer Ltd	
G-LCYJ	Embraer ERJ190-100SR	BA Cityflyer Ltd	
G-LCYK	Embraer ERJ190-100SR	BA Cityflyer Ltd	
G-LCYL	Embraer ERJ190-100SR	BA Cityflyer Ltd	
G-LCYM	Embraer ERJ190-100SR	BA Cityflyer Ltd	
G-LCYN	Embraer ERJ190-100SR	BA Cityflyer Ltd	
G-LCYO	Embraer ERJ190-100SR	BA Cityflyer Ltd	
G-LCYP	Embraer ERJ190-100SR	BA Cityflyer Ltd	
G-LCYR	Embraer ERJ190-100SR	BA Cityflyer Ltd	
G-LCYS	Embraer ERJ190-100SR	BA Cityflyer Ltd	
G-LCYT	Embraer ERJ190-100SR	BA Cityflyer Ltd	
G-LCYU	Embraer ERJ190-100SR	BA Cityflyer Ltd	
G-LCYV	Embraer ERJ190-100SR	BA Cityflyer Ltd	
G-LCYW	Embraer ERJ190-100SR	BA Cityflyer Ltd	
G-LCYX	Embraer ERJ190-100SR	BA Cityflyer Ltd	
G-LCYY	Embraer ERJ190-100SR	BA Cityflyer Ltd	
G-LCYZ	Embraer ERJ190-100LR	BA Cityflyer Ltd	
G-LDAH	Skyranger 912 (2)	L. Dickinson & K. R. Mason	
G-LDER	Schleicher ASW-22	P. Shrosbree & D. Starer	
G-LDSA	TAF Sting 4	L. J. d'Sa	
G-LDVO	Europa Aviation Europa XS	D. J. Park	
G-LDWS	Jodel D.150	A. L. Hall-Carpenter (G-BKSS)	
G-LDYS	Colt 56A balloon	M. J. Myddelton	
G-LEAC	Cessna 510 Citation Mustang	London Executive Aviation Ltd	
G-LEAF	Cessna F.406	Reconnaisance Ventures Ltd	
G-LEAH	Alpi Pioneer 300	A. Bortolan	
G-LEAM	PA-28-236 Dakota	G-LEAM Group (G-BHLS)	
G-LEAS	Sky 90-24 balloon	C. I. Humphrey	
G-LEAT	Ultramagic B-70 balloon	A. M. Holly	
G-LEAU	Cameron N-31 balloon	P. L. Mossman	
G-LEAX	Cessna 560XL Citation XLS	London Executive Aviation Ltd	
G-LEBE	Shaw Europa	J. E. Fallis	
G-LEDE	Zenair CH.601UL Zodiac	R. Vicary	
G-LEED	Denney Kitfox Mk 2	O. C. Rash	
G-LEEE	Avtech Jabiru UL-450	T. Bailey	
G-LEEH	Ultramagic M-90 balloon	Sport Promotion SRL/Italy	

Notes	Reg	Type	Owner or Operator
	G-LEEK	Reality Escapade	G-LEEK Phoenix Flying Group
	G-LEEN	Aero Designs Pulsar XP	R. B. Hemsworth (G-BZMP/G-DESI)
	G-LEEZ	Bell 206L-1 LongRanger 2	Heli-Lift Services (G-BPCT)
	G-LEGC	Embraer EMB-135BJ Legacy	London Executive Aviation Ltd
	G-LEGG	Cessna F.182Q	W. A. L. Mitchell (G-GOOS)
	G-LEGO	Cameron O-77 balloon	P. M. Traviss
	G-LEGY	Flight Design CTLS	T. R. Grief
	G-LELE	Lindstrand LBL-31A balloon	D. S. Wilson
	G-LEMI	Van's RV-8	The Lord Rotherwick
	G-LEMM	Ultramagic Z-90 balloon	M. Maranoni/Italy
	G-LEMP	P & M Quik R	E. M. & A. M. Brewis
	G-LENI	AS.355F1 Twin Squirrel	Grid Defence Systems Ltd (G-ZFDB/G-BLEV)
	G-LENN	Cameron V-56 balloon	D. J. Groombridge
	G-LENZ	Cirrus SR20	Renneta Ltd
	G-LEOD	Pietenpol Aircamper	I. D. McCleod
	G-LEOG	Airbus Helicopters AS.350B3 Ecureuil	Leo Group Ltd (G-CIRG)
	G-LEOS	Robin DR.400/120	J. M. Minion
	G-LERE	Aerospatiale ATR-72-212A	Aurigny Air Services Ltd
	G-LESH	BB Microlight BB03 Trya/Alien	L. R. Hodgson
	G-LESZ	Denney Kitfox Mk 5	G. M. Park
	G-LETS	Van's RV-7	M. O'Hearne
	G-LEVI	Aeronca 7AC Champion	G-LEVI Group
	G-LEXS	Agusta A.109E Power	Blade 5 Ltd (G-IVJM/G-MOMO)
	G-LEXX	Van's RV-8	S. Emery
	G-LEXY	Van's RV-8	R. McCarthy
	G-LEYA	PA-32R-301T Saratoga II TC	Gamit Ltd
	G-LEZE	Rutan LongEz	Bill Allen's Autos Ltd
	G-LFBD	Cessna 525A Citationjet CJ2	Centreline AV Ltd
	G-LFES	AB Sportine LAK-17B FES	C. J. Tooze
	G-LFEZ	AB Sportine LAK-17B FES	Baltic Sailplanes Ltd
	G-LFIX	VS.509 Spitfire T.IX (ML407)	Air Leasing Ltd
	G-LFSA	PA-38-112 Tomahawk	Liverpool Flying School Ltd (G-BSFC)
	G-LFSB	PA-38-112 Tomahawk	J. D. Burford
	G-LFSC	PA-28 Cherokee 140	G-LFSC Flying Group (G-BGTR)
	G-LFSG	PA-28 Cherokee 180E	Liverpool Flying School Ltd (G-AYAA)
	G-LFSH	PA-38-112 Tomahawk	Liverpool Flying School Ltd (G-BOZM)
	G-LFSI	PA-28 Cherokee 140	G-LFSI Group (G-AYKV)
	G-LFSJ	PA-28-161 Warrior II	B. J. Rawlings
	G-LFSM	PA-38-112 Tomahawk	Liverpool Flying School Ltd (G-BWNR)
	G-LFSN	PA-38-112 Tomahawk	Liverpool Flying School Ltd (G-BNYV)
	G-LFSR	PA-28RT-201 Arrow IV	S. A. Breslaw
	G-LFSW	PA-28-161 Warrior II	Liverpool Flying School Ltd (G-BSGL)
	G-LFVB	VS.349 Spitfire LF.Vb (EP120)	Patina Ltd
	G-LFVC	VS.349 Spitfire VC	Comanche Warbirds Ltd
	G-LGCA	Robin DR.400/180R	London Gliding Club Proprietary Ltd
	G-LGCB	Robin DR.400/180R	London Gliding Club Proprietary Ltd
	G-LGCC	Robin DR 400/180R	London Gliding Club Proprietary Ltd (G-BNXI)
	G-LGEZ	Rutan Long-EZ	P. C. Elliott
	G-LGIS	Dornier 228-202K	Aurigny Air Services Ltd
	G-LGLG	Cameron Z-210 balloon	Flying Circus SRL/Spain
	G-LGNA	SAAB SF.340B	Loganair Ltd
	G-LGNB	SAAB SF.340B	Loganair Ltd
	G-LGNC	SAAB SF.340B	Loganair Ltd
	G-LGND	SAAB SF.340B	Loganair Ltd (G-GNTH)
	G-LGNE	SAAB SF.340B	Loganair Ltd (G-GNTI)
	G-LGNF	SAAB SF.340B	Loganair Ltd (G-GNTJ)
	G-LGNG	SAAB SF.340B	Loganair Ltd
	G-LGNH	SAAB SF.340B	Loganair Ltd
	G-LGNI	SAAB SF.340B	Loganair Ltd
	G-LGNJ	SAAB SF.340B	Loganair Ltd
	G-LGNK	SAAB SF.340B	Loganair Ltd
	G-LGNM	SAAB SF.340B	Loganair Ltd
	G-LGNN	SAAB SF.340B	Loganair Ltd
	G-LGNO	SAAB 2000	Loganair Ltd
	G-LGNP	SAAB 2000	Loganair Ltd
	G-LGNR	SAAB 2000	Loganair Ltd
	G-LGNS	SAAB 2000	Loganair Ltd
	G-LGNT	SAAB 2000	Loganair Ltd
	G-LGNU	SAAB SF.340B	Loganair Ltd

Reg	Type	Owner or Operator	Notes
G-LGNZ	SAAB SF.340B	Loganair Ltd	
G-LGOC	Aero AT-3 R100	Propeller Film SP ZOO	
G-LHAB	TAF Sling 2	A. P. Beggin	
G-LHCB	Robinson R22 Beta	Helipower Hire Ltd (G-SIVX)	
G-LHCI	Bell 47G-5	Heli-Highland Ltd (G-SOLH/G-AZMB)	
G-LHEL	AS.355F2 Twin Squirrel	Beechview Aviation Ltd	
G-LHER	Czech Sport Aircraft Piper Sport	M. P. Lhermette	
G-LIBB	Cameron V-77 balloon	R. J. Mercer	
G-LIBI	Glasflugel Standard Libelle 201B	O. Spreckley	
G-LIBS	Hughes 369HS	R. J. H. Strong	
G-LIBY	Glasflugel Standard Libelle 201B	R. P. Hardcastle	
G-LICK	Cessna 172N II	Sky Back Ltd (G-BNTR)	
G-LIDA	Hoffmann H36 Dimona	Bidford Airfield Ltd	
G-LIDE	PA-31-350 Navajo Chieftain	Blue Sky Investments Ltd	
G-LIKE	Europa	N. G. Henry (G-CHAV)	
G-LIKY	Aviat A-1C-180 Husky	L. W. H. Griffith	
G-LILY	Bell 206B JetRanger 3	T. S. Brown (G-NTBI)	
G-LIMO	Bell 206L-1 LongRanger	Aerospeed Ltd	
G-LIMP	Cameron C-80 balloon	Balloons over Yorkshire Ltd	
G-LINE	AS.355N Twin Squirrel	Cheshire Helicopters Ltd	
G-LINN	Shaw Europa XS	T. Pond	
G-LINY	Robinson R44 II	Helicentre Aviation Ltd	
G-LINZ	Robinson R44 II	Helicentre Aviation Ltd	
G-LIOA	Lockheed 10A ElectraH (NC5171N) ★	Science Museum/South Kensington	
G-LION	PA-18 Super Cub 135 (R-167)	JG Jones Haulage Ltd	
G-LIOT	Cameron O-77 balloon	N. D. Eliot	
G-LIPS	Cameron 90 Lips SS balloon	Reach For The Sky Ltd (G-BZBV)	
G-LISS	AutogGyro UK Calidus	Gyronauts Flying Club Ltd	
G-LITE	Rockwell Commander 112A	B. G. Rhodes	
G-LITO	Agusta A109S Grand	Castle Air Ltd	
G-LITS	P & M Quik R	A. Dixon	
G-LITZ	Pitts S-1E Special	H. J. Morton	
G-LIVH	Piper J-3C-65 Cub (330238:A-24)	B. L. Procter	
G-LIVS	Schleicher ASH-26E	P. O. Sturley	
G-LIZI	PA-28 Cherokee 160	Peterborough Flying School Ltd (G-ARRP)	
G-LIZY	Westland Lysander III (V9673) ★	G. A. Warner/Duxford	
G-LJCC	Murphy Rebel	P. H. Hyde	
G-LLBE	Lindstrand LBL-360A balloon	Adventure Balloons Ltd	
G-LLCH	Cessna 172S	Bristol Flying Club Ltd (G-PLBI)	
G-LLEW	Aeromot AMT-200S Super Ximango	Echo Whiskey Ximango Syndicate	
G-LLGE	Lindstrand LBL-360A balloon	Adventure Balloons Ltd	
G-LLIZ	Robinson R44 II	HQ Aviation Ltd	
G-LLLL	Rolladen-Schneider LS8-18	P. C. Fritche	
G-LLMW	Diamond DA42 Twin Star	Ming W. L.	
G-LLNT	Schleicher ASW-27-18E	N. D. Tillett	
G-LLOO	SOCATA TB.20 Trinidad	J-P Nicoletti/Belgium	
G-LLOY	Alpi Pioneer 300	M. R. Foreman	
G-LLLY	Enstrom 480B	J. P. Ball	
G-LMAO	Cessna F.172N	M. G. Schlumberger	
G-LMBO	Robinson R44	Thurston Helicopters Ltd	
G-LMCB	Raj Hamsa X'Air Hawk	B. N. Thresher	
G-LMLV	Dyn'Aéro MCR-01	G-LMLV Flying Group	
G-LNAC	Leonardo AW169	Specialist Aviation Services Ltd	
G-LNCT	MDH MD-900 Explorer	Specialist Aviation Services Ltd	
G-LNDN	MDH MD-900 Explorer	London's Air Ambulance Ltd	
G-LNIG	Flylight Dragonfly	P. J. Cheyney	
G-LOAD	Dan Rihn DR.107 One Design	M. J. Clark	
G-LOAM	Flylight MotorFloater	A. W. Nancarrow	
G-LOAN	Cameron N-77 balloon	P. Lawman	
G-LOBO	Cameron O-120 balloon	Solo Aerostatics	
G-LOCH	Piper J-3C-65 Cub	M. C. & M. R. Greenland	
G-LOFM	Maule MX-7-180A	C. M. Brittlebank	
G-LOFT	Cessna 500 Citation I	Fox Tango (Jersey) Ltd	
G-LOGN	PA-28-181 Cherokee Archer III	I. P. Logan	

Notes	Reg	Type	Owner or Operator
	G-LOIS	Avtech Jabiru UL	C. Conidaris
	G-LOKI	Ultramagic M-77C balloon	Border Ballooning Ltd
	G-LOLA	Beech A36 Bonanza	Lima Alfa Limited
	G-LOLI	DG Flugzeugbau DG-1000M	P. Crawley
	G-LOLL	Cameron V-77 balloon	P. Spellward
	G-LOLZ	Robinson R22 Beta	Swift Helicopter Services Ltd
	G-LOMN	Cessna 152	North Weald Flying Group Ltd
	G-LONE	Bell 206L-1 LongRanger	Central Helicopters Ltd
	G-LOOC	Cessna 172S	Goodwood Road Racing Co.Ltd
	G-LOON	Cameron C-60 balloon	T. Lex/Germany
	G-LOOP	Pitts S-1D Special	D. Shutter
	G-LORC	PA-28-161 Cadet	Advanced Flight Training Ltd
	G-LORD	PA-34-200T Seneca II	H. E. Held-Ruf
	G-LORN	Avions Mudry CAP-10B	Cole Aviation Ltd
	G-LORR	PA-28-181 Archer III	Shropshire Aero Club Ltd
	G-LORY	Thunder Ax4-31Z balloon	M. J. Woodcock
	G-LOSM	Gloster Meteor NF.11 (WM167)	Aviation Heritage Ltd
	G-LOST	Denney Kitfox Mk 3	J. T. Lister
	G-LOSY	Aerotechnik EV-97 Eurostar	M. L. Willmington
	G-LOTE	PA-28-161 Cadet	AJW Construction Ltd
	G-LOTI	Bleriot XI (replica) ★	Brooklands Museum Trust Ltd
	G-LOTY	P & M Aviation Pegasus Quik	L. Hewitt
	G-LOUD	Schleicher ASW-27-18E	T. Stuart
	G-LOUS	EV-97 Eurostar SL	S. E. Bettley & M. D. Jealous
	G-LOWE	Monett Sonerai I	P. A. Hall & A. R. Lewis
	G-LOWS	Sky 77-24 balloon	A. J. Byrne & D. J. Bellinger
	G-LOWZ	P & M Quik GT450	R. E. J. Pattenden
	G-LOYA	Cessna FR.172J	Mid America (UK) Ltd (G-BLVT)
	G-LOYD	Aérospatiale SA.341G Gazelle 1	S. Athgerton (G-SFTC)
	G-LPAD	Lindstrand LBL-105A balloon	G. R. Down
	G-LPIN	P & M Aviation Quik R	Arnold Gilpin Associates Ltd
	G-LRBW	Lindstrand LBL HS-110 Hot-Air Airship	C. J. Sanger-Davies
	G-LREE	Grob G.109B	G-LREE Group
	G-LROK	Robinson R66	London Rock Supplies Ltd
	G-LSAA	Boeing 757-236	Jet 2.com (G-BNSF)
	G-LSAB	Boeing 757-27B	Jet 2.com (G-OAHF)
	G-LSAC	Boeing 757-23A	Jet 2.com
	G-LSAD	Boeing 757-236	Jet 2.com (G-OOOS/G-BRJD)
	G-LSAE	Boeing 757-27B	Jet 2.com
	G-LSAG	Boeing 757-21B	Jet 2.com
	G-LSAH	Boeing 757-21B	Jet 2.com
	G-LSAI	Boeing 757-21B	Jet 2.com
	G-LSAJ	Boeing 757-236	Jet 2.com (G-CDUP/G-OOOT/G-BRJJ)
	G-LSAK	Boeing 757-23N	Jet 2.com
	G-LSAN	Boeing 757-2K2	Jet 2.com
	G-LSCM	Cessna 172S	Pooler-LMT Ltd
	G-LSCP	Rolladen-Schneider LS6-18W	M. F. Collins & L. G. Blows
	G-LSCW	Gulfstream 550	Langley Aviation Ltd
	G-LSED	Rolladen-Schneider LS6-c	K. Atkinson & T. Faver
	G-LSFB	Rolladen-Schneider LS7-WL	P. Thomson
	G-LSFR	Rolladen-Schneider LS4-a	A. Mulder
	G-LSFT	PA-28-161 Warrior II	Biggin Hill Flying Club Ltd (G-BXTX)
	G-LSGB	Rolladen-Schneider LS6-b	A. Rieder
	G-LSGM	Rolladen-Schneider LS3-17	M. R. W. Crook
	G-LSHI	Colt 77A balloon	J. H. Dobson
	G-LSIF	Rolladen-Schneider LS1-f	R. C. Godden
	G-LSIV	Rolladen-Schneider LS4	264 Syndicate
	G-LSIX	Rolladen-Schneider LS6-18W	D. P. Masson
	G-LSJE	Escapade Jabiru(1)	L. S. J. Webb
	G-LSKS	Robinson R66	Heli-Air Ltd
	G-LSKV	Rolladen-Schneider LS8-18	J. R. W. Luxton, C. E. Garner & P. A. Binnee
	G-LSKY	Mainair Pegasus Quik	M. Gudgeon
	G-LSLS	Rolladen-Schneider LS4	288 Syndicate
	G-LSPH	Van's RV-8	R. S. Partridge-Hicks
	G-LSTR	Stoddard-Hamilton Glastar	D. I. Waller
	G-LSVI	Rolladen-Schneider LS6-c18	R. Hanks
	G-LSZA	Diamond DA.42NG Twin Star	J. Molen
	G-LTFB	PA-28-140 Cherokee	I. Fereday

G-ACMA DH.85 Leopard Moth *Peter R. March*

G-ADYS Aeronca C.3 *Peter R. March*

G-AHKX Avro 19 Anson *Peter R. March*

G-AIXN Benes –Miraz M.1C Sokol *Peter R. March*

G-AKIN Miles M.38 Messenger *Peter R. March*

G-ARNG Piper PA.22-108 Colt *Allan S. Wright*

G-BTRG Aeronca 65C Super Chief *Peter R. March*

G-BYXH Grob G.115E Tutor *Peter R. March*

G-CBJV Rotorway Executive 162F *Allan S. Wright*

G-CGOA Cessna 550 Citation II *Tom Cole*

G-CIYD Sikorsky S-92A *Allan S. Wright**

G-GDFD Boeing 737-8K5 of Jet 2 *Allan S. Wright*

G-IACE Sikorsky S-92A *Allan S Wright**

G-JABJ Jabiru J400 *Allan S. Wright*

G-KIMZ PA-28-160 Cherokee D *Allan S. Wright*

G-LLOY Alpi Pioneer 300 *Peter R. March*

G-MAJW Jetstream 41 of Eastern Airways *Allan S. Wright*

G-MARL Autogyro Calidus *Tom Cole*

G-PMIZ Pitts Model 12 *Peter R. March*

G-SCOL Gippsland GA-8 Airvan *Peter R. March*

G-UWEB Cameron Z-120 balloon *Peter R. March*

WL419/G-JSMA Gloster Meteor T.Mk.7.5 *Peter R. March*

D-ASTB Airbus A.319-112 of Germania *Allan S. Wright*

ER-AXL Airbus A.319-112 of Air Moldova *Allan S. Wright*

F-HBXO Embraer ERJ170-100LR of HOP! *Allan S. Wright*

HB-JBB Bombardier CS100 of Swiss Global Airlines *Peter R. March*

LN-WDI DHC.8Q-402 Dash Eight of Wideroe's Flyveselskap *Allan S. Wright*

N845MH Boeing 767-432ER of Delta Air Lines *Peter R. March*

OE-IQC Airbus A.320-214 of Eurowings *Peter R. March*

PH-CXC Boeing 747-406ERF of KLM Cargo *Allan S. Wright*

PH-EXM Embraer ERJ170-200STD of KLM Cityhopper *Allan S. Wright*

Reg	Type	Owner or Operator	Notes
G-LTFC	PA-28-140 Cherokee	N. M. G. Pearson (G-AXTI)	
G-LTSB	Cameron LTSB-90 balloon	ABC Flights Ltd	
G-LTSK	Bombardier CL600-2B16 Challenger	TAG Aviation (UK) Ltd	
G-LTWA	Robinson R44	L. T. W. Alderman	
G-LUBB	Cessna 525 Citationjet	Surrey Heli Charters LLP	
G-LUBY	Jabiru J430	K. Luby	
G-LUCK	Cessna F.150M	A. W. C. Knight	
G-LUCL	Colomban MC-30 Luciole	R. C. Teverson	
G-LUDM	Van's RV-8	A. G. Ransom	
G-LUED	Aero Designs Pulsar	J. C. Anderson	
G-LUEK	Cessna 182T	S. R. Greenall	
G-LUEY	Rans S-7S Courier	S. Garfield	
G-LUGS	Agusta A109S Grand	Volare Aviation Ltd (G-FRZN)	
G-LUKA	Beech G.58 Baron	Bentley O-S Ltd	
G-LUKE	Rutan LongEz	R. A. Pearson	
G-LULA	Cameron C-90 balloon	S. D. Davis	
G-LULU	Grob G.109	B. M. E. Loth	
G-LULV	Diamond DA-42 Twin Star	Deltabond Ltd	
G-LUNE	Mainair Pegasus Quik	D. Muir	
G-LUNG	Rotorsport UK MT-03	P. Krysiak	
G-LUNY	Pitts S-1S Special	G-LUNY Group	
G-LUON	Schleicher ASW-27-18E	P. C. Naegeli	
G-LUPY	Marganski Swift S-1	G. S. S. Rizk	
G-LUSC	Luscombe 8E Silvaire	M. Fowler	
G-LUSI	Luscombe 8F Silvaire	P. H. Isherwood	
G-LUSK	Luscombe 8F Silvaire	M. A. Lamprell & P. J. Laycock (G-BRGG)	
G-LUST	Luscombe 8E Silvaire	C. J. Watson & M. R. Griffiths	
G-LUUP	Pilatus B4-PC11AF	B. L. Coopere (G-ECSW)	
G-LUXE	BAe 146-301	Natural Environment Research Council (G-SSSH)	
G-LVCY	Colomban MC-30 Luciole	C. Wright	
G-LVDC	Bell 206L Long Ranger III	WAG Aviation Ltd (G-OFST/G-BXIB)	
G-LVES	Cessna 182S	R. W. & A. M. Glaves (G-ELIE)	
G-LVME	Cessna F.152 II	Superior Air SA/Greece (G-BGHI)	
G-LVPL	Edge XT912 B/Streak III/B	C. D. Connor	
G-LVRS	PA-28-181 Archer II	L. V. Liveras (G-ZMAM/G-BNPN)	
G-LWLW	Diamond DA.40D Star	M. P. Wilkinson (G-CCLV)	
G-LWNG	Aero Designs Pulsar	A. B. Wood (G-OMKF)	
G-LXUS	Alpi Pioneer 300	A. & J. Oswald	
G-LXVI	Schempp-Hirth Arcus T	A. Aveling	
G-LXWD	Cessna 560XL Citation XLS	Catreus AOC Ltd	
G-LYDA	Hoffmann H-36 Dimona	G-LYDA Flying Group	
G-LYDF	PA-31-350 Navajo Chieftain	Atlantic Bridge Aviation Ltd	
G-LYFA	IDABacau Yakovlev Yak-52	Fox Alpha Group	
G-LYNC	Robinson R22 Beta II	Hummingford Helicopters Ltd	
G-LYND	PA-25 Pawnee 235	York Gliding Centre Ltd (G-ASFX/G-BSFZ)	
G-LYNI	Aerotechnik EV-97 Eurostar	M. W. Holmes & A. C. Thomson	
G-LYNK	CFM Shadow Srs DD	P. R. Dalton	
G-LYNX	Westland WG.13 Lynx (ZB500)	IHM/Weston-super-Mare	
G-LYPG	Avtech Jabiru UL	A. J. Geary	
G-LYPH	Rolladen-Schneider LS8-18-st	S. & S. Barter	
G-LYTE	Thunder Ax7-77 balloon	R. G. Turnbull	
G-LYZA	Guimbal Cabri G2	Lyza Aviation Ltd (G-IZOO)	
G-LZED	AutoGyro MTO Sport	L. Zivanovic	
G-LZII	Laser Z200	K. G. Begley	
G-MAAM	CFM Shadow Srs.C	R. Sinclair-Brown (G-MTCA)	
G-MAAN	Shaw Europa XS	P. S. Mann	
G-MAAS	PA-28-181 II	Skies Aviation Academy PC/Greece	
G-MABE	Cessna F.150L	Aviolease Ltd (G-BLJP)	
G-MABL	Quik GTR	G. J. P. Skinner & M. Finch	
G-MACA	Robinson R22 Beta	Jepar Rotorcraft	
G-MACH	SIAI-Marchetti SF.260	Cheyne Motors Ltd	
G-MACI	Van's RV-7	N. J. F. Campbell	
G-MADA	Boeing 737-548	Opel Investments Ltd	

Notes	Reg	Type	Owner or Operator
	G-MADV	P & M Quik GT450	G. Colby
	G-MAFA	Cessna F.406	Directflight Ltd (G-DFLT)
	G-MAFB	Cessna F.406	Directflight Ltd
	G-MAFF	BN-2T Turbine Islander	Islander Aircraft Ltd (G-BJED)
	G-MAFI	Dornier 228-202K	RUAG Aerospace Services GmbH/Germany
	G-MAFT	Diamond DA.40 Star	Airways Aviation Academy Ltd
	G-MAGC	Cameron Grand Illusion SS balloon	Magical Adventures Ltd
	G-MAGG	Pitts S-1SE Special	R. G. Gee
	G-MAGK	Schleicher ASW-20L	A. G. K. Mackenzie
	G-MAGL	Sky 77-24 balloon	RCM SRL/Luxembourg
	G-MAGN	Magni M-24C	Net2Net IPS Ltd
	G-MAGZ	Robin DR.400/500	T. J. Thomas
	G-MAHY	Cessna 182T	Keyboard Print Solutions Ltd (G-SKEN)
	G-MAIE	PA-32RT-301T Turbo Saratoga II TC	Rainbow Self Storage Ltd
	G-MAIN	Mainair Blade 912	J. G. Parkin
	G-MAIR	PA-34-200T Seneca II	Ravenair Aircraft Ltd
	G-MAJA	BAe Jetstream 4102	Eastern Airways
	G-MAJB	BAe Jetstream 4102	Eastern Airways (G-BVKT)
	G-MAJC	BAe Jetstream 4102	Eastern Airways (G-LOGJ)
	G-MAJD	BAe Jetstream 4102	Eastern Airways (G-WAWR)
	G-MAJE	BAe Jetstream 4102	Eastern Airways (G-LOGK)
	G-MAJF	BAe Jetstream 4102	Eastern Airways (G-WAWL)
	G-MAJG	BAe Jetstream 4102	Eastern Airways (G-LOGL)
	G-MAJH	BAe Jetstream 4102	Eastern Airways (G-WAYR)
	G-MAJI	BAe Jetstream 4102	Eastern Airways (G-WAND)
	G-MAJJ	BAe Jetstream 4102	Eastern Airways (G-WAFT)
	G-MAJK	BAe Jetstream 4102	Eastern Airways
	G-MAJL	BAe Jetstream 4102	Eastern Airways
	G-MAJR	DHC.1 Chipmunk 22 (WP805)	C. Adams
	G-MAJT	BAe Jetstream 4100	Eastern Airways
	G-MAJU	BAe Jetstream 4100	Eastern Airways
	G-MAJW	BAe Jetstream 4100	Eastern Airways
	G-MAJY	BAe Jetstream 4100	Eastern Airways
	G-MAJZ	BAe Jetstream 4100	Eastern Airways
	G-MAKE	Rotorsport UK Calidus	P. M. Ford
	G-MAKI	Robinson R44	ACS Engineering Ltd
	G-MAKK	Aeroprakt A22-L Foxbat	M. A. McKillop
	G-MAKN	Pilatus PC-12/47E	Ravenair Aircraft Ltd
	G-MAKS	Cirrus SR22	J. P. Briggs
	G-MALA	PA-28-181 Archer II	Energies Ltd (G-BIIU)
	G-MALC	AA-5 Traveler	M. A. Ray (G-BCPM)
	G-MALE	Balony Kubicek BB-S Skyballs SS balloon	A. M. Holly
	G-MALS	Mooney M.20K-231	P. Mouterde
	G-MALT	Colt Flying Hop SS balloon	P. J. Stapley
	G-MAMM	Ikarus C42 FB80	Mid Anglia Microlights Ltd
	G-MANC	BAe ATP	West Atlantic Aircraft Management AB (G-LOGF)
	G-MANH	BAe ATP	Atlantic Airlines Ltd (G-LOGC/G-OLCC)
	G-MANX	FRED Srs 2	S. Styles
	G-MANZ	Robinson R44 II	S. M. Hill
	G-MAOL	Agusta AW109SP Grand New	Sloane Helicopters Ltd
	G-MAPR	Beech A36 Bonanza	C. B. Gufler
	G-MAPY	PA-31-350 Chieftain	Blue Sky Investments Ltd (G-BXUV)
	G-MARA	Airbus A.321-231	SASOF III (A5) Aviation Ireland DAC
	G-MARE	Schweizer 269C	The Earl of Caledon
	G-MARL	Autogyro Calidus	M. R. Love
	G-MARO	Skyranger J2.2 (2)	G-MARO Flying Group
	G-MARZ	Thruster T.600N 450	A. S. R. Czajka
	G-MASC	Jodel 150A	K. F. & R. Richardson
	G-MASF	PA-28-181 Archer II	Mid-Anglia School of Flying
	G-MASH	Westland-Bell 47G-4A	A. J. E. Smith (G-AXKU)
	G-MASS	Cessna 152 II	MK Aero Support Ltd (G-BSHN)
	G-MATB	Robin DR.400-160	J. C. Bacon (G-BAFP)
	G-MATO	Dassault Falcon 7X	SDI Aviation Ltd
	G-MATS	Colt GA-42 airship	P. A. Lindstrand
	G-MATT	Robin R.2160	Swift Flying Group (G-BKRC)
	G-MATW	Cessna 182P	Subados SL/Spain
	G-MATZ	PA-28 Cherokee 140	Midland Air Training School (G-BASI)
	G-MAUS	Shaw Europa XS	A. P. Ringrose
	G-MAUX	Raj Hamsa X'Air Hawk	M. A. Urch
	G-MAVK	Pitts S-1S	M. O'Leary

Reg	Type	Owner or Operator	Notes
G-MAVV	Aero AT-3 R100	KN Singles and Twins Aviation Consultants BV/Netherlands	
G-MAXA	PA-32-301FT	L. Bennett & Son Ltd	
G-MAXD	Robinson R44 1	RSM Aviation Ltd	
G-MAXG	Pitts S-1S Special	The Assets of G-MAXG Group	
G-MAXI	PA-34-200T Seneca II	Draycott Seneca Syndicate Ltd	
G-MAXS	Mainair Pegasus Quik 912S	W. J. Walker	
G-MAXT	PA-28RT-201T Turbo Arrow IV	M. Toninelli/Italy	
G-MAXV	Van's RV-4	S. B. Shirley	
G-MAZA	Rotorsport UK MT-03	N. Crownshaw & M. Manson	
G-MAZY†	DH.82A Tiger Moth ★	Newark Air Museum	
G-MAZZ	Cirrus SR22	Nosig Services BV/Netherlands	
G-MBAA	Hiway Skytrike Mk 2	M. J. Aubrey	
G-MBAB	Hovey Whing-Ding II	M. J. Aubrey	
G-MBAD	Weedhopper JC-24A	M. Stott	
G-MBAF	R. J. Swift 3	C. G. Wrzesien	
G-MBAL	Ultrasports Tripace/Hiway Demon	D. M. Pecheur	
G-MBAW	Pterodactyl Ptraveller	J. C. K. Scardifield	
G-MBBJ	Hiway Demon	M. J. Aubrey	
G-MBCJ	Mainair Sports Tri-Flyer	R. A. Smith	
G-MBCL	Sky-Trike/Typhoon	P. J. Callis	
G-MBCX	Airwave Nimrod 165	M. Maylor	
G-MBDG	Eurowing Goldwing	A. J. Glynn	
G-MBDL	AES Lone Ranger ★	North East Aircraft Museum	
G-MBDM	Southdown Sigma Trike	A. R. Prentice	
G-MBET	MEA Mistral Trainer	B. H. Stephens	
G-MBFO	Eipper Quicksilver MX	R. A. Szczepanik	
G-MBGF	Twamley Trike	T. B. Woolley	
G-MBHE	American Aerolights Eagle	R. J. Osborne	
G-MBHK	Flexiform Skytrike	A. L. Virgoe	
G-MBHZ	Pterodactyl Ptraveller	J. C. K. Scardifield	
G-MBIO	American Eagle 215B	D. J. Lewis	
G-MBIT	Hiway Demon Skytrike	K. S. Hodgson	
G-MBIZ	Mainair Tri-Flyer	D. M. A. Templeman/E. F. C. Clapham/ S. P. Slade/W. B. S. Dobie	
G-MBJK	American Aerolights Eagle	B. W. Olley	
G-MBKY	American Aerolight Eagle	M. J. Aubrey	
G-MBKZ	Hiway Skytrike	L. Magill	
G-MBLU	Southdown Lightning L.195	C. R. Franklin	
G-MBMG	Rotec Rally 2B	J. R. Pyper	
G-MBOF	Pakes Jackdaw	M. J. Aubrey	
G-MBOH	Microlight Engineering Mistral	T. J. Gayton-Polley	
G-MBPB	Pterodactyl Ptraveller	T. D. Dawson	
G-MBPX	Eurowing Goldwing SP	V. H. Hallam	
G-MBRB	Electraflyer Eagle 1	R. C. Bott	
G-MBRD	American Aerolights Eagle	R. J. Osborne	
G-MBRH	Ultraflight Mirage Mk II	R. W. F. Boarder	
G-MBSJ	American Aerolights Eagle 215B	T. J. Gayton-Polley	
G-MBSX	Ultraflight Mirage II	A. D. Russell	
G-MBTJ	Solar Wings Microlight	H. A. Comber	
G-MBWL	Huntair Pathfinder Mk.1	A. D. Russell	
G-MBZO	Tri-Pacer 330	A. N. Burrows	
G-MBZV	American Aerolights Eagle	M. J. Aubrey	
G-MCAB	Gardan GY-201 Minicab	P. G. Hooper	
G-MCAN	Agusta A109S Grand	Cannon Air LLP	
G-MCAP	Cameron C-80 balloon	L. D. Pickup	
G-MCAZ	Robinson R44 II	M. C. Allen	
G-MCCF	Thruster T.600N	C. C. F. Fuller	
G-MCDB	VS.361 Spitfire LF.IX	M. Collenette	
G-MCEL	Pegasus Quantum 15-912	F. Hodgson	
G-MCFK	P & M Quik GT450	F. A. A. Kay	
G-MCGA	Sikorsky S-92A	Bristow Helicopters Ltd	
G-MCGB	Sikorsky S-92A	Bristow Helicopters Ltd	
G-MCGC	Sikorsky S-92A	Bristow Helicopters Ltd	
G-MCGD	Sikorsky S-92A	Bristow Helicopters Ltd	
G-MCGE	Sikorsky S-92A	Bristow Helicopters Ltd	
G-MCGF	Sikorsky S-92A	Bristow Helicopters Ltd	
G-MCGG	Sikorsky S-92A	Bristow Helicopters Ltd	
G-MCGH	Sikorsky S-92A	Bristow Helicopters Ltd	

Notes	Reg	Type	Owner or Operator
	G-MCGI	Sikorsky S-92A	Bristow Helicopters Ltd
	G-MCGJ	Sikorsky S-92A	Bristow Helicopters Ltd
	G-MCGK	Sikorsky S-92A	Bristow Helicopters Ltd
	G-MCGL	Sikorsky S-92A	Bristow Helicopters Ltd
	G-MCGM	Agusta AW189	Bristow Helicopters Ltd
	G-MCGN	Agusta AW189	Bristow Helicopters Ltd (G-CJNV)
	G-MCGO	Agusta AW189	Bristow Helicopters Ltd
	G-MCGP	Agusta AW189	Bristow Helicopters Ltd
	G-MCGR	Agusta AW189	Bristow Helicopters Ltd
	G-MCGS	Agusta AW189	Bristow Helicopters Ltd
	G-MCGT	Agusta AW189	Bristow Helicopters Ltd
	G-MCGU	Leonardo AW189	Leonardo MW Ltd
	G-MCGV	Leonardo AW189	Leonardo MW Ltd
	G-MCGW	Leonardo AW189	Leonardo MW Ltd
	G-MCGX	Leonardo MW189	Leonardo MW Ltd
	G-MCGY	Sikorsky S-92A	Bristow Helicopters Ltd
	G-MCGZ	Sikorsky S-92A	Bristow Helicopters Ltd
	G-MCJL	Pegasus Quantum 15-912	RM Aviation Ltd
	G-MCLK	Van's RV-10	M. W. Clarke
	G-MCLN	Cirrus SR20	Laminair Flight Ltd
	G-MCLY	Cessna 172P	McAully Flying Group Ltd
	G-MCOW	Lindstrand LBL-77A balloon	S. & S. Villiers
	G-MCOX	Fuji FA.200-180AO	A. M. Cox
	G-MCPR	PA-32-301T Turbo Saratoga	M. C. Plomer-Roberts (G-MOLL)
	G-MCRO	Dyn'Aero MCR-01	J. M. Keane
	G-MCSA	Sikorsky S-92A	Babcock Mission Critical Services Offshore Ltd
	G-MCSB	Sikorsky S-92A	Babcock Mission Critical Services Offshore Ltd
	G-MCSC	Agusta Westland AW139	Babcock Mission Critical Services Offshore Ltd
	G-MCSD	Agusta Westland AW139	Babcock Mission Critical Services Offshore Ltd
	G-MCSE	Airbus Helicopters EC175B	Babcock Mission Critical Services Offshore Ltd
	G-MCSF	Airbus Helicopters EC175B	Babcock Mission Critical Services Offshore Ltd
	G-MCSG	Airbus Helicopters EC175B	Babcock Mission Critical Services Offshore Ltd
	G-MCTO	Flylight Dragon Chaser	B. J. Syson
	G-MCUB	Reality Escapade	M. A. Appleby
	G-MCVE	Ikarus C42 FB80	A. & J. McVey
	G-MCVY	Flight Design CT2K	A. & J. McVey (G-CBNA)
	G-MDAC	PA-28-181 Archer II	S. A. Nicklen
	G-MDAY	Cessna 170B	M. Day
	G-MDBC	Pegasus Quantum 15-912	J. D. Ryan
	G-MDBD	Airbus A.330-243	Thomas Cook Airlines Ltd
	G-MDDE	Hughes 369E	Draper Gain Aviation Ltd
	G-MDJE	Cessna 208 Caravan 1 (amphibian)	Holcombe Ltd
	G-MDKD	Robinson R22 Beta	M. A. & M. L. Mulcahy
	G-MDLE	MD Helicopters MD500N	Loxwood Holdings Ltd
	G-MDME	Diamond DA.62	Flight Calibration Services Ltd
	G-MDPI	Agusta A109A-II	Castle Air Ltd (G-PERI/G-EXEK/G-SLNE/ G-EEVS/G-OTSL)
	G-MECK	TL2000UK Sting Carbon S4	M. J. Seemann
	G-MEDF	Airbus A.321-231	British Airways PLC
	G-MEDG	Airbus A.321-231	British Airways PLC
	G-MEDJ	Airbus A.321-232	British Airways PLC
	G-MEDK	Airbus A.320-232	British Airways PLC
	G-MEDL	Airbus A.321-231	British Airways PLC
	G-MEDM	Airbus A.321-231	British Airways PLC
	G-MEDN	Airbus A.321-231	British Airways PLC
	G-MEDU	Airbus A.321-231	British Airways PLC
	G-MEDX	Agusta A109E Power	Sloane Helicopters Ltd
	G-MEEE	Schleicher ASW-20L	T. E. Macfadyen
	G-MEGG	Shaw Europa XS	R. L. Hitchcock
	G-MEGN	Beech B200 Super King Air	Dragonfly Aviation Services Ltd
	G-MEGS	Cessna 172S	The Cambridge Aero Club Ltd
	G-MEGZ	Ikarus C42 FB100	J. M. Mooney
	G-MEIS	CASA 1-133 Jungmeister	B. S. Charters
	G-MELL	CZAW Sportcruiser	G. A. & J. A. Mellins
	G-MELS	PA-28-181 Archer III	P. J. Sowood
	G-MELT	Cessna F.172H	Falcon Aviation Ltd (G-AWTI)
	G-MEME	PA-28R-201 Arrow III	Henry J. Clare Ltd
	G-MENU	Robinson R44 II	HQ Aviation Ltd
	G-MEOW	CFM Streak Shadow	G. J. Moor

Reg	Type	Owner or Operator	Notes
G-MEPS	Embraer EMB-500 Phenom 100	Affinity Flying Training Services Ltd	
G-MEPT	Embraer EMB-500 Phenom 100	Affinity Flying Training Services Ltd	
G-MERC	Colt 56A balloon	A. F. & C. D. Selby	
G-MERE	Lindstrand LBL-77A balloon	R. D. Baker	
G-MERF	Grob G.115A	G-MERF Group	
G-MERL	PA-28RT-201 Arrow IV	J. Gubbay & D. Brennan	
G-MESH	CZAW Sportcruiser	M. E. S. Heaton	
G-METH	Cameron C-90 balloon	A. & D. Methley	
G-MEUP	Cameron A-120 balloon	J. M. Woodhouse	
G-MFAC	Cessna F.172H	G. Y. Phillips (G-AVGZ)	
G-MFEF	Cessna FR.172J	Campaign Creative Ltd	
G-MFHI	Shaw Europa	Hi Fliers	
G-MFLA	Robin HR200/120B	R. J. Williamson (G-HHUK)	
G-MFLE	Robin HR200/120B	R. J. Williamson (G-BYLH)	
G-MFLI	Cameron V-90 balloon	J. M. Percival	
G-MFLJ	P & M Quik GT450	M. F. Jakeman	
G-MFLM	Cessna F.152 II	Pilot Training and Testing Ltd (G-BFFC)	
G-MFLT	Eurocopter AS.365N3 Dauphin II	Ven Air ULC	
G-MFLY	Mainair Rapier	J. J. Tierney	
G-MFMF	Bell 206B JetRanger 3	Polo Aviation Ltd (G-BJNJ)	
G-MFMM	Scheibe SF.25C Falke	J. E. Selman	
G-MFOX	Aeropro Eurofox 912(1)	D. W. & M. L. Squire	
G-MGBG	Cessna 310Q	Cotswold Aero Maintenance Ltd (G-AYND)	
G-MGCA	Jabiru Aircraft Jabiru UL	K. D. Pearce	
G-MGCK	Whittaker MW6-S FT	M. W. Hampton	
G-MGDL	Pegasus Quantum 15	M. J. Buchanan	
G-MGEC	Rans S.6-ESD-XL Coyote II	D. Williams & S. P. Tkaczyk	
G-MGEF	Pegasus Quantum 15	M. A. Steadman	
G-MGFC	Aeropro Eurofox 912(1)	M. G. F. Cawson	
G-MGFK	Pegasus Quantum 15	J. R. Willment	
G-MGGG	Pegasus Quantum 15	R. A. Beauchamp	
G-MGGT	CFM Streak Shadow SAM	G. von Wilcken	
G-MGGV	Pegasus Quantum 15-912	I. S. Duffy	
G-MGIC	Ace Magic Cyclone	N. I. Garland	
G-MGMM	PA-18 Super Cub 150	Alice's Flying Group	
G-MGNI	Magni M.16C Tandem Trainer	Gyromania Ltd	
G-MGOD	Medway Raven	N. R. Andrew, A. Wherrett & D. J. Millward	
G-MGOO	Renegade Spirit UK Ltd	J. Aley	
G-MGPA	Ikarus C42 FB100	S. Ashley	
G-MGPD	Pegasus XL-R	T. A. Dockrell	
G-MGPH	CFM Streak Shadow	V. C. Readhead (G-RSPH)	
G-MGPX	Kolb Twinstar Mk.3 Extra	T. R. Fawcett	
G-MGTG	Pegasus Quantum 15	F. B. Oram (G-MZIO)	
G-MGTR	Hunt Wing	A. C. Ryall	
G-MGTV	Thruster T.600N 450	R. Bingham	
G-MGTW	CFM Shadow Srs DD	G. T. Webster	
G-MGUN	Cyclone AX2000	M. A. Boffin	
G-MGUY	CFM Shadow Srs BD	Shadow Flight Centre Ltd	
G-MGWH	Thruster T.300	J. B. Silverstone	
G-MGWI	Robinson R44	Ed Murray and Sons Ltd (G-BZEF)	
G-MHAR	PA-42-720 Cheyenne IIIA	BAE Systems (Operations) Ltd	
G-MHCE	Enstrom F-28A	M. P. Larsen (G-BBHD)	
G-MHCM	Enstrom 280FX	Dave Tinsley Ltd (G-IBWF/G-ZZWW/G-BSIE)	
G-MHGS	Stoddard-Hamilton Glastar	H. D. Jones	
G-MHMR	Pegasus Quantum 15-912	Hadair	
G-MHPS	Glasair Sportsman	Hardmead Ltd	
G-MHRV	Van's RV-6A	M. R. Harris	
G-MIAN	Skyranger Nynja 912S(1)	I. P. Stubbins	
G-MICH	Robinson R22 Beta	Tiger Helicopters Ltd (G-BNKY)	
G-MICI	Cessna 182S	Magic Carpet Flying Company (G-WARF)	
G-MICK	Cessna F.172N	D. H. G. Penney	
G-MICX	Air Creation Tanarg/Bionix 13 912S(1)	M. J. Moulton	
G-MICY	Everett Srs 1 gyroplane	G. M. V. Richardson	
G-MIDD	PA-28 Cherokee 140	Midland Air Training School (G-BBDD)	
G-MIDG	Midget Mustang	C. E. Bellhouse	
G-MIDO	Airbus A.320-232	British Airways PLC	
G-MIDS	Airbus A.320-232	British Airways PLC	

Notes	Reg	Type	Owner or Operator
	G-MIDT	Airbus A.320-232	British Airways PLC
	G-MIDX	Airbus A.320-232	British Airways PLC
	G-MIDY	Airbus A.320-232	British Airways PLC
	G-MIFF	Robin DR.400/180	G. E. Snushall
	G-MIGG	WSK-Mielec LiM-5 (1211) ★	D. Miles (G-BWUF)
	G-MIII	Extra EA.300/L	Angels High Ltd
	G-MIKE	Brookland Hornet	M. H. J. Goldring
	G-MIKI	Rans S.6-ESA Coyote II	S. P. Slade
	G-MILD	Scheibe SF.25C Falke	P. G. Marks
	G-MILE	Cameron N-77 balloon	Miles Air Ltd
	G-MILF	Harmon Rocket II	E. Stinton
	G-MILR	Aeroprakt A22-LS Foxbat	Myrtlegrove Aviation Services
	G-MIME	Shaw Europa	A. I. & A. S. Findlay
	G-MIMU	CFM Shadow Series CD	N. M. Barriskell (G-MYXY)
	G-MIND	Cessna 404	Reconnaissance Ventures Ltd
	G-MINN	Lindstrand LBL-90A balloon	S. M. & D. Johnson (G-SKKC/G-OHUB)
	G-MINS	Nicollier HN.700 Menestrel II	R. Fenion
	G-MINT	Pitts S-1S Special	T. R. G. Barnby
	G-MIOO	M.100 Student ★	Museum of Berkshire Aviation/Woodley (G-APLK)
	G-MIRA	Jabiru SP-340	C. P. L. Helson/Belgium (G-LUMA)
	G-MIRN	Remos GX	M. Kurkic
	G-MIRV	Van's RV-8	E. R. J. Hicks & S. P. Ayres
	G-MISG	Boeing 737-3L9	Cello Aviation Ltd (G-OGBD)
	G-MISH	Cessna 182R	A. C. Hill & A. A. D. McKerrell (G-RFAB/G-BIXT)
	G-MISJ	CZAW Sportcruiser	SJ Aviators Ltd
	G-MISK	Robinson R44	H. W. Euridge (G-BYCE)
	G-MISS	Taylor JT.2 Titch	D. Beale
	G-MITE	Raj Hamsa X'Air Falcon	D. M. Lonnen
	G-MITY	Mole Mite	R. H. Mole
	G-MITZ	Cameron N-77 balloon	Colt Car Co Ltd
	G-MJAD	Eipper Quicksilver MX	J. McCullough
	G-MJAE	American Aerolights Eagle	T. B. Woolley
	G-MJAJ	Eurowing Goldwing	M. J. Aubrey
	G-MJAM	Eipper Quicksilver MX	P. R. Szczepanik
	G-MJAN	Hiway Skytrike	G. M. Sutcliffe
	G-MJBK	Swallow AeroPlane Swallow B	M. A. Newbould
	G-MJBL	American Aerolights Eagle	B. W. Olley
	G-MJCU	Tarjani	J. K. Ewing
	G-MJDE	Huntair Pathfinder	P. Rayson
	G-MJDJ	Hiway Skytrike Demon	A. J. Cowan
	G-MJDP	Eurowing Goldwing	A. D. Russell
	G-MJEO	American Aerolights Eagle	A. M. Shaw
	G-MJER	Flexiform Striker	D. S. Simpson
	G-MJFM	Huntair Pathfinder	M. J. Aubrey
	G-MJFX	Skyhook TR-1	M. R. Dean
	G-MJFZ	Hiway Demon/Tri-flyer	A. W. Lowrie
	G-MJHV	Hiway Demon 250	A. G. Griffiths
	G-MJJA	Huntair Pathfinder	J. M. Watkins & R. D. Bateman
	G-MJJK	Eipper Quicksilver MXII	J. McCullough
	G-MJKP	Super Scorpion/Sky-Trike ★	Aero Venture
	G-MJKX	Ultralight Skyrider Phantom	L. R. Graham
	G-MJOC	Huntair Pathfinder	A. J. Glynn
	G-MJOE	Eurowing Goldwing	R. J. Osborne
	G-MJPE	Hiway Demon Skytrike	T. G. Elmhirst
	G-MJPV	Eipper Quicksilver MX	F. W. Ellis
	G-MJSE	Skyrider Airsports Phantom	R. P. Tribe
	G-MJSF	Skyrider Airsports Phantom	R. P. Stonor
	G-MJSL	Dragon 200	M. J. Aubrey
	G-MJSO	Hiway Skytrike	D. C. Read
	G-MJSP	Romain Tiger Cub 440	A. R. Sunley
	G-MJST	Pterodactyl Ptraveller	T. D. Dawson
	G-MJSY	Eurowing Goldwing	A. J. Rex
	G-MJSZ	DH Wasp	J. J. Hill
	G-MJTM	Aerostructure Pipistrelle 2B	A. M. Sirant
	G-MJTX	Skyrider Airsports Phantom	P. D. Coppin
	G-MJTY	Huntair Pathfinder Mk.1	A. S. Macdonald
	G-MJTZ	Skyrider Airsports Phantom	B. J. Towers
	G-MJUF	MBA Super Tiger Cub 440	D. G. Palmer

Reg	Type	Owner or Operator	Notes
G-MJUR	Skyrider Aviation Phantom	M. J. Whiteman-Haywood	
G-MJUW	MBA Tiger Cub 440	D. G. Palmer	
G-MJUX	Skyrider Airsports Phantom	T. J. Searle	
G-MJVF	CFM Shadow series CD	J. A. Cook	
G-MJVN	Ultrasports Puma 440	R. McGookin	
G-MJVP	Eipper Quicksilver MX II	G. J. Ward	
G-MJVU	Eipper Quicksilver MX II	F. J. Griffith	
G-MJVY	Dragon Srs 150	J. C. Craddock	
G-MJWB	Eurowing Goldwing	D. G. Palmer	
G-MJWF	Tiger Cub 440	R. A. & T. Maycock	
G-MJYV	Mainair Triflyer 2 Seat	H. L. Phillips	
G-MJYW	Wasp Gryphon III	P. D. Lawrence	
G-MJYX	Mainair Tri-Flyer/Hiway Demon	K. G. Grayson & R. D. Leigh	
G-MJZK	Southdown Puma Sprint 440	R. J. Osborne	
G-MJZX	Hummer TX	M. J. Aubrey	
G-MKAK	Colt 77A balloon	M. A. Webb & P. M. Davies	
G-MKAS	PA-28 Cherokee 140	3G's Flying Group (G-BKVR)	
G-MKER	P & M QuikR	M. C. Kerr	
G-MKEV	EV-96 Eurostar	K. Laud	
G-MKHB	Aeropro Eurofox 912(iS)	Ascent Industries Ltd	
G-MKVB	VS.349 Spitfire LF.VB (BM597)	Historic Aircraft Collection	
G-MKXI	VS.365 Spitfire PR.XI (PL624:R)	Hangar 11 Collection	
G-MKZG	Super Marine Spitfire Mk.26	D. G. Richardson	
G-MLAL	Jabiru J400	G-MLAL Group	
G-MLAP	Agusta Westland AW169	Starspeed Ltd	
G-MLAS	Cessna 182E ★	Parachute jump trainer/St. Merryn	
G-MLAW	P & M Quik GT450	J. R. Payne	
G-MLHI	Maule MX-7-180 Star Rocket	Maulehigh Group (G-BTMJ)	
G-MLJL	Airbus A.330-243	Thomas Cook Airlines Ltd	
G-MLKE	P & M Aviation Quik R	G. Oliver	
G-MLLE	CEA DR.200A-B	M. Jurig	
G-MLLI	PA-32RT-300 Lance II	T. Steward (G-JUPP/G-BNJF)	
G-MLTA	UltraMagic M-77 balloon	T. J. Gouder	
G-MLWI	Thunder Ax7-77 balloon	C. A. Butter	
G-MLXP	Europa	M. Davies	
G-MLZZ	Best Off Sky Ranger Swift 912S(1)	I. D. Grossart	
G-MMAC	Dragon Srs.200	J. F. Ashton & J. P. Kirwan	
G-MMAG	MBA Tiger Cub 440	M. J. Aubrey	
G-MMAM	MBA Tiger Cub 440	I. Pearson	
G-MMAR	Mainair Gemini/Southdown Puma Sprint	B. A. Fawkes	
G-MMBE	MBA Tiger Cub 440	A. Gannon	
G-MMBU	Eipper Quicksilver MX II	D. A. Norwood	
G-MMCV	Solar Wings Typhoon III	G. Addison	
G-MMEK	Medway Hybred 44XL	West Country Wings	
G-MMFE	Flexiform Striker	W. Camm	
G-MMFV	Flexiform Striker	R. A. Walton	
G-MMGF	MBA Tiger Cub 440	I. J. Webb	
G-MMGL	MBA Tiger Cub 440	H. E. Dunning	
G-MMGS	Solar Wings Panther XL	G. C. Read	
G-MMGT	Solar Wings Typhoon	H. Cook	
G-MMGV	Whittaker MW5 Sorcerer	M. W. J. Whittaker & G. N. Haffey	
G-MMHN	MBA Tiger Cub 440	M. J. Aubrey	
G-MMHS	SMD Viper	C. J. Meadows	
G-MMIE	MBA Tiger Cub 440	B. M. Olliver	
G-MMIH	MBA Tiger Cub 440	T. Barnby	
G-MMJD	Southdown Puma Sprint	M. P. Robertshaw	
G-MMJV	MBA Tiger Cub 440	D. G. Palmer	
G-MMKA	Ultrasports Panther Dual	R. S. Wood	
G-MMKM	Flexiform Dual Striker	S. W. Hutchinson	
G-MMKP	MBA Tiger Cub 440	J. W. Beaty	
G-MMKR	Southdown Lightning DS/Tri-Flyer 440	C. R. Madden	
G-MMKT	MBA Tiger Cub 440	A. R. Sunley	
G-MMKX	Skyrider Phantom 330	G. J. Lampitt	
G-MMLE	Eurowing Goldwing SP	M. J. Aubrey	
G-MMLK	MBA Tiger Cub 440	M. J. Aubrey	
G-MMMG	Eipper Quicksilver MXL	L. Swift	
G-MMMH	Hadland Willow	M. J. Hadland	
G-MMML	Dragon 150	M. J. Aubrey	

Notes	Reg	Type	Owner or Operator
	G-MMMN	Ultrasports Panther Dual 440	C. Downton
	G-MMNA	Eipper Quicksilver MXII	G. A. Marples
	G-MMNB	Eipper Quicksilver MX	M. J. Lindop
	G-MMNC	Eipper Quicksilver MX	W. S. Toulmin
	G-MMNH	Dragon 150	T. J. Barlow
	G-MMOB	Southdown Sprint	D. Woolcock
	G-MMOK	Solar Wings Panther XL	R. F. & A. J. Foster
	G-MMPH	Southdown Puma Sprint	J. Siddle
	G-MMPL	Lanashire Micro-Trike 440/Flexiform Dual Striker (modified)	P. D. Lawrence
	G-MMPZ	Teman Mono-Fly	H. Smith
	G-MMRH	Highway Skytrike	A. M. Sirant
	G-MMRL	Solar Wings Panther XL	R. J. Hood
	G-MMRN	Southdown Puma Sprint	D. C. Read
	G-MMRP	Mainair Gemini	J. C. S. Jones
	G-MMRW	Flexiform Dual Striker	M. D. Hinge
	G-MMSG	Solar Wings Panther XL-S	R. W. McKee
	G-MMSH	Solar Wings Panther XL	I. J. Drake
	G-MMSP	Mainair Gemini/Flash	J. Whiteford
	G-MMSS	Lightning/Tri-Pacer	G. A. Hazell
	G-MMSZ	Medway Half Pint/Aerial Arts 130SX	A. M. Sutton
	G-MMTD	Mainair Tri-Flyer 330	W. E. Teare
	G-MMTL	Mainair Gemini	K. Birkett
	G-MMTR	Ultrasports Panther	P. M. Kelsey
	G-MMTY	Fisher FP.202U	M. A. Welch
	G-MMUA	Southdown Puma Sprint	M. R. Crowhurst
	G-MMUO	Mainair Gemini/Flash	D. M. Pecheur
	G-MMUV	Southdown Puma Sprint	D. C. Read
	G-MMUW	Mainair Gemini/Flash	J. C. K. Scardifield
	G-MMUX	Gemini Sprint	D. R. Gregson
	G-MMVI	Southdown Puma Sprint	G. R. Williams
	G-MMVS	Skyhook Pixie	B. W. Olley
	G-MMWG	Greenslade Mono-Trike	G-MMWG Group
	G-MMWS	Mainair Tri-Flyer	P. H. Risdale
	G-MMWX	Southdown Puma Sprint	G. A. Webb
	G-MMXO	Southdown Puma Sprint	I. White
	G-MMXU	Mainair Gemini/Flash	T. J. Franklin
	G-MMXV	Mainair Gemini/Flash	M. A. Boffin
	G-MMZA	Mainair Gemini/Flash	G. T. Johnston
	G-MMZD	Mainair Gemini/Flash	S. McDonnell
	G-MMZW	Southdown Puma Sprint	M. G. Ashbee
	G-MNAE	Mainair Gemini/Flash	G. C. luddington
	G-MNAI	Ultrasports Panther XL-S	R. G. Cameron
	G-MNAZ	Solar Wings Pegasus XL-R	R. W. houldsworth
	G-MNBA	Solar Wings Pegasus XL-R	V. C. Chambers
	G-MNBB	Solar Wings Pegasus XL-R	A. A. Sawera
	G-MNBC	Solar Wings Pegasus XL-R	R. T. Parry
	G-MNBI	Solar Wings Panther XL-S	M. O'Connell
	G-MNBP	Mainair Gemini/Flash	B. J. James
	G-MNBS	Mainair Gemini/Flash	P. A. Comins
	G-MNCA	Hiway Demon 175	M. A. Sirant
	G-MNCF	Mainair Gemini/Flash	C. F. Janes
	G-MNCG	Mainair Gemini/Flash	T. Lynch
	G-MNCM	CFM Shadow Srs C	A. Gibson
	G-MNCP	Southdown Puma Sprint	D. A. Payne
	G-MNCS	Skyrider Airsports Phantom	J. A. Harris
	G-MNCU	Medway Hybred 44XL	J. E. Evans
	G-MNCV	Medway Hybred 44XL	M. J. Turland
	G-MNDD	Mainair Scorcher	S. F. Winter
	G-MNDE	Medway Half Pint	Delta Echo Half Pint Group
	G-MNDU	Midland Sirocco 377GB	M. A. Collins
	G-MNDY	Southdown Puma Sprint	A. M. Coupland
	G-MNEG	Mainair Gemini/Flash	A. Sexton/Ireland
	G-MNER	CFM Shadow Srs B	P. A. Taylor
	G-MNEY	Mainair Gemini/Flash	D. A. Spiers
	G-MNFF	Mainair Gemini/Flash	C. H. Spencer & R. P. Cook
	G-MNFG	Southdown Puma Sprint	M. Ingleton
	G-MNFL	AMF Chevvron	J. Pool
	G-MNFM	Mainair Gemini/Flash	P. M. Fidell
	G-MNFN	Mainair Gemini/Flash	J. R. Martin

Reg	Type	Owner or Operator	Notes
G-MNGK	Mainair Gemini/Flash	G. P. Warnes	
G-MNHD	Solar Wings Pegasus XL-R	A. Evans	
G-MNHH	Solar Wings Panther XL-S	F. J. Williams	
G-MNHI	Solar Wings Pegasus XL-R	B. R. Claughton	
G-MNHJ	Solar Wings Pegasus XL-R	C. Council	
G-MNHK	Solar Wings Pegasus XL-R	C. Parkinson	
G-MNHL	Solar Wings Pegasus XL-R	The Microlight School (Lichfield) Ltd	
G-MNHM	Solar Wings Pegasus XL-R	P. A. Howell	
G-MNHR	Solar Wings Pegasus XL-R	B. D. Jackson	
G-MNHZ	Mainair Gemini/Flash	I. O. S. Ross	
G-MNIA	Mainair Gemini/Flash	W. R. Furness	
G-MNIG	Mainair Gemini/Flash	M. Grimes	
G-MNII	Mainair Gemini/Flash	R. F. Finnis	
G-MNIK	Pegasus Photon	M. Belemet	
G-MNJD	Southdown Puma Sprint	S. D. Smith	
G-MNJJ	Solar Wings Pegasus Flash	P. A. Shelley	
G-MNJR	Solar Wings Pegasus Flash	M. G. Ashbee	
G-MNJS	Southdown Puma Sprint	E. A. Frost	
G-MNJX	Medway Hybred 44XL	H. A. Stewart	
G-MNKB	Solar Wings Pegasus Photon	I. E. Wallace	
G-MNKC	Solar Wings Pegasus Photon	K. B. Woods	
G-MNKD	Solar Wings Pegasus Photon	A. M. Sirant	
G-MNKE	Solar Wings Pegasus Photon	H. C. Lowther	
G-MNKG	Solar Wings Pegasus Photon	S. N. Robson	
G-MNKK	Solar Wings Pegasus Photon	M. E. Gilbert	
G-MNKM	MBA Tiger Cub 440	A. R. Sunley	
G-MNKN	Skycraft Scout Mk.3-3R	M. A. Aubrey	
G-MNKP	Solar Wings Pegasus Flash	I. N. Miller	
G-MNKW	Solar Wings Pegasus Flash	G. J. Eaton	
G-MNKX	Solar Wings Pegasus Flash	T. A. Newton	
G-MNLT	Southdown Raven	J. L. Stachini	
G-MNMC	Mainair Gemini Sprint	J. C. Peat	
G-MNMG	Mainair Gemini/Flash	N. A. M. Beyer-Kay	
G-MNMK	Solar Wings Pegasus XL-R	A. F. Smallacombe	
G-MNMM	Aerotech MW5 Sorcerer	S. F. N. Warnell	
G-MNMU	Southdown Raven	M. J. Curley	
G-MNMV	Mainair Gemini/Flash	S. Staig	
G-MNMW	Aerotech MW6 Merlin	E. F. Clapham	
G-MNMY	Cyclone 70	N. R. Beale	
G-MNNA	Southdown Raven	D. & G. D. Palfrey	
G-MNNF	Mainair Gemini/Flash	W. J. Gunn	
G-MNNG	Solar Wings Photon	K. B. Woods	
G-MNNJ	Mainair Gemini/Flash II	L. J. Nelson	
G-MNNL	Mainair Gemini/Flash II	C. L. Rumney	
G-MNNM	Mainair Scorcher Solo	S. R. Leeper	
G-MNNO	Southdown Raven	M. J. Robbins	
G-MNNS	Eurowing Goldwing	N. K. Geddes	
G-MNPY	Mainair Scorcher Solo	R. J. Turner	
G-MNPZ	Mainair Scorcher Solo	S. Stevens	
G-MNRD	Ultraflight Lazair IIIE	Sywell Lazair Group	
G-MNRE	Mainair Scorcher Solo	R. D. Leigh	
G-MNRM	Hornet Dual Trainer	I. C. Cannan	
G-MNRS	Southdown Raven	M. C. Newman	
G-MNRX	Mainair Gemini/Flash II	R. Downham	
G-MNRZ	Mainair Scorcher Solo	R. D. Leigh	
G-MNSJ	Mainair Gemini/Flash	P. Cooney	
G-MNSL	Southdown Raven X	P. B. Robinson	
G-MNSY	Southdown Raven X	L. A. Hosegood	
G-MNTD	Aerial Arts Chaser 110SX	B. Richardson	
G-MNTK	CFM Shadow Srs B	K. Davies	
G-MNTP	CFM Shadow Srs B	C. Lockwood	
G-MNTV	Mainair Gemini/Flash II	A.M. Sirant	
G-MNUF	Mainair Gemini/Flash II	K. Jones	
G-MNUI	Skyhook Cutlass Dual	M. Holling	
G-MNUR	Mainair Gemini/Flash II	J. S. Hawkins	
G-MNVE	Solar Wings Pegasus XL-R	M. P. Aris	
G-MNVG	Solar Wings Pegasus Flash II	D. J. Ward	
G-MNVI	CFM Shadow Srs B	D. R. C. Pugh	
G-MNVJ	CFM Shadow Srs CD	A. H. Dyer	
G-MNVK	CFM Shadow Srs B	A. K. Atwell	
G-MNVO	Hovey Whing-Ding II	C. Wilson	

Notes	Reg	Type	Owner or Operator
	G-MNVT	Mainair Gemini/Flash II	S. P. Barker
	G-MNVW	Mainair Gemini/Flash II	J. C. Munro-Hunt
	G-MNVZ	Solar Wings Pegasus Photon	J. J. Russ
	G-MNWB	Thruster TST	B. Donnelly
	G-MNWG	Southdown Raven X	D. Murray
	G-MNWI	Mainair Gemini/Flash II	P. Dickinson
	G-MNWL	Aerial Arts 130SX	E. H. Snook
	G-MNWW	Solar Wings Pegasus XL-R	G-MNWW Group
	G-MNWY	CFM Shadow Srs C	R. R. L. & S. R. Potts
	G-MNXE	Southdown Raven X	A. E. Silvey
	G-MNXO	Medway Hybred 44XLR	R. P. Taylor
	G-MNXU	Mainair Gemini/Flash II	J. M. Hucker
	G-MNXX	CFM Shadow Srs BD	R. Sinclair-Brown
	G-MNXZ	Whittaker MW5 Sorcerer	A. J. Glynn
	G-MNYC	Solar Wings Pegasus XL-R	J. S. Hawkins
	G-MNYD	Aerial Arts 110SX Chaser	B. Richardson
	G-MNYF	Aerial Arts 110SX Chaser	R. W. Twamley
	G-MNYP	Southdown Raven X	A. G. Davies
	G-MNYU	Pegasus XL-R	G. L. Turner
	G-MNZD	Mainair Gemini/Flash II	N. D. Carter
	G-MNZJ	CFM Shadow Srs BD	W. Hepburn
	G-MNZK	Solar Wings Pegasus XL-R	P. J. Appleby
	G-MNZU	Eurowing Goldwing	P. D. Coppin & P. R. Millen
	G-MNZW	Southdown Raven X	T. A. Willcox
	G-MNZZ	CFM Shadow Srs B	Shadow Aviation Ltd
	G-MOAC	Beech F33A Bonanza	R. M. Camrass
	G-MOAL	Agusta Westland AW109SP Grand New	SDI Aviation Ltd
	G-MOAN	Aeromot AMT-200S Super Ximango	T. Boin/Switzerland
	G-MOCL	Bombardier CL600-2B16 Challenger 604	London Executive Aviation Ltd
	G-MODE	Eurocopter EC 120B	P. G. Barker
	G-MOFB	Cameron O-120 balloon	D. M. Moffat
	G-MOGS	CZAW Sportcruiser	J. M. Oliver
	G-MOKE	Cameron V-77 balloon	G-MOKE ASBC/Luxembourg
	G-MOLA	Evektor EV-97 TeamEurostar UK	A. Szczepanek
	G-MOMA	Thruster T.600N 450	Compton Abbas Microlight Group (G-CCIB)
	G-MONI	Monnett Moni	P. N. Stacey
	G-MONK	Boeing 757-2T7	Icelandair/Iceland
	G-MOOD	Ikarus C42 FB100	R. Moody (G-HARL)
	G-MOOR	SOCATA TB10 Tobago	P. D. Kirkham (G-MILK)
	G-MOOS	P.56 Provost T.1 (XF690)	YeoPro Group (G-BGKA)
	G-MOOV	CZAW Sportcruiser	G-MOOV Syndicate
	G-MOPS	Best Off Sky Ranger Swift 912S	S. Dixon
	G-MORG	Balony Kubicek BB-SS balloon	A. M. Holly
	G-MOSA	Morane Saulnier MS317	A. C. Whitehead
	G-MOSH	PA-28R-201 Arrow	3 Greens Flying Group
	G-MOSJ	Beech C90 GTI King Air	NalJets
	G-MOSY	Cameron O-84 balloon	P. L. Mossman
	G-MOTA	Bell 206B JetRanger 3	J. W. Sandle
	G-MOTH	DH.82A Tiger Moth (K2567)	P. T. Szluha
	G-MOTI	Robin DR.400/500	Tango India Flying Group
	G-MOTO	PA-24 Comanche 180	B. Spiralke (G-EDHE/G-ASFH)
	G-MOTW	Meyers OTW-145	J. K. Padden
	G-MOUL	Maule M6-235	H. G. Meyer
	G-MOUR	HS. Gnat T.1 (XR991)	Heritage Aircraft Ltd
	G-MOUT	Cessna 182T	C. Mountain
	G-MOUZ	Cameron O-26 balloon	T. J. Orchard & M. E. Banks
	G-MOVI	PA-32R-301 Saratoga SP	J. E. Bray (G-MARI)
	G-MOWG	Aeroprakt A22-L Foxbat	J. Smith
	G-MOYR	Aeropro Eurofox 912(S)	The Northumbria Gliding Club Ltd
	G-MOZE	P & M Quik GTR	M. R. Mosley
	G-MOZI	Glasflugel Mosquito	J. Christensen & P. Smith
	G-MOZZ	Avions Mudry CAP-10B	N. Skipworth & P. M. Wells
	G-MPAA	PA-28-181 Archer III	Shropshire Aero Club Ltd
	G-MPAC	Ultravia Pelican PL	J. J. Bodnarec
	G-MPAT	EV-97 TeamEurostar UK	P. J. Dale
	G-MPFC	Grumman AA-5B	MPFC Ltd (G-ZARI/G-BHVY)
	G-MPHY	Ikarus C42 FB100	P. Murphy
	G-MPLA	Cessna 182T	AJW Construction Ltd
	G-MPLB	Cessna 182T	Colne Valley Electrical Ltd

Reg	Type	Owner or Operator	Notes
G-MPLC	Cessna 182T	Oxford Aviation Academy (Oxford) Ltd	
G-MPLD	Cessna 182T	Cropspray Ltd	
G-MPLE	Cessna 182T	Oxford Aviation Academy (Oxford) Ltd	
G-MPLF	Cessna 182T	Oxford Aviation Academy (Oxford) Ltd	
G-MPRL	Cessna 210M	Mike Stapleton & Co.Ltd	
G-MPSA	Eurocopter MBB BK-117C-2	Police & Crime Commissioner for West Yorkshire	
G-MPSB	Eurocopter MBB BK-117C-2	Police & Crime Commissioner for West Yorkshire	
G-MPSC	Eurocopter MBB BK-117C-2	Police & Crime Commissioner for West Yorkshire	
G-MPWI	Robin HR.100/210	P. G. Clarkson & S. King	
G-MRAG	Cessna 182T	A. S. Gardner	
G-MRAJ	Hughes 369E	A. Jardine	
G-MRAM	Mignet HM.1000 Balerit	R. A. Marven	
G-MRDS	CZAW Sportcruiser	P. Wood	
G-MRED	Christavia Mk 1	Mister Ed Group	
G-MRGT	Skyranger Swift 912S(1)	G. I. Taylor	
G-MRJC	AutoGyro Cavalon	Tipjets UK Ltd	
G-MRJJ	Mainair Pegasus Quik	J.H. Sparks	
G-MRJP	Silence Twister	J. P. Marriott	
G-MRKS	Robinson R44	TJD Trade Ltd (G-RAYC)	
G-MRKT	Lindstrand LBL-90A balloon	R. M. Stanley	
G-MRLI	Sikorsky S-92A	Bristow Helicopters Ltd (G-CKGZ)	
G-MRLN	Sky 240-24 balloon	Merlin Balloons	
G-MRLS	AutoGyro Calidus	C. N. Fleming	
G-MRLX	Gulfstream 550	Saxonair Charter Ltd	
G-MRLZ	Robinson R44 II	Catedra Services XXI SRL/Spain	
G-MRME	Gefa-Flug AS 105 GD airship	Airship Over Atlanta Ltd	
G-MROC	Pegasus Quantum 15-912	P. Hill	
G-MROD	Van's RV-7A	K. R. Emery	
G-MRPH	Murphy Rebel	P. & B. S. Metson	
G-MRPT	Cessna 172S	Sands Wealth Management Ltd & TWC Facilities Ltd (G-UFCC)	
G-MRSN	Robinson R22 Beta	Yorkshire Helicopters Ltd	
G-MRSS	Ikarus C42 FB80	North East Aviation Ltd	
G-MRST	PA-28 RT-201 Arrow IV	G. de Beaufort & P. de Grove/France	
G-MRSW	Lindstrand LBL-90A balloon	D. S. Wilson (G-CHWU)	
G-MRTN	SOCATA TB10 Tobago	G. C. Jarvis (G-BHET)	
G-MRTY	Cameron N-77 balloon	R. A. Vale & ptnrs	
G-MRVK	Czech Sport Aircraft Pipersport	M. Farrugia	
G-MRVL	Van's RV-7	T. W. Wielkopolski	
G-MRVN	PZL-Bielsko SZD-50-3	The Bath, Wilts and North Dorset Gliding Club Ltd	
G-MRVP	Van's RV-6	M. R. Parker	
G-MSAL	MS.733 Alcyon (143)	M. Isbister t/a Alcyon Flying Group	
G-MSCL	AutoGyro Cavalon	Power Management Engineering Ltd	
G-MSES	Cessna 150L	Go Fly Oxford Aircraft Rentals Ltd	
G-MSFT	PA-28-161 Warrior II	Western Air (Thruxton) Ltd (G-MUMS)	
G-MSGI	Magni M-24C Orion	M. S. Gregory	
G-MSIX	Glaser-Dirks DG.800B	G-MSIX Group	
G-MSKY	Ikarus C.42 FB100 VLA	G-MSKY Group	
G-MSOF	Cessna 172N	Excelis Ltd	
G-MSON	Cameron Z-90 balloon	Regional Property Services Ltd	
G-MSOO	Revolution Mini 500 helicopter	R. H. Ryan	
G-MSPT	Eurocopter EC 135T2	S. J. Golding	
G-MSPY	Pegasus Quantum 15-912	B. E. Wagenhauser	
G-MSTG	NA P-51D Mustang (414419:LH-F)	M. Hammond	
G-MSTR	Cameron 110 Monster SS Balloon	Monster Syndicate (G-OJOB)	
G-MSVI	Agusta A.109S Grand	JPM Ltd (G-ETOU)	
G-MTAB	Mainair Gemini/Flash II	M. J. Thompson	
G-MTAC	Mainair Gemini/Flash II	B. T. Bradshaw	
G-MTAF	Mainair Gemini/Flash II	A. G. Lister	
G-MTAH	Mainair Gemini/Flash II	A. J. Rowe	
G-MTAL	Solar Wings Pegasus Photon	I. T. Callaghan	
G-MTAP	Southdown Raven X	M. C. Newman	
G-MTAS	Whittaker MW5 Sorcerer	C. D. Wills	
G-MTAV	Solar Wings Pegasus XL-R	S. Fairweather	
G-MTAW	Solar Wings Pegasus XL-R	M. G. Ralph	
G-MTAY	Solar Wings Pegasus XL-R	S. A. McLatchie	
G-MTAZ	Solar Wings Pegasus XL-R	M. O'Connell	

Notes	Reg	Type	Owner or Operator
	G-MTBB	Southdown Raven X	A. Miller
	G-MTBD	Mainair Gemini/Flash II	J. G. Jones
	G-MTBE	CFM Shadow Srs BD	P. J. Mogg
	G-MTBJ	Mainair Gemini/Flash II	P. J. & R. M. Perry
	G-MTBL	Solar Wings Pegasus XL-R	R. N. Whiting
	G-MTBN	Southdown Raven X	A. J. & S. E. Crosby-Jones
	G-MTBO	Southdown Raven X	J. Liversuch
	G-MTBP	Aerotech MW5B Sorcerer	
	G-MTBR	Aerotech MW5B Sorcerer	R. Poulter
	G-MTBS	Aerotech MW5B Sorcerer	D. J. Pike
	G-MTCM	Southdown Raven X	J. C. Rose
	G-MTCP	Aerial Arts Chaser 110SX	B. Richardson
	G-MTCU	Mainair Gemini/Flash II	T. J. Philip
	G-MTDD	Aerial Arts Chaser 110SX	B. Richardson
	G-MTDE	American Aerolights 110SX	J. T. Meager
	G-MTDF	Mainair Gemini/Flash II	P. G. Barnes
	G-MTDK	Aerotech MW5B Sorcerer	C. C. Wright
	G-MTDO	Eipper Quicksilver MXII	D. L. Ham
	G-MTDR	Mainair Gemini/Flash II	D. J. Morriss
	G-MTDU	CFM Shadow Srs BD	M. Lowe
	G-MTDW	Mainair Gemini/Flash II	S. R. Leeper
	G-MTDY	Mainair Gemini/Flash IIA	S. Penoyre
	G-MTEE	Solar Wings Pegasus XL-R	The Microlight School (Lichfield) Ltd
	G-MTEK	Mainair Gemini/Flash II	M. O'Hearne
	G-MTER	Solar Wings Pegasus XL-R	S. J. Nix
	G-MTES	Solar Wings Pegasus XL-R	N. P. Read
	G-MTEU	Solar Wings Pegasus XL-R	T. E. Thomas
	G-MTEY	Mainair Gemini/Flash II	E. Jackson
	G-MTFC	Medway Hybred 44XLR	J. K. Masters
	G-MTFG	AMF Chevvron 232	J. Pool
	G-MTFN	Aerotech MW5 Sorcerer	S. M. King
	G-MTFU	CFM Shadow Srs CD	J. E. Course
	G-MTGB	Thruster TST Mk 1	M. J. Aubrey
	G-MTGD	Thruster TST Mk 1	B. A. Janaway
	G-MTGF	Thruster TST Mk 1	B. Swindon
	G-MTGL	Solar Wings Pegasus XL-R	R. & P. J. Openshaw
	G-MTGO	Mainair Gemini/Flash	J. Ouru
	G-MTGR	Thruster TST Mk 1	The Vulture Squadron
	G-MTGS	Thruster TST Mk 1	R. J. Nelson
	G-MTGV	CFM Shadow Srs BD	V. R. Riley
	G-MTGW	CFM Shadow Srs CD	G. N. Smith
	G-MTHH	Solar Wings Pegasus XL-R	J. Palmer
	G-MTHN	Solar Wings Pegasus XL-R	M. T. Seal
	G-MTHT	CFM Shadow Srs BD	A. P. Jones
	G-MTHV	CFM Shadow Srs CD	S. J. Ellis
	G-MTIB	Mainair Gemini/Flash IIA	M. D. Maclagan
	G-MTIE	Solar Wings Pegasus XL-R	P. Wibberley
	G-MTIJ	Solar Wings Pegasus XL-R	M. J. F. Gilbody
	G-MTIL	Mainair Gemlni/Flash IIA	M. Ward
	G-MTIM	Mainair Gemini/Flash II	T. M. Swan
	G-MTIR	Solar Wings Pegasus XL-R	P. Jolley
	G-MTIW	Solar Wings Pegasus XL-R	S. G. Hutchinson
	G-MTIZ	Solar Wings Pegasus XL-R	S. L. Blount
	G-MTJB	Mainair Gemini/Flash IIA	B. Skidmore
	G-MTJC	Mainair Gemini/Flash IIA	T. A. Dockrell
	G-MTJE	Mainair Gemini/Flash IIA	C. I. Hemingway
	G-MTJG	Medway Hybred 44XLR	M. A. Trodden
	G-MTJH	SW Pegasus Flash	C. G. Ludgate
	G-MTJL	Mainair Gemini/Flash IIA	R. Thompson
	G-MTJT	Mainair Gemini/Flash IIA	P. J. Barratt
	G-MTJV	Mainair Gemini/Flash IIA	D. C. Dunn
	G-MTJX	Hornet Dual Trainer/Raven	J. P. Kirwan
	G-MTKA	Thruster TST Mk 1	M. J. Coles & S. R. Williams
	G-MTKH	Solar Wings Pegasus XL-R	B. P. Hoare
	G-MTKI	Solar Wings Pegasus XL-R	M. Wady
	G-MTKR	CFM Shadow Srs CD	D. P. Eichhorn
	G-MTKW	Mainair Gemini/Flash IIA	J. H. McIvor
	G-MTKX	Mainair Gemini/Flash IIA	S. P. Disney
	G-MTLB	Mainair Gemini/Flash IIA	C. R. Partington
	G-MTLC	Mainair Gemini/Flash IIA	R. J. Alston
	G-MTLG	Solar Wings Pegasus XL-R	D. Young

Reg	Type	Owner or Operator	Notes
G-MTLL	Mainair Gemini/Flash IIA	M. S. Lawrence	
G-MTLM	Thruster TST Mk 1	R.J. Nelson	
G-MTLN	Thruster TST Mk 1	P. W. Taylor	
G-MTLT	Solar Wings Pegasus XL-R	K. M. Mayling	
G-MTLV	Solar Wings Pegasus XL-R	W. D. Foster	
G-MTLX	Medway Hybred 44XLR	D. A. Coupland	
G-MTLY	Solar Wings Pegasus XL-R	G. J. Prisk	
G-MTMA	Mainair Gemini/Flash IIA	S. Cunningham	
G-MTMC	Mainair Gemini/Flash IIA	A. Shearer	
G-MTMF	Solar Wings Pegasus XL-R	H. T. M. Smith	
G-MTMG	Solar Wings Pegasus XL-R	C. W. & P. E. F. Suckling	
G-MTML	Mainair Gemini/Flash IIA	J. F. Ashton	
G-MTMR	Hornet Dual Trainer/Raven	D. J. Smith	
G-MTMW	Mainair Gemini/Flash IIA	D. J. Boulton	
G-MTMX	CFM Shadow Srs BD	D. R. White	
G-MTNC	Mainair Gemini/Flash IIA	K. R. Emery	
G-MTND	Medway Hybred 44XLR	Butty Boys Flying Group	
G-MTNE	Medway Hybred 44XLR	A. G. Rodenburg	
G-MTNF	Medway Hybred 44XLR	P. A. Bedford	
G-MTNI	Mainair Gemini/Flash IIA	D. R. McDougall	
G-MTNK	Weedhopper JC-24B	G. R. Moore	
G-MTNO	Solar Wings Pegasus XL-Q	P. J. Knibb & G. J. Rowe	
G-MTNR	Thruster TST Mk 1	A. M. Sirant	
G-MTNU	Thruster TST Mk 1	T. H. Brearley	
G-MTNV	Thruster TST Mk 1	J. B. Russell	
G-MTOA	Solar Wings Pegasus XL-R	R. A. Bird	
G-MTOH	Solar Wings Pegasus XL-R	H. Cook	
G-MTOJ	Solar Wings Pegasus XL-R	J. Hennessy	
G-MTON	Solar Wings Pegasus XL-R	D. J. Willett	
G-MTOY	Solar Wings Pegasus XL-R	G-MTOY Group	
G-MTPB	Mainair Gemini/Flash IIA	G. von Wilcken	
G-MTPF	Solar Wings Pegasus XL-R	G-MTPF Group	
G-MTPH	Solar Wings Pegasus XL-R	G. Barker & L. Blight	
G-MTPL	Solar Wings Pegasus XL-R	C. J. Jones	
G-MTPM	Solar Wings Pegasus XL-R	D. K. Seal	
G-MTPU	Thruster TST Mk 1	N. Hay	
G-MTPW	Thruster TST Mk 1	D. W. Tewson	
G-MTPX	Thruster TST Mk 1	T. Snook	
G-MTRC	Midlands Ultralights Sirocco 377G	D. Thorpe	
G-MTRM	Solar Wings Pegasus XL-R	C. H. Edwards	
G-MTRS	Solar Wings Pegasus XL-R	W. R. Edwards	
G-MTRX	Whittaker MW5 Sorceror	W. Turner	
G-MTRZ	Mainair Gemini/Flash IIA	D. S. Lally	
G-MTSC	Mainair Gemini/Flash IIA	J. Kilpatrick	
G-MTSH	Thruster TST Mk 1	R. R. Orr	
G-MTSJ	Thruster TST Mk 1	J. D. Buchanan	
G-MTSM	Thruster TST Mk 1	M. A. Horton	
G-MTSP	Solar Wings Pegasus XL-R	P. L. Wilkinson	
G-MTSS	Solar Wings Pegasus XL-R	V. Marchant	
G-MTSZ	Solar Wings Pegasus XL-R	D. L. Pickover	
G-MTTA	Solar Wings Pegasus XL-R	D. Hall	
G-MTTE	Solar Wings Pegasus XL-R	C. F. Barnard	
G-MTTF	Aerotech MW6 Merlin	P. Cotton	
G-MTTI	Mainair Gemini/Flash IIA	G-MTTI Flying Group	
G-MTTM	Mainair Gemini/Flash IIA	M. E. Porter	
G-MTTN	Ultralight Flight Phantom	F. P. Welsh	
G-MTTP	Mainair Gemini/Flash IIA	A. Ormson	
G-MTTU	Solar Wings Pegasus XL-R	A. Friend	
G-MTTZ	Solar Wings Pegasus XL-Q	M. O. Bloy	
G-MTUA	Solar Wings Pegasus XL-R	J. & S. Bunyan	
G-MTUC	Thruster TST Mk 1	N. S. Chittenden	
G-MTUK	Solar Wings Pegasus XL-R	G. McLaughlin	
G-MTUN	Solar Wings Pegasus XL-Q	M. J. O'Connor	
G-MTUP	Solar Wings Pegasus XL-Q	F. Dethridge	
G-MTUR	Solar Wings Pegasus XL-Q	G. Ball	
G-MTUS	Solar Wings Pegasus XL-Q	P. W. Davidson	
G-MTUT	Solar Wings Pegasus XL-Q (modified)	R. E. Bull	
G-MTUV	Mainair Gemini/Flash IIA	T. R. Parsons	
G-MTUY	Solar Wings Pegasus XL-Q	H. C. Lowther	
G-MTVC	Solar Wings Pegasus XL-R	A. Duffy	
G-MTVH	Mainair Gemini/Flash IIA	P. H. Statham	

Notes	Reg	Type	Owner or Operator
	G-MTVI	Mainair Gemini/Flash IIA	J. A. Hewitt
	G-MTVJ	Mainair Gemini/Flash IIA	M. Gibson
	G-MTVP	Thruster TST Mk 1	J. M. Evans
	G-MTVT	Thruster TST Mk.1	W. H. J. Knowles
	G-MTVX	Solar Wings Pegasus XL-Q	D. A. Foster
	G-MTWK	CFM Shadow Srs BD	M. Cooper
	G-MTWR	Mainair Gemini/Flash IIA	J. B. Hodson
	G-MTWS	Mainair Gemini/Flash IIA	A. Robins
	G-MTWX	Mainair Gemini/Flash IIA	K. Walsh
	G-MTWZ	Thruster TST Mk 1	M. J. Aubrey
	G-MTXA	Thruster TST Mk 1	M. A. Franklin
	G-MTXB	Thruster TST Mk 1	J. J. Hill
	G-MTXD	Thruster TST Mk 1	D. Newton
	G-MTXJ	Solar Wings Pegasus XL-Q	E. W. Laidlaw
	G-MTXK	Solar Wings Pegasus XL-Q	D. R. G. Whitelaw
	G-MTXM	Mainair Gemini/Flash IIA	H. J. Vinning
	G-MTXO	Whittaker MW6	C. A. Harper & R. E. Arnold
	G-MTXR	CFM Shadow Srs BD	G. E. Arnott
	G-MTXU	Noble Hardman Snowbird Mk.IV	P. Asbridge
	G-MTXZ	Mainair Gemini/Flash IIA	J. S. Hawkins
	G-MTYC	Solar Wings Pegasus XL-Q	C. I. D. H. Garrison
	G-MTYI	Solar Wings Pegasus XL-Q	M. A. Cox
	G-MTYL	Solar Wings Pegasus XL-Q	S. Cooper
	G-MTYR	Solar Wings Pegasus XL-Q	D. T. Evans
	G-MTYS	Solar Wings Pegasus XL-Q	R. G. Wall
	G-MTYV	Southdown Raven X	S. R. Jones
	G-MTYW	Raven X	R. Solomons
	G-MTYY	Solar Wings Pegasus XL-R	L. A. Hosegood
	G-MTZA	Thruster TST Mk 1	J. F. Gallagher
	G-MTZB	Thruster TST Mk 1	J. E. Davies
	G-MTZC	Thruster TST Mk 1	R. S. O'Carroll
	G-MTZE	Thruster TST Mk 1	B. S. P. Finch
	G-MTZF	Thruster TST Mk 1	J. D. Buchanan
	G-MTZG	Mainair Gemini/Flash IIA	A. P. Fenn
	G-MTZH	Mainair Gemini/Flash IIA	D. C. Hughes
	G-MTZL	Mainair Gemini/Flash IIA	N. S. Brayn
	G-MTZM	Mainair Gemini/Flash IIA	G. Burns
	G-MTZS	Solar Wings Pegasus XL-Q	S. Danby
	G-MTZV	Mainair Gemini/Flash IIA	P. Robinson
	G-MTZW	Mainair Gemini/Flash IIA	M. Devlin
	G-MTZX	Mainair Gemini/Flash IIA	N. Musgrave
	G-MTZY	Mainair Gemini/Flash IIA	M. D. Leslie
	G-MTZZ	Mainair Gemini/Flash IIA	G. J. Cadden
	G-MUCK	Lindstrand LBL 77A	C. J. Wootton
	G-MUDD	Hughes 369E	Derwen Plant Co.Ltd
	G-MUDX	AutoGyro Cavalon	P. R. Biggs (G-CJVT)
	G-MUDY	PA-18-150 Super Cub	C. J. de Sousa e Morgado (G-OTUG)
	G-MUIR	Cameron V-65 balloon	Border Ballooning Ltd
	G-MUJD	Van's RV-12	M. F. El-Deen
	G-MUKY	Van's RV-8	I. E. K. Mackay
	G-MULT	Beech 76 Duchess	Southern Counties Aviation Ltd
	G-MUMM	Colt 180A balloon	D. K. Hempleman-Davis
	G-MUMY	Vans RV-4	S. D. Howes
	G-MUNI	Mooney M.20J	P. R. Williams
	G-MUPP	Lindstrand LBL-90A balloon	J. A. Viner
	G-MURG	Van's RV-6	Cadmium Lake Ltd
	G-MUSH	Robinson R44 II	Degould Helicopters Ltd
	G-MUSO	Rutan LongEz	D. J. Gay
	G-MUTT	CZAW Sportcruiser	A. M. Griffin
	G-MUTS	Jurca MJ.100 Spitfire	S. M. Johnston & J. E. D. Rogerson (G-CDPM)
	G-MUTZ	Avtech Jabiru J430	N. C. Dean
	G-MUZY	Titan T-51 Mustang (472218:WZ-I)	A. D. Bales
	G-MUZZ	Agusta AW.109SP Grand	Hagondale Ltd
	G-MVAC	CFM Shadow Srs BD	R. G. Place
	G-MVAH	Thruster TST Mk 1	M. W. H. Henton
	G-MVAI	Thruster TST Mk 1	P. J. Houtman
	G-MVAJ	Thruster TST Mk 1	D. Watson
	G-MVAM	CFM Shadow Srs BD	C. P. Barber
	G-MVAN	CFM Shadow Srs BD	R. W. Frost

Reg	Type	Owner or Operator	Notes
G-MVAO	Mainair Gemini/Flash IIA	S. W. Grainger	
G-MVAR	Solar Wings Pegasus XL-R	A. J. Thomas	
G-MVAV	Solar Wings Pegasus XL-R	D. J. Utting	
G-MVAX	Solar Wings Pegasus XL-Q	J. H. Cuthbertson	
G-MVAY	Solar Wings Pegasus XL-Q	V. O. Morris	
G-MVBC	Aerial Arts Tri-Flyer 130SX	D. Beer	
G-MVBJ	Solar Wings Pegasus XL-R	M. Sims	
G-MVBK	Mainair Gemini/Flash IIA	B. R. McLoughlin	
G-MVBN	Mainair Gemini/Flash IIA	S. R. Potts	
G-MVBO	Mainair Gemini/Flash IIA	M. Bailey	
G-MVCA	Solar Wings Pegasus XL-R	R. Walker	
G-MVCC	CFM Shadow Srs BD	Walpole Shadow Group	
G-MVCD	Medway Hybred 44XLR	V. W. Beynon	
G-MVCF	Mainair Gemini/Flash IIA	R. C. Hinds	
G-MVCL	Solar Wings Pegasus XL-Q	T. E. Robinson	
G-MVCR	Solar Wings Pegasus XL-Q	P. Hoeft	
G-MVCS	Solar Wings Pegasus XL-Q	J. J. Sparrow	
G-MVCT	Solar Wings Pegasus XL-Q	G. S. Lampitt	
G-MVCV	Solar Wings Pegasus XL-Q	G. Stewart	
G-MVCW	CFM Shadow Srs BD	D. A. Coupland	
G-MVCZ	Mainair Gemini/Flash IIA	S. G. Roberts	
G-MVDA	Mainair Gemini/Flash IIA	C. Tweedley	
G-MVDE	Thruster TST Mk 1	T. S. Walker	
G-MVDF	Thruster TST Mk 1	G-MVDF Syndicate	
G-MVDH	Thruster TST Mk 1	R. J. Whettem	
G-MVDJ	Medway Hybred 44XLR	W. D. Hutchins	
G-MVDL	Aerial Arts Chaser S	N. P. Lloyd	
G-MVDP	Aerial Arts Chaser S	G. J. Slater	
G-MVDT	Mainair Gemini/Flash IIA	D. C. Stephens	
G-MVDY	Solar Wings Pegasus XL-R	C. G. Murphy	
G-MVEF	Solar Wings Pegasus XL-R	D. M. Pecheur	
G-MVEG	Solar Wings Pegasus XL-R	A. M. Shaw	
G-MVEH	Mainair Gemini/Flash IIA	D. Evans	
G-MVEI	CFM Shadow Srs BD	R. L. Morgan	
G-MVEL	Mainair Gemini/Flash IIA	M. R. Starling	
G-MVEN	CFM Shadow Srs BD	M. R. Garwood	
G-MVER	Mainair Gemini/Flash IIA	J. R. Davis	
G-MVES	Mainair Gemini/Flash IIA	R. M. Rose	
G-MVET	Mainair Gemini/Flash IIA	J. R. Kendall	
G-MVEV	Mainair Gemini/Flash IIA	K. Davies	
G-MVFB	Solar Wings Pegasus XL-Q	M. O. Bloy	
G-MVFD	Solar Wings Pegasus XL-Q	C. D. Humphries	
G-MVFE	Solar Wings Pegasus XL-Q	S. J. Weeks	
G-MVFF	Solar Wings Pegasus XL-Q	A. Makepiece	
G-MVFH	CFM Shadow Srs BD	M. D. Goad	
G-MVFJ	Thruster TST Mk 1	B. E. Reneham	
G-MVFL	Thruster TST Mk 1	E. J. Wallington	
G-MVFM	Thruster TST Mk 1	G. J. Boyer	
G-MVFO	Thruster TST Mk 1	A. Whittaker	
G-MVFX	Thruster TST Mk 1	A. M. Dalgetty	
G-MVGA	Aerial Arts Chaser S	Golf Alpha Group	
G-MVGC	AMF Chevvron 2-32	W. Fletcher	
G-MVGD	AMF Chevvron 2-32	S. C. B. Bruton	
G-MVGF	Aerial Arts Chaser S	P. J. Higgins	
G-MVGG	Aerial Arts Chaser S	J. A. Horn	
G-MVGI	Aerial Arts Chaser S	J. M. Mooney	
G-MVGK	Aerial Arts Chaser S	D. J. Smith	
G-MVGN	Solar Wings Pegasus XL-R	M. J. Smith	
G-MVGO	Solar Wings Pegasus XL-R	J. B. Peacock	
G-MVGP	Solar Wings Pegasus XL-R	J. W. Norman	
G-MVGY	Medway Hybred 44XL	M. Vines	
G-MVGZ	Ultraflight Lazair IIIE	D. M. Broom	
G-MVHB	Powerchute Raider	G. A. Marples	
G-MVHE	Mainair Gemini/Flash IIA	T. J. McMenamin	
G-MVHH	Mainair Gemini/Flash IIA	D. Rowland	
G-MVHI	Thruster TST Mk 1	G. L. Roberts	
G-MVHJ	Thruster TST Mk 1	T. Welch	
G-MVHK	Thruster TST Mk 1	D. J. Gordon	
G-MVHP	Solar Wings Pegasus XL-Q	J. B. Gasson	
G-MVHR	Solar Wings Pegasus XL-Q	J. M. Hucker	
G-MVIB	Mainair Gemini/Flash IIA	LSA Systems	

Notes	Reg	Type	Owner or Operator
	G-MVIE	Aerial Arts Chaser S	C. J. Meadows
	G-MVIF	Medway Raven X	R. J. Webb
	G-MVIG	CFM Shadow Srs BD	M. Roberts
	G-MVIH	Mainair Gemini/Flash IIA	T. M. Gilesnan
	G-MVIL	Noble Hardman Snowbird Mk IV	S. J. Reid
	G-MVIN	Noble Hardman Snowbird Mk.IV	C. P. Dawes
	G-MVIO	Noble Hardman Snowbird Mk.IV	C. R. Taylor
	G-MVIP	AMF Chevvron 232	J. Pool
	G-MVIR	Thruster TST Mk 1	T. Dziadkiewicz
	G-MVIU	Thruster TST Mk 1	G. L. Roberts
	G-MVIV	Thruster TST Mk 1	G. Rainey
	G-MVIX	Mainair Gemini/Flash IIA	S. G. A. Milburn
	G-MVJC	Mainair Gemini/Flash IIA	B. Temple
	G-MVJF	Aerial Arts Chaser S	V. S. Rudham
	G-MVJG	Aerial Arts Chaser S	T. H. Scott
	G-MVJJ	Aerial Arts Chaser S	C. W. Potts
	G-MVJK	Aerial Arts Chaser S	M. P. Lomax
	G-MVJN	Solar Wings Pegasus XL-Q	L. P. Geer
	G-MVJP	Solar Wings Pegasus XL-Q	S. H. Bakowski
	G-MVJU	Solar Wings Pegasus XL-Q	J. C. Sutton
	G-MVKH	Solar Wings Pegasus XL-R	D. J. Higham
	G-MVKJ	Solar Wings Pegasus XL-R	G. V. Warner
	G-MVKK	Solar Wings Pegasus XL-R	G. P. Burns
	G-MVKL	Solar Wings Pegasus XL-R	B. J. Morton
	G-MVKN	Solar Wings Pegasus XL-Q	D. Seiler
	G-MVKO	Solar Wings Pegasus XL-Q	A. R. Hughes
	G-MVKP	Solar Wings Pegasus XL-Q	K. R. Emery
	G-MVKT	Solar Wings Pegasus XL-Q	A. P. Love
	G-MVKU	Solar Wings Pegasus XL-Q	I. K. Priestley
	G-MVKW	Solar Wings Pegasus XL-Q	R. J. Humphries
	G-MVLA	Aerial Arts Chaser S	K. R. Emery
	G-MVLB	Aerial Arts Chaser S	R. P. Wilkinson
	G-MVLC	Aerial Arts Chaser S	B. R. Barnes
	G-MVLD	Aerial Arts Chaser S	J. D. Doran
	G-MVLE	Aerial Arts Chaser S	J. M. Hucker
	G-MVLF	Chaser S 508	A. Matheu/Spain
	G-MVLJ	CFM Shadow Srs B	D. R. C. Pugh
	G-MVLL	Mainair Gemeni/Flash IIA	A. A. Sawera
	G-MVLS	Aerial Arts Chaser S	P. K. Dale
	G-MVLT	Aerial Arts Chaser S	P. H. Newson
	G-MVLX	Solar Wings Pegasus XL-Q	D. J. Harber
	G-MVLY	Solar Wings Pegasus XL-Q	I. B. Osborn
	G-MVMA	Solar Wings Pegasus XL-Q	M. Peters
	G-MVMC	Solar Wings Pegasus XL-Q	I. W. Barlow
	G-MVMG	Thruster TST Mk 1	A. D. McCaldin
	G-MVMI	Thruster TST Mk 1	L. Mayo
	G-MVML	Aerial Arts Chaser S	G. C. Luddington
	G-MVMM	Aerial Arts Chaser S	D. Margereson
	G-MVMR	Mainair Gemini/Flash IIA	P. W. Ramage
	G-MVMT	Mainair Gemini/Flash IIA	R. F. Sanders
	G-MVMW	Mainair Gemini/Flash IIA	G. Jones
	G-MVMX	Mainair Gemini/Flash IIA	E. A. Dygutowicz
	G-MVNA	Powerchute Raider	J. McGoldrick
	G-MVNC	Powerchute Raider	S. T. P. Askew
	G-MVNE	Powerchute Raider	A. E. Askew
	G-MVNK	Powerchute Raider	A. E. Askew
	G-MVNL	Powerchute Raider	E. C. Rhodes
	G-MVNM	Gemini/Flash IIA	C. D. Phillips
	G-MVNP	Aerotech MW5 (K) Sorcerer	A. M. Edwards
	G-MVNR	Aerotech MW5 (K) Sorcerer	E. I. Rowlands-Jones
	G-MVNS	Aerotech MW5 (K) Sorcerer	A. M. Sirant
	G-MVNW	Mainair Gemini/Flash IIA	D. J. Furey
	G-MVNX	Mainair Gemini/Flash IIA	A. R. Lynn
	G-MVNY	Mainair Gemini/Flash IIA	M. K. Buckland
	G-MVNZ	Mainair Gemini/Flash IIA	D. A. Ballard
	G-MVOD	Aerial Arts Chaser 110SX	N. R. Beale
	G-MVOJ	Noble Hardman Snowbird Mk IV	C. D. Beetham
	G-MVON	Mainair Gemini/Flash IIA	D. S. Lally
	G-MVOO	AMF Chevvron 2-32	M. K. Field
	G-MVOP	Aerial Arts Chaser S	D. Thorpe
	G-MVOR	Mainair Gemini/Flash IIA	P. T. & R. M. Jenkins

Reg	Type	Owner or Operator	Notes
G-MVOT	Thruster TST Mk 1	Doyt Ltd	
G-MVOV	Thruster TST Mk 1	I. Garforth	
G-MVPA	Mainair Gemini/Flash IIA	D. Hume	
G-MVPB	Mainair Gemini/Flash IIA	J. M. Breaks	
G-MVPC	Mainair Gemini/Flash IIA	W. O. Flannery	
G-MVPD	Mainair Gemini/Flash IIA	P. Thelwel	
G-MVPF	Medway Hybred 44XLR	G. H. Crick	
G-MVPK	CFM Shadow Srs B	P. Sarfas	
G-MVPM	Whittaker MW6 Merlin	K. W. Curry	
G-MVPN	Whittaker MW6 Merlin	A. M. Field	
G-MVPR	Solar Wings Pegasus XL-Q	D. A. Karniewicz	
G-MVPS	Solar Wings Pegasus XL-Q	G. W. F. J. Dear	
G-MVPW	Solar Wings Pegasus XL-R	C. A. Mitchell	
G-MVPX	Solar Wings Pegasus XL-Q	J. R. Appleton	
G-MVRD	Mainair Gemini/Flash IIA	J. D. Pearce	
G-MVRG	Aerial Arts Chaser S	T. M. Stiles	
G-MVRH	Solar Wings Pegasus XL-Q	K. Farr	
G-MVRI	Solar Wings Pegasus XL-Q	R. J. Pattinson	
G-MVRM	Mainair Gemini/Flash IIA	M. Davidson	
G-MVRO	CFM Shadow Srs CD	K. H. Creed	
G-MVRR	CFM Shadow Srs BD	S. P. Christian	
G-MVRS	CFM Shadow Srs BD ★	Aero Venture	
G-MVRT	CFM Shadow Srs CD	G. M. Cruise-Smith & J. Campbell	
G-MVRW	Solar Wings Pegasus XL-Q	C. A. Hamps	
G-MVRZ	Medway Hybred 44XLR	P. J. Higgins	
G-MVSE	Solar Wings Pegasus XL-Q	T. Wilbor	
G-MVSG	Aerial Arts Chaser S	M. Roberts	
G-MVSI	Medway Hybred 44XLR	R. J. Hood	
G-MVSJ	Aviasud Mistral 532	R. J. Taylor	
G-MVSL	Aerial Arts Chaser 5	D. M. Pearson	
G-MVSO	Mainair Gemini/Flash IIA	M. Larrad	
G-MVSP	Mainair Gemini/Flash IIA	D. R. Buchanan	
G-MVST	Mainair Gemini/Flash IIA	S. R. Stockley	
G-MVTD	Whittaker MW6 Merlin	G. R. Reynolds	
G-MVTF	Aerial Arts Chaser S 447	D. A. Morgan	
G-MVTJ	Solar Wings Pegasus XL-Q	M. P. & R. A. Wells	
G-MVTL	Aerial Arts Chaser S	N. D. Meer	
G-MVTM	Aerial Arts Chaser S	G. L. Davies	
G-MVUA	Mainair Gemini/Flash IIA	K. D. Sinclair-Russell	
G-MVUB	Thruster T.300	A. K. Grayson	
G-MVUC	Medway Hybred 44XLR	B. Pounder	
G-MVUF	Solar Wings Pegasus XL-Q	G. P. Blakemore	
G-MVUG	Solar Wings Pegasus XL-Q	R. A. Allen	
G-MVUI	Solar Wings Pegasus XL-Q	P. E. Hadley & K. Casserley	
G-MVUJ	Solar Wings Pegasus XL-Q	N. Huxtable	
G-MVUO	AMF Chevvron 2-32	W. D. M. Turtle	
G-MVUP	Aviasud Mistral 532GB	D. J. Brightman	
G-MVUS	Aerial Arts Chaser S	H. Poyzer	
G-MVUU	Hornet ZA	K. W. Warn	
G-MVVI	Medway Hybred 44XLR	C. J. Turner	
G-MVVK	Solar Wings Pegasus XL-R	A. J. Weir	
G-MVVO	Solar Wings Pegasus XL-Q	A. L. Scarlett	
G-MVVT	CFM Shadow Srs CD	P. L. Naylor	
G-MVVV	AMF Chevvron 2-32	J. S. Firth	
G-MVVZ	Powerchute Raider	G. A. Marples	
G-MVWJ	Powerchute Raider	N. J. Doubek	
G-MVWN	Thruster T.300	R. D. Leigh	
G-MVWR	Thruster T.300	G. Rainey	
G-MVWS	Thruster T.300	R. J. Hunphries	
G-MVWW	Aviasud Mistral	S. Wood & S. G. A. Milburn	
G-MVXA	Brewster I MW6 (modified SS)	J. C. Gates	
G-MVXC	Mainair Gemini/Flash IIA	A. Worthington	
G-MVXJ	Medway Hybred 44XLR	P. J. Wilks	
G-MVXN	Aviasud Mistral	P. W. Cade	
G-MVXP	Aerial Arts Chaser S	C. Surman	
G-MVXR	Mainair Gemini/Flash IIA	D. M. Bayne	
G-MVXV	Aviasud Mistral	D. L. Chalk & G. S. Jefferies	
G-MVXX	AMF Chevvron 232	T. R. James	
G-MVYC	Solar Wings Pegasus XL-Q	P. E. L. Street	
G-MVYD	Solar Wings Pegasus XL-Q	J. S. Hawkins	
G-MVYE	Thruster TST Mk 1	M. J. Aubrey	

Notes	Reg	Type	Owner or Operator
	G-MVYI	Hornet R-ZA	K. W. Warn
	G-MVYT	Noble Hardman Snowbird Mk IV	P. Asbridge
	G-MVYU	Snowbird MV.IV (modified)	R. P. Tribe
	G-MVYV	Noble Hardman Snowbird Mk IV	D. W. Hayden
	G-MVYW	Noble Hardman Snowbird Mk IV	T. J. Harrison
	G-MVYX	Noble Hardman Snowbird Mk IV	R. McBlain
	G-MVYY	Aerial Arts Chaser S508	G. H. Crick
	G-MVYZ	CFM Shadow Series BD	D. H. Lewis
	G-MVZA	Thruster T.300	A. I. Milne
	G-MVZC	Thruster T.300	S. Dougan
	G-MVZD	Thruster T.300	J. Chapman
	G-MVZE	Thruster T.300	T. L. Davis
	G-MVZI	Thruster T.300	R. W. Skelton
	G-MVZL	Solar Wings Pegasus XL-Q	P. R. Dobson
	G-MVZM	Aerial Arts Chaser S	P. Leigh
	G-MVZO	Medway Hybred 44XLR	S. J. Taft
	G-MVZP	Murphy Renegade Spirit UK	The North American Syndicate
	G-MVZS	Mainair Gemini/Flash IIA	R. L. Beese
	G-MVZT	Solar Wings Pegasus XL-Q	C. J. Meadows
	G-MVZU	Solar Wings Pegasus XL-Q	R. D. Proctor
	G-MVZV	Solar Wings Pegasus XL-Q	K. Mudra
	G-MVZX	Renegade Spirit UK	G. Holmes
	G-MVZZ	AMF Chevvron 232	W. A. L. Mitchell
	G-MWAB	Mainair Gemini/Flash IIA	J. E. Buckley
	G-MWAC	Solar Wings Pegasus XL-Q	H. Lloyd-Hughes & D. Jones
	G-MWAE	CFM Shadow Srs BD	M. D. Brown
	G-MWAJ	Murphy Renegade Spirit UK	L. D. Blair
	G-MWAN	Thruster T.300	M. Jady
	G-MWAT	Solar Wings Pegasus XL-Q	C. A. Reid
	G-MWBI	Medway Hybred 44XLR	G. E. Coates
	G-MWBJ	Medway Sprint	C. C. Strong
	G-MWBP	Hornet R-ZA	Foston Hornet Group
	G-MWBS	Hornet RS-ZA	P. D. Jaques
	G-MWBT	Hornet R-ZA	W. Finley & K. W. Warn
	G-MWBY	Hornet RS-ZA	IP Rights Ltd
	G-MWCC	Solar Wings Pegasus XL-R	I. K. Priestley
	G-MWCE	Mainair Gemini/Flash IIA	B. A. Tooze
	G-MWCF	Solar Wings Pegasus XL-R	S. P. Tkaczyk
	G-MWCG	Microflight Spectrum (modified)	C. Ricketts
	G-MWCH	Rans S.6 Coyote	D. C. & P. R. Smith
	G-MWCK	Powerchute Kestrel	A. E. Askew
	G-MWCL	Powerchute Kestrel	R. W. Twamley
	G-MWCM	Powerchute Kestrel	J. R. Hewitt
	G-MWCN	Powerchute Kestrel	A. E. Askew
	G-MWCO	Powerchute Kestrel	J. R. E. Gladstone
	G-MWCP	Powerchute Kestrel	A. E. Askew
	G-MWCS	Powerchute Kestrel	S. T. P. Askew
	G-MWCY	Medway Hybred 44XLR	J. K. Masters
	G-MWCZ	Medway Hybed 44XLR	D. Botha
	G-MWDB	CFM Shadow Srs BD	T. D. Dawson
	G-MWDI	Hornet RS-ZA	K. W. Warn
	G-MWDK	Solar Wings Pegasus XL-R	J. E. Merriman & D. R. Western
	G-MWDL	Solar Wings Pegasus XL-R	M. J. Pearson
	G-MWDN	CFM Shadow Srs BD	J. P. Bath
	G-MWDS	Thruster T.300	A. W. Nancarrow
	G-MWDZ	Eipper Quicksilver MXL II	R. G. Cook
	G-MWEG	Solar Wings Pegasus XL-Q	S. P. Michlig
	G-MWEH	Solar Wings Pegasus XL-Q	K. A. Davidson
	G-MWEK	Whittaker MW5 Sorcerer	D. W. & M. L. Squire
	G-MWEL	Mainair Gemini/Flash IIA	D. R. Spencer
	G-MWEN	CFM Shadow Srs BD	C. Dawn
	G-MWEO	Whittaker MW5 Sorcerer	P. M. Quinn
	G-MWEP	Rans S.4 Coyote	E. J. Wallington
	G-MWER	Solar Wings Pegasus XL-Q	The Microlight School (Lichfield) Ltd
	G-MWES	Rans S.4 Coyote	A. R. Dobrowolski
	G-MWEZ	CFM Shadow Srs CD	G-MWEZ Group
	G-MWFA	Solar Wings Pegasus XL-R	D. G. Shaw
	G-MWFD	TEAM mini-MAX	J. T. Blackburn
	G-MWFF	Rans S.4 Coyote	P. J. Greenrod
	G-MWFL	Powerchute Kestrel	G. A. Marples

Reg	Type	Owner or Operator	Notes
G-MWFS	Solar Wings Pegasus XL-Q	D. R. Williams	
G-MWFT	MBA Tiger Cub 440	J. R. Ravenhill	
G-MWFU	Quad City Challenger II UK	C. J. Whittaker	
G-MWFV	Quad City Challenger II UK	M. Liptrot	
G-MWFW	Rans S.4 Coyote	C. Dewhurst	
G-MWFX	Quad City Challenger II UK	I. M. Walton	
G-MWFY	Quad City Challenger II UK	C. C. B. Soden	
G-MWGI	Whittaker MW5 (K) Sorcerer	J. Aley	
G-MWGJ	Whittaker MW5 (K) Sorcerer	I. Pearson	
G-MWGK	Whittaker MW5 (K) Sorcerer	R. J. Cook	
G-MWGL	Solar Wings Pegasus XL-Q	F. McGlynn	
G-MWGM	Solar Wings Pegasus XL-Q	I. Davis	
G-MWGN	Rans S.4 Coyote II	V. Hallam	
G-MWGR	Solar Wings Pegasus XL-Q	M. Jady	
G-MWHF	Solar Wings Pegasus XL-Q	N. J. Troke	
G-MWHG	Solar Wings Pegasus XL-Q	M. D. Morris	
G-MWHH	TEAM mini-MAX	R. J. Hood	
G-MWHI	Mainair Gemini/Flash	P. Harwood	
G-MWHL	Solar Wings Pegasus XL-Q	G. J. Eaton	
G-MWHM	Whittaker MW6-6	K. R. Emery	
G-MWHO	Mainair Gemini/Flash IIA	J. J. Jackson	
G-MWHP	Rans S.6-ESD Coyote	P. G. Angus	
G-MWHR	Mainair Gemini/Flash IIA	J. E. S. Harter	
G-MWHX	Solar Wings Pegasus XL-Q	N. P. Kelly	
G-MWIA	Mainair Gemini/Flash IIA	A. Evans	
G-MWIB	Aviasud Mistral	P. Brady	
G-MWIC	Whittaker MW5-C Sorcerer	P. J. Cheyney	
G-MWIF	Rans S.6-ESD Coyote II	K. Kelly	
G-MWIG	Mainair Gemini/Flash IIA	A. P. Purbrick	
G-MWIM	Solar Wings Pegasus Quasar	M. C. Keeley	
G-MWIP	Whittaker MW6 Merlin	B. J. Merret & D. Beer	
G-MWIS	Solar Wings Pegasus XL-Q	P. G. Strangward	
G-MWIU	Pegasus Quasar TC	W. Hepburn	
G-MWIX	Solar Wings Pegasus Quasar	G. Hawes	
G-MWIZ	CFM Shadow Srs BD	T. A. England	
G-MWJF	CFM Shadow Srs BD	T. de B. Gardner	
G-MWJH	Solar Wings Pegasus Quasar	L. A. Hosegood	
G-MWJI	Solar Wings Pegasus Quasar	M. G. J. Bridges	
G-MWJJ	Solar Wings Pegasus Quasar	P. Darcy	
G-MWJN	Solar Wings Pegasus XL-Q	J. C. Corrall	
G-MWJR	Medway Hybred 44XLR	T. G. Almond	
G-MWJT	Solar Wings Pegasus Quasar	F. McGlynn	
G-MWKE	Hornet R-ZA	D. R. Stapleton	
G-MWKX	Microflight Spectrum	C. R. Ions	
G-MWLD	CFM Shadow Srs BD	M. P. Holdstock	
G-MWLE	Solar Wings Pegasus XL-R	D. Stevenson	
G-MWLG	Solar Wings Pegasus XL-R	C. Cohen	
G-MWLK	Solar Wings Pegasus Quasar	D. T. Page	
G-MWLL	Solar Wings Pegasus XL-Q	A. J. Bacon	
G-MWLN	Whittaker MW6-S Fatboy Flyer	S. J. Field	
G-MWLP	Mainair Gemini/Flash IIA	K. M. Husecken	
G-MWLS	Medway Hybred 44XLR	M. A. Oliver	
G-MWLU	Solar Wings Pegasus XL-R	T. P. G. Ward	
G-MWLW	TEAM mini-MAX	E. J. Oteng	
G-MWLX	Mainair Gemini/Flash IIA	G-MWLX Syndicate	
G-MWLZ	Rans S.4 Coyote	Hedge Hopper Flying Group	
G-MWMB	Powerchute Kestrel	S. T. P. Askew	
G-MWMC	Powerchute Kestrel	S. T. P. Askew	
G-MWMD	Powerchute Kestrel	S. T. P. Askew	
G-MWMF	Powerchute Kestrel	P. J. Blundell	
G-MWMH	Powerchute Kestrel	E. W. Potts	
G-MWMI	SolarWings Pegasus Quasar	R. A. Khosravi	
G-MWML	SolarWings Pegasus Quasar	F. A. Collar	
G-MWMM	Mainair Gemini/Flash IIA	D. R. Langton	
G-MWMN	Solar Wings Pegasus XL-Q	P. A. Arnold & N. A. Rathbone	
G-MWMO	Solar Wings Pegasus XL-Q	D. S. F. McNair	
G-MWMV	Solar Wings Pegasus XL-R	M. Nutting	
G-MWMW	Renegade Spirit UK	D. M. Casey	
G-MWMX	Mainair Gemini/Flash IIA	P. G. Hughes/Ireland	
G-MWMY	Mainair Gemini/Flash IIA	G. R. Walker	
G-MWNB	Solar Wings Pegasus XL-Q	P. F. J. Rogers	

Notes	Reg	Type	Owner or Operator
	G-MWND	Tiger Cub Developments RL.5A	D. A. Pike
	G-MWNE	Mainair Gemini/Flash IIA	D. N. Brocklesby & S. D. P. Bridge
	G-MWNF	Renegade Spirit UK	R. Haslam
	G-MWNK	Solar Wings Pegasus Quasar	N. Brigginshaw
	G-MWNL	Solar Wings Pegasus Quasar	N. H. S. Install
	G-MWNO	AMF Chevvron 232	J. R. Milnes
	G-MWNP	AMF Chevvron 232	M. K. Field
	G-MWNR	Renegade Spirit UK	RJR Flying Group
	G-MWNS	Mainair Gemini/Flash IIA	P. Carroll
	G-MWNU	Mainair Gemini/Flash IIA	C. C. Muir
	G-MWOC	Powerchute Kestrel	A. Evans
	G-MWOD	Powerchute Kestrel	T. Morgan
	G-MWOI	Solar Wings Pegasus XL-R	B. T. Geoghegan
	G-MWON	CFM Shadow Series CD	D. A. Crosbie
	G-MWOO	Renegade Spirit UK	R. C. Wood
	G-MWOR	Solar Wings Pegasus XL-Q	G. W. F. J. Dear
	G-MWOV	Whittaker MW6 Merlin	D. J. Brown
	G-MWPB	Mainair Gemini/Flash IIA	J. Fenton & S. G. Roberts
	G-MWPD	Mainair Gemini/Flash IIA	A. Vaughan
	G-MWPE	Solar Wings Pegasus XL-Q	E. C. R. Hudson
	G-MWPF	Mainair Gemini/Flash IIA	G. P. Taggart
	G-MWPH	Microflight Spectrum	C. G. Chambers
	G-MWPN	CFM Shadow Srs CD	W. R. H. Thomas
	G-MWPO	Mainair Gemini/Flash IIA	W. Anderson
	G-MWPP	CFM Streak Shadow	P. A. Wilman
	G-MWPR	Whittaker MW6 Merlin	S. F. N. Warnell
	G-MWPU	Solar Wings Pegasus Quasar TC	P. R. Murdock
	G-MWPX	Solar Wings Pegasus XL-R	R. J. Wheeler
	G-MWPZ	Renegade Spirit UK	J. levers
	G-MWRC	Mainair Gemini/Flash IIA	T. Karczewski
	G-MWRD	Mainair Gemini/Flash IIA	D. Morton
	G-MWRE	Mainair Gemini/Flash IIA	Kendal College
	G-MWRF	Mainair Gemini/Flash IIA	N. Hay
	G-MWRH	Mainair Gemini/Flash IIA	K. J. Hughes
	G-MWRJ	Mainair Gemini/Flash IIA	M. Dibben
	G-MWRL	CFM Shadow Srs.CD	A. M. Morris
	G-MWRN	Solar Wings Pegasus XL-R	Malvern Aerotow Club
	G-MWRS	Ultravia Super Pelican	T. B. Woolley
	G-MWRT	Solar Wings Pegasus XL-R	G. L. Gunnell
	G-MWRY	CFM Shadow Srs CD	A. T. Armstrong
	G-MWSA	TEAM mini-MAX	A. R. Stratton
	G-MWSC	Rans S.6-ESD Coyote II	E. J. D. Heathfield
	G-MWSD	Solar Wings Pegasus XL-Q	A. M. Harley
	G-MWSF	Solar Wings Pegasus XL-R	J. J. Freeman
	G-MWSI	Solar Wings Pegasus Quasar TC	M. B. Sears
	G-MWSJ	Solar Wings Pegasus XL-Q	R. J. Collison
	G-MWSK	Solar Wings Pegasus XL-Q	J. Doogan
	G-MWSM	Mainair Gemini/Flash IIA	R. M. Wall
	G-MWSO	Solar Wings Pegasus XL-R	M. A. Clayton
	G-MWSP	Solar Wings Pegasus XL-R	J. S. Hawkins
	G-MWST	Medway Hybred 44XLR	A. Ferguson
	G-MWSU	Medway Hybred 44XLR	T. De Landro
	G-MWSW	Whittaker MW6 Merlin	S. F. N. Warnell
	G-MWSX	Whittaker MW5 Sorcerer	A. T. Armstrong
	G-MWSY	Whittaker MW5 Sorcerer	J. E. Holloway
	G-MWSZ	CFM Shadow Srs CD	M. W. W. Clotworthy
	G-MWTC	Solar Wings Pegasus XL-Q	M. M. Chittenden
	G-MWTI	Solar Wings Pegasus XL-Q	J. G. Hilliard
	G-MWTJ	CFM Shadow Srs CS	Shadow Tango Juliet Group
	G-MWTL	Solar Wings Pegasus XL-R	B. Lindsay
	G-MWTN	CFM Shadow Srs CD	M. J. Broom
	G-MWTO	Mainair Gemini/Flash IIA	M. B. Ryder-Jarvis
	G-MWTP	CFM Shadow Srs CD	P. J. F. Spedding
	G-MWTT	Rans S.6-ESD Coyote II	L. E. Duffin
	G-MWTZ	Mainair Gemini/Flash IIA	C. W. R. Felce
	G-MWUA	CFM Shadow Srs CD	P. A. James
	G-MWUD	Solar Wings Pegasus XL-R	A. J. Weir
	G-MWUI	AMF Chevvron 2-32C	Group G-MWUI
	G-MWUK	Rans S.6-ESD Coyote II	G. K. Hoult
	G-MWUL	Rans S.6-ESD Coyote II	D. M. Bayne
	G-MWUN	Rans S.6-ESD Coyote II	J. Parke

Reg	Type	Owner or Operator	Notes
G-MWUR	Solar Wings Pegasus XL-R	Scottish Hang Gliding Club	
G-MWUU	Solar Wings Pegasus XL-R	B. R. Underwood	
G-MWUV	Solar Wings Pegasus XL-R	XL Group	
G-MWUW	Solar Wings Pegasus XL-R	Ultraflight Microlights Ltd	
G-MWUX	Solar Wings Pegasus XL-Q	B. D. Attwell	
G-MWVA	Solar Wings Pegasus XL-Q	W. Frosina	
G-MWVE	Solar Wings Pegasus XL-R	W. A. Keel-Stocker	
G-MWVF	Solar Wings Pegasus XL-R	J. B. Wright	
G-MWVG	CFM Shadow Srs CD	Shadow Aviation Ltd	
G-MWVH	CFM Shadow Srs CD	M. McKenzie	
G-MWVL	Rans S.6-ESD Coyote II	J. C. Gates	
G-MWVM	Solar Wings Pegasus Quasar II	A. A. Edmonds	
G-MWVO	Mainair Gemini/Flash IIA	W. W. Hammond	
G-MWVP	Renegade Spirit UK	P. D. Mickleburgh	
G-MWVT	Mainair Gemini/Flash IIA	P. J. Newman	
G-MWVZ	Mainair Gemini/Flash IIA	R. W. Twamley	
G-MWWB	Mainair Gemini/Flash IIA	W. P. Seward	
G-MWWC	Mainair Gemini/Flash IIA	D. & A. Margereson	
G-MWWD	Renegade Spirit	T. P. Nettleton	
G-MWWH	Solar Wings Pegasus XL-Q	R. G. Wall	
G-MWWI	Mainair Gemini/Flash IIA	M. A. S. Nesbitt	
G-MWWN	Mainair Gemini/Flash IIA	M. M. Pope	
G-MWWS	Thruster T.300	J. H. Milne	
G-MWWV	Solar Wings Pegasus XL-Q	R. W. Livingstone	
G-MWWZ	Cyclone Chaser S	P. K. Dale	
G-MWXF	Mainair Mercury	D. McAuley	
G-MWXH	Solar Wings Pegasus Quasar IITC	R. P. Wilkinson	
G-MWXJ	Mainair Mercury	P. J. Taylor	
G-MWXK	Mainair Mercury	M. P. Wilkinson	
G-MWXP	Solar Wings Pegasus XL-Q	A. P. Attfield	
G-MWXV	Mainair Gemini/Flash IIA	T. A. Daniel	
G-MWXX	Cyclone Chaser S 447	P. I. Frost	
G-MWXY	Cyclone Chaser S 447	D. Curtis	
G-MWXZ	Cyclone Chaser S 508	D. L. Hadley	
G-MWYA	Mainair Gemini/Flash IIA	R. F. Hunt	
G-MWYC	Solar Wings Pegasus XL-Q (modified)	D. W. Curtis	
G-MWYD	CFM Shadow Srs C	W. J. I. Robb	
G-MWYE	Rans S.6-ESD Coyote II	G. A. M. Moffat	
G-MWYG	Mainair Gemini/Flash IIA	J. H. McIvor	
G-MWYI	Solar Wings Pegasus Quasar II	T. J. Lundie	
G-MWYJ	Solar Wings Pegasus Quasar II	A. Clarke & L. B. Hughes	
G-MWYL	Mainair Gemini/Flash IIA	A. J. Hinks	
G-MWYM	Cyclone Chaser S 1000	C. J. Meadows	
G-MWYS	CGS Hawk 1 Arrow	Civilair	
G-MWYT	Mainair Gemini/Flash IIA	P. K. Morley & A. J. Geary	
G-MWYU	Solar Wings Pegasus XL-Q	J. S. Hawkins	
G-MWYV	Mainair Gemini/Flash IIA	R. Bricknell	
G-MWYY	Mainair Gemini/Flash IIA	R. D. Allard	
G-MWZA	Mainair Mercury	M. Willan	
G-MWZB	AMF Microlight Chevvron 2-32C	E. Ratcliffe	
G-MWZF	Solar Wings Pegasus Quasar IITC	I. A. Macadam	
G-MWZJ	Solar Wings Pegasus XL-R	P. Kitchen	
G-MWZL	Mainair Gemini/Flash IIA	D. Renton	
G-MWZO	Solar Wings Pegasus Quasar IITC	A. Robinson	
G-MWZP	Solar Wings Pegasus Quasar IITC	C. Garton	
G-MWZR	Solar Wings Pegasus Quasar IITC	R. Veart	
G-MWZS	Solar Wings Pegasus Quasar IITC	A. M. Charlton	
G-MWZU	Solar Wings Pegasus XL-R	K. J. Slater	
G-MWZY	Solar Wings Pegasus XL-R	Darley Moor Airsports Club Ltd	
G-MWZZ	Solar Wings Pegasus XL-R	The Microlight School (Lichfield) Ltd	
G-MXII	Pitts Model 12	P. T. Borchert	
G-MXMX	PA-46R-350T Malibu Matrix	Feabrex Ltd	
G-MXPH	BAC.167 Strikemaster Mk 84 (311)	R. S. Partridge-Hicks (G-SARK)	
G-MXPI	Robinson R44 II	MG Group Ltd (G-CGAE)	
G-MXVI	VS.361 Spitfire LF.XVIe (TE184:D)	S. R. Stead	
G-MYAB	Solar Wings Pegasus XL-R	A. N. F. Stewart	
G-MYAC	Solar Wings Pegasus XL-Q	M. E. Gilman	
G-MYAF	Solar Wings Pegasus XL-Q	J. H. S. Booth	
G-MYAH	Whittaker MW5 Sorcerer	A. R. Hawes	

Notes	Reg	Type	Owner or Operator
	G-MYAI	Mainair Mercury	J. Ellerton
	G-MYAN	Whittaker MW5 (K) Sorcerer	A. F. Reid
	G-MYAO	Mainair Gemini/Flash IIA	K. R. Emery
	G-MYAR	Thruster T.300	G. Hawkins
	G-MYAS	Mainair Gemini/Flash IIA	J. R. Davis
	G-MYAT	TEAM mini-MAX	T. J. Bates
	G-MYAZ	Renegade Spirit UK	R. Smith
	G-MYBA	Rans S.6-ESD Coyote II	A. M. Hughes
	G-MYBB	Maxair UK Drifter	M. Ingleton
	G-MYBC	CFM Shadow Srs CD	P. C. H. Clarke
	G-MYBF	Solar Wings Pegasus XL-Q	S. J. Hillyard
	G-MYBJ	Mainair Gemini/Flash IIA	G. C. Bowers
	G-MYBM	TEAM mini-MAX	B. Hunter
	G-MYBR	Solar Wings Pegasus XL-Q	M. J. Larbey & G. T. Hunt
	G-MYBT	Solar Wings Pegasus Quasar IITC	G. A. Rainbow-Ockwell
	G-MYBU	Cyclone Chaser S 447	P. L. Wilkinson
	G-MYBW	Solar Wings Pegasus XL-Q	J. S. Chapman
	G-MYCA	Whittaker MW6 Merlin	C. M. Byford
	G-MYCB	Cyclone Chaser S 447	S. D. Voysey
	G-MYCE	Solar Wings Pegasus Quasar IITC	S. W. Barker
	G-MYCJ	Mainair Mercury	D. W. B. Aitken
	G-MYCK	Mainair Gemini/Flash IIA	A. W. Dunn
	G-MYCL	Mainair Mercury	P. B. Cole
	G-MYCM	CFM Shadow Srs CD	A. K. Robinson
	G-MYCO	Renegade Spirit UK	T. P. Williams
	G-MYCP	Whittaker MW6 Merlin	K. R. Emery
	G-MYCR	Mainair Gemini/Flash IIA	A. P. King
	G-MYCS	Mainair Gemini/Flash IIA	M. J. Rankin
	G-MYCT	Team Minimax 91	N. L. Owen
	G-MYCX	Powerchute Kestrel	S. J. Pugh-Jones
	G-MYDA	Powerchute Kestrel	A. E. Askew
	G-MYDC	Mainair Mercury	D. Moore
	G-MYDD	CFM Shadow Srs CD	C. H. Gem/Spain
	G-MYDE	CFM Shadow Srs CD	D. N. L. Howell
	G-MYDF	TEAM mini-MAX	J. L. Barker
	G-MYDJ	Solar Wings Pegasus XL-R	Cambridgeshire Aerotow Club
	G-MYDK	Rans S.6-ESD Coyote II	J. W. Caush & K. Southam
	G-MYDN	Quad City Challenger II	J. E. Barlow
	G-MYDP	Kolb Twinstar Mk 3	Norberts Flying Group
	G-MYDR	Thruster Tn.300	H. G. Soper
	G-MYDT	Thruster T.300	A. J. L. Eves
	G-MYDU	Thruster T.300	S. Collins
	G-MYDV	Mainair Gemini /Flash IIA	S. J. Mazilis
	G-MYDX	Rans S.6-ESD Coyote II	A. Tucker
	G-MYDZ	Mignet HM.1000 Balerit	D. S. Simpson
	G-MYEA	Solar Wings Pegasus XL-Q	A. M. Taylor
	G-MYEI	Cyclone Chaser S447	D. J. Hyatt
	G-MYEJ	Cyclone Chaser S447	A. W. Lowrie
	G-MYEK	Solar Wings Pegasus Quasar IITC	The Microlight School (Lichfield) Ltd
	G-MYEM	Solar Wings Pegasus Quasar IITC	D. J. Moore
	G-MYEN	Solar Wings Pegasus Quasar IITC	T. J. Feeney
	G-MYEO	Solar Wings Pegasus Quasar IITC	A. R. Young
	G-MYEP	CFM Shadow Srs. CD	S. A. Taylor
	G-MYER	Cyclone AX3/503	T. F. Horrocks
	G-MYFA	Powerchute Kestrel	M. Phillips
	G-MYFL	Solar Wings Pegasus Quasar IITC	C. C. Wright
	G-MYFO	Cyclone Airsports Chaser S	M. H. Broadbent
	G-MYFP	Mainair Gemini/Flash IIA	A. O'Connor
	G-MYFT	Mainair Scorcher	E. Kirkby
	G-MYFV	Cyclone AX3/503	I. J. Webb
	G-MYFW	Cyclone AX3/503	Microlight School (Lichfield) Ltd
	G-MYGD	Cyclone AX3/503	G. M. R. Keenan
	G-MYGF	TEAM mini-MAX	W. P. Seward
	G-MYGK	Cyclone Chaser S 508	P. C. Collins
	G-MYGM	Quad City Challenger II	S. J. Luck
	G-MYGO	CFM ShadowSrs CD	D. B. Bullard
	G-MYGP	Rans S.6-ESD Coyote II	J. Cook
	G-MYGR	Rans S.6-ESD Coyote II	F. C. J. Denton
	G-MYGT	Solar Wings Pegasus XL-R	Condors Aerotow Syndicate
	G-MYGU	Solar Wings Pegasus XL-R	J. A. Sims
	G-MYGV	Solar Wings Pegasus XL-R	J. A. Crofts & G. M. Birkett

Reg	Type	Owner or Operator	Notes
G-MYGZ	Mainair Gemini/Flash IIA	I. N. Blanchard	
G-MYHG	Cyclone AX/503	N. P. Thomson	
G-MYHI	Rans S.6-ESD Coyote II	I. J. Steele	
G-MYHJ	Cyclone AX3/503	M. J. Buchanan	
G-MYHK	Rans S.6-ESD Coyote II	M. R. Williamson	
G-MYHL	Mainair Gemini/Flash IIA	O. G. Houghton	
G-MYHM	Cyclone AX3/503	G-MYHM Group	
G-MYHN	Mainair Gemini/Flash IIA	H. J. Timms	
G-MYHP	Rans S.6-ESD Coyote II	D. M. Smith	
G-MYHR	Cyclone AX3/503	C. W. Williams	
G-MYIA	Quad City Challenger II	I. Pearson	
G-MYIF	CFM Shadow Srs CD	P. J. Edwards	
G-MYIH	Mainair Gemini/Flash IIA	T. L. T. Sheldrick	
G-MYII	TEAM mini-MAX	G. H. Crick	
G-MYIK	Kolb Twinstar Mk 3	M. Khalid	
G-MYIL	Cyclone Chaser S 508	R. A. Rawes	
G-MYIN	Solar Wings Pegasus Quasar IITC	W. P. Hughes	
G-MYIP	CFM Shadow Srs CD	D. R. G. Whitelaw	
G-MYIR	Rans S.6-ESD Coyote II	M. L. Foden	
G-MYIS	Rans S.6-ESD Coyote II	I. S. Everett & M. Stott	
G-MYIT	Cyclone Chaser S 508	R. Barringer	
G-MYIU	Cyclone AX3/503	Ulster Seaplane Association Ltd	
G-MYIV	Mainair Gemini/Flash IIA	P. Norton & T. Williams	
G-MYIY	Mainair Gemini/Flash IIA	D. Jackson	
G-MYIZ	TEAM mini-MAX 2	J. C. Longmore	
G-MYJC	Mainair Gemini/Flash IIA	M. N. Irven	
G-MYJD	Rans S.6-ESD Coyote II	A. G. Vallis	
G-MYJF	Thruster T.300	P. F. McConville	
G-MYJG	Thruster T.300	J. W. Rice	
G-MYJJ	Solar Wings Pegasus Quasar IITC	S. J. Reader	
G-MYJK	Solar Wings Pegasus Quasar IITC	The Microlight School (Lichfield) Ltd	
G-MYJM	Mainair Gemini/Flash IIA	J. G. Treanor	
G-MYJT	Solar Wings Pegasus Quasar IITC	S. Ferguson	
G-MYJU	Solar Wings Pegasus Quasar IITC	C. Lamb	
G-MYJZ	Whittaker MW5D Sorcerer	P. A. Aston	
G-MYKB	Kolb Twinstar Mk 3	T. Antell	
G-MYKD	Cyclone Chaser S 508	S. D. Pain	
G-MYKE	CFM Shadow Srs BD	MKH Engineering	
G-MYKF	Cyclone AX3/503	M. A. Collins	
G-MYKG	Mainair Gemini/Flash IIA	B. D. Walker	
G-MYKH	Mainair Gemini/Flash IIA	A. W. Leadley	
G-MYKJ	TEAM mini-MAX	D. R. Baker	
G-MYKO	Whittaker MW6-S Fat Boy Flyer	J. A. Weston	
G-MYKR	Solar Wings Pegasus Quasar IITC	C. Stallard	
G-MYKS	Solar Wings Pegasus Quasar IITC	D. J. Oskis	
G-MYKV	Mainair Gemini/Flash IIA	P. J. Gulliver	
G-MYKX	Mainair Mercury	K. Medd	
G-MYKY	Mainair Mercury	P. M. Kelsey	
G-MYKZ	TEAM mini-MAX	J. Batchelor	
G-MYLC	Solar Wings Pegasus Quantum 15	C. McKay	
G-MYLD	Rans S.6-ESD Coyote II	A. W. Nancarrow	
G-MYLE	Solar Wings Pegasus Quantum 15	Quantum Quartet	
G-MYLF	Rans S.6-ESD Coyote II	A. J. Spencer	
G-MYLG	Mainair Gemini/Flash IIA	N. J. Axworthy	
G-MYLH	Solar Wings Pegasus Quantum 15	D. Parsons	
G-MYLI	Solar Wings Pegasus Quantum 15	A. M. Keyte	
G-MYLM	Solar Wings Pegasus Quasar IITC	R. G. Hearsey	
G-MYLN	Kolb Twinstar Mk 3	J. F. Joyes	
G-MYLO	Rans S.6-ESD Coyote II	M. D. Morris	
G-MYLR	Mainair Gemini/Flash IIA	A. L. Lyall	
G-MYLS	Mainair Mercury	W. K. C. Davies	
G-MYLT	Mainair Blade	T. D. Hall	
G-MYLV	CFM Shadow Srs CD	Aviation for Paraplegics and Tetraplegics Trust	
G-MYLW	Rans S6-ESD	A. D. Dias	
G-MYLX	Medway Raven	K. Hayley	
G-MYMB	Solar Wings Pegasus Quantum 15	D. B. Jones	
G-MYMC	Solar Wings Pegasus Quantum 15	I. A. Macadam	
G-MYMH	Rans S.6-ESD Coyote II	R. W. Keene	
G-MYMI	Kolb Twinstar Mk.3	F. J. Brown	
G-MYMJ	Medway Raven	N. Brigginshaw	
G-MYMK	Mainair Gemini/Flash IIA	C. L. M. Haywood	

Notes	Reg	Type	Owner or Operator
	G-MYML	Mainair Mercury	D. J. Dalley
	G-MYMM	Ultraflight Fun 18S	N. P. Power
	G-MYMN	Whittaker MW6 Merlin	R. E. Arnold
	G-MYMS	Rans S.6-ESD Coyote II	C. G. Chambers
	G-MYMV	Mainair Gemini/Flash IIA	A. J. Evans
	G-MYMW	Cyclone AX3/503	D. I. Lee
	G-MYMZ	Cyclone AX3/503	Microlight School (Lichfield) Ltd
	G-MYNB	Solar Wings Pegasus Quantum 15	L. Myford
	G-MYND	Mainair Gemini/Flash IIA	D. J. Morrell
	G-MYNE	Rans S.6 Coyote II	J. L. Smoker
	G-MYNF	Mainair Mercury	S. Carter
	G-MYNI	TEAM mini-MAX	I. Pearson
	G-MYNK	Solar Wings Pegasus Quantum 15	M. T. Cain
	G-MYNL	Solar Wings Pegasus Quantum 15	I. J. Rawlingson
	G-MYNN	Solar Wings Pegasus Quantum 15	V. Loy
	G-MYNP	Solar Wings Pegasus Quantum 15	K. A. Davidson
	G-MYNR	Solar Wings Pegasus Quantum 15	S. F. Winter
	G-MYNS	Solar Wings Pegasus Quantum 15	W. R. Furness
	G-MYNT	Solar Wings Pegasus Quantum 15	N. Ionita
	G-MYNV	Solar Wings Pegasus Quantum 15	J. Goldsmith-Ryan
	G-MYNX	CFM Streak Shadow SA	S. P. Fletcher
	G-MYNY	Kolb Twinstar Mk 3	A. Vaughan
	G-MYNZ	Solar Wings Pegasus Quantum 15	P. W. Rogers
	G-MYOA	Rans S6-ESD Coyote II	T. Briton
	G-MYOG	Kolb Twinstar Mk 3	T. A. Womersley
	G-MYOH	CFM Shadow Srs CD	D. R. Sutton
	G-MYOL	Air Creation Fun 18S GTBIS	S. N. Bond
	G-MYON	CFM Shadow Srs CD	D. J. Shaw
	G-MYOO	Kolb Twinstar Mk 3	G. C. Dixon
	G-MYOS	CFM Shadow Srs CD	C. A. & E. J. Bowles
	G-MYOU	Solar Wings Pegasus Quantum 15	D. J. Tasker
	G-MYOX	Mainair Mercury	K. Driver
	G-MYPA	Rans S.6-ESD Coyote II	G. J. Jones
	G-MYPE	Mainair Gemini/Flash IIA	A. Matthews
	G-MYPH	Solar Wings Pegasus Quantum 15	I. E. Chapman
	G-MYPI	Solar Wings Pegasus Quantum 15	P. L. Jarvis & D. S. Ross
	G-MYPJ	Rans S.6-ESD Coyote II	K. A. Eden
	G-MYPL	CFM Shadow Srs CD	G. I. Madden
	G-MYPM	Cyclone AX3/503	A. A. Ahmed
	G-MYPN	Solar Wings Pegasus Quantum 15	C. M. Boswell
	G-MYPP	Whittaker MW6-S Fat Boy Flyer	G. Everett & D. Smith
	G-MYPR	Cyclone AX3/503	D. H. Baker
	G-MYPS	Whittaker MW6 Merlin	I. S. Bishop
	G-MYPT	CFM Shadow Srs CD	R. Gray
	G-MYPV	Mainair Mercury	R. Whitworth
	G-MYPW	Mainair Gemini/Flash IIA	P. Lacon & K. Tunnicliff
	G-MYPX	Solar Wings Pegasus Quantum 15	M. M. P. Evans
	G-MYPZ	BFC Challenger II	J. I. Gledhill & J. Harvard
	G-MYRD	Mainair Blade	A. J. Roberts
	G-MYRE	Cyclone Chaser S	S. W. Barker
	G-MYRF	Solar Wings Pegasus Quantum 15	S. D. Dempsey
	G-MYRG	TEAM mini-MAX	A. R. Hawes
	G-MYRH	BFC Challenger II	B. Dillon-White
	G-MYRJ	BFC Challenger II	R. A. Allen
	G-MYRK	Renegade Spirit UK	B. J. Palfreyman
	G-MYRL	TEAM mini-MAX	J. N. Hanson
	G-MYRN	Solar Wings Pegasus Quantum 15	I. L. Waghorn
	G-MYRP	Letov LK-2M Sluka	R. M. C. Hunter
	G-MYRS	Solar Wings Pegasus Quantum 15	B. P. & . L. A. Perkins
	G-MYRT	Solar Wings Pegasus Quantum 15	G. P. Preston
	G-MYRW	Mainair Mercury	G. C. Hobson
	G-MYRY	Solar Wings Pegasus Quantum 15	N. J. Lindsay
	G-MYRZ	Solar Wings Pegasus Quantum 15	R. E. Forbes
	G-MYSA	Cyclone Chaser S508	P. W. Dunn & A. R. Vincent
	G-MYSB	Solar Wings Pegasus Quantum 15	H. G. Reid
	G-MYSC	Solar Wings Pegasus Quantum 15	K. R. White
	G-MYSD	BFC Challlenger II	C. W. Udale
	G-MYSJ	Mainair Gemini/Flash IIA	A. Warnock
	G-MYSK	Team Minimax 91	T. D. Wolstenholme
	G-MYSL	Aviasud Mistral	R. D. Ainley
	G-MYSO	Cyclone AX3/50	J. P. Gilroy

Reg	Type	Owner or Operator	Notes
G-MYSR	Solar Wings Pegasus Quantum 15	M. P. Bawden	
G-MYSU	Rans S.6-ESD Coyote II	R. Warriner	
G-MYSV	Aerial Arts Chaser	G. S. Highley	
G-MYSW	Solar Wings Pegasus Quantum 1	M. Richardson	
G-MYSY	Solar Wings Pegasus Quantum 15	B. D. S. Vere	
G-MYSZ	Mainair Mercury	W. Fletcher	
G-MYTB	Mainair Mercury	P. J. Higgins	
G-MYTD	Mainair Blade	B. E. Warburton & D. B. Meades	
G-MYTE	Rans S.6-ESD Coyote II	M. F. Hadley	
G-MYTH	CFM Shadow Srs CD	W. J. I. Robb	
G-MYTI	Solar Wings Pegasus Quantum 15	K. M. Gaffney	
G-MYTJ	Solar Wings Pegasus Quantum 15	L. Blight	
G-MYTK	Mainair Mercury	D. A. Holroyd	
G-MYTL	Mainair Blade	S. Gibson	
G-MYTN	Solar Wings Pegasus Quantum 15	M. Humphries	
G-MYTO	Quad City Challenger II	A. Studley	
G-MYTP	Arrowflight Hawk II	R. J. Turner	
G-MYTT	Quad City Challenger II	P. W. Brush	
G-MYTU	Mainair Blade	A. Worthington	
G-MYTY	CFM Streak Shadow Srs M	Adventurer's SSDR Group	
G-MYUA	Air Creation Fun 18S GTBIS	A. Davis & G. Evans	
G-MYUC	Mainair Blade	C. J. Ashton	
G-MYUD	Mainair Mercury	P. W. Margetson	
G-MYUF	Renegade Spirit	B. W. Webb	
G-MYUH	Solar Wings Pegasus XL-Q	K. S. Daniels	
G-MYUI	Cyclone AX3/503	R. J. Humphries	
G-MYUJ	Murphy Maverick 430	P. J. Porter (G-ONFL)	
G-MYUL	Quad City Challenger II UK	N. V. & B. M. R. Van Cleve	
G-MYUN	Mainair Blade	G. A. Barratt	
G-MYUO	Solar Wings Pegasus Quantum 15	E. J. Hughes	
G-MYUP	Letov LK-2M Sluka	F. Overall	
G-MYUV	Pegasus Quantum 15	S. E. Lyden	
G-MYUW	Mainair Mercury	G. C. Hobson	
G-MYVA	Kolb Twinstar Mk 3	E. Bayliss	
G-MYVB	Mainair Blade	P. Mountain	
G-MYVC	Pegasus Quantum 15	D. D'Arcy-Ewing	
G-MYVG	Letov LK-2M Sluka	S. P. Halford	
G-MYVH	Mainair Mercury	R. H. de C. Ribeiro	
G-MYVI	Air Creation Fun 18S GTBIS	D. Rowland	
G-MYVJ	Pegasus Quantum 15	A. I. McPherson & P. W. Davidson	
G-MYVK	Pegasus Quantum 15	T. P. C. Hague	
G-MYVL	Mainair Mercury	P. J. Judge	
G-MYVM	Pegasus Quantum 15	G. J. Gibson	
G-MYVN	Cyclone AX3/503	F. Watt	
G-MYVO	Mainair Blade	Victor Oscar Group	
G-MYVP	Rans S.6-ESD Coyote II	M. Jady	
G-MYVR	Pegasus Quantum 15	J. M. Webster & M. Winwood	
G-MYVV	Medway Hybred 44XLRR	S. Perity	
G-MYVZ	Mainair Blade	W. C. Hyner	
G-MYWC	Hunt Wing Avon Skytrike	D. Dales	
G-MYWE	Thruster T.600	J. K. Avis	
G-MYWF	CFM Shadow Srs CD	J. Preller	
G-MYWG	Pegasus Quantum 15	S. L. Greene	
G-MYWI	Pegasus Quantum 15	C. Elliott	
G-MYWJ	Pegasus Quantum 15	L. M. Sams & I. Clarkson	
G-MYWK	Pegasus Quantum 15	J. R. Bluett	
G-MYWL	Pegasus Quantum 15	R. P. McGuffie	
G-MYWM	CFM Shadow Srs CD	N. McKinley	
G-MYWN	Cyclone Chaser S 508	R. A. Rawes	
G-MYWO	Pegasus Quantum 15	J. Featherstone	
G-MYWR	Pegasus Quantum 15	The Microlight School (Lichfield) Ltd	
G-MYWS	Cyclone Chaser S 447	M. H. Broadbent	
G-MYWU	Pegasus Quantum 15	P. L. Owen	
G-MYWV	Rans S.4C Coyote	P. G. Anthony & D. A. Crouchman	
G-MYWW	Pegasus Quantum 15	B. Mandley	
G-MYWY	Pegasus Quantum 15	P. Byrne	
G-MYXA	TEAM mini-MAX 91	D. C. Marsh	
G-MYXB	Rans S.6-ESD Coyote II	M. Gaffney	
G-MYXC	BFC Challenger II	B. Plunkett	
G-MYXD	Pegasus Quasar IITC	A. Knight	
G-MYXE	Pegasus Quantum 15	J. F. Bolton	

Notes	Reg	Type	Owner or Operator
	G-MYXH	Cyclone AX3/503	T. de Breffe Gardner
	G-MYXI	Aries 1	H. Cook
	G-MYXJ	Mainair Blade	S. N. Robson
	G-MYXL	Mignet HM.1000 Baleri	R. W. Hollamby
	G-MYXM	Mainair Blade	C. Johnson
	G-MYXN	Mainair Blade	J. C. Birkbeck
	G-MYXO	Letov LK-2M Sluka	J. R. Surbey & A. Furness
	G-MYXT	Pegasus Quantum 15	L. A. Washer
	G-MYXU	Thruster T.300	D. W. Wilson
	G-MYXV	Quad City Challenger II	T. S. Savage
	G-MYXW	Pegasus Quantum 15	J. Uttley
	G-MYXX	Pegasus Quantum 15	G. Fish
	G-MYXZ	Pegasus Quantum 15	A. K. Hole
	G-MYYA	Mainair Blade	S. J. Ward
	G-MYYB	Pegasus Quantum 15	A. L. Johnson & D. S. Ross
	G-MYYC	Pegasus Quantum 15	T. R. E. Goldfield
	G-MYYD	Cyclone Chaser S 447	J. V. Clewer
	G-MYYF	Quad City Challenger II	L. E. J. Wojciechowski
	G-MYYH	Mainair Blade	D. J. Dodd
	G-MYYI	Pegasus Quantum 15	C. M. Day
	G-MYYJ	Hunt Wing	R. M. Jarvis
	G-MYYK	Pegasus Quantum 15	N. Ionita
	G-MYYL	Cyclone AX3/503	D. Roach
	G-MYYR	TEAM mini-MAX 91	M. A. Field
	G-MYYS	TEAM mini-MAX	J. G. Burns
	G-MYYV	Rans S.6-ESD XL Coyote II	A. B. Mousley
	G-MYYW	Mainair Blade	M. D. Kirby
	G-MYYX	Pegasus Quantum 15	S. J. Tennant
	G-MYYY	Mainair Blade	E. D. Lockie
	G-MYYZ	Medway Raven X	J. W. Leaper
	G-MYZB	Pegasus Quantum 15	I. K. Priestley
	G-MYZC	Cyclone AX3/503	AX3-Musketeers
	G-MYZF	Cyclone AX3/503	Microflight (Ireland) Ltd
	G-MYZG	Cyclone AX3/503	I. J. Webb
	G-MYZH	Chargus Titan 38	T. J. Gayton-Polley
	G-MYZJ	Pegasus Quantum 15	J. Urwin
	G-MYZL	Pegasus Quantum 15	R. F. Greaves
	G-MYZP	CFM Shadow Srs DD	H. T. Cook
	G-MYZR	Rans S.6-ESD XL Coyote II	N. R. Beale
	G-MYZV	Rans S.6-ESD XL Coyote II	I. M. Charlwood
	G-MYZY	Pegasus Quantum 15	C. Chapman
	G-MZAB	Mainair Blade	D. Brennan
	G-MZAC	Quad City Challenger II	T. R. Gregory
	G-MZAE	Mainair Blade	A. P. Finn
	G-MZAF	Mainair Blade	P. F. Mayes
	G-MZAG	Mainair Blade	M. J. P. Sanderson
	G-MZAK	Mainair Mercury	I. Rawson
	G-MZAM	Mainair Blade	R. J. Coppin
	G-MZAN	Pegasus Quantum 15	P. M. Leahy
	G-MZAP	Mainair Blade	K. D. Adams
	G-MZAR	Mainair Blade	D. Reston
	G-MZAS	Mainair Blade	T. Carter
	G-MZAT	Mainair Blade	S. Elmazouri
	G-MZAU	Mainair Blade	A. F. Glover
	G-MZAW	Pegasus Quantum 15	O. O'Donnell
	G-MZAZ	Mainair Blade	A. Evans
	G-MZBC	Pegasus Quantum 15	B. M. Quinn
	G-MZBD	Rans S-6-ESD-XL Coyote II	W. E. Tinsley
	G-MZBF	Letov LK-2M Sluka	V. Simpson
	G-MZBG	Hodder MW6-A	E. I. Rowlands-Jons & M. W. Kilvert
	G-MZBH	Rans S.6-ESD Coyote II	G. L. Campbell
	G-MZBK	Letov LK-2M Sluka	R. M. C. Hunter
	G-MZBL	Mainair Blade	C. J. Rubery
	G-MZBN	CFM Shadow Srs B	W. J. Buskell
	G-MZBS	CFM Shadow Srs D	T. P. Ryan
	G-MZBT	Pegasus Quantum 15	M. L. Saunders
	G-MZBU	Rans S.6-ESD Coyote II	R. S. Marriott
	G-MZBW	Quad City Challenger II UK	R. M. C. Hunter
	G-MZBY	Pegasus Quantum 15	P. L. Wilkinson
	G-MZBZ	Quad City Challenger II UK	T. R. Gregory

Reg	Type	Owner or Operator	Notes
G-MZCB	Cyclone Chaser S 447	A. R. Vincent & P. W. Dunn	
G-MZCC	Mainair Blade 912	K. S. Rissmann	
G-MZCE	Mainair Blade	I. C. Hindle	
G-MZCF	Mainair Blade	C. Hannanby	
G-MZCI	Pegasus Quantum 15	P. H. Risdale	
G-MZCJ	Pegasus Quantum 15	T. N. Jerry	
G-MZCK	AMF Chevvron 2-32C	S. Mebarki	
G-MZCM	Pegasus Quantum 15	J. E. Bullock	
G-MZCN	Mainair Blade	G. M. Munoz	
G-MZCS	TEAM mini-MAX	J. Aley	
G-MZCT	CFM Shadow Srs CD	W. G. Gill	
G-MZCU	Mainair Blade	C. E. Pearce	
G-MZCV	Pegasus Quantum 15	F. Raveau-Violette	
G-MZCW	Pegasus Quantum 15	K. L. Baldwin	
G-MZCX	Huntwing Avon Skytrike	Easter Airfield Microlight Flying Group	
G-MZCY	Pegasus Quantum 15	G. Murphy	
G-MZDA	Rans S.6-ESD Coyote IIXL	R. Plummer	
G-MZDB	Pegasus Quantum 15	Scottish Hang Gliding Club	
G-MZDC	Pegasus Quantum 15	C. Garton	
G-MZDD	Pegasus Quantum 15	A. J. Todd	
G-MZDE	Pegasus Quantum 15	R. G. Hedley	
G-MZDF	Mainair Blade	M. Liptrot	
G-MZDG	Rans S.6-ESD Coyote IIXL	P. Coates	
G-MZDH	Pegasus Quantum 15	G-MZDH Flying Group	
G-MZDI	Whittaker MW6-S Fat Boy Flyer	C. M. Byford (G-BUNN)	
G-MZDJ	Medway Raven X	R. Bryan & S. Digby	
G-MZDK	Mainair Blade	J. Bunyan	
G-MZDM	Rans S.6-ESD Coyote II	M. E. Nicholas	
G-MZDN	Pegasus Quantum 15	N. Cross	
G-MZDS	Cyclone AX3/503	M. J. Cooper	
G-MZDT	Mainair Blade	R. L. Beese	
G-MZDU	Pegasus Quantum 15	J. J. D. Firmino do Carmo	
G-MZDV	Pegasus Quantum 15	Griffin Toomes Consulting Engineers Ltd	
G-MZDX	Letov LK-2M Sluka	J. L. Barker	
G-MZDY	Pegasus Quantum 15	R. J. Deeth	
G-MZDZ	Hunt Wing	E. W. Laidlaw	
G-MZEA	BFC Challenger II	G. S. Cridland	
G-MZEB	Mainair Blade	R. A. Campbell	
G-MZEC	Pegasus Quantum 15	A. B. Godber	
G-MZEE	Pegasus Quantum 15	I. W. & J. R. King	
G-MZEG	Mainair Blade	G. Cole	
G-MZEH	Pegasus Quantum 15	P. S. Hall	
G-MZEK	Mainair Mercury	G. Crane	
G-MZEL	Cyclone Airsports AX3/503	L. M. Jackson & R. I. Simpson	
G-MZEM	Pegasus Quantum 15	L. H. Black	
G-MZEN	Rans S.6-ESD Coyote II	R. Mills	
G-MZEP	Mainair Rapier	A. G. Bird	
G-MZEU	Rans S-6-ESD XL Coyote II	P. Wilcox	
G-MZEV	Mainair Rapier	W. T. Gardner	
G-MZEW	Mainair Blade	T. D. Holder	
G-MZEX	Pegasus Quantum 15	D. A. Eastough	
G-MZEZ	Pegasus Quantum 15	M. J. Ing	
G-MZFA	Cyclone AX2000	G. S. Highley	
G-MZFB	Mainair Blade	A. J. Plant	
G-MZFC	Letov LK-2M Sluka	R. J. Turner	
G-MZFD	Mainair Rapier	A. Hayward	
G-MZFE	Hunt Wing	G. J. Latham	
G-MZFF	Hunt Wing	B. J. Adamson	
G-MZFH	AMF Chevvron 2-32C	Eagle Flying Group	
G-MZFL	Rans S.6-ESD Coyote IIXL	J. J. Lynch	
G-MZFM	Pegasus Quantum 15	N. Musgrave	
G-MZFN	Rans S.6-ESD Coyote IIXL	C. J. & W. R. Wallbank	
G-MZFO	Thruster T.600N	S. J. P. Stevenson	
G-MZFS	Mainair Blade	P. L. E. Zelazowski	
G-MZFT	Pegasus Quantum 15	G. R. Smith	
G-MZFU	Thruster T.600N	A. J. Pickup	
G-MZFX	Cyclone AX2000	AX Group	
G-MZFY	Rans S.6-ESD Coyote IIXL	L. G. Tserkezos	
G-MZFZ	Mainair Blade	D. J. Bateman	
G-MZGA	Cyclone AX2000	R. D. Leigh	
G-MZGC	Cyclone AX2000	T. J. McMenamin	

Notes	Reg	Type	Owner or Operator
	G-MZGD	Rans S.5 Coyote II	P. J. Greenrod
	G-MZGF	Letov LK-2M Sluka	T. W. Thiele
	G-MZGG	Pegasus Quantum 15	J. M. Chapman
	G-MZGH	Hunt Wing/Avon 462(3)	J. H. Cole
	G-MZGI	Mainair Blade 912	H. M. Roberts
	G-MZGL	Mainair Rapier	T. H. Abraham-Roth
	G-MZGM	Cyclone AX2000	A. F. Smallacombe
	G-MZGN	Pegasus Quantum 15	B. J. Youngs
	G-MZGO	Pegasus Quantum 15	S. F. G. Allen
	G-MZGP	Cyclone AX2000	Buchan Light Aeroplane Club
	G-MZGR	TEAM mini-MAX	K. G. Seeley
	G-MZGU	Arrowflight Hawk II (UK)	J. N. Holden
	G-MZGV	Pegasus Quantum 15	G. Rokita
	G-MZGW	Mainair Blade	R. C. Ford
	G-MZGX	Thruster T.600N	Fen Tiger Flying Group
	G-MZGY	Thruster T.600N 450	K. J. Brooker
	G-MZHA	Thruster T.600N	P. Stark
	G-MZHB	Mainair Blade	R. R. Till
	G-MZHD	Thruster T.600N	B. E. Foster
	G-MZHF	Thruster T.600N	C. Carmichael
	G-MZHG	Whittaker MW6-T Merlin	D. R. Thompson
	G-MZHI	Pegasus Quantum 15	M. A. Gardiner
	G-MZHJ	Mainair Rapier	G. Standish
	G-MZHM	Team Himax 1700R	M. H. McKeown
	G-MZHN	Pegasus Quantum 15	F. W. Ferichs
	G-MZHO	Quad City Challenger II	J. Pavelin
	G-MZHP	Pegasus Quantum 15	W. J. Flood
	G-MZHR	Cyclone AX2000	J. P. Jones
	G-MZHS	Thruster T.600T	G-MZHS Group
	G-MZHT	Whittaker MW6 Merlin	G. J. Chadwick
	G-MZHV	Thruster T.600T	H. G. Denton
	G-MZHW	Thruster T.600N	A. J. Glynn
	G-MZHY	Thruster T.600N	B. W. Webster
	G-MZIB	Pegasus Quantum 15	S. Murphy
	G-MZID	Whittaker MW6 Merlin	C. P. F. Sheppard
	G-MZIE	Pegasus Quantum 15	Flylight Airsports Ltd
	G-MZIH	Mainair Blade 912	N. J. Waller
	G-MZIJ	Pegasus Quantum 15	D. L. Wright
	G-MZIK	Pegasus Quantum 15	C. M. Wilkinson
	G-MZIL	Mainair Rapier	B. L. Cook
	G-MZIM	Mainair Rapier	M. J. McKegney
	G-MZIR	Mainair Blade	S. Connor
	G-MZIS	Mainair Blade	M. K. Richings
	G-MZIT	Mainair Blade 912	M. A. Robinson
	G-MZIU	Pegasus Quantum 15-912	M. G. Chalmers
	G-MZIV	Cyclone AX2000	G-MZIV Syndicate
	G-MZIW	Mainair Blade	J. C. Boyd
	G-MZIZ	Renegade Spirit UK (G-MWGP)	C. B. Hopkins
	G-MZJA	Mainair Blade	D. M. Whelan
	G-MZJD	Mainair Blade	M. Howard
	G-MZJE	Mainair Rapier	A. P. Pearce
	G-MZJF	Cyclone AX2000	D. J. Lewis
	G-MZJG	Pegasus Quantum 15	S. A. Holmes
	G-MZJH	Pegasus Quantum 15	P. Copping
	G-MZJI	Rans S-6-ESD-XL Coyote II	J. P. Hunsdale
	G-MZJJ	Murphy Maverick	M. F. Farrer
	G-MZJK	Mainair Blade	P. G. Angus
	G-MZJL	Cyclone AX2000	M. H. Owen
	G-MZJM	Rans S.6-ESD Coyote IIXL	B. Lorriane
	G-MZJO	Pegasus Quantum 15	D. J. Cook
	G-MZJP	Whittaker MW6-S Fatboy Flyer	R. C. Funnell & D. J. Burton
	G-MZJT	Pegasus Quantum 15	M. A. McClelland
	G-MZJV	Mainair Blade 912	M. A. Roberts
	G-MZJW	Pegasus Quantum 15	G. A. & G. E. Blackstone
	G-MZJX	Mainair Blade	H. Mercer
	G-MZJY	Pegasus Quantum 15	R. G. Wyatt
	G-MZJZ	Mainair Blade	Lima Zulu Owner Syndicate
	G-MZKA	Pegasus Quantum 15	S. P. Tkaczyk
	G-MZKC	Cyclone AX2000	D. J. Pike
	G-MZKD	Pegasus Quantum 15	T. M. Frost
	G-MZKE	Rans S.6-ESD Coyote IIXL	P. A. Flaherty

Reg	Type	Owner or Operator	Notes
G-MZKF	Pegasus Quantum 15	A. H., D. P. & V. J. Tidmas	
G-MZKG	Mainair Blade	N. S. Rigby	
G-MZKH	CFM Shadow Srs DD	S. P. H. Calvert	
G-MZKI	Mainair Rapier	D. L. Aspinall	
G-MZKJ	Mainair Blade	The G-MZKJ Group	
G-MZKL	Pegasus Quantum 15	Kilo Lima Group	
G-MZKN	Mainair Rapier	O. P. Farrell	
G-MZKR	Thruster T.600N	R. J. Arnett	
G-MZKS	Thruster T.600N	M. I. Garner	
G-MZKU	Thruster T.600N	A. S. Day	
G-MZKW	Quad City Challenger II	R. A. Allen	
G-MZKY	Pegasus Quantum 15	P. S. Constable	
G-MZKZ	Mainair Blade	R. P. Wolstenholme	
G-MZLA	Pegasus Quantum 15	A. C. Hodges	
G-MZLD	Pegasus Quantum 15	L. Sokoli	
G-MZLE	Maverick (G-BXSZ)	M. W. Hands	
G-MZLF	Pegasus Quantum 15	S. Seymour	
G-MZLG	Rans S.6-ESD Coyote IIXL	A. M. Beale	
G-MZLI	Mignet HM.1000 Balerit	A. G. Barr	
G-MZLJ	Pegasus Quantum 15	R. M. Williams	
G-MZLL	Rans S.6-ESD Coyote II	D. W. Adams	
G-MZLM	Cyclone AX2000	P. E. Hadley	
G-MZLN	Pegasus Quantum 15	P. A. Greening	
G-MZLP	CFM Shadow Srs D	D. J. Gordon	
G-MZLT	Pegasus Quantum 15	B. Jackson	
G-MZLU	Cyclone AX2000	E. Pashley	
G-MZLV	Pegasus Quantum 15	M. K. Ballard	
G-MZLW	Pegasus Quantum 15	R. W. R. Crevel & D. P. Hampson	
G-MZLX	Micro Aviation B.22S Bantam	V. J. Vaughan	
G-MZLY	Letov LK-2M Sluka	W. McCarthy	
G-MZLZ	Mainair Blade	D. Round	
G-MZMA	Solar Wings Pegasus Quasar IITC	G. Burns	
G-MZMC	Pegasus Quantum 15	J. J. Baker	
G-MZME	Medway Eclipser	T. A. Dobbins	
G-MZMF	Pegasus Quantum 15	A. J. Tranter	
G-MZMG	Pegasus Quantum 15	M. S. Ahmadu	
G-MZMH	Pegasus Quantum 15	L. Hogan & W. Gray	
G-MZMJ	Mainair Blade	D. Wilson	
G-MZMK	Chevvron 2-32C	P. M. Waller	
G-MZML	Mainair Blade 912	C. J. Meadows	
G-MZMM	Mainair Blade 912	A. M. Donkin	
G-MZMN	Pegasus Quantum 912	G-MZMN Group	
G-MZMO	TEAM mini-MAX 91	North East Flight Training Ltd	
G-MZMT	Pegasus Quantum 15	J. A. Davies	
G-MZMU	Rans S.6-ESD Coyote II	WEZ Group	
G-MZMV	Mainair Blade	S. P. Allen & C. J. Tomlin	
G-MZMW	Mignet HM.1000 Balerit	M. E. Whapham	
G-MZMY	Mainair Blade	C. J. Millership	
G-MZMZ	Mainair Blade	M. Lewis	
G-MZNA	Quad City Challenger II UK	S. Hennessy	
G-MZNB	Pegasus Quantum 15	S. J. Metters	
G-MZNC	Mainair Blade 912	A. J. Harrison	
G-MZND	Mainair Rapier	D. W. Stamp	
G-MZNG	Pegasus Quantum 15	The Scottish Flying Club	
G-MZNH	CFM Shadow Srs DD	P. A. James	
G-MZNJ	Mainair Blade	R. A. Hardy	
G-MZNM	TEAM mini-MAX	S. M. Williams	
G-MZNN	TEAM mini-MAX	P. J. Bishop	
G-MZNO	Mainair Blade 912	G. Burns	
G-MZNR	Pegasus Quantum 15	N. J. Clemens	
G-MZNS	Pegasus Quantum 15	S. Uzochukwu	
G-MZNT	Pegasus Quantum 15-912	N. W. Barnett	
G-MZNU	Mainair Rapier	B. Johnson	
G-MZNV	Rans S.6-ESD Coyote II	A. P. Thomas	
G-MZNX	Thruster T.600N	J. B. Silverstone	
G-MZNY	Thruster T.600N	Cheshire Flying School Ltd	
G-MZOC	Mainair Blade	A. S. Davies	
G-MZOD	Pegasus Quantum 15	G. P. Burns	
G-MZOE	Cyclone AX2000	B. E. Wagenhauser	
G-MZOF	Mainair Blade	R. M. Ellis	
G-MZOG	Pegasus Quantum 15-912	D. Smith	

Notes	Reg	Type	Owner or Operator
	G-MZOH	Whittaker MW5D Sorcerer	I. Pearson
	G-MZOI	Letov LK-2M Sluka	J. G. Burns
	G-MZOK	Whittaker MW6 Merlin	G-MZOK Syndicate
	G-MZOP	Mainair Blade 912	K. M. Thorogood
	G-MZOS	Pegasus Quantum 15-912	T. G. Ryan
	G-MZOV	Pegasus Quantum 15	G-MZOV Group
	G-MZOW	Pegasus Quantum 15-912	G. P. Burns
	G-MZOX	Letov LK-2M Sluka	N. R. Beale
	G-MZOY	TEAM Mini-MAX 91	P. R. & S. E. Whitehouse
	G-MZOZ	Rans S.6-ESA Coyote II	G. L. Daniels
	G-MZPH	Mainair Blade	A. M. Donkin
	G-MZPJ	TEAM mini-MAX	J. Aubert
	G-MZRC	Pegasus Quantum 15	M. Hopkins
	G-MZRM	Pegasus Quantum 15	R. Milwain
	G-MZRS	CFM Shadow Srs CD	C. J. Tomlin
	G-MZSP	Spacek SD-1 Minisport	A. M. Hughes
	G-MZTG	Titan T-51 Mustang	A. R. Evans
	G-MZUB	Rans S.6-ESD Coyote IIXL	R. E. Main
	G-MZZT	Kolb Twinstar Mk 3	F. Omaraie-Hamdanie
	G-MZZY	Mainair Blade 912	A. Mucznik
	G-NACA	Norman NAC-2 Freelance 180	A. R. Norman & P. J. L. Caruth
	G-NACI	Norman NAC-1 Srs 100	M. D. Gorlov (G-AXFB)
	G-NACL	Norman NAC-6 Fieldmaster	EPA Aircraft Co Ltd (G-BNEG)
	G-NACO	Norman NAC-6 Fieldmaster	EPA Aircraft Co Ltd
	G-NACP	Norman NAC-6 Fieldmaster	EPA Aircraft Co Ltd
	G-NADN	PA-23-250 Aztec F	N. M. T. Sparks (G-XSFT/G-CPPC/G-BGBH)
	G-NADO	Titan Tornado SS	Euro Aviation LLP
	G-NADS	TEAM mini-MAX 91	C. D. Cheese
	G-NAGG	Rotorsport UK MT-03	C. A. Clements
	G-NALA	Cessna 172S	NAL Asset Management Ltd (G-GFEA/G-CEDY)
	G-NANI	Robinson R44 II	Mega Parquet SL/Spain
	G-NANO	Avid Speed Wing	D. N. Smith & G. Everett
	G-NAPO	Pegasus Quantum 15-912	J. K. Kerr & K. S. Henderson
	G-NAPP	Van's RV-7	R. C. Meek
	G-NARG	Tanarg/Ixess 15 912S (1)	K. Kirby
	G-NATI	Corby CJ-1 Starlet	S. P. Evans
	G-NATT	Rockwell Commander 114A	Northgleam Ltd
	G-NATY	HS. Gnat T.1 (XR537) ★	DS Aviation (UK) Ltd
	G-NBCA	Pilatus PC-12/47E	Narm Aviation Ltd
	G-NBDD	Robin DR.400/180	Delta Delta Group
	G-NBOX	Ikarus C42 FB100 Bravo	Natterbox Ltd
	G-NBSI	Cameron N-77 balloon	Nottingham Hot-Air Balloon Club
	G-NCFC	PA-38-112 Tomahawk II	A. M. Heynen
	G-NCUB	Piper J-3C-65 Cub	R. J. Willies (G-BGXV)
	G-NDAD	Medway SLA100 Executive	R. D. Pyne
	G-NDIA	Robinson R22	EBG (Helicopters) Ltd & Altitude Consultants Ltd (G-CCGE)
	G-NDJS	Jonker JS1-C Revelation	A. J. Davis
	G-NDOT	Thruster T.600N	P. C. Bailey
	G-NDPA	Ikarus C42 FB UK	Grandpa's Flying Group
	G-NEAL	PA-32-260 Cherokee Six	H. J. Samples (G-BFPY)
	G-NEAT	Europa	P. F. D. Foden
	G-NEAU	Eurocopter EC 135T2+	Police & Crime Commissioner for West Yorkshire
	G-NEDS	Skyranger Nynja 912S(1)	H. Van Allen
	G-NEEE	Cessna F.172M	St. Athan 172 Flying Group (G-BCZM)
	G-NEEL	Rotorway Executive 90	I. C. Bedford
	G-NEII	Montgomerie-Bensen B8MR	Dept of Doing Ltd (G-BVJF)
	G-NEIL	Thunder Ax3 balloon	R. M. Powell
	G-NELI	PA-28R Cherokee Arrow 180	MK Aero Support Ltd
	G-NELS	Robinson R44	Heliwarms Aviation Ltd
	G-NEMO	Raj Hamsa X'Air Jabiru (4)	G. F. Allen
	G-NEON	PA-32 Cherokee Six 300B	T. F. Rowley
	G-NESA	Shaw Europa XS	A. M. Kay
	G-NESE	Tecnam P2002-JF	N. & S. Easton

Reg	Type	Owner or Operator	Notes
G-NESH	Robinson R44 II	Helicentre Aviation Ltd	
G-NEST	Christen Eagle II	P. J. Nonat	
G-NESW	PA-34-220T Seneca III	G. C. U. Guida	
G-NESY	PA-18 Super Cub 95	V. Featherstone	
G-NETR	AS.355F1 Twin Squirrel	PLM Dollar Group Ltd (G-JARV/G-OGHL)	
G-NETT	Cessna 172S	Aero-Club Rhein-Nahe EV	
G-NETY	PA-18 Super Cub 150	S. de Sutter	
G-NEVE	Ikarus C42 FB100	M. Neve	
G-NEWA	Rans S-6-ES Coyote II	Royal Aeronautical Society	
G-NEWT	Beech 35 Bonanza	J. S. Allison (G-APVW)	
G-NEWZ	Bell 206B JetRanger 3	H. P. L. Frost	
G-NFLA	BAe Jetstream 3102	Cranfield University (G-BRGN/G-BLHC)	
G-NFLC	HP.137 Jetstream 1H (G-AXUI) ★	Instructional airframe/Perth	
G-NFLY	Tecnam P2002-EA Sierra	C. N. Hodgson	
G-NFNF	Robin DR.400/180	M. Child, W. Cobb & J. Archer	
G-NFON	Van's RV-8	N. F. O'Neill	
G-NFOX	Aeropro Eurofox 912(S)	A. E. Mayhew	
G-NFVB	Cameron Z-105 balloon	Ballooning Network Ltd	
G-NGAA	Bristell NG5 Speed Wing	F. Sayyah & A. J. Palmer	
G-NGCC	Bristell NG5 Speed Wing	G. C. Coull	
G-NGII	Bristell NG5 Speed Wing	F. Sayyah & A. J. Palmer	
G-NHAA	AS.365N-2 Dauphin 2	The Great North Air Ambulance Service (G-MLTY)	
G-NHAB	AS.365N-2 Dauphin 2	The Great North Air Ambulance Service (G-DAUF)	
G-NHAC	AS.365N-2 Dauphin 2	The Great North Air Ambulance Service	
G-NHEM	Eurocopter EC.135T2	Babcock Mission Critical Services Onshore Ltd (G-KRNW)	
G-NHRH	PA-28 Cherokee 140	C. J. Milsom	
G-NHRJ	Shaw Europa XS	R. J. Dawson	
G-NIAA	Beech B.200 Super King Air	Blue Sky Investments Ltd	
G-NIAB	Beech B.200 Super King Air	Blue Sky Investments Ltd	
G-NICC	Aerotechnik EV-97 Team Eurostar UK	Pickup and Son Ltd	
G-NICI	Robinson R44	David Fishwick Vehicles Sales Ltd	
G-NICS	Best Off Sky Ranger Swift 912S(1)	I. A. Forrest & C. K. Richardson	
G-NICX	Europa XS	N. Kenney	
G-NIDG	Aerotechnik EV-97 Eurostar	Skydrive Ltd	
G-NIEN	Van's RV-9A	K. N. P. Higgs	
G-NIFE	SNCAN Stampe SV.4A (156)	Tiger Airways	
G-NIGC	Avtech Jabiru UL-450	C. K. Fry	
G-NIGE	Luscombe 8E Silvaire	Garden Party Ltd (G-BSHG)	
G-NIGL	Shaw Europa	N. M. Graham	
G-NIGS	Thunder Ax7-65 balloon	S. D. Annett	
G-NIHM	Eurocopter EC135 T2+	Babcock Mission Critical Services Onshore Ltd (G-SASA)	
G-NIKE	PA-28-181 Archer II	Key Properties Ltd	
G-NIKK	Diamond Katana DA20-C1	Cubair Flight Training Ltd	
G-NIKO	Airbus A.321-211	Thomas Cook Airlines Ltd	
G-NIKS	Aeropro Eurofox 912(1)	Gosk Ltd	
G-NILT	EV-97 Eurostar SL Microlight	Take 2 Events Ltd	
G-NIMA	Balóny Kubíček BB30Z balloon	C. Williamson	
G-NIMB	Schempp-Hirth Nimbus 2C	W. J. Winthrop & W. P. Stephen	
G-NIME	Cessna T.206H Turbo Stationair	Whitby Seafoods Ltd	
G-NINA	PA-28-161 Warrior II	Global Aviation SA (G-BEUC)	
G-NINC	PA-28-180 Cherokee	NWMAS Leasing Ltd	
G-NIND	PA-28-180 Cherokee	Aquarelle Investments Ltd	
G-NINJ	Best Off Skyranger Nynja 912S(1)	G-NINJ Group	
G-NIOG	Robinson R44 II	Helicopter Sharing Ltd	
G-NIOS	PA-32R-301 Saratoga SP	Plant Aviation	
G-NIPA	Slingsby T.66 Nipper 3	R. J. O. Walker (G-AWDD)	
G-NIPL	Eurocopter AS.350B3 Ecureuil	Pacific Helicopters Ltd	
G-NIPP	Slingsby T.66 Nipper 3	North East Flight Training Ltd (G-AVKJ)	
G-NIPR	Slingsby T.66 Nipper 3	P. A. Gibbs (G-AVXC)	
G-NIPS	Tipsy T.66 Nipper 2	B. W. Faulkner	
G-NISA	Robinson R44 II	Antinori Agricola SRL/Italy (G-HTMT)	
G-NISH	Van's RV-8	N. H. F. Hampton & S. R. Whitling	
G-NIUS	Cessna F.172N	M. Lee	

BRITISH CIVIL AIRCRAFT MARKINGS

Notes	Reg	Type	Owner or Operator
	G-NIVA	Eurocopter EC 155B1	Lanthwaite Aviation Ltd
	G-NIXX	Best Off Skyranger 912(1)	R. E. Parker & B. Cook (G-CDYJ)
	G-NJBA	Rotorway Executive 162F	British Waterproofing Ltd
	G-NJCZ	Czech Sport Pipersport	Aerocruz Ltd
	G-NJET	Schempp-Hirth Ventus cT	P. S. Carder
	G-NJNH	Robinson R66	Hawesbates LLP
	G-NJOY	PA-28-181 Archer III	M. J. Groves
	G-NJPG	Best Off Skyranger Nynja 912S(1)	P. Gibbs
	G-NJPW	P & M Quik GT450	Golf Papa Whiskey Group
	G-NJSH	Robinson R22 Beta	Hawesbates LLP
	G-NJSP	Jabiru J430	N. J. S. Pitman
	G-NJTC	Aeroprakt A22-L Foxbat	I. R. Russell & P. A. Henretty
	G-NKEL	Robinson R44 II	Avio Service
	G-NLCH	Lindstrand LBL-35A balloon	S. A. Lacey
	G-NLDR	AS.355F2 Ecureuil 2	PDG Helicopters (G-PDGS)
	G-NLEE	Cessna 182Q	R. J. Houghton
	G-NLMB	Zenair CH.601UL Zodiac	N. Lamb
	G-NLSE	AS.355F2 Ecureuil 2	PLM Dollar Group Ltd (G-ULES/G-OBHL/G-HARO/G-DAFT/G-BNNN)
	G-NLYB	Cameron N-105 balloon	P. H. E. Van Overwalle/Belgium
	G-NMCL	Eurofox 912(S)	N. R. McLeod
	G-NMMB	Van's RV-10	M. S. Bamber & N. R. MacLennan
	G-NMOS	Cameron C-80 balloon	C. J. Thomas & M. C. East
	G-NMRV	Van's RV-6	R. L. N. & S. C. Lucey
	G-NMUS	Steen Skybolt	N. Musgrave
	G-NNAC	PA-18 Super Cub 135	PAW Flying Services Ltd
	G-NNON	Mainair Blade	D. R. Kennedy
	G-NOAH	Airbus A.319-115CJ	Acropolis Aviation Ltd
	G-NOCK	Cessna FR.182RG II	M. K. Aves (G-BGTK)
	G-NODE	AA-5 Tiger	Ultranomad Sro
	G-NOIL	BN-2A-26 Islander	Aerospace Resources Ltd (G-BJWO/G-BAXC)
	G-NOMZ	Balony Kubicek BB-S Gnome SS balloon	A. M. Holly
	G-NONE	Dyn'Aéro MCR-01 ULC	M. A. Collins
	G-NONI	AA-5 Traveler	I. H. Molesworth (G-BBDA)
	G-NORA	Ikarus C.42 FB UK	N. A. Rathbone
	G-NORB	Saturne S110K hang glider	R. N. Pearce
	G-NORD	SNCAN NC.854	A. D. Pearce
	G-NORG	Gefa-Flug AS105GD airship	Fairfax Aviation Ltd (G-BZUR)
	G-NORK	Bell 206B-3 JetRanger III	R. S. Forsyth
	G-NOSE	Cessna 402B	Reconnaissance Ventures Ltd (G-MPCU)
	G-NOTE	PA-28-181 Archer III	J. Beach
	G-NOTS	Skyranger 912S(1)	S. F. N. Warnell
	G-NOTT	Nott ULD-2 balloon	J. R. P. Nott
	G-NOTY	Westland Scout AH.Mk.1	Kennet Aviation
	G-NOWW	Mainair Blade 912	R. S. Sanby
	G-NOXY	Robinson R44	T A Knox Shopfitters Ltd (G-VALV)
	G-NPKJ	Van's RV-6	M. R. Turner
	G-NPPL	Comco Ikarus C.42 FB.100	Papa Lima Group
	G-NPTV	AS.355NP Ecureuil II	Arena Aviation Ltd
	G-NPTY	Boeing 737-436F	West Atlantic UK Ltd (G-DOCA)
	G-NRFK	Van's RV-8	C. N. Harper & P. G. Peal
	G-NRMA	Dan Rihn DR.107 One Design	A. W. Brown
	G-NROY	PA-32RT-300 Lance II	B. Nedjati-Gilani (G-LYNN/G-BGNY)
	G-NRRA	SIAI-Marchetti SF.260 ★	G. Boot
	G-NRWY	Boeing 737-8JP	Norwegian Air UK Ltd
	G-NSBB	Ikarus C.42 FB-100 VLA	Bravo Bravo Flying Group
	G-NSEW	Robinson R44	Styl SC/Poland
	G-NSEY	Embraer ERJ190-200STD	Aurigny Air Services Ltd
	G-NSKB	Aeroprakt A22-L Foxbat	N. F. Smith
	G-NSKY	Alpi Pioneer 400	A. P. Sellars
	G-NSSA	TLAC Sherwood Ranger XP	A. R. Stanley
	G-NSTG	Cessna F.150F	Westair Flying Services Ltd (G-ATNI)

Reg	Type	Owner or Operator	Notes
G-NSYS	Eurocopter EC135 T1	Novas Aerospace Ltd (G-CEYF/G-HARP)	
G-NTAR	MD Helicopters MD.600N	Eastern Atlantic Helicopters Ltd	
G-NTPS	BRM Aero Bristell NG5	N. D. H. Stokes	
G-NTVE	Beagle A-61 Terrier 3	D. Capon (G-ASIE)	
G-NTWK	AS.355F2 Twin Squirrel	PLM Dollar Group (G-FTWO/G-OJOR/G-BMUS)	
G-NUFC	Best Off Skyranger 912S(1)	C. R. Rosby	
G-NUGC	Grob G.103A Twin II Acro	The University of Nottingham Students Union	
G-NUKA	PA-28-181 Archer II	N. Ibrahim	
G-NULA	Flight Design CT2K	R. E. Antell	
G-NUNI	Lindstrand LBL-77A balloon	The University of Nottingham	
G-NUTA	Christen Eagle II	A. R. Whincup	
G-NUTT	Mainair Pegasus Quik	NUTT Syndicate	
G-NVBF	Lindstrand LBL-210A balloon	Virgin Balloon Flights	
G-NWAA	Eurocopter EC.135T2	Babcock Mission Critical Services Onshore Ltd	
G-NWAE	Eurocopter EC.135T2	Babcock Mission Critical Services Onshore Ltd (G-DAAT)	
G-NWEM	Eurocopter EC.135T2	Babcock Mission Critical Services Onshore Ltd (G-SSXX/G-SSSX)	
G-NWFA	Cessna 150M	North Weald Flying Group Ltd (G-CFBD)	
G-NWFC	Cessna 172P	North Weald Flying Group Ltd	
G-NWFG	Cessna 172P	North Weald Flying Group Ltd	
G-NWFS	Cessna 172P	North Weald Flying Group Ltd (G-TYMS)	
G-NWFT	Cessna F.172N	North Weald Flying Training Ltd (G-BURD)	
G-NWOI	Eurocopter EC135 P2+	Police & Crime Commissioner for West Yorkshire	
G-NWPR	Cameron N-77 balloon	D. B. Court	
G-NWPS	Eurocopter EC 135T1	Patriot Aviation Ltd	
G-NXOE	Cessna 172S	Goodwood Road Racing Co.Ltd	
G-NYKS	Cessna 182T	M. Lapidus	
G-NYMB	Schempp-Hirth Nimbus 3	Nimbus Syndicate	
G-NYMF	PA-25 Pawnee 235D	Bristol Gliding Club Pty Ltd	
G-NYNA	Van's RV-9A	B. Greathead & S. Hiscox	
G-NYNE	Schleicher ASW-27-18E	R. C. W. Ellis	
G-NYNJ	Best Off Skyranger Nynja 912S)1)	N. J. Sutherland	
G-NZGL	Cameron O-105 balloon	R. A. Vale & ptnrs	
G-NZSS	Boeing Stearman N2S-5 (43517:227)	R. W. Davies	
G-OAAA	PA-28-161 Warrior II	Red Hill Air Services Ltd	
G-OAAM	Cameron C-90 balloon	A. M. Holly	
G-OABB	Jodel D.150	K. Manley	
G-OABC	Colt 69A balloon	P. A. C. Stuart-Kregor	
G-OABO	Enstrom F-28A	C. R. Taylor (G-BAIB)	
G-OABR	AG-5B Tiger	A. J. Neale	
G-OACE	Valentin Taifun 17E	I. F. Wells	
G-OACI	MS.893E Rallye 180GT	J. M. & S. Bain	
G-OACJ	Airbus A.319-133ACJ	TAG Aviation (UK) Ltd	
G-OADY	Beech 76 Duchess	Skies Airlines Training AB/Sweden	
G-OAGA	Eurocopter EC.225LP Super Puma	CHC Scotia Ltd	
G-OAER	Lindstrand LBL-105A balloon	M. P. Rowley	
G-OAFA	Cessna F.172M	The Army Flying Association (G-BFZV)	
G-OAFF	Cessna 208 Caravan 1	FSSD GmbH/Germany	
G-OAGA	Eurocopter EC.225LP Super Puma	Element Capital Corp	
G-OAGC	Eurocopter EC.225LP Super Puma	Wilmington Trust SP Services (Dublin) Ltd	
G-OAGD	Eurocopter EC.225LP Super Puma	Vertical Aviation No.1 Ltd (G-JENZ)	
G-OAGE	Eurocopter EC.225LP Super Puma	Wilmington Trust SP Services (Dublin) Ltd	
G-OAGI	FLS Aerospace Sprint 160	A. L. Breckell (G-FLSI)	
G-OAHC	Beech F33C Bonanza	Cirrus Aviation Ltd (G-BTTF)	
G-OAJL	Ikarus C.42 FB100	G. D. M. McCulloch	
G-OAJS	PA-39 Twin Comanche 160 C/R	M. C. Bellamy (G-BCIO)	
G-OALD	SOCATA TB20 Trinidad	Gold Aviation	
G-OALE	Balony Kubicek BB22XR balloon	Belvoir Brewery Ltd	
G-OALH	Tecnam P92-EA Echo	A. Pritchard	

Notes	Reg	Type	Owner or Operator
	G-OALI	AS.355F1 Ecureuil II	Atlas Helicopters Ltd (G-WDKR/G-NEXT/ G-OMAV)
	G-OALP	Alpi Pioneer 300 Hawk	Cavendish Aviation UK Ltd
	G-OAMF	Pegasus Quantum 15-912	G. A. Viquerat
	G-OAML	Cameron AML-105 balloon	Stratton Motor Co (Norfolk) Ltd
	G-OAMP	Cessna F.177RG	P. Denegre (G-AYPF)
	G-OANI	PA-28-161 Warrior II	Falcon Flying Services
	G-OANN	Zenair CH.601HD	R. Torrie
	G-OAPR	Brantly B.2B	Helicopter International Magazine
	G-OARA	PA-28R-201 Arrow III	Dorian & Brunning Holdings LLP
	G-OARC	PA-28RT-201 Arrow IV	Norton Systems (G-BMVE)
	G-OARI	PA-28R-201 Arrow III	D. J. Hockings
	G-OARS	Cessna 172S	De Hertog Juweeldesign GCV/Belgium
	G-OART	PA-23 Aztec 250D	Prescribing Services Ltd (G-AXKD)
	G-OARU	PA-28R-201 Arrow III	M. Oliver
	G-OASA	Flight Design CTSW	O. E. W. & S. M. Achurch (G-CGHE)
	G-OASH	Robinson R22 Beta	J. C. Lane
	G-OASJ	Thruster T.600N 450	J. Hennessy
	G-OASK	Aeropro Eurofox 912(S)	Aero Space Scientific Educational Trust
	G-OASP	AS.355F2 Twin Squirrel	Helicopter & Pilot Services Ltd
	G-OASW	Schleicher ASW-27	M. P. W. Mee
	G-OATE	Mainair Pegasus Quantum 15-912	A. Roberts
	G-OATV	Cameron V-77 balloon	A. W. & E. P. Braund-Smith
	G-OATZ	Van's RV-12	J. Jones & J. W. Armstrong
	G-OAUD	Robinson R44	Pinpoint 3D Ltd (G-CDHV)
	G-OAUR	Dornier 228-212	Aurigny Air Services Ltd
	G-OAVA	Robinson R22 Beta	Phoenix Helicopter Academy Ltd
	G-OAWM	Cirrus SR20	AWM General Aviation Ltd (G-GCDD)
	G-OAWS	Colt 77A balloon	P. Lawman
	G-OAYJ	PA-28-180 Cherokee	Airborne Adventures Ltd (G-AXZF)
	G-OBAB	Lindstrand LBL-35A Cloudhopper balloon	A. J. Gregory
	G-OBAD	EV-97 Eurostar SL	M. J. Robbins
	G-OBAK	PA-28R-201T Turbo Arrow III	G-OBAK Group
	G-OBAL	Mooney M.20J	G-OBAL Group
	G-OBAN	Jodel D.140B	L. P. Keegan (G-ATSU)
	G-OBAP	Zenair CH.701SP	J. L. Adams
	G-OBAX	Thruster T.600N 450-JAB	Hilton Estates
	G-OBAZ	Best Off Skyranger 912(2)	B. J. Marsh
	G-OBBO	Cessna 182S	A. E. Kedros
	G-OBDA	Diamond Katana DA20-A1	Oscar Papa Ltd
	G-OBDN	PA-28-161 Warrior II	R. M. Bennett
	G-OBEE	Boeing Stearman A75N-1 (3397:174)	P. G. Smith
	G-OBEI	SOCATA TB200 Tobago XL	K. Stoter
	G-OBEN	Cessna 152 II	Globibussola Lda (G-NALI/G-BHVM)
	G-OBET	Sky 77-24 balloon	P. M. Watkins & S. M. Carden
	G-OBFE	Sky 120-24 balloon	J. Sonnabend
	G-OBFS	PA-28-161 Warrior III	KN Singles & Twins Aviation Consultants BV/Netherlands
	G-OBHE	Robinson R44	The BHE Hub Ltd (G-PRET)
	G-OBIL	Robinson R22 Beta	Helicopter & Pilot Services Ltd
	G-OBIO	Robinson R22 Beta	SD Helicopters LLP
	G-OBJB	Lindstrand LBL-90A balloon	B. J. Bower
	G-OBJM	Taylor JT.1 Monoplane	R. K. Thomas
	G-OBJP	Pegasus Quantum 15-912	G. I. Somers
	G-OBJT	Shaw Europa	A. Burill (G-MUZO)
	G-OBLC	Beech 76 Duchess	Air Navigation & Trading Company Ltd
	G-OBMI	Mainair Blade	R. G. Jeffery
	G-OBMS	Cessna F.172N	Mike Sierra Group
	G-OBNA	PA-34-220T Seneca V	O. R. & P. M. Saiman
	G-OBNC	BN-2B-20 Islander	Britten-Norman Aircraft Ltd
	G-OBOF	Remos GX	D. Hawkins
	G-OBPP	Schleicher ASG-29E	M. H. Patel
	G-OBRO	Alpi Pioneer 200M	A. Brown
	G-OBRY	Cameron N-180 balloon	A. C. K. Rawson & J. J. Rudoni
	G-OBSM	Robinson R44 Raven	NT Aviation (G-CDSE)
	G-OBSR	Partenavia P68	Ravenair Aircraft Ltd
	G-OBTS	Cameron C-90 balloon	Skydive Chatteris Club Ltd
	G-OBUC	PA-34-220T Seneca III	Tamara Trading SL
	G-OBUP	DG Flugzeugbau DG-808C	C. J. Lowrie
	G-OBUU	Replica Comper CLA Swift	J. A. Pothecary & R. H. Hunt

Reg	Type	Owner or Operator	Notes
G-OBUY	Colt 69A balloon	T. G. Read	
G-OBUZ	Van's RV-6	A. F. Hall	
G-OBWP	BAe ATP	West Atlantic Aircraft Management AB (G-BTPO)	
G-OBYF	Boeing 767-304ER	TUI Airways Ltd	
G-OBYG	Boeing 767-304ER	TUI Airways Ltd	
G-OBYH	Boeing 767-304ER	TUI Airways Ltd	
G-OBYK	Boeing 767-38AER	TUI Airways Ltd (G-OOAL)	
G-OBYT	Agusta-Bell 206A JetRanger	R. J. Everett (G-BNRC)	
G-OBZR	Aerostyle Breezer LSA	P. Coomber	
G-OCAC	Robin R-2112	The Cotswold Aero Club Ltd (G-EWHT)	
G-OCAD	Sequoia F.8L Falco	D. R. Vale	
G-OCAK	Bombardier BD700-1A10 Global Express	Gama Aviation (UK) Ltd	
G-OCAM	AA-5A Cheetah	J. Khambatta & G. Fenton (G-BLHO)	
G-OCBI	Schweizer 269C-1	Alpha Properties (London) Ltd	
G-OCCF	Diamond DA40D Star	Flying Time Ltd	
G-OCCG	Diamond DA40D Star	Flying Time Ltd	
G-OCCH	Diamond DA40D Star	Innovative Aviation (Leeds) Ltd	
G-OCCN	Diamond DA40D Star	Flying Time Ltd	
G-OCCU	Diamond DA40D Star	Chalrey Ltd	
G-OCCX	Diamond DA42 Twin Star	Smart People Dont Buy Ltd	
G-OCDC	Best Off Sky Ranger Nynja 912S(1)	C. D. Church	
G-OCDO	Guimbal Cabri G2	Vantage Aviation Ltd	
G-OCDP	Flight Design CTSW	M. A. Beadman	
G-OCDW	Jabiru UL-450	D. Goodman & S. S. Aujla	
G-OCFD	Bell 206B JetRanger 3	Rushmere Helicopters LLP (G-WGAL/ G-OICS)	
G-OCFM	PA-34-200 Seneca II	Stapleford Flying Club Ltd (G-ELBC/G-BANS)	
G-OCFT	Bombardier CL600-2B16 Challenger	Air Link One Ltd	
G-OCGC	Robin DR.400-180R	Cambridge Gliding Club Ltd	
G-OCGD	Cameron O-26 balloon	C. G. Dobson	
G-OCHM	Robinson R44	Westleigh Developments Ltd	
G-OCJZ	Cessna 525A Citationjet CJ2	Centreline AV Ltd	
G-OCLC	Aviat A-1B Husky	U. Heissel	
G-OCMM	Agusta A109A II	Castle Air Ltd (G-BXCB/G-ISEB/G-IADT/ G-HBCA)	
G-OCMS	EV-97 TeamEurostar UK	C. M. Saysell	
G-OCMT	EV-97 TeamEurostar UK	P. Crowhurst	
G-OCOK	American Champion 8KCAB Super Decathlon	L. Levinson	
G-OCON	Robinson R44	P. Kelly	
G-OCOV	Robinson R22 Beta	Turner Helicopter Company Ltd	
G-OCPC	Cessna FA.152	Devon & Somerset Flight Training Ltd	
G-OCRI	Colomban MC.15 Cri-Cri	M. J. J. Dunning	
G-OCRL	Europa	R. J. Lewis (G-OBEV)	
G-OCRM	Slingsby T.67M Firefly II	CRM Aviation Europe Ltd (G-BUUB)	
G-OCRZ	CZAW Sportcruiser	P. Marsden	
G-OCTI	PA-32 Cherokee Six 260	M. B. Dyos (G-BGZX)	
G-OCTO	Van's RV-8	A. P. S. Maynard & A. Stokes	
G-OCTS	Cameron Z-90 balloon	A. Collett	
G-OCTU	PA-28-161 Cadet	Glenn Aviation Ltd	
G-OCUB	Piper J-3C-90 Cub	Zebedee Flying Group	
G-OCXI	Van's RV-8	P. S. Gilmour	
G-OCZA	CZAW Sportcruiser	S. M. Dawson	
G-ODAC	Cessna F.152 II	T. M. Jones (G-BITG)	
G-ODAF	Lindstrand LBL-105A balloon	T. J. Horne	
G-ODAK	PA-28-236 Dakota	Flydak LLP	
G-ODAY	Cameron N-56 balloon	British Balloon Museum & Library	
G-ODAZ	Robinson R44 II	S. L. Walton	
G-ODBN	Lindstrand LBL Flowers SS balloon	Magical Adventures Ltd	
G-ODCH	Schleicher ASW-20L	P. J. Stratten	
G-ODDD	Agusta A.109A II	Jetworx Ltd (G-JBRG/G-TMUR/G-CEPO)	
G-ODDF	Siren PIK-30	G. F. Bailey, J. D. Sorrell & D. M. Thomas	
G-ODDS	Aerotek Pitts S-2A	A. C. Cassidy	
G-ODDZ	Schempp-Hirth Duo Discus T	P. A. King	
G-ODEE	Van's RV-6	J. Redfearn	
G-ODEL	Falconar F-11-3	G. F. Brummell	
G-ODGC	Aeropro Eurofox 912(iS)	Dorset Gliding Club Ltd	
G-ODGS	Avtech Jabiru UL-450	W. K. Evans	
G-ODHB	Robinson R44	A. J. Mossop	

Notes	Reg	Type	Owner or Operator
	G-ODHC	DHC.1B-2-S5 Chipmunk	P. M. Wells
	G-ODIN	Avions Mudry CAP-10B	CAP Ten
	G-ODIP	Aviat A-1C-180 Husky	A. J. White
	G-ODIZ	AutoGyro Cavalon	P. Williams
	G-ODJD	Raj Hamsa X'Air 582 (7)	N. M. Toulson
	G-ODJF	Lindstrand LBL-90B balloon	Helena Dos Santos SA/Portugal
	G-ODJG	Shaw Europa	K. R. Challis & C. S. Andersson
	G-ODJH	Mooney M.20C	R. M. Schweitzer/Netherlands (G-BMLH)
	G-ODOC	Robinson R44	E. Theben/Germany
	G-ODOG	PA-28R Cherokee Arrow 200-II	M. Brancart (G-BAAR)
	G-ODPJ	VPM M-16 Tandem Trainer	S. Palmer (G-BVWX)
	G-ODRT	Cameron Z-105 balloon	N. W. N. Townshend
	G-ODSA	Bell 429	Starspeed Ltd
	G-ODTW	Shaw Europa	D. T. Walters
	G-ODUD	PA-28-181 Archer II	S. Barlow, R. N. Ingle & R. J. Murray (G-IBBO)
	G-ODUO	Schempp-Hirth Duo Discus	3D Syndicate
	G-ODUR	Raytheon Hawker 900XP	Sable Air APS
	G-ODVB	CFM Shadow Srs DD	L. J. E. Moss
	G-ODWS	Silence SA.180 Twister	T. R. Dews
	G-OEAC	Mooney M.20J	S. Lovatt
	G-OEAT	Robinson R22 Beta	Leamington Hobby Centre Ltd (G-RACH)
	G-OECM	Commander 114B	R. G. Macdowall
	G-OECO	Flylight Dragonfly	P. A. & M. W. Aston
	G-OEDB	PA-38-112 Tomahawk	BS Offshore Ltd (G-BGGJ)
	G-OEDP	Cameron N-77 balloon	M. J. Betts
	G-OEFT	PA-38-112 Tomahawk	M. Lee
	G-OEGG	Cameron Egg-65 SS balloon	Mobberley Balloon Collection
	G-OEGL	Christen Eagle II	G. G. Ferriman & C. Butler
	G-OEGO	E-Go	Cambridge Business Travel
	G-OEKS	Ikarus C42 FB80	J. D. Smith
	G-OELZ	Wassmer WA.52 Europa	J. A. Simms
	G-OEMT	MBB BK-117 C-1	RCR Aviation Ltd
	G-OEMZ	Pietenpol Air Camper	C. Brockis (G-IMBY)
	G-OENA	Agusta Westland AW.139	Bristow Helicopters Ltd
	G-OENB	Agusta Westland AW.189	Bristow Helicopters Ltd
	G-OENC	Agusta Westland AW.189	Bristow Helicopters Ltd
	G-OERR	Lindstrand LBL-60A balloon	P. C. Gooch
	G-OERS	Cessna 172N	N. J. Smith & A. Stevens (G-SSRS)
	G-OESC	Aquila AT01	Osterreichischer Sportflieger/Austria (G-OZIO)
	G-OESP	Robinson R44 II	MJL Plant Hire (Cornwall) Ltd (G-CGND)
	G-OESY	Easy Raider J2.2 (1)	J. Gray
	G-OETI	Bell 206B JetRanger 3	Jaspa (G-RMIE/G-BPIE)
	G-OETV	PA-31-350 Navajo Chieftain	Atlantic Bridge Aviation Ltd
	G-OEVA	PA-32-260 Cherokee Six	Enterprise Purchasing Ltd (G-FLJA/G-AVTJ)
	G-OEWD	Raytheon 390 Premier 1	Avidus Jet Management Ltd
	G-OEZI	Easy Raider J2.2(2)	S. E. J. M. McDonald
	G-OEZY	Shaw Europa	A. W. Wakefield
	G-OFAA	Cameron Z-105 balloon	R. A. Schwab
	G-OFAL	Ozone Roadster/Bailey Quattro	Malcolm Roberts Heating, Plumbing and Electrical Ltd
	G-OFAS	Robinson R22 Beta	Advance Helicopters Ltd
	G-OFBT	Cameron O-84 balloon	A. A. & W. S. Calvert
	G-OFBU	Ikarus C.42 FB UK	Old Sarum C42 Group
	G-OFCM	Cessna F.172L	Sirius Aviation Ltd (G-AZUN)
	G-OFDR	PA-28-161 Cadet	Electric Scribe 2000 Ltd
	G-OFDT	Mainair Pegasus Quik	R. M. Tomlins
	G-OFER	PA-18 Super Cub 150	White Watham Airfield Ltd
	G-OFES	Alisport Silent 2 Electro	N. D. A. Graham
	G-OFFA	Pietenpol Air Camper	C. Brockis & P. A. Hall
	G-OFFO	Extra EA.300/L	2 Excel Aviation Ltd
	G-OFFS	PA-38-112 Tomahawk	NWMAS Leasing Ltd (G-BMSF)
	G-OFGC	Aeroprakt A22-L Foxbat	J. M. Fearn
	G-OFIT	SOCATA TB10 Tobago	GFI Aviation Group (G-BRIU)
	G-OFIX	Grob G.109B	T. R. Dews
	G-OFJC	Eiriavion PIK-20E	G. Bailey, J. D. Sorrell & D. Thomas
	G-OFLI	Colt 105A balloon	Virgin Airship & Balloon Co Ltd
	G-OFLT	EMB-110P1 Bandeirante ★	Rescue trainer/Aveley, Essex (G-MOBL/ G-BGCS)
	G-OFLY	Cessna 210M	A. P. Mothew
	G-OFNC	Balony Kubicek BB17XR balloon	M. R. Jeynes

Reg	Type	Owner or Operator	Notes
G-OFOM	BAe 146-100	Formula One Management Ltd (G-BSLP/G-BRLM)	
G-OFRB	Everett gyroplane	T. N. Holcroft-Smith	
G-OFRY	Cessna 152	Devon and Somerset Flight Training Ltd	
G-OFSP	CZAW Sportcruiser	L. Dempsey	
G-OFTI	PA-28 Cherokee 140	Startrade Heli GmbH & Co KG	
G-OGAN	Europa	R. K. W. Moss	
G-OGAR	PZL SZD-45A Ogar	J. F. C. Sergeant	
G-OGAS	Westland WG.30 Srs 100 ★	(stored)/Yeovil (G-BKNW)	
G-OGEM	PA-28-181 Archer II	GEM Integrated Solutions Ltd	
G-OGEO	Aérospatiale SA.341G Gazelle 1	G. Steel (G-BXJK)	
G-OGES	Enstrom 280FX	AWB SAS/France (G-CBYL)	
G-OGGB	Grob G.102 Astir CS	M. P. Webb	
G-OGGI	Aviat A-1C-180 Husky	E. D. Fern	
G-OGGM	Cirrus SR22	Morson Human Resources Ltd	
G-OGGS	Thunder Ax8-84 balloon	G. Gamble & Sons (Quorn) Ltd	
G-OGGY	Aviat A.1B	M. J. Medland	
G-OGIL	Short SD3-30 Variant 100 ★	North East Aircraft Museum/Usworth (G-BITV)	
G-OGJC	Robinson R44 II	Telecom Advertising & Promotions Ltd	
G-OGJM	Cameron C-80 balloon	G. F. Madelin	
G-OGJP	Commander 114B	M. J. Church	
G-OGJS	Puffer Cozy	G. J. Stamper	
G-OGLE	AS.350B3 Ecureuil	Freshair UK Ltd (G-CIEU)	
G-OGLY	Cameron Z-105 balloon	H. M. Ogston	
G-OGOD	P & M Quik GT450	L. McIlwaine	
G-OGOS	Everett gyroplane	N. A. Seymour	
G-OGPN	Cassutt Special	S. Alexander (G-OMFI/G-BKCH)	
G-OGRL	Van's RV-7	M. A. Wyer	
G-OGSA	Avtech Jabiru SPL-450	G-OGSA Group	
G-OGSE	Gulfstream V-SP	TAG Aviation (UK) Ltd	
G-OGTR	P & M Quik GTR	K. J. Bowles	
G-OGUN	Eurocopter AS.350B2 Ecureuil	Go Exclusive Ltd (G-SMDJ)	
G-OHAC	Cessna F.182Q	MaguireIzatt LLP	
G-OHAL	Pietenpol Air Camper	A. Ryan-Fecitt	
G-OHAM	Robinson R44 II	Hamsters Wheel Productions Ltd (G-GBEN/G-CDJZ)	
G-OHAS	Robinson R66	Heli Air Scotland Ltd	
G-OHAV	ATG Ltd HAV-3	Hybrid Air Vehicles Ltd	
G-OHCP	AS.355F1 Twin Squirrel	Staske Construction Ltd (G-BTVS/G-STVE/G-TOFF/G-BKJX)	
G-OHDC	Colt Film Cassette SS balloon ★	Balloon Preservation Group	
G-OHDK	Glasflugel 304S Shark	The Shark Syndicate	
G-OHGA	Hughes O-6A (69-16011)	MSS Holdings (UK) Ltd	
G-OHGC	Scheibe SF.25C Falke	Heron Gliding Club	
G-OHIG	EMB-110P1 Bandeirante ★	Air Salvage International/Alton (G-OPPP)	
G-OHIO	Dyn'Aero MCR-01	J. M. Keane	
G-OHJE	Alpi Pioneer 300 Hawk	Abergavenny Flying Group	
G-OHJV	Robinson R44	I. Taylor	
G-OHKS	Pegasus Quantum 15-912	L. J. Nelson	
G-OHLI	Robinson R44 II	NCS Partnership	
G-OHLV	Sackville BM-65 balloon	H. & L. D. Vaughan	
G-OHMS	AS.355F1 Twin Squirrel	HFS (Aviation) Ltd	
G-OHOV	Rotorway Executive 162F	M. G. Bird	
G-OHPC	Cessna 208 Caravan 1	S. Ulrich	
G-OHPH	HpH Glasflugel 304MS	A. D. Wood & A. D. Le Roux	
G-OHUR	Hurricane 315	M. Ingleton	
G-OHWK	Bell 206L-1 LongRanger	Hawk Site Facilities Ltd (G-PWIT/G-DWMI)	
G-OHWV	Raj Hamsa X'Air 582(6)	S. A. Mercer	
G-OHYE	Thruster T.600N 450	T. Kossakowski (G-CCRO)	
G-OHZO	Aviat A-1A Husky	Neil's Seaplanes Ltd	
G-OIBO	PA-28 Cherokee 180	M. Kraemer & J. G. C. Schneider (G-AVAZ)	
G-OIFM	Cameron 90 Dude SS balloon	Magical Adventures Ltd	
G-OIHC	PA-32R-301 Saratoga IIHP	N. J. Lipczynski (G-PUSK)	
G-OIIO	Robinson R22 Beta	Whizzard Helicopters (G-ULAB)	
G-OIIY	Ultramagic S-70 balloon	M. Cowling	
G-OIMC	Cessna 152 II	East Midlands Flying School Ltd	
G-OIMF	Dassault Falcon 7X	TAG Aviation (UK) Ltd	
G-OINN	UltraMagic H-31 balloon	G. Everett	

Notes	Reg	Type	Owner or Operator
	G-OINT	Balony Kubicek BB20XR balloon	M. A. Green
	G-OIOB	Mudry CAP.10B	Rolls-Royce PLC
	G-OIOZ	Thunder Ax9-120 S2 balloon	R. H. Etherington
	G-OITV	Enstrom 280C-UK-2	C. W. Brierley Jones (G-HRVY/G-DUGY/ G-BEEL)
	G-OIVN	Liberty XL-2	I. Shaw
	G-OJAB	Avtech Jabiru SK	J. D. Winder
	G-OJAC	Mooney M.20J	Hornet Engineering Ltd
	G-OJAG	Cessna 172S	Valhalla Aviation LLP
	G-OJAN	Robinson R22 Beta	J. C. Lane (G-SANS/G-BUHX)
	G-OJAS	Auster J/1U Workmaster	D. S. Hunt
	G-OJBB	Enstrom 280FX	M. Jones
	G-OJBM	Cameron N-90 balloon	B. J. Bettin
	G-OJBS	Cameron N-105A balloon	J. Bennett & Son (Insurance Brokers) Ltd
	G-OJBW	Lindstrand LBL J & B Bottle SS balloon	G. Gray
	G-OJCL	Robinson R22	JCL Aviation (G-HRHE/G-BTWP)
	G-OJCS	BRM Bristell NG5 Speed Wing	J. C. Simpson
	G-OJCW	PA-32RT-300 Lance II	P. G. Dobson
	G-OJDA	EAA Acrosport II	D. B. Almey
	G-OJDC	Thunder Ax7-77 balloon	A. Heginbottom
	G-OJEG	Airbus A.321-231	SASOF III (A10) Aviation Ireland DAC
	G-OJEH	PA-28-181 Archer II	P. C. Lilley
	G-OJEN	Cameron V-77 balloon	S. D. Wrighton
	G-OJER	Cessna 560XL Citation XLS	Aviation Beauport
	G-OJGC	Van's RV-4	J. G. Claridge
	G-OJGT	Maule M.5-235C	Newnham Joint Flying Syndicate
	G-OJHC	Cessna 182P	N. Foster
	G-OJHL	Shaw Europa	M. D. Burns & G. Rainey
	G-OJIM	PA-28R-201T Turbo Arrow III	Black Star Aviation Ltd
	G-OJJV	P & M Pegasus Quik	J. J. Valentine
	G-OJKM	Rans S.7 Courier	A. J. Owen
	G-OJLD	Van's RV-7	J. L. Dixon
	G-OJLH	TEAM mini-MAX 91	P. D. Parry (G-MYAW)
	G-OJMP	Cessna 208B Grand Caravan	Parachuting Aircraft Ltd
	G-OJMS	Cameron Z-90 balloon	Joinerysoft Ltd
	G-OJNB	Linsdstrand LBL-21A balloon	M. J. Axtell
	G-OJNE	Schempp-Hirth Nimbus 3T	M. R. Garwood
	G-OJON	Taylor JT.2 Titch	Freelance Aviation Ltd
	G-OJPS	Bell 206B JetRanger 2	C & L Fairburn Property Developments Ltd (G-UEST/G-ROYB/G-BLWU)
	G-OJRM	Cessna T.182T	Romeo Mike Group
	G-OJSD	Aeropro Eurofox 912(S)	J. D. Sinclair-Day
	G-OJSH	Thruster T.600N 450 JAB	G-OJSH Group
	G-OJVA	Van's RV-6	J. A. Village
	G-OJVL	Van's RV-6	S. E. Tomlinson
	G-OJWB	Hawker 800XP	Langford Lane Ltd
	G-OJWS	PA-28-161 Warrior II	P. J. Ward
	G-OKAY	Pitts S-1E Special	S. R. S. Evans
	G-OKCC	Cameron N-90 balloon	D. J. Head
	G-OKCP	Lindstrand LBL Battery SS balloon	Lindstrand-Asia Ltd (G-MAXX)
	G-OKED	Cessna 150L	M. J. Fogarty
	G-OKEN	PA-28R-201T Turbo Arrow III	L. James
	G-OKER	Van's RV-7	R. M. Johnson
	G-OKEV	Shaw Europa	K. A. Kedward
	G-OKEW	UltraMagic M-65C balloon	Hampshire Balloons Ltd
	G-OKEY	Robinson R22 Beta	Heliservices
	G-OKID	Reality Escapade Kid	V. H. Hallam
	G-OKIM	Best Off Sykyranger 912 (2)	K. P. Taylor
	G-OKIS	Tri-R Kis	M. R. Cleveley
	G-OKLY	Cessna F.150K	J. L. Sparks (G-ECBH)
	G-OKMA	Tri-R Kis	K. Miller
	G-OKPW	Tri-R Kis	P. J. Reilly
	G-OKTA	Ikarus C42 FB80	Avion Training & Consultancy Ltd
	G-OKTI	Aquila AT01	P. H. Ferdinand
	G-OKUB	TLAC Sherwood Kub	The Light Aircraft Company Ltd
	G-OKYA	Cameron V-77 balloon	R. J. Pearce
	G-OKYM	PA-28 Cherokee 140	R. B. Petrie (G-AVLS)
	G-OLAA	Alpi Pioneer 300 Hawk	G. G. Hammond

Reg	Type	Owner or Operator	Notes
G-OLAU	Robinson R22 Beta	Carriag Homes Ltd	
G-OLAW	Lindstrand LBL-25A balloon	George Law Plant Ltd	
G-OLCP	AS.355N Twin Squirrel	Cheshire Helicopters Ltd (G-CLIP)	
G-OLCY	Lindstrand LTL Series 1-105 balloon	A. M. Holly	
G-OLDG	Cessna T.182T	H. W. Palmer (G-CBTJ)	
G-OLDH	Aérospatiale SA.341G Gazelle 1	MW Helicopters Ltd (G-UTZY/G-BKLV)	
G-OLDM	Pegasus Quantum 15-912	J. W. Holme	
G-OLDO	Eurocopter EC.120B Colibri	Gold Group International Ltd (G-HIGI)	
G-OLDP	Mainair Pegasus Quik	G. J. Gibson	
G-OLEA	PA-28-151 Cherokee Warrior	London School of Flying Ltd	
G-OLEC	Alisport Silent 2 Electro	Lleweni Parc Ltd	
G-OLEE	Cessna F.152	Redhill Air Services Ltd	
G-OLEG	Yakovlev Yak-3UA	W. H. Greenwood	
G-OLEM	Jodel D.18	G. E. Roe (G-BSBP)	
G-OLEW	Vans RV-7A	A. Burani	
G-OLEZ	Piper J-3C-65 Cub	L. Powell (G-BSAX)	
G-OLFA	AS.350B3 Ecureuil	Twin Otter International Ltd	
G-OLFB	Pegasus Quantum 15-912	M. S. McGimpsey	
G-OLFE	Dassault Falcon 20-E5	Green Go Aircraft KFT	
G-OLFT	Rockwell Commander 114	D. A. Tubby (G-WJMN)	
G-OLFY	Breezer B600 LSA	S. Thomson	
G-OLFZ	P & M Quik GT450	A. J. Boyd	
G-OLGA	Starstreak Shadow SA-II	G. L. Turner	
G-OLHR	Cassutt Racer IIIM	P. A. Hall & A. R. Lewis (G-BNJZ)	
G-OLIC	Tecnam P2008-JC	Stapleford Flying Club Ltd	
G-OLIV	Beech B.200 Super King Air	Dragonfly Aviation Services Ltd (G-RAFN)	
G-OLLI	Cameron O-31 SS balloon	The British Balloon Museum & Library Ltd	
G-OLNT	SA.365N1 Dauphin 2	LNT Aviation Ltd (G-POAV/G-BOPI)	
G-OLPE	AS.350BA Ecureuil	G. Martinelli	
G-OLPM	P & M Quik R	M. D. Freeman	
G-OLSF	PA-28-161 Cadet	Flew LLP (G-OTYJ)	
G-OLUD	Extra EA.300/200	A. P. Walsh	
G-OMAA	Eurocopter EC.135 T2+	Babcock Mission Critical Services Onshore Ltd	
G-OMAF	Dornier 228-200	RUAG Aerospace Services GmbH/Germany	
G-OMAG	Cessna 182B	Bodmin Light Aeroplane Services Ltd	
G-OMAL	Thruster T.600N 450	M. Howland	
G-OMAO	SOCATA TB-20 Trinidad	Alpha Oscar Group (G-GDGR)	
G-OMAS	Cessna A.150M	M. A. Segar (G-BTFS)	
G-OMAT	PA-28 Cherokee 140	Midland Air Training School (G-JIMY/G-AYUG)	
G-OMCB	TL2000UK Sting Carbon S4	M. C. Bayley	
G-OMCC	AS.350B Ecureuil	Airbourne Solutions Ltd (G-JTCM/G-HLEN/ G-LOLY)	
G-OMCH	PA-28-161 Warrior III	Chalrey Ltd	
G-OMDB	Van's V-6A	D. A. Roseblade	
G-OMDD	Thunder Ax8-90 S2 balloon	M. D. Dickinson	
G-OMDH	Hughes 369E	Stilgate Ltd	
G-OMDR	Agusta-Bell 206B JetRanger II	Castle Air Ltd (G-HRAY/G-VANG/G-BIZA)	
G-OMEM	Eurocopter EC 120B	Go Exclusive Ltd (G-BXYD)	
G-OMEN	Cameron Z-90 balloon	M. G. Howard	
G-OMER	Avtech Jabiru UL-450	B. P. Bradley (G-GPAS)	
G-OMEX	Zenair CH.701 UL	D. I. Waller	
G-OMEZ	Zenair CH.601HDS	A. D. Sutton	
G-OMGR	Cameron Z-105 balloon	Omega Resource Group PLC	
G-OMHC	PA-28RT-201 Arrow IV	J. W. Tonge	
G-OMHD	EE Canberra PR.Mk.9 (XH134)	Kemble Airfield Estates Ltd	
G-OMHI	Mills MH-1	J. P. Mills	
G-OMHP	Avtech Jabiru UL	J. Livingstone	
G-OMIA	MS.893A Rallye Commodore 180	D. Perryman	
G-OMIK	Shaw Europa	Mikite Flying Group	
G-OMIW	Pegasus Quik	A. J. Ladell	
G-OMJA	PA-28-181 Archer II	P. R. Monk	
G-OMJT	Rutan LongEz	D. A. Daniel	
G-OMMG	Robinson R22 Beta	Sky Touch GmbH & Co KG/Germany (G-BPYX)	
G-OMMM	Colt 90A balloon	A. & M. Frayling	
G-OMNI	PA-28R Cherokee Arrow 200D	Cotswold Aviation Services Ltd (G-BAWA)	
G-OMPH	Van's RV-7	R. J. Luke	
G-OMPW	Mainair Pegasus Quik	M. P. Wimsey	
G-OMRB	Cameron V-77 balloon	I. J. Jevons	
G-OMRC	Van's RV-10	A. W. Collett	

Notes	Reg	Type	Owner or Operator
	G-OMRP	Flight Design CTSW	M. E. Parker
	G-OMSA	Flight Design CTSW	Microlight Sport Aviation Ltd
	G-OMST	PA-28-161 Warrior III	Mid-Sussex Timber Co Ltd (G-BZUA)
	G-OMUM	Rockwell Commander 114	M. J. P. Lynch
	G-OMYT	Airbus A.330-243	Thomas Cook Airlines Ltd (G-MOJO)
	G-ONAA	North American Rockwell OV-10B Bronco (99+18)	Liberty Aviation Ltd
	G-ONAF	Naval Aircraft Factory N3N-3 (4406:12)	J. P. Birnie
	G-ONAT	Grob G.102 Astir CS77	N. A. Toogood
	G-ONAV	PA-31-310 Turbo Navajo C	Panther Aviation Ltd (G-IGAR)
	G-ONCB	Lindstrand LBL-31A balloon	M. D. Freeston & S. Mitchell
	G-ONCS	Slingsby T.66 Nipper 3	C. Swann & N. J. Riddin (G-AZBA)
	G-ONES	Slingsby T.67M Firefly 200	Aquaman Aviation Ltd
	G-ONET	PA-28 Cherokee 180E	N. Z. Ali & T. Mahmood (G-AYAU)
	G-ONEZ	Glaser-Dirks DG-200/17	One Zulu Group
	G-ONGC	Robin DR.400/180R	Norfolk Gliding Club Ltd
	G-ONHH	Forney F-1A Aircoupe	R. D. I. Tarry (G-ARHA)
	G-ONIC	Evektor EV-97 Sportstar Max	D. M. Jack
	G-ONIG	Murphy Elite	N. S. Smith
	G-ONKA	Aeronca K	N. J. R. Minchin
	G-ONNE	Westland Gazelle HT.3 (XW858:C)	A. M. Parkes (G-DMSS)
	G-ONSW	Skyranger Swift 912S(1)	N. S. Wells
	G-ONTV	Agusta-Bell 206B-3 JetRanger III	Adventure 001 Ltd (G-GOUL)
	G-ONUN	Van's RV-6A	D. Atkinson
	G-ONVG	Guimbal Cabri G2	Vantage Aviation Ltd
	G-ONYX	Bell 206B-3 JetRanger III	CBM Aviation Ltd (G-BXPN)
	G-OOBA	Boeing 757-26N	TUI Airways Ltd
	G-OOBB	Boeing 757-28A	TUI Airways Ltd
	G-OOBC	Boeing 757-28A	TUI Airways Ltd
	G-OOBD	Boeing 757-28A	TUI Airways Ltd
	G-OOBE	Boeing 757-28A	TUI Airways Ltd
	G-OOBF	Boeing 757-28A	TUI Airways Ltd
	G-OOBG	Boeing 757-236	TUI Airways Ltd
	G-OOBH	Boeing 757-236	TUI Airways Ltd
	G-OOBN	Boeing 757-2G5	TUI Airways Ltd
	G-OOBP	Boeing 757-2G5	TUI Airways Ltd
	G-OOCP	SOCATA TB-10 Tobago	R. M. Briggs (G-BZRL)
	G-OODD	Robinson R44 II	S. K. Miles
	G-OODE	SNCAN Stampe SV.4C (modified)	G-OODE Flying Group (G-AZNN)
	G-OODI	Pitts S-1D Special	C. Hutson & R. S. Wood (G-BBBU)
	G-OODW	PA-28-181 Archer II	Redhill Air Services Ltd
	G-OODX	Robinson R22	HQ Aviation Ltd (G-BXXN)
	G-OOEY	Balony Kubicek BB-222 balloon	A. W. Holly
	G-OOFE	Thruster T.600N 450	D. Dance
	G-OOFT	PA-28-161 Warrior III	Aerodynamics Malaga SL/Spain
	G-OOGO	GA-7 Cougar	CCB Servicos Aereos Lda/Portugal
	G-OOGS	GA-7 Cougar	P. Wilkinson (G-BGJW)
	G-OOGY	P & M Quik R	Cambridge Road Professional Services Ltd
	G-OOIO	AS.350B3 Ecureuil	Hovering Ltd
	G-OOJP	Commander 114B	R. J. Rother
	G-OOLE	Cessna 172M	J. Edmondson (G-BOSI)
	G-OOMA	PA-28-161 Warrior II	Aviation Advice and Consulting Ltd (G-BRBB)
	G-OOMF	PA-18-150 Super Cub	C. G. Bell
	G-OONA	Robinson R44 II	Malaika Developments LLP
	G-OONE	Mooney M.20J	M. Kalyuzhny, C. Hollis & T. Slotover
	G-OONY	PA-28-161 Warrior II	J. R. Golding
	G-OONZ	P & M Aviation Quik	G-OONZ Group
	G-OOON	PA-34-220T Seneca III	R. Paris
	G-OOPY	CSA PS-28 Cruiser	V. Barnes
	G-OORV	Van's RV-6	C. Sharples
	G-OOSE	Rutan Vari-Eze	B. O. Smith & J. A. Towers
	G-OOSH	Zenair CH.601UL Zodiac	J. R. C. Brightman & J. P. Batty
	G-OOSY	DH.82A Tiger Moth (DE971)	S. Philpott & C. Stopher
	G-OOTC	PA-28R-201T Turbo Arrow III	G-OOTC Group (G-CLIV)
	G-OOTT	Eurocopter AS.350B3 Ecureuil	R. J. Green
	G-OOUK	Cirrus SR22	P. R. D. Smith
	G-OOWS	Eurocopter AS.350B3 Ecureuil	Millburn World Travel Services Ltd
	G-OOXP	Aero Designs Pulsar XP	P. C. Avery

Reg	Type	Owner or Operator	Notes
G-OPAG	PA-34-200 Seneca II	A. H. Lavender (G-BNGB)	
G-OPAH	Eurocopter EC135 T2 +	Pure Leisure Air (North West) LLP (G-RWLA)	
G-OPAM	Cessna F.152 II (tailwheel)	PJC Leasing Ltd (G-BFZS)	
G-OPAR	Van's RV-6	R. Parr (G-CGNR)	
G-OPAT	Beech 76 Duchess	Golf Alpha Tango Ltd	
G-OPAZ	Pazmany PL.2	A. D. Wood	
G-OPBW	Cameron nZ-150 balloon	Polar Bear Windows Ltd	
G-OPCG	Cessna 182T	S. K. Pomfret	
G-OPDA	Aquila AT01	Go PDA Ltd	
G-OPEJ	TEAM Minimax 91A	A. W. McBlain	
G-OPEN	Bell 206B	Gazelle Aviation LLP	
G-OPEP	PA-28RT-201T Turbo Arrow IV	S. Denham	
G-OPER	Lindstrand LTL Series 1-70 balloon	Lindstrand Technologies Ltd	
G-OPET	PA-28-181 Archer II	Cambrian Flying Group Ltd	
G-OPFA	Pioneer 300	S. Eddison & R. Minett	
G-OPFR	Diamond DA.42 Twin Star	P. F. Rothwell	
G-OPHT	Schleicher ASH-26E	J. S. Wand	
G-OPIC	Cessna FRA.150L	A. V. Harmer (G-BGNZ)	
G-OPIK	Eiri PIK-20E	G-OPIK Syndicate	
G-OPIT	CFM Streak Shadow Srs SA	I. J. Guy	
G-OPJD	PA-28RT-201T Turbo Arrow IV	J. M. McMillan	
G-OPJK	Shaw Europa	P. J. Kember	
G-OPJS	Pietenpol Air Camper	P. J. Shenton	
G-OPKF	Cameron 90 Bowler SS balloon	D. K. Fish	
G-OPLC	DH.104 Dove 8	Columba Aviation Ltd (G-BLRB)	
G-OPME	PA-23 Aztec 250D	R. G. Pardo (G-ODIR/G-AZGB)	
G-OPMJ	Cessna F.172M	Jefferson Air Photography (G-BIIB)	
G-OPMT	Lindstrand LBL-105A balloon	K. R. Karlstrom	
G-OPOT	Agusta A.109S Grand	Sundorne Properties (Llanidloes) Ltd (G-EMHD/G-STGR)	
G-OPPO	Groppo Trail	A. C. Hampson	
G-OPRC	Shaw Europa XS	M. J. Ashby-Arnold & D. Lee	
G-OPSF	PA-38-112 Tomahawk	P. I. Higham (G-BGZI)	
G-OPSG	Aeropro Eurofox 912(S)	P. S. Gregory	
G-OPSL	PA-32R-301 Saratoga SP	Defence Vision Systems Pte Ltd (G-IMPW)	
G-OPSP	Diamond DA.40D Star	Lindsky Aviation Training & Services NV/Belgium (G-OCCR)	
G-OPSS	Cirrus SR20	Clifton Aviation Ltd	
G-OPST	Cessna 182R	Just Plane Trading Ltd	
G-OPTI	PA-28-161 Warrior II	Rio Leon Services Ltd	
G-OPTZ	Pitts S-2A Special	J. L. Dixon (G—SKNT/G-PEAL)	
G-OPUB	Slingsby T.67M Firefly 160	A. L. Barker (G-DLTA/G-SFTX)	
G-OPUK	PA-28-161 Warrior III	D. J. King	
G-OPUP	Beagle B.121 Pup 2	F. A. Zubiel (G-AXEU)	
G-OPVM	Van's RV-9A	R. M. Cochran	
G-OPWR	Cameron Z-90 balloon	Flying Enterprises	
G-OPWS	Mooney M.20K	J. C. Woolard	
G-OPYE	Cessna 172S	Quarry Garage (Rotherham) Ltd	
G-OPYO	Alpi Pioneer 300 Hawk	T. J. Franklin & D. S. Simpson	
G-ORAC	Cameron 110 Van SS balloon	T. G. Church	
G-ORAE	Van's RV-7	R. W. Eaton	
G-ORAF	CFM Streak Shadow	G. A. Carter	
G-ORAM	Thruster T600N 450	D. W. Wilson	
G-ORAR	PA-28-181 Archer III	P. N. & S. M. Thornton	
G-ORAS	Clutton FRED Srs 2	A. I. Sutherland	
G-ORAU	Evektor EV-97A Eurostar	W. R. C. Williams-Wynne	
G-ORAW	Cessna 525 Citation M2	Catreus AOC Ltd	
G-ORAY	Cessna F.182Q II	S. Bonham (G-BHDN)	
G-ORBK	Robinson R44 II	T2 Technology Ltd (G-CCNO)	
G-ORBS	Mainair Blade	J. W. Dodson	
G-ORCA	Van's RV-4	I. A. Harding	
G-ORCC	AutoGyro Calidus	R. P. Churchill-Coleman	
G-ORCW	Schempp-Hirth Ventus 2cT	J. C. A. Garland & M. S. Hawkins	
G-ORDA	Cessna F.172N	D. G. Martinez	
G-ORDH	AS.355N Twin Squirrel	Atlas Helicopters Ltd	
G-ORDM	Cessna 182T	The Cambridge Aero Club Ltd (G-KEMY)	
G-ORDS	Thruster T.600N 450	G. J. Pill	
G-ORED	BN-2T Turbine Islander	Britten-Norman Ltd (G-BJYW)	
G-OREZ	Cessna 525 Citation M2	Helitrip Charter LLP	
G-ORIB	Aeropro Eurofox 912(IS)	J. McAlpine	

Notes	Reg	Type	Owner or Operator
	G-ORIG	Glaser-Dirks DG.800A	M. Bond & R. Kalin
	G-ORIX	ARV K1 Super 2	T. M. Lyons (G-BUXH/G-BNVK)
	G-ORJW	Laverda F.8L Falco Srs 4	Viking BV/Netherlands
	G-ORKY	AS.350B2 Ecureuil	PLM Dollar Group Ltd
	G-ORLA	P & M Pegasus Quik	J. Summers
	G-ORMB	Robinson R22 Beta	Heli Air Scotland Ltd
	G-ORMW	Ikarus C.42 FB100	A. J. Dixon & J. W. D. Blythe
	G-OROA	PA-28RT-201T Turbo Arrow IV	J. C. Lafontaine
	G-OROD	PA-18 Super Cub 150	B. W. Faulkner
	G-OROS	Ikarus C.42 FB80	R. I. Simpson
	G-ORPC	Shaw Europa XS	P. W. Churms
	G-ORPR	Cameron O-77 balloon	S. R. Vining
	G-ORRG	Robin DR.400-180 Regent	Radley Robin Group
	G-ORSE	Ikarus C42 FB100 Bravo	D. S. Murrell
	G-ORST	Airbus EC.135 T3	Babcock Mission Critical Services Onshore Ltd (G-DEWF)
	G-ORTH	Beech E90 King Air	Gorthair Ltd
	G-ORUG	Thruster T.600N 450	D. J. N. Brown
	G-ORUN	Reality Escapade	M. J. Clark
	G-ORVE	Van's RV-6	R. J. F. Swain & F. M. Sperryn
	G-ORVG	Van's RV-6	RV Group
	G-ORVI	Van's RV-6	J. D. B. Paines
	G-ORVR	Partenavia P.68B	Ravenair Aircraft Ltd (G-BFBD)
	G-ORVS	Van's RV-9	C. J. Marsh
	G-ORVX	Van's RV-10	C. D. Meek (G-OHIY)
	G-ORVZ	Van's RV-7	C. Taylor
	G-ORYG	Rotorsport UK Cavalon	M. P. L. Dowie
	G-OSAR	Bell 206L-1 LongRanger	Vantage Aviation Ltd
	G-OSAT	Cameron Z-105 balloon	A. V. & M. R. Noyce
	G-OSAW	QAC Quickie Q.2	S. A. Wilson (G-BVYT)
	G-OSAZ	Robinson R22	W. Oswald (G-DERB/G-BPYH)
	G-OSCC	PA-32 Cherokee Six 300	BG & G Airlines Ltd (G-BGFD)
	G-OSCO	TEAM mini-MAX 91	S. H. Slade
	G-OSDF	Schempp-Hirth Ventus a	S. D. Foster
	G-OSEA	BN-2B-26 Islander	W. T. Johnson & Sons (Huddersfield) Ltd (G-BKOL)
	G-OSEM	Robinson R44 II	Sloane Charter
	G-OSEP	Mainair Blade 912	J. D. Smith
	G-OSFB	Diamond HK.36TTC Super Dimona	Oxfordshire Sportflying Ltd
	G-OSFS	Cessan F.177RG	D. G. Wright
	G-OSGU	Aeropro Eurofox 912(S)	Scottish Gliding Union Ltd
	G-OSHK	Schempp-Hirth SHK-1	P. B. Hibbard
	G-OSHL	Robinson R22 Beta	Sloane Helicopters Ltd
	G-OSIC	Pitts S-1C Special	P. J. Hebdon (G-BUAW)
	G-OSII	Cessna 172N	G-OSII Group (G-BIVY)
	G-OSIS	Pitts S-1S Special	P. J. Burgess
	G-OSIT	Pitts S-1T Special	C. J. J. Robertson
	G-OSKR	Skyranger 912 (2)	J. E. O. Larsson
	G-OSKY	Cessna 172M	Skyhawk Leasing Ltd
	G-OSLD	Shaw Europa XS	S. Percy & C. Davies
	G-OSLO	Schweizer 269C	A. H. Helicopter Services Ltd
	G-OSMD	Bell 206B JetRanger 2	TR Aviation Services Ltd (G-LTEK/G-BMIB)
	G-OSND	Cessna FRA.150M	Group G-OSND (G-BDOU)
	G-OSNX	Grob G.109B	R. J. Barsby
	G-OSOD	P & M Quik GTR	R. Gellert
	G-OSON	P & M QuikR	R. Parr
	G-OSOR	DG Flugzeugbau DG-1000M	Lleweni Parc Ltd
	G-OSPD	Aerotechnik EV-97 TeamEurostar UK	R. A. Stewart-Jones
	G-OSPH	Ikarus C42 FB100	J. Bainbridge
	G-OSPP	Robinson R44	Foton Ltd
	G-OSPS	PA-18 Super Cub 95	R. C. Lough
	G-OSPX	Grob G.109B	Aerosparx (G-BMHR)
	G-OSPY	Cirrus SR20	J. & R. K. Hyatt
	G-OSRA	Boeing 727-2S2F	T2 Aviation Ltd
	G-OSRB	Boeing 727-2S2F	T2 Aviation Ltd
	G-OSRL	Learjet 45	S. R. Lloyd
	G-OSRS	Cameron A-375 balloon	Wickers World Ltd
	G-OSSA	Cessna Tu.206B	Skydive St.Andrews Ltd
	G-OSST	Colt 77A balloon	A. A. Brown
	G-OSTC	AA-5A Cheetah	5th Generation Designs Ltd

Reg	Type	Owner or Operator	Notes
G-OSTL	Ikarus C.42 FB 100	G. P. Curtis	
G-OSUS	Mooney M.20K	K. D. Leifert	
G-OSUT	Scheibe SF-25C Rotax-Falke	Yorkshire Gliding Club (Pty.) Ltd	
G-OSVN	AutoGyro Cavalon	Engetel Ltd	
G-OSZA	Aerotek Pitts S-2A	Septieme Ciel	
G-OSZB	Christen Pitts S-2B Special	K. A. Fitton & A. M. Gent (G-OGEE)	
G-OSZS	Pitts S-2S Special	G-OSZS Group	
G-OTAL	ARV Super 2	J. M. Cullen (G-BNGZ)	
G-OTAM	Cessna 172M	G. V. White	
G-OTAN	PA-18 Super Cub 135 (54-2445)	A. & J. D. Owen	
G-OTAY	Tecnam P2006T	Nyuki Ltd (G-ZOOG)	
G-OTCH	Streak Shadow	R. M. M. & A. G. Moura	
G-OTCT	Cameron Z-105 balloon	Lighter Than Air Ltd	
G-OTCV	Skyranger 912S (1)	M. B. Lowe	
G-OTCZ	Schempp-Hirth Ventus 2cT	A. J. Rees	
G-OTEA	Balony Kubicek BB17XR balloon	A. M. Holly	
G-OTEC	Tecnam P2002 Sierra Deluxe	C. W. Thirtle	
G-OTEL	Thunder Ax8-90 balloon	J. W. Adkins	
G-OTFL	Eurocopter EC 120B	J. Henshall (G-IBRI)	
G-OTFT	PA-38-112 Tomahawk	P. Tribble (G-BNKW)	
G-OTGA	PA-28R-201 Arrow III	TG Aviation Ltd	
G-OTHE	Enstrom 280C-UK Shark	K. P. Groves (G-OPJT/G-BKCO)	
G-OTIB	Robin DR.400/180R	The Windrushers Gliding Club Ltd	
G-OTIG	AA-5B Tiger	L. Burke (G-PENN)	
G-OTIM	Bensen B.8MV	T. J. Deane	
G-OTIV	Aerospool Dynamic WT9 UK	D. P. Pactor & P. O'Donohue	
G-OTJH	Pegasus Quantum 15-912	L. R. Gartside	
G-OTJS	Robinson R44 II	Kuki Helicopter Sales Ltd	
G-OTJT	Glasflugel 304SJ Shark	N. J. L. Busvine	
G-OTLC	Grumman AA-5 Traveller	L. P. Keegan & S. R. Cameron (G-BBUF)	
G-OTME	SNCAN Nord 1002 Pingouin	S. H. O'Connell	
G-OTNA	Robinson R44 Raven II	Abel Developments Ltd	
G-OTNM	Tecnam P2008-LC	Tog Aviation Ltd	
G-OTOE	Aeronca 7AC Champion	D. Cheney (G-BRWW)	
G-OTOO	Stolp SA.300 Starduster Too	I. M. Castle	
G-OTOP	P & M Quik R	M. I. White	
G-OTRT	Robinson R44 II	Seasail (UK) Ltd (G-CFEC)	
G-OTRV	Van's RV-6	D. C. Crossan	
G-OTRY	Schleicher ASW-24	A. H. Beckingham	
G-OTSP	AS.355F1 Twin Squirrel	MW Helicopters Ltd (G-XPOL/G-BPRF)	
G-OTTI	Cameron Otti-34 balloon	P. Spellward	
G-OTTS	Ikarus C42 FB100 Bravo	B. C. Gotts	
G-OTTY	Rotorsport UK Calidus	GS Aviation (Europe) Ltd	
G-OTUI	SOCATA TB20 Trinidad	H. Graff (G-KKDL/G-BSHU)	
G-OTUM	Skyranger Nynja LS 912S(1)	D. W. Wallington	
G-OTUN	EV-97A Eurostar	L. R. Morris & K. R. Annett	
G-OTVR	PA-34-220T Seneca V	Brinor International Shipping & Forwarding Ltd	
G-OTWS	Schempp-Hirth Duo Discus XLT	T. W. Slater	
G-OTYE	Aerotechnik EV-97 Eurostar	A. B. Godber	
G-OTYP	PA-28 Cherokee 180	T. C. Lewis	
G-OTZZ	AutoGyro Cavalon	B. C. Gotts	
G-OUAV	TLAC Sherwood Scout	University of Southampton	
G-OUCP	PA-31 Navajo C	2 Excel Aviation Ltd (G-GURN/G-BHGA)	
G-OUDA	Aeroprakt A22-L Foxbat	A. R. Cattell	
G-OUGH	Yakovlev Yak-52	I. M. Gough (G-LAOK)	
G-OUHI	Shaw Europa XS	N. M. Graham	
G-OUIK	Mainair Pegasus Quik	M. D. Evans	
G-OURO	Shaw Europa	I. M. Mackay	
G-OURT	Lindstrand LTL Series Racer 56 balloon	A. B. Court	
G-OUVI	Cameron O-105 balloon	Bristol University Hot Air Ballooning Society	
G-OVAL	Ikarus C.42 FB100	N. G. Tomes	
G-OVBF	Cameron A-250 balloon	Virgin Balloon Flights	
G-OVBL	Lindstrand LBL-150A balloon	R. J. Henderson	
G-OVEG	Diamond DA.20-C1 Katana	Tungsten Group Ltd	
G-OVET	Cameron O-56 balloon	B. D. Close	
G-OVFM	Cessna 120	T. B. Parmenter	
G-OVFR	Cessna F.172N	Marine and Aviation Ltd	
G-OVII	Van's RV-7	T. J. Richardson	

Notes	Reg	Type	Owner or Operator
	G-OVIN	Rockwell Commander 112TC	L. C. Branfield
	G-OVIV	Aerostyle Breezer LSA	P. & V. Lynch
	G-OVLA	Ikarus C.42 FB	Propeller Owners Ltd
	G-OVMC	Cessna F.152 II	Swiftair Maintenance Ltd
	G-OVNE	Cessna 401A H	Norwich Aviation Museum
	G-OVNR	Robinson R22 Beta	HQ Aviation Ltd
	G-OVOL	Skyranger 912S(1)	A. S. Docherty
	G-OVON	PA-18-95 Super Cub	V. F. A. Stanley
	G-OVPM	Europa NG	P. Munford
	G-OWAG	Cameron TR-70 balloon	M. G. Howard
	G-OWAI	Schleicher ASK-21	Scottish Gliding Union
	G-OWAL	PA-34-220T Seneca III	G-OWAL Group
	G-OWAP	PA-28-161 Cherokee Warrior II	Tayside Aviation Ltd (G-BXNH)
	G-OWAR	PA-28-161 Warrior II	Bickertons Aerodromes Ltd
	G-OWAZ	Pitts S-1C Special	P. E. S. Latham (G-BRPI)
	G-OWBA	Alpi Pioneer 300 Hawk	A. H. Lloyd
	G-OWEN	K & S Jungster	R. C. Owen
	G-OWGC	Slingsby T.61F Venture T.2	Wolds Gliding Club Ltd
	G-OWLL	Ultramagic M-105 balloon	J. A. Lawton
	G-OWLY	Cameron C-70 balloon	
	G-OWMC	Thruster T.600N	Wilts Microlight Centre
	G-OWOW	Cessna 152 II	M. D. Perry (G-BMSZ)
	G-OWPS	Ikarus C42 FB100	Webb Plant Sales
	G-OWRC	Cessna F.152 II	Unimat SA/France
	G-OWRT	Cessna 182G	Tripacer Group
	G-OWST	Cessna 172S	Westair Flying Services Ltd (G-WABH)
	G-OWTF	Pitts S-2B Special	D. P. Curtis (G-BRVT)
	G-OWTN	Embraer EMB-145EP	BAE Systems (Corporate Air Travel) Ltd
	G-OWWW	Shaw Europa	R. F. W. Holder
	G-OWYN	Aviamilano F.14 Nibbio	Karpol Sp zoo/Poland
	G-OXBA	Cameron Z-160 balloon	J. E. Rose
	G-OXBC	Cameron A-140 balloon	J. E. Rose
	G-OXBY	Cameron N-90 balloon	C. A. Oxby
	G-OXFA	PA-34-220T Seneca V	Oxford Aviation Academy (Oxford) Ltd
	G-OXFB	PA-34-220T Seneca V	Oxford Aviation Academy (Oxford) Ltd
	G-OXFC	PA-34-220T Seneca V	Oxford Aviation Academy (Oxford) Ltd
	G-OXFD	PA-34-220T Seneca V	Oxford Aviation Academy (Oxford) Ltd
	G-OXFE	PA-34-220T Seneca V	Oxford Aviation Academy (Oxford) Ltd
	G-OXFF	PA-34-220T Seneca V	Oxford Aviation Academy (Oxford) Ltd
	G-OXFG	PA-34-220T Seneca V	Oxford Aviation Academy (Oxford) Ltd
	G-OXII	Van's RV-12	J. A. King
	G-OXIV	Van's RV-14	M. A. N. Newall
	G-OXOM	PA-28-161 Cadet	AJW Construction Ltd (G-BRSG)
	G-OXPS	Falcon XPS	J. C. Greenslade (G-BUXP)
	G-OXRS	Bombardier BD700 1A10 Global Express	TAG Aviation (UK) Ltd
	G-OXVI	VS.361 Spitfire LF.XVIe (TD248:CR-S)	Spitfire Ltd
	G-OYAK	Yakovlev C-11 (9 white)	A. H. Soper
	G-OYES	Mainair Blade 912	C. R. Chapman
	G-OYGC	Aeropro Eurofox 912(iS)	York Gliding Centre Ltd
	G-OYIO	Robin DR.400/120	Exeter Aviation Ltd
	G-OYTE	Rans S.6ES Coyote II	K. C. Noakes
	G-OZAM	PA-28-161 Warrior II	G. Hussain
	G-OZBG	Airbus A.321-231	Archway Aviation (Ireland) 2 Ltd
	G-OZBH	Airbus A.321-231	Archway Aviation (Ireland) 3 Ltd
	G-OZBL	Airbus A.321-231	Aercap Dutch Aircraft Leasing 1 BV (G-MIDE)
	G-OZBM	Airbus A.321-231	Philharmonic Aircraft Leasing Ltd (G-MIDJ)
	G-OZBN	Airbus A.321-231	ALS Irish Aircraft Leasing MSN 1153 Ltd (G-MIDK)
	G-OZBO	Airbus A.321-231	Aergen Aircraft Three Ltd (G-MIDM)
	G-OZBT	Airbus A.321-231	Wells Fargo Bank Northwest, NA (G-TTIH)
	G-OZBU	Airbus A.321-231	Aergen Aircraft Twenty Two Ltd (G-TTII)
	G-OZBW	Airbus A.320-214	DCAL 4 Leasing Ltd (G-OOPP/G-OOAS)
	G-OZBX	Airbus A.320-214	SASOF II © Aviation Ireland Ltd (G-OOPU/ G-OOAU)
	G-OZBZ	Airbus A.321-231	Wilmington Trust SP Services (Dublin) Ltd
	G-OZEE	Light Aero Avid Speedwing Mk 4	G. D. Bailey
	G-OZIE	Jabiru J400	S. A. Bowkett

Reg	Type	Owner or Operator	Notes
G-OZIP	Christen Eagle II	J. D. N. Cooke	
G-OZOI	Cessna R.182	J. R. G. & F. L. G. Fleming (G-ROBK)	
G-OZON	PA-32R-301T Saratoga II TC	P. J. Pilkington	
IG-OZOZ	Schempp-Hirth Nimbus 3DT	G-OZOZ Flying Group	
G-OZSB	Geta-Flug AS.105GD airship	Cheers Airships Ltd	
G-OZZE	Lambert Mission M108	Lambert Aircraft Engineering BVBA/Belgium	
G-OZZI	Jabiru SK	A. H. Godfrey	
G-OZZT	Cirrus SR-22T	H. G. Dilloway	
G-PACE	Robin R.1180T	C. A. C. Bontet/France	
G-PACO	Sikorsky S-76C	Cardinal Helicopter Services	
G-PACT	PA-28-181 Archer III	A. Parsons	
G-PADE	Escapade 912 (2)	F. Overall	
G-PAFF	AutoGyro MTO Sport	S. R. Paffett	
G-PAIG	Grob G.109B	M. E. Baker	
G-PAIZ	PA-12 Super Cruiser	B. R. Pearson	
G-PALI	Czech Sport Aircraft Piper Sport	P. A. Langley	
G-PALT	AutoGyro MTO Sport	D. A. Jordan	
G-PAMY	Robinson R44 II	Batchelor Aviation Ltd	
G-PAOL	Cessna 525B Citationjet CJ3	Blu Halkin Ltd	
G-PAPE	Diamond DA42 Twin Star	Diamond Executive Aviation Ltd	
G-PAPI	Ikarus C42 FB80	Avon Training and Consultancy Ltd	
G-PARG	Pitts S-1C Special	R. J. Dolby	
G-PARI	Cessna 172RG Cutlass	Mannion Automation Ltd	
G-PASH	AS.355F1 Twin Squirrel	MW Helicopters Ltd	
G-PASL	AS.355F2 Ecureuil 2	C-E. Giblain/France	
G-PASN	Enstrom F-28F	N. Pasha (G-BSHZ)	
G-PATF	Shaw Europa	Condor Aviation International Ltd	
G-PATG	Cameron O-90 balloon	S. Neighbour & N. Symonds	
G-PATJ	Ikarus C42 FB80	P. J. Oakey	
G-PATN	SOCATA TB10 Tobago	J. D. C. Pritchard (G-LUAR)	
G-PATO	Zenair CH.601UL Zodiac	R. Duckett	
G-PATP	Lindstrand LBL-77A balloon	P. Pruchnickyj	
G-PATS	Shaw Europa	G-PATS Flying Group	
G-PATX	Lindstrand LBL-90A balloon	M. R. Noyce & R. P. E. Phillips	
G-PATZ	Shaw Europa	H. P. H. Griffin	
G-PAVL	Robin R.3000/120	MintLPG Ltd	
G-PAWS	AA-5A Cheetah	Close Encounters	
G-PAWZ	Best Off Sky Ranger Swift 912S(1)	G-PAWZ Syndicate	
G-PAXX	PA-20 Pacer 135 (modified)	C. W. Monsell	
G-PAYD	Robin DR.400/180	M. J. Bennett	
G-PAZY	Pazmany PL.4A	M. Richardson (G-BLAJ)	
G-PBAL	Autogyro MTOsport	P. S. Ball	
G-PBAT	Czech Sport Aircraft Sportcruiser	P. M. W. Bath	
G-PBCL	Cessna 182P	Kammon BV/Netherlands	
G-PBEC	Van's RV-7	P. G. Reid	
G-PBEE	Robinson R44	Echo Echo Syndicate	
G-PBEL	CFM Shadow Srs DD	S. Fairweather	
G-PBIG	Airbus EC.130 T2	Airbus Helicopters UK Ltd (G-CJYT)	
G-PBIX	VS.361 Spitfire LF XVI E (RW382)	Downlock Ltd (G-XVIA)	
G-PBWR	Agusta A109S Grand	Helix Helicopters Ltd	
G-PBWS	Schleicher ASH-31MI	P. B. Walker	
G-PBYA	Consolidated PBY-5A Catalina (433915)	Catalina Aircraft Ltd	
G-PBYY	Enstrom 280FX	S. Craske (G-BXKV)	
G-PCAT	SOCATA TB10 Tobago	G-PCAT Group (G-BHER)	
G-PCCC	Alpi Pioneer 300	R. Pidcock	
G-PCCM	Alpi Pioneer 200M	M. G. Freeman	
G-PCDP	Zlin Z.526F Trener Master	D. J. Lee	
G-PCGC	Allstar PZL SZD-54-2 Perkoz	Cambridge Gliding Club Ltd	
G-PCJS	Diamond DA.42NG Twin Star	P. J. Cooper & G. E. J. Sealey	
G-PCMC	P & M Quik R	G. Charman	
G-PCOP	Beech B200 Super King Air	Albert Batlett and Sons (Airdrie) Ltd	
G-PCPC	AutoGyro Calidus	P. E. Churchill	
G-PCTW	Pilatus PC-12/47E	Yellow Skies LLP	
G-PDGF	AS.350B2 Ecureuil	PLM Dollar Group Ltd (G-FROH)	
G-PDGG	Aeromere F.8L Falco Srs 3	S. R. Stead	
G-PDGI	AS.350B2 Ecureuil	PLM Dollar Group Ltd (G-BVJE)	
G-PDGN	SA.365N Dauphin 2	PLM Dollar Group Ltd (G-TRAF/G-BLDR)	

Notes	Reg	Type	Owner or Operator
	G-PDGO	AS.365N2 Dauphin II	PLM Dollar Group Ltd
	G-PDGR	AS.350B2 Ecureuil	PLM Dollar Group Ltd (G-RICC/G-BTXA)
	G-PDGT	AS.355F2 Ecureuil 2	PLM Dollar Group Ltd (G-BOOV)
	G-PDGV	Vulcanair P.68C-TC	PLM Dollar Group Ltd
	G-PDOC	PA-44-180 Seminole	Medicare (G-PVAF)
	G-PDOG	Cessna O-1E Bird Dog (24550)	J. D. Needham
	G-PDRO	Schleicher ASH-31 Mi	P. Crawley
	G-PDSI	Cessna 172N	DA Flying Group
	G-PEAR	P &M Pegasus Quik	N. D. Major
	G-PECK	PA-32-300 Cherokee Six D	K. H. McCune (G-ETAV/G-MCAR/G-LADA/G-AYWK)
	G-PECX	Eurofox 912S(2)	SAE Systems Ltd
	G-PEGA	Pegasus Quantum 15-912	M. Konisti
	G-PEGE	Skyranger 912	A. N. Hughes
	G-PEGI	PA-34-200T Seneca II	ACS Aviation Ltd
	G-PEGY	Shaw Europa	A. Carter
	G-PEJM	PA-28-181 Archer III	S. J. Clark
	G-PEKT	SOCATA TB20 Trinidad	The WERY Flying Group
	G-PEPI	Embraer EMB-135BJ Legacy	London Executive Aviation Ltd
	G-PERC	Cameron N-90 balloon	I. R. Warrington
	G-PERD	Agusta Westland AW.139	Babcock Mission Critical Services Offshore Ltd
	G-PERE	Robinson R22 Beta	Phoenix Helicopter Academy Ltd
	G-PERG	Embraer EMB-505 Phenom 300	Air Charter Scotland Ltd (G-POWO)
	G-PERH	Guimbal Cabri G2	M. Munson
	G-PERR	Cameron 60 Bottle SS balloon ★	British Balloon Museum/Newbury
	G-PERU	Guimbal Cabri G2	M. Munson
	G-PERX	Airbus AS.355NP Ecureuil 2	Heligroup Operations Ltd
	G-PEST	Hawker Tempest II (MW401)	Anglia Aircraft Restorations Ltd
	G-PETH	PA-24-260C Comanche	J. V. Hutchinson & W. T. G. Ponnet
	G-PETO	Hughes 369HM	P. E. Tornberg (G-HAUS/G-KBOT/G-RAMM)
	G-PETR	PA-28-140 Cherokee	P. Stamp (G-BCJL)
	G-PFAA	EAA Biplane Model P	T. A. Fulcher
	G-PFAF	FRED Srs 2	M. S. Perkins
	G-PFAH	Evans VP-1	J. A. Scott
	G-PFAP	Currie Wot/SE-5A (C1904:Z)	J. H. Seed
	G-PFAR	Isaacs Fury II (K2059)	C. C. Silk & D. J. Phillips
	G-PFAT	Monnett Sonerai II	H. B. Carter
	G-PFAW	Evans VP-1	R. F. Shingler
	G-PFCL	Cessna 172S	C. H. S. Carpenter
	G-PFKD	Yakovlev Yak-12M	R. D. Bade
	G-PFSL	Cessna F.152	P. A. Simon
	G-PGAC	MCR-01	G. A. Coatesworth
	G-PGFG	Tecnam P92-EM Echo	P. G. Fitzgerald
	G-PGGY	Robinson R44	EBG (Helicopters) Ltd
	G-PGHM	Air Creation 582(2)/Kiss 450	R. J. Turner
	G-PGSA	Thruster T.600N	D. S. Elliston
	G-PGSI	Pierre Robin R2160	M. A. Spencer
	G-PHAA	Cessna F.150M	W. B. Bateson (G-BCPE)
	G-PHAB	Cirrus SR22	G3 Aviation Ltd (G-MACL)
	G-PHAT	Cirrus SR20	T. W. Wielkopolski
	G-PHNX	Schempp-Hirth Duo Discus Xt	72 Syndicate
	G-PHOR	Cessna FRA.150L Aerobat	M. Bonsall (G-BACC)
	G-PHOX	Aeroprakt A22-L Foxbat	J. D. Webb
	G-PHRG	Hybrid Air Vehicles Airlander 10 airship	Hybrid Air Vehicles Ltd
	G-PHSE	Balony Kubicek BB26Z balloon	The Packhouse Ltd
	G-PHSI	Colt 90A balloon	P. H. Strickland
	G-PHTG	SOCATA TB10 Tobago	A. J. Baggarley
	G-PHUN	Cessna FRA.150L Aerobat	M. Bonsall (G-BAIN)
	G-PHVM	Van's RV-8	G. P. Howes & A. Leviston
	G-PHYL	Denney Kitfox Mk 4	G-PHYL Group
	G-PHYS	Jabiru SP-470	C. Mayer
	G-PIAF	Thunder Ax7-65 balloon	L. Battersley
	G-PICO	Cameron O-31 balloon	J. F. Trehern
	G-PICU	Leonardo AW169	Specialist Aviation Services Ltd
	G-PICX	P & M Aviation QuikR	G. L. Muizelaar

Reg	Type	Owner or Operator	Notes
G-PIEL	CP.301A Emeraude	E. B. Atalay (G-BARY)	
G-PIES	Thunder Ax7-77Z balloon	M. K. Bellamy	
G-PIET	Pietenpol Air Camper	A. R. Wyatt	
G-PIFZ	Agusta Westland AW109SP Grand New	Alba Aviation Partnership	
G-PIGI	Aerotechnik EV-97 Eurostar	Pigs Might Fly Group	
G-PIGS	SOCATA Rallye 150ST	Boonhill Flying Group (G-BDWB)	
G-PIGY	Short SC.7 Skyvan Srs 3A Variant 100	Liberty Aviation Ltd	
G-PIGZ	Cameron Z-315 balloon	Wickers World Ltd	
G-PIII	Pitts S-1D Special	On A Roll Aerobatics Group (G-BETI)	
G-PIIT	Pitts S-2 Special	J. Law	
G-PIKD	Eiriavion PIK-20D-78	M. C. Hayes	
G-PIKE	Robinson R22 Mariner	Sloane Helicopters Ltd	
G-PIKK	PA-28 Cherokee 140	V. Vieira (G-AVLA)	
G-PILE	Rotorway Executive 90	J. B. Russell	
G-PILL	Light Aero Avid Flyer Mk 4	D. R. Meston	
G-PILY	Pilatus B4 PC-11	J. Hunt	
G-PILZ	AutoGyro MT-03	Gyrocopter Flying Club	
G-PIMM	Ultramagic M-77 balloon	G. Everett	
G-PIMP	Robinson R44	A. Ferrari	
G-PING	AA-5A Cheetah	D. Byrne	
G-PINO	AutoGyro MTO Sport	N. Crighton	
G-PINT	Cameron 65 Barrel SS balloon	D. K. Fish	
G-PINX	Lindstrand Pink Panther SS balloon	Magical Adventures Ltd/USA	
G-PION	Alpi Pioneer 300	A. A. Mortimer	
G-PIPB	AS.355F1 Ecureuil 2	Heli Air Ltd (G-NBEL/G-SKYW/G-BTIS/G-TALI)	
G-PIPI	Mainair Pegasus Quik	R. E. Forbes	
G-PIPR	PA-18 Super Cub 95	R. & T. Kellett (G-BCDC)	
G-PIPS	Van's RV-4	P. N. Davis	
G-PIPZ	BRM Aero Bristell NG5 Speed Wing	D. T. White	
G-PITS	Pitts S-2AE Special	P. N. A. & S. N. Whithead	
G-PITZ	Pitts S-2A Special	M. J. Wood	
G-PIVI	Pipistrel Virus SW127 912S(1)	Pipistrel Virus UK Group	
G-PIXE	Colt 31A balloon	A. D. McCutcheon	
G-PIXI	Pegasus Quantum 15-912	K. J. Rexter	
G-PIXL	Robinson R44 II	Flying TV Ltd	
G-PIXX	Robinson R44 II	Flying TV Ltd	
G-PIXY	Supermarine Aircraft Spitfire Mk.26 (RK855)	R. Collenette	
G-PJMT	Lancair 320	K. A. & P. P. Gilroy	
G-PJSY	Van's RV-6	P. J. York	
G-PJTM	Cessna FR.172K II	R. & J. R. Emery (G-BFIF)	
G-PKPK	Schweizer 269C	C. H. Dobson & M. R. Golden	
G-PLAD	Kolb Twinstar Mk.111 Xtra	A. R. Smith	
G-PLAN	Cessna F.150L	J. Emmett	
G-PLAR	Vans RV-9A	M. P. Board	
G-PLAY	Robin R.2112	S. J. Wilson	
G-PLAZ	Rockwell Commander 112	I. Hunt (G-RDCI/G-BFWG)	
G-PLEE	Cessna 182Q	Peterlee Parachute Centre	
G-PLIP	Diamond DA.40D Star	C. A. & D. R. Ho	
G-PLJR	Pietenpol Air Camper	P. E. Taylor	
G-PLLT	Lindstrand Box SS balloon	Lindstrand Media Ltd	
G-PLMH	AS.350B2 Ecureuil	PLM Dollar Group Ltd	
G-PLOP	Magni M-24C	R. S. Bird	
G-PLOW	Hughes 269B	C. Walton Ltd (G-AVUM)	
G-PLPC	Schweizer Hughes 269C	A. R. Baker	
G-PLPM	Shaw Europa XS	P. L. P. Mansfield	
G-PLSR	P & M PulsR	P and M Aviation Ltd	
G-PMAM	Cameron V-65 balloon	P. A. Meecham	
G-PMGG	Agusta-Bell 206A JetRanger	P. M. Gallagher & S. Perry (G-EEGO/G-PELS/ G-DNCN)	
G-PMIZ	Pitts Model 12	I. S. Smith (G-DEWD/G-CGRP)	
G-PMNF	VS.361 Spitfire HF.IX (TA805:FX-M)	P. R. Monk	
G-PNEU	Colt 110 Bibendum SS balloon	P. A. Rowley	
G-PNGB	Partenavia P-68B	P. Morton	
G-PNGC	Schleicher ASK-21	Portsmouth Naval Gliding Centre	
G-PNIX	Cessna FRA.150L	Dukeries Aviation (G-BBEO)	

271

Notes	Reg	Type	Owner or Operator
	G-PODD	Robinson R66	Jamiroquai Ltd
	G-POET	Robinson R44 II	GP Owen Ltd
	G-POGO	Flight Design CT2K	L. I. Bailey
	G-POLA	Eurocopter EC 135 P2+	Police & Crime Commissioner for West Yorkshire
	G-POLB	Eurocopter EC 135 T2+	Police & Crime Commissioner for West Yorkshire
	G-POLC	Eurocopter EC 135 T2+	Police & Crime Commissioner for West Yorkshire (G-CPSH)
	G-POLD	Eurocopter EC 135 T2+	Police & Crime Commissioner for West Yorkshire (G-NMID)
	G-POLF	Eurocopter EC 135 T2+	Police & Crime Commissioner for West Yorkshire (G-ESEX)
	G-POLG	Eurocopter EC 135 T2+	Police & Crime Commissioner for West Yorkshire (G-LASU)
	G-POLH	Eurocopter EC 135 T2+	Police & Crime Commissioner for West Yorkshire (G-WCAO)
	G-POLL	Skyranger 912 (1)	J. Hunter & D. Allan
	G-POLR	P & M Quik R	D. Sykes
	G-POLS	Airbus Helicopters EC 135 T3	Babcock Mission Critical Services Onshore Ltd
	G-POLY	Cameron N-77 balloon	S. Church & S. Jenkins
	G-POMP	Cameron Bearskin 100 balloon	Lighter Than Air Ltd
	G-POND	Oldfield Baby Lakes	J. Maehringer/Germany
	G-POOH	Piper J-3C-65 Cub	P. L. Beckwith
	G-POOL	ARV Super 2	E. Stinton (G-BNHA)
	G-POPA	Beech A36 Bonanza	S. F. Payne
	G-POPE	Eiri PIK-20E-1	G-POPE Syndicate
	G-POPG	Aeropro Eurofox 2K	C. M. Hoyle
	G-POPW	Cessna 182S	D. L. Price
	G-POPY	Best Off Sky Ranger Swift 912S(1)	S. G. Penk
	G-POPZ	Druine D.31A Turbulent	S. A. Blanchard
	G-PORG	AB Sportine LAK-17AT	R. M. Garden
	G-PORK	AA-5B Tiger	Miss P Flying Group (G-BFHS)
	G-POSH	Colt 56A balloon	B. K. Rippon (G-BMPT)
	G-POTA	Extra EA.300/LT	M. Frizza & L. Franceschetti
	G-POTR	Agusta 109E Power	Castle Air Ltd (G-OFTC)
	G-POUX	Pou du Ciel-Bifly	G. D. Priest
	G-POWC	Boeing 737-33A	Titan Airways Ltd
	G-POWD	Boeing 767-36N	Titan Airways Ltd
	G-POWH	Boeing 757-256	Titan Airways Ltd
	G-POWI	Airbus A.320-233	Aero Capital Solutions Inc
	G-POWK	Airbus A.320-233	Titan Airways Ltd
	G-POWL	Cessna 182R	Oxford Aeroplane Company Ltd
	G-POWM	Airbus A.320-232	Titan Airways Ltd
	G-POWN	Airbus A.321-211	Titan Airways Ltd
	G-POWP	Boeing 737-436	Titan Airways Ltd (G-DOCY/G-BVBY)
	G-POWS	Boeing 737-436	Titan Airways Ltd (G-DOCT)
	G-POZA	Escapade Jabiru ULP (2)	M. R. Jones
	G-PPBZ	Autogyro Calidus	Dept of Doing Ltd
	G-PPFS	Cessna FRA.150L	M. Bonsall (G-AZJY)
	G-PPIO	Cameron C-90 balloon	A. G. Martin
	G-PPLG	Rotorsport UK MT-03	Gyro Syndicate PPLG
	G-PPLL	Van's RV-7A	D. Bull
	G-PPLS	Cessna F.152	Devon & Somerset Flight Training Ltd
	G-PPOD	Europa Aviation Europa XS	S. Easom
	G-PPPP	Denney Kitfox Mk 3	C. J. Thompson
	G-PRAG	Brügger MB.2 Colibri	Colibri Flying Group
	G-PRAH	Flight Design CT2K	P. A. Banks
	G-PRAY	Lindstrand LTL Series 2-60 balloon	Trinity Balloons
	G-PRBB	HpH Glasflugel 304ES	P. J. Belcher & R. I. Brickwood
	G-PRDH	AS.355F2 Ecureuil 2	Claremont Air Services
	G-PREY	Pereira Osprey II	Condor Aviation International Ltd (G-BEPB)
	G-PRII	Hawker Hunter PR.11 (WT723:692/LM)	Horizon Aircraft Engineering Ltd
	G-PRIM	PA-38-112 Tomahawk	Braddock Ltd
	G-PRIV	VS.353 Spitfire PR.IV	P. R. Arnold
	G-PRKZ	Allstar PZL SZD-54-2 Perkoz	Buckminster Gliding Club Ltd
	G-PRLY	Avtech Jabiru SK	J. McVey (G-BYKY)
	G-PROO	Hawker 4000 Horizon	EJME (Portugal) Aircraft Management Lda/Portugal
	G-PROS	Van's RV-7A	A. J. & S. A. Sutcliffe

Reg	Type	Owner or Operator	Notes
G-PROV	P.84 Jet Provost T.52A (T.4)	Provost Group	
G-PROW	EV-97A Eurostar	Fly Hire Ltd	
G-PRPA	DHC.8-402Q Dash Eight	Flybe.com	
G-PRPB	DHC.8-402Q Dash Eight	Flybe.com	
G-PRPC	DHC.8-402Q Dash Eight	Flybe.com	
G-PRPD	DHC.8-402Q Dash Eight	Flybe.com	
G-PRPE	DHC.8-402Q Dash Eight	Flybe.com	
G-PRPF	DHC.8-402Q Dash Eight	Flybe.com	
G-PRPG	DHC.8-402Q Dash Eight	Flybe.com	
G-PRPH	DHC.8-402Q Dash Eight	Flybe.com	
G-PRPI	DHC.8-402Q Dash Eight	Flybe.com (G-CJFN)	
G-PRPJ	DHC.8-402Q Dash Eight	Flybe.com	
G-PRPK	DHC.8-402Q Dash Eight	Flybe.com	
G-PRPL	DHC.8-402Q Dash Eight	Flybe.com	
G-PRPM	DHC.8-402Q Dash Eight	Flybe.com	
G-PRPN	DHC.8-402Q Dash Eight	Flybe.com	
G-PRPO	DHC.8-402Q Dash Eight	Flybe.com	
G-PRXI	VS.365 Spitfire PR.XI (PL983)	Propshop Ltd	
G-PRZI	Cameron A-375 balloon	Red Letter Days Ltd	
G-PSAX	Lindstrand LBL-77B balloon	M. V. Farrant & I. Risbridger	
G-PSFG	Robin R.21601	Mardenair Ltd (G-COVD/G-BYOF)	
G-PSGC	PA-25 Pawnee 260C (modified)	Peterborough & Spalding Gliding Club Ltd (G-BDDT)	
G-PSHK	Schempp-Hirth SHK-1	P. Gentil	
G-PSHU	Eurocopter EC135 T2+	Babcock Mission Critical Services Onshore Ltd (G-WONN)	
G-PSIR	Jurca MJ.77 Gnatsum (474008 'VF-R')	P. W. Carlton & D. F. P. Finan	
G-PSJS	Robinson R22 II	G. E. J. Sealey (G-PBRL)	
G-PSKY	Skyranger 912S(1)	P. W. Curnock & J. W. Wilcox	
G-PSMS	Aeropro Eurofox 912(S)	P. V. Stevens	
G-PSNI	Eurocopter EC 135T2	Police Service of Northern Ireland	
G-PSNO	Eurocopter MBB BK-117C-2	Police Service of Northern Ireland	
G-PSNR	MBB-BK 117 C-2	Police Service of Northern Ireland (G-LFRS)	
G-PSON	Colt Cylinder One SS balloon	Flintnine Fasteners Ltd	
G-PSRT	PA-28-151 Warrior	R. W. Nash (G-BSGN)	
G-PSUE	CFM Shadow Srs CD	D. A. Crosbie (G-MYAA)	
G-PSUK	Thruster T.600N 450	K. Edwards	
G-PTAG	Shaw Europa	R. C. Harrison	
G-PTAR	Best Off Skyranger 912S(1)	P. Vergette	
G-PTBA	Boeing Stearman A-75	Mach Eight 3 Ltd	
G-PTCA	Cessna F.172P	B. O'Donnchu	
G-PTCC	PA-28RT-201 ArrowIV	B. O'Donnchu (G-BXYS)	
G-PTDP	Bücker Bü133C Jungmeister	T. J. Reeve & M. S. Pettit (G-AEZX)	
G-PTEA	PA-46-350P Malibu Mirage	K. Buchberger	
G-PTEK	Van's RV-9A	P. K. Eckersley	
G-PTFE	Bristell NG5 Speed Wing	P. R. Thody	
G-PTIX	VS.361 Spitfire IX (PT879)	Hangar 11 Collection (G-AYDE)	
G-PTOO	Bell 206L-4 LongRanger 4	Helicompany Ltd	
G-PTRE	SOCATA TB20 Trinidad	W. M. Chesson (G-BNKU)	
G-PTTA	Cessna F.152	Pilot Training and Testing Ltd (G-BJVT)	
G-PTTB	Cessna F.152	Pilot Training and Testing Ltd (G-WACT/ G-BKFT)	
G-PTTC	Cessna F.152 II	Pilot Training and Testing Ltd (G-BKWY)	
G-PTTD	Cessna F.152 II	Pilot Training and Testing Ltd (G-BIXH)	
G-PTTS	Aerotek Pitts S-2A	P. & J. Voce	
G-PUDL	PA-18 Super Cub 150	C. M. Edwards	
G-PUDS	Shaw Europa	C. R. A. Spirit	
G-PUFF	Thunder Ax7-77A balloon	Intervarsity Balloon Club	
G-PUGS	Cessna 182H	D. Waterhouse	
G-PUGZ	P & M Aviation Quik GT450	A. E. Hill	
G-PUKA	Jabiru Aircraft Jabiru J400	D. P. Harris	
G-PULA	Dassault Falcon 2000EX	Centreline AV Ltd	
G-PULR	Pitts S-2AE	The Waddington Flying Club	
G-PUMB	AS.332L Super Puma	CHC Scotia Ltd	
G-PUMM	AS.332L Super Puma	Element Capital Corp	
G-PUMN	AS.332L Super Puma	CHC Scotia Ltd	
G-PUMO	AS.332L-2 Super Puma	Element Capital Corp	
G-PUMS	AS.332L-2 Super Puma	Element Capital Corp	

Notes	Reg	Type	Owner or Operator
	G-PUNK	Thunder Ax8-105 balloon	S. C. Kinsey
	G-PUNT	Robinson R44 II	R. D. Cameron
	G-PUPP	Beagle B.121 Pup 2	M. G. Evans (G-BASD)
	G-PUPY	Shaw Europa XS	D. A. Cameron
	G-PURE	Cameron can 70 SS balloon	Mobberley Balloon Collection
	G-PURL	PA-32R-301 Saratoga II	A. P.H. & E. Hay
	G-PURP	Lindstrand LBL-90 balloon	C. & P. Mackley
	G-PURR	AA-5A Cheetah	G-PURR Group (G-BJDN)
	G-PURS	Rotorway Executive	J. & D. Parke
	G-PUSA	Gefa-Flug AS105GD Hot Air Airship	Skyking Aviation Ltd
	G-PUSH	Rutan Long-Ez	W. S. Allen
	G-PUSI	Cessna T.303	C. Smith & S. Devin
	G-PUSS	Cameron N-77 balloon	B. D. Close
	G-PUTT	Cameron Golfball 76 SS balloon	Lakeside Lodge Golf Centre
	G-PVBF	Lindstrand LBL-260S balloon	Virgin Balloon Flights
	G-PVCV	Robin DR400/140	Bustard Flying Club Ltd
	G-PVET	DHC.1 Chipmunk 22 (WB565)	Connect Properties Ltd
	G-PVIP	Cessna 421C	Passion 4 Autos Ltd
	G-PVML	Robin DR400/140B	Weald Air Services Ltd
	G-PVSS	P & M Quik GT450	M. Winship
	G-PWAL	Aeropro Eurofox 912(1)	P. Walton
	G-PWBE	DH.82A Tiger Moth	K. M. Perkins
	G-PWUL	Van's RV-6	D. C. Arnold
	G-PYAK	Yakovlev Yak-18T	P. S. Beardsell
	G-PYNE	Thruster T.600N 450	R. Dereham
	G-PYPE	Van's RV-7	R. & L. Pyper
	G-PYRO	Cameron N-65 balloon	A. C. Booth
	G-PZAS	Schleicher ASW-27-18	A. P. C. Sampson
	G-PZPZ	P & M Aviation Pegasus Quantum 15-912	J. Urrutia
	G-RAAF	VS.359 Spitfire VIII	Composite Mast Engineering and Technology Ltd
	G-RAAM	PA-28-161 Warrior II	Falcon Flying Services Ltd (G-BRSE)
	G-RAAY	Taylor JT.1 Monoplane	R. Bowden (G-BEHM)
	G-RABB	Pilatus PC-12/47E	Oriens Leasing Ltd
	G-RABS	Alpi Pioneer 300	J. Mullen
	G-RACA	P.57 Sea Prince T.1 (571/CU) ★	(stored)/Long Marston
	G-RACK	Ikarus C42 FB80	G. P. Burns (G-CFIY)
	G-RACO	PA-28R Cherokee Arrow 200-II	Graco Group Ltd
	G-RACR	Ultramagic M-65C balloon	R. A. Vale
	G-RACY	Cessna 182S	C. M. Bishop
	G-RADA	Soko P-2 Kraguj	S. M. Johnston
	G-RADI	PA-28-181 Archer II	I. Davidson
	G-RADR	Douglas AD-4NA Skyraider (126922:503)	Orion Enterprises Ltd (G-RAID)
	G-RADY	Bombardier CL600-2B19 Challenger 850	TAG Aviation (UK) Ltd
	G-RAEF	Schempp-Hirth SHK-1	R. A. Earnshaw-Fretwell
	G-RAEM	Rutan LongEz	Cambridge Business Travel
	G-RAES	Boeing 777-236	British Airways
	G-RAFA	Grob G.115	K. J. Peacock & S. F. Turner
	G-RAFB	Grob G.115	RAF College Flying Club Ltd
	G-RAFC	Robin R.2112	RAF Charlie Group
	G-RAFE	Thunder Ax7-77 balloon	Giraffe Balloon Syndicate
	G-RAFG	Slingsby T.67C Firefly	R. C. P. Brookhouse
	G-RAFH	Thruster T.600N 450	G-RAFH Group
	G-RAFR	Skyranger 912S(1)	M. Ellis
	G-RAFS	Thruster T.600N 450	Hoveton Flying Group
	G-RAFT	Rutan LongEz	H. M. & S. Roberts
	G-RAFV	Avid Speedwing	Fox Victor Group (G-MOTT)
	G-RAFW	Mooney M.20E	Vinola (Knitwear) Manufacturing Co Ltd (G-ATHW)
	G-RAFY	Best Off Sky Ranger Swift 912S(1)	A. P. Portsmouth
	G-RAFZ	RAF 2000 GTX-SE	John Pavitt (Engineers) Ltd
	G-RAGE	Wilson Cassutt IIIM	R. S. Grace (G-BEUN)
	G-RAGS	Pietenpol Air Camper	S. H. Leonard
	G-RAGT	PA-32-301FT Cherokee Six	Oxhill Aviation
	G-RAHA	Schempp-Hirth Standard Cirrus	G. C. Stallard
	G-RAIR	Schleicher ASH-25	P. T. Reading
	G-RAIX	CCF AT-16 Harvard 4 (KF584)	J. G. Mainka (G-BIWX)

Reg	Type	Owner or Operator	Notes
G-RAJA	Raj Hamsa X'Air 582 (2)	C. Roadnight	
G-RAJJ	BAe 146-200	Cello Aviation Ltd (G-CFDH)	
G-RALF	Rotorway Executive 162F	I. C. Bedford (G-BZOM)	
G-RAMI	Bell 206B JetRanger 3	Yorkshire Helicopters	
G-RAML	PA-34-220T Seneca III	P. d'Costa (G-BWDT/G-BKHS)	
G-RAMP	Piper J-3C-65 Cub	J. A. Gibson	
G-RAMS	PA-32R-301 Saratoga SP	Mike Sierra LLP	
G-RANN	Beech B.300 Super King Air 350	Flycorp Aviation LLP	
G-RAPH	Cameron O-77 balloon	P. A. Sweatman	
G-RAPL	Schempp-Hirth Duo Discus T	G-RAPL Duo XLT Syndicate	
G-RARA	AutoGyro MTO Sport	Gyro School Pro Ltd	
G-RARB	Cessna 172N	H. C. R. Page	
G-RARE	Thunder Ax5-42 SS balloon ★	Balloon Preservation Group	
G-RASA	Diamond DA42 Twin Star	C. D. Hill	
G-RASC	Evans VP-2	R. F. Powell	
G-RASH	Grob G.109E	G-RASH Syndicate	
G-RATC	Van's RV-4	A. F. Ratcliffe	
G-RATD	Van's RV-8	J. R. Pike	
G-RATE	AA-5A Cheetah	G-RATE Flying Group (G-BIFF)	
G-RATH	Rotorway Executive 162F	W. H. Cole	
G-RATI	Cessna F.172M	N. F. Collins (G-PATI/G-WACZ/G-BCUK)	
G-RATT	Aeropro Eurofox 912(S)	Rattlesden Gliding Club Ltd	
G-RATV	PA-28RT-201T Turbo Arrow IV	Tango Victor Ltd (G-WILS)	
G-RATZ	Shaw Europa	W. Goldsmith	
G-RAVE	Southdown Raven X	M. J. Robbins (G-MNZV)	
G-RAVN	Robinson R44	Brambledown Aircraft Hire	
G-RAWS	Rotorway Executive 162F	R. P. Robinson & D. D. Saint	
G-RAYB	P & M Quik GT450	R. Blatchford	
G-RAYH	Zenair CH.701UL	R. Horner	
G-RAYM	SOCATA TB-20 Trinidad GT	West Wales Airport Ltd	
G-RAYO	Lindstrand LBL-90A balloon	R. Owen	
G-RAYY	Cirrus SR22	Alquiler de Veleros SL/Spain	
G-RAYZ	Tecnam P2002-EA Sierra	R. Wells	
G-RAZY	PA-28-181 Archer II	T. H. Pemberton (G-REXS)	
G-RAZZ	Maule MX-7-180	R. Giles	
G-RBBB	Shaw Europa	T. J. Hartwell	
G-RBCA	Agusta A109A II	R. Bauer (G-TBGL/G-VJCB/G-BOUA)	
G-RBCT	Schempp-Hirth Ventus 2Ct	M. J. Weston & J. D. Huband	
G-RBIL	SA.341D Gazelle HT Mk.3	R. B. Illingworth (G-CGJY)	
G-RBLU	PA-28RT-201 Arrow IV	M. & C. Busoni	
G-RBMV	Cameron O-31 balloon	P. D. Griffiths	
G-RBOS	Colt AS-105 airship ★	Science Museum/Wroughton	
G-RBOW	Thunder Ax-7-65 balloon	R. S. McDonald	
G-RBRI	Robinson R44 II	Helicentre Aviation Ltd (G-RWGS)	
G-RBSN	Ikarus C.42 FB80	P. B. & M. Robinson	
G-RBWW	BRM Aero Bristell NG5 Speed Wing	W. Woods & R. J. Baker	
G-RCAV	Bombardier CL600-2B16 Challenger	Gama Aviation (UK) Ltd	
G-RCED	Rockwell Commander 114	D. J. and D. Pitman	
G-RCHE	Cessna 182T	R. S. Bentley (G-PTRI)	
G-RCHL	P & M Quik GT450	R. M. Broughton	
G-RCHY	Aerotechnik EV-97 Eurostar	N. McKenzie	
G-RCIE	J-3C-65 Cub	R. P. Marks (G-CCOX)	
G-RCKT	Harmon Rocket II	K. E. Armstrong	
G-RCMC	Murphy Renegade 912	The Renegades	
G-RCMF	Cameron V-77 balloon	J. M. Percival	
G-RCMP	PA-28RT-201T Turbo Arrow IV	Southeast Air Ltd	
G-RCNB	Eurocopter EC.120B	C. B. Ellis	
G-RCOH	Cameron Cube 105 SS balloon	A. M. Holly	
G-RCRC	P & M Quik	R. M. Brown	
G-RCSR	Replica de Havilland DH.88 Comet	K. Fern	
G-RCST	Jabiru J430	P. M. Jones	
G-RCUB	PA-18-95 Super Cub	R. F. L. Cuypers (G-BPJH)	
G-RCUS	Schempp-Hirth Arcus T	Arcus G-RCUS Syndicate	
G-RDAD	Reality Escapade ULP(1)	F. Overall	
G-RDAS	Cessna 172M	J. Martin	
G-RDAY	Van's RV-9	R. M. Day	
G-RDCO	Avtech Jabiru J430	A. H. & F. A. Macaskill	
G-RDDM	Cessna 182T	Optum Global Ltd	

Notes	Reg	Type	Owner or Operator
	G-RDEN	Cameron Z-105 balloon	Hillmount Bangor Ltd
	G-RDFX	Aero AT-3	M. W. Richardson
	G-RDHS	Shaw Europa XS	R. D. H. Spencer
	G-RDNS	Rans S.6-S Super Coyote	S. R. Green
	G-RDNY	AutoGyro Cavalon	C. Rodney
	G-RDPH	P & M Quik R	R. S. Partidge-Hicks
	G-RDRL	Reaction Drive Rotorcraft	Genesis Aerotech Ltd
	G-READ	Colt 77A balloon	Intervarsity Balloon Club
	G-REAF	Jabiru J400	R. E. Afia
	G-REAR	Lindstrand LBL-69X balloon	A. M. Holly
	G-REAS	Van's RV-6A	T. J. Smith
	G-REBB	Murphy Rebel	M. Stow
	G-RECW	PA-28-181 Archer II	R. E. C. Washington (G-BOBZ)
	G-REDC	Pegasus Quantum 15-912	S. Houghton
	G-REDF	Eurocopter AS.365N3 Dauphin 2	Babcock Mission Critical Services Offshore Ltd
	G-REDJ	Eurocopter AS.332L-2 Super Puma	Babcock Mission Critical Services Leasing Ltd
	G-REDK	Eurocopter AS.332L-2 Super Puma	Babcock Mission Critical Services Leasing Ltd
	G-REDM	Eurocopter AS.332L-2 Super Puma	Babcock Mission Critical Services Leasing Ltd
	G-REDN	Eurocopter AS.332L-2 Super Puma	Babcock Mission Critical Services Leasing Ltd
	G-REDO	Eurocopter AS.332L-2 Super Puma	Babcock Mission Critical Services Leasing Ltd
	G-REDP	Eurocopter AS.332L-2 Super Puma	Babcock Mission Critical Services Leasing Ltd
	G-REDR	Eurocopter AS.225LP Super Puma	Babcock Mission Critical Services Leasing Ltd
	G-REDT	Eurocopter EC.225LP Super Puma	Babcock Mission Critical Services Leasing Ltd
	G-REDX	Experimental Aviation Berkut	G. V. Waters
	G-REDZ	Thruster T.600T 450	N. S. Dell
	G-REEC	Sequoia F.8L Falco	K. J. E. Augustinus/Belgium
	G-REED	Mainair Blade 912S	D. J. Kaye
	G-REEF	Mainair Blade 912S	B. Skidmore
	G-REEM	AS.355F1 Twin Squirrel	Heliking Ltd (G-EMAN/G-WEKR/G-CHLA)
	G-REER	Centrair 101A Pegase	R. L. Howorth & G. C. Stinchcombe
	G-REES	Jodel D.140C	G-REES Flying Group
	G-REEV	Robinson R44 II	SNG Aviation Ltd
	G-REFO	Gulfstream 650	TAG Aviation (UK) Ltd
	G-REGC	Zenair CH.601XL Zodiac	G. P. Coutie
	G-REGJ	Robinson R44 II	HQ Aviation Ltd (G-OPTF)
	G-REGZ	Aeroprakt A-22L Foxbat	L. Campbell
	G-REJP	Europa XS	A. Milner
	G-REKO	Pegasus Quasar IITC	M. Carter (G-MWWA)
	G-RELL	D.62B Condor	M. J. Golder (G-OPJH/G-AVDW)
	G-REMH	Bell 206B-3 JetRanger III	Flightpath Ltd
	G-RENI	Balony Kubicek BB-30Z balloon	A. M. Holly
	G-RESG	Dyn'Aéro MCR-01 Club	R. E. S. Greenwood
	G-REST	Beech P35 Bonanza	C. R. Taylor (G-ASFJ)
	G-RESU	Airbus Helicopters MBB BK-117D-2	Babcock Mission Critical Services Onshore Ltd
	G-RETA	CASA 1.131 Jungmann 2000	A. N. R. Houghton (G-BGZC)
	G-REVE	Van's RV-6	S. D. Foster
	G-REVO	Skyranger 912(2)	H. Murray & D. A. Wilson
	G-REYE	Robinson R44 I	Redeye.com Ltd
	G-REYS	Canadair CL600-2B16 Challenger 604	Locally Applied Solutions Ltd
	G-RFAD	Sportavia-Putzer Fournier RF4D	M. P. Dentith
	G-RFCA	Tecnam P2008-JC	The Waddington Flying Club
	G-RFCB	Tecnam P2008-JC	The Waddington Flying Club
	G-RFIO	Aeromot AMT-200 Super Ximango	M. D. Evans
	G-RFLO	Ultramagic M-105 balloon	Flying Enterprises
	G-RFLY	Extra EA.300/L	H. B. Sauer
	G-RFOX	Denney Kitfox Mk 3	D. A. Jackson
	G-RFSB	Sportavia RF-5B	G-RFSB Group
	G-RGTS	Schempp-Hirth Discus b	G. R. & L. R. Green
	G-RGUS	Fairchild 24A-46A Argus III (44-83184)	R. Ellingworth
	G-RGWY	Bell 206B-3 Jet Ranger III	Ridgway Aviation Ltd (G-OAGL/G-CORN/G-BHTR)
	G-RGZT	Cirrus SR20	M. Presenti
	G-RHAM	Skyranger 582(1)	L. Smart & P. Gibson
	G-RHCB	Schweizer 269C-1	AH Helicopter Services Ltd
	G-RHML	Robinson R22	C. Lescure

Reg	Type	Owner or Operator	Notes
G-RHMS	Embraer EMB-135BJ Legacy	TAG Aviation (UK) Ltd	
G-RHOD	Just Superstol	C. S. & K. D. Rhodes	
G-RHOS	ICP MXP-740 Savannah VG Jabiru(1)	J. C. Munro-Hunt	
G-RHYM	PA-31-310 Turbo Navajo B	2 Excel Aviation Ltd (G-BJLO)	
G-RHYS	Rotorway Executive 90	A. K. Voase	
G-RIAM	SOCATA TB10 Tobago	TB10 Group	
G-RIBA	P & M Quik GT450	R. J. Murphy	
G-RICO	AG-5B Tiger	Delta Lima Flying Group	
G-RICS	Shaw Europa	The Flying Property Doctor	
G-RIDA	Eurocopter AS.355NP Ecureuil 2	National Grid Electricity Transmission PLC	
G-RIDB	Bell 429	National Grid Electricity Transmission PLC	
G-RIDE	Stephens Akro	R. Mitchell	
G-RIDG	Van's RV-7	G-RIDG Flying Group	
G-RIEF	DG Flugzeugbau DG-1000T	EF Gliding Group	
G-RIET	Hoffmann H.36 Dimona	Dimona Syndicate	
G-RIEV	Rolladen-Schneider LS8-18	R. D. Grieve	
G-RIFB	Hughes 269C	Findelta Pty Ltd	
G-RIFD	HpH Glasflugel 304ES	D. Griffiths	
G-RIFN	Avion Mudry CAP-10B	D. E. Starkey & R. A. J. Spurrell	
G-RIFO	Schempp-Hirth Standard Cirrus 75-VTC	A. Mura (G-CKGT)	
G-RIFY	Christen Eagle II	G-RIFY Flying Group	
G-RIGB	Thunder Ax7-77 balloon	N. J. Bettin	
G-RIGH	PA-32R-301 Saratoga IIHP	A. Brinkley	
G-RIGS	PA-60 Aerostar 601P	G. G. Caravatti & P. G. Penati/Italy	
G-RIHN	Dan Rihn DR.107 One Design	P. J. Burgess	
G-RIII	Vans RV-3B	J. F. Dowe	
G-RIIV	Van's RV-4	M. R. Overall	
G-RIKI	Mainair Blade 912	C. M. Mackinnon	
G-RIKS	Shaw Europa XS	H. Foster	
G-RIKY	Mainair Pegasus Quik	S. Clarke	
G-RILA	Flight Design CTSW	P. A. Mahony	
G-RILY	Monnett Sonnerai 2L	A Sharp	
G-RIMB	Lindstrand LBL-105A balloon	D. Grimshaw	
G-RIME	Lindstrand LBL-25A balloon	N. Ivison	
G-RIMM	Westland Wasp HAS.1 (XT435:430)	G. P. Hinkley	
G-RINN	Mainair Blade	P. Hind	
G-RINO	Thunder Ax7-77 balloon	D. J. Head	
G-RINS	Rans S.6-ESA Coyote II	R. W. Hocking	
G-RINT	CFM Streak Shadow	D. Grint	
G-RINZ	Van's RV-7	R. C. May (G-UZZL)	
G-RIOT	Silence SA.180 Twister	Zulu Glasstek Ltd (G-SWIP)	
G-RIPA	Partenavia P68 Observer 2	Apem Ltd	
G-RIPH	VS.384 Seafire F.XVII	Seafire Displays Ltd (G-CDTM)	
G-RISA	PA-28-180 Cherokee C	D. B. Riseborough (G-ATZK)	
G-RISH	Rotorway Exeecutive 162F	M. H. Hoffman	
G-RISY	Van's RV-7	D. I. Scott	
G-RITS	Pitts S-1C	J. H. D. Newman	
G-RITT	P & M Quik	T. H. Parr	
G-RIVA	SOCATA TBM-700N	MSV GmbH & Co KG/Germany	
G-RIVE	Jodel D.153	M. J. Applewhite	
G-RIVR	Thruster T.600N 450	S. W. Turley	
G-RIVT	Van's RV-6	R. Howard	
G-RIXA	J-3C-65 Cub	J. J. Rix	
G-RIXS	Shaw Europa XS	T. J. Houlihan	
G-RIXY	Cameron Z-77 balloon	Rix Petroleum (Hull) Ltd	
G-RIZE	Cameron O-90 balloon	S. F. Burden/Netherlands	
G-RIZI	Cameron N-90 balloon	R. Wiles	
G-RIZK	Schleicher ASW-27-18E	G. S. S. Rizk	
G-RIZZ	PA-28-161 Warrior II	W. Ali	
G-RJAM	Sequoia F.8L Falco	D. G. Drew	
G-RJCC	Cessna 172S	R. J. Chapman	
G-RJIT	Groppo Trail Mk.2	Dragon Trail Group	
G-RJMS	PA-28R-201 Arrow III	M. G. Hill	
G-RJRC	Commander114B	R. M. Jowitt	
G-RJRJ	Evektor EV-97A Eurostar	D. P. Myatt	
G-RJVH	Guimbal Cabri G2	RJV Holdings Ltd	
G-RJWW	Maule M5-235C Lunar Rocket	D. E. Priest (G-BRWG)	
G-RJWX	Shaw Europa XS	D. S. P. Disney	
G-RJXA	Embraer RJ145EP	bmi regional	

Notes	Reg	Type	Owner or Operator
	G-RJXB	Embraer RJ145EP	bmi regional
	G-RJXC	Embraer RJ145EP	bmi regional
	G-RJXD	Embraer RJ145EP	bmi regional
	G-RJXE	Embraer RJ145EP	bmi regional
	G-RJXF	Embraer RJ145EP	bmi regional
	G-RJXG	Embraer RJ145EP	bmi regional
	G-RJXH	Embraer RJ145EP	bmi regional
	G-RJXI	Embraer RJ145EP	bmi regional
	G-RJXJ	Embraer RJ135LR	bmi regional
	G-RJXK	Embraer RJ135LR	bmi regional
	G-RJXL	Embraer RJ135LR	bmi regional
	G-RJXM	Embraer RJ145MP	bmi regional
	G-RJXP	Embraer RJ135ER	bmi regional (G-CDFS)
	G-RJXR	Embraer RJ145EP	bmi regional (G-CCYH)
	G-RKAF	Diamond DA.40D Star	Airways Aviation Academy Ltd
	G-RKAG	Diamond DA.40D Star	Airways Aviation Academy Ltd
	G-RKAH	Diamond DA.40D Star	Airways Aviation Academy Ltd
	G-RKAI	Diamond DA.40D Star	Airways Aviation Academy Ltd
	G-RKBD	Diamond DA.42 Twin Star	Airways Aviation Academy Ltd
	G-RKEL	Agusta-Bell 206B JetRanger 3	Nunkeeling Ltd
	G-RKID	Van's RV-6A	I. Shaw
	G-RKKT	Cessna FR.172G	K. L. Irvine (G-AYJW)
	G-RKUS	Arcus T	Arcus Syndicate
	G-RLDS	Cameron A-315 balloon	Red Letter Days Ltd
	G-RLDX	Cameron A-375 balloon	Red Letter Days Ltd
	G-RLDZ	Cameron A-315 balloon	Red Letter Days Ltd
	G-RLMW	Tecnam P2002-EA Sierra	S. P. Hoskins
	G-RLON	BN-2A Mk III-2 Trislander	Aurigny Air Services Ltd (G-ITEX/G-OCTA/G-BCXW)
	G-RLWG	Ryan ST3KR	R. A. Fleming
	G-RMAA	Airbus MBB BK117 D-2	Babcock Mission Critical Services Onshore Ltd
	G-RMAC	Shaw Europa	P. J. Lawless
	G-RMAN	Aero Designs Pulsar	J. M. Angiolini & G. Melling
	G-RMAR	Robinson R66	Marfleet Civil Engineering Ltd (G-NSEV)
	G-RMAV	Ikarus C42 FB80	RM Aviation Ltd
	G-RMAX	Cameron C-80 balloon	J. Kenny
	G-RMCS	Cessna 182R	R. W. C. Sears
	G-RMHE	Aerospool Dynamic WT9 UK	D. R. Lewis
	G-RMIT	Van's RV-4	J. P. Kloos
	G-RMMA	Dassault Falcon 900EX	TAG Aviation (UK) Ltd
	G-RMMT	Europa XS	N. Schmitt
	G-RMPI	Whittaker MW5D Sorcerer	R. W. Twamley
	G-RMPS	Van's RV-12	K. D. Boardman
	G-RMPY	Aerotechnik EV-97 Eurostar	N. R. Beale
	G-RMRV	Van's RV-7A	R. Morris
	G-RMUG	Cameron Nescafe Mug 90 SS balloon	The British Balloon Museum & Library Ltd
	G-RNAC	IDA Bacau Yakovlev Yak-52	Chewton Glen Aviation
	G-RNAS	DH.104 Sea Devon C.20 (XK896) ★	Airport Fire Service/Filton
	G-RNBW	Bell 206B JetRanger 2	Rainbow Helicopters Ltd
	G-RNCH	PA-28-181 Archer II	Airborne Adventures Ltd
	G-RNDD	Robin DR.400/500	Witham (Specialist Vehicles) Ltd
	G-RNER	Cessna 510 Citation Mustang	S. J. Davies
	G-RNFR	Bombardier CL600-2B16 Challenger 605	TAG Aviation (UK) Ltd
	G-RNGD	Murphy Renegade Spirit UK	Spirit Flying Group
	G-RNHF	Hawker Sea Fury T.Mk.20 (VX281)	Naval Aviation Ltd (G-BCOW)
	G-RNIE	Cameron 70 Ball SS balloon	N. J. Bland
	G-RNJP	Bombardier CL600-2B16 Challenger 605	TAG Aviation (UK) Ltd
	G-RNLI	VS.236 Walrus I (W2718) ★	Walrus Aviation Ltd
	G-RNRM	Cessna A.185F	Skydive St. Andrews Ltd
	G-ROAD	Robinson R44 II	Aztec Aviators Ltd
	G-ROAT	Robinson R44 II	R. D. Jordan
	G-ROBA	Grob G.115D-2 Heron	Social Infrastructure Ltd (G-BVHF)
	G-ROBD	Shaw Europa	Condor Aviation International Ltd
	G-ROBG	P & M Quik GT450	Exodus Airsports Ltd
	G-ROBJ	Robin DR.500/200i	D. R. L. Jones

Reg	Type	Owner or Operator	Notes
G-ROBN	Pierre Robin R1180T	N. D. Anderson	
G-ROBT	Hawker Hurricane I (P2902:DX-X)	Anglia Aircraft Restorations Ltd	
G-ROBZ	Grob G109B	Bravo Zulu Group	
G-ROCH	Cessna T.303	R. S. Bentley	
G-ROCK	Thunder Ax7-77 balloon	M. A. Green	
G-ROCR	Schweizer 269C	K. Abel, E. Beard, C. Hayles & N. Pringle	
G-ROCT	Robinson R44 II	A. von Liechtenstein	
G-RODC	Steen Skybolt	D. G. Girling	
G-RODD	Cessna 310R II	Alpha Properties (London) Ltd (G-TEDD/ G-MADI)	
G-RODG	Avtech Jabiru UL	G-RODG Group	
G-RODI	Isaacs Fury (K3731)	M. J. Bond	
G-RODJ	Ikarus C42 FB80	P. M. Yeoman	
G-RODO	Shaw Europa XS	R. M. Carson (G-ROWI)	
G-RODZ	Van's RV-3A	D. Williams	
G-ROEI	Avro Roe 1 Replica	Brooklands Museum Trust Ltd	
G-ROEN	Cameron C-70 balloon	R. M. W. Romans	
G-ROFS	Groppo Trail	R. F. Bond	
G-ROGY	Cameron 60 Concept balloon	S. A. Laing	
G-ROKO	Roko-Aero NG-4HD	C. D. Sidoli	
G-ROKS	Robinson R44 II	R. Starling (G-WEGO)	
G-ROKT	Cessna FR.172E	R. N. R. Bellamy	
G-ROKY	Groppo Trail	J. Webb	
G-ROLF	PA-32R-301 Saratoga SP	P. F. Larkins	
G-ROLL	Pitts S-2A Special	N. Lamb	
G-ROLY	Cessna F.172N	M. Bonsall (G-BHIH)	
G-ROME	I.I.I. Sky Arrow 650TC	Sky Arrow (Kits) UK Ltd	
G-ROMP	Extra 230H	D. G. Cowden & S. C. Hipwell	
G-ROMT	Robinson R44 II	DYDB Marketing Ltd (G-RALA)	
G-ROMW	Cyclone AX2000	K. V. Falvey	
G-RONA	Shaw Europa	C. M. Noakes	
G-RONG	PA-28R Cherokee Arrow 200-II	R. W. Hinton	
G-RONI	Cameron V-77 balloon	R. E. Simpson	
G-RONS	Robin DR.400/180	Robin Flying Club Ltd	
G-RONW	FRED Srs 2	F. J. Keitch	
G-RONZ	Ikarus C42 FB80 Bravo	R. F. Dean	
G-ROOG	Extra EA.300/LT	M. J. Coward	
G-ROOK	Cessna F.172P	Rolim Ltd	
G-ROON	Sikorsky S-76C	Rooney Air Ltd	
G-ROOO	Jabiru J430	H. S. A. Brewis (G-HJZN)	
G-ROOV	Shaw Europa XS	P. W. Hawkins & K. Siggery	
G-ROPO	Groppo Trail	J. M. Chapman	
G-ROPP	Groppo Trail	J. M. Cubley	
G-RORA	Embraer EMB-550 Legacy 500	Centreline	
G-RORB	Spitfire Mk.26	Bertha Property LLP	
G-RORI	Folland Gnat T.1 (XR538)	Heritage Aircraft Ltd	
G-RORY	Piaggio FWP.149D	M. Edwards (G-TOWN)	
G-ROSI	Thunder Ax7-77 balloon	J. E. Rose	
G-ROSK	Ultramagic M-90 balloon	N. Roskell	
G-ROSS	Practavia Pilot Sprite	A. N. Barley	
G-ROTI	Luscombe 8A Silvaire	R. Ludgate & L. Prebble	
G-ROTS	CFM Streak Shadow Srs SA	J. Edwards	
G-ROUS	PA-34-200T Seneca II	R. Pedersen	
G-ROVA	Aviat A-1B Husky Pup	Aviat Aircraft (UK) Ltd	
G-ROVE	PA-18 Super Cub 135 (R-156)	S. J. Gaveston	
G-ROVY	Robinson R22 Beta	R. F. McLachlan	
G-ROWA	Aquila AT01	R. Simpson	
G-ROWL	AA-5B Tiger	Box MR Ltd	
G-ROWS	PA-28-151 Warrior	Air Academy	
G-ROXI	Cameron C-90 balloon	D. Marshall	
G-ROYC	Avtech Jabiru UL450	G-ROYC Flying Group	
G-ROYM	Robinson R44 II	HQ Aviation Ltd	
G-ROYP	Robinson R22	Startrade Heli GmbH/Germany	
G-ROZE	Magni M-24C	R. I. Simpson	
G-ROZZ	Ikarus C.42 FB 80	A. J. Blackwell	
G-RPAF	Europa XS	G-RPAF Group	
G-RPAX	CASA 1-133 Jungmeister	A. J. E. Smith	
G-RPCC	Europa XS	R. P. Churchill-Coleman	
G-RPEZ	Rutan LongEz	M. P. Dunlop	
G-RPPO	Groppo Trail	G. N. Smith	

Notes	Reg	Type	Owner or Operator
	G-RPRV	Van's RV-9A	T. A. Willcox
	G-RRAK	Enstrom 480B	C. A. Reed (G-RIBZ)
	G-RRAT	CZAW Sportcruiser	G. Sipson
	G-RRCU	CEA DR.221B Dauphin	Merlin Flying Club Ltd
	G-RRED	PA-28-181 Archer II	J. P. Reddington
	G-RRFF	VS.329 Spitfire Mk.IIB	Retro Track & Air (UK) Ltd
	G-RRGN	VS.390 Spitfire PR.XIX (PS853)	Rolls-Royce PLC (G-MXIX)
	G-RROB	Robinson R44 II	R. S. Rai
	G-RRRV	Van's RV-6	C. St. J. Hall
	G-RRRZ	Van's RV-8	J. Bate
	G-RRSR	Piper J-3C-65 Cub (480173:57-H)	R. W. Roberts
	G-RRVX	Van's RV-10	T. Booth
	G-RSAF	BAC.167 Strikemaster 80A	M. A. Petrie
	G-RSAM	P & M Quik GTR	J. W. Foster
	G-RSCU	Agusta A.109E	Sloane Helicopters Ltd
	G-RSHI	PA-34-220T Seneca V	R. S. Hill and Sons
	G-RSKR	PA-28-161 Warrior II	Aviation, Advice & Consulting Ltd (G-BOJY)
	G-RSKY	Skyranger 912(2)	C. H. Tregonning
	G-RSMC	Medway SLA 100 Executive	W. S. C. Toulmin
	G-RSSF	Denney Kitfox Mk 2	C. Bingham
	G-RSWO	Cessna 172R	G. Fischer
	G-RSXP	Cessna 560 Citation XLS	Fly Vectra Ltd
	G-RTFM	Jabiru J400	M. Ekaratcharoenchai
	G-RTHS	Rans S-6-ES Coyote II	R. G. Hughes
	G-RTIN	Rotorsport UK MT-03	C. J. Morton
	G-RTMS	Rans S.6 ES Coyote II	C. J. Arthur
	G-RTMY	Ikarus C.42 FB 100	Mike Yankee Group
	G-RTRV	V an's RV-9A	R. Taylor
	G-RUBB	AA-5B Tiger	D. E. Gee
	G-RUBY	PA-28RT-201T Turbo Arrow IV	Arrow Aircraft Group (G-BROU)
	G-RUCK	Bell 206B-3 JetRanger III	J. A. Ruck
	G-RUES	Robin HR.100/210	R. H. R. Rue
	G-RUFF	Mainair Blade 912	P. Mulvey
	G-RUFS	Avtech Jabiru UL	M. Bastin
	G-RUGS	Campbell Cricket Mk 4 gyroplane	J. L. G. McLane
	G-RUIA	Cessna F.172N	D. R. Clyde
	G-RULE	Robinson R44 Raven II	Huckair
	G-RUMI	Noble Harman Snowbird Mk.IV	G. Crossley (G-MVOI)
	G-RUMM	Grumman F8F-2P Bearcat (121714:201B)	Patina Ltd
	G-RUMN	AA-1A Trainer	A. M. Leahy
	G-RUMW	Grumman FM-2 Wildcat (JV579:F)	Patina Ltd
	G-RUNS	P & M Quik GT450	S. Nicol
	G-RUNT	Cassutt Racer IIIM	D. P. Lightfoot
	G-RUPS	Cameron TR-70 balloon	R. M. Stanley
	G-RUSL	Van's RV-6A	G. R. Russell
	G-RUSO	Robinson R22 Beta	R. M. Barnes-Gorell
	G-RUSS	Cessna 172N ★	Leisure Lease (stored)/Southend
	G-RUVE	Van's RV-8	J. P. Brady & D. J. Taylor
	G-RUVI	Zenair CH.601UL	P. G. Depper
	G-RUVY	Van's RV-9A	R. D. Taylor
	G-RVAA	Van's RV-7	A. J. Almosawi
	G-RVAB	Van's RV-7	I. M. Belmore & A. T. Banks
	G-RVAC	Van's RV-7	A. F. S. & B. Caldecourt
	G-RVAH	Van's RV-7	Regent Group
	G-RVAL	Van's RV-8	P. D. Scandrett
	G-RVAN	Van's RV-6	C. Richards
	G-RVAR	Van's RV-8	B. A. Ridgway
	G-RVAT	Van's RV-8	T. R. Grief
	G-RVAW	Van's RV-6	C. Rawlings & R. J. Tomlinson
	G-RVBA	Van's RV-8A	D. P. Richard
	G-RVBC	Van's RV-6A	B. J. Clifford
	G-RVBF	Cameron A-340 balloon	Virgin Balloon Flights
	G-RVBI	Van's RV-8	K. R. H. Wingate
	G-RVCE	Van's RV-6A	C. & M. D. Barnard
	G-RVCH	Van's RV-8A	B. F. Hill
	G-RVCL	Van's RV-6	N. Halsall

Reg	Type	Owner or Operator	Notes
G-RVDB	Van's RV-7	D. Broom	
G-RVDC	Van's RV-8	D. P. Catt	
G-RVDG	Van's RV-9	D. M. Gill	
G-RVDH	Van's RV-8	D. J. Harrison (G-ONER)	
G-RVDJ	Van's RV-6	C. S. & P. S. Foster	
G-RVDP	Van's RV-4	O. Florin	
G-RVDR	Van's RV-6A	P. R. Redfern	
G-RVDX	Van's RV-4	P. Musso (G-FTUO)	
G-RVEA	BRM Aero Bristell NG5 Speed Wing	R. V. Emerson	
G-RVEE	Van's RV-6	J. C. A. Wheeler	
G-RVEI	Van's RV-8	D. Stephens	
G-RVEM	Van's RV-7A	D. A. Cowan (G-CBJU)	
G-RVER	Van's RV-4	G-RVER Flying Group	
G-RVET	Van's RV-6	D. R. Coleman	
G-RVGA	Van's RV-6A	R. Emery	
G-RVGO	Van's RV-10	D. C. Arnold	
G-RVHD	Van's RV-7	D. J. Mountain & H. W. Hall	
G-RVIA	Van's RV-6A	K. R. W. Scull & J. Watkins	
G-RVIB	Van's RV-6	P. D. Gorman	
G-RVIC	Van's RV-6A	I. T. Corse	
G-RVII	Van's RV-7	P. H. C. Hall	
G-RVIL	Van's RV-4	S. C. Hipwell	
G-RVIN	Van's RV-6	M. Lawton	
G-RVIO	Van's RV-10	G-RVIO Group	
G-RVIS	Van's RV-8	M. W. Edwards	
G-RVIT	Van's RV-6	P. J. Shotbolt	
G-RVIV	Van's RV-4	S. B. Robson	
G-RVIW	Van's RV-9	C. R. James	
G-RVIX	Van's RV-9A	J. R. Holt & C. S. Simmons	
G-RVIZ	Van's RV-12	Chelwood Flying Group	
G-RVJG	Van's RV-7	J. W. Ellis (G-JTEM)	
G-RVJM	Van's RV-6	M. D. Challoner	
G-RVJO	Van's RV-9A	P. D. Chandler	
G-RVJP	Van's RV-9A	R. M. Palmer	
G-RVJW	Van's RV-4	J. M. Williams	
G-RVLC	Van's RV-9A	L. J. Clark	
G-RVLW	Cessna F.406 Caravan II	RVL Aviation Ltd	
G-RVLX	Cessna F.406 Caravan II	RVL Aviation Ltd	
G-RVLY	Cessna F.406 Caravan II	RVL Aviation Ltd (G-BPSX)	
G-RVLZ	Cessna 310R	RVL Aviation Ltd	
G-RVMB	Van's RV-9A	M. James	
G-RVMT	Van's RV-6	P. I. Lewis	
G-RVMZ	Van's RV-8	A. E. Kay	
G-RVNA	PA-38-112 Tomahawk	Ravenair Aircraft Ltd (G-DFLY)	
G-RVNC	PA-38-112 Tomahawk	Ravenair Aircraft Ltd (G-BTJK)	
G-RVND	PA-38-112 Tomahawk	NPA Aviation (G-BTAS)	
G-RVNE	Partenavia P.68B	Ravenair Aircraft Ltd (G-SAMJ)	
G-RVNG	Partenavia P.68B	Ravenair Aircraft Ltd (G-BMOI)	
G-RVNH	Van's RV-9A	N. R. Haines	
G-RVNI	Van's RV-6A	G-RVNI Group	
G-RVNJ	Partenavia P.68B	Ravenair Aircraft Ltd	
G-RVNK	Partenavia P.68B	Ravenair Aircraft Ltd (G-BHBZ)	
G-RVNM	Partenavia P.68B	Ravenair Aircraft Ltd (G-BFBU)	
G-RVNO	PA-34-200T Seneca II	Ravenair Aircraft Ltd (G-VVBK/G-BSBS/ G-BDRI)	
G-RVNP	Partenavia P.68B	Ravenair Aircraft Ltd	
G-RVNS	Van's RV-4	D. R. Cairns & K. A. Beetson (G-CBGN)	
G-RVOM	Van's RV-8	O. D. Mihalop	
G-RVPH	Van's RV-8	J. C. P. Herbert	
G-RVPL	Van's RV-8	B. J. Summers	
G-RVPM	Van's RV-4	D. P. Lightfoot (G-RVDS)	
G-RVPW	Van's RV-6A	C. G. Deeley	
G-RVRA	PA-28 Cherokee 140	Par Contractors Ltd (G-OWVA)	
G-RVRB	PA-34-200T Seneca II	Ravenair Aircraft Ltd (G-BTAJ)	
G-RVRC	PA-23 Aztec 250E	B. J. Green (G-BNPD)	
G-RVRE	Partenavia P.68B	Ravenair Aircraft Ltd	
G-RVRJ	PA-E23 Aztec 250E	Ravenair Aircraft Ltd (G-BBGB)	
G-RVRK	PA-38-112 Tomahawk	Ravenair Aircraft Ltd (G-BGZW)	
G-RVRL	PA-38-112 Tomahawk	Aviation South West Ltd (G-BGZW/G-BGBY)	
G-RVRM	PA-38-112 Tomahawk	Ravenair Aircraft Ltd (G-BGEK)	
G-RVRN	PA-28-161 Warrior II	Ravenair Aircraft Ltd (G-BPID)	

Notes	Reg	Type	Owner or Operator
	G-RVRO	PA-38-112 Tomahawk II	Ravenair Aircraft Ltd (G-BOUD)
	G-RVRP	Van's RV-7	R. C. Parris
	G-RVRR	PA-38-112 Tomahawk	Aviation South West Ltd (G-BRHT)
	G-RVRT	PA-28-140 Cherokee C	Full Sutton Flying Centre Ltd (G-AYKX)
	G-RVRU	PA-38-112 Tomahawk	Ravenair Aircraft Ltd (G-NCFE/G-BKMK)
	G-RVRV	Van's RV-4	P. Jenkins
	G-RVRW	PA-23 Aztec 250E	Ravenair Aircraft Ltd (G-BAVZ)
	G-RVRX	Partenavia P.68B	Ravenair Aircraft Ltd (G-PART)
	G-RVRY	PA-38-112 Tomahawk	Ravenair Aircraft Ltd (G-BTND)
	G-RVRZ	PA-23-250 Aztec E	Ravenair Aircraft Ltd (G-NRSC/G-BSFL)
	G-RVSA	Van's RV-6A	J. Stevenson
	G-RVSB	Van's RV-6	S. Beard
	G-RVSD	Van's RV-9A	S. W. Damarell
	G-RVSG	Van's RV-9A	S. Gerrish
	G-RVSH	Van's RV-6A	S. F. A. Madi
	G-RVSK	Van's RV-9A	D. A. Kenworthy
	G-RVSR	Van's RV-8	R. K. & S. W. Elders
	G-RVST	Van's RV-6	A. F. Vizoso (G-BXYX)
	G-RVSX	Van's RV-6	R. L. & V. A. West
	G-RVTA	Van's RV-7	A. G. Andrew
	G-RVTB	Van's RV-7	T. M. Bootyman (G-CIWM)
	G-RVTE	Van's RV-6	E. McShane & T. Feeny
	G-RVTN	Van's RV-10	C. I. Law
	G-RVTT	Van's RV-7	R. L. Mitcham
	G-RVTW	Van's RV-12	A. P. Watkins
	G-RVTX	Van's RV-8	M. N. Stannard
	G-RVUK	Van's RV-7	P. D. G. Grist
	G-RVVI	Van's RV-6	P. R. Thorne
	G-RVWJ	Van's RV-9A	N. J. Williams-Jones
	G-RVXP	Van's RV-3B	A. N. Buchan
	G-RWAY	Rotorway Executive 162F	C. R. Johnson (G-URCH)
	G-RWCA	PA-18-150 Super Cub	R. J. Williamson
	G-RWEW	Robinson R44	Pilot Training and Testing Ltd
	G-RWIA	Robinson R22 Beta	S. A. Wolski (G-BOEZ)
	G-RWIN	Rearwin 175	A. B. Bourne & N. D. Battye
	G-RWOD	Dan Rihn DR.107 One Design	R. S. Wood
	G-RWSS	Denney Kitfox Mk 2	J. I. V. Hill
	G-RWWW	WS-55 Whirlwind HCC.12 (XR486)★	IHM/Weston-super-Mare
	G-RXTV	Agusta A.109E Power	Arena Aviation Ltd (G-GCMM)
	G-RXUK	Lindstrand LBL-105A balloon	C. C. & R. K. Scott
	G-RYAL	Avtech Jabiru UL	G. R. Oscroft
	G-RYDR	Rotorsport UK MT-03	H. W. Parsons & U. Junger
	G-RYNS	PA-32-301FT Cherokee Six	D. A. Earle
	G-RYPE	DG Flugzeugbau DG-1000T	DG-1000T Partners
	G-RYPH	Mainair Blade 912	A. R. Young
	G-RYSE	Cessna TR.182 RG	E. Tattam (G-BZVO)
	G-RYZZ	Robinson R44 II	Rivermead Aviation Ltd
	G-RZEE	Schleicher ASW-19B	R. Christopherson
	G-RZLY	Flight Design CTSW	J. D. Macnamara
	G-SAAA	Flight Design CTSW	Comunica Industries International Ltd
	G-SAAR	Agusta Westland AW-189	British International Helicopter Services Ltd
	G-SABA	PA-28R-201T Turbo Arrow III	C. A. Burton (G-BFEN)
	G-SACH	Stoddard-Hamilton Glastar	R. S. Holt
	G-SACI	PA-28-161 Warrior II	PJC (Leasing) Ltd
	G-SACL	Tecnam P2006T	Surrey Aero Club Ltd
	G-SACM	TL2000UK Sting Carbon	M. Clare
	G-SACN	Scheibe SF-25C Falke	The RAF Gliding and Soaring Association
	G-SACO	PA-28-161 Warrior II	Stapleford Flying Club Ltd
	G-SACP	Aero AT-3 R100	Sherburn Aero Club Ltd
	G-SACR	PA-28-161 Cadet	Sherburn Aero Club Ltd
	G-SACS	PA-28-161 Cadet	Sherburn Aero Club Ltd
	G-SACT	PA-28-161 Cadet	Sherburn Aero Club Ltd
	G-SACW	Aero AT-3 R100	Sherburn Aero Club Ltd
	G-SACX	Aero AT-3 R100	Sherburn Aero Club Ltd
	G-SADD	EV-97 Eurostar SL	T. R. Southall
	G-SAEA	Spitfire LF XVIE	M. Harris

Reg	Type	Owner or Operator	Notes
G-SAFE	Cameron N-77 balloon	P. J. Waller	
G-SAFI	CP.1320 Super Emeraude	C. S. Carleton-Smith	
G-SAGA	Grob G.109B	M. C. Downey	
G-SAGE	Luscombe 8A Silvaire	C. Howell (G-AKTL)	
G-SAHI	Trago Mills SAH-1	Hotel India Group	
G-SAIG	Robinson R44 II	Torfield Aviation Ltd	
G-SAJA	Schempp-Hirth Discus 2	J. G. Arnold	
G-SALD	Bombardier BD700-1A10 Global 6000	Gama Aviation (UK) Ltd	
G-SALE	Cameron Z-90 balloon	R. D. Baker	
G-SAMC	Ikarus C42 FB80	E. B. S. Farmer	
G-SAMG	Grob G.109B	The Royal Air Force Gliding and Soaring Association	
G-SAMY	Shaw Europa	K. R. Tallent	
G-SAMZ	Cessna 150D	A. J. Taylor (G-ASSO)	
G-SANT	Schempp-Hirth Discus bT	S. Cervantes (G-JPIP)	
G-SAOC	Schempp-Hirth Discus 2cT	The Royal Air Force Gliding and Soaring Association	
G-SAPI	PA-28-181 Archer II	Biggleswade Flying Group Ltd	
G-SAPM	SOCATA TB20 Trinidad	G-SAPM Ltd (G-EWFN)	
G-SARA	PA-28-181 Archer II	C. P. W. Villa	
G-SARD	Agusta Westland AW139	CHC Scotia Ltd	
G-SARJ	P & M Quik GT450	A. R. Jones	
G-SARM	Ikarus C.42 FB80	G-SARM Group	
G-SARP	Cessna R182RG	Aerobatica Lda/Portugal	
G-SARV	Van's RV-4	Hinton Flying Group	
G-SASC	Beech B200C Super King Air	Gama Aviation (UK) Ltd	
G-SASD	Beech B200C Super King Air	Gama Aviation (UK) Ltd	
G-SASF	Scheibe SF-25C Rotor-Falke	The RAF Gliding and Soaring Association	
G-SASG	Schleicher ASW-27-18E	C. Jackson & P. T. Reading	
G-SASI	CZAW Sportcruiser	K. W. Allan	
G-SASK	PA-31P Pressurised Navajo	Middle East Business Club Ltd (G-BFAM)	
G-SASM	Westland Scout AH.Mk.1 (XV138)	C. J. Marsden	
G-SASN	MBB-BK 117D-2	Babcock Mission Critical Services Onshore Ltd	
G-SASO	MD Helicopters MD.900 Explorer	Specialist Aviation Services Ltd	
G-SASR	MDH MD-900 Explorer	Specialist Aviation Services Ltd (G-LNAA)	
G-SASS	MBB-BK 117D-2	Babcock Mission Critical Services Onshore Ltd	
G-SASY	Eurocopter EC.130 B4	R. J. H. Smith	
G-SATI	Cameron Sphere 105 SS balloon	T. G. Read, S. J. Roake & M. A. Sterling	
G-SATL	Cameron Sphere 105 SS balloon	T. G. Read, S. J. Roake & M. A. Sterling	
G-SATN	PA-25-260 Pawnee C	The Royal Gliding and Soaring Association	
G-SAUF	Colt 90A balloon	K. H. Medau	
G-SAUK	Rans S6-ES Coyote II	J. M. A. Juanos	
G-SAUL	Robin HR.200-160	R. A. Smith & J. C. Wignall	
G-SAUO	Cessna A.185F	T. G. Lloyd	
G-SAVY	Savannah VG Jabiru(1)	S. P. Yardley	
G-SAWG	Scheibe SF.25C Falke	The RAF Gliding and Soaring Association Ltd	
G-SAWI	PA-32RT-300T Turbo Lance II	D. Pye	
G-SAXL	Schempp-Hirth Duo Discus T	The Royal Air Force Gliding and Soaring Association	
G-SAXT	Schempp-Hirth Duo Discus Xt	The Royal Air Force Gliding and Soaring Association	
G-SAYE	Dornier 228-200	Aurigny Air Services Ltd	
G-SAYS	RAF 2000 GTX-SE gyroplane	G. D. Prebble	
G-SAYX	Cessna 152	Aero Club de Portugal/Portugal	
G-SAZM	Piper J-3C-65 Cub	I. E. M. J. Van Vuuren	
G-SAZY	Avtech Jabiru J400	S.M. Pink	
G-SAZZ	CP.328 Super Emeraude	D. J. Long	
G-SBAG	Phoenix Currie Wot	R. W. Clarke (G-BFAH)	
G-SBCB	Cirrus SR22T	C. R. Barr (G-CKNH)	
G-SBDB	Remos GX	G-SBDB Group	
G-SBII	Steen Skybolt	K. G., P. D. & P. J. Begley	
G-SBIZ	Cameron Z-90 balloon	Snow Business International Ltd	
G-SBKR	SOCATA TB10 Tobago	Profit Invest Sp.Z.O.O	
G-SBLT	Steen Skybolt	Skybolt Group	
G-SBOL	Steen Skybolt	M. J. Tetlow	
G-SBRK	Aero AT-3 R100	Sywell Aerodrome Ltd	
G-SBSB	Diamond DA.40NG Star	Diamond Aviation Training Ltd	
G-SBUS	BN-2A-26 Islander	Isles of Scilly Skybus Ltd (G-BMMH)	

283

Notes	Reg	Type	Owner or Operator
	G-SCAA	Eurocopter EC135 T2	Babcock Mission Critical Services Onshore Ltd (G-SASB)
	G-SCBI	SOCATA TB20 Trinidad	G. & J. Steven
	G-SCCA	Cessna 510 Citation Mustang	Airplay Ltd
	G-SCCZ	CZAW Sportcruiser	J. W. Ellis & M. P. Hill
	G-SCFC	Ultramagic S-90 balloon	J. S. Russon
	G-SCHI	AS.350B2 Ecureuil	Patriot Aviation Ltd
	G-SCHZ	Eurocopter AS.355N Ecureuil 2	Patriot Aviation Ltd (G-STON)
	G-SCII	Agusta A109C	Plattreid Ltd (G-JONA)
	G-SCIP	SOCATA TB20 Trinidad GT	The Studio People Ltd
	G-SCIR	PA-31 Navajo C	2 Excel Aviation Ltd
	G-SCLX	FLS Aerospace Sprint 160	Aero Sprint Group (G-PLYM)
	G-SCMG	Ikarus C42 FB80	C. J. Cooper
	G-SCMR	PA-31 Navajo	2 Excel Aviation Ltd
	G-SCNN	Schempp-Hirth Standard Cirrus	G. C. Short
	G-SCOL	Gippsland GA-8 Airvan	Parachuting Aircraft Ltd
	G-SCOR	Eurocopter EC.155 B1	Starspeed Ltd
	G-SCPD	Escapade 912 (1)	C. W. Potts
	G-SCPI	CZAW Sportcruiser	I. M. Speight & P. F. J. Burton
	G-SCPJ	Hawker 900XP	Saxonair Charter Ltd (G-KTIA)
	G-SCPL	PA-28 Cherokee 140	Aeros Leasing Ltd (G-BPVL)
	G-SCRZ	CZAW Sportcruiser	R. Vora
	G-SCSC	CZAW Sportcruiser	G. Chalmers
	G-SCTA	Westland Scout AH.1	G. R. Harrison
	G-SCTR	PA-31 Navajo C	2 Excel Aviation Ltd
	G-SCUB	PA-18 Super Cub 135 (542447)	J. D. Needham
	G-SCUL	Rutan Cozy	K. R. W. Scull
	G-SCZR	CZAW Sportcruiser	G. Farrar
	G-SDAT	Flight Design CTSW	S. P. Pearson
	G-SDCI	Bell 206B JetRanger 2	Heliwork (Services) Ltd (G-GHCL/G-SHVV)
	G-SDEV	DH. 104 Sea Devon C.20 (XK895)	Aviation Heritage Ltd
	G-SDFM	Aerotechnik EV-97 Eurostar	G-SDFM Eurostar Group
	G-SDII	Eurocopter AS.350B2 Ecureuil	Airbourne Solutions Ltd (G-PROB/G-PROD)
	G-SDNI	VS.361 Spitfire LF.IX E	P. M. Andrews
	G-SDOB	Tecnam P2002-EA Sierra	A. B. Dean
	G-SDOI	Aeroprakt A.22 Foxbat	S. A. Owen
	G-SDOZ	Tecnam P92-EA Echo Super	Cumbernauld Flyers G-SDOZ
	G-SDRV	Van's RV-8	S. M. Dawson
	G-SDRY	Cessna 525C CitationJet CJ4	Dowdeswell Aviation LLP
	G-SDTL	Guimbal Cabri G2	The Gazelle Squadron Display Team Ltd
	G-SEAF	Hawker Sea Fury FB.11	Patina Ltd (G-BWOL)
	G-SEAI	Cessna U.206G (amphibian)	K. O'Conner
	G-SEAL	Robinson R44 II	A. Soria (G-KLNJ)
	G-SEAT	Colt 42A balloon	T. G. Read
	G-SEBN	Skyranger 912S(1)	C. M. James
	G-SEDO	Cameron N-105 balloon	I. M. Ashpole
	G-SEED	Piper J-3C-65 Cub	J. H. Seed
	G-SEEE	Pegasus Quik GT450	I. M. Spence
	G-SEEK	Cessna T.210N	A. Hopper
	G-SEFA	PA-38-112 Tomahawk	Ace Line Ltd
	G-SEHK	Cessna 182T	Golf HK Ltd
	G-SEJW	PA-28-161 Warrior II	Tor Financial Consulting Ltd
	G-SELA	Cessna 152	Cloud Global Ltd (G-FLOP)
	G-SELB	PA-28-161 Warrior II	POM Flight Training Ltd (G-LFSK)
	G-SELC	Diamond DA42 Twin Star	Stapleford Flying Club Ltd
	G-SELF	Shaw Europa	N. D. Crisp & ptnrs
	G-SELL	Robin DR.400/180	C. R. Beard Farmers Ltd
	G-SELY	Agusta-Bell 206B JetRanger 3	M. D. Tracey
	G-SEMI	PA-44-180 Seminole	J. Benfell & M. Djukic (G-DENW)
	G-SEMR	Cessna T206H Turbo Stationair	Semer LLP
	G-SENA	Rutan LongEz	G. Bennett
	G-SEND	Colt 90A balloon	Air du Vent/France
	G-SENE	PA-34-200T Seneca II	HK Asset Management Ltd
	G-SENS	Eurocopter EC.135T2+	Saville Air Services
	G-SENX	PA-34-200T Seneca II	First Air Ltd (G-DARE/G-WOTS/G-SEVL)
	G-SEPT	Cameron N-105 balloon	A. G. Merry
	G-SERE	Diamond DA42 Twin Star	Sere Ltd
	G-SERL	SOCATA TB10 Tobago	G. C. Jarvis (G-LANA)
	G-SERV	Cameron N-105 balloon	Servo & Electronic Sales Ltd

Reg	Type	Owner or Operator	Notes
G-SESA	RAF SE.5A 75 replica	D. J. Calvert	
G-SETI	Cameron Sky 80-16 balloon	R. P. Allan	
G-SEUK	Cameron TV-80 ss balloon	Mobberley Balloon Collection	
G-SEVA	SE-5A (replica) (F141:G)	G-SEVA Trust	
G-SEVE	Cessna 172N	Imagineer London Ltd	
G-SEVN	Van's RV-7	N. Reddish	
G-SEXE	Scheibe SF.25C Falke	SF25C G-SESE Syndicate	
G-SEXX	PA-28-161 Warrior II	Weald Air Services Ltd	
G-SEXY	AA-1 Yankee ★	Jetstream Club, Liverpool Marriott Hotel South, Speke (G-AYLM)	
G-SEZA	Schleicher ASW-20C	A. H. Brown	
G-SFAR	Ikarus C42 FB100	R. Moore	
G-SFCM	P & M PulsR	J. D. Harrison	
G-SFLA	Ikarus C42 FB80	Solent Flight Ltd	
G-SFLB	Ikarus C42 FB80	Solent Flight Ltd	
G-SFLY	Diamond DA40 Star	L. & N. P. L. Turner	
G-SFRY	Thunder Ax7-77 balloon	M. Rowlands	
G-SFSL	Cameron Z-105 balloon	A. J. Gregory	
G-SFTZ	Slingsby T.67M Firefly 160	Slingsby T.67M Group	
G-SGEN	Ikarus C.42 FB 80	G. A. Arturi	
G-SGFE	Liberty XL-2	I. Fidler (G-OLAR)	
G-SGNT	Skylark	N. H. Townsend	
G-SGRP	Agusta AW.109SP Grand New	Apollo Air Services Ltd	
G-SGSE	PA-28-181 Archer II	U. Patel (G-BOJX)	
G-SGSG	Bombardier BD700-1A11 Global 5000	TAG Aviation (UK) Ltd	
G-SGTS	Viking DHC.6-400 Twin Otter	Loganair Ltd	
G-SHAA	Enstrom 280-UK	D. McCann	
G-SHAF	Robinson R44 II	H. S. Thirsk & Son	
G-SHAK	Cameron Cabin SS balloon	Magical Adventures Ltd (G-ODIS)	
G-SHAR	Cessna 182T Skylane	G. N. Clarkson	
G-SHAY	PA-28R-201T Turbo Arrow III	Alpha Yankee Flying Group (G-BFDG/G-JEFS)	
G-SHBA	Cessna F.152	Paul's Planes Ltd	
G-SHCK	Ikarus C42 FB80	F. S. Group Ltd	
G-SHED	PA-28-181 Archer II	G-SHED Flying Group (G-BRAU)	
G-SHEE	P & M Quik GT450	C. J. Millership	
G-SHEZ	Mainair Pegasus Quik	R. & S. Wells	
G-SHHH	Glaser-Dirks DG-100G	Bristol and Gloucestershire Gliding Club	
G-SHIM	CFM Streak Shadow	P. D. Babin	
G-SHIP	PA-23 Aztec 250F ★	Midland Air Museum/Coventry	
G-SHKI	Ikarus C42 FB80	Poet Pilot (UK) Ltd	
G-SHMI	Evektor EV-97 Team EuroStar UK	Mike India Flying Group	
G-SHMN	Alpi Pioneer 300 Hawk	E. G. Shimmin (G-GKEV)	
G-SHOG	Colomban MC.15 Cri-Cri	K. D. & C. S. Rhodes (G-PFAB)	
G-SHOW	MS.733 Alcyon	P. Cartwright & F. A. Forster	
G-SHRD	Eurocopter AS.350B2 Ecureuil	Jet Helicopters Ltd (G-LHTB)	
G-SHRK	Enstrom 280C-UK	Shark Helicopters Ltd (G-BGMX)	
G-SHRN	Schweizer 269C-1	CSL Industrial Ltd	
G-SHRT	Robinson R44 II	Hingley Aviation Ltd	
G-SHSH	Shaw Europa	S. G. Hayman & J. Price	
G-SHSP	Cessna 172S	Shropshire Aero Club Ltd	
G-SHUC	Rans S-6-ESD Coyote II	P. Robichaud & B. J. Colburn (G-MYKN)	
G-SHUF	Mainair Blade	G. Holdcroft	
G-SHUG	PA-28R-201T Turbo Arrow III	G-SHUG Ltd	
G-SHUI	Cessna 680A Citation Latitude	Air Charter Scotland Ltd	
G-SHUU	Enstrom 280C-UK-2	Gewerbepark Siegerland GmbH/Germany (G-OMCP/G-KENY/G-BJFG)	
G-SHUV	Aerosport Woody Pusher	J. R. Wraigh	
G-SHWK	Cessna 172S	Cambridge Aero Club Ltd	
G-SHWN	P-51D Mustang (KH774/GA-S)	Sharkmouth Ltd	
G-SIBK	Raytheon Beech A36 Bonanza	W. Robson	
G-SICA	BN-2B-20 Islander	Shetland Leasing and Property Development Ltd (G-SLAP)	
G-SICB	BN-2B-20 Islander	Shetlands Islands Council (G-NESU/G-BTVN)	
G-SIGN	PA-39 Twin Comanche 160 C/R	D. Buttle	
G-SIIE	Christen Pitts S-2B Special	Wild Thing (G-SKYD)	
G-SIII	Extra EA.300	Owners of G-SIII	
G-SIJJ	North American P-51D-NA Mustang (472035)	Hangar II Collection	

Notes	Reg	Type	Owner or Operator
	G-SIJW	SA Bulldog Srs 120/121 (XX630:5)	M. Miles
	G-SILS	Pietenpol Skyscout	D. Silsbury
	G-SILY	Pegasus Quantum 15	S. D. Sparrow
	G-SIMM	Ikarus C.42 FB 100 VLA	D. Simmons
	G-SIMY	PA-32-300 Cherokee Six	I. Simpson (G-OCPF/G-BOCH)
	G-SINK	Schleicher ASH-25	G-SINK Group
	G-SINN	EV-97 Eurostar SL microlight	J. C. Miller
	G-SIPA	SIPA 903	A. C. Leak & G. S. Dilland (G-BGBM)
	G-SIPP	Lindstrand lbl-35a Cloudhopper balloon	A. R. Rich
	G-SIRD	Robinson R44 II	Peglington Productions Ltd
	G-SIRE	Best Off Sky Ranger Swift 912S(1)	P. W. F. Coleman
	G-SIRO	Dassault Falcon 900EX	Condor Aviation LLP
	G-SIRS	Cessna 560XL Citation Excel	London Executive Aviation Ltd
	G-SISI	Schempp-Hirth Duo Discus	Glider Sierra India
	G-SISU	P & M Quik GT450	Executive and Business Aviation Support Ltd
	G-SITA	Pegasus Quantum 15-912	P. N. Thompson
	G-SIVJ	Westland Gazelle HT.2	Skytrace (UK) Ltd (G-CBSG)
	G-SIVK	MBB Bolkow Bo.105DBS-4	Eastern Atlantic Helicopters Ltd (G-PASX)
	G-SIXC	Douglas DC-6B★	The DC-6 Diner/Coventry
	G-SIXD	PA-32 Cherokee Six 300D	M. B. Paine & I. Gordon
	G-SIXT	PA-28-161 Warrior II	Airways Aero Associations Ltd (G-BSSX)
	G-SIXX	Colt 77A balloon	S. Drawbridge
	G-SIXY	Van's RV-6	C. J. Hall & C. R. P. Hamlett
	G-SIZZ	Jabiru J400	K. J. Betteley
	G-SJBI	Pitts S-2C Special	S. L. Walton
	G-SJEF	AutoGyro Cavalon	J. Smith
	G-SJES	Evektor EV-97 TeamEurostar UK	North East Aviation Ltd
	G-SJKR	Lindstrand LBL-90A balloon	P. Richardson
	G-SJMH	Robin DR.400-140B	Flugsportclub Odenwald EV/Germany
	G-SJPI	Dynamic WT9 UK	S. R. Wilkinson
	G-SKAN	Cessna F.172M	M. Richardson & J. Williams (G-BFKT)
	G-SKAZ	Aero AT-3 R100	G-SKAZ Flying Group
	G-SKBD	Raytheon Beech 400A	Sky Border Logistics Ltd
	G-SKBH	Agusta Westland AW109SP Grand New	Sky Border Logistics Ltd
	G-SKBL	Agusta A109S Grand	Sky Border Logistics Ltd (G-PDAY/G-CDWY)
	G-SKCI	Rutan Vari-Eze	C. Boyd
	G-SKEW	Mudry CAP-232	G. Haye
	G-SKFY	Robinson R44 II	Skyfly Air Ltd (G-GRGE)
	G-SKIE	Steen Skybolt	G-SKIE Group
	G-SKKY	Cessna 172S Skyhawk	J. Herbert & G. P. Turner
	G-SKNY	FD Composites Arrowcopter AC20	C. J. Rose
	G-SKOT	Cameron V-42 balloon	S. A. Laing
	G-SKPG	Best Off Skyranger 912 (2)	T. Farncombe
	G-SKPH	Yakovlev Yak-50	R. S. Partridge-Hicks & I. C. Austin (G-BWWH)
	G-SKPP	Eurocopter EC.120B Colbri	Bliss Aviation Ltd (G-MKII)
	G-SKRA	Best Off Skyranger 912S (1)	SKRA Flying Group
	G-SKRG	Best Off Skyranger 912 (2)	M. J. Kingsley
	G-SKSW	Best Off Sky Ranger Swift 912S	J. & J. A. Pegram
	G-SKTN	Avro 696 Shackleton MR.Mk.2 (WR963)	Shackleton Preservation Trust
	G-SKUA	Stoddard-Hamilton Glastar	F. P. Smiddy (G-LEZZ/G-BYCR)
	G-SKYC	Slingsby T.67M Firefly	K. Taylor (G-BLDP)
	G-SKYF	SOCATA TB10 Tobago	W. L. McNeil
	G-SKYL	Cessna 182S	G. A. Gee
	G-SKYN	AS.355F1 Twin Squirrel	Arena Aviation Ltd (G-OGRK/G-BWZC/G-MODZ)
	G-SKYO	Slingsby T.67M-200	VG Flight Ltd
	G-SKYT	I.I.I. Sky Arrow 650TC	W. M. Bell & S. J. Brooks
	G-SKYV	PA-28RT-201T Turbo Arrow IV	North Yorks Properties Ltd (G-BNZG)
	G-SLAC	Cameron N-77 balloon	A. Barnes
	G-SLAK	Thruster T.600N 450	P. R. Howson (G-CBXH)
	G-SLAR	Agusta A109C	MW Helicopters Ltd (G-OWRD/G-USTC/G-LAXO)
	G-SLCC	EV-97 Eurostar SL	E. S. A. McMahon
	G-SLCE	Cameron C-80 balloon	A. M. Holly
	G-SLCT	Diamond DA42NG Twin Star	Stapleford Flying Club Ltd
	G-SLEA	Mudry/CAARP CAP-10B	M. J. M. Jenkins, N. R. Thorburn & R. Harris
	G-SLIP	Easy Raider	D. R. Squires
	G-SLIV	TAF Sling 4	D. J. Pilkington

Reg	Type	Owner or Operator	Notes
G-SLMG	Diamond HK.36 TTC Super Dimona	G-SLMG Syndicate	
G-SLNG	TAF Sling 4	R. S. D. Wheeler & R. J. H. Davis	
G-SLNT	Flight Design CTSW	K. Kirby	
G-SLNW	Robinson R22 Beta	Sky Helicopters Ltd (G-LNIC)	
G-SLYR	Gnat Mk.1	Heritage Aircraft Ltd	
G-SMAJ	DG Flugzeugbau DG-808C	S. Marriott (G-TRTM)	
G-SMAR	Schempp-Hirth Arcus M	Alpha Syndicate	
G-SMBM	Pegasus Quantum 15-912	M. Gudgeon	
G-SMDH	Shaw Europa XS	S. W. Pitt	
G-SMIG	Cameron O-65 balloon	R. D. Parry	
G-SMIL	Lindstrand LBL-105A balloon	A. L. Wade	
G-SMKR	Eurofox 912(S)	S. M. Kenyon-Roberts	
G-SMLA	BAe.146-200	Meteor Aero Ltd (G-OZRH)	
G-SMLE	Robinson R44 II	English Braids Ltd	
G-SMLI	Groppo Trail	A. M. Wilson	
G-SMLZ	Groppo Trail Mk.2	A. M. Wilson	
G-SMMA	Cessna F.406 Caravan II	Secretary of State for Scotland per Environmental and Rural Affairs Department	
G-SMMB	Cessna F.406 Caravan II	Secretary of State for Scotland per Environmental and Rural Affairs Department	
G-SMMF	Lindstrand LBL-77A balloon	S. Mitchell & M. D. Freeston	
G-SMON	Cessna A.152	North Weald Flying Group Ltd (G-BNJE/ G-OWFS/G-DESY)	
G-SMRS	Cessna 172F	M. R. Sarling	
G-SMSM	Dassault Falcon 2000LX	London Executive Aviation Ltd	
G-SMSP	Super Marine Spitfire Mk.26B	S. J. D. Hall	
G-SMYK	PZL-Swidnik PW-5 Smyk	PW-5 Syndicate	
G-SNAL	Cessna 182T	N. S. Lyndhurst	
G-SNCA	PA-34-200T Seneca II	Social Infrastructure Ltd	
G-SNEV	CFM Streak Shadow SA	A. Child	
G-SNIF	Cameron A-300 balloon	A. C. K. Rowson & Sudoni	
G-SNOG	Kiss 400-582 (1)	B. H. Ashman	
G-SNOP	Shaw Europa	A. Graham (G-DESL/G-WWWG)	
G-SNOW	Cameron V-77 balloon	I. Welsford	
G-SNOZ	Shaw Europa	P. O. Bayliss (G-DONZ)	
G-SNSA	Agusta Westland AW139	CHC Scotia Ltd	
G-SNSB	Agusta Westland AW139	Waypoint Asset Co 6 Ltd	
G-SNSE	Agusta Westland AW139	CHC Scotia Ltd	
G-SNSF	Agusta Westland AW139	CHC Scotia Ltd	
G-SNSG	Agusta Westland AW139	Waypoint Asset Co.3 Ltd	
G-SNSH	Agusta Westland AW139	CHC Scotia Ltd (G-LLOV)	
G-SNSI	Agusta Westland AW139	CHC Scotia Ltd (G-FTOM)	
G-SNSJ	Agusta Westland AW139	CHC Scotia Ltd	
G-SNSK	Agusta Westland AW139	CHC Scotia Ltd	
G-SNUG	Best Off Skyranger 912S(1)	J. C. Mundy & J. D. Fielding	
G-SNUZ	PA-28-161 Warrior II	Freedom Aviation Ltd	
G-SNXA	Sonex	S. J. Moody	
G-SOAF	BAC.167 Strikemaster Mk. 82A (425)	Strikemaster Flying Club	
G-SOBI	PA-28-181 Archer II	G-SOBI Flying Group	
G-SOCK	Mainair Pegasus Quik	K. R. McCartney	
G-SOCT	Yakovlev Yak-50 (AR-B)	M. J. Gadsby	
G-SOKO	Soko P-2 Kraguj (30149)	P. C. Avery (G-BRXK)	
G-SOLA	Aero Designs Star-Lite SL.1	G. P. Thomas	
G-SONA	SOCATA TB10 Tobago	J. Freeman (G-BIBI)	
G-SONE	Cessna 525A Citationjet	Centreline AV Ltd	
G-SONX	Sonex	C. S. Rayner	
G-SOOC	Hughes 369HS	R.J.H. Strong (G-BRRX)	
G-SOOM	Glaser-Dirks DG-500M	A. M. Wensing & J. A. van Gorp	
G-SOOS	Colt 21A balloon	P. J. Stapley	
G-SOOT	PA-28 Cherokee 180	R. J. Hunter (G-AVNM)	
G-SOOZ	Rans S-6-ES Coyote II	R. E. Cotterell	
G-SOPC	Replica Sopwith Camel	C. I. Law & P. Hoeft	
G-SORA	Glaser-Dirks DG.500/22	DG Syndicate	
G-SOUL	Cessna 310R	Reconnaissance Ventures Ltd	
G-SOUT	Van's RV-8	J. M. Southern (G-CDPJ)	
G-SOVB	Learjet 45	Zenith Aviation Ltd (G-OLDJ)	
G-SPAM	Avid Aerobat (modified)	M. Durcan	

Notes	Reg	Type	Owner or Operator
	G-SPAT	Aero AT-3 R100	S2T Aero Ltd
	G-SPCI	Cessna 182P	K. Brady (G-GUMS/G-CBMN)
	G-SPCM	Mooney M.20K Model 231	A. E. Vigueras
	G-SPCY	Embraer EMB-135BJ Legacy 650	London Executive Aviation Ltd (G-OTGL)
	G-SPCZ	CZAW Sportcruiser	R. J. Robinson
	G-SPDY	Raj Hamsa X'Air Hawk	K. J. Underwood
	G-SPED	Alpi Pioneer 300	C. F. Garrod
	G-SPEL	Sky 220-24 balloon	T. G. Church
	G-SPEY	Agusta-Bell 206B JetRanger 3	Castle Air Ltd (G-BIGO)
	G-SPFX	Rutan Cozy	B. D. Tutty
	G-SPHU	Eurocopter EC 135T2+	Babcock Mission Critical Services Onshore Ltd
	G-SPID	Ultramagic S-90 balloon	A. Fawcett
	G-SPIN	Pitts S-2A Special	P. Avery
	G-SPIP	SNCAN Stampe SV.4C	A. G. & P. M. Solleveld (G-BTIO)
	G-SPIT	VS.379 Spitfire FR.XIV (MV268)	Anglia Aircraft Restorations Ltd (G-BGHB)
	G-SPJE	Robinson R44 II	Abel Alarm Co.Ltd
	G-SPMM	Best Off Sky Ranger Swift 912S(1)	A. W. Paterson
	G-SPOG	Jodel DR.1050	G-SPOG Group (G-AXVS)
	G-SPRC	Van's RV-8	A. P. & C. Durston & J. C. Gowdy
	G-SPRE	Cessna 550 Citation Bravo	XJC Ltd
	G-SPRK	Van's RV-4	Jack Aviation Ltd
	G-SPRX	Van's RV-4	Jack Aviation Ltd
	G-SPTR	Robinson R44 II	Heli Air Ltd
	G-SPTT	Diamond DA.40D Star	G. Trotter (G-OCCS)
	G-SPUR	Cessna 550 Citation II	London Executive Aviation Ltd
	G-SPUT	Yakovlev Yak-52	D. J. Hopkinson (G-BXAV)
	G-SPVI	SOCATA TB.20 Trinidad	Teegee Group
	G-SPVK	AS.350B3 Ecureuil	SD Helicopters LLP (G-CERU)
	G-SPWP	Cirrus SR22	S. Pope
	G-SPXX	VS.356 Spitfire F.22	P. R. Arnold
	G-SPYS	Robinson R44 II	SKB Partners LLP
	G-SRAH	Schempp-Hirth Mini-Nimbus C	Sarah Group
	G-SRBM	Beech B350 Super King Air	Skyhopper LLP
	G-SRDG	Dassault Falcon 7X	Triair (Bermuda) Ltd
	G-SRFA	Embraer EMB-505 Phenom 300	Surf Air Europe Ltd
	G-SRII	Easy Raider 503	K. Myles
	G-SRNE	Eurocopter MBB BK-117C-2	Starspeed Ltd
	G-SROE	Westland Scout AH.1 (XP907)	Saunders-Roe Helicopter Ltd
	G-SRRA	Tecnam P2002-EA Sierra	J. Dunn
	G-SRTT	Cirrus SR22	S. A. Breslaw
	G-SRWN	PA-28-161 Warrior II	A. J. Bell (G-MAND/G-BRKT)
	G-SRYY	Shaw Europa XS	I. O'Brien
	G-SRZZ	Cirrus SR22	A. Bodaghi
	G-SSCA	Diamond DA.42NG Twin Star	S. C. Horwood
	G-SSCL	MDH Hughes 369E	Shaun Stevens Contractors Ltd
	G-SSDI	SD-1 Minisport	P. C. Piggott & B. A. Fairston
	G-SSDR	Scooter	J. Attard
	G-SSIX	Rans S.6-116 Coyote II	R. I. Kelly
	G-SSKP	Airbus Helicopters AS.365N3 Dauphin 2	Starspeed Ltd (G-CIUC)
	G-SSKY	BN-2B-26 Islander	Isles of Scilly Skybus Ltd (G-BSWT)
	G-SSRD	Balony Kubicek BB17XR balloon	A. M. Holly
	G-SSTI	Cameron N-105 balloon	A. A. Brown
	G-SSTL	Just Superstol	Avalanche Aviation Ltd
	G-SSVB	VS.349 Spitfire LF.Vb	I. D. Ward (G-CGBI)
	G-SSWV	Sportavia Fournier RF-5B	Fournier Flying Group
	G-SSXL	Just Superstol XL	P. T. Price
	G-STAV	Cameron O-84 balloon	A. Pollock
	G-STAY	Cessna FR.172K	J. M. Wilkins
	G-STBA	Boeing 777-336ER	British Airways
	G-STBB	Boeing 777-36NER	British Airways
	G-STBC	Boeing 777-36NER	British Airways
	G-STBD	Boeing 777-36NER	British Airways
	G-STBE	Boeing 777-36NER	British Airways
	G-STBF	Boeing 777-336ER	British Airways
	G-STBG	Boeing 777-336ER	British Airways
	G-STBH	Boeing 777-336ER	British Airways
	G-STBI	Boeing 777-336ER	British Airways

Reg	Type	Owner or Operator	Notes
G-STBJ	Boeing 777-336ER	British Airways	
G-STBK	Boeing 777-336ER	British Airways	
G-STBL	Boeing 777-336ER	British Airways	
G-STBT	Cameron N-42 balloon	D. Sjokvist (G-BVLC)	
G-STBY	Flylight MotorFloater	M. P. Wimsey	
G-STCH	Fiesler Fi 156A-1 Storch (GM+AI)	P. R. Holloway	
G-STDO	BRM Aero Bristell NG Speed Wing	S. M. Wade & J. A. Strong	
G-STEA	PA-28R Cherokee Arrow 200	D. W. Breden	
G-STEE	EV-97 Eurostar	S. G. Beeson	
G-STEL	BRM Aero Bristell NG5	I. Archer	
G-STEM	Stemme S.10V	A. M. Booth	
G-STEN	Stemme S.10 (4)	G-STEN Syndicate	
G-STEU	Rolladen-Schneider LS6-18W	F. K. Russell	
G-STEV	Jodel DR.221	B. J-P. Cordiez	
G-STFO	TL.2000UK Sting Carbon S4	I. H. Foster	
G-STHA	PA-31-350 Navajo Chieftain	Atlantic Bridge Aviation Ltd (G-GLUG/ G-BLOE/ G-NITE)	
G-STIN	TL 2000UK Sting Carbon	N. A. Smith	
G-STIX	Van's RV-7	R. D. S. Jackson	
G-STMA	PA-32RT-201T Turbo Arrow IV	S. Zanone	
G-STME	Stemme S 10-VT	A. Jeske & J. Vad	
G-STMP	SNCAN Stampe SV.4A	A. C. Thorne	
G-STMT	Dassault Falcon 7X	TAG Aviation (UK) Ltd	
G-STNG	TL2000UK Sting Carbon	Geesting 3 Syndicate	
G-STNK	Pitts S-1-11 Super Stinker	T. H. Castle	
G-STNR	IDA Bacau Yakovlev Yak-52	D. J. Hopkinson (G-BWOD)	
G-STNS	Agusta A109A-II	Hevolution Eood	
G-STOD	ICP MXP-740 Savannah VG Jabiru(1)	M. P. Avison & L. J. Boardman	
G-STOK	Colt 77B balloon	A. C. Booth	
G-STOO	Stolp Starduster Too	A. K. Robinson	
G-STOP	Robinson R44 Raven II	HLQ Services Ltd/Ireland	
G-STOW	Cameron 90 Wine Box SS balloon	Flying Enterprises	
G-STPK	Lambert Mission M108	S. T. P. Kember	
G-STRG	Cyclone AX2000	J. L. Jordan	
G-STRK	CFM Streak Shadow SA	E. J. Hadley	
G-STRL	AS.355N Twin Squirrel	Mettwees BV/Netherlands	
G-STSN	Stinson 108-3 Voyager	M. S. Colebrook (G-BHMR)	
G-STUA	Aerotek Pitts S-2A Special (modified)	G-STUA Group	
G-STUE	Europa	F. Xuereb	
G-STUI	Pitts S-2AE	S. L. Goldspink	
G-STUN	TL2000UK Sting Carbon	D. Russell (G-KEVT)	
G-STUU	Bristell NG5 Speed Wing	S. M. Spencer	
G-STUY	Robinson R44 II	Central Helicopters Ltd	
G-STUZ	Lambert Mission M108	S. A. Blanchard	
G-STVL	Lindstrand LBL-77A balloon	S. J. Donkin	
G-STVT	CZAW Sportcruiser	S. Taylor	
G-STVZ	Bell 206B Jet Ranger 3	Mediatech Consulting Ltd (G-XBCI)	
G-STWO	ARV Super 2	R. E. Griffiths	
G-STZZ	TL2000UK Sting Carbon	Dorset Aviation Group	
G-SUAU	Cameron C-90 balloon	A. Heginbottom	
G-SUCK	Cameron Z-105 balloon	R. P. Wade	
G-SUCT	Robinson R22	Irwin Plant Sales	
G-SUED	Thunder Ax8-90 balloon	E. C. Lubbock & S. A. Kidd (G-PINE)	
G-SUEI	Diamond DA.42 Twin Star	Sue Air	
G-SUEJ	Embraer EMB-550 Legacy 500	Saxonair Charter Ltd	
G-SUEL	P & M Quik GT450	D. A. Ellis	
G-SUEM	Diamond DA.42 Twin Star	Sue Air	
G-SUEO	Diamond DA.40NG Star	Sue Air	
G-SUER	Bell 206B JetRanger	Aerospeed Ltd (G-CBYX)	
G-SUET	Bell 206B JetRanger	Aerospeed Ltd (G-BLZN)	
G-SUEY	Bell 206L-1 Long Ranger	Aerospeed Ltd	
G-SUEZ	Agusta-Bell 206B JetRanger 2	Aerospeed Ltd	
G-SUFK	Eurocopter EC 135P2+	Police & Crime Commissioner for West Yorkshire	
G-SUGR	Embraer EMB-135BJ Legacy 650	Air Charter Scotland Ltd	
G-SUKI	PA-38-112 Tomahawk	Merseyflight Ltd (G-RVNB/G-BPNV)	
G-SUKK	Sukhoi Su-29	M. Benshemesh	
G-SULU	Best Off Sky Ranger 912(2)	S. Marathe (G-SOPH)	
G-SUMM	Skyranger Nynja LS912(1)	A. Summers	
G-SUMX	Robinson R22 Beta	Bickerstaffe Aviation Ltd	

Notes	Reg	Type	Owner or Operator
	G-SUNN	Robinson R44	R. Purchase
	G-SUPA	PA-18 Super Cub 150	S. E. Leach
	G-SURY	Eurocopter EC 135T2+	Police & Crime Commissioner for West Yorkshire
	G-SUSE	Shaw Europa XS	P. R. Tunney
	G-SUSI	Cameron V-77 balloon	J. H. Dryden
	G-SUSX	MDH MD-902 Explorer	Specialist Aviation Services Ltd
	G-SUTD	Jabiru UL-D	W. J. Lister & R. F. G. Bermudez
	G-SUTE	Van's RV-8	G. N. Fraser & A. H. Brown
	G-SUTN	I.I.I. Sky Arrow 650TC	D. J. Goldsmith
	G-SUUK	Sukhoi Su-29	D. J. Barke
	G-SUZN	PA-28-161 Warrior II	Pilot Training & Testing Ltd
	G-SVAS	PA-18-150 Super Cub	Richard Shuttleworth Trustees
	G-SVDG	Jabiru SK	R. Tellegen
	G-SVEA	PA-28-161 Warrior II	G-SVEA Group
	G-SVEN	Centrair 101A Pegase	G7 Group
	G-SVET	Yakovlev Yak-50	The Assets of the Svetlana Group
	G-SVGL	SNCAN Stampe SV-4A	G. W. Lynch
	G-SVIP	Cessna 421B Golden Eagle II	R. P. Bateman
	G-SVIV	SNCAN Stampe SV.4C	J. E. Keighley
	G-SVNH	Savannah VG Jabiru(1)	K. Harmston (G-CFKV)
	G-SVNX	Dassault Falcon 7X	Executive Jet Charter Ltd
	G-SVPN	PA-32R-301T Turbo Saratoga	Stratton Motor Company (Norfolk) Ltd
	G-SVRN	Embraer EMB-500 Phenom 100	TD Aviation Ltd
	G-SWAB	Tiger Cub RL5A Sherwood Ranger XP	D. S. Brown
	G-SWAI	Swift SWO1A	Swift Aircraft Ltd
	G-SWAK	Oldfield Baby Lakes	B. Bryan
	G-SWAT	Robinson R44 II	Unique Helicopters (NI) Ltd
	G-SWAY	PA-18-150 Super Cub	S. J. Gaveston & R. L. Brinklow
	G-SWCT	Flight Design CTSW	J. A. Shufflebotham
	G-SWEE	Beech 95-B55 Baron	Orman (Carrolls Farm) Ltd (G-AZDK)
	G-SWEL	Hughes 369HS	M. A. Crook & A. E. Wright (G-RBUT)
	G-SWIF	VS.541 Swift F.7 (XF114) ★	Solent Sky, Southampton
	G-SWIG	Robinson R44	S. Goddard
	G-SWLL	Aero AT-3 R100	Sywell Aerodrome Ltd
	G-SWNG	Eurocopter EC.120B	J. G. Jones
	G-SWNS	Robinson R44 II	Swan Staff Recruitment Ltd (G-PROJ)
	G-SWON	Pitts S-1S Special	S. L. Goldspink
	G-SWOT	Currie Wot (C3011:S)	P. N. Davis
	G-SWRD	Boeing 737-3L9	Onexp 2006 ApS & TAG Aviation (Stansted) Ltd (G-OGBE)
	G-SWRE	Tecnam P2002-EA Sierra	W. Swire
	G-SWSW	Schempp-Hirth Ventus bT	R. Kalin
	G-SWYF	Best Off Skyranger Swift 912(1)	C. Moore & K. J. Bradley
	G-SWYM	CZAW Sportcruiser	R. W. Beal
	G-SXIX	Rans S.19	D. J. Thomas
	G-SYDH	Bell 206B-3 Jet Ranger III	SJH North West Ltd (G-BXNT)
	G-SYEL	Aero AT-3 R100	Sywell Aerodrome Ltd
	G-SYES	Robinson R66	LSET Hire LLP
	G-SYFW	Focke-Wulf Fw.190 replica (2+1)	A. Collins
	G-SYLJ	Embraer RJ135BJ	Blue Wings Ltd
	G-SYLV	Cessna 208B Grand Caravan	WAS Aircraft Leasing Ltd
	G-SYPS	MDH MD.900 Explorer	Specialist Aviation Services Ltd
	G-SYWL	Aero AT-3 R100	Sywell Aerodrome Ltd
	G-SZDA	PZL SZD-59 Acro	P. C. Sharphouse
	G-TAAB	Cirrus SR22	Alpha Bravo Aviation Ltd
	G-TAAC	Cirrus SR20	Pegasus Grab Hire Ltd
	G-TAAS	Agusta AW.109SP Grand New	Sloane Helicopters Ltd
	G-TAAT	PA-32-301FT	A. D. Trotter
	G-TACK	Grob G.109B	A. P. Mayne
	G-TADS	Mead BM-77 balloon	D. J. Stagg
	G-TAFF	CASA 1.131E Jungmann 1000	R. A. Fleming (G-BFNE)
	G-TAJF	Lindstrand LBL-77A balloon	T. A. J. Fowles
	G-TAKE	AS.355F1 Ecureuil II	Arena Aviation Ltd (G-OITN)
	G-TALA	Cessna 152 II	Tatenhill Aviation Ltd (G-BNPZ)

Reg	Type	Owner or Operator	Notes
G-TALB	Cessna 152 II	Tatenhill Aviation Ltd (G-BORO)	
G-TALC	Cessna 152	Tatenhill Aviation Ltd (G-BPBG)	
G-TALD	Cessna F.152	Tatenhill Aviation Ltd (G-BHRM)	
G-TALE	PA-28-181 Archer II	Tatenhill Aviation Ltd (G-BJOA)	
G-TALF	PA-24-250 Comanche	Tatenhill Aviation Ltd (G-APUZ)	
G-TALG	PA-28-151 Warrior	Tatenhill Aviation Ltd (G-BELP)	
G-TALH	PA-28-181 Archer II	Tatenhill Aviation Ltd (G-CIFR)	
G-TALJ	Grumman AA-5 Traveler	The Lima Juliet Group (G-BBUE)	
G-TALN	Rotorway A600 Talon	Southern Helicopters Ltd	
G-TALO	Cessna FA.152	Tatenhill Aviation Ltd (G-BFZU)	
G-TAMI	Diamond DA.40 Star	AJW Construction Ltd	
G-TAMR	Cessna 172S	Caledonian Air Surveys Ltd	
G-TAMS	Beech A23-24 Musketeer Super	C. P. Allen	
G-TANA	Tanarg 912S(2)/Ixess 15	S. S. Smy	
G-TANG	Tanarg 912S(2)/Ixess 15	N. L. Stammers	
G-TANJ	Raj Hamsa X'Air 582(5)	K. P. Smith	
G-TANO	Rolladen-Schneider LS3-a	T. Cavattoni	
G-TANY	EAA Acrosport 2	P. J. Tanulak	
G-TAPS	PA-28RT-201T Turbo Arrow IV	R. L. Nunn & T. R. Edwards	
G-TARN	Pietenpol Air Camper	P. J. Heilbron	
G-TARR	P & M Quik	A. Edwards	
G-TART	PA-28-236 Dakota	N. K. G. Prescot	
G-TASK	Cessna 404	Reconnaissance Ventures Ltd	
G-TATS	Replica Travelair R Type	R. A. Seeley	
G-TATS	AS.350BA Ecureuil	Helitrain Ltd	
G-TATT	Gardan GY-20 Minicab	Tatt's Group	
G-TAWA	Boeing 737-8K5	TUI Airways Ltd	
G-TAWB	Boeing 737-8K5	TUI Airways Ltd	
G-TAWC	Boeing 737-8K5	TUI Airways Ltd	
G-TAWD	Boeing 737-8K5	TUI Airways Ltd	
G-TAWF	Boeing 737-8K5	TUI Airways Ltd	
G-TAWG	Boeing 737-8K5	TUI Airways Ltd	
G-TAWH	Boeing 737-8K5	TUI Airways Ltd	
G-TAWI	Boeing 737-8K5	TUI Airways Ltd	
G-TAWJ	Boeing 737-8K5	TUI Airways Ltd	
G-TAWK	Boeing 737-8K5	TUI Airways Ltd	
G-TAWL	Boeing 737-8K5	TUI Airways Ltd	
G-TAWM	Boeing 737-8K5	TUI Airways Ltd	
G-TAWN	Boeing 737-8K5	TUI Airways Ltd	
G-TAWO	Boeing 737-8K5	TUI Airways Ltd	
G-TAWS	Boeing 737-8K5	TUI Airways Ltd	
G-TAWU	Boeing 737-8K5	TUI Airways Ltd	
G-TAWV	Boeing 737-8K5	TUI Airways Ltd	
G-TAWW	Boeing 737-8K5	TUI Airways Ltd	
G-TAXI	PA-23-250 Aztec E	S. Waite	
G-TAYC	Gulfstream G450	Executive Jet Charter Ltd	
G-TAYI	Grob G.115	K. P. Widdowson (G-DODO)	
G-TAYL	Pitts S-1S Special	R. S. Taylor	
G-TAZZ	Dan Rihn DR.107 One Design	N. J. Riddin	
G-TBAG	Murphy Renegade II	M. R. Tetley	
G-TBET	Ultramagic M-77 balloon	H. Crawley & P. Dopson	
G-TBGT	SOCATA TB-20 Trinidad GT	A. J. Maitland-Robinson	
G-TBHH	AS355F2 Twin Squirrel	Alpha Properties (London) Ltd (G-HOOT/ G-SCOW/ G-POON/G-MCAL)	
G-TBIO	SOCATA TB10 Tobago	RPR Associates Ltd	
G-TBJP	Mainair Pegasus Quik	D. J. Bromley	
G-TBLB	P & M Quik GT450	L. Chesworth	
G-TBLC	Rans S-6-ES Coyote II	Royal Aeronautical Society	
G-TBLY	Eurocopter EC 120B	AD Bly Aircraft Leasing Ltd	
G-TBMR	P & M Aviation Quik GT450	G-TBMR Syndicate	
G-TBOK	SOCATA TB10 Tobago	TB10 Ltd	
G-TBSV	SOCATA TB20 Trinidad GT	Condron Concrete Ltd	
G-TBTN	SOCATA TB10 Tobago	Airways International Ltd (G-BKIA)	
G-TBUC	Airbus Helicopters EC155 B1	Noirmont (EC155) Ltd	
G-TBXX	SOCATA TB20 Trinidad	Aeroplane Ltd	
G-TBYD	Raj Hamsa X'Air Falcon D(1)	T. Ansari	
G-TBZO	SOCATA TB20 Trinidad	J. P. Bechu & J. L. Auberget	
G-TCAA	Leonardo AW169	Specialist Aviation Services Ltd	
G-TCAE	Airbus A.320-214	Thomas Cook Airlines Ltd (G-YLBM)	

Notes	Reg	Type	Owner or Operator
	G-TCAL	Robinson R44 II	Barhale PLC
	G-TCAN	Colt 69A balloon	H. C. J. Williams
	G-TCDA	Airbus A.321-211	Thomas Cook Airlines Ltd (G-JOEE)
	G-TCDB	Airbus A.321-211	Thomas Cook Airlines Ltd
	G-TCDC	Airbus A.321-211	Thomas Cook Airlines Ltd
	G-TCDD	Airbus A.321-211	Thomas Cook Airlines Ltd
	G-TCDE	Airbus A.321-211	Thomas Cook Airlines Ltd
	G-TCDF	Airbus A.321-211	Thomas Cook Airlines Ltd
	G-TCDG	Airbus A.321-211	Thomas Cook Airlines Ltd
	G-TCDH	Airbus A.321-211	Thomas Cook Airlines Ltd
	G-TCDJ	Airbus A.321-211	Thomas Cook Airlines Ltd
	G-TCDK	Airbus A.321-211	Thomas Cook Airlines Ltd
	G-TCDL	Airbus A.321-211	Thomas Cook Airlines Ltd
	G-TCDM	Airbus A.321-211	Thomas Cook Airlines Ltd
	G-TCDN	Airbus A.321-211	Thomas Cook Airlines Ltd
	G-TCDO	Airbus A.321-211	Thomas Cook Airlines Ltd
	G-TCDV	Airbus A.321-211	Thomas Cook Airlines Ltd (G-SMTJ)
	G-TCDW	Airbus A.321-211	Thomas Cook Airlines Ltd
	G-TCDX	Airbus A.321-211	Thomas Cook Airlines Ltd (G-CTLA)
	G-TCDY	Airbus A.321-211	Thomas Cook Airlines Ltd
	G-TCDZ	Airbus A.321-211	Thomas Cook Airlines Ltd (G-OOAI)
	G-TCEE	Hughes 369HS	A. M. E. Castro (G-AZVM)
	G-TCHI	VS.509 Spitfire Tr.9	M. B. Phillips
	G-TCHO	VS Spitfire Mk.IX	B. Phillips
	G-TCHZ	VS.329 Spitfire IIA	M. B. Phillips
	G-TCMC	Embraer EMB-135BJ Legacy 650	London Executive Aviation Ltd
	G-TCNM	Tecnam P92-EA Echo	M. Kolev
	G-TCNY	Mainair Pegasus Quik	G-TCNY Group
	G-TCSX	Boeing 757-2K2	TAF Aviation (UK) Ltd
	G-TCTC	PA-28RT-200 Arrow IV	P. Salemis
	G-TCUB	Piper J-3C-65 Cub (modified)	C. Kirk
	G-TCXB	Airbus A.330-243	Thomas Cook Airlines Ltd (G-CINS)
	G-TCXC	Airbus A.330-243	Thomas Cook Airlines Ltd (G-CIUJ)
	G-TDJN	North American AT-6D Harvard III	D. J. Nock
	G-TDJP	Van's RV-8	D. J. Pearson
	G-TDOG	SA Bulldog Srs 120/121 (XX538:O)	G. S. Taylor
	G-TDSA	Cessna F.406 Caravan II	Nor Leasing
	G-TDVB	Dyn' Aero MCR-01ULC	D. V. Brunt
	G-TDYN	Aerospool Dynamic WT9 UK	N. Lilley & N. C. Herrington
	G-TEBZ	PA-28R-201 Arrow III	Smart People Don't Buy Ltd
	G-TECA	Tecnam P2002-JF	Aeros Holdings Ltd
	G-TECB	Tecnam P2006T	Aeros Holdings Ltd
	G-TECC	Aeronca 7AC Champion	N. J. Orchard-Armitage
	G-TECH	Rockwell Commander 114	A. S. Turner (G-BEDH)
	G-TECI	Tecnam P2002-JF	G-TECI Flying Club Ltd
	G-TECM	Tecnam P92-EM Echo	G-TECM Group
	G-TECO	Tecnam P92-EM Echo	A. N. Buchan
	G-TECS	Tecnam P2002-EA Sierra	D. A. Lawrence
	G-TECT	Tecnam P2006T	Cabledraw Ltd
	G-TEDB	Cessna F.150L	R. Nightingale (G-AZLZ)
	G-TEDI	Best Off Skyranger J2.2(1)	P. W. Reid
	G-TEDW	Kiss 450-582 (2)	G. Frost
	G-TEDY	Evans VP-1	N. K. Marston (G-BHGN)
	G-TEFC	PA-28 Cherokee 140	Foxtrot Charlie Flyers
	G-TEGS	Bell 206B JetRanger III	HC Services Ltd
	G-TEHL	CFM Streak Shadow SA-M	D. W. Allen (G-MYJE)
	G-TELY	Agusta A109A-II	Castle Air Ltd
	G-TEMB	Tecnam P2000-EA Sierra	M. B. Hill
	G-TEMP	PA-28 Cherokee 180	F. R. Busch & M. Khoshkou (G-AYBK)
	G-TEMT	Hawker Tempest II (MW763)	Anglia Aircraft Restorations Ltd
	G-TENG	Extra EA.300/L	D. C. Mowat
	G-TENN	Van's RV-10	RV10 Group
	G-TENT	Auster J/1N Alpha	R. Callaway-Lewis (G-AKJU)
	G-TERN	Shaw Europa	J. Smith
	G-TERO	Van's RV-7	A. Phillips
	G-TERR	Mainair Pegasus Quik	M. Faulkner
	G-TERY	PA-28-181 Archer II	J. R. Bratherton (G-BOXZ)
	G-TESI	Tecnam P2002 EA Sierra	C. C. Burgess
	G-TESR	Tecnam P2002-RG Sierra	Tecnam RG Group

Reg	Type	Owner or Operator	Notes
G-TEST	PA-34-200 Seneca	Stapleford Flying Club Ltd (G-BLCD)	
G-TEWS	PA-28-140 Cherokee	G-TEWS Group (G-KEAN/G-AWTM)	
G-TEXN	North American T-6G Texan (3072:72)	Boultbee Vintage LLP (G-BHTH)	
G-TEZZ	CZAW Sportcruiser	M. A. Lomas	
G-TFAM	PA-46-350T Malibu Matrix	Take Flight Aviation Ltd (G-UDMS)	
G-TFCC	Cub Crafters Carbon Cub SS CC11-160	Patina Ltd	
G-TFIX	Mainair Pegasus Quantum 15-912	T. G. Jones	
G-TFLX	P & M Quik GT450	I. M. Lane	
G-TFLY	Air Creation Kiss 450-582 (1)	A. J. Ladell	
G-TFOG	Best Off Skyranger 912(2)	T. J. Fogg	
G-TFRA	Cessna 525 Citationjet CJ1+	Blu Halkin Ltd	
G-TFRB	Air Command 532 Elite	F. R. Blennerhassett	
G-TFSI	NA TF-51D Mustang (44-14561/CY-D)	Anglia Aircraft Restorations Ltd	
G-TFUN	Valentin Taifun 17E	North West Taifun Group	
G-TGER	AA-5B Tiger	D. T. Pangbourne (G-BFZP)	
G-TGGR	Eurocopter EC 120B	Messiah Corporation Ltd	
G-TGJH	Evans VP-1 series 2	Condor Aviation International Ltd	
G-TGLG	AutoGyro Calidus	T. R. Galloway	
G-TGPG	Boeing 737-3YO	21T Ltd	
G-TGRA	Agusta A109A	Tiger Helicopters Ltd	
G-TGRC	Robinson R22 Beta	Tiger Aviation Ltd (G-RSWW)	
G-TGRD	Robinson R22 Beta II	Tiger Helicopters Ltd (G-OPTS)	
G-TGRE	Robinson R22 Alpha	Tiger Helicopters Ltd (G-SOLD)	
G-TGRS	Robinson R22 Beta	Tiger Aviation Ltd (G-DELL)	
G-TGRZ	Bell 206B JetRanger 3	Tiger Aviation Ltd (G-BXZX)	
G-TGTT	Robinson R44 II	Smart People UK Ltd	
G-TGUN	Aero AT-3 R100	KN Singles and Twins Aviation Consultants BV/Netherlands	
G-TGVP	Cunliffe-Owen Seafire Mk.XV	T. A. V. Percy	
G-THAT	Raj Hamsa X'Air Falcon 912 (1)	M. C. Sawyer	
G-THEO	TEAM mini-MAX 91	D. R. Western	
G-THFC	Embraer RJ135BJ Legacy	Raz Air Ltd (G-RRAZ/G-RUBN)	
G-THFW	Bell 206B-3 JetRanger III	Fly Heli Wales Ltd	
G-THIN	Cessna FR.172E	I. C. A. Ussher (G-BXYY)	
G-THOM	Thunder Ax-6-56 balloon	T. H. Wilson	
G-THOT	Avtech Jabiru SK	S. G. Holton	
G-THRE	Cessna 182S	J. P. Monjalet	
G-THRM	Schleicher ASW-27	B. Freddy (G-CJWC)	
G-THSL	PA-28R-201 Arrow III	D. M. Markscheffe	
G-THYA	Cessna 172S	Atlantic Flight Training Academy Ltd	
G-THYB	Cessna 172S	Atlantic Flight Training Ltd	
G-TIAC	Tiger Cub RL5A LW Sherwood Ranger	The Light Aircraft Co.Ltd	
G-TIBF	Balony Kubicek BB34Z balloon	G. B.Lescott	
G-TIBS	SOCATA TB.20 Trinidad	C. C. Jewell	
G-TICH	Taylor JT.2 Titch	J. W. Graham-White	
G-TICO	Cameron O-77 balloon	J. F. Trehern	
G-TIDS	Jodel 150	M. R. Parker	
G-TIDY	Sky Ranger Nynja 912S(1)	J. M. Stables	
G-TIFG	Ikarus C42 FB80	The Ikarus Flying Group	
G-TIGA	DH.82A Tiger Moth	D. E. Leatherland (G-AOEG)	
G-TIGC	AS.332L Super Puma	Airbus Helicopters (G-BJYH)	
G-TIGS	AS.332L Super Puma	Airbus Helicopters	
G-TIGV	AS.332L Super Puma	Vector Aerospace Financial Services Ireland Ltd	
G-TIII	Aerotek Pitts S-2A Special	D. D. & D. S. Welch	
G-TILE	Robinson R22 Beta	Heli Air Ltd	
G-TIMC	Robinson R44	T. Clark Aviation LLP (G-CDUR)	
G-TIMI	BRM Aero Bristell NG5	A. I. D. Rich	
G-TIMK	PA-28-181 Archer II	Minimal Risk Consultancy Ltd	
G-TIMP	Aeronca 7BCM Champion	R. B. Valler	
G-TIMS	Falconar F-12A	T. Sheridan	
G-TIMX	Head AX8-88B balloon	J. Edwards & S. McMahon	
G-TIMY	Gardan GY-80 Horizon 160	A. R. Whyte	
G-TINK	Robinson R22 Beta	Omega Helicopters	
G-TINS	Cameron N-90 balloon	J. R. Clifton	
G-TINT	Aerotechnik EV-97 Team Eurostar UK	I. A. Cunningham	
G-TINY	Z.526F Trener Master	D. Evans	
G-TIPJ	Cameron Z-77 balloon	Servowarm Balloon Syndicate	

Notes	Reg	Type	Owner or Operator
	G-TIPP	Aeroprakt A22-LS Foxbat	E. Fogarty
	G-TIPR	Eurocopter AS.350B2 Ecureuil	Thames Materials Holdings Ltd (G-PATM)
	G-TIPS	Nipper T.66 Srs.3	F. V. Neefs
	G-TIPY	Czech Sport PS-28 Cruiser	I. C. Tandy
	G-TIVV	Aerotechnik EV-97 Team Eurostar UK	G-TIVV Group
	G-TJAL	Jabiru SPL-430	D. W. Cross
	G-TJAV	Mainair Pegasus Quik	Access Anywhere Ltd
	G-TJAY	PA-22 Tri-Pacer 135	D. Pegley
	G-TJCL	P &M QuikR	B. R. Dale
	G-TJDM	Van's RV-6A	J. D. Michie
	G-TKAY	Shaw Europa	A. M. Kay
	G-TKEV	P & M Quik R	S. J. Thompson
	G-TKIS	Tri-R Kis	T. J. Bone
	G-TKNO	UltraMagic S-50 balloon	P. Dickinson
	G-TLAC	Sherwood Ranger ST	The Light Aircraft Co.Ltd
	G-TLDL	Medway SLA 100 Executive	Woodfern Associates Ltd
	G-TLET	PA-28-161 Cadet	ADR Aviation (G-GFCF/G-RHBH)
	G-TLMA	Lindstrand LTL 1-105 balloon	A. M. Holly
	G-TLST	TL 2000UK Sting Carbon	W. H. J. Knowles
	G-TLTL	Schempp-Hirth Discus CS	E. K. Armitage
	G-TMAN	Roadster/Adventure Funflyer Quattro	P. A. Mahony
	G-TMAX	Evektor EV-97 Sportstar Max	G-TMAX Group
	G-TMCB	Best Off Skyranger 912 (2)	J. R. Davis
	G-TMCC	Cameron N-90 balloon	M. S. Jennings
	G-TMHK	PA-38-112 Tomahawk	Smart People Don't Buy Ltd (G-GALL/G-BTEV)
	G-TMPV	Hawker Tempest V	Anglia Aircraft Restorations Ltd
	G-TNAM	Tecnam P2006T	Tog Aviation Ltd
	G-TNGO	Van's RV-6	J. D. M. Willis
	G-TNIK	Dassault Falcon 2000	Blu Halkin Ltd
	G-TNJB	P & M Quik R	C. J. Shorter
	G-TNRG	Tanarg/Ixess 15 912S(2)	L. A. Read
	G-TNTN	Thunder Ax6-56 balloon	H. M. Savage & A. A. Leggate
	G-TOBA	SOCATA TB10 Tobago	E. Downing
	G-TOBI	Cessna F.172K	The TOBI Group (G-AYVB)
	G-TODD	ICA IS-28M2A	C. I. Roberts & C. D. King
	G-TOES	PA-28-161 Warrior II	Freedom Aviation Ltd
	G-TOFT	Colt 90A balloon	C. S. Perceval
	G-TOGO	Van's RV-6	I. R. Thomas
	G-TOLL	PA-28R-201 Arrow III	Arrow Aircraft Ltd
	G-TOLS	Robinson R44	K. N. Tolley (G-CBOT)
	G-TOLY	Robinson R22 Beta	Helicopter & Pilot Services Ltd (G-NSHR)
	G-TOMC	NA AT-6D Harvard III	A. A. Marshall
	G-TOMJ	Flight Design CT2K	Avair Ltd
	G-TOMX	MCR-01 VLA Sportster	P. T. Knight
	G-TONE	Pazmany PL-4	P. I. Morgans
	G-TONN	Mainair Pegasus Quik	T. D. Evans
	G-TOOB	Schempp-Hirth Discus 2b	M. F. Evans
	G-TOOL	Thunder Ax8-105 balloon	D. V. Howard
	G-TOOO	Guimbal Cabri G2	Helicentre Aviation Ltd
	G-TOOZ	Eurocopter EC 120B Colibri	C. J. Toohy (G-GTJM)
	G-TOPB	Cameron Z-140 balloon	Anana Ltd
	G-TOPC	AS.355F1 Twin Squirrel	Kinetic Avionics Ltd
	G-TOPI	Bell 407	Top Flight Helicopters Isle of Man Ltd
	G-TOPK	Shaw Europa XS	P. J. Kember
	G-TOPM	Agusta-Bell 206B-2 JetRanger 2	Topflight Helicopters (G-CCBL)
	G-TOPO	PA-23-250 Turbo Aztec	Ravenair Aircraft Ltd (G-BGWW)
	G-TOPP	Van's RV-10	D. Topp & S. E. Coles
	G-TOPS	AS.355F1 Twin Squirrel	RCR Aviation Ltd (G-BPRH)
	G-TORC	PA-28R Cherokee Arrow 200	Pure Aviation Support Services Ltd
	G-TORE	P.84 Jet Provost T.3A ★	Instructional airframe/City University, Islington
	G-TORI	Zenair CH.701SP	A. Johnston & J. D. Hayward (G-CCSK)
	G-TORK	Cameron Z-105 balloon	M. E. Dunstan-Sewell
	G-TORN	Flight Design CTSW	N. C. Harper
	G-TORO	Skyranger Nynja 912S(1)	L. J. E. Moss & C. Fenwick
	G-TOSH	Robinson R22 Beta	Choicecircle Ltd

Reg	Type	Owner or Operator	Notes
G-TOTN	Cessna 210M	Quay Financial Strategies Ltd (G-BVZM)	
G-TOTO	Cessna F.177RG	Airspeed Aviation Ltd (G-OADE/G-AZKH)	
G-TOUR	Robin R.2112	R. M. Wade	
G-TOWS	PA-25 Pawnee 260	Lasham Gliding Society Ltd	
G-TOYZ	Bell 206B JetRanger 3	G-TOYZ Ltd (G-RGER)	
G-TPAL	P & M Aviation Quik GT450	R. Robertson	
G-TPGR	Ultramagic F-25 Futbol balloon	A. M. Holly	
G-TPPW	Van's RV-7	P. Wright	
G-TPSL	Cessna 182S	A. N. Purslow	
G-TPSY	Champion 8KCAB Super Decathlon	MCRS Aviation (G-CEOE)	
G-TPTP	Robinson R44	A. N. Purslow	
G-TPWL	P & M Quik GT450	The G-TPWL Group	
G-TPWX	Heliopolis Gomhouria Mk.6 (TP+WX)	W. H. Greenwood	
G-TRAC	Robinson R44	C. J. Sharples	
G-TRAM	Pegasus Quantum 15-912	G-TRAM Group	
G-TRAN	Beech 76 Duchess	Pan Aero Services LLC (G-NIFR)	
G-TRAT	Pilatus PC-12/45	Flew LLP	
G-TRBN	HpH Glasflugel 304S Shark	A. Cluskey	
G-TRBO	Schleicher ASW-28-18E	M. P. & R. W. Weaver	
G-TRCY	Robinson R44	Marman Aviation Ltd	
G-TRDS	Guimbal Cabri G2	W. R. Harford	
G-TREB	Cessna 182T	Camel Aviation Ltd	
G-TREC	Cessna 421C	Sovereign Business Integration PLC (G-TLOL)	
G-TREE	Bell 206B JetRanger 3	Heliflight (UK) Ltd	
G-TREK	Jodel D.18	R. H. Mole	
G-TREX	Alpi Pioneer 300	S. R. Winter	
G-TRIG	Cameron Z-90 balloon	Hedge Hoppers Balloon Group	
G-TRIM	Monnett Moni	E. A. Brotherton-Ratcliffe	
G-TRIN	SOCATA TB20 Trinidad	M. J. Porter	
G-TRJB	Beech A36 Bonanza	G. A. J. Bowles	
G-TRLL	Groppo Trail	P. M. Grant	
G-TRMP	Sikorsky S-76B	DT Connect Europe Ltd	
G-TRNG	Agusta A109E Power	G. Walters (Leasing) Ltd (G-NWOY/G-JMXA)	
G-TRON	Robinson R66	PFR Aviation Ltd	
G-TROY	NA T-28A Fennec (51-7692)	S. G. Howell & S. Tilling	
G-TRTL	Skyranger Nynja LS 912S(1)	J. T. & J. W. Whicher	
G-TRUE	MDH Hughes 369E	N. E. Bailey	
G-TRUK	Stoddard-Hamilton Glasair RG	S. Moore	
G-TRUU	PA-34-220T Seneca III	Omega Sky Taxi Ltd (G-BOJK/G-BRUF)	
G-TRUX	Colt 77A balloon	J. R. Lawson	
G-TRVR	Van's RV-7	The Richard Ormonde Shuttleworth Remembrance Trust	
G-TSAC	Tecnam P2002-EA Sierra	A. G. Cozens	
G-TSDA	Aquila AT-01-100A	Tayside Aviation Ltd	
G-TSDB	Aquila AT-01-100A	Tayside Aviation Ltd	
G-TSDC	Aquila AT-01-100A	Tayside Aviation Ltd	
G-TSDE	Aquila AT-01-100A	Tayside Aviation Ltd	
G-TSDS	PA-32R-301 Saratoga SP	I. R. Jones (G-TRIP/G-HOSK)	
G-TSFC	Tecnam P2008-JC	Stapleford Flying Club Ltd	
G-TSGA	PA-28R-201 Arrow III	I. R. Lockhart & J. N. Bailey (G-ONSF/ G-EMAK)	
G-TSGJ	PA-28-181 Archer II	Golf Juliet Flying Club	
G-TSHO	Ikarus C42 FB80	A. P. Shoobert	
G-TSIM	Titan T-51 Mustang	B. J. Chester-Master	
G-TSIX	AT-6C Harvard IIA (111836:JZ-6)	Century Aviation Ltd	
G-TSKD	Raj Hamsa X'Air Jabiru J.2.2.	T. Sexton & K. B. Dupuy	
G-TSKS	EV-97 TeamEurostar UK	North East Aviation Ltd	
G-TSKY	Beagle B.121 Pup 2	Osprey Group (G-AWDY)	
G-TSLC	Schweizer 269C-1	C. J. Cox Ltd	
G-TSOB	Rans S.6-ES Coyote II	G-TSOB Syndicate	
G-TSOG	TLAC Sherwood Ranger XP	The Spirit of Goole	
G-TSOL	EAA Acrosport 1	D. F. Cumberlidge & H. Stuart (G-BPKI)	
G-TSUE	Shaw Europa	H. J. C. Maclean	
G-TSWI	Lindstrand LBL-90A balloon	R. J. Gahan	
G-TSWZ	Cameron Z-77 balloon	Business First Centre	
G-TTAT	ICP MXP-740 Savannah VG Jabiru(1)	D. Varley & D. J. Broughall	
G-TTEC	PA-32-301FT 6X	Taytech Environmental Ltd	
G-TTEN	Tecnam P2010	R. C. Mincik	

Notes	Reg	Type	Owner or Operator
	G-TTFG	Colt 77B balloon	T. J. & M. J. Turner (G-BUZF)
	G-TTGV	Bell 206L-4 LongRanger IV	Langley Aviation Ltd (G-JACI)
	G-TTJF	Dassault Falcon 2000S	TAG Aviation (UK) Ltd
	G-TTNA	Airbus A.320-251N	British Airways PLC
	G-TTNB	Airbus A.320-251N	British Airways PLC
	G-TTNC	Airbus A.320-251N	British Airways PLC
	G-TTOB	Airbus A.320-232	British Airways PLC
	G-TTOE	Airbus A.320-232	British Airways PLC
	G-TTOM	Zenair CH.601HD Zodiac	G-TTOM Group
	G-TTOY	CFM Streak Shadow SA	J. Softley
	G-TTRL	Van's RV-9A	J. E. Gattrell
	G-TTUG	Aeropro Eurofox 912(IS)	Buckminster Gliding Club Ltd (G-WTUG)
	G-TUBB	Avtech Jabiru UL	A. H. Bower
	G-TUCK	Van's RV-8	N. G. R. Moffat
	G-TUGG	PA-18 Super Cub 150	Ulster Gliding Club Ltd
	G-TUGI	CZAW Sportcruiser	T. J. Wilson
	G-TUGY	Robin DR.400/180	TUGY Group
	G-TUGZ	Robin DR.400/180R	M. J. Aldridge
	G-TUIA	Boeing 787-8	TUI Airways Ltd
	G-TUIB	Boeing 787-8	TUI Airways Ltd
	G-TUIC	Boeing 787-8	TUI Airways Ltd
	G-TUID	Boeing 787-8	TUI Airways Ltd
	G-TUIE	Boeing 787-8	TUI Airways Ltd
	G-TUIF	Boeing 787-8	TUI Airways Ltd
	G-TUIG	Boeing 787-8	TUI Airways Ltd
	G-TUIH	Boeing 787-8	TUI Airways Ltd
	G-TUII	Boeing 787-8	TUI Airways Ltd
	G-TUIJ	Boeing 787-9	TUI Airways Ltd
	G-TUIK	Boeing 787-9	TUI Airways Ltd
	G-TUIL	Boeing 787-9	TUI Airways Ltd
	G-TUKU	Stemme S 10-VT	Stemme UK Ltd
	G-TULA	Diamond DA.40D Star	AJW Construction Ltd
	G-TUNE	Robinson R22 Beta	Heli Air Ltd (G-OJVI)
	G-TURF	Cessna F.406	Reconnaissance Ventures Ltd
	G-TUTU	Cameron O-105 balloon	A. C. K. Rawson & J. J. Rudoni
	G-TVAL	Airbus Helicopters EC 135 T3	Babcock Mission Critical Services Onshore Ltd
	G-TVAM	MBB Bo105DBS-4	South Georgis Heritage Trust (G-SPOL)
	G-TVBF	Lindstrand LBL-310A balloon	Virgin Balloons Flights
	G-TVCO	Gippsland GA-8 Airvan	P. Ligertwood
	G-TVGC	Schempp-Hirth Janus A	Trent Valley Gliding Club Ltd
	G-TVHB	Eurocopter EC 135 P2+	Police & Crime Commissioner for West Yorkshire
	G-TVHD	AS.355F2 Ecureuil 2	Arena Aviation Ltd
	G-TVIJ	CCF Harvard IV (T-6J) (28521:TA-521)	R. W. Davies (G-BSBE)
	G-TVSI	Campbell Cricket Replica	G. Smith
	G-TWAL	Rutan Long-Ez	T. Walsh (G-BNCZ)
	G-TWAZ	Rolladen-Schneider LS7-WL	S. Derwin
	G-TWEL	PA-28-181 Archer II	International Aerospace Engineering Ltd
	G-TWIS	Silence Twister	C. S. & K. D. Rhodes
	G-TWIY	Hawker 750	Saxonair Charter Ltd (G-NLPA)
	G-TWIZ	Rockwell Commander 114	B. C. & P. M. Cox
	G-TWLV	Van's RV-12	G-TWLV Group
	G-TWNN	Beech 76 Duchess	M. Magrabi
	G-TWOA	Schempp-Hirth Discus 2a	S. Briel
	G-TWOC	Schempp-Hirth Ventus 2cT	G. C. Lewis
	G-TWOO	Extra EA.300/200	Skyboard Aerobatics Ltd (G-MRKI)
	G-TWOP	Cessna 525A Citationjet CJ2	Centreline AV Ltd (G-ODAG)
	G-TWRL	Pitts S-1S Special	C. Dennis
	G-TWSR	Silence Twister	J. A. Hallam
	G-TWSS	Silence Twister	T. R. Dews
	G-TWST	Silence Twister	Zulu Glasstek Ltd (G-ZWIP)
	G-TWTR	Robinson R44 II	Volitant Aviation Ltd
	G-TWTW	Denney Kitfox Mk.2	R. M. Bremner
	G-TXAN	AT-6D Harvard III (51970)	K-F Grimminger (G-JUDI)
	G-TXAS	Cessna A.150L	Tango Xray Alpha Sierra Group (G-HFCA)
	G-TXTV	AgustaWestland A.109E Power	Arena Aviation Ltd

Reg	Type	Owner or Operator	Notes
G-TYAK	IDA Bacau Yakovlev Yak-52	S. J. Ducker	
G-TYER	Robin DR.400/500	Robin Group	
G-TYGA	AA-5B Tiger	Three Musketeers Flying Group (G-BHNZ)	
G-TYGR	Best Off Skyranger Swift 912S(1)	B. W. G. Stanbridge	
G-TYKE	Avtech Jabiru UL-450	B. McGuire	
G-TYNE	SOCATA TB20 Trinidad	N. V. Price	
G-TYPH	BAe.146-200	BAE Systems (Corporate Air Travel) Ltd (G-BTVT)	
G-TYRE	Cessna F.172M	J. S. C. English	
G-TYRO	AutoGyro MTOSport	I. Bryant (G-CINT)	
G-TZED	SOCATA TB-200 Tobago XL	Zytech Ltd	
G-TZII	Thorp T.211B	M. J. Newton	
G-UACA	Best Off Skyranger Swift 912(1)	R. G. Hicks	
G-UAKE	NA P-51D-5-NA Mustang	P. S. Warner	
G-UANO	DHC.1 Chipmunk 22	Advanced Flight Training Ltd (G-BYYW)	
G-UANT	PA-28 Cherokee 140	Air Navigation & Trading Co Ltd	
G-UAPA	Robin DR.400/140B	Sor Air Sociedade de Aeronautica SA/Portugal	
G-UAPO	Ruschmeyer R.90-230RG	P. Randall	
G-UART	Moravan Zlin Z-242L	Oxford Aviation Academy (Oxford) Ltd (G-EKMN)	
G-UAVA	PA-30 Twin Comanche	Small World Aviation Ltd	
G-UCAM	PA-31-350 Navajo Chieftain	Blue Sky Investments Ltd (G-NERC/G-BBXX)	
G-UCAN	Tecnam P2002-JF Sierra	Aerobility	
G-UCCC	Cameron 90 Sign SS balloon	Unipart Group of Companies Ltd	
G-UCLU	Schleicher ASK-21	University College London Union	
G-UCRM	Slingsby T.67M Firefly II	CRM Aviation Europe Ltd (G-BONT)	
G-UDET	Replica Fokker E.111 (105/15)	M. J. Clark	
G-UDGE	Thruster T.600N	G-UDGE Syndicate (G-BYPI)	
G-UDIX	Schempp-Hirth Duo Discus T	R. Banks	
G-UDOG	SA Bulldog Srs 120/121 (XX518:S)	M. van den Broek	
G-UFAW	Raj Hamsa X'Air 582 (5)	P. Batchelor	
G-UFCB	Cessna 172S	The Cambridge Aero Club Ltd	
G-UFCG	Cessna 172S	Ulster Flying Club (1961) Ltd	
G-UFCI	Cessna 172S	Ulster Flying Club (1961) Ltd	
G-UFCL	Tecnam P2002-JF Sierra	Tecair Ltd	
G-UFCN	Cessna 152	Ulster Flying Club (1961) Ltd	
G-UFCO	Cessna 152	Ulster Flying Club (1961) Ltd	
G-UFLY	Cessna F.150H	Westair Flying Services Ltd (G-AVVY)	
G-UFOE	Grob G.115	Swiftair Maintenance Ltd	
G-UFOX	Aeropro Eurofox 912(1)	G-UFOX Group	
G-UHIH	Bell UH-1H Iroquois (21509)	MSS Holdings Ltd	
G-UHOP	UltraMagic H-31 balloon	A. R. Brown	
G-UIII	Extra EA.300/200	M. Thomas	
G-UIKR	P & M Quik R	A. M. Sirant	
G-UILD	Grob G.109B	K. Butterfield	
G-UILE	Lancair 320	R. J. Martin	
G-UILT	Cessna T.303	D. L. Tucker (G-EDRY)	
G-UIMB	Guimbal Cabri G2	Helitrain Ltd	
G-UINN	Stolp SA.300 Starduster Too	A. Dunne	
G-UINS	Ultramagic B-70 balloon	A. M. Holly	
G-UINZ	Ultramagic B-70 balloon	A. M. Holly	
G-UIRI	Aeropro Eurofox 912(S)	P. Crawley	
G-UIRO	AutoGyro MT-03	S. D. Kellner (G-CFAG)	
G-UISE	Van's RV-8	J. A. Green	
G-UJAB	Avtech Jabiru UL	C. A. Thomas	
G-UJET	Learjet 45	Patriot Aviation Ltd (G-PFCT/G-GOMO/ G-OLDF/G-JRJR)	
G-UJGK	Avtech Jabiru UL	W. G. Upton & J. G. Kosak	
G-UKAL	Cessna F.406 Caravan II	Aero Lease UK	
G-UKAW	Agusta A.109E	Agusta Westland Ltd	
G-UKCS	PA-31 Navajo	2 Excel Aviation Ltd	
G-UKOZ	Avtech Jabiru SK	D. J. Burnett	
G-UKPB	Cessna 208B Grand Caravan	UK Parachute Services Ltd	

Notes	Reg	Type	Owner or Operator
	G-UKPS	Cessna 208 Caravan 1	UK Parachute Services Ltd
	G-UKRB	Colt 105A balloon	Virgin Airship & Balloon Co Ltd
	G-UKRV	Van's RV-7A	Netwasp.net Ltd
	G-UKTV	AS.355F2 Ecureuil 2	Arena Aviation Ltd (G-JESE/G-EMHH/G-BYKH)
	G-UKUK	Head Ax8-105 balloon	P. A. George
	G-ULAS	DHC.1 Chipmunk 22 (WK517)	M. B. Phillips
	G-ULCC	Schleicher ASH-30 MI	G-ULCC Flying Club
	G-ULFM	Gulfstream 450	Pendley Aviation LLP
	G-ULHI	SA Bulldog Srs.100/101	Kryten Systems Ltd (G-OPOD/G-AZMS)
	G-ULIA	Cameron V-77 balloon	J. T. Wilkinson
	G-ULPS	Everett Srs 1 gyroplane	I. Pearson (G-BMNY)
	G-ULRK	Sequoia F.8L Falco	U. K. S. S. N. M. Lawson
	G-ULSY	Ikarus C.42 FB 80	M. L. Cade
	G-ULTA	Ultramagic M-65C	G. A. Board
	G-ULTR	Cameron A-105 balloon	P. Glydon
	G-ULUL	Rotorsport UK Calidus	R. S. Payne (G-HTBT)
	G-ULZE	Robinson R22	HQ Aviation Ltd (G-BUBW)
	G-UMBL	Guimbal Cabri G2	European Helicopter Importers Ltd
	G-UMBO	Thunder Ax7-77A balloon	Virgin Airship & Balloon Co Ltd
	G-UMBY	Hughes 369E	HQ Aviation Ltd
	G-UMMI	PA-31-310 Turbo Navajo	2 Excel Aviation Ltd (G-BGSO)
	G-UMMS	EV-97 TeamEurostar UK	G. W. Carwardine (G-ODRY)
	G-UMMY	Best Off Skyranger J2.2(2)	D. A. Tibbals
	G-UMPY	Shaw Europa	GDBMK Ltd
	G-UNAC	PA-32R-301T Saratoga II TC	A. C. Campbell
	G-UNDD	PA-23 Aztec 250E	G. J. & D. P. Deadman (G-BATX)
	G-UNER	Lindstrand LBL-90A balloon	Blind Veterans UK
	G-UNES	Van's RV-6	C. A. Greatrex
	G-UNGE	Lindstrand LBL-90A balloon	Silver Ghost Balloon Club (G-BVPJ)
	G-UNGO	Pietenpol Air Camper	A. R. Wyatt
	G-UNIN	Schempp-Hirth Ventus b	U9 Syndicate
	G-UNIX	VPM M16 Tandem Trainer	A. P. Wilkinson
	G-UNKY	Ultramagic S-50 balloon	A. M. Holly
	G-UNNA	Jabiru UL-450WW	J. F. Heath
	G-UNRL	Lindstrand LBL-RR21 balloon	Lindstrand Media Ltd
	G-UORO	Shaw Europa	D. Dufton
	G-UPFS	Waco UPS-7	D. N. Peters & N. R. Finlayson
	G-UPHI	Best Off Skyranger Swift 912S(1)	C. E. Walsh & M. B. Harper
	G-UPID	Bowers Fly Baby 1A	R. D. Taylor
	G-UPIZ	BRM Aero Bristell NG5 Speed Wing	C. P. & K. J. Faint
	G-UPOI	Cameron TR-84 S1 balloon	Cameron Balloons Ltd
	G-UPRT	Slingsby T.67M-260 Firefly	L3 CTS Airline and Academy Training Ltd (G-BWXU)
	G-UPTA	Skyranger 912S (1)	S. J. Joseph
	G-UPUP	Cameron V-77 balloon	S. F. Burden/Netherlands
	G-UPUZ	Lindstrand LBL-120A balloon	C.J. Sanger-Davies
	G-URMS	Europa	C. Parkinson (G-DEBR)
	G-UROP	Beech 95-B55 Baron	Just Plane Trading Ltd
	G-URRR	Air Command 582 Sport	L. Armes
	G-URSA	Sikorsky S-76C	Capital Air Services Ltd (G-URSS)
	G-URUH	Robinson R44	Heli Air Ltd
	G-USAA	Cessna F.150G	Aeros Holdings Ltd (G-OIDW)
	G-USAR	Cessna 441 Conquest	I. Annenskiy
	G-USCO	Hughes 269C	C. R. Colquhoun (G-CECO)
	G-USHA	Learjet 75	Essexjets Ltd
	G-USIL	Thunder Ax7-77 balloon	Window On The World Ltd
	G-USKY	Aviat A-1B Husky	D. J. Nock
	G-USRV	Van's RV-6	C. Ramshaw
	G-USSY	PA-28-181 Archer II	The Leicestershire Aero Club Ltd
	G-USTH	Agusta A109A-II	Stratton Motor Co.(Norfolk) Ltd
	G-USTS	Agusta A109A-II	Eagle Helicopters & Tedham Ltd (G-MKSF)
	G-USTY	FRED Srs 2	I. Pearson

Reg	Type	Owner or Operator	Notes
G-UTRA	Ultramagic M-77 balloon	Ultrait Ltd	
G-UTSI	Rand-Robinson KR-2	K. B. Gutridge	
G-UUPP	Cameron Z-70 balloon	Cameron Balloons Ltd	
G-UURO	Aerotechnik EV-97 Eurostar	Romeo Oscar Syndicate	
G-UUUU	Ikarus C42 FB100	R. Engelhard	
G-UVBF	Lindstrand LBL-400A balloon	Virgin Balloon Flights	
G-UVIP	Cessna 421C	Aerodata International Surveys (G-BSKH)	
G-UWAS	SA Bulldog Srs 120/121 (XX625)	Mid America (UK) Ltd (G-CBAB)	
G-UWEB	Cameron Z-120 balloon	GWE Business West Ltd	
G-UYAK	Yakovlev Yak-18T	C. A. Brightwell	
G-UZHA	Airbus A.320-251N	easyJet Airline Co.Ltd	
G-UZHB	Airbus A.320-251N	easyJet Airline Co.Ltd	
G-UZHC	Airbus A.320-251N	easyJet Airline Co.Ltd	
G-UZHD	Airbus A.320-251N	easyJet Airline Co.Ltd	
G-UZHE	Airbus A.320-251N	easyJet Airline Co.Ltd	
G-UZHF	Airbus A.320-251N	easyJet Airline Co.Ltd	
G-UZLE	Colt 77A balloon	G. B. Davies	
G-UZUP	Aerotechnik EV-97A Eurostar	G-UZUP Flying Group	
G-UZZI	Lancair LC41-550FG Corvalis TT	The Lord Rotherwick	
G-UZZY	Enstrom 480	N. Shakespeare	
G-VAAC	PA-28-181 Archer III	J. N. D. de Jager (G-CCDN)	
G-VAAV	P & M Quik R	M. Kent	
G-VAGA	PA-15 Vagabond	N. S. Lomax (G-CCEE)	
G-VAHH	Boeing 787-9	Virgin Atlantic Airways Ltd	
G-VALG	Evektor EV-97 Eurostar SL	J. A. Ganderton	
G-VALS	Pietenpol Air Camper	G-VALS Flying Group	
G-VALY	SOCATA TB21 Trinidad GT Turbo	Richard Thwaites Aviation Ltd	
G-VALZ	Cameron N-120 balloon	J. D. & K. Griffiths	
G-VANA	Gippsland GA-8 Airvan	P. Marsden	
G-VANC	Gippsland GA-8 Airvan	Irish Skydiving Club Ltd	
G-VAND	Gippsland GA-8 Airvan	Irish Skydiving Club Ltd	
G-VANN	Van's RV-7A	G-VANN Flying Group	
G-VANS	Van's RV-4	R. J. Marshall	
G-VANX	Gippsland GA-8 Airvan	Airkix Aircraft Ltd	
G-VANZ	Van's RV-6A	M. Wright	
G-VARG	Varga 2150A Kachina	R. A. Denton	
G-VARK	Van's RV-7	D. A. Sadler	
G-VAST	Boeing 747-41R	Virgin Atlantic Airways Ltd *Ladybird*	
G-VBAA	Cameron A-400 balloon	Virgin Balloon Flights	
G-VBAB	Cameron A-400 balloon	Virgin Balloon Flights	
G-VBAD	Cameron A-300 balloon	Virgin Balloon Flights	
G-VBAE	Cameron A-400 balloon	Virgin Balloon Flights	
G-VBAF	Cameron A-300 balloon	Virgin Balloon Flights	
G-VBAG	Cameron A-400 balloon	Virgin Balloon Flights	
G-VBAH	Cameron A-400 balloon	Virgin Balloon Flights	
G-VBAI	Cameron A-400 balloon	Virgin Balloon Flights	
G-VBAJ	Cameron A-400 balloon	Virgin Balloon Flights	
G-VBAK	Cameron A-400 balloon	Virgin Balloon Flights	
G-VBAL	Cameron A-400 balloon	Virgin Balloon Flights	
G-VBAM	Cameron A-400 balloon	Virgin Balloon Flights	
G-VBAN	Cameron A-400 balloon	Virgin Balloon Flights	
G-VBAO	Cameron A-400 balloon	Virgin Balloon Flights	
G-VBAP	Cameron A-400 balloon	Virgin Balloon Flights	
G-VBAR	Cameron A-400 balloon	Airxcite Ltd	
G-VBAS	Cameron A-400 balloon	Airxcite Ltd	
G-VBCA	Cirrus SR22	C. A. S. Atha	
G-VBFA	Ultramagic N-250 balloon	Virgin Balloon Flights	
G-VBFB	Ultramagic N-355 balloon	Virgin Balloon Flights	
G-VBFC	Ultramagic N-250 balloon	Virgin Balloon Flights	
G-VBFD	Ultramagic N-250 balloon	Virgin Balloon Flights	
G-VBFE	Ultramagic N-255 balloon	Virgin Balloon Flights	
G-VBFF	Lindstrand LBL-360A balloon	Virgin Balloon Flights	
G-VBFG	Cameron Z-350 balloon	Virgin Balloon Flights	
G-VBFH	Cameron Z-350 balloon	Virgin Balloon Flights	

Notes	Reg	Type	Owner or Operator
	G-VBFI	Cameron Z-350 balloon	Virgin Balloon Flights
	G-VBFJ	Cameron Z-350 balloon	Virgin Balloon Flights
	G-VBFK	Cameron Z-350 balloon	Virgin Balloon Flights
	G-VBFL	Cameron Z-400 balloon	Virgin Balloon Flights
	G-VBFM	Cameron Z-375 balloon	Virgin Balloon Flights
	G-VBFN	Cameron Z-375 balloon	Virgin Balloon Flights
	G-VBFO	Cameron Z-375 balloon	Virgin Balloon Flights
	G-VBFP	Ultramagic N-425 balloon	Virgin Balloon Flights
	G-VBFR	Cameron Z-375 balloon	Virgin Balloon Flights
	G-VBFS	Cameron Z-375 balloon	Virgin Balloon Flights
	G-VBFT	Cameron Z-375 balloon	Virgin Balloon Flights
	G-VBFU	Cameron A-400 balloon	Virgin Balloon Flights
	G-VBFV	Cameron Z-400 balloon	Virgin Balloon Flights
	G-VBFW	Cameron Z-77 balloon	Virgin Balloon Flights
	G-VBFX	Cameron Z-400 balloon	Virgin Balloon Flights
	G-VBFY	Cameron Z-400 balloon	Virgin Balloon Flights
	G-VBFZ	Cameron A-300 balloon	Virgin Balloon Flights
	G-VBIG	Boeing 747-4Q8	Virgin Atlantic Airways Ltd *Tinkerbelle*
	G-VBOW	Boeing 787-9	Virgin Atlantic Airways Ltd *Pearly Queen*
	G-VBPM	Cirrus SR22	S. Perkes
	G-VBUG	Airbus A.340-642	Virgin Atlantic Airways Ltd *Olivia Rae*
	G-VBZZ	Boeing 787-9	Virgin Atlantic Airways Ltd
	G-VCIO	EAA Acro Sport II	C. M. Knight
	G-VCJH	Robinson R22 Beta	Nedroc Ltd
	G-VCML	Beech 58 Baron	St. Angelo Aviation Ltd
	G-VCRU	Boeing 787-9	Virgin Atlantic Airways Ltd
	G-VCUB	PA-18-150 Super Cub	N. J. Morgan
	G-VCXT	Schempp-Hirth Ventus 2cT	R. F. Aldous/Germany
	G-VDIA	Boeing 787-9	Virgin Atlantic Airways Ltd
	G-VDIR	Cessna T.310R	J. Driver
	G-VDOG	Cessna 305C Bird Dog (24582)	J. A. Watt
	G-VECD	Robin R.1180T	B. Lee
	G-VEGA	Slingsby T.65A Vega	R. A. Rice (G-BFZN)
	G-VELA	SIAI-Marchetti S.205-22R	G-VELA Group
	G-VENC	Schempp-Hirth Ventus 2cT	J. B. Giddins
	G-VENM	DH.112 Venom FB.50 (WK436)	Aviation Heritage Ltd (G-BLIE)
	G-VERA	Gardan GY-201 Minicab	D. K. Shipton
	G-VETC	Lambert Mission M108	C. J. Cheetham
	G-VETS	Enstrom 280C-UK Shark	B. G. Rhodes (G-FSDC/G-BKTG)
	G-VETT	Guimbal Cabri G2	Farm Veterinary Aviation Ltd
	G-VEYE	Robinson R22	K. A. Jones (G-BPTP)
	G-VEZE	Rutan Vari-Eze	Go Eze Flying
	G-VFAN	Boeing 787-9	Virgin Atlantic Airways Ltd *Pin Up Girl*
	G-VFAS	PA-28R-200 Cherokee Arrow	P. Wood (G-MEAH/G-BSNM)
	G-VFDS	Van's RV-8	J. Ratford & K. Treskonova
	G-VFIT	Airbus A.340-642	Virgin Atlantic Airways Ltd *Dancing Queen*
	G-VFIZ	Airbus A.340-642	Virgin Atlantic Airways Ltd *Bubbles*
	G-VGAG	Cirrus SR20 GTS	C. M. O'Connell
	G-VGAL	Boeing 747-443	Virgin Atlantic Airways Ltd *Jersey Girl*
	G-VGBR	Airbus A.330-343	Virgin Atlantic Airways Ltd
	G-VGEM	Airbus A.330-343	Virgin Atlantic Airways Ltd
	G-VGFS	Cameron Z-90 balloon	Western Commodities Ltd
	G-VGMC	Eurocopter AS.355N Ecureuil II	Cheshire Helicopters Ltd (G-HEMH)
	G-VGML	AS.350B3 Ecureuil	Starspeed Ltd
	G-VGVG	Savannah VG Jabiru(1)	M. A. Jones
	G-VICC	PA-28-161 Warrior II	Freedom Aviation Ltd (G-JFHL)
	G-VICM	Beech F33C Bonanza	Velocity Engineering Ltd
	G-VIIA	Boeing 777-236	British Airways
	G-VIIB	Boeing 777-236	British Airways
	G-VIIC	Boeing 777-236	British Airways
	G-VIID	Boeing 777-236	British Airways
	G-VIIE	Boeing 777-236	British Airways
	G-VIIF	Boeing 777-236	British Airways
	G-VIIG	Boeing 777-236	British Airways
	G-VIIH	Boeing 777-236	British Airways

Reg	Type	Owner or Operator	Notes
G-VIIJ	Boeing 777-236	British Airways	
G-VIIK	Boeing 777-236	British Airways	
G-VIIL	Boeing 777-236	British Airways	
G-VIIM	Boeing 777-236	British Airways	
G-VIIN	Boeing 777-236	British Airways	
G-VIIO	Boeing 777-236	British Airways	
G-VIIP	Boeing 777-236	British Airways	
G-VIIR	Boeing 777-236	British Airways	
G-VIIS	Boeing 777-236	British Airways	
G-VIIT	Boeing 777-236	British Airways	
G-VIIU	Boeing 777-236	British Airways	
G-VIIV	Boeing 777-236	British Airways	
G-VIIW	Boeing 777-236	British Airways	
G-VIIX	Boeing 777-236	British Airways	
G-VIIY	Boeing 777-236	British Airways	
G-VIIZ	CZAW Sportcruiser	Skyview Systems Ltd	
G-VIKE	Bellanca 1730A Viking	R. Waas	
G-VILL	Lazer Z.200 (modified)	S. A. Youngman (G-BOYZ)	
G-VINA	Aeroprakt A-22L Foxbat	J. M. Davidson	
G-VINB	Agusta AW.139	Babcock Mission Critical Services Offshore Ltd	
G-VINC	Agusta AW.139	Babcock Mission Critical Services Offshore Ltd	
G-VIND	Sikorsky S-92A	Babcock Mission Critical Services Offshore Ltd	
G-VINE	Airbus A.330-343	Virgin Atlantic Airways Ltd	
G-VINF	Sikorsky S-92A	Babcock Mission Critical Services Offshore Ltd	
G-VING	Sikorsky S-92A	Babcock Mission Critical Services Offshore Ltd	
G-VINI	Sikorsky S-92A	Babcock Mission Critical Services Offshore Ltd	
G-VINJ	Agusta AW.139	Babcock Mission Critical Services Offshore Ltd	
G-VINK	Sikorsky S-92A	Babcock Mission Critical Services Offshore Ltd	
G-VINL	Sikorsky S-92A	Babcock Mission Critical Services Offshore Ltd	
G-VINM	EC.225LP Super Puma	Babcock Mission Critical Services Offshore Ltd	
G-VINP	Sikorsky S-92A	Babcock Mission Critical Services Offshore Ltd	
G-VINR	Sikorsky S-92A	Vertical Aviation No.1 Ltd	
G-VINT	Sikorsky S-92A	Babcock Mission Critical Services Offshore Ltd	
G-VIPA	Cessna 182S	Stallingborough Aviation Ltd	
G-VIPH	Agusta A109C	Cheqair Ltd(G-BVNH/G-LAXO)	
G-VIPI	BAe 125 Srs 800B	Castle Air Services Ltd	
G-VIPR	Eurocopter EC 120B Colibri	EFL Helicopters Ltd	
G-VIPU	PA-31-350 Navajo Chieftain	Capital Air Ambulance Ltd	
G-VIPV	PA-31-350 Navajo Chieftain	Capital Air Ambulance Ltd	
G-VIPW	PA-31-350 Navajo Chieftain	Capital Air Ambulance Ltd	
G-VIPX	PA-31-350 Navajo Chieftain	Capital Air Ambulance Ltd	
G-VIPY	PA-31-350 Navajo Chieftain	Capital Air Ambulance Ltd	
G-VITE	Robin R.1180T	G-VITE Flying Group	
G-VITL	Lindstrand LBL-105A balloon	M. J. Axtell	
G-VIVA	Thunder Ax7-65 balloon	R. J. Mitchener	
G-VIVI	Taylor JT.2 Titch	P. J. Hebdon & C. S. Hales	
G-VIVM	P.84 Jet Provost T.5	Victor Mike Group (G-BVWF)	
G-VIVO	Nicollier HN700 Menestrel II	D. G. Tucker	
G-VIXN	DH.110 Sea Vixen FAW.2 (XS587) ★	P. G. Vallance Ltd/Charlwood	
G-VIXX	Alpi Pioneer 300	N. Harrison (G-CESE/G-CERJ)	
G-VIZZ	Sportavia RS.180 Sportsman	The Exeter Fournier Group	
G-VJET	Avro 698 Vulcan B.2 (XL426) ★	Vulcan Restoration Trust	
G-VKSS	Airbus A.330-343	Virgin Atlantic Airways Ltd *Mademoiselle Rouge*	
G-VKUP	Cameron Z-90 balloon	T. P. E. Y. Eyckerman	
G-VLCN	Avro 698 Vulcan B.2 (XH558) ★	Vulcan to the Sky Trust	
G-VLIP	Boeing 747-443	Virgin Atlantic Airways Ltd *Hot Lips*	
G-VLTT	Diamond DA.42 Twin Star	R. H. Butterfield	
G-VLUV	Airbus A.330-343	Virgin Atlantic Airways Ltd	
G-VMAP	Boeing 787-9	Virgin Atlantic Airways Ltd *West End Girl*	
G-VMCG	PA-38-112 Tomahawk	Pure Aviation Support Services Ltd (G-BSVX)	
G-VMIK	Airbus A.330-223	Virgin Atlantic Airways Ltd	
G-VMJM	SOCATA TB10 Tobago	D. J. Bryan (G-BTOK)	
G-VMNK	Airbus A.330-223	Virgin Atlantic Airways Ltd	
G-VMOZ	Van's RV-8	V. Millard (G-CIKP)	
G-VMSF	Robinson R22	Alcam International Ltd	
G-VMVM	Cessna Z-77 balloon	Virgin Balloon Flights	

Notes	Reg	Type	Owner or Operator
	G-VNAM	Cessna 305A Bird Dog	O-1 Aviation Ltd
	G-VNAP	Airbus A.340-642	Virgin Atlantic Airways Ltd
	G-VNEW	Boeing 787-9	Virgin Atlantic Airways Ltd
	G-VNOM	DH.112 Venom FB.50 (J-1632) ★	de Havilland Heritage Museum/London Colney
	G-VNON	Escapade Jabiru (5)	P. A. Vernon
	G-VNTS	Schempp-Hirth Ventus bT	911 Syndicatem
	G-VNYC	Airbus A.330-343	Virgin Atlantic Airways Ltd
	G-VOAR	PA-28-181 Archer III	Carlisle Flight Training Ltd
	G-VOCE	Robinson R22	J. J. Voce (G-BSCL)
	G-VODA	Cameron N-77 balloon	H. Cusden
	G-VOID	PA-28RT-201 Arrow IV	Doublecube Aviation LLP
	G-VOIP	Westland SA.341G Gazelle	E. K. Coventry
	G-VOLO	Alpi Pioneer 300	J. Buglass
	G-VONG	AS.355F1 Twin Squirrel	Hoban Ltd (G-OILX/G-RMGN/G-BMCY)
	G-VONK	AS.355F1 Squirrel	Airbourne Solutions Ltd (G-BLRI/G-NUTZ)
	G-VONS	PA-32R-301T Saratoga IITC	Vox Filemaker Solutions SRL/Romania
	G-VONY	Cessna T182T	W. S. Stanley
	G-VOOH	Boeing 787-9	Virgin Atlantic Airways Ltd
	G-VOOM	Pitts S-1S Special	VOOM Syndicate
	G-VORN	Aerotechnik EV-97 Eurostar	J. Parker (G-ODAV)
	G-VOUS	Cessna 172S	Flyglass Ltd
	G-VOWS	Boeing 787-9	Virgin Atlantic Airways Ltd *Maid Marion*
	G-VPAT	Evans VP-1 Srs 2	A. P. Twort
	G-VPCM	Dassault Falcon 2000LX	Executive Jet Charter Ltd
	G-VPPL	SOCATA TB20 Trinidad	J. M. Thorpe (G-BPAS)
	G-VPSJ	Shaw Europa	J. D. Bean
	G-VRAY	Airbus A.330-343	Virgin Atlantic Airways Ltd
	G-VRED	Airbus A.340-642	Virgin Atlantic Airways Ltd *Scarlet Lady*
	G-VROE	Avro 652A Anson T.21 (WD413)	G. G. L. James (G-BFIR)
	G-VROM	Boeing 747-443	Virgin Atlantic Airways Ltd
	G-VROS	Boeing 747-443	Virgin Atlantic Airways Ltd *English Rose*
	G-VROY	Boeing 747-443	Virgin Atlantic Airways Ltd *Pretty Woman*
	G-VRRV	Van's RV-12	J. F. Edmunds
	G-VRVB	Van's RV-8	R. J. Verrall (G-CETI)
	G-VRVI	Cameron O-90 balloon	Air Events BVBA/Belgium
	G-VSGE	Cameron O-105 balloon	P. M. Oggioni/Italy
	G-VSGG	Schempp-Hirth Ventus 2b	S. G. Gaunt
	G-VSKP	AgustaWestland AW169	Foxborough Ltd
	G-VSIX	Schempp-Hirth Ventus 2cT	V6 Group
	G-VSOZ	Yakovlev Yak-18T	N. R. Parsons & J. Dodd
	G-VSPY	Boeing 787-9	Virgin Atlantic Airways Ltd *Miss Moneypenny*
	G-VSTR	Stolp SA-900 V-Star	R. L. Hanreck
	G-VSXY	Airbus A.330-343	Virgin Atlantic Airways Ltd *Beauty Queen*
	G-VTAL	Beech V35 Bonanza	M. Elsey
	G-VTCT	Schempp-Hirth Ventus-2cT	V26 Syndicate
	G-VTEW	Schempp-Hirth Ventus-2a	O. M. McCormack
	G-VTGE	Bell 206L LongRanger	Vantage Helicopters Ltd (G-ELIT)
	G-VTII	DH.115 Vampire T.11 (XX507:74)	Vampire Preservation Group, Bournemouth
	G-VTOL	Hawker Siddeley Harrier T.52 ★	Brooklands Museum of Aviation/Weybridge
	G-VTUS	Schempp-Hirth Ventus 2cT	Ventus 02 Syndicate
	G-VTWO	Schempp-Hirth Ventus 2c	S. G. Jones
	G-VUFO	Airbus A.330-343	Virgin Atlantic Airways Ltd
	G-VULC	Avro 698 Vulcan B.2A (XM655) ★	Radarmoor Ltd/Wellesbourne
	G-VVBA	AS.355F2 Ecureuil II	Hudson Aviation Ltd (G-DBOK)
	G-VVBE	Robinson R22 Beta	Heli Air Ltd (G-OTOY/G-BPEW)
	G-VVBF	Colt 315A balloon	Virgin Balloon Flights
	G-VVBH	Guimbal Cabri G2	S. D. Evans
	G-VVBL	Robinson R44 II	Phoenix Helicopter Academy Ltd
	G-VVBO	Bell 206L-3 LongRanger III	Hudson Aviation Ltd
	G-VVBR	Robinson R22	A & M Helicopters Ltd (G-SIMS)
	G-VVBZ	Guimbal Cabri G2	Hudson Aviation Ltd
	G-VVIP	Cessna 421C	Cranfield Aerospace Solutions Ltd (G-BMWB)
	G-VVTV	Diamond DA42 Twin Star	A. D. R. Northeast

Reg	Type	Owner or Operator	Notes
G-VVVV	Skyranger 912 (2)	J. Thomas	
G-VWWW	Enstrom 280C Shark	P. J. Odendaal	
G-VWAG	Airbus A.330-343	Virgin Atlantic Airways Ltd	
G-VWEB	Airbus A.340-642	Virgin Atlantic Airways Ltd *Surfer Girl*	
G-VWET	Lake LA-4-200 Buccaneer	Belgian Seaplane Aeroclub/Belgium	
G-VWHO	Boeing 787-9	Virgin Atlantic Airways Ltd	
G-VWIN	Airbus A.340-642	Virgin Atlantic Airways Ltd *Lady Luck*	
G-VWND	Airbus A.330-223	Virgin Atlantic Airways Ltd	
G-VWOO	Boeing 787-9	Virgin Atlantic Airways Ltd *Leading Lady*	
G-VXLG	Boeing 747-41R	Virgin Atlantic Airways Ltd *Ruby Tuesday*	
G-VYAK	Yakovlev Yak-18T	A. I. McRobbie	
G-VYGJ	Airbus A.330-243	Air Tanker Ltd	
G-VYGK	Airbus A.330-243	Air Tanker Ltd	
G-VYGL	Airbus A.330-243	Air Tanker Ltd	
G-VYGM	Airbus A.330-243	Air Tanker Ltd	
G-VYOU	Airbus A.340-642	Virgin Atlantic Airways Ltd *Emmeline Heaney born August 2006*	
G-VYUM	Boeing 787-9	Virgin Atlantic Airways Ltd	
G-VZIG	Boeing 787-9	Virgin Atlantic Airways Ltd	
G-VZIM	Alpha R2160	I. M. Hollingsworth	
G-VZON	ATR-72-212A	Aurigny Air Services Ltd	
G-VZSF	Hawker Sea Fury T.Mk.20	Patina Ltd	
G-WAAS	MBB Bö.105DBS-4	South Georgia Heritage Trust (G-ESAM/ G-BUIB/G-BDYZ)	
G-WACB	Cessna F.152 II	Airways Aero Associations Ltd	
G-WACE	Cessna F.152 II	Airways Aero Associations Ltd	
G-WACF	Cessna 152 II	Airways Aero Associations Ltd	
G-WACG	Cessna 152 II	Airways Aero Associations Ltd	
G-WACH	Cessna FA.152 II	Airways Aero Associations Ltd	
G-WACU	Cessna FA.152	Airways Aero Associations Ltd (G-BJZU)	
G-WACW	Cessna 172P	Civil Service Flying Club (Biggin Hill) Ltd	
G-WACY	Cessna F.172P	The Vintage Wings Aviation Co.Ltd	
G-WADD	Airbus Helicopters EC120B Colibri	GGR Group Ltd	
G-WADF	Tanarg/Bionix 13 912S(2)	W. O. Fogden	
G-WADS	Robinson R22 Beta	Whizzard Helicopters (G-NICO)	
G-WADZ	Lindstrand LBL-90A balloon	A. K. C., J. E. H., M. H. & Y. K. Wadsworth (G-CGVN)	
G-WAGA	Wag-Aero Wagabond	A. I. Sutherland (G-BNJA)	
G-WAGG	Robinson R22 Beta II	Aztec Aviators Ltd	
G-WAGN	Stinson 108-3 Voyager	S. E. H. Ellcome	
G-WAHL	QAC Quickie	M. P. Wimsey	
G-WAIR	PA-32-301 Saratoga	Finningley Aviation	
G-WAIT	Cameron V-77 balloon	C. P. Brown	
G-WAKE	Mainair Blade 912	G. J. Molloy	
G-WAKY	Cyclone AX2000	E. E. & R. J. Hunt	
G-WALI	Robinson R44 II	G. Reidy	
G-WALY	Maule MX-7-180	J. R. Colthurst	
G-WALZ	Best Off Sky Ranger Nynja 912S(1)	R. J. Thomas	
G-WAMS	PA-28R-201 Arrow	Stapleford Flying Club Ltd	
G-WANA	P & M Quik	A. Lord	
G-WAPA	Robinson R44 II	Aerocorp Ltd	
G-WARA	PA-28-161 Warrior III	KN Singles & Twins Aviation Consultants BV/Netherlands	
G-WARB	PA-28-161 Warrior III	OSF Ltd	
G-WARD	Taylor JT.1 Monoplane	R. P. J. Hunter	
G-WARE	PA-28-161 Warrior II	I. D. Wakeling	
G-WARH	PA-28-161 Warrior II	KN Singles & Twins Aviation Consultants BV	
G-WARO	PA-28-161 Warrior III	T. G. D. Leasing Ltd	
G-WARP	Cessna 182F Sylane	R. D. Fowden (G-ASHB)	
G-WARR	PA-28-161 Warrior II	R. N. Brown	
G-WARS	PA-28-161 Warrior III	London School of Flying Ltd	
G-WARU	PA-28-161 Warrior III	Smart People Don't Buy Ltd	
G-WARV	PA-28-161 Warrior III	Bickertons Aerodromes Ltd	
G-WARW	PA-28-161 Warrior III	J. G. McVey & P. Lodge	
G-WARX	PA-28-161 Warrior III	White Waltham Airfield Ltd	
G-WARY	PA-28-161 Warrior III	Target Aviation Ltd	

303

Notes	Reg	Type	Owner or Operator
	G-WARZ	PA-28-161 Warrior III	Target Aviation Ltd
	G-WASC	Eurocopter EC.135 T2+	Babcock Mission Critical Services Onshore Ltd
	G-WASS	Eurocopter EC.135 T2+	Babcock Mission Critical Services Onshore Ltd
	G-WATR	Christen A1 Husky	Clipper Aviation Ltd
	G-WAVA	Robin HR.200/120B	Carlisle Flight Training Ltd
	G-WAVE	Grob G.109B	C. G. Wray
	G-WAVS	PA-28-161 Warrior III	TGD Leasing Ltd (G-WARC)
	G-WAVV	Robon HR200/120B	Carlisle Flight Training Ltd (G-GORF)
	G-WAVY	Grob G.109B	G-WAVY Group
	G-WAWW	P & M Quik GT450	O. P. Gall
	G-WAYS	Lindstrand LBL-105A balloon	D. B. Green
	G-WAZP	Skyranger 912 (2)	M. Gilson & P. C. Terry
	G-WBEV	Cameron N-77 balloon	T. J. & M. Turner (G-PVCU)
	G-WBLY	Mainair Pegasus Quik	A. J. Lindsey
	G-WBRD	Avro Curtiss 1911 Replica	Cooper Aerial Surveys Engineering Ltd & The Lakes Flying Company Ltd
	G-WBTS	Falconar F-11	M. K. Field (G-BDPL)
	G-WBVS	Diamond DA.4D Star	G. W. Beavis
	G-WCAT	Colt Flying Mitt SS balloon	I. Chadwick
	G-WCCP	Beech B200 Super King Air	GCP Aviation Ltd
	G-WCKM	Best Off Sky Ranger 912(1)	D. R. Hardy
	G-WCME	Grumman FM-2 Wildcat	Wildcat WP Ltd
	G-WCMI	Grumman FM-2 Wildcat	Wildcat WP Ltd
	G-WCMO	Grumman FM-2 Wildcat	Wildcat WP Ltd
	G-WCUB	PA-18 Super Cub 150	P. A. Walley
	G-WDCL	Agusta A.109E Power	Wickford Development Company Ltd (G-WELY)
	G-WDEB	Thunder Ax-7-77 balloon	A. Heginbottom
	G-WDGC	Rolladen-Schneider LS8-18	W. D. G. Chappel (G-CEWJ)
	G-WEAT	Robinson R44 II	R. F. Brook
	G-WEBY	Ace Magic Cyclone	B. W. Webster
	G-WEBS	American Champion 7ECA Citabria	Flugsportclub Odenwald
	G-WECG	AS.355NP Ecureuil 2	WEC Group Ltd (G-MXCO)
	G-WEEK	Skyranger 912(2)	D. J. Prothero
	G-WEFR	Alpi Pioneer 200-M	S. G. Llewelyn
	G-WEND	PA-28RT-201 Arrow IV	Tayside Aviation Ltd
	G-WENN	Hoffmann H-36 Dimona	L. Ingram & N. Clarke
	G-WENU	Airbus Helicopters MBB-BK117 D-2	Babcock Mission Critical Services Onshore Ltd
	G-WERY	SOCATA TB20 Trinidad	R-Aviation SARL/France
	G-WESX	CFM Streak Shadow	M. Catania
	G-WETI	Cameron N-31 balloon	C. A. Butter & J. J. T. Cooke
	G-WEWI	Cessna 172	T. J. Wassell (G-BSEP)
	G-WEZZ	Taylor JT.1 Monoplane	W. A. Tierney (G-BDRF)
	G-WFFW	PA-28-161 Warrior II	S. Letheren & D. Jelly
	G-WFLY	Mainair Pegasus Quik	S. Turton
	G-WFWA	PA-28-161 Cherokee Warrior II	Wings for Warriors (G-BPMR)
	G-WFWS	Robinson R22	Wings for Warriors (G-LINS/G-DMCD/G-OOLI)
	G-WGCS	PA-18 Super Cub 95	S. C. Thompson
	G-WGSI	Tanarg/Ixess 13 912S(1)	M. Nazm
	G-WHAT	Colt 77A balloon	M. A. Scholes
	G-WHEE	Pegasus Quantum 15-912	Airways Airsports Ltd
	G-WHEN	Tecnam P92-EM Echo	F. G. Walker
	G-WHIL	Balony Kubicek BB-S Cup SS balloon	A. M. Holly
	G-WHIM	Colt 77A balloon	D. L. Morgan
	G-WHOG	CFM Streak Shadow	B. R. Cannell
	G-WHOO	Rotorway Executive 162F	J. White
	G-WHPG	Ikarus C42 FB80	T. Penn & C. P. Roche
	G-WHRL	Schweizer 269C	P. A. Adams & T. S. Davies
	G-WHST	AS.350B2 Ecureuil	Cheshire Helicopters Ltd (G-BWYA)
	G-WHYS	ICP MXP-740 Savannah VG Jabiru(1)	R. W. Swift

Reg	Type	Owner or Operator	Notes
G-WIBB	Jodel D.18	C. J. Bragg	
G-WIBS	CASA 1-131E Jungmann 2000	C. Willoughby	
G-WICH	Clutton FRED Srs II	D. R. G. Griffith	
G-WIFE	Cessna R.182 RG II	Wife 182 Group (G-BGVT)	
G-WIFI	Cameron Z-90 balloon	A. R. Rich	
G-WIGS	Yeoman Dynamic WT9 UK	A. Wiggins (G-DYMC)	
G-WIGY	Pitts S-1S Special	R. E. Welch (G-ITTI)	
G-WIII	Schempp-Hirth Ventus bT	I. G. Carrick	
G-WIIZ	Augusta-Bell 206B JetRanger 2	Bradawl Ltd	
G-WIKD	Van's RV-8	E. P. Morrow	
G-WIKI	Europa XS	A. H. Smith & S. P. Kirton	
G-WILB	Ultramagic M-105 balloon	Nottingham & Derby Hot Air Balloon Club	
G-WILD	Pitts S-1T Special	S. L. Goldspink	
G-WILG	PZL-104 Wilga 35	M. H. Bletsoe-Brown (G-AZYJ)	
G-WILN	Tecnam P2006T	W Flight Hire Ltd	
G-WILT	Ikarus C42 FB80	V. J. P. R. Denecker	
G-WIMP	Colt 56A balloon	D. M. Wade	
G-WINE	Thunder Ax7-77Z balloon ★	Balloon Preservation Group/Lancing	
G-WINH	EV-97 TeamEurostar UK	J. A. Warters	
G-WINI	SA Bulldog Srs.120/121 (XX546:03)	A. Bole (G-CBCO)	
G-WINK	AA-5B Tiger	B. St. J. Cooke	
G-WINN	Stolp SA.300 Starduster Too	H. Feeney	
G-WINO	Aeropro Eurofox 912S(1)	M. A. J. Spiers	
G-WINR	Robinson R22	Heli Air Ltd (G-BTHG)	
G-WINS	PA-32 Cherokee Six 300	Cheyenne Ltd	
G-WINX	Tecnam P2010	CR Flight Hire Ltd	
G-WINZ	Lindstrand LTL Penguin balloon	A. M. Holly	
G-WIRG	Embraer EMB-135BJ Legacy 650	Air Charter Scotland Ltd	
G-WIRL	Robinson R22 Beta	Rivermead Aviation Ltd/Switzerland	
G-WISZ	Steen Skybolt	G. S. Reid	
G-WIXI	Avions Mudry CAP-10B	A. R. Harris	
G-WIZG	Agusta A.109E Power	Tycoon Aviation Ltd (G-TYCN/G-VMCO)	
G-WIZI	Enstrom 280FX	Cloud Telematics LLP	
G-WIZR	Robinson R22 Beta II	Helimech Ltd	
G-WIZS	Mainair Pegasus Quik	Oban Air Sports	
G-WIZZ	Agusta-Bell 206B JetRanger 2	Rivermead Aviation Ltd	
G-WJAC	Cameron TR-70 balloon	S. J. & J. A. Bellaby	
G-WJCM	CASA 1.131E Jungmann 2000 (S5+B06)	G. W. Lynch (G-BSFB)	
G-WJET	HpH Glasflugel 304 S Shark	P. Thomson	
G-WJSG	P & M Quik GT450	W. J. Hardy	
G-WKNS	Shaw Europa XS	A. L. Wickens	
G-WLAC	PA-18 Super Cub 150	White Waltham Airfield Ltd (G-HAHA/G-BSWE)	
G-WLDN	Robinson R44 Raven	M. R. J. Pearson	
G-WLGC	PA-28-181 Archer III	E. F. Mangion (G-FLUX)	
G-WLKI	Lindstrand LBL-105A balloon	C. Wilkinson	
G-WLKS	Schleicher ASW-20L	S. E. Wilks (G-IUMB)	
G-WLLS	Rolladen-Schneider LS8-18	L & A Wells	
G-WLMS	Mainair Blade 912	G. Zerrun	
G-WLSN	Best Off Skyranger 912S (1)	A. R. Wilson	
G-WLTS	Bell 429	Helicharter Ltd	
G-WLVE	Cameron Buddy-90 SS balloon	C. J. Freeman & A. E. Austin	
G-WMBL	P & M Quik R	W M Buchanan Ltd	
G-WMRN	SOCATA TBM-900	Ravenair	
G-WMTM	AA-5B Tiger	G. R. Balls	
G-WNCH	Beech B200 Super King Air	Synergy Aircraft Leasing Ltd (G-OMGI)	
G-WNSC	Eurocopter AS.332L2 Super Puma	Airbus Helicopters Ltd	
G-WNSD	Sikorsky S-92A	CHC Scotia Ltd	
G-WNSE	Sikorsky S-92A	CHC Scotia Ltd	
G-WNSF	Sikorsky S-92A	CHC Scotia Ltd	
G-WNSG	Sikorsky S-92A	CHC Scotia Ltd	
G-WNSI	Sikorsky S-92A	CHC Scotia Ltd	
G-WNSJ	Sikorsky S-92A	CHC Scotia Ltd	
G-WNSL	Sikorsky S-92A	CHC Scotia Ltd	
G-WNSM	Sikorsky S-92A	CHC Scotia Ltd	
G-WNSN	Eurocopter EC.225LP Super Puma	Lombard North Central PLC	

Notes	Reg	Type	Owner or Operator
	G-WNSO	Eurocopter EC.225LP Super Puma	Wilmington Trust SP Services (Dublin) Ltd (G-PNEO)
	G-WNSP	Eurocopter EC.225LP Super Puma	Lombard North Central PLC
	G-WNSR	Sikorsky S-92A	CHC Scotia Ltd
	G-WNST	Sikorsky S-92A	CHC Scotia Ltd
	G-WNSU	Sikorsky S-92A	CHC Scotia Ltd
	G-WNSV	Sikorsky S-92A	CHC Scotia Ltd
	G-WNSW	Sikorsky S-92A	CHC Scotia Ltd
	G-WNTR	PA-28-161 Warrior II	Fleetlands Flying Group (G-BFNJ)
	G-WOFM	Agusta A109E Power	Quinnasette Ltd (G-NWRR)
	G-WOLF	PA-28 Cherokee 140	G-WOLF Group
	G-WONE	Schempp-Hirth Ventus 2cT	J. P. Wright
	G-WOOD	Beech 95-B55A Baron	M. S. Choskey (G-AYID)
	G-WOOF	Enstrom 480	Netcopter.co.uk Ltd & Curvature Ltd
	G-WOOL	Colt 77A balloon	T. D. Gibbs
	G-WOOO	CZAW Sportcruiser	J. J. Nicholson
	G-WORM	Thruster T.600N	WORM Group
	G-WOTW	Ultramagic M-77 balloon	Window on the World Ltd
	G-WOWI	Van's RV-7	P. J. Wood
	G-WPDA	Eurocopter EC135 P1	WPD Helicopter Unit
	G-WPDB	Eurocopter EC135 P1	WPD Helicopter Unit
	G-WPDC	Eurocopter EC135 P1	WPD Helicopter Unit
	G-WPDD	Eurocopter EC135 P1	WPD Helicopter Unit
	G-WPDE	Eurocopter EC135P2+	WPD Helicopter Unit
	G-WPKR	Enstrom 280FX Shark	N. Ker (G-WPIE/G-RCAR/G-BXRD)
	G-WPNS	BN-2T-4S Defender 4000	Britten-Norman Ltd (G-GMPB/G-BWPU)
	G-WREN	Pitts S-2A Special	W. Ali
	G-WRFM	Enstrom 280C-UK Shark	A. J. Clark (G-CTSI/G-BKIO)
	G-WRIT	Thunder Ax7-77A balloon	G. Pusey
	G-WRLY	Robinson R22 Beta	Burman Aviation Ltd (G-OFJS/G-BNXJ)
	G-WROL	MBB-BK 117 D-2	Babcock Mission Critical Services Onshore Ltd (G-OLWG)
	G-WSKY	Enstrom 280C-UK-2 Shark	B. J. Rutterford (G-BEEK)
	G-WSMW	Robinson R44	M. Wass (G-SGPL)
	G-WSSX	Ikarus C42 FB100	J. M. Crane
	G-WSTY	Lindstrand LBL-77A balloon	C. & C. Westwood
	G-WTAV	Robinson R44 II	T. Levitan
	G-WTAY	Robinson R44 II	William Taylor Aviation Ltd
	G-WTFH	Van's RV-6	N. M. R. Richards
	G-WTSN	Van's RV-8	S. R. Watson
	G-WTWO	Aquila AT01	J. P. Wright
	G-WUFF	Shaw Europa	W. H. Bliss
	G-WULF	Replica WAR Focke-Wulf 190	B. Hunter
	G-WVBF	Lindstrand LBL-210A balloon	Virgin Balloon Flights Ltd
	G-WVEN	Extra EA300/200	R. J. Hunter
	G-WVIP	Beech B.200 Super King Air	Capital Air Ambulance Ltd
	G-WWAL	PA-28R Cherokee Arrow 180	White Waltham Airfield Ltd (G-AZSH)
	G-WWAY	Piper PA-28-181 Archer II	R. A. Witchell
	G-WWLF	Extra EA.300/L	P. Sapignoli
	G-WWZZ	CZAW Sportcruiser	L. Hogan
	G-WXYZ	Zenair CH.750	P. W. Porter
	G-WYAT	CFM Streak Shadow Srs SA	J. L. Wolstenholme
	G-WYDE	Schleicher ASW-20BL	461 Syndicate
	G-WYKD	Tanarg/Ixess 15 912S(2)	J. L. V. Lowry-Corry
	G-WYLD	Cessna T.210N Turbo Centurion II	R. M. de Roeck (G-EEWS)
	G-WYMM	PA-15 Vagabond	N. G. Busschau (G-AWOF)
	G-WYND	Wittman W.8 Tailwind	R. S. Marriott
	G-WYNT	Cameron N-56 balloon	P. Richardson
	G-WYSZ	Robin DR.400/100	Exavia Ltd (G-FTIM)
	G-WYVN	DG Flugzeugbau DG-1000S	Army Gliding Association

Reg	Type	Owner or Operator	Notes
G-WZAP	Embraer EMB-505 Phenom 300	Hagondale Ltd/Titan Airways	
G-WZOL	RL.5B LWS Sherwood Ranger	D. Lentell (G-MZOL)	
G-WZOY	Rans S.6-ESA Coyote II	M. J. Laundy	
G-WZRD	Eurocopter EC 120B Colibri	Conductia Enterprises Ltd	
G-XAIM	Ultramagic H-31 balloon	G. Everett	
G-XALT	PA-38-112 Tomahawk	D. R. Clyde	
G-XALZ	Rans S6S-116 Super Six	D. G. I. Wheldon	
G-XARA	Czech Sport PS-28 Cruiser	Andrew English PS-28 Group	
G-XARV	ARV Super 2	C. M. Rose (G-OPIG/G-BMSJ)	
G-XASH	Schleicher ASH-31 MI	R. C. Wilson	
G-XAVB	Cessna 510 Citation Mustang	Aviation Beauport	
G-XAVI	PA-28-161 Warrior II	Freedom Aviation Ltd (G-SACZ)	
G-XAVV	Schempp-Hirth Ventus 2c	R. G. Corbin & S. E. Buckley	
G-XBAL	Skyringer Nynja 912S(1)	W. G. Gill & N. D. Ewer	
G-XBGA	Glaser-Dirks DG500/22 Elan	N. Kelly	
G-XBJT	Aerotechnik EV-97 Eurostar	C. J. & J. A. Aldous (G-WHOA/G-DATH)	
G-XBLD	MBB Bo.105DB	PLM Dollar Group Ltd	
G-XBOX	Bell 206B JetRanger 3	Castle Air Ltd (G-OOHO/G-OCHC/G-KLEE/ G-SIZL/G-BOSW)	
G-XCCC	Extra EA.300/L	P. T. Fellows	
G-XCID	SAAB 91D Safir	J. T. Hunter	
G-XCIT	Alpi Pioneer 300	A. Thomas	
G-XCRI	Coloman MC-15 Cri-Cri	P. A. Harvie	
G-XCRJ	Van's RV-9A	Romeo Juliet Group	
G-XCUB	PA-18 Super Cub 150	White Waltham Airfield Ltd	
G-XDEA	Diamond DA.42 Twin Star	J. M. Pirrie	
G-XDUO	Schempp-Hirth Duo Discus xT	G-XDUO Group	
G-XDWE	P & M Quik GT450	G. J. Prisk	
G-XELL	Schleicher ASW-27-18E	S. R. Ell	
G-XENA	PA-28-161 Warrior II	P. Brewer	
G-XERK	Van's RV-7	C. A. Morris	
G-XERO	CZAW Sportcruiser	M. R. Mosley	
G-XFLY	Lambert Mission M212-100	Lambert Aircraft Engineering BVBA	
G-XFOX	Aeropro Eurofox 912(S)	Fox Five Group	
G-XFTF	BRM Aero Bristell NG5	R. O'Donnell	
G-XHOT	Cameron Z-105 balloon	S. F. Burden	
G-XIFR	Lambert Mission M108	Lambert Aircraft Engineering BVBA	
G-XIII	Van's RV-7	Icarus Flying Group	
G-XIIX	Robinson R22 Beta ★	(Static exhibit)/Blackbushe	
G-XILM	TL-3000 Sirius	Orbis Management Ltd	
G-XINE	PA-28-161 Warrior II	P. Tee (G-BPAC)	
G-XION	Dassault Falcon 8X	Execujet (UK) Ltd	
G-XIOO	Raj Hamsa X'Air 133 (1)	G. M. R. Keenan	
G-XIXI	Evektor EV-97 TeamEurostar UK	J. A. C. Cockfield	
G-XIXT	AB Sportine LAK-19T	P. R. Thomas & W. M. Kay	
G-XIXX	Glaser-Dirks DG-300 Elan	S. D. Black	
G-XJCI	Cessna 550 Citation Bravo	XJC Ltd	
G-XJCJ	Cessna 550 Citation Bravo	XJC Ltd	
G-XJET	Learjet 45	Patriot Aviation Ltd (G-IZAP/G-OLDK)	
G-XJON	Schempp-Hirth Ventus 2b	J. C. Bastin	
G-XKKA	Diamond KH36 Super Dimona	G-XKKA Group	
G-XKRV	Best Off Skyranger Nynja LS 912S(1)	A. V. Francis	
G-XLAM	Best Off Skyranger 912S	X-LAM Skyranger Syndicate	
G-XLEA	Airbus A.380-841	British Airways	
G-XLEB	Airbus A.380-841	British Airways	
G-XLEC	Airbus A.380-841	British Airways	
G-XLED	Airbus A.380-841	British Airways	
G-XLEE	Airbus A.380-841	British Airways	
G-XLEF	Airbus A.380-841	British Airways	
G-XLEG	Airbus A.380-841	British Airways	

Notes	Reg	Type	Owner or Operator
	G-XLEH	Airbus A.380-841	British Airways
	G-XLEI	Airbus A.380-841	British Airways
	G-XLEJ	Airbus A.380-841	British Airways
	G-XLEK	Airbus A.380-841	British Airways
	G-XLEL	Airbus A.380-841	British Airways
	G-XLII	Schleicher ASW-27-18E	P. M. Wells
	G-XLLL	AS.355F1 Twin Squirrel	MW Helicopters Ltd (G-PASF/G-SCHU)
	G-XLNT	Zenair CH.601XL	Zenair G-XLNT Group
	G-XLTG	Cessna 182S	The G-XLTG Flying Group
	G-XLXL	Robin DR.400/160	L. R. Marchant (G-BAUD)
	G-XMGO	Aeromot AMT-200S Super Ximango	G. McLean & R. P. Beck
	G-XONE	Canadair CL600-2B16	Gama Aviation (UK) Ltd
	G-XPBI	Letov LK-2M Sluka	R. M. C. Hunter
	G-XPDA	Cameron Z-120 balloon	M. Cowling
	G-XPII	Cessna R.172K	The Crew Flying Group (G-DIVA)
	G-XPTV	Embraer EMB-135BJ Legacy 600	Arena Aviation Ltd
	G-XPWW	Cameron TR-77 balloon	Chalmers Ballong Corps/Sweden
	G-XPXP	Aero Designs Pulsar XP	B. J. Edwards
	G-XRAF	Raj Hamsa X'Air 582(5)	D. Brunton
	G-XRAY	Rand-Robinson KR-2	R. S. Smith
	G-XRED	Pitts S-1C Special	J. E. Rands (G-SWUN/G-BSXH)
	G-XRLD	Cameron A-250 balloon	Aeolus Aviation GmbH/Germany
	G-XRVB	Van's RV-8	R. E. Kelly
	G-XRVX	Van's RV-10	N. K. Lamping
	G-XRXR	Raj Hamsa X'Air 582 (1)	J. E. Merriman
	G-XSAM	Van's RV-9A	Parachuting Aircraft Ltd
	G-XSDJ	Europa XS	D. N. Joyce
	G-XSEA	Van's RV-8	H. M. Darlington
	G-XSEL	Silence Twister	Skyview Systems Ltd
	G-XSRF	Europa XS	R. L. W. Frank
	G-XSTV	Cessna 560XL Citation XLS	Arena Aviation Ltd
	G-XTAZ	Van's RV-7	G-XTAZ Group
	G-XTEE	Edge XT912-B/Streak III	Shropshire Bush Pilots
	G-XTNI	AirBorne XT912-B/Streak	A. J. Parry
	G-XTRA	Extra EA.230	C. Butler
	G-XTUN	Westland-Bell 47G-3B1 (XT223)	P. A. Rogers (G-BGZK)
	G-XVAX	Tecnam P2006T	D. J. Lee & M. A. Baldwin
	G-XVII	Schleicher ASW-17	C. A. & S. C. Noujaim (G-DCTE)
	G-XVIP	Beech 200 Super King Air	Patriot Aviation Ltd (G-OCEG)
	G-XVOM	Van's RV-6	A. Baker-Munton
	G-XWEB	Best Off Skyranger 912 (2)	A. P. Dalgetty & M. Chambers
	G-XWON	Rolladen-Schneider LS8-18	G-XWON Syndicate
	G-XXBH	Agusta-Bell 206B JetRanger 3	Temchu Ltd (G-BYBA/G-BHXV/G-OWJM)
	G-XXEB	Sikorsky S-76C	The Queen's Helicopter Flight
	G-XXEC	Agusta A.109S Grand	A. Reid, Keeper of the Privy Purse
	G-XXHP	Extra EA.300/L	H. Poulson (G-BZFR)
	G-XXIV	Agusta-Bell 206B JetRanger 3	Castle Air Ltd
	G-XXIX	Schleicher ASW-27-18E	P. R. & A. H. Pentecost
	G-XXRS	Bombardier BD-700 Global Express	TAG Aviation (UK) Ltd
	G-XXRV	Van's RV-9	D. R. Gilbert & D. Slabbert
	G-XXTB	SOCATA TB20 Trinidad	N. Schaefer (G-KPTT)
	G-XXTR	Extra EA.300/L	The Shoreham Extra Group (G-ECCC)
	G-XXVB	Schempp-Hirth Ventus b	R. Johnson
	G-XYJY	Best Off Skyranger 912(1)	A. V. Francis
	G-XYZT	Aeromot AMT-200S Super Ximango	Betav BV/Netherlands
	G-XZXZ	Robinson R44 II	Ashley Martin Ltd
	G-YAAC	Airbus Helicopters MBB-BK117 D-2	Yorkshire Air Ambulance Ltd
	G-YAAK	Yakovlev Yak-50 (20)	D. J. Hopkinson (G-BWJT)
	G-YADA	Ikarus C42 FB100	Ikarus Flying Syndicate

Reg	Type	Owner or Operator	Notes
G-YAKC	Yakovlev Yak-52	Airborne Services Ltd	
G-YAKE	Yakovlev Yak-52	D. J. Hopkinson (G-BVVA)	
G-YAKF	Aerostar Yakovlev Yak-52	Yak-Attack Ltd	
G-YAKG	Yakovlev Yak-18T	M. P. Blokland	
G-YAKH	IDA Bacau Yakovlev Yak-52	Plus 7 minus 5 Ltd	
G-YAKI	IDA Bacau Yakovlev Yak-52 (100 blue)	Yak One Ltd	
G-YAKJ	Yakovlev Yak-18T	Teshka Aviation Syndicate	
G-YAKM	IDA Bacau Yakovlev Yak-50 (61 red)	Airborne Services Ltd	
G-YAKN	IDA Bacau Yakovlev Yak-52 (66 red)	Airborne Services Ltd	
G-YAKP	Yakovlev Yak-9	M. V. Rijkse & N. M. R. Richards	
G-YAKU	IDA Bacau Yakovlev Yak-50 (49 red)	D. J. Hopkinson (G-BXND)	
G-YAKX	IDA Bacau Yakovlev Yak-52 (27 red)	The X-Flyers Ltd	
G-YAKY	Aerostar Yakovlev Yak-52	W. T. Marriott	
G-YAKZ	IDA Bacau Yakovlev Yak-50 (33 red)	Airborne Services Ltd	
G-YANK	PA-28-181 Archer II	G-YANK Flying Group	
G-YARD	Robinson R44 II	Caffco Ltd	
G-YARR	Mainair Rapier	D. Yarr	
G-YARV	ARV Super 2	A. M. Oliver (G-BMDO)	
G-YAWW	PA-28RT-201T Turbo Arrow IV	Barton Aviation Ltd	
G-YBAA	Cessna FR.172J	G-YBAA Flying Group	
G-YCKF	Dassault Falcon 900EX	Concierge U Ltd	
G-YCMI	Sonex	D. R. D. H. Mobbs	
G-YCUB	PA-18 Super Cub 150	F. W. Rogers	
G-YDEA	DA-42 Twin Star	Diamond Executive Aviation Ltd	
G-YEDC	Cessna 525B Citationjet CJ3	Air Charter Scotland Ltd	
G-YEHA	Schleicher ASW-27	B. L. Cooper	
G-YELL	Murphy Rebel	A. H. Godfrey	
G-YELP	RL5A Sherwood Ranger ST	C. Blount	
G-YEOM	PA-31-350 Navajo Chieftain	Oxcis Aviation Ltd	
G-YETI	Europa	C. G. Sutton (G-CILF)	
G-YEWS	Rotorway Executive 152	R. Turrell & P. Mason	
G-YFOX	Dassault Falcon 2000EX	London Executive Aviation Ltd	
G-YIPI	Cessan FR.172K	J. Francis & M. T. Hodgson	
G-YIRO	Campbell Cricket Mk.4	R. Boese (G-KGED)	
G-YJET	Montgomerie-Bensen B.8MR	P. D. Davis-Ratcliffe (G-BMUH)	
G-YKSO	Yakovlev Yak-50 (23)	A. M. Holman-West	
G-YKSS	Yakovlev Yak-55	T. Ollivier	
G-YKSZ	Aerostar Yakovlev Yak-52 (01 yellow)	M. Stavjarsky	
G-YMFC	Waco YMF	S. J. Brenchley	
G-YMKH	Embraer EMB-135BJ Legacy 650	TAG Aviation (UK) Ltd	
G-YMMA	Boeing 777-236ER	British Airways	
G-YMMB	Boeing 777-236ER	British Airways	
G-YMMC	Boeing 777-236ER	British Airways	
G-YMMD	Boeing 777-236ER	British Airways	
G-YMME	Boeing 777-236ER	British Airways	
G-YMMF	Boeing 777-236ER	British Airways	
G-YMMG	Boeing 777-236ER	British Airways	
G-YMMH	Boeing 777-236ER	British Airways	
G-YMMI	Boeing 777-236ER	British Airways	
G-YMMJ	Boeing 777-236ER	British Airways	
G-YMMK	Boeing 777-236ER	British Airways	
G-YMML	Boeing 777-236ER	British Airways	
G-YMMN	Boeing 777-236ER	British Airways	
G-YMMO	Boeing 777-236ER	British Airways	
G-YMMP	Boeing 777-236ER	British Airways	
G-YMMR	Boeing 777-236ER	British Airways	
G-YMMS	Boeing 777-236ER	British Airways	
G-YMMT	Boeing 777-236ER	British Airways	
G-YMMU	Boeing 777-236ER	British Airways	
G-YNOT	D.62B Condor	T. Littlefair (G-AYFH)	
G-YNYS	Cessna 172S Skyhawk	T. V. Hughes	

Notes	Reg	Type	Owner or Operator
	G-YOAA	Airbus Helicopters MBB BK117 D-2	Yorkshire Air Ambulance Ltd
	G-YOBI	Schleicher ASH-25	J. Kangurs
	G-YODA	Schempp-Hirth Ventus 2cT	J. W. M. Gijrath
	G-YOGI	Robin DR.400/140B	G-YOGI Flying Group (G-BDME)
	G-YOLK	P & M Aviation Quik GT450	G. J. Wright
	G-YOLO	Aeroprakt A22-L2 Foxbat	J. W. Mann
	G-YORC	Cirrus SR-22	A. P. Von Croy
	G-YORK	Cessna F.172M	EIMH-Flying Group
	G-YOTS	IDA Bacau Yakovlev Yak-52	G-YOTS Group
	G-YOYO	Pitts S-1E Special	P. M. Jarvis (G-OTSW/G-BLHE)
	G-YPDN	Rotorsport UK MT-03	T. M. Jones
	G-YPOL	MDH MD-900 Explorer	Specialist Aviation Services Ltd
	G-YPSY	Andreasson BA-4B	J. P. Burrill
	G-YRAF	RAF 2000 GTX-SE gyroplane	J. R. Cooper
	G-YRAX	Magni M-24C	R. Whiteley
	G-YRIL	Luscombe 8E Silvaire	C. Potter
	G-YROA	Rotorsport UK MTO Sport	S. Smith
	G-YROC	Rotorsport UK MT-03	C. V. Catherall
	G-YROF	Magni M22 Voyager	Clocktower Fund Management Ltd
	G-YROG	Magni M24C Orion	A. D. Mann & A. J. Brent
	G-YROH	Rotorsport UK MTO Sport	M. Winship
	G-YROI	Air Command 532 Elite	W. B. Lumb
	G-YROK	Magni M-16C	K. J. Yeadon
	G-YROL	Rotorsport UK Cavalon	C. G. Gilbert
	G-YROM	Rotorsport UK MT-03	A. Wallace
	G-YRON	Magni M-16C Tandem Trainer	H. E. Simons
	G-YROO	RAF 2000 GTX-SE gyroplane	L. Goodison
	G-YROP	Magni M-16C Tandem Trainer	Clocktower Fund Management Ltd
	G-YROR	Magni M.24C	R. M. Stanley
	G-YROU	Magni M24C Orion	Fairoaks Gyros Ltd
	G-YROV	Rotorsport UK MT-03	PKPS Aviation Ltd (G-UMAS)
	G-YROX	Rotorsport UK MT-03	Surplus Art
	G-YROY	Montgomerie-Bensen B.8MR	S. S. Wilson
	G-YROZ	Rotorsport UK Calidus	A. M. Mackey
	G-YRRO	Rotorsport UK Calidus	C. M. Leivers
	G-YRTE	Agusta A.109S Grand	Galegrove 2 LBG
	G-YRUS	Jodel D.140E	W. E. Massam (G-YRNS)
	G-YSIR	Van's RV-8	The Lord Rotherwick
	G-YSMO	Mainair Pegasus Quik	T. Southwell
	G-YTLY	Rans S-6-ES Coyote II	D. M. Geddes
	G-YUGE	Schempp-Hirth Ventus cT	E. P. Lambert (G-CFNN)
	G-YUGO	HS.125 Srs 1B/R-522 ★	Fire Section/Dunsfold (G-ATWH)
	G-YULL	PA-28 Cherokee 180E	C. J. Varley (G-BEAJ)
	G-YUMM	Cameron N-90 balloon	H. Stringer
	G-YUPI	Cameron N-90 balloon	MCVH SA/Belgium
	G-YURO	Shaw Europa ★	Yorkshire Air Museum/Elvington
	G-YVES	Alpi Pioneer 300	A. P. Anderson
	G-YXLX	ISF Mistral C	R. R. Penman
	G-YYAK	Aerostar SA Yak-52	Repxper SARL/France
	G-YYRO	Magni M-16C Tandem Trainer	Willy Rose Technology Ltd
	G-YYYY	MH.1521C-1 Broussard	Aerosuperbatics Ltd
	G-YZYZ	Mainair Blade 912	A. M. Beale
	G-ZAAP	CZAW Sportcruiser	H. Page
	G-ZAAZ	Van's RV-8	P. A. Soper
	G-ZABC	Sky 90-24 balloon	P. Donnelly
	G-ZACE	Cessna 172S	Sywell Aerodrome Ltd
	G-ZACH	Robin DR.400/100	A. P. Wellings (G-FTIO)
	G-ZACK	Cirrus SR20	Modern Air (UK) Ltd
	G-ZADA	Best Off Skyranger 912S(1)	C. P. Lincoln
	G-ZAIR	Zenair CH 601HD	A. D. Brown
	G-ZANY	Diamond DA40D Star	Altair Aviation Ltd

Reg	Type	Owner or Operator	Notes
G-ZAPX	Boeing 757-256	Titan Airways Ltd	
G-ZAPY	Robinson R22 Beta	HQ Aviation Ltd (G-INGB)	
G-ZARV	ARV Super 2	P. R. Snowden	
G-ZASH	Ikarus C42 FB80	J. W. D. Blythe	
G-ZAST	Christen A-1 Husky	E. Marinoni/Italy	
G-ZATG	Diamond DA.42M Twin Star	Directflight Ltd (G-DOSA)	
G-ZAVI	Ikarus C42 FB100	M. de Cleen & M. J. Hawkins	
G-ZAZA	PA-18 Super Cub 95	G. J. Harry, The Viscount Goschen	
G-ZAZU	Diamond DA.42 Twin Star	NAL Asset Management Ltd (G-GFDA/G-CEFX)	
G-ZAZZ	Lindstrand LBL-120A balloon	Idea Balloon SAS Di Stefano Travaglia and Co./ Italy	
G-ZBAD	Airbus A.321-231	Bank of Utah as Owner Trustee	
G-ZBAE	Airbus A.321-231	Bank of Utah as Owner Trustee	
G-ZBAF	Airbus A.321-231	Monarch Airlines Ltd	
G-ZBAG	Airbus A.321-231	Wilmington Trust SP Services (Dublin) Ltd	
G-ZBAH	Airbus A.320-214	Wells Fargo Bank Northwest, NA as Owner Trustee	
G-ZBAI	Airbus A.321-231	Wilmington Trust SP Services (Dublin) Ltd	
G-ZBAJ	Airbus A.321-231	Wilmington Trust SP Services (Dublin) Ltd	
G-ZBAK	Airbus A.321-231	Constitution Aircraft Leasing	
G-ZBAM	Airbus A.321-231	Bank of Utah as Owner Trustee	
G-ZBAO	Airbus A.321-231	Bank of Utah as Owner Trustee	
G-ZBAP	Airbus A.320-214	First Star Speir Aviation 1 Ltd (G-OOPT/ G-OOAT)	
G-ZBAU	Airbus A.320-214	IGAL MSN 3293 Ltd	
G-ZBAV	Boeing 737-82R	ALC B378 40874 LLC	
G-ZBED	Robinson R22 Beta	M. J. Wearing	
G-ZBEN	IAV Bacau Yakovlev Yak-52	B. A. Nicholson	
G-ZBJA	Boeing 787-8	British Airways	
G-ZBJB	Boeing 787-8	British Airways	
G-ZBJC	Boeing 787-8	British Airways	
G-ZBJD	Boeing 787-8	British Airways	
G-ZBJE	Boeing 787-8	British Airways	
G-ZBJF	Boeing 787-8	British Airways	
G-ZBJG	Boeing 787-8	British Airways	
G-ZBJH	Boeing 787-8	British Airways	
G-ZBJI	Boeing 787-8	British Airways	
G-ZBKA	Boeing 787-9	British Airways	
G-ZBKB	Boeing 787-9	British Airways	
G-ZBKC	Boeing 787-9	British Airways	
G-ZBKD	Boeing 787-9	British Airways	
G-ZBKE	Boeing 787-9	British Airways	
G-ZBKF	Boeing 787-9	British Airways	
G-ZBKG	Boeing 787-9	British Airways	
G-ZBKH	Boeing 787-9	British Airways	
G-ZBKI	Boeing 787-9	British Airways	
G-ZBKJ	Boeing 787-9	British Airways	
G-ZBKK	Boeing 787-9	British Airways	
G-ZBKL	Boeing 787-9	British Airways	
G-ZBKM	Boeing 787-9	British Airways	
G-ZBKN	Boeing 787-9	British Airways	
G-ZBKO	Boeing 787-9	British Airways	
G-ZBKP	Boeing 787-9	British Airways	
G-ZBLT	Cessna 182S Skylane	Cessna 182S Group/Ireland	
G-ZBOP	PZL-Bielsko SZD-36A Cobra 15	S. Bruce	
G-ZDEA	Diamond DA.42 Twin Star	Diamond Executive Aviation Ltd	
G-ZEBY	PA-28-140 Cherokee	N. Wright (G-BFBF)	
G-ZECH	CZAW Sportcruiser	Sportcruiser UK015	
G-ZEIN	Slingsby T.67M Firefly 260	R. C. P. Brookhouse	
G-ZENA	Zenair CH.701UL	I. E. Bentley	
G-ZENI	Zenair CH.601HD Zodiac	P. P. Plumley	
G-ZENR	Zenair CH.601HD Zodiac	N. G. Bumford (G-BRJB)	
G-ZENT	Cessna 560XL Citation XLS	Jet Aircraft Ltd	
G-ZENY	Zenair CH.601HD Zodiac	T. R. & B. K. Pugh	
G-ZEPI	Colt GA-42 gas airship	P. A. Lindstrand (G-ISPY/G-BPRB)	
G-ZERO	AA-5B Tiger	N. R. Evans & D. K. Rose	
G-ZEXL	Extra EA.300/L	2 Excel Aviation Ltd	

Notes	Reg	Type	Owner or Operator
	G-ZFOO	Tucano Replica	A. J. Palmer & D. Sayyah
	G-ZFOX	Denney Kitfox Mk.2	S. M. Hall
	G-ZGAB	BRM Aero Bristell NG5 Speed Wing	G. A. Beale
	G-ZGZG	Cessna 182T	J. Noble
	G-ZGTK	Schleicher ASH-26E	P. M. Wells (G-BWBY)
	G-ZHKF	Escapade 912(2)	C. D. & C. M. Wills
	G-ZHWH	Rotorway Executive 162F	B. Alexander
	G-ZIGI	Robin DR.400/180	Aeroclub du Bassin D'Arcachon/France
	G-ZIGY	Europa XS	K. D. Weston
	G-ZIII	Pitts S-2B	W. A. Cruickshank (G-CDBH)
	G-ZINC	Cessna 182S	M. Mears (G-VALI)
	G-ZINT	Cameron Z-77 balloon	G. Bogliaccino/Italy
	G-ZION	Cessna 177B	J. Tully
	G-ZIPA	Rockwell Commander 114A	R. Robson (G-BHRA)
	G-ZIPE	Agusta A109E Power Elite	Noble Foods Ltd
	G-ZIPI	Robin DR.400/180	A. J. Cooper
	G-ZIPY	Wittman W.8 Tailwind	K. J. Nurcombe
	G-ZIRA	Z-1RA Stummelflitzer	P. J. Dale
	G-ZITZ	AS.355F2 Twin Squirrel	Heli Aviation Ltd
	G-ZIZI	Cessna 525 CitationJet	Ortac Air Ltd
	G-ZIZY	TL2000UK Sting Carbon S4	C. E. & R. P. Reeves
	G-ZLLE	Aérospatiale SA.341G Gazelle	MW Helicopters Ltd
	G-ZLOJ	Beech A36 Bonanza	C. J. Parker
	G-ZNTH	Learjet 75	Zenith Aircraft Ltd
	G-ZODY	Zenair CH.601UL Zodiac	Sarum AX2000 Group
	G-ZOIZ	Ultramagic M-105 balloon	British Telecommunications PLC
	G-ZOMB	Ikarus C42 FB100	Apocalypse Aviation Ltd
	G-ZOOB	Tecnam P2008-JC	Century Aviation Ltd
	G-ZOOL	Cessna FA.152	A. S. C. Rathmell-Davey (G-BGXZ)
	G-ZORO	Shaw Europa	N. T. Read
	G-ZOSA	Champion 7GCAA	R. McQueen
	G-ZPPY	PA-18-95 Super Cub	R. Sims (G-NICK)
	G-ZRZZ	Cirrus SR22	Zoehrer-Gradwohl GmbH/Austria
	G-ZSDB	PA-28-236 Dakota	Dakota Air Services LLP (G-BPCX)
	G-ZSIX	Schleicher ASW-17-18E	C. Cowley & F. J. Davies
	G-ZSKD	Cameron Z-90 balloon	M. J. Gunston
	G-ZSKY	Best Off Sky Ranger Swift 912S(1)	J. E. Lipinski
	G-ZTED	Shaw Europa	J. J. Kennedy
	G-ZTOO	Staaken Z-2 Flitzer	E. B. Toulson
	G-ZTUG	Aeropro Eurofox 914	P. J. Tiller (G-CICX)
	G-ZTWO	Staaken Z-2 Flitzer	S. J. Randle
	G-ZUFL	Lindstrand LBL-90A balloon	Zuffle Dog Balloon Team (G-CHLL)
	G-ZUMI	Van's RV-8	D. R. CairnsT
	G-ZVIP	Beech 200 Super King Air	Capital Air Ambulance Ltd (G-SAXN/G-OMNH)
	G-ZVKO	Edge 360	R. J. Allan, N. Jones & A. J. Maxwell
	G-ZXCL	Extra EA.300/L	2 Excel Aviation Ltd
	G-ZXEL	Extra EA.300/L	2 Excel Aviation Ltd
	G-ZXLL	Extra EA.300/L	2 Excel Aviation Ltd
	G-ZZAC	Aerotechnik EV-97 Eurostar	N. R. Beale
	G-ZZAJ	Schleicher ASH-26E	A. T. Johnstone
	G-ZZDD	Schweizer 269C	C. D. Reeves (G-OCJK)
	G-ZZDG	Cirrus SR20 G2	B. Lane & N. Deeks
	G-ZZEL	Westland Gazelle AH.1	The Gazelle Squadron Display Team Ltd
	G-ZZIJ	PA-28-180 Cherokee C	G-ZZIJ Group (G-AVGK)
	G-ZZLE	Westland Gazelle AH.2 (XX436)	A. Moorhouse, S. Qardan & P. J. Whitaker
	G-ZZMM	Enstrom 480B	Fly 7 Helicopters LLP (G-TOIL)
	G-ZZOE	Eurocopter EC 120B	J. F. H. James
	G-ZZOT	PA-34-220T Seneca V	Cheshire Aircraft Leasing Ltd

Reg	Type	Owner or Operator	Notes
G-ZZOW	Medway Eclipse	M. Belemet	
G-ZZSA	Eurocopter EC.225LP Super Puma	Bristow Helicopters Ltd	
G-ZZSB	Eurocopter EC.225LP Super Puma	Bristow Helicopters Ltd	
G-ZZSC	Eurocopter EC.225LP Super Puma	Bristow Helicopters Ltd	
G-ZZSD	Eurocopter EC.225LP Super Puma	Bristow Helicopters Ltd	
G-ZZSE	Eurocopter EC.225LP Super Puma	Bristow Helicopters Ltd	
G-ZZSF	Eurocopter EC.225LP Super Puma	Bristow Helicopters Ltd	
G-ZZSG	Eurocopter EC.225LP Super Puma	Bristow Helicopters Ltd	
G-ZZSI	Eurocopter EC.225LP Super Puma	Bristow Helicopters Ltd (G-CGES)	
G-ZZSK	Eurocopter EC.225LP Super Puma	Bristow Helicopters Ltd	
G-ZZSL	Eurocopter EC.225LP Super Puma	Bristow Helicopters Ltd	
G-ZZSM	Eurocopter EC.225LP Super Puma	Bristow Helicopters Ltd	
G-ZZSN	Eurocopter EC.225LP Super Puma	Bristow Helicopters Ltd	
G-ZZTT	Schweizer 269C	Heli Andaluz SL/Spain	
G-ZZXX	P & M Quik GT450	B. B. Seabridge	
G-ZZZA	Boeing 777-236	British Airways	
G-ZZZB	Boeing 777-236	British Airways	
G-ZZZC	Boeing 777-236	British Airways	
G-ZZZS	Eurocopter EC.120B Colibri	Rosegate Helicopter Services Ltd	

ISLE OF MAN REGISTER

Reg	Type	Owner or Operator	Notes
M-AAAA	Bombardier CL600-2B16 Challenger	Lee Fai International Ltd	
M-AAAL	Gulfstream 650	ALM New Jet Ltd	
M-AAAM	Bombardier CL600-2B16 Challenger	Durstwell Ltd	
M-AABG	Bombardier BD700-1A11 Global 5000	AB Air Holdings	
M-AAKV	Embraer EMB-135BJ Legacy	AAK Company Ltd	
M-AAMM	Gulfstream 45	Al-Sahab G450 Ltd	
M-ABCC	Bombardier BD700-1A10 Global 6000	Global Aviation Partners LP Inc	
M-ABDP	Hawker 800XP	Kitlan Ltd	
M-ABDQ	Eurocopter EC.135 P2+	Knightspeed Ltd	
M-ABEC	Embraer EMB-135BJ Legacy 600	Carys Investment Group Ltd	
M-ABEF	ATR-72-202	Aircraft Solutions Lux V-B SARL	
M-ABEU	Learjet 45	Aviation Leasing (IOM) Ltd	
M-ABFD	Aerospatiale ATR-72-212A	KP Aero	
M-ABFE	Aerospatiale ATR-72-212A	KP Aero	
M-ABFI	Aerospatiale ATR-72-212A	Plateau Aviation Ltd	
M-ABFQ	Bombardier BD700-1A10 Global 6000	AGT International GmbH	
M-ABFR	Bombardier BD700-1A10 Global 6000	AGT International GmbH	
M-ABGG	Bombardier CL600-2B16 Challenger	Zarox Holdings Ltd	
M-ABGS	Bombardier CL600-2B16 Challenger 605	Viking Travel Services Ltd	
M-ABGV	Learjet 45	Aviation Leasing (IOM) Ltd	
M-ABIY	Airbus A.320-232	CIT Aerospace International	
M-ABJA	Learjet 45	Aviation Leasing (IOM) Ltd	
M-ABJE	Airbus A-319-133CJ	GE European Equipment Finance (Aircraft No.2) Ltd	
M-ABJX	Eurocopter EC.225LP Super Puma	Parilease SAS	
M-ABJZ	Eurocopter EC.225LP Super Puma	Parilease SAS	
M-ABKA	Eurocopter EC-225LP Super Puma	Parilease SAS	
M-ABKB	Eurocopter EC.225LP Super Puma	Parilease SAS	
M-ABKC	Eurocopter EC.225LP Super Puma	Parilease SAS	
M-ABKD	Eurocopter EC.225LP Super Puma	Parilease SAS	
M-ABKE	Eurocopter EC.225LP Super Puma	Parilease SAS	
M-ABKF	Eurocopter EC.225LP Super Puma	Parilease SAS	
M-ABKG	Eurocopter EC.225LP Super Puma	Parilease SAS	
M-ABKH	Eurocopter EC.225LP Super Puma	Parilease SAS	
M-ABKI	Eurocopter EC.225LP Super Puma	Parilease SAS	
M-ABKJ	Eurocopter EC.225LP Super Puma	Parilease SAS	
M-ABKK	Eurocopter EC.225LP Super Puma	Parilease SAS	
M-ABKM	Aerospatiale ATR-72-212A	Elix Assets 7 Ltd	
M-ABKN	Aerospatiale ATR-72-212A	Elix Assets 7 Ltd	
M-ABKR	Embraer ERJ170-200LR	Celestial Aviation Trading 71 Ltd	
M-ABKT	Embraer ERJ170-200LR	Celestial Aviation Trading 71 Ltd	
M-ABKU	Embraer ERJ190-100LR	Celestial Aviation Trading 63 Ltd	
M-ABKY	Avro RJ100	M. A. Elobeid	
M-ABKZ	Avro RJ100	M. A. Elobeid	
M-ACPT	BAe. 125 Srs.1000	Remo Investments Ltd	
M-ACRO	Eurocopter AS.350B3 Ecureuil	F. Allani	

Notes	Reg	Type	Owner or Operator
	M-AERO	Dassault Falcon 2000LX	Rirox Ltd
	M-AFAJ	Dassault Falcon 900EX	Elan Finance Management SA
	M-AGGY	Cessna 550 Citation II	Maudib GmbH Deutschland
	M-AGIK	Dassault Falcon 900LX	Amboy Overseas Ltd
	M-AGMA	Bombardier BD700-IA10 Global Express XRS	Sugar Mama Ltd
	M-AGRI	Bombardier BD700-1A11 Global 5000	Blezir Invest Ltd
	M-AHAA	Bombardier BD700-IA10 Global 6000	AH Aviation Ltd
	M-AJOR	Leonardo AW139	Major Aviation LLP
	M-AKAL	Bombardier CL600-2B16 Challenger 604	A and A Aviation Ltd
	M-AKAR	Sikorsky S-76C	Starspeed Ltd
	M-ALAY	Gulfstream VP	Stonefel Trade & Invest Ltd
	M-ALCB	Pilatus PC-12/47E	M. S. Bartlett
	M-ALEN	Embraer EMB-135BJ Legacy	ATT Aviation Ltd
	M-ALFA	Eurocopter MBB BK-117C-2	ALF Air International Ltd
	M-ALMA	Dassault Falcon 7X	Armad Ltd
	M-ALSH	Bombardier BD700-1A10 Global Express	Mirgab Aviation Ltd
	M-ALTI	Bombardier CL600-2B16 Challenger 605	Hartsage International Ltd
	M-ALUN	BAe 125 Srs.700A	Briarwood Products Ltd
	M-AMAN	Pilatus PC-12	Pilatus PC-12 Centre UK Ltd
	M-AMRM	ATR-72-212A	Fastjet Air Four Ltd
	M-ANAP	Embraer EMB-505 Phenom	Equiom (Isle of Man) Ltd
	M-ANGA	Embraer EMB-135BJ Legacy 600	Max Air Ltd
	M-ANGO	Bombardier BD700-1A11 Global 5000	Waylawn Ltd
	M-ANNA	Bombardier CL600-2B16 Challenger	Generativity Ltd
	M-ANTA	Bombardier CL600-2B190 Challenger	Tathra International Holdings Inc
	M-ORIS	Embraer EMB-550 Legacy 500	Legacy 500 Ltd
	M-AQUA	Bombardier BD700-1A11 Global 5000	Theberton Ltd
	M-ARDA	Embraer EMB-135BJ Legacy 600	MRH IOM Ltd
	M-ARDI	Gulfstream V-SP	LGM Property Services Ltd
	M-AREA	Hawker 900XP	Area Plus JV Ltd
	M-ARGO	Bombardier BD700-1A10 Global 6000	Sun Burst Invest & Finance Inc
	M-ARIA	Dassault Falcon 2000LX	Group Murr Aviation IM Ltd
	M-ARIE	Hawker 800XP	Surf-Air Ltd
	M-ARKZ	Bombardier CL600-2B16 Challenger	Markz Jet Ltd
	M-ARRH	Bombardier BD100-1A10 Challenger 300	Eagle Aviation Ltd
	M-ARTY	Pilatus PC-12/47E	Creston (UK) Ltd
	M-ARUB	Bombardier CL600-2B16 Challenger 650	Setfair Aviation Ltd
	M-ARVY	Dassault Falcon 7X	Almondine Ltd
	M-ASHI	Bombardier CL600-2B16 Challenger	Beckett Holding Ltd
	M-ASRI	Bombardier BD700-1A10 Globa Expressl	YYA Aviation Ltd
	M-ASTR	Dornier 328-300	Sino Europe Aircraft Ltd
	M-ATAR	Bombardier BD700-1A10 Global	AV West Aircraft Pty.Ltd
	M-ATEX	Dassault Falcon 8X	Maritime Investment and Shipping Company Ltd
	M-ATPS	Gulfstream V-SP	Tarona Ltd
	M-AVIR	Bombardier BD700-1A10 Global 6000	Anjet Co. Ltd
	M-AXIM	CessnaT.206H Turbo Stationair	C. D. B. Cope
	M-AYBE	Gulfstream 280	Maybe Aviation Ltd
	M-AYRU	Bombardier CL600-2B16 Challenger	Setfair Aviation Ltd
	M-AZIA	Cessna 525C CitationJet CJ4	Hunting Star Ltd
	M-BADU	Gulfstream VI	BH2 Aviation Ltd
	M-BAEP	Bombardier CL600-2B16 Challenger	Swift Cloud Aviation Services Ltd
	M-BASH	Bombardier CL600-2B16 Challenger 605	Channel IT Isle of Man Ltd
	M-BEST	Cessna 750 Citation X	Lanara Ltd
	M-BETS	Rockwell Commander 695A	Aldersey Aviation Ltd
	M-BETY	Dornier Do.328-310	Funfte XR-GmbH
	M-BHBH	Gulfstream 650	Caldana Holding and Invest Ltd
	M-BIGG	Bombardier BD700-1A11 Global 5000	Harley Airlines Ltd
	M-BIRD	Embraer EMB-135BJ Legacy 600	YH Aviation Ltd
	M-BJEP	Gulfstream 550	M-BJEP Ltd
	M-BLUE	Bombardier BD700-1A11 Global 5000	Tetran Assets Ltd
	M-BONO	Cessna 172N Skyhawk II	J. McCandless
	M-BRAB	Diamond DA.42M Twin Star	Bravura Group of Companies Ltd
	M-BRAC	Diamond DA.42M Twin Star	Bravura Group of Companies Ltd
	M-BTAR	Bombardier BD700-1A10 Global Express	AVWest Aircraft Pty.Ltd
	M-BULL	Cessna S550 Citation II	Bulltofta Aviation
	M-CARA	Cessna 525 Citation M2	Anam Cara Aviation
	M-CCCP	Bombardier BD700-1A11 Global 5000	Heda Airlines Ltd
	M-CDFY	Beech B.200 Super King Air	BAE Systems Marine Ltd
	M-CDJC	Beech B.200GT Super King Air	BAE Systems Marine Ltd
	M-CDOM	Aerospatiale ATR-72-212A	Fastjet Air Four Ltd
	M-CDZT	Beech B.200 Super King Air	BAE Systems Marine Ltd

Reg	Type	Owner or Operator	Notes
M-CELT	Dassault Falcon 7X	Cravant Ltd	
M-CESC	Cessna 560XL	Cessna Spanish Citation Service Center SL	
M-CESD	Cessna 560XL	Cessna Spanish Citation Service Center SL	
M-CHEM	Dassault Falcon 200EX	Hampshire Aviation LLP	
M-CICO	Dassault Falcon 50	BZ Air Ltd	
M-CIMO	Dassault Falcon 2000EX	Dassault Aviation SA	
M-CITI	Bomvbardier BD700-1A11 Global 5000	Global 9683 Ltd	
M-CKSB	Dassault Falcon 2000	John Mason Aircraft Management Services	
M-CLAB	Bombardier BD100-1A10 Challenger 300	Shamrock Trading Ltd	
M-COOL	Cessna 510 Citation Mustang	E. Keats	
M-CPRS	Embraer EMB-135BJ Legacy 600	Puru Aviation Ltd	
M-CRAO	Beech B.300 Super King Air 350	Dr. A. Oetker	
M-CSMS	Learjet 45	SMS Aviation Service SA	
M-CVGL	Bombardier BD700-1A11 Global 5000	Aircraft Operations Ltd	
M-DADA	Bombardier BD700-1A10 Global 6000	STC Aviation Services Ltd	
M-DADI	Dassault Falcon 900DX	Rubicon Capital Consulting Co.Ltd	
M-DKVL	Gulfstream 450	Fiordani Holding Ltd	
M-DMBP	Learjet 40	VEN Air	
M-DRIL	Pilatus PC-12/47E	Pilatus Centre (BIS) Ltd	
M-DSCL	Embraer 135BJ Legacy	Legacy Aviation Ltd	
M-DSKY	SOCATA TBM.930	Sterna Aviation Ltd	
M-DSML	BAe.125-800B	St. Francis Group (Aviation) Ltd	
M-DSTZ	Bombardiewer CL600-2B16 Challenger 650	Cameron Industries Consult Inc	
M-DSUN	Bombardier BD700-1A10 Global 6000	Splendiferous Global Ltd	
M-DUBS	Dassult Falcon 2000EX	Six Daughters Ltd	
M-DWWW	Bombardier CL600-2B19 Challenger	Dragon Asset Global Investment Group Ltd	
M-EAGL	Dassault Falcon 900EX	Faycroft Finance	
M-EASY	Leajet 35A	PM Lutfahrzeugvermietung GmbH & Co KG	
M-ECJI	Dassault Falcon 10	Fleet International Aviation and Finance Ltd	
M-EDIA	Dassault Falcon 7X	M-EDIA Aviation Ltd	
M-EGGA	Beech B200 Super King Air	Langley Aviation Ltd	
M-ELAS	Gulfstream 280	Aventurine Aviation Ltd	
M-ELON	Embraer EMB-505 Phenom 300	Sleepwell Aviation Ltd	
M-ENTA	Dassault Falcon 200	Riviera Invest und Services SA	
M-ETAL	Piaggio P.180 Avanti	GFG Aviation Ltd	
M-EVAN	Bombardier BD100-1A10 Challenger 300	Marcus Evans (Aviation) Ltd	
M-EXPL	Eurocopter AS.355N Ecureuil 2	Select Plant Hire Co.Ltd	
M-FALC	Dassault Falcon 7X	Premier Aircraft Leasing Ltd	
M-FALZ	Dassault Falcon 7X	Pacelli Beteiligungs GmbH & Company KG	
M-FASH	Dassault Falcon 900B	Al Hokair Aviation Ltd	
M-FAST	IAI Gulfstream 150	G-150 Aeronautics Ltd	
M-FINE	Bombardier BD700-1A11 Global 5000	Noristevo Investments Ltd	
M-FINK	BAe. 125 Srs.1000B	B. T. Fink	
M-FISH	Gulfstream V	Osprey Wings SRO	
M-FLCN	Dassault Falcon 2000EX	Omega Aviation Ltd	
M-FLSN	Agusta Westland AW.139	Boutique Aviation Ltd	
M-FLYI	Cessna 525 Citationjet CJ4	Avtrade Ltd	
M-FROG	Beech 390 Premier 1	White and Cope Aviation LLP	
M-FRZN	Bombardier CL600-2B16 Challenger	Iceland Foods Ltd	
M-FTHD	Dassault Falcon 2000EX	Eagle Reach Group Ltd	
M-FUAD	Gulfstream 550	Future Pipe Aviation Ltd	
M-FZMH	Bombardier CL600-2B19 Global Express	AK VI Ltd	
M-GACB	Dassault Falcon 10	Valiant Aviation Ltd	
M-GAGA	Gulfstream 650ER	Advance Global Development Ltd	
M-GASG	Gulfstream 150	PIV Global Holding Ltd	
M-GCAP	Piaggio P.180 Avanti	Greensill Capital (IOM) Ltd	
M-GCCC	Beech B.350i King Air	NG2 SA	
M-GDRS	Hawker 850XP	Surf-Air Ltd	
M-GETS	Pilatus PC-12/47E	3FS Aviation Ltd	
M-GLEX	Bombardier BD700-1A10 Global Express	Pytonian Trade & Invest SA	
M-GMKM	Dassault Falcon 7X	MKAir7X Pty Ltd	
M-GOLF	Cessna FR.182RG	P. R. Piggin & C. J. Harding	
M-GRAN	Bombardier BD700-1A11 Global 5000	Starflight Investments Ltd	
M-GSIR	Dassault Falcon 900DX	Sublime Holdings Ltd	
M-GSKY	Bombardier BD700-1A10 Global Express	Jerand Holdings Ltd	
M-HAWK	Bombardier BD700-1A10 Global 6000	Genetechma Finance Ltd	
M-HELI	Eurocopter EC.155-B1	Flambards Ltd	
M-HHHH	Airbus A.318-112CJ	Kutus Ltd	
M-HKND	Dassault Falcon 7X	Skyrizon Aircraft Holdings Ltd	
M-HLAN	Bombardier CL600-2B19 Challenger 850	Wonder Air International Ltd	
M-HNDA	Honda HA-420 Hondajet	Marshall Aircraft Sales Ltd	

Notes	Reg	Type	Owner or Operator
	M-HOME	Bombardier BD700-1A10 Global 6000	Symphony Master (IOM) Ltd
	M-HOTB	Gulfstream V SP	Darwin Air Ltd
	M-HSNT	Bombardier BD100-1A10 Challenger 300	Unisky Ltd
	M-HSXP	Hawker 800XP	HEWE Ltd
	M-IABU	Airbus A.340-313	Klaret Aviation Ltd
	M-IAMI	Falcon 7X	Delane Finance Ltd
	M-IBAJ	Aerospatiale ATR-72-212A	KF Turbo Leasing Ltd
	M-IBAL	Airbus A.320-232	TC Skyward Aviation Ireland Ltd
	M-ICRC	Cessna 525A Citationjet CJ2	Pektron Group Ltd
	M-ICRO	Cessna 525C Citationjet CJ4	Pektron Group Ltd
	M-IDAS	Agusta A109E Power	Trustair Ltd
	M-IFFY	Cessna 510 Citation Mustang	Xead Aviation Ltd
	M-IFLY	Pilatus PC-12/47E	N. J. Vetch
	M-IGHT	Learjet 60	High Wing Aviation Ltd
	M-IGWT	Bombardier BD700-1A10	Business Encore (IOM) Ltd
	M-IKEY	Airbus Helicopters AS.365N3	Whirligig Ltd
	M-ILAN	Embraer EMB-135BJ Legacy 650	Artjet Ltd
	M-ILLA	Beech 400XP	Sunshine Aviation Ltd
	M-ILTA	Dassault Falcon 900LX	Delta Technical Services Ltd
	M-INER	Bombardier BD700-1A10 Global 6000	ICC Aviation Ltd
	M-INNI	Learjet 60	M-INNI Aviation Ltd
	M-INOR	Bell 429	Major Aviation LLP
	M-INSK	GulfstreamVI	Skyfort Aviation Ltd
	M-INTY	IAI Gulfstream 280	Hampshire Aviation LLP
	M-IPHS	Gulfstream 550	Islands Aviation Ltd
	M-IRAS	Bombardier BD700-1A10 Global 6000	STC Jet Ltd
	M-IRNE	Hawker 850XP	R. N. Edmiston
	M-IRTH	Pilatus PC-12/47E	Wingmen Ltd
	M-ISTY	IAI Gulfstream 280	Hampshire Aviation LLP
	M-IUNI	Bombardier BD700-1A11 Global 5000	Unitrans Management Ltd
	M-JACK	Beech B200GT King Air	Jetstream Aviation Ltd
	M-JCBA	Sikorsky S-76C	J C Bamford Excavators Ltd
	M-JCBB	Gulfstream 650	J C Bamford Excavators Ltd
	M-JCBC	Sikorsky S-76C	J C Bamford Excavators Ltd
	M-JCCA	Embraer EMB-135BJ Legacy	Jeju China Castle Ltd
	M-JETT	Dassault Falcon 200	Piraeus Leasing Chrimatodotikes Mishoseis SA
	M-JETZ	Dassault Falcon 2000EX	Avtorita Holdings Ltd
	M-JGVJ	Bombardier BD700-1A11	Aquatics Ventures Holdings Ltd
	M-JJTL	Pilatus PC-12/47E	L. Uggia, J. P. Huth & K. Giannamore
	M-JNJL	Bombardier BD700-1A11 Global Express	Global Thirteen Worldwide Resources Ltd
	M-JSMN	Bombardier BD700-1A11 Global 5000	Jasmin Aviation Ltd
	M-JSTA	Bombardier CL600-2B16 Challenger	Jetsteff Aviation Ltd
	M-KATE	Airbus A.319-133	Sophar Property Holding
	M-KBBG	Gulfstream 450	Golden Global Aviation Ltd
	M-KBSD	Bombardier BD700-1A11 Global 5000	Faraotis Holdings Ltd
	M-KELY	Embraer EMB-500 Phenom 100	Kelly Air Ltd
	M-KGTS	Embraer EMB-505 Phenom 300	VTS Sp z.o.o.
	M-KKCO	Gulfstream 450	ATAC Ltd
	M-KSSN	Gulfstream 650	NS Aviation Ltd
	M-LAAA	Bombardier BD700-1A10 Global Express	ALM Jet Ltd
	M-LANG	Dassault Falcon 900LX	Longest Day International Ltd
	M-LCFC	Boeing 737-7EI	Ceilo Del Rey Co.Ltd
	M-LDME	ATR-72-212A	Elix Assets 7 Ltd
	M-LEFB	Cessna 550	Patagonia Assets Ltd
	M-LEKT	Robin DR.400/180	T. D. Allan, P. & J. P. Bromley
	M-LENR	Beech B.200GT Super King Air	BAE Systems Marine Ltd
	M-LEYS	Beech C.90GT King Air	Heres Aviation Ltd
	M-LFBB	Gulfstream 450	Oviation Two Ltd
	M-LILJ	Bombardier CL600-2B19 Challenger 850	Raise in Development Ltd
	M-LILY	Bombardier CL600-2B19 Challenger 850	Bright Loysal Ltd/Offshore Incorporations (Cayman) Ltd
	M-LION	Hawker 900XP	Lion Invest and Trade Ltd
	M-LIZI	Eurocopter EC.155 B1	Ledzone Investments Ltd
	M-LJGI	Dassault Falcon 7X	Milestown
	M-LLIN	Bombardier BD700-1A10 Global 6000	Tian Yi Ltd
	M-LLMW	Beech Super King Air 300	Trosa Ltd
	M-LOOK	Bombardier CL600-2B16 Challenger	Kennington Ltd
	M-LRLR	Bombardier CL600-2B16 Challenger	L & B Conveyjet Ltd
	M-LUNA	Eurocopter MBB BK-117C-2	Flambards Ltd
	M-LVIA	Eurocopter AS.365N3 Dauphin 2	Flambards Ltd
	M-LVNA	Eurocopter EC.155 B1	Lucy Ltd

Reg	Type	Owner or Operator	Notes
M-LWSA	Bombardier BD700-1A10 Global Express	Lynx Aviation (Isle of Man) Ltd	
M-LWSG	Bombardier BD700-1A10 Global 6000	Lynx Aircraft Ltd	
M-MAEE	Gulfstream 450	Royston Sky Holdings Ltd	
M-MANX	Cessna 425 Conquest	Suas Investments Ltd	
M-MARI	Learjet 60XR	Rumit Aviation Ltd	
M-MAVP	Bombardier BD700-1A10 Global 6000	Sentonian Investments Ltd	
M-MAXX	Bombardier BD700-1A10 Global 6000	Max Smart Development Ltd	
M-MDBD	Bombardier BD700-1A10 Global Express	Cozuro Holdings Ltd	
M-MDMH	Embraer EMB-550 Legacy 500	Herrenkneckt Aviation GmbH	
M-MEVA	Cessna 560 Citation Ultra	AVEM'R	
M-MHFZ	Embraer EMB-135BJ Legacy	AK VI Ltd	
M-MICS	Bombardier BD700-1A11 Global 5000	Challenger-Mondel Ltd	
M-MIDY	Dassault Falcon 900EX	Midy Aviation Ltd	
M-MIKE	Cessna 525C Citationjet CJ4	Aviation by Westminster Ltd	
M-MJLD	Cessna 680A Citation Latitude	CCC Isle of Man Ltd	
M-MBLY	Bombardier BD700-1A10 Global 6000	Asaj Holdings LLC	
M-MNDG	Gulfstream 550	Oviation Ltd	
M-MOMO	Gulfstream V SP	Fayair (Jersey) Co Ltd	
M-MOON	Cessna 750	Bambara Holding SA	
M-MRBB	Learjet 45	Boultbee Aviation 3 LLP	
M-MSGG	Bombardier CL600-2B16 Challenger 605	Toyna Ltd	
M-MSVI	Cessna 525B Citationjet CJ3	JPM Ltd	
M-MTOO	Bombardier BD100-1A10 Challenger 300	Nadremal Air Holding Ltd	
M-MYNA	Bombardier BD700-1A10 Global 6000	Tibit Ltd	
M-NALE	Bombardier BD700-1A10 Global Express	Jover Ltd	
M-NAME	Bombardier BD700-1A10 Global 6000	Blezir Aircraft Leasing (IOM) Ltd	
M-NELS	Gulfstream 450	Citylink Partners Ltd	
M-NGNG	Gulfstream 650	Infinity Sky Ltd	
M-NGSN	Pilatus PC-12/47E	N. Stolt-Nielsen	
M-NHOI	Bombardier CL600-2B16 Challenger	Hatta Investments Ltd	
M-NICE	Gulfstream 200	M-NICE Ltd	
M-NJSS	Embraer EMB-135BJ Legacy	Saby Finance Ltd	
M-NLYY	PA-42-1000 Cheyenne 400LS	Factory Leasing Ltd	
M-NNNN	Gulfstream 650	Matrix Aviation 650 Ltd	
M-NONA	Avro RJ100	Nona Trade Corporation GmbH	
M-NTOS	Cessna 525bCitationjet CJ4	Selementos Ltd	
M-OBIL	Cessna 525C Citationjet C14	Popken Fashion Services GmbH	
M-OCNY	Bombardier BD100-1A10 Challenger 350	RH-Flugdienst GmbH & Co KG	
M-OCOM	Bombardier CL600-2B16 Challenger 604	Focus Holdings Ltd	
M-ODKZ	Dassault Falcon 900EX	Skylane LP	
M-OEPL	Dassault Falcon 7X	Cloud Services Ltd	
M-OGUL	Agusta A109S Grand	Medway Leasing Ltd	
M-OIWA	Bombardier BD100-1A10 Challenger	Delta A/S	
M-OLEG	Embraer 135BJ Legacy	Hermitage Air Ltd	
M-OLJM	Agusta Westland AW.139	Boutique Aviation Ltd	
M-OLLY	Cessna 525 Citationjet CJ1	MBK Maschinenbau GmbH/Bohnet GmbH	
M-OLOT	Bombardier CL600-2B16 Challenger	Kellie Aviation Ltd	
M-OLTT	Pilatus PC-12/47E	One Luxury Travel LLP	
M-OMAN	Dassault Falcon 7X	RUWI Ltd	
M-ONAV	Hawker 900XP	Monavia Ltd	
M-ONDE	Eurocopter MBB BK.117C2	Peyton Ltd	
M-ONEM	Gulfstream 550	G550 Ltd	
M-ONTE	Piaggio P.180 Avanti II	Scotia Aviation Ltd	
M-ONTY	Sikorsky S-76C	Trustair Ltd	
M-OPED	PA-32-301XTC Saratoga	Hock Lai Cham	
M-ORAD	Dassault Falcon 7X	Swift New Jet Ltd	
M-ORZE	Eurocopter EC135 P2+	G650 Management Ltd	
M-OTOR	Beech B200GT Super King Air	Pektron Group Ltd	
M-OUNT	Dassault Falcon 7X	Abelia Ltd	
M-OUSE	Cessna 510 Citation Mustang	Mouse (IOM) Ltd	
M-OUTH	Diamond DA.42 Twin Star	Sky Fly LP Inc	
M-OVIE	Gulfstream 650	Hampshire Aviation LLP	
M-OZZA	Bombardier BD100-1A10 Challenger 300	Casam International Ltd	
M-PACF	Eurocopter EC135 P2+	Starspeed Ltd	
M-PAPA	Airbus EC130 T2	Papa Fly Ltd	
M-PCPC	Pilatus PC-12/45	Treetops Aviation LLP	
M-PDCS	Dassault Falcon 2000EX	Six Daughters Ltd	
M-PHML	American General AG-5B Tiger	I. J. Ross & J. R. Shannon	
M-PIRE	Piaggio P180 Avanti	Northside Aviation Ltd	
M-PLUS	Gulfstream 650	650 Management Ltd	
M-POWR	Beech C.90A King Air	Northside Aviation Ltd	

Notes	Reg	Type	Owner or Operator
	M-PREI	Raytheon RB390 Premier 1	Craft Air SA
	M-PZPZ	Gulfstream IV	A. I. Eze
	M-RAYS	Bombardier CL600-2B16 Challenger 650	Gufo Lines Ltd
	M-RBIG	Learjet 45	Volantair LP Inc
	M-RBUS	Airbus A.319-115CJ	Belville Investment Ltd
	M-RCCG	Embraer EMB-135BJ Legacy 650	Russian Copper Co. Holdings Ltd
	M-RCCH	Embraer EMB135BJ Legacy 650	Russian Copper Company Holdings Ltd
	M-REEE	Dassault Falcon 7X	B. C. Ecclestone
	M-RENT	Cessna 525 Citation M2	Sixt Air GmbH
	M-RISE	Boeing 757-23N	Talos Aviation Ltd
	M-RKAY	Raytheon 390 Premier 1A	Sunseeker Corporate Aviation Ltd
	M-RLIV	Bombardier CL600-2B16 Challenger	Mobyhold Ltd
	M-RONE	Dassault Falcon 2000EX	Ocean Sky Aircraft Management Ltd
	M-RRRR	Bombardier BD700-1A11 Global 6000	Prestige Investments Ltd
	M-RSKL	Bombardier BD700-1A10 Global 6000	Angel Aviation Ltd
	M-RTFS	Dassault Falcon 7X	CIM Corporate Services Ltd
	M-RZDC	Gulfstream 550	KRP Aviation Ltd
	M-SAID	Bombardier BD700-IA11 Global 5000	S & K Aviation Ltd
	M-SAIL	Pilatus PC-12/47E	G. G. & L. G. Gordon
	M-SAIR	Falcon 900B	W. A. Developments International Ltd
	M-SAJJ	Gulfstream V-SP	Horizon Aviation Ltd
	M-SAMA	Bombardier BD700-1A10 Global 6000	Fanar Aviation Ltd
	M-SAPT	Bombardier BD700-1A11 Global 5000	Sapetro Aviation Ltd
	M-SASS	IAI Gulfstream 200	Falcon Crest Resources Inc
	M-SAWO	Gulfstream V-SP	Cloud Air Services Ltd
	M-SAXY	Pilatus PC12/45	Saxon Logistics Ltd
	M-SBUR	IAI Gulfstream 200	Quinzol Ventures Ltd
	M-SCMG	Dassault Falcon 7X	BlueSky International Management Ltd
	M-SCOT	Dassault 7X	Arirang Aviation IOM Ltd
	M-SETT	Bombardier BD700-1A11 Global 5000	Lodging 2020 LP Inc
	M-SEVN	Bombardier CL600-2B16 Challenger	Persimmon Trading Ltd
	M-SEXY	Embraer EMB-135BJ Legacy 650	Gerfaut Capital Ltd
	M-SFAM	McDonnell Douglas MD-87	Montavachi Ltd
	M-SFOZ	Dassault Falcon 2000	Alaman for Jets Ltd
	M-SGCR	Cessna 550 Citation Bravo	Labraid Ltd
	M-SGJS	Bombardier BD100-1A10 Challenger 350	Twenty 27 (IOM) Ltd
	M-SHRM	AgustaWestlandAW139	Frozendale Ltd
	M-SIRI	Bombardier BD700-1A10 Global Express	Supreme Sun Ltd
	M-SIXT	Cessna 525C Citationjet CJ4	Sixt Air GmbH
	M-SKSM	Bombardier BD700-1A11 Global Express	Tesker Management Ltd
	M-SNER	Dassault Falcon 2000EX	Wincor Aviation Establishment
	M-SOBM	Gulfstream 450	Sobha Aviation Ltd
	M-SOBR	Gulfstream 450	Sobha & BR Aviation Ltd
	M-SPBM	Bombardier CL600-2B16 Challenger 605	G200 Ltd
	M-SPEC	Beech B300 Super King Air	Specsavers Corporate Aircraft Leasing Ltd
	M-SPEK	Beech B300 Super King Air	Specsavers Corporate Aircraft Leasing Ltd
	M-SPOR	Beech B200 King Air	Select Plant Hire Co.Ltd
	M-SQAR	Gulfstream V-SP	M Square Aviation Ltd
	M-SSYS	Cessna 525C CitationJet CJ4	Fimway Asset Holdings Ltd
	M-STAR	Boeing 727-2X8	Starling Aviation Ltd
	M-STCO	Dassault Falcon 2000LX	STC IOM Ltd
	M-STRY	Avro RJ70	B. C. Ecclestone
	M-SURE	Dassault Falcon 7X	Arirang Aviation IOM Ltd
	M-SVGN	Cessna 680 Citation Sovereign	Vocalion Ltd
	M-TAKE	Bombardier CL600-2B19 Challenger 850	Caropan Company SA
	M-TBEA	Cessna 525A Citationjet CJ2	Bealaw (Man) 8 Ltd
	M-TECH	Bombardier BD100-1A10 Challenger 350	Primelock Investments Ltd
	M-TELE	Gulfstream 400	Arena Aviation Ltd
	M-TFFS	Dassault Falcon 900LX	Astira Holdings Ltd
	M-TINK	Dassault Falcon 7X	Stark Limited
	M-TOMS	Pilatus PC-12/47E	C J Airways Ltd
	M-TOPI	Bombardier CL600-2B16 Challenger	Gladiator Flight Ltd
	M-TRBS	Bombardier CL600-2B16 Challenger	Arrow Management Property Corp
	M-TSKW	Dassault Falcon 900C	Boutique Aviation Ltd
	M-TSLT	Bombardier BD700-1A10 Global 6000	VL9762 Ltd
	M-TSRI	Beech C.90GTI King Air	Timpson Ltd
	M-TYRA	Bombardier BD700-1A11 Global 5000	KKCO Ltd
	M-UGIC	Gulfstream 550	Cityville Capital Ltd
	M-ULTI	Bombardier BD700-1A10 Global Express XRS	Multibird Overseas Ltd
	M-UNIS	Bombardier BD700-1A10 Global Express	Lapwing Ltd
	M-URRY	Hawker 800XP	Corporate Sealandair Ltd

Reg	Type	Owner or Operator	Notes
M-URUS	Boeing 737-7GC	Ingram Services Ltd	
M-USBA	Gulfstream V	Shukra Ltd	
M-USCA	SOCATA TBM-850	Sterna Aviation Ltd	
M-USHY	Cessna 441 Conquest	Flying Dogs Ltd	
M-USIC	Gulfstream 550	Hampshire Aviation Ltd	
M-USIK	Gulfstream 650	OS Aviation Ltd	
M-USTG	Cessna 510 Citation Mustang	OSM Aviation Ltd	
M-VGAL	Dassault Falcon F900EX	Charter Air Ltd	
M-VITB	Gulfstream 650	Matrix Aviation 650 III Ltd	
M-VITC	Dassault Falcon 8X	Aerolus Air Ltd	
M-VITO	Hawker 800XP	Beratex Group Ltd	
M-VQBI	Bombardier BD700-1A10 Global Express	Altitude X3 Ltd	
M-VRNY	Gulfstream 550	Mirtos Ltd	
M-WANG	Dassault Falcon 7X	Keystone International Co.Ltd	
M-WATJ	Beech B.200GT Super King Air	Saxonhenge Ltd	
M-WHAT	Eurocopter EC.135T2+	Starspeed Ltd	
M-WIND	Gulfstream 650	Nursam Invest SA	
M-WINT	Pilatus PC-12/43E	Air Winton Ltd	
M-WMWM	Cessna 525A Citationjet CJ2	Standard Aviation Ltd	
M-WONE	Gulfstream IV-X	RYT Aviation LP Inc	
M-XHEC	Eurocopter EC155B	Flambards Ltd	
M-YAKW	Pilatus PC-12/47E	Limbourne Ltd	
M-YANG	Gulfstream 450	DJM Holding Ltd	
M-YBBJ	Boeing 737-7HE BBJ	Hamilton Jets Ltd	
M-YBLS	Pilatus PC-12/45	B. L. Schroder	
M-YBUS	Airbus A.320-214ACJ	STC Flight Ltd	
M-YCYS	Learjet 60	CYS Ltd	
M-YFLY	Pilatus PC-12/47E	Fly High Ltd	
M-YFTA	Bombardier BD700-1A10 Global 6000	Carolina Ltd	
M-YGJL	Bombardier BD700-1A10 Global Express	Ansakl Aviation Two Ltd	
M-YJET	Dassault Falcon 7	M-EDIA Aviation Ltd	
M-YKBO	Embraer EMB-135BJ Legacy	Transeurope Air Establishment	
M-YMCM	Bell 429	T. J. Morris Ltd	
M-YNNS	Gulfstream 650	Aviation One Ltd	
M-YOIL	Bombardier BD700-1A10 Global 6000	Shelf Support Shiphold Ltd	
M-YRGL	Aerospatiale ATR-72-212A	Turbo 72-500 Leasing Ltd	
M-YSAI	Bombardier BD700-1A10 Global 5000	Capital Investment Worldwide	
M-YSIX	Gulfstream 650	AC Executive Aircraft (2016) Ltd	
M-YSSF	Bombardier BD700-1A10 Global 6000	Springtime Ltd	
M-YTAF	Beech B.36TC Bonanza	FBS Aviation Ltd	
M-YULI	Bombardier BD700-1A10 Global 6000	Woodlock Holdings Ltd	
M-YVVF	Bombardier BD700-1A10 Global 5000	Lightstar Aviation Ltd	
M-YWAY	Gulfstream IV	Blue Sky Leasing Ltd	
M-ZELL	Cessna 208 Caravan	Ridler Verwaltungs und Vermittlungs GmbH	
M-ZJBT	Dassault Falcon 7X	Thrive Star Global Ltd	
M-ZMDZ	Bombardier BD700-1A10 Global Express XRS	Zhong Jia Global Ltd	

Reg	Type	Owner or Operator	Notes
2-AERA	Boeing 777-28EER	Fortress Ireland Leasing Ltd	
2-AERD	Airbus A.330-223	Aircraft Lotus Inc	
2-AERE	Airbus A.319-132	AerCap Ireland Ltd	
2-AKOP	Commander 114B	M. A. Perry	
2-ALOU	Sud Aviation 3130 Alouette II	S. Atherton	
2-ANLD	PA-34-220T Seneca V	D. & L. Medcraft	
2-ASIA	ATR-72-212A	Aircraft Solutions XIX SARL	
2-AUER	Cirrus Vision SF-50	Euro Aircraft Leasing Ltd	
2-AVCO	Canadair CRJ200	Avionco Ltd	
2-AWBN	PA-30-160 Twin Comanche	Bravo November Ltd	
2-AZFR	Cessna 401B	R. E. H. Wragg	
2-BASG	Boeing 737-73W	Business Aviation Services Guernsey Ltd	
2-BEST	Commander 114B	D. W. R. Best	
2-BHXG	Airbus A.340-313	Aerfin Ltd	
2-BLUE	Bombardier CL600-2B16 Challenger 601	Sable Air ApS	
2-BOYS	Commander 114B	I. Barker	
2-BREM	MBB Bolkow BO.105 DBS-5	Wessex Aviation Ltd	
2-BYDF	Sikorsky S-76	Brecqhou Development Company	
2-CAUL	DHC.8-402 Dash Eight	Aero Century Corp	

Notes	Reg	Type	Owner or Operator
	2-CAUY	DHC.8-402 Dash Eight	Aero Century Corp
	2-CFFV	Canadair CRJ200ER	Regional One Inc
	2-CFML	Canadair CRJ200ER	Regional One Inc
	2-CHEZ	PA-28-161 Warrior II	Fletcher Aviation Ltd
	2-CHIU	Gulfstream 300	Business Aviation Services Guernsey Ltd
	2-CREW	Cessna 208B Grand Caravan	ASL NV
	2-CUTE	Bombardier CL600-2B16 Challenger 601-3A	Springbok Holdings Ltd
	2-CYAJ	Embraer ERJ190-100LR	Aldus Portfolio T Ltd
	2-CYAS	Embraer ERJ190-200IGW	Aldus Portfolio T Ltd
	2-DARE	Pilatus PC-12/47E	Brightling Services Ltd
	2-DCBU	ATR-72-212A	Elix Assets 14 Ltd
	2-DCBV	ATR-72-500	Elix Assets 14 Ltd
	2-DEER	Boeing 787-8(BBJ)	Ocean Transportation Facility Investment Ltd
	2-DITO	PA-46-500TP Malibu Meridian	Citavia BV
	2-DOLU	Beech 95-58 Baron	R. A. Perrot
	2-DRPA	Airbus A.380-841	Flagship Three Ltd
	2-EACA	ATR-72-212A	Elix Assets 7 Ltd
	2-ESKA	Boeing 737-301	European Aviation Ltd
	2-ESKB	Boeing 737-301	European Aviation Ltd
	2-FIEX	Airbus A.340-642	European Aviation Ltd
	2-FIFI	PA-46-500TP Malibu Meridian	Springhaven Ltd
	2-FINA	Embraer ERJ170-200	AerFin Ltd
	2-FIXP	Airbus A.340-642	European Aviation Ltd
	2-FLUX	PA-32R-301T Saratoga II TC	Fluxitech Consulting
	2-FLYE	ATR-42-320	Airtrails Leasing 1 GmbH
	2-FLYY	Pilatus PC-12/47E	M. Ozmerter
	2-FPLF	Beech B.350 Super King Air	Miralty Holdings Ltd
	2-GECA	Sikorsky S-76C	Wilmington Trust SP Services (Dublin) Ltd
	2-GECB	Sikorsky S-76C	Wilmington Trust SP Services (Dublin) Ltd
	2-GECC	Sikorsky S-76C	Wilmington Trust SP Services (Dublin) Ltd
	2-GIAR	Bombardier CL600-2B19 CRJ200ER	Sky Swallows Capital Ltd
	2-GJSA	ATR-42-500	Flair Aviation GmbH
	2-GJSB	ATR-42-500	Flair Aviation GmbH
	2-GNSY	Cammander Aircraft Commander 114B	J. Tostevin
	2-GODS	Cirrus SR22T	Jetworx Ltd
	2-GOLF	Cessna 525A Citationjet CJ2+	MTEAM Ltd
	2-GOOD	PA-32-301T Saratoga II TC	S. R. Miller
	2-GSYJ	Diamond DA.42 Twin Star	Crosby Aviation (Jersey) Ltd
	2-GULF	Gulfstream IVSP	Travcorp Transportation Ltd
	2-GZEH	Airbus A.319-111	SAP Meridian 7 LP
	2-HAUL	Boeing 737-3YO	European Aviation Ltd
	2-HELO	Agusta A109C	Helicopter (Seychelles) Ltd
	2-ITLG	Boeing 737-8K5	ILFC Ireland Ltd
	2-ITLH	Boeing 737-8K5	ILFC Ireland Ltd
	2-JACK	PA-46-500TP Malibu Meridian	Icaris Ventura SA
	2-JBMF	Embraer EMB-500 Phenom 100	JB Feggair ApS
	2-JEFS	PA-32R-301T Turbo Saratoga SP	J. Barnet
	2-JFJC	Bombardier BD700-1A10 Global Express	Shanbeth Limited Partnership
	2-JSEG	Eclipse EA500	Truly Classic LP Inc
	2-KOOL	PA-28-181 Archer II	Charlie Alpha Ltd
	2-LAND	Rockwell Commander 114B	88 Zulu Ltd
	2-LCXO	BAe Jetstream 3102	J. Ibbotson
	2-LFEA	Aerospatiale ATR-42-500	Phoenix Aircraft Leasing PTE Ltd
	2-LIFE	Eclipse EA500	B. Vonk
	2-LIFT	Agusta A109A II	Lift West Ltd
	2-LIVE	Pilatus PC-12/47E	Stammair Guernsey
	2-LOVE	Beech A.36 Bonanza	Immuno Biotech Ltd
	2-MAPP	Cessna 421C	MBA Aviation Ltd
	2-MATO	Bombardier CL600-2B16 Challenger	Volare Aviation Ltd
	2-MIKE	Commander 114B	M. A. Perry
	2-MMTT	Boeing 727-76	Platinum Services Ltd
	2-MOVE	Boeing 737-382QC	European Aviation Ltd
	2-MSTG	Cessna 510 Citation Mustang	Mustang Sally Aviation Ltd
	2-MUST	Cessna 510 Citation Mustang	W. F. McSweeney
	2-NOOR	Commander 114B	As-Al Ltd
	2-NOVA	Beech 95-B55 Baron	Novatrust Agency SRL
	2-NYAW	Dassault Falcon 50	H2M
	2-OCST	Agusta-Bell 206B-3 Jet Ranger 3	Lift West Ltd
	2-ODAY	Bombardier CL600-2B16 Challenger 601	Pixwood Limited Partnership
	2-OFUS	Cirrus SR22	L. J. Murray
	2-OSJN	Airbus A.320-231	Craftlease Ltd

Reg	Type	Owner or Operator	Notes
2-OWLC	PA-31 Turbo Navajo	Channel Airways Ltd	
2-PDPD	Agusta-Bell 206B-3 Jet Ranger III	Pink Time Ltd	
2-PETE	PA-32-300 Cherokee Six	P. Biggins	
2-PGSI	Boeing 737-55D	European Aviation Ltd	
2-PJBA	Aerospatiale SA.341G Gazelle	S. Atherton	
2-PKSG	ATR-72-212A	NAC Aviation 8 Ltd	
2-PLAY	SOCATA TBM-700C-1	N700 VB Ltd	
2-POSH	Cessna 525B Citationjet CJ3	Danish Aircraft Management ApS	
2-PROP	Beech 58 Baron	L. Moore	
2-PSFI	Boeing 737-33A	European Aviation Ltd	
2-QWEA	Boeing 737-8H6	Alip No.36 Co.Ltd	
2-QWEB	Boeing 737-8H6	Alip No.37 Co.Ltd	
2-RACE	Commander 114B	M. A. Perry	
2-RAYM	PA-31T Cheyenne II	Helijet	
2-RICH	PA-46-500TP Malibu Meridian	M K Homes Ltd	
2-RIOH	Navion H Rangemaster	M K Homes Ltd	
2-RLAD	Embraer EMB-145LI	Komiaviatrans	
2-RLAS	Boeing 777-31H	SASOF III(B) Aviation Ireland DAC	
2-RLAT	Boeing 777-31H	SASOF III(B) Aviation Ireland DAC	
2-ROCK	Cirrus SR22	Fletcher Aviation Ltd	
2-RODS	Cessna 310Q	Formalhaut Ltd	
2-ROMA	Boeing 737-524	A. Drevs	
2-RPDA	ATR-72-212A	NAC Aviation 29 Ltd	
2-RPDC	ATR-72-212A	NAC Aviation 29 Ltd	
2-SAIL	Agusta-Bell 206B Jet Ranger II	L. E. V. Knifton	
2-SALA	PA-32-300 Cherokee Six	R. M. Harrison & J. W. A. Portch	
2-SALE	Diamond DA.62	Morson Group Ltd	
2-SEVN	Boeing 727-281A	TAG Aviation (Stansted) Ltd	
2-SEXY	Agusta A.109E Power	Volare Aviation Ltd	
2-SMKM	Cirrus SR20	K. Mallet	
2-STEJ	Airbus A.330-322	AerCap Dutch Aircraft Leasing IV BV	
2-SWKE	ATR-72-212A	Elix Assets 12 Ltd	
2-TBMI	SOCATA TBM-930	TBM Aviation Ltd	
2-TAXI	PA-34-200T Seneca II	Quantstellation Investment Management (Guernsey)	
2-TGHA	Embraer EMB-145LR	Airbus SAS	
2-TGHB	Embraer EMB-145LR	Airbus SAS	
2-TGHC	Embraer EMB-145LR	Airbus SAS	
2-TGHD	Embraer EMB-145LR	Airbus SAS	
2-TGHE	Embraer EMB-145LI	Airbus SAS	
2-TGHF	Embraer EMB-145LR	Airbus SAS	
2-TGHG	Embraer EMB-145LR	Airbus SAS	
2-TGHH	Embraer EMB-145LR	Alphastream Ltd	
2-TGHI	Embraer EMB-145LR	Alphastream Ltd	
2-TRAV	Gulfstream 550	Travcorp Air Transportation 2 (IOM) Ltd	
2-WFBA	ATR-42-320	Wells Fargo Bank Northwest National Association	
2-WILD	Aerospatiale SA.342J Gazelle	X. de Tracy	
2-WMAN	Aerospatiale SA.341G Gazelle	J. Wightman	
2-WOOD	Cessna 550 Citation Bravo	Horizon Air LLP	
2-WORK	Boeing 737-3L9	European Aviation Ltd	
2-XAVT	ATR-72-212A	KA1 P/S	
2-YAGY	Canadair CRJ200LR		
2-YULL	PA-28R-201 Arrow	G. Watkinson-Yull	
2-ZOOM	Commander 114B	Bagair (Guernsey) Ltd	

Reg	Type	Owner or Operator	Notes
ZJ-HLH	Eurocopter EC135 P2	GAMA Aviation Ltd	
ZJ-THC	Cessna 525c Citationjet CJ4	Tower House Consultants	

Serial Carried	Civil Identity	Serial Carried	Civil Identity
001	G-BYPY	503 (Hungarian AF)	G-BRAM
1	G-BPVE	540 (USAAF)	G-BCNX
1 (Soviet AF)	G-BZMY	556/17 (Luftwaffe)	G-CFHY
6	G-CAMM	669 (USAAC)	G-CCXA
6G+ED (Lutwaffe)	G-BZOB	687	G-AWYI
9 (Soviet AF)	G-OYAK	781-32 (Spanish AF)	G-BPDM
01 (Soviet AF)	G-YKSZ	854 (USAAC)	G-BTBH
03 (Soviet AF)	G-CEIB	897:E (USN)	G-BJEV
07 (Soviet AF)	G-BMJY	99+18 (Luftwaffe)	G-ONAA
10 (DOSAAF)	G-BTZB	99+26 (Luftwaffe)	G-BZGL
10 (DOSAAF)	G-CBMD	99+32 (Luftwaffe)	G-BZGK
14 (USAAC)	G-ISDN	1018 (Polish AF)	G-ISKA
20 (Soviet AF)	G-YAAK	1102:102 (USN)	G-AZLE
21 (Soviet AF)	G-CDBJ	1130 (Royal Saudi AF)	G-VPER
23 (Soviet AF)	G-YKSO	1164:64 (USAAC)	G-BKGL
26 (USAAC)	G-BAVO	1211(North Korean AF)	G-MIGG
26 (DOSAAF)	G-BVXK	1264	G-FDHB
27 (Soviet AF)	G-YAKX	1342 (Soviet AF)	G-BTZD
27 (USN)	G-BRVG	1350 (Portuguese AF)	G-CGAO
27 (USAAC)	G-AGYY	1365 (Portuguese AF)	G-DHPM
27 (Soviet AF)	G-YAKX	1373 (Portuguese AF)	G-CBJG
28 (Soviet AF)	G-BSSY	1377 (Portuguese AF)	G-BARS
33 (grey) (Soviet AF)	G-YAKH	1747 (Portuguese AF)	G-BGPB
33 (red) (Soviet AF)	G-YAKZ	1801/18 (Luftwaffe)	G-BNPV
42 (Soviet AF)	G-CBRU	1803/18 (Luftwaffe)	G-BUYU
43 (Soviet AF)	G-BWSV	2345 (RFC)	G-ATVP
43:SC (USAF)	G-AZSC	3066	G-AETA
44 (USAAC)	G-DINS	3072:72 (USN)	G-TEXN
44 (DOSAAF)	G-BXAK	3303 (Portuguese AF)	G-CBGL
49 (USAAF)	G-KITT	3349 (RCAF)	G-BYNF
49 (Soviet AF)	G-YAKU	3397:174 (USN)	G-OBEE
50 (DOSAAF)	G-CBPM	3681 (USAAC)	G-AXGP
50 (DOSAAF)	G-CBRW	4034 (Luftwaffe)	G-CDTI
50 (DOSAAF)	G-EYAK	4406:12 (USN)	G-ONAF
52 (DOSAAF)	G-BWVR	4513:1 (French AF)	G-BFYO
52 (Soviet AF)	G-BTZE	51970(USN)	G-TXAN
52 (Soviet AF)	G-CCJK	5964 (RFC)	G-BFVH
52 (Soviet AF)	G-YAKY	6136:205 (USN)	G-BRUJ
61 (Soviet AF)	G-YAKM	7198/18 (Luftwaffe)	G-AANJ
66 (Soviet AF)	G-YAKN	7797 (USAAF)	G-BFAF
67 (DOSAAF)	G-CBSL	8084 (USAAF)	G-KAMY
68 (Chinese AF)	G-BVVG	8449M (RAF)	G-ASWJ
78 (French Army)	G-BIZK	9917	G-EBKY
82:8 (French AF)	G-CCVH	01420 (Polish AF but in Korean colours)	G-BMZF
100 (DOSAAF)	G-CGXG	14863 (USAAF)	G-BGOR
100 (DOSAAF)	G-YAKI	16037 (USAAC)	G-BSFD
104 (South Arabian AF)	G-PROV	16693:693 (RCAF)	G-BLPG
105/15 (Luftwaffe)	G-UDET	18393:393 (RCAF)	G-BCYK
112 (USAAC)	G-BSWC	18671:671 (RCAF)	G-BNZC
113 (Kuwait AF)	G-CFBK	20310:310 (RCAF)	G-BSBG
118 (USAAC)	G-BSDS	21261:261 (RCAF)	G-TBRD
124 (French Army)	G-BOSJ	21509 (US Army)	G-UHIH
143 (French AF)	G-MSAL	24541:BMG (French Army)	G-JDOG
152/17 (Luftwaffe)	G-BVGZ	24550 (US Army)	G-PDOG
156 (French AF)	G-NIFE	24582 (US Army)	G-VDOG
161 (Irish Air Corps)	G-CCCA	28521:TA-521 (USAF)	G-TVIJ
168 (RFC)	G-BFDE	30146 (Yugoslav Army)	G-BSXD
174 (Royal Netherlands Navy)	G-BEPV	30149 (Yugoslav Army)	G-SOKO
309 (USAAC)	G-IIIG	31145:G-26 (USAAF)	G-BBLH
311 (Singapore AF)	G-MXPH	3-1923 (USAAF)	G-BRHP
317 (USAAC)	G-CIJN	31952 (USAAF)	G-BRPR
354	G-BZNK	39-160:160 10AB (USAAF)	G-CIIO
379 (USAAC)	G-ILLE	43517:227 (USN)	G-NZSS
403/17 (Luftwaffe)	G-CDXR	56321:U-AB (Royal Norwegian AF)	G-BKPY
416/15 (Luftwaffe)	G-GSAL	61367	G-CGHB
422/15 (Luftwaffe)	G-AVJO	66-374:EO (USAAF)	G-BAGT
422/15 (Luftwaffe)	G-FOKR	80105 (US Air Service)	G-CCBN
423 / 427 (Royal Norwegian AF)	G-AMRK	80425:WT-4 (USN)	G-RUMT
425 (Oman AF)	G-SOAF	85061:7F-061 (USN)	G-CHIA
441 (USN)	G-BTFG	111836:JZ-6 (USN)	G-TSIX
477/17 (Luftwaffe)	G-FOKK	115042:TA-042 (USAF)	G-BGHU

Serial Carried	Civil Identity	Serial Carried	Civil Identity
115227 (USN)	G-BKRA	51-15555 (US Army)	G-OSPS
115302:TP (USMC)	G-BJTP	54-2445 (USAF)	G-OTAN
115373 (USAAF)	G-AYPM	69-16011 (USAAF)	G-OHGA
115684 (USAAF)	G-BKVM	108-1601 (USAAF)	G-CFGE
121714:201-B (USN)	G-RUMM	A-10 (Swiss AF)	G-BECW
124485:DF-A (USAAF)	G-BEDF	A11-301 (RAN)	G-ARKG
126922:503 (USN)	G-RADR	A16-199:SF-R (RAAF)	G-BEOX
150225:123 (USMC)	G-AWOX	A17-48 (RAAF)	G-BPHR
18-2001 (USAAF)	G-BIZV	A-57 (Swiss AF)	G-BECT
18-5395:CDG (French Army)	G-CUBJ	A-806 (Swiss AF)	G-BTLL
2106638:E9-R (USAAF)	G-CIFD	A126	G-CILI
236657:D-72 (USAAF)	G-BGSJ	A8226	G-BIDW
238410:A-44 (USAAF)	G-BHPK	B595:W	G-BUOD
314887 (USAAF)	G-AJPI	B1807	G-EAVX
315509:W7-S (USAAF)	G-BHUB	B2458:R	G-BPOB
329405:A-23 (USAAF)	G-BCOB	B6401	G-AWYY
329417 (USAAF)	G-BDHK	C1904:Z	G-PFAP
329471:F-44 (USAAF)	G-BGXA	C3009	G-BFWD
329601:D-44 (USAAF)	G-AXHR	C3011:S	G-SWOT
329707:S-44 (USAAF)	G-BFBY	C4918	G-BWJM
329854:R-44 (USAAF)	G-BMKC	C4994	G-BLWM
329934:B-72 (USAAF)	G-BCPH	C5430	G-CCXG
330238:A-24 (USAAF)	G-LIVH	C9533:M	G-BUWE
330244:C-46 (USAAF)	G-CGIY	D-692	G-BVAW
330314 (USAAF)	G-BAET	D1851	G-BZSC
330372 (USAAF)	G-AISX	D5397/17 (Luftwaffe)	G-BFXL
330485:C-44 (USAAF)	G-AJES	D7889	G-AANM
379994:J-52 (USAAF)	G-BPUR	D8084	G-ACAA
413926: E2-S (USAAF)	G-CGOI	D8096:D	G-AEPH
414419:LH-F (USAAF)	G-MSTG	E-15 (Royal Netherlands AF)	G-BIYU
414673:LH-I (USAAF)	G-BDWM	E3B-143 (Spanish AF)	G-JUNG
414907:CY-S (USAAF)	G-DHYS	E3B-153:781-75 (Spanish AF)	G-BPTS
433915 (USAAF)	G-PBYA	E3B-350:05-97 (Spanish AF)	G-BHPL
436021 (USAAF)	G-BWEZ	E449	G-EBJE
454467:J-44 (USAAF)	G-BILI	E3273	G-ADEV
454537:J-04 (USAAF)	G-BFDL	E8894	G-CDLI
461748:Y (USAF)	G-BHDK	F141:G	G-SEVA
472035 (USAAF)	G-SIJJ	F235:B	G-BMDB
472216:HO-M (USAAF)	G-BIXL	F904	G-EBIA
472218:WZ-I (USAAF)	G-MUZY	F938	G-EBIC
474008:VF-R (USAAF)	G-PSIR	F943	G-BIHF
479712:8-R (USAAF)	G-AHIP	F943	G-BKDT
479744:M-49 (USAAF)	G-BGPD	F5447:N	G-BKER
479766:D-63 (USAAF)	G-BKHG	F5459:Y	G-INNY
479897:JD(USAAF)	G-BOXJ	F8010:Z	G-BDWJ
480015:M-44 (USAAF)	G-AKIB	F8614	G-AWAU
480133:B-44 (USAAF)	G-BDCD	G-48-1 (Class B)	G-ALSX
480173:57-H (USAAF)	G-RRSR	J-1605 (Swiss AF)	G-BLID
480321:H-44 (USAAF)	G-FRAN	J-1632 (Swiss AF)	G-VNOM
480480:E-44 (USAAF)	G-BECN	J-1758 (Swiss AF)	G-BLSD
480636:A-58 (USAAF)	G-AXHP	J-4021 (Swiss AF)	G-HHAC
480723:E5-J (USAAF)	G-BFZB	J7326	G-EBQP
480752:E-39 (USAAF)	G-BCXJ	J9941:57	G-ABMR
493209 (US ANG)	G-DDMV	K1786	G-AFTA
542447 (USAF)	G-SCUB	K1930	G-BKBB
2632019 (Chinese AF)	G-BXZB	K2048	G-BZNW
41-19841:X-17	G-CGZP	K2050	G-ASCM
41-33275:CE (USAAF)	G-BICE	K2059	G-PFAR
42-35870:129 (USN)	G-BWLJ	K2075	G-BEER
42-58678:IY (USAAF)	G-BRIY	K2227	G-ABBB
42-78044 (USAAF)	G-BRXL	K2567	G-MOTH
42-84555:EP-H (USAAF)	G-ELMH	K2572	G-AOZH
43-35943 (USN)	G-BKRN	K2587	G-BJAP
44-14561:CY-D (USAAF)	G-TFSI	K3241	G-AHSA
44-79609:44-S (USAAF)	G-BHXY	K3661	G-BURZ
44-79790 (USAAF)	G-BJAY	K3731	G-RODI
44-80594 (USAAF)	G-BEDJ	K4259:71	G-ANMO
44-83184 (USAAF)	G-RGUS	K5054	G-BRDV
51-7692 (French AF)	G-TROY	K5414:XV	G-AENP
51-15319 (USAAF)	G-FUZZ	K5600	G-BVVI
51-15527 (USN)	G-BKRA	K5673	G-BZAS

Serial Carried	Civil Identity	Serial Carried	Civil Identity
K5682	G-BBVO	T9768	G-AIUA
K5674	G-CBZP	U-0247 (Class B identity)	G-AGOY
K7271	G-CCKV	U-80 (Swiss AF)	G-BUKK
K7985	G-AMRK	U-95 (Swiss AF)	G-BVGP
K8203	G-BTVE	U-99 (Swiss AF)	G-AXMT
K8303:D	G-BWWN	U-108 (Swiss AF)	G-BJAX
L2301	G-AIZG	U-110 (Swiss AF)	G-PTWO
L6739:YP-Q	G-BPIV	V-54 (Swiss AF)	G-BVSD
L6906	G-AKKY	V3388	G-AHTW
N-294 (RNeth AF)	G-KAXF	V7497	G-HRLI
N500	G-BWRA	V9312	G-CCOM
N1854	G-AIBE	V9367:MA-B	G-AZWT
N1977:8 (French AF)	G-BWMJ	V9673:MA-J	G-LIZY
N3200	G-CFGJ	W2718	G-RNLI
N3788	G-AKPF	W5856:A2A	G-BMGC
N4877:MK-V	G-AMDA	W9385:YG-L	G-ADND
N5182	G-APUP	X4276	G-CDGU
N5195	G-ABOX	X4650	G-CGUK
N5199	G-BZND	Z2033:N/275	G-ASTL
N5719	G-CBHO	Z5207	G-BYDL
N5903:H	G-GLAD	Z5252:GO-B	G-BWHA
N6290	G-BOCK	Z7015:7-L	G-BKTH
N6452	G-BIAU	Z7197	G-AKZN
N6466	G-ANKZ	AB196	G-CCGH
N6537	G-AOHY	AD370 : PJ-C	G-CHBW
N6720:VX	G-BYTN	AG244	G-CBOE
N6797	G-ANEH	AP506	G-ACWM
N6847	G-APAL	AP507:KX-P	G-ACWP
N6965:FL-J	G-AJTW	AR501:NN-A	G-AWII
N9191	G-ALND	BB697	G-ADGT
N9192:RCO-N	G-DHZF	BB803	G-ADWJ
N9328	G-ALWS	BB807	G-ADWO
N9389	G-ANJA	BE505:XP-L	G-HHII
N9503	G-ANFP	BI-005 (RNethAF)	G-BUVN
P2902:DX-X	G-ROBT	BL735 (BT-A)	G-HABT
P2921:GZ-L	G-CHTK	BL927 (JH-I)	G-CGWI
P3700:RF-E	G-HURI	BM597:JH-C	G-MKVB
P3717:SW-P	G-HITT	CW-BG (Luftwaffe)	G-BXBD
P6382:C	G-AJRS	DE208	G-AGYU
P7308:XR-D	G-AIST	DE470	G-ANMY
P9398	G-CEPL	DE623	G-ANFI
R-55 (RNethAF)	G-BLMI	DE673	G-ADNZ
R-151 (RNethAF)	G-BIYR	DE971	G-OOSY
R-156 (RNethAF)	G-ROVE	DE974	G-ANZZ
R-167 (RNethAF)	G-LION	DE992	G-AXXV
R1914	G-AHUJ	DF112	G-ANRM
R4118:UP-W	G-HUPW	DF128:RCO-U	G-AOJJ
R4922	G-APAO	DF198	G-BBRB
R4959:59	G-ARAZ	DG590	G-ADMW
R5136	G-APAP	EE602:DV-V	G-IBSY
R5172:FIJ-E	G-AOIS	EM720	G-AXAN
R5250	G-AODT	EM726	G-ANDE
R9649	G-CISV	EN130 : FN-A	G-ENAA
S1287	G-BEYB	EN224	G-FXII
S1581:573	G-BWWK	EN961:SD-X	G-CGIK
T5854	G-ANKK	EP120:AE-A	G-LFVB
T5879:RUC-W	G-AXBW	ES.1-4 (Spanish AF)	G-BUTX
T6562	G-ANTE	FE695:94	G-BTXI
T6818	G-ANKT	FE788	G-CTKL
T6953	G-ANNI	FH153	G-BBHK
T7281	G-ARTL	FJ777 (RCAF)	G-BIXN
T7290	G-ANNK	FR886	G-BDMS
T7793	G-ANKV	FS628	G-AIZE
T7794	G-ASPV	FT391	G-AZBN
T7798	G-ANZT	FZ626:YS-DH	G-AMPO
T7842	G-AMTF	HB275	G-BKGM
T7909	G-ANON	HB751	G-BCBL
T7997	G-AHUF	HD-75 (R Belgian AF)	G-AFDX
T8191	G-BWMK	HG691	G-AIYR
T9707	G-AKKR	HM580	G-ACUU
T9738	G-AKAT	JV579:F	G-RUMW

Serial Carried	Civil Identity	Serial Carried	Civil Identity
KB889:NA-I	G-LANC	SM969:D-A	G-BRAF
KD345:130-A	G-FGID	SX336:105-VL	G-KASX
KF584:RAI-X	G-RAIX	SR661	G-CBEL
KF729	G-BJST	TA634:8K-K	G-AWJV
KG651	G-AMHJ	TA719:6T	G-ASKC
KH570:5J-X	G-CIXK	TA805:FX-M	G-PMNF
KH774:GA-S	G-SHWN	TD248:CR-S	G-OXVI
KK116	G-AMPY	TD314:FX-P	G-CGYJ
KN353	G-AMYJ	TE184:D	G-MXVI
LB264	G-AIXA	TE517	G-JGCA
LB312	G-AHXE	TJ207	G-AKPI
LB323	G-AHSD	TJ343	G-AJXC
LB367	G-AHGZ	TJ518	G-AJIH
LB375	G-AHGW	TJ534	G-AKSY
LF858	G-BLUZ	TJ565	G-AMVD
LZ766	G-ALCK	TJ569	G-AKOW
LZ842:EF-F	G-CGZU	TJ672:TS-D	G-ANIJ
MH434:ZD-B	G-ASJV	TJ704:JA	G-ASCD
MJ627:9G-P	G-BMSB	TS798	G-AGNV
MJ772:NL-R	G-AVAV	TW439	G-ANRP
MK912:SH-L	G-BRRA	TW467	G-ANIE
ML407:OU-V	G-LFIX	TW501	G-ALBJ
MP425	G-AITB	TW511	G-APAF
MS824 (French AF)	G-AWBU	TW519	G-ANHX
MT182	G-AJDY	TW536:TS-V	G-BNGE
MT197	G-ANHS	TW591:N	G-ARIH
MT438	G-AREI	TW641	G-ATDN
MT818	G-AIDN	TX213	G-AWRS
MV268:JE-J	G-SPIT	TX310	G-AIDL
MW401	G-PEST	TZ164:OI-A	G-ISAC
MW763:HF-A	G-TEMT	VF512:PF-M	G-ARRX
NJ633	G-AKXP	VF516	G-ASMZ
NJ673	G-AOCR	VF526:T	G-ARXU
NJ689	G-ALXZ	VF557:H	G-ARHM
NJ695	G-AJXV	VL348	G-AVVO
NJ719	G-ANFU	VL349	G-AWSA
NJ728	G-AIKE	VM360	G-APHV
NJ889	G-AHLK	VN799	G-CDSX
NL750	G-AOBH	VP955	G-DVON
NL985	G-BWIK	VP981	G-DHDV
NM138	G-ANEW	VR192	G-APIT
NM181	G-AZGZ	VR249:FA-EL	G-APIY
NX534	G-BUDL	VR259:M	G-APJB
NX611:LE-C/DX-C	G-ASXX	VS356	G-AOLU
PG657	G-AGPK	VS610:K-L	G-AOKL
PL788	G-CIEN	VS623	G-AOKZ
PL793	G-CIXM	VX113	G-ARNO
PL965:R	G-MKXI	VX118	G-ASNB
PL983	G-PRXI	VX147	G-AVIL
PP972 : II-5	G-BUAR	VX281	G-RNHF
PS853:C	G-RRGN	VX927	G-ASYG
PT462:SW-A	G-CTIX	VZ638:HF	G-JETM
PT879	G-PTIX	VZ728	G-AGOS
PV202U	G-CCCA	WA576	G-ALSS
PV303:ON-B	G-CCJL	WA577	G-ALST
RB142:DW-B	G-CEFC	WA591:FMK-Q	G-BWMF
RG333	G-AIEK	WB565:X	G-PVET
RG333	G-AKEZ	WB569:R	G-BYSJ
RH377	G-ALAH	WB585:M	G-AOSY
RK855	G-PIXY	WB588:D	G-AOTD
RL962	G-AHED	WB615:E	G-BXIA
RM221	G-ANXR	WB652:V	G-CHPY
RN218:N	G-BBJI	WB654:U	G-BXGO
RR232	G-BRSF	WB671:910	G-BWTG
RT486:PF-A	G-AJGJ	WB697:95	G-BXCT
RT520	G-ALYB	WB702	G-AOFE
RT610	G-AKWS	WB703	G-ARMC
RW382:3W-P	G-PBIX	WB711	G-APPM
RX168	G-BWEM	WB726:E	G-AOSK
SM520:KJ-1	G-ILDA	WB763:14	G-BBMR
SM845:R	G-BUOS	WD286	G-BBND

Serial Carried	Civil Identity	Serial Carried	Civil Identity
WD292	G-BCRX	WP930:J	G-BXHF
WD310:B	G-BWUN	WP964	G-HDAE
WD327	G-ATVF	WP971	G-ATHD
WD331:J	G-BXDH	WP973	G-BCPU
WD363:5	G-BCIH	WP983:B	G-BXNN
WD373:12	G-BXDI	WP984:H	G-BWTO
WD379:K	G-APLO	WR410:N	G-BLKA
WD390:68	G-BWNK	WR963	G-SKTN
WD413	G-VROE	WT333	G-BVXC
WE569	G-ASAJ	WT723:692/LM	G-PRII
WE724:062	G-BUCM	WT933	G-ALSW
WF118	G-DACA	WV198:K	G-BJWY
WF877	G-BPOA	WV318:D	G-FFOX
WG308:8	G-BYHL	WV322:Y	G-BZSE
WG316	G-BCAH	WV493:29	G-BDYG
WG321:G	G-DHCC	WV514	G-BLIW
WG348	G-BBMV	WV740	G-BNPH
WG350	G-BPAL	WV783	G-ALSP
WG407:67	G-BWMX	WZ507:74	G-VTII
WG422:16	G-BFAX	WZ662	G-BKVK
WG465	G-BCEY	WZ679	G-CIUX
WG469:72	G-BWJY	WZ706	G-BURR
WG472	G-AOTY	WZ847:F	G-CPMK
WG655	G-CHFP	WZ868:H	G-ARMF
WG719	G-BRMA	WZ872:E	G-BZGB
WJ358	G-ARYD	WZ879	G-BWUT
WJ368	G-ASZX	WZ882:K	G-BXGP
WJ404	G-ASOI	XD693:Z-Q	G-AOBU
WJ945:21	G-BEDV	XE489	G-JETH
WK163	G-CTTS	XE685:861/VL	G-GAII
WK436	G-VENM	XE856	G-DUSK
WK512:A	G-BXIM	XE956	G-OBLN
WK514	G-BBMO	XF114	G-SWIF
WK517	G-ULAS	XF597:AH	G-BKFW
WK522	G-BCOU	XF603	G-KAPW
WK549	G-BTWF	XF690	G-MOOS
WK558:DH	G-ARMG	XF785	G-ALBN
WK577	G-BCYM	XF836:J-G	G-AWRY
WK585	G-BZGA	XG160:U	G-BWAF
WK586:V	G-BXGX	XG452	G-BRMB
WK590:69	G-BWVZ	XH134	G-OMHD
WK609:93	G-BXDN	XH558	G-VLCN
WK611	G-ARWB	XJ389	G-AJJP
WK624	G-BWHI	XJ398	G-BDBZ
WK628	G-BBMW	XJ615	G-BWGL
WK630	G-BXDG	XJ729	G-BVGE
WK633:A	G-BXEC	XK417	G-AVXY
WK634:902	G-CIGE	XK895:19/CU	G-SDEV
WK635	G-HFRH	XK896	G-RNAS
WK640:C	G-BWUV	XK940:911	G-AYXT
WL419	G-JSMA	XL426	G-VJET
WL626:P	G-BHDD	XL500	G-KAEW
WM167	G-LOSM	XL502	G-BMYP
WP308:572CU	G-GACA	XL571:V	G-HNTR
WP321	G-BRFC	XL573	G-BVGH
WP788	G-BCHL	XL587	G-HPUX
WP790:T	G-BBNC	XL602	G-BWFT
WP795:901	G-BVZZ	XL621	G-BNCX
WP800:2	G-BCXN	XL714	G-AOGR
WP803	G-HAPY	XL809	G-BLIX
WP805:D	G-MAJR	XL929	G-BNPU
WP809:78 RN	G-BVTX	XL954	G-BXES
WP848	G-BFAW	XM223:J	G-BWWC
WP860:6	G-BXDA	XM424	G-BWDS
WP870:12	G-BCOI	XM479:54	G-BVEZ
WP896	G-BWVY	XM553	G-AWSV
WP901:B	G-BWNT	XM575	G-BLMC
WP903	G-BCGC	XM655	G-VULC
WP925:C	G-BXHA	XM685:513/PO	G-AYZJ
WP928:D	G-BXGM	XM819	G-APXW
WP929:F	G-BXCV	XN351	G-BKSC

Serial Carried	Civil Identity	Serial Carried	Civil Identity
XN437	G-AXWA	XX546:03	G-WINI
XN441	G-BGKT	XX549:6	G-CBID
XN498	G-BWSH	XX550:Z	G-CBBL
XN637:03	G-BKOU	XX551:E	G-BZDP
XP242	G-BUCI	XX554	G-BZMD
XP254	G-ASCC	XX561:7	G-BZEP
XP282	G-BGTC	XX611:7	G-CBDK
XP355	G-BEBC	XX612:A, 03	G-BZXC
XP820	G-CICP	XX614:V	G-GGRR
XP907	G-SROE	XX619:T	G-CBBW
XP924	G-CVIX	XX621:H	G-CBEF
XR240	G-BDFH	XX622:B	G-CBGZ
XR241	G-AXRR	XX624:E	G-KDOG
XR244	G-CICR	XX625	G-UWAS
XR246	G-AZBU	XX626:02, W	G-CDVV
XR267	G-BJXR	XX628:9	G-CBFU
XR486	G-RWWW	XX629:V	G-BZXZ
XR537:T	G-NATY	XX630:5	G-SIJW
XR538:01	G-RORI	XX631:W	G-BZXS
XR595:M	G-BWHU	XX636:Y	G-CBFP
XR673:L	G-BXLO	XX638	G-DOGG
XR724	G-BTSY	XX658:07	G-BZPS
XR944	G-ATTB	XX667:16	G-BZFN
XR991	G-MOUR	XX668:1	G-CBAN
XS104	G-FRCE	XX692:A	G-BZMH
XS165:37	G-ASAZ	XX693:07	G-BZML
XS235	G-CPDA	XX694:E	G-CBBS
XS587	G-VIXN	XX695:3	G-CBBT
XS765	G-BSET	XX698:9	G-BZME
XT131	G-CICN	XX699:F	G-CBCV
XT223	G-XTUN	XX700:17	G-CBEK
XT420:606	G-CBUI	XX702:P	G-CBCR
XT435:430	G-RIMM	XX704	G-BCUV
XT626	G-CIBW	XX885	G-HHAA
XT634	G-BYRX	XZ329	G-BZYD
XT671	G-BYRC	XZ933	G-CGJZ
XT787	G-KAXT	XZ934:U	G-CBSI
XT788:316	G-BMIR	XZ937:Y	G-CBKA
XV134:P	G-BWLX	ZA250	G-VTOL
XV137	G-CRUM	ZA634:C	G-BUHA
XV138	G-SASM	ZA652	G-BUDC
XV268	G-BVER	ZA656	G-BTWC
XW283	G-CIMX	ZA730	G-FUKM
XW293:Z	G-BWCS	ZB500	G-LYNX
XW324:K	G-BWSG	ZB627:A	G-CBSK
XW325:E	G-BWGF	ZB646:59/CU	G-CBGZ
XW333:79	G-BVTC	HKG-5 (Royal Hong Kong AAF)	G-BULL
XW354	G-JPTV	HKG-6 (Royal Hong Kong AAF)	G-BPCL
XW422:3	G-BWEB	HKG-11 (Royal Hong Kong AAF)	G-BYRY
XW423:14	G-BWUW	HKG-13 (Royal Hong Kong AAF)	G-BXKW
XW433	G-JPRO	2+1:7334 Luftwaffe)	G-SYFW
XW612	G-KAXW	3+ (Luftwaffe)	G-BAYV
XW613	G-BXRS	4+ (Luftwaffe)	G-BSLX
XW635	G-AWSW	07 (Russian AF)	G-BMJY
XW784:VL	G-BBRN	F+IS (Luftwaffe)	G-BIRW
XW853	G-IBNH	BG+KM (Luftwaffe)	G-ASTG
XW854:46/CU	G-TIZZ	BU+CC (Luftwaffe)	G-BUCC
XW858:C	G-ONNE	BU+CK (Luftwaffe)	G-BUCK
XX432	G-CDNO	CF+HF (Luftwaffe)	EI-AUY
XX436	G-ZZLE	CG+EV (Luftwaffe)	G-CGEV
XX513:10	G-KKKK	DM+BK (Luftwaffe)	G-BPHZ
XX514	G-BWIB	GM+AI (Luftwaffe)	G-STCH
XX515:4	G-CBBC	LG+01 (Luftwaffe)	G-CIJV
XX518:S	G-UDOG	LG+03 (Luftwaffe)	G-AEZX
XX521:H	G-CBEH	KG+EM (Luftwaffe)	G-ETME
XX522:06	G-DAWG	NJ+C11 (Luftwaffe)	G-ATBG
XX524:04	G-DDOG	S4+A07 (Luftwaffe)	G-BWHP
XX528:D	G-BZON	S5+B06 (Luftwaffe)	G-WJCM
XX534:B	G-EDAV	TP+WX (Luftwaffe)	G-TPWX
XX537:C	G-CBCB	6J+PR (Luftwaffe)	G-AWHB
XX538:O	G-TDOG	57-H (USAAC)	G-AKAZ

327

Serial Carried	Civil Identity	Serial Carried	Civil Identity
+14 (Luftwaffe)	G-BSMD		
146-11083 (5)	G-BNAI		

39-160/G-CII0 Curtis P-40C Warhawk *Peter R. March*

D8096/G-AEPH Bristol F.2B *Peter R. March*

Reg	Type († False registration)	Owner or Operator	Notes
EI-ABI	DH.84 Dragon	Aer Lingus Charitable Foundation (EI-FBK)	
EI-AED	Cessna 120	E. McNeill & P. O'Reilly	
EI-AEE	Auster 3/1 Autocrat	O. & N. A. O'Sullivan	
EI-AEF	Cessna 120	J. Halligan	
EI-AEH	Luscombe 8F	D. Kelly	
EI-AEI	Aeronca 65-TACS	Hudson &Partners	
EI-AEJ	PA-16	G. Dolan	
EI-AEL	PA-16	G. Dolan	
EI-AEM	Cessna 140	D. J. Whittaker	
EI-AET	Piper J3C-65 Cub	S. T. Scully	
EI-AFE	Piper J3C-65 Cub	4 of Cubs Flying Group	
EI-AFZ	DHC.1 Chipmunk 22	Gipsy Captains Group	
EI-AGD	Taylorcraft Plus D	B. & K. O'Sullivan	
EI-AGJ	Auster J/1 Autocrat	T. G. Rafter	
EI-AHI	DH.82A Tiger Moth	High Fidelity Flyers	
EI-AII	Cessna 150F	L. Bagnell	
EI-AKM	Piper J-3C-65 Cub	J. A. Kent	
EI-ALP	Avro 643 Cadet	J. C. O'Loughlin	
EI-AMK	Auster J/1 Autocrat	Iona National Airways	
EI-ANT	Champion 7ECA Citabria	T. Croke & ptnrs	
EI-ANY	PA-18 Super Cub 95	Bogavia Group	
EI-AOB	PA-28 Cherokee 140	Knock Flying Group	
EI-APS	Schleicher ASK.14	E. Shiel & ptnrs	
EI-ARW	Jodel D.R.1050	J. Davy	
EI-ATJ	B.121 Pup Srs 2	C. Barrett & N. James	
EI-AUM	Auster J/1 Autocrat	T. G. Rafter	
EI-AUO	Cessna FA.150K Aerobat	S. Burke & L. Bagnell	
EI-AVM	Cessna F.150L	J. Nugent	
EI-AWH	Cessna 210J	Rathcoole Flying Club	
EI-AWP	DH.82A Tiger Moth	A. P. Bruton	
EI-AWR	Malmö MFI-9 Junior	L. P. Murray	
EI-AYB	GY-80 Horizon 180	J. B. Smith	
EI-AYI	MS.880B Rallye Club	J. McNamara	
EI-AYN	BN-2A-8 Islander	Aer Arann	
EI-AYR	Schleicher ASK-16	B. O'Broin & ptnrs	
EI-AYT	MS.894A Rallye Minerva	K. A. O'Connor	
EI-AYY	Evans VP-1	Ballyboughal VP-1 Flying Group	
EI-BAJ	Stampe SV.4C	W. Rafter & Partners	
EI-BAT	Cessna F.150M	J. Nugent	
EI-BAV	PA-22 Colt 108	E. Finnamore	
EI-BBC	PA-28 Cherokee 180C	A. Milhaud	
EI-BBE	Champion 7FC Tri-Traveler	P. Ryan	
EI-BBV	Piper J-3C-65 Cub	A. N. Johnston	
EI-BCE	BN-2A-26 Islander	Aer Arann	
EI-BCF	Bensen B.8M	P. Flanagan	
EI-BCJ	Aeromere F.8L Falco 1 Srs 3	M. P. McLoughlin	
EI-BCK	Cessna F.172N II	K. A. O'Connor	
EI-BCM	Piper J-3C-65 Cub	M. Bergin & Partners	
EI-BCN	Piper J-3C-65 Cub	H. Diver	
EI-BCP	D.62B Condor	T. Delaney	
EI-BDL	Evans VP-2	P. Buggle	
EI-BDR	PA-28 Cherokee 180	Cherokee Group	
EI-BDX	D.62B Condor	The Brian Douglas Trust BDX Group	
EI-BEN	Piper J-3C-65 Cub	Capt. J. J. Sullivan	
EI-BHV	Champion 7EC Traveler	P. O'Donnell & ptnrs	
EI-BIB	Cessna F.152	Sligo Aeronautical Club Ltd	
EI-BID	PA-18 Super Cub 95	A. Connaire & Partners	
EI-BIK	PA-18 Super Cub 180	Dublin Gliding Club	
EI-BIO	Piper J-3C-65 Cub	H. Duggan & Partners	
EI-BIR	Cessna F.172M	Figile Flying Group	
EI-BIV	Bellanca 8KCAB	Atlantic Flight Training Ltd	
EI-BJB	Aeronca 7AC Champion	A. W. Kennedy	
EI-BJC	Aeronca 7AC Champion	A. E. Griffin	
EI-BJK	MS.880B Rallye 110ST	M. Keenen	
EI-BJM	Cessna A.152	K. A. O'Connor	
EI-BJO	Cessna R.172K	The XP Group	
EI-BKC	Aeronca 15AC Sedan	G. Hendrick & M. Farrell	
EI-BKK	Taylor JT.1 Monoplane	D. Doyle	
EI-BMI	SOCATA TB9 Tampico	A. Breslin	
EI-BMN	Cessna F.152 II	K. A. O'Connor	
EI-BMU	Monnet Sonerai IIL	N. O'Donnell	

REPUBLIC OF IRELAND CIVIL REGISTRATIONS

Notes	Reg	Type († False registration)	Owner or Operator
	EI-BNL	Rand-Robinson KR-2	K. Hayes
	EI-BNU	MS.880B Rallye Club	J. Cooke
	EI-BOV	Rand-Robinson KR-2	G. O'Hara & G. Callan
	EI-BPL	Cessna F.172K	Phoenix Flying
	EI-BPP	Quicksilver MX	J. A. Smith
	EI-BRU	Evans VP-1	C. O'Shea
	EI-BSB	Wassmer Jodel D.112	T. Darmody
	EI-BSG	Bensen B.80	J. Todd
	EI-BSK	SOCATA TB9 Tampico	J. Byrne
	EI-BSL	PA-34-220T Seneca III	P. Sreenan
	EI-BSN	Cameron O-65 balloon	L. Duncan
	EI-BSO	PA-28 Cherokee 140B	S. Brazil
	EI-BSW	Solar Wings Pegasus XL-R	E. Fitzgerald
	EI-BSX	J-3C-65 Cub	J. O'Dwyer
	EI-BUC	Jodel D.9 Bébé	B. Lyons & M. Blake
	EI-BUF	Cessna 210N	210 Group
	EI-BUG	SOCATA ST.10 Diplomate	J. Cooke
	EI-BUL	Whittaker MW5 Sorcerer	J. Culleton
	EI-BUN	Beech 76 Duchess	K. A. O'Connor
	EI-BUT	MS.893A Commodore 180	T. Keating
	EI-BVJ	AMF Chevvron 232	A. Dunn
	EI-BVK	PA-38-112 Tomahawk	B. Lowe
	EI-BVT	Evans VP-2	P. Morrison
	EI-BVY	Zenith 200AA-RW	J. Matthews & M. Skelly
	EI-BYL	Zenith CH.250	I. Calton
	EI-BYX	Champion 7GCAA	P. J. Gallagher
	EI-BYY	Piper J-3C-85 Cub	The Cub Club
	EI-CAC	Grob G.115A	C. Phillips
	EI-CAD	Grob G.115A	C. Phillips
	EI-CAE	Grob G.115A	R. M. Davies
	EI-CAN	Aerotech MW5 Sorcerer	V. A. Vaughan
	EI-CAP	Cessna R.182RG	EICAP Ltd
	EI-CAU	AMF Chevvron 232	J. Tarrant
	EI-CAX	Cessna P.210N	K. A. O'Connor
	EI-CBK	Aérospatiale ATR-42-310	Stobart Air/Aer Lingus Regional
	EI-CCF	Aeronca 11AC Chief	G. McGuinness
	EI-CCM	Cessna 152 II	E. Hopkins
	EI-CDP	Cessna 182L	Irish Parachute Club
	EI-CDV	Cessna 150G	K. A. O'Connor
	EI-CEG	MS.893A Rallye 180GT	M. Jarrett
	EI-CES	Taylorcraft BC-65	G. Higgins & Partners
	EI-CFF	PA-12 Super Cruiser	J. & T. O'Dwyer
	EI-CFG	CP.301B Emeraude	F. Doyle
	EI-CFH	PA-12 Super Cruiser	G. Treacy
	EI-CFO	Piper J-3C-65 Cub	B. Reilly
	EI-CFY	Cessna 172N	K. A. O'Connor
	EI-CGF	Luton LA-5 Major	B. Doyle
	EI-CGH	Cessna 210N	J. Smith
	EI-CGP	PA-28 Cherokee 140C	L. A. Tattan
	EI-CHR	CFM Shadow Srs BD	B. Kelly
	EI-CIF	PA-28 Cherokee 180C	AA Flying Group
	EI-CIG	PA-18 Super Cub 150	K. A. O'Connor
	EI-CIM	Avid Flyer Mk IV	P. Swan
	EI-CIN	Cessna 150K	K. A. O'Connor
	EI-CJJ	Slingsby T-31M	J. J. Sullivan
	EI-CJS	Jodel D.120A	A. Flood
	EI-CJT	Slingsby Motor Cadet III	J. Tarrant
	EI-CJX	Boeing 757-2YOF	ASL Airlines (Ireland) Ltd
	EI-CJY	Boeing 757-2YO	I-Fly
	EI-CKH	PA-18 Super Cub 95	G. Brady
	EI-CKI	Thruster TST Mk 1	S. Woodgates
	EI-CKJ	Cameron N-77 balloon	A. F. Meldon
	EI-CKZ	Jodel D.18	J. O'Brien
	EI-CLQ	Cessna F.172N	E. Finnamore
	EI-CMB	PA-28 Cherokee 140	K. Furnell & Partners
	EI-CMD	Boeing 767-324ER	Blue Panorama
	EI-CML	Cessna 150M	P. Donohoe
	EI-CMN	PA-12 Super Cruiser	A. McNamee & ptnrs
	EI-CMR	Rutan LongEz	F. & C. O'Caoimh
	EI-CMT	PA-34-200T Seneca II	Atlantic Flight Training

Reg	Type († False registration)	Owner or Operator	Notes
EI-CMU	Mainair Mercury	Bill O'Neill	
EI-CMW	Rotorway Executive	B. McNamee	
EI-CNG	Air & Space 18A gyroplane	P. Joyce	
EI-CNU	Pegasus Quantum 15-912	M. Ffrench	
EI-COT	Cessna F.172N	Tojo Air Leasing	
EI-COY	Piper J-3C-65 Cub	W. Flood	
EI-CPE	Airbus A.321-211	Aer Lingus St Enda	
EI-CPG	Airbus A.321-211	Aer Lingus St Aidan	
EI-CPH	Airbus A.321-211	Aer Lingus St Dervilla	
EI-CPI	Rutan LongEz	D. J. Ryan	
EI-CPP	Piper J-3C-65 Cub	W. Kennedy	
EI-CPX	I.I.I. Sky Arrow 650T	M. McCarthy	
EI-CRB	Lindstrand LBL-90A balloon	J. & C. Concannon	
EI-CRG	Robin DR.400/180R	D. & B. Lodge	
EI-CRR	Aeronca 11AC Chief	L. Maddock & ptnrs	
EI-CRV	Hoffman H-36 Dimona	The Dimona Group	
EI-CRX	SOCATA TB-9 Tampico	Hotel Bravo Flying Club	
EI-CSG	Boeing 737-8AS	CIT Aerospace International	
EI-CSI	Boeing 737-8AS	CIT Aerospace International	
EI-CTL	Aerotech MW-5B Sorcerer	M. Wade	
EI-CUJ	Cessna 172N	Atlantic Flight Training Ltd	
EI-CUS	AB-206B JetRanger 3	R. Lyons	
EI-CUW	BN-2B-20 Islander	Aer Arann	
EI-CVA	Airbus A.320-214	Aer Lingus St Schira	
EI-CVB	Airbus A.320-214	Aer Lingus St Mobhi	
EI-CVC	Airbus A.320-214	Aer Lingus St Kealin	
EI-CVL	Ercoupe 415CD	V. O'Rourke	
EI-CVW	Bensen B.8M	F. Kavanagh	
EI-CXC	Raj Hamsa X'Air 502T	R. Dunleavy	
EI-CXN	Boeing 737-329	Transalpine Leasing Ltd	
EI-CXR	Boeing 737-329	Transalpine Leasing Ltd	
EI-CXV	Boeing 737-8CX	MASL Ireland(14)Ltd/MIAT Mongolian Airlines	
EI-CXY	Evektor EV-97 Eurostar	G. Doody & ptnrs	
EI-CXZ	Boeing 767-216ER	Transalpine Leasing Ltd	
EI-CZA	ATEC Zephyr 2000	D. Cassidy	
EI-CZC	CFM Streak Shadow Srs II	R. Camp	
EI-CZP	Schweizer 269C-1	T. Ng Kam	
EI-DAA	Airbus A.330-202	Aer Lingus St Keeva	
EI-DAC	Boeing 737-8AS	Ryanair	
EI-DAD	Boeing 737-8AS	Ryanair	
EI-DAE	Boeing 737-8AS	Ryanair	
EI-DAF	Boeing 737-8AS	Ryanair	
EI-DAG	Boeing 737-8AS	Ryanair	
EI-DAH	Boeing 737-8AS	Ryanair	
EI-DAI	Boeing 737-8AS	Ryanair	
EI-DAJ	Boeing 737-8AS	Ryanair	
EI-DAK	Boeing 737-8AS	Ryanair	
EI-DAL	Boeing 737-8AS	Ryanair	
EI-DAM	Boeing 737-8AS	Ryanair	
EI-DAN	Boeing 737-8AS	Ryanair	
EI-DAO	Boeing 737-8AS	Ryanair	
EI-DAP	Boeing 737-8AS	Ryanair	
EI-DAR	Boeing 737-8AS	Ryanair	
EI-DAS	Boeing 737-8AS	Ryanair	
EI-DBI	Raj Hamsa X'Air Mk.2 Falcon	D. Cornally	
EI-DBJ	Huntwing Pegasus XL Classic	P. A. McMahon	
EI-DBK	Boeing 777-243ER	Alitalia	
EI-DBL	Boeing 777-243ER	Alitalia	
EI-DBM	Boeing 777-243ER	Alitalia	
EI-DBO	Air Creation Kiss 400	E. Spain	
EI-DBP	Boeing 767-35H	Blue Panorama Airlines	
EI-DBV	Rand Kar X' Air 602T	S. Scanlon	
EI-DCA	Raj Hamsa X'Air	S. Cahill	
EI-DCF	Boeing 737-8AS	Ryanair	
Ei-DCG	Boeing 737-8AS	Ryanair	
EI-DCH	Boeing 737-8AS	Ryanair	
EI-DCI	Boeing 737-8AS	Ryanair	
EI-DCJ	Boeing 737-8AS	Ryanair	
EI-DCK	Boeing 737-8AS	Ryanair	
EI-DCL	Boeing 737-8AS	Ryanair	
EI-DCM	Boeing 737-8AS	Ryanair	

Notes	Reg	Type († False registration)	Owner or Operator
	EI-DCN	Boeing 737-8AS	Ryanair
	EI-DCO	Boeing 737-8AS	Ryanair
	EI-DCP	Boeing 737-8AS	Ryanair
	EI-DCR	Boeing 737-8AS	Ryanair
	EI-DCW	Boeing 737-8AS	Ryanair
	EI-DCX	Boeing 737-8AS	Ryanair
	EI-DCY	Boeing 737-8AS	Ryanair
	EI-DCZ	Boeing 737-8AS	Ryanair
	EI-DDC	Cessna F.172M	Trim Flying Club
	EI-DDD	Aeronca 7AC	J. Sullivan & M. Quinn
	EI-DDH	Boeing 777-243ER	Alitalia
	EI-DDJ	Raj Hamsa X'Air 582	I. Talt
	EI-DDP	Southdown International microlight	M. Mannion
	EI-DDR	Bensen B8V	P. MacCabe & Partners
	EI-DDU	Airbus A.330-203	Celestial Aviation Trading Ltd
	EI-DDX	Cessna 172S	Atlantic Flight Training
	EI-DEA	Airbus A.320-214	Aer Lingus St Fidelma
	EI-DEB	Airbus A.320-214	Aer Lingus St Nathy
	EI-DEC	Airbus A.320-214	Aer Lingus St Fergal
	EI-DEE	Airbus A.320-214	Aer Lingus St Fintan
	EI-DEF	Airbus A.320-214	Aer Lingus St Declan
	EI-DEG	Airbus A.320-214	Aer Lingus St Fachtna
	EI-DEH	Airbus A.320-214	Aer Lingus St Malachy
	EI-DEI	Airbus A.320-214	Aer Lingus St Kilian
	EI-DEJ	Airbus A.320-214	Aer Lingus St Oliver Plunkett
	EI-DEK	Airbus A.320-214	Aer Lingus St Eunan
	EI-DEL	Airbus A.320-214	Aer Lingus St Ibar
	EI-DEM	Airbus A.320-214	Aer Lingus St Canice
	EI-DEN	Airbus A.320-214	Aer Lingus St Kieran
	EI-DEO	Airbus A.320-214	Aer Lingus St Senan
	EI-DEP	Airbus A.320-214	Aer Lingus St Eugene
	EI-DER	Airbus A.320-214	Aer Lingus St Mel
	EI-DES	Airbus A.320-214	Aer Lingus St Pappin
	EI-DFM	Evektor EV-97 Eurostar	J. Gibbons
	EI-DFO	Airbus A.320-211	Windjet
	EI-DFS	Boeing 767-33AER	Transalpine Leasing Ltd
	EI-DFX	Air Creation Kiss 400	L. Daly
	EI-DFY	Raj Hamsa R100 (2)	P. McGirr & R Gillespie
	EI-DGA	Urban Air UFM-11UK Lambada	Dr. P. & D. Durkin
	EI-DGG	Raj Hamsa X'Air 582	P. A. Weldon
	EI-DGH	Raj Hamsa X'Air 582	K. & K. Kiernan
	EI-DGJ	Raj Hamsa X'Air 582	N. Brereton
	EI-DGK	Raj Hamsa X'Air 133	B. Chambers
	EI-DGP	Urban Air UFM-11 Lambada	R. Linehan
	EI-DGT	Urban Air UFM-11UK Lambada	P. Walsh & Partners
	EI-DGU	Airbus A.300-622R	ASL Airlines (Ireland) Ltd
	EI-DGV	ATEC Zephyr 2000	K. Higgins
	EI-DGW	Cameron Z-90 balloon	J. Leahy
	EI-DGX	Cessna 152 II	K. A. O'Connor
	EI-DGY	Urban Air UFM-11 Lambada	D. McMorrow
	EI-DHA	Boeing 737-8AS	Ryanair
	EI-DHB	Boeing 737-8AS	Ryanair
	EI-DHC	Boeing 737-8AS	Ryanair
	EI-DHD	Boeing 737-8AS	Ryanair
	EI-DHE	Boeing 737-8AS	Ryanair
	EI-DHF	Boeing 737-8AS	Ryanair
	EI-DHG	Boeing 737-8AS	Ryanair
	EI-DHH	Boeing 737-8AS	Ryanair
	EI-DHN	Boeing 737-8AS	Ryanair
	EI-DHO	Boeing 737-8AS	Ryanair
	EI-DHP	Boeing 737-8AS	Ryanair
	EI-DHR	Boeing 737-8AS	Ryanair
	EI-DHS	Boeing 737-8AS	Ryanair
	EI-DHT	Boeing 737-8AS	Ryanair
	EI-DHV	Boeing 737-8AS	Ryanair
	EI-DHW	Boeing 737-8AS	Ryanair
	EI-DHX	Boeing 737-8AS	Ryanair
	EI-DHY	Boeing 737-8AS	Ryanair
	EI-DHZ	Boeing 737-8AS	Ryanair
	EI-DIA	Solar Wings Pegasus XL-Q	P. Byrne
	EI-DIF	PA-31-350 Navajo Chieftain	Flightwise Aviation Ltd & Partners

Reg	Type († False registration)	Owner or Operator	Notes
EI-DIP	Airbus A.330-202	Alitalia	
EI-DIR	Airbus A.330-202	Alitalia	
EI-DIY	Van's RV-4	J. A. Kent	
EI-DJM	PA-28-161 Warrior II	Waterford Aero Club	
EI-DKE	Air Creation Kiss 450-582	J. Bennett	
EI-DKJ	Thruster T.600N	C. Brogan	
EI-DKK	Raj Hamsa X'Air Jabiru	M. Tolan	
EI-DKT	Raj Hamsa X'Air 582 (11)	S. Kiernan & S. Newlands	
EI-DKU	Air Creation Kiss 450-582 (1)	P. Kirwan	
EI-DKW	Evektor EV-97 Eurostar	Ormand Flying Club	
EI-DKY	Raj Hamsa X'Air 582	M. Clarke	
EI-DKZ	Reality Aircraft Escapade 912 (1)	J. Deegan	
EI-DLB	Boeing 737-8AS	Ryanair	
EI-DLC	Boeing 737-8AS	Ryanair	
EI-DLD	Boeing 737-8AS	Ryanair	
EI-DLE	Boeing 737-8AS	Ryanair	
EI-DLF	Boeing 737-8AS	Ryanair	
EI-DLG	Boeing 737-8AS	Ryanair	
EI-DLH	Boeing 737-8AS	Ryanair	
EI-DLI	Boeing 737-8AS	Ryanair	
EI-DLJ	Boeing 737-8AS	Ryanair	
EI-DLK	Boeing 737-8AS	Ryanair	
EI-DLN	Boeing 737-8AS	Ryanair	
EI-DLO	Boeing 737-8AS	Ryanair	
EI-DLR	Boeing 737-8AS	Ryanair	
EI-DLV	Boeing 737-8AS	Ryanair	
EI-DLW	Boeing 737-8AS	Ryanair	
EI-DLX	Boeing 737-8AS	Ryanair	
EI-DLY	Boeing 737-8AS	Ryanair	
EI-DMA	MS.892E Rallye 150	J. Lynn & Partners	
EI-DMB	Best Off Skyranger 912S (1)	E. Spain	
EI-DMG	Cessna 441	Dawn Meats Group	
EI-DMU	Whittaker MW6S Merlin	M. Heaton	
EI-DNM	Boeing 737-4S3	Transaero	
EI-DNR	Raj Hamsa X'Air 582 (5)	N. Furlong & J. Grattan	
EI-DNV	Urban Air UFM-11UK Lambada	F. Maughan	
EI-DOB	Zenair CH-701	D. O'Brien	
EI-DOW	Mainair Blade 912	G. D. Fortune	
EI-DOY	PZL Koliber 150A	T. J. Britton	
EI-DPB	Boeing 737-8AS	Ryanair	
EI-DPC	Boeing 737-8AS	Ryanair	
EI-DPD	Boeing 737-8AS	Ryanair	
EI-DPF	Boeing 737-8AS	Ryanair	
EI-DPG	Boeing 737-8AS	Ryanair	
EI-DPH	Boeing 737-8AS	Ryanair	
EI-DPI	Boeing 737-8AS	Ryanair	
EI-DPJ	Boeing 737-8AS	Ryanair	
EI-DPK	Boeing 737-8AS	Ryanair	
EI-DPL	Boeing 737-8AS	Ryanair	
EI-DPM	Boeing 737-8AS	Ryanair	
EI-DPN	Boeing 737-8AS	Ryanair	
EI-DPO	Boeing 737-8AS	Ryanair	
EI-DPP	Boeing 737-8AS	Ryanair	
EI-DPR	Boeing 737-8AS	Ryanair	
EI-DPT	Boeing 737-8AS	Ryanair	
EI-DPV	Boeing 737-8AS	Ryanair	
EI-DPW	Boeing 737-8AS	Ryanair	
EI-DPX	Boeing 737-8AS	Ryanair	
EI-DPY	Boeing 737-8AS	Ryanair	
EI-DPZ	Boeing 737-8AS	Ryanair	
EI-DRA	Boeing 737-852	Aeromexico	
EI-DRC	Boeing 737-852	Aeromexico	
EI-DRD	Boeing 737-852	Aeromexico	
EI-DRE	Boeing 737-752	Aeromexico	
EI-DRH	Mainair Blade	J. McErlain	
EI-DRL	Raj Hamsa X'Air Jabiru	N. Brunton	
EI-DRM	Urban Air UFM-10 Samba	K. Haslett	
EI-DRT	Air Creation Tanarg 912	P. McMahon	
EI-DRU	Tecnam P92/EM Echo	P. Gallogly	
EI-DRW	Evektor EV-97R Eurostar	Eurostar Flying Club	
EI-DRX	Raj Hamsa X'Air 582 (5)	M. Sheelan & D. McShane	

Notes	Reg	Type († False registration)	Owner or Operator
	EI-DSA	Airbus A.320-216	Alitalia
	EI-DSG	Airbus A.320-216	Alitalia
	EI-DSL	Airbus A.320-216	Alitalia
	EI-DSU	Airbus A.320-216	Alitalia
	EI-DSV	Airbus A.320-216	Alitalia
	EI-DSW	Airbus A.320-216	Alitalia
	EI-DSX	Airbus A.320-216	Alitalia
	EI-DSY	Airbus A.320-216	Alitalia
	EI-DSZ	Airbus A.320-216	Alitalia
	EI-DTA	Airbus A.320-216	Alitalia
	EI-DTB	Airbus A.320-216	Alitalia
	EI-DTD	Airbus A.320-216	Alitalia
	EI-DTE	Airbus A.320-216	Alitalia
	EI-DTF	Airbus A.320-216	Alitalia
	EI-DTG	Airbus A.320-216	Alitalia
	EI-DTH	Airbus A.320-216	Alitalia
	EI-DTI	Airbus A.320-216	Alitalia
	EI-DTJ	Airbus A.320-216	Alitalia
	EI-DTK	Airbus A.320-216	Alitalia
	EI-DTL	Airbus A.320-216	Alitalia
	EI-DTM	Airbus A.320-216	Alitalia
	EI-DTN	Airbus A.320-216	Alitalia
	EI-DTO	Airbus A.320-216	Alitalia
	EI-DTR	Robinson R44	R & M Quarries Ltd
	EI-DTS	PA-18 Super Cub	M. D. Murphy
	EI-DTT	ELA-07 R-100 Gyrocopter	N. Steele
	EI-DUH	Scintex CP.1310C3 Emeraude	W. Kennedy
	EI-DUJ	Evektor EV-97 Eurostar	E. Fitzpatrick
	EI-DUL	Alpi Aviation Pioneer	W. Flood
	EI-DUO	Airbus A.330-203	Aer Lingus
	EI-DUV	Beech 55	J. Given
	EI-DUZ	Airbus A.330-203	Aer Lingus
	EI-DVE	Airbus A.320-214	Aer Lingus
	EI-DVG	Airbus A.320-214	Aer Lingus
	EI-DVH	Airbus A.320-214	Aer Lingus
	EI-DVI	Airbus A.320-214	Aer Lingus
	EI-DVJ	Airbus A.320-214	Aer Lingus
	EI-DVK	Airbus A.320-214	Aer Lingus
	EI-DVL	Airbus A.320-214	Aer Lingus
	EI-DVM	Airbus A.320-214	Aer Lingus
	EI-DVN	Airbus A.320-214	Aer Lingus
	EI-DVO	Barnett J4B2	T. Brennan
	EI-DVZ	Robinson R44 II	M. O'Donovan
	EI-DWA	Boeing 737-8AS	Ryanair
	EI-DWB	Boeing 737-8AS	Ryanair
	EI-DWC	Boeing 737-8AS	Ryanair
	EI-DWD	Boeing 737-8AS	Ryanair
	EI-DWE	Boeing 737-8AS	Ryanair
	EI-DWF	Boeing 737-8AS	Ryanair
	EI-DWG	Boeing 737-8AS	Ryanair
	EI-DWH	Boeing 737-8AS	Ryanair
	EI-DWI	Boeing 737-8AS	Ryanair
	EI-DWJ	Boeing 737-8AS	Ryanair
	EI-DWK	Boeing 737-8AS	Ryanair
	EI-DWL	Boeing 737-8AS	Ryanair
	EI-DWM	Boeing 737-8AS	Ryanair
	EI-DWO	Boeing 737-8AS	Ryanair
	EI-DWP	Boeing 737-8AS	Ryanair
	EI-DWR	Boeing 737-8AS	Ryanair
	EI-DWS	Boeing 737-8AS	Ryanair
	EI-DWT	Boeing 737-8AS	Ryanair
	EI-DWV	Boeing 737-8AS	Ryanair
	EI-DWW	Boeing 737-8AS	Ryanair
	EI-DWX	Boeing 737-8AS	Ryanair
	EI-DWY	Boeing 737-8AS	Ryanair
	EI-DWZ	Boeing 737-8AS	Ryanair
	EI-DXA	Ikarus C42	S. Ryan
	EI-DXL	CFM Shadow	F. Lynch
	EI-DXM	Raj Hamsa X'Air 582	B. Nugent
	EI-DXN	Zenair CH.601HD	N. Gallagher
	EI-DXP	Cyclone AX3/503	J. Hennessey

Reg	Type († False registration)	Owner or Operator	Notes
EI-DXS	CFM Shadow	R. W. Frost	
EI-DXT	UrbanAir UFM-10 Samba	N. Irwin	
EI-DXV	Thruster T.600N	P. Higgins	
EI-DXX	Raj Hamsa X'AIR 582(5)	E. D. Hanly & S. Macsweeney	
EI-DXZ	UrbanAir UFM-10 Samba	D. O'Leary	
EI-DYA	Boeing 737-8AS	Ryanair	
EI-DYB	Boeing 737-8AS	Ryanair	
EI-DYC	Boeing 737-8AS	Ryanair	
EI-DYD	Boeing 737-8AS	Ryanair	
EI-DYE	Boeing 737-8AS	Ryanair	
EI-DYF	Boeing 737-8AS	Ryanair	
EI-DYL	Boeing 737-8AS	Ryanair	
EI-DYM	Boeing 737-8AS	Ryanair	
EI-DYN	Boeing 737-8AS	Ryanair	
EI-DYO	Boeing 737-8AS	Ryanair	
EI-DYP	Boeing 737-8AS	Ryanair	
EI-DYR	Boeing 737-8AS	Ryanair	
EI-DYV	Boeing 737-8AS	Ryanair	
EI-DYW	Boeing 737-8AS	Ryanair	
EI-DYX	Boeing 737-8AS	Ryanair	
EI-DYY	Boeing 737-8AS	Ryanair	
EI-DYZ	Boeing 737-8AS	Ryanair	
EI-DZA	Colt 21A balloon	P. Baker	
EI-DZB	Colt 21A balloon	P. Baker	
EI-DZE	UrbanAir UFM-10 Samba	P. Keane	
EI-DZF	Pipistrel Sinus 912	Light Sport Aviation Ltd	
EI-DZK	Robinson R22B2 Beta	Skywest Aviation Ltd	
EI-DZL	Urban Air Samba XXL	M. Tormey	
EI-DZM	Robinson R44 II	A. & G. Thomond Builders Ltd	
EI-DZN	Bell 222	B. McCarty & A. Dalton	
EI-DZO	Dominator Gyroplane Ultrawhite	P. O'Reilly	
EI-DZS	BRM Land Africa	M. Whyte	
EI-EAJ	RAF-2000GTX-SE	J. P. Henry	
EI-EAK	Airborne Windsports Edge XT	M. O'Brien	
EI-EAM	Cessna 172R	Atlantic Flight Training Ltd	
EI-EAV	Airbus A.330-302	Aer Lingus	
EI-EAY	Raj Hamsa X'Air 582 (5)	West-Tech Aviation Ltd	
EI-EAZ	Cessna 172R	Atlantic Flight Training Ltd	
EI-EBA	Boeing 737-8AS	Ryanair	
EI-EBC	Boeing 737-8AS	Ryanair	
EI-EBD	Boeing 737-8AS	Ryanair	
EI-EBE	Boeing 737-8AS	Ryanair	
EI-EBF	Boeing 737-8AS	Ryanair	
EI-EBG	Boeing 737-8AS	Ryanair	
EI-EBH	Boeing 737-8AS	Ryanair	
EI-EBI	Boeing 737-8AS	Ryanair	
EI-EBK	Boeing 737-8AS	Ryanair	
EI-EBL	Boeing 737-8AS	Ryanair	
EI-EBM	Boeing 737-8AS	Ryanair	
EI-EBN	Boeing 737-8AS	Ryanair	
EI-EBO	Boeing 737-8AS	Ryanair	
EI-EBP	Boeing 737-8AS	Ryanair	
EI-EBR	Boeing 737-8AS	Ryanair	
EI-EBS	Boeing 737-8AS	Ryanair	
EI-EBV	Boeing 737-8AS	Ryanair	
EI-EBW	Boeing 737-8AS	Ryanair	
EI-EBX	Boeing 737-8AS	Ryanair	
EI-EBY	Boeing 737-8AS	Ryanair	
EI-EBZ	Boeing 737-8AS	Ryanair	
EI-ECC	Cameron Z-90 balloon	J. J. Daly	
EI-ECG	BRM Land Africa	J. McGuinness	
EI-ECK	Raj Hamsa X'Air Hawk	N. Geh	
EI-ECL	Boeing 737-86N	Rise Aviation 1 (Ireland) Ltd	
EI-ECM	Boeing 737-86N	Celestial Aviation Trading 26 Ltd	
EI-ECP	Raj Hamsa X'Air Hawk	R. Gillespie & Partners	
EI-ECR	Cessna 525	Aircraft International Renting Ltd	
EI-ECZ	Raj Hamsa X'Air Hawk	M. Tolan	
EI-EDB	Cessna 152	K. O'Connor	
EI-EDC	Cessna FA.152	National Flight Centre Ltd	
EI-EDI	Ikarus C42	M. Owens	
EI-EDJ	CZAW Sportcruiser	Croftal Ltd	

Notes	Reg	Type († False registration)	Owner or Operator
	EI-EDP	Airbus A.320-214	Aer Lingus
	EI-EDR	PA-28R Cherokee Arrow 200	Dublin Flyers
	EI-EDS	Airbus A.320-214	Aer Lingus
	EI-EDY	Airbus A.330-302	Aer Lingus
	EI-EEH	BRM Land Africa	R. Duffy
	EI-EEO	Van's RV-7	A. Butler
	EI-EES	ELA-07R	D. Doyle & Partners
	EI-EEU	Osprey II	P. Forde & S. Coughlan
	EI-EFC	Boeing 737-8AS	Ryanair
	EI-EFD	Boeing 737-8AS	Ryanair
	EI-EFE	Boeing 737-8AS	Ryanair
	EI-EFF	Boeing 737-8AS	Ryanair
	EI-EFG	Boeing 737-8AS	Ryanair
	EI-EFH	Boeing 737-8AS	Ryanair
	EI-EFI	Boeing 737-8AS	Ryanair
	EI-EFJ	Boeing 737-8AS	Ryanair
	EI-EFK	Boeing 737-8AS	Ryanair
	EI-EFN	Boeing 737-8AS	Ryanair
	EI-EFO	Boeing 737-8AS	Ryanair
	EI-EFX	Boeing 737-8AS	Ryanair
	EI-EFY	Boeing 737-8AS	Ryanair
	EI-EFZ	Boeing 737-8AS	Ryanair
	EI-EGA	Boeing 737-8AS	Ryanair
	EI-EGB	Boeing 737-8AS	Ryanair
	EI-EGC	Boeing 737-8AS	Ryanair
	EI-EGD	Boeing 737-8AS	Ryanair
	EI-EHF	Aeroprakt A22 Foxbat	K. Glynn
	EI-EHG	Robinson R22 Beta	G. Jordan
	EI-EHH	Aerospatiale ATR-42-300	Aer Arran
	EI-EHK	Magni Gyro M-22 Voyager	M. Concannon
	EI-EHL	Air Creation Tanarg/Ixess 15 912S	S. Woods
	EI-EHM	Rand KR-2T	A. Lagun
	EI-EHY	Urban Air Samba XXL	J. K. Woodville
	EI-EIA	Airbus A.320-216	Alitalia
	EI-EIB	Airbus A.320-216	Alitalia
	EI-EIC	Airbus A.320-216	Alitalia
	EI-EID	Airbus A.320-216	Alitalia
	EI-EIE	Airbus A.320-216	Alitalia
	EI-EJG	Airbus A.330-202	Alitalia
	EI-EJH	Airbus A.330-202	Alitalia
	EI-EJI	Airbus A.330-202	Alitalia
	EI-EJJ	Airbus A.330-202	Alitalia
	EI-EJK	Airbus A.330-202	Alitalia
	EI-EJL	Airbus A.330-202	Alitalia
	EI-EJM	Airbus A.330-202	Alitalia
	EI-EJN	Airbus A.330-202	Alitalia
	EI-EJO	Airbus A.330-202	Alitalia
	EI-EJP	Airbus A.330-202	Alitalia
	EI-EJZ	Airbus A.330-223	Amentum Aircraft Leasing No.6 Ltd
	EI-EKA	Boeing 737-8AS	Ryanair
	EI-EKB	Boeing 737-8AS	Ryanair
	EI-EKC	Boeing 737-8AS	Ryanair
	EI-EKD	Boeing 737-8AS	Ryanair
	EI-EKE	Boeing 737-8AS	Ryanair
	EI-EKF	Boeing 737-8AS	Ryanair
	EI-EKG	Boeing 737-8AS	Ryanair
	EI-EKH	Boeing 737-8AS	Ryanair
	EI-EKI	Boeing 737-8AS	Ryanair
	EI-EKJ	Boeing 737-8AS	Ryanair
	EI-EKK	Boeing 737-8AS	Ryanair
	EI-EKL	Boeing 737-8AS	Ryanair
	EI-EKM	Boeing 737-8AS	Ryanair
	EI-EKN	Boeing 737-8AS	Ryanair
	EI-EKO	Boeing 737-8AS	Ryanair
	EI-EKP	Boeing 737-8AS	Ryanair
	EI-EKR	Boeing 737-8AS	Ryanair
	EI-EKS	Boeing 737-8AS	Ryanair
	EI-EKT	Boeing 737-8AS	Ryanair
	EI-EKV	Boeing 737-8AS	Ryanair
	EI-EKW	Boeing 737-8AS	Ryanair
	EI-EKX	Boeing 737-8AS	Ryanair

Reg	Type († False registration)	Owner or Operator	Notes
EI-EKY	Boeing 737-8AS	Ryanair	
EI-EKZ	Boeing 737-8AS	Ryanair	
EI-ELA	Airbus A.330-302	Aer Lingus	
EI-ELB	Raj Hamsa X'Air 582 (1)	G. McLaughlin	
EI-ELC	Ikarus C42B	A. Kilpatrick & M. Mullin	
EI-ELL	Medway Eclipser	P. McMahon	
EI-ELM	PA-18-95 Super Cub	S. Coughlan	
EI-EMA	Boeing 737-8AS	Ryanair	
EI-EMB	Boeing 737-8AS	Ryanair	
EI-EMC	Boeing 737-8AS	Ryanair	
EI-EMD	Boeing 737-8AS	Ryanair	
EI-EME	Boeing 737-8AS	Ryanair	
EI-EMF	Boeing 737-8AS	Ryanair	
EI-EMH	Boeing 737-8AS	Ryanair	
EI-EMI	Boeing 737-8AS	Ryanair	
EI-EMJ	Boeing 737-8AS	Ryanair	
EI-EMK	Boeing 737-8AS	Ryanair	
EI-EML	Boeing 737-8AS	Ryanair	
EI-EMM	Boeing 737-8AS	Ryanair	
EI-EMN	Boeing 737-8AS	Ryanair	
EI-EMO	Boeing 737-8AS	Ryanair	
EI-EMP	Boeing 737-8AS	Ryanair	
EI-EMR	Boeing 737-8AS	Ryanair	
EI-EMT	PA-16 Clipper	G. Dolan	
EI-EMU	Cessna F.152	K. O'Connor	
EI-EMV	CZAW Sportcruiser	L. Doherty & partners	
EI-ENA	Boeing 737-8AS	Ryanair	
EI-ENB	Boeing 737-8AS	Ryanair	
EI-ENC	Boeing 737-8AS	Ryanair	
EI-ENE	Boeing 737-8AS	Ryanair	
EI-ENF	Boeing 737-8AS	Ryanair	
EI-ENG	Boeing 737-8AS	Ryanair	
EI-ENH	Boeing 737-8AS	Ryanair	
EI-ENI	Boeing 737-8AS	Ryanair	
EI-ENJ	Boeing 737-8AS	Ryanair	
EI-ENK	Boeing 737-8AS	Ryanair	
EI-ENL	Boeing 737-8AS	Ryanair	
EI-ENM	Boeing 737-8AS	Ryanair	
EI-ENN	Boeing 737-8AS	Ryanair	
EI-ENO	Boeing 737-8AS	Ryanair	
EI-ENP	Boeing 737-8AS	Ryanair	
EI-ENR	Boeing 737-8AS	Ryanair	
EI-ENS	Boeing 737-8AS	Ryanair	
EI-ENT	Boeing 737-8AS	Ryanair	
EI-ENV	Boeing 737-8AS	Ryanair	
EI-ENW	Boeing 737-8AS	Ryanair	
EI-ENX	Boeing 737-8AS	Ryanair	
EI-ENY	Boeing 737-8AS	Ryanair	
EI-ENZ	Boeing 737-8AS	Ryanair	
EI-EOA	Raj Hamsa X'Air Jabiru	B. Lynch Jnr	
EI-EOB	Cameron Z-69 balloon	J. Leahy	
EI-EOC	Van's RV-6	V. P. & N. O'Brien	
EI-EOF	Jabiru SP430	J. Bermingham	
EI-EOH	BRM Land Africa	M. McCarrick	
EI-EOI	Take Off Merlin 1100	N. Fitzmaurice	
EI-EOO	Ikarus C42 FB UK	B. Gurnett & Partners	
EI-EOU	Evektor EV-97 Eurostar SL	S. Kearney	
EI-EOW	Flight Design CTSW	J. Moriarty	
EI-EPA	Boeing 737-8AS	Ryanair	
EI-EPB	Boeing 737-8AS	Ryanair	
EI-EPC	Boeing 737-8AS	Ryanair	
EI-EPD	Boeing 737-8AS	Ryanair	
EI-EPE	Boeing 737-8AS	Ryanair	
EI-EPF	Boeing 737-8AS	Ryanair	
EI-EPG	Boeing 737-8AS	Ryanair	
EI-EPH	Boeing 737-8AS	Ryanair	
EI-EPI	Medway Hybred 44XLR	H. J. Long	
EI-EPJ	Mainair/Gemini Flash IIA	L. Flannery	
EI-EPK	Pegasus Quantum 15-912	H. J. Long	
EI-EPP	PA-22-160	P. McCabe	
EI-EPW	MXP-740 Savannah Jabiru(5)	L. Reilly	

Notes	Reg	Type († False registration)	Owner or Operator
	EI-EPY	UFM-11 Lambada	P. Kearney
	EI-EPZ	Jodel DR.1050M1	A. Dunne & Partners
	EI-ERE	Pegasus Quantum 15-912	M. Carter
	EI-ERH	Airbus A.320-232	CRA Aircraft No.1 Ltd
	EI-ERI	Air Creation Clipper/Kiss 400-582(1)	E. Thompson
	EI-ERJ	Southdown Raven X	M. Hanley
	EI-ERL	Best Off Sky Ranger 912	B. Chambers
	EI-ERM	Ikarus C42B	C42 Club
	EI-ERO	Pegasus XL-R	M. Doyle
	EI-ERZ	Flight Design CT-2K	M. Bowden
	EI-ESA	Airbus A.330-223	Amentum Aircraft Leasing No.7 Ltd
	EI-ESB	Urban Air Samba XXL	G. Creegan
	EI-ESC	BRM Land Africa	D. Killian
	EI-ESD	Mainair Blade	O. Farrell
	EI-ESE	Zenair CH.601XL Zodiac	C. O'Connell
	EI-ESF	PA-22-160	G. Dolan
	EI-ESL	Boeing 737-8AS	Ryanair
	EI-ESM	Boeing 737-8AS	Ryanair
	EI-ESN	Boeing 737-8AS	Ryanair
	EI-ESO	Boeing 737-8AS	Ryanair
	EI-ESP	Boeing 737-8AS	Ryanair
	EI-ESR	Boeing 737-8AS	Ryanair
	EI-ESS	Boeing 737-8AS	Ryanair
	EI-EST	Boeing 737-8AS	Ryanair
	EI-ESV	Boeing 737-8AS	Ryanair
	EI-ESW	Boeing 737-8AS	Ryanair
	EI-ESX	Boeing 737-8AS	Ryanair
	EI-ESY	Boeing 737-8AS	Ryanair
	EI-ESZ	Boeing 737-8AS	Ryanair
	EI-ETB	Ikarus C42B	P. Connolly
	EI-ETD	Raj Hamsa X'Air Hawk	T. McDevitt
	EI-ETE	MS.880B Rallye	Wicklow Wings Ltd
	EI-ETF	Samba XXL	V. Vaughan
	EI-ETV	Raj Hamsa X'Air Hawk	P. Higgins & Partners
	EI-EUA	Airbus A.320-232	GASL Leasing Ireland No.1 Ltd
	EI-EVA	Boeing 737-8AS	Ryanair
	EI-EVB	Boeing 737-8AS	Ryanair
	EI-EVC	Boeing 737-8AS	Ryanair
	EI-EVD	Boeing 737-8AS	Ryanair
	EI-EVE	Boeing 737-8AS	Ryanair
	EI-EVF	Boeing 737-8AS	Ryanair
	EI-EVG	Boeing 737-8AS	Ryanair
	EI-EVH	Boeing 737-8AS	Ryanair
	EI-EVI	Boeing 737-8AS	Ryanair
	EI-EVJ	Boeing 737-8AS	Ryanair
	EI-EVK	Boeing 737-8AS	Ryanair
	EI-EVL	Boeing 737-8AS	Ryanair
	EI-EVM	Boeing 737-8AS	Ryanair
	EI-EVN	Boeing 737-8AS	Ryanair
	EI-EVO	Boeing 737-8AS	Ryanair
	EI-EVP	Boeing 737-8AS	Ryanair
	EI-EVR	Boeing 737-8AS	Ryanair
	EI-EVS	Boeing 737-8AS	Ryanair
	EI-EVT	Boeing 737-8AS	Ryanair
	EI-EVV	Boeing 737-8AS	Ryanair
	EI-EVW	Boeing 737-8AS	Ryanair
	EI-EVX	Boeing 737-8AS	Ryanair
	EI-EVY	Boeing 737-8AS	Ryanair
	EI-EVZ	Boeing 737-8AS	Ryanair
	EI-EWB	Ikarus C42B	P. O'Reilly
	EI-EWC	Beech 76	K. A. O'Connor
	EI-EWG	Airbus A.330-223	Nightjar Ltd
	EI-EWH	Airbus A.330-223	Skua Ltd
	EI-EWI	Boeing 717-2BL	Volotea Airlines
	EI-EWJ	Boeing 717-2BL	Volotea Airlines
	EI-EWR	Airbus A.330-202	Aer Lingus
	EI-EWV	Ikarus C42 FB100 VLA	D. Parke
	EI-EWX	Aeropro Eurofox 912	E. J. Symes
	EI-EWY	Van's RV-6A	D. McKendrick
	EI-EWZ	MB-2 Colibri	Colibri Group
	EI-EXA	Boeing 717-2BL	Volotea Airlines

Reg	Type († False registration)	Owner or Operator	Notes
EI-EXB	Boeing 717-2BL	Volotea Airlines	
EI-EXD	Boeing 737-8AS	Ryanair	
EI-EXE	Boeing 737-8AS	Ryanair	
EI-EXF	Boeing 737-8AS	Ryanair	
EI-EXI	Boeing 717-2BL	Volotea Airlines	
EI-EXJ	Boeing 717-2BL	Volotea Airlines	
EI-EXR	Airbus A.300-B4622RF	Air Contractors (Ireland) Ltd	
EI-EXY	Urban Air Samba XXL	M. Tormey	
EI-EYI	PA-28-181	C. Rooney	
EI-EYJ	Cessna F.172N	Trim Flying Club Ltd	
EI-EYK	Airbus A.300B4-622R	Air Contractors (Ireland) Ltd	
EI-EYL	Airbus A.319-111	Rossiya	
EI-EYM	Airbus A.319-111	Rossiya	
EI-EYT	Ikarus C42B	Croom C42 Club	
EI-EYW	Thruster T600N 450	M. O'Carroll & B. Corrigan	
EI-EZC	Airbus A.319-112	Rossiya	
EI-EZD	Airbus A.319-112	Rossiya	
EI-EZU	Cessna FR.172K	The Hawk Group	
EI-EZX	PA-22-108 Colt	A. Fenton	
EI-EZY	Dominator Ultrawhite	J. Dowling	
EI-FAB	Eurocopter EC.120B	Billy Jet Ltd	
EI-FAD	Van's RV-7A	J. Lynch & Partners	
EI-FAM	Rans S-6ES Coyote II	N. Blair	
EI-FAS	Aerospatiale ATR-72-212A	Stobart Air	
EI-FAT	Aerospatiale ATR-72-600	Stobart Air	
EI-FAU	Aerospatiale ATR-72-600	Stobart Air	
EI-FAV	Aerospatiale ATR-72-600	Stobart Air	
EI-FAW	Aerospatiale ATR-72-600	Stobart Air	
EI-FAX	Aerospatiale ATR-72-600	Stobart Air	
EI-FAZ	Urban Air UFM-10 Samba	J. Halpin	
EI-FBC	Cessna 172N	K. O'Connor	
EI-FBJ	Boeing 717-200	Volotea Airlines	
EI-FBL	Boeing 717-200	Volotea Airlines	
EI-FBM	Boeing 717-2BL	Volotea Airlines	
EI-FBU	Airbus A.330-322	IFTI Aviation Ireland Ltd	
EI-FBW	BRM Land Africa	J. O'Connor	
EI-FBX	BRM Land Africa Citius	P. Higgins	
EI-FBY	BRM Land Africa Citius	S. Smith	
EI-FBZ	Thruster T.600N	V. Vaughan	
EI-FCA	Urban Air UFM-11 Lambada	S. Walshe	
EI-FCB	Boeing 717-200	Volotea Airlines	
EI-FCH	Boeing 737-83N	Alrosa Airlines	
EI-FCI	Zenair CH-601HD	J. Kenny	
EI-FCT	Embraer ERJ190-100STD	Celestial Aviation Trading Ltd	
EI-FCU	Boeing 717-2BL	Volotea Airlines	
EI-FCY	Aerospatiale ATR-72-600	Aer Arran	
EI-FCZ	Aerospatiale ATR-72-600	Aer Arran	
EI-FDC	PZL-110 Koliber 150	A. D. Brennan	
EI-FDD	Cameron Z-105 balloon	The Travel Department	
EI-FDF	Urban Air Samba XXL	K. Dardis	
EI-FDJ	Embraer ERJ190-100STD	Celestial Aviation Trading Ltd	
EI-FDO	Jabiru UL-D	O. Matthews	
EI-FDR	Bombardier CL600-2B16 Challenger	P. Collins	
EI-FDS	Boeing 737-86N	Air Italy/Meridiana	
EI-FDY	Ikarus C42	N. Dockery	
EI-FED	Boeing 737-8KN	AWAS 402 36 Ireland LTD	
EI-FEE	Boeing 737-8AS	Ryanair Ltd	
EI-FEF	Boeing 737-8AS	Ryanair Ltd	
EI-FEG	Boeing 737-8AS	Ryanair Ltd	
EI-FEH	Boeing 737-8AS	Ryanair Ltd	
EI-FEI	Boeing 737-8AS	Ryanair Ltd	
EI-FEJ	Pipistrel Virus 912	R. Armstrong	
EI-FEO	ELA-07S	H. Graham	
EI-FEP	Aviatika MAI-890	H. A. Humphreys	
EI-FET	Raj Hamsa X'Air 502T	A. Cunningham	
EI-FEU	Aviatika MAI-890	P. O'Donnell	
EI-FEV	Raj Hamsa X'Air 582	J. Marbach	
EI-FEW	Van's RV-7	P. Hayes	
EI-FFK	Boeing 737-81Q	Air Italy/Meridiana	
EI-FFM	Boeing 737-73S	Air Italy/Meridiana	
EI-FFN	Raj Hamsa X'Air 582	P. J. Gleeson	

Notes	Reg	Type († False registration)	Owner or Operator
	EI-FFV	AA-5 Traveler	K. A. J. O'Doherty
	EI-FFW	Boeing 737-85F	Air Italy/Meridiana
	EI-FFZ	Magni M16	S. Brennan
	EI-FGB	BRM Land Africa	P J Piling Contracts Ltd
	EI-FGF	Ikarus C42	Tibohine Flying Club
	EI-FGG	Ikarus C42	M. Murphy
	EI-FGH	Boeing 717-2BL	Volotea Airlines
	EI-FGI	Boeing 717-2BL	Volotea Airlines
	EI-FGN	Boeing 767-3BGER	Canas Leasing Ltd
	EI-FGU	Sky Ranger 912S(1)	A. Ryan
	EI-FGW	PA-22-108	W. H. Worrell
	EI-FGX	Boeing 737-3Q8	Aircraft 23810 QC Holdings Ltd
	EI-FHA	Boeing 737-8JP	Norwegian Air International Ltd
	EI-FHD	Boeing 737-8JP	Norwegian Air International Ltd
	EI-FHE	Boeing 737-8JP	Norwegian Air International Ltd
	EI-FHG	Boeing 737-8JP	Norwegian Air International Ltd
	EI-FHH	Boeing 737-8JP	Norwegian Air International Ltd
	EI-FHJ	Boeing 737-8JP	Norwegian Air International Ltd
	EI-FHK	Boeing 737-8JP	Norwegian Air International Ltd
	EI-FHL	Boeing 737-8JP	Norwegian Air International Ltd
	EI-FHM	Boeing 737-8JP	Norwegian Air International Ltd
	EI-FHN	Boeing 737-8JP	Norwegian Air International Ltd
	EI-FHP	Boeing 737-8JP	Norwegian Air International Ltd
	EI-FHR	Boeing 737-8JP	Norwegian Air International Ltd
	EI-FHS	Boeing 737-8JP	Norwegian Air International Ltd
	EI-FHT	Boeing 737-8JP	Norwegian Air International Ltd
	EI-FHU	Boeing 737-8JP	Norwegian Air International Ltd
	EI-FHV	Boeing 737-8JP	Norwegian Air International Ltd
	EI-FHW	Boeing 737-8JP	Norwegian Air International Ltd
	EI-FHX	Boeing 737-8JP	Norwegian Air International Ltd
	EI-FHY	Boeing 737-8JP	Norwegian Air International Ltd
	EI-FHZ	Boeing 737-8JP	Norwegian Air International Ltd
	EI-FIA	Boeing 737-8AS	Ryanair
	EI-FIB	Boeing 737-8AS	Ryanair
	EI-FIC	Boeing 737-8AS	Ryanair
	EI-FID	Boeing 737-8AS	Ryanair
	EI-FIE	Boeing 737-8AS	Ryanair
	EI-FIF	Boeing 737-8AS	Ryanair
	EI-FIG	Boeing 737-8AS	Ryanair
	EI-FIH	Boeing 737-8AS	Ryanair
	EI-FII	Cessna 172RG	K. O'Connor
	EI-FIJ	Boeing 737-8AS	Ryanair
	EI-FIK	Boeing 737-8AS	Ryanair
	EI-FIL	Boeing 737-8AS	Ryanair
	EI-FIM	Boeing 737-8AS	Ryanair
	EI-FIN	Boeing 737-8AS	Ryanair
	EI-FIO	Boeing 737-8AS	Ryanair
	EI-FIP	Boeing 737-8AS	Ryanair
	EI-FIR	Boeing 737-8AS	Ryanair
	EI-FIS	Boeing 737-8AS	Ryanair
	EI-FIT	Boeing 737-8AS	Ryanair
	EI-FIV	Boeing 737-8AS	Ryanair
	EI-FIW	Boeing 737-8AS	Ryanair
	EI-FIY	Boeing 737-8AS	Ryanair
	EI-FIZ	Boeing 737-8AS	Ryanair
	EI-FJA	Boeing 737-8JP	Norwegian Air International Ltd
	EI-FJB	Boeing 737-8JP	Norwegian Air International Ltd
	EI-FJC	Boeing 737-8JP	Norwegian Air International Ltd
	EI-FJD	Boeing 737-8JP	Norwegian Air International Ltd
	EI-FJE	Boeing 737-8JP	Norwegian Air International Ltd
	EI-FJG	Boeing 737-8JP	Norwegian Air International Ltd
	EI-FJH	Boeing 737-8JP	Norwegian Air International Ltd
	EI-FJI	Boeing 737-8JP	Norwegian Air International Ltd
	EI-FJJ	Boeing 737-8JP	Norwegian Air International Ltd
	EI-FJK	Boeing 737-8JP	Norwegian Air International Ltd
	EI-FJL	Boeing 737-8JP	Norwegian Air International Ltd
	EI-FJM	Boeing 737-8JP	Norwegian Air International Ltd
	EI-FJN	Boeing 737-8JP	Norwegian Air International Ltd
	EI-FJO	Boeing 737-8JP	Norwegian Air International Ltd
	EI-FJP	Boeing 737-8JP	Norwegian Air International Ltd
	EI-FJR	Boeing 737-8JP	Norwegian Air International Ltd

Reg	Type († False registration)	Owner or Operator	Notes
EI-FJS	Boeing 737-8JP	Norwegian Air International Ltd	
EI-FJT	Boeing 737-8JP	Norwegian Air International Ltd	
EI-FJU	Boeing 737-8JP	Norwegian Air International Ltd	
EI-FJV	Boeing 737-8JP	Norwegian Air International Ltd	
EI-FJW	Boeing 737-8JP	Norwegian Air International Ltd	
EI-FJX	Boeing 737-8JP	Norwegian Air International Ltd	
EI-FJY	Boeing 737-8JP	Norwegian Air International Ltd	
EI-FJZ	Boeing 737-8JP	Norwegian Air International Ltd	
EI-FLA	Rotor Flight Dominator	P. Flanagan	
EI-FLH	BRM Land Africa	M. P. Dwyer	
EI-FLI	Urban Air Samba XXL	M. Tormey	
EI-FLK	BRM Land Africa	Lough Sheelin Aero	
EI-FLL	Ikarus C42	A. Clarke	
EI-FLM	Boeing 737-85F	Meridiana	
EI-FLO	Kitfox Mk.IV	M. Nee	
EI-FLR	Embraer ERJ190-200IGW	Celestial Aviation Trading 2 Ltd	
EI-FLS	Ikarus C42	J. & O. Houlihan	
EI-FLU	PA-22-108	M. Bergin	
EI-FLW	Ikarus C42	D. Browne	
EI-FLX	Raj Hamsa X'Air 582(5)	P. M. Noons, I. Bennett & P. J. Keating	
EI-FMA	Aeropro Eurofox 912 3K	P. Reilly	
EI-FMF	Bellanca 7GCAA	V. J. Vaughan	
EI-FMG	Solar Wings Pegasus XL-R	T. Noonan	
EI-FMJ	Aerospatiale ATR-72-212A	Stobart Air	
EI-FMK	Aerospatiale ATR-72-212A	Stobart Air	
EI-FMO	BRM Land Africa	Laois Flying Club Ltd	
EI-FMP	Agusta AW.169	LCI Helicopters Eleven Ltd	
EI-FMR	Boeing 767-304ER	Meridiana	
EI-FMZ	Boeing 777-312ER	Inishgort Leasing Ltd	
EI-FNA	Aerospatiale ATR-72-600	Stobart Air	
EI-FNC	BRM Land Africa Citius	R. F. Gibney	
EI-FNE	Javron PA-18	P. J. McKenna	
EI-FNG	Airbus A.330-302	Aer Lingus Ltd	
EI-FNH	Airbus A.330-302	Aer Lingus Ltd	
EI-FNI	Boeing 777-2Q8ER	Alitalia	
EI-FNJ	Airbus A.320-214	Aer Lingus Ltd	
EI-FNO	Aeropro Eurofox	A. Donnelly	
EI-FNS	Ikarus C42	M. J. Brady	
EI-FNT	Agusta AW.169	Como Aviation Ltd	
EI-FNU	Boeing 737-86N	Meridiana	
EI-FNW	Boeing 737-86N	Meridiana	
EI-FNX	Airbus A.330-243	DAE Leasing (Ireland) Ltd	
EI-FOA	Boeing 737-8AS	Ryanair	
EI-FOB	Boeing 737-8AS	Ryanair	
EI-FOC	Boeing 737-8AS	Ryanair	
EI-FOD	Boeing 737-8AS	Ryanair	
EI-FOE	Boeing 737-8AS	Ryanair	
EI-FOF	Boeing 737-8AS	Ryanair	
EI-FOG	Boeing 737-8AS	Ryanair	
EI-FOH	Boeing 737-8AS	Ryanair	
EI-FOI	Boeing 737-8AS	Ryanair	
EI-FOJ	Boeing 737-8AS	Ryanair	
EI-FOK	Boeing 737-8AS	Ryanair	
EI-FOL	Boeing 737-8AS	Ryanair	
EI-FOM	Boeing 737-8AS	Ryanair	
EI-FON	Boeing 737-8AS	Ryanair	
EI-FOO	Boeing 737-8AS	Ryanair	
EI-FOP	Boeing 737-8AS	Ryanair	
EI-FOR	Boeing 737-8AS	Ryanair	
EI-FOS	Boeing 737-8AS	Ryanair	
EI-FOT	Boeing 737-8AS	Ryanair	
EI-FOV	Boeing 737-8AS	Ryanair	
EI-FOW	Boeing 737-8AS	Ryanair	
EI-FOY	Boeing 737-8AS	Ryanair	
EI-FOZ	Boeing 737-8AS	Ryanair	
EI-FPA	Canadair CRJ900LR	Cityjet/SAS	
EI-FPB	Canadair CRJ900LR	Cityjet/SAS	
Ei-FPC	Canadair CRJ900LR	Cityjet/SAS	
EI-FPD	Canadair CRJ900LR	Cityjet/SAS	
EI-FPE	Canadair CRJ900LR	Cityjet/SAS	
EI-FPF	Canadair CRJ900LR	Cityjet/SAS	

Notes	Reg	Type († False registration)	Owner or Operator
	EI-FPG	Canadair CRJ900LR	Cityjet/SAS
	EI-FPH	Canadair CRJ900LR	Cityjet/SAS
	EI-FPI	Canadair CRJ900LR	Cityjet/SAS
	EI-FPJ	Canadair CRJ900LR	Cityjet/SAS
	EI-FPK	Canadair CRJ900LR	Cityjet/SAS
	EI-FPM	Canadair CRJ900LR	Cityjet/SAS
	EI-FPN	Canadair CRJ900LR	Cityjet/SAS
	EI-FPO	Canadair CRJ900LR	Cityjet/SAS
	EI-FPP	Canadair CRJ900LR	Cityjet/SAS
	EI-FPR	Canadair CRJ900LR	Cityjet/SAS
	EI-FPS	Canadair CRJ900LR	Cityjet/SAS
	EI-FPT	Canadair CRJ900LR	Cityjet/SAS
	EI-FPU	Canadair CRJ900LR	Cityjet/SAS
	EI-FPV	Canadair CRJ900LR	Cityjet/SAS
	EI-FRB	Boeing 737-8AS	Ryanair
	EI-FRC	Boeing 737-8AS	Ryanair
	EI-FRD	Boeing 737-8AS	Ryanair
	EI-FRE	Boeing 737-8AS	Ryanair
	EI-FRF	Boeing 737-8AS	Ryanair
	EI-FRG	Boeing 737-8AS	Ryanair
	EI-FRH	Boeing 737-8AS	Ryanair
	EI-FRI	Boeing 737-8AS	Ryanair
	EI-FRJ	Boeing 737-8AS	Ryanair
	EI-FRK	Boeing 737-8AS	Ryanair
	EI-FRL	Boeing 737-8AS	Ryanair
	EI-FRM	Boeing 737-8AS	Ryanair
	EI-FRN	Boeing 737-8AS	Ryanair
	EI-FRO	Boeing 737-8AS	Ryanair
	EI-FRP	Boeing 737-8AS	Ryanair
	EI-FRR	Boeing 737-8AS	Ryanair
	EI-FRS	Boeing 737-8AS	Ryanair
	EI-FRT	Boeing 737-8AS	Ryanair
	EI-FRV	Boeing 737-8AS	Ryanair
	EI-FRW	Boeing 737-8AS	Ryanair
	EI-FRX	Boeing 737-800	Ryanair
	EI-FRY	Boeing 737-800	Ryanair
	EI-FRZ	Boeing 737-800	Ryanair
	EI-FSA	TL3000 Sirius	M. J. Kirrane
	EI-FSE	Airbus A.330-243	DAE Leasing (Ireland) Ltd
	EI-FSF	Airbus A.330-243	DAE Leasing (Ireland) 16 Ltd
	EI-FSJ	Boeing 737-86N	Blue Panorama
	EI-FSK	Aerospatiale ATR-72-600	Stobart Air
	EI-FSL	Aerospatiale ATR-72-600	Stobart Air
	EI-FSP	Airbus A.330-322	Aviation Ireland Designated Activity Company
	EI-FSR	ELA Aviacion ELA-07S	J. Heffernan
	EI-FSS	Boeing 777-2Q8ER	MASL Ireland (11) Ltd
	EI-FST	Ikarus C42	Ikarus Aviation Ireland Ltd
	EI-FSU	Airbus A.321-231	ACG Acquisition 2004-1 Ireland Ltd
	EI-FSW	Rans S-6 ESD	A. J., A. & J. Cunningham
	EI-FSX	Pegasus Quantum 15	G. Hanna
	EI-FSZ	Pipistrel Virus 912	N. Armstrong
	EI-FTA	Boeing 737-8AS	Ryanair
	EI-FTB	Boeing 737-8AS	Ryanair
	EI-FTC	Boeing 737-8AS	Ryanair
	EI-FTD	Boeing 737-8AS	Ryanair
	EI-FTE	Boeing 737-8AS	Ryanair
	EI-FTF	Boeing 737-8AS	Ryanair
	EI-FTG	Boeing 737-8AS	Ryanair
	EI-FTH	Boeing 737-8AS	Ryanair
	EI-FTI	Boeing 737-8AS	Ryanair
	EI-FTJ	Boeing 737-8AS	Ryanair
	EI-FTK	Boeing 737-8AS	Ryanair
	EI-FTL	Boeing 737-8AS	Ryanair
	EI-FTM	Boeing 737-8AS	Ryanair
	EI-FTN	Boeing 737-8AS	Ryanair
	EI-FTO	Boeing 737-8AS	Ryanair
	EI-FTP	Boeing 737-8AS	Ryanair
	EI-FTR	Boeing 737-8AS	Ryanair
	EI-FTS	Boeing 737-8AS	Ryanair
	EI-FTT	Boeing 737-8AS	Ryanair
	EI-FTV	Boeing 737-8AS	Ryanair

Reg	Type († False registration)	Owner or Operator	Notes
EI-FTW	Boeing 737-8AS	Ryanair	
EI-FTX	Rans S-6ES Coyote II	N. Blair	
EI-FTY	Boeing 737-8AS	Ryanair	
EI-FTZ	Boeing 737-8AS	Ryanair	
EI-FVA	Boeing 737-4Q8	Blue Panorama	
EI-FVF	Raj Hamsa X'Air 582(1)	K. Kiernan	
EI-FVG	Airbus A.319-111	Ernest Airlines	
EI-FVH	Boeing 737-800	Norwegian Air International Ltd	
EI-FVI	Boeing 737-800	Norwegian Air International Ltd	
EI-FVJ	Boeing 737-800	Norwegian Air International Ltd	
EI-FVK	Boeing 737-800	Norwegian Air International Ltd	
EI-FVL	Boeing 737-800	Norwegian Air International Ltd	
EI-FVM	Boeing 737-800	Norwegian Air International Ltd	
EI-FVN	Boeing 737-800	Norwegian Air International Ltd	
EI-FVP	Boeing 737-800	Norwegian Air International Ltd	
EI-FVR	Boeing 737-800	Norwegian Air International Ltd	
EI-FVS	Boeing 737-800	Norwegian Air International Ltd	
EI-FVT	Boeing 737-800	Norwegian Air International Ltd	
EI-FVU	Boeing 737-800	Norwegian Air International Ltd	
EI-FVV	Boeing 737-800	Norwegian Air International Ltd	
EI-FVW	Boeing 737-800	Norwegian Air International Ltd	
EI-FVX	Boeing 737-800	Norwegian Air International Ltd	
EI-FVY	Boeing 737-800	Norwegian Air International Ltd	
EI-FVZ	Boeing 737-800	Norwegian Air International Ltd	
EI-FWA	Sukhoi RRJ95B	Cityjet	
EI-FWB	Sukhoi RRJ95B	Cityjet	
EI-FWC	Sukhoi RRJ95B	Cityjet	
EI-FWD	Sukhoi RRJ95B	Cityjet	
EI-FWE	Sukhoi RRJ95B	Cityjet	
EI-FWF	Sukhoi RRJ95B	Cityjet	
EI-FXA	Aérospatiale ATR-42-300	Air Contractors (Ireland) Ltd	
EI-FXB	Aérospatiale ATR-42-300	Air Contractors (Ireland) Ltd	
EI-FXC	Aérospatiale ATR-42-300	Air Contractors (Ireland) Ltd	
EI-FXD	Aérospatiale ATR-42-300	Air Contractors (Ireland) Ltd	
EI-FXE	Aérospatiale ATR-42-300	Air Contractors (Ireland) Ltd	
EI-FXG	Aérospatiale ATR-72-202	Air Contractors (Ireland) Ltd	
EI-FXH	Aérospatiale ATR-72-202	Air Contractors (Ireland) Ltd	
EI-FXI	Aérospatiale ATR-72-202	Air Contractors (Ireland) Ltd	
EI-FXJ	Aérospatiale ATR-72-202	Air Contractors (Ireland) Ltd	
EI-FXK	Aerospatiale ATR-72-202	Air Contractors (Ireland) Ltd	
EI-FXL	Robinson R44	Skywest Aviation Ltd	
EI-FXO	Airbus A.320-214	LATAM Ireland DAC	
EI-FXU	Aerospatiale ATR-72-212A	Aircraft International Renting (A.I.R.) Ltd	
EI-FXV	Best Off Sky Ranger Nynja 912S(1)	M. Brereton & M. P. Dwyer	
EI-FXW	Best Off Sky Ranger Swift 912(2)	P. Marnane	
EI-FXZ	Roko Aero NG 4UL	Fly Hubair Ltd	
EI-FYA	Boeing 737-800	Norwegian Air International Ltd	
EI-FYB	Boeing 737-800	Norwegian Air International Ltd	
EI-FYC	Boeing 737-MAX8	Norwegian Air International Ltd	
EI-FYD	Boeing 737-MAX8	Norwegian Air International Ltd	
EI-FYE	Boeing 737-MAX8	Norwegian Air International Ltd	
EI-FYF	Boeing 737-MAX8	Norwegian Air International Ltd	
EI-FZA	Boeing 737-800	Ryanair	
EI-FZB	Boeing 737-800	Ryanair	
EI-FZC	Boeing 737-800	Ryanair	
EI-FZD	Boeing 737-800	Ryanair	
EI-FZE	Boeing 737-800	Ryanair	
EI-FZF	Boeing 737-800	Ryanair	
EI-FZG	Boeing 737-800	Ryanair	
EI-FZH	Boeing 737-800	Ryanair	
EI-FZI	Boeing 737-800	Ryanair	
EI-FZJ	Boeing 737-800	Ryanair	
EI-FZK	Boeing 737-800	Ryanair	
EI-FZL	Boeing 737-800	Ryanair	
EI-FZM	Boeing 737-800	Ryanair	
EI-FZN	Boeing 737-800	Ryanair	
EI-FZO	Boeing 737-800	Ryanair	
EI-FZP	Boeing 737-800	Ryanair	
EI-FZR	Boeing 737-800	Ryanair	
EI-FZS	Boeing 737-800	Ryanair	
EI-FZT	Boeing 737-800	Ryanair	

Notes	Reg	Type († False registration)	Owner or Operator
	EI-FZV	Boeing 737-800	Ryanair
	EI-FZW	Boeing 737-800	Ryanair
	EI-FZX	Boeing 737-800	Ryanair
	EI-FZY	Boeing 737-800	Ryanair
	EI-FZZ	Boeing 737-800	Ryanair
	EI-GAH	Ikarus C42B	Tibohine Flying Club Ltd
	EI-GAJ	Airbus A.330-302	Aer Lingus
	EI-GAL	Airbus A.320-214	Aer Lingus
	EI-GAM	Airbus A.320-214	Aer Lingus
	EI-GAW	Boeing 737-8ZO	Blue Panorama Airlines
	EI-GAX	Boeing 737-8ZO	Blue Panorama Airlines
	EI-GAZ	Embraer ERJ190-200LR	Celestial Aviation Trading 5 Ltd
	EI-GBB	Boeing 737-86N	Norwegian Air International Ltd
	EI-GBF	Boeing 737-8JP	Norwegian Air International Ltd
	EI-GBG	Boeing 737-8JP	Norwegian Air International Ltd
	EI-GBI	Boeing 737-8JP	Norwegian Air International Ltd
	EI-GCA	Embraer ERJ190-200LR	Celestial Aviation Trading 69 Ltd
	EI-GCB	Embraer ERJ190-200LR	Celestial Aviation Trading 5 Ltd
	EI-GCC	Airbus A.320-233	MASL Ireland (35) Ltd
	EI-GCF	Airbus A.330-302	Aer Lingus
	EI-GCH	Embraer ERJ190-100IGW	Aldus Portfolio Leasing Ltd
	EI-GCI	Embraer ERJ190-100IGW	Aldus Portfolio Leasing Ltd
	EI-GCJ	CSA Sportcruiser	S. Meagher, N. Mulligan, D. O'Reilly & M. D. Ryan
	EI-GCP	Sky Ranger 912(2)	J. Marbach
	EI-GCT	ATEC Zephyr 2000	C. S. Kilpatrick & S. R. McGirr
	EI-GCU	Airbus A.330-223	DAE Leasing (Ireland) 31 Ltd
	EI-GCV	Boeing 737-7CT	Wilmington Trust SP Services (Dublin) Ltd/Alrosa Air
	EI-GCX	Airbus A.320-214	SMBC Aviation Capital Ireland Leasing 3 Ltd
	EI-GDA	Boeing 737-800	Ryanair
	EI-GDB	Boeing 737-800	Ryanair
	EI-GDC	Boeing 737-800	Ryanair
	EI-GDD	Boeing 737-800	Ryanair
	EI-GDE	Boeing 737-800	Ryanair
	EI-GDF	Boeing 737-800	Ryanair
	EI-GDG	Boeing 737-800	Ryanair
	EI-GDH	Boeing 737-800	Ryanair
	EI-GDI	Boeing 737-800	Ryanair
	EI-GDJ	Piper J-4E	Ballyboughal J4 Flying Group
	EI-GDK	Boeing 737-800	Ryanair
	EI-GDM	Boeing 737-800	Ryanair
	EI-GDN	Boeing 737-800	Ryanair
	EI-GDO	Boeing 737-800	Ryanair
	EI-GDP	Boeing 737-800	Ryanair
	EI-GDR	Boeing 737-800	Ryanair
	EI-GDS	Boeing 737-800	Ryanair
	EI-GDT	Boeing 737-800	Ryanair
	EI-GDV	Boeing 737-800	Ryanair
	EI-GDW	Boeing 737-800	Ryanair
	EI-GDX	Boeing 737-800	Ryanair
	EI-GDY	Boeing 737-800	Ryanair
	EI-GEK	Airbus A.320-232	Chameli Aircraft Leasing Ltd
	EI-GEL	Airbus A.320-232	Fifi Aircraft Leasing Ltd
	EI-GEO	ICP MXP-740 Savannah S	M. Brereton
	EI-GER	Maule MX7-180A	R. Lanigan & J.Patrick
	EI-GEV	Aerospatiale ATR-42-600	Aer Lingus Regional
	EI-GFD	Airbus A.330-223	ILFC Aircraft 33A-444 Ltd
	EI-GFE	Airbus A.330-223	ILFC Aircraft 33A-454 Ltd
	EI-GFF	Airbus A.330-223	ILFC Aircraft 33A-469 Ltd
	EI-GFG	Airbus A.330-223	Fortress Ireland Leasing Ltd
	EI-GFH	Airbus A.330-223	Whitney Ireland Leasing Ltd
	EI-GFI	Airbus A.330-223	ILFC Aircraft 33A-822 Ltd
	EI-GFJ	Airbus A.330-223	Blowfishfunding Ltd
	EI-GFK	Airbus A.330-223	ILFC Aircraft 33-911 Ltd
	EI-GFL	Airbus A.330-223	Cielofunding Ltd
	EI-GFM	Airbus A.330-223	Aircraft Portfolio Holding Company No.2 Ltd
	EI-GJA	Boeing 737-800	Ryanair
	EI-GJB	Boeing 737-800	Ryanair
	EI-GJC	Boeing 737-800	Ryanair
	EI-GJD	Boeing 737-800	Ryanair

Reg	Type († False registration)	Owner or Operator	Notes
EI-GJE	Boeing 737-800	Ryanair	
EI-GJF	Boeing 737-800	Ryanair	
EI-GJG	Boeing 737-800	Ryanair	
EI-GJH	Boeing 737-800	Ryanair	
EI-GJI	Boeing 737-800	Ryanair	
EI-GJJ	Boeing 737-800	Ryanair	
EI-GJK	Boeing 737-800	Ryanair	
EI-GJL	AS.365N3	Anglo Beef Processors Ireland	
EI-GLA	Schleicher ASK-21	Dublin Gliding Club Ltd	
EI-GLB	Schleicher ASK-21	Dublin Gliding Club Ltd	
EI-GLC	Centrair 101A Pegase	Dublin Gliding Club Ltd	
EI-GLD	Schleicher ASK-13	Dublin Gliding Club Ltd	
EI-GLF	Schleicher K-8B	Dublin Gliding Club Ltd	
EI-GLG	Schleicher Ka 6CR	C. Sinclair	
EI-GLH	AB Sportine LAK-17A	S. Kinnear & K. Commins	
EI-GLL	Glaser-Dirks DG-200	P. Denman & C. Craig	
EI-GLM	Schleicher Ka-6CR	P. Denman, C. Craig & J. Finnan	
EI-GLO	Scheibe Zugvogel IIIB	J. Walsh, J. Murphy & N. Short	
EI-GLP	Olympia 2B	J. Cashin	
EI-GLT	Schempp-Hirth Discus b	D. Thomas	
EI-GLU	Schleicher Ka-6CR	K. Cullen & Partners	
EI-GLV	Schleicher ASW-19B	C. Sinclair & B. O'Neill	
EI-GMB	Schleicher ASW-17	ASW-17 Group	
EI-GMC	Schleicher ASK-18	The Eighteen Group	
EI-GMD	Phoebus C	F. McDonnell & Partners	
EI-GMF	Schleicher ASK-13	Dublin Gliding Club Ltd	
EI-GMH	WAG-Aero Sport Trainer	J. Matthews	
EI-GMO	Schleicher Ka 6E	C. Ainclair & W. Kilroy	
EI-GPT	Robinson R22 Beta	Treaty Plant & Tool (Hire & Sales)	
EI-GSM	Cessna 182S	Westpoint Flying Group	
EI-GVM	Robinson R22 Beta	B. A. Derham	
EI-GWY	Cessna 172R	Atlantic Flight Training	
EI-HAA	Boeing 737-4YOF	ASL Airlines (Ireland) Ltd	
EI-HEA	Airbus A.330-322F	ASL Airlines (Ireland) Ltd	
EI-HFA	DHC-1 Chipmunk 22	Irish Historic Flight Foundation Ltd	
EI-HFB	DHC-1 Chipmunk 22	Irish Historic Flight Foundation Ltd	
EI-HFC	DHC-1 Chipmunk 22	Irish Historic Flight Foundation Ltd	
EI-HFD	Boeing E75 Stearman	Irish Historic Flight Foundation Ltd	
EI-HUM	Van's RV-7	G. Humphreys	
EI-IAL	Agusta AW.109SP	Ion Aviation Ltd	
EI-IAN	Pilatus PC-6/B2-H4	Irish Parachute Club	
EI-ICA	Sikorsky S-92A	CHC Ireland Ltd	
EI-ICD	Sikorsky S-92A	CHC Ireland Ltd	
EI-ICG	Sikorsky S-92A	CHC Ireland Ltd	
EI-ICR	Sikorsky S-92A	CHC Ireland Ltd	
EI-ICS	Sikorsky S-92A	CHC Ireland Ltd	
EI-ICU	Sikorsky S-92A	CHC Ireland Ltd	
EI-IKB	Airbus A.320-214	Alitalia	
EI-IKF	Airbus A.320-214	Alitalia	
EI-IKG	Airbus A.320-214	Alitalia	
EI-IKL	Airbus A.320-214	Alitalia	
EI-IKU	Airbus A.320-214	Alitalia	
EI-IMB	Airbus A.319-112	Alitalia	
EI-IMC	Airbus A.319-112	Alitalia	
EI-IMD	Airbus A.319-112	Alitalia	
EI-IME	Airbus A.319-112	Alitalia	
EI-IMF	Airbus A.319-112	Alitalia	
EI-IMG	Airbus A.319-112	Alitalia	
EI-IMH	Airbus A.319-112	Alitalia	
EI-IMI	Airbus A.319-112	Alitalia	
EI-IMJ	Airbus A.319-112	Alitalia	
EI-IML	Airbus A.319-112	Alitalia	
EI-IMM	Airbus A.319-112	Alitalia	
EI-IMN	Airbus A.319-111	Alitalia	
EI-IMO	Airbus A.319-112	Alitalia	
EI-IMP	Airbus A.319-111	Alitalia	
EI-IMR	Airbus A.319-111	Alitalia	
EI-IMS	Airbus A.319-111	Alitalia	
EI-IMT	Airbus A.319-111	Alitalia	
EI-IMU	Airbus A.319-111	Alitalia	
EI-IMV	Airbus A.319-111	Alitalia	

Notes	Reg	Type († False registration)	Owner or Operator
	EI-IMW	Airbus A.319-111	Alitalia
	EI-IMX	Airbus A.319-111	Alitalia
	EI-ING	Cessna F.172P	21st Century Flyers
	EI-ISA	Boeing 777-243ER	Alitalia
	EI-ISB	Boeing 777-243ER	Alitalia
	EI-ISD	Boeing 777-243ER	Alitalia
	EI-ISE	Boeing 777-243ER	Alitalia
	EI-ISO	Boeing 777-243ER	Alitalia
	EI-ITN	Bombardier BD700-1A10	Airlink Airways
	EI-IXH	Airbus A.321-112	Alitalia
	EI-IXJ	Airbus A.321-112	Alitalia
	EI-IXV	Airbus A.321-112	Alitalia
	EI-IXZ	Airbus A.321-112	Alitalia
	EI-JIM	Urban Air Samba XLA	J. Smith
	EI-JOR	Robinson R44 II	Bluebrook Investments Ltd
	EI-JPK	Tecnam P2002-JF	Limerick Flying Club (Coonagh) Ltd
	EI-JSK	Gulfstream VI	Westair Aviation
	EI-KDH	PA-28-181 Archer II	K. O'Driscoll & D. Harris
	EI-KEL	Eurocopter EC.135T2+	Bond Air Services (Ireland) Ltd
	EI-KEV	Raj Hamsa X'Air Jabiru(3)	P. Kearney
	EI-KMA	Canadair CL600-2B16	Gain Jet Ireland Ltd
	EI-LAD	Robinson R44 II	Helicopter Support Ireland Ltd
	EI-LAX	Airbus A.330-202	Aer Lingus St Mella
	EI-LBR	Boeing 757-2Q8	Air Contractors (Ireland) Ltd
	EI-LBS	Boeing 757-2Q8	Air Contractors (Ireland) Ltd
	EI-LBT	Boeing 757-2Q8	Air Contractors (Ireland) Ltd
	EI-LCM	TBM-700N	G. Power
	EI-LEO	Cessna 750	Gain Jet Ireland Ltd
	EI-LFC	Tecnam P.2002-JF	Limerick Flying Club (Coonagh) Ltd
	EI-LID	Agusta AW.169	Vertical Aviation No.1 Ltd
	EI-LIM	Agusta AW.139	Westair Aviation
	EI-LOW	AS.355N	Executive Helicopter Maintenance Ltd
	EI-LSA	Cub Crafters CC11-160	Directsky Aviation Ltd
	EI-LSN	Gulfstream VI	Gain Jet Ireland Ltd
	EI-LSY	Gulfstream V-SP	Gain Jet (Ireland) Ltd
	EI-MCF	Cessna 172R	K. O'Connor
	EI-MCG	Cessna 172R	Galway Flying Club
	EI-MIK	Eurocopter EC.120B	Executive Helicopter Maintenance Ltd
	EI-MIR	Roko Aero NG 4HD	A. Fegan
	EI-MPW	Robinson R44	Connacht Helicopters
	EI-MRB	Denney Kitfox Mk.2	D. Doyle
	EI-MTZ	Urban Air Samba XXL	M. Motz
	EI-NEO	Boeing 787-9	Neos
	EI-NFW	Cessna 172S	Galway Flying Club
	EI-NJA	Robinson R44 II	Nojo Aviation Ltd
	EI-NVL	Jora spol S. R. O. Jora	A. McAllister & partners
	EI-ODD	Bell 206B JetRanger	Dwyer Nolan Developments Ltd
	EI-OFM	Cessna F.172N	C. Phillips
	EI-OOR	Cessna 172S	M. Casey
	EI-OZL	Airbus A.300B4-622R	ASL Airlines (Ireland) Ltd
	EI-OZM	Airbus A.300B4-622R	ASL Airlines (Ireland) Ltd
	EI-PGA	Dudek Hadron XX	F. Taylor
	EI-PGB	Dudek Hadron 28	C. Fowler
	EI-PGH	Dudek Sytnthesis LT	R. Leslie
	EI-PGI	Dudek Hadron 28	J. McGovern
	EI-PGJ	Swing Sting 2	A. Auffret
	EI-PGK	Ozone Power Spyder 26	O. Creagh
	EI-PGL	Dudek Synthesis 34	K. Sullivan
	EI-PGM	Dudek Nucleon XX	L. Graham
	EI-PGN	ITV Boxer	N. Burke
	EI-PGO	Fly Market Relax 25	M. N. Bendon
	EI-PGP	Paramania Reflex Wings Fusion 26	E. DeKhors
	EI-PMI	Agusta-Bell 206B JetRanger III	Eirland Ltd
	EI-POK	Robinson R44	Skywest Aviation Ltd
	EI-POP	Cameron Z-90 balloon	The Travel Department
	EI-PRO	Airbus Helicopters AS.365N2	Executive Helicopter Maintenance Ltd
	EI-PWC	Magni M-24 Orion	R. Macnioclais
	EI-RCA	Roko Aero NG4UL	A. Breslin
	EI-RDA	Embraer ERJ170-200LR	Alitalia Cityliner
	EI-RDB	Embraer ERJ170-200LR	Alitalia Cityliner
	EI-RDC	Embraer ERJ170-200LR	Alitalia Cityliner

Reg	Type († False registration)	Owner or Operator	Notes
EI-RDD	Embraer ERJ170-200LR	Alitalia Cityliner	
EI-RDE	Embraer ERJ170-200LR	Alitalia Cityliner	
EI-RDF	Embraer ERJ170-200LR	Alitalia Cityliner	
EI-RDG	Embraer ERJ170-200LR	Alitalia Cityliner	
EI-RDH	Embraer ERJ170-200LR	Alitalia Cityliner	
EI-RDI	Embraer ERJ170-200LR	Alitalia Cityliner	
EI-RDJ	Embraer ERJ170-200LR	Alitalia Cityliner	
EI-RDK	Embraer ERJ170-200LR	Alitalia Cityliner	
EI-RDL	Embraer ERJ170-200LR	Alitalia Cityliner	
EI-RDM	Embraer ERJ170-200LR	Alitalia Cityliner	
EI-RDN	Embraer ERJ170-200LR	Alitalia Cityliner	
EI-RDO	Embraer ERJ170-200LR	Alitalia Cityliner	
EI-REJ	Aérospatiale ATR-72-201	Air Contractors (Ireland) Ltd	
EI-REL	Aerospatiale ATR-72-212	Aer Arann	
EI-REM	Aerospatiale ATR-72-212	Aer Arann	
EI-RJD	Avro RJ85	Cityjet	
EI-RJF	Avro RJ85	Cityjet	
EI-RJH	Avro RJ85	Cityjet	
EI-RJI	Avro RJ85	Cityjet	
EI-RJN	Avro RJ85	Cityjet	
EI-RJO	Avro RJ85	Cityjet	
EI-RJR	Avro RJ85	Cityjet	
EI-RJT	Avro RJ85	Cityjet	
EI-RJU	Avro RJ85	Cityjet	
EI-RJW	Avro RJ85	Cityjet Garinish Island	
EI-RJX	Avro RJ85	Cityjet	
EI-RJY	Avro RJ85	Cityjet	
EI-RJZ	Avro RJ85	Cityjet	
EI-RNA	Embraer ERJ190-100STD	Alitalia Cityliner	
EI-RNB	Embraer ERJ190-100STD	Alitalia Cityliner	
EI-RNC	Embraer ERJ190-100STD	Alitalia Cityliner	
EI-RND	Embraer ERJ190-100STD	Alitalia Cityliner	
EI-RNE	Embraer ERJ190-100STD	Alitalia Cityliner	
EI-ROK	Roko Aero NG 4UL	K. Harley	
EI-RUH	Boeing 737-8K5	VEBL-767-300 Ltd	
EI-RUI	Boeing 737-85P	VEBL-767-300 Ltd	
EI-RUJ	Boeing 737-81Q	VEBL-767-300 Ltd	
EI-RUK	Boeing 737-86N	VEBL-767-300 Ltd	
EI-RUN	Boeing 737-808	Vardy Ltd	
EI-RUO	Boeing 737-808	Vardy Ltd	
EI-SAC	Cessna 172P	Sligo Aero Club	
EI-SEA	SeaRey	J. Brennan	
EI-SEV	Boeing 737-73S	Ryanair	
EI-SIA	Airbus A.320-251N	Scandinavian Airlines Ireland Ltd	
EI-SIB	Airbus A.320-251N	Scandinavian Airlines Ireland Ltd	
EI-SIC	Airbus A.320-251N	Scandinavian Airlines Ireland Ltd	
EI-SID	Airbus A.320-251N	Scandinavian Airlines Ireland Ltd	
EI-SIE	Airbus A.320-251N	Scandinavian Airlines Ireland Ltd	
EI-SIF	Airbus A.320-251N	Scandinavian Airlines Ireland Ltd	
EI-SKS	Robin R.2160	Shemburn Ltd	
EI-SKV	Robin R.2160	Shemburn Ltd	
EI-SKW	PA-28-161 Warrior II	Shemburn Ltd	
EI-SLF	Aérospatiale ATR-72-201	ASL Airlines (Ireland) Ltd	
EI-SLG	Aérospatiale ATR-72-202	ASL Airlines (Ireland) Ltd	
EI-SLJ	Aerospatiale ATR-72-201	ASL Airlines (Ireland) Ltd	
EI-SLO	Aerospatiale ATR-42-320	ASL Airlines (Ireland) Ltd	
EI-SLP	Aerospatiale ATR-72-212	ASL Airlines (Ireland) Ltd	
EI-SLS	Aerospatiale ATR-72-201	ASL Airlines (Ireland) Ltd	
EI-SLT	Aerospatiale ATR-72-201	ASL Airlines (Ireland) Ltd	
EI-SLU	Aerospatiale ATR-72-202	ASL Airlines (Ireland) Ltd	
EI-SLV	Aerospatiale ATR-72-202	ASL Airlines (Ireland) Ltd	
EI-SLW	Aerospatiale ATR-72-202	ASL Airlines (Ireland) Ltd	
EI-SLX	Aerospatiale ATR-72-202	ASL Airlines (Ireland) Ltd	
EI-SLY	Aerospatiale ATR-72-202	ASL Airlines (Ireland) Ltd	
EI-SLZ	Aerospatiale ATR-72-202	ASL Airlines (Ireland) Ltd	
EI-SMK	Zenair CH701	S. King	
EI-SOA	Aerospatiale ATR-72-202	ASL Airlines (Ireland) Ltd	
EI-SOO	Aerospatiale ATR-72-212A	ASL Airlines (Ireland) Ltd	
EI-SOP	Aerospatiale ATR-72-212A	ASL Airlines (Ireland) Ltd	
EI-STA	Boeing 737-31S	ASL Airlines (Ireland) Ltd	
EI-STJ	Boeing 737-490F	ASL Airlines (Ireland) Ltd	

REPUBLIC OF IRELAND CIVIL REGISTRATIONS

Notes	Reg	Type († False registration)	Owner or Operator
	EI-STK	Boeing 737-448	ASL Airlines (Ireland) Ltd
	EI-STL	Boeing 737-42C	ASL Airlines (Ireland) Ltd
	EI-STM	Boeing 737-4Z9F	ASL Airlines (Ireland) Ltd
	EI-STN	Boeing 737-4Q8	ASL Airlines (Ireland) Ltd
	EI-STO	Boeing 737-43Q	ASL Airlines (Ireland) Ltd
	EI-SYM	Van's RV-7	E. Symes
	EI-TAT	Bombardier CL600-2B16	Bandon Aircraft Leasing Ltd
	EI-TIM	Piper J-5A	N. & P. Murphy
	EI-TKI	Robinson R22 Beta	J. McDaid
	EI-TON	M. B. Cooke 582 (5)	T. Merrigan
	EI-TVG	Boeing 737-7ZF	Hansel Jet Ireland Ltd
	EI-UFO	PA-22 Tri-Pacer 150 (tailwheel)	W. Treacy
	EI-UNH	Boeing 737-524	TFM Aviation Ltd
	EI-UNL	Boeing 777-312	Stecker Ltd
	EI-UNM	Boeing 777-312	VEBL-767-300 Ltd
	EI-UNN	Boeing 777-312	Stecker Ltd
	EI-UNP	Boeing 777-312	VEBL-767-300 Ltd
	EI-UNR	Boeing 777-212ER	VEBL-767-300 Ltd
	EI-UNU	Boeing 777-222ER	VEBL-767-300 Ltd
	EI-VII	Vans RV-7	B. Sheane
	EI-VLN	PA-18A-150	D. O'Mahony
	EI-WAC	PA-23 Aztec 250E	Westair Aviation
	EI-WAT	Tecnam P.2002-JF	Waterford Aero Club Ltd
	EI-WFD	Tecnam P.2002-JF	Waterford Aero Club Ltd
	EI-WFI	Bombardier CL600-2B16 Challenger	Midwest Atlantic/Westair
	EI-WIG	Sky Ranger 912	K. Lannery
	EI-WLA	Boeing 777-3Q8ER	Alitalia
	EI-WMN	PA-23 Aztec 250F	Westair Aviation
	EI-WOT	Currie Wot	D. Doyle & Partners
	EI-WWI	Robinson R44 II	Ourville Ltd
	EI-WXA	Avro RJ85	Cityjet Ltd
	EI-WXP	Hawker 800XP	Westair Aviation Ltd
	EI-XLB	Boeing 747-446	VEBL-767-300 Ltd
	EI-XLC	Boeing 747-446	SB Leasing Ireland Ltd
	EI-XLD	Boeing 747-446	VEBL-767-300 Ltd
	EI-XLE	Boeing 747-446	SB Leasing Ireland Ltd
	EI-XLF	Boeing 747-446	SB Leasing Ireland Ltd
	EI-XLG	Boeing 747-446	SB Leasing Ireland Ltd
	EI-XLH	Boeing 747-446	Pembroke Exchanges Ltd
	EI-XLI	Boeing 747-446	Pembroke Exchanges Ltd
	EI-XLJ	Boeing 747-446	Richdale Investments Ltd
	EI-XLK	Boeing 747-412	VEBL-767-300 Ltd
	EI-XLL	Boeing 747-412	VEBL-767-300 Ltd
	EI-XLM	Boeing 747-412	Richdale Investments Ltd
	EI-XLN	Boeing 747-412	VEBL-767-300 Ltd
	EI-XLO	Boeing 747-412	VEBL-767-300 Ltd
	EI-XLP	Boeing 777-312	VEBL-767-300 Ltd
	EI-XLZ	Boeing 747-444	VEBL-767-300 Ltd
	EI-YLG	Robin HR.200/120B	Leinster Aero Club
	EI-ZEU	Cessna 525A	Airlink Airways Ltd
	EI-ZMA	Falcon 900EX	Airlink Airways Ltd
	EI-ZZZ	Bell222	Executive Helicopter Maintenance Ltd

EI-DVM Airbus A.320-214 of Aer Lingus *Allan S. Wright*

EI-FWA Sukhoi SU95 of Cityjet *Allan S. Wright*

Notes	Reg	Type	Owner or Operator
	A6 (United Arab Emirates)		
	A6-APA	Airbus A.380-861	Etihad Airways
	A6-APB	Airbus A.380-861	Etihad Airways
	A6-APC	Airbus A.380-861	Etihad Airways
	A6-APD	Airbus A.380-861	Etihad Airways
	A6-APE	Airbus A.380-861	Etihad Airways
	A6-APF	Airbus A.380-861	Etihad Airways
	A6-APG	Airbus A.380-861	Etihad Airways
	A6-APH	Airbus A.380-861	Etihad Airways
	A6-API	Airbus A.380-861	Etihad Airways
	A6-APJ	Airbus A.380-861	Etihad Airways
	A6-DDA	Boeing 777-FFX	Etihad Airways Cargo
	A6-DDB	Boeing 777-FFX	Etihad Airways Cargo
	A6-DDC	Boeing 777-FFX	Etihad Airways Cargo
	A6-DDD	Boeing 777-FFX	Etihad Airways Cargo
	A6-DDE	Boeing 777-FFX	Etihad Airways Cargo
	A6-EBA	Boeing 777-31HER	Emirates Airlines
	A6-EBB	Boeing 777-31HER	Emirates Airlines
	A6-EBC	Boeing 777-31HER	Emirates Airlines
	A6-EBE	Boeing 777-36NER	Emirates Airlines
	A6-EBF	Boeing 777-31HER	Emirates Airlines
	A6-EBG	Boeing 777-36NER	Emirates Airlines
	A6-EBH	Boeing 777-31HER	Emirates Airlines
	A6-EBI	Boeing 777-36NER	Emirates Airlines
	A6-EBJ	Boeing 777-36NER	Emirates Airlines
	A6-EBK	Boeing 777-36NER	Emirates Airlines
	A6-EBL	Boeing 777-31HER	Emirates Airlines
	A6-EBM	Boeing 777-31HER	Emirates Airlines
	A6-EBN	Boeing 777-36NER	Emirates Airlines
	A6-EBO	Boeing 777-36NER	Emirates Airlines
	A6-EBP	Boeing 777-31HER	Emirates Airlines
	A6-EBR	Boeing 777-36NER	Emirates Airlines
	A6-EBQ	Boeing 777-36NER	Emirates Airlines
	A6-EBS	Boeing 777-31HER	Emirates Airlines
	A6-EBT	Boeing 777-31HER	Emirates Airlines
	A6-EBU	Boeing 777-31HER	Emirates Airlines
	A6-EBV	Boeing 777-31HER	Emirates Airlines
	A6-EBW	Boeing 777-36NER	Emirates Airlines
	A6-EBX	Boeing 777-31HER	Emirates Airlines
	A6-EBY	Boeing 777-36NER	Emirates Airlines
	A6-EBZ	Boeing 777-31HER	Emirates Airlines
	A6-ECA	Boeing 777-36NER	Emirates Airlines
	A6-ECB	Boeing 777-31HER	Emirates Airlines
	A6-ECC	Boeing 777-36NER	Emirates Airlines
	A6-ECD	Boeing 777-36NER	Emirates Airlines
	A6-ECE	Boeing 777-31HER	Emirates Airlines
	A6-ECF	Boeing 777-31HER	Emirates Airlines
	A6-ECG	Boeing 777-31HER	Emirates Airlines
	A6-ECH	Boeing 777-31HER	Emirates Airlines
	A6-ECI	Boeing 777-31HER	Emirates Airlines
	A6-ECJ	Boeing 777-31HER	Emirates Airlines
	A6-ECK	Boeing 777-31HER	Emirates Airlines
	A6-ECL	Boeing 777-31NER	Emirates Airlines
	A6-ECM	Boeing 777-31NER	Emirates Airlines
	A6-ECN	Boeing 777-31NER	Emirates Airlines
	A6-ECO	Boeinb 777-31NER	Emirates Airlines
	A6-ECP	Boeing 777-31NER	Emirates Airlines
	A6-ECQ	Boeing 777-31HER	Emirates Airlines
	A6-ECR	Boeing 777-31HER	Emirates Airlines
	A6-ECS	Boeing 777-31HER	Emirates Airlines
	A6-ECT	Boeing 777-31HER	Emirates Airlines
	A6-ECU	Boeing 777-31HER	Emirates Airlines
	A6-ECV	Boeing 777-31HER	Emirates Airlines
	A6-ECW	Boeing 777-31HER	Emirates Airlines
	A6-ECX	Boeing 777-31HER	Emirates Airlines
	A6-ECY	Boeing 777-31HER	Emirates Airlines
	A6-ECZ	Boeing 777-31HER	Emirates Airlines
	A6-EDA	Airbus A.380-861	Emirates Airlines

Reg	Type	Owner or Operator	Notes
A6-EDB	Airbus A.380-861	Emirates Airlines	
A6-EDC	Airbus A.380-861	Emirates Airlines	
A6-EDD	Airbus A.380-861	Emirates Airlines	
A6-EDE	Airbus A.380-861	Emirates Airlines	
A6-EDF	Airbus A.380-861	Emirates Airlines	
A6-EDG	Airbus A.380-861	Emirates Airlines	
A6-EDH	Airbus A.380-861	Emirates Airlines	
A6-EDI	Airbus A.380-861	Emirates Airlines	
A6-EDJ	Airbus A.380-861	Emirates Airlines	
A6-EDK	Airbus A.380-861	Emirates Airlines	
A6-EDL	Airbus A.380-861	Emirates Airlines	
A6-EDM	Airbus A.380-861	Emirates Airlines	
A6-EDN	Airbus A.380-861	Emirates Airlines	
A6-EDO	Airbus A.380-861	Emirates Airlines	
A6-EDP	Airbus A.380-861	Emirates Airlines	
A6-EDQ	Airbus A.380-861	Emirates Airlines	
A6-EDR	Airbus A.380-861	Emirates Airlines	
A6-EDS	Airbus A.380-861	Emirates Airlines	
A6-EDT	Airbus A.380-861	Emirates Airlines	
A6-EDU	Airbus A.380-861	Emirates Airlines	
A6-EDV	Airbus A.380-861	Emirates Airlines	
A6-EDW	Airbus A.380-861	Emirates Airlines	
A6-EDX	Airbus A.380-861	Emirates Airlines	
A6-EDY	Airbus A.380-861	Emirates Airlines	
A6-EDZ	Airbus A.380-861	Emirates Airlines	
A6-EEA	Airbus A.380-861	Emirates Airlines	
A6-EEB	Airbus A.380-861	Emirates Airlines	
A6-EEC	Airbus A.380-861	Emirates Airlines	
A6-EED	Airbus A.380-861	Emirates Airlines	
A6-EEE	Airbus A.380-861	Emirates Airlines	
A6-EEF	Airbus A.380-861	Emirates Airlines	
A6-EEG	Airbus A.380-861	Emirates Airlines	
A6-EEH	Airbus A.380-861	Emirates Airlines	
A6-EEI	Airbus A.380-861	Emirates Airlines	
A6-EEJ	Airbus A.380-861	Emirates Airlines	
A6-EEK	Airbus A.380-861	Emirates Airlines	
A6-EEL	Airbus A.380-861	Emirates Airlines	
A6-EEM	Airbus A.380-861	Emirates Airlines	
A6-EEN	Airbus A.380-861	Emirates Airlines	
A6-EEO	Airbus A.380-861	Emirates Airlines	
A6-EEP	Airbus A.380-861	Emirates Airlines	
A6-EEQ	Airbus A.380-861	Emirates Airlines	
A6-EER	Airbus A.380-861	Emirates Airlines	
A6-EES	Airbus A.380-861	Emirates Airlines	
A6-EET	Airbus A.380-861	Emirates Airlines	
A6-EEU	Airbus A.380-861	Emirates Airlines	
A6-EEV	Airbus A.380-861	Emirates Airlines	
A6-EEW	Airbus A.380-861	Emirates Airlines	
A6-EEX	Airbus A.380-861	Emirates Airlines	
A6-EEY	Airbus A.380-861	Emirates Airlines	
A6-EEZ	Airbus A.380-861	Emirates Airlines	
A6-EGA	Boeing 777-31HER	Emirates Airlines	
A6-EGB	Boeing 777-31HER	Emirates Airlines	
A6-EGC	Boeing 777-31HER	Emirates Airlines	
A6-EGD	Boeing 777-31HER	Emirates Airlines	
A6-EGE	Boeing 777-31HER	Emirates Airlines	
A6-EGF	Boeing 777-31HER	Emirates Airlines	
A6-EGG	Boeing 777-31HER	Emirates Airlines	
A6-EGH	Boeing 777-31HER	Emirates Airlines	
A6-EGI	Boeing 777-31HER	Emirates Airlines	
A6-EGJ	Boeing 777-31HER	Emirates Airlines	
A6-EGK	Boeing 777-31HER	Emirates Airlines	
A6-EGL	Boeing 777-31HER	Emirates Airlines	
A6-EGM	Boeing 777-31HER	Emirates Airlines	
A6-EGN	Boeing 777-31HER	Emirates Airlines	
A6-EGO	Boeing 777-31HER	Emirates Airlines	
A6-EGP	Boeing 777-31HER	Emirates Airlines	
A6-EGQ	Boeing 777-31HER	Emirates Airlines	
A6-EGR	Boeing 777-31HER	Emirates Airlines	
A6-EGS	Boeing 777-31HER	Emirates Airlines	
A6-EGT	Boeing 777-31HER	Emirates Airlines	

Notes	Reg	Type	Owner or Operator
	A6-EGU	Boeing 777-31HER	Emirates Airlines
	A6-EGV	Boeing 777-31HER	Emirates Airlines
	A6-EGW	Boeing 777-31HER	Emirates Airlines
	A6-EGX	Boeing 777-31HER	Emirates Airlines
	A6-EGY	Boeing 777-31HER	Emirates Airlines
	A6-EGZ	Boeing 777-31HER	Emirates Airlines
	A6-ENA	Boeing 777-31HER	Emirates Airlines
	A6-ENB	Boeing 777-31HER	Emirates Airlines
	A6-ENC	Boeing 777-31HER	Emirates Airlines
	A6-END	Boeing 777-31HER	Emirates Airlines
	A6-ENE	Boeing 777-31HER	Emirates Airlines
	A6-ENF	Boeing 777-31HER	Emirates Airlines
	A6-ENG	Boeing 777-31HER	Emirates Airlines
	A6-ENH	Boeing 777-31HER	Emirates Airlines
	A6-ENI	Boeing 777-31HER	Emirates Airlines
	A6-ENJ	Boeing 777-31HER	Emirates Airlines
	A6-ENK	Boeing 777-31HER	Emirates Airlines
	A6-ENL	Boeing 777-31HER	Emirates Airlines
	A6-ENM	Boeing 777-31HER	Emirates Airlines
	A6-ENN	Boeing 777-31HER	Emirates Airlines
	A6-ENO	Boeing 777-31HER	Emirates Airlines
	A6-ENP	Boeing 777-31HER	Emirates Airlines
	A6-ENQ	Boeing 777-31HER	Emirates Airlines
	A6-ENR	Boeing 777-31HER	Emirates Airlines
	A6-ENS	Boeing 777-31HER	Emirates Airlines
	A6-ENT	Boeing 777-31HER	Emirates Airlines
	A6-ENU	Boeing 777-31HER	Emirates Airlines
	A6-ENV	Boeing 777-31HER	Emirates Airlines
	A6-ENW	Boeing 777-31HER	Emirates Airlines
	A6-ENX	Boeing 777-31HER	Emirates Airlines
	A6-ENY	Boeing 777-31HER	Emirates Airlines
	A6-ENZ	Boeing 777-31HER	Emirates Airlines
	A6-EOA	Airbus A.380-861	Emirates Airlines
	A6-EOB	Airbus A.380-861	Emirates Airlines
	A6-EOC	Airbus A.380-861	Emirates Airlines
	A6-EOD	Airbus A.380-861	Emirates Airlines
	A6-EOE	Airbus A.380-861	Emirates Airlines
	A6-EOF	Airbus A.380-861	Emirates Airlines
	A6-EOG	Airbus A.380-861	Emirates Airlines
	A6-EOH	Airbus A.380-861	Emirates Airlines
	A6-EOI	Airbus A.380-861	Emirates Airlines
	A6-EOJ	Airbus A.380-861	Emirates Airlines
	A6-EOK	Airbus A.380-861	Emirates Airlines
	A6-EOL	Airbus A.380-861	Emirates Airlines
	A6-EOM	Airbus A.380-861	Emirates Airlines
	A6-EON	Airbus A.380-861	Emirates Airlines
	A6-EOO	Airbus A.380-861	Emirates Airlines
	A6-EOP	Airbus A.380-861	Emirates Airlines
	A6-EOQ	Airbus A.380-861	Emirates Airlines
	A6-EOR	Airbus A.380-861	Emirates Airlines
	A6-EOS	Airbus A.380-861	Emirates Airlines
	A6-EOT	Airbus A.380-861	Emirates Airlines
	A6-EOU	Airbus A.380-861	Emirates Airlines
	A6-EOV	Airbus A.380-861	Emirates Airlines
	A6-EOW	Airbus A.380-861	Emirates Airlines
	A6-EOX	Airbus A.380-861	Emirates Airlines
	A6-EOY	Airbus A.380-861	Emirates Airlines
	A6-EOZ	Airbus A.380-861	Emirates Airlines
	A6-EPA	Boeing 777-31HER	Emirates Airlines
	A6-EPB	Boeing 777-31HER	Emirates Airlines
	A6-EPC	Boeing 777-31HER	Emirates Airlines
	A6-EPD	Boeing 777-31HER	Emirates Airlines
	A6-EPE	Boeing 777-31HER	Emirates Airlines
	A6-EPF	Boeing 777-31HER	Emirates Airlines
	A6-EPG	Boeing 777-31HER	Emirates Airlines
	A6-EPH	Boeing 777-31HER	Emirates Airlines
	A6-EPI	Boeing 777-31HER	Emirates Airlines
	A6-EPJ	Boeing 777-31HER	Emirates Airlines
	A6-EPK	Boeing 777-31HER	Emirates Airlines
	A6-EPL	Boeing 777-31HER	Emirates Airlines
	A6-EPM	Boeing 777-31HER	Emirates Airlines

Reg	Type	Owner or Operator	Notes
A6-EPN	Boeing 777-31HER	Emirates Airlines	
A6-EPO	Boeing 777-31HER	Emirates Airlines	
A6-EPP	Boeing 777-31HER	Emirates Airlines	
A6-EPQ	Boeing 777-31HER	Emirates Airlines	
A6-EPR	Boeing 777-31HER	Emirates Airlines	
A6-EPS	Boeing 777-31HER	Emirates Airlines	
A6-EPT	Boeing 777-31HER	Emirates Airlines	
A6-EPU	Boeing 777-31HER	Emirates Airlines	
A6-EPV	Boeing 777-31HER	Emirates Airlines	
A6-EPW	Boeing 777-31HER	Emirates Airlines	
A6-EPX	Boeing 777-31HER	Emirates Airlines	
A6-EPY	Boeing 777-31HER	Emirates Airlines	
A6-EPZ	Boeing 777-31HER	Emirates Airlines	
A6-EQA	Boeing 777-31HER	Emirates Airlines	
A6-EQB	Boeing 777-31HER	Emirates Airlines	
A6-EQC	Boeing 777-31HER	Emirates Airlines	
A6-EQD	Boeing 777-31HER	Emirates Airlines	
A6-EQE	Boeing 777-31HER	Emirates Airlines	
A6-EQF	Boeing 777-31HER	Emirates Airlines	
A6-EQG	Boeing 777-31HER	Emirates Airlines	
A6-EQH	Boeing 777-31HER	Emirates Airlines	
A6-EQI	Boeing 777-31HER	Emirates Airlines	
A6-EQJ	Boeing 777-31HER	Emirates Airlines	
A6-ETA	Boeing 777-3FXER	Etihad Airways	
A6-ETB	Boeing 777-3FXER	Etihad Airways	
A6-ETC	Boeing 777-3FXER	Etihad Airways	
A6-ETD	Boeing 777-3FXER	Etihad Airways	
A6-ETE	Boeing 777-3FXER	Etihad Airways	
A6-ETF	Boeing 777-3FXER	Etihad Airways	
A6-ETG	Boeing 777-3FXER	Etihad Airways	
A6-ETH	Boeing 777-3FXER	Etihad Airways	
A6-ETI	Boeing 777-3FXER	Etihad Airways	
A6-ETJ	Boeing 777-3FXER	Etihad Airways	
A6-ETK	Boeing 777-3FXER	Etihad Airways	
A6-ETL	Boeing 777-3FXER	Etihad Airways	
A6-ETM	Boeing 777-3FXER	Etihad Airways	
A6-ETN	Boeing 777-3FXER	Etihad Airways	
A6-ETO	Boeing 777-3FXER	Etihad Airways	
A6-ETP	Boeing 777-3FXER	Etihad Airways	
A6-ETQ	Boeing 777-3FXER	Etihad Airways	
A6-ETR	Boeing 777-3FXER	Etihad Airways	
A6-ETS	Boeing 777-3FXER	Etihad Airways	
A6-EUA	Airbus A.380-861	Emirates Airlines	
A6-EUB	Airbus A.380-861	Emirates Airlines	
A6-EUC	Airbus A.380-861	Emirates Airlines	
A6-EUD	Airbus A.380-861	Emirates Airlines	
A6-EUE	Airbus A.380-861	Emirates Airlines	
A6-EUF	Airbus A.380-861	Emirates Airlines	
A6-EUG	Airbus A.380-861	Emirates Airlines	
A6-EUH	Airbus A.380-861	Emirates Airlines	
A6-EUI	Airbus A.380-861	Emirates Airlines	
A6-EUJ	Airbus A.380-861	Emirates Airlines	
A6-EUK	Airbus A.380-861	Emirates Airlines	
A6-EUL	Airbus A.380-861	Emirates Airlines	
A6-EUM	Airbus A.380-861	Emirates Airlines	
A6-EUN	Airbus A.380-861	Emirates Airlines	
A6-EUO	Airbus A.380-861	Emirates Airlines	
A6-EUP	Airbus A.380-861	Emirates Airlines	
A6-EUQ	Airbus A.380-861	Emirates Airlines	
A6-EUR	Airbus A.380-861	Emirates Airlines	
A6-EUS	Airbus A.380-861	Emirates Airlines	
A6-EUT	Airbus A.380-861	Emirates Airlines	
A6-EUU	Airbus A.380-861	Emirates Airlines	
A6-EUV	Airbus A.380-861	Emirates Airlines	
A6-EUW	Airbus A.380-861	Emirates Airlines	
A6-EUX	Airbus A.380-861	Emirates Airlines	
A6-EUY	Airbus A.380-861	Emirates Airlines	
A6-EUZ	Airbus A.380-861	Emirates Airlines	
A6-EVA	Airbus A.380-842	Emirates Airlines	
A6-EVB	Airbus A.380-842	Emirates Airlines	
A6-EYD	Airbus A.330-243	Etihad Airways	

Notes	Reg	Type	Owner or Operator
	A6-EYE	Airbus A.330-243	Etihad Airways
	A6-EYF	Airbus A.330-243	Etihad Airways
	A6-EYG	Airbus A.330-243	Etihad Airways
	A6-EYH	Airbus A.330-243	Etihad Airways
	A6-EYI	Airbus A.330-243	Etihad Airways
	A6-EYJ	Airbus A.330-243	Etihad Airways
	A6-EYK	Airbus A.330-243	Etihad Airways
	A6-EYL	Airbus A.330-243	Etihad Airways
	A6-EYM	Airbus A.330-243	Etihad Airways
	A6-EYN	Airbus A.330-243	Etihad Airways
	A6-EYO	Airbus A.330-243	Etihad Airways
	A6-EYP	Airbus A.330-243	Etihad Airways
	A6-EYQ	Airbus A.330-243	Etihad Airways
	A6-EYR	Airbus A.330-243	Etihad Airways
	A6-EYS	Airbus A.330-243	Etihad Airways
	A6-EYT	Airbus A.330-243	Etihad Airways
	A6-EYU	Airbus A.330-243	Ethiad Airways

A7 (Qatar)

Notes	Reg	Type	Owner or Operator
	A7-AFF	Airbus A.330-243F	Qatar Airways Cargo
	A7-AFG	Airbus A.330-243F	Qatar Airways Cargo
	A7-AFH	Airbus A.330-243F	Qatar Airways Cargo
	A7-AFI	Airbus A.330-243F	Qatar Airways Cargo
	A7-AFJ	Airbus A.330-243F	Qatar Airways Cargo
	A7-AFV	Airbus A.330-243F	Qatar Airways Cargo
	A7-AFY	Airbus A.330-243F	Qatar Airways Cargo
	A7-AFZ	Airbus A.330-243F	Qatar Airways Cargo
	A7-ALA	Airbus A.350-941	Qatar Airways
	A7-ALB	Airbus A.350-941	Qatar Airways
	A7-ALC	Airbus A.350-941	Qatar Airways
	A7-ALD	Airbus A.350-941	Qatar Airways
	A7-ALE	Airbus A.350-941	Qatar Airways
	A7-ALF	Airbus A.350-941	Qatar Airways
	A7-ALG	Airbus A.350-941	Qatar Airways
	A7-ALH	Airbus A.350-941	Qatar Airways
	A7-ALI	Airbus A.350-941	Qatar Airways
	A7-ALJ	Airbus A.350-941	Qatar Airways
	A7-ALK	Airbus A.350-941	Qatar Airways
	A7-ALL	Airbus A.350-941	Qatar Airways
	A7-ALM	Airbus A.350-941	Qatar Airways
	A7-ALN	Airbus A.350-941	Qatar Airways
	A7-ALO	Airbus A.350-941	Qatar Airways
	A7-ALP	Airbus A.350-941	Qatar Airways
	A7-ALQ	Airbus A.350-941	Qatar Airways
	A7-ALR	Airbus A.350-941	Qatar Airways
	A7-ALS	Airbus A.350-941	Qatar Airways
	A7-ALT	Airbus A.350-941	Qatar Airways
	A7-ALU	Airbus A.350-941	Qatar Airways
	A7-ALV	Airbus A.350-941	Qatar Airways
	A7-ALW	Airbus A.350-941	Qatar Airways
	A7-ALX	Airbus A.350-941	Qatar Airways
	A7-ALY	Airbus A.350-941	Qatar Airways
	A7-ALZ	Airbus A.350-941	Qatar Airways
	A7-ANA	Airbus A.350-1041	Qatar Airways
	A7-ANC	Airbus A.350-1041	Qatar Airways
	A7-AND	Airbus A.350-1041	Qatar Airways
	A7-ANE	Airbus A.350-1041	Qatar Airways
	A7-ANF	Airbus A.350-1041	Qatar Airways
	A7-APA	Airbus A.380-861	Qatar Airways
	A7-APB	Airbus A.380-861	Qatar Airways
	A7-APC	Airbus A.380-861	Qatar Airways
	A7-APD	Airbus A.380-861	Qatar Airways
	A7-APE	Airbus A.380-861	Qatar Airways
	A7-APF	Airbus A.380-861	Qatar Airways
	A7-APG	Airbus A.380-861	Qatar Airways
	A7-APH	Airbus A.380-861	Qatar Airways
	A7-API	Airbus A.380-861	Qatar Airways
	A7-APJ	Airbus A.380-861	Qatar Airways
	A7-BAA	Boeing 777-3DZ ER	Qatar Airways
	A7-BAB	Boeing 777-3DZ ER	Qatar Airways

Reg	Type	Owner or Operator	Notes
A7-BAC	Boeing 777-3DZ ER	Qatar Airways	
A7-BAE	Boeing 777-3DZ ER	Qatar Airways	
A7-BAF	Boeing 777-3DZ ER	Qatar Airways	
A7-BAG	Boeing 777-3DZ ER	Qatar Airways	
A7-BAH	Boeing 777-3DZ ER	Qatar Airways	
A7-BAI	Boeing 777-3DZ ER	Qatar Airways	
A7-BAJ	Boeing 777-3DZ ER	Qatar Airways	
A7-BAK	Boeing 777-3DZ ER	Qatar Airways	
A7-BAL	Boeing 777-3DZ ER	Qatar Airways	
A7-BAM	Boeing 777-3DZ ER	Qatar Airways	
A7-BAN	Boeing 777-3DZ ER	Qatar Airways	
A7-BAO	Boeing 777-3DZ ER	Qatar Airways	
A7-BAP	Boeing 777-3DZ ER	Qatar Airways *Al Qattard*	
A7-BAQ	Boeing 777-3DZ ER	Qatar Airways	
A7-BAS	Boeing 777-3DZ ER	Qatar Airways	
A7-BAT	Boeing 777-3DZ ER	Qatar Airways	
A7-BAV	Boeing 777-3DZ ER	Qatar Airways	
A7-BAW	Boeing 777-3DZ ER	Qatar Airways	
A7-BAX	Boeing 777-3DZ ER	Qatar Airways	
A7-BAY	Boeing 777-3DZ ER	Qatar Airways	
A7-BAZ	Boeing 777-3DZ ER	Qatar Airways	
A7-BBA	Boeing 777-2DZ LR	Qatar Airways	
A7-BBB	Boeing 777-2DZ LR	Qatar Airways	
A7-BBC	Boeing 777-2DZ LR	Qatar Airways	
A7-BBD	Boeing 777-2DZ LR	Qatar Airways	
A7-BBE	Boeing 777-2DZ LR	Qatar Airways	
A7-BBF	Boeing 777-2DZ LR	Qatar Airways	
A7-BBG	Boeing 777-2DZ LR	Qatar Airways	
A7-BBH	Boeing 777-2DZ LR	Qatar Airways *A.Calail*	
A7-BBI	Boeing 777-2DZ LR	Qatar Airways *Jaow Alsalam*	
A7-BBJ	Boeing 777-2DZ LR	Qatar Airways	
A7-BCA	Boeing 787-8	Qatar Airways	
A7-BCB	Boeing 787-8	Qatar Airways	
A7-BCC	Boeing 787-8	Qatar Airways	
A7-BCD	Boeing 787-8	Qatar Airways	
A7-BCE	Boeing 787-8	Qatar Airways	
A7-BCF	Boeing 787-8	Qatar Airways	
A7-BCG	Boeing 787-8	Qatar Airways	
A7-BCH	Boeing 787-8	Qatar Airways	
A7-BCI	Boeing 787-8	Qatar Airways	
A7-BCJ	Boeing 787-8	Qatar Airways	
A7-BCK	Boeing 787-8	Qatar Airways	
A7-BCL	Boeing 787-8	Qatar Airways	
A7-BCM	Boeing 787-8	Qatar Airways	
A7-BCN	Boeing 787-8	Qatar Airways	
A7-BCO	Boeing 787-8	Qatar Airways	
A7-BCP	Boeing 787-8	Qatar Airways	
A7-BCQ	Boeing 787-8	Qatar Airways	
A7-BCR	Boeing 787-8	Qatar Airways	
A7-BCS	Boeing 787-8	Qatar Airways	
A7-BCT	Boeing 787-8	Qatar Airways	
A7-BCU	Boeing 787-8	Qatar Airways	
A7-BCV	Boeing 787-8	Qatar Airways	
A7-BCW	Boeing 787-8	Qatar Airways	
A7-BCX	Boeing 787-8	Qatar Airways	
A7-BCY	Boeing 787-8	Qatar Airways	
A7-BCZ	Boeing 787-8	Qatar Airways	
A7-BDA	Boeing 787-8	Qatar Airways	
A7-BDB	Boeing 787-8	Qatar Airways	
A7-BDC	Boeing 787-8	Qatar Airways	
A7-BDD	Boeing 787-8	Qatar Airways	
A7-BEA	Boeing 777-3DZER	Qatar Airways	
A7-BEB	Boeing 777-3DZER	Qatar Airways	
A7-BEC	Boeing 777-3DZER	Qatar Airways	
A7-BED	Boeing 777-3DZER	Qatar Airways	
A7-BEE	Boeing 777-3DZER	Qatar Airways	
A7-BEF	Boeing 777-3DZER	Qatar Airways	
A7-BEG	Boeing 777-3DZER	Qatar Airways	
A7-BEH	Boeing 777-3DZER	Qatar Airways	
A7-BEI	Boeing 777-3DZER	Qatar Airways	
A7-BEJ	Boeing 777-3DZER	Qatar Airways	

Notes	Reg	Type	Owner or Operator
	A7-BEK	Boeing 777-3DZER	Qatar Airways
	A7-BEL	Boeing 777-3DZER	Qatar Airways
	A7-BEM	Boeing 777-3DZER	Qatar Airways
	A7-BEN	Boeing 777-3DZER	Qatar Airways
	A7-BEO	Boeing 777-3DZER	Qatar Airways
	A7-BEP	Boeing 777-3DZER	Qatar Airways
	A7-BEQ	Boeing 777-3DZER	Qatar Airways
	A7-BER	Boeing 777-3DZER	Qatar Airways
	A7-BES	Boeing 777-3DZER	Qatar Airways
	A7-BFA	Boeing 777-FDZ	Qatar Airways Cargo
	A7-BFB	Boeing 777-FDZ	Qatar Airways Cargo
	A7-BFC	Boeing 777-FDZ	Qatar Airways Cargo
	A7-BFD	Boeing 777-FDZ	Qatar Airways Cargo
	A7-BFE	Boeing 777-FDZ	Qatar Airways Cargo
	A7-BFF	Boeing 777-FDZ	Qatar Airways Cargo
	A7-BFG	Boeing 777-FDZ	Qatar Airways Cargo
	A7-BFH	Boeing 777-FDZ	Qatar Airways Cargo
	A7-BFI	Boeing 777-FDZ	Qatar Airways Cargo
	A7-BFJ	Boeing 777-FDZ	Qatar Airways Cargo
	A7-BFK	Boeing 777-FDZ	Qatar Airways Cargo
	A7-BFL	Boeing 777-FDZ	Qatar Airways Cargo
	A7-BFM	Boeing 777-FDZ	Qatar Airways Cargo

A9C (Bahrain)

Notes	Reg	Type	Owner or Operator
	A9C-KA	Airbus A.330-243 (501)	Gulf Air
	A9C-KB	Airbus A.330-243 (502)	Gulf Air
	A9C-KC	Airbus A.330-243 (503)	Gulf Air
	A9C-KD	Airbus A.330-243 (504)	Gulf Air
	A9C-KE	Airbus A.330-243 (505)	Gulf Air
	A9C-KF	Airbus A.330-243 (506)	Gulf Air

A4O (Oman)

Notes	Reg	Type	Owner or Operator
	A4O-DA	Airbus A.330-243	Oman Air
	A4O-DB	Airbus A.330-243	Oman Air
	A4O-DC	Airbus A.330-243	Oman Air
	A4O-DD	Airbus A.330-343	Oman Air
	A4O-DE	Airbus A.330-343	Oman Air
	A4O-DF	Airbus A.330-243	Oman Air
	A4O-DG	Airbus A.330-243	Oman Air
	A4O-DH	Airbus A.330-343	Oman Air
	A4O-DI	Airbus A.330-343	Oman Air
	A4O-DJ	Airbus A.330-343	Oman Air
	A4O-SA	Boeing 787-8	Oman Air
	A4O-SB	Boeing 787-8	Oman Air
	A4O-SC	Boeing 787-9	Oman Air
	A4O-SD	Boeing 787-9	Oman Air
	A4O-SE	Boeing 787-9	Oman Air
	A4O-SY	Boeing 787-8	Oman Air
	A4O-SZ	Boeing 787-8	Oman Air

AP (Pakistan)

Notes	Reg	Type	Owner or Operator
	AP-BGJ	Boeing 777-240ER	Pakistan International Airlines
	AP-BGK	Boeing 777-240ER	Pakistan International Airlines
	AP-BGL	Boeing 777-240ER	Pakistan International Airlines
	AP-BGY	Boeing 777-240LR	Pakistan International Airlines
	AP-BGZ	Boeing 777-240LR	Pakistan International Airlines
	AP-BHV	Boeing 777-340ER	Pakistan International Airlines
	AP-BHW	Boeing 777-340ER	Pakistan International Airlines
	AP-BHX	Boeing 777-240ER	Pakistan International Airlines
	AP-BID	Boeing 777-340ER	Pakistan International Airlines
	AP-BMG	Boeing 777-2Q8ER	Pakistan International Airlines
	AP-BMH	Boeing 777-2Q8ER	Pakistan International Airlines
	AP-BMS	Boeing 777-3Q8ER	Pakistan International Airlines

Reg	Type	Owner or Operator	Notes

B (China/Taiwan/Hong Kong)

Reg	Type	Owner or Operator	Notes
B-HNR	Boeing 777-367ER	Cathay Pacific Airways	
B-KPA	Boeing 777-367ER	Cathay Pacific Airways	
B-KPB	Boeing 777-367ER	Cathay Pacific Airways	
B-KPC	Boeing 777-367ER	Cathay Pacific Airways	
B-KPD	Boeing 777-367ER	Cathay Pacific Airways	
B-KPE	Boeing 777-367ER	Cathay Pacific Airways	
B-KPF	Boeing 777-367ER	Cathay Pacific Airways	
B-KPG	Boeing 777-367ER	Cathay Pacific Airways	
B-KPH	Boeing 777-367ER	Cathay Pacific Airways	
B-KPI	Boeing 777-367ER	Cathay Pacific Airways	
B-KPJ	Boeing 777-367ER	Cathay Pacific Airways	
B-KPK	Boeing 777-367ER	Cathay Pacific Airways	
B-KPL	Boeing 777-367ER	Cathay Pacific Airways	
B-KPM	Boeing 777-367ER	Cathay Pacific Airways	
B-KPN	Boeing 777-367ER	Cathay Pacific Airways	
B-KPO	Boeing 777-367ER	Cathay Pacific Airways	
B-KPP	Boeing 777-367ER	Cathay Pacific Airways	
B-KPQ	Boeing 777-367ER	Cathay Pacific Airways	
B-KPR	Boeing 777-367ER	Cathay Pacific Airways	
B-KPS	Boeing 777-367ER	Cathay Pacific Airways	
B-KPT	Boeing 777-367ER	Cathay Pacific Airways	
B-KPU	Boeing 777-367ER	Cathay Pacific Airways	
B-KPV	Boeing 777-367ER	Cathay Pacific Airways	
B-KPW	Boeing 777-367ER	Cathay Pacific Airways	
B-KPX	Boeing 777-367ER	Cathay Pacific Airways	
B-KPY	Boeing 777-367ER	Cathay Pacific Airways	
B-KPZ	Boeing 777-367ER	Cathay Pacific Airways	
B-KQA	Boeing 777-367ER	Cathay Pacific Airways	
B-KQB	Boeing 777-367ER	Cathay Pacific Airways	
B-KQC	Boeing 777-367ER	Cathay Pacific Airways	
B-KQD	Boeing 777-367ER	Cathay Pacific Airways	
B-KQE	Boeing 777-367ER	Cathay Pacific Airways	
B-KQF	Boeing 777-367ER	Cathay Pacific Airways	
B-KQG	Boeing 777-367ER	Cathay Pacific Airways	
B-KQH	Boeing 777-367ER	Cathay Pacific Airways	
B-KQI	Boeing 777-367ER	Cathay Pacific Airways	
B-KQJ	Boeing 777-367ER	Cathay Pacific Airways	
B-KQK	Boeing 777-367ER	Cathay Pacific Airways	
B-KQL	Boeing 777-367ER	Cathay Pacific Airways	
B-KQM	Boeing 777-367ER	Cathay Pacific Airways	
B-KQN	Boeing 777-367ER	Cathay Pacific Airways	
B-KQO	Boeing 777-367ER	Cathay Pacific Airways	
B-KQP	Boeing 777-367ER	Cathay Pacific Airways	
B-KQQ	Boeing 777-367ER	Cathay Pacific Airways	
B-KQR	Boeing 777-367ER	Cathay Pacific Airways	
B-KQS	Boeing 777-367ER	Cathay Pacific Airways	
B-KQT	Boeing 777-367ER	Cathay Pacific Airways	
B-KQU	Boeing 777-367ER	Cathay Pacific Airways	
B-KQV	Boeing 777-367ER	Cathay Pacific Airways	
B-KQW	Boeing 777-367ER	Cathay Pacific Airways	
B-KQX	Boeing 777-367ER	Cathay Pacific Airways	
B-KQY	Boeing 777-367ER	Cathay Pacific Airways	
B-KQZ	Boeing 777-367ER	Cathay Pacific Airways	
B-LIA	Boeing 747-467ERF	Cathay Pacific Airways	
B-LIB	Boeing 747-467ERF	Cathay Pacific Airways	
B-LIC	Boeing 747-467ERF	Cathay Pacific Airways	
B-LID	Boeing 747-467ERF	Cathay Pacific Airways	
B-LIE	Boeing 747-467ERF	Cathay Pacific Airways	
B-LIF	Boeing 747-467ERF	Cathay Pacific Airways	
B-LJA	Boeing 747-867F	Cathay Pacific Airways	
B-LJB	Boeing 747-867F	Cathay Pacific Airways	
B-LJC	Boeing 747-867F	Cathay Pacific Airways	
B-LJD	Boeing 747-867F	Cathay Pacific Airways	
B-LJE	Boeing 747-867F	Cathay Pacific Airways	
B-LJF	Boeing 747-867F	Cathay Pacific Airways	
B-LJG	Boeing 747-867F	Cathay Pacific Airways	
B-LJH	Boeing 747-867F	Cathay Pacific Airways	
B-LJI	Boeing 747-867F	Cathay Pacific Airways	
B-LJJ	Boeing 747-867F	Cathay Pacific Airways	

Notes	Reg	Type	Owner or Operator
	B-LJK	Boeing 747-867F	Cathay Pacific Airways
	B-LJL	Boeing 747-867F	Cathay Pacific Airways
	B-LJM	Boeing 747-867F	Cathay Pacific Airways
	B-LJN	Boeing 747-867F	Cathay Pacific Airways
	B-LRA	Airbus A.350-941	Cathay Pacific Airways
	B-LRB	Airbus A.350-941	Cathay Pacific Airways
	B-LRC	Airbus A.350-941	Cathay Pacific Airways
	B-LRD	Airbus A.350-941	Cathay Pacific Airways
	B-LRE	Airbus A.350-941	Cathay Pacific Airways
	B-LRF	Airbus A.350-941	Cathay Pacific Airways
	B-LRG	Airbus A.350-941	Cathay Pacific Airways
	B-LRI	Airbus A.350-941	Cathay Pacific Airways
	B-LRJ	Airbus A.350-941	Cathay Pacific Airways
	B-LRK	Airbus A.350-941	Cathay Pacific Airways
	B-LRL	Airbus A.350-941	Cathay Pacific Airways
	B-LRM	Airbus A.350-941	Cathay Pacific Airways
	B-LRN	Airbus A.350-941	Cathay Pacific Airways
	B-LRO	Airbus A.350-941	Cathay Pacific Airways
	B-LRP	Airbus A.350-941	Cathay Pacific Airways
	B-LRQ	Airbus A.350-941	Cathay Pacific Airways
	B-LRR	Airbus A.350-941	Cathay Pacific Airways
	B-LRS	Airbus A.350-941	Cathay Pacific Airways
	B-LRT	Airbus A.350-941	Cathay Pacific Airways
	B-LRU	Airbus A.350-941	Cathay Pacific Airways
	B-LRV	Airbus A.350-941	Cathay Pacific Airways
	B-LRX	Airbus A.350-941	Cathay Pacific Airways
	B-1020	Airbus A.330-343	Hainan Airlines
	B-1021	Airbus A.330-343	Hainan Airlines
	B-1022	Airbus A.330-343	Hainan Airlines
	B-1048	Airbus A.330-343	Hainan Airlines
	B-1323	Boeing 787-9	Hainan Airlines
	B-1341	Boeing 787-9	Hainan Airlines
	B-1342	Boeing 787-9	Hainan Airlines
	B-1343	Boeing 787-9	Hainan Airlines
	B-1345	Boeing 787-9	Hainan Airlines
	B-1356	Boeing 787-9	Hainan Airlines
	B-1428	Boeing 777-39LER	Air China
	B-1429	Boeing 777-39LER	Air China
	B-1430	Boeing 777-39LER	Air China
	B-1499	Boeing 787-9	Hainan Airlines
	B-1539	Boeing 787-9	Hainan Airlines
	B-1540	Boeing 787-9	Hainan Airlines
	B-1543	Boeing 787-9	Hainan Airlines
	B-1546	Boeing 787-9	Hainan Airlines
	B-2001	Boeing 777-39PER	China Eastern Airlines
	B-2002	Boeing 777-39PER	China Eastern Airlines
	B-2003	Boeing 777-39PER	China Eastern Airlines
	B-2005	Boeing 777-2PER	China Eastern Airlines
	B-2006	Boeing 777-39LER	Air China
	B-2010	Boeing 777-F1B	China Southern Airlines Cargo
	B-2020	Boeing 777-39PER	China Eastern Airlines
	B-2021	Boeing 777-39PER	China Eastern Airlines
	B-2022	Boeing 777-39PER	China Eastern Airlines
	B-2023	Boeing 777-39PER	China Eastern Airlines
	B-2025	Boeing 777-39PER	China Eastern Airlines
	B-2026	Boeing 777-F1B	China Southern Airlines Cargo
	B-2027	Boeing 777-F1B	China Southern Airlines Cargo
	B-2028	Boeing 777-F1B	China Southern Airlines Cargo
	B-2031	Boeing 777-39LER	Air China
	B-2032	Boeing 777-39LER	Air China
	B-2033	Boeing 777-39LER	Air China
	B-2035	Boeing 777-39LER	Air China
	B-2036	Boeing 777-39LER	Air China
	B-2037	Boeing 777-39LER	Air China
	B-2038	Boeing 777-39LER	Air China
	B-2039	Boeing 777-39LER	Air China
	B-2040	Boeing 777-39LER	Air China
	B-2041	Boeing 777-F1B	China Southern Airlines Cargo
	B-2042	Boeing 777-F1B	China Southern Airlines Cargo
	B-2043	Boeing 777-39LER	Air China
	B-2045	Boeing 777-39LER	Air China

Reg	Type	Owner or Operator	Notes
B-2046	Boeing 777-39LER	Air China	
B-2047	Boeing 777-39LER	Air China	
B-2071	Boeing 777-F1B	China Southern Airlines Cargo	
B-2072	Boeing 777-F1B	China Southern Airlines Cargo	
B-2073	Boeing 777-F1B	China Southern Airlines Cargo	
B-2075	Boeing 777-F1B	China Southern Airlines Cargo	
B-2080	Boeing 777-F1B	China Southern Airlines Cargo	
B-2081	Boeing 777-F1B	China Southern Airlines Cargo	
B-2085	Boeing 777-39LER	Air China	
B-2086	Boeing 777-39LER	Air China	
B-2087	Boeing 777-39LER	Air China	
B-2088	Boeing 777-39LER	Air China	
B-2089	Boeing 777-39LER	Air China	
B-2090	Boeing 777-39LER	Air China	
B-2722	Boeing 787-8	Hainan Airlines	
B-2723	Boeing 787-8	Hainan Airlines	
B-2725	Boeing 787-8	China Southern Airlines	
B-2726	Boeing 787-8	China Southern Airlines	
B-2727	Boeing 787-8	China Southern Airlines	
B-2728	Boeing 787-8	Hainan Airlines	
B-2729	Boeing 787-8	Hainan Airlines	
B-2730	Boeing 787-8	Hainan Airlines	
B-2731	Boeing 787-8	Hainan Airlines	
B-2732	Boeing 787-8	China Southern Airlines	
B-2733	Boeing 787-8	China Southern Airlines	
B-2735	Boeing 787-8	China Southern Airlines	
B-2736	Boeing 787-8	China Southern Airlines	
B-2737	Boeing 787-8	China Southern Airlines	
B-2739	Boeing 787-8	Hainan Airlines	
B-2750	Boeing 787-8	Hainan Airlines	
B-2759	Boeing 787-8	Hainan Airlines	
B-2787	Boeing 787-8	China Southern Airlines	
B-2788	Boeing 787-8	China Southern Airlines	
B-5902	Airbus A.330-243	China Eastern Airlines	
B-5903	Airbus A.330-243	China Eastern Airlines	
B-5905	Airbus A.330-343	Hainan Airlines	
B-5908	Airbus A.330-243	China Eastern Airlines	
B-5918	Airbus A.330-243	Air China	
B-5920	Airbus A.330-243	China Eastern Airlines	
B-5921	Airbus A.330-243	China Eastern Airlines	
B-5925	Airbus A.330-243	Air China	
B-5926	Airbus A.330-243	China Eastern Airlines	
B-5927	Airbus A.330-243	Air China	
B-5930	Airbus A.330-243	China Eastern Airlines	
B-5931	Airbus A.330-243	China Eastern Airlines	
B-5932	Airbus A.330-243	Air China	
B-5933	Airbus A.330-243	Air China	
B-5935	Airbus A.330-343	Hainan Airlines	
B-5936	Airbus A.330-243	China Eastern Airlines	
B-5937	Airbus A.330-243	China Eastern Airlines	
B-5938	Airbus A.330-243	China Eastern Airlines	
B-5941	Airbus A.330-243	China Eastern Airlines	
B-5942	Airbus A.330-243	China Eastern Airlines	
B-5943	Airbus A.330-243	China Eastern Airlines	
B-5949	Airbus A.330-243	China Eastern Airlines	
B-5950	Airbus A.330-343	Hainan Airlines	
B-5952	Airbus A.330-243	China Eastern Airlines	
B-5955	Airbus A.330-243	Hainan Airlines	
B-5961	Airbus A.330-243	China Eastern Airlines	
B-5962	Airbus A.330-243	China Eastern Airlines	
B-5963	Airbus A.330-243	Hainan Airlines	
B-5968	Airbus A.330-243	China Eastern Airlines	
B-5972	Airbus A.330-343	Hainan Airlines	
B-5973	Airbus A.330-243	China Eastern Airlines	
B-5975	Airbus A.330-243	China Eastern Airlines	
B-5979	Airbus A.330-243	Hainan Airlines	
B-6070	Airbus A.330-243	Air China	
B-6071	Airbus A.330-243	Air China	
B-6072	Airbus A.330-243	Air China	
B-6073	Airbus A.330-243	Air China	
B-6075	Airbus A.330-243	Air China	

Notes	Reg	Type	Owner or Operator
	B-6076	Airbus A.330-243	Air China
	B-6079	Airbus A.330-243	Air China
	B-6080	Airbus A.330-243	Air China
	B-6081	Airbus A.330-243	Air China
	B-6082	Airbus A.330-243	China Eastern Airlines
	B-6088	Airbus A.330-243	Hainan Airlines
	B-6089	Airbus A.330-243	Hainan Airlines
	B-6090	Airbus A.330-243	Air China
	B-6091	Airbus A.330-243	Air China
	B-6092	Airbus A.330-243	Air China
	B-6093	Airbus A.330-243	Air China
	B-6099	Airbus A.330-243	China Eastern Airlines
	B-6113	Airbus A.330-243	Air China
	B-6115	Airbus A.330-243	Air China
	B-6116	Airbus A.330-243	Hainan Airlines
	B-6117	Airbus A.330-243	Air China
	B-6118	Airbus A.330-243	Hainan Airlines
	B-6121	Airbus A.330-243	China Eastern Airlines
	B-6122	Airbus A.330-243	China Eastern Airlines
	B-6123	Airbus A.330-243	China Eastern Airlines
	B-6130	Airbus A.330-243	Air China
	B-6131	Airbus A.330-243	Air China
	B-6132	Airbus A.330-243	Air China
	B-6133	Airbus A.330-243	Hainan Airlines
	B-6135	Airbus A.330-223	China Southern Airlines
	B-6505	Airbus A.330-243	Air China
	B-6515	Airbus A.330-223	China Southern Airlines
	B-6516	Airbus A.330-223	China Southern Airlines
	B-6519	Airbus A.330-243	Hainan Airlines
	B-6520	Airbus A.330-343	Hainan Airlines
	B-6526	Airbus A.330-223	China Southern Airlines
	B-6527	Airbus A.330-343	Hainan Airlines
	B-6528	Airbus A.330-223	China Southern Airlines
	B-6529	Airbus A.330-343	Hainan Airlines
	B-6531	Airbus A.330-223	China Southern Airlines
	B-6532	Airbus A.330-223	China Southern Airlines
	B-6533	Airbus A.330-243	Air China
	B-6536	Airbus A.330-243	Air China
	B-6537	Airbus A.330-243	China Eastern Airlines
	B-6538	Airbus A.330-243	China Eastern Airlines
	B-6539	Airbus A.330-343	Hainan Airlines
	B-6540	Airbus A.330-243	Air China
	B-6541	Airbus A.330-243	Air China
	B-6542	Airbus A.330-223	China Southern Airlines
	B-6543	Airbus A.330-243	China Eastern Airlines
	B-6547	Airbus A.330-223	China Southern Airlines
	B-6548	Airbus A.330-223	China Southern Airlines
	B-6549	Airbus A.330-243	Air China
	B-6969	Boeing 787-9	Hainan Airlines
	B-6998	Boeing 787-9	Hainan Airlines
	B-7302	Boeing 787-9	Hainan Airlines
	B-7343	Boeing 777-39PER	China Eastern Airlines
	B-7347	Boeing 777-39PER	China Eastern Airlines
	B-7349	Boeing 777-39PER	China Eastern Airlines
	B-7365	Boeing 777-39PER	China Eastern Airlines
	B-7367	Boeing 777-39PER	China Eastern Airlines
	B-7368	Boeing 777-39PER	China Eastern Airlines
	B-7369	Boeing 777-39PER	China Eastern Airlines
	B-7667	Boeing 787-9	Hainan Airlines
	B-7835	Boeing 787-9	Hainan Airlines
	B-7837	Boeing 787-9	Hainan Airlines
	B-7839	Boeing 787-9	Hainan Airlines
	B-7868	Boeing 777-39PER	China Eastern Airlines
	B-7880	Boeing 787-9	Hainan Airlines
	B-7881	Boeing 777-39PER	China Eastern Airlines
	B-7882	Boeing 777-39PER	China Eastern Airlines
	B-7883	Boeing 777-39PER	China Eastern Airlines
	B-8015	Airbus A.330-343	Hainan Airlines
	B-8016	Airbus A.330-343	Hainan Airlines
	B-8117	Airbus A.330-343	Hainan Airlines
	B-8118	Airbus A.330-343	Hainan Airlines

Reg	Type	Owner or Operator	Notes
B-8226	Airbus A.330-243	China Eastern Airlines	
B-8231	Airbus A.330-243	China Eastern Airlines	
B-8287	Airbus A.330-343	Hainan Airlines	
B-8596	Airbus A.330-243	Tianjin Airlines	
B-8659	Airbus A.330-243	Tianjin Airlines	
B-8776	Airbus A.330-243	Tianjin Airlines	
B-8959	Airbus A.330-243	Tianjin Airlines	
B-16703	Boeing 777-35EER	EVA Airways	
B-16705	Boeing 777-35EER	EVA Airways	
B-16706	Boeing 777-35EER	EVA Airways	
B-16707	Boeing 777-35EER	EVA Airways	
B-16708	Boeing 777-35EER	EVA Airways	
B-16709	Boeing 777-35EER	EVA Airways	
B-16710	Boeing 777-35EER	EVA Airways	
B-16711	Boeing 777-35EER	EVA Airways	
B-16712	Boeing 777-35EER	EVA Airways	
B-16713	Boeing 777-35EER	EVA Airways	
B-16715	Boeing 777-35EER	EVA Airways	
B-16716	Boeing 777-35EER	EVA Airways	
B-16717	Boeing 777-35EER	EVA Airways	
B-16718	Boeing 777-35EER	EVA Airways	
B-16719	Boeing 777-35EER	EVA Airways	
B-16720	Boeing 777-35EER	EVA Airways	
B-16721	Boeing 777-35EER	EVA Airways	
B-16722	Boeing 777-36NER	EVA Airways	
B-16723	Boeing 777-36NER	EVA Airways	
B-16725	Boeing 777-35EER	EVA Airways	
B-16726	Boeing 777-35EER	EVA Airways	
B-16727	Boeing 777-35EER	EVA Airways	
B-16728	Boeing 777-36NER	EVA Airways	
B-16729	Boeing 777-36NER	EVA Airways	
B-16730	Boeing 777-36NER	EVA Airways	
B-16731	Boeing 777-36NER	EVA Airways	
B-16732	Boeing 777-36NER	EVA Airways	
B-16733	Boeing 777-36NER	EVA Airways	
B-16735	Boeing 777-36NER	EVA Airways	
B-16736	Boeing 777-36NER	EVA Airways	
B-16737	Boeing 777-36NER	EVA Airways	
B-16738	Boeing 777-36NER	EVA Airways	
B-16739	Boeing 777-36NER	EVA Airways	
B-16740	Boeing 777-36NER	EVA Airways	
B-18901	Airbus A.350-941	China Airlines	
B-18902	Airbus A.350-941	China Airlines	
B-18903	Airbus A.350-941	China Airlines	
B-18905	Airbus A.350-941	China Airlines	
B-18906	Airbus A.350-941	China Airlines	
B-18907	Airbus A.350-941	China Airlines	
B-18908	Airbus A.350-941	China Airlines	
B-18909	Airbus A.350-941	China Airlines	
B-18910	Airbus A.350-941	China Airlines	
B-18912	Airbus A.350-941	China Airlines	
B-18915	Airbus A.350-941	China Airlines	
B-18916	Airbus A.350-941	China Airlines	

C (Canada)

Reg	Type	Owner or Operator	Notes
C-FCAE	Boeing 767-375ER (682)	Air Canada	
C-FCAF	Boeing 767-375ER (683)	Air Canada	
C-FCAG	Boeing 767-375ER (684)	Air Canada	
C-FDAT	Airbus A.310-308 (305)	Air Transat	
C-FGDT	Boeing 787-9	Air Canada	
C-FGDX	Boeing 787-9	Air Canada	
C-FGDZ	Boeing 787-9	Air Canada	
C-FGEI	Boeing 787-9 (838)	Air Canada	
C-FGEO	Boeing 787-9 (839)	Air Canada	
C-FGFZ	Boeing 787-9 (840)	Air Canada	
C-FGHZ	Boeing 787-9	Air Canada	
C-FITL	Boeing 777-333ER (731)	Air Canada	
C-FITU	Boeing 777-333ER (732)	Air Canada	
C-FITW	Boeing 777-3Q8ER (733)	Air Canada	
C-FIUA	Boeing 777-233LR (701)	Air Canada	

Notes	Reg	Type	Owner or Operator
	C-FIUF	Boeing 777-233LR (702)	Air Canada
	C-FIUJ	Boeing 777-233LR (703)	Air Canada
	C-FIUL	Boeing 777-333ER (734)	Air Canada
	C-FIUR	Boeing 777-333ER (735)	Air Canada
	C-FIUV	Boeing 777-333ER (736)	Air Canada
	C-FIUW	Boeing 777-333ER (737)	Air Canada
	C-FIVK	Boeing 777-233LR (704)	Air Canada
	C-FIVM	Boeing 777-333ER (738)	Air Canada
	C-FIVQ	Boeing 777-333ER (740)	Air Canada
	C-FIVR	Boeing 777-333ER (741)	Air Canada
	C-FIVS	Boeing 777-333ER (742)	Air Canada
	C-FIVW	Boeing 777-333ER (743)	Air Canada
	C-FIVX	Boeing 777-333ER (744)	Air Canada
	C-FIYA	Boeing 767-33AER	Air Canada Rouge
	C-FIYE	Boeing 767-33AER	Air Canada Rouge
	C-FJZK	Boeing 767-3Q8ER	Air Canada Rouge
	C-FJZS	Boeing 777-333ER (748)	Air Canada
	C-FKAU	Boeing 777-333ER (749)	Air Canada
	C-FKSV	Boeing 787-9	Air Canada
	C-FMLV	Boeing 767-316ER	Air Canada Rouge
	C-FMLZ	Boeing 767-316ER	Air Canada Rouge
	C-FMWP	Boeing 767-333ER (631)	Air Canada Rouge
	C-FMWQ	Boeing 767-333ER (632)	Air Canada Rouge
	C-FMWU	Boeing 767-333ER (633)	Air Canada Rouge
	C-FMWV	Boeing 767-333ER (634)	Air Canada Rouge
	C-FMWY	Boeing 767-333ER (635)	Air Canada Rouge
	C-FMXC	Boeing 767-333ER (636)	Air Canada Rouge
	C-FNAX	Boeing 737-8MAX	Westjet
	C-FNND	Boeing 777-233LR (705)	Air Canada
	C-FNNH	Boeing 777-233LR (706)	Air Canada
	C-FNNQ	Boeing 777-333ER (745)	Air Canada
	C-FNNU	Boeing 777-333ER (746)	Air Canada
	C-FNNW	Boeing 777-333ER	Air Canada
	C-FNOE	Boeing 787-9	Air Canada
	C-FNOG	Boeing 787-9	Air Canada
	C-FNOH	Boeing 787-9	Air Canada
	C-FNOI	Boeing 787-9	Air Canada
	C-FOCA	Boeing 767-375ER (640)	Air Canada
	C-FOGJ	Boeing 767-338ER	Westjet
	C-FOGT	Boeing 767-338ER	Westjet
	C-FPCA	Boeing 767-375ER (637)	Air Canada
	C-FPQB	Boeing 787-9 (841)	Air Canada
	C-FRAM	Boeing 777-333ER (739)	Air Canada
	C-FRAX	Boeing 737-MAX8	Westjet
	C-FRSA	Boeing 787-9	Air Canada
	C-FRSE	Boeing 787-9	Air Canada
	C-FRSI	Boeing 787-9	Air Canada
	C-FRSO	Boeing 787-9	Air Canada
	C-FRSR	Boeing 787-9 (848)	Air Canada
	C-FRTG	Boeing 787-9 (849)	Air Canada
	C-FRTU	Boeing 787-9 (850)	Air Canada
	C-FRTW	Boeing 787-9(851)	Air Canada
	C-FRYV	Boeing 737-MAX8	Westjet
	C-FSBV	Boeing 787-9	Air Canada
	C-FTCA	Boeing 767-375ER (638)	Air Canada
	C-FVLQ	Boeing 787-9 (853)	Air Canada
	C-FVLU	Boeing 787-9 (854)	Air Canada
	C-FVLX	Boeing 787-9 (855)	Air Canada
	C-FWAD	Boeing 767-338ER	Westjet
	C-FWSK	Boeing 737-7CT	Westjet
	C-FXCA	Boeing 767-375ER (639)	Air Canada Rouge
	C-GBZR	Boeing 767-38EER (645)	Air Canada Rouge
	C-GCTS	Airbus A.330-342	Air Transat
	C-GDUZ	Boeing 767-38EER (646)	Air Canada Rouge
	C-GEOQ	Boeing 767-375ER (647)	Air Canada Rouge
	C-GEOU	Boeing 767-375ER (648)	Air Canada Rouge
	C-GFAF	Airbus A.330-343X (931)	Air Canada
	C-GFAH	Airbus A.330-343X (932)	Air Canada
	C-GFAJ	Airbus A.330-343X (933)	Air Canada
	C-GFAT	Airbus A.310-304 (301)	Air Transat
	C-GFUR	Airbus A.330-343X (934)	Air Canada

Reg	Type	Owner or Operator	Notes
C-GGTS	Airbus A.330-243 (101)	Air Transat	
C-GHKR	Airbus A.330-343X (935)	Air Canada	
C-GHKW	Airbus A.330-343X (936)	Air Canada	
C-GHKX	Airbus A.330-343X (937)	Air Canada	
C-GHLA	Boeing 767-35HER	Air Canada Rouge	
C-GHLK	Boeing 767-35HER (657)	Air Canada Rouge	
C-GHLM	Airbus A.330-343X (938)	Air Canada	
C-GHLQ	Boeing 767-333ER	Air Canada Rouge	
C-GHLT	Boeing 767-333ER	Air Canada Rouge	
C-GHLU	Boeing 767-333ER	Air Canada Rouge	
C-GHLV	Boeing 767-333ER	Air Canada Rouge	
C-GHOZ	Boeing 767-375ER (685)	Air Canada	
C-GHPE	Boeing 767-33AER	Air Canada Rouge	
C-GHPN	Boeing 767-33AER	Air Canada Rouge	
C-GHPQ	Boeing 787-8	Air Canada	
C-GHPT	Boeing 787-8	Air Canada	
C-GHPU	Boeing 787-8	Air Canada	
C-GHPV	Boeing 787-8	Air Canada	
C-GHPX	Boeing 787-8	Air Canada	
C-GHPY	Boeing 787-8	Air Canada	
C-GHQQ	Boeing 787-8	Air Canada	
C-GHQY	Boeing 787-8	Air Canada	
C-GITS	Airbus A.330-243 (102)	Air Transat	
C-GJDA	Airbus A.330-243	Air Transat	
C-GKTS	Airbus A.330-342 (100)	Air Transat	
C-GLAT	Airbus A.310-308 (302)	Air Transat	
C-GLCA	Boeing 767-375ER (641)	Air Canada	
C-GMWJ	Boeing 737-7CT	Westjet	
C-GOGN	Boeing 767-338ER	Westjet	
C-GPAT	Airbus A.310-308 (303)	Air Transat	
C-GPTS	Airbus A.330-243 (103)	Air Transat	
C-GQWJ	Boeing 737-7CT	Westjet	
C-GRAX	Boeing 737-MAX8	Westjet	
C-GSAT	Airbus A.310-308 (304)	Air Transat	
C-GSCA	Boeing 767-375ER (642)	Air Canada Rouge	
C-GTSD	Airbus A.330-343	Air Transat	
C-GTSF	Airbus A.310-304 (345)	Air Transat	
C-GTSH	Airbus A.310-304 (343)	Air Transat	
C-GTSI	Airbus A.330-243	Air Transat	
C-GTSJ	Airbus A.330-243	Air Transat	
C-GTSN	Airbus A.330-243	Air Transat	
C-GTSO	Airbus A.330-342	Air Transat	
C-GTSR	Airbus A.330-243	Air Transat	
C-GTSW	Airbus A.310-304	Air Transat	
C-GTSY	Airbus A.310-304 (344)	Air Transat	
C-GTSZ	Airbus A.330-243	Air Transat	
C-GUBD	Airbus A.330-243	Air Transat	
C-GUBF	Airbus A.330-243	Air Transat	
C-GUBH	Airbus A.330-243	Air Transat	
C-GUFR	Airbus A.330-243	Air Transat	
C-GUWJ	Boeing 737-7CT	Westjet	
C-GVWJ	Boeing 737-7CT	Westjet	
C-GWCN	Boeing 737-7CT	Westjet	
C-GWJG	Boeing 737-7CT	Westjet	
C-GXAX	Boeing 737-MAX8	Westjet	
C-GYWJ	Boeing 737-7CT	Westjet	

Note: Airline fleet number when carried on aircraft is shown in parentheses.

CN (Morocco)

CN-NMF	Airbus A.320-214	Air Arabia Maroc	
CN-NMG	Airbus A.320-214	Air Arabia Maroc	
CN-NMH	Airbus A.320-214	Air Arabia Maroc	
CN-NMI	Airbus A.320-214	Air Arabia Maroc	
CN-NMJ	Airbus A.320-214	Air Arabia Maroc	
CN-NMK	Airbus A.320-214	Air Arabia Maroc	
CN-NML	Airbus A.320-214	Air Arabia Maroc	
CN-NMM	Airbus A.320-214	Air Arabia Maroc	
CN-RGE	Boeing 737-86N	Royal Air Maroc	
CN-RGF	Boeing 737-86N	Royal Air Maroc	

Notes	Reg	Type	Owner or Operator
	CN-RGG	Boeing 737-86N	Royal Air Maroc
	CN-RGH	Boeing 737-86N	Royal Air Maroc
	CN-RGI	Boeing 737-86N	Royal Air Maroc
	CN-RGJ	Boeing 737-8B6	Royal Air Maroc
	CN-RGK	Boeing 737-8B6	Royal Air Maroc
	CN-RGM	Boeing 737-8B6	Royal Air Maroc
	CN-RGN	Boeing 737-8B6	Royal Air Maroc
	CN-RGO	Embraer ERJ190-100AR	Royal Air Maroc
	CN-RGP	Embraer ERJ190-100AR	Royal Air Maroc
	CN-RGQ	Embraer ERJ190-100AR	Royal Air Maroc
	CN-RGR	Embraer ERJ190-100AR	Royal Air Maroc
	CN-RGV	Boeing 737-85P	Royal Air Maroc
	CN-RNJ	Boeing 737-8B6	Royal Air Maroc
	CN-RNK	Boeing 737-8B6	Royal Air Maroc
	CN-RNL	Boeing 737-7B6	Royal Air Maroc
	CN-RNM	Boeing 737-7B6	Royal Air Maroc
	CN-RNP	Boeing 737-8B6	Royal Air Maroc
	CN-RNQ	Boeing 737-7B6	Royal Air Maroc
	CN-RNR	Boeing 737-7B6	Royal Air Maroc
	CN-RNU	Boeing 737-8B6	Royal Air Maroc
	CN-RNV	Boeing 737-7B6	Royal Air Maroc
	CN-RNW	Boeing 737-8B6	Royal Air Maroc
	CN-RNZ	Boeing 737-8B6	Royal Air Maroc
	CN-ROA	Boeing 737-8B6	Royal Air Maroc
	CN-ROB	Boeing 737-8B6	Royal Air Maroc
	CN-ROC	Boeing 737-8B6	Royal Air Maroc
	CN-ROD	Boeing 737-7B6	Royal Air Maroc
	CN-ROE	Boeing 737-8B6	Royal Air Maroc
	CN-ROH	Boeing 737-8B6	Royal Air Maroc
	CN-ROJ	Boeing 737-8B6	Royal Air Maroc
	CN-ROK	Boeing 737-8B6	Royal Air Maroc
	CN-ROL	Boeing 737-8B6	Royal Air Maroc
	CN-ROP	Boeing 737-8B6	Royal Air Maroc
	CN-ROR	Boeing 737-8B6	Royal Air Maroc
	CN-ROS	Boeing 737-8B6	Royal Air Maroc
	CN-ROT	Boeing 737-8B6	Royal Air Maroc
	CN-ROU	Boeing 737-8B6	Royal Air Maroc
	CN-ROY	Boeing 737-8B6	Royal Air Maroc
	CN-ROZ	Boeing 737-8B6	Royal Air Maroc

CS (Portugal)

Notes	Reg	Type	Owner or Operator
	CS-FAF	Boeing 737-8FB	White Airways
	CS-TFM	Boeing 777-212ER	Euro Atlantic Airways
	CS-TFU	Airbus A.319-115	White Airways/PrivatAir
	CS-TFX	Airbus A.340-542	Hi Fly
	CS-TFZ	Airbus A.330-243	Hi Fly
	CS-TJE	Airbus A.321-211	TAP Air Portugal *Pero Vaz de Caminha*
	CS-TJF	Airbus A.321-211	TAP Air Portugal *Luis Vaz de Cameos*
	CS-TJG	Airbus A.321-211	TAP Air Portugal *Amelia Rodrigues*
	CS-TJH	Airbus A.321-211	TAP Air Portugal *Manuel de Oliveira*
	CS-TKK	Airbus A.320-214	Azores Airlines
	CS-TKP	Airbus A.320-214	Azores Airlines
	CS-TKQ	Airbus A.320-214	Azores Airlines
	CS-TKR	Boeing 767-36NER	Euro Atlantic Airways
	CS-TKS	Boeing 767-36NER	Euro Atlantic Airways
	CS-TKT	Boeing 767-36NER	Euro Atlantic Airways
	CS-TKW	Airbus A.330-322	Hi Fly
	CS-TMW	Airbus A.320-214	TAP Air Portugal *Luisa Todi*
	CS-TNG	Airbus A.320-214	TAP Air Portugal *Mouzinho da Silveira*
	CS-TNH	Airbus A.320-214	TAP Air Portugal *Almada Negreiros*
	CS-TNI	Airbus A.320-214	TAP Air Portugal *Aquilino Ribiera*
	CS-TNJ	Airbus A.320-214	TAP Air Portugal *Florbela Espanca*
	CS-TNK	Airbus A.320-214	TAP Air Portugal *Teofilo Braga*
	CS-TNL	Airbus A.320-214	TAP Air Portugal *Vitorino Nermesio*
	CS-TNM	Airbus A.320-214	TAP Air Portugal *Natalia Correia*
	CS-TNN	Airbus A.320-214	TAP Air Portugal *Gil Vicente*
	CS-TNP	Airbus A.320-214	TAP Air Portugal *Alexandre O'Neill*
	CS-TNQ	Airbus A.320-214	TAP Air Portugal *Jose Regio*
	CS-TNR	Airbus A.320-214	TAP Air Portugal *Luis de Freitas Branco*
	CS-TNS	Airbus A.320-214	TAP Air Portugal *D.Alfonso Henriques*

Reg	Type	Owner or Operator	Notes
CS-TNT	Airbus A.320-214	TAP Air Portugal *Rafael Bordaio Pinheiro*	
CS-TNU	Airbus A.320-214	TAP Air Portugal *Columbano Bordalo Pinheiro*	
CS-TNV	Airbus A.320-214	TAP Air Portugal *Grao Vasco*	
CS-TNW	Airbus A.320-214	TAP Air Portugal *Jose Saramago*	
CS-TNX	Airbus A.320-214	TAP Air Portugal *Malangatana*	
CS-TNY	Airbus A.320-214	TAP Air Portugal *Dominigos Sequeira*	
CS-TOA	Airbus A.340-312	TAP Air Portugal *Fernao Mendes Pinto*	
CS-TOB	Airbus A.340-312	TAP Air Portugal *D Joao de Castro*	
CS-TOC	Airbus A.340-312	TAP Air Portugal *Wenceslau de Moraes*	
CS-TOD	Airbus A.340-312	TAP Air Portugal *D Francisco de Almeida*	
CS-TOE	Airbus A.330-223	TAP Air Portugal *Pedro Alvares Cabal*	
CS-TOF	Airbus A.330-223	TAP Air Portugal *Infante D Henrique*	
CS-TOG	Airbus A.330-223	TAP Air Portugal *Bartolomeu de Gusmão*	
CS-TOH	Airbus A.330-223	TAP Air Portugal *Nuno Gongalves*	
CS-TOI	Airbus A.330-223	TAP Air Portugal *Damiao de Gois*	
CS-TOJ	Airbus A.330-223	TAP Air Portugal *D. Joao II O. Principe Perfeito*	
CS-TOK	Airbus A.330-223	TAP Air Portugal *Padre Antonio Vieira*	
CS-TOL	Airbus A.330-202	TAP Air Portugal *Joao Goncalves Zarco*	
CS-TOM	Airbus A.330-202	TAP Air Portugal *Vasco da Gama*	
CS-TON	Airbus A.330-202	TAP Air Portugal *Ja-o XXI*	
CS-TOO	Airbus A.330-202	TAP Air Portugal *Fernao de Magalhaes*	
CS-TOP	Airbus A.330-202	TAP Air Portugal *Pedro Nunes*	
CS-TOQ	Airbus A.330-203	TAP Air Portugal *Pedro Teixeira*	
CS-TOR	Airbus A.330-203	TAP Air Portugal *Bartolomeu Dias*	
CS-TOU	Airbus A.330-343E	TAP Air Portugal *John dos Passos*	
CS-TOV	Airbus A.330-343E	TAP Air Portugal *Portugal*	
CS-TOW	Airbus A.330-343E	TAP Air Portugal *Joao Vaz Corte-real*	
CS-TOX	Airbus A.330-343E	TAP Air Portugal *D. Maria Ii*	
CS-TPO	Embraer ERJ190-100LR	TAP Express	
CS-TPP	Embraer ERJ190-100LR	TAP Express	
CS-TPQ	Embraer ERJ190-100LR	TAP Express	
CS-TPR	Embraer ERJ190-100LR	TAP Express	
CS-TPS	Embraer ERJ190-100LR	TAP Express	
CS-TPT	Embraer ERJ190-100LR	TAP Express	
CS-TPU	Embraer ERJ190-100LR	TAP Express	
CS-TPV	Embraer ERJ190-100LR	TAP Express	
CS-TPW	Embraer ERJ190-100LR	TAP Express	
CS-TQD	Airbus A.320-214	TAP Air Portugal *Eugenio de Andrade*	
CS-TQP	Airbus A.330-202	Hi Fly	
CS-TQU	Boeing 737-8K2	Euro Atlantic Airways/Med-View Airline	
CS-TQW	Airbus A.330-223	Hi Fly	
CS-TQY	Airbus A.340-313X	Hi Fly	
CS-TQZ	Airbus A.340-313	Hi Fly	
CS-TRO	Airbus A.320-214	White Airways	
CS-TSF	Airbus A.321-253N	Azores Airlines	
CS-TSG	Airbus A.321-253N	Azores Airlines	
CS-TTA	Airbus A.319-111	TAP Air Portugal *Vieira da Silva*	
CS-TTB	Airbus A.319-111	TAP Air Portugal *Gago Coutinho*	
CS-TTC	Airbus A.319-111	TAP Air Portugal *Fernando Pessoa*	
CS-TTD	Airbus A.319-111	TAP Air Portugal *Amadeo de Souza-Cardoso*	
CS-TTE	Airbus A.319-111	TAP Air Portugal *Francisco d'Ollanda*	
CS-TTF	Airbus A.319-111	TAP Air Portugal *Calouste Gulbenkian*	
CS-TTG	Airbus A.319-111	TAP Air Portugal *Humberto Delgado*	
CS-TTH	Airbus A.319-111	TAP Air Portugal *Antonio Sergio*	
CS-TTI	Airbus A.319-111	TAP Air Portugal *Eca de Queiros*	
CS-TTJ	Airbus A.319-111	TAP Air Portugal *Eusebio*	
CS-TTK	Airbus A.319-111	TAP Air Portugal *Miguel Torga*	
CS-TTL	Airbus A.319-111	TAP Air Portugal *Almeida Garrett*	
CS-TTM	Airbus A.319-111	TAP Air Portugal *Alexandre Herculano*	
CS-TTN	Airbus A.319-111	TAP Air Portugal *Camilo Castelo Branco*	
CS-TTO	Airbus A.319-111	TAP Air Portugal *Antero de Quental*	
CS-TTP	Airbus A.319-111	TAP Air Portugal *Josefa d'Obidos*	
CS-TTQ	Airbus A.319-112	TAP Air Portugal *Agostinho da Silva*	
CS-TTR	Airbus A.319-112	TAP Air Portugal *Soares dos Reis*	
CS-TTS	Airbus A.319-112	TAP Air Portugal *Guilhermina Suggia*	
CS-TTU	Airbus A.319-112	TAP Air Portugal *Sophia de Mello Breyner*	
CS-TTV	Airbus A.319-112	TAP Air Portugal *Aristides de Sousa Mendes*	
CS-TTW	Embraer ERJ190-200IGW	TAP Express	
CS-TTX	Embraer ERJ190-200IGW	TAP Express	
CS-TTY	Embraer ERJ190-200IGW	TAP Express	
CS-TTZ	Embraer ERJ190-200IGW	TAP Express	

Notes	Reg	Type	Owner or Operator
	CS-TUA	Airbus A.330-941	TAP Air Portugal
	CS-TUB	Airbus A.330-941	TAP Air Portugal
	CS-TUC	Airbus A.330-941	TAP Air Portugal

D (Germany)

Notes	Reg	Type	Owner or Operator
	D-AALA	Boeing 777-FZN	AeroLogic
	D-AALB	Boeing 777-FZN	AeroLogic
	D-AALC	Boeing 777-FZN	AeroLogic
	D-AALD	Boeing 777-FZN	AeroLogic
	D-AALE	Boeing 777-FZN	AeroLogic
	D-AALF	Boeing 777-FZN	AeroLogic
	D-AALG	Boeing 777-FZN	AeroLogic
	D-AALH	Boeing 777-FZN	AeroLogic
	D-AALI	Boeing 777-FZN	AeroLogic
	D-AALJ	Boeing 777-FZN	AeroLogic
	D-ABAF	Boeing 737-86J	TUIfly
	D-ABAG	Boeing 737-86J	TUIfly
	D-ABBD	Boeing 737-86J	Eurowings
	D-ABFO	Airbus A.320-214	Eurowings
	D-ABGH	Airbus A.319-112	Eurowings
	D-ABGJ	Airbus A.319-112	Eurowings
	D-ABGN	Airbus A.319-112	Eurowings
	D-ABGQ	Airbus A.319-112	Eurowings
	D-ABHA	Airbus A.320-214	Eurowings
	D-ABHC	Airbus A.320-214	Eurowings
	D-ABHF	Airbus A.320-214	Eurowings
	D-ABHG	Airbus A.320-214	Eurowings
	D-ABHN	Airbus A.320-214	Eurowings
	D-ABKA	Boeing 737-82R	TUIfly
	D-ABKI	Boeing 737-86J	TUIfly
	D-ABKJ	Boeing 737-86J	TUIfly
	D-ABKM	Boeing 737-86J	Eurowings
	D-ABKN	Boeing 737-86J	Eurowings
	D-ABLA	Boeing 737-76J	Germania
	D-ABLB	Boeing 737-76J	Germania
	D-ABMQ	Boeing 737-86J	Eurowings
	D-ABMV	Boeing 737-86J	TUIfly
	D-ABNI	Airbus A.320-214	Eurowings
	D-ABNN	Airbus A.320-214	Eurowings
	D-ABNT	Airbus A.320-214	Eurowings
	D-ABNU	Airbus A.320-214	Eurowings
	D-ABOA	Boeing 757-330	Condor
	D-ABOB	Boeing 757-330	Condor
	D-ABOC	Boeing 757-330	Condor
	D-ABOE	Boeing 757-330	Condor
	D-ABOF	Boeing 757-330	Condor
	D-ABOH	Boeing 757-330	Condor
	D-ABOI	Boeing 757-330	Condor
	D-ABOJ	Boeing 757-330	Condor
	D-ABOK	Boeing 757-330	Condor
	D-ABOL	Boeing 757-330	Condor
	D-ABOM	Boeing 757-330	Condor
	D-ABON	Boeing 757-330	Condor
	D-ABQA	DHC.8Q-402 Dash Eight	Eurowings
	D-ABQB	DHC.8Q-402 Dash Eight	Eurowings
	D-ABQC	DHC.8Q-402 Dash Eight	Eurowings
	D-ABQD	DHC.8Q-402 Dash Eight	Eurowings
	D-ABQE	DHC.8Q-402 Dash Eight	Eurowings
	D-ABQF	DHC.8Q-402 Dash Eight	Eurowings
	D-ABQG	DHC.8Q-402 Dash Eight	Eurowings
	D-ABQH	DHC.8Q-402 Dash Eight	Eurowings
	D-ABQI	DHC.8Q-402 Dash Eight	Eurowings
	D-ABQJ	DHC.8Q-402 Dash Eight	Eurowings
	D-ABQK	DHC.8Q-402 Dash Eight	Eurowings
	D-ABQL	DHC.8Q-402 Dash Eight	Eurowings
	D-ABQM	DHC.8Q-402 Dash Eight	Eurowings
	D-ABQN	DHC.8Q-402 Dash Eight	Eurowings
	D-ABQO	DHC.8Q-402 Dash Eight	Eurowings
	D-ABQP	DHC.8Q-402 Dash Eight	Eurowings
	D-ABQQ	DHC.8Q-402 Dash Eight	Eurowings

Reg	Type	Owner or Operator	Notes
D-ABQR	DHC.8Q-402 Dash Eight	Eurowings	
D-ABQS	DHC.8Q-402 Dash Eight	Eurowings	
D-ABQT	DHC.8Q-402 Dash Eight	Eurowings	
D-ABTK	Boeing 747-430 (SCD)	Lufthansa Kiel	
D-ABTL	Boeing 747-430 (SCD)	Lufthansa	
D-ABUA	Boeing 767-330ER	Condor	
D-ABUB	Boeing 767-330ER	Condor	
D-ABUC	Boeing 767-330ER	Condor	
D-ABUD	Boeing 767-330ER	Condor	
D-ABUE	Boeing 767-330ER	Condor	
D-ABUF	Boeing 767-330ER	Condor	
D-ABUH	Boeing 767-330ER	Condor	
D-ABUI	Boeing 767-330ER	Condor	
D-ABUK	Boeing 767-343ER	Condor	
D-ABUL	Boeing 767-31BER	Condor	
D-ABUM	Boeing 767-31BER	Condor	
D-ABUO	Boeing 767-3Q8ER	Condor	
D-ABUP	Boeing 767-3Q8ER	Condor	
D-ABUS	Boeing 767-38EER	Condor	
D-ABUT	Boeing 767-3Q8ER	Condor	
D-ABUX	Boeing 767-31KER	Condor	
D-ABUY	Boeing 767-31KER	Condor	
D-ABUZ	Boeing 767-330ER	Condor	
D-ABVO	Boeing 747-430	Lufthansa Mulheim a.d.Ruhr	
D-ABVP	Boeing 747-430	Lufthansa Bremen	
D-ABVR	Boeing 747-430	Lufthansa Koln	
D-ABVS	Boeing 747-430	Lufthansa Saarland	
D-ABVT	Boeing 747-430	Lufthansa Rheinland Pfalz	
D-ABVU	Boeing 747-430	Lufthansa Bayern	
D-ABVW	Boeing 747-430	Lufthansa Wolfsburg	
D-ABVX	Boeing 747-430	Lufthansa Schleswig-Holstein	
D-ABVY	Boeing 747-430	Lufthansa Nordrhein Westfalen	
D-ABVZ	Boeing 747-430	Lufthansa	
D-ABYA	Boeing 747-830	Lufthansa Brandenberg	
D-ABYC	Boeing 747-830	Lufthansa Sachsen	
D-ABYD	Boeing 747-830	Lufthansa Mecklenburg-Vorpommern	
D-ABYF	Boeing 747-830	Lufthansa Sachsen-Anhalt	
D-ABYG	Boeing 747-830	Lufthansa Baden-Wurttemberg	
D-ABYH	Boeing 747-830	Lufthansa Thuringen	
D-ABYI	Boeing 747-830	Lufthansa Potsdam	
D-ABYJ	Boeing 747-830	Lufthansa Hannover	
D-ABYK	Boeing 747-830	Lufthansa Rheinland-Pfalz	
D-ABYL	Boeing 747-830	Lufthansa Hessen	
D-ABYM	Boeing 747-830	Lufthansa Bayern	
D-ABYN	Boeing 747-830	Lufthansa Niedersachsen	
D-ABYO	Boeing 747-830	Lufthansa Saarland	
D-ABYP	Boeing 747-830	Lufthansa Nordrhein-Westfalen	
D-ABYQ	Boeing 747-830	Lufthansa Schleswig-Holstein	
D-ABYR	Boeing 747-830	Lufthansa Bremen	
D-ABYS	Boeing 747-830	Lufthansa Dresden	
D-ABYT	Boeing 747-830	Lufthansa Koln	
D-ABYU	Boeing 747-830	Lufthansa	
D-ABZE	Airbus A.320-216	Eurowings	
D-ABZK	Airbus A.320-216	Eurowings	
D-ABZL	Airbus A.320-216	Eurowings	
D-ABZN	Airbus A.320-216	Eurowings	
D-ACKA	Canadair CRJ900ER	Lufthansa Regional Pfaffenhofen a.d.ilm	
D-ACKB	Canadair CRJ900ER	Lufthansa Regional Schliersee	
D-ACKC	Canadair CRJ900ER	Lufthansa Regional Mettmann	
D-ACKD	Canadair CRJ900ER	Lufthansa Regional Wittlich	
D-ACKE	Canadair CRJ900ER	Lufthansa Regional Weningerode	
D-ACKF	Canadair CRJ900ER	Lufthansa Regional Prenzlau	
D-ACKG	Canadair CRJ900ER	Lufthansa Regional Glucksburg	
D-ACKH	Canadair CRJ900ER	Lufthansa Regional Radebuel	
D-ACKI	Canadair CRJ900ER	Lufthansa Regional Tuttlingen	
D-ACKJ	Canadair CRJ900ER	Lufthansa Regional Ilmenau	
D-ACKK	Canadair CRJ900ER	Lufthansa Regional Furstenwalde	
D-ACKL	Canadair CRJ900ER	Lufthansa Regional Bad Bergzabern	
D-ACNA	Canadair CRJ900ER	Lufthansa Regional	
D-ACNB	Canadair CRJ900ER	Lufthansa Regional	
D-ACNC	Canadair CRJ900ER	Lufthansa Regional	

Notes	Reg	Type	Owner or Operator
	D-ACND	Canadair CRJ900ER	Lufthansa Regional
	D-ACNE	Canadair CRJ900ER	Lufthansa Regional
	D-ACNF	Canadair CRJ900ER	Lufthansa Regional
	D-ACNG	Canadair CRJ900ER	Lufthansa Regional
	D-ACNH	Canadair CRJ900ER	Lufthansa Regional
	D-ACNI	Canadair CRJ900ER	Lufthansa Regional
	D-ACNJ	Canadair CRJ900ER	Lufthansa Regional
	D-ACNK	Canadair CRJ900ER	Lufthansa Regional
	D-ACNL	Canadair CRJ900ER	Lufthansa Regional
	D-ACNM	Canadair CRJ900ER	Lufthansa Regional
	D-ACNN	Canadair CRJ900ER	Lufthansa Regional
	D-ACNO	Canadair CRJ900ER	Lufthansa Regional
	D-ACNP	Canadair CRJ900ER	Lufthansa Regional
	D-ACNQ	Canadair CRJ900ER	Lufthansa Regional
	D-ACNR	Canadair CRJ900ER	Lufthansa Regional
	D-ACNT	Canadair CRJ900ER	Lufthansa Regional
	D-ACNU	Canadair CRJ900ER	Lufthansa Regional
	D-ACNV	Canadair CRJ900ER	Lufthansa Regional
	D-ACNW	Canadair CRJ900ER	Lufthansa Regional
	D-ACNX	Canadair CRJ900ER	Lufthansa Regional
	D-AEAA	Airbus A.300B4-622R	EAT Leipzig/DHL
	D-AEAB	Airbus A.300B4-622R	EAT Leipzig/DHL
	D-AEAC	Airbus A.300B4-622R	EAT Leipzig/DHL
	D-AEAD	Airbus A.300B4-622R	EAT Leipzig/DHL
	D-AEAE	Airbus A.300B4-622R	EAT Leipzig/DHL
	D-AEAF	Airbus A.300B4-622R	EAT Leipzig/DHL
	D-AEAG	Airbus A.300B4-622R	EAT Leipzig/DHL
	D-AEAH	Airbus A.300B4-622R	EAT Leipzig/DHL
	D-AEAI	Airbus A.300B4-622R	EAT Leipzig/DHL
	D-AEAJ	Airbus A.300B4-622R	EAT Leipzig/DHL
	D-AEAK	Airbus A.300B4-622R	EAT Leipzig/DHL
	D-AEAL	Airbus A.300B4-622R	EAT Leipzig/DHL
	D-AEAM	Airbus A.300B4-622R	EAT Leipzig/DHL
	D-AEAN	Airbus A.300B4-622R	EAT Leipzig/DHL
	D-AEAO	Airbus A.300B4-622R	EAT Leipzig/DHL
	D-AEAP	Airbus A.300B4-622R	EAT Leipzig/DHL
	D-AEAQ	Airbus A.300B4-622R	EAT Leipzig/DHL
	D-AEAR	Airbus A.300B4-622R	EAT Leipzig/DHL
	D-AEAS	Airbus A.300B4-622R	EAT Leipzig/DHL
	D-AEAT	Airbus A.300B4-622R	EAT Leipzig/DHL
	D-AEBB	Embraer ERJ190-200LR	Lufthansa Regional
	D-AEBC	Embraer ERJ190-200LR	Lufthansa Regional
	D-AECA	Embraer ERJ190-100LR	Lufthansa Regional *Deidesheim*
	D-AECB	Embraer ERJ190-100LR	Lufthansa Regional *Meiben*
	D-AECC	Embraer ERJ190-100LR	Lufthansa Regional *Eisleben*
	D-AECD	Embraer ERJ190-100LR	Lufthansa Regional *Schkeuditz*
	D-AECE	Embraer ERJ190-100LR	Lufthansa Regional *Kronach*
	D-AECF	Embraer ERJ190-100LR	Lufthansa Regional
	D-AECG	Embraer ERJ190-100LR	Lufthansa Regional
	D-AECH	Embraer ERJ190-100LR	Lufthansa Regional
	D-AECI	Embraer ERJ190-100LR	Lufthansa Regional
	D-AEJS	BAe146-300	WDL Aviation
	D-AEMB	Embraer ERJ190-200LR	Lufthansa Regional
	D-AEMD	Embraer ERJ190-200LR	Lufthansa Regional
	D-AEME	Embraer ERJ190-200LR	Lufthansa Regional
	D-AEWF	Airbus A.320-214	Eurowings
	D-AEWG	Airbus A.320-214	Eurowings
	D-AEWI	Airbus A.320-214	Eurowings
	D-AEWJ	Airbus A.320-214	Eurowings
	D-AEWK	Airbus A.320-214	Eurowings
	D-AEWL	Airbus A.320-214	Eurowings
	D-AEWM	Airbus A.320-214	Eurowings
	D-AEWN	Airbus A.320-214	Eurowings
	D-AEWO	Airbus A.320-214	Eurowings
	D-AEWP	Airbus A.320-214	Eurowings
	D-AEWQ	Airbus A.320-214	Eurowings
	D-AEWR	Airbus A.320-214	Eurowings
	D-AEWS	Airbus A.320-214	Eurowings
	D-AEWT	Airbus A.320-214	Eurowings
	D-AEWU	Airbus A.320-214	Eurowings
	D-AEWV	Airbus A.320-214	Eurowings

Reg	Type	Owner or Operator	Notes
D-AEWW	Airbus A.320-214	Eurowings	
D-AGEL	Boeing 737-75B	Germania	
D-AGEN	Boeing 737-75B	Germania	
D-AGEP	Boeing 737-75B	Germania	
D-AGEQ	Boeing 737-75B	Germania	
D-AGER	Boeing 737-75B	Germania	
D-AGES	Boeing 737-75B	Germania	
D-AGET	Boeing 737-75B	Germania	
D-AGEU	Boeing 737-75B	Germania	
D-AGWA	Airbus A.319-132	Eurowings	
D-AGWB	Airbus A.319-132	Eurowings	
D-AGWC	Airbus A.319-132	Eurowings	
D-AGWD	Airbus A.319-132	Eurowings	
D-AGWE	Airbus A.319-132	Eurowings	
D-AGWF	Airbus A.319-132	Eurowings	
D-AGWG	Airbus A.319-132	Eurowings	
D-AGWH	Airbus A.319-132	Eurowings	
D-AGWI	Airbus A.319-132	Eurowings	
D-AGWK	Airbus A.319-132	Eurowings	
D-AGWL	Airbus A.319-132	Eurowings	
D-AGWM	Airbus A.319-132	Eurowings	
D-AGWN	Airbus A.319-132	Eurowings	
D-AGWO	Airbus A.319-132	Eurowings	
D-AGWS	Airbus A.319-132	Eurowings	
D-AGWT	Airbus A.319-132	Eurowings	
D-AGWU	Airbus A.319-132	Eurowings	
D-AGWV	Airbus A.319-132	Eurowings	
D-AGWW	Airbus A.319-132	Eurowings	
D-AGWX	Airbus A.319-132	Eurowings	
D-AGWY	Airbus A.319-132	Eurowings	
D-AGWZ	Airbus A.319-132	Eurowings	
D-AHFT	Boeing 737-8K5	TUIfly	
D-AHLK	Boeing 737-8K5	TUIfly	
D-AHXE	Boeing 737-7K5	TUIfly	
D-AHXF	Boeing 737-7K5	TUIfly	
D-AHXG	Boeing 737-7K5	TUIfly	
D-AHXJ	Boeing 737-7K5	TUIfly	
D-AIAA	Airbus A.321-211	Condor	
D-AIAC	Airbus A.321-211	Condor	
D-AIAD	Airbus A.321-211	Condor	
D-AIAE	Airbus A.321-211	Condor	
D-AIAF	Airbus A.321-211	Condor	
D-AIAG	Airbus A.321-211	Condor	
D-AIAH	Airbus A.321-211	Condor	
D-AIBA	Airbus A.319-114	Lufthansa	
D-AIBB	Airbus A.319-114	Lufthansa	
D-AIBC	Airbus A.319-114	Lufthansa	
D-AIBD	Airbus A.319-114	Lufthansa	
D-AIBE	Airbus A.319-114	Lufthansa	
D-AIBF	Airbus A.319-112	Lufthansa	
D-AIBG	Airbus A.319-112	Lufthansa	
D-AIBH	Airbus A.319-112	Lufthansa	
D-AIBI	Airbus A.319-112	Lufthansa	
D-AIBJ	Airbus A.319-112	Lufthansa	
D-AICA	Airbus A.320-212	Condor	
D-AICC	Airbus A.320-212	Condor	
D-AICD	Airbus A.320-212	Condor	
D-AICE	Airbus A.320-212	Condor	
D-AICF	Airbus A.320-212	Condor	
D-AICG	Airbus A.320-212	Condor	
D-AICH	Airbus A.320-212	Condor	
D-AICK	Airbus A.320-212	Condor	
D-AICL	Airbus A.320-212	Condor	
D-AIDA	Airbus A.321-231	Lufthansa	
D-AIDB	Airbus A.321-231	Lufthansa	
D-AIDC	Airbus A.321-231	Lufthansa	
D-AIDD	Airbus A.321-231	Lufthansa	
D-AIDE	Airbus A.321-231	Lufthansa	
D-AIDF	Airbus A.321-231	Lufthansa	
D-AIDG	Airbus A.321-231	Lufthansa	
D-AIDH	Airbus A.321-231	Lufthansa	

Notes	Reg	Type	Owner or Operator
	D-AIDI	Airbus A.321-231	Lufthansa
	D-AIDJ	Airbus A.321-231	Lufthansa
	D-AIDK	Airbus A.321-231	Lufthansa
	D-AIDL	Airbus A.321-231	Lufthansa
	D-AIDM	Airbus A.321-231	Lufthansa
	D-AIDN	Airbus A.321-231	Lufthansa
	D-AIDO	Airbus A.321-231	Lufthansa
	D-AIDP	Airbus A.321-231	Lufthansa
	D-AIDQ	Airbus A.321-231	Lufthansa
	D-AIDT	Airbus A.321-231	Lufthansa
	D-AIDU	Airbus A.321-231	Lufthansa
	D-AIDV	Airbus A.321-231	Lufthansa
	D-AIDW	Airbus A.321-231	Lufthansa
	D-AIDX	Airbus A.321-231	Lufthansa
	D-AIFA	Airbus A.340-313X	Lufthansa *Dorsten*
	D-AIFC	Airbus A.340-313X	Lufthansa *Gander/Halifax*
	D-AIFD	Airbus A.340-313X	Lufthansa *Giessen*
	D-AIFE	Airbus A.340-313X	Lufthansa *Passau*
	D-AIFF	Airbus A.340-313X	Lufthansa *Delmenhorst*
	D-AIGL	Airbus A.340-313X	Lufthansa *Herne*
	D-AIGM	Airbus A.340-313X	Lufthansa *Görlitz*
	D-AIGN	Airbus A.340-313X	Lufthansa *Solingen*
	D-AIGO	Airbus A.340-313X	Lufthansa *Offenbach*
	D-AIGP	Airbus A.340-313X	Lufthansa *Paderborn*
	D-AIGS	Airbus A.340-313X	Lufthansa *Bergisch-Gladbach*
	D-AIGT	Airbus A.340-313X	Lufthansa *Viersen*
	D-AIGU	Airbus A.340-313X	Lufthansa *Castrop-Rauxei*
	D-AIGV	Airbus A.340-313X	Lufthansa *Dinslaken*
	D-AIGW	Airbus A.340-313X	Lufthansa *Gladbeck*
	D-AIGX	Airbus A.340-313X	Lufthansa *Duren*
	D-AIGZ	Airbus A.340-313X	Lufthansa *Villingen-Schwenningen*
	D-AIHA	Airbus A.340-642	Lufthansa *Nurnberg*
	D-AIHB	Airbus A.340-642	Lufthansa *Bremerhaven*
	D-AIHC	Airbus A.340-642	Lufthansa *Essen*
	D-AIHE	Airbus A.340-642	Lufthansa *Leverkusen*
	D-AIHF	Airbus A.340-642	Lufthansa *Lübeck*
	D-AIHI	Airbus A.340-642	Lufthansa *Monchengladbach*
	D-AIHK	Airbus A.340-642	Lufthansa *Mainz*
	D-AIHL	Airbus A.340-642	Lufthansa *Saarbrucken*
	D-AIHT	Airbus A.340-642	Lufthansa
	D-AIHV	Airbus A.340-642	Lufthansa
	D-AIHW	Airbus A.340-642	Lufthansa
	D-AIHX	Airbus A.340-642	Lufthansa
	D-AIHY	Airbus A.340-642	Lufthansa
	D-AIHZ	Airbus A.340-642	Lufthansa *Leipzig*
	D-AIKA	Airbus A.330-343X	Lufthansa *Minden*
	D-AIKB	Airbus A.330-343X	Lufthansa *Cuxhaven*
	D-AIKC	Airbus A.330-343X	Lufthansa *Hamm*
	D-AIKD	Airbus A.330-343X	Lufthansa *Siegen*
	D-AIKE	Airbus A.330-343X	Lufthansa *Landshut*
	D-AIKF	Airbus A.330-343X	Lufthansa *Witten*
	D-AIKG	Airbus A.330-343X	Lufthansa *Ludwigsburg*
	D-AIKH	Airbus A.330-343X	Lufthansa
	D-AIKI	Airbus A.330-343X	Lufthansa
	D-AIKJ	Airbus A.330-343X	Lufthansa *Bottrop*
	D-AIKK	Airbus A.330-343X	Lufthansa *Furth*
	D-AIKL	Airbus A.330-343X	Lufthansa *Ingolstadt*
	D-AIKM	Airbus A.330-343X	Lufthansa
	D-AIKN	Airbus A.330-343X	Lufthansa
	D-AIKO	Airbus A.330-343X	Lufthansa
	D-AIKP	Airbus A.330-343X	Lufthansa
	D-AIKQ	Airbus A.330-343X	Lufthansa
	D-AIKR	Airbus A.330-343X	Lufthansa
	D-AIKS	Airbus A.330-343X	Lufthansa
	D-AILA	Airbus A.319-114	Lufthansa *Frankfurt (Oder)*
	D-AILB	Airbus A.319-114	Lufthansa *Lutherstadt Wittenburg*
	D-AILC	Airbus A.319-114	Lufthansa *Russelsheim*
	D-AILD	Airbus A.319-114	Lufthansa *Dinkelsbühl*
	D-AILE	Airbus A.319-114	Lufthansa *Kelsterbach*
	D-AILF	Airbus A.319-114	Lufthansa Italia
	D-AILH	Airbus A.319-114	Lufthansa Italia *Norderstedt*

Reg	Type	Owner or Operator	Notes
D-AILI	Airbus A.319-114	Lufthansa Italia *Roma*	
D-AILK	Airbus A.319-114	Lufthansa *Landshut*	
D-AILL	Airbus A.319-114	Lufthansa *Marburg*	
D-AILM	Airbus A.319-114	Lufthansa *Friedrichshafen*	
D-AILN	Airbus A.319-114	Lufthansa *Idar-Oberstein*	
D-AILP	Airbus A.319-114	Lufthansa *Tubingen*	
D-AILR	Airbus A.319-114	Lufthansa *Tegernsee*	
D-AILS	Airbus A.319-114	Lufthansa *Heide*	
D-AILT	Airbus A.319-114	Lufthansa *Straubing*	
D-AILU	Airbus A.319-114	Lufthansa *Verden*	
D-AILW	Airbus A.319-114	Lufthansa *Donaueschingen*	
D-AILX	Airbus A.319-114	Lufthansa *Feilbach*	
D-AILY	Airbus A.319-114	Lufthansa *Schweinfurt*	
D-AIMA	Airbus A.380-841	Lufthansa *Frankfurt am Main*	
D-AIMB	Airbus A.380-841	Lufthansa *Munchen*	
D-AIMC	Airbus A.380-841	Lufthansa *Peking*	
D-AIMD	Airbus A.380-841	Lufthansa *Tokio*	
D-AIME	Airbus A.380-841	Lufthansa *Johannesburg*	
D-AIMF	Airbus A.380-841	Lufthansa *Zurich*	
D-AIMG	Airbus A.380-841	Lufthansa *Wien*	
D-AIMH	Airbus A.380-841	Lufthansa *New York*	
D-AIMI	Airbus A.380-841	Lufthansa *Berlin*	
D-AIMJ	Airbus A.380-841	Lufthansa *Brussel*	
D-AIMK	Airbus A.380-841	Lufthansa *Dusseldorf*	
D-AIML	Airbus A.380-841	Lufthansa *Hamburg*	
D-AIMM	Airbus A.380-841	Lufthansa *Delhi*	
D-AIMN	Airbus A.380-841	Lufthansa *San Francisco*	
D-AINA	Airbus A.320-271N	Lufthansa	
D-AINB	Airbus A.320-271N	Lufthansa	
D-AINC	Airbus A.320-271N	Lufthansa	
D-AIND	Airbus A.320-271N	Lufthansa	
D-AINE	Airbus A.320-271N	Lufthansa	
D-AINF	Airbus A.320-271N	Lufthansa	
D-AING	Airbus A.320-271N	Lufthansa	
D-AINH	Airbus A.320-271N	Lufthansa	
D-AINI	Airbus A.320-271N	Lufthansa	
D-AINJ	Airbus A.320-271N	Lufthansa	
D-AINK	Airbus A.320-271N	Lufthansa	
D-AIPA	Airbus A.320-211	Lufthansa *Buxtehude*	
D-AIPB	Airbus A.320-211	Lufthansa *Heidelberg*	
D-AIPC	Airbus A.320-211	Lufthansa *Braunschweig*	
D-AIPD	Airbus A.320-211	Lufthansa *Freiburg*	
D-AIPE	Airbus A.320-211	Lufthansa *Kassel*	
D-AIPF	Airbus A.320-211	Lufthansa *Deggendorf*	
D-AIPH	Airbus A.320-211	Lufthansa *Munster*	
D-AIPK	Airbus A.320-211	Lufthansa *Wiesbaden*	
D-AIPL	Airbus A.320-211	Lufthansa	
D-AIPM	Airbus A.320-211	Lufthansa *Troisdorf*	
D-AIPP	Airbus A.320-211	Lufthansa *Starnberg*	
D-AIPR	Airbus A.320-211	Lufthansa *Kaufbeuren*	
D-AIPS	Airbus A.320-211	Lufthansa	
D-AIPT	Airbus A.320-211	Lufthansa	
D-AIPU	Airbus A.320-211	Eurowings	
D-AIPW	Airbus A.320-211	Eurowings	
D-AIPY	Airbus A.320-211	Lufthansa	
D-AIPZ	Airbus A.320-211	Lufthansa *Erfurt*	
D-AIQA	Airbus A.320-211	Lufthansa	
D-AIQB	Airbus A.320-211	Eurowings	
D-AIQC	Airbus A.320-211	Eurowings	
D-AIQD	Airbus A.320-211	Lufthansa	
D-AIQE	Airbus A.320-211	Eurowings	
D-AIQF	Airbus A.320-211	Lufthansa	
D-AIQK	Airbus A.320-211	Eurowings	
D-AIQL	Airbus A.320-211	Eurowings	
D-AIQN	Airbus A.320-211	Eurowings	
D-AIQT	Airbus A.320-211	Lufthansa *Gotha*	
D-AIQU	Airbus A.320-211	Lufthansa *Backnang*	
D-AIQW	Airbus A.320-211	Lufthansa *Kleve*	
D-AIRA	Airbus A.321-131	Lufthansa *Finkenwerder*	
D-AIRB	Airbus A.321-131	Lufthansa *Baden-Baden*	
D-AIRC	Airbus A.321-131	Lufthansa *Erlangen*	

OVERSEAS AIRLINERS

Notes	Reg	Type	Owner or Operator
	D-AIRD	Airbus A.321-131	Lufthansa *Coburg*
	D-AIRE	Airbus A.321-131	Lufthansa *Osnabrueck*
	D-AIRF	Airbus A.321-131	Lufthansa *Kempten*
	D-AIRH	Airbus A.321-131	Lufthansa *Garmisch-Partenkirchen*
	D-AIRK	Airbus A.321-131	Lufthansa *Freudenstadt/Schwarzwald*
	D-AIRL	Airbus A.321-131	Lufthansa *Kulmbach*
	D-AIRM	Airbus A.321-131	Lufthansa *Darmstadt*
	D-AIRN	Airbus A.321-131	Lufthansa *Kaiserslautern*
	D-AIRO	Airbus A.321-131	Lufthansa *Konstanz*
	D-AIRP	Airbus A.321-131	Lufthansa *Lüneburg*
	D-AIRR	Airbus A.321-131	Lufthansa *Wismar*
	D-AIRS	Airbus A.321-131	Lufthansa *Husum*
	D-AIRT	Airbus A.321-131	Lufthansa *Regensburg*
	D-AIRU	Airbus A.321-131	Lufthansa *Würzburg*
	D-AIRW	Airbus A.321-131	Lufthansa *Heilbronn*
	D-AIRX	Airbus A.321-131	Lufthansa *Weimar*
	D-AIRY	Airbus A.321-131	Lufthansa *Flensburg*
	D-AISB	Airbus A.321-231	Lufthansa *Hameln*
	D-AISC	Airbus A.321-231	Lufthansa *Speyer*
	D-AISD	Airbus A.321-231	Lufthansa *Chemnitz*
	D-AISF	Airbus A.321-231	Lufthansa *Lippstadt*
	D-AISG	Airbus A.321-231	Lufthansa *Dormagen*
	D-AISH	Airbus A.321-231	Lufthansa *Wetzlar*
	D-AISI	Airbus A.321-231	Lufthansa *Bergheim*
	D-AISJ	Airbus A.321-231	Lufthansa *Gutersloh*
	D-AISK	Airbus A.321-231	Lufthansa *Emden*
	D-AISL	Airbus A.321-231	Lufthansa *Arnsberg*
	D-AISN	Airbus A.321-231	Lufthansa *Goppingen*
	D-AISO	Airbus A.321-231	Lufthansa *Bocholt*
	D-AISP	Airbus A.321-231	Lufthansa *Rosenheim*
	D-AISQ	Airbus A.321-231	Lufthansa *Lindau*
	D-AISR	Airbus A.321-231	Lufthansa *Donauworth*
	D-AIST	Airbus A.321-231	Lufthansa *Erbach*
	D-AISU	Airbus A.321-231	Lufthansa *Nordlingen*
	D-AISV	Airbus A.321-231	Lufthansa *Bingen*
	D-AISW	Airbus A.321-231	Lufthansa *Stade*
	D-AISX	Airbus A.321-231	Lufthansa *Celle*
	D-AISZ	Airbus A.321-231	Lufthansa *Eberswalde*
	D-AIUA	Airbus A.320-214	Lufthansa
	D-AIUB	Airbus A.320-214	Lufthansa
	D-AIUC	Airbus A.320-214	Lufthansa
	D-AIUD	Airbus A.320-214	Lufthansa
	D-AIUE	Airbus A.320-214	Lufthansa
	D-AIUF	Airbus A.320-214	Lufthansa
	D-AIUG	Airbus A.320-214	Lufthansa
	D-AIUH	Airbus A.320-214	Lufthansa
	D-AIUI	Airbus A.320-214	Lufthansa
	D-AIUJ	Airbus A.320-214	Lufthansa
	D-AIUK	Airbus A.320-214	Lufthansa
	D-AIUL	Airbus A.320-214	Lufthansa
	D-AIUM	Airbus A.320-214	Lufthansa
	D-AIUN	Airbus A.320-214	Lufthansa
	D-AIUO	Airbus A.320-214	Lufthansa
	D-AIUP	Airbus A.320-214	Lufthansa
	D-AIUQ	Airbus A.320-214	Lufthansa
	D-AIUR	Airbus A.320-214	Lufthansa
	D-AIUS	Airbus A.320-214	Lufthansa
	D-AIUT	Airbus A.320-214	Lufthansa
	D-AIUU	Airbus A.320-214	Lufthansa
	D-AIUV	Airbus A.320-214	Lufthansa
	D-AIUW	Airbus A.320-214	Lufthansa
	D-AIUX	Airbus A.320-214	Lufthansa
	D-AIUY	Airbus A.320-214	Lufthansa
	D-AIUZ	Airbus A.320-214	Lufthansa
	D-AIWA	Airbus A.320-214	Lufthansa
	D-AIWB	Airbus A.320-214	Lufthansa
	D-AIXA	Airbus A.350-941	Lufthansa
	D-AIXB	Airbus A.350-941	Lufthansa
	D-AIXC	Airbus A.350-941	Lufthansa
	D-AIXD	Airbus A.350-941	Lufthansa
	D-AIXE	Airbus A.350-941	Lufthansa

Reg	Type	Owner or Operator	Notes
D-AIXF	Airbus A.350-941	Lufthansa	
D-AIXG	Airbus A.350-941	Lufthansa	
D-AIXH	Airbus A.350-941	Lufthansa	
D-AIXI	Airbus A.350-941	Lufthansa	
D-AIXJ	Airbus A.350-941	Lufthansa	
D-AIXK	Airbus A.350-941	Lufthansa	
D-AIZA	Airbus A.320-214	Lufthansa	
D-AIZB	Airbus A.320-214	Lufthansa	
D-AIZC	Airbus A.320-214	Lufthansa	
D-AIZD	Airbus A.320-214	Lufthansa	
D-AIZE	Airbus A.320-214	Lufthansa	
D-AIZF	Airbus A.320-214	Lufthansa	
D-AIZG	Airbus A.320-214	Lufthansa	
D-AIZH	Airbus A.320-214	Lufthansa	
D-AIZI	Airbus A.320-214	Lufthansa	
D-AIZJ	Airbus A.320-214	Lufthansa	
D-AIZM	Airbus A.320-214	Lufthansa	
D-AIZN	Airbus A.320-214	Lufthansa	
D-AIZO	Airbus A.320-214	Lufthansa	
D-AIZP	Airbus A.320-214	Lufthansa	
D-AIZQ	Airbus A.320-214	Eurowings	
D-AIZR	Airbus A.320-214	Eurowings	
D-AIZS	Airbus A.320-214	Eurowings	
D-AIZT	Airbus A.320-214	Eurowings	
D-AIZU	Airbus A.320-214	Eurowings	
D-AIZV	Airbus A.320-214	Eurowings	
D-AIZW	Airbus A.320-214	Lufthansa	
D-AIZX	Airbus A.320-214	Lufthansa	
D-AIZY	Airbus A.320-214	Lufthansa	
D-AIZZ	Airbus A.320-214	Lufthansa	
D-AKNF	Airbus A.319-112	Eurowings	
D-AKNG	Airbus A.319-112	Eurowings	
D-AKNH	Airbus A.319-112	Eurowings	
D-AKNI	Airbus A.319-112	Eurowings	
D-AKNJ	Airbus A.319-112	Eurowings	
D-AKNK	Airbus A.319-112	Eurowings	
D-AKNL	Airbus A.319-112	Eurowings	
D-AKNM	Airbus A.319-112	Eurowings	
D-AKNN	Airbus A.319-112	Eurowings	
D-AKNO	Airbus A.319-112	Eurowings	
D-AKNP	Airbus A.319-112	Eurowings	
D-AKNQ	Airbus A.319-112	Eurowings	
D-AKNR	Airbus A.319-112	Eurowings	
D-AKNS	Airbus A.319-112	Eurowings	
D-AKNT	Airbus A.319-112	Eurowings	
D-AKNU	Airbus A.319-112	Eurowings	
D-AKNV	Airbus A.319-112	Eurowings	
D-ALCA	McD Douglas MD-11F	Lufthansa Cargo	
D-ALCB	McD Douglas MD-11F	Lufthansa Cargo	
D-ALCC	McD Douglas MD-11F	Lufthansa Cargo	
D-ALCD	McD Douglas MD-11F	Lufthansa Cargo	
D-ALCE	McD Douglas MD-11F	Lufthansa Cargo	
D-ALCF	McD Douglas MD-11F	Lufthansa Cargo	
D-ALCH	McD Douglas MD-11F	Lufthansa Cargo	
D-ALCI	McD Douglas MD-11F	Lufthansa Cargo	
D-ALCJ	McD Douglas MD-11F	Lufthansa Cargo	
D-ALCK	McD Douglas MD-11F	Lufthansa Cargo	
D-ALCM	McD Douglas MD-11F	Lufthansa Cargo	
D-ALCN	McD Douglas MD-11F	Lufthansa Cargo	
D-ALEG	Boeing 757-236SF	EAT Leipzig/DHL	
D-ALEH	Boeing 757-236SF	EAT Leipzig/DHL	
D-ALEK	Boeing 757-236SF	EAT Leipzig/DHL	
D-ALEN	Boeing 757-2Q8F	EAT Leipzig/DHL	
D-ALEO	Boeing 757-2Q8F	EAT Leipzig/DHL	
D-ALEP	Boeing 757-2Q8F	EAT Leipzig/DHL	
D-ALEQ	Boeing 757-2Q8F	EAT Leipzig/DHL	
D-ALER	Boeing 757-2Q8F	EAT Leipzig/DHL	
D-ALES	Boeing 757-2Q8F	EAT Leipzig/DHL	
D-ALEV	Boeing 757-236SF	EAT Leipzig/DHL	
D-ALEW	Boeing 757-236SF	EAT Leipzig/DHL	
D-ALEZ	Boeing 757-236SF	EAT Leipzig/DHL	

Notes	Reg	Type	Owner or Operator
	D-ALFA	Boeing 777FBT	Lufthansa Cargo
	D-ALFB	Boeing 777FBT	Lufthansa Cargo
	D-ALFC	Boeing 777FBT	Lufthansa Cargo
	D-ALFD	Boeing 777FBT	Lufthansa Cargo
	D-ALFE	Boeing 777FBT	Lufthansa Cargo
	D-AMGL	BAe 146-200A	WDL Aviation
	D-ASTA	Airbus A.319-112	Germania
	D-ASTB	Airbus A.319-112	Germania
	D-ASTC	Airbus A.319-112	Germania
	D-ASTE	Airbus A.321-211	Germania
	D-ASTF	Airbus A.319-112	Germania
	D-ASTJ	Airbus A.319-111	Germania
	D-ASTK	Airbus A.319-112	Germania
	D-ASTL	Airbus A.319-112	Germania
	D-ASTP	Airbus A.321-211	Germania
	D-ASTQ	Airbus A.319-111	Germania
	D-ASTR	Airbus A.319-112	Germania
	D-ASTT	Airbus A.319-112	Germania
	D-ASTU	Airbus A.319-112	Germania
	D-ASTV	Airbus A.321-211	Germania
	D-ASTW	Airbus A.321-211	Germania
	D-ASTX	Airbus A.319-112	Eurowings
	D-ASTY	Airbus A.319-112	Germania
	D-ASTZ	Airbus A.319-112	Germania
	D-ASUN	Boeing 737-8BK	TUIfly
	D-ATCA	Airbus A.321-211	Condor
	D-ATCB	Airbus A.321-211	Condor
	D-ATCC	Airbus A.321-211	Condor
	D-ATCD	Airbus A.321-211	Condor
	D-ATCE	Airbus A.321-211	Condor
	D-ATUA	Boeing 737-8K5	TUIfly
	D-ATUB	Boeing 737-8K5	TUIfly
	D-ATUC	Boeing 737-8K5	TUIfly
	D-ATUD	Boeing 737-8K5	TUIfly
	D-ATUE	Boeing 737-8K5	TUIfly
	D-ATUF	Boeing 737-8K5	TUIfly
	D-ATUG	Boeing 737-8K5	TUIfly
	D-ATUH	Boeing 737-8K5	TUIfly
	D-ATUI	Boeing 737-8K5	TUIfly
	D-ATUJ	Boeing 737-8K5	TUIfly
	D-ATUK	Boeing 737-8K5	TUIfly
	D-ATUL	Boeing 737-8K5	TUIfly
	D-ATUM	Boeing 737-8K5	TUIfly
	D-ATUN	Boeing 737-8K5	TUIfly
	D-ATUO	Boeing 737-8K5	TUIfly
	D-ATUR	Boeing 737-8K5	TUIfly
	D-ATUZ	Boeing 737-8K5	TUIfly
	D-ATYA	Boeing 737-8K5	TUIfly
	D-ATYB	Boeing 737-8K5	TUIfly
	D-ATYC	Boeing 737-8K5	TUIfly
	D-AWBA	BAe 146-300	WDL Aviation
	D-AWUE	BAe 146-200	WDL Aviation
	D-AZMO	Airbus A.300F4-622R	EAT Leipzig/DHL
	D-CIRP	Dornier 328-120	Sun-Air/British Airways

EC (Spain)

	EC-HDS	Boeing 757-256	Privilege Style
	EC-HQI	Airbus A.320-214	Vueling Airlines *Merce Sune*
	EC-HQJ	Airbus A.320-214	Vueling Airlines
	EC-HQL	Airbus A.320-214	Vueling Airlines *Click on Vueling*
	EC-HTD	Airbus A.320-214	Vueling Airlines *Unos Vuelan,otros Vueling*
	EC-HUH	Airbus A.321-211	Iberia *Benidorm*
	EC-HUI	Airbus A.321-211	Iberia *Comunidad Autonoma de la Rioja*
	EC-IDA	Boeing 737-86Q	Air Europa
	EC-IDT	Boeing 737-86Q	Air Europa
	EC-IEF	Airbus A.320-214	Iberia *Castillo de Loarre*
	EC-IEG	Airbus A.320-214	Iberia *Costa Brava*
	EC-IGK	Airbus A.321-213	Iberia *Costa Calida*
	EC-III	Boeing 737-86Q	Air Europa
	EC-IJN	Airbus A.321-212	Iberia *Merida*

Reg	Type	Owner or Operator	Notes
EC-ILO	Airbus A.321-211	Iberia *Cueva de Nerja*	
EC-ILP	Airbus A.321-211	Iberia *Peniscola*	
EC-ILQ	Airbus A.320-214	Iberia Express	
EC-ILR	Airbus A.320-214	Iberia *San Juan de la Pena*	
EC-ILS	Airbus A.320-214	Iberia *Sierra de Cameros*	
EC-INO	Airbus A.340-642	Iberia *Gaudi*	
EC-IOB	Airbus A.340-642	Iberia *Julio Romanes de Torres*	
EC-IQR	Airbus A.340-642	Iberia *Salvador Dali*	
EC-ISN	Boeing 737-86Q	Air Europa	
EC-ISY	Boeing 757-256	Privilege Style	
EC-IXD	Airbus A.321-212	Iberia *Vall d'Aran*	
EC-IZH	Airbus A.320-214	Iberia *San Pere de Roda*	
EC-IZR	Airbus A.320-214	Iberia *Urkiola*	
EC-IZX	Airbus A.340-642	Iberia *Mariano Benlliure*	
EC-IZY	Airbus A.340-642	Iberia *I. Zuloaga*	
EC-JAZ	Airbus A.319-111	Iberia *Las Medulas*	
EC-JBA	Airbus A.340-642	Iberia *Joaquin Rodrigo*	
EC-JCY	Airbus A.340-642	Iberia *Andrés Segovia*	
EC-JCZ	Airbus A.340-642	Iberia *Vicente Aleixandre*	
EC-JDL	Airbus A.319-111	Iberia *Los Llanos de Aridane*	
EC-JDM	Airbus A.321-213	Iberia Express	
EC-JDR	Airbus A.321-213	Iberia *Sierra Cebollera*	
EC-JEI	Airbus A.319-111	Iberia *Xátiva*	
EC-JEJ	Airbus A.321-231	Iberia Express	
EC-JFF	Airbus A.320-214	Vueling Airlines *Vueling the world*	
EC-JFG	Airbus A.320-214	Iberia Express	
EC-JFH	Airbus A.320-214	Iberia Express	
EC-JFN	Airbus A.320-214	Iberia *Sirrea de las Nieves*	
EC-JFX	Airbus A.340-642	Iberia *Jacinto Benavente*	
EC-JGM	Airbus A.320-214	Vueling Airlines *The joy of vueling*	
EC-JGS	Airbus A.321-213	Iberia *Guadelupe*	
EC-JLE	Airbus A.340-642	Iberia *Santiago Ramon y Cajal*	
EC-JLI	Airbus A.321-211	Iberia Express	
EC-JNF	Boeing 737-85P	Air Europa *Mutua Madrileqa*	
EC-JNQ	Airbus A.340-642	Iberia *Antonio Machado*	
EC-JPF	Airbus A.330-202	Air Europa	
EC-JPU	Airbus A.340-642	Iberia *Pio Baroja*	
EC-JQG	Airbus A.330-202	Air Europa *Estepona – Costa del Sol*	
EC-JQQ	Airbus A.330-202	Air Europa	
EC-JQZ	Airbus A.321-211	Iberia *Generalife*	
EC-JRE	Airbus A.321-211	Iberia *Villa de Uncastillo*	
EC-JSK	Airbus A.320-214	Iberia Express	
EC-JSY	Airbus A.320-214	Vueling Airlines	
EC-JTQ	Airbus A.320-214	Vueling Airlines *Vueling, que es gerundio*	
EC-JTR	Airbus A.320-214	Vueling Airlines *No Vueling no party*	
EC-JVE	Airbus A.319-111	Iberia *Puerto de la Cruz*	
EC-JXJ	Airbus A.319-111	Iberia	
EC-JXV	Airbus A.319-112	Iberia	
EC-JYX	Airbus A.320-214	Vueling Airlines *Elisenda Masana*	
EC-JZI	Airbus A.320-214	Vueling Airlines *Vueling in love*	
EC-JZL	Airbus A.330-202	Air Europa	
EC-JZM	Airbus A.321-211	Iberia *Águila Imperial Ibérica*	
EC-KBX	Airbus A.319-111	Iberia *Oso Pardo*	
EC-KCG	Boeing 737-85P	Air Europa	
EC-KCU	Airbus A.320-216	Vueling Airlines	
EC-KDG	Airbus A.320-214	Vueling Airlines	
EC-KDH	Airbus A.320-214	Vueling Airlines *Ain't no Vueling high enough*	
EC-KDT	Airbus A.320-216	Vueling Airlines	
EC-KDX	Airbus A.320-216	Vueling Airlines *Francisco Jose Ruiz Cortizo*	
EC-KHM	Airbus A.319-111	Iberia *Buho Real*	
EC-KHN	Airbus A.320-216	Vueling Airlines	
EC-KJD	Airbus A.320-216	Vueling Airlines	
EC-KKS	Airbus A.319-111	Iberia *Halcon Peregrino*	
EC-KLB	Airbus A.320-214	Vueling Airlines *Vuela Punto*	
EC-KLT	Airbus A.320-214	Vueling Airlines	
EC-KMD	Airbus A.319-111	Iberia *Petirrojo*	
EC-KMI	Airbus A.320-216	Vueling Airlines *How are you? I'm Vueling!*	
EC-KOH	Airbus A.320-214	Iberia *Fontibre*	
EC-KOM	Airbus A.330-202	Air Europa	
EC-KOY	Airbus A.319-111	Iberia *Vencejo*	
EC-KRH	Airbus A.320-214	Vueling Airlines *Vueling me softly*	

Notes	Reg	Type	Owner or Operator
	EC-KTG	Airbus A.330-203	Air Europa
	EC-KUB	Airbus A.319-111	Iberia *Flamenco*
	EC-KZI	Airbus A.340-642	Iberia *Miguel Hernandez*
	EC-LAA	Airbus A.320-214	Vueling Airlines
	EC-LAB	Airbus A.320-214	Vueling Airlines
	EC-LCZ	Airbus A.340-642	Iberia *Miguel Servet*
	EC-LEA	Airbus A.320-214	Iberia Express
	EC-LEI	Airbus A.319-111	Iberia *Vison Europeo*
	EC-LEU	Airbus A.340-642	Iberia *Rio Amazonas*
	EC-LEV	Airbus A.340-642	Iberia *Isaac Albeniz*
	EC-LFS	Airbus A.340-642	Iberia *Ciudad de Mexico*
	EC-LKG	Airbus A.320-214	Iberia Express
	EC-LKH	Airbus A.320-214	Iberia Express
	EC-LLE	Airbus A.320-214	Iberia Express
	EC-LLJ	Airbus A.320-214	Vueling Airlines
	EC-LLM	Airbus A.320-216	Vueling Airlines *Be happy, be Vueling*
	EC-LMR	BAe 146-300QT	ASL Airlines Spain
	EC-LOB	Airbus A.320-232	Vueling Airlines
	EC-LOC	Airbus A.320-232	Vueling Airlines *Vueling on heaven's door*
	EC-LOF	BAe 146-300QT	ASL Airlines Spain
	EC-LOP	Airbus A.320-214	Vueling Airlines
	EC-LPQ	Boeing 737-85P	Air Europa
	EC-LPR	Boeing 737-85P	Air Europa
	EC-LQK	Airbus A.320-232	Vueling Airlines
	EC-LQL	Airbus A.320-232	Vueling Airlines
	EC-LQM	Airbus A.320-232	Vueling Airlines
	EC-LQN	Airbus A.320-232	Vueling Airlines
	EC-LQO	Airbus A.330-243	Air Europa
	EC-LQP	Airbus A.330-243	Air Europa
	EC-LQX	Boeing 737-85P	Air Europa
	EC-LQZ	Airbus A.320-232	Vueling Airlines
	EC-LRE	Airbus A.320-232	Vueling Airlines
	EC-LRG	Airbus A.320-214	Iberia
	EC-LRM	Airbus A.320-232	Vueling Airlines
	EC-LRY	Airbus A.320-232	Vueling Airlines
	EC-LTG	Boeing 737-4K5	AlbaStar
	EC-LTM	Boeing 737-85P	Air Europa
	EC-LUB	Airbus A.330-302	Iberia *Tikal*
	EC-LUC	Airbus A.320-214	Iberia Express
	EC-LUD	Airbus A.320-214	Iberia Express
	EC-LUK	Airbus A.330-302E	Iberia *Costa Rica*
	EC-LUL	Airbus A.320-216	Iberia *Cangas de Onis*
	EC-LUN	Airbus A.320-232	Vueling Airlines
	EC-LUO	Airbus A.320-232	Vueling Airlines
	EC-LUS	Airbus A.320-216	Iberia Express
	EC-LUT	Boeing 737-85P	Air Europa
	EC-LUX	Airbus A.330-302E	Iberia *Panama*
	EC-LVD	Airbus A.320-216	Iberia *Valle de Mena*
	EC-LVL	Airbus A.320-243	Air Europa
	EC-LVO	Airbus A.320-214	Vueling Airlines
	EC-LVP	Airbus A.320-214	Vueling Airlines
	EC-LVQ	Airbus A.320-216	Iberia Express
	EC-LVR	Boeing 737-85P	Air Europa
	EC-LVS	Airbus A.320-214	Vueling Airlines
	EC-LVT	Airbus A.320-214	Vueling Airlines
	EC-LVU	Airbus A.320-214	Vueling Airlines
	EC-LVV	Airbus A.320-214	Vueling Airlines
	EC-LVX	Airbus A.320-214	Vueling Airlines *Vuelingsgefuhle*
	EC-LXK	Airbus A.330-302E	Iberia *El Salvador*
	EC-LXQ	Airbus A.320-216	Iberia *Penon de Ifach*
	EC-LXR	Airbus A.330-343	Air Europa
	EC-LXV	Boeing 737-86N	Air Europa
	EC-LYE	Airbus A.320-216	Iberia Express
	EC-LYF	Airbus A.330-302E	Iberia *Juan Carlos I*
	EC-LYM	Airbus A.320-216	Iberia Express
	EC-LYR	Boeing 737-85P	Air Europa
	EC-LZD	Airbus A.320-214	Evelop Airlines
	EC-LZJ	Airbus A.330-302E	Iberia *Miami*
	EC-LZN	Airbus A.320-214	Vueling Airlines
	EC-LZO	Boeing 767-35DER	Privilege Style
	EC-LZX	Airbus A.330-302E	Iberia *Madrid*

Reg	Type	Owner or Operator	Notes
EC-LZZ	Airbus A.320-214	Vueling Airlines	
EC-MAA	Airbus A.330-302	Iberia *Rio de Janeiro*	
EC-MAD	Boeing 737-4YOF	Swiftair	
EC-MAH	Airbus A.320-214	Vueling Airlines	
EC-MAI	Airbus A.320-214	Vueling Airlines	
EC-MAJ	Airbus A.330-243	Air Europa	
EC-MAN	Airbus A.320-214	Vueling Airlines	
EC-MAO	Airbus A.320-214	Vueling Airlines	
EC-MAX	Airbus A.320-214	Vueling Airlines	
EC-MBD	Airbus A.320-214	Vueling Airlines	
EC-MBE	Airbus A.320-214	Vueling Airlines	
EC-MBF	Airbus A.320-214	Vueling Airlines	
EC-MBK	Airbus A.320-214	Vueling Airlines	
EC-MBL	Airbus A.320-214	Vueling Airlines	
EC-MBM	Airbus A.320-232	Vueling Airlines	
EC-MBS	Airbus A.320-214	Vueling Airlines	
EC-MBT	Airbus A.320-214	Iberia Express	
EC-MBU	Airbus A.320-214	Vueling Airlines	
EC-MBY	Airbus A.320-214	Iberia Express	
EC-MCB	Airbus A.320-214	Iberia Express	
EC-MCI	Boeing 737-4Q8F	Swiftair	
EC-MCK	BAe 146-300QT	ASL Airlines Spain	
EC-MCL	BAe 146-300QT	ASL Airlines Spain	
EC-MCS	Airbus A.320-216	Iberia *Playa de Los Lances*	
EC-MCU	Airbus A.320-214	Vueling Airlines	
EC-MDK	Airbus A.320-214	Iberia *P.N.Picas de Europa*	
EC-MDZ	Airbus A.320-232	Vueling Airlines	
EC-MEA	Airbus A.320-232	Vueling Airlines	
EC-MEG	Airbus A.320-214	Iberia Express	
EC-MEH	Airbus A.320-214	Iberia Express	
EC-MEL	Airbus A.320-232	Vueling Airlines	
EC-MEO	BAe 146-300QT	ASL Airlines Spain	
EC-MEQ	Airbus A.320-232	Vueling Airlines	
EC-MER	Airbus A.320-232	Vueling Airlines	
EC-MES	Airbus A.320-232	Vueling Airlines	
EC-MEY	Boeing 737-476F	Swiftair	
EC-MEZ	Boeing 717-2CM	Volotea Airlines	
EC-MFE	Boeing 737-476F	Swiftair	
EC-MFJ	Boeing 717-2CM	Volotea Airlines	
EC-MFK	Airbus A.320-232	Vueling Airlines	
EC-MFL	Airbus A.320-232	Vueling Airlines	
EC-MFM	Airbus A.320-232	Vueling Airlines	
EC-MFN	Airbus A.320-232	Vueling Airlines	
EC-MFO	Airbus A.319-111	Iberia	
EC-MFP	Airbus A.319-111	Iberia	
EC-MFT	BAe 146-300QT	ASL Airlines Spain	
EC-MGE	Airbus A.320-232	Vueling Airlines	
EC-MGF	Airbus A.319-111	Vueling Airlines	
EC-MGS	Boeing 717-2CM	Volotea Airlines	
EC-MGT	Boeing 717-23S	Volotea Airlines	
EC-MGY	Airbus A.321-231	Vueling Airlines	
EC-MGZ	Airbus A.321-231	Vueling Airlines	
EC-MHA	Airbus A.321-231	Vueling Airlines *Good Sense and Rebelliousness*	
EC-MHB	Airbus A.321-231	Vueling Airlines	
EC-MHL	Airbus A.330-343	Air Europa	
EC-MHR	BAe 146-300QT	ASL Airlines Spain	
EC-MHS	Airbus A.321-231	Vueling Airlines *Vuelissimo*	
EC-MIA	Boeing 777-28EER	Privilege Style	
EC-MID	BAe 146-300QT	ASL Airlines Spain	
EC-MIE	Boeing 737-4YOF	Swiftair	
EC-MIL	Airbus A.330-202	Iberia *Oaxaca*	
EC-MIQ	Airbus A.319-112	Vueling Airlines	
EC-MIR	Airbus A.319-112	Vueling Airlines	
EC-MJA	Airbus A.330-202	Iberia *Buenos Aires*	
EC-MJB	Airbus A.320-232	Vueling Airlines *Alex Cruz 5.0*	
EC-MJC	Airbus A.320-232	Vueling Airlines	
EC-MJR	Airbus A.321-231	Vueling Airlines	
EC-MJT	Airbus A.330-202	Iberia *La Habana*	
EC-MJU	Boeing 737-85P	Air Europa	
EC-MKI	Airbus A.330-202	Iberia *Buenos Aires*	

Notes	Reg	Type	Owner or Operator
	EC-MKJ	Airbus A.330-202	Iberia *Montevideo*
	EC-MKL	Boeing 737-85P	Air Europa
	EC-MKM	Airbus A.320-232	Vueling Airlines *Miguel Angel Galan*
	EC-MKN	Airbus A.320-232	Vueling Airlines *Arelis & Carlos*
	EC-MKO	Airbus A.320-232	Vueling Airlines *The Tutu Project*
	EC-MKV	Airbus A.319-112	Vueling Airlines
	EC-MKX	Airbus A.319-112	Vueling Airlines
	EC-MLB	Airbus A.330-202	Iberia *Iberoamerica*
	EC-MLD	Airbus A.321-231	Vueling Airlines
	EC-MLE	Airbus A.320-232	Vueling Airlines *Amrani-Bus*
	EC-MLM	Airbus A.321-231	Vueling Airlines
	EC-MLP	Airbus A.330-202	Iberia *Lima*
	EC-MMG	Airbus A.330-202	Iberia *Santiago de Chile*
	EC-MMH	Airbus A.321-231	Vueling Airlines *Ryan's Well*
	EC-MMU	Airbus A.321-231	Vueling Airlines *Mason Wartman*
	EC-MNK	Airbus A.330-202	Iberia *Bogota*
	EC-MNL	Airbus A.330-202	Iberia *Tokio*
	EC-MNM	Boeing 737-4YOF	Swiftair
	EC-MNY	Airbus A.330-243	Wamos Air
	EC-MNZ	Airbus A.320-232	Vueling Airlines
	EC-MOG	Airbus A.320-232	Vueling Airlines
	EC-MOO	Airbus A.321-231	Vueling Airlines
	EC-MOU	Airbus A.330-202	Iberia
	EC-MOY	Airbus A.330-202	Iberia
	EC-MPG	Boeing 737-85P	Air Europa
	EC-MPS	Boeing 737-85P	Air Europa
	EC-MPV	Airbus A.321-231	Vueling Airlines
	EC-MQB	Airbus A.321-231	Vueling Airlines *Biciclown*
	EC-MQE	Airbus A.320-232	Vueling Airlines
	EC-MQH	Airbus A.320-214	Iberia Express
	EC-MQL	Airbus A.321-231	Vueling Airlines *Klaus' Angels*
	EC-MQP	Boeing 737-85P	Air Europa
	EC-MRF	Airbus A.321-231	Vueling Airlines *Flavia Carvalho*
	EC-MSY	Airbus A.330-202	Iberia
	EC-MTB	Airbus A.319-111	Volotea Airlines
	EC-MTC	Airbus A.319-111	Volotea Airlines
	EC-MTD	Airbus A.319-111	Volotea Airlines
	EC-MTE	Airbus A.319-112	Volotea Airlines
	EC-MTF	Airbus A.319-112	Volotea Airlines
	EC-MTJ	Airbus A.320-214	Thomas Cook Airlines Balearics
	EC-MTL	Airbus A.319-111	Volotea Airlines
	EC-MTM	Airbus A.319-111	Volotea Airlines
	EC-MTN	Airbus A.319-111	Volotea Airlines
	EC-MTV	Boeing 737-86J	AlbaStar
	EC-MUB	Boeing 737-86J	AlbaStar
	EC-MUC	Airbus A.319-112	Volotea Airlines
	EC-MUD	Airbus A.330-302	Iberia
	EC-MUF	Airbus A.320-214	Iberia
	EC-MUK	Airbus A.320-214	Vueling Airlines
	EC-MUM	Airbus A.320-214	Vueling Airlines
	EC-MUT	Airbus A.319-111	Volotea Airlines
	EC-MUU	Airbus A.319-111	Volotea Airlines
	EC-MUZ	Boeing 737-85P	Air Europa
	EC-MVD	Airbus A.320-214	Vueling Airlines
	EC-MVE	Airbus A.320-214	Vueling Airlines
	EC-MVF	Airbus A.320-214	Thomas Cook Airlines Balearics
	EC-MVG	Airbus A.320-214	Thomas Cook Airlines Balearics
	EC-MVH	Airbus A.320-214	Thomas Cook Airlines Balearics

EP (Iran)

Notes	Reg	Type	Owner or Operator
	EP-IBA	Airbus A.300B4-605R	Iran Air
	EP-IBB	Airbus A.300B4-605R	Iran Air
	EP-IBC	Airbus A.300B4-605R	Iran Air
	EP-IBD	Airbus A.300B4-605R	Iran Air
	EP-IBK	Airbus A.310-304	Iran Air
	EP-IBL	Airbus A.310-304	Iran Air
	EP-IJA	Airbus A.330-243	Iran Air
	EP-IJB	Airbus A.330-243	Iran Air
	EP-IJC	Airbus A.330-243	Iran Air

Reg	Type	Owner or Operator	Notes

ER (Moldova)

ER-00001	Airbus A.320-233	Fly One	
ER-00002	Airbus A.319-112	Fly One	
ER-AXL	Airbus A.319-112	Air Moldova	
ER-AXM	Airbus A.319-112	Air Moldova	
ER-AXP	Airbus A.320-211	Air Moldova	
ER-AXV	Airbus A.320-211	Air Moldova	
ER-ECB	Embraer ERJ190-100AR	Air Moldova	
ER-ECC	Embraer ERJ190-100AR	Air Moldova	
ER-ECD	Embraer ERJ190-100AR	Air Moldova	

ET (Ethiopia)

ET-ATQ	Airbus A.350-941	Ethiopian Airlines	
ET-ATR	Airbus A.350-941	Ethiopian Airlines	
ET-ATY	Airbus A.350-941	Ethiopian Airlines	
ET-AUA	Airbus A.350-941	Ethiopian Airlines	
ET-AUB	Airbus A.350-941	Ethiopian Airlines	
ET-AUC	Airbus A.350-941	Ethiopian Airlines	
ET-AVB	Airbus A.350-941	Ethiopian Airlines	
ET-AVC	Airbus A.350-941	Ethiopian Airlines	

EW (Belarus)

EW-250PA	Boeing 737-524	Belavia	
EW-251PA	Boeing 737-5Q8	Belavia	
EW-252PA	Boeing 737-524	Belavia	
EW-253PA	Boeing 737-524	Belavia	
EW-254PA	Boeing 737-3Q8	Belavia	
EW-282PA	Boeing 737-3Q8	Belavia	
EW-290PA	Boeing 737-5Q8	Belavia	
EW-294PA	Boeing 737-505	Belavia	
EW-308PA	Boeing 737-3K2	Belavia	
EW-336PA	Boeing 737-3Q8	Belavia	
EW-340PO	Embraer ERJ170-200LR	Belavia	
EW-341PO	Embraer ERJ170-200LR	Belavia	
EW-366PA	Boeing 737-31S	Belavia	
EW-399PO	Embraer ERJ190-200LR	Belavia	
EW-400PO	Embraer ERJ190-200LR	Belavia	
EW-404PA	Boeing 737-3L9	Belavia	
EW-407PA	Boeing 737-36M	Belavia	
EW-437PA	Boeing 737-8K5	Belavia	
EW-438PA	Boeing 737-86Q	Belavia	
EW-455PA	Boeing 737-8ZM	Belavia	
EW-456PA	Boeing 737-8ZM	Belavia	
EW-457PA	Boeing 737-8ZM	Belavia	

EZ (Turkmenistan)

EZ-A004	Boeing 737-82K	Turkmenistan Airlines	
EZ-A005	Boeing 737-82K	Turkmenistan Airlines	
EZ-A011	Boeing 757-22K	Turkmenistan Airlines	
EZ-A014	Boeing 757-22K	Turkmenistan Airlines	
EZ-A015	Boeing 737-82K	Turkmenistan Airlines	
EZ-A016	Boeing 737-82K	Turkmenistan Airlines	
EZ-A017	Boeing 737-82K	Turkmenistan Airlines	
EZ-A018	Boeing 737-82K	Turkmenistan Airlines	
EZ-A019	Boeing 737-82K	Turkmenistan Airlines	
EZ-A020	Boeing 737-82K	Turkmenistan Airlines	
EZ-A778	Boeing 777-22K	Turkmenistan Airlines	
EZ-A779	Boeing 777-22K	Turkmenistan Airlines	

F (France)

F-GIXB	Boeing 737-33AF	ASL Airlines France	
F-GIXC	Boeing 737-38B	ASL Airlines France	
F-GIXN	Boeing 737-4YOF	ASL Airlines France	
F-GIXT	Boeing 737-39M	ASL Airlines France	
F-GKXC	Airbus A.320-214	Air France	

Notes	Reg	Type	Owner or Operator
	F-GKXE	Airbus A.320-214	Air France
	F-GKXG	Airbus A.320-214	Air France
	F-GKXI	Airbus A.320-214	Air France
	F-GKXJ	Airbus A.320-214	Air France
	F-GKXK	Airbus A.320-214	Air France
	F-GKXL	Airbus A.320-214	Air France
	F-GKXM	Airbus A.320-214	Air France
	F-GKXO	Airbus A.320-214	Air France
	F-GKXP	Airbus A.320-214	Air France
	F-GKXQ	Airbus A.320-214	Air France
	F-GKXS	Airbus A.320-214	Air France
	F-GKXU	Airbus A.320-214	Air France
	F-GKXZ	Airbus A.320-214	Air France
	F-GLZJ	Airbus A.340-313X	Air France
	F-GLZK	Airbus A.340-313X	Air France
	F-GLZN	Airbus A.340-313X	Air France
	F-GLZO	Airbus A.340-313X	Air France
	F-GLZP	Airbus A.340-313X	Air France
	F-GLZS	Airbus A.340-313X	Air France
	F-GLZU	Airbus A.340-313X	Air France
	F-GMZA	Airbus A.321-111	Air France
	F-GMZB	Airbus A.321-111	Air France
	F-GMZC	Airbus A.321-111	Air France
	F-GMZD	Airbus A.321-111	Air France
	F-GMZE	Airbus A.321-111	Air France
	F-GPEK	Boeing 757-236	Open Skies
	F-GPMA	Airbus A.319-113	Air France
	F-GPMB	Airbus A.319-113	Air France
	F-GPMC	Airbus A.319-113	Air France
	F-GPMD	Airbus A.319-113	Air France
	F-GPME	Airbus A.319-113	Air France
	F-GPMF	Airbus A.319-113	Air France
	F-GRGC	Embraer RJ145EU	HOP !
	F-GRGD	Embraer RJ145EU	HOP !
	F-GRGF	Embraer RJ145EU	HOP !
	F-GRGG	Embraer RJ145EU	HOP !
	F-GRGH	Embraer RJ145EU	HOP !
	F-GRGI	Embraer RJ145EU	HOP !
	F-GRGJ	Embraer RJ145EU	HOP !
	F-GRGK	Embraer RJ145EU	HOP !
	F-GRGL	Embraer RJ145EU	HOP !
	F-GRHB	Airbus A.319-111	Air France
	F-GRHE	Airbus A.319-111	Air France
	F-GRHF	Airbus A.319-111	Air France
	F-GRHG	Airbus A.319-111	Air France
	F-GRHH	Airbus A.319-111	Air France
	F-GRHI	Airbus A.319-111	Air France
	F-GRHJ	Airbus A.319-111	Air France
	F-GRHK	Airbus A.319-111	Air France
	F-GRHL	Airbus A.319-111	Air France
	F-GRHM	Airbus A.319-111	Air France
	F-GRHN	Airbus A.319-111	Air France
	F-GRHO	Airbus A.319-111	Air France
	F-GRHP	Airbus A.319-111	Air France
	F-GRHQ	Airbus A.319-111	Air France
	F-GRHR	Airbus A.319-111	Air France
	F-GRHS	Airbus A.319-111	Air France
	F-GRHT	Airbus A.319-111	Air France
	F-GRHU	Airbus A.319-111	Air France
	F-GRHV	Airbus A.319-111	Air France
	F-GRHX	Airbus A.319-111	Air France
	F-GRHY	Airbus A.319-111	Air France
	F-GRHZ	Airbus A.319-111	Air France
	F-GRXA	Airbus A.319-111	Air France
	F-GRXB	Airbus A.319-111	Air France
	F-GRXC	Airbus A.319-111	Air France
	F-GRXD	Airbus A.319-111	Air France
	F-GRXE	Airbus A.319-111	Air France
	F-GRXF	Airbus A.319-111	Air France
	F-GRXJ	Airbus A.319-111LR	Air France
	F-GRXK	Airbus A.319-111LR	Air France

Reg	Type	Owner or Operator	Notes
F-GRXL	Airbus A.319-111	Air France	
F-GRXM	Airbus A.319-111	Air France	
F-GRZE	Canadair CRJ700	HOP !	
F-GRZF	Canadair CRJ700	HOP !	
F-GRZG	Canadair CRJ700	HOP !	
F-GRZH	Canadair CRJ700	HOP !	
F-GRZI	Canadair CRJ700	HOP !	
F-GRZJ	Canadair CRJ700	HOP !	
F-GRZK	Canadair CRJ700	HOP !	
F-GRZL	Canadair CRJ700	HOP !	
F-GRZM	Canadair CRJ700	HOP !	
F-GRZN	Canadair CRJ700	HOP !	
F-GRZO	Canadair CRJ700	HOP !	
F-GSPA	Boeing 777-228ER	Air France	
F-GSPB	Boeing 777-228ER	Air France	
F-GSPC	Boeing 777-228ER	Air France	
F-GSPD	Boeing 777-228ER	Air France	
F-GSPE	Boeing 777-228ER	Air France	
F-GSPF	Boeing 777-228ER	Air France	
F-GSPG	Boeing 777-228ER	Air France	
F-GSPH	Boeing 777-228ER	Air France	
F-GSPI	Boeing 777-228ER	Air France	
F-GSPJ	Boeing 777-228ER	Air France	
F-GSPK	Boeing 777-228ER	Air France	
F-GSPL	Boeing 777-228ER	Air France	
F-GSPM	Boeing 777-228ER	Air France	
F-GSPN	Boeing 777-228ER	Air France	
F-GSPO	Boeing 777-228ER	Air France	
F-GSPP	Boeing 777-228ER	Air France	
F-GSPQ	Boeing 777-228ER	Air France	
F-GSPR	Boeing 777-228ER	Air France	
F-GSPS	Boeing 777-228ER	Air France	
F-GSPT	Boeing 777-228ER	Air France	
F-GSPU	Boeing 777-228ER	Air France	
F-GSPV	Boeing 777-228ER	Air France	
F-GSPX	Boeing 777-228ER	Air France	
F-GSPY	Boeing 777-228ER	Air France	
F-GSPZ	Boeing 777-228ER	Air France	
F-GSQA	Boeing 777-328ER	Air France	
F-GSQB	Boeing 777-328ER	Air France	
F-GSQC	Boeing 777-328ER	Air France	
F-GSQD	Boeing 777-328ER	Air France	
F-GSQE	Boeing 777-328ER	Air France	
F-GSQF	Boeing 777-328ER	Air France	
F-GSQG	Boeing 777-328ER	Air France	
F-GSQH	Boeing 777-328ER	Air France	
F-GSQI	Boeing 777-328ER	Air France	
F-GSQJ	Boeing 777-328ER	Air France	
F-GSQK	Boeing 777-328ER	Air France	
F-GSQL	Boeing 777-328ER	Air France	
F-GSQM	Boeing 777-328ER	Air France	
F-GSQN	Boeing 777-328ER	Air France	
F-GSQO	Boeing 777-328ER	Air France	
F-GSQP	Boeing 777-328ER	Air France	
F-GSQR	Boeing 777-328ER	Air France	
F-GSQS	Boeing 777-328ER	Air France	
F-GSQT	Boeing 777-328ER	Air France	
F-GSQU	Boeing 777-328ER	Air France	
F-GSQV	Boeing 777-328ER	Air France	
F-GSQX	Boeing 777-328ER	Air France	
F-GSQY	Boeing 777-328ER	Air France	
F-GSTA	Airbus A.300-608ST Beluga (1)	Airbus Transport International	
F-GSTB	Airbus A.300-608ST Beluga (2)	Airbus Transport International	
F-GSTC	Airbus A.300-608ST Beluga (3)	Airbus Transport International	
F-GSTD	Airbus A.300-608ST Beluga (4)	Airbus Transport International	
F-GSTF	Airbus A.300-608ST Beluga (5)	Airbus Transport International	
F-GTAD	Airbus A.321-211	Air France	
F-GTAE	Airbus A.321-211	Air France	
F-GTAH	Airbus A.321-211	Air France	
F-GTAJ	Airbus A.321-211	Air France	
F-GTAK	Airbus A.321-211	Air France	

Notes	Reg	Type	Owner or Operator
	F-GTAM	Airbus A.321-211	Air France
	F-GTAO	Airbus A.321-211	Air France
	F-GTAP	Airbus A.321-212	Air France
	F-GTAQ	Airbus A.321-211	Air France
	F-GTAS	Airbus A.321-211	Air France
	F-GTAT	Airbus A.321-211	Air France
	F-GTAU	Airbus A.321-211	Air France
	F-GTAX	Airbus A.321-211	Air France
	F-GTAY	Airbus A.321-211	Air France
	F-GTAZ	Airbus A.321-211	Air France
	F-GUBC	Embraer RJ145MP	HOP !
	F-GUBE	Embraer RJ145MP	HOP !
	F-GUBF	Embraer RJ145MP	HOP !
	F-GUBG	Embraer RJ145MP	HOP !
	F-GUEA	Embraer RJ145MP	HOP !
	F-GUGA	Airbus A.318-111	Air France
	F-GUGB	Airbus A.318-111	Air France
	F-GUGC	Airbus A.318-111	Air France
	F-GUGD	Airbus A.318-111	Air France
	F-GUGE	Airbus A.318-111	Air France
	F-GUGF	Airbus A.318-111	Air France
	F-GUGG	Airbus A.318-111	Air France
	F-GUGH	Airbus A.318-111	Air France
	F-GUGI	Airbus A.318-111	Air France
	F-GUGJ	Airbus A.318-111	Air France
	F-GUGK	Airbus A.318-111	Air France
	F-GUGL	Airbus A.318-111	Air France
	F-GUGM	Airbus A.318-111	Air France
	F-GUGN	Airbus A.318-111	Air France
	F-GUGO	Airbus A.318-111	Air France
	F-GUGP	Airbus A.318-111	Air France
	F-GUGQ	Airbus A.318-111	Air France
	F-GUGR	Airbus A.318-111	Air France
	F-GUOB	Boeing 777-F28	Air France Cargo
	F-GUOC	Boeing 777-F28	Air France Cargo
	F-GVHD	Embraer RJ145MP	HOP !
	F-GZCA	Airbus A.330-203	Air France
	F-GZCB	Airbus A.330-203	Air France
	F-GZCC	Airbus A.330-203	Air France
	F-GZCD	Airbus A.330-203	Air France
	F-GZCE	Airbus A.330-203	Air France
	F-GZCF	Airbus A.330-203	Air France
	F-GZCG	Airbus A.330-203	Air France
	F-GZCH	Airbus A.330-203	Air France
	F-GZCI	Airbus A.330-203	Air France
	F-GZCJ	Airbus A.330-203	Air France
	F-GZCK	Airbus A.330-203	Air France
	F-GZCL	Airbus A.330-203	Air France
	F-GZCM	Airbus A.330-203	Air France
	F-GZCN	Airbus A.330-203	Air France
	F-GZCO	Airbus A.330-203	Air France
	F-GZHA	Boeing 737-8GJ	Transavia France
	F-GZHB	Boeing 737-8GJ	Transavia France
	F-GZHC	Boeing 737-8GJ	Transavia France
	F-GZHD	Boeing 737-8K2	Transavia France
	F-GZHE	Boeing 737-8K2	Transavia France
	F-GZHF	Boeing 737-8HX	Transavia France
	F-GZHI	Boeing 737-8K2	Transavia France
	F-GZHJ	Boeing 737-8K2	Transavia France
	F-GZHK	Boeing 737-8K2	Transavia France
	F-GZHL	Boeing 737-8K2	Transavia France
	F-GZHM	Boeing 737-8K2	Transavia France
	F-GZHN	Boeing 737-8K2	Transavia France
	F-GZHO	Boeing 737-8K2	Transavia France
	F-GZHP	Boeing 737-8K2	Transavia France
	F-GZHQ	Boeing 737-8K2	Transavia France
	F-GZHR	Boeing 737-8K2	Transavia France
	F-GZHS	Boeing 737-84P	Transavia France
	F-GZHT	Boeing 737-8K2	Transavia France
	F-GZHU	Boeing 737-8K2	Transavia France
	F-GZHV	Boeing 737-85H	Transavia France

Reg	Type	Owner or Operator	Notes
F-GZHX	Boeing 737-8K2	Transavia France	
F-GZHY	Boeing 737-8K2	Transavia France	
F-GZNA	Boeing 777-328ER	Air France	
F-GZNB	Boeing 777-328ER	Air France	
F-GZNC	Boeing 777-328ER	Air France	
F-GZND	Boeing 777-328ER	Air France	
F-GZNE	Boeing 777-328ER	Air France	
F-GZNF	Boeing 777-328ER	Air France	
F-GZNG	Boeing 777-328ER	Air France	
F-GZNH	Boeing 777-328ER	Air France	
F-GZNI	Boeing 777-328ER	Air France	
F-GZNJ	Boeing 777-328ER	Air France	
F-GZNK	Boeing 777-328ER	Air France	
F-GZNL	Boeing 777-328ER	Air France	
F-GZNN	Boeing 777-328ER	Air France	
F-GZNO	Boeing 777-328ER	Air France	
F-GZNP	Boeing 777-328ER	Air France	
F-GZNQ	Boeing 777-328ER	Air France	
F-GZNR	Boeing 777-328ER	Air France	
F-GZNS	Boeing 777-328ER	Air France	
F-GZNT	Boeing 777-328ER	Air France	
F-GZNU	Boeing 777-328ER	Air France	
F-GZTA	Boeing 737-33V	ASL Airlines France	
F-GZTB	Boeing 737-33V	ASL Airlines France	
F-GZTC	Boeing 737-73V	ASL Airlines France	
F-GZTD	Boeing 737-73V	ASL Airlines France	
F-GZTI	Boeing 737-408F	ASL Airlines France	
F-GZTJ	Boeing 737-4S3F	ASL Airlines France	
F-GZTK	Boeing 737-4Q8F	ASL Airlines France	
F-GZTN	Boeing 737-73S	ASL Airlines France	
F-GZTO	Boeing 737-73S	ASL Airlines France	
F-GZTP	Boeing 737-71B	ASL Airlines France	
F-GZTQ	Boeing 737-73S	ASL Airlines France	
F-GZTS	Boeing 737-73V	ASL Airlines France	
F-GZTU	Boeing 737-73V	ASL Airlines France	
F-HAVI	Boeing 757-26D	Open Skies *Violette*	
F-HAVN	Boeing 757-230	Open Skies *Gloria*	
F-HBEV	Airbus A.320-216	Air Corsica	
F-HBLA	Embraer RJ190-100LR	HOP !	
F-HBLB	Embraer RJ190-100LR	HOP !	
F-HBLC	Embraer RJ190-100LR	HOP !	
F-HBLD	Embraer RJ190-100LR	HOP !	
F-HBLE	Embraer RJ190-100LR	HOP !	
F-HBLF	Embraer RJ190-100LR	HOP !	
F-HBLG	Embraer RJ190-100LR	HOP !	
F-HBLH	Embraer RJ190-100LR	HOP !	
F-HBLI	Embraer RJ190-100LR	HOP !	
F-HBLJ	Embraer RJ190-100LR	HOP !	
F-HBNA	Airbus A.320-214	Air France	
F-HBNB	Airbus A.320-214	Air France	
F-HBNC	Airbus A.320-214	Air France	
F-HBND	Airbus A.320-214	Air France	
F-HBNE	Airbus A.320-214	Air France	
F-HBNF	Airbus A.320-214	Air France	
F-HBNG	Airbus A.320-214	Air France	
F-HBNH	Airbus A.320-214	Air France	
F-HBNI	Airbus A.320-214	Air France	
F-HBNJ	Airbus A.320-214	Air France	
F-HBNK	Airbus A.320-214	Air France	
F-HBNL	Airbus A.320-214	Air France	
F-HBSA	Airbus A.320-216	Air Corsica	
F-HBXA	Embraer RJ170-100LR	HOP !	
F-HBXB	Embraer RJ170-100LR	HOP !	
F-HBXC	Embraer RJ170-100LR	HOP !	
F-HBXD	Embraer RJ170-100LR	HOP !	
F-HBXE	Embraer RJ170-100LR	HOP !	
F-HBXF	Embraer RJ170-100LR	HOP !	
F-HBXG	Embraer RJ170-100LR	HOP !	
F-HBXH	Embraer RJ170-100LR	HOP !	
F-HBXI	Embraer RJ170-100LR	HOP !	
F-HBXJ	Embraer RJ170-100LR	HOP !	

Reg	Type	Owner or Operator
F-HBXK	Embraer RJ170-100LR	HOP !
F-HBXL	Embraer RJ170-100LR	HOP !
F-HBXM	Embraer RJ170-100LR	HOP !
F-HBXN	Embraer RJ170-100LR	HOP !
F-HBXO	Embraer RJ170-100LR	HOP !
F-HEPA	Airbus A.320-214	Air France
F-HEPB	Airbus A.320-214	Air France
F-HEPD	Airbus A.320-214	Air France
F-HEPE	Airbus A.320-214	Air France
F-HEPF	Airbus A.320-214	Air France
F-HEPG	Airbus A.320-214	Air France
F-HEPH	Airbus A.320-214	Air France
F-HEPI	Airbus A.320-214	Air France
F-HEPJ	Airbus A.320-214	Air France
F-HEPK	Airbus A.320-214	Air France
F-HILU	Boeing 767-336ER	Open Skies
F-HMLA	Canadair CRJ1000	HOP !
F-HMLC	Canadair CRJ1000	HOP !
F-HMLD	Canadair CRJ1000	HOP !
F-HMLE	Canadair CRJ1000	HOP !
F-HMLF	Canadair CRJ1000	HOP !
F-HMLG	Canadair CRJ1000	HOP !
F-HMLH	Canadair CRJ1000	HOP !
F-HMLI	Canadair CRJ1000	HOP !
F-HMLJ	Canadair CRJ1000	HOP !
F-HMLK	Canadair CRJ1000	HOP !
F-HMLL	Canadair CRJ1000	HOP !
F-HMLM	Canadair CRJ1000	HOP !
F-HMLN	Canadair CRJ1000	HOP !
F-HMLO	Canadair CRJ1000	HOP !
F-HPJA	Airbus A.380-861	Air France
F-HPJB	Airbus A.380-861	Air France
F-HPJC	Airbus A.380-861	Air France
F-HPJD	Airbus A.380-861	Air France
F-HPJE	Airbus A.380-861	Air France
F-HPJF	Airbus A.380-861	Air France
F-HPJG	Airbus A.380-861	Air France
F-HPJH	Airbus A.380-861	Air France
F-HPJI	Airbus A.380-861	Air France
F-HPJJ	Airbus A.380-861	Air France
F-HPJK	Airbus A.380-861	Air France
F-HRBA	Boeing 787-9	Air France
F-HRBB	Boeing 787-9	Air France
F-HRBC	Boeing 787-9	Air France
F-HRBD	Boeing 787-9	Air France
F-HRBE	Boeing 787-9	Air France
F-HTVA	Boeing 737-8K2	Transavia France
F-HTVB	Boeing 737-8K2	Transavia France
F-HTVC	Boeing 737-8K2	Transavia France
F-HTVD	Boeing 737-8K2	Transavia France
F-HTVE	Boeing 737-8K2	Transavia France
F-HTVF	Boeing 737-8K2	Transavia France
F-HTVG	Boeing 737-8K2	Transavia France
F-HTVH	Boeing 737-8K2	Transavia France
F-HTVI	Boeing 737-8K2	Transavia France
F-HTVJ	Boeing 737-8K2	Transavia France
F-HZDP	Airbus A.320-214	Air Corsica
F-HZFM	Airbus A.320-214	Air Corsica
F-HZPG	Airbus A.320-214	Air Corsica

HA (Hungary)

Reg	Type	Owner or Operator
HA-FAU	Boeing 737-43QF	ASL Airlines Hungary
HA-FAW	Boeing 737-476F	ASL Airlines Hungary
HA-FAZ	Boeing 737-476SF	ASL Airlines Hungary
HA-KAD	Boeing 737-4YOSF	ASL Airlines Hungary
HA-LKG	Boeing 737-8CX	Travel Service Airlines
HA-LPJ	Airbus A.320-232	Wizz Air
HA-LPK	Airbus A.320-231	Wizz Air
HA-LPL	Airbus A.320-232	Wizz Air
HA-LPM	Airbus A.320-232	Wizz Air

Reg	Type	Owner or Operator	Notes
HA-LPN	Airbus A.320-232	Wizz Air	
HA-LPO	Airbus A.320-232	Wizz Air	
HA-LPQ	Airbus A.320-232	Wizz Air	
HA-LPR	Airbus A.320-232	Wizz Air	
HA-LPS	Airbus A.320-232	Wizz Air	
HA-LPT	Airbus A.320-232	Wizz Air	
HA-LPU	Airbus A.320-232	Wizz Air	
HA-LPV	Airbus A.320-232	Wizz Air	
HA-LPW	Airbus A.320-232	Wizz Air	
HA-LPX	Airbus A.320-232	Wizz Air	
HA-LPY	Airbus A.320-232	Wizz Air	
HA-LPZ	Airbus A.320-232	Wizz Air	
HA-LWA	Airbus A.320-232	Wizz Air	
HA-LWB	Airbus A.320-232	Wizz Air	
HA-LWC	Airbus A.320-232	Wizz Air	
HA-LWD	Airbus A.320-232	Wizz Air	
HA-LWE	Airbus A.320-232	Wizz Air	
HA-LWF	Airbus A.320-232	Wizz Air	
HA-LWG	Airbus A.320-232	Wizz Air	
HA-LWH	Airbus A.320-232	Wizz Air	
HA-LWI	Airbus A.320-214	Wizz Air	
HA-LWJ	Airbus A.320-214	Wizz Air	
HA-LWK	Airbus A.320-232	Wizz Air	
HA-LWL	Airbus A.320-232	Wizz Air	
HA-LWM	Airbus A.320-232	Wizz Air	
HA-LWN	Airbus A.320-232	Wizz Air	
HA-LWO	Airbus A.320-232	Wizz Air	
HA-LWP	Airbus A.320-232	Wizz Air	
HA-LWQ	Airbus A.320-232	Wizz Air	
HA-LWR	Airbus A.320-232	Wizz Air	
HA-LWS	Airbus A.320-232	Wizz Air	
HA-LWT	Airbus A.320-232	Wizz Air	
HA-LWU	Airbus A.320-232	Wizz Air	
HA-LWV	Airbus A.320-232	Wizz Air	
HA-LWX	Airbus A.320-232	Wizz Air	
HA-LWY	Airbus A.320-232	Wizz Air	
HA-LWZ	Airbus A.320-232	Wizz Air	
HA-LXA	Airbus A.321-231	Wizz Air	
HA-LXB	Airbus A.321-231	Wizz Air	
HA-LXC	Airbus A.321-231	Wizz Air	
HA-LXD	Airbus A.321-231	Wizz Air	
HA-LXE	Airbus A.321-231	Wizz Air	
HA-LXF	Airbus A.321-231	Wizz Air	
HA-LXG	Airbus A.321-231	Wizz Air	
HA-LXH	Airbus A.321-231	Wizz Air	
HA-LXI	Airbus A.321-231	Wizz Air	
HA-LXJ	Airbus A.321-231	Wizz Air	
HA-LXK	Airbus A.321-231	Wizz Air	
HA-LXL	Airbus A.321-231	Wizz Air	
HA-LXM	Airbus A.321-231	Wizz Air	
HA-LXN	Airbus A.321-231	Wizz Air	
HA-LXO	Airbus A.321-231	Wizz Air	
HA-LXP	Airbus A.321-231	Wizz Air	
HA-LXQ	Airbus A.321-231	Wizz Air	
HA-LXR	Airbus A.321-231	Wizz Air	
HA-LXS	Airbus A.321-231	Wizz Air	
HA-LXT	Airbus A.321-211	Wizz Air	
HA-LXU	Airbus A.321-231	Wizz Air	
HA-LXV	Airbus A.321-231	Wizz Air	
HA-LXW	Airbus A.321-231	Wizz Air	
HA-LXY	Airbus A.321-231	Wizz Air	
HA-LXZ	Airbus A.321-231	Wizz Air	
HA-LYA	Airbus A.320-232	Wizz Air	
HA-LYB	Airbus A.320-232	Wizz Air	
HA-LYC	Airbus A.320-232	Wizz Air	
HA-LYD	Airbus A.320-232	Wizz Air	
HA-LYE	Airbus A.320-232	Wizz Air	
HA-LYF	Airbus A.320-232	Wizz Air	
HA-LYG	Airbus A.320-232	Wizz Air	
HA-LYH	Airbus A.320-232	Wizz Air	
HA-LYI	Airbus A.320-232	Wizz Air	

Reg	Type	Owner or Operator
HA-LYJ	Airbus A.320-232	Wizz Air
HA-LYK	Airbus A.320-232	Wizz Air
HA-LYL	Airbus A.320-232	Wizz Air
HA-LYM	Airbus A.320-232	Wizz Air
HA-LYN	Airbus A.320-232	Wizz Air
HA-LYO	Airbus A.320-232	Wizz Air
HA-LYP	Airbus A.320-232	Wizz Air
HA-LYQ	Airbus A.320-232	Wizz Air
HA-LYR	Airbus A.320-232	Wizz Air
HA-LYS	Airbus A.320-232	Wizz Air
HA-LYT	Airbus A.320-232	Wizz Air
HA-LYU	Airbus A.320-232	Wizz Air
HA-LYV	Airbus A.320-232	Wizz Air
HA-LYW	Airbus A.320-232	Wizz Air
HA-LYX	Airbus A.320-232	Wizz Air

HB (Switzerland)

Reg	Type	Owner or Operator
HB-AEO	Dornier 328-110	Sky Work Airlines
HB-IHX	Airbus A.320-214	Edelweiss Air *Calvaro*
HB-IHY	Airbus A.320-214	Edelweiss Air *Bluemlisalp*
HB-IHZ	Airbus A.320-214	Edelweiss Air *Viktoria*
HB-IJD	Airbus A.320-214	Swiss International
HB-IJE	Airbus A.320-214	Swiss International *Arosa*
HB-IJH	Airbus A.320-214	Swiss International *Dubendorf*
HB-IJI	Airbus A.320-214	Swiss International *Basodino*
HB-IJJ	Airbus A.320-214	Swiss International *Les Diablerets*
HB-IJK	Airbus A.320-214	Swiss International *Wissigstock*
HB-IJL	Airbus A.320-214	Swiss International *Pizol*
HB-IJM	Airbus A.320-214	Swiss International *Schilthorn*
HB-IJN	Airbus A.320-214	Swiss International *Vanil Noir*
HB-IJO	Airbus A.320-214	Swiss International *Lissengrat*
HB-IJP	Airbus A.320-214	Swiss International *Nollen*
HB-IJQ	Airbus A.320-214	Swiss International *Agassizhorn*
HB-IJR	Airbus A.320-214	Swiss International *Dammastock*
HB-IJS	Airbus A.320-214	Swiss International *Creux du Van*
HB-IJU	Airbus A.320-214	Edelweiss Air
HB-IJV	Airbus A.320-214	Edelweiss Air
HB-IJW	Airbus A.320-214	Edelweiss Air
HB-IOC	Airbus A.321-111	Swiss International *Eiger*
HB-IOD	Airbus A.321-111	Swiss International *Zermatt*
HB-IOF	Airbus A.321-111	Swiss International *Winterthur*
HB-IOH	Airbus A.321-111	Swiss International *Wengen*
HB-IOK	Airbus A.321-111	Swiss International *Biefertenstock*
HB-IOL	Airbus A.321-111	Swiss International *Kaiseregg*
HB-IOM	Airbus A.321-212	Swiss International *Biel/Bienne*
HB-ION	Airbus A.321-212	Swiss International *Lugano*
HB-IOO	Airbus A.321-212	Swiss International
HB-IPT	Airbus A.319-112	Swiss International *Stadel*
HB-IPU	Airbus A.319-112	Swiss International *Hochfelden*
HB-IPV	Airbus A.319-112	Swiss International *Rumlang*
HB-IPX	Airbus A.319-112	Swiss International *Steinmaur*
HB-IPY	Airbus A.319-112	Swiss International *Hori*
HB-IYA	Saab 2000	Sky Work Airlines
HB-IZB	Saab 2000	Sky Work Airlines
HB-IZD	Saab 2000	Sky Work Airlines
HB-IZS	Saab 2000	Sky Work Airlines
HB-JBA	Bombardier CS100	Swiss Global Airlines *Kanton Zurich*
HB-JBB	Bombardier CS100	Swiss Global Airlines *Kanton de Geneve*
HB-JBC	Bombardier CS100	Swiss Global Airlines
HB-JBD	Bombardier CS100	Swiss Global Airlines
HB-JBE	Bombardier CS100	Swiss Global Airlines
HB-JBF	Bombardier CS100	Swiss Global Airlines
HB-JBG	Bombardier CS100	Swiss Global Airlines
HB-JBH	Bombardier CS100	Swiss Global Airlines
HB-JCA	Bombardier CS300	Swiss Global Airlines
HB-JCB	Bombardier CS300	Swiss Global Airlines
HB-JCC	Bombardier CS300	Swiss Global Airlines
HB-JCD	Bombardier CS300	Swiss Global Airlines
HB-JCE	Bombardier CS300	Swiss Global Airlines
HB-JCF	Bombardier CS300	Swiss Global Airlines

Reg	Type	Owner or Operator	Notes
HB-JCG	Bombardier CS300	Swiss Global Airlines	
HB-JCH	Bombardier CS300	Swiss Global Airlines	
HB-JHA	Airbus A.330-343	Swiss International	
HB-JHB	Airbus A.330-343	Swiss International *Sion*	
HB-JHC	Airbus A.330-343	Swiss International *Bellinzona*	
HB-JHD	Airbus A.330-343	Swiss International *St.Gallen*	
HB-JHE	Airbus A.330-343	Swiss International *Fribourg*	
HB-JHF	Airbus A.330-343	Swiss International *Bern*	
HB-JHG	Airbus A.330-343	Swiss International *Glarus*	
HB-JHH	Airbus A.330-343	Swiss International *Neuchatel*	
HB-JHI	Airbus A.330-343	Swiss International *Geneve*	
HB-JHJ	Airbus A.330-343	Swiss International *Appenzell*	
HB-JHK	Airbus A.330-343	Swiss International *Herisau*	
HB-JHL	Airbus A.330-343	Swiss International *Sarnen*	
HB-JHM	Airbus A.330-343	Swiss International	
HB-JHN	Airbus A.330-343	Swiss International	
HB-JJL	Airbus A.320-214	Edelweiss Air	
HB-JJM	Airbus A.320-214	Edelweiss Air	
HB-JLP	Airbus A.320-214	Swiss International *Allschwil*	
HB-JLQ	Airbus A.320-214	Swiss International *Bllach*	
HB-JLR	Airbus A.320-214	Swiss International *Bassersdorf*	
HB-JLS	Airbus A.320-214	Swiss International *Niederhasli*	
HB-JLT	Airbus A.320-214	Swiss International *Grenchen*	
HB-JMA	Airbus A.340-313X	Swiss International *Matterhorn*	
HB-JMB	Airbus A.340-313X	Swiss International *Zurich*	
HB-JMC	Airbus A.340-313X	Swiss International *Basel*	
HB-JMD	Airbus A.340-313X	Swiss International *Liestal*	
HB-JME	Airbus A.340-313X	Swiss International *Dom*	
HB-JMH	Airbus A.340-313X	Swiss International *Chur*	
HB-JMI	Airbus A.340-313X	Swiss International *Schaffhausen*	
HB-JNA	Boeing 777-3DEER	Swiss Global Airlines	
HB-JNB	Boeing 777-3DEER	Swiss Global Airlines	
HB-JNC	Boeing 777-3DEER	Swiss Global Airlines	
HB-JND	Boeing 777-3DEER	Swiss Global Airlines	
HB-JNE	Boeing 777-3DEER	Swiss Global Airlines	
HB-JNF	Boeing 777-3DEER	Swiss Global Airlines	
HB-JNG	Boeing 777-3DEER	Swiss Global Airlines	
HB-JNH	Boeing 777-3DEER	Swiss Global Airlines	
HB-JNI	Boeing 777-3DEER	Swiss Global Airlines	
HB-JNJ	Boeing 777-3DEER	Swiss Global Airlines	
HB-JOG	Airbus A.319-112	Germania	
HB-JOH	Airbus A.319-112	Germania	
HB-JOI	Airbus A.321-211	Germania	
HB-JVC	Fokker 100	Helvetic Airways	
HB-JVE	Fokker 100	Helvetic Airways	
HB-JVF	Fokker 100	Helvetic Airways	
HB-JVG	Fokker 100	Helvetic Airways	
HB-JVH	Fokker 100	Helvetic Airways	
HB-JVL	Embraer ERJ190-100LR	Helvetic Airways	
HB-JVM	Embraer ERJ190-100LR	Helvetic Airways	
HB-JVN	Embraer ERJ190-100LR	Helvetic Airways	
HB-JVO	Embraer ERJ190-100LR	Helvetic Airways	
HB-JVP	Embraer ERJ190-100LR	Helvetic Airways	
HB-JVQ	Embraer ERJ190-100LR	Helvetic Airways	
HB-JVR	Embraer ERJ190-100LR	Helvetic Airways	
HB-JXA	Airbus A.320-214	easyJet Switzerland	
HB-JXB	Airbus A.320-214	easyJet Switzerland	
HB-JXC	Airbus A.320-214	easyJet Switzerland	
HB-JXD	Airbus A.320-214	easyJet Switzerland	
HB-JXE	Airbus A.320-214	easyJet Switzerland	
HB-JXF	Airbus A.320-214	easyJet Switzerland	
HB-JXI	Airbus A.320-214	easyJet Switzerland	
HB-JYA	Airbus A.320-214	easyJet Switzerland	
HB-JYB	Airbus A.319-111	easyJet Switzerland	
HB-JYC	Airbus A.319-111	easyJet Switzerland	
HB-JYD	Airbus A.320-214	easyJet Switzerland	
HB-JYE	Airbus A.320-214	easyJet Switzerland	
HB-JYF	Airbus A.319-111	easyJet Switzerland	
HB-JYG	Airbus A.319-111	easyJet Switzerland	
HB-JYH	Airbus A.319-111	easyJet Switzerland	
HB-JYI	Airbus A.319-111	easyJet Switzerland	

Notes	Reg	Type	Owner or Operator
	HB-JYJ	Airbus A.319-111	easyJet Switzerland
	HB-JYK	Airbus A.319-111	easyJet Switzerland
	HB-JYL	Airbus A.319-111	easyJet Switzerland
	HB-JYM	Airbus A.319-111	easyJet Switzerland
	HB-JYN	Airbus A.319-111	easyJet Switzerland
	HB-JZR	Airbus A.320-214	easyJet Switzerland
	HB-JZX	Airbus A.320-214	easyJet Switzerland
	HB-JZY	Airbus A.320-214	easyJet Switzerland
	HB-JZZ	Airbus A.320-214	easyJet Switzerland

HL (Korea)

Notes	Reg	Type	Owner or Operator
	HL7202	Boeing 777-3B5EER	Korean Air
	HL7203	Boeing 777-3B5EER	Korean Air
	HL7413	Boeing 747-48EBCF	Asiana Airlines Cargo
	HL7415	Boeing 747-48EBCF	Asiana Airlines Cargo
	HL7417	Boeing 747-48EBCF	Asiana Airlines Cargo
	HL7418	Boeing 747-4BEBCF	Asiana Airlines Cargo
	HL7419	Boeing 747-48EF (SCD)	Asiana Airlines Cargo
	HL7420	Boeing 747-48EF (SCD)	Asiana Airlines Cargo
	HL7421	Boeing 747-48EBSF	Asiana Airlines Cargo
	HL7423	Boeing 747-48EBSF	Asiana Airlines Cargo
	HL7436	Boeing 747-48EF (SCD)	Asiana Airlines Cargo
	HL7578	Airbus A.350-941	Asiana Airlines
	HL7579	Airbus A.350-941	Asiana Airlines
	HL7611	Airbus A.380-861	Korean Air
	HL7612	Airbus A.380-861	Korean Air
	HL7613	Airbus A.380-861	Korean Air
	HL7614	Airbus A.380-861	Korean Air
	HL7615	Airbus A.380-861	Korean Air
	HL7616	Boeing 747-446F	Asiana Airlines Cargo
	HL7618	Boeing 747-446F	Asiana Airlines Cargo
	HL7619	Airbus A.380-861	Korean Air
	HL7620	Boeing 747-419F	Asiana Airlines Cargo
	HL7621	Airbus A.380-861	Korean Air
	HL7622	Airbus A.380-861	Korean Air
	HL7627	Airbus A.380-861	Korean Air
	HL7628	Airbus A.380-861	Korean Air
	HL7700	Boeing 777-28EER	Asiana Airlines
	HL7732	Boeing 777-28EER	Asiana Airlines
	HL7739	Boeing 777-28EER	Asiana Airlines
	HL7755	Boeing 777-28EER	Asiana Airlines
	HL7756	Boeing 777-28EER	Asiana Airlines
	HL7775	Boeing 777-28EER	Asiana Airlines
	HL7782	Boeing 777-3B5ER	Korean Air
	HL7783	Boeing 777-3B5ER	Korean Air
	HL7784	Boeing 777-3B5ER	Korean Air
	HL7791	Boeing 777-28EER	Asiana Airlines
	HL8005	Boeing 777-FB5	Korean Air Cargo
	HL8006	Boeing 777-3B5ER	Korean Air
	HL8007	Boeing 777-3B5ER	Korean Air
	HL8008	Boeing 777-3B5ER	Korean Air
	HL8009	Boeing 777-3B5ER	Korean Air
	HL8010	Boeing 777-3B5ER	Korean Air
	HL8011	Boeing 777-3B5ER	Korean Air
	HL8041	Boeing 777-3B5ER	Korean Air
	HL8042	Boeing 777-3B5ER	Korean Air
	HL8043	Boeing 777-FB5	Korean Air Cargo
	HL8044	Boeing 777-FB5	Korean Air Cargo
	HL8045	Boeing 777-FB5	Korean Air Cargo
	HL8046	Boeing 777-FB5	Korean Air Cargo
	HL8075	Boeing 777-FB5	Korean Air Cargo
	HL8076	Boeing 777-FB5	Korean Air Cargo
	HL8077	Boeing 777-FB5	Korean Air Cargo
	HL8078	Airbus A.350-941	Asiana Airlines
	HL8079	Airbus A.350-941	Asiana Airlines
	HL8208	Boeing 777-3B5ER	Korean Air
	HL8209	Boeing 777-3B5ER	Korean Air
	HL8210	Boeing 777-3B5ER	Korean Air
	HL8216	Boeing 777-3B5ER	Korean Air
	HL8217	Boeing 777-3B5ER	Korean Air

Reg	Type	Owner or Operator	Notes
HL8218	Boeing 777-3B5ER	Korean Air	
HL8226	Boeing 777-FB5	Korean Air Cargo	
HL8250	Boeing 777-3B5ER	Korean Air	
HL8251	Boeing 777-FB5	Korean Air Cargo	
HL8252	Boeing 777-FB5	Korean Air Cargo	
HL8254	Boeing 777-28EER	Asiana Airlines	
HL8274	Boeing 777-3B5ER	Korean Air	
HL8275	Boeing 777-3B5ER	Korean Air	
HL8284	Boeing 777-28EER	Asiana Airlines	
HL8285	Boeing 777-FB5	Korean Air Cargo	

HS (Thailand)

Reg	Type	Owner or Operator	Notes
HS-THB	Airbus A.350-941	Thai Airways International	
HS-THC	Airbus A.350-941	Thai Airways International	
HS-THD	Airbus A.350-941	Thai Airways International	
HS-THE	Airbus A.350-941	Thai Airways International	
HS-THF	Airbus A.350-941	Thai Airways International	
HS-THG	Airbus A.350-941	Thai Airways International	
HS-THH	Airbus A.350-941	Thai Airways International	
HS-THJ	Airbus A.350-941	Thai Airways International	
HS-THK	Airbus A.350-941	Thai Airways International	
HS-THL	Airbus A.350-941	Thai Airways International	
HS-THM	Airbus A.350-941	Thai Airways International	
HS-THN	Airbus A.350-941	Thai Airways International	
HS-TKK	Boeing 777-3ALER	Thai Airways International	
HS-TKL	Boeing 777-3ALER	Thai Airways International	
HS-TKM	Boeing 777-3ALER	Thai Airways International	
HS-TKN	Boeing 777-3ALER	Thai Airways International	
HS-TKO	Boeing 777-3ALER	Thai Airways International	
HS-TKP	Boeing 777-3ALER	Thai Airways International	
HS-TKQ	Boeing 777-3ALER	Thai Airways International	
HS-TKR	Boeing 777-3ALER	Thai Airways International	
HS-TKU	Boeing 777-3D7ER	Thai Airways International	
HS-TKV	Boeing 777-3D7ER	Thai Airways International	
HS-TKW	Boeing 777-3D7ER	Thai Airways International	
HS-TKX	Boeing 777-3D7ER	Thai Airways International	
HS-TKY	Boeing 777-3D7ER	Thai Airways International	
HS-TKZ	Boeing 777-3D7ER	Thai Airways International	
HS-TUA	Airbus A.380-841	Thai Airways International	
HS-TUB	Airbus A.380-841	Thai Airways International	
HS-TUC	Airbus A.380-841	Thai Airways International	
HS-TUD	Airbus A.380-861	Thai Airways International	
HS-TUE	Airbus A.380-861	Thai Airways International	
HS-TUF	Airbus A.380-861	Thai Airways International	

HZ (Saudi Arabia)

Reg	Type	Owner or Operator	Notes
HZ-AK11	Boeing 777-368ER	Saudi Arabian Airlines	
HZ-AK12	Boeing 777-368ER	Saudi Arabian Airlines	
HZ-AK13	Boeing 777-368ER	Saudi Arabian Airlines	
HZ-AK14	Boeing 777-368ER	Saudi Arabian Airlines	
HZ-AK15	Boeing 777-368ER	Saudi Arabian Airlines	
HZ-AK16	Boeing 777-368ER	Saudi Arabian Airlines	
HZ-AK17	Boeing 777-368ER	Saudi Arabian Airlines	
HZ-AK18	Boeing 777-368ER	Saudi Arabian Airlines	
HZ-AK19	Boeing 777-368ER	Saudi Arabian Airlines	
HZ-AK20	Boeing 777-368ER	Saudi Arabian Airlines	
HZ-AK21	Boeing 777-368ER	Saudi Arabian Airlines	
HZ-AK22	Boeing 777-368ER	Saudi Arabian Airlines	
HZ-AK23	Boeing 777-368ER	Saudi Arabian Airlines	
HZ-AK24	Boeing 777-368ER	Saudi Arabian Airlines	
HZ-AK25	Boeing 777-368ER	Saudi Arabian Airlines	
HZ-AK26	Boeing 777-368ER	Saudi Arabian Airlines	
HZ-AK27	Boeing 777-368ER	Saudi Arabian Airlines	
HZ-AK28	Boeing 777-368ER	Saudi Arabian Airlines	
HZ-AK29	Boeing 777-368ER	Saudi Arabian Airlines	
HZ-AK30	Boeing 777-368ER	Saudi Arabian Airlines	
HZ-AK31	Boeing 777-3FGER	Saudi Arabian Airlines	
HZ-AK32	Boeing 777-3FGER	Saudi Arabian Airlines	

OVERSEAS AIRLINERS

Notes	Reg	Type	Owner or Operator
	HZ-AK33	Boeing 777-3FGER	Saudi Arabian Airlines
	HZ-AK34	Boeing 777-3FGER	Saudi Arabian Airlines
	HZ-AK35	Boeing 777-3FGER	Saudi Arabian Airlines
	HZ-AK36	Boeing 777-3FGER	Saudi Arabian Airlines
	HZ-AK37	Boeing 777-3FGER	Saudi Arabian Airlines
	HZ-AK38	Boeing 777-3FGER	Saudi Arabian Airlines
	HZ-AK39	Boeing 777-3FGER	Saudi Arabian Airlines
	HZ-AK40	Boeing 777-3FGER	Saudi Arabian Airlines
	HZ-AK41	Boeing 777-3FGER	Saudi Arabian Airlines
	HZ-AK42	Boeing 777-3FGER	Saudi Arabian Airlines
	HZ-AK43	Boeing 777-3FGER	Saudi Arabian Airlines
	HZ-AK44	Boeing 777-3FGER	Saudi Arabian Airlines
	HZ-AK45	Boeing 777-3FGER	Saudi Arabian Airlines
	HZ-AR11	Boeing 787-9	Saudi Arabian Airlines
	HZ-AR12	Boeing 787-9	Saudi Arabian Airlines
	HZ-AR13	Boeing 787-9	Saudi Arabian Airlines
	HZ-AR14	Boeing 787-9	Saudi Arabian Airlines
	HZ-ARA	Boeing 787-9	Saudi Arabian Airlines
	HZ-ARB	Boeing 787-9	Saudi Arabian Airlines
	HZ-ARC	Boeing 787-9	Saudi Arabian Airlines
	HZ-ARD	Boeing 787-9	Saudi Arabian Airlines
	HZ-ARE	Boeing 787-9	Saudi Arabian Airlines
	HZ-ARF	Boeing 787-9	Saudi Arabian Airlines
	HZ-ARG	Boeing 787-9	Saudi Arabian Airlines
	HZ-ARH	Boeing 787-9	Saudi Arabian Airlines

I (Italy)

Notes	Reg	Type	Owner or Operator
	I-ADJK	Embraer ERJ190-200LR	Air Dolomiti
	I-ADJL	Embraer ERJ190-200LR	Air Dolomiti
	I-ADJM	Embraer ERJ190-200LR	Air Dolomiti
	I-ADJN	Embraer ERJ190-200LR	Air Dolomiti
	I-ADJO	Embraer ERJ190-200LR	Air Dolomiti
	I-ADJP	Embraer ERJ190-200LR	Air Dolomiti
	I-ADJQ	Embraer ERJ190-200LR	Air Dolomiti
	I-ADJR	Embraer ERJ190-200LR	Air Dolomiti
	I-ADJS	Embraer ERJ190-200LR	Air Dolomiti
	I-ADJT	Embraer ERJ190-200LR	Air Dolomiti
	I-ADJU	Embraer ERJ190-200LR	Air Dolomiti
	I-BIKA	Airbus A.320-214	Alitalia *Johann Sebastian Bach*
	I-BIKC	Airbus A.320-214	Alitalia *Zefiro*
	I-BIKD	Airbus A.320-214	Alitalia *Maestrale*
	I-BIKI	Airbus A.320-214	Alitalia *Girolamo Frescobaldi*
	I-BIKO	Airbus A.320-214	Alitalia *George Bizet*
	I-BIMA	Airbus A.319-112	Alitalia *Isola d'Elba*
	I-BIXK	Airbus A.321-112	Alitalia *Piazza Ducale Vigevano*
	I-BIXL	Airbus A.321-112	Alitalia *Piazza del Duomo Lecce*
	I-BIXM	Airbus A.321-112	Alitalia *Piazza di San Franceso Assisi*
	I-BIXN	Airbus A.321-112	Alitalia *Piazza del Duomo Catania*
	I-BIXP	Airbus A.321-112	Alitalia *Carlo Morelli*
	I-BIXQ	Airbus A.321-112	Alitalia *Domenico Colapietro*
	I-BIXR	Airbus A.321-112	Alitalia *Piazza dell Campidoglio-Roma*
	I-BIXS	Airbus A.321-112	Alitalia *Piazza San Martino-Lucca*
	I-DISU	Boeing 777-243ER	Alitalia *Madonna di Campiglio*
	I-EJGA	Airbus A.330-202	Alitalia
	I-EJGB	Airbus A.330-202	Alitalia
	I-NDDL	Boeing 767-324ER	Neos
	I-NDMJ	Boeing 767-306ER	Neos
	I-NDOF	Boeing 767-306ER	Neos
	I-NEOT	Boeing 737-86N	Neos
	I-NEOU	Boeing 737-86N	Neos
	I-NEOW	Boeing 737-86N	Neos
	I-NEOX	Boeing 737-86N	Neos
	I-NEOZ	Boeing 737-86N	Neos *Monte Rosa*
	I-SWIA	Boeing 747-4R7F	Silk Way Italia Airlines
	I-SWIB	Boeing 747-4R7F	Silk Way Italia Airlines

JA (Japan)

Notes	Reg	Type	Owner or Operator
	JA731A	Boeing 777-381ER	All Nippon Airways

Reg	Type	Owner or Operator	Notes
JA731J	Boeing 777-346ER	Japan Airlines	
JA732A	Boeing 777-381ER	All Nippon Airways	
JA732J	Boeing 777-346ER	Japan Airlines	
JA733A	Boeing 777-381ER	All Nippon Airways	
JA733J	Boeing 777-346ER	Japan Airlines	
JA734A	Boeing 777-381ER	All Nippon Airways	
JA734J	Boeing 777-346ER	Japan Airlines	
JA735A	Boeing 777-381ER	All Nippon Airways	
JA735J	Boeing 777-346ER	Japan Airlines	
JA736A	Boeing 777-381ER	All Nippon Airways	
JA736J	Boeing 777-346ER	Japan Airlines	
JA737J	Boeing 777-346ER	Japan Airlines	
JA738J	Boeing 777-346ER	Japan Airlines	
JA739J	Boeing 777-346ER	Japan Airlines	
JA740J	Boeing 777-346ER	Japan Airlines	
JA741J	Boeing 777-346ER	Japan Airlines	
JA742J	Boeing 777-346ER	Japan Airlines	
JA743J	Boeing 777-346ER	Japan Airlines	
JA777A	Boeing 777-381ER	All Nippon Airways	
JA778A	Boeing 777-381ER	All Nippon Airways	
JA779A	Boeing 777-381ER	All Nippon Airways	
JA780A	Boeing 777-381ER	All Nippon Airways	
JA781A	Boeing 777-381ER	All Nippon Airways	
JA782A	Boeing 777-381ER	All Nippon Airways	
JA783A	Boeing 777-381ER	All Nippon Airways	
JA784A	Boeing 777-381ER	All Nippon Airways	
JA785A	Boeing 777-381ER	All Nippon Airways	
JA786A	Boeing 777-381ER	All Nippon Airways	
JA787A	Boeing 777-381ER	All Nippon Airways	
JA788A	Boeing 777-381ER	All Nippon Airways	
JA789A	Boeing 777-381ER	All Nippon Airways	
JA790A	Boeing 777-381ER	All Nippon Airways	
JA791A	Boeing 777-381ER	All Nippon Airways	
JA792A	Boeing 777-381ER	All Nippon Airways	
JA837J	Boeing 787-8	Japan Airlines	
JA839J	Boeing 787-8	Japan Airlines	
JA841J	Boeing 787-8	Japan Airlines	
JA842J	Boeing 787-8	Japan Airlines	
JA845J	Boeing 787-8	Japan Airlines	

JY (Jordan)

Reg	Type	Owner or Operator	Notes
JY-AYL	Airbus A.319-132	Royal Jordanian	
JY-AYM	Airbus A.319-132	Royal Jordanian	
JY-AYN	Airbus A.319-132	Royal Jordanian	
JY-AYP	Airbus A.319-132	Royal Jordanian	
JY-AYQ	Airbus A.320-232	Royal Jordanian	
JY-AYR	Airbus A.320-232	Royal Jordanian	
JY-AYS	Airbus A.320-232	Royal Jordanian	
JY-AYT	Aitbus A.321-231	Royal Jordanian	
JY-AYU	Airbus A.320-232	Royal Jordanian	
JY-AYV	Airbus A.321-231	Royal Jordanian	
JY-AYW	Airbus A.320-232	Royal Jordanian	
JY-AYX	Airbus A.320-232	Royal Jordanian	
JY-BAA	Boeing 787-8	Royal Jordanian	
JY-BAB	Boeing 787-8	Royal Jordanian	
JY-BAC	Boeing 787-8	Royal Jordanian	
JY-BAE	Boeing 787-8	Royal Jordanian	
JY-BAF	Boeing 787-8	Royal Jordanian	
JY-BAG	Boeing 787-8	Royal Jordanian	
JY-BAH	Boeing 787-8	Royal Jordanian	
JY-BAI	Boeing 787-9	Royal Jordanian	

LN (Norway)

Reg	Type	Owner or Operator	Notes
LN-DYA	Boeing 737-8JP	Norwegian Air Shuttle *Erik Bye*	
LN-DYB	Boeing 737-8JP	Norwegian Air Shuttle *Bjornstjerne Bjornson*	
LN-DYC	Boeing 737-8JP	Norwegian Air Shuttle Max Manus	
LN-DYD	Boeing 737-8JP	Norwegian Air Shuttle *Hans Christian Andersen*	
LN-DYE	Boeing 737-8JP	Norwegian Air Shuttle *Arne Jacobsen*	

OVERSEAS AIRLINERS

Notes	Reg	Type	Owner or Operator
	LN-DYF	Boeing 737-8JP	Norwegian Air Shuttle *Fridtjof Nansen*
	LN-DYG	Boeing 737-8JP	Norwegian Air Shuttle *Jenny Lind*
	LN-DYN	Boeing 737-8JP	Norwegian Air Shuttle *Karen Blixen*
	LN-DYO	Boeing 737-8JP	Norwegian Air Shuttle *Otto Sverdrup*
	LN-DYP	Boeing 737-8JP	Norwegian Air Shuttle *Aksel Sandemose*
	LN-DYQ	Boeing 737-8JP	Norwegian Air Shuttle *Helge Ingstad*
	LN-DYT	Boeing 737-8JP	Norwegian Air Shuttle *Kirsten Flagstad*
	LN-DYU	Boeing 737-8JP	Norwegian Air Shuttle *Jorn Utzon*
	LN-DYV	Boeing 737-8JP	Norwegian Air Shuttle *Elsa Beskow*
	LN-DYW	Boeing 737-8JP	Norwegian Air Shuttle *Thorbjorn Egner*
	LN-DYZ	Boeing 737-8JP	Norwegian Air Shuttle *Aril Edvardsen*
	LN-LNA	Boeing 787-8	Norwegian Air International
	LN-LNB	Boeing 787-8	Norwegian Air International
	LN-LNC	Boeing 787-8	Norwegian Air International
	LN-LND	Boeing 787-8	Norwegian Air International
	LN-LNE	Boeing 787-8	Norwegian Air International
	LN-LNF	Boeing 787-8	Norwegian Air International
	LN-LNG	Boeing 787-8	Norwegian Air International
	LN-LNH	Boeing 787-8	Norwegian Air International
	LN-LNI	Boeing 787-9	Norwegian Air International
	LN-LNJ	Boeing 787-9	Norwegian Air International
	LN-LNK	Boeing 787-9	Norwegian Air International
	LN-LNL	Boeing 787-9	Norwegian Air International
	LN-LNN	Boeing 787-9	Norwegian Air International
	LN-NGA	Boeing 737-8JP	Norwegian Air Shuttle *Ludwig Walentin Karlsen*
	LN-NGB	Boeing 737-8JP	Norwegian Air Shuttle *Geirr Tveitt*
	LN-NGC	Boeing 737-8JP	Norwegian Air Shuttle *Jens Glad Balchen*
	LN-NGD	Boeing 737-8JP	Norwegian Air Shuttle *Ivo Caprino*
	LN-NGE	Boeing 737-8JP	Norwegian Air Shuttle
	LN-NGF	Boeing 737-8JP	Norwegian Air Shuttle *H. C. Orsted*
	LN-NGG	Boeing 737-8JP	Norwegian Air Shuttle *Gunnar Sonsteby*
	LN-NGN	Boeing 737-8JP	Norwegian Air Shuttle *Georg Sverdrup*
	LN-NGO	Boeing 737-8JP	Norwegian Air Shuttle *Victor Borge*
	LN-NGP	Boeing 737-8JP	Norwegian Air Shuttle *Ivar Aasen*
	LN-NGQ	Boeing 737-8JP	Norwegian Air Shuttle
	LN-NGR	Boeing 737-8JP	Norwegian Air Shuttle
	LN-NGS	Boeing 737-8JP	Norwegian Air Shuttle *Regine Normann*
	LN-NGT	Boeing 737-8JP	Norwegian Air Shuttle *Anton K. H. Jakobsen*
	LN-NGU	Boeing 737-8JP	Norwegian Air Shuttle *Harry S. Pettersen*
	LN-NGV	Boeing 737-8JP	Norwegian Air Shuttle
	LN-NGW	Boeing 737-8JP	Norwegian Air Shuttle *Theodor Kittelsen*
	LN-NGX	Boeing 737-8JP	Norwegian Air Shuttle
	LN-NGY	Boeing 737-8JP	Norwegian Air Shuttle *Sigrid Undset*
	LN-NGZ	Boeing 737-8JP	Norwegian Air Shuttle
	LN-NHA	Boeing 737-8JP	Norwegian Air Shuttle
	LN-NHB	Boeing 737-8JP	Norwegian Air Shuttle
	LN-NHC	Boeing 737-8JP	Norwegian Air Shuttle
	LN-NHD	Boeing 737-8JP	Norwegian Air Shuttle
	LN-NHE	Boeing 737-8JP	Norwegian Air Shuttle
	LN-NHF	Boeing 737-8JP	Norwegian Air Shuttle
	LN-NHG	Boeing 737-8JP	Norwegian Air Shuttle
	LN-NIA	Boeing 737-8JP	Norwegian Air Shuttle *Johan Ludwig Runeberg*
	LN-NIB	Boeing 737-8JP	Norwegian Air Shuttle *Helmer Hanssen*
	LN-NIC	Boeing 737-8JP	Norwegian Air Shuttle *Fredrikke Marie Qvam*
	LN-NID	Boeing 737-8JP	Norwegian Air Shuttle
	LN-NIE	Boeing 737-8JP	Norwegian Air Shuttle *Asta Nielsen*
	LN-NIG	Boeing 737-8JP	Norwegian Air Shuttle *Juan Sebastian Elcano*
	LN-NIH	Boeing 737-8JP	Norwegian Air Shuttle *Cristopher Columbus*
	LN-NII	Boeing 737-8JP	Norwegian Air Shuttle *Jacob Ellehammer*
	LN-NIJ	Boeing 737-8JP	Norwegian Air Shuttle
	LN-RCN	Boeing 737-883	SAS *Hedrun Viking*
	LN-RCT	Boeing 737-683	SAS *Fridlev Viking*
	LN-RCX	Boeing 737-883	SAS *Hottur Viking*
	LN-RCY	Boeing 737-883	SAS *Eylime Viking*
	LN-RCZ	Boeing 737-883	SAS *Glitne Viking*
	LN-RDV	DHC.8-402 Dash Eight	Wideroe's Flyveselskap
	LN-RDY	DHC.8-402 Dash Eight	Wideroe's Flyveselskap
	LN-RDZ	DHC.8-402 Dash Eight	Wideroe's Flyveselskap
	LN-RGA	Boeing 737-883	SAS *Svarthofde Viking*
	LN-RGB	Boeing 737-883	SAS *Benedicte Viking*
	LN-RGC	Boeing 737-883	SAS *Cecilia Viking*

Reg	Type	Owner or Operator	Notes
LN-RGD	Boeing 737-883	SAS *Dygve Viking*	
LN-RGE	Boeing 737-883	SAS *Egil Viking*	
LN-RGF	Boeing 737-883	SAS *Torolf Viking*	
LN-RGG	Boeing 737-883	SAS *Asgerd Viking*	
LN-RGH	Boeing 737-883	SAS *Odvar Viking*	
LN-RGI	Boeing 737-883	SAS *Turid Viking*	
LN-RGK	Boeing 737-683	SAS *Vile Viking*	
LN-RGL	Airbus A.320-251N	SAS *Sol Viking*	
LN-RGM	Airbus A.320-251N	SAS *Silje Viking*	
LN-RGN	Airbus A.320-251N	SAS *Ulrik Viking*	
LN-RGO	Airbus A.320-251N	SAS *Brage Viking*	
LN-RKF	Airbus A.340-313X	SAS *Godfred Viking*	
LN-RKG	Airbus A.340-313X	SAS *Gudrod Viking*	
LN-RKH	Airbus A.330-343X	SAS *Emund Viking*	
LN-RKI	Airbus A.321-231	SAS *Gunnhild Viking*	
LN-RKK	Airbus A.321-231	SAS *Svipdag Viking*	
LN-RKM	Airbus A.330-343	SAS *Eystein Viking*	
LN-RKN	Airbus A.330-343	SAS *Erik Viking*	
LN-RKO	Airbus A.330-343	SAS *Sigrid Viking*	
LN-RKP	Airbus A.340-313	SAS *Torfinn Viking*	
LN-RKR	Airbus A.330-343	SAS *Tore Viking*	
LN-RKS	Airbus A.330-343	SAS *Frithiof Viking*	
LN-RKT	Airbus A.330-343	SAS *Bele Viking*	
LN-RKU	Airbus A.330-343	SAS *Helge Viking*	
LN-RNN	Boeing 737-783	SAS *Borgny Viking*	
LN-RNO	Boeing 737-783	SAS *Gjuke Viking*	
LN-RNU	Boeing 737-783	SAS *Hans Viking*	
LN-RNW	Boeing 737-783	SAS *Granmar Viking*	
LN-RPE	Boeing 737-683	SAS *Edla Viking*	
LN-RPF	Boeing 737-683	SAS *Frede Viking*	
LN-RPG	Boeing 737-683	SAS *Geirmund Viking*	
LN-RPJ	Boeing 737-783	SAS *Grimhild Viking*	
LN-RPK	Boeing 737-783	SAS *Heimer Viking*	
LN-RPL	Boeing 737-883	SAS *Svanevit Viking*	
LN-RPM	Boeing 737-883	SAS *Frigg Viking*	
LN-RPN	Boeing 737-883	SAS *Bergfora Viking*	
LN-RPO	Boeing 737-883	SAS *Thorleif Viking*	
LN-RPR	Boeing 737-883	SAS *Ore Viking*	
LN-RRA	Boeing 737-783	SAS *Steinar Viking*	
LN-RRB	Boeing 737-783	SAS *Cecilia Viking*	
LN-RRD	Boeing 737-683	SAS *Embla Viking*	
LN-RRE	Boeing 737-883	SAS *Knut Viking*	
LN-RRF	Boeing 737-883	SAS *Froydis Viking*	
LN-RRG	Boeing 737-883	SAS *Einar Viking*	
LN-RRH	Boeing 737-883	SAS *Freja Viking*	
LN-RRJ	Boeing 737-883	SAS *Frida Viking*	
LN-RRK	Boeing 737-883	SAS *Gerud Viking*	
LN-RRL	Boeing 737-883	SAS *Jarlabanke Viking*	
LN-RRM	Boeing 737-783	SAS *Erland Viking*	
LN-RRN	Boeing 737-783	SAS *Solveig Viking*	
LN-RRO	Boeing 737-683	SAS *Bernt Viking*	
LN-RRP	Boeing 737-683	SAS *Vilborg Viking*	
LN-RRS	Boeing 737-883	SAS *Ymir Viking*	
LN-RRT	Boeing 737-883	SAS *Lodyn Viking*	
LN-RRU	Boeing 737-883	SAS *Vingolf Viking*	
LN-RRW	Boeing 737-883	SAS *Saga Viking*	
LN-RRX	Boeing 737-683	SAS *Ragnfast Viking*	
LN-RRY	Boeing 737-683	SAS *Signe Viking*	
LN-RRZ	Boeing 737-683	SAS *Gisla Viking*	
LN-TUA	Boeing 737-705	SAS *Ingeborg Eriksdatter*	
LN-TUF	Boeing 737-705	SAS *Tyra Haraldsdatter*	
LN-TUJ	Boeing 737-705	SAS *Eirik Blodoks*	
LN-TUK	Boeing 737-705	SAS *Inge Bardsson*	
LN-TUL	Boeing 737-705	SAS *Haakon IV Haakonson*	
LN-TUM	Boeing 737-705	SAS *Oystein Magnusson*	
LN-WDE	DHC.8-402 Dash Eight	Wideroe's Flyveselskap	
LN-WDF	DHC.8-402 Dash Eight	Wideroe's Flyveselskap	
LN-WDG	DHC.8-402 Dash Eight	Wideroe's Flyveselskap	
LN-WDH	DHC.8-402 Dash Eight	Wideroe's Flyveselskap	
LN-WDI	DHC.8-402 Dash Eight	Wideroe's Flyveselskap	
LN-WDJ	DHC.8-402 Dash Eight	Wideroe's Flyveselskap	

OVERSEAS AIRLINERS

Notes	Reg	Type	Owner or Operator
	LN-WDK	DHC.8-402 Dash Eight	Wideroe's Flyveselskap
	LN-WDL	DHC.8-402 Dash Eight	Wideroe's Flyveselskap
	LN-WFC	DHC.8-311 Dash Eight	Wideroe's Flyveselskap
	LN-WFH	DHC.8-311 Dash Eight	Wideroe's Flyveselskap
	LN-WFO	DHC.8Q-311 Dash Eight	Wideroe's Flyveselskap
	LN-WFP	DHC.8Q-311 Dash Eight	Wideroe's Flyveselskap
	LN-WFS	DHC.8Q-311 Dash Eight	Wideroe's Flyveselskap
	LN-WFT	DHC.8Q-311 Dash Eight	Wideroe's Flyveselskap
	LN-WFU	DHC.8Q-311 Dash Eight	Wideroe's Flyveselskap

LX (Luxembourg)

Notes	Reg	Type	Owner or Operator
	LX-ECV	Boeing 747-4HQERF	Cargolux
	LX-FCL	Boeing 747-467F	Cargolux
	LX-GCL	Boeing 747-467F	Cargolux
	LX-ICL	Boeing 747-467F	Cargolux
	LX-JCV	Boeing 747-4EVERF	Cargolux
	LX-LBA	Boeing 737-8C9	Luxair
	LX-LBB	Boeing 737-86J	Luxair
	LX-LGE	DHC.8Q-402 Dash Eight	Luxair
	LX-LGF	DHC.8Q-402 Dash Eight	Luxair
	LX-LGG	DHC.8Q-402 Dash Eight	Luxair
	LX-LGM	DHC.8Q-402 Dash Eight	Luxair
	LX-LGN	DHC.8Q-402 Dash Eight	Luxair
	LX-LGQ	Boeing 737-7C9	Luxair *Chateau de Burg*
	LX-LGS	Boeing 737-7C9	Luxair *Chateau de Senningen*
	LX-LGU	Boeing 737-8C9	Luxair
	LX-LGV	Boeing 737-8C9	Luxair
	LX-LQA	DHC.8Q-402 Dash Eight	Luxair
	LX-LQB	DHC.8Q-402 Dash Eight	Luxair
	LX-LQC	DHC.8Q-402 Dash Eight	Luxair
	LX-LQD	DHC.8Q-402 Dash Eight	Luxair
	LX-LQI	DHC.8Q-402 Dash Eight	Luxair
	LX-LQJ	DHC.8Q-402 Dash Eight	Luxair
	LX-OCV	Boeing 747-4R7F (SCD)	Cargolux Italia
	LX-RCV	Boeing 747-4R7F (SCD)	Cargolux Italia
	LX-SCV	Boeing 747-4R7F (SCD)	Cargolux *City of Niederanven*
	LX-TCV	Boeing 747-4R7F (SCD)	Cargolux Italia
	LX-UCV	Boeing 747-4R7F (SCD)	Cargolux *City of Bertragne*
	LX-VCA	Boeing 747-8R7F	Cargolux *City of Vianden*
	LX-VCB	Boeing 747-8R7F	Cargolux *City of Esch-sur-Aizette*
	LX-VCC	Boeing 747-8R7F	Cargolux *City of Ettelbruck*
	LX-VCD	Boeing 747-8R7F	Cargolux *City of Luxembourg*
	LX-VCE	Boeing 747-8R7F	Cargolux *City of Echternach*
	LX-VCF	Boeing 747-8R7F	Cargolux *City of Grevenmacher*
	LX-VCG	Boeing 747-8R7F	Cargolux *City of Diekirch*
	LX-VCH	Boeing 747-8R7F	Cargolux *City of Dudelange*
	LX-VCI	Boeing 747-8R7F	Cargolux *City of Troisvierges*
	LX-VCJ	Boeing 747-8R7F	Cargolux *City of Zhengzhou*
	LX-VCK	Boeing 747-8R7F	Cargolux *City of Contern*
	LX-VCL	Boeing 747-8R7F	Cargolux *Joe Sutter-Father of the Boeing 747*
	LX-VCM	Boeing 747-8R7F	Cargolux*City of Redange-sur-Attert*
	LX-VCN	Boeing 747-8R7F	Cargolux *Spirit of Schengen*
	LX-VCV	Boeing 747-4R7F (SCD)	Cargolux *City of Walferdange*
	LX-WCV	Boeing 747-4R7F (SCD)	Cargolux *City of Petange*
	LX-YCV	Boeing 747-4R7F	Cargolux Italia

LY (Lithuania)

Notes	Reg	Type	Owner or Operator
	LY-GGC	Boeing 737-3Q8	Grand Cru Airlines
	LY-LGC	Boeing 737-382	Grand Cru Airlines
	LY-MGC	Boeing 737-4YO	Grand Cru Airlines
	LY-ONJ	Airbus A.320-214	Small Planet Airlines
	LY-ONL	Airbus A.320-214	Small Planet Airlines
	LY-SPA	Airbus A.320-232	Small Planet Airlines
	LY-SPB	Airbus A.320-232	Small Planet Airlines
	LY-SPC	Airbus A.320-231	Grand Cru Airlines
	LY-SPD	Airbus A.320-232	Small Planet Airlines
	LY-SPF	Airbus A.320-214	Small Planet Airlines
	LY-SPH	Airbus A.320-214	Small Planet Airlines

Reg	Type	Owner or Operator	Notes
LY-SPI	Airbus A.320-214	Small Planet Airlines	
LY-VEE	Airbus A.321-211	Avion Express	
LY-VEF	Airbus A.321-211	Avion Express	
LY-VEG	Airbus A.321-211	Avion Express	
LY-VEI	Airbus A.320-233	Avion Express	
LY-VEL	Airbus A.320-232	Avion Express	
LY-VEN	Airbus A.320-233	Avion Express	
LY-VEO	Airbus A.320-233	Avion Express	
LY-VEP	Airbus A.320-233	Avion Express	
LY-VEV	Airbus A.320-211	Avion Express	

LZ (Bulgaria)

LZ-AOA	Airbus A.319-112	Bulgarian Eagle	
LZ-BHG	Airbus A.320-232	BH Air	
LZ-BHH	Airbus A.320-232	BH Air	
LZ-BHI	Airbus A.320-232	BH Air	
LZ-BUR	Embraer ERJ190-100IGW	Bulgaria Air	
LZ-FBA	Airbus A.319-112	Bulgaria Air	
LZ-FBB	Airbus A.319-112	Bulgaria Air	
LZ-FBC	Airbus A.320-214	Bulgaria Air	
LZ-FBD	Airbus A.320-214	Bulgaria Air	
LZ-FBE	Airbus A.320-214	Bulgaria Air	
LZ-PLO	Embraer ERJ190-100STD	Bulgaria Air	
LZ-SOF	Embraer ERJ190-100IGW	Bulgaria Air	
LZ-VAR	Embraer ERJ190-100IGW	Bulgaria Air	

N (USA)

N152DL	Boeing 767-3P6ER	Delta Air Lines	
N153DL	Boeing 767-3P6ER	Delta Air Lines	
N154DL	Boeing 767-3P6ER	Delta Air Lines	
N155DL	Boeing 767-3P6ER	Delta Air Lines	
N156DL	Boeing 767-3P6ER	Delta Air Lines	
N169DZ	Boeing 767-332ER	Delta Air Lines	
N171DN	Boeing 767-332ER	Delta Air Lines	
N171DZ	Boeing 767-332ER	Delta Air Lines	
N172DN	Boeing 767-332ER	Delta Air Lines	
N172DZ	Boeing 767-332ER	Delta Air Lines	
N173DZ	Boeing 767-332ER	Delta Air Lines	
N174DN	Boeing 767-332ER	Delta Air Lines	
N174DZ	Boeing 767-332ER	Delta Air Lines	
N175DN	Boeing 767-332ER	Delta Air Lines	
N175DZ	Boeing 767-332ER	Delta Air Lines	
N176DN	Boeing 767-332ER	Delta Air Lines	
N176DZ	Boeing 767-332ER	Delta Air Lines	
N177DN	Boeing 767-332ER	Delta Air Lines	
N177DZ	Boeing 767-332ER	Delta Air Lines	
N178DN	Boeing 767-332ER	Delta Air Lines	
N178DZ	Boeing 767-332ER	Delta Air Lines	
N179DN	Boeing 767-332ER	Delta Air Lines	
N180DN	Boeing 767-332ER	Delta Air Lines	
N181DN	Boeing 767-332ER	Delta Air Lines	
N182DN	Boeing 767-332ER	Delta Air Lines	
N183AM	Boeing 787-9	Aeromexico	
N183DN	Boeing 767-332ER	Delta Air Lines	
N184DN	Boeing 767-332ER	Delta Air Lines	
N185DN	Boeing 767-332ER	Delta Air Lines	
N186DN	Boeing 767-332ER	Delta Air Lines	
N187DN	Boeing 767-332ER	Delta Air Lines	
N188DN	Boeing 767-332ER	Delta Air Lines	
N189DN	Boeing 767-332ER	Delta Air Lines	
N190DN	Boeing 767-332ER	Delta Air Lines	
N191DN	Boeing 767-332ER	Delta Air Lines	
N192DN	Boeing 767-332ER	Delta Air Lines	
N193DN	Boeing 767-332ER	Delta Air Lines	
N194DN	Boeing 767-332ER	Delta Air Lines	
N195DN	Boeing 767-332ER	Delta Air Lines	
N196DN	Boeing 767-332ER	Delta Air Lines	
N197DN	Boeing 767-332ER	Delta Air Lines	

Notes	Reg	Type	Owner or Operator
	N198DN	Boeing 767-332ER	Delta Air Lines
	N199DN	Boeing 767-332ER	Delta Air Lines
	N204UA	Boeing 777-222ER	United Airlines
	N206UA	Boeing 777-222ER	United Airlines
	N209UA	Boeing 777-222ER	United Airlines
	N216UA	Boeing 777-222ER	United Airlines
	N217UA	Boeing 777-222ER	United Airlines
	N218UA	Boeing 777-222ER	United Airlines
	N219UA	Boeing 777-222ER	United Airlines
	N220UA	Boeing 777-222ER	United Airlines
	N221UA	Boeing 777-222ER	United Airlines
	N222UA	Boeing 777-222ER	United Airlines
	N223UA	Boeing 777-222ER	United Airlines
	N224UA	Boeing 777-222ER	United Airlines
	N225UA	Boeing 777-222ER	United Airlines
	N226UA	Boeing 777-222ER	United Airlines
	N227UA	Boeing 777-222ER	United Airlines
	N228UA	Boeing 777-222ER	United Airlines
	N229UA	Boeing 777-222ER	United Airlines
	N270AY	Airbus A.330-323X	American Airlines
	N271AY	Airbus A.330-323X	American Airlines
	N272AY	Airbus A.330-323X	American Airlines
	N273AY	Airbus A.330-323X	American Airlines
	N274AY	Airbus A.330-323X	American Airlines
	N275AY	Airbus A.330-323X	American Airlines
	N276AY	Airbus A.330-323X	American Airlines
	N277AY	Airbus A.330-323X	American Airlines
	N278AY	Airbus A.330-323X	American Airlines
	N279AY	Airbus A.330-243	American Airlines
	N280AY	Airbus A.330-243	American Airlines
	N281AY	Airbus A.330-243	American Airlines
	N282AY	Airbus A.330-243	American Airlines
	N283AY	Airbus A.330-243	American Airlines
	N284AY	Airbus A.330-243	American Airlines
	N285AY	Airbus A.330-243	American Airlines
	N286AY	Airbus A.330-243	American Airlines
	N287AY	Airbus A.330-243	American Airlines
	N288AY	Airbus A.330-243	American Airlines
	N289AY	Airbus A.330-243	American Airlines
	N290AY	Airbus A.330-243	American Airlines
	N291AY	Airbus A.330-243	American Airlines
	N292AY	Airbus A.330-243	American Airlines
	N293AY	Airbus A.330-243	American Airlines
	N301UP	Boeing 767-34AFER	United Parcel Service
	N302UP	Boeing 767-34AFER	United Parcel Service
	N303UP	Boeing 767-34AFER	United Parcel Service
	N304UP	Boeing 767-34AFER	United Parcel Service
	N305UP	Boeing 767-34AFER	United Parcel Service
	N306UP	Boeing 767-34AFER	United Parcel Service
	N307UP	Boeing 767-34AFER	United Parcel Service
	N308UP	Boeing 767-34AFER	United Parcel Service
	N309UP	Boeing 767-34AFER	United Parcel Service
	N310UP	Boeing 767-34AFER	United Parcel Service
	N311UP	Boeing 767-34AFER	United Parcel Service
	N312UP	Boeing 767-34AFER	United Parcel Service
	N313UP	Boeing 767-34AFER	United Parcel Service
	N314UP	Boeing 767-34AFER	United Parcel Service
	N315UP	Boeing 767-34AFER	United Parcel Service
	N316UP	Boeing 767-34AFER	United Parcel Service
	N317UP	Boeing 767-34AFER	United Parcel Service
	N318UP	Boeing 767-34AFER	United Parcel Service
	N319UP	Boeing 767-34AFER	United Parcel Service
	N320UP	Boeing 767-34AFER	United Parcel Service
	N322UP	Boeing 767-34AFER	United Parcel Service
	N323UP	Boeing 767-34AFER	United Parcel Service
	N324UP	Boeing 767-34AFER	United Parcel Service
	N325UP	Boeing 767-34AFER	United Parcel Service
	N326UP	Boeing 767-34AFER	United Parcel Service
	N327UP	Boeing 767-34AFER	United Parcel Service
	N328UP	Boeing 767-34AFER	United Parcel Service
	N329UP	Boeing 767-34AER	United Parcel Service

Reg	Type	Owner or Operator	Notes
N330UP	Boeing 767-34AER	United Parcel Service	
N331UP	Boeing 767-34AER	United Parcel Service	
N332UP	Boeing 767-34AER	United Parcel Service	
N334UP	Boeing 767-34AER	United Parcel Service	
N335UP	Boeing 767-34AF	United Parcel Service	
N336UP	Boeing 767-34AF	United Parcel Service	
N337UP	Boeing 767-34AF	United Parcel Service	
N338UP	Boeing 767-34AF	United Parcel Service	
N339UP	Boeing 767-34AF	United Parcel Service	
N340UP	Boeing 767-34AF	United Parcel Service	
N341UP	Boeing 767-34AF	United Parcel Service	
N342AN	Boeing 767-323ER	American Airlines	
N342UP	Boeing 767-34AF	United Parcel Service	
N343AN	Boeing 767-323ER	American Airlines	
N343UP	Boeing 767-34AF	United Parcel Service	
N344AN	Boeing 767-323ER	American Airlines	
N344UP	Boeing 767-34AF	United Parcel Service	
N345UP	Boeing 767-34AF	United Parcel Service	
N346AN	Boeing 767-323ER	American Airlines	
N346UP	Boeing 767-34AF	United Parcel Service	
N347AN	Boeing 767-323ER	American Airlines	
N347UP	Boeing 767-34AF	United Parcel Service	
N348AN	Boeing 767-323ER	American Airlines	
N348UP	Boeing 767-34AF	United Parcel Service	
N349AN	Boeing 767-323ER	American Airlines	
N349UP	Boeing 767-34AF	United Parcel Service	
N350AN	Boeing 767-323ER	American Airlines	
N350UP	Boeing 767-34AF	United Parcel Service	
N351UP	Boeing 767-34AF	United Parcel Service	
N352UP	Boeing 767-34AF	United Parcel Service	
N353UP	Boeing 767-34AF	United Parcel Service	
N354UP	Boeing 767-34AF	United Parcel Service	
N355UP	Boeing 767-34AF	United Parcel Service	
N356UP	Boeing 767-34AF	United Parcel Service	
N357UP	Boeing 767-34AF	United Parcel Service	
N358UP	Boeing 767-34AF	United Parcel Service	
N359UP	Boeing 767-34AF	United Parcel Service	
N360UP	Boeing 767-34AF	United Parcel Service	
N361UP	Boeing 767-34AF	United Parcel Service	
N363UP	Boeing 767-346ER	United Parcel Service	
N381AN	Boeing 767-323ER	American Airlines	
N384AA	Boeing 767-323ER	American Airlines	
N385AM	Boeing 767-323ER	American Airlines	
N388AA	Boeing 767-323ER	American Airlines	
N390AA	Boeing 767-323ER	American Airlines	
N391AA	Boeing 767-323ER	American Airlines	
N392AN	Boeing 767-323ER	American Airlines	
N393AN	Boeing 767-323ER	American Airlines	
N394AN	Boeing 767-323ER	American Airlines	
N394DL	Boeing 767-324ER	Delta Air Lines	
N395AN	Boeing 767-323ER	American Airlines	
N396AN	Boeing 767-323ER	American Airlines	
N397AN	Boeing 767-323ER	American Airlines	
N398AN	Boeing 767-323ER	American Airlines	
N399AN	Boeing 767-323ER	American Airlines	
N401KZ	Boeing 747-481F	Kalitta Air	
N402KZ	Boeing 747-481F	Kalitta Air	
N403KZ	Boeing 747-481F	Kalitta Air	
N407KZ	Boeing 747-4KZF	Atlas Air	
N409MC	Boeing 747-47UF	Atlas Air	
N412MC	Boeing 747-47UF	Atlas Air	
N415MC	Boeing 747-47UF	Atlas Air	
N418MC	Boeing 747-47UF	Atlas Air	
N419MC	Boeing 747-48EF	Atlas Air	
N429MC	Boeing 747-481	Atlas Air	
N438AM	Boeing 787-8	Aeromexico	
N446MC	Boeing 747-4B5ERF	Atlas Air	
N472MC	Boeing 747-45EF	Atlas Air	
N473MC	Boeing 747-45EF	Atlas Air	
N475MC	Boeing 747-47U	Atlas Air	
N476MC	Boeing 747-47U	Atlas Air	

Notes	Reg	Type	Owner or Operator
	N477MC	Boeing 747-47U	Atlas Air
	N492MC	Boeing 747-47UF	Atlas Air
	N493MC	Boeing 747-47UF	Atlas Air
	N496BC	Boeing 747-4B5	Kalitta Air
	N496MC	Boeing 747-47UF	Atlas Air
	N497MC	Boeing 747-47UF	Atlas Air
	N498MC	Boeing 747-47UF	Atlas Air/Polar Air Cargo
	N499MC	Boeing 747-47UF	Atlas Air/Polar Air Cargo
	N521FE	McD Douglas MD-11F	Federal Express
	N522FE	McD Douglas MD-11F	Federal Express
	N523FE	McD Douglas MD-11F	Federal Express
	N525FE	McD Douglas MD-11F	Federal Express
	N528FE	McD Douglas MD-11F	Federal Express
	N529FE	McD Douglas MD-11F	Federal Express
	N539BC	Boeing 747-4B5BCF	Kalitta Air
	N572FE	McD Douglas MD-11F	Federal Express
	N573FE	McD Douglas MD-11F	Federal Express
	N574FE	McD Douglas MD-11F	Federal Express
	N575FE	McD Douglas MD-11F	Federal Express
	N576FE	McD Douglas MD-11F	Federal Express
	N578FE	McD Douglas MD-11F	Federal Express *Stephen*
	N582FE	McD Douglas MD-11F	Federal Express *Jamie*
	N583FE	McD Douglas MD-11F	Federal Express *Nancy*
	N584FE	McD Douglas MD-11F	Federal Express *Jeffrey Wellington*
	N585FE	McD Douglas MD-11F	Federal Express *Katherine*
	N586FE	McD Douglas MD-11F	Federal Express *Dylan*
	N587FE	McD Douglas MD-11F	Federal Express *Jeanna*
	N588FE	McD Douglas MD-11F	Federal Express *Kendra*
	N589FE	McD Douglas MD-11F	Federal Express *Shaun*
	N590FE	McD Douglas MD-11F	Federal Express
	N591FE	McD Douglas MD-11F	Federal Express *Giovanni*
	N592FE	McD Douglas MD-11F	Federal Express *Joshua*
	N593FE	McD Douglas MD-11F	Federal Express *Harrison*
	N594FE	McD Douglas MD-11F	Federal Express
	N595FE	McD Douglas MD-11F	Federal Express *Avery*
	N596FE	McD Douglas MD-11F	Federal Express
	N597FE	McD Douglas MD-11F	Federal Express
	N598FE	McD Douglas MD-11F	Federal Express
	N599FE	McD Douglas MD-11F	Federal Express *Mariana*
	N601FE	McD Douglas MD-11F	Federal Express *Jim Riedmeyer*
	N602FE	McD Douglas MD-11F	Federal Express *Malcolm Baldridge 1990*
	N603FE	McD Douglas MD-11F	Federal Express
	N604FE	McD Douglas MD-11F	Federal Express *Hollis*
	N605FE	McD Douglas MD-11F	Federal Express *April Star*
	N606FE	McD Douglas MD-11F	Federal Express *Charles & Theresa*
	N607FE	McD Douglas MD-11F	Federal Express *Christina*
	N608FE	McD Douglas MD-11F	Federal Express *Karen*
	N609FE	McD Douglas MD-11F	Federal Express *Scott*
	N610FE	McD Douglas MD-11F	Federal Express *Marisa*
	N612FE	McD Douglas MD-11F	Federal Express *Alyssa*
	N613FE	McD Douglas MD-11F	Federal Express *Krista*
	N614FE	McD Douglas MD-11F	Federal Express *Christy Allison*
	N615FE	McD Douglas MD-11F	Federal Express *Max*
	N616FE	McD Douglas MD-11F	Federal Express *Shanita*
	N617FE	McD Douglas MD-11F	Federal Express *Travis*
	N618FE	McD Douglas MD-11F	Federal Express *Justin*
	N619FE	McD Douglas MD-11F	Federal Express *Lyndon*
	N620FE	McD Douglas MD-11F	Federal Express
	N621FE	McD Douglas MD-11F	Federal Express *Connor*
	N623FE	McD Douglas MD-11F	Federal Express *Meghan*
	N624AG	Boeing 757-2Q8	Delta Air Lines
	N624FE	McD Douglas MD-11F	Federal Express
	N625FE	McD Douglas MD-11F	Federal Express
	N628FE	McD Douglas MD-11F	Federal Express
	N631FE	McD Douglas MD-11F	Federal Express
	N641UA	Boeing 767-322ER	United Airlines
	N642FE	McD Douglas MD-11F	Federal Express
	N642UA	Boeing 767-322ER	United Airlines
	N643FE	McD Douglas MD-11F	Federal Express
	N643UA	Boeing 767-322ER	United Airlines
	N644UA	Boeing 767-322ER	United Airlines

Reg	Type	Owner or Operator	Notes
N646UA	Boeing 767-322ER	United Airlines	
N647UA	Boeing 767-322ER	United Airlines	
N648UA	Boeing 767-322ER	United Airlines	
N649UA	Boeing 767-322ER	United Airlines	
N651UA	Boeing 767-322ER	United Airlines	
N652UA	Boeing 767-322ER	United Airlines	
N653UA	Boeing 767-322ER	United Airlines	
N654UA	Boeing 767-322ER	United Airlines	
N655UA	Boeing 767-322ER	United Airlines	
N656UA	Boeing 767-322ER	United Airlines	
N657UA	Boeing 767-322ER	United Airlines	
N658UA	Boeing 767-322ER	United Airlines	
N659UA	Boeing 767-322ER	United Airlines	
N660UA	Boeing 767-322ER	United Airlines	
N661UA	Boeing 767-322ER	United Airlines	
N662UA	Boeing 767-322ER	United Airlines	
N663UA	Boeing 767-322ER	United Airlines	
N664UA	Boeing 767-322ER	United Airlines	
N665UA	Boeing 767-322ER	United Airlines	
N666UA	Boeing 767-322ER	United Airlines	
N667UA	Boeing 767-322ER	United Airlines	
N668UA	Boeing 767-322ER	United Airlines	
N669UA	Boeing 767-322ER	United Airlines	
N670UA	Boeing 767-322ER	United Airlines	
N671UA	Boeing 767-322ER	United Airlines	
N672UA	Boeing 767-322ER	United Airlines	
N673UA	Boeing 767-322ER	United Airlines	
N674UA	Boeing 767-322ER	United Airlines	
N675UA	Boeing 767-322ER	United Airlines	
N676UA	Boeing 767-322ER	United Airlines	
N677UA	Boeing 767-322ER	United Airlines	
N700CK	Boeing 747-4R7F	Kalitta Air	
N701CK	Boeing 747-4B5F	Kalitta Air	
N702CK	Boeing 747-4B5F	Kalitta Air	
N702TW	Boeing 757-2Q8	Delta Air Lines	
N703TW	Boeing 757-2Q8	Delta Air Lines	
N704X	Boeing 757-2Q8	Delta Air Lines	
N705CK	Boeing 747-4B5F	Kalitta Air	
N705TW	Boeing 757-231	Delta Air Lines	
N706CK	Boeing 747-4B5F	Kalitta Air	
N706TW	Boeing 757-2Q8	Delta Air Lines	
N707TW	Boeing 757-2Q8	Delta Air Lines	
N709TW	Boeing 757-2Q8	Delta Air Lines	
N710TW	Boeing 757-2Q8	Delta Air Lines	
N711ZX	Boeing 757-231	Delta Air Lines	
N712TW	Boeing 757-2Q8	Delta Air Lines	
N713TW	Boeing 757-2Q8	Delta Air Lines	
N714SA	Boeing 777-FZB	Southern Air	
N717AN	Boeing 777-323ER	American Airlines	
N717TW	Boeing 757-231	Delta Air Lines	
N718AN	Boeing 777-323ER	American Airlines	
N718TW	Boeing 757-231	Delta Air Lines	
N719AN	Boeing 777-323ER	American Airlines	
N720AN	Boeing 777-323ER	American Airlines	
N721AN	Boeing 777-323ER	American Airlines	
N721TW	Boeing 757-231	Delta Air Lines	
N722AN	Boeing 777-323ER	American Airlines	
N722FD	Airbus A.300B4-622RF	Federal Express	
N722TW	Boeing 757-231	Delta Air Lines	
N723AN	Boeing 777-323ER	American Airlines	
N723TW	Boeing 757-231	Delta Air Lines	
N724AN	Boeing 777-323ER	American Airlines	
N724FD	Airbus A.300B4-622RF	Federal Express	
N725AN	Boeing 777-323ER	American Airlines	
N726AN	Boeing 777-323ER	American Airlines	
N727AN	Boeing 777-323ER	American Airlines	
N727TW	Boeing 757-231	Delta Air Lines	
N728AN	Boeing 777-323ER	American Airlines	
N729AN	Boeing 777-323ER	American Airlines	
N730AN	Boeing 777-323ER	American Airlines	
N731AN	Boeing 777-323ER	American Airlines	

Notes	Reg	Type	Owner or Operator
	N732AN	Boeing 777-323ER	American Airlines
	N733AR	Boeing 777-323ER	American Airlines
	N734AR	Boeing 777-323ER	American Airlines
	N735AT	Boeing 777-323ER	American Airlines
	N736AT	Boeing 777-323ER	American Airlines
	N740CK	Boeing 747-4H6BCF	Kalitta Air
	N741CK	Boeing 747-4H6F	Kalitta Air
	N742CK	Boeing 747-446BCF	Kalitta Air
	N740FD	Airbus A.300B4-622RF	Federal Express
	N743CK	Boeing 747-446BCF	Kalitta Air
	N743FD	Airbus A.300B4-622RF	Federal Express
	N744CK	Boeing 747-446BCF	Kalitta Air
	N745CK	Boeing 747-446BCF	Kalitta Air
	N750AN	Boeing 777-223ER	American Airlines
	N751AN	Boeing 777-223ER	American Airlines
	N752AN	Boeing 777-223ER	American Airlines
	N753AN	Boeing 777-223ER	American Airlines
	N754AN	Boeing 777-223ER	American Airlines
	N755AN	Boeing 777-223ER	American Airlines
	N756AM	Boeing 777-223ER	American Airlines
	N757AN	Boeing 777-223ER	American Airlines
	N758AN	Boeing 777-223ER	American Airlines
	N759AN	Boeing 777-223ER	American Airlines
	N760AN	Boeing 777-223ER	American Airlines
	N761AJ	Boeing 777-223ER	American Airlines
	N762AN	Boeing 777-223ER	American Airlines
	N765AN	Boeing 777-223ER	American Airlines
	N766AN	Boeing 777-223ER	American Airlines
	N767AJ	Boeing 777-223ER	American Airlines
	N768AA	Boeing 777-223ER	American Airlines
	N769UA	Boeing 777-222	United Airlines
	N770AN	Boeing 777-223ER	American Airlines
	N771AN	Boeing 777-223ER	American Airlines
	N771UA	Boeing 777-222	United Airlines
	N772AN	Boeing 777-223ER	American Airlines
	N772UA	Boeing 777-222	United Airlines
	N773AN	Boeing 777-223ER	American Airlines
	N773UA	Boeing 777-222	United Airlines
	N774AN	Boeing 777-223ER	American Airlines
	N774SA	Boeing 777-FZB	Southern Air
	N774UA	Boeing 777-222	United Airlines
	N775AN	Boeing 777-223ER	American Airlines
	N775SA	Boeing 777-FZB	Southern Air
	N775UA	Boeing 777-222	United Airlines
	N776AN	Boeing 777-223ER	American Airlines
	N776UA	Boeing 777-222	United Airlines
	N777AN	Boeing 777-223ER	American Airlines
	N777SA	Boeing 777-FZB	Southern Air
	N777UA	Boeing 777-222	United Airlines
	N778AN	Boeing 777-223ER	American Airlines
	N778LA	Boeing 777-F16	Southern Air
	N778UA	Boeing 777-222	United Airlines
	N779AN	Boeing 777-223ER	American Airlines
	N779UA	Boeing 777-222	United Airlines
	N780AN	Boeing 777-223ER	American Airlines
	N780AV	Boeing 787-8	AVIANCA
	N780UA	Boeing 777-222	United Airlines
	N781AN	Boeing 777-223ER	American Airlines
	N781AV	Boeing 787-8	AVIANCA
	N781UA	Boeing 777-222	United Airlines
	N782AM	Boeing 787-8	Aeromexico
	N782AN	Boeing 777-223ER	American Airlines
	N782AV	Boeing 787-8	AVIANCA
	N782CK	Boeing 747-4HQF	Kalitta Air
	N782UA	Boeing 777-222ER	United Airlines
	N783AM	Boeing 787-8	Aeromexico
	N783AN	Boeing 777-223ER	American Airlines
	N783AV	Boeing 787-8	AVIANCA
	N783UA	Boeing 777-222ER	United Airlines
	N784AN	Boeing 777-223ER	American Airlines
	N784AV	Boeing 787-8	AVIANCA

Reg	Type	Owner or Operator	Notes
N784UA	Boeing 777-222ER	United Airlines	
N785AN	Boeing 777-223ER	American Airlines	
N785AV	Boeing 787-8	AVIANCA	
N785UA	Boeing 777-222ER	United Airlines	
N786AN	Boeing 777-223ER	American Airlines	
N786AV	Boeing 787-8	AVIANCA	
N786UA	Boeing 777-222ER	United Airlines	
N787AL	Boeing 777-223ER	American Airlines	
N787UA	Boeing 777-222ER	United Airlines	
N788AN	Boeing 777-223ER	American Airlines	
N788UA	Boeing 777-222ER	United Airlines	
N789AN	Boeing 777-223ER	American Airlines	
N790AN	Boeing 777-223ER	American Airlines	
N790AV	Boeing 787-8	AVIANCA	
N791AN	Boeing 777-223ER	American Airlines	
N791AV	Boeing 787-8	AVIANCA	
N791UA	Boeing 777-222ER	United Airlines	
N792AN	Boeing 777-223ER	American Airlines	
N792AV	Boeing 787-8	AVIANCA	
N792UA	Boeing 777-222ER	United Airlines	
N793AN	Boeing 777-223ER	American Airlines	
N793AV	Boeing 787-8	AVIANCA	
N793UA	Boeing 777-222ER	United Airlines	
N794AN	Boeing 777-223ER	American Airlines	
N794AV	Boeing 787-8	AVIANCA	
N794UA	Boeing 777-222ER	United Airlines	
N795AN	Boeing 777-223ER	American Airlines	
N795AV	Boeing 787-8	AVIANCA	
N795UA	Boeing 777-222ER	United Airlines	
N796AN	Boeing 777-223ER	American Airlines	
N796UA	Boeing 777-222ER	United Airlines	
N797AN	Boeing 777-223ER	American Airlines	
N797UA	Boeing 777-222ER	United Airlines	
N798AN	Boeing 777-223ER	American Airlines	
N798UA	Boeing 777-222ER	United Airlines	
N799AN	Boeing 777-223ER	American Airlines	
N799UA	Boeing 777-222ER	United Airlines	
N800AN	Boeing 787-8	American Airlines	
N801AC	Boeing 787-8	American Airlines	
N801NW	Airbus A.330-323X	Delta Airlines	
N802AN	Boeing 787-8	American Airlines	
N802NW	Airbus A.330-323X	Delta Airlines	
N803AL	Boeing 787-8	American Airlines	
N803NW	Airbus A.330-323X	Delta Air Lines	
N804AN	Boeing 787-8	American Airlines	
N804NW	Airbus A.330-323X	Delta Air Lines	
N805AN	Boeing 787-8	American Airlines	
N805NW	Airbus A.330-323X	Delta Air Lines	
N806AA	Boeing 787-8	American Airlines	
N806NW	Airbus A.330-323X	Delta Air Lines	
N807AA	Boeing 787-8	American Airlines	
N807NW	Airbus A.330-323X	Delta Air Lines	
N808AN	Boeing 787-8	American Airlines	
N808NW	Airbus A.330-323X	Delta Air Lines	
N809AA	Boeing 787-8	American Airlines	
N809NW	Airbus A.330-323E	Delta Air Lines	
N810AN	Boeing 787-8	American Airlines	
N810NW	Airbus A.330-323E	Delta Air Lines	
N811AB	Boeing 787-8	American Airlines	
N811NW	Airbus A.330-323E	Delta Air Lines	
N812AA	Boeing 787-8	American Airlines	
N812NW	Airbus A.330-323E	Delta Air Lines	
N813AN	Boeing 787-8	American Airlines	
N813NW	Airbus A.330-323E	Delta Air Lines	
N814AA	Boeing 787-8	American Airlines	
N814NW	Airbus A.330-323E	Delta Air Lines	
N815AA	Boeing 787-8	American Airlines	
N815NW	Airbus A.330-323E	Delta Air Lines	
N816AA	Boeing 787-8	American Airlines	
N816NW	Airbus A.330-323E	Delta Air Lines	
N817AN	Boeing 787-8	American Airlines	

Notes	Reg	Type	Owner or Operator
	N817NW	Airbus A.330-323E	Delta Air Lines
	N818AL	Boeing 787-8	American Airlines
	N818NW	Airbus A.330-323E	Delta Air Lines
	N819AN	Boeing 787-8	American Airlines
	N819NW	Airbus A.330-323E	Delta Air Lines
	N820AL	Boeing 787-9	American Airlines
	N820NW	Airbus A.330-323E	Delta Air Lines
	N821AN	Boeing 787-9	American Airlines
	N821NW	Airbus A.330-323E	Delta Air Lines
	N822AN	Boeing 787-9	American Airlines
	N822NW	Airbus A.330-323E	Delta Air Lines
	N823AN	Boeing 787-9	American Airlines
	N823NW	Airbus A.330-302	Delta Air Lines
	N824AN	Boeing 787-9	American Airlines
	N824NW	Airbus A.330-302	Delta Air Lines
	N825AA	Boeing 787-9	American Airlines
	N825MH	Boeing 767-432ER (1801)	Delta Air Lines
	N825NW	Airbus A.330-302	Delta Air Lines
	N826AN	Boeing 787-9	American Airlines
	N826MH	Boeing 767-432ER (1802)	Delta Air Lines
	N826NW	Airbus A.330-302	Delta Air Lines
	N827AN	Boeing 787-9	American Airlines
	N827MH	Boeing 767-432ER (1803)	Delta Air Lines
	N827NW	Airbus A.330-302	Delta Air Lines
	N828AA	Boeing 787-9	American Airlines
	N828MH	Boeing 767-432ER (1804)	Delta Air Lines
	N828NW	Airbus A.330-302	Delta Air Lines
	N829AN	Boeing 787-9	American Airlines
	N829MH	Boeing 767-432ER (1805)	Delta Air Lines
	N829NW	Airbus A.330-302	Delta Air Lines
	N830AN	Boeing 787-9	American Airlines
	N830MH	Boeing 767-432ER (1806)	Delta Air Lines
	N830NW	Airbus A.330-302	Delta Air Lines
	N831AA	Boeing 787-9	American Airlines
	N831MH	Boeing 767-432ER (1807)	Delta Air Lines
	N831NW	Airbus A.330-302	Delta Air Lines
	N832AA	Boeing 787-9	American Airlines
	N832MH	Boeing 767-432ER (1808)	Delta Air Lines
	N833AA	Boeing 787-9	American Airlines
	N833MH	Boeing 767-432ER (1809)	Delta Air Lines
	N834AA	Boeing 787-9	American Airlines
	N834MH	Boeing 767-432ER (1810)	Delta Air Lines
	N835AN	Boeing 787-9	American Airlines
	N835MH	Boeing 767-432ER (1811)	Delta Air Lines
	N836MH	Boeing 767-432ER (1812)	Delta Air Lines
	N837MH	Boeing 767-432ER (1813)	Delta Air Lines
	N838MH	Boeing 767-432ER (1814)	Delta Air Lines
	N839MH	Boeing 767-432ER (1815)	Delta Air Lines
	N840MH	Boeing 767-432ER (1816)	Delta Air Lines
	N841MH	Boeing 767-432ER (1817)	Delta Air Lines
	N842FD	Boeing 777-FHT	Federal Express
	N842MH	Boeing 767-432ER (1818	Delta Air Lines
	N843FD	Boeing 777-FHT	Federal Express
	N843MH	Boeing 767-432ER (1819)	Delta Air Lines
	N844FD	Boeing 777-FHT	Federal Express
	N844MH	Boeing 767-432ER (1820)	Delta Air Lines
	N845MH	Boeing 767-432ER (1821)	Delta Air Lines
	N850FD	Boeing 777-2S2LRF	Federal Express
	N850GT	Boeing 747-87UF	Atlas Air/Panalpina World Transport
	N851FD	Boeing 777-2S2LRF	Federal Express
	N851GT	Boeing 747-87UF	Atlas Air/Panalpina World Transport
	N851NW	Airbus A.330-223	Delta Air Lines
	N852FD	Boeing 777-2S2LRF	Federal Express
	N852GT	Boeing 747-87UF	Atlas Air/Polar Air Cargo
	N852NW	Airbus A.330-223	Delta Air Lines
	N853FD	Boeing 777-2S2LRF	Federal Express
	N853GT	Boeing 747-87UF	Atlas Air/Polar Air Cargo
	N853NW	Airbus A.330-223	Delta Air Lines
	N854FD	Boeing 777-2S2LRF	Federal Express
	N854GT	Boeing 747-87UF	Atlas Air
	N854NW	Airbus A.330-223	Delta Air Lines

Reg	Type	Owner or Operator	Notes
N855FD	Boeing 777-2S2LRF	Federal Express	
N855GT	Boeing 747-87UF	Atlas Air	
N855NW	Airbus A.330-223	Delta Air Lines	
N856FD	Boeing 777-2S2LRF	Federal Express	
N856GT	Boeing 747-87UF	Atlas Air/Polar Air Cargo	
N856NW	Airbus A.330-223	Delta Air Lines	
N857FD	Boeing 777-2S2LRF	Federal Express	
N857GT	Boeing 747-87UF	Atlas Air/Polar Air Cargo	
N857NW	Airbus A.330-223	Delta Air Lines	
N858FD	Boeing 777-2S2LRF	Federal Express	
N858GT	Boeing 747-87UF	Atlas Air/Polar Air Cargo	
N858NW	Airbus A.330-223	Delta Air Lines	
N859FD	Boeing 777-2S2LRF	Federal Express	
N859GT	Boeing 747-87UF	Atlas Air	
N859NW	Airbus A.330-223	Delta Air Lines	
N860NW	Airbus A.330-223	Delta Air Lines	
N861FD	Boeing 777-2S2LRF	Federal Express	
N861NW	Airbus A.330-223	Delta Air Lines	
N862FD	Boeing 777-2S2LRF	Federal Express	
N863FD	Boeing 777-2S2LRF	Federal Express	
N864FD	Boeing 777-2S2LRF	Federal Express	
N868FD	Boeing 777-2S2LRF	Federal Express	
N869FD	Boeing 777-2S2LRF	Federal Express	
N877FD	Boeing 777-2S2LRF	Federal Express	
N878FD	Boeing 777-2S2LRF	Federal Express	
N880FD	Boeing 777-2S2LRF	Federal Express	
N882FD	Boeing 777-2S2LRF	Federal Express	
N883FD	Boeing 777-2S2LRF	Federal Express	
N884FD	Boeing 777-2S2LRF	Federal Express	
N885FD	Boeing 777-2S2LRF	Federal Express	
N886FD	Boeing 777-2S2LRF	Federal Express	
N887FD	Boeing 777-2S2LRF	Federal Express	
N888FD	Boeing 777-2S2LRF	Federal Express	
N889FD	Boeing 777-2S2LRF	Federal Express	
N890FD	Boeing 777-2S2LRF	Federal Express	
N891FD	Boeing 777-2S2LRF	Federal Express	
N892FD	Boeing 777-2S2LRF	Federal Express	
N895FD	Boeing 777-2S2LRF	Federal Express	
N897FD	Boeing 777-2S2LRF	Federal Express	
N901FD	Boeing 757-2B7	Federal Express	
N903FD	Boeing 757-2B7	Federal Express	
N910FD	Boeing 757-28A	Federal Express	
N913FD	Boeing 757-28A	Federal Express	
N915FD	Boeing 757-236	Federal Express	
N916FD	Boeing 757-27B	Federal Express	
N917FD	Boeing 757-23A	Federal Express	
N918FD	Boeing 757-23A	Federal Express	
N919CA	Boeing 747-428BCF	National Airlines	
N919FD	Boeing 757-23A	Federal Express	
N920FD	Boeing 757-23A	Federal Express	
N922FD	Boeing 757-23A	Federal Express	
N923FD	Boeing 757-204	Federal Express	
N939FD	Boeing 757-23A	Federal Express	
N952CA	Boeing 747-428BCF	National Airlines	
N961AM	Boeing 787-8	Aeromexico	
N964AM	Boeing 787-8	Aeromexico	
N965AM	Boeing 787-8	Aeromexico	
N966AM	Boeing 787-8	Aeromexico	
N967AM	Boeing 787-8	Aeromexico	
N972FD	Boeing 757-28A	Federal Express	
N976BA	Boeing 747-4B5CF	Kalitta Air	
N1200K	Boeing 767-332ER (200)	Delta Air Lines	
N1201P	Boeing 767-332ER (201)	Delta Air Lines	
N1602	Boeing 767-332ER (1602)	Delta Air Lines	
N1603	Boeing 767-332ER (1603)	Delta Air Lines	
N1604R	Boeing 767-332ER (1604)	Delta Air Lines	
N1605	Boeing 767-332ER (1605)	Delta Air Lines	
N1607B	Boeing 767-332ER (1607)	Atlas Air Lines	
N1608	Boeing 767-332ER (1608)	Delta Air Lines	
N1609	Boeing 767-332ER (1609)	Delta Air Lines	
N1610D	Boeing 767-332ER (1610)	Delta Air Lines	

Notes	Reg	Type	Owner or Operator
	N1611B	Boeing 767-332ER (1611)	Delta Air Lines
	N1612T	Boeing 767-332ER (1612)	Delta Air Lines
	N1613B	Boeing 767-332ER (1613)	Delta Air Lines
	N2135U	Boeing 777-322ER	United Airlines
	N2136U	Boeing 777-322ER	United Airlines
	N2138U	Boeing 777-322ER	United Airlines
	N2140U	Boeing 777-322ER	United Airlines
	N2142U	Boeing 777-322ER	United Airlines
	N2243U	Boeing 777-322ER	United Airlines
	N2331U	Boeing 777-322ER	United Airlines
	N2332U	Boeing 777-322ER	United Airlines
	N2333U	Boeing 777-322ER	United Airlines
	N2341U	Boeing 777-322ER	United Airlines
	N2534U	Boeing 777-322ER	United Airlines
	N2639U	Boeing 777-322ER	United Airlines
	N2644U	Boeing 777-322ER	United Airlines
	N2645U	Boeing 777-322ER	United Airlines
	N2737U	Boeing 777-322ER	United Airlines
	N2846U	Boeing 777-322ER	United Airlines
	N12109	Boeing 757-224	United Airlines
	N12114	Boeing 757-224	United Airlines
	N12116	Boeing 757-224	United Airlines
	N12125	Boeing 757-224	United Airlines
	N13110	Boeing 757-224	United Airlines
	N13113	Boeing 757-224	United Airlines
	N13138	Boeing 757-224	United Airlines
	N13954	Boeing 787-9	United Airlines
	N14102	Boeing 757-224	United Airlines
	N14106	Boeing 757-224	United Airlines
	N14107	Boeing 757-224	United Airlines
	N14115	Boeing 757-224	United Airlines
	N14118	Boeing 757-224	United Airlines
	N14120	Boeing 757-224	United Airlines
	N14121	Boeing 757-224	United Airlines
	N15969	Boeing 787-9	United Airlines
	N16065	Boeing 767-332ER (1606)	Delta Air Lines
	N17104	Boeing 757-224	United Airlines
	N17105	Boeing 757-224	United Airlines
	N17122	Boeing 757-224	United Airlines
	N17126	Boeing 757-224	United Airlines
	N17128	Boeing 757-224	United Airlines
	N17133	Boeing 757-224	United Airlines
	N17139	Boeing 757-224	United Airlines
	N17963	Boeing 787-9	United Airlines
	N18112	Boeing 757-224	United Airlines
	N18119	Boeing 757-224	United Airlines
	N19117	Boeing 757-224	United Airlines
	N19130	Boeing 757-224	United Airlines
	N19136	Boeing 757-224	United Airlines
	N19141	Boeing 757-224	United Airlines
	N19951	Boeing 787-9	United Airlines
	N20904	Boeing 787-8	United Airlines
	N21108	Boeing 757-224	United Airlines
	N24972	Boeing 787-9	United Airlines
	N24973	Boeing 787-9	United Airlines
	N24974	Boeing 787-9	United Airlines
	N26123	Boeing 757-224	United Airlines
	N26902	Boeing 787-8	United Airlines
	N26906	Boeing 787-8	United Airlines
	N26909	Boeing 787-8	United Airlines
	N26910	Boeing 787-8	United Airlines
	N26952	Boeing 787-9	United Airlines
	N26960	Boeing 787-9	United Airlines
	N26966	Boeing 787-9	United Airlines
	N26967	Boeing 787-9	United Airlines
	N26970	Boeing 787-9	United Airlines
	N27015	Boeing 777-224ER	United Airlines
	N27901	Boeing 787-8	United Airlines
	N27903	Boeing 787-8	United Airlines
	N27908	Boeing 787-8	United Airlines
	N27957	Boeing 787-9	United Airlines

Reg	Type	Owner or Operator	Notes
N27958	Boeing 787-9	United Airlines	
N27959	Boeing 787-9	United Airlines	
N27964	Boeing 787-9	United Airlines	
N27965	Boeing 787-9	United Airlines	
N28912	Boeing 787-8	United Airlines	
N29124	Boeing 757-224	United Airlines	
N29129	Boeing 757-224	United Airlines	
N29907	Boeing 787-8	United Airlines	
N29961	Boeing 787-9	United Airlines	
N29968	Boeing 787-9	United Airlines	
N29971	Boeing 787-9	United Airlines	
N30913	Boeing 787-8	United Airlines	
N33103	Boeing 757-224	United Airlines	
N33132	Boeing 757-224	United Airlines	
N34131	Boeing 757-224	United Airlines	
N34137	Boeing 757-224	United Airlines	
N35953	Boeing 787-9	United Airlines	
N36962	Boeing 787-9	United Airlines	
N37018	Boeing 777-224ER	United Airlines	
N38950	Boeing 787-9	United Airlines	
N38955	Boeing 787-9	United Airlines	
N41135	Boeing 757-224	United Airlines	
N41140	Boeing 757-224	United Airlines	
N45905	Boeing 787-8	United Airlines	
N45956	Boeing 787-9	United Airlines	
N48127	Boeing 757-224	United Airlines	
N57016	Boeing 777-224ER	United Airlines	
N57111	Boeing 757-224	United Airlines	
N58031	Boeing 777-322ER	United Airlines	
N58101	Boeing 757-224	United Airlines	
N59053	Boeing 767-424ER	United Airlines	
N66051	Boeing 767-424ER	United Airlines	
N66056	Boeing 767-424ER	United Airlines	
N66057	Boeing 767-424ER	United Airlines	
N67052	Boeing 767-424ER	United Airlines	
N67058	Boeing 767-424ER	United Airlines	
N67134	Boeing 757-224	United Airlines	
N68061	Boeing 767-424ER	United Airlines	
N68091	McD Douglas MD-11F	Federal Express	
N69020	Boeing 777-224ER	United Airlines	
N69059	Boeing 767-424ER	United Airlines	
N69063	Boeing 767-424ER	United Airlines	
N74007	Boeing 777-224ER	United Airlines	
N76010	Boeing 777-224ER	United Airlines	
N76021	Boeing 777-224ER	United Airlines	
N76054	Boeing 767-424ER	United Airlines	
N76055	Boeing 767-424ER	United Airlines	
N76062	Boeing 767-424ER	United Airlines	
N76064	Boeing 767-424ER	United Airlines	
N76065	Boeing 767-424ER	United Airlines	
N77006	Boeing 777-224ER	United Airlines	
N77012	Boeing 777-224ER	United Airlines	
N77014	Boeing 777-224ER	United Airlines	
N77019	Boeing 777-224ER	United Airlines	
N77022	Boeing 777-224ER	United Airlines	
N77066	Boeing 767-424ER	United Airlines	
N78001	Boeing 777-224ER	United Airlines	
N78002	Boeing 777-224ER	United Airlines	
N78003	Boeing 777-224ER	United Airlines	
N78004	Boeing 777-224ER	United Airlines	
N78005	Boeing 777-224ER	United Airlines	
N78008	Boeing 777-224ER	United Airlines	
N78009	Boeing 777-224ER	United Airlines	
N78013	Boeing 777-224ER	United Airlines	
N78017	Boeing 777-224ER	United Airlines	
N78060	Boeing 767-424ER	United Airlines	
N79011	Boeing 777-224ER	United Airlines	

OD (Lebanon)

OD-MEA	Airbus A.330-243	Middle East Airlines	

OVERSEAS AIRLINERS

Notes	Reg	Type	Owner or Operator
	OD-MEB	Airbus A.330-243	Middle East Airlines
	OD-MEC	Airbus A.330-243	Middle East Airlines
	OD-MED	Airbus A.330-243	Middle East Airlines
	OD-MEE	Airbus A.330-243	Middle East Airlines
	OD-MRL	Airbus A.320-232	Middle East Airlines
	OD-MRM	Airbus A.320-232	Middle East Airlines
	OD-MRN	Airbus A.320-232	Middle East Airlines
	OD-MRO	Airbus A.320-232	Middle East Airlines
	OD-MRR	Airbus A.320-232	Middle East Airlines
	OD-MRS	Airbus A.320-232	Middle East Airlines
	OD-MRT	Airbus A.320-232	Middle East Airlines

OE (Austria)

Notes	Reg	Type	Owner or Operator
	OE-IAB	Boeing 737-4Z9	ASL Airlines Belgium
	OE-IAC	Boeing 737-4MO	ASL Airlines Belgium
	OE-IAE	Boeing 737-4Q8	ASL Airlines Belgium
	OE-IAF	Boeing 737-4YO	ASL Airlines Belgium
	OE-IAG	Boeing 737-4Q8	ASL Airlines Belgium
	OE-IAJ	Boeing 737-476F	ASL Airlines Belgium
	OE-IAP	Boeing 737-4MO	ASL Airlines Belgium
	OE-IAQ	Boeing 737-4MO	ASL Airlines Belgium
	OE-IAR	Boeing 737-4MO	ASL Airlines Belgium
	OE-IAT	Boeing 737-4MO	ASL Airlines Belgium
	OE-IAX	Boeing 737-48EF	ASL Airlines Belgium
	OE-IAY	Boeing 737-4Q8	ASL Airlines Belgium
	OE-IAZ	Boeing 737-4Q8F	ASL Airlines Belgium
	OE-IBW	Boeing 737-4Q8F	ASL Airlines Belgium
	OE-ICT	Airbus A.320-214	easyJet Europe
	OE-IEU	Airbus A.320-214	Eurowings Europe
	OE-IEW	Airbus A.320-214	Eurowings Europe
	OE-IJA	Airbus A.320-214	easyJet Europe
	OE-IJB	Airbus A.320-214	easyJet Europe
	OE-IJD	Airbus A.320-214	easyJet Europe
	OE-IJE	Airbus A.320-214	easyJet Europe
	OE-IJF	Airbus A.320-214	easyJet Europe
	OE-IJG	Airbus A.320-214	easyJet Europe
	OE-IJH	Airbus A.320-214	easyJet Europe
	OE-IJI	Airbus A.320-214	easyJet Europe
	OE-IJJ	Airbus A.320-214	easyJet Europe
	OE-IJK	Airbus A.320-214	easyJet Europe
	OE-IJL	Airbus A.320-214	easyJet Europe
	OE-IJN	Airbus A.320-214	easyJet Europe
	OE-IJO	Airbus A.320-214	easyJet Europe
	OE-IJP	Airbus A.320-214	easyJet Europe
	OE-IJQ	Airbus A.320-214	easyJet Europe
	OE-IJR	Airbus A.320-214	easyJet Europe
	OE-IJS	Airbus A.320-214	easyJet Europe
	OE-IJU	Airbus A.320-214	easyJet Europe
	OE-IJV	Airbus A.320-214	easyJet Europe
	OE-IJW	Airbus A.320-214	easyJet Europe
	OE-IQA	Airbus A.320-214	Eurowings Europe
	OE-IQB	Airbus A.320-214	Eurowings Europe
	OE-IQC	Airbus A.320-214	Eurowings Europe
	OE-IQD	Airbus A.320-214	Eurowings Europe
	OE-IVA	Airbus A.320-214	easyJet Europe
	OE-IVB	Airbus A.320-214	easyJet Europe
	OE-IVC	Airbus A.320-214	easyJet Europe
	OE-IVD	Airbus A.320-214	easyJet Europe
	OE-IVE	Airbus A.320-214	easyJet Europe
	OE-IVF	Airbus A.320-214	easyJet Europe
	OE-IVH	Airbus A.320-214	easyJet Europe
	OE-IVI	Airbus A.320-214	easyJet Europe
	OE-IVJ	Airbus A.320-214	easyJet Europe
	OE-IVK	Airbus A.320-214	easyJet Europe
	OE-IVL	Airbus A.320-214	easyJet Europe
	OE-IVM	Airbus A.320-214	easyJet Europe
	OE-IVN	Airbus A.320-214	easyJet Europe
	OE-IVO	Airbus A.320-214	easyJet Europe
	OE-IVQ	Airbus A.320-214	easyJet Europe
	OE-IVR	Airbus A.320-214	easyJet Europe

Reg	Type	Owner or Operator	Notes
OE-IVS	Airbus A.320-214	easyJet Europe	
OE-IVT	Airbus A.320-214	easyJet Europe	
OE-IVU	Airbus A.320-214	easyJet Europe	
OE-IVV	Airbus A.320-214	easyJet Europe	
OE-IVW	Airbus A.320-214	easyJet Europe	
OE-IVX	Airbus A.320-214	easyJet Europe	
OE-IVZ	Airbus A.320-214	easyJet Europe	
OE-IZB	Airbus A.320-214	easyJet Europe	
OE-IZC	Airbus A.320-214	easyJet Europe	
OE-IZD	Airbus A.320-214	easyJet Europe	
OE-IZE	Airbus A.320-214	easyJet Europe	
OE-IZF	Airbus A.320-214	easyJet Europe	
OE-IZG	Airbus A.320-214	easyJet Europe	
OE-IZH	Airbus A.320-214	easyJet Europe	
OE-IZJ	Airbus A.320-214	easyJet Europe	
OE-IZL	Airbus A.320-214	easyJet Europe	
OE-IZN	Airbus A.320-214	easyJet Europe	
OE-IZO	Airbus A.320-214	easyJet Europe	
OE-IZP	Airbus A.320-214	easyJet Europe	
OE-IZQ	Airbus A.320-214	easyJet Europe	
OE-IZS	Airbus A.320-214	easyJet Europe	
OE-IZT	Airbus A.320-214	easyJet Europe	
OE-IZU	Airbus A.320-214	easyJet Europe	
OE-IZV	Airbus A.320-214	easyJet Europe	
OE-IZW	Airbus A.320-214	easyJet Europe	
OE-LAE	Boeing 767-3Z9ER	Austrian Airlines *Malaysia*	
OE-LAT	Boeing 767-31AER	Austrian Airlines *Enzo Ferrari*	
OE-LAW	Boeing 767-3Z9ER	Austrian Airlines *China*	
OE-LAX	Boeing 767-3Z9ER	Austrian Airlines *Thailand*	
OE-LAY	Boeing 767-3Z9ER	Austrian Airlines *Japan*	
OE-LAZ	Boeing 767-3Z9ER	Austrian Airlines *India*	
OE-LBA	Airbus A.321-111	Austrian Airlines *Salzkammergut*	
OE-LBB	Airbus A.321-111	Austrian Airlines *Pinzgau*	
OE-LBC	Airbus A.321-111	Austrian Airlines *Sudtirol*	
OE-LBD	Airbus A.321-111	Austrian Airlines *Steirisches Weinland*	
OE-LBE	Airbus A.321-111	Austrian Airlines *Wachau*	
OE-LBF	Airbus A.321-111	Austrian Airlines *Wien*	
OE-LBI	Airbus A.320-214	Austrian Airlines *Marchfeld*	
OE-LBJ	Airbus A.320-212	Austrian Airlines *Hohe Tauern*	
OE-LBK	Airbus A.320-214	Austrian Airlines *Sterisches Thermenland*	
OE-LBL	Airbus A.320-214	Austrian Airlines *Ausseerland*	
OE-LBM	Airbus A.320-214	Austrian Airlines *Arlberg*	
OE-LBN	Airbus A.320-214	Austrian Airlines *Osttirol*	
OE-LBO	Airbus A.320-214	Austrian Airlines *Pyhrn-Eisenwurzen*	
OE-LBP	Airbus A.320-214	Austrian Airlines *Neusiedler See*	
OE-LBQ	Airbus A.320-214	Austrian Airlines *Wienerwald*	
OE-LBR	Airbus A.320-214	Austrian Airlines *Frida Kahle*	
OE-LBS	Airbus A.320-214	Austrian Airlines *Waldviertel*	
OE-LBT	Airbus A.320-214	Austrian Airlines *Worthersee*	
OE-LBU	Airbus A.320-214	Austrian Airlines *Muhlviertel*	
OE-LBV	Airbus A.320-214	Austrian Airlines *Weinviertel*	
OE-LBW	Airbus A.320-214	Austrian Airlines *Innviertel*	
OE-LBX	Airbus A.320-214	Austrian Airlines *Mostviertel*	
OE-LBY	Airbus A.320-214	Austrian Airlines *Carnuntum*	
OE-LBZ	Airbus A.320-214	Austrian Airlines *Obertauern*	
OE-LDA	Airbus A.319-112	Austrian Airlines *Sofia*	
OE-LDB	Airbus A.319-112	Austrian Airlines *Bucharest*	
OE-LDC	Airbus A.319-112	Austrian Airlines *Kiev*	
OE-LDD	Airbus A.319-112	Austrian Airlines *Moscow*	
OE-LDE	Airbus A.319-112	Austrian Airlines *Baku*	
OE-LDF	Airbus A.319-112	Austrian Airlines *Sarajevo*	
OE-LDG	Airbus A.319-112	Austrian Airlines *Tbilisi*	
OE-LFB	Boeiung 757-23APF	ASL Airlines Belgium	
OE-LGA	DHC.8Q-402 Dash Eight	Austrian Airlines *Karnten*	
OE-LGB	DHC.8Q-402 Dash Eight	Austrian Airlines *Tirol*	
OE-LGC	DHC.8Q-402 Dash Eight	Austrian Airlines	
OE-LGD	DHC.8Q-402 Dash Eight	Austrian Airlines *Steiermark*	
OE-LGE	DHC.8Q-402 Dash Eight	Austrian Airlines *Oberosterreich*	
OE-LGF	DHC.8Q-402 Dash Eight	Austrian Airlines *Niederosterreich*	
OE-LGG	DHC.8Q-402 Dash Eight	Austrian Airlines *Budapest*	
OE-LGH	DHC.8Q-402 Dash Eight	Austrian Airlines *Vorarlberg*	

Notes	Reg	Type	Owner or Operator
	OE-LGI	DHC.8Q-402 Dash Eight	Austrian Airlines *Eisenstadt*
	OE-LGJ	DHC.8Q-402 Dash Eight	Austrian Airlines *St Pölten*
	OE-LGK	DHC.8Q-402 Dash Eight	Austrian Airlines *Burgenland*
	OE-LGL	DHC.8Q-402 Dash Eight	Austrian Airlines *Altenrhein*
	OE-LGM	DHC.8Q-402 Dash Eight	Austrian Airlines *Villach*
	OE-LGN	DHC.8Q-402 Dash Eight	Austrian Airlines *Gmunden*
	OE-LGO	DHC.8Q-402 Dash Eight	Austrian Airlines *Innsbruck*
	OE-LGP	DHC.8Q-402 Dash Eight	Austrian Airlines *Spirit of Alpach*
	OE-LGQ	DHC.8Q-402 Dash Eight	Austrian Airlines *Wilder Kaiser*
	OE-LGR	DHC.8Q-402 Dash Eight	Austrian Airlines *Tyrolean Spirit*
	OE-LKD	Airbus A.319-111	easyJet Europe
	OE-LKE	Airbus A.319-111	easyJet Europe
	OE-LKF	Airbus A.319-111	easyJet Europe
	OE-LKG	Airbus A.319-111	easyJet Europe
	OE-LKH	Airbus A.319-111	easyJet Europe
	OE-LKI	Airbus A.319-111	easyJet Europe
	OE-LKJ	Airbus A.319-111	easyJet Europe
	OE-LKK	Airbus A.319-111	easyJet Europe
	OE-LKL	Airbus A.319-111	easyJet Europe
	OE-LKM	Airbus A.319-111	easyJet Europe
	OE-LPA	Boeing 777-2Z9	Austrian Airlines *Melbourne*
	OE-LPB	Boeing 777-2Z9	Austrian Airlines *Sydney*
	OE-LPC	Boeing 777-2Z9ER	Austrian Airlines *Donald Bradman*
	OE-LPD	Boeing 777-2Z9ER	Austrian Airlines *America*
	OE-LPE	Boeing 777-2Q8ER	Austrian Airlines *Blue Danube*
	OE-LPF	Boeing 777-2Q8ER	Austrian Airlines
	OE-LQA	Airbus A.319-111	easyJet Europe
	OE-LQB	Airbus A.319-111	easyJet Europe
	OE-LQC	Airbus A.319-111	easyJet Europe
	OE-LQD	Airbus A.319-111	easyJet Europe
	OE-LQE	Airbus A.319-111	easyJet Europe
	OE-LQF	Airbus A.319-111	easyJet Europe
	OE-LQG	Airbus A.319-111	easyJet Europe
	OE-LQH	Airbus A.319-111	easyJet Europe
	OE-LQI	Airbus A.319-111	easyJet Europe
	OE-LQJ	Airbus A.319-111	easyJet Europe
	OE-LQK	Airbus A.319-111	easyJet Europe
	OE-LQL	Airbus A.319-111	easyJet Europe
	OE-LQM	Airbus A.319-111	easyJet Europe
	OE-LQN	Airbus A.319-111	easyJet Europe
	OE-LQO	Airbus A.319-111	easyJet Europe
	OE-LQP	Airbus A.319-111	easyJet Europe
	OE-LQQ	Airbus A.319-111	easyJet Europe
	OE-LQR	Airbus A.319-111	easyJet Europe
	OE-LQS	Airbus A.319-111	easyJet Europe
	OE-LQT	Airbus A.319-111	easyJet Europe
	OE-LQU	Airbus A.319-111	easyJet Europe
	OE-LQV	Airbus A.319-111	easyJet Europe
	OE-LQW	Airbus A.319-111	easyJet Europe
	OE-LQX	Airbus A.319-111	easyJet Europe
	OE-LQY	Airbus A.319-111	easyJet Europe
	OE-LQZ	Airbus A.319-111	easyJet Europe
	OE-LWA	Embraer ERJ190-200LR	Austrian Airlines
	OE-LWB	Embraer ERJ190-200LR	Austrian Airlines
	OE-LWC	Embraer ERJ190-200LR	Austrian Airlines
	OE-LWD	Embraer ERJ190-200LR	Austrian Airlines *Central Europe*
	OE-LWE	Embraer ERJ190-200LR	Austrian Airlines
	OE-LWF	Embraer ERJ190-200LR	Austrian Airlines
	OE-LWG	Embraer ERJ190-200LR	Austrian Airlines
	OE-LWH	Embraer ERJ190-200LR	Austrian Airlines
	OE-LWI	Embraer ERJ190-200LR	Austrian Airlines
	OE-LWJ	Embraer ERJ190-200LR	Austrian Airlines
	OE-LWK	Embraer ERJ190-200LR	Austrian Airlines
	OE-LWL	Embraer ERJ190-200LR	Austrian Airlines
	OE-LWM	Embraer ERJ190-200LR	Austrian Airlines
	OE-LWN	Embraer ERJ190-200LR	Austrian Airlines
	OE-LWO	Embraer ERJ190-200LR	Austrian Airlines
	OE-LWP	Embraer ERJ190-200LR	Austrian Airlines
	OE-LWQ	Embraer ERJ190-200LR	Austrian Airlines
	OE-LXA	Airbus A.320-216	Austrian Airlines
	OE-LXB	Airbus A.320-216	Austrian Airlines

408

Reg	Type	Owner or Operator	Notes
OE-LXC	Airbus A.320-216	Austrian Airlines	
OE-LXD	Airbus A.320-216	Austrian Airlines	
OE-LXE	Airbus A.320-216	Austrian Airlines	
OE-LYX	Airbus A.319-132	Eurowings Europe	
OE-LYY	Airbus A.319-132	Eurowings Europe	
OE-LYZ	Airbus A.319-132	Eurowings Europe	

OH (Finland)

Reg	Type	Owner or Operator	Notes
OH-JTZ	Boeing 737-73S	Jet Time Finland	
OH-LKE	Embraer RJ190-100LR	Nordic Regional Airlines/Finnair	
OH-LKF	Embraer RJ190-100LR	Nordic Regional Airlines/Finnair	
OH-LKG	Embraer RJ190-100LR	Nordic Regional Airlines/Finnair	
OH-LKH	Embraer RJ190-100LR	Nordic Regional Airlines/Finnair	
OH-LKI	Embraer RJ190-100LR	Nordic Regional Airlines/Finnair	
OH-LKK	Embraer RJ190-100LR	Nordic Regional Airlines/Finnair	
OH-LKL	Embraer RJ190-100LR	Nordic Regional Airlines/Finnair	
OH-LKM	Embraer RJ190-100LR	Nordic Regional Airlines/Finnair	
OH-LKN	Embraer RJ190-100LR	Nordic Regional Airlines/Finnair	
OH-LKO	Embraer RJ190-100LR	Nordic Regional Airlines/Finnair	
OH-LKP	Embraer RJ190-100LR	Nordic Regional Airlines/Finnair	
OH-LKR	Embraer RJ190-100LR	Nordic Regional Airlines/Finnair	
OH-LTM	Airbus A.330-302	Finnair	
OH-LTN	Airbus A.330-302	Finnair	
OH-LTO	Airbus A.330-302	Finnair	
OH-LTP	Airbus A.330-302	Finnair	
OH-LTR	Airbus A.330-302	Finnair	
OH-LTS	Airbus A.330-302	Finnair	
OH-LTT	Airbus A.330-302	Finnair	
OH-LTU	Airbus A.330-302	Finnair	
OH-LVA	Airbus A.319-112	Finnair	
OH-LVB	Airbus A.319-112	Finnair	
OH-LVC	Airbus A.319-112	Finnair	
OH-LVD	Airbus A.319-112	Finnair	
OH-LVH	Airbus A.319-112	Finnair	
OH-LVI	Airbus A.319-112	Finnair	
OH-LVK	Airbus A.319-112	Finnair	
OH-LVL	Airbus A.319-112	Finnair	
OH-LWA	Airbus A.350-941	Finnair	
OH-LWB	Airbus A.350-941	Finnair	
OH-LWC	Airbus A.350-941	Finnair	
OH-LWD	Airbus A.350-941	Finnair	
OH-LWE	Airbus A.350-941	Finnair	
OH-LWF	Airbus A.350-941	Finnair	
OH-LWG	Airbus A.350-941	Finnair	
OH-LWH	Airbus A.350-941	Finnair	
OH-LWI	Airbus A.350-941	Finnair	
OH-LWK	Airbus A.350-941	Finnair	
OH-LWL	Airbus A.350-941	Finnair	
OH-LXA	Airbus A.320-214	Finnair	
OH-LXB	Airbus A.320-214	Finnair	
OH-LXC	Airbus A.320-214	Finnair	
OH-LXD	Airbus A.320-214	Finnair	
OH-LXF	Airbus A.320-214	Finnair	
OH-LXH	Airbus A.320-214	Finnair	
OH-LXI	Airbus A.320-214	Finnair	
OH-LXK	Airbus A.320-214	Finnair	
OH-LXL	Airbus A.320-214	Finnair	
OH-LXM	Airbus A.320-214	Finnair	
OH-LZA	Airbus A.321-211	Finnair	
OH-LZB	Airbus A.321-211	Finnair	
OH-LZC	Airbus A.321-211	Finnair	
OH-LZD	Airbus A.321-211	Finnair	
OH-LZE	Airbus A.321-211	Finnair	
OH-LZF	Airbus A.321-211	Finnair	
OH-LZG	Airbus A.321-231	Finnair	
OH-LZH	Airbus A.321-231	Finnair	
OH-LZI	Airbus A.321-231	Finnair	
OH-LZK	Airbus A.321-231	Finnair	
OH-LZL	Airbus A.321-231	Finnair	
OH-LZM	Airbus A.321-231	Finnair	

Notes	Reg	Type	Owner or Operator
	OH-LZN	Airbus A.321-231	Finnair
	OH-LZO	Airbus A.321-231	Finnair
	OH-LZP	Airbus A.321-231	Finnair
	OH-LZR	Airbus A.321-231	Finnair
	OH-LZS	Airbus A.321-231	Finnair
	OH-LZT	Airbus A.321-231	Finnair

OK (Czech Republic)

	OK-MEK	Airbus A.319-112	CSA Czech Airlines
	OK-MEL	Airbus A.319-112	CSA Czech Airlines
	OK-NEM	Airbus A,319-112	CSA Czech Airlines
	OK-NEN	Airbus A.319-112	CSA Czech Airlines
	OK-NEO	Airbus A.319-112	CSA Czech Airlines
	OK-NEP	Airbus A.319-112	CSA Czech Airlines
	OK-OER	Airbus A.319-112	CSA Czech Airlines
	OK-PET	Airbus A.319-112	CSA Czech Airlines
	OK-REQ	Airbus A.319-112	CSA Czech Airlines
	OK-SWA	Boeing 737-8MAX	Smart Wings
	OK-SWB	Boeing 737-8MAX	Smart Wings
	OK-SWT	Boeing 737-7Q8	Smart Wings
	OK-SWW	Boeing 737-7Q8	Smart Wings
	OK-TSC	Boeing 737-8FH	Smart Wings
	OK-TSD	Boeing 737-8Q8	Travel Service Airlines
	OK-TSE	Boeing 737-81D	Travel Service Airlines
	OK-TSF	Boeing 737-8GJ	Smart Wings
	OK-TSH	Boeing 737-804	Smart Wings
	OK-TSI	Boeing 737-9GJ	Travel Service Airlines
	OK-TSM	Boeing 737-9GJ	Travel Service Airlines
	OK-TSO	Boeing 737-8GQ	Smart Wings
	OK-TSR	Boeing 737-82R	Smart Wings
	OK-TSS	Boeing 737-8Q8	Travel Service Airlines
	OK-TST	Boeing 737-8JP	Travel Service Airlines
	OK-TVE	Boeing 737-86Q	Travel Service Airlines
	OK-TVF	Boeing 737-8FH	Travel Service Airlines
	OK-TVG	Boeing 737-8Q8	Smart Wings
	OK-TVH	Boeing 737-8Q8	Smart Wings
	OK-TVJ	Boeing 737-8Q8	Smart Wings
	OK-TVL	Boeing 737-8FN	Travel Service Airlines
	OK-TVM	Boeing 737-8FN	Travel Service Airlines
	OK-TVO	Boeing 737-8CX	Travel Service Airlines
	OK-TVP	Boeing 737-8K5	Smart Wings
	OK-TVR	Boeing 737-86N	Smart Wings
	OK-TVS	Boeing 737-86N	Travel Service Airlines
	OK-TVT	Boeing 737-86N	Travel Service Airlines
	OK-TVU	Boeing 737-86N	Smart Wings
	OK-TVV	Boeing 737-86N	Travel Service Airlines
	OK-TVW	Boeing 737-86Q	Smart Wings
	OK-TVX	Boeing 737-8Z9	Smart Wings
	OK-TVY	Boeing 737-8Q8	Smart Wings

OM (Slovakia)

	OM-FEX	Boeing 737-8Q8	AirExplore
	OM-GEX	Boeing 737-8AS	AirExplore
	OM-GTB	Boeing 737-49R	Go2Sky
	OM-GTD	Boeing 737-46J	Go2Sky
	OM-GTE	Boeing 737-8AS	Go2Sky
	OM-GTF	Boeing 737-86J	Go2Sky
	OM-IEX	Boeing 737-8BK	AirExplore
	OM-JEX	Boeing 737-8AS	AirExplore
	OM-TSG	Boeing 737-82R	Smart Wings

OO (Belgium)

	OO-JAA	Boeing 737-8BK	TUI Airlines Belgium
	OO-JAD	Boeing 737-8K5	TUI Airlines Belgium
	OO-JAF	Boeing 737-8K5	TUI Airlines Belgium
	OO-JAH	Boeing 737-8K5	TUI Airlines Belgium
	OO-JAL	Boeing 737-7K2	TUI Airlines Belgium

Reg	Type	Owner or Operator	Notes
OO-JAO	Boeing 737-7K5	TUI Airlines Belgium	
OO-JAQ	Boeing 737-8K5	TUI Airlines Belgium	
OO-JAR	Boeing 737-7K5	TUI Airlines Belgium	
OO-JAS	Boeing 737-7K5	TUI Airlines Belgium	
OO-JAU	Boeing 737-8K5	TUI Airlines Belgium	
OO-JAV	Boeing 737-8K5	TUI Airlines Belgium	
OO-JAX	Boeing 737-8K5	TUI Airlines Belgium	
OO-JAY	Boeing 737-8K5	TUI Airlines Belgium	
OO-JBG	Boeing 737-8K5	TUI Airlines Belgium	
OO-JDL	Boeing 787-8K5	TUI Airlines Belgium	
OO-JEB	Embraer ERJ190-100STD	TUI Airlines Belgium	
OO-JEF	Boeing 737-8K5	TUI Airlines Belgium	
OO-JEM	Embraer ERJ190-100STD	TUI Airlines Belgium	
OO-JLO	Boeing 737-8K5	TUI Airlines Belgium	
OO-JNL	Boeing 767-304ER	TUI Airlines Belgium	
OO-JOS	Boeing 737-7K5	TUI Airlines Belgium	
OO-JVA	Embraer ERJ190-100STD	TUI Airlines Belgium	
OO-MAX	Boeing 737-8MAX	TUI Airlines Belgium	
OO-SFM	Airbus A.330-301	Brussels Airlines	
OO-SFN	Airbus A.330-301	Brussels Airlines	
OO-SFO	Airbus A.330-301	Brussels Airlines	
OO-SFT	Airbus A.330-223	Brussels Airlines	
OO-SFU	Airbus A.330-223	Brussels Airlines	
OO-SFV	Airbus A.330-322	Brussels Airlines	
OO-SFW	Airbus A.330-322	Brussels Airlines	
OO-SFX	Airbus A.330-343E	Brussels Airlines	
OO-SFY	Airbus A.330-223	Brussels Airlines	
OO-SFZ	Airbus A.330-223	Brussels Airlines	
OO-SNA	Airbus A.320-214	Brussels Airlines	
OO-SNB	Airbus A.320-214	Brussels Airlines	
OO-SNC	Airbus A.320-214	Brussels Airlines	
OO-SND	Airbus A.320-214	Brussels Airlines	
OO-SNE	Airbus A.320-214	Brussels Airlines	
OO-SNF	Airbus A.320-214	Brussels Airlines	
OO-SNG	Airbus A.320-214	Brussels Airlines	
OO-SNH	Airbus A.320-214	Brussels Airlines	
OO-SNI	Airbus A.320-214	Brussels Airlines	
OO-SNJ	Airbus A.320-214	Brussels Airlines	
OO-SNK	Airbus A.320-214	Brussels Airlines	
OO-SNL	Airbus A.320-214	Brussels Airlines	
OO-SNM	Airbus A.320-214	Brussels Airlines	
OO-SSA	Airbus A.319-111	Brussels Airlines	
OO-SSB	Airbus A.319-111	Brussels Airlines	
OO-SSC	Airbus A.319-112	Brussels Airlines	
OO-SSD	Airbus A.319-112	Brussels Airlines	
OO-SSE	Airbus A.319-111	Brussels Airlines	
OO-SSF	Airbus A.319-111	Brussels Airlines	
OO-SSG	Airbus A.319-112	Brussels Airlines	
OO-SSH	Airbus A.319-112	Brussels Airlines	
OO-SSI	Airbus A.319-112	Brussels Airlines	
OO-SSJ	Airbus A.319-111	Brussels Airlines	
OO-SSK	Airbus A.319-112	Brussels Airlines	
OO-SSL	Airbus A.319-112	Brussels Airlines	
OO-SSM	Airbus A.319-112	Brussels Airlines	
OO-SSN	Airbus A.319-112	Brussels Airlines	
OO-SSO	Airbus A.319-111	Brussels Airlines	
OO-SSQ	Airbus A.319-112	Brussels Airlines	
OO-SSR	Airbus A.319-112	Brussels Airlines	
OO-SSS	Airbus A.319-111	Brussels Airlines	
OO-SSU	Airbus A.319-111	Brussels Airlines	
OO-SSV	Airbus A.319-111	Brussels Airlines	
OO-SSW	Airbus A.319-111	Brussels Airlines	
OO-SSX	Airbus A.319-111	Brussels Airlines	
OO-TCH	Airbus A.320-214	Brussels Airlines	
OO-TCQ	Airbus A.320-214	Brussels Airlines	
OO-TCT	Airbus A.320-212	VLM Airlines	
OO-TCV	Airbus A.320-212	Brussels Airlines	
OO-TCX	Airbus A.320-212	VLM Airlines	
OO-TEA	Embraer ERJ190-100LR	TUI Airlines Belgium	
OO-TFA	Boeing 757-28A	ASL Airlines Belgium	
OO-TFC	Boeing 757-222	ASL Airlines Belgium	

Notes	Reg	Type	Owner or Operator
	OO-TMA	Boeing 737-MAX8	TUI Airlines Belgium
	OO-TNN	Boeing 737-45D	ASL Airlines Belgium/Federal Express
	OO-TNO	Boeing 737-49RF	ASL Airlines Belgium
	OO-TNP	Boeing 737-45D	ASL Airlines Belgium/Federal Express
	OO-TNQ	Boeing 737-4MOF	ASL Airlines Belgium
	OO-TUK	Boeing 737-86J	TUI Airlines Belgium
	OO-TUP	Boeing 737-85P	TUI Airlines Belgium
	OO-TUV	Boeing 737-86J	TUI Airlines Belgium
	OO-TUX	Boeing 737-86N	TUI Airlines Belgium
	OO-VLI	Fokker 50	VLM Airlines
	OO-VLN	Fokker 50	VLM Airlines
	OO-VLQ	Fokker 50	VLM Airlines
	OO-VLS	Fokker 50	VLM Airlines
	OO-VLZ	Fokker 50	VLM Airlines

OY (Denmark)

Notes	Reg	Type	Owner or Operator
	OY-JRK	Airbus A.320-231	Danish Air Transport
	OY-JRZ	Airbus A.320-233	Danish Air Transport
	OY-JTP	Boeing 737-79L	Jet Time
	OY-JTR	Boeing 737-73A	Jet Time
	OY-JTS	Boeing 737-7K2	Jet Time
	OY-JTT	Boeing 737-73S	Jet Time
	OY-JTY	Boeing 737-7Q8	Jet Time
	OY-JTZ	Boeing 737-73S	Jet Time
	OY-KAL	Airbus A.320-232	SAS Jon Viking
	OY-KAM	Airbus A.320-232	SAS Randver Viking
	OY-KAN	Airbus A.320-232	SAS Refil Viking
	OY-KAO	Airbus A.320-232	SAS Amled Viking
	OY-KAP	Airbus A.320-232	SAS Viglek Viking
	OY-KAR	Airbus A.320-232	SAS Vermund Viking
	OY-KAS	Airbus A.320-232	SAS Igulfsast Viking
	OY-KAT	Airbus A.320-232	SAS Hildegun Viking
	OY-KAU	Airbus A.320-232	SAS Hjorvard Viking
	OY-KAW	Airbus A.320-232	SAS Tyke Viking
	OY-KAY	Airbus A.320-232	SAS Runar Viking
	OY-KBA	Airbus A.340-313X	SAS Adalstein Viking
	OY-KBB	Airbus A.321-231	SAS Hjorulf Viking
	OY-KBC	Airbus A.340-313X	SAS Fredis Viking
	OY-KBD	Airbus A.340-313X	SAS Toste Viking
	OY-KBE	Airbus A.321-231	SAS Emma Viking
	OY-KBF	Airbus A.321-231	SAS Skapti Viking
	OY-KBH	Airbus A.321-231	SAS Sulke Viking
	OY-KBI	Airbus A.340-313X	SAS Rurik Viking
	OY-KBK	Airbus A.321-231	SAS Arne Viking
	OY-KBL	Airbus A.321-231	SAS Gynnbjorn Viking
	OY-KBM	Airbus A.340-313X	SAS Astrid Viking
	OY-KBO	Airbus A.319-131	SAS Christian Valdemar Viking
	OY-KBP	Airbus A.319-131	SAS Viger Viking
	OY-KBR	Airbus A.319-132	SAS Finnboge Viking
	OY-KBT	Airbus A.319-132	SAS Ragnvald Viking
	OY-KFD	Canadair CRJ900ER	SAS Estrid Viking
	OY-KFE	Canadair CRJ900ER	SAS Ingemar Viking
	OY-KFF	Canadair CRJ900ER	SAS Karl Viking
	OY-KFG	Canadair CRJ900ER	SAS Maria Viking
	OY-KFH	Canadair CRJ900ER	SAS Ella Viking
	OY-KFI	Canadair CRJ900ER	SAS Rolf Viking
	OY-KFK	Canadair CRJ900ER	SAS Hardeknud Viking
	OY-KFL	Canadair CRJ900ER	SAS Regin Viking
	OY-LHD	Airbus A.320-231	Danish Air Transport
	OY-NCL	Dornier 328-300 JET	Sun-Air/British Airways
	OY-NCM	Dornier 328-300 JET	Sun-Air/British Airways
	OY-NCN	Dornier 328-300 JET	Sun-Air/British Airways
	OY-NCO	Dornier 328-300 JET	Sun-Air/British Airways
	OY-NCP	Dornier 328-300 JET	Sun-Air/British Airways
	OY-NCU	Dornier 328-300 JET	Sun-Air/British Airways
	OY-NCW	Dornier 328-300 JET	Sun-Air/British Airways
	OY-PAA	Airbus A.321-251N	Primera Air
	OY-PAB	Airbus A.321-251N	Primera Air
	OY-PSA	Boeing 737-8Q8	Primera Air
	OY-PSE	Boeing 737-809	Primera Air

Reg	Type	Owner or Operator	Notes
OY-RCG	Airbus A.319-112	Atlantic Airways	
OY-RCI	Airbus A.319-112	Atlantic Airways	
OY-RCJ	Airbus A.320-214	Atlantic Airways	
OY-RUE	McD Douglas MD-83	Danish Air Transport	
OY-RUS	Airbus A.320-231	Danish Air Transport	
OY-SRF	Boeing 767-219 (SF)	Star Air	
OY-SRG	Boeing 767-219 (SF)	Star Air	
OY-SRH	Boeing 767-204 (SF)	Star Air	
OY-SRI	Boeing 767-25E (SF)	Star Air	
OY-SRJ	Boeing 767-25E (SF)	Star Air	
OY-SRK	Boeing 767-204 (SF)	Star Air	
OY-SRL	Boeing 767-232 (SF)	Star Air	
OY-SRM	Boeing 767-25E (SF)	Star Air	
OY-SRN	Boeing 767-219 (SF)	Star Air	
OY-SRO	Boeing 767-25E (SF)	Star Air	
OY-SRP	Boeing 767-232 (SF)	Star Air	
OY-SRU	Boeing 767-36NER	Star Air	
OY-SRV	Boeing 767-346ERF	Star Air	
OY-SRW	Boeing 767-346ERF	Star Air	
OY-TCD	Airbus A.321-211	Thomas Cook Airlines	
OY-TCE	Airbus A.321-211	Thomas Cook Airlines	
OY-TCF	Airbus A.321-211	Thomas Cook Airlines	
OY-TCG	Airbus A.321-211	Thomas Cook Airlines	
OY-TCH	Airbus A.321-211	Thomas Cook Airlines	
OY-TCI	Airbus A.321-211	Thomas Cook Airlines	
OY-VKC	Airbus A.321-211	Thomas Cook Airlines	
OY-VKD	Airbus A.321-211	Thomas Cook Airlines	
OY-VKF	Airbus A.330-243	Thomas Cook Airlines	
OY-VKG	Airbus A.330-343X	Thomas Cook Airlines	
OY-VKH	Airbus A.330-343X	Thomas Cook Airlines	
OY-VKI	Airbus A.330-343X	Thomas Cook Airlines	

P4 (Aruba)

Reg	Type	Owner or Operator	Notes
P4-EAS	Boeing 757-2G5	Air Astana	
P4-FAS	Boeing 757-2G5	Air Astana	
P4-GAS	Boeing 757-2G5	Air Astana	
P4-KCU	Boeing 757-23N	Air Astana	
P4-MAS	Boeing 757-28A	Air Astana	

PH (Netherlands)

Reg	Type	Owner or Operator	Notes
PH-AKA	Airbus A.330-303	KLM *Times Square – New York*	
PH-AKB	Airbus A.330-303	KLM *Piazza Navona-Roma*	
PH-AKD	Airbus A.330-303	KLM *Plaza de la Catedral-La Habana*	
PH-AKE	Airbus A.330-303	KLM *Pracia de Rossio-Lisboa*	
PH-AKF	Airbus A.330-303	KLM *Hofplein-Rotterdam*	
PH-AOA	Airbus A.330-203	KLM *Dam – Amsterdam*	
PH-AOB	Airbus A.330-203	KLM *Potsdamer Platz - Berlin*	
PH-AOC	Airbus A.330-203	KLM *Place de la Concorde – Paris*	
PH-AOD	Airbus A.330-203	KLM *Plazza del Duomo – Milano*	
PH-AOE	Airbus A.330-203	KLM *Parliament Square - Edinburgh*	
PH-AOF	Airbus A.330-203	KLM *Federation Square – Melbourne*	
PH-AOM	Airbus A.330-203	KLM *Piazza San Marco-Venezia*	
PH-AON	Airbus A.330-203	KLM *Museumplein-Amsterdam*	
PH-BCA	Boeing 737-8K2	KLM *Flamingo*	
PH-BCB	Boeing 737-8BK	KLM *Grote Pijlstormvogel/Great Shearwater*	
PH-BCD	Boeing 737-8BK	KLM	
PH-BCE	Boeing 737-8CK	KLM *Blauwborst/Bluethroat*	
PH-BFB	Boeing 747-406	KLM *City of Bangkok*	
PH-BFC	Boeing 747-406 (SCD)	KLM *City of Calgary*	
PH-BFG	Boeing 747-406	KLM *City of Guayaquil*	
PH-BFH	Boeing 747-406 (SCD)	KLM *City of Hong Kong*	
PH-BFI	Boeing 747-406 (SCD)	KLM *City of Jakarta*	
PH-BFL	Boeing 747-406	KLM *City of Lima*	
PH-BFN	Boeing 747-406	KLM *City of Nairobi*	
PH-BFS	Boeing 747-406 (SCD)	KLM *City of Seoul*	
PH-BFT	Boeing 747-406 (SCD)	KLM *City of Tokyo*	
PH-BFU	Boeing 747-406 (SCD)	KLM *City of Beijing*	
PH-BFV	Boeing 747-406	KLM *City of Vancouver*	

Notes	Reg	Type	Owner or Operator
	PH-BFW	Boeing 747-406	KLM *City of Shanghai*
	PH-BFY	Boeing 747-406	KLM *City of Johannesburg*
	PH-BGA	Boeing 737-8K2	KLM *Tureluur/Redshank*
	PH-BGB	Boeing 737-8K2	KLM *Whimbrel/Regenwulg*
	PH-BGC	Boeing 737-8K2	KLM *Pijlstaart/Pintail*
	PH-BGD	Boeing 737-706	KLM *Goldcrest/Goadhaantje*
	PH-BGE	Boeing 737-706	KLM *Ortolan Bunting/Ortolaan*
	PH-BGF	Boeing 737-7K2	KLM *Great White Heron/Grote Ziverreiger*
	PH-BGG	Boeing 737-706	KLM *King Eider/Koening Seider*
	PH-BGH	Boeing 737-7K2	KLM *Grutto/Godwit*
	PH-BGI	Boeing 737-7K2	KLM *Vink/Finch*
	PH-BGK	Boeing 737-7K2	KLM *Noordse Stormvogel/Fulmar*
	PH-BGL	Boeing 737-7K2	KLM *Rietzangler/Warbler*
	PH-BGM	Boeing 737-7K2	KLM *Aabscholver/Cormorant*
	PH-BGN	Boeing 737-7K2	KLM *Jan van Gent/Gannet*
	PH-BGO	Boeing 737-7K2	KLM *Paradijsvogel/Bird of Paradise*
	PH-BGP	Boeing 737-7K2	KLM *Pelikaan/Pelican*
	PH-BGQ	Boeing 737-7K2	KLM *Wielewaal/Golden Oriole*
	PH-BGR	Boeing 737-7K2	KLM *Zwarte Wouw/Black Kite*
	PH-BGT	Boeing 737-7K2	KLM *Zanglijster/Song Thrush*
	PH-BGU	Boeing 737-7K2	KLM *Koekoek/Cuckoo*
	PH-BGW	Boeing 737-7K2	KLM *Zanglijster/Song Thrush*
	PH-BGX	Boeing 737-7K2	KLM *Scholekster/Oystercatcher*
	PH-BHA	Boeing 787-9	KLM *Anjer/Crnation*
	PH-BHC	Boeing 787-9	KLM *Zonnebloem/Sunflower*
	PH-BHD	Boeing 787-9	KLM
	PH-BHE	Boeing 787-9	KLM *Dahlia*
	PH-BHF	Boeing 787-9	KLM *Hisbiscus*
	PH-BHG	Boeing 787-9	KLM *Mimosa*
	PH-BHH	Boeing 787-9	KLM *Jasmine*
	PH-BHI	Boeing 787-9	KLM *Lavender*
	PH-BHL	Boeing 787-9	KLM *Lily*
	PH-BHM	Boeing 787-9	KLM *Marguerite*
	PH-BHN	Boeing 787-9	KLM
	PH-BQA	Boeing 777-206ER	KLM *Albert Plesman*
	PH-BQB	Boeing 777-206ER	KLM *Borobudur*
	PH-BQC	Boeing 777-206ER	KLM *Chichen-Itza*
	PH-BQD	Boeing 777-206ER	KLM *Darjeeling Highway*
	PH-BQE	Boeing 777-206ER	KLM *Epidaurus*
	PH-BQF	Boeing 777-206ER	KLM *Ferrara City*
	PH-BQG	Boeing 777-206ER	KLM *Galapagos Islands*
	PH-BQH	Boeing 777-206ER	KLM *Hadrian's Wall*
	PH-BQI	Boeing 777-206ER	KLM *Iguazu Falls*
	PH-BQK	Boeing 777-206ER	KLM *Mount Kilimanjaro*
	PH-BQL	Boeing 777-206ER	KLM *Litomysl Castle*
	PH-BQM	Boeing 777-206ER	KLM *Macchu Picchu*
	PH-BQN	Boeing 777-206ER	KLM *Nahanni National Park*
	PH-BQO	Boeing 777-206ER	KLM *Old Rauma*
	PH-BQP	Boeing 777-206ER	KLM *Pont du Gard*
	PH-BVA	Boeing 777-306ER	KLM *National Park De Hoge Veluwe*
	PH-BVB	Boeing 777-306ER	KLM *Fulufjallet National Park*
	PH-BVC	Boeing 777-306ER	KLM *National ParkSian Ka'an*
	PH-BVD	Boeing 777-306ER	KLM *Amboseli National Park*
	PH-BVF	Boeing 777-306ER	KLM *Yakushima*
	PH-BVG	Boeing 777-306ER	KLM *National Park Wolong*
	PH-BVI	Boeing 777-306ER	KLM *Nationaal Park Vuurland*
	PH-BVK	Boeing 777-306ER	KLM *Yellowstone National Park*
	PH-BVN	Boeing 777-306ER	KLM *Tijuca National Park*
	PH-BVO	Boeing 777-306ER	KLM *Kaziranga National Park*
	PH-BVP	Boeing 777-306ER	KLM *Jasper National Park*
	PH-BVR	Boeing 777-306ER	KLM *Gunung Mulu National Park*
	PH-BVS	Boeing 777-306ER	KLM *National Park Darien*
	PH-BVU	Boeing 777-306ER	KLM
	PH-BXA	Boeing 737-8K2	KLM *Zwaan/Swan*
	PH-BXB	Boeing 737-8K2	KLM *Valk/Falcon*
	PH-BXC	Boeing 737-8K2	KLM *Korhoen/Grouse*
	PH-BXD	Boeing 737-8K2	KLM *Arend/Eagle*
	PH-BXE	Boeing 737-8K2	KLM *Harvik/Hawk*
	PH-BXF	Boeing 737-8K2	KLM *Zwallou/Swallow*
	PH-BXG	Boeing 737-8K2	KLM *Kraanvogel/Crane*
	PH-BXH	Boeing 737-8K2	KLM *Gans/Goose*

Reg	Type	Owner or Operator	Notes
PH-BXI	Boeing 737-8K2	KLM *Zilvermeeuw*	
PH-BXK	Boeing 737-8K2	KLM *Gierzwallou/Swift*	
PH-BXL	Boeing 737-8K2	KLM *Sperwer/Sparrow*	
PH-BXM	Boeing 737-8K2	KLM *Kluut/Avocet*	
PH-BXN	Boeing 737-8K2	KLM *Merel/Blackbird*	
PH-BXO	Boeing 737-9K2	KLM *Plevier/Plover*	
PH-BXP	Boeing 737-9K2	KLM *Meerkoet/Crested Coot*	
PH-BXR	Boeing 737-9K2	KLM *Nachtegaal/Nightingale*	
PH-BXS	Boeing 737-9K2	KLM *Buizerd/Buzzard*	
PH-BXT	Boeing 737-9K2	KLM *Zeestern/Sea Tern*	
PH-BXU	Boeing 737-8BK	KLM *Albatros/Albatross*	
PH-BXV	Boeing 737-8K2	KLM *Roodborstje*	
PH-BXW	Boeing 737-8K2	KLM *Patrijs/Partridge*	
PH-BXY	Boeing 737-8K2	KLM *Fuut/Grebe*	
PH-BXZ	Boeing 737-8K2	KLM *Uil/Owl*	
PH-CKA	Boeing 747-406ERF	KLM Cargo *Eendracht*	
PH-CKB	Boeing 747-406ERF	KLM Cargo *Leeuwin*	
PH-CKC	Boeing 747-406ERF	KLM Cargo *Oranje*	
PH-EXA	Embraer ERJ190-100STD	KLM Cityhopper	
PH-EXB	Embraer ERJ190-100STD	KLM Cityhopper	
PH-EXC	Embraer ERJ190-100STD	KLM Cityhopper	
PH-EXD	Embraer ERJ190-100STD	KLM Cityhopper	
PH-EXE	Embraer ERJ190-100STD	KLM Cityhopper	
PH-EXF	Embraer ERJ190-100STD	KLM Cityhopper	
PH-EXG	Embraer ERJ170-200STD	KLM Cityhopper	
PH-EXH	Embraer ERJ170-200STD	KLM Cityhopper	
PH-EXI	Embraer ERJ170-200STD	KLM Cityhopper	
PH-EXJ	Embraer ERJ170-200STD	KLM Cityhopper	
PH-EXK	Embraer ERJ170-200STD	KLM Cityhopper	
PH-EXL	Embraer ERJ170-200STD	KLM Cityhopper	
PH-EXM	Embraer ERJ170-200STD	KLM Cityhopper	
PH-EXN	Embraer ERJ170-200STD	KLM Cityhopper	
PH-EXO	Embraer ERJ170-200STD	KLM Cityhopper	
PH-EXP	Embraer ERJ170-200STD	KLM Cityhopper	
PH-EXR	Embraer ERJ170-200STD	KLM Cityhopper	
PH-EXS	Embraer ERJ170-200STD	KLM Cityhopper	
PH-EXT	Embraer ERJ170-200STD	KLM Cityhopper	
PH-EXU	Embraer ERJ170-200STD	KLM Cityhopper	
PH-EXV	Embraer ERJ170-200STD	KLM Cityhopper	
PH-EXW	Embraer ERJ170-200STD	KLM Cityhopper	
PH-EXX	Embraer ERJ170-200STD	KLM Cityhopper	
PH-EXY	Embraer ERJ170-200STD	KLM Cityhopper	
PH-EZA	Embraer ERJ190-100STD	KLM Cityhopper	
PH-EZB	Embraer ERJ190-100STD	KLM Cityhopper	
PH-EZC	Embraer ERJ190-100STD	KLM Cityhopper	
PH-EZD	Embraer ERJ190-100STD	KLM Cityhopper	
PH-EZE	Embraer ERJ190-100STD	KLM Cityhopper	
PH-EZF	Embraer ERJ190-100STD	KLM Cityhopper	
PH-EZG	Embraer ERJ190-100STD	KLM Cityhopper	
PH-EZH	Embraer ERJ190-100STD	KLM Cityhopper	
PH-EZI	Embraer ERJ190-100STD	KLM Cityhopper	
PH-EZK	Embraer ERJ190-100STD	KLM Cityhopper	
PH-EZL	Embraer ERJ190-100STD	KLM Cityhopper	
PH-EZM	Embraer ERJ190-100STD	KLM Cityhopper	
PH-EZN	Embraer ERJ190-100STD	KLM Cityhopper	
PH-EZO	Embraer ERJ190-100STD	KLM Cityhopper	
PH-EZP	Embraer ERJ190-100STD	KLM Cityhopper	
PH-EZR	Embraer ERJ190-100STD	KLM Cityhopper	
PH-EZS	Embraer ERJ190-100STD	KLM Cityhopper	
PH-EZT	Embraer ERJ190-100STD	KLM Cityhopper	
PH-EZU	Embraer ERJ190-100STD	KLM Cityhopper	
PH-EZV	Embraer ERJ190-100STD	KLM Cityhopper	
PH-EZW	Embraer ERJ190-100STD	KLM Cityhopper	
PH-EZX	Embraer ERJ190-100STD	KLM Cityhopper	
PH-EZY	Embraer ERJ190-100STD	KLM Cityhopper	
PH-EZZ	Embraer ERJ190-100STD	KLM Cityhopper	
PH-GGX	Boeing 737-8EH	Transavia	
PH-GGY	Boeing 737-8EH	Transavia	
PH-HSA	Boeing 737-8K2	Transavia	
PH-HSB	Boeing 737-8K2	Transavia	
PH-HSC	Boeing 737-8K2	Transavia	

Notes	Reg	Type	Owner or Operator
	PH-HSD	Boeing 737-8K2	KLM *Groene Specht*
	PH-HSE	Boeing 737-8K2	KLM *Blauwstaart*
	PH-HSF	Boeing 737-8K2	Transavia
	PH-HSG	Boeing 737-8K2	Transavia
	PH-HSI	Boeing 737-8K2	Transavia
	PH-HSJ	Boeing 737-8K2	Transavia
	PH-HSK	Boeing 737-8K2	Transavia
	PH-HSM	Boeing 737-8K2	Transavia
	PH-HSW	Boeing 737-8K2	Transavia
	PH-HXA	Boeing 737-8K2	Transavia
	PH-HXB	Boeing 737-8K2	Transavia
	PH-HXC	Boeing 737-8K2	Transavia
	PH-HXD	Boeing 737-8K2	Transavia
	PH-HXE	Boeing 737-8K2	Transavia
	PH-HXF	Boeing 737-8K2	Transavia
	PH-HXG	Boeing 737-8K2	Transavia
	PH-HXI	Boeing 737-8K2	Transavia
	PH-HXJ	Boeing 737-8K2	Transavia
	PH-HXK	Boeing 737-8K2	Transavia
	PH-HXL	Boeing 737-8K2	Transavia
	PH-HZD	Boeing 737-8K2	Transavia
	PH-HZE	Boeing 737-8K2	Transavia
	PH-HZG	Boeing 737-8K2	Transavia
	PH-HZI	Boeing 737-8K2	Transavia
	PH-HZJ	Boeing 737-8K2	Transavia
	PH-HZL	Boeing 737-8K2	Transavia
	PH-HZN	Boeing 737-8K2	Transavia
	PH-HZO	Boeing 737-8K2	Transavia
	PH-HZV	Boeing 737-8K2	Transavia
	PH-HZW	Boeing 737-8K2	Transavia
	PH-HZX	Boeing 737-8K2	Transavia
	PH-MPS	Boeing 747-412BCF	Martinair Cargo
	PH-OYI	Boeing 767-304ER	TUI Airlines Nederland
	PH-TFA	Boeing 737-8FH	TUI Airlines Nederland
	PH-TFB	Boeing 737-8K5	TUI Airlines Nederland
	PH-TFC	Boeing 737-8K5	TUI Airlines Nederland
	PH-TFD	Boeing 737-86N	TUI Airlines Nederland
	PH-TFF	Boeing 737-86N	TUI Airlines Nederland
	PH-TFK	Boeing 787-8	TUI Airlines Nederland
	PH-TFL	Boeing 787-8	TUI Airlines Nederland
	PH-TFM	Boeing 787-8	TUI Airlines Nederland
	PH-XRA	Boeing 737-7K2	Transavia
	PH-XRB	Boeing 737-7K2	Transavia
	PH-XRC	Boeing 737-7K2	Transavia
	PH-XRD	Boeing 737-7K2	Transavia
	PH-XRV	Boeing 737-7K2	Transavia
	PH-XRX	Boeing 737-7K2	Transavia
	PH-XRY	Boeing 737-7K2	Transavia
	PH-XRZ	Boeing 737-7K2	Transavia

PK (Indonesia)

Notes	Reg	Type	Owner or Operator
	PK-GIA	Boeing 777-3U3ER	Garuda Indonesia
	PK-GIC	Boeing 777-3U3ER	Garuda Indonesia
	PK-GID	Boeing 777-3U3ER	Garuda Indonesia
	PK-GIE	Boeing 777-3U3ER	Garuda Indonesia
	PK-GIF	Boeing 777-3U3ER	Garuda Indonesia
	PK-GIG	Boeing 777-3U3ER	Garuda Indonesia
	PK-GIH	Boeing 777-3U3ER	Garuda Indonesia
	PK-GII	Boeing 777-3U3ER	Garuda Indonesia
	PK-GIJ	Boeing 777-3U3ER	Garuda Indonesia
	PK-GIK	Boeing 777-3U3ER	Garuda Indonesia

PP/PR/PT (Brazil)

Notes	Reg	Type	Owner or Operator
	PT-MUA	Boeing 777-32WER	LATAM Airlines
	PT-MUB	Boeing 777-32WER	LATAM Airlines
	PT-MUC	Boeing 777-32WER	LATAM Airlines
	PT-MUD	Boeing 777-32WER	LATAM Airlines
	PT-MUE	Boeing 777-32WER	LATAM Airlines

Reg	Type	Owner or Operator	Notes
PT-MUF	Boeing 777-32WER	LATAM Airlines	
PT-MUG	Boeing 777-32WER	LATAM Airlines	
PT-MUH	Boeing 777-32WER	LATAM Airlines	
PT-MUI	Boeing 777-32WER	LATAM Airlines	
PT-MUJ	Boeing 777-32WER	LATAM Airlines	

RA (Russia)

Reg	Type	Owner or Operator	Notes
RA-82042	An-124	Volga-Dnepr	
RA-82043	An-124	Volga-Dnepr	
RA-82044	An-124	Volga-Dnepr	
RA-82045	An-124	Volga-Dnepr	
RA-82046	An-124	Volga-Dnepr	
RA-82047	An-124	Volga-Dnepr	
RA-82068	An-124	Volga-Dnepr	
RA-82074	An-124	Volga-Dnepr	
RA-82077	An-124	Volga-Dnepr	
RA-82078	An-124	Volga-Dnepr	
RA-82079	An-124	Volga-Dnepr	
RA-82081	An-124	Volga-Dnepr	
RA-76503	Ilyushin Il-76TD	Volga-Dnepr	
RA-76511	Ilyushin Il-76TD	Volga-Dnepr	
RA-76950	Ilyushin Il-76TD	Volga-Dnepr	
RA-76951	Ilyushin Il-76TD	Volga-Dnepr	
RA-76952	Ilyushin Il-76TD	Volga-Dnepr	

RP (Philippines)

Reg	Type	Owner or Operator	Notes
RP-C7772	Boeing 777-3F6ER	Philippine Airlines	
RP-C7773	Boeing 777-3F6ER	Philippine Airlines	
RP-C7774	Boeing 777-3F6ER	Philippine Airlines	
RP-C7775	Boeing 777-3F6ER	Philippine Airlines	
RP-C7776	Boeing 777-3F6ER	Philippine Airlines	
RP-C7777	Boeing 777-3F6ER	Philippine Airlines	
RP-C7778	Boeing 777-3F6ER	Philippine Airlines	
RP-C7779	Boeing 777-3F6ER	Philippine Airlines	
RP-C7781	Boeing 777-3F6ER	Philippine Airlines	
RP-C7782	Boeing 777-3F6ER	Philippine Airlines	

S2 (Bangladesh)

Reg	Type	Owner or Operator	Notes
S2-AFO	Boeing 777-3E9ER	Bangladesh Biman	
S2-AFP	Boeing 777-3E9FR	Bangladesh Biman	
S2-AHM	Boeing 777-3E9FR	Bangladesh Biman	
S2-AHN	Boeing 777-3E9FR	Bangladesh Biman	

S5 (Slovenia)

Reg	Type	Owner or Operator	Notes
S5-AAK	Canadair CRJ900LR	Adria Airways	
S5-AAL	Canadair CRJ900LR	Adria Airways	
S5-AAN	Canadair CRJ900LR	Adria Airways	
S5-AAO	Canadair CRJ900LR	Adria Airways	
S5-AAP	Airbus A.319-132	Adria Airways	
S5-AAR	Airbus A.319-132	Adria Airways	
S5-AAU	Canadair CRJ900LR	Adria Airways	
S5-AAV	Canadair CRJ900LR	Adria Airways	
S5-AAW	Canadair CRJ700ER	Adria Airways	
S5-AAX	Airbus A.319-111	Adria Airways	
S5-AAY	Canadair CRJ700ER	Adria Airways	
S5-AAZ	Canadair CRJ700ER	Adria Airways/Luxair	
S5-AFA	Canadair CRJ900LR	Adria Airways	

SE (Sweden)

Reg	Type	Owner or Operator	Notes
SE-DOX	Airbus A.320-251N	SAS *Torarve Viking*	
SE-DOY	Airbus A.320-251N	SAS *Markus Viking*	
SE-DOZ	Airbus A.320-251N	SAS *Jarngerd Viking*	
SE-DZV	Boeing 737-804	TUIfly Nordic	
SE-KXP	BAe ATP	West Air Sweden	

Notes	Reg	Type	Owner or Operator
	SE-LGX	BAe ATP	West Air Sweden
	SE-LGZ	BAe ATP	West Air Sweden
	SE-LHZ	BAe ATP	West Air Sweden
	SE-LNX	BAe ATP	West Air Sweden
	SE-LNY	BAe ATP	West Air Sweden
	SE-LPR	BAe ATP	West Air Sweden
	SE-LPS	BAe ATP	West Air Sweden
	SE-LPT	BAe ATP	West Air Sweden
	SE-LPX	BAe ATP	West Air Sweden
	SE-MAI	BAe ATP	West Air Sweden
	SE-MAJ	BAe ATP	West Air Sweden
	SE-MAM	BAe ATP	West Air Sweden
	SE-MAN	BAe ATP	West Air Sweden
	SE-MAO	BAe ATP	West Air Sweden
	SE-MAP	BAe ATP	West Air Sweden
	SE-MAR	BAe ATP	West Air Sweden
	SE-MHD	BAe ATP	West Air Sweden
	SE-MHE	BAe ATP	West Air Sweden
	SE-MHF	BAe ATP	West Air Sweden
	SE-MHG	BAe ATP	West Air Sweden
	SE-MHH	BAe ATP	West Air Sweden
	SE-MHI	BAe ATP	West Air Sweden
	SE-MHK	BAe ATP	West Air Sweden
	SE-RER	Boeing 737-7BX	SAS *Svein Viking*
	SE-RES	Boeing 737-7BX	SAS *Rut Viking*
	SE-RET	Boeing 737-76N	SAS *Katarina Viking*
	SE-REU	Boeing 737-76N	SAS *Folke Viking*
	SE-REX	Boeing 737-76N	SAS *Lodin Viking*
	SE-REY	Boeing 737-76N	SAS *Kristina Viking*
	SE-REZ	Boeing 737-76N	SAS *Margareta Viking*
	SE-RFT	Boeing 737-8K5	TUIfly Nordic
	SE-RFV	Boeing 737-86N	TUIfly Nordic
	SE-RFX	Boeing 737-8K5	TUIfly Nordic
	SE-RFY	Boeing 737-8K5	TUIfly Nordic
	SE-RJR	Boeing 737-76N	SAS *Styrbjorn Viking*
	SE-RJS	Boeing 737-76N	SAS *Sigvalde Viking*
	SE-RJT	Boeing 737-76N	SAS *Tora Viking*
	SE-RJU	Boeing 737-76N	SAS *Ubbe Viking*
	SE-RJX	Boeing 737-76N	SAS *Vagn Viking*
	SE-RKA	Airbus A.321-251N	Novair
	SE-RKB	Airbus A.321-251N	Novair
	SE-RLA	Boeing 767-232F	West Air Sweden
	SE-RLB	Boeing 767-232F	West Air Sweden
	SE-RLC	Boeing 767-232F	West Air Sweden
	SE-RNA	Boeing 737-MAX8	TUIfly Nordic
	SE-RNB	Boeing 737-MAX8	TUIfly Nordic
	SE-RNC	Boeing 737-MAX8	TUIfly Nordic
	SE-ROA	Airbus A.320-251N	SAS *Jake Viking*
	SE-ROB	Airbus A.320-251N	SAS *Towa Viking*
	SE-ROC	Airbus A.320-251N	SAS *Torarin Viking*
	SE-ROD	Airbus A.320-251N	SAS *Ingolf Viking*
	SE-ROE	Airbus A.320-251N	SAS

SP (Poland)

	SP-ENG	Boeing 737-8CX	Enter Air
	SP-ENL	Boeing 737-8CX	Enter Air
	SP-ENM	Boeing 737-8CX	Enter Air
	SP-ENN	Boeing 737-8CX	Enter Air
	SP-ENO	Boeing 737-8AS	Enter Air
	SP-ENP	Boeing 737-8AS	Enter Air
	SP-ENQ	Boeing 737-85R	Enter Air
	SP-ENR	Boeing 737-8Q8	Enter Air
	SP-ENT	Boeing 737-8AS	Enter Air
	SP-ENU	Boeing 737-83N	Enter Air
	SP-ENV	Boeing 737-8BK	Enter Air
	SP-ENW	Boeing 737-86J	Enter Air
	SP-ENX	Boeing 737-8Q8	Enter Air
	SP-ENZ	Boeing 737-85F	Enter Air
	SP-ESA	Boeing 737-8AL	Enter Air
	SP-ESB	Boeing 737-86N	Enter Air

Reg	Type	Owner or Operator	Notes
SP-HAB	Airbus A.320-232	Small Planet Airlines	
SP-HAD	Airbus A.320-232	Small Planet Airlines	
SP-HAG	Airbus A.320-232	Small Planet Airlines	
SP-HAH	Airbus A.320-233	Small Planet Airlines	
SP-HAI	Airbus A.320-233	Small Planet Airlines	
SP-HAW	Airbus A.321-211	Small Planet Airlines	
SP-HAX	Airbus A.321-211	Small Planet Airlines	
SP-HAY	Airbus A.321-211	Small Planet Airlines	
SP-HAZ	Airbus A.321-211	Small Planet Airlines	
SP-LDE	Embraer RJ170 100LR	LOT	
SP-LDF	Embraer RJ170 100LR	LOT	
SP-LDG	Embraer RJ170 100LR	LOT	
SP-LDH	Embraer RJ170 100LR	LOT	
SP-LDI	Embraer RJ170 100LR	LOT	
SP-LDK	Embraer RJ170 100LR	LOT	
SP-LIA	Embraer RJ170-200STD	LOT	
SP-LIB	Embraer RJ170-200STD	LOT	
SP-LIC	Embraer RJ170-200STD	LOT	
SP-LID	Embraer RJ170-200STD	LOT	
SP-LII	Embraer RJ170-200STD	LOT	
SP-LIK	Embraer RJ170-200STD	LOT	
SP-LIL	Embraer RJ170-200STD	LOT	
SP-LIM	Embraer RJ170-200STD	LOT	
SP-LIN	Embraer RJ170-200STD	LOT	
SP-LIO	Embraer RJ170-200STD	LOT	
SP-LLE	Boeing 737-45D	LOT	
SP-LLF	Boeing 737-45D	LOT	
SP-LLG	Boeing 737-45D	LOT	
SP-LNA	Embraer RJ190-200LR	LOT	
SP-LNB	Embraer RJ190-200LR	LOT	
SP-LNC	Embraer RJ190-200LR	LOT	
SP-LND	Embraer RJ190-200LR	LOT	
SP-LNE	Embraer RJ190-200LR	LOT	
SP-LNF	Embraer RJ190-200LR	LOT	
SP-LRA	Boeing 787-8	LOT	
SP-LRB	Boeing 787-8	LOT	
SP-LRC	Boeing 787-8	LOT	
SP-LRD	Boeing 787-8	LOT	
SP-LRE	Boeing 787-8	LOT	
SP-LRF	Boeing 787-8	LOT	
SP-LRG	Boeing 787-8	LOT	
SP-LRH	Boeing 787-8	LOT	
SP-LSA	Boeing 787-9	LOT	
SP-LSD	Boeing 787-9	LOT	
SP-LVA	Boeing 737-MAX8	LOT	
SP-LVB	Boeing 737-MAX8	LOT	
SP-LWA	Boeing 737-89P	LOT	
SP-LWB	Boeing 737-89P	LOT	
SP-LWC	Boeing 737-89P	LOT	
SP-LWD	Boeing 737-89P	LOT	

SU (Egypt)

Reg	Type	Owner or Operator	Notes
SU-GAC	Airbus A.300B4-203F	EgyptAir Cargo New Valley	
SU-GAS	Airbus A.300F4-622RF	EgyptAir Cargo Cheops	
SU-GAY	Airbus A.300B4-622RF	EgyptAir Cargo Seti I	
SU-GBS	Boeing 777-266ER	EgyptAir Tyie	
SU-GCF	Airbus A.330-243	EgyptAir	
SU-GCG	Airbus A.330-243	Egyptair	
SU-GCH	Airbus A.330-243	EgyptAir	
SU-GCI	Airbus A.330-243	EgyptAir	
SU-GCJ	Airbus A.330-243	EgyptAir	
SU-GCK	Airbus A.330-243	EgyptAir	
SU-GCM	Boeing 737-866WIN	EgyptAir	
SU-GCN	Boeing 737-866WIN	EgyptAir	
SU-GCO	Boeing 737-866WIN	EgyptAir	
SU-GCP	Boeing 737-866WIN	EgyptAir	
SU-GCR	Boeing 737-866WIN	EgyptAir	
SU-GCS	Boeing 737-866WIN	EgyptAir	
SU-GCZ	Boeing 737-866WIN	EgyptAir	
SU-GDA	Boeing 737-866WIN	EgyptAir	

Notes	Reg	Type	Owner or Operator
	SU-GDB	Boeing 737-866WIN	EgyptAir
	SU-GDC	Boeing 737-866WIN	EgyptAir
	SU-GDD	Boeing 737-866WIN	EgyptAir
	SU-GDE	Boeing 737-866WIN	EgyptAir
	SU-GDL	Boeing 777-36NER	EgyptAir
	SU-GDM	Boeing 777-36NER	EgyptAir
	SU-GDN	Boeing 777-36NER	EgyptAir
	SU-GDO	Boeing 777-36NER	EgyptAir
	SU-GDP	Boeing 777-36NER	EgyptAir
	SU-GDR	Boeing 777-36NER	EgyptAir
	SU-GDS	Airbus A.330-343X	EgyptAir
	SU-GDT	Airbus A.330-343X	EgyptAir
	SU-GDU	Airbus A.330-343X	EgyptAir
	SU-GDV	Airbus A.330-343X	EgyptAir
	SU-GDX	Boeing 737-866WIN	EgyptAir
	SU-GDY	Boeing 737-866WIN	EgyptAir
	SU-GDZ	Boeing 737-866WIN	EgyptAir
	SU-GEA	Boeing 737-866WIN	EgyptAir
	SU-GEB	Boeing 737-866WIN	EgyptAir
	SU-GEC	Boeing 737-866WIN	EgyptAir
	SU-GED	Boeing 737-866WIN	EgyptAir
	SU-GEE	Boeing 737-866WIN	EgyptAir
	SU-GEF	Boeing 737-866WIN	EgyptAir
	SU-GEG	Boeing 737-866WIN	EgyptAir
	SU-GEH	Boeing 737-866WIN	EgyptAir
	SU-GEI	Boeing 737-866WIN	EgyptAir
	SU-GEJ	Boeing 737-866WIN	EgyptAir
	SU-GEK	Boeing 737-866WIN	EgyptAir
	SU-GEL	Boeing 737-866WIN	EgyptAir
	SU-GEM	Boeing 737-866WIN	EgyptAir
	SU-GEN	Boeing 737-866WIN	EgyptAir

SX (Greece)

Notes	Reg	Type	Owner or Operator
	SX-ABY	Airbus A.321-231	Olympus Airways
	SX-ACP	Airbus A.321-231	Olympus Airways
	SX-DGA	Airbus A.321-231	Aegean Airlines
	SX-DGB	Airbus A.320-232	Aegean Airlines
	SX-DGC	Airbus A.320-232	Aegean Airlines
	SX-DGD	Airbus A.320-232	Aegean Airlines
	SX-DGE	Airbus A.320-232	Aegean Airlines
	SX-DGF	Airbus A.319-132	Aegean Airlines
	SX-DGI	Airbus A.320-232	Aegean Airlines
	SX-DGJ	Airbus A.320-232	Aegean Airlines
	SX-DGK	Airbus A.320-232	Aegean Airlines
	SX-DGL	Airbus A.320-232	Aegean Airlines
	SX-DGN	Airbus A.320-232	Aegean Airlines
	SX-DGO	Airbus A.320-232	Aegean Airlines
	SX-DGP	Airbus A.321-232	Aegean Airlines
	SX-DGQ	Airbus A.321-232	Aegean Airlines
	SX-DGR	Airbus A.320-232	Aegean Airlines
	SX-DGS	Airbus A.321-231	Aegean Airlines
	SX-DGT	Airbus A.321-231	Aegean Airlines
	SX-DGV	Airbus A.320-232	Aegean Airlines
	SX-DGX	Airbus A.320-232	Aegean Airlines
	SX-DGY	Airbus A.320-232	Aegean Airlines
	SX-DGZ	Airbus A.320-232	Aegean Airlines
	SX-DNA	Airbus A.320-232	Aegean Airlines
	SX-DNB	Airbus A.320-232	Aegean Airlines
	SX-DNC	Airbus A.320-232	Aegean Airlines
	SX-DND	Airbus A.320-232	Aegean Airlines
	SX-DNE	Airbus A.320-232	Aegean Airlines
	SX-DNF	Airbus A.321-231	Aegean Airlines
	SX-DNG	Airbus A.321-231	Aegean Airlines
	SX-DVG	Airbus A.320-232	Aegean Airlines
	SX-DVH	Airbus A.320-232	Aegean Airlines
	SX-DVI	Airbus A.320-232	Aegean Airlines
	SX-DVJ	Airbus A.320-232	Aegean Airlines
	SX-DVK	Airbus A.320-232	Aegean Airlines
	SX-DVL	Airbus A.320-232	Aegean Airlines
	SX-DVM	Airbus A.320-232	Aegean Airlines

Reg	Type	Owner or Operator	Notes
SX-DVN	Airbus A.320-232	Aegean Airlines	
SX-DVO	Airbus A.321-232	Aegean Airlines	
SX-DVP	Airbus A.321-232	Aegean Airlines	
SX-DVQ	Airbus A.320-232	Aegean Airlines	
SX-DVR	Airbus A.320-232	Aegean Airlines	
SX-DVS	Airbus A.320-232	Aegean Airlines	
SX-DVT	Airbus A.320-232	Aegean Airlines	
SX-DVU	Airbus A.320-232	Aegean Airlines	
SX-DVV	Airbus A.320-232	Aegean Airlines	
SX-DVW	Airbus A.320-232	Aegean Airlines	
SX-DVX	Airbus A.320-232	Aegean Airlines	
SX-DVY	Airbus A.320-232	Aegean Airlines	
SX-DVZ	Airbus A.321-232	Aegean Airlines	
SX-MAH	Boeing 737-405	Air Mediterranean	
SX-MAI	Boeing 737-4K5	Air Mediterranean	

T7 (San Marino)

Reg	Type	Owner or Operator	Notes
T7-MRA	Airbus A.320-214	Middle East Airlines	
T7-MRB	Airbus A.320-214	Middle East Airlines	
T7-MRC	Airbus A.320-214	Middle East Airlines	
T7-MRD	Airbus A.320-214	Middle East Airlines	
T7-MRE	Airbus A.320-214	Middle East Airlines	
T7-MRF	Airbus A.320-214	Middle East Airlines	

TC (Turkey)

Reg	Type	Owner or Operator	Notes
TC-AAO	Boeing 737-86N	Pegasus Airlines	
TC-AAR	Boeing 737-86N	Pegasus Airlines	
TC-AAU	Boeing 737-82R	Pegasus Airlines	
TC-ABL	Airbus A.320-214	AtlasGlobal	
TC-ADP	Boeing 737-82R	Pegasus Airlines	
TC-AEP	Boeing 737-82R	Pegasus Airlines	
TC-AGG	Airbus A.321-231	AtlasGlobal	
TC-AGI	Airbus A.321-131	AtlasGlobal	
TC-AGS	Airbus A.321-231	AtlasGlobal	
TC-AIP	Boeing 737-82R	Pegasus Airlines	
TC-AIS	Boeing 737-82R	Pegasus Airlines	
TC-AJP	Boeing 737-82R	Pegasus Airlines	
TC-AMP	Boeing 737-82R	Pegasus Airlines	
TC-ANP	Boeing 737-82R	Pegasus Airlines	
TC-ARP	Boeing 737-82R	Pegasus Airlines	
TC-ASP	Boeing 737-82R	Pegasus Airlines	
TC-ATB	Airbus A.321-211	AtlasGlobal	
TC-ATD	Airbus A.319-112	AtlasGlobal	
TC-ATE	Airbus A.321-211	AtlasGlobal	
TC-ATF	Airbus A.321-211	AtlasGlobal	
TC-ATH	Airbus A.321-231	AtlasGlobal	
TC-ATR	Airbus A.321-211	AtlasGlobal	
TC-ATT	Airbus A.320-233	AtlasGlobal	
TC-AVP	Boeing 737-82R	Pegasus Airlines	
TC-AZP	Boeing 737-82R	Pegasus Airlines	
TC-CCJ	Boeing 737-82R	Pegasus Airlines	
TC-COR	Boeing 737-800	Corendon Air	
TC-CPA	Boeing 737-82R	Pegasus Airlines	
TC-CPB	Boeing 737-82R	Pegasus Airlines	
TC-CPC	Boeing 737-82R	Pegasus Airlines	
TC-CPD	Boeing 737-82R	Pegasus Airlines	
TC-CPE	Boeing 737-82R	Pegasus Airlines	
TC-CPG	Boeing 737-82R	Pegasus Airlines	
TC-CPI	Boeing 737-82R	Pegasus Airlines	
TC-CPJ	Boeing 737-82R	Pegasus Airlines	
TC-CPK	Boeing 737-82R	Pegasus Airlines	
TC-CPL	Boeing 737-82R	Pegasus Airlines	
TC-CPM	Boeing 737-82R	Pegasus Airlines	
TC-CPN	Boeing 737-82R	Pegasus Airlines	
TC-CPO	Boeing 737-8AS	Pegasus Airlines	
TC-CPP	Boeing 737-804	Pegasus Airlines	
TC-CPR	Boeing 737-8GJ	Pegasus Airlines	
TC-CPS	Boeing 737-8GJ	Pegasus Airlines	

Notes	Reg	Type	Owner or Operator
	TC-CPU	Boeing 737-86N	Pegasus Airlines
	TC-CPV	Boeing 737-86J	Pegasus Airlines
	TC-CPY	Boeing 737-8H6	Pegasus Airlines
	TC-CPZ	Boeing 737-8H6	Pegasus Airlines
	TC-CRA	Boeing 737-8H6	Pegasus Airlines
	TC-CRB	Boeing 737-8H6	Pegasus Airlines
	TC-DCA	Airbus A.320-214	Pegasus Airlines
	TC-DCB	Airbus A.320-214	Pegasus Airlines
	TC-DCC	Airbus A.320-214	Pegasus Airlines
	TC-DCD	Airbus A.320-214	Pegasus Airlines
	TC-DCE	Airbus A.320-214	Pegasus Airlines
	TC-DCF	Airbus A.320-214	Pegasus Airlines
	TC-DCG	Airbus A.320-214	Pegasus Airlines
	TC-DCH	Airbus A.320-214	Pegasus Airlines
	TC-DCI	Airbus A.320-216	Pegasus Airlines
	TC-DCJ	Airbus A.320-214	Pegasus Airlines
	TC-DCL	Airbus A.320-214	Pegasus Airlines
	TC-DCM	Airbus A.320-214	Pegasus Airlines
	TC-ETF	Airbus A.321-211	AtlasGlobal
	TC-ETM	Airbus A.321-131	AtlasGlobal
	TC-ETN	Airbus A.321-131	AtlasGlobal
	TC-ETV	Airbus A.321-211	AtlasGlobal
	TC-FBH	Airbus A.320-214	Freebird Airlines
	TC-FBO	Airbus A.320-214	Freebird Airlines
	TC-FBR	Airbus A.320-232	Freebird Airlines/AtlasGlobal
	TC-FBV	Airbus A.320-214	Freebird Airlines
	TC-FHB	Airbus A.320-214	Freebird Airlines
	TC-FHC	Airbus A.320-214	Freebird Airlines
	TC-FHY	Airbus A.320-214	Freebird Airlines
	TC-IZD	Boeing 737-83N	Pegasus Airlines
	TC-IZE	Boeing 737-86J	Pegasus Airlines
	TC-IZG	Boeing 737-8AS	Pegasus Airlines
	TC-IZI	Boeing 737-8GJ	Pegasus Airlines
	TC-IZJ	Boeing 737-82R	Pegasus Airlines
	TC-IZK	Boeing 737-86J	Pegasus Airlines
	TC-JAI	Airbus A.320-232	Turkish Airlines
	TC-JDM	Airbus A.340-311	Turkish Airlines
	TC-JDN	Airbus A.340-311	Turkish Airlines
	TC-JFC	Boeing 737-8F2	AnadoluJet
	TC-JFD	Boeing 737-8F2	AnadoluJet
	TC-JFE	Boeing 737-8F2	AnadoluJet
	TC-JFF	Boeing 737-8F2	AnadoluJet
	TC-JFG	Boeing 737-8F2	AnadoluJet
	TC-JFH	Boeing 737-8F2	AnadoluJet
	TC-JFI	Boeing 737-8F2	AnadoluJet
	TC-JFJ	Boeing 737-8F2	AnadoluJet
	TC-JFK	Boeing 737-8F2	AnadoluJet
	TC-JFL	Boeing 737-8F2	Turkish Airlines
	TC-JFM	Boeing 737-8F2	Turkish Airlines
	TC-JFN	Boeing 737-8F2	AnadoluJet
	TC-JFO	Boeing 737-8F2	AnadoluJet
	TC-JFP	Boeing 737-8F2	AnadoluJet
	TC-JFR	Boeing 737-8F2	AnadoluJet
	TC-JFT	Boeing 737-8F2	AnadoluJet
	TC-JFU	Boeing 737-8F2	Turkish Airlines
	TC-JFV	Boeing 737-8F2	Turkish Airlines
	TC-JFY	Boeing 737-8F2	AnadoluJet
	TC-JFZ	Boeing 737-8F2	AnadoluJet
	TC-JGA	Boeing 737-8F2	Turkish Airlines
	TC-JGB	Boeing 737-8F2	AnadoluJet
	TC-JGC	Boeing 737-8F2	Turkish Airlines
	TC-JGD	Boeing 737-8F2	Turkish Airlines
	TC-JGF	Boeing 737-8F2	AnadoluJet
	TC-JGG	Boeing 737-8F2	Turkish Airlines
	TC-JGH	Boeing 737-8F2	Turkish Airlines
	TC-JGI	Boeing 737-8F2	Turkish Airlines
	TC-JGK	Boeing 737-8F2	Turkish Airlines
	TC-JGL	Boeing 737-8F2	Turkish Airlines
	TC-JGM	Boeing 737-8F2	Turkish Airlines
	TC-JGN	Boeing 737-8F2	Turkish Airlines
	TC-JGO	Boeing 737-8F2	Turkish Airlines

Reg	Type	Owner or Operator	Notes
TC-JGP	Boeing 737-8F2	Turkish Airlines	
TC-JGR	Boeing 737-8F2	Turkish Airlines	
TC-JGS	Boeing 737-8F2	Turkish Airlines	
TC-JGT	Boeing 737-8F2	Turkish Airlines	
TC-JGU	Boeing 737-8F2	Turkish Airlines	
TC-JGV	Boeing 737-8F2	Turkish Airlines	
TC-JGY	Boeing 737-8F2	Turkish Airlines	
TC-JGZ	Boeing 737-8F2	Turkish Airlines	
TC-JHA	Boeing 737-8F2	Turkish Airlines	
TC-JHB	Boeing 737-8F2	Turkish Airlines	
TC-JHC	Boeing 737-8F2	Turkish Airlines	
TC-JHD	Boeing 737-8F2	Turkish Airlines	
TC-JHE	Boeing 737-8F2	Turkish Airlines	
TC-JHF	Boeing 737-8F2	Turkish Airlines	
TC-JHK	Boeing 737-8F2	Turkish Airlines	
TC-JHL	Boeing 737-8F2	Turkish Airlines	
TC-JHM	Boeing 737-8F2	Turkish Airlines	
TC-JHN	Boeing 737-8F2	Turkish Airlines	
TC-JHO	Boeing 737-8F2	Turkish Airlines	
TC-JHP	Boeing 737-8F2	Turkish Airlines	
TC-JHR	Boeing 737-8F2	Turkish Airlines	
TC-JHS	Boeing 737-8F2	Turkish Airlines	
TC-JHT	Boeing 737-8F2	Turkish Airlines	
TC-JHU	Boeing 737-8F2	Turkish Airlines	
TC-JHV	Boeing 737-8F2	Turkish Airlines	
TC-JHY	Boeing 737-8F2	Turkish Airlines	
TC-JHZ	Boeing 737-8F2	Turkish Airlines	
TC-JIH	Airbus A.340-313X	Turkish Airlines	
TC-JII	Airbus A.340-313X	Turkish Airlines	
TC-JIL	Airbus A.330-202	Turkish Airlines	
TC-JIM	Airbus A.330-202	Turkish Airlines	
TC-JIN	Airbus A.330-202	Turkish Airlines	
TC-JIO	Airbus A.330-223	Turkish Airlines	
TC-JIP	Airbus A.330-223	Turkish Airlines	
TC-JIR	Airbus A.330-223	Turkish Airlines	
TC-JIS	Airbus A.330-223	Turkish Airlines	
TC-JIT	Airbus A.330-223	Turkish Airlines	
TC-JIZ	Airbus A.330-223	Turkish Airlines	
TC-JJE	Boeing 777-3F2ER	Turkish Airlines	
TC-JJF	Boeing 777-3F2ER	Turkish Airlines	
TC-JJG	Boeing 777-3F2ER	Turkish Airlines	
TC-JJH	Boeing 777-3F2ER	Turkish Airlines	
TC-JJI	Boeing 777-3F2ER	Turkish Airlines	
TC-JJJ	Boeing 777-3F2ER	Turkish Airlines	
TC-JJK	Boeing 777-3F2ER	Turkish Airlines	
TC-JJL	Boeing 777-3F2ER	Turkish Airlines	
TC-JJM	Boeing 777-3F2ER	Turkish Airlines	
TC-JJN	Boeing 777-3F2ER	Turkish Airlines	
TC-JJO	Boeing 777-3F2ER	Turkish Airlines	
TC-JJP	Boeing 777-3F2ER	Turkish Airlines	
TC-JJR	Boeing 777-3F2ER	Turkish Airlines	
TC-JJS	Boeing 777-3F2ER	Turkish Airlines	
TC-JJT	Boeing 777-3F2ER	Turkish Airlines	
TC-JJU	Boeing 777-3F2ER	Turkish Airlines	
TC-JJV	Boeing 777-3F2ER	Turkish Airlines	
TC-JJY	Boeing 777-3F2ER	Turkish Airlines	
TC-JJZ	Boeing 777-3F2ER	Turkish Airlines	
TC-JKO	Boeing 737-752	Turkish Airlines	
TC-JLS	Airbus A.319-132	Turkish Airlines	
TC-JLT	Airbus A.319-132	Turkish Airlines	
TC-JLU	Airbus A.319-132	Turkish Airlines	
TC-JLV	Airbus A.319-132	Turkish Airlines	
TC-JLY	Airbus A.319-132	Turkish Airlines	
TC-JLZ	Airbus A.319-132	Turkish Airlines	
TC-JMH	Airbus A.321-232	Turkish Airlines	
TC-JMI	Airbus A.321-232	Turkish Airlines	
TC-JMJ	Airbus A.321-232	Turkish Airlines	
TC-JMK	Airbus A.321-232	Turkish Airlines	
TC-JML	Airbus A.321-231	Turkish Airlines	
TC-JMM	Airbus A.321-232	Turkish Airlines	
TC-JMN	Airbus A.321-232	Turkish Airlines	

Notes	Reg	Type	Owner or Operator
	TC-JNA	Airbus A.330-203	Turkish Airlines
	TC-JNB	Airbus A.330-203	Turkish Airlines
	TC-JNC	Airbus A.330-203	Turkish Airlines
	TC-JND	Airbus A.330-203	Turkish Airlines
	TC-JNE	Airbus A.330-203	Turkish Airlines
	TC-JNH	Airbus A.330-343X	Turkish Airlines
	TC-JNI	Airbus A.330-343X	Turkish Airlines
	TC-JNJ	Airbus A.330-343X	Turkish Airlines
	TC-JNK	Airbus A.330-343X	Turkish Airlines
	TC-JNL	Airbus A.330-343E	Turkish Airlines
	TC-JNM	Airbus A.330-343X	Turkish Airlines
	TC-JNN	Airbus A.330-343	Turkish Airlines
	TC-JNO	Airbus A.330-343	Turkish Airlines
	TC-JNP	Airbus A.330-343	Turkish Airlines
	TC-JNR	Airbus A.330-343	Turkish Airlines
	TC-JNS	Airbus A.330-303	Turkish Airlines
	TC-JNT	Airbus A.330-303	Turkish Airlines
	TC-JNZ	Airbus A.330-303	Turkish Airlines
	TC-JOA	Airbus A.330-303	Turkish Airlines
	TC-JOB	Airbus A.330-303	Turkish Airlines
	TC-JOD	Airbus A.330-303	Turkish Airlines
	TC-JOE	Airbus A.330-303	Turkish Airlines
	TC-JOF	Airbus A.330-303	Turkish Airlines
	TC-JOG	Airbus A.330-303	Turkish Airlines
	TC-JOH	Airbus A.330-303	Turkish Airlines
	TC-JOI	Airbus A.330-303	Turkish Airlines
	TC-JOJ	Airbus A.330-303	Turkish Airlines
	TC-JOK	Airbus A.330-303	Turkish Airlines
	TC-JOL	Airbus A.330-303	Turkish Airlines
	TC-JOM	Airbus A.330-302	Turkish Airlines
	TC-JPA	Airbus A.320-232	Turkish Airlines
	TC-JPC	Airbus A.320-232	Turkish Airlines
	TC-JPD	Airbus A.320-232	Turkish Airlines
	TC-JPF	Airbus A.320-232	Turkish Airlines
	TC-JPG	Airbus A.320-232	Turkish Airlines
	TC-JPH	Airbus A.320-232	Turkish Airlines
	TC-JPI	Airbus A.320-232	Turkish Airlines
	TC-JPJ	Airbus A.320-232	Turkish Airlines
	TC-JPK	Airbus A.320-232	Turkish Airlines
	TC-JPL	Airbus A.320-232	Turkish Airlines
	TC-JPM	Airbus A.320-232	Turkish Airlines
	TC-JPN	Airbus A.320-232	Turkish Airlines
	TC-JPO	Airbus A.320-232	Turkish Airlines
	TC-JPP	Airbus A.320-232	Turkish Airlines
	TC-JPR	Airbus A.320-232	Turkish Airlines
	TC-JPS	Airbus A.320-232	Turkish Airlines
	TC-JPT	Airbus A.320-232	Turkish Airlines
	TC-JRA	Airbus A.321-231	Turkish Airlines
	TC-JRB	Airbus A.321-231	Turkish Airlines
	TC-JRC	Airbus A.321-231	Turkish Airlines
	TC-JRD	Airbus A.321-231	Turkish Airlines
	TC-JRE	Airbus A.321-231	Turkish Airlines
	TC-JRF	Airbus A.321-231	Turkish Airlines
	TC-JRG	Airbus A.321-231	Turkish Airlines
	TC-JRH	Airbus A.321-231	Turkish Airlines
	TC-JRI	Airbus A.321-232	Turkish Airlines
	TC-JRJ	Airbus A.321-232	Turkish Airlines
	TC-JRK	Airbus A.321-231	Turkish Airlines
	TC-JRL	Airbus A.321-231	Turkish Airlines
	TC-JRM	Airbus A.321-232	Turkish Airlines
	TC-JRN	Airbus A.321-232	Turkish Airlines
	TC-JRO	Airbus A.321-231	Turkish Airlines
	TC-JRP	Airbus A.321-231	Turkish Airlines
	TC-JRR	Airbus A.321-231	Turkish Airlines
	TC-JRS	Airbus A.321-231	Turkish Airlines
	TC-JRT	Airbus A.321-231	Turkish Airlines
	TC-JRU	Airbus A.321-231	Turkish Airlines
	TC-JRV	Airbus A.321-232	Turkish Airlines
	TC-JRY	Airbus A.321-232	Turkish Airlines
	TC-JRZ	Airbus A.321-232	Turkish Airlines
	TC-JSA	Airbus A.321-232	Turkish Airlines

Reg	Type	Owner or Operator	Notes
TC-JSB	Airbus A.321-231	Turkish Airlines	
TC-JSC	Airbus A.321-231	Turkish Airlines	
TC-JSD	Airbus A.321-231	Turkish Airlines	
TC-JSE	Airbus A.321-231	Turkish Airlines	
TC-JSF	Airbus A.321-231	Turkish Airlines	
TC-JSG	Airbus A.321-231	Turkish Airlines	
TC-JSH	Airbus A.321-231	Turkish Airlines	
TC-JSI	Airbus A.321-231	Turkish Airlines	
TC-JSJ	Airbus A.321-232	Turkish Airlines	
TC-JSK	Airbus A.321-232	Turkish Airlines	
TC-JSL	Airbus A.321-232	Turkish Airlines	
TC-JSM	Airbus A.321-231	Turkish Airlines	
TC-JSN	Airbus A.321-231	Turkish Airlines	
TC-JSO	Airbus A.321-231	Turkish Airlines	
TC-JSP	Airbus A.321-231	Turkish Airlines	
TC-JSR	Airbus A.321-231	Turkish Airlines	
TC-JSS	Airbus A.321-231	Turkish Airlines	
TC-JST	Airbus A.321-231	Turkish Airlines	
TC-JSU	Airbus A.321-231	Turkish Airlines	
TC-JSV	Airbus A.321-231	Turkish Airlines	
TC-JSY	Airbus A.321-231	Turkish Airlines	
TC-JSZ	Airbus A.321-231	Turkish Airlines	
TC-JTA	Airbus A.321-231	Turkish Airlines	
TC-JTD	Airbus A.321-231	Turkish Airlines	
TC-JTE	Airbus A.321-231	Turkish Airlines	
TC-JTF	Airbus A.321-231	Turkish Airlines	
TC-JTG	Airbus A.321-231	Turkish Airlines	
TC-JTH	Airbus A.321-231	Turkish Airlines	
TC-JTI	Airbus A.321-231	Turkish Airlines	
TC-JTJ	Airbus A.321-231	Turkish Airlines	
TC-JTK	Airbus A.321-231	Turkish Airlines	
TC-JTL	Airbus A.321-231	Turkish Airlines	
TC-JTM	Airbus A.321-231	Turkish Airlines	
TC-JTN	Airbus A.321-231	Turkish Airlines	
TC-JTO	Airbus A.321-231	Turkish Airlines	
TC-JTP	Airbus A.321-231	Turkish Airlines	
TC-JTR	Airbus A.321-231	Turkish Airlines	
TC-JUE	Airbus A.320-232	Turkish Airlines	
TC-JUF	Airbus A.320-232	Turkish Airlines	
TC-JUG	Airbus A.320-232	Turkish Airlines	
TC-JUI	Airbus A.320-232	Turkish Airlines	
TC-JUJ	Airbus A.320-232	Turkish Airlines	
TC-JUK	Airbus A.320-232	Turkish Airlines	
TC-JVA	Boeing 737-8F2	Turkish Airlines	
TC-JVB	Boeing 737-8F2	Turkish Airlines	
TC-JVC	Boeing 737-8F2	Turkish Airlines	
TC-JVD	Boeing 737-8F2	Turkish Airlines	
TC-JVE	Boeing 737-8F2	Turkish Airlines	
TC-JVF	Boeing 737-8F2	Turkish Airlines	
TC-JVG	Boeing 737-8F2	Turkish Airlines	
TC-JVH	Boeing 737-8F2	Turkish Airlines	
TC-JVI	Boeing 737-8F2	Turkish Airlines	
TC-JVJ	Boeing 737-8F2	Turkish Airlines	
TC-JVK	Boeing 737-8F2	Turkish Airlines	
TC-JVL	Boeing 737-8F2	Turkish Airlines	
TC-JVM	Boeing 737-8F2	Turkish Airlines	
TC-JVN	Boeing 737-8F2	Turkish Airlines	
TC-JVO	Boeing 737-8F2	Turkish Airlines	
TC-JVP	Boeing 737-8F2	Turkish Airlines	
TC-JVR	Boeing 737-8F2	Turkish Airlines	
TC-JVS	Boeing 737-8F2	Turkish Airlines	
TC-JVT	Boeing 737-8F2	Turkish Airlines	
TC-JVU	Boeing 737-8F2	Turkish Airlines	
TC-JVV	Boeing 737-8F2	Turkish Airlines	
TC-JVY	Boeing 737-8F2	Turkish Airlines	
TC-JVZ	Boeing 737-8F2	Turkish Airlines	
TC-JYA	Boeing 737-9F2ER	Turkish Airlines	
TC-JYB	Boeing 737-9F2ER	Turkish Airlines	
TC-JYC	Boeing 737-9F2ER	Turkish Airlines	
TC-JYD	Boeing 737-9F2ER	Turkish Airlines	
TC-JYE	Boeing 737-9F2ER	Turkish Airlines	

Notes	Reg	Type	Owner or Operator
	TC-JYF	Boeing 737-9F2ER	Turkish Airlines
	TC-JYG	Boeing 737-9F2ER	Turkish Airlines
	TC-JYH	Boeing 737-9F2ER	Turkish Airlines
	TC-JYI	Boeing 737-9F2ER	Turkish Airlines
	TC-JYJ	Boeing 737-9F2ER	Turkish Airlines
	TC-JYL	Boeing 737-9F2ER	Turkish Airlines
	TC-JYM	Boeing 737-9F2ER	Turkish Airlines
	TC-JYN	Boeing 737-9F2ER	Turkish Airlines
	TC-JYO	Boeing 737-9F2ER	Turkish Airlines
	TC-JYP	Boeing 737-9F2ER	Turkish Airlines
	TC-JZE	Boeing 737-8F2	Turkish Airlines
	TC-JZF	Boeing 737-8F2	Turkish Airlines
	TC-JZG	Boeing 737-8F2	Turkish Airlines
	TC-JZH	Boeing 737-8F2	Turkish Airlines
	TC-LJA	Boeing 777-3F2ER	Turkish Airlines
	TC-LJB	Boeing 777-3F2ER	Turkish Airlines
	TC-LJC	Boeing 777-3F2ER	Turkish Airlines
	TC-LJD	Boeing 777-3F2ER	Turkish Airlines
	TC-LJE	Boeing 777-3F2ER	Turkish Airlines
	TC-LJF	Boeing 777-3F2ER	Turkish Airlines
	TC-LJG	Boeing 777-3F2ER	Turkish Airlines
	TC-LJH	Boeing 777-3F2ER	Turkish Airlines
	TC-LJI	Boeing 777-3F2ER	Turkish Airlines
	TC-LJJ	Boeing 777-3F2ER	Turkish Airlines
	TC-LJK	Boeing 777-3F2ER	Turkish Airlines
	TC-LJL	Boeing 777-3F2ER	Turkish Airlines
	TC-LJM	Boeing 777-3F2ER	Turkish Airlines
	TC-LKA	Boeing 777-36NER	Turkish Airlines
	TC-LKB	Boeing 777-36NER	Turkish Airlines
	TC-LKC	Boeing 777-3U8ER	Turkish Airlines
	TC-LNA	Airbus A.330-223	Turkish Airlines
	TC-LNB	Airbus A.330-223	Turkish Airlines
	TC-LNC	Airbus A.330-303	Turkish Airlines
	TC-LND	Airbus A.330-303	Turkish Airlines
	TC-LNE	Airbus A.330-303	Turkish Airlines
	TC-LNF	Airbus A.330-303	Turkish Airlines
	TC-LNG	Airbus A.330-303	Turkish Airlines
	TC-LOA	Airbus A.330-343	Turkish Airlines
	TC-LOD	Airbus A.330-343	Turkish Airlines
	TC-LOE	Airbus A.330-343	Turkish Airlines
	TC-LOF	Airbus A.330-343	Turkish Airlines
	TC-LOG	Airbus A.330-343	Turkish Airlines
	TC-MCC	Airbus A.300B4-622RF	MNG Cargo
	TC-MCD	Airbus A.300B4-605RF	MNG Cargo
	TC-MCE	Airbus A.300B4-605R	MNG Cargo
	TC-MCG	Airbus A.300B4-622RF	MNG Cargo
	TC-MCH	Airbus A.300B4-622RF	MNG Cargo
	TC-MCZ	Airbus A.330-243F	MNG Cargo
	TC-MNV	Airbus A.300B4-605R	MNG Cargo
	TC-NBA	Airbus A.320-251N	Pegasus Airlines
	TC-NBB	Airbus A.320-251N	Pegasus Airlines
	TC-NBC	Airbus A.320-251N	Pegasus Airlines
	TC-NBD	Airbus A.320-251N	Pegasus Airlines
	TC-NBE	Airbus A.320-251N	Pegasus Airlines
	TC-NBF	Airbus A.320-251N	Pegasus Airlines
	TC-NBG	Airbus A.320-251N	Pegasus Airlines
	TC-NBH	Airbus A.320-251N	Pegasus Airlines
	TC-NBI	Airbus A.320-251N	Pegasus Airlines
	TC-NBJ	Airbus A.320-251N	Pegasus Airlines
	TC-NBK	Airbus A.320-251N	Pegasus Airlines
	TC-NBL	Airbus A.320-251N	Pegasus Airlines
	TC-NBM	Airbus A.320-251N	Pegasus Airlines
	TC-NBN	Airbus A.320-251N	Pegasus Airlines
	TC-NBO	Airbus A.320-251N	Pegasus Airlines
	TC-NBP	Airbus A.320-251N	Pegasus Airlines
	TC-NBR	Airbus A.320-251N	Pegasus Airlines
	TC-NBS	Airbus A.320-251N	Pegasus Airlines
	TC-NBT	Airbus A.320-251N	Pegasus Airlines
	TC-OBG	Airbus A.320-233	Onur Air
	TC-OBJ	Airbus A.321-231	Onur Air
	TC-OBK	Airbus A.321-231	Onur Air

Reg	Type	Owner or Operator	Notes
TC-OBL	Airbus A.320-232	Onur Air	
TC-OBM	Airbus A.320-232	Onur Air	
TC-OBS	Airbus A.320-232	Onur Air	
TC-OBU	Airbus A.320-231	Onur Air	
TC-OBZ	Airbus A.321-231	Onur Air	
TC-ODA	Airbus A.320-233	Onur Air	
TC-ODB	Airbus A.320-232	Onur Air	
TC-OEA	Airbus A.321-131	Onur Air	
TC-ONJ	Airbus A.321-131	Onur Air	
TC-ONS	Airbus A.321-131	Onur Air	
TC-SAH	Boeing 737-8FH	AnadoluJet	
TC-SAI	Boeing 737-8AS	AnadoluJet	
TC-SAJ	Boeing 737-8AS	AnadoluJet	
TC-SAK	Boeing 737-8AS	AnadoluJet	
TC-SBE	Boeing 737-8BK	AnadoluJet	
TC-SBF	Boeing 737-86Q	AnadoluJet	
TC-SBI	Boeing 737-8AS	AnadoluJet	
TC-SBJ	Boeing 737-8AS	AnadoluJet	
TC-SBM	Boeing 737-8AS	AnadoluJet	
TC-SBN	Boeing 737-86N	AnadoluJet	
TC-SBP	Boeing 737-86N	AnadoluJet	
TC-SBR	Boeing 737-86N	AnadoluJet	
TC-SBS	Boeing 737-8AS	AnadoluJet	
TC-SBV	Boeing 737-86N	AnadoluJet	
TC-SBZ	Boeing 737-86N	AnadoluJet	
TC-SCF	Boeing 737-8AL	AnadoluJet	
TC-SCG	Boeing 737-8AL	AnadoluJet	
TC-SCK	Boeing 737-8GJ	AnadoluJet	
TC-SCL	Boeing 737-8GJ	AnadoluJet	
TC-SED	Boeing 737-86N	SunExpress	
TC-SEE	Boeing 737-86N	SunExpress	
TC-SEI	Boeing 737-8Q8	SunExpress	
TC-SEJ	Boeing 737-8HC	SunExpress	
TC-SEK	Boeing 737-8HC	SunExpress	
TC-SEM	Boeing 737-8HC	SunExpress	
TC-SEN	Boeing 737-8HC	SunExpress	
TC-SEO	Boeing 737-8HC	SunExpress	
TC-SEP	Boeing 737-8HC	SunExpress	
TC-SEU	Boeing 737-8HC	SunExpress	
TC-SEY	Boeing 737-8HC	SunExpress	
TC-SEZ	Boeing 737-8HC	SunExpress	
TC-SNG	Boeing 737-8HC	SunExpress	
TC-SNN	Boeing 737-8HC	SunExpress	
TC-SNO	Boeing 737-8HC	SunExpress	
TC-SNP	Boeing 737-8HC	SunExpress	
TC-SNR	Boeing 737-8HC	SunExpress	
TC-SNU	Boeing 737-8HC	SunExpress	
TC-SNV	Boeing 737-86J	SunExpress	
TC-SNY	Boeing 737-8K5	SunExpress	
TC-SNZ	Boeing 737-86N	SunExpress	
TC-SOA	Boeing 737-86N	SunExpress	
TC-SOB	Boeing 737-8HC	SunExpress	
TC-SOC	Boeing 737-8HC	SunExpress	
TC-SOD	Boeing 737-8HC	SunExpress	
TC-SOE	Boeing 737-8HC	SunExpress	
TC-SOF	Boeing 737-8HC	SunExpress	
TC-SOG	Boeing 737-8HC	SunExpress	
TC-SOH	Boeing 737-8HC	SunExpress	
TC-SUO	Boeing 737-86Q	SunExpress	
TC-SUU	Boeing 737-86Q	SunExpress	
TC-TJI	Boeing 737-8S3	Corendon Air	
TC-TJJ	Boeing 737-8S3	Corendon Air	
TC-TJM	Boeing 737-8Q8	Corendon Air	
TC-TJN	Boeing 737-8Q8	Corendon Air	
TC-TJO	Boeing 737-86N	Corendon Air	
TC-TJP	Boeing 737-8BK	Corendon Air	
TC-TJS	Boeing 737-86N	Corendon Air	
TC-TJT	Boeing 737-8HC	Corendon Air	
TC-TJU	Boeing 737-8HX	Corendon Air	
TC-TLA	Boeing 737-4Q8	Tailwind Airlines	
TC-TLB	Boeing 737-4Q8	Tailwind Airlines	

Notes	Reg	Type	Owner or Operator
	TC-TLC	Boeing 737-4Q8	Tailwind Airlines
	TC-TLD	Boeing 737-4Q8	Tailwind Airlines
	TC-TLE	Boeing 737-4Q8	Tailwind Airlines

TF (Iceland)

Notes	Reg	Type	Owner or Operator
	TF-AAC	Boeing 747-481	Air Atlanta Icelandic/Saudi Arabian Airlines
	TF-AAD	Boeing 747-4H6	Air Atlanta Icelandic/Saudi Arabian Airlines
	TF-AAH	Boeing 747-4H6	Air Atlanta Icelandic/Saudi Arabian Airlines
	TF-AAJ	Boeing 747-428	Air Atlanta Icelandic/Saudi Arabian Airlines
	TF-AAK	Boeing 747-428	Air Atlanta Icelandic/Saudi Arabian Airlines
	TF-AAL	Boeing 747-428	Air Atlanta Icelandic/Saudi Arabian Airlines
	TF-AAM	Boeing 747-4H6	Air Atlanta Icelandic/Saudi Arabian Airlines
	TF-AMI	Boeing 747-412BCF	Air Atlanta Icelandic/Saudi Arabian Airlines
	TF-AMM	Boeing 747-4H6BCF	Air Atlanta Icelandic/Saudi Arabian Airlines
	TF-AMN	Boeing 747-4F6SF	Air Atlanta Icelandic/Saudi Arabian Airlines
	TF-AMP	Boeing 747-481BCF	Air Atlanta Icelandic
	TF-AMQ	Boeing 747-412F	Air Atlanta Icelandic
	TF-BBD	Boeing 737-3Y0F	Bluebird Cargo
	TF-BBE	Boeing 737-36EF	Bluebird Cargo
	TF-BBF	Boeing 737-36EF	Bluebird Cargo
	TF-BBG	Boeing 737-36EF	Bluebird Cargo
	TF-BBH	Boeing 737-4YO	Bluebird Cargo
	TF-BBJ	Boeing 737-476F	Bluebird Cargo
	TF-BBK	Boeing 737-4Q8SF	Bluebird Cargo
	TF-BRO	Airbus A.320-232	WOW Air
	TF-CAT	Airbus A.321-211	WOW Air
	TF-DAD	Airbus A.321-211	WOW Air
	TF-DOG	Airbus A.321-211	WOW Air
	TF-FIA	Boeing 757-256	Icelandair
	TF-FIC	Boeing 757-23N	Icelandair
	TF-FIG	Boeing 757-23APF	Icelandair Cargo
	TF-FIH	Boeing 757-208PCF	Icelandair Cargo
	TF-FIJ	Boeing 757-208	Icelandair
	TF-FIK	Boeing 757-256	Icelandair
	TF-FIN	Boeing 757-208	Icelandair
	TF-FIO	Boeing 757-208	Icelandair
	TF-FIP	Boeing 757-208	Icelandair
	TF-FIR	Boeing 757-256	Icelandair
	TF-FIS	Boeing 757-256	Icelandair
	TF-FIT	Boeing 757-256	Icelandair
	TF-FIU	Boeing 757-256	Icelandair
	TF-FIV	Boeing 757-208	Icelandair
	TF-FIX	Boeing 757-308	Icelandair
	TF-FXA	DHC.8-402 Dash Eight	Air Iceland
	TF-FXB	DHC.8-402 Dash Eight	Air Iceland
	TF-FXI	DHC.8-402 Dash Eight	Air Iceland
	TF-FXL	DHC.8-402 Dash Eight	Air Iceland
	TF-GAY	Airbus A.330-343E	WOW Air
	TF-GMA	Airbus A.321-211	WOW Air
	TF-GPA	Airbus A.321-211	WOW Air
	TF-ICE	Boeing 737-MAX8	Icelandair
	TF-ICU	Boeing 737-MAX8	Icelandair
	TF-ICY	Boeing 737-MAX8	Icelandair
	TF-ISD	Boeing 757-223	Icelandair
	TF-ISF	Boeing 757-223	Icelandair
	TF-ISJ	Boeing 757-256	Icelandair
	TF-ISK	Boeing 757-223	Icelandair
	TF-ISL	Boeing 757-223	Icelandair
	TF-ISN	Boeing 767-319ER	Icelandair
	TF-ISO	Boeing 767-319ER	Icelandair
	TF-ISP	Boeing 767-319ER	Icelandair
	TF-ISR	Boeing 757-256	Icelandair
	TF-ISS	Boeing 757-223	Icelandair
	TF-ISV	Boeing 757-256	Icelandair
	TF-ISW	Boeing 767-319ER	Icelandair
	TF-ISY	Boeing 757-223	Icelandair
	TF-ISZ	Boeing 757-223	Icelandair
	TF-JOY	Airbus A.321-211	WOW Air
	TF-KID	Airbus A.321-211	WOW Air
	TF-LLX	Boeing 757-256	Icelandair

Reg	Type	Owner or Operator	Notes
TF-LOV	Airbus A.321-251N	WOW Air	
TF-LUV	Airbus A.330-343	WOW Air	
TF-MOM	Airbus A.321-211	WOW Air	
TF-NEO	Airbus A.320-251N	WOW Air	
TF-NOW	Airbus A.321-211	WOW Air	
TF-PRO	Airbus A.321-211	WOW Air	
TF-SIS	Airbus A.320-232	WOW Air	
TF-SKY	Airbus A.321-253N	WOW Air	
TF-SON	Airbus A.321-211	WOW Air	
TF-WIN	Airbus A.321-211	WOW Air	
TF-WOW	Airbus A.330-343	WOW Air	

TS (Tunisia)

Reg	Type	Owner or Operator	Notes
TS-IMC	Airbus A.320-211	Tunis Air *7 Novembre*	
TS-IMD	Airbus A.320-211	Tunis Air *Khereddine*	
TS-IME	Airbus A.320-211	Tunis Air *Tabarka*	
TS-IMF	Airbus A.320-211	Tunis Air *Djerba*	
TS-IMG	Airbus A.320-211	Tunis Air *Abou el Kacem Chebbi*	
TS-IMH	Airbus A.320-211	Tunis Air *Ali Belhaouane*	
TS-IMI	Airbus A.320-211	Tunis Air *Jughurta*	
TS-IMJ	Airbus A.319-114	Tunis Air *El Kantaoui*	
TS-IMK	Airbus A.319-114	Tunis Air *Kerkenah*	
TS-IML	Airbus A.320-211	Tunis Air *Gafsa el Ksar*	
TS-IMM	Airbus A.320-211	Tunis Air *Le Bardo*	
TS-IMN	Airbus A.320-211	Tunis Air *Ibn Khaldoun*	
TS-IMO	Airbus A.319-114	Tunis Air *Hannibal*	
TS-IMP	Airbus A.320-211	Tunis Air *La Galite*	
TS-IMQ	Airbus A.319-114	Tunis Air *Alyssa*	
TS-IMR	Airbus A.320-211	Tunis Air *Habib Bourguiba*	
TS-IMS	Airbus A.320-214	Tunis Air *Dougga*	
TS-IMT	Airbus A.320-214	Tunis Air *Aziza Othmana*	
TS-IMU	Airbus A.320-214	Tunis Air *Sousse*	
TS-IMV	Airbus A.320-214	Tunis Air *Ibn Eljazzar*	
TS-IMW	Airbus A.320-214	Tunis Air *Farhat Hached*	
TS-INA	Airbus A.320-214	Nouvelair	
TS-INB	Airbus A.320-214	Nouvelair	
TS-INC	Airbus A.320-214	Nouvelair/Royal Air Maroc	
TS-INH	Airbus A.320-214	Nouvelair	
TS-INO	Airbus A.320-214	Nouvelair	
TS-INP	Airbus A.320-214	Nouvelair	
TS-INQ	Airbus A.320-214	Nouvelair	
TS-INR	Airbus A.320-214	Nouvelair	
TS-IOK	Boeing 737-6H3	Tunis Air *Kairouan*	
TS-IOL	Boeing 737-6H3	Tunis Air *Tozeur-Nefta*	
TS-IOM	Boeing 737-6H3	Tunis Air *Carthage*	
TS-ION	Boeing 737-6H3	Tunis Air *Utique*	
TS-IOP	Boeing 737-6H3	Tunis Air *El Jem*	
TS-IOQ	Boeing 737-6H3	Tunis Air *Bizerte*	
TS-IOR	Boeing 737-6H3	Tunis Air *Tahar Haddad*	

UK (Uzbekistan)

Reg	Type	Owner or Operator	Notes
UK-75701	Boeing 757-23P	Uzbekistan Airways	
UK-78701	Boeing 787-8	Uzbekistan Airways	
UK-78702	Boeing 787-8	Uzbekistan Airways	

UN (Kazakhstan)

Note: Air Astana operates P4- registered Boeing 757s.

UR (Ukraine)

Reg	Type	Owner or Operator	Notes
UR-PSA	Boeing 737-8HX	Ukraine International	
UR-PSB	Boeing 737-8HX	Ukraine International	
UR-PSC	Boeing 737-8HX	Ukraine International	
UR-PSD	Boeing 737-89P	Ukraine International	
UR-PSE	Boeing 737-84R	Ukraine International	
UR-PSF	Boeing 737-84R	Ukraine International	
UR-PSG	Boeing 737-85R	Ukraine International	

Notes	Reg	Type	Owner or Operator
	UR-PSH	Boeing 737-85R	Ukraine International
	UR-PSI	Boeing 737-9KVER	Ukraine International
	UR-PSJ	Boeing 737-9KVER	Ukraine International
	UR-PSK	Boeing 737-94XER	Ukraine International
	UR-PSL	Boeing 737-94XER	Ukraine International
	UR-PSM	Boeing 737-8FZ	Ukraine International
	UR-PSN	Boeing 737-86N	Ukraine International
	UR-PSO	Boeing 737-8Q8	Ukraine International
	UR-PSP	Boeing 737-8Q8	Ukraine International
	UR-PSQ	Boeing 737-86N	Ukraine International
	UR-PSR	Boeing 737-8KV	Ukraine International
	UR-PSS	Boeing 737-8AS	Ukraine International
	UR-PST	Boeing 737-8AS	Ukraine International
	UR-PSU	Boeing 737-8AS	Ukraine International
	UR-PSV	Boeing 737-8AS	Ukraine International
	UR-PSW	Boeing 737-8AS	Ukraine International
	UR-PSX	Boeing 737-8EH	Ukraine International
	UR-PSY	Boeing 737-8EH	Ukraine International
	UR-PSZ	Boeing 737-8EH	Ukraine International
	UR-UIA	Boeing 737-8KV	Ukraine International
	UR-UIC	Boeing 737-800	Ukraine International
	UR-82007	Antonov An-124	Antonov Airlines
	UR-82008	Antonov An-124	Antonov Airlines
	UR-82009	Antonov An-124	Antonov Airlines
	UR-82027	Antonov An-124	Antonov Airlines
	UR-82029	Antonov An-124	Antonov Airlines
	UR-82060	Antonov An-225	Antonov Airlines
	UR-82072	Antonov An-124	Antonov Airlines
	UR-82073	Antonov An-124	Antonov Airlines

V8 (Brunei)

	V8-DLA	Boeing 787-8	Royal Brunei Airlines
	V8-DLB	Boeing 787-8	Royal Brunei Airlines
	V8-DLC	Boeing 787-8	Royal Brunei Airlines
	V8-DLD	Boeing 787-8	Royal Brunei Airlines
	V8-DLE	Boeing 787-8	Royal Brunei Airlines

VH (Australia)

	VH-OQA	Airbus A.380-841	QANTAS
	VH-OQB	Airbus A.380-841	QANTAS
	VH-OQC	Airbus A.380-841	QANTAS
	VH-OQD	Airbus A.380-841	QANTAS
	VH-OQE	Airbus A.380-841	QANTAS
	VH-OQF	Airbus A.380-841	QANTAS
	VH-OQG	Airbus A.380-841	QANTAS
	VH-OQH	Airbus A.380-841	QANTAS
	VH-OQI	Airbus A.380-841	QANTAS
	VH-OQJ	Airbus A.380-841	QANTAS
	VH-OQK	Airbus A.380-841	QANTAS
	VH-OQL	Airbus A.380-841	QANTAS
	VH-ZNA	Boeing 787-9	QANTAS
	VH-ZNB	Boeing 787-9	QANTAS
	VH-ZNC	Boeing 787-9	QANTAS
	VH-ZND	Boeing 787-9	QANTAS
	VH-ZNE	Boeing 787-9	QANTAS
	VH-ZNF	Boeing 787-9	QANTAS
	VH-ZNG	Boeing 787-9	QANTAS
	VH-ZNH	Boeing 787-9	QANTAS

VN (Vietnam)

	VN-A861	Boeing 787-9	Vietnam Airlines
	VN-A862	Boeing 787-9	Vietnam Airlines
	VN-A863	Boeing 787-9	Vietnam Airlines
	VN-A864	Boeing 787-9	Vietnam Airlines
	VN-A865	Boeing 787-9	Vietnam Airlines
	VN-A866	Boeing 787-9	Vietnam Airlines
	VN-A867	Boeing 787-9	Vietnam Airlines

Reg	Type	Owner or Operator	Notes
VN-A868	Boeing 787-9	Vietnam Airlines	
VN-A869	Boeing 787-9	Vietnam Airlines	
VN-A870	Boeing 787-9	Vietnam Airlines	
VN-A871	Boeing 787-9	Vietnam Airlines	

VP-B/VP-Q (Bermuda)

Reg	Type	Owner or Operator	Notes
VP-BAC	Airbus A.320-214	Aeroflot Russian International *L. Tolstoy*	
VP-BAD	Airbus A.320-214	Aeroflot Russian International *A. Ioffe*	
VP-BAE	Airbus A.321-211	Aeroflot Russian International *S. Bondarchuk*	
VP-BAF	Airbus A.321-211	Aeroflot Russian International *A. Tarkovsky*	
VP-BAV	Airbus A.321-211	Aeroflot Russian International *F. Ushakov*	
VP-BAX	Airbus A.321-211	Aeroflot Russian International *S. Richter*	
VP-BAY	Airbus A.321-211	Aeroflot Russian International *V. Shukshin*	
VP-BAZ	Airbus A.321-211	Aeroflot Russian International *Y. Levitan*	
VP-BBR	Boeing 787-8	Azerbaijan Airlines	
VP-BBS	Boeing 787-8	Azerbaijan Airlines	
VP-BBT	Airbus A.319-112	Rossiya	
VP-BBU	Airbus A.319-112	Rossiya	
VP-BCA	Airbus A.320-214	Aeroflot Russian International *A. German*	
VP-BCB	Airbus A.320-214	Aeroflot Russian International *S. Gerasimov*	
VP-BCD	Boeing 737-8LJ	Aeroflot Russian International *N. Karamzin*	
VP-BCE	Airbus A.320-214	Aeroflot Russian International *F. Dostoevsky*	
VP-BCF	Boeing 737-8LJ	Aeroflot Russian International *I. Krylov*	
VP-BCG	Boeing 737-8LJ	Aeroflot Russian International *N. Ieskov*	
VP-BDC	Airbus A.321-211	Aeroflot Russian International *V.Alekseev*	
VP-BDD	Airbus A.321-211	Aeroflot Russian International *A. Mozhaysky*	
VP-BDE	Airbus A.330-343	Aeroflot Russian International *L. Kantorovich*	
VP-BDK	Airbus A.320-214	Aeroflot Russian International *G. Sviridov*	
VP-BEA	Airbus A.321-211	Aeroflot Russian International *I. Dunayevsky*	
VP-BEE	Airbus A.321-211	Aeroflot Russian International *Y. Lyubimov*	
VP-BEG	Airbus A.321-211	Aeroflot Russian International *V. Nemirovich-Danchenko*	
VP-BEO	Airbus A.320-214	Aeroflot Russian International	
VP-BES	Airbus A.321-211	Aeroflot Russian International	
VP-BET	Airbus A.320-214	Aeroflot Russian International *A. Voznesensky*	
VP-BEW	Airbus A.321-211	Aeroflot Russian International *M. Zoschenko*	
VP-BFA	Airbus A.320-214	Aeroflot Russian International	
VP-BFB	Boeing 737-800	Aeroflot Russian International	
VP-BFE	Airbus A.320-214	Aeroflot Russian International *I. Levitan*	
VP-BFF	Airbus A.321-211	Aeroflot Russian International	
VP-BFG	Airbus A.320-214	Aeroflot Russian International	
VP-BFH	Airbus A.320-214	Aeroflot Russian International *K. Malevich*	
VP-BFK	Airbus A.320-214	Aeroflot Russian International *F. Volkov*	
VP-BFQ	Airbus A.321-211	*Aeroflot Russian International A. Alexandrov*	
VP-BFX	Airbus A.321-211	Aeroflot Russian International *I. Shishkin*	
VP-BGG	Boeing 737-8LJ	Aeroflot Russian International *G. Sviridov*	
VP-BGI	Boeing 737-8LJ	Aeroflot Russian International *Mikhail Vrubel*	
VP-BGN	Boeing 737-8LJ	Aeroflot Russian International *L. Utesov*	
VP-BID	Airbus A.320-214	Aeroflot Russian International *I. Tamm*	
VP-BIF	Airbus A.320-214	Aeroflot Russian International	
VP-BIG	Boeing 747-46NERF	AirBridge Cargo Airlines	
VP-BII	Airbus A.320-214	Aeroflot Russian International	
VP-BIK	Boeing 747-46NERF	AirBridge Cargo Airlines	
VP-BIL	Airbus A.320-214	Aeroflot Russian International	
VP-BIM	Boeing 747-4HAERF	AirBridge Cargo Airlines	
VP-BIQ	Airbus A.319-111	Rossiya	
VP-BIS	Airbus A.319-111	Rossiya	
VP-BIT	Airbus A.319-111	Rossiya	
VP-BIU	Airbus A.319-114	Rossiya	
VP-BIV	Airbus A.319-115	Rossiya	
VP-BIW	Airbus A.320-214	Aeroflot Russian International	
VP-BIY	Airbus A.320-214	Aeroflot Russian International	
VP-BJA	Airbus A.320-214	Aeroflot Russian International *L. Mechnikov*	
VP-BJW	Airbus A.320-214	Aeroflot Russian International *K. Paustovsky*	
VP-BJX	Airbus A.321-211	Aeroflot Russian International *I. Goncharov*	
VP-BJY	Airbus A.320-214	Aeroflot Russian International *S. Marshak*	
VP-BKA	Boeing 737-800	Aeroflot Russian International *M. Magomaev*	
VP-BKC	Airbus A.320-214	Aeroflot Russian International	
VP-BKE	Boeing 737-800	Aeroflot Russian International	
VP-BKF	Boeing 737-800	Aeroflot Russian International	

Notes	Reg	Type	Owner or Operator
	VP-BKI	Airbus A.321-211	Aeroflot Russian International D. Ryabushinsky
	VP-BKJ	Airbus A.321-211	Aeroflot Russian International
	VP-BKK	Boeing 737-800	Aeroflot Russian International M. Botvinnik
	VP-BKN	Boeing 737-800	Aeroflot Russian International B. Okudzhava
	VP-BKP	Airbus A.320-214	Aeroflot Russian International S. Prokofiev
	VP-BKQ	Airbus A.321-211	Aeroflot Russian International D. Mendeleev
	VP-BKR	Airbus A.321-211	Aeroflot Russian International S. Rachmaninoff
	VP-BKY	Airbus A.320-214	Aeroflot Russian International M. Rostropovich
	VP-BKZ	Airbus A.321-211	Aeroflot Russian International
	VP-BLH	Airbus A.320-214	Aeroflot Russian International P. Cherenkov
	VP-BLL	Airbus A.320-214	Aeroflot Russian International N. Basov
	VP-BLN	Airbus A.320-214	Aeroflot Russian International A. Tarasov
	VP-BLO	Airbus A.320-214	Aeroflot Russian International I. Repin
	VP-BLP	Airbus A.320-214	Aeroflot Russian International A. Popov
	VP-BLR	Airbus A.320-214	Aeroflot Russian International P. Yablochkov
	VP-BLX	Airbus A.330-243	Aeroflot Russian International E. Svetlanov
	VP-BLY	Airbus A.330-243	Aeroflot Russian International V. Vysotskiy
	VP-BMB	Boeing 737-8LJ	Aeroflot Russian International
	VP-BMD	Boeing 737-800	Aeroflot Russian International Igor Stravinsky
	VP-BME	Airbus A.320-214	Aeroflot Russian International N. Mikluho-Maklay
	VP-BMF	Airbus A.320-214	Aeroflot Russian International G. Shelihov
	VP-BMI	Boeing 737-800	Aeroflot Russian International A. Dargomyzhsky
	VP-BML	Boeing 737-800	Aeroflot Russian International
	VP-BMM	Boeing 737-800	Aeroflot Russian International
	VP-BMO	Boeing 737-800	Aeroflot Russian International
	VP-BNB	Airbus A.319-111	Rossiya
	VP-BNC	Boeing 737-800	Aeroflot Russian International V. Serov
	VP-BNJ	Airbus A.319-111	Rossiya
	VP-BNL	Airbus A.320-214	Aeroflot Russian International
	VP-BNN	Airbus A.319-111	Rossiya
	VP-BNP	Boeing 737-800	Aeroflot Russian International I. Ayvazovsky
	VP-BNQ	Boeing 737-800	Aeroflot Russian International
	VP-BNT	Airbus A.320-214	Aeroflot Russian International Dobrolet
	VP-BOA	Boeing 737-800	Aeroflot Russian International
	VP-BOB	Boeing 737-800	Aeroflot Russian International
	VP-BOC	Airbus A.321-231	Aeroflot Russian International S. Mikhalkov
	VP-BOE	Airbus A.321-211	Aeroflot Russian International G. Vishnevskaya
	VP-BON	Boeing 737-8LJ	Aeroflot Russian International N. Berdyaev
	VP-BPF	Boeing 737-800	Aeroflot Russian International N. Rerih
	VP-BQK	Airbus A.319-111	Rossiya
	VP-BRF	Boeing 737-8LJ	Aeroflot Russian International Sergey Obraztsov
	VP-BRH	Boeing 737-8LJ	Aeroflot Russian International B. Kustodiev
	VP-BRR	Boeing 737-8LJ	Aeroflot Russian International Alexander Solzhenitsin
	VP-BSB	Boeing 737-800	Aeroflot Russian International
	VP-BTA	Airbus A.320-214	Aeroflot Russian International A. Borodin
	VP-BTC	Airbus A.320-214	Aeroflot Russian International
	VP-BTG	Airbus A.321-211	Aeroflot Russian International K. Stanivlaskey
	VP-BTH	Airbus A.321-211	Aeroflot Russian International
	VP-BTI	Airbus A.320-214	Aeroflot Russian International V. Meyerhold
	VP-BTJ	Airbus A.320-214	Aeroflot Russian International A. Rublev
	VP-BTK	Airbus A.321-211	Aeroflot Russian International
	VP-BTL	Airbus A.321-211	Aeroflot Russian International E. Vakhtangov
	VP-BTO	Airbus A.320-214	Aeroflot Russian International
	VP-BTR	Airbus A.321-211	Aeroflot Russian International S. Diaghilev
	VP-BUH	Boeing 757-231	Uzbekistan Airways
	VP-BUM	Airbus A.321-211	Aeroflot Russian International A. Deineka
	VP-BUP	Airbus A.321-211	Aeroflot Russian International M. Shagal
	VP-BWD	Airbus A.320-214	Aeroflot Russian International A. Aliabiev
	VP-BWE	Airbus A.320-214	Aeroflot Russian International H. Rimsky-Korsakov
	VP-BWF	Airbus A.320-214	Aeroflot Russian International D. Shostakovich
	VP-BWG	Airbus A.319-111	Rossiya
	VP-BWH	Airbus A.320-214	Aeroflot Russian International M. Balakirev
	VP-BWI	Airbus A.320-214	Aeroflot Russian International A. Glazunov
	VP-BWJ	Airbus A.319-111	Rossiya
	VP-BZA	Boeing 737-8LJ	Aeroflot Russian International Ch.Aytmatov
	VP-BZB	Boeing 737-8LJ	Aeroflot Russian International K. Simonov
	VP-BZO	Airbus A.320-214	Aeroflot Russian International V. Bering
	VP-BZP	Airbus A.320-214	Aeroflot Russian International E. Habarov
	VP-BZQ	Airbus A.320-214	Aeroflot Russian International Yu. Lisiansky

Reg	Type	Owner or Operator	Notes
VP-BZR	Airbus A.320-214	Aeroflot Russian International *F. Bellinsgauzen*	
VP-BZS	Airbus A.320-214	Aeroflot Russian International *M. Lazarev*	
VQ-BAQ	Airbus A.319-111	Rossiya	
VQ-BAR	Airbus A.319-111	Rossiya	
VQ-BAS	Airbus A.319-111	Rossiya	
VQ-BAT	Airbus A.319-111	Rossiya	
VQ-BAU	Airbus A.319-111	Rossiya	
VQ-BAV	Airbus A.319-111	Rossiya	
VQ-BAX	Airbus A.320-214	Aeroflot Russian International *G. Nevelskoy*	
VQ-BAY	Airbus A.320-214	Aeroflot Russian International *S. Krasheninnikov*	
VQ-BBA	Airbus A.319-111	Rossiya	
VQ-BBC	Airbus A.320-214	Aeroflot Russian International *N. Przhevalsky*	
VQ-BBE	Airbus A.330-243	Aeroflot Russian International *I. Brodsky*	
VQ-BBF	Airbus A.330-243	Aeroflot Russian International *A. Griboedov*	
VQ-BBG	Airbus A.330-243	Aeroflot Russian International *N. Gogol*	
VQ-BCM	Airbus A.320-214	Aeroflot Russian International *G. Titov*	
VQ-BCN	Airbus A.320-214	Aeroflot Russian International *V. Chelomey*	
VQ-BCO	Airbus A.319-112	Rossiya	
VQ-BCP	Airbus A.319-112	Rossiya	
VQ-BCQ	Airbus A.330-343	Aeroflot Russian International	
VQ-BCU	Airbus A.330-343	Aeroflot Russian International *W. Majakowski*	
VQ-BCV	Airbus A.330-343	Aeroflot Russian International *B. Paster*	
VQ-BEA	Airbus A.321-211	Aeroflot Russian International *I. Michurin*	
VQ-BED	Airbus A.321-211	Aeroflot Russian International *N. Pirogov*	
VQ-BEE	Airbus A.321-211	Aeroflot Russian International *I. Sechenov*	
VQ-BEF	Airbus A.321-211	Aeroflot Russian International *N. Zhukovsky*	
VQ-BEG	Airbus A.321-211	Aeroflot Russian International *K. Tsiolkovsky*	
VQ-BEH	Airbus A.320-214	Aeroflot Russian International *I. Pavlov*	
VQ-BEI	Airbus A.321-211	Aeroflot Russian International *S. Korolev*	
VQ-BEJ	Airbus A.320-214	Aeroflot Russian International *I. Kurchatov*	
VQ-BEK	Airbus A.330-343	Aeroflot Russian International *A. Tvardovsky*	
VQ-BEL	Airbus A.330-343	Aeroflot Russian International *F. Tyutchev*	
VQ-BHB	Boeing 737-800	Aeroflot Russian International *N. Nekrasov*	
VQ-BHC	Boeing 737-800	Aeroflot Russian International	
VQ-BHE	Boeing 747-4KZF	AirBridge Cargo Airlines	
VQ-BHK	Airbus A.321-211	Aeroflot Russian International *M. Keldysh*	
VQ-BHL	Airbus A.320-214	Aeroflot Russian International *S. Vavilov*	
VQ-BHM	Airbus A.321-211	Aeroflot Russian International *N. Vavilov*	
VQ-BHN	Airbus A.320-214	Aeroflot Russian International *N. Lobachevsky*	
VQ-BHE	Boeing 747-4KZF	AirBridge Cargo Airlines	
VQ-BIA	Boeing 747-4KZF	AirBridge Cargo Airlines	
VQ-BIR	Airbus A.320-214	Aeroflot Russian International *S. Kovalevskaya*	
VQ-BIT	Airbus A.320-214	Aeroflot Russian International *L. Landau*	
VQ-BIU	Airbus A.320-214	Aeroflot Russian International *K. Timiryazev*	
VQ-BIV	Airbus A.320-214	Aeroflot Russian International *A. Kolmogorov*	
VQ-BIW	Airbus A.320-214	Aeroflot Russian International *V. Glushko*	
VQ-BJW	Airbus A.320-214	Aeroflot Russian International	
VQ-BJY	Airbus A.320-214	Aeroflot Russian International	
VQ-BKS	Airbus A.320-214	Aeroflot Russian International *A. Chivhevsky*	
VQ-BKT	Airbus A.320-214	Aeroflot Russian International *V. Vernadsky*	
VQ-BKU	Airbus A.320-214	Aeroflot Russian International *A. Nikolaev*	
VQ-BMV	Airbus A.330-343	Aeroflot Russian International *P. Kapitsa*	
VQ-BMX	Airbus A.330-343	Aeroflot Russian International *A. Sakharov*	
VQ-BMY	Airbus A.330-343	Aeroflot Russian International *Ilya Frank*	
VQ-BNS	Airbus A.330-343	Aeroflot Russian International *A. Bakulev*	
VQ-BOH	Airbus A.321-211	Aeroflot Russian International *A. Prokhorov*	
VQ-BOI	Airbus A.321-211	Aeroflot Russian International *N. Semenov*	
VQ-BPI	Airbus A.330-343	Aeroflot Russian International *L. Yashin*	
VQ-BPJ	Airbus A.330-343	Aeroflot Russian International *V. Brumel*	
VQ-BPK	Airbus A.330-343	Aeroflot Russian International *L. Kulibin*	
VQ-BPU	Airbus A.320-214	Aeroflot Russian International	
VQ-BPV	Airbus A.320-214	Aeroflot Russian International	
VQ-BPW	Airbus A.320-214	Aeroflot Russian International	
VQ-BQX	Airbus A.330-343	Aeroflot Russian International	
VQ-BQY	Airbus A.330-343	Aeroflot Russian International *M. Sholohov*	
VQ-BQZ	Airbus A.330-343	Aeroflot Russian International *N. Burdenko*	
VQ-BRV	Airbus A.320-214	Aeroflot Russian International	
VQ-BRW	Airbus A.320-214	Aeroflot Russian International	
VQ-BSE	Airbus A.320-214	Aeroflot Russian International	
VQ-BSG	Airbus A.320-214	Aeroflot Russian International	
VQ-BSH	Airbus A.320-214	Aeroflot Russian International	

Notes	Reg	Type	Owner or Operator
	VQ-BSI	Airbus A.320-214	Aeroflot Russian International
	VQ-BSJ	Airbus A.320-214	Aeroflot Russian International
	VQ-BSL	Airbus A.320-214	Aeroflot Russian International *K. Feoktistov*
	VQ-BST	Airbus A.320-214	Aeroflot Russian International *P. Popovich*
	VQ-BSU	Airbus A.320-214	Aeroflot Russian International
	VQ-BUU	Boeing 747-4EVERF	AirBridge Cargo Airlines
	VQ-BVO	Boeing 737-8LJ	Aeroflot Russian International *V. Belinsky*
	VQ-BVP	Boeing 737-8LJ	Aeroflot Russian International *L. Gumilev*
	VQ-BWA	Boeing 737-8LJ	Aeroflot Russian International *V. Dahl*
	VQ-BWB	Boeing 737-8LJ	Aeroflot Russian International *S. Ozhegov*
	VQ-BWC	Boeing 737-8LJ	Aeroflot Russian International *S. Soloviev*
	VQ-BWD	Boeing 737-8LJ	Aeroflot Russian International *G. Tovstonogov*
	VQ-BWE	Boeing 737-8LJ	Aeroflot Russian International *M. Shchepkin*
	VQ-BWF	Boeing 737-8LJ	Aeroflot Russian International *S. Eisenstein*
	VQ-BWW	Boeing 747-4EVERF	AirBridge Cargo Airlines
	VT (India)		
	VT-ALJ	Boeing 777-337ER	Air India
	VT-ALK	Boeing 777-337ER	Air India
	VT-ALL	Boeing 777-337ER	Air-India
	VT-ALM	Boeing 777-337ER	Air India
	VT-ALN	Boeing 777-337ER	Air India
	VT-ALO	Boeing 777-337ER	Air India
	VT-ALP	Boeing 777-337ER	Air India
	VT-ALQ	Boeing 777-337ER	Air India
	VT-ALR	Boeing 777-337ER	Air India
	VT-ALS	Boeing 777-337ER	Air India
	VT-ALT	Boeing 777-337ER	Air India
	VT-ALU	Boeing 777-337ER	Air India
	VT-ALV	Boeing 777-337ER	Air India
	VT-ALW	Boeing 777-337ER	Air India
	VT-ALX	Boeing 777-337ER	Air India
	VT-ANA	Boeing 787-8	Air India
	VT-ANB	Boeing 787-8	Air India
	VT-ANC	Boeing 787-8	Air India
	VT-AND	Boeing 787-8	Air India
	VT-ANE	Boeing 787-8	Air India
	VT-ANG	Boeing 787-8	Air India
	VT-ANH	Boeing 787-8	Air India
	VT-ANI	Boeing 787-8	Air India
	VT-ANJ	Boeing 787-8	Air India
	VT-ANK	Boeing 787-8	Air India
	VT-ANL	Boeing 787-8	Air India
	VT-ANM	Boeing 787-8	Air India
	VT-ANN	Boeing 787-8	Air India
	VT-ANO	Boeing 787-8	Air India
	VT-ANP	Boeing 787-8	Air India
	VT-ANQ	Boeing 787-8	Air India
	VT-ANR	Boeing 787-8	Air India
	VT-ANS	Boeing 787-8	Air India
	VT-ANT	Boeing 787-8	Air India
	VT-ANU	Boeing 787-8	Air India
	VT-ANV	Boeing 787-8	Air India
	VT-ANW	Boeing 787-8	Air India
	VT-ANX	Boeing 787-8	Air India
	VT-ANY	Boeing 787-8	Air India
	VT-ANZ	Boeing 787-8	Air India
	VT-JEH	Boeing 777-35RER	Jet Airways
	VT-JEK	Boeing 777-35RER	Jet Airways
	VT-JEM	Boeing 777-35RER	Jet Airways
	VT-JEQ	Boeing 777-35RER	Jet Airways
	VT-JES	Boeing 777-35RER	Jet Airways
	VT-JET	Boeing 777-35RER	Jet Airways
	VT-JEU	Boeing 777-35RER	Jet Airways
	VT-JEV	Boeing 777-35RER	Jet Airways
	VT-JEW	Boeing 777-35RER	Jet Airways
	VT-JEX	Boeing 777-35RER	Jet Airways
	VT-NAA	Boeing 787-8	Air India
	VT-NAC	Boeing 787-8	Air India

Reg	Type	Owner or Operator	Notes

XA (Mexico)

XA-ADC	Boeing 787-9	Aeromexico	
XA-ADD	Boeing 787-9	Aeromexico	
XA-ADG	Boeing 787-9	Aeromexico	
XA-ADH	Boeing 787-9	Aeromexico	
XA-ADL	Boeing 787-9	Aeromexico	
XA-AMR	Boeing 787-8	Aeromexico	
XA-AMX	Boeing 787-8	Aeromexico	

YI (Iraq)

YI-ARA	Airbus A.320-214	Iraqi Airways	
YI-ARB	Airbus A.320-214	Iraqi Airways	
YI-ARD	Airbus A.320-214	Iraqi Airways	

YL (Latvia)

YL-BBD	Boeing 737-53S	Air Baltic	
YL-BBE	Boeing 737-53S	Air Baltic	
YL-BBI	Boeing 737-33A	Air Baltic	
YL-BBJ	Boeing 737-36Q	Air Baltic	
YL-BBM	Boeing 737-522	Air Baltic	
YL-BBN	Boeing 737-522	Air Baltic	
YL-BBQ	Boeing 737-522	Air Baltic	
YL-BBR	Boeing 737-31S	Air Baltic	
YL-BBS	Boeing 737-31S	Air Baltic	
YL-BBX	Boeing 737-36Q	Air Baltic	
YL-BBY	Boeing 737-36Q	Air Baltic	
YL-CSA	Bombardier CS300	Air Baltic	
YL-CSB	Bombardier CS300	Air Baltic	
YL-CSC	Bombardier CS300	Air Baltic	
YL-CSD	Bombardier CS300	Air Baltic	
YL-CSE	Bombardier CS300	Air Baltic	
YL-CSF	Bombardier CS300	Air Baltic	
YL-CSG	Bombardier CS300	Air Baltic	
YL-CSH	Bombardier CS300	Air Baltic	
YL-LCL	Airbus A.320-214	Smart Lynx Airlines	
YL-LCN	Airbus A.320-233	Smart Lynx Airlines	
YL-LCO	Airbus A.320-214	Smart Lynx Airlines	
YL-LCQ	Airbus A.321-231	Smart Lynx Airlines	
YL-LCS	Airbus A.320-214	Smart Lynx Airlines	
YL-LCT	Airbus A.320-214	Smart Lynx Airlines	
YL-LCU	Airbus A.320-214	Smart Lynx Airlines	
YL-LCV	Airbus A.321-231	Smart Lynx Airlines	

YR (Romania)

YR-AMA	Boeing 737-530	Blue Air	
YR-AMB	Boeing 737-530	Blue Air	
YR-AMC	Boeing 737-530	Blue Air	
YR-AMD	Boeing 737-530	Blue Air	
YR-AME	Boeing 737-530	Blue Air	
YR-ASA	Airbus A.318-111	Tarom	
YR-ASB	Airbus A.318-111	Tarom	
YR-ASC	Airbus A.318-111	Tarom	
YR-ASD	Airbus A.318-111	Tarom	
YR-BAE	Boeing 737-46N	Blue Air	
YR-BAF	Boeing 737-322	Blue Air	
YR-BAG	Boeing 737-5L9	Blue Air	
YR-BAO	Boeing 737-42C	Blue Air	
YR-BAP	Boeing 737-3YO	Blue Air	
YR-BAQ	Boeing 737-4D7	Blue Air	
YR-BAS	Boeing 737-430	Blue Air	
YR-BAU	Boeing 737-4YO	Blue Air	
YR-BAZ	Boeing 737-405	Blue Air	
YR-BGA	Boeing 737-38J	Tarom *Alba Iulia*	
YR-BGB	Boeing 737-38J	Tarom *Bucuresti*	
YR-BGD	Boeing 737-38J	Tarom *Deva*	
YR-BGE	Boeing 737-38J	Tarom *Timisoara*	

Notes	Reg	Type	Owner or Operator
	YR-BGF	Boeing 737-78J	Tarom *Braila*
	YR-BGG	Boeing 737-78J	Tarom *Craiova*
	YR-BGH	Boeing 737-78J	Tarom *Hunedoara*
	YR-BGI	Boeing 737-78J	Tarom *Iasi*
	YR-BGJ	Boeing 737-82R	Tarom *Sarmizegetusa*
	YR-BGK	Boeing 737-82R	Tarom *Marea Unire*
	YR-BMA	Boeing 737-79P	Blue Air
	YR-BMB	Boeing 737-85R	Blue Air
	YR-BMC	Boeing 737-85F	Blue Air
	YR-BMD	Boeing 737-85F	Blue Air
	YR-BME	Boeing 737-86N	Blue Air
	YR-BMF	Boeing 737-8Q8	Blue Air
	YR-BMG	Boeing 737-86N	Blue Air
	YR-BMH	Boeing 737-8K5	Blue Air
	YR-BMI	Boeing 737-8K5	Blue Air
	YR-BMJ	Boeing 737-82R	Blue Air
	YR-BMK	Boeing 737-82R	Blue Air/LOT
	YR-BML	Boeing 737-82R	Blue Air
	YR-BMM	Boeing 737-82R	Blue Air
	YR-BMN	Boeing 737-82R	Blue Air/LOT

YU (Serbia and Montenegro)

	YU-APA	Airbus A.319-132	Air Serbia
	YU-APB	Airbus A.319-132	Air Serbia
	YU-APC	Airbus A.319-131	Air Serbia
	YU-APD	Airbus A.319-132	Air Serbia
	YU-APE	Airbus A.319-132	Air Serbia
	YU-APF	Airbus A.319-131	Air Serbia
	YU-APG	Airbus A.320-232	Air Serbia
	YU-APH	Airbus A.320-232	Air Serbia
	YU-API	Airbus A.319-132	Air Serbia
	YU-APJ	Airbus A.319-132	Air Serbia

ZA (Albania)

	ZA-AWA	Boeing 737-5K5	Albawings
	ZA-AWB	Boeing 737-408	Albawings

ZK (New Zealand)

	ZK-OKA	Boeing 777-219ER	Air New Zealand
	ZK-OKB	Boeing 777-219ER	Air New Zealand
	ZK-OKC	Boeing 777-219ER	Air New Zealand
	ZK-OKD	Boeing 777-219ER	Air New Zealand
	ZK-OKE	Boeing 777-219ER	Air New Zealand
	ZK-OKF	Boeing 777-219ER	Air New Zealand
	ZK-OKG	Boeing 777-219ER	Air New Zealand
	ZK-OKH	Boeing 777-219ER	Air New Zealand
	ZK-OKM	Boeing 777-319ER	Air New Zealand
	ZK-OKN	Boeing 777-319ER	Air New Zealand
	ZK-OKO	Boeing 777-319ER	Air New Zealand
	ZK-OKP	Boeing 777-319ER	Air New Zealand
	ZK-OKQ	Boeing 777-319ER	Air New Zealand
	ZK-OKR	Boeing 777-319ER	Air New Zealand
	ZK-OKS	Boeing 777-319ER	Air New Zealand

ZS (South Africa)

	ZS-SNA	Airbus A.340-642	South African Airways
	ZS-SNB	Airbus A.340-642	South African Airways
	ZS-SNC	Airbus A.340-642	South African Airways
	ZS-SND	Airbus A.340-642	South African Airways
	ZS-SNE	Airbus A.340-642	South African Airways
	ZS-SNF	Airbus A.340-642	South African Airways
	ZS-SNG	Airbus A.340-642	South African Airways
	ZS-SNH	Airbus A.340-642	South African Airways
	ZS-SNI	Airbus A.340-642	South African Airways
	ZS-SXA	Airbus A.340-313E	South African Airways
	ZS-SXB	Airbus A.340-313E	South African Airways

Reg	Type	Owner or Operator	Notes
ZS-SXC	Airbus A.340-313E	South African Airways	
ZS-SXD	Airbus A.340-313E	South African Airways	
ZS-SXE	Airbus A.340-313E	South African Airways	
ZS-SXF	Airbus A.340-313E	South African Airways	
ZS-SXG	Airbus A.340-313X	South African Airways	
ZS-SXH	Airbus A.340-313X	South African Airways	
ZS-SXI	Airbus A.330-343E	South African Airways	
ZS-SXJ	Airbus A.330-343E	South African Airways	
ZS-SXK	Airbus A.330-343E	South African Airways	
ZS-SXL	Airbus A.330-343E	South African Airways	
ZS-SXM	Airbus A.330-343E	South African Airways	
ZS-SXU	Airbus A.330-243	South African Airways	
ZS-SXV	Airbus A.330-243	South African Airways	
ZS-SXW	Airbus A.330-243	South African Airways	
ZS-SXX	Airbus A.330-243	South African Airways	
ZS-SXY	Airbus A.330-243	South African Airways	
ZS-SXZ	Airbus A.330-243	South African Airways	

3B (Mauritius)

3B-NAU	Airbus A.340-312	Air Mauritius *Pink Pigeon*	
3B-NAY	Airbus A.340-313X	Air Mauritius *Cardinal*	
3B-NBD	Airbus A.340-313X	Air Mauritius *Parakeet*	
3B-NBE	Airbus A.340-313X	Air Mauritius *Paille en Queue*	
3B-NBJ	Airbus A.340-313E	Air Mauritius *Le Chamarel*	

4K (Azerbaijan)

4K-AZ81	Boeing 767-32LER	Azerbaijan Airlines	
4K-AZ82	Boeing 767-32LER	Azerbaijan Airlines	
4K-AZ85	Airbus A.340-542	Azerbaijan Airlines	
4K-AZ86	Airbus A.340-542	Azerbaijan Airlines	

4L (Georgia)

4L-TGN	Boeing 737-7BK	Georgian Airways	
4L-TGO	Boeing 737-7CT	Georgian Airways	
4L-TGU	Embraer ERJ190-100AR	Georgian Airways	
4L-TGV	Embraer ERJ190-100AR	Georgian Airways	

4O (Montenegro)

4O-AOA	Embraer ERJ190-200LR	Montenegro Airlines	
4O-AOB	Embraer ERJ190-200LR	Montenegro Airlines	
4O-AOC	Embraer ERJ190-200LR	Montenegro Airlines	
4O-AOM	Fokker 100	Montenegro Airlines	
4O-AOP	Fokker 100	Montenegro Airlines	

4R (Sri Lanka)

4R-ALA	Airbus A.330-243	SriLankan Airlines	
4R-ALB	Airbus A.330-243	SriLankan Airlines	
4R-ALC	Airbus A.330-243	SriLankan Airlines	
4R-ALD	Airbus A.330-243	SriLankan Airlines	
4R-ALH	Airbus A.330-243	SriLankan Airlines	
4R-ALJ	Airbus A.330-243	SriLankan Airlines	
4R-ALL	Airbus A.330-343	SriLankan Airlines	
4R-ALM	Airbus A.330-343	SriLankan Airlines	
4R-ALN	Airbus A.330-343	SriLankan Airlines	
4R-ALO	Airbus A.330-343	SriLankan Airlines	
4R-ALP	Airbus A.330-343	SriLankan Airlines	
4R-ALQ	Airbus A.330-343	SriLankan Airlines	
4R-ALR	Airbus A.330-343	SriLankan Airlines	

4X (Israel)

4X-ABF	Airbus A.320-232	Israir	
4X-ABG	Airbus A.320-232	Israir	
4X-ABI	Airbus A.320-232	Israir	

Notes	Reg	Type	Owner or Operator
	4X-EAJ	Boeing 767-330ER	El Al
	4X-EAK	Boeing 767-3Q8ER	El Al
	4X-EAL	Boeing 767-33AER	El Al
	4X-EAM	Boeing 767-3Q8ER	El Al
	4X-EAN	Boeing 767-3Q8ER	El Al
	4X-EAP	Boeing 767-3Y0ER	El Al
	4X-EAR	Boeing 767-352ER	El Al
	4X-ECA	Boeing 777-258ER	El Al
	4X-ECB	Boeing 777-258ER	El Al
	4X-ECC	Boeing 777-258ER	El Al
	4X-ECD	Boeing 777-258ER	El Al
	4X-ECE	Boeing 777-258ER	El Al
	4X-ECF	Boeing 777-258ER	El Al
	4X-EDA	Boeing 787-9	El Al
	4X-EDB	Boeing 787-9	El Al
	4X-EDC	Boeing 787-9	El Al
	4X-EDD	Boeing 787-9	El Al
	4X-EDE	Boeing 787-9	El Al
	4X-EDF	Boeing 787-9	El Al
	4X-EDH	Boeing 787-9	El Al
	4X-EDI	Boeing 787-9	El Al
	4X-EHA	Boeing 737-958ER	El Al
	4X-EHB	Boeing 737-958ER	El Al
	4X-EHC	Boeing 737-958ER	El Al
	4X-EHD	Boeing 737-958ER	El Al
	4X-EHE	Boeing 737-958ER	El Al
	4X-EHF	Boeing 737-958ER	El Al
	4X-EHH	Boeing 737-958ER	El Al
	4X-EHI	Boeing 737-958ER	El Al
	4X-EKA	Boeing 737-858	El Al
	4X-EKB	Boeing 737-858	El Al
	4X-EKC	Boeing 737-858	El Al
	4X-EKF	Boeing 737-858	El Al
	4X-EKH	Boeing 737-85P	El Al
	4X-EKI	Boeing 737-86N	El Al
	4X-EKJ	Boeing 737-85P	El Al
	4X-EKL	Boeing 737-85P	El Al
	4X-EKP	Boeing 737-8Q8	El Al
	4X-EKS	Boeing 737-8Q8	El Al
	4X-ELA	Boeing 747-458	El Al
	4X-ELB	Boeing 747-458	El Al
	4X-ELC	Boeing 747-458	El Al
	4X-ELD	Boeing 747-458	El Al
	4X-ELE	Boeing 747-458	El Al
	4X-ELF	Boeing 747-412F	El Al Cargo

5B (Cyprus)

	5B-DCR	Airbus A.320-232	Cobalt Air
	5B-DCU	Airbus A.319-112	Cobalt Air
	5B-DCV	Airbus A.319-132	Cobalt Air
	5B-DCW	Airbus A.319-114	Cyprus Airways
	5B-DCY	Airbus A.320-214	Cobalt Air
	5B-DCZ	Airbus A.320-214	Cobalt Air
	5B-DDC	Airbus A.320-232	Cobalt Air

5Y (Kenya)

	5Y-KZA	Boeing 787-8	Kenya Airways
	5Y-KZB	Boeing 787-8	Kenya Airways
	5Y-KZC	Boeing 787-8	Kenya Airways
	5Y-KZD	Boeing 787-8	Kenya Airlines
	5Y-KZE	Boeing 787-8	Kenya Airways
	5Y-KZF	Boeing 787-8	Kenya Airways
	5Y-KZG	Boeing 787-8	Kenya Airways

7T (Algeria)

	7T-VJA	Airbus A.330-202	Air Algerie
	7T-VJB	Airbus A.330-202	Air Algerie

Reg	Type	Owner or Operator	Notes
7T-VJC	Airbus A.330-202	Air Algerie	
7T-VJK	Boeing 737-8D6	Air Algerie *Mansourah*	
7T-VJL	Boeing 737-8D6	Air Algerie *Illizi*	
7T-VJM	Boeing 737-8D6	Air Algerie	
7T-VJN	Boeing 737-8D6	Air Algerie	
7T-VJO	Boeing 737-8D6	Air Algerie	
7T-VJP	Boeing 737-8D6	Air Algerie	
7T-VJQ	Boeing 737-6D6	Air Algerie *Kasbah d'Alger*	
7T-VJR	Boeing 737-6D6	Air Algerie	
7T-VJS	Boeing 737-6D6	Air Algerie	
7T-VJT	Boeing 737-6D6	Air Algerie	
7T-VJU	Boeing 737-6D6	Air Algerie	
7T-VJV	Airbus A.330-202	Air Algerie *Tinhinan*	
7T-VJW	Airbus A.330-202	Air Algerie *Lalla Setti*	
7T-VJX	Airbus A.330-202	Air Algerie *Mers el Kebir*	
7T-VJY	Airbus A.330-202	Air Algerie *Monts des Beni Chougrane*	
7T-VJZ	Airbus A.330-202	Air Algerie *Teddis*	
7T-VKA	Boeing 737-8D6	Air Algerie	
7T-VKB	Boeing 737-8D6	Air Algerie	
7T-VKC	Boeing 737-8D6	Air Algerie	
7T-VKD	Boeing 737-8D6	Air Algerie	
7T-VKE	Boeing 737-8D6	Air Algerie	
7T-VKF	Boeing 737-8D6	Air Algerie	
7T-VKG	Boeing 737-8D6	Air Algerie	
7T-VKH	Boeing 737-8D6	Air Algerie	
7T-VKI	Boeing 737-8D6	Air Algerie	
7T-VKJ	Boeing 737-8D6	Air Algerie	
7T-VKK	Boeing 737-8D6	Air Algerie	
7T-VKL	Boeing 737-8D6	Air Algerie	
7T-VKM	Boeing 737-8D6	Air Algerie	
7T-VKN	Boeing 737-8D6	Air Algerie	
7T-VKO	Boeing 737-8D6	Air Algerie	
7T-VKP	Boeing 737-8D6	Air Algerie	
7T-VKQ	Boeing 737-8D6	Air Algerie	
7T-VKR	Boeing 737-8D6	Air Algerie	
7T-VKS	Boeing 737-7D6	Air Algerie	
7T-VKT	Boeing 737-7D6	Air Algerie	

9A (Croatia)

Reg	Type	Owner or Operator	Notes
9A-CTG	Airbus A.319-112	Croatia Airlines *Zadar*	
9A-CTH	Airbus A.319-112	Croatia Airlines *Zagreb*	
9A-CTI	Airbus A.319-112	Croatia Airlines *Vukovar*	
9A-CTJ	Airbus A.320-214	Croatia Airlines *Dubrovnik*	
9A-CTK	Airbus A.320-214	Croatia Airlines *Split*	
9A-CTL	Airbus A.319-112	Croatia Airlines *Pula*	

9H (Malta)

Reg	Type	Owner or Operator	Notes
9H-AEI	Airbus A.320-214	Air Malta	
9H-AEJ	Airbus A.319-112	Air Malta	
9H-AEK	Airbus A.320-214	Air Malta	
9H-AEN	Airbus A.320-214	Air Malta	
9H-AEO	Airbus A.320-214	Air Malta	
9H-AEP	Airbus A.320-214	Air Malta	
9H-AEQ	Airbus A.320-214	Air Malta	
9H-AHR	Airbus A.320-232	Air Malta	

9K (Kuwait)

Reg	Type	Owner or Operator	Notes
9K-AOA	Boeing 777-269ER	Kuwait Airways *Al-Grain*	
9K-AOB	Boeing 777-269ER	Kuwait Airways *Garouh*	
9K-AOC	Boeing 777-369ER	Kuwait Airways *Failaka*	
9K-AOD	Boeing 777-369ER	Kuwait Airways *Ul Almaradim*	
9K-AOE	Boeing 777-369ER	Kuwait Airways *Kathma*	
9K-AOF	Boeing 777-369ER	Kuwait Airways *Kubbar*	
9K-AOH	Boeing 777-369ER	Kuwait Airways *Warbah*	
9K-AOI	Boeing 777-369ER	Kuwait Airways *Meskan*	
9K-AOJ	Boeing 777-369ER	Kuwait Airways *Bubiyan*	
9K-AOK	Boeing 777-369ER	Kuwait Airways *Auhah*	

Notes	Reg	Type	Owner or Operator
	9K-AOL	Boeing 777-369ER	Kuwait Airways *Al Wafrah*
	9K-AOM	Boeing 777-369ER	Kuwait Airways *Garouh*

9M (Malaysia)

Notes	Reg	Type	Owner or Operator
	9M-MAB	Airbus A.350-941	Malaysian Airlines
	9M-MAC	Airbus A.350-941	Malaysian Airlines
	9M-MAD	Airbus A.350-941	Malaysian Airlines
	9M-MNA	Airbus A.380-841	Malaysian Airlines
	9M-MNB	Airbus A.380-841	Malaysian Airlines
	9M-MNC	Airbus A.380-841	Malaysian Airlines
	9M-MND	Airbus A.380-841	Malaysian Airlines
	9M-MNE	Airbus A.380-841	Malaysian Airlines
	9M-MNF	Airbus A.380-841	Malaysian Airlines

9V (Singapore)

Notes	Reg	Type	Owner or Operator
	9V-SFI	Boeing 747-412F	Singapore Airlines Cargo
	9V-SFK	Boeing 747-412F	Singapore Airlines Cargo
	9V-SFM	Boeing 747-412F	Singapore Airlines Cargo
	9V-SFN	Boeing 747-412F	Singapore Airlines Cargo
	9V-SFO	Boeing 747-412F	Singapore Airlines Cargo
	9V-SFP	Boeing 747-412F	Singapore Airlines Cargo
	9V-SFQ	Boeing 747-412F	Singapore Airlines Cargo
	9V-SKE	Airbus A.380-841	Singapore Airlines
	9V-SKF	Airbus A.380-841	Singapore Airlines
	9V-SKG	Airbus A.380-841	Singapore Airlines
	9V-SKH	Airbus A.380-841	Singapore Airlines
	9V-SKI	Airbus A.380-841	Singapore Airlines
	9V-SKJ	Airbus A.380-841	Singapore Airlines
	9V-SKK	Airbus A.380-841	Singapore Airlines
	9V-SKL	Airbus A.380-841	Singapore Airlines
	9V-SKM	Airbus A.380-841	Singapore Airlines
	9V-SKN	Airbus A.380-841	Singapore Airlines
	9V-SKP	Airbus A.380-841	Singapore Airlines
	9V-SKQ	Airbus A.380-841	Singapore Airlines
	9V-SKR	Airbus A.380-841	Singapore Airlines
	9V-SKS	Airbus A.380-841	Singapore Airlines
	9V-SKT	Airbus A.380-841	Singapore Airlines
	9V-SKU	Airbus A.380-841	Singapore Airlines
	9V-SKV	Airbus A.380-841	Singapore Airlines
	9V-SKW	Airbus A.380-841	Singapore Airlines
	9V-SKY	Airbus A.380-841	Singapore Airlines
	9V-SKZ	Airbus A.380-841	Singapore Airlines
	9V-SMA	Airbus A.350-941	Singapore Airlines
	9V-SMB	Airbus A.350-941	Singapore Airlines
	9V-SMC	Airbus A.350-941	Singapore Airlines
	9V-SMD	Airbus A.350-941	Singapore Airlines
	9V-SME	Airbus A.350-941	Singapore Airlines
	9V-SMF	Airbus A.350-941	Singapore Airlines
	9V-SMG	Airbus A.350-941	Singapore Airlines
	9V-SMH	Airbus A.350-941	Singapore Airlines
	9V-SMI	Airbus A.350-941	Singapore Airlines
	9V-SMJ	Airbus A.350-941	Singapore Airlines
	9V-SMK	Airbus A.350-941	Singapore Airlines
	9V-SML	Airbus A.350-941	Singapore Airlines
	9V-SMM	Airbus A.350-941	Singapore Airlines
	9V-SMN	Airbus A.350-941	Singapore Airlines
	9V-SMO	Airbus A.350-941	Singapore Airlines
	9V-SMP	Airbus A.350-941	Singapore Airlines
	9V-SMQ	Airbus A.350-941	Singapore Airlines
	9V-SMR	Airbus A.350-941	Singapore Airlines
	9V-SMS	Airbus A.350-941	Singapore Airlines
	9V-SMT	Airbus A.350-941	Singapore Airlines
	9V-SMU	Airbus A.350-941	Singapore Airlines
	9V-SNA	Boeing 777-312ER	Singapore Airlines
	9V-SNB	Boeing 777-312ER	Singapore Airlines
	9V-SNC	Boeing 777-312ER	Singapore Airlines
	9V-SWA	Boeing 777-312ER	Singapore Airlines
	9V-SWB	Boeing 777-312ER	Singapore Airlines

Reg	Type	Owner or Operator	Notes
9V-SWD	Boeing 777-312ER	Singapore Airlines	
9V-SWE	Boeing 777-312ER	Singapore Airlines	
9V-SWF	Boeing 777-312ER	Singapore Airlines	
9V-SWG	Boeing 777-312ER	Singapore Airlines	
9V-SWH	Boeing 777-312ER	Singapore Airlines	
9V-SWI	Boeing 777-312ER	Singapore Airlines	
9V-SWJ	Boeing 777-312ER	Singapore Airlines	
9V-SWK	Boeing 777-312ER	Singapore Airlines	
9V-SWL	Boeing 777-312ER	Singapore Airlines	
9V-SWM	Boeing 777-312ER	Singapore Airlines	
9V-SWN	Boeing 777-312ER	Singapore Airlines	
9V-SWO	Boeing 777-312ER	Singapore Airlines	
9V-SWP	Boeing 777-312ER	Singapore Airlines	
9V-SWQ	Boeing 777-312ER	Singapore Airlines	
9V-SWR	Boeing 777-312ER	Singapore Airlines	
9V-SWS	Boeing 777-312ER	Singapore Airlines	
9V-SWT	Boeing 777-312ER	Singapore Airlines	
9V-SWU	Boeing 777-312ER	Singapore Airlines	
9V-SWV	Boeing 777-312ER	Singapore Airlines	
9V-SWW	Boeing 777-312ER	Singapore Airlines	
9V-SWY	Boeing 777-312ER	Singapore Airlines	
9V-SWZ	Boeing 777-312ER	Singapore Airlines	

9XR (Rwanda)

Reg	Type	Owner or Operator	Notes
9XR-WN	Airbus A.330-343E	Rwand Air	
9XR-WP	Airbus A.330-343E	Rwand Air	

B-LRQ Airbus A.350-941 of Cathay Pacific Airways *Allan S. Wright*

LN-LNF Boeing 787-8 of Norwegian Long Haul *Peter R. March*

The frequencies used by the larger airfields and airports are listed below.
Abbreviations used: TWR – Tower, APP – Approach, A/G – Air/Ground advisory.
It is possible that changes will be made from time to time with the frequencies allocated, all of which are quoted in Megahertz (MHz).

	TWR	APP	A/G		TWR	APP	A/G
Aberdeen	118.1	119.05		Leeds Bradford	120.3	134.575	
Alderney	125.35	128.65		Leicester			122.125
Andrewsfield			130.55	Liverpool	126.35	119.85	
Barrow			123.2	London City	118.075	132.7	
Beccles			120.375	London Gatwick		124.225	126.825
Belfast International	118.3	128.5		London Heathrow	118.5	119.725	
Belfast City	122.825	130.85		London Stansted	123.8	120.625	
Bembridge			123.25	Luton	132.55	129.55	
Biggin Hill	134.8	129.4		Lydd	119.375	120.700	
Birmingham	118.3	118.05		Manchester (Barton)			120.25
Blackbushe			122.3	Manchester	118.625	118.575	
Blackpool	118.400	119.95		Netherthorpe			123.275
Bodmin			122.7	Newcastle	119.7	124.375	
Bourn			124.35	Newquay	134.375	133.40	
Bournemouth	125.6	119.475		North Weald			123.525
Breighton			129.80	Norwich	124.25	119.35	
Bristol	133.85	125.65		Nottingham			134.875
Bruntingthorpe			122.825	Old Warden			130.7
Caernarfon			122.25	Oxford	133.425	127.750	
Cambridge	125.900	123.6		Perth			119.8
Cardiff	133.	125.85		Peterborough Conington			129.725
Carlisle			123.6	Peterborough Sibson			122.3
Clacton			118.15	Popham			129.8
Compton Abbas			122.7	Prestwick	118.15	129.45	
Cosford	128.65	135.875		Redhill			119.6
Coventry	123.825	119.25		Rochester			122.25
Cranfield	134.925	122.85		Ronaldsway IOM	122.6	120.85	
Cumbernauld			120.6	Sandown IOW			119.275
Denham			130.725	Sandtoft			130.425
Doncaster RHA	128.775	126.225		Scilly Isles			124.875
Dundee	122.9			Seething			122.6
Dunkeswell		123.475		Sherburn			122.6
Durham Tees Valley	119.8	118.85		Shipdham			132.23
Duxford			122.075	Shobdon			123.5
East Midlands	134.175	124.0		Shoreham	125.4	123.15	
Earls Colne			122.425	Sleap			122.45
Edinburgh	118.7	121.2		Southampton	118.2	122.725	
Elstree			122.4	Southend	127.725	130.775	
Exeter	119.8	128.975		Stapleford			122.8
Fairoaks			123.425	Sumburgh	118.25	131.3	
Farnborough	122.5	134.35		Swansea			119.7
Fenland			122.925	Sywell			122.7
Fowlmere			135.7	Tatenhill			124.075
Gamston			130.475	Thruxton			130.45
Glasgow	118.8	119.1		Wellesbourne			124.025
Gloucester/Staverton	122.9	128.55		Welshpool			128.0
Goodwood			122.45	White Waltham			122.6
Guernsey	119.95	128.65		Wick			119.7
Haverfordwest			122.2	Wickenby			122.45
Hawarden	124.95	123.35		Wolverhampton			123.000
Henstridge			130.25	Woodvale	119.75	121.0	
Headcorn			122.0	Wycombe Air Park			126.55
Humberside	124.9	119.125		Yeovil	125.4	130.8	
Inverness	118.40	122.6					
Jersey	119.45	120.3					
Kemble			118.9				
Land's End			120.25				
Lasham			131.025				

Those listed below identify many of the UK and overseas carriers appearing in the book

Code	Airline	Reg		Code	Airline	Reg		Code	Airline	Reg
AAF	Aigle Azur	F		CSA	CSA Czech Airlines	OK		LOT	LOT Polish Airlines	SP
AAL	American Airlines	N		CSN	China Southern Airlines	B		LTC	Smart Lynx Airlines	YL
AAR	Asiana Airlines	HL		CSW	Silkway Italia	I		LZB	Bulgaria Air	LZ
ABO	Air Atlanta Icelandic	TF		CTN	Croatia Airlines	9A		MAC	Air Arabia Maroc	CN
ABR	ASL Airlines Ireland	EI		DAH	Air Algerie	7T		MAR	Air Mediterreanean	SX
ABW	AirBridge Cargo	RA		DAL	Delta Air Lines	N		MAS	Malaysian Airlines	9M
ACA	Air Canada	C		DHK	DHL Air	D/G		MAU	Air Mauritius	3B
ADR	Adria Airways	S5		DLA	Air Dolomiti	I		MEA	Middle East Airlines	OD
AEE	Aegean Airlines	SX		DLH	Lufthansa	D		MEV	Med-View Airline	5N
AFL	Aeroflot	RA		DTR	Danish Air Transport	OY		MGX	Montenegro Airlines	4O
AFR	Air France	F		EDW	Edelweiss Air	HB		MLD	Air Moldova	ER
AHY	Azerbaijan Airlines	4K		EEZ	Meridiana	I		MMZ	Euro Atlantic Airways	CS
AIC	Air-India	VT		EIN	Aer Lingus	EI		MNG	MNG Airlines	TC
AIZ	Arkia Israel Airlines	4X		ELY	El Al	4X		MPH	Martinair	PH
AJA	Anadolujet	TC		ENT	Enter Air	SP		MSR	EgyptAir	SU
ALK	SriLankan Airlines	4R		ETD	Etihad Airways	A6		NAX	Norwegian Air Shuttle	LN
AMC	Air Malta	9H		ETH	Ethiopian Airlines	ET		NCA	Nippon Cargo Airlines	JA
AMX	Aeromexico	XA		EVA	EVA Airways	B		NOS	Neos	I
ANA	All Nippon Airways	JA		EWG	Eurowings	D		NPT	West Atlantic Airlines	G
ANE	Air Nostrum	EC		EXS	Jet 2.com	G		NRS	Norwegian Air UK	G
ANZ	Air New Zealand	ZK		EZE	Eastern Airways	G		NVD	Avion Express	LY
ASL	Air Serbia	YU		EZS	easyJet Switzerland	HB		NVQ	Nouvelair	TS
AUA	Austrian Airlines	OE		EZY	easyJet	G		NVR	Novair Airlines	SE
AUI	Ukraine International	UR		FAH	ASL Airlines Hungary	HA		OAE	Omni Air International	N
AUR	Aurigny A/S	G		FCB	Cobalt Air	5B		OAW	Helvetic Airways	HB
AVA	AVIANCA	HK		FDX	Federal Express	N		OHY	Onur Air	TC
AWC	Titan Airways	G		FHY	Freebird Airlines	TC		OMA	Oman Air	A4O
AWT	Albawings	ZA		FIN	Finnair	OH		OVA	Air Europa	EC
AXE	AirExplore	OM		FLI	Atlantic Airways	OY		PAC	Polar Air Cargo	N
AZA	Alitalia	I		FPO	ASL Airlines France	F		PAL	Philippine Airlines	RP
BAW	British Airways	G		FXI	Air Iceland	TF		PGT	Pegasus Airlines	TC
BBC	Biman Bangladesh	S2		GCA	Grand Cru Airlines	LY		PIA	Pakistan International	AP
BBD	Bluebird Cargo	TF		GCR	Tianjin Airlines	B		PLM	Wamos Air	EC
BCI	Blue Islands	G		GEC	Lufthansa Cargo	D		PRI	Primera Air Scandinavia	OY
BCS	European A/T	OO		GFA	Gulf Air	A9C		PTI	PrivatAir	HB
BCY	CityJet	EI		GIA	Garuda Indonesia Airlines	PK		PVG	Privilege Style	EC
BEE	Flybe	G		GMI	Germania	D		QFA	QANTAS	VH
BEL	Brussels Airlines	OO		GTI	Atlas Air	N		QTR	Qatar Airways	A7
BGA	Airbus Tpt International	F		GWI	Germanwings	D		RAM	Royal Air Maroc	CN
BGH	BH Air	LZ		HFY	HiFly	CS		RBA	Royal Brunei Airlines	V8
BID	Binair	D		HOP	HOP!	F		RJA	Royal Jordanian	JY
BLC	TAM Linhas Aereas	PT		HVN	Vietnam Airlines	VN		ROT	Tarom	YR
BLX	TUIfly Nordic	SE		IAW	Iraqi Airways	YI		ROU	Air Canada Rouge	C
BMR	bmi regional	G		IBE	Iberia	EC		RWD	RwandAir	9XR
BOS	Open Skies	F		IBS	Iberia Express	EC		RYR	Ryanair	EI
BOX	AeroLogic	D		ICE	Icelandair	TF		RZO	Azores Airlines	CS
BPA	Blue Panorama	I		ICV	Cargolux Italia	I		SAA	South African Airways	ZS
BRU	Belavia	EW		IOS	Isles of Scilly Skybus	G		SAS	SAS	SE/ OY/ LN
BTI	Air Baltic	YL		IRA	Iran Air	EP		SIA	Singapore Airlines	9V
BUC	Bulgarian Air Charter	LZ		JAF	TUI Airlines Belgium	OO		SQC	Singapore Airlines Cargo	9V
CAI	Corendon Airlines	TC		JAI	Jet Airways	VT		SRK	SkyWork Airlines	HB
CAL	China Airlines	B		JAL	Japan Airlines	JA		SRR	Star Air	OY
CCA	Air China	B		JOR	Blue Air	YR		STK	Stobart Air	EI
CCM	Air Corsica	F		JTG	Jet Time	OY		SUS	Sun-Air	OY
CES	China Eastern	B		KAC	Kuwait Airways	9K		SVA	Saudi Arabian Airlines	HZ
CFE	BA Cityflyer	G		KAL	Korean Air	HL		SWN	West Atlantic Airlines	SE
CFG	Condor	D		KKK	Atlas Global Airlines	TC		SWR	Swiss International	HB
CGF	Cargo Air	LZ		KLC	KLM CityHopper	PH		SXS	SunExpress	TC
CHH	Hainan Airlines	B		KLM	KLM	PH		TAM	TAM Linhas Aereas	PT
CKS	Kalitta Air	N		KQA	Kenya Airways	5Y		TAP	TAP Portugal	CS
CLH	Lufthansa CityLine	D		KZR	Air Astana	UN		TAR	Tunis Air	TS
CLJ	Cello Aviation	G		LAV	Alba Star	EC		TAY	ASL Airlines Belgium	OO
CLU	CargoLogicAir	G		LBT	Nouvelair	TS		TCX	Thomas Cook Airlines	G
CLX	Cargolux	LX		LGL	Luxair	LX		TFL	TUIfly	PH
CPA	Cathay Pacific	B		LLC	Small Planet Airlines	LY		TGZ	Georgian Airways	4L
CRL	Corsair	F		LOG	Loganair	G		THA	Thai Airways International	HS

THY	Turkish Airlines	TC	TWI	Tailwind Airlines	TC	VLG	Vueling Airlines	EC
TOM	TUIfly	G	UAE	Emirates Airlines	A6	VOE	Volotea Airlines	EC
TRA	Transavia	PH	UAL	United Airlines	N	WDL	WDL Aviation	D
TSC	Air Transat	C	UPS	United Parcel Service	N	WHT	White Airways	CS
TUA	Turkmenistan Airlines	EZ	UZB	Uzbekistan Airways	UK	WIF	Wideroe's	LN
TUI	TUIfly	D,G	VDA	Volga-Dnepr Airlines	RA	WOW	WOW Air	TF
TVF	Transavia France	F	VIR	Virgin Atlantic Airways	G	WZZ	Wizz Air	HA
TVS	Travel Service/Smart Wings	OK	VKG	Thomas Cook Airlines	OY			

EC-MGZ Airbus A.321-231 of Vueling Airlines *Allan S. Wright*

TC-LOC Airbus A.330-343 of Turkish Airlines *Peter R. March*

The British Aircraft Preservation Council was formed in 1967 to co-ordinate the works of all bodies involved in the preservation, restoration and display of historical aircraft. Membership covers the whole spectrum of national, Service, commercial and voluntary groups, and meetings are held regularly at the bases of member organisations. The Council is able to provide a means of communication, helping to resolve any misunderstandings or duplication of effort. Every effort is taken to encourage the raising of standards of both organisation and technical capacity amongst the member groups to the benefit of everyone interested in aviation. To assist historians, the B.A.P.C. register has been set up and provides an identity for those aircraft which do not qualify for a Service serial or inclusion in the UK Civil Register.

Note: Registrations/Serials carried are mostly false identities.

FSM = Full Scale Model, MPA = Man Powered Aircraft, IHM = International Helicopter Museum.

The aircraft, listed as 'models' are generally intended for exhibition purposes and are not airworthy although they are full scale replicas. However, in a few cases the machines have the ability to taxi when used for film work.

Aircraft on the current B.A.P.C. Register are as follows:

Reg	Type	Owner or Operator	Notes
1	Roe Triplane Type 4 (replica)	Shuttleworth Collection as G-ARSG (not carried)	
2	Bristol Boxkite (replica)	Shuttleworth Collection as G-ASPP (not carried)	
3	Bleriot Type XI	Shuttleworth Collection as G-AANG (not carried)	
4	Deperdussin Monoplane	Shuttleworth Collection as G-AANH (not carried)	
5	Blackburn Monoplasne	Shuttleworth Collection as G-AANI (not carried)	
6	Roe Triplane Type IV (replica)	Manchester Museum of Science & Industry	
7	Southampton University MPA	Solent Sky, Southampton	
8	Dixon ornithopter	Shuttleworth Collection	
9	Humber Monoplane (replica)	Midland Air Museum (Coventry)	
10	Hafner R.11 Revoplane	International Helicopter Museum/Weston-Super-Mare	
11	English Electric Wren Composite	Shuttleworth Collection	
12	Mignet HM.14	Manchester Museum of Science and Industry	
13	Mignet HM.14	Brimpex Metal Treatments	
14	Addyman Standard Training Glider	A. Lindsay & N. H. Ponsford	
15	Addyman Standard Training Glider	The Aeroplane Collection	
16	Addyman ultra-light aircraft	N. H. Ponsford	
17	Woodhams Sprite	BB Aviation/Canterbury	
18	Killick MP gyroplane	A. Lindsay & N. H. Ponsford	
19	Bristol F.2b Fighter	Musee Royal de l'Armee Brussels	
20	Lee-Richards annular biplane (replica)	Visitor Centre Shoreham Airport	
21	D. H. 82A Tiger Moth	Newark Air Museum	
22	Mignet HM.14 (G-AEOF)	Aviodome, Netherlands	
23	SE-5A Scale Model	Newark Air Museum	
24	Currie Wot (replica)	Newark Air Museum	
25	Nyborg TGN-III glider	Warwick	
28	Wright Flyer (replica)	Yorkshire Air Museum Elvington	
29	Mignet HM.14 (replica) (G-ADRY)	Brooklands Museum of Aviation/Weybridge	
32	Crossley Tom Thumb	Midland Air Museum	
33	DFS.108-49 Grunau Baby IIb	Denmark	
34	DFS.108-49 Grunau Baby IIb	D. Elsdon	
35	EoN primary glider	–	
36	Fieseler Fi 103 (V-1) (replica)	Kent Battle of Britain Museum/Hawkinge	
37	Blake Bluetit (G-BXIY)	The Shuttleworth Collection/Old Warden	
38	Bristol Scout replica (A1742)	Shuttleworth Trust	
39	Addyman Zephyr sailplane	A. Lindsay & N. H. Ponsford	
40	Bristol Boxkite (replica)	Bristol City Museum	
41	B.E.2C (replica) (6232)	Yorkshire Air Museum/Elvington	
42	Avro 504 (replica) (H1968)	Yorkshire Air Museum/Elvington	
43	Mignet HM.14	Newark Air Museum/Winthorpe	
44	Miles Magister (L6906)	Museum of Berkshire Aviation (G-AKKY)/Woodley	
45	Pilcher Hawk (replica)	Percy Pilcher Museum Rugby	
47	Watkins Monoplane	National Waterfront Museum Swansea	
48	Pilcher Hawk (replica)	Glasgow Museum of Transport	
49	Pilcher Hawk	Royal Scottish Museum/East Fortune	

Notes	Reg	Type	Owner or Operator
	50	Roe Triplane Type 1	Science Museum/South Kensington
	51	Vickers Vimy IV	Science Museum/South Kensington
	52	Lilienthal glider	National Museum of Science and Industry/Wroughton
	53	Wright Flyer (replica)	Science Museum/South Kensington
	54	JAP-Harding monoplane	Science Museum/South Kensington
	55	Levavasseur Antoinette VII	Science Museum/South Kensington
	56	Fokker E.III (210/16)	Science Museum/South Kensington
	57	Pilcher Hawk (replica)	Duxford
	58	Yokosuka MXY7 Ohka II (15-1585)	F.A.A. Museum/Yeovilton
	59	Sopwith Camel (replica) (D3419)	East Fortune
	60	Murray M.1 helicopter	International Helicopter Museum/Weston-super-Mare
	61	Stewart man-powered ornithopter	Boston Lincolnshire
	62	Cody Biplane (304)	Science Museum/South Kensington
	63	Hurricane (replica) (P3208)	Kent Battle of Britain Museum/Hawkinge
	64	Hurricane (replica) (P3059)	Kent Battle of Britain Museum/Hawkinge
	65	Spitfire (replica) (N3289)	Kent Battle of Britain Museum/Hawkinge
	66	Bf 109 (replica) (1480)	Kent Battle of Britain Museum/Hawkinge
	67	Bf 109 (replica) (14)	Kent Battle of Britain Museum/Hawkinge
	68	Hurricane (replica) (H3426)	–
	69	Spitfire (replica) (N3313)	Kent Battle of Britain Museum/Hawkinge
	70	Auster AOP.5 (TJ398)	North East Aircraft Museum/Usworth
	71	Spitfire (replica) (P8140)	Norfolk & Suffolk Aviation Museum
	72	Hurricane (model) (V6779)	Gloucestershire Aviation Collection
	73	Hurricane (replica)	New Zealand
	74	Bf 109 (replica) (6357)	Kent Battle of Britain Museum/Hawkinge
	75	Mignet HM.14 (G-AEFG)	N. H. Ponsford
	76	Mignet HM.14 (G-AFFI)	Yorkshire Air Museum/Elvington
	77	Mignet HM.14 (replica) (G-ADRG)	Lower Stondon Transport Museum
	78	Hawker Hind (K5414) (G-AENP)	The Shuttleworth Collection/Old Warden
	79	Fiat G.46-4B (MM53211)	Norfolk
	80	Airspeed Horsa (KJ351)	Museum of Army Flying/Middle Wallop
	81	Hawkridge Dagling	stored Bedford
	82	Hawker Hind (Afghan)	RAF Museum/Cosford
	83	Kawasaki Ki-100-1b (24)	RAF Museum/Hendon
	84	Nakajima Ki-46 (Dinah II)(5439)	RAF Museum/Cosford
	85	Weir W-2 autogyro	Museum of Flight/East Fortune
	86	de Havilland Tiger Moth (replica)	Yorkshire Aircraft Preservation Society
	87	Bristol Babe (replica) (G-EASQ)	Bristol Aero Collection/Kemble
	88	Fokker Dr 1 (replica) (102/17)	F.A.A. Museum/Yeovilton
	89	Cayley glider (replica)	Yorkshire Air Museum/Elvington
	90	Colditz Cock (replica)	Imperial War Museum/South Lambeth
	91	Fieseler Fi 103 (V-1)	Germany
	92	Fieseler Fi 103 (V-1)	RAF Museum/Hendon
	93	Fieseler Fi 103 (V-1)	Imperial War Museum/Duxford
	94	Fieseler Fi 103 (V-1)	RAF Museum/Cosford
	95	Gizmor autogyro	F. Fewsdale
	96	Brown helicopter	North East Aircraft Museum
	97	Luton L.A.4A Minor	North East Aircraft Museum
	98	Yokosuka MXY7 Ohka II (997)	Manchester Museum of Science & Industry
	99	Yokosuka MXY7 Ohka II (8486M)	RAF Museum/Cosford
	100	Clarke Chanute biplane gliderr	RAF Museum/Hendon
	101	Mignet HM.14	Newark Air Museum/Winthorpe
	102	Mignet HM.14	Not completed
	103	Hulton hang glider (replica)	Personal Plane Services Ltd
	105	Blériot XI (replica)	San Diego Aerospace Museum
	106	Blériot XI (164)	RAF Museum/Hendon
	107	Blériot XXVII	RAF Museum/Hendon
	108	Fairey Swordfish IV (HS503)	Stafford
	109	Slingsby Kirby Cadet TX.1	–
	110	Fokker D.VII replica (static) (5125)	USA
	111	Sopwith Triplane replica (static) (N5492)	F.A.A. Museum/Yeovilton
	112	DH.2 replica (static) (5964)	Museum of Army Flying/Middle Wallop
	113	S.E.5A replica (static) (B4863)	Orlando Florida
	114	Vickers Type 60 Viking (static) (G-EBED)	Brooklands Museum of Aviation/Weybridge

Reg	Type	Owner or Operator	Notes
115	Mignet HM.14	Norfolk & Suffolk Aviation Museum/Flixton	
116	Santos-Dumont Demoiselle (replica)	–	
117	B.E.2C (replica)(1701)	Stored Hawkinge	
119	Bensen B.7	North East Aircraft Museum	
120	Mignet HM.14 (G-AEJZ)	South Yorkshire Aviation Museum/Doncaster	
121	Mignet HM.14 (G-AEKR)	South Yorkshire Aviation Society	
122	Avro 504 (replica) (1881)	Stored	
123	Vickers FB.5 Gunbus (replica)	A. Topen (stored)/Cranfield	
124	Lilienthal Glider Type XI (replica)	Science Museum/South Kensington	
126	D.31 Turbulent (static)	Midland Air Museum/Coventry	
127	Halton Jupiter MPA	Wannock Eastbourne	
128	Watkinson Cyclogyroplane Mk IV	IHM/Weston-super-Mare	
129	Blackburn 1911 Monoplane (replica)	–	
130	Blackburn 1912 Monoplane (replica)	Yorkshire Air Museum/Elvington	
131	Pilcher Hawk (replica)	C. Paton	
132	Blériot XI (G-BLXI)	Montelimar France	
133	Fokker Dr 1 (replica) (425/17)	Kent Battle of Britain Museum/Hawkinge	
134	Pitts S-2A static (G-AXNZ)	Istanbul Turkey	
135	Bristol M.1C (replica) (C4912)	Stored	
136	Deperdussin Seaplane (replica)	Planes of Fame Musem Chino/USA	
137	Sopwith Baby Floatplane (replica) (8151)	Stored	
138	Hansa Brandenburg W.29 Floatplane (replica) (2292)	Stored	
139	Fokker Dr 1 (replica) 150/17	Orlando Florida	
140	Curtiss 42A (replica)	Planes of Fame Museum Chino USA	
141	Macchi M39 (replica)	Planes of Fame Museum Chino USA	
142	SE-5A (replica) (F5459)	Switzerland	
143	Paxton MPA	–	
144	Weybridge Mercury MPA	–	
145	Oliver MPA	Stored	
146	Pedal Aeronauts Toucan MPA	Stored	
147	Bensen B.7	Norfolk & Suffolk Aviation Museum/Flixton	
148	Hawker Fury II (replica) (K7271)	High Ercall Aviation Museum	
149	Short S.27 (replica)	F.A.A. Museum (stored)/Yeovilton	
150	SEPECAT Jaguar GR.1 (replica) (XX728)	Oman	
151	SEPECAT Jaguar GR.1 (replica) (XZ363)	RAF M & R Unit/St. Athan	
152	BAe Hawk T.1 (replica) (XX227)	RAF M & R Unit/Bottesford	
153	Westland WG.33	IHM/Weston-super-Mare	
154	D.31 Turbulent	Lincolnshire Aviation Museum/E. Kirkby	
155	Panavia Tornado GR.1 (model) (ZA556)	RAF M & R Unit/St. Athan	
156	Supermarine S-6B (replica)	Planes of Fame Museum Chino/USA	
157	Waco CG-4A(237123)	Yorkshire Air Museum/Elvington	
158	Fieseler Fi 103 (V-1)	Defence Ordnance Disposal School/Chattenden	
159	Yokosuka MXY7 Ohka II	Imperial War Museum/Duxford	
160	Chargus 18/50 hang glider	Museum of Flight/East Fortune	
161	Stewart Ornithopter Coppelia	stored Louth	
162	Goodhart MPA	Science Museum/Wroughton	
163	AFEE 10/42 Rotabuggy (replica)	Museum of Army Flying/Middle Wallop	
164	Wight Quadruplane Type 1 (replica)	Solent Sky, Southampton	
165	Bristol F.2b (E2466)	RAF Museum/Hendon	
166	Bristol F.2b (D7889)	Canada	
167	Bristol SE-5A	USA	
168	DH.60G Moth (static replica)	Stored Hawkinge (G-AAAH)	
169	BAC/Sepecat Jaguar GR.1 (XX110)	RAF Training School/Cosford	
170	Pilcher Hawk (replica)	–	
171	BAe Hawk T.1 (model) (XX308)	RAF Marketing & Recruitment Unit/Bottesford	
172	Chargus Midas Super 8 hang glider	Science Museum/Wroughton	
173	Birdman Promotions Grasshopper	Science Museum/Wroughton	
174	Bensen B.7	Science Museum/Wroughton	
175	Volmer VJ-23 Swingwing	Manchester Museum of Science & Industry	
176	SE-5A (replica) (A4850)	Bygone Times Antiques Warehouse/Eccleston	
177	Avro 504K (replica) (G-AACA)	Brooklands Museum of Aviation/Weybridge	
178	Avro 504K (replica) (E373)	–	
179	Sopwith Pup (replica) (A7317)	Sywell	
180	McCurdy Silver Dart (replica)	Reynolds Pioneer Museum/Canada	

Notes	Reg	Type	Owner or Operator
	181	RAF B.E.2b (replica) (687)	RAF Museum/Hendon
	182	Wood Ornithopter	Manchester Museum of Science & Industry
	183	Zurowski ZP.1 helicopter	Newark Air Museum/Winthorpe
	184	Spitfire IX (replica) (EN398)	Sleap
	185	Waco CG-4A (243809)	Museum of Army Flying/Middle Wallop
	186	DH.82B Queen Bee (LF789)	de Havilland Aircraft Heritage Museum/ London Colney
	187	Roe Type 1 biplane (replica)	Brooklands Museum of Aviation/Weybridge
	188	McBroom Cobra 88	Science Museum/Wroughton
	189	Bleriot XI (replica)	Stored
	190	Spitfire (replica) (K5054)	P. Smith/Hawkinge
	191	BAe Harrier GR.7 (model) (ZH139)	RAF M & R Unit/St. Athan
	192	Weedhopper JC-24	The Aeroplane Collection
	193	Hovey WD-11 Whing Ding	The Aeroplane Collection
	194	Santos Dumont Demoiselle (replica)	Deutches Technikmuseum/Berlin
	195	Moonraker 77 hang glider	Museum of Flight/East Fortune
	196	Sigma 2M hang glider	Museum of Flight/East Fortune
	197	Scotkites Cirrus III hang glider	Museum of Flight/East Fortune
	198	Fieseler Fi 103 (V-1)	Imperial War Museum/Duxford
	199	Fieseler Fi 103 (V-1)	Science Museum/South Kensington
	200	Bensen B.7	stored Leeds
	201	Mignet HM.14	stored Hooton Park
	202	Spitfire V (model) (MAV467)	–
	203	Chrislea LC.1 Airguard (G-AFIN)	stored Dunkeswell
	204	McBroom hang glider	stored Hooton Park
	205	Hurricane (replica) (Z3427)	RAF Museum/Hendon
	206	Spitfire (replica) (MH486)	RAF Museum/Hendon
	207	Austin Whippet (replica) (K.158)	South Yorkshire Aviation Museum/Doncaster
	208	SE-5A (replica) (D276)	Prince's Mead Shopping Precinct/Farnborough
	209	Spitfire IX (replica) (MJ751)	Niagara Falls Canada
	210	Avro 504J (replica) (C4451)	Solent Sky, Southampton
	211	Mignet HM.14 (replica) (G-ADVU)	North East Aircraft Museum
	212	Bensen B.8	IHM/Weston-super-Mare
	213	Vertigo MPA	IHM/Weston-super-Mare
	214	Spitfire prototype (replica) (K5054)	Tangmere Military Aviation Museum
	215	Airwave hang-glider prototype	Solent Sky, Southampton
	216	DH.88 Comet (replica) (G-ACSS)	de Havilland Heritage Museum/London Colney
	217	Spitfire (replica) (K9926)	RAF Museum/Bentley Priory
	218	Hurricane (replica) (P3386)	RAF Museum/Bentley Priory
	219	Hurricane (replica) (L1710)	Northolt
	220	Spitfire 1 (replica) (N3194)	Shirleywich
	221	Spitfire LF.IX (replica) (MH777)	RAF Museum/Northolt
	222	Spitfire IX (replica) (BR600)	RAF Museum/Uxbridge
	223	Hurricane 1 (replica) (V7467)	RAF High Wycombe
	224	Spitfire V (replica) (BR600)	National Air Force Museum Trenton Canada
	225	Spitfire IX (replica) (P8448)	RAF Museum/Cranwell
	226	Spitfire XI (replica) (EN343)	RAF Museum/Benson
	227	Spitfire 1A (replica) (L1070)	RAF Museum/Turnhouse
	228	Olympus hang-glider	North East Aircraft Museum/Usworth
	229	Spitfire IX (replica) (MJ832)	RAF Museum/Digby
	230	Spitfire (replica) (AA550)	Eden Camp/Malton
	231	Mignet HM.14 (G-ADRX)	South Copeland Aviation Group
	232	AS.58 Horsa I/II	de Havilland Heritage Museum/London Colney
	233	Broburn Wanderlust sailplane	Museum of Berkshire Aviation/Woodley
	234	Vickers FB.5 Gunbus (replica)	Sywell
	235	Fieseler Fi 103 (V-1) (replica)	Eden Camp Wartime Museum
	237	Fieseler Fi 103 (V-1)	Netherlands
	238	Waxflatter ornithopter	Wycombe Air Park
	239	Fokker D.VIII 5/8 scale replica	Norfolk & Suffolk Aviation Museum/Flixton
	240	Messerschmitt Bf.109G (replica)	Yorkshire Air Museum/Elvington
	241	Hurricane 1 (replica) (L1679)	Tangmere Military Aviation Museum
	242	Spitfire Vb (replica) (BL924)	Tangmere Military Aviation Museum
	243	Mignet HM.14 (replica) (G-ADYV)	stored Malvern Wells
	244	Solar Wings Typhoon	Museum of Flight/East Fortune
	245	Electraflyer Floater hang glider	Museum of Flight/East Fortune
	246	Hiway Cloudbase hang glider	Museum of Flight/East Fortune

Reg	Type	Owner or Operator	Notes
247	Albatross ASG.21 hang glider	Museum of Flight/East Fortune	
248	McBroom hang glider	Museum of Berkshire Aviation/Woodley	
249	Hawker Fury 1 (replica) (K5673)	Brooklands Museum of Aviation/Weybridge	
250	RAF SE-5A (replica) (F5475)	Brooklands Museum of Aviation/Weybridge	
251	Hiway Spectrum hang glider (replica)	Manchester Museum of Science & Industry	
252	Flexiform Wing hang glider	Manchester Museum of Science & Industry	
253	Mignet HM.14 (G-ADZW)	Solent Sky/Southampton	
254	Hawker Hurricane (P3873)	Yorkshire Air Museum/Elvington	
255	NA P-51D Mustang (replica) (463209)	American Air Museum/Duxford	
256	Santos Dumont Type 20 (replica)	Brooklands Museum of Aviation/Weybridge	
257	DH.88 Comet (G-ACSS)	Sywell	
258	Adams balloon	British Balloon Museum	
259	Gloster Gamecock (replica)	Jet Age Museum Gloucestershire	
260	Mignet HM280	–	
261	GAL Hotspur (replica)	Museum of Army Flying/ Middle Wallop	
262	Catto CP-16	Museum of Flight/East Fortune	
263	Chargus Cyclone	Ulster Aviation Heritage/Langford Lodge	
264	Bensen B.8M	IHM/Weston-super-Mare	
265	Spitfire 1 (P3873)	Yorkshire Air Museum/Elvington	
266	Rogallo hang glider	Ulster Aviation Heritage	
267	Hurricane (model)	Imperial War Museum/Duxford	
268	Spifire (model)	stored St.Mawgan	
269	Spitfire (model) USAF	RAF Lakenheath	
270	DH.60 Moth (model)	Yorkshire Air Museum/Elvington	
271	Messerschmitt Me 163B	Shuttleworth Collection/Old Warden	
272	Hurricane (model)	Kent Battle of Britain Museum/Hawkinge	
273	Hurricane (model)	Kent Battle of Britain Museum/Hawkinge	
274	Boulton & Paul P.6 (model)	Pendeford Wolverhampton	
275	Bensen B.7 gyroglider	Doncaster Museum	
276	Hartman Ornithopter	Science Museum/Wroughton	
277	Mignet HM.14	Visitor Centre Shoreham Airport	
278	Hurricane (model)	Kent Battle of Britain Museum/Hawkinge	
279	Airspeed Horsa	RAF Shawbury	
280	DH.89A Dragon Rapide (model)	Crowne Plaza Hotel Speke	
281	Boulton & Paul Defiant (model)	Pendeford	
282	Manx Elder Duck	Isle of Man Airport Terminal	
283	Spitfire (model	Jurby, Isle of Man	
284	Gloster E.28/39 (model)	Lutterworth Leics	
285	Gloster E.28/39 (model)	Farnborough	
286	Mignet HM.14	Caernarfon Air Museum	
287	Blackburn F.2 Lincock (model)	Street Life Museum/Hull	
288	Hurricane (model)	Wonderland Pleasure Park, Mansfield	
289	Gyro Boat	IHM Weston-super-Mare	
290	Fieseler Fi 103 (V1) (model)	Dover Museum	
291	Hurricane (model)	National Battle of Britain Memorial, Capel-le-Ferne, Kent	
292	Eurofighter Typhoon (model)	RAF Museum/Hendon	
293	Spitfire (model)	RAF Museum/Hendon	
294	Fairchild Argus (model)	Visitor Centre, Thorpe Camp, Woodhall Spa	
295	Da Vinci hang glider (replica)	Skysport Engineering	
296	Army Balloon Factory NullI (replica)	RAF Museum, Hendon	
297	Spitfire (replica)	Kent Battle of Britain Museum/Hawkinge	
298	Spitfire IX (Model)	RAF Cosford Parade Ground	
299	Spitfire 1 (model).	National Battle of Britain Memorial, Capel-le-Ferne, Kent	
300	Hummingbird (replica)	Shoreham Airport Historical Association	
301	Spitfire V FSM (replica)	Thornaby Aerodrome Memorial, Thornaby-on-Tees	
302	Mignet HM.14 reproduction	Shoreham Airport Historical Association	
303	Goldfinch 161 Amphibian	Norfolk and Suffolk Aviation Museum, Flixton	
304	Supermaine Spitfire FSM		
305	Mersnier pedal powered airship Reproduction	British Balloon Museum and Library	
306	Lovegrove Autogyro trainer	Norfolk and Suffolk Aviation Museum, Flixton	
307	Bleriot XI (replica)		
308	Supermarine Spitfire 1 FSM		

Notes	Reg	Type	Owner or Operator
	309	Fairey Gannet T.2 cockpit	The Aeroplane Collection, Hooton Park
	310	Miles Wings (Engineers) Ltd Gulp 100A Hang Glider	The Aeroplane Collection, Hooton Park
	311	GEC-Ferranti Phoenix UAV	National Museum of Flight, East Fortune
	312	Airwave Magic Kiss Hang Glider	National Museum of Flight, East Fortune
	313	Firebird Sierra Hang Glider	National Museum of Flight, East Fortune
	314	Gold Marque Gyr Hang Glider	National Museum of Flight, East Fortune
	315	Bensen B.8 Gyroglider	APSS/National Museum of Flight (Store), East Fortune
	316	Pilcher Bat Replica	Riverside Museum, Glasgow
	317	WACO CG-4A Hadrian cockpit	National Museum of Flight, East Fortune
	318	Supermarine Spitfire FSM (PT462)	H. Macleod, Moffatt, Dumfries and Galloway
	319	Supermarine Spitfire FSM (X4859)	No.1333 Sqn. Air Training Corps, Grangemouth
	320	Supermarine Spitfire FSM (EP121)	Air Station Heritage Centre, Montrose
	321	Royal Aircraft Factory BE.2c FSM	Air Station Heritage Centre, Montrose
	322	Handley Page Halifax III cockpit replica	Dumfries & Galloway Aviation Museum, Tinwald Downs
	323	Supermarine Spitfire Vb FSM (W3644)	Fairhaven Lake, Lytham St. Annes
	324	Supermarine Spitfire IX FSM (BS435)	Lytham Spitfire Display Team, Blackpool
	325	Supermarine Spitfire FSM (PL256)	Lytham Spitfire Display Team, Blackpool
	326	Supermaine Spitfire II FSM (X4253)	Lytham Spitfire Display Team, Blackpool
	327	Fiesler Fi.103 (FZG-76) FSM	Simon Pulford
	328	Avro F Type cabin reproduction	Museum of Science and Industry, Manchester
	329	Mignet HM.14 Pou-du-Ciel	Breighton
	330	Ward Gnome	Newark Air Museum, Winthorpe
	331	Gloster E28/39 FSM (W4041)	
	332	Royal Aircraft Factory BE.2b reproduction (2783)	Boscombe Down Aviation Collection, Old Sarum
	333	Supermarine Spitfire II FSM (RG904)	Royal Air Force Museum, RAF Cosford
	334	Hawker Hurricane FSM (R4229)	Alexandra Park, Windsor
	335	Supermarine Spitfire IIa FSM (P7666)	RAF High Wycombe
	336	Northrop F-5E Tiger II FSM (01532)	RAF Alconbury
	337	Pilcher Bat Mk.3 reproduction	The Shuttleworth Collection, Old Warden
	338	Halton Aero Club Mayfly reproduction	Trenchard Museum, RAF Halton
	339	Husband Modac 500 Hornet Gyroplane	The Helicopter Museum, Weston-Super-Mare
	340	Dickson Primary Glider	Nigel Ponsford Collection
	341	Lockheed-Martin F-35 Lightning II FSM	Royal Air Force Museum, Hendon
	342	Lockheed-Martin F-35 Lightning II FSM	Royal Air Force
	343	Lockheed-Martin F-35 Lightning II FSM	Royal Air Force
	344	Fiesler Fi.103 (FZG-76/V-1)	Cornwall Aviation Heritage Centre, Newquay
	345	Fiesler Fi.103 (FZG-76/V-1)	Cornwall At War Museum, Davidstow Moor
	346	Hawker Hurricane (V7313)	Gate Guard, North Weald
	347	Colditz Cock reproduction	Gliding Heritage Centre, Lasham
	348	Sopwith 7F.1 Snipe reproduction	Royal Air Force Museum, Hendon
	349	de Havilland DH.103 Hornet F.1 cockpit composite	DH Hornet Project, Chelmsford
	350	TEAM Minimax Hi-MAX	LAA Build-A-Plane Project mobile exhibit
	351	Airspeed Horsa replica	Cobbaton Combat Collection, Chittlehampton
	352	Hawker Sea Hawk cockpit	Graham Sparkes/Fort Perch Museum, stored Hooton Park
	353	Sopwith 5F1 Dolphin composite (C3988)	Royal Air Force Museum, Hendon
	354	Sopwith Tabloid Floatplane reproduction	Brooklands Museum, Weybridge
	355	Slingsby T.7 Cadet (PD685)	Tettenhall Transport Heritage Centre, Wolverhampton
	356	BAe Systems Phoenix UAV composite	Medway Aircraft Preservation Society, Rochester
	357	BAC Lightning	BAe Systems, Salmesbury
	358	Boulton-Paul Overstrand cockpit reproduction (K4556)	Norfolk & Suffolk Aviation Museum, Flixton
	359	Cody Army Aeroplane No.1A reproduction	Farnborough Air Sciences Trust, Farnborough
	360	Eurofighter Typhoon FGR.4 FSM (IR106)	RAF Exhibition Unit
	361	Boeing-Vertol CH-47 Chinook HC.2 FSM (IR108)	RAF Exhibition Unit
	362	Hawker Fury reproduction (L1639)	Cambridge Bomber and Fighter Society, Cambridge
	363	Hawker Typhoon cockpit	Jet Age Museum, Staverton
	364	Kiceniuk Icsarus II	Norfolk & Suffolk Aviation Museum, Flixton

Reg	Type	Owner or Operator	Notes
365	Northrop MQM-36 Shelduck D.1 UAV (XT005)	Medway Aircraft Preservation Society, Rochester	
366	Percival E.2H Mew Gull reproduction (G-AEXF)	Royal Air Force Museum, Hendon	
367	Percival E.2H Mew Gull reproduction (G-AEXF)	Thorpe Camp Visitor Centre, Woodhall Spa	
368	Supermarine 361 Spitfire LF.XVIe (TD248)	Norfolk & Suffolk Aviation Museum, Flixton	
369	Supermarine Spitfire FSM (P7895)	Ulster Aviation Collection, Long Kesh	
370	WACO CG-4A reproduction (241079)	Royal Air Force Museum, RAF Cosford	
371	Westland Lysander FSM (V9875)		
372	Wasp Falcon 4 Hang Glider	Norfolk & Suffolk Aviation Museum, Flixton	
373	Westland Whirlwind Mk.1 reproduction	Whirlwind Fighter Project	
374	Antonov C.12 Hang Glider	Norfolk & Suffolk Aviation Museum, Flixton	
375	Boeing Stearman PT-27 composite	Norfolk & Suffolk Aviation Museum, Flixton	
376	Messerschmidt Bf.109 FSM	Northern Forties Re-enactment Group	
377	Supermarine Spitfire IX FSM (EN398)	Northern Forties Re-enactment Group	
378	Hawker Hurricane IIc FSM (V7467)	Gate Guard, RAF High Wycombe	
379	Supermarine Spitfire FSM	Formerly with Dumfries & Galloway Aviation Museum, Tinwald Downs	
380	Vlackburn Triplane reproduction	Fort Paull Museum	
381	Westland Wallace reproduction		
382	BAe 125 forward fuselage	Deeside College, Connah's Quay	
383	Airspeed Horsa cockpit reproduction	Jet Age Museum, Staverton	
384	Flight Refuelling Ltd Falconet UAV	Mark Oliver, Knutsford	
385	Sopwith F.1 Camel reproduction (D6447)	Mark Oliver, Knutsford	
386	Bristol F.28 Fighter replica (A7228)	Bristol Aero Collection, Filton	
387	Bristol F.2B Fighter replica	Bristol Aero Collection, Filton	
388	Short Stirling B.III composite	The Stirling Project, Alconbury	
389	Heinkel He.111 Recreation	Lincolnshire Aviation Heritage Centre, East Kirkby	
390	Felixstowe F.5 cockpit	Norfolk and Suffolk Aviation Museum, Flixton	
391	Cody Type V Bi-Plane reproduction	Farnborough Air Sciences Trust, Farnborough	
392	Avro RJX100	Bristol Aero Collection, Filton	
393	Supermarine Spitfire FSM (N3310/N3320)	Lodge Hill Garage, Abingdon	
394	Supermarine Spitfire 1 FSM (X4178)	Imperial War Museum, Duxford	
395	Pilatus P2-05 replica	Personal Plane Services, Booker	
396	Airspeed AS.51 Horsa II cockpit	Imperial War Museum, Duxford	
397	General Aircraft GAL.48 Hotspur II	cockpit Imperial War Museum, Duxford	
398	Bristol 156 Beaufighter VI cockpit	Midland Air Museum, Coventry	
399	Hawker Hurricane FSM (P2793)	Eden Camp Wartime Museum, Old Malton	
400	RAF FE.2b reproduction (A6526)	Royal Air Force Museum, Hendon	
401	Mignet HM.14 Pou-du-Ciel	Catford Independent Air Force	
402	Hawker Hurricane I composite (L1639)	Cambridge Bomber and Fighter Society, Cambridge	
403	Fieseler Fi.103 FSM (FZG-76/V-1)	Ulster Aviation Museum, Long Kesh	
404	Civilian Aircraft Company Coupe (incomplete)	Shipping and Airlines Ltd, Biggin Hill	
405	BGA.178 Manuel Crested Wing	Gliding Heritage Centre, Lasham	
406	Electro Flight Lightning P.1E FSM	Stroud	
407	DH.2 7/8 scale model	Great War Aerodrome, Stow Maries	
408	BAe Systems Phoenix UAV composite	Larkhill	
409	DH.82A Tiger Moth composite	Thorpe Camp Visitor Centre, Woodhall Spa	
410	Supermarine Spitfire FSM (P7370)	War and Peace, Ash	
411	Hawker Hurricane FSM (V6555)	War and Peace, Ash	
412	Gotha G.V. cockpit reproduction	Great War Aerodrome, Stow Maries	
413	Sopwith Strutter reproduction (A8274)	Great War Aerodrome, Stow Maries	
414	Sopwith F.1 Camel reproduction	Great War Aerodrome, Stow Maries	
415	ML Aviation Sprite UAV	Museum of Berkshire Aviation, Woodley	
416	ML Aviation Sprite UAV	Museum of Army Flying, Middle Wallop	
417	Airspeed Horsa replica	Museum of Army Flying, Middle Wallop	
418	Airspeed Horsa cockpit replica	Museum of Army Flying, Middle Wallop	
419	Fieseler Fi.103 (FZG-76/V-1) FSM	North East Land Sea and Air Museum, Usworth	
420	Vickers FB.27A Vimy cockpit	Brooklands Museum, Weybridge	
421	Vickers Wellington forward fuselage	Brooklands Museum, Weybridge	
422	Avro 683 Lancaster Composite cockpit	Avro Heritage Trust, Woodford	

Notes	Reg	Type	Owner or Operator
	423	EoN AP.5 Primary	Aircraft Restoration Group, Fishburn-Morgansfield
	424	Manchester University BAe. JAVA UAV	Museum of Science and Industry, Manchester
	425	Avro 683 Lancaster cockpit	Pitstone Museum
	426	Supermarine Spitfire IX FSM (MK805)	Simply Spitfires, Lowestoft
	427	Skyhook Safari powered hang glider	The Science Museum, Wroughton
	428	Cody man-lifting kite reproduction	Museum of Science and Industry, Manchester
	429	Bleriot XI cockpit	The Science Museum, South Kensington
	430	Army Balloon Factory Airship Beta II	The Science Museum, South Kensington
	431	Supermarine Spitfire FSM (K9998)	RAF Chapel, Biggin Hill
	432	Breen hang glider	Tettenhall Transport Heritage Collection, Wolverhampton
	433	Westland Whirlwind Mk.1 cockpit	City of Norwich Aviation Museum
	434	DH.98 Mosquito recreation (HJ711)	Yorkshire Air Museum, Elvington
	435	WACO CG-4A Hadrian cockpit	Museum of Military Life, Carlisle
	436	Bristol 152 Beaufort composite (DD931)	Royal Air Force Museum, Hendon
	437	Lilienthal Kleiner Doppeldecker reproduction	Shuttleworth Collection
	438	Lilienthal Normal Apparatus reproduction	Shuttleworth Collection
	439	Lilienthal Type XI glider reproduction	Shuttleworth Collection
	440	Lovegrove Rota-Glida Gyro-Glider	The Gyrocopter Experience, Rufforth
	441	Pilcher Triplane reproduction	Shuttleworth Collection
	442	Sopwith Baby Composite (N2078)	Fleet Air Arm Museum, Yeovilton
	443	WACO CG-4A Hadrian cockpit reproduction	South Yorkshire Aviation Museum, Doncaster
	444	Westland WG-25 Mote remotely piloted helicopter	The Helicopter Museum, Weston-Super-Mare
	445	Westland WG-25 Wideye remotely piloted	The Helicopter Museum, Weston-Super-Mare helicopter
	446	Westland WG-25 Wisp remotely piloted	The Helicopter Museum, Weston-Super-Mare helicopter
	447	Yamaha Motors remotely piloted helicopter	The Helicopter Museum, Weston-Super-Mare
	448	Bleriot XI reproduction	Caernafon Airworld Museum
	449	HP.61 Halifax B.III composite(LV907/NP763)	Yorkshire Air Museum, Elvington
	450	Hawker Siddeley Harrier composite	The Helicopter Museum, Weston-Super-Mare
	451	Westland WG-25 Sharpeye remotely	The Helicopter Museum, Weston-Super-Mare piloted helicopter
	452	Sopwith Strutter replica (N5177/B9708)	In store, Mersham, Surrey
	453	F-35B Lightning II ground training aid	Fleet Air Arm, RNAS Culdrose
	454	F-35B Lightning II ground training aid	Fleet Air Arm, RNAS Culsrose
	455	F-35B Lightning FSM	Fleet Air Arm, RNAS Culdrose
	456	Supermarine Spitfire FSM	Seymour-Johnson AFB, USA
	457	Supermarine Spitfire Mk.VIII FSM (A58-492)	RAAF Museum, Point Cook, Victoria
	458	P-51D Mustang FSM	Business Park, Auckland, New Zealand
	459	Levasseur PL.8 biplane 7/8 scale FSM	Peninsular Hotel, Paris
	460	Supermarine Spitfire V FSM	Oxfordshire
	461	Supermarine Spitfire cockpit FSM	
	462	Supermarine Spitfire cockpit FSM	
	463	Bristol 156 Beaufighter IIF cockpit	Royal Air Force Museum, Hendon
	464	P-51D Mustang FSM 'Duchess Arlene'	Tuskegee, Alabama, USA
	465	Fieseler Fi.103 FSM (FZG-76/V-1)	RAF Manston Museum
	466	Huntair Pathfinder 2	RAF Manston Museum
	467	Nieuport 17 reproduction (A213)	RAF Manston Museum
	468	Sopwith Strutter reproduction (B619)	RAF Manston Museum
	469	Nieuport 17 reproduction	RAF Manston Museum
	470	DH.60G Gipsy Moth FSM (G-AAAH)	Paragon Station, Hull
	471	Avro 683 Lancaster cockpit reproduction	Mobile exhibit, Lincolnshire
	472	Morane-Saulnier N reproduction	North-East Land Sea Air Museum, Usworth
	473	Messerschmitt Bf.109 FSM	War and Peace, Ash, Kent
	474	Philips British Matchless Flying Machine	Shuttleworth Collection
	475	Hawker Hurricane 1 FSM	The Battle of Britain Bunker, Uxbridge
	476	Supermarine Spitfire cockpit reproduction (TB885)	Biggin Hill Heritage Limited
	477	Hawker Hurricane FSM	St. George's Chapel of Remembrance, Biggin Hill
	478	Supermarine Spitfire cockpit reproduction	RAF Elsham Wolds Memorial Garden
	479	Bleriot XI reproduction	Under construction, Ipswich

Reg	Type	Owner or Operator	Notes
480	Ferranti/Slingsby T.68 Phoenix UAV	National Museum of Flight Scotland, East Fortune	
481	Mignet HM.14 Pou-du-Ciel ('G-ADRZ')	Aircraft Restoration Group, Masham	
482	Avro Lancaster cockpit reproduction	Staffordshire	
483	Supermarine Spitfire II cockpit reproduction	Staffordshire	

Reg	Type	Owner or Operator

Reg	Type	Owner or Operator

BRITISH CIVIL AIRCRAFT REGISTRATIONS

Reg	Type	Owner or Operator
G-CKUT	Eurocopter EC.155B1	Waypoint Asset Euro 1A Ltd
G-CKUY	Eurocopter EC.155B1	Waypoint Asset Euro 1A Ltd
G-CKVW	Robinson R22	Startrade Heli GmbH and Co KG
G-CKWA	Boeing 787-9	Norwegian Air UK Ltd
G-CKWG	SD1 Minisport	R. Y. Kendal
G-CKWJ	Lindstrand LBL-77A balloon	D. W. Torrington
G-CKWR	Magni M.16C	Willy Rose Technology Ltd
G-IACZ	Aerospatiale ATR-72-212A	Eastern Airways
G-TCVD	Airbus A.321-231	Thomas Cook Airlines Ltd
G-WUKA	Airbus A.320-232	Wizz Air UK

OVERSEAS AIRLINER REGISTRATIONS

Reg	Type	Owner or Operator
A6-EQK	Boeing 777-31HER	Emirates Airlines
A6-EQL	Boeing 777-31HER	Emirates Airlines
A7-BEU	Boeing 777-3DZER	Qatar Airways
A7-BEV	Boeing 777-3DZER	Qatar Airways
D-ASTI	Airbus A.319-112	Germania
HL7204	Boeing 777-3B5EER	Korean Airlines
HL7205	Boeing 777-3B5EER	Korean Airlines
N7274U	Boeing 777-322ER	United Airlines
TC-LOB	Airbus A.330-223	Turkish Airlines
TC-LOC	Airbus A.330-223	Turkish Airlines